D0984961

FEDERAL ANTITRUST POLICY

THE LAW OF COMPETITION AND ITS PRACTICE

Second Edition

By

HERBERT HOVENKAMP

Ben V. & Dorothy Willie Professor
University of Iowa, College of Law

HORNBOOK SERIES®

ST. PAUL, MINN., 1999

610 Opperman Drive
P.O. Box 64526
St. Paul, MN 55164–0526
1–800–328–9352

Printed in the United States of America

ISBN 0–314–23180–3

*TEXT IS PRINTED ON 10% POST
CONSUMER RECYCLED PAPER*

Preface

This second edition of Federal Antitrust Policy: the Law of Competition and its Practice is a complete revision of the first and is current with all case law through the summer of 1999.

Today the union of antitrust and economics is so complete that one cannot study antitrust seriously without at least some exposure to economics. *Federal Antitrust Policy* uses economics in a modestly technical way. I assume that the reader has no background in economics, and thus that each step must be explained. For those whose economics is more advanced, the footnotes cite to more technical literature in the applied economics of antitrust. However, the book is designed in such a way that its substance can be fully understood by a reader with no economic training and no inclination to learn even the little that is presented here. The small number of equations are merely illustrative, and almost always in footnotes. The geometric figures illustrate only what the text explains.

Law school antitrust curricula vary considerably, with some classes focusing only on questions of substance, some involving many questions of enforcement and procedure, and some being quite creative in their application of economics. I have tried to accommodate all of these to one degree or another. I have also attempted to provide a level of detail and analysis that makes this book a useful resource for the practitioner, judge or other antitrust scholar.

I chose the word "policy" for the title, since this book attempts both to state the "black letter" law and to present policy arguments for alternatives. Although I frequently disagree with court decisions, in all cases I have tried to state clearly what the legal rule is, and then give the reasons for my disagreement. Of course, I have my own ideological views. But here I have tried to present alternative views fairly, and to uncover the premises upon which they rely.

HERBERT HOVENKAMP

Iowa City, Iowa
November, 1999

*

WESTLAW® Overview

Federal Antitrust Policy: The Law of Competition and Its Practice, by Herbert Hovenkamp, offers a detailed and comprehensive treatment of basic rules, principles and issues relating to antitrust law. To supplement the information contained in this book, you can access Westlaw, a computer-assisted legal research service of West Group. Westlaw contains a broad array of legal resources, including case law, statutes, administrative decisions, rules, expert commentary, current developments and various other types of information.

Learning how to use these materials effectively will enhance your legal research abilities. To help you coordinate the information in the book with your Westlaw research, this volume contains an appendix listing Westlaw databases, search techniques and sample problems.

THE PUBLISHER

*

Summary of Contents

Summary of Contents

Table of Contents

FEDERAL ANTITRUST POLICY

Second Edition

*

Part I

FOUNDATIONS: POLICY AND MEASUREMENT

Chapter 1

THE BASIC ECONOMICS OF ANTITRUST

Table of Sections

---

§ 1.1 Price Theory: Economic Behavior and Perfect Competition

Those who make antitrust policy are consumers, not usually creators, of economic theory. Further, antitrust policy makers are quite stodgy about adopting new theory. The economics applied in antitrust decision making is quite conventional, "applied" economics. The economics literature as a whole is more technical, more venturesome and speculative, much more stylized, and at the margins much more controversial than most of the economics that is applied by the antitrust policy maker.[1] What follows is a brief presentation of relatively orthodox economics that forms the basis of federal antitrust policy.

§ 1.1

1. For example, consider the literature on game theory that now forms the center of industrial organization analysis in economics departments, but is barely beginning to make inroads in applied antitrust economics. Further, the game theory being applied in antitrust is simple and quite uncontroversial. See 1 Handbook of Industrial Organization, chs. 5–7 (R. Schmalensee & R. Willig, eds. 1989). But see S. Peltzman, The Handbook of Industrial Organization: a Review Article, 99 J.Pol.Econ. 201 (1991), arguing that very little in game theory offers useful predictions; *pro tanto*, it is of little use to the policy maker. Accord T. Muris, Economics and Antitrust, 5 Geo. Mason L. Rev. 303 (1997).

Market economies are dedicated to the principle that in the first instance people are responsible for their own welfare. Further, they are best off if they can make voluntary exchanges of goods and services in competitive markets.[2] If all exchanges are voluntary, each person will continue to exchange goods and services until she can make herself no better off by an exchange that is voluntary for both parties to the transaction. If all exchanges occur at competitive prices, society as a whole is wealthier than if some occur at a higher or lower price. An important goal of antitrust law—arguably its only goal—is to ensure that markets are competitive.

1.1a. The Perfectly Competitive Market

A competitive market is one in which 1) every good is priced at the cost of producing it, giving the producers and sellers only enough profit to maintain investment in the industry; and 2) every person willing to pay this price will be able to buy it.

Most customers prefer to purchase things at the lowest possible price—even, if possible, at less than the cost of producing them. By contrast, sellers prefer to sell at a price that will give them the highest possible profits. As a result competition is not an absolutely natural state of affairs; both buyers and sellers must be forced to compete.

The conditions most conducive to competition, and which obtain perfectly in an economic model of "perfect competition," are: 1) All sellers make an absolutely homogenous product, so that customers are indifferent as to which seller they purchase from, provided that the price is the same; 2) each seller in the market is so small in proportion to the entire market that the seller's increase or decrease in output, or even its exit from the market, will not affect the decisions of other sellers in that market; 3) all resources are completely mobile, or alternatively, all sellers have the same access to needed inputs; 4) all participants in the market have good knowledge about price, output and other information about the market. As a general rule, the closer a market comes to fulfilling these conditions, the more competitively it will perform.

The perfect competition model generally assumes "constant returns to scale"—that is, that costs of production per unit remain constant at all practical rates of output. As we shall see in § 1.4, the presence of substantial economies of scale—that is, of per unit costs that decrease as output increases—can undermine the perfect competition model, particularly if a firm must acquire a large market share in order to take advantage of these scale economies.

The most important rule governing price is the law of supply and demand. Price setting in any market is a function of the relationship between the amount of a product available and the amount that consumers, at the margin, are willing to pay. If the supply is not infinite, the market allocates goods to customers based on their individual willingness to pay. For example, if all the world's steel mills produced only 1000 pounds of steel per year, customers would likely bid a very high price for the steel, which would naturally be sold to the highest bidder. The price would be determined by the marginal customer's willingness to pay—that is, by the amount that some buyer would be willing to pay for the 1000th pound. Perhaps orthodontists, who put one half ounce of steel in a set of $800 braces, would be willing to buy all the steel at $3000 per pound. In that case no steel would be sold at a lower price. If the supply of steel increased 1000–fold, however, there might be far more steel than orthodontists could use at a price of $3000 per pound. The price of steel would drop so that the market could take in additional customers who place a high value on steel but are not willing to pay $3000 per pound.

2. For a normative defense of the free market, see R. Posner, The Economics of Justice (1981). The discussion of price theory that appears in this chapter is very spare, and some may be frustrated by the brevity, the lack of mathematical proof, or the paucity of examples. Those persons are referred to any modern text on microeconomics. Good current examples are J. M. Perloff, Microeconomics (1999); R. S. Pindyck & D.L. Rubinfeld, Microeconomics (4th ed. 1998). A classic and quite technical text is G. Stigler, The Theory of Price (3d ed. 1966).

As more and more steel is produced, the market price must drop further in order to reach customers who have lower "reservation" prices. A reservation price is the highest amount that a consumer is willing to pay for a product. As the price of steel drops those customers with very high reservation prices, such as the orthodontists, can also buy steel at the lower price. In the perfect competition model all sales tend to be made at the same price, even though different groups of consumers have vastly different reservation prices. If the seller attempted to charge orthodontists $3000 per pound but automakers $3 per pound, the seller's plan would be frustrated by "arbitrage." That is, automakers would buy steel at $3.00 per pound and resell some steel to orthodontists at a price higher than $3.00 per pound but lower than $3000 per pound. If all buyers have complete information about the market, all of them will pay the same price, regardless of their reservation prices. When a market reaches this condition, it is said to be in "equilibrium."[3]

Assume that the market contains 100 sellers of steel. Each seller wants to make as much money as possible, and every buyer (regardless of his reservation price) wants to purchase steel at the lowest possible price. How much steel will be produced in the market and what will be its price?

Figure 1 illustrates how a perfectly competitive market arrives at equilibrium, or the point at which supply and demand are perfectly balanced and will not change unless the market is disturbed. The figure illustrates the market demand curve (D) and the market supply curve (S) for a single product. Since both price and output are generally positive numbers, it is common to display only the upper right quadrant of the standard two-axis graph. The vertical axis represents price, which increases from 0 as one moves upward. The horizontal axis represents output (or quantity), which increases from 0 as one moves from the origin to the right.

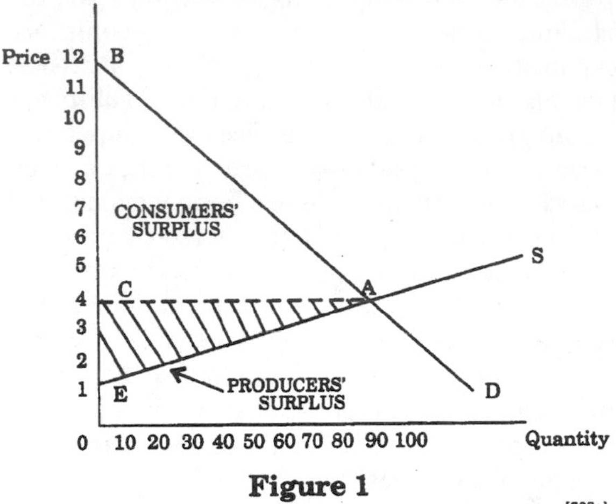

Figure 1

[608a]

The graph shows that at low levels of quantity, or output, the market price is quite high. Since few units are being produced, the good is sold only to customers who have very high reservation prices. Sellers will be earning enormous profits on their output. Profit, which is revenue (or price times quantity sold) minus cost, is measured by the vertical distance between the supply curve and the demand curve at any point. The supply curve itself includes "competitive" or "normal" profits. Any vertical distance between the supply curve and the demand curve is referred to as "economic" or "monopoly" profits. These are profits in excess of those earned by a competitive industry, and in excess of the amount needed to maintain investment in the industry.

If profits per unit of output are extremely high, as they are when output is very low, two things will happen. First, existing sellers will be encouraged by the very high profits to increase their output. Suppose current output is twenty units, the cost of production is approximately $2.00, but the price is on the order of $10.00. Each additional unit that the firm produces will give it economic profits of $8.00. Secondly, and for the same reason, new firms will come into the market. People with money to invest invariably seek opportunities where the expected return is highest.

The figure shows an upward sloping supply curve. A horizontal supply curve would imply

3. In real world markets, however, price discrimination, or obtaining higher profits from one set of customers than from another set, is both possible and common. See §§ 14.1–14.3.

that the costs of producing additional units are the same at all levels of market output. However, this is not always the case. As firms increase their output, the cost of producing the final units of output may rise. The new production must make use of increasingly marginal (less attractive) resources. The first units of steel, for example, will be produced from the iron ore that is the cheapest to obtain and refine. As output increases, however, these firms must turn to more marginal ore. Likewise, as new steel producers enter the market they will buy up the best remaining ore reserves, and firms that come in later will have to take more marginal reserves. As the market grows, increasingly marginal materials will be used and the cost of producing steel will tend to rise.[4]

As output increases, the market price will fall as customers with lower and lower reservation prices must be drawn in. The market will finally stabilize at point A. At any point on the supply curve to the left of A, an increase in output of one unit will generate positive economic profits—that is, more in revenue than the cost of producing that unit. At least one firm will increase its output or at least one new firm will enter the market and start producing. This process will continue until the supply curve and demand curve intersect.

By contrast, if production is at some point on the supply curve to the right of A, then at least some steel is being produced at less than the price than can be obtained for it. In that case the least efficient firms will exit from the market or some firms will close down their least efficient mines and plants or reduce their output until the quantity supplied falls back to the intersection with the demand curve at A. The market constantly moves toward this "equilibrium."

As noted above, in a competitive market all buyers pay the market price, even if their individual reservation prices are higher. The difference between the buyers' reservation prices and the price they actually pay is called "consumers' surplus." The size of the consumers' surplus in Figure 1 is represented by triangle ABC. A competitive market tends to maximize the size of the consumers' surplus: the consumers' surplus cannot be larger than ABC without at least one sale being unprofitable.

Some firms in the market are likely to have lower costs than others. They may have the richest veins of ore or the lowest energy, labor, or distribution costs. Cross-hatched triangle ACE represents "producers' surplus:" the difference between total revenue at the competitive price and the sum of the producers' costs. Only at the margin does a firm earn zero profits. Such a marginal firm is the one with the highest costs that is still capable of earning a competitive rate of return when the product is sold at a competitive price. If the market shifts in a way that is unfavorable to sellers, this marginal firm is likely to be the first, or one of the first, to go out of business.

The supply and demand curves in Figure 1 can assume an infinite variety of shapes. The figure shows them as straight lines, suggesting that the quantity demanded increases at a uniform rate as price falls, and that production costs rise at a uniform rate as output increases. But in most markets the two lines are nonlinear, and may often be quite irregular. Drawing them as straight lines is a useful analytic device, however, that often does not affect analysis.

The relationships expressed by the supply and demand curves can be quantified and expressed in formulas. One formula, for *price elasticity of demand*, is simply a short-hand expression for the relationship between a particular change in the price of a product and the corresponding change in demand for it. That formula is:[5]

4. If these costs differences result from new entry by additional firms, they are usually diagrammed by a supply curve that shifts to reflect higher costs. If they are the increasing costs of a single firm or group of firms, they are generally diagrammed by a curve that has an upward slope, as in Figure 1.

5. The importance of dividing δQ by Q, and δP by P in the formula is to ensure that we are talking about percentage changes, which can be expressed in any possible units of measure. That is, we might wish to express elasticity of demand simply as $\delta Q/\delta P$; but in that case the ratio would appear to change if we changed the unit in which Q is measured from, say, gallons to quarts.

$$\varepsilon = \frac{\delta Q}{Q} \div \frac{\delta P}{P}$$[5]

or alternatively,

$$\varepsilon = \frac{\delta Q}{\delta P} \cdot \frac{P}{Q}$$

in which δQ and δP are equal to changes in quantity demanded and market clearing price, respectively, and Q and P are the base quantity and price from which the changes took place. Since quantity and price change in opposite directions (quantity demanded goes up as price goes down) this number is negative. As a matter of convention, however, it is common to take the absolute value, or drop the negative sign.

If at an output of 200 the market-clearing price per unit is $100, and at an output of 240 the market-clearing price drops to $90, we can compute price elasticity of demand as follows: change in output = 40; change in price = 10. The elasticity of demand equals:

$$\frac{40}{10} \cdot \frac{100}{200} = \frac{4000}{2000} = 2.$$

A simpler way of describing price elasticity of demand is that it is the relationship between the percentage change in quantity of a good demanded when the price of the good changes by a certain percentage. In the above example, a 10% drop in price elicits a 20% increase in market demand, yielding an elasticity of demand of 20%/10%, or 2.

The elasticity of demand along any curve is different than the slope of the curve, which in the case of a straight line is the ratio of the vertical axis to the horizontal axis. While the slope of a linear curve is the same at all points, the price elasticity of demand represented by a straight line demand curve is different at all points. If a demand curve stretching from the price axis to the output axis is a straight line, the elasticity of demand will be one at the line's midpoint, higher than one at all points above the midpoint, and lower than one at all points below. Whenever the elasticity of demand in a market is greater than one, we term the demand "elastic." In that case a price increase of X% will yield a decrease in quantity demanded of greater than X%. When the elasticity of demand is less than one we term the demand "inelastic." In that case a price increase of X% yields a decrease in quantity of less than X%. As you might guess, a seller would prefer to face an inelastic rather than an elastic demand: if demand is very inelastic, a relatively large price increase will yield a relatively small decrease in demand.

Elasticity of *supply* is a relationship between changes in the price of a product and the amount produced. As the price of a product rises, more of it will be produced because existing firms will increase their output or new firms will enter the market and start producing. The elasticity of supply is measured by the percentage change in the amount supplied that results from a certain percentage change in pricc. For cxample, if a 10% price increase yields a 30% increase in supply, the elasticity of supply in the market is 3. If a 30% price increase yields a 15% supply increase, the market's elasticity of supply is .5. Elasticity of supply is a positive number.

For antitrust policy one must consider not only the absolute elasticity of supply, but also the amount of time it takes for supply to increase in response to a price increase. Suppose that the elasticity of supply in a market is 3, which is very high. If price goes up by 10%, the quantity supplied to the market will increase by 30%. But suppose that the construction of the additional plants that account for the 30% supply increase takes 10 years. A seller attempting to raise its price to a monopoly level will eventually lose sales to this increased output by competitors. But during the ten year construction period the seller will earn monopoly profits. Further, the expense and time required to build a competing plant may enable the incumbent to engage in certain "strategic" behavior. For example, if prospective competitors know that the incumbent has substantial excess capacity and can increase output and drop price at will, the large investment and long wait for an uncertain return may look unprofitable.[6]

Time can also be a factor in antitrust analysis of elasticity of demand. Often customers facing a price increase can switch to a different seller more quickly than suppliers can expand output or enter the market, but this is not always the case. For example, customers may be constrained by long-term contracts, or their technology may tie them to a given supplier or group of suppliers. For example, an electric utility that uses uranium for its power plant might wish to switch to coal if the uranium market is cartelized. However, changing over is both costly and time-consuming. Eventually, when the nuclear plant wears out, the utility may switch to coal if the uranium cartel is still in existence. In its *Kodak* decision, the Supreme Court spoke of "locked-in" customers who have a large investment in a durable piece of equipment such as a photocopier, and must thus buy its specially designed replacement parts until the machine wears out or becomes obsolete.[7] Economists generally speak of these time factors by distinguishing between "long-run" and "short-run" elasticities of supply and demand. The "long-run" elasticity of supply is generally said to be higher than the "short-run" elasticity. The same is true of elasticity of demand.

The importance of time in antitrust analysis results from the fact that the policy maker is necessarily concerned with *short*-run dislocations in the market. We could presume that all markets will eventually become competitive, but antitrust is concerned with ensuring that this occurs sooner rather than later. The concern is not unique to antitrust. For example, we would not need contract law in competitive markets if our only concern was with the long run. Firms who break their contracts would be shunned by buyers and sellers who have other alternatives. Likewise, in the long run all of us will be dead. But that fact does not undermine the state's concern to protect us from murderers or see to it that we are provided with nutrition and health care.

The previous discussion of the relationship between supply and demand assumes that the market is unaffected by changes imposed from outside. If relative consumer income rises or falls, new technology makes a product obsolete or the country goes to war, however, demand for any good may rise or fall regardless of available supply or costs of production. In such cases we talk, not about changes *along* a demand (or supply) curve, but about *shifts* in the curve. For example, the invention of the electronic calculator had no effect on the cost of production of a slide rule or on the capacity of slide rule factories. Nevertheless, when the electronic calculator was invented the demand for slide rules dropped precipitously. We diagram that change by saying that the demand curve for slide rules shifted to the left. As Figure 2 suggests, if a shift to the left is dramatic enough, a product may simply cease to exist. If the lowest possible cost of producing a slide rule by the most efficient producer is $20, but even the consumer with the highest reservation price is unwilling to pay $20 (perhaps because she can obtain an equivalent electronic calculator for $16.00), then no one can make slide rules profitably. They will go the way of the quill pen, the vacuum tube, and the washboard. The shifted demand curve (D_2 in Figure 2) illustrates this: it never intersects the supply curve.

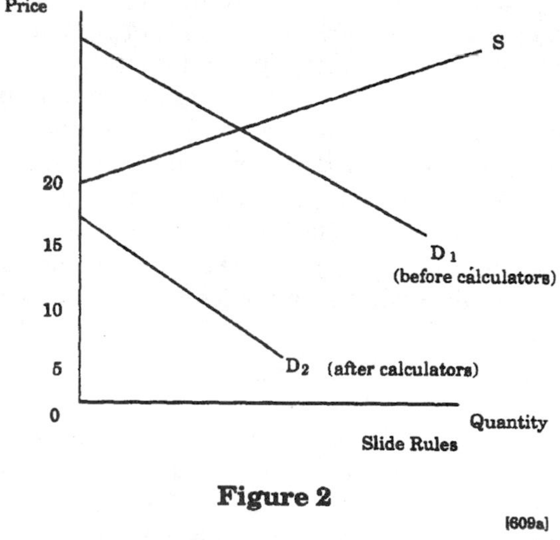

Figure 2

[609a]

6. See § 7.3.

7. Eastman Kodak Co. v. Image Technical Services, 504 U.S. 451, 112 S.Ct. 2072 (1992). See § 7.6a.

Supply curves may shift just as demand curves do. The invention of the microprocessor in a silicone chip reduced the cost of building computers by a factor of one hundred. The result is that the new supply curve for computers in the 1990's is much lower than the supply curve of the 1960's, and equilibrium output is much higher.

1.1b. Behavior of the Competitive Firm

We have considered the competitive, multi-firm market, and can now examine the behavior of the individual firm in that market. We assume a market with a large number of sellers, into which entry is relatively easy and can be accomplished in a short time. How will an individual firm in that market decide how much to produce and what price to charge?

Even though the steel market's equilibrium price is $3.00 per pound, there are still individual buyers, such as the orthodontists, whose reservation price is far higher than $3.00. Suppose that the individual firm attempts to charge a higher price than $3.00—perhaps $4.00—for a pound of steel. The orthodontists are certainly willing to pay $4.00, but if they can buy for $3.00 they will do so. When one firm in a 100–firm market attempts to charge $4.00, a buyer who knows that the "going" price is $3.00 will look for a different seller. In a perfectly competitive market in which all buyers have complete price information, all the sellers will be "price takers"—they must simply accept the market price as given. No single firm is large enough to influence either the total amount produced or the market price. As a result, the individual firm can sell as little or as much as it pleases at the market price, but it will lose all sales if it attempts to charge more.

The situation facing the perfect competitor can be described in two ways. First, the firm faces a perfectly horizontal demand curve, as is illustrated in Figure 3. For the perfect competitor the market price is the same at all rates of output. Alternatively, the individual competitor faces extremely high firm elasticities of supply and demand. In response to a very small price increase, alternative suppliers will immediately offer substitute products to the price raiser's customers, and all customers will switch to those substitutes. The firm will lose all of its sales.

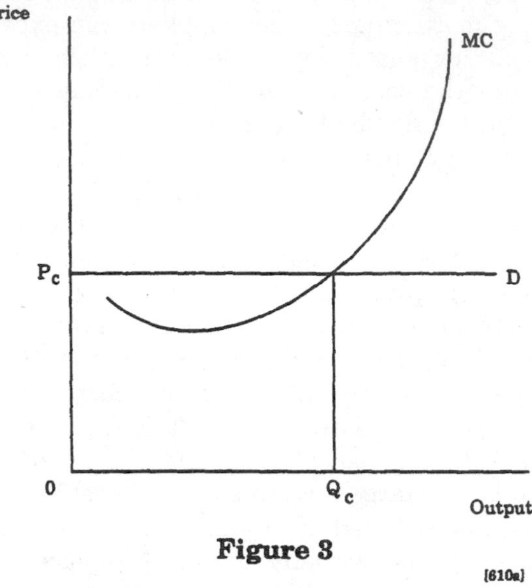

Figure 3

[610a]

One must therefore distinguish between *market* elasticities of supply and demand, and individual *firm* elasticities of supply and demand. Except for the pure monopolist (whose output is the same as the output of the entire market) the individual firm faces higher elasticities of supply and demand than does the market as a whole. This is because *within* a market substitution is easy and quick. If the market contains 100 producers of identical steel, then A's steel is indistinguishable from B's steel, which is indistinguishable from C's, and so on. The fact that customers are indifferent as to whose steel they buy means that they will switch immediately to B or C if A attempts to increase price; conversely, B or C will happily provide the steel.

The firms in a perfectly competitive market have little discretion about what price to charge. They do make individual decisions, however, about the amount to produce. Even in a perfectly competitive market with an established single market price, different firms are of different sizes and produce differing amounts.

The individual competitor's output decision is a function of its marginal costs. Marginal cost is the additional cost that a firm incurs in the production of one additional unit of output. The best way to understand marginal cost is to consider several related cost curves. A firm's costs can be divided into two broad categories, fixed and variable. Fixed costs are those costs that do not change with output over the short-run, which is some finite period of time, usually less than the lifetime of the plant. Land costs, property taxes, management salaries, plant and durable equipment all generally fall into the category of fixed costs. Once the money for fixed cost items is invested it must be paid whether or not the plant produces anything, and the costs do not vary with the amount the plant produces.

Variable costs, by contrast, are costs that change with output. For the steel mill, the costs of iron ore and other raw materials are variable costs, as are fuel to burn in the refining furnaces, hourly wages, and transportation. If a firm increases its output by, say 10%, the cost of all these things rises because the firm must purchase more. The cost of the plant, durable equipment and the president's salary are likely to stay the same. Over the long-run, however, even these "fixed" costs must be considered variable. Eventually plant and durable equipment will have to be replaced. The firm will then decide whether to increase capacity, decrease it, or perhaps even go out of business.

Both fixed and variable costs are generally expressed as costs per unit of output. These are illustrated in Figure 4. "Average fixed cost" (AFC) is the amount of fixed cost divided by the amount of output. Since total fixed costs remain constant, average fixed costs decline as output increases. "Average variable cost" (AVC) is total variable cost divided by the amount of output the firm produces. The behavior of the average variable cost curve is more complex. Every established plant has some particular range of output in which it is most efficient. For example, a plant properly designed to produce 80–100 units per year will perform at lowest cost when output is in that range. If output drops to 50 the plant will perform less efficiently and per unit costs will rise. Thus the AVC curve shows higher than minimum AVC at low outputs. Blast furnaces, to give just one example, cost the same amount to heat whether they are used at capacity or only at half capacity. The same thing generally holds true for output that exceeds the plant's "optimal capacity." For example, a plant and work force designed to produce 80 units per week may be able to increase output to 100 units per week only if workers are paid overtime wages, which may be twice their normal wages, or if equipment is used at a level at which its breakdown rate is high. Thus, the AVC curve increases to the right of the minimum point as output increases.

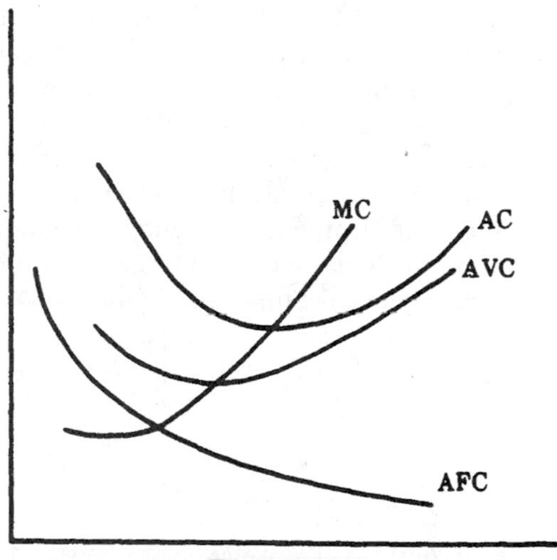

Figure 4

The average variable cost curve (AVC) of the plant tends to be U-shaped. Average variable cost declines as output increases toward the optimal output for the plant. AVC is at the lowest point when the plant is producing the optimal output for which it was designed, and increases when the plant's output exceeds optimal capacity. The AVC curve often has a relatively flat bottom, because many plants are efficient over a fairly broad range of output.

Just above the AVC curve in Figure 4 is the average total cost curve (AC), usually called the average cost curve, which is nothing more than the *sum* of all fixed and variable costs divided by output. Since all costs are either fixed or variable, the AC curve represents the total costs that a firm incurs. As a result the AC curve is important in determining the firm's profitability. In order to be profitable the firm must obtain an average price per unit equal to or greater than AC. The AC curve is shaped roughly like the AVC curve, except that the two converge as output increases.[8]

Once again, *marginal* cost is the additional cost that a firm incurs in producing one additional unit of output.[9] Since a firm incurs no increased *fixed* costs in expanding output in the short run, marginal cost is a function of variable costs alone. The marginal cost curve (MC) falls and rises more dramatically than the average variable cost curve does, because the marginal cost curve considers merely the additional costs of one added unit of output. By contrast, the AVC curve averages that difference over the entire output being produced.[10] Importantly, the marginal cost curve always intersects the AVC curve at its lowest point. A minute's reflection about averages will tell you why. Suppose that you are averaging the height of United States Supreme Court Justices and you have managed to gather eight of them, and have computed their average height as 6′0″. Now the ninth Justice walks in the door and happens to be 5′3″ tall. The average height will decline. But if the ninth Justice happens to be 6′7″ the average will increase. Whether the average falls or rises is a function of the height of the "marginal" Justice. As long as the marginal Justice is below the average, the average will decline; as soon as the marginal Justice is above the average, the average will increase.

The relationship between the cost curves is illustrated in Table A. Notice that as output increases total fixed costs remain constant at 120. As a result, average fixed costs decline steadily, but at a decreasing rate. Total variable costs increase constantly as output increases; however, they increase more slowly as the plant approaches optimal capacity (in the 3–5 output range), and more rapidly again as the plant exceeds optimal capacity. As a result, *average* variable cost bottoms out at an output of about 5 and then increases.

Output	Total Fixed Cost	Average Fixed Cost	Total Variable Cost	AVC	MC	AC
1	120	120	200	200	200	320
2	120	60	240	120	40	180
3	120	40	270	90	30	130
4	120	30	320	80	50	110
5	120	24	375	75	55	99
6	120	20	510	85	135	105
7	120	17.14	700	100	190	117.14

TABLE A

How will the competitive firm make its output decision? Suppose the market price is $100.00 per unit. At its current rate of production the firm has marginal costs of only $60.00 per unit. That is, if it produced one additional unit it would incur $60.00 in additional costs. The production of the additional unit will generate profits of $40.00. A profit-maximizing firm will increase production by one additional unit. However, suppose that the firm's marginal cost at its current rate of output is $120.00. If it produced one fewer unit it would spend $120.00 less. In that case the production of the last unit is generating $20.00 in losses: the firm could make $20.00 more by producing one unit less.

8. The AC and AVC curves converge because AC is equal to the vertical sum of AVC and AFC; as output increases AFC continually decreases, approaching zero.

9. Or, $MC = AC_j - AC_i$, where the difference between output i and output j at any level is one unit. In the short run, it is also true that $MC = AVC_j - AVC_i$; that is, short-run marginal cost is a function of variable costs alone.

10. For example, suppose that AVC for 100 units is 3, and at that point marginal cost is 6. When unit 101 is produced, marginal cost is 6, but AVC would rise only to 306/101, or 3.029.

Look back at Figure 3 to see the relationship between the competitive firm's marginal cost curve and the demand curve that it faces. The firm will always try to produce at a rate of output at which its marginal cost equals the market price. If it is producing more than that, it can increase profits by decreasing production. If it is producing less it can increase profits by increasing production. The competitive rate of output in Figure 3 is Q_c.

Two observations are important. First, although economists sometimes say that a firm's efficiency is a function of its marginal costs, all competitive firms have the same marginal cost at current output levels. If the current market price of widgets is $100.00, and the market is perfectly competitive, all firms at their current output rate will have marginal costs of $100.00. (If marginal costs never drop to $100.00, then the firm is so inefficient that it will not produce at all.) The efficiency differences show up, not in the marginal costs, but in the rate of output. That is, a more efficient firm will produce more units of output than a less efficient firm produces at the same marginal cost level.

Second, not every firm in a competitive market is necessarily profitable. The fact that every firm has a point on its marginal cost curve which is lower than $100.00 does not tell us anything about the firm's profitability when the market price is $100.00. In order for the firm to be profitable, that point on the marginal cost curve must be at or above the firm's average (total) cost curve. Even if the firm is losing money, however, if it produces at all it will produce at the rate at which price equals marginal cost. In that case that rate of output will be the "loss-minimizing" rather than the "profit-maximizing" rate of output.

Although the market price might be less than a firm's average total cost at any output level, the firm will not necessarily cease production. The fixed costs may have been "sunk"—that is, the firm may not be able to recover them if it goes out of business. Further, the fixed costs must be paid whether or not the plant produces. As a general rule, the firm will be able to cut its losses as long as the market price is above its average variable costs, and it will continue to produce. However, when the plant wears out and needs to be replaced, the firm may then decide to go out of business, or else to build a more efficient plant.

Perfectly competitive markets are generally thought to be "efficient" because they do the best job of providing consumers with goods at the cost of producing them. As a result, competition maximizes the total value of goods produced in society. In a competitive market no single firm has the power to reduce the available supply of goods, and no firm has the power to increase the price above the market level.

The world contains no perfectly competitive markets, and many markets do not even come close. Firms often differentiate their products from other firms; as a result, customers are no longer indifferent to the identity of the seller. Information about market conditions is always less than perfect; as a result many transactions take place at some price other than the market price, and some socially valuable transactions never occur at all.[11] "Economies of scale"—the ability of larger firms to produce at a lower cost than smaller firms—may result in markets that have fewer than the number of sellers required for perfect competition to occur.[12] In short, like all scientific models, the model of perfect competition applies only imperfectly in the real world; nevertheless it can be of great service to the antitrust policy maker in predicting the consequences of a certain action or legal rule.

§ 1.2 Monopoly

1.2a. Price and Output of the Protected Monopolist

The monopolist—the only firm selling in a particular market—faces a different array of

11. In general, the more expensive it is for consumers to search out relevant information about prices and markets, the more likely they will make a less than optimal transaction. As a result, prices tend to vary more in markets where search costs are high in relation to the value of the product. See G. Stigler, The Economics of Information, 69 J. Pol. Econ. 213 (1961); G. Stigler, The Theory of Price 2–6 (3d ed. 1966).

12. See § 1.4a.

price and output decisions than those that confront the perfect competitor. For this formal analysis we assume that the market contains only one firm, whose demand curve is therefore identical with the market demand curve. Second, the formal monopolist does not need to worry about new entry by a competitor. These assumptions often will not apply to the *de facto* "monopolist" that exists in most antitrust litigation. The antitrust "monopolist" is a dominant firm, but the market may contain a competitive "fringe" of smaller competitors.[1] Second, the antitrust monopolist ordinarily has no legal protection from competitive entry. If either formal assumption is relaxed the monopolist will face a certain amount of "competition" and will vary its behavior accordingly.[2] Assuming, however, that the monopolist has a 100% share of a market and no concern about entry by a competitor, how much will it sell and what price will it charge?

The monopolist has one power that the perfect competitor does not have. If the monopolist reduces output, total market output will decline, for the monopolist is the only producer in the market. As total market output goes down, the market-clearing price goes up. As a result, the monopolist, unlike the competitor, can obtain a higher price per unit of output by producing less.

However, the monopolist will not be able to charge an infinite price for its product. Even the orthodontists may be unwilling to pay more than $3000 per pound for steel; if the price goes higher they will change to silver or some other alternative.

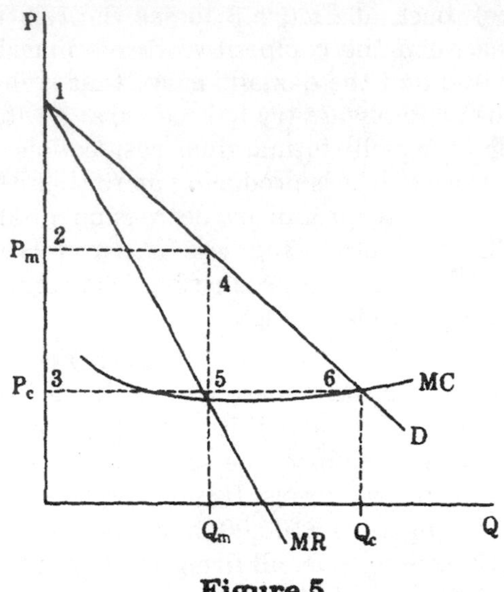

Figure 5

Figure 5 introduces the marginal revenue curve (MR), which represents the additional revenue that the monopolist obtains when it produces one additional unit of output. As Figure 5 shows, the marginal revenue curve facing the monopolist is steeper than the demand curve.[3] This is because the monopolist must sell all units of output at the same price. Thus the marginal revenue curve shows not only that increases in market output reduce the market clearing price (which is what the demand curve shows), but also that less revenue is obtained from sales of all units, not just the incremental unit. This is easy to see in Table B. At output of one unit, the price is $20 and the seller's marginal revenue—the difference between the amount it obtains from one unit and the amount it obtains from zero units—is also $20. When output increases to 2 units, price drops to $18. However, the monopolist must sell both the first and the second units for $18.00. While the price drops by $2.00, marginal revenue drops by $4.00—$2.00 for each of the two units. This process continues and yields the MR curve in Figure 5.[4]

§ 1.2

1. Economists generally speak of such firms not as "monopolists," but rather as "dominant firms."

2. For example, it may charge a lower, or "limit" price, calculated to make entry by outsiders less attractive. See § 8.3b.

3. If the demand curve is linear, the marginal revenue curve is also linear and exactly twice as steep as the demand curve. For a simple proof, see F. M. Scherer & D. Ross, Industrial Market Structure and Economic Performance 21 & n. 13 (3d ed. 1990).

4. Marginal revenue can also be expressed as:

$MR = \delta R/\delta Q$,

where δR equals the change in total revenue and δQ equals the corresponding change in quantity. As a result, marginal revenue can also be written as $MR = P + Q(\delta P/\delta Q)$, where P equals the price paid by the marginal consumer, and $\delta P/\delta Q$ equals the change in price necessary

The profit-maximizing monopolist, just as the profit-maximizing competitor, will expand production to the point that one additional unit will produce greater additional costs than additional revenues. It will produce at point Q_m on the graph in Figure 5 and charge price P_m. If the monopolist expands output beyond Q_m the additional revenue, shown by the MR curve, will be less than the additional costs, shown by the marginal cost curve (MC). P_m is known as the "monopoly price," or as the monopolist's "profit-maximizing price."

Output	Price	Total Revenue	Marginal Revenue
1	$20	$20	$20
2	$18	$36	$16
3	$16	$48	$12
4	$14	$56	$8
5	$12	$60	$4
6	$10	$60	0
7	$8	$56	$−4
8	$6	$48	$−8

TABLE B

Both the perfect competitor and the monopolist maximize profits by equating marginal revenue and marginal cost. For the competitor, the marginal revenue curve is identical with the demand curve, and therefore with the market price.[5] For the monopolist, by contrast, the marginal revenue curve and marginal cost curve intersect to the left of the marginal cost curve's intersection with the demand curve. The monopolist produces at a lower rate than would a perfect competitor in the same market, and its profit-maximizing price is higher.

The difference between the monopolist's profit-maximizing price, P_m, and the competitor's profit-maximizing price, P_c tells us something about the degree of power that the monopolist has. If P_c is $1.00, a monopolist whose profit-maximizing price is $1.50 has more monopoly power than one whose profit-maximizing price is $1.02. The Lerner Index, discussed in § 3.1a, expresses market power in this way through the use of a simply derived formula relating the firm's marginal cost to its profit-maximizing price.

A monopolist's market power is a function of the elasticity of demand for its product. If the elasticity of demand for pistachios at the competitive price is high, consumers will be sensitive to changes in the price. If the price goes too high many will buy a substitute, such as almonds or cashews. In that case, the "spread" between the competitive price and the monopolist's profit-maximizing price will be relatively small. However, if the elasticity of demand is low, then consumers view the product as having few good substitutes. The monopolist will be able to extract a much higher price without losing too many sales.

Market power can also be computed directly from a firm's price elasticity of demand. The formulas are also discussed in § 3.1. The formulas offer several insights about the relevant variables in market power measurement. In general, however, the formal analysis of market power is of little use to a court because the elasticity of demand a firm faces cannot be computed in litigation.

1.2b. Monopsony; Output Effects; Policy Implications

The mirror image of monopoly is "monopsony." A monopsonist is a monopoly buyer

to attract the marginal consumer. For example, assume that at a price of 11, 20 units are sold; at a price of 10, 21 units are sold. In that case marginal revenue per unit, going from a price of 11 to a price of 10 equals:

$$10 + 20(-1/1) = -10$$

That is to say, marginal revenue equals the price paid by the new, or marginal consumer (10), plus the change in revenue that accrues as a result of the price change to the 20 existing consumers. In this case, the twenty existing customers pay $1 less apiece.

This equation enables us to relate a firm's market power to the elasticity of demand facing it. See the discussion of technical measurement of market power in § 3.1a.

5. This is so because the competitive price remains constant at all rates of output. For example, if price is $20, each additional sale at any output level the competitive firm chooses will generate an additional $20, and marginal revenue will remain constant at $20.

rather than seller. Although most antitrust litigation of market power offenses has involved monopoly sellers rather than buyers, monopsony can impose social costs on society similar to those caused by monopoly.[6]

By reducing its demand for a product, a monopsonist can force suppliers to sell to it at a lower price than would prevail in a competitive market. Some people are skeptical about this conclusion. No supplier would stay in business if it were forced to sell to the monopsonist at a price lower than its average costs, and price would tend toward average cost in a competitive market. Can a monopsonist actually force suppliers to engage in continuous loss selling?

The answer is no, of course. However, not all suppliers have the same costs, and many suppliers will have lower average costs if they reduce their output. When the price in a competitive market is $1.00, then the average costs of the least efficient, or "marginal," supplier are near $1.00. However, there may be other sellers who have lower costs. If the monopsonist announces that it will pay only 90¢ in the future, then the marginal sellers in the market—those with costs in the 90¢ to $1.00 range—will drop out, at least if the 90¢ price persists and they are unable to reduce their costs. Likewise, when prices are at the competitive level most firms have a rising marginal cost curve. If the price is suppressed they will reduce output to a level that once again equals their marginal costs. In any event, both price and output will fall below the competitive level when the buyer is a monopsonist. Some productive assets will be assigned to products that would have been the supplier's second choice in a competitive market. As a result, monopsony allocates resources inefficiently just as monopoly does.[7]

The important policy implication of monopsony is that it *reduces* rather than increases output in the monopsonized market. Many federal judges have failed to see this. The consumer welfare principle in antitrust, or the notion that the central goal of antitrust policy should be low prices,[8] has often suggested to courts that monopsony is not all that important an antitrust policy concern. For example, in *Balmoral* the court faced an agreement among theater operators not to bid against each other for motion pictures.[9] As a result, the prices they paid for the pictures were lower than if they had bid competitively. The court suggested that such an agreement could result in lower prices to consumers and concluded that the agreement might "serve rather than undermine consumer welfare."[10] Likewise, in the *Kartell* case,[11] the First Circuit refused to condemn as monopolistic a health insurer's policy of setting the maximum price it was willing to pay for health care services used by its insureds. The court noted that "the prices at issue here are low prices, not high prices * * *. [T]he Congress that enacted the Sherman Act saw it as a way of protecting consumers against prices that were too *high*,

6. For a thorough, readable study of the law and economics of monopsony, see R. Blair & J. Harrison, Monopsony: Antitrust Law & Economics (1993). On the law of buying cartels, see 12 Antitrust Law ¶¶ 2010–2015 (1999).

7. There is some ambiguous legislative history suggesting that Senator Sherman did not intend his proposed statute to apply to monopsony or buyers' cartels.

> Senator George (D.Miss.): Upon the formation of [the] bagging trust the cotton farmers * * * agreed that they would not purchase jute bagging, and by that agreement * * * the rich rewards anticipated by the * * * trust were defeated. The fact that the bill * * * applied to all arrangements * * * by whomsoever made, would bring within its reach all defensive agreements made by farmers for the purpose of enhancing the price of their products * * *.

* * *

> Senator Sherman: That is a very extraordinary proposition. There is nothing in the bill to prevent a refusal by anybody to buy something. All that it says is that the people producing or selling a particular article shall not make combinations to advance the price of the necessaries of life.

20 Cong.Rec. 1458 (1889).

8. See §§ 2.2–2.3.

9. Balmoral Cinema v. Allied Artists Pictures Corp., 885 F.2d 313 (6th Cir.1989).

10. Id. at 317. The court approved the lower court's instruction to the jury to apply the rule of reason, and its subsequent judgment for the defendants.

11. Kartell v. Blue Shield (Mass.), 749 F.2d 922 (1st Cir.1984), cert. denied, 471 U.S. 1029, 105 S.Ct. 2040 (1985).

not too low."[12]

These decisions suggest that monopsony buyers will generally pass their lower costs on to their consumers. But that is not necessarily the case. The monopsonist reduces its buying price by *reducing* the amount of some input that it purchases. If the input is used in the output in fixed proportions, then the output must be reduced is well. This suggests two things: (1) the monopsony buyer that resells in a competitive market will charge the same price, but its output will be lower than if it were a competitive purchaser; (2) the monopsony buyer (or cartel) that resells in a monopolized (or cartelized) market will actually charge a *higher* price than if it were a competitive purchaser.

Consider this illustration. A monopoly manufacturer of aluminum is also a monopsony purchaser of bauxite. Bauxite is an ingredient in aluminum, and one ton of bauxite, when mixed with other ingredients, yields two tons of aluminum. In a competitive market bauxite sells for $25 per ton and the producer would purchase 1000 tons, which it would then use to make 2000 tons of aluminum. The aluminum would be sold at the monopoly price of $80 per ton. In the monopsonized bauxite market, however, the monopsonist/monopolist reduces its purchases of bauxite to 700 tons, which it purchases at $20 per ton. If it uses bauxite and other ingredients in fixed proportions of one ton of bauxite to two tons of aluminum, then it must also reduce the output of aluminum to 1400 tons. In that case, the market clearing price of the aluminum will rise to, say, $105.00. In sum, even though the monopsonist/monopolist buys an input at a lower price, the lower output entails a higher, not a lower, resale price.[13] If the monopsonist/monopolist can change the proportion of bauxite in its aluminum the story becomes more complicated. But in general two things will be true. First, the price of aluminum will not go down and will almost always go up anyway. Second, consumers will not get the aluminum alloy that they would have gotten in a competitive market.[14]

12. Id. at 930–931.

13. Although the monopsonist purchases at a lower absolute price, it has a higher effective marginal cost (actually, marginal outlay) than the buyer in a competitive market. Each incremental unit that the monopsonist purchases, assuming it cannot price discriminate in its buying, entails a higher price for all previously purchased units as well. For example, assume that if the monopsonist purchases 100 units the price is 25¢, but if it purchases 101 units the price rises to 26¢. The marginal outlay for the move from 100 units to 101 units is 100 × 1¢ + 26¢, or a total of $1.26. By contrast, the marginal cost of unit 101 is only 26¢. "Marginal outlay" refers to the total additional cost that the monopsonist incurs when it purchases one more unit. By contrast, "marginal cost" refers to the cost of the one additionally purchased unit. While the monopolist generally maximizes profits by equating marginal cost and marginal revenue, the monopolist that is also a monopsonist in an input market maximizes profits by equating marginal outlay and marginal revenue.

Figure 6 illustrates. It shows the relevant demand (D), marginal revenue (MR), marginal cost (MC) and marginal outlay (MO) curves of a firm that purchases a single input in a monopsonized market and resells this input in a monopolized market. Considering the firm simply as a monopolist in the output market, it would equate MC and MR. The monopoly price would be P_m and monopoly output would be Q_m. However, if the monopolist is also a monopsonist in the market for the input and its marginal cost curve slopes upward, then its marginal outlay curve will slope upward as well, only twice as steeply. That is, the relation between marginal cost and marginal outlay is exactly the same as the relation between demand and marginal revenue, except turned upside down. The monopolist/monopsonist maximizes its profits by equating MO and MR. This yields a monopoly/monopsony price of P_{mm}, and an output of Q_{mm}.

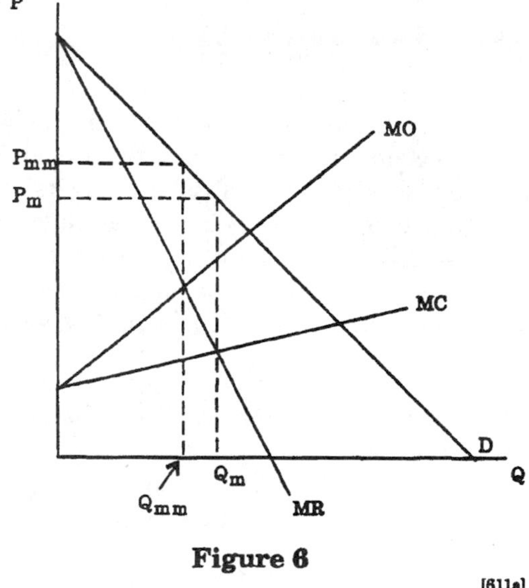

Figure 6

[611a]

14. For a more technical explanation, see R. Blair & J. Harrison, Antitrust Policy and Monopsony, 76 Cornell L. Rev. 297, 299–300 (1991).

The foregoing suggests two things. First, monopsony is an important antitrust concern and is just as inconsistent with consumer welfare as monopoly is. Indeed, one should *never* presume that the lower prices paid by a monopsonist are passed on to consumers as lower resale prices. Second, however, the antitrust policy maker must distinguish between lower buying prices that result from reduced transaction costs or the elimination of upstream market power, and lower buying prices that result from monopsony. If a large buyer is able to obtain lower prices by reducing transaction costs, the buyer will generally buy *more* rather than less.[15] The result will be lower resale prices, even if the large buyer resells in a monopolized market. Further, as § 9.2 illustrates, the firm that purchases at a lower price by eliminating an upstream monopolist or cartel virtually always charges a lower price on resale. Once again, this is true for both the competitor and the monopolist in the resale market.

A principal difficulty of antitrust policy toward monopsony is distinguishing between the efficient low purchase prices that result from reduced transaction costs or elimination of upstream monopoly, and the inefficient low purchase prices that result from monopsony. Perhaps the most problematic area is joint purchasing arrangements, which create a significant potential for cost savings but may also facilitate buyer price fixing.[16] In such a case the decision maker should try to determine whether the defendants' managers are encouraging members to purchase as much as possible, which is generally inconsistent with buyer price-fixing; or encouraging them to suppress their buying, which is highly suspicious.

1.2c. De Facto Monopolies in Real World Markets

The analysis of monopoly in this section was predicated on two assumptions—namely, that the monopolist had 100% of its market and that new entry was impossible. Such monopolies do exist in the real world, but most of them are price-regulated public utilities, such as electric companies. The rationale for the legal recognition of such "natural monopolies" is discussed below in § 1.4. Most antitrust policy concerning monopolies is directed at the *de facto* monopolist, which has no such legal protection. The *de facto* monopolist most generally does not have 100% of its relevant market, although the percentage may be close. Furthermore, the *de facto* monopolist must consider the possibility of entry by new firms.

Once these two assumptions of pure monopoly are relaxed, analyzing the monopolist's output and price decisions becomes more difficult. The *de facto* monopolist behaves strategically. In making a price or output decision it must either take the current output of competitors into account, or else it must try to anticipate responses by small competitors or potential competitors. It may also strategize a price or output decision designed to eliminate a competitor or potential competitor from the market. Much of antitrust law is concerned with the strategic decisions of the *de facto* monopolist trying to enlarge or protect its monopoly position.

The *de facto* monopolist may deter or delay competitive entry by setting a lower price than the one determined by the intersection of its marginal cost and marginal revenue curves. In general, the *de facto* monopolist has two choices. On the one hand, it can forget about new entry and earn as much as possible right now. In that case the monopolist will make maximum monopoly profits in the immediate future, but its monopoly position will be more quickly eroded by competitors and new entrants who are attracted by the high profits. On the other hand, the monopolist might set a

15. See, for example, Northwest Wholesale Stationers v. Pacific Stationery and Printing Co., 472 U.S. 284, 105 S.Ct. 2613 (1985), where the Supreme Court noted that joint buying is most generally efficient—a claim that the courts can test by assessing the venturers' market share of the market in which they buy. See also All Care Nursing Service, v. High Tech Staffing Services, 135 F.3d 740 (11th Cir.1998), cert. denied, ___ U.S. ___, 119 S.Ct. 1250 (1999), which approved a joint venture among hospitals to take bids from nursing service providers. The court cited the absence of any evidence of market power.

16. See § 4.1d. See also 13 *Antitrust Law* ¶ 2135 (1999).

lower "entry deterring" or "limit" price. Under limit pricing the monopolist will earn lower profits today, but its stream of profits will last longer, because new firms will not be as eager to enter the market. Which alternative the monopolist takes varies from case to case, and economists have different opinions about the circumstances under which each will occur.[17] Much of this debate is relevant to antitrust policy, and is discussed in chapters 6–8.

Whichever decision the firm makes, it will likely be attempting to maximize its profits. That is to say, a firm's monopoly profits are a function not only of their magnitude at any instant, but also of their duration. Thus we speak of a "short run" profit-maximizing price, determined by the intersection of marginal cost and marginal revenue, which maximizes the monopolist's profits in the immediate instant. But we can also speak of a "long run" profit-maximizing price that takes the duration of monopoly profits into account as well. The latter price will often be significantly lower than the former.

§ 1.3 Antitrust Policy and the Social Cost of Monopoly

1.3a. Monopoly as a Status; Monopolization as a Process

A *social cost* is a net loss that society suffers as a result of a particular transaction. A *social benefit* is a net gain. If A gives B $100, B is $100 richer and A is $100 poorer. Disregarding the costs of the transaction itself, such "transfer payments" produce neither a social cost nor a social benefit. By contrast, if A produces for $100 a widget that B values at $150, society may become $50 richer. B might pay $150 for the widget. In that case B will be neither better nor worse off, for he valued the widget by just what he paid for it. But A will be $50 richer, for his costs were only $100. Alternatively, if A sells the widget at $100, A will be neither better nor worse off, but B will be $50 better off.

If A holds out for a price of $150 and B is willing to pay only $140, however, the transaction will not occur. In that case no one will be better off. B may then enter into a transaction with C and purchase a substitute that B values at perhaps $130, and which costs C, say, $110. The price will be between $110 and $130. Even if that alternative transaction occurs, however, society will be only $20 better off. The substitute transaction is less favorable to both B and society as a whole than B's preferred transaction would have been.

Social costs can also result when transactions injure someone who was not a party to the transaction. For example, the builder of a factory may not bother to negotiate with neighbors for the right to pollute their air, particularly if he thinks the neighbors have no legal right to protect their air from pollution. However, the neighbors are worse off. The common law of nuisance and the National Environmental Policy Act are both attempts to force the factory to "internalize" and pay at least a part of this cost.[1]

For antitrust purposes, the *social cost* of monopoly is equal to the loss produced by monopoly pricing and monopoly behavior, minus any social gains that monopoly produces. *Monopolization*—or the antitrust offense of creating or maintaining a monopoly by means of anticompetitive exclusionary practices—is a process rather than merely an outcome. We sometimes distinguish the two when we call

17. For example, if entry will occur in ten years at any price higher than marginal cost, the incumbent would be best off to charge its short-run profit-maximizing price. So a patent monopolist, for example, who knows entry will occur immediately after its patent expires would probably equate marginal cost and marginal revenue today. By contrast, a firm whose short run profit-maximizing price of $1.50 will encourage entry in one year, while a price of $1.40 will delay entry indefinitely, will likely charge the latter price. The less a firm knows about the rate at which others will enter, or the more volatile the market, the more likely that the firm will charge its short-run profit maximizing price. In such cases the value of entry-deterrent pricing must be discounted by the uncertainty of the profits it will produce over the future.

On limit pricing, see W. Kip Viscusi, John M. Vernon & Joseph E. Harrington, Jr., Economics of Regulation and Antitrust 166–179 (2d ed. 1995).

§ 1.3

1. See 42 U.S.C.A. §§ 4321–47; and see R. Coase, The Problem of Social Cost, 3 J.L. & Econ. 1 (1960); A.M. Polinsky, An Introduction to Law and Economics 11–26 (2d ed. 1989).

the outcome "monopoly," and the process by which it is created by a term such as "monopolization," or "rent seeking." For any antitrust policy concerned with minimizing the social cost of harmful activity, both the process and the outcome are properly counted as a part of the activity's social cost, and part of the reasons for prevention. This is generally true of the economic theory of criminal behavior. For example, the social cost of theft is not merely the money value of the stolen object—indeed, the theft itself is only a wealth transfer. The social cost must also include the collateral damage that the thief inflicts on society, as well as the costs of the elaborate mechanisms that we use to deter theft.[2]

To be sure, some of the processes that create monopoly are efficient. For example, monopoly can be created by research and development. So we must have rules that distinguish harmful from beneficial practices that create monopoly. But this problem of definition or characterization is quite different from the question whether losses caused by harmful exclusionary practices should be counted as part of monopoly's social costs.

The *policy* question of monopoly's social cost always trades off relative gains and losses. Every state of affairs includes some positive social costs. Even vigorous competition entails costs that monopoly might avoid, such as the costs of making and interpreting competitive bids, or the inefficient duplication of productive assets or processes. One can always imagine a system with lower social costs than the present situation. So when we ask whether something is a social cost, we must always consider "relative to what?"

The earliest measures of the social cost of monopoly in the American economy took a kind of "public utility" approach to monopoly. The authors dealt with monopoly as if it were a given equilibrium condition, giving no consideration to the method by which the monopoly was created or preserved, or the mechanisms by which it might eventually be destroyed. In such a static situation, the only social cost of monopoly is the "deadweight" loss that it produces—a loss caused principally by the fact that consumers make inefficient substitutions in order to avoid paying monopoly prices.

But antitrust law is not frequently concerned with such equilibrium monopolies, for they are generally the product of legislation. Further, even those that result from legislation can impose social costs that the traditional deadweight loss triangle fails to capture. For example, if the owner of a shopping mall bribes a city council into refusing to rezone nearby property at the request of a potential competitor, the social cost of the monopoly will be (1) the deadweight loss caused by the incumbent's monopoly output restriction and price increase; (2) at least part of the expenses paid by the shopping mall owner in influencing the city council, and (3) the investment in planning a competing development that the potential entrant will now lose as a result of the incumbent's bribery.

Antitrust law's concern with this *process* of monopolization, rather than merely with the outcome, is quite apparent from the statutory scheme. The law of monopolization requires not only a monopoly position, but also the commission of one or more anticompetitive "exclusionary practices," thus signalling that the process by which monopoly is to be created determines its legality.[3] We condemn collusion, attempts and conspiracies to monopolize, tying arrangements, exclusive dealing, mergers and other practices only because we believe that these tend to facilitate the creation of monopoly. We may sometimes be wrong about our underlying facts or even about the economic theories we employ, but the basic premise remains the same: the principal target of the antitrust laws is not static monopoly as such, but rather the manifold mechanisms by which monopoly is created or preserved. Indeed, there is no law of "no fault" monopoly; the innocent monopolist does not violate the antitrust laws simply by charging its profit-max-

2. See G. Becker, Crime and Punishment: An Economic Approach, 76 J.Pol.Econ. 169 (1968).

3. See chs. 6–8.

imizing price.[4]

One possible explanation of antitrust's focus on process is that the real concern of the antitrust laws is the final outcome, but we need to deter, and deterrence is most effective if we hit things in the process of their creation. But the very fact that we fail to condemn the completed result *ipso facto* belies this claim. Antitrusters often say that their principal concern is monopoly, but that is not quite true. Their principal concern is monopoly created by certain means. Indeed the costs of the means by which monopoly is created and preserved may dwarf the costs of any misallocation caused by the monopoly pricing and output reduction themselves.

With these premises in mind, let us consider first the social cost of monopoly as economists have defined it, and then the expanded concerns of American antitrust policy with the social cost of monopoly's consequences and of the means by which monopoly is created and maintained.[5]

1.3b. The Deadweight Loss Caused by Monopoly

Monopoly forces some people to forego the transaction that was their first choice and would have produced the largest benefit. Rather, they take their second choice, which produces a smaller benefit.

Although monopoly imposes a social cost, society is not necessarily poorer because the monopolist exists. For example, society was clearly better off because Alcoa existed than if no aluminum producer existed at all, even if for many years Alcoa was a monopolist. Monopolist Alcoa produced a product that buyers valued more than the cost of producing it. Otherwise there would have been no market for aluminum. We talk about the "social cost" of the aluminum monopoly in order to underscore the fact that the production and sale of aluminum would have produced even greater social benefits had the market been competitive. The social cost of monopoly is the difference in social value between a monopolized market and a competitive market. It is not the difference in social value between a monopolized market and no market at all. For that reason the patent laws may be socially valuable, even though they create monopolies.[6]

In Figure 7, on page 20, P_c and Q_c show price and output in a competitive market. P_m shows the price for the same product in a market dominated by a monopolist, and Q_m shows the monopoly rate of output. Rectangle 2–3–5–4 represents a wealth transfer to the monopolist (the monopolist's output multiplied by the difference between the monopoly and competitive prices). Triangle 1–2–4 at the top of the diagram represents consumers' surplus, which is substantially less than it would be in a competitive market, where it would be triangle 1–3–6.

4. See 3 Antitrust Law ¶ ¶ 630–650 (rev. ed. 1996); and see § 6.3.

5. See H. Hovenkamp, Antitrust's Protected Classes, 88 Mich.L.Rev. 1 (1989).

6. See L. Kaplow, The Patent–Antitrust Intersection: A Reappraisal, 97 Harv.L.Rev. 1813 (1984).

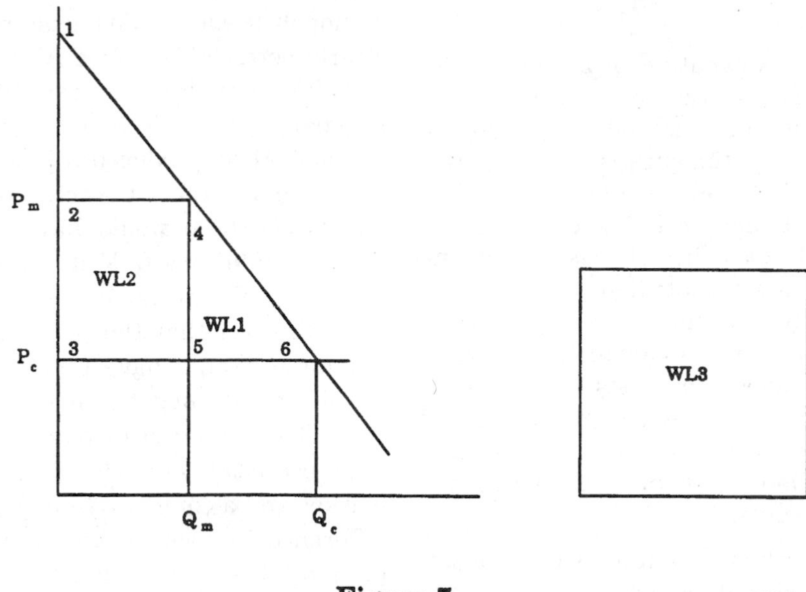

Figure 7 [620a]

Finally, triangle 4–5–6 represents the "deadweight loss" of monopoly. Consumers located along the demand curve between points 4 and 6 are not willing to purchase the monopolized product at the monopoly price, even though they are willing to buy it at the competitive price. Instead, they substitute to something that would have been their second choice in a competitive market. This inefficient substitution is traditionally spoken of as the social cost of monopoly. It is labeled "WL1," or welfare loss 1, in the Figure, for it is the oldest and most universally recognized of monopoly's social costs.[7]

Importantly, the traditional deadweight loss of monopoly does not derive from the fact that consumers pay higher prices. Within the pure monopoly model that loss to consumers is offset by an equal gain to the monopolist and from an efficiency standpoint is a "neutral" transfer of wealth. The deadweight loss arises because the monopoly encourages some customers to engage in an alternative transaction that produces less social value than would their first choice. A monopoly in the brick market may force a builder to switch to aluminum siding, even though he preferred bricks and was willing to pay the competitive price for them.

1.3c. The Social Cost of Monopoly: Rent–Seeking

At one time economists regarded triangle 4–5–6 as the only social cost of monopoly. But triangle 4–5–6 may understate the social cost of monopoly in real world markets. The discussion of monopoly in the previous section assumed that the monopolist was unconcerned about competitive entry. When that assumption is removed, as it is for *de facto* monopolists, then the social costs of monopoly are likely to loom larger.[8]

The *de facto* monopolist—the firm that does not have legal protection from new entry—must continually exclude competitors, who would increase output and drive prices down to the competitive level. In fact, the more profitable the monopoly, the more that potential entrants will be willing to spend in

7. A large literature on the size of the deadweight loss triangle of an individual monopolist and on the total deadweight loss caused by monopoly in the American economy is summarized in F. Scherer & D. Ross, Industrial Market Structure and Economic Performance 661–665 (3d ed. 1990).

8. See R. Posner, The Social Costs of Monopoly and Regulation, 83 J.Pol.Econ. 807 (1975). Other literature is summarized in Hovenkamp, Antitrust's Protected Classes, note 5.

order to enter the market, and the more the monopolist will spend to keep them out. Part or perhaps even all of rectangle 2–3–5–4 in Figure 7, which we characterized as a "wealth transfer," may not be a wealth transfer at all because the monopolist uses it up in entrenching its monopoly. At the outer limit the monopolist would spend *all* its expected monopoly profits in protecting its position, and would end up with no more than a competitive rate of return. This rectangle is labeled "WL2" in Figure 7.

With a linear demand curve and constant marginal costs, the area of the WL2 rectangle is precisely double the area of WL1.[9] But this hardly suggests that WL2 losses are always twice as large as WL1 losses. First, if the marginal cost curve is not horizontal (usually, it is rising through this range) and if the demand curve is nonlinear, then WL2 could be either less than or greater than WL1. Second, a monopolist does not necessarily spend all of WL2 in inefficient exclusionary practices. Presumably, at least part is paid to the owners as monopoly profits; another part is paid in efficient, rather than inefficient, attempts to secure or perpetuate the monopoly. In order to quantify the true social cost of monopoly, we must know something about how the monopolist spends these resources. So WL2 is best characterized as the outer limit of welfare losses of this type.

As the previous section observed, one way the monopolist might deter competition is by charging a price lower than its short-run profit-maximizing price. Although full analysis of such entry-deterring pricing is complex,[10] the short-run consequence is to make both the "wealth transfer" rectangle and the "deadweight loss" triangle smaller than they would be under short-run profit-maximizing pricing. Whether such entry-deterring pricing reduces the social cost of monopoly in the long run, however, depends on the effect of the pricing on the duration of the monopoly. A large deadweight loss that lasts for one year may still be less costly than a relatively small deadweight loss that lasts for ten.

A firm might also deter new entry by spending part of its monopoly profits in research and development (R & D), thus keeping ahead of its industry and making it more difficult for competitors to keep up. Throughout the 1970's, for example, IBM Corp. probably retained a dominant position in the computer market by being an aggressive innovator.[11] R & D may reduce the net deadweight loss of monopoly if society values the product of the R & D by an amount that exceeds its costs plus the increased social costs of any additional monopoly power that the R & D creates. Nevertheless, one effect of R & D will be to make new entry by competitors more difficult.

The relationship between R & D expenditures and monopoly is controversial, and has produced a number of conflicting theories. At one end is Joseph Schumpeter's argument that since research is both expensive and risky, firms in competition will not be able to afford it. A large amount of money spent without an assured return may be enough to deter a competitive firm from innovating.[12] A common rebuttal to this argument is that all new investment entails risk. Some research investments are rational and others are not. The consequences for a competitive firm of falling behind other competitors are just as serious as the consequences of spending R & D money unprofitably. Furthermore, competitors research in order to *acquire* market power. If they can somehow distinguish their product and make it more attractive than the product offered by others, the difference may show up as monopoly profits.

The monopolist unconcerned about competitive entry may not innovate very much. For

9. This is true because when the demand curve is linear, the marginal revenue curve is linear and twice as steep as the demand curve. If MC is also linear, this generates a "deadweight loss" triangle and a "wealth transfer" rectangle that have precisely the same base and height, but the area of a right triangle is one-half of base times height.

10. See § 8.3b.

11. But see L. Sullivan, Monopolization: Corporate Strategy, the IBM Cases, and the Transformation of the Law, 60 Tex.L.Rev. 587 (1982).

12. See J. Schumpeter, Capitalism, Socialism, and Democracy 106 (3d ed. 1950).

example, a monopoly public utility may have little incentive to innovate, particularly if cost-saving technology will reduce the base from which its rate of return is calculated.[13] By contrast, a monopolist threatened by competitive entry may spend a great deal on entry-deterring innovation. It has been argued that the monopolist may even engage in inefficient "predatory" innovation—that is, innovation reasonably calculated to preserve the monopolist's dominance, and whose monopoly efficiency losses will exceed any efficiency gains that result from the innovation itself.[14] Whether or not this theory has any economic merit, it has been popular among antitrust plaintiffs. Many monopolization cases in the late 1970's and early 1980's involved allegations that the defendant injured the plaintiff or drove it out of business by predatory product innovation.[15] The claim is still recognized today, although less frequently.[16]

Arguments have also been made that large firms can engage in research more cheaply than small firms because the larger firm can distribute the costs of R & D over a larger volume of production.[17] Likewise, a firm that operates in many markets might profit more from research and development than a single market firm because often research yields unanticipated or tangential benefits in markets other than the one for which it was undertaken. Neither of these arguments, it should be noted, depends on the firm's market power, but only on its large absolute size or on its operation in many markets. Furthermore, both arguments tend to be undermined by the fact that literally thousands of small firms engage daily and profitably in relatively sophisticated types of research and development. The computer revolution of the late 1970's and early 1980's, for example, involved the research activity of many tiny firms. Finally, there is a healthy market for the products of innovation. A small firm that is unable to take advantage of the consequences of innovation in an adjacent market will probably be able to license the innovation to someone else who can.

The ambiguous relationship between monopoly and innovation has been apparent in the case law since soon after the Sherman Act was passed. In the *American Can* case,[18] the court faced the defense that a monopoly created by merger should be preserved because the monopolist could afford research and development activities that had not occurred before the monopoly came into existence. The judge was "reluctant to destroy so finely adjusted an industrial machine * * *." Thirty years later Judge Learned Hand wrote that monopoly was bad because it "deadens initiative * * * and depresses energy," and because "immunity from competition is a narcotic, and rivalry is a stimulant, to industrial progress." In the very same opinion, however, Judge Hand found that Alcoa had illegally monopolized the market because it aggressively "embrace[d] each new opportunity as it opened" and faced "every newcomer with new capacity already geared into a great organization, having the advantage of experience, trade connections and the elite of personnel."[19]

Before criticizing judges for being unclear about the relationship between monopolization and innovation, however, one should note that economists have not done much better. Even

13. In general, the utility will not innovate if any cost reductions or increased revenues are immediately passed on to customers. In most cases, however, the utility will be able to keep the increased profits, at least for a time, and this will give it some incentive to innovate.

14. See J. Ordover & R. Willig, An Economic Definition of Predation: Pricing and Product Innovation, 91 Yale L.J. 8 (1981).

15. For example, Berkey Photo, Inc. v. Eastman Kodak Co., 603 F.2d 263 (2d Cir.1979), cert. denied, 444 U.S. 1093, 100 S.Ct. 1061 (1980); California Computer Prod., Inc. v. IBM Corp., 613 F.2d 727 (9th Cir.1979). Both plaintiffs lost on the innovation issue. Claims of anticompetitive product innovation are discussed in § 7.8a.

16. See, e.g., C.R. Bard, Inc. v. M3 Sys., Inc., 157 F.3d 1340 (Fed.Cir.1998), in which a divided panel condemned a patent monopolist's reconfiguration of its tissue sampling machine so that it was compatible only with the defendant's disposable needles rather than those of others.

17. See J.K. Galbraith, American Capitalism 86 (Rev. Ed.1956).

18. United States v. American Can Co., 230 Fed. 859, 903 (D.Md.1916), appeal dismissed, 256 U.S. 706, 41 S.Ct. 624 (1921). See 11 Antitrust Law ¶ 1801a (1998).

19. United States v. Aluminum Co. of America (Alcoa), 148 F.2d 416, 427 (2d Cir.1945).

today there is widespread disagreement about whether monopoly encourages or discourages research and development and, if monopoly encourages development, whether that fact increases or decreases the social costs of monopoly.[20] No easy generalizations have been forthcoming.

The monopolist threatened with new entry may also spend part of its monopoly returns in less ambiguous entry-deterring practices which increase the social costs of monopoly. Properly defined predatory pricing,[21] sabotage, espionage, vexatious litigation,[22] false and misleading advertising can all have the effect of prolonging the period during which a *de facto* monopoly exists and thereby increase the social cost of the monopoly.

Monopoly may also yield certain inefficiencies that are not planned but which appear to accompany the absence of competition in a market. For one thing, the monopolist is a "price maker" rather than a "price taker." The monopolist, unlike the competitor, must calculate its profit-maximizing price by predicting how the market will respond to a price increase of a certain size. If the monopolist predicts incorrectly and sets its price too high, the deadweight loss triangle will become larger and increase the social cost of the monopoly.

Finally, some economists have attempted to evaluate and quantify Learned Hand's dictum in the *Alcoa* case that monopoly "deadens initiative" and results in less efficient use of resources than would prevail in competitive markets. Monopolists may not have the same incentives to reduce costs; their managers may not operate under the same "crisis" conditions that affect competitors; they may become comfortable. Such phenomena undoubtedly exist in many firms. The extent to which they are more prevalent among monopolists than among competitors is difficult to quantify.[23]

1.3d. The Social Cost of Monopoly: Lost Competitor Investment

Figure 7 above also describes a third kind of welfare loss, denominated WL3. The WL3 rectangle is drawn away from the demand curve because it is an "externality"—something that shows up in neither the formation of the demand curve nor in the firm's calculation of its costs and profits. WL3's definition, existence or size is not clearly related to any of the cost or revenue functions that explain a firm's behavior.

Exclusionary practices, or rent-seeking, by the monopolist generally impose costs on the monopolist itself. The costs can be diagrammed, for their outer limit is determined by the wealth transfer, which is itself a function of the demand curve and the monopolist's marginal cost curve. A firm will not spend more in acquiring or maintaining a monopoly than the expected value of the monopoly. Thus the outer boundaries of monopoly rent-seeking are determined by the potential wealth transfer (WL2).

But monopoly rent-seeking also imposes inefficient losses on competitors or perhaps others, and these losses are potentially unlimited. They can certainly be larger than either the traditional deadweight loss (WL1) or the loss that results from rent-seeking (WL2). To take an extreme example, suppose that the world market contains two manufacturers of aircraft, each of which has a single plant. The CEO of one of the firms creates a monopoly by visiting the other firm's plant one night with a can of gasoline and a match, and burning it down. In this case WL1 is indeterminate, WL2 is the cost of the match, the gasoline, the opportunity cost of the CEO's time, and the risk and expected consequences of getting caught. At the very least, WL3 is the cost of the victim's destroyed plant, inventory and perhaps good-

20. One study finding that firms become less efficient internally as the industries in which they operate become more oligopolistic is R. Caves & D. Barton, Efficiency in U.S. Manufacturing Industries (1990).

21. See ch. 8.

22. See ch. 18.

23. See H. Leibenstein, Allocative Efficiency vs. "X–Efficiency," 56 Amer.Econ.Rev. 392 (1966); L. De Alessi, Property Rights, Transaction Costs, and X–Efficiency: An Essay in Economic Theory, 73 Amer.Econ.Rev. 64 (1983). A good survey of the literature relating to productive inefficiency and monopoly is J. Siegfried & E. Wheeler, Cost Efficiency and Monopoly Power: A Survey, 21 Q.Rev. Econ. & Bus. 25 (1981).

will, of retraining employees whose jobs have been lost, and of reliance interests lost by broken contracts.[24]

What is the size of WL3 losses in real world monopolization or cartel cases? Generalizing is difficult, but it could be substantial.[25] Consider, for example, the Supreme Court's *Allied Tube* decision.[26] The plaintiff, Indian Head, had developed a plastic electrical conduit that threatened substantial injury to the market for traditional steel conduit. Defendant Allied, a manufacturer of steel conduit, conspired with others to "pack" a meeting of a standard setting organization with the result that approval of the plastic conduit was successfully delayed for several years. Because government building codes generally incorporated the organization's standards and numerous private contractors followed them voluntarily, the effect was that the plaintiff's plastic conduit could not be used in most construction.

In *Indian Head*, WL1 is the deadweight loss caused by any monopoly perpetuated by Allied's conduct.[26] WL2 includes the costs of packing the meeting and campaigning for disapproval of the plastic conduit, and the risk of a lawsuit and its costs. WL3 is the lost investment that accrued to Indian Head in research and development of a product that now has no market, or whose introduction into the market has been delayed. If Allied had succeeded in delaying plastic conduit indefinitely, Indian Head's entire investment in researching and developing a socially valuable product would have been lost.

Actually, the *Indian Head* situation may be a little more complex. Presumably, the demand curve for steel conduit would shift to the left in response to the introduction of Indian Head's product, which is a substitute for steel conduit. This would make steel conduit less profitable. The result of the conspiracy was to delay this shift, and this would yield a deadweight loss analogous to that caused by monopolization of a market in which no technological change was occurring.

Most bona fide monopolization cases produce substantial WL3 losses. Often the amount of WL3 loss will be proportional to the plausibility of the basic offense. For example, monopolizing conduct is most likely to succeed in markets where assets are specialized, durable and costly, because new entry into such markets can most easily be deterred. These markets are said to be subject to high barriers to entry.[27] WL3 loss is also most likely to be larger in such markets, because there is more likely to be investment that cannot be recovered in the event of failure. One important exception to this is strategic entry deterrence, or exclusionary conduct directed at potential, rather than actual, competitors. Potential competitors may be deterred easily precisely because they have not yet made irreversible investments in a market. WL3 losses in such situations are accordingly smaller.[28]

The model of WL3 losses limits the reach of arguments that antitrust should do away with competitor lawsuits, or at least severely circumscribe their role.[29] To be sure, most mar-

24. For example, if a supplier has invested heavily in a contractual commitment to supply the victim firm with some input, that investment is now lost.

25. WL3 losses might also include practices that raise the marginal costs of rivals, thus causing deadweight losses in secondary markets. See I. Ayres, Rationalizing Antitrust Cluster Markets, 95 Yale L.J. 109, 117 n.42, Fig. 4 (1985); S. Salop & D. Scheffman, Raising Rivals' Costs, 73 Am. Econ. rev. 267 (1983).

26. Allied Tube & Conduit Corp. v. Indian Head, 486 U.S. 492, 108 S.Ct. 1931 (1988). A similar case is American Soc. of Mechanical Engineers v. Hydrolevel Corp., 456 U.S. 556, 102 S.Ct. 1935 (1982). For further discussion of *Indian Head*, see § 18.5; and see 13 Antitrust Law ¶¶ 2220, 2231 (1999).

27. See 2A Antitrust Law Ch. 4C (Rev. ed. 1995)

28. See S. Salop, Strategic Entry Deterrence, 69 Am. Econ. Rev. 335 (1979); O. Williamson, Predatory Pricing: A Strategic and Welfare Analysis, 87 Yale L.J. 284 (1977). For further analysis of WL3 and its implications for antitrust policy, see Hovenkamp, Antitrust's Protected Classes, note 5. For critiques, see W. Page, Optimal Antitrust Penalties and Competitors' Injury, 88 Mich.L.Rev. 2151 (1990); R. Markovits, Second Best Theory and the Standard Analysis of Monopoly–Rent–Seeking: A Generalizable Critique, a "Sociological" Account, and Some Illustrative Stories, 78 Iowa L.Rev. 327 (1993).

29. See E. Snyder & T. Kauper, Misuse of the Antitrust Laws: the Competitor Plaintiff, 90 Mich. L. Rev. 551 (1991). For a response, see R. Blair & W. Page, Controlling the Competitor Plaintiff in Antitrust Litigation, 91 Mich. L. Rev. 111 (1992).

ket injuries to competitors result from the increased efficiency of rivals—a theme to which this book often returns. Nevertheless, inefficient competitor injuries are real social costs and an important part of antitrust concern. Further, consumers are often not well positioned to redress these injuries, because they have inadequate information or face extremely difficult problems of organization or proof. (For example, the injured consumers in *Indian Head* are those that would have purchased plastic conduit but for Allied's antitrust violation.). By contrast, competitor injuries are often quite easy to quantify and known to competitors the instant they occur. This means that competitors may be in a better position to bring certain antitrust actions. They can sue earlier, when the social cost of inefficient monopoly is still rather small, and they may have a better knowledge base.[30]

The model of WL3 losses does suggest that the focus of the antitrust laws on lost profits in competitor suits is often misplaced. Lost profits are notoriously difficult to measure, especially when the plaintiff never had a chance to get into the market in the first place. Further, the real social burden of WL3 losses is lost *investment*—in the case of *Indian Head*, the resources spent in developing a product that cannot be marketed because of Allied's antitrust violation.

The question whether lost investments of this sort should form the basis of antitrust violations is controversial. First, because they do not show up in the "market," economists have been inclined not to calculate them as part of the social cost of monopoly. Second, natural free market forces, without the intervention of any anticompetitive practices, produce a great deal of lost investment. For example, much of the research and development engaged in by business firms fails to produce products that can be profitably produced.

But antitrust's concern is not with eliminating unproductive research and development, measured *ex post*. Rather, it is concerned with ensuring that, measured *ex ante*, the competitive incentives to R & D are maintained. For example, consider two firms racing to invent and patent a useable plastic conduit. First of all, a research joint venture might be a superior way to go about developing such a project, for it would entail one set of research expenditures rather than two. But our economy and the state of our legal policy is such that not every efficiency enhancing joint venture will be formed. As a result, two firms may be engaged in the highly inefficient activity of researching and developing the identical product. The winner gets a patent and twenty year monopoly, which will outlast the product's life; the loser gets nothing and its investment is lost. Presumably this loss is *not* a social cost of monopoly that the antitrust laws should take into account. Rather, it is a result of the kinds of inefficiencies that are an everyday occurrence in robustly competitive markets.

Suppose one of the firms wins the research race, not by doing better research, but rather by sabotaging the research of the rival, or perhaps by using ill-founded litigation strategically.[31] The differences between competitive behavior and noncompetitive behavior under such circumstances is that the competitive behavior (1) rewards the person who gets there first (and a product innovated today produces more social value than a product innovated tomorrow); and (2) the competitive behavior permits the *market* (or at least, the market as qualified by our patent laws) to determine whether there is room for both products or only one. By contrast, the anticompetitive behavior, such as sabotaging another's research, is calculated *ex ante* to yield the inferior solution. Normally, the person winning the patent race does not need to sabotage the person who is losing; it works the other way around. Considered *ex ante*, the monopoly created by the person who sabotages his competitor's research is not the kind of monopoly whose costs are offset by the increased incentive to research. Quite to the contrary. For policy reasons, then, we count this particular loss as a qualifying social cost that can raise antitrust's

30. See § 2.2c.

31. On the latter, see § 18.3b.

concern.[32]

One does not need to look at markets that are the subject of government intervention, such as the market for patents, in order to come up with analogous situations. Completely unregulated markets can produce a duplication of expenditures that might be regarded as a qualifying social cost when they are used for one purpose, but not when they are used for another. Consider the market for complex, high priced, and perhaps technically sophisticated structures. The developer who wishes to have such a structure may take competitive bids from intending builders. Looking *ex ante*, the cost of making a bid on a complicated project can be high—perhaps 2% or more of the product's final cost. Suppose that five bidders enter the contest, and the cost of making a bid is $100,000, but only one of the bidders can win. Further, the cost of making the bid is presumably sunk. A sunk cost is an investment that a firm will not be able to recover in the event of failure. In this case, the bid itself has no value to the loser. If all firms behave competitively, the process will yield a deadweight loss of $400,000 in bidding costs as compared with a process under which a single firm were asked to build the project and did so at the competitive price. The competitive bidding process is certainly wasteful of resources. Nonetheless, looking *ex ante* we can easily conclude that the bidding process is more efficient than any alternative mechanism for getting the project completed at a competitive price. We would not expect that the four losers would have a "damages action" against either the winning bidder or the developer.

Suppose, however, that four of the bidders had formed a cartel. When the fifth bidder refused to join in, the four undertook some exclusionary practice designed to make the fifth firm's bid unacceptable.[33] In this case the fifth firm would have an antitrust damages action.[34] Damages should be based on the fifth firm's lost investment—in this case, the $100,000 that the firm invested in a bid that it would have won, but for the cartel's exclusionary practice.

§ 1.4 Industrial Organization Theory and Economies of Scale

The field of economics known as industrial organization performs two important functions in antitrust analysis.[1] First, it can help us decide whether the perfect competition model is optimal for a particular market. Second, industrial organization can help us understand whether a particular firm's activities that affect market structure are efficient and should be encouraged, or inefficient and ought to be condemned. Indeed, the field of industrial organization developed in response to increasing policy concerns about the rise of "big business" in the late nineteenth century, and the resulting debate among lawyers concerning when antitrust condemnation is in order. Many of the basic doctrines of industrial organization theory were suggested first by lawyers in the context of litigation, and later adopted and formalized by economists.[2]

32. See H. Hovenkamp, Antitrust Policy and the Social Cost of Monopoly, 78 Iowa L. Rev. 371 (1993).

33. For example, the four might bribe a government official to refuse the fifth firm a license, or in the case of a public developer to reject the fifth firm's bid. They might also bring ill-founded litigation against the fifth firm, or bribe one or more of the fifth firm's employees to upset the bid; or they might agree with the fifth firm's suppliers to deny the fifth firm access to an essential input.

34. If the project were actually built at the higher bid price, the buyer of the project would also have a damage action for the monopoly overcharge.

§ 1.4

1. The classic text on industrial organization is E.A.G. Robinson's The Structure of Competitive Industry (rev. ed. 1958). A very useful and comprehensive contemporary text is F.M. Scherer & D. Ross, Industrial Market Structure and Economic Performance (3d ed. 1990). More technical accounts of the cutting edge of industrial organization theory are Handbook of Industrial Organization (R. Schmalensee & R. Willig, eds. 1989, 2 vols.); J. Tirole, The Theory of Industrial Organization (1988), which is particularly good on applications of game theory. A good beginners text is S. Martin, Industrial Economics: Economic Analysis and Public Policy (2d ed. 1994). A good economic introduction to the relationship between industrial organization and various regulatory and policy concerns is W. Kip Viscusi, John M. Vernon & Joseph E. Harrington, Jr., Economics of Regulation and Antitrust 166–179 (2d ed. 1995).

2. See H. Hovenkamp, Enterprise and American Law, 1836–1937 at chs. 22–25 (1991).

Many real world markets do not come very close to the classical model of perfect competition. In some markets this failure is an antitrust problem: the market would perform more efficiently if the firms behaved more competitively. In other markets, competition among large numbers of incumbents producing undifferentiated products is simply not the optimal structure.

1.4a. The General Case of Economies of Scale

The single largest factor tending to undermine perfect competition is economies of scale. The model of perfect competition is premised on the notion of a market containing many equally efficient firms, each indifferent to the output decisions of others. Within this model, firm size is not a factor in competitor decisions, because the model assumes constant returns to scale: production and distribution costs do not vary with size. A small firm can thus compete quite effectively with a large one. Suppose, however, that one firm develops a new process that enables it to produce the product at substantially lower cost. In order to take advantage of this new process, however, the firm must build a plant capable of serving one half of the existing market. Now incumbent firms can no longer be indifferent to the price and output decisions of the innovator.

Most economies of scale are not as dramatic as the illustration suggests. However, economies of scale obtain in most industries, and they range from the trivial to the very substantial. Technically, an economy of scale exists whenever the costs per unit of some input decrease as volume increases.[3] The following examples illustrate the manifold presence of scale economies in a wide variety of industries.

1) To drive a truck from point A to point B costs $100, whether the truck is full or half empty. As a result, the full truck can transport its cargo at a lower cost per pound than the half empty truck.

2) A 30–second television commercial advertising automobiles costs $100,000, whether the manufacturer has 4,000 dealerships across the country and produces 10,000,000 cars per year, or has 300 dealerships and produces 90,000 cars per year.

3) To set up an automatic metal lathe to turn out a particular machine part costs $100 in labor. Once the lathe is set up, the costs of turning out the parts is $1.00 each. If the lathe is set up to turn out a single part, its cost will be $101.00. If the lathe is set up to turn out 10,000 parts, their cost will be $1.01 each.

4) A procurement department and legal staff spend $2000 to negotiate and draft a contract to purchase an essential raw material, whether the company is buying 50 units of the material or 5000 units.

5) A manufacturer of essential medical or industrial supplies must always keep one production machine in reserve, so that a breakdown will not interrupt production. If it produces with a single machine operating at a time, it must therefore maintain capacity equal to twice its actual output. If it produces with eight machines, however, it needs to maintain only nine machines, a capacity equal to 12% more than output.

6) A production process requires 40 discrete functions. If a firm has ten employees, each must perform, on average, four different functions. If the firm has 4000 employees, no single employee will have to perform more than one function, in which she will be a specialist. If she becomes ill, another specialist in the same function will replace her.

7) The transaction costs of borrowing money (or raising equity capital) are 2% for blocks of $1,000,000; 1% for blocks of $10,000,000; or .5% for blocks of $100,000,000.

8) The development of a new manufacturing process reduces the cost of manufacturing widgets by 50¢ per unit. The research and development costs for inventing the new pro-

3. By contrast, an economy of *scope* exists when there are economies to performing two different economic activities at the same time. For example, if corn starch and corn flakes are separate products from a kernel of corn, a company that produced both products simultaneously in the same plant might have lower costs than individual companies that produced each in separate plants. For a brief technical discussion, see J. Panzar & R. Willig, Economies of Scope, 71 Am. Econ. Rev. Pap. & Proc. 268 (1981).

cess are $1,000,000, regardless of the amount of production to which the process is applied. If the firm produces 1,000,000 units per year, the new process will pay for itself in 2 years and thereafter the firm will save $500,000 per year. If the firm produces 12,000,000 units per year the new process will pay for itself in two months and thereafter the firm will save $6,000,000 per year.

This list is only a tiny sampling of the economies of scale that can exist.[4] Traditionally atomized industries, such as farming, are no exception. An automatic milking machine may greatly reduce the cost of milking dairy cows, but the basic cost of the machine is such that the farmer will not reach the "break-even" point unless he milks at least 100 cows.

Economies of scale are largely a function of technology, which both creates and destroys economies of scale. The invention of the milking machine meant that the large farmer could obtain a cost advantage over the farmer too small to use the machine profitably. As a result dairy farms tended to become larger. By contrast, the invention of the microprocessor (the tiny silicone chip that is the heart of the modern computer) made it possible for much smaller firms to manufacture computers efficiently.

The above list also reflects that not all economies of scale need to be attained within a single plant. Certain "multi-plant" economies can also give a cost advantage to the operator of multiple plants. Other economies, such as advertising, may obtain as output increases, whether or not the output comes from a single plant. As a result, it is often impossible to determine the most efficient minimum size of a single plant and conclude that a firm that operates such a plant has attained all available economies of scale. A firm that operates two or more such plants may have even lower costs.

The term Minimum Efficient Scale (MES) refers to the smallest production unit capable of achieving all relevant economies of scale. If a firm or plant operates at MES, no other firm or plant can be more efficient because of its scale of operation (although it may be more efficient for other reasons; for example, it may have better management).

MES in any particular industry is difficult to measure. In a multi-step production process, different steps may attain MES at different levels of output. Suppose, for example, that a plant manufactures clocks, which consist of three parts: motor, face and cabinet. The face is printed, and the largest cost of producing faces is drafting the design and setting up the printing press. Once the press is ready to roll it can produce ten million units as easily as ten. As a result MES in the production of clock faces is very high—say 10,000,000 units per year. The motor is a relatively standard item in which significant economies obtain; a plant of MES would produce about 100,000 motors per year. Finally, the cabinet involves a great deal of individual work, and economies of scale are less substantial. All available economies in producing the cabinet can be attained at an output of 10,000 units per year. How many clocks will the firm produce?

It probably will not produce 10,000,000 clocks per year, even though at that rate of output it would be taking maximum advantage of the economies available in the printing of the clock faces. In fact, the printing of a particular clock face is likely to be a natural monopoly. Once the face has been designed and the printing press set up, the press will turn out copies of the face until it wears out: the more faces produced, the lower the cost per face. This is frequently true of printed products. The *Kansas City Star* could probably produce 10,000,000 copies of its Wednesday morning newspaper at a lower cost per copy than it could produce 400,000 copies. It produces 400,000 copies, not because of economies of scale, but because the market is not capable of absorbing more than 400,000 copies. Likewise, the market may not be able to absorb 10,000,000 clock faces of a particular style.

The firm will probably be content to manufacture less than the optimal number of clock faces. The problem with motors and cabinets is more substantial, however, because they make

4. For a fuller discussion, see Scherer & Ross, note 1 at 97–151.

up a larger percentage of the clock's costs. The firm has some options. It can manufacture both motors and cabinets itself and produce 10,000 units per year. In that case it would achieve all available economies in cabinets, but it would have higher costs in the production of motors. Alternatively, it could manufacture only the cabinets and purchase the motors from an independent motor manufacturing company that is large enough to attain MES. The firm's choice depends on overall costs. On one side are the increased costs of manufacturing motors at an inefficiently low rate. On the other side are the transaction costs of using the marketplace—of negotiating a contract that covers the motors' detailed specifications, of trusting the motor manufacturer to produce a good product on time, etc. If the clock manufacturer believes that the motor manufacturers are untrustworthy, or that they are charging monopoly prices, it may conclude that it is cheaper to manufacture the motors itself, even at an inefficiently low rate.[5]

The other alternative open to the firm is to expand output to 100,000 units per year, in which case it could manufacture both motors and cabinets at MES. Then, however, it must discern whether the market will absorb all this increased production. A tenfold increase in output will probably force the market-clearing price to drop substantially. Any economies achieved by manufacturing both motors and cabinets at MES might be more than lost in the price decrease.

Even the relatively simple problem of a clockmaker with three inputs (most firms, even clockmakers, have far more) makes MES difficult to determine. Several economists suggest that there is no reliable way of determining *all* relevant economies of scale in any real world industry. Importantly, a determination that overlooks just one nontrivial economy of scale may understate the minimum efficient size of the firms in that market.[6]

In a competitive market firms will gravitate toward MES, perhaps through trial and error. One firm will grow to a larger size or begin performing for itself a service that it previously purchased in the market. If the change creates no economies, the balance of the market will remain unaffected. If the change gives the firm lower costs, however, the firm will likely expand output and increase its market share at the expense of competitors. These competitors will then be forced to achieve these economies for themselves or eventually be forced out of business. By making a few qualifying assumptions, economists have been able to guess MES in certain industries by a rule of "natural selection": firms that have attained all important economies of scale tend to survive; those that fail to attain important economies tend not to.[7]

The best way to visualize how firms gravitate toward MES is to consider the long-run average cost curve. The average cost curve discussed in § 1.1b is the sum of average variable and average fixed costs. Over the long run, however, almost all costs are variable. For example, when the plant wears out the firm will have a number of options: it can retire the plant and not replace it, or it can replace the plant with a plant of smaller, equal or greater size. A profit-maximizing firm will select the most profitable option.

The term "long-run average cost" refers to a firm's average costs when the firm is in a position to select the optimum size of a plant or other long-term investment. Once the plant is in place, of course, its costs are sunk and must be considered fixed for the period during which the plant is used.

As a competitive market approaches equilibrium, it will force firms not only to price their products at marginal cost, but also to operate plants of the most efficient size. A moment's thought will bear this out. As noted above, each firm in a perfectly competitive

5. See R. Coase, The Nature of the Firm, 4 Economica (n.s.) 386 (1937).

6. See the debate between Professors F.M. Scherer and John S. McGee in H.J. Goldschmid, H.M. Mann, & J. Fred Weston, Industrial Concentration: the New Learning 15–113 (1974).

7. See G. Stigler, The Economies of Scale, 1 J.L. & Econ. 54 (1958); L. Weiss, The Survival Technique and the Extent of Suboptimal Capacity, 72 J.Pol.Econ. 246 (1964).

market faces a very high elasticity of demand. If the prevailing market price is $1.00 and a firm tries to charge $1.10, it will make no sales. Likewise, if the market price is $1.00 but one firm faces substantial production inefficiencies and must charge $1.10, it will also lose all its sales. Customers are generally both ignorant and indifferent as to whether a firm's price is too high because it is trying to earn monopoly profits or because it is an inefficient firm. They will buy from someone selling for less. As one firm attains new economies it will enlarge its output. This will force competitors to copy the cost saving innovation. Competition among the innovators will drive the price down and remaining firms will be forced to copy the innovation as well.

The long-run average cost curve determines the minimum size a firm must be in order to achieve available economies. The curve generally slopes downward and then levels off at some minimum efficient level of output. Whether the curve eventually slopes upward again—that is, whether there are long-run diseconomies of large size—is debatable and generally irrelevant to antitrust policy for reasons explained below. However, the long-run average cost curve in most industries has a flat bottom across a relatively broad range. For example, if MES in a particular industry is 5% of total market output, it is likely that a much larger firm, producing perhaps 25% of market output, is equally efficient. If this is true, then in any given industry at a certain time we would expect to see plants or firms in a variety of sizes equal to or greater than MES. This is likely to be true for a number of reasons. First, not all firms of minimum efficient size are equally efficient firms. Some will have better management and grow larger. Others will simply have better luck. If a new industry came into existence today with twenty firms of equal and optimal size, we could anticipate a different market structure a half century from now. Some firms would go out of business. Others would merge. Others would grow internally. The end result might well be two or three firms with 20%–30% of the market, two with 10% of the market each and two or three with 5% each.[8]

If the market is monopolized or cartelized, some fringe firms may be able to survive even if they are not of MES. For example, suppose that MES in a particular industry is 20% of the market, and an MES firm can produce widgets for $1.00 each. A firm with 10% of the market has costs of $1.20. But what if three firms, each with 30% of the market, are engaged in price fixing and charging $1.30? The inefficiently small firm will find it quite easy to survive, because the cartel has created a price "umbrella" which protects the small firm from its inefficiency. If the cartel ever falls apart the small firm may be in trouble. That same thing is true of oligopoly, or tacit collusion. Among the relatively few beneficiaries of collusion and oligopoly are fringe competitors.

What role does the notion of economies of scale play in antitrust? First, it suggests that much of antitrust's historic preoccupation with bigness *per se* was ill-advised, at least if low prices are an important goal of antitrust policy. Firms frequently become big because large firms are more efficient than small firms. The unfortunate result, of course, is that the small firms become unprofitable and are forced either to become big themselves or else to exit the market. Invariably, the minimum efficient *size* of firms in a particular market dictates the optimal maximum *number* of firms in the market. If MES is 25% of the market, the market will not have room for more than four MES firms. High market concentration, with all its possible attendant evils, is often a function of economies of scale.

Second, knowledge of economies of scale in a market can help a policy maker evaluate the consequences of certain practices alleged to be

8. See Scherer & Ross, note 1, at 141–146. It is important to distinguish the question whether the long-run average cost curve rises, and whether the average cost curve does. The average cost curve—which represents the output of an established plant—eventually rises in most industries. That is, when an individual plant produces more than its optimal capacity it operates inefficiently and incurs higher costs. The long-run average cost curve, however, reflects the fact that the firm has the option of building a different size plant or of operating multiple plants.

monopolistic. Many such practices, such as vertical integration, may be nothing more than a means of attaining economies. Likewise, knowledge of scale economies may help predict the consequences of mergers.

Third, knowledge of scale economies and optimal market structure can help a policy maker determine the appropriateness of "structural" relief in certain cases. When a firm has been found guilty of monopolization or illegal merger, should the court respond by ordering divestiture—judicially enforced break-up of the defendant into two or more smaller firms? What if the new firms are too small to achieve important economies of scale? The result might be that prices would be higher in the new "competitive" market than they were in the old "monopolized" market. In such cases a more efficient solution may be to tolerate the highly concentrated, "oligopoly" market and use the antitrust laws to force the firms to compete with each other as much as possible.[9]

As noted above, there is some debate about whether firms might become inefficiently large—that is, whether the long-run average cost curve slopes upward at high levels of output. The relevance of that debate to antitrust depends in part on whether we believe "self-deterring" conduct should be condemned. For example, should antitrust enforcers take a policy position against mergers creating firms above a certain size, on the theory that such firms are inefficiently large?

The argument against antitrust intervention is that the market itself disciplines firms that became too large, for the inefficiencies show up as reduced profits. Smaller rivals will have lower costs and earn larger profits. To be sure, stockholders and managers may not have the same set of interests. Managers may wish to pursue high output, while stockholders prefer high profits. But the protection of high stockholder profits is not an antitrust concern. Further, even if these concerns are legitimate, there does not seem to be any way that antitrust can make them operational at the present time. Our empirical knowledge of the size at which firms become inefficient is severely limited. Further, if stockholders cannot effectively discipline managers, that problem lies with the structure of the corporation or of corporate law, not with antitrust. Not every inefficient managerial decision is an antitrust problem. Finally, mergers creating firms that are too large may stimulate competition as often as they impair it. Such mergers may give second and third largest firms a chance to compete with the industry leader more effectively.

1.4b. Persistent Scale Economies, Natural Monopoly, Franchise Bidding and Contestability

Substantial economies of scale can strain the perfect competition model to the breaking point. For example, if the long-run average cost curve slopes downward to a point equal to one-half of market demand, then the market has room for only two MES firms. Any firm whose output is less than 50% of the market will face higher costs. But a market with two or three firms is far more conducive to monopolization or collusion than a market containing dozens of firms.

The extreme example of economies of scale is natural monopoly, which occurs when a firm's costs decline as output increases all the way to the market's saturation point. Figure 8 (on the following page) illustrates such a market. The long-run average cost curve (AC) slopes down continuously until it intersects the demand curve. A single plant of MES would be large enough to satisfy the entire market demand at a price sufficient to cover the firm's costs. Any firm producing a smaller amount would face higher per unit costs.

9. The problems of high concentration and oligopoly pricing are discussed in § 4.4a.

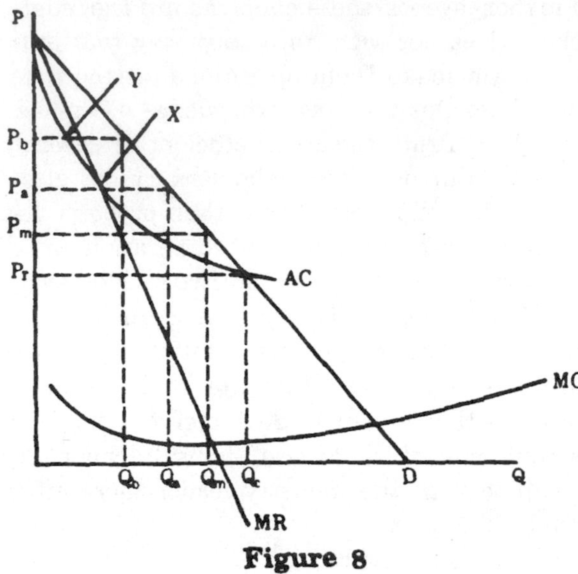

Figure 8

Suppose that the market in Figure 8 were divided between two firms of equal size and efficiency, and that each charged a price equal to its average costs (the same as a competitive market in equilibrium). Each firm would fill one-half the demand, so the costs of each would be determined by a point on the AC curve halfway between the vertical axis and the demand curve: point X. At that point each firm would recover its costs. However, their joint output would be reduced to Q_a and price would be P_a. If three identical firms shared the market each would have costs equal to that point on the AC curve one-third of the horizontal distance from the vertical axis to the demand curve: point Y. For three firms, combined output would be even lower and price even higher.

The classic example of natural monopoly is the toll bridge. Suppose that a bridge costs $1000 to build and lasts ten years, so fixed costs are $100 per year. Average variable costs are 10¢ per crossing, which include maintenance and the costs of collecting the toll. The bridge is large enough to accommodate any number of crossers. If 1000 people cross the bridge annually, a toll of 20¢ will cover the average total cost of a crossing—10¢ for average variable costs and $100 ÷ 1000, or 10¢ for average fixed costs.

Suppose that a competitor builds a second toll bridge next to the first. Variable costs for each bridge remain at 10¢ per crossing,[10] but now there are only 500 crossers on each bridge annually. The fixed costs jump from 10¢ per crosser to 20¢ per crosser, and average total costs are 30¢. Worse yet, when the price rises some of the 1000 people willing to cross at a toll of 20¢ opt not to cross at all (or to swim across), rather than pay 30¢. Suppose only 800 people make crossings—400 on each bridge. Then the fixed costs jump to 25¢ per crosser rather than 20¢. As a result of the second bridge, 200 fewer people cross, creating a deadweight loss similar to the loss caused by monopoly,[11] and the price of a crossing rises from 20¢ to 35¢. If a third bridge came in, the toll would have to rise even higher before all three bridges could remain profitable.

Natural monopoly markets perform optimally when they are occupied by a single firm that charges a competitive price. The last part of that statement is critical, however. A natural monopolist is a monopolist. Like any monopolist, the natural monopolist will seek out its profit-maximizing price at the intersection of its marginal cost and marginal revenue curves. Sometimes the natural monopolist's profit-maximizing price will be higher than the price charged by multiple competitors in the natural monopoly market and sometimes lower.

The problem of natural monopoly is easily stated: if the market is occupied by a single firm, the firm will charge a monopoly price. If it is occupied by multiple firms, even assuming that the firms behave competitively,[12] they will

10. Actually, maintenance costs per crosser would also rise, unless maintenance is directly proportional to the number of crossers.

11. See § 1.3.

12. Competitors in natural monopoly markets have very strong incentives to collude. In the bridge example, each bridge operator has constant variable costs of 10¢ per crosser—that is, one additional crosser imposes 10¢ in additional costs on the bridge. In this case, since average variable costs are constant, marginal costs and average variable costs are the same. Each bridge operator will therefore be better off obtaining additional crossers at any price above 10¢. The likely result will be a toll war in which prices are driven to marginal costs without enough

have higher costs and will charge higher prices.

The traditional solution to the problem of persistent, recognized natural monopoly is price regulation. A single firm is permitted to occupy the market and is protected by law from competitive entry. In exchange, the firm's prices are set by a regulatory agency designed to ensure that pricing approaches P_r in Figure 8 rather than P_m.[13] Whether the regulation is socially beneficial depends upon the accuracy of the regulatory agency's cost determinations, whether the cost of regulating is greater than or less than the cost of monopoly pricing or of ceding the market to multiple firms, and whether the regulation process changes the firm's incentives to behave efficiently.

When a natural monopoly is recognized as such and subjected to price regulation, it acquires at least a limited immunity from the federal antitrust laws. For some time this has been true of local telecommunications, electric companies, gas companies, and other price regulated utilities. The result has been the development of a complex doctrine of antitrust in the regulated industries.[14] Other natural monopolies are not recognized as such and are treated no differently than competitive firms. Newspapers, newspaper delivery routes and court reporting services, for example, may be natural monopolies. Failure to recognize this fact has occasionally led courts astray in their analysis of antitrust problems in those markets.[15]

More than any time since the New Deal policy makers in the 1980s and 1990s have questioned accepted beliefs about the costs, benefits and proper scope of price regulation. In particular, they have become critical of the large costs of operating the regulatory system and of the failure of most regulatory systems to approximate competitive behavior in price-regulated markets. A by-product of this criticism has been a great deal of reinterpretation of the proper scope of the antitrust laws in price-regulated industries.[16]

Another important by-product is a broad attack on the traditional perfect competition model and on the model for natural monopoly. This attack, sometimes called the theory of contestable markets, creates a "competition model" for markets, including natural monopolies, where the given wisdom has been that competition will not work. Despite substantial shortcomings in implementation, the theory has opened the way for greater enforcement of the antitrust laws in markets that were once price regulated but are now being deregulated.[17]

Contestability theory starts with the premise that the perfect competition and natural monopoly models have one deficiency: although they describe competition *in* the market quite well, they ignore the phenomenon of competition *for* the market. Even though a market may have room for only one firm, someone must decide which firm will have the right to enter, how long it may stay, and what price it will charge. Competition can play an important role in this decision process. Furthermore, if the process is constructed properly, a market with a single seller can perform

remaining to cover fixed costs. One of two things will probably happen: one of the bridges will go out of business or else the two bridges will expressly or tacitly fix prices. During the nineteenth century the railroad industry, which contained many natural monopoly markets, was rife with collusion. See H. Hovenkamp, Enterprise and American Law: 1836–1937, ch. 12 (1991).

13. P_r is not the economically "competitive" price, because it exceeds marginal cost; but it is the regulatory agency's approximation of a price that will enable a natural monopoly utility to earn a competitive rate of return.

14. See Chapter 19 (federally regulated industries) and Chapter 20 (state and local regulated industries).

15. For example, see Albrecht v. Herald Co., 390 U.S. 145, 88 S.Ct. 869 (1968), overruled by State Oil Co. v. Khan, 522 U.S. 3, 118 S.Ct. 275 (1997); H. Hovenkamp, Vertical Integration by the Newspaper Monopolist, 69 Iowa L. Rev. 451 (1984).

16. For good discussions of these problems, see S. Breyer, Regulation and its Reform (1982); C. Sunstein, After the Rights Revolution: Reconceiving the Regulatory State (1990). On the general problem of antitrust in newly deregulated industries, see 1A Antitrust Law ¶¶ 240–241 (rev. ed. 1997).

17. For discussion, see D. I. Baker & B. Baker, Antitrust and Communications Deregulation, 28 Antitrust Bull. 1 (1983); M. Cohen, The Antitrust Implications of Airline Deregulation, 28 Antitrust Bull. 131 (1983).

just as competitively as a traditional perfectly competitive market.[18]

An important precursor to the theory of contestable markets is the idea of franchise bidding.[19] The notion that a single firm wins a competitive bid is commonplace. If the city of San Francisco decides to build a sports arena, the "market" for the construction of the arena is probably a natural monopoly—the city would prefer to have a single contractor take charge of the entire project. The city will identify the contractor and the price of the project by taking competitive bids, with the offer generally going to the lowest qualified bidder. Although a single firm ends up building the arena, the process of competitive bidding helps ensure that the firm will not charge a monopoly price.

Franchise bidding in natural monopoly utilities presents some difficult problems, however, because fixed cost items are especially durable. For example, a natural gas pipeline from El Paso to Los Angeles might last fifty years. It would not be practical to ask competing natural gas companies to bid for the right to build the pipeline and supply gas from El Paso to Los Angeles for fifty years. The firms would have to calculate an enormous risk premium into their bids, because they cannot accurately determine the price, supply or demand for gas over such long periods.

One solution to this problem is to divide the period into small intervals and renew the bidding periodically. Suppose bids were taken for the right to build the pipeline and sell natural gas to Los Angeles for a period of one year. After that year the bidding would be renewed. Suppose firm A wins the bid, builds the pipeline and supplies the gas for one year. The original bid might yield a price fairly close to the cost of building the pipeline and supplying the gas for one year, assuming there are many bidders and that they do not collude.

But what will happen the second year? A is now in a much different position than other bidders: A already owns a pipeline which has forty-nine years of life remaining. The pipeline cannot costlessly be moved and used for other purposes; so other bidders must calculate its installation costs into their bids. These additional costs, which have already been "sunk" by A, give A considerable latitude for monopolistic pricing. If the pipeline cost $1,000,000, A will be able to add some amount under $1,000,000 to his bid and still underbid all competitors. The higher A's sunk costs—that is, the costs of durable items that can be used throughout the subsequent bid period and that cannot easily be transferred elsewhere—the more latitude A will have to charge a monopoly price.

In some natural monopoly markets sunk costs are far lower and franchise bidding more workable than in the natural gas market. For example, a particular airline route may be a natural monopoly if it has room for only one round trip per day. If two different airline companies tried to offer daily planes on this route, each would fly with many empty seats and average costs would be very high.

The largest expense of establishing an air route between two points is the cost of the plane. The plane itself, however, is easily transferable from route to route. If a potential entrant who already owns a plane moves into the route to compete with the incumbent, the incumbent will not have any particular advantage over the newcomer. Any potential entrant could enter the market cheaply and exit cheaply, taking his plane with him. Theoretically, natural monopoly airline routes should be more practically contestable than natural monopoly pipelines. If the only airline operating along a route sets a monopoly price, other airlines will quickly bid to come in.[20]

18. Unlike the perfect competition model, the theory of contestable markets applies equally to natural monopolies and to multi-seller markets. The most comprehensive, but very technical, statement of the theory is W.J. Baumol, J.C. Panzar & R.D. Willig, Contestable Markets and the Theory of Industry Structure (1982). A good survey of the literature is J. Brock, Contestable Markets and the Theory of Industry Structure: A Review Article, 91 J.Pol.Econ. 1055 (1983). The theory is criticized in W. Shepherd, "Contestability" vs. Competition, 74 Am.Econ.Rev. 572 (1984).

19. The seminal article is H. Demsetz, Why Regulate Utilities?, 11 J.L. & Econ. 55 (1968).

20. See J. Brodley, Antitrust Policy Under Deregulation: Airline Mergers and the Theory of Contestable Markets, 61 Boston Univ.L.Rev. 823 (1981).

Airline routes, newspaper delivery routes, bus lines and direct satellite television seem to be relatively well suited for franchise bidding. Electric utilities, cable television and natural gas pipelines are not, unless expensive, durable items can be made transferable from one winning bidder to the next. For example, if the pipeline in the above example was publicly owned, and competitive bidding were used to determine only who would deliver the gas and what the price would be, then the market might be contestable. The same result would obtain if the initial winning bidder were forced to transfer the pipeline to the second-term winning bidder at some previously agreed price. Although these methods for awarding natural monopolies on the basis of competitive bidding have been tried, they have not been particularly successful.[21]

The theory of contestable markets takes the insights of franchise bidding analysis one step further. Even without franchise bidding, a sole provider may be constrained to charge a monopoly price if the instant it tries to charge more it faces "hit-and-run" entry by competitors. For example, we may not need to award airline routes through a bidding process at all. Assume that the route from Topeka, Kansas, to Madison, Wisconsin, has room for only one flight per day. The current sole supplier of that flight has no franchise, and thus has no protection from entry by competitors. If that firm attempts to charge more than the competitive price, however, it will immediately lose its business to a firm who can come in, provide the service, and exit costlessly if need be. This contestability theory provided a major economic justification for airline deregulation even where there was no franchise bidding for periodic monopoly rights.

Unfortunately, airline markets have proved to be far less contestable than the theory originally predicted. Although the routes themselves are highly contestable, space at airport gates is not. Gate space is strategically located (it must be in the airport terminal) and is quite scarce.[22] Presumably, gate space itself could be made more contestable than it is.[23] Unfortunately, airports have the wrong incentives: the more rents they can make from leasing gate space, the less they have to look to unpopular taxes or more visible airport user fees in order to pay airport operating expenses.

A major factor preventing markets from being contestable is "sunk" costs—or investments that a firm must make to get into a market, but that cannot be recovered in the event the firm must later exit. The more

21. See O. Williamson, Franchise Bidding for Natural Monopolies—in General and With Respect to CATV, 7 Bell J. Econ. & Management Science 73 (1976).

22. One reason gate space is at such a premium is that "hubbing" is so efficient. For example, suppose there are four eastern cities (Boston, New York, Washington and Philadelphia) and four western cities (Phoenix, Los Angeles, San Francisco, and Seattle). On any given day 50 people from each eastern city wish to travel to each of the western cities, and the distance between any eastern city and any western city is 3000 miles. Further, an airplane holds 200 passengers. City-pair routing would then require 16 trips, or a total of 48,000 air miles, from each eastern city to each of the four western cities, and each plane would be one-fourth full. However, suppose the airline placed a hub in Chicago, the midway point. It could then fly four full planes from the four cities to Chicago. At that point all the people would transfer, and then four full planes would fly from Chicago to the four western cities. The result would be eight 1500 mile trips with full planes, or a total of 12,000 air miles. As the route system becomes more complex and takes more locations into account, the advantage of hubbing over city pair routing becomes even more pronounced.

As a general matter, and not considering the costs of externalities such as increased traffic, the more traffic that can be hubbed into a single terminal, the lower the cost of running the transportation system. For example, overnight courier services such as Federal Express may fly all their parcels nationwide into a single central location, such as Memphis, sort them, and then fly them out to their destinations.

Gate space restrictions and the existence of hubbing suggest that the airline industry is in fact much less contestable, and thus much less competitive, than first appears. See S. Borenstein, The Evolution of U.S. Airline Competition, 6 J. Econ. Perspectives 45 (1992) (contestability "no substitute for actual competition"); P. Dempsey, Flying Blind: the Failure of Airline Deregulation (1990); S. Morrison & C. Winston, Empirical Implications and Tests of the Contestability Hypothesis, 30 J.L. & Econ. 53 (1987) (contestability highly imperfect).

23. For example, airport authorities could give rather short term leases—say, three years—and make sure that no carrier acquired a dominant share of gates; or sufficient gates could be built to produce ample capacity. In several European airports the airport authorities rather than the carriers control the gates. The gates are assigned on a per-arrival basis to incoming planes, and any carrier willing to pay the fee can request a gate for its inbound flight.

cheaply an incumbent can exit the market without abandoning durable and expensive sunk cost items, the more contestable the market and the more competitively it will perform, even though it might have room for only one seller at any given time. The very notion of "hit-and-run" entry implies that the prospective firm cannot count on staying in the contested market for a long period of time. For that reason, any amount of irreversible investment acts as a deterrent to contestability.

Further, a market is perfectly contestable only if entry is instantaneous and the incumbent firm is unable to react. In the airline example, if the prospective firm must announce its entry even one day in advance, the incumbent firm may respond by lowering its prices to the competitive level or to a level just below the announced prices of the prospective entrant. In that case passengers will stay with the incumbent and entry will be unprofitable.

The minimum conditions for contestability (costless exit and instantaneous entry) must obtain very strictly, and contestable market performance deteriorates very quickly in response to minor imperfections. For this reason, contestable market theory is not nearly as robust as the traditional theory of competition, which suggests fairly competitive behavior in spite of a wide variety of imperfections. This lack of robustness may have made contestability a flash in the pan, so to speak, as economic theories of industrial organization go.

Whether or not contestable market theory proves durable, the consequences of deregulation will likely be with us for some time. Most deregulation has occurred in areas where sunk costs are relatively low, durable and expensive assets are easily transferable, and there are already multiple firms operating in the markets. Long-distance telecommunications by satellite and microwave, trucking, and airline routes are only three important examples. As these industries become governed less by statutory price regulation, and as entry is opened to more firms, antitrust will have an increasingly important role to play. These matters are developed more fully in Chapter 19.

§ 1.5 Less–Than–Perfect Competition

Antitrust economics is "applied" economics, which means that it must accept real world markets as given and consider any deviations from the perfect competition model. Economies of scale, discussed in the previous section, are only one of the important differences between the assumptions of perfect competition and the markets encountered by antitrust tribunals. Although some markets contain hundreds of small competitors selling indistinguishable products, many others do not. The real world contains not widgets but automobiles, hot dogs, and stereo sets, and these come in several varieties.

Two theories have attempted to apply the perfect competition model to the more complex situations found in real world markets. These models are called "imperfect competition"[1] and "monopolistic competition."[2] These formal theories have not had much explicit effect on antitrust policy, although judges must often consider the degree that competition in the real world appears to deviate from the given models.

The theories are not formally presented in this chapter. Rather, as they are relevant they are discussed in various sections of this book, particularly those on oligopoly and price discrimination.[3] The list of imperfections described in the following discussion is useful to keep in mind, however, for it can often help explain the motive or effect of certain litigated practices.

1.5a. Product Differentiation

Many products in markets that appear competitive are nevertheless differentiated from one another. Although Ford and Chrysler automobiles compete, some buyers prefer one to the other and are willing to pay more

§ 1.5

1. See J. Robinson, The Economics of Imperfect Competition (1933).

2. See E. Chamberlin, The Theory of Monopolistic Competition (1933).

3. See chs. 4 & 14.

for their first choice. To the extent this is true the manufacturer faces a slightly downward sloping demand curve and may charge a price higher than marginal cost. Total output in such markets may be less than optimal. More importantly for antitrust analysis, product differentiation may explain many vertical restrictions on distribution, tying arrangements, exclusive dealing or other allegedly anticompetitive practices.

Product differentiation plays a complex role in modern antitrust economics, however. Although it does give individual firms small amounts of market power, it also has one other important effect: it makes collusion and some kinds of oligopoly far more difficult.[4] Sellers find it harder to agree on price and output when they do not produce precisely the same product, or they have different costs.

As a result, the policy implications of product differentiation pull in two different directions. One rough generalization is possible: when we are concerned with the market power of a single firm, product differentiation tends to be an aggravating factor. It creates or enlarges market power individually held, although frequently in amounts too low to be of antitrust concern. By contrast, when we are focusing on practices that might facilitate collusion, as in traditional merger policy, product differentiation tends to be a mitigating factor.[5]

1.5b. Price Discrimination

In the perfect competition model price discrimination is impossible. In the real world it occurs daily. The two imperfections that facilitate most price discrimination are information costs and transportation costs. If one group of buyers does not know enough about market conditions or about the contents of the product, they may pay a higher price than more knowledgeable buyers. Likewise, high transportation costs make it possible for firms to earn higher profits from near-by "captive" purchasers than from more remote purchasers.

Relatively small amounts of market power can facilitate price discrimination, and it is more widespread in product differentiated markets. It is particularly common in markets for intellectual property, such as franchising and patent licensing. Most price discrimination is not illegal, and it generally benefits rather than harms consumers in the aggregate.

1.5c. Oligopoly

When markets are highly concentrated, because of economies of scale or for other reasons, a firm cannot reasonably ignore the price and output decisions of competitors. Ford Motor Co., for example, would be unwise *not* to respond to General Motors' price reduction or output increase.[6]

Oligopoly has become a major concern of American antitrust policy. The laws against price fixing, expressed mainly in § 1 of the Sherman Act, have generally proved ineffectual.[7] So the focus has shifted to merger policy, an important goal of which is to prevent mergers that may facilitate various kinds of oligopoly pricing.[8]

1.5d. Transaction Costs

Transaction costs, which are the costs of using the market, can distort our picture of any market. Behavior that appears irrational when transaction costs are ignored becomes rational when they are taken into account.[9]

One can generalize that avoidable transaction costs are a substantial source of inefficiency in the economy. Indeed, the business firm itself can be viewed as nothing more than a device for reducing the transaction costs of engaging in business.[10] Reduction or avoidance

4. See § 4.1a.

5. See § 12.1b, which is concerned with mergers that might facilitate collusion. Contrast § 12.3, which is concerned with unilateral anticompetitive effects of mergers.

6. See § 4.2.

7. See §§ 4.4, 4.6.

8. See Ch. 12.

9. On the importance of transaction costs in economic analysis of law, see O. Williamson, Transaction Cost Economics Meets Posnerian Law and Economics, Univ. of California Law School Law and Economics Working Paper 92–18 (1993).

10. As in R. Coase, The Nature of the Firm, 4 Economica 386 (1937).

of transaction costs explains many phenomena that have been made subject to antitrust scrutiny. Among these are mergers, vertical price and nonprice restrictions, tying arrangements and exclusive dealing.

Importantly for antitrust analysis, many practices that look suspicious at first appear more benign when transaction costs are considered.[11] Vertical mergers and numerous forms of vertical contracting are a good example. For many years antitrust policy makers tended to look at these practices with great suspicion, viewing them principally as mechanisms for permitting firms to enhance their market power, or perhaps to "leverage" a second monopoly in another market.[12] But in most cases these practices are nothing other than devices by which firms reduce the costs of doing business, by making transactions less risky, less costly, or eliminating them altogether.

1.5e. Less–Than–Perfect Competition and "Second Best"

The complex economic theory of "second best" begins with the premise that real world markets never satisfy all the assumptions of the perfect competition model. Economies of scale, cartelization and monopoly, imperfect competition, market imperfections created by the patent system and many other phenomena taint all aspects of the general market system. Given that all markets are imperfect, will improvement of competition in one market necessarily make the entire system more efficient? The answer is ambiguous, but may often be no.[13]

Suppose, for example, that copper and aluminum can both be used to make a particular type of tubing. The competitive price of copper tubing is $2.00 per foot and the competitive price of aluminum tubing is $1.50 per foot. At those prices most buyers prefer the aluminum and will buy it. However, both tubing markets are monopolized. The monopoly price of the copper tubing is $3.00 per foot and of the aluminum tubing is $2.50 per foot. In this doubly monopolized market most customers who would buy aluminum in the competitive market continue to buy it.

Suppose the government intervenes under the antitrust laws and destroys the copper monopoly but not the aluminum monopoly. The price of copper drops to $2.00, but the price of aluminum remains at $2.50. Now most of these customers switch to copper. The destruction of only the copper monopoly may actually be inefficient—that is, more inefficient substitutions are made after the monopoly is destroyed than when both products were monopolized. This is because the welfare effects of these two monopolies tended to cancel each other out, insofar as the substitution between copper and aluminum was concerned. Of course, under the double monopoly less of both was consumed, and there were still distortions as between copper and aluminum on the one hand, and alternatives on the other.

The overall welfare effects of monopoly cannot be known unless we have complete information about every market affected by the change from monopoly to competition, or vice-versa. This fact makes second best problems extraordinarily complex, and its practical consideration in antitrust litigation is generally out of the question.[14]

The theory of second best illustrates one thing well: the model of perfect competition is highly artificial, and the real world satisfies its conditions only imperfectly. However, this fact does not distinguish economics from physics, chemistry or genetics. Model building is endemic in science, and in all cases the model is an abstraction based on simplifying assump-

11. See, e.g., P. Joskow, The Role of Transaction Cost Economics in Antitrust and Public Utility Regulatory Policies, 7 J.L.,Econ. & Org. 53 (1991).

12. See §§ 9.3–9.4.

13. See F.M. Scherer & D. Ross, Industrial Market Structure and Economic Performance 33–38 (3d ed. 1990); R. Lipsey & R. Lancaster, The General Theory of Second Best, 24 Rev.Econ.Stud. 11 (1956).

14. For an argument disagreeing with this proposition, see R. Markovits, Second Best Theory and the Standard Analysis of Monopoly–Rent–Seeking: A Generalizable Critique, a "Sociological" Account, and Some Illustrative Stories, 78 Iowa L.Rev. 327 (1993). For a response, see H. Hovenkamp, Antitrust Policy and the Social Cost of Monopoly, 78 Iowa L. Rev. 371 (1993).

tions. Just as the real world contains no perfectly competitive markets, so too it contains no perfectly equilateral triangles. Furthermore, once one line or angle is inaccurate, at least one other line or angle must be inaccurate as well. However, the engineer's imperfect triangle functions very well in most real world applications, from astrodomes to space shuttles.

The value of any model lies not in the absolute fidelity of each element to real world phenomena, but in the model's ability to make useful predictions and, more importantly, its ability to give us meaningful verbal accounts of our observations. In general, antitrust analysis has confined itself to relatively uncontroversial uses of economic models in which their record as explanatory devices is good (but not perfect). In those areas second best analysis is properly ignored, unless it is obvious that antitrust enforcement in one sector will have adverse consequences in another.[15]

The chief use of second-best analysis in antitrust theory has been ideological. The theory has enabled some scholars to argue for limiting the use of economic analysis in antitrust by presenting the theory of second best as a fatal objection to economic analysis of real world markets.[16]

The use of second best analysis in this way is troublesome. It is impossible to have a little bit of second best: if the theory disqualifies economics as an analytic tool for antitrust, it disqualifies *all* economic analysis. Nevertheless, those who rely on second best as an argument against pervasive economic analysis of antitrust problems continue themselves to give economic justifications for some policies, such as the rules against price fixing. If the implications of second best analysis are accepted however, then even the simple economic argument against cartels loses its force.

§ 1.6 Barriers to Entry

For antitrust purposes, a barrier to entry is some factor in a market that permits firms already in the market to earn monopoly profits, while deterring outsiders from coming in.[1] More formally, entry barriers measure "the extent to which, in the long run, established firms can elevate their selling prices above the minimal average costs of production and distribution" without "inducing potential entrants to enter the industry."[2]

Economists have not been unanimous in accepting the foregoing definition of entry barriers, which is sometimes called "Bainian" after the economist Joe S. Bain who developed it. Many prefer the "Stiglerian" definition that entry barriers are costs that a prospective entrant must incur at or after entry, that those already in the market did not have to incur when they entered. More technically, an entry barrier under this definition is "a cost of producing (at some or every rate of output) which must be borne by a firm which seeks to enter an industry but is not borne by firms already in the industry."[3]

The difference between the two definitions of entry barriers can be quite substantial. For

15. The fact that it is logically possible that correction of monopoly in one market will lead to a general welfare loss because of increased imperfections in other markets does not mean that such losses occur very often, or even that they occur at all. Most interrelationships between distinct markets are weak enough to be ignored. If they are strong enough to be considered, the interrelationships will usually be obvious. See O. Williamson, Assessing Vertical Market Restrictions: Antitrust Ramifications of the Transaction Cost Approach, 127 U.Pa.L.Rev. 953, 987 (1979); W. Baumol, Informed Judgment, Rigorous Theory and Public Policy, 32 S.Econ.J. 137 (1965).

16. For Example, see L. Sullivan, Handbook of the Law of Antitrust 3–5, 21, 153–54 (1977).

§ 1.6

1. J. Bain, Barriers to New Competition: Their Character and Consequences in Manufacturing Industries (1962).

2. J. Bain, Industrial Organization 252 (1968). Others have suggested that marginal cost rather than minimum average cost should be the correct measure. See J. M. Ferguson, Advertising and Competition: Theory, Measurement, Fact 10 (1974) (an entry barrier is a factor making "entry unprofitable while permitting established firms to set prices above marginal cost, and to persistently earn monopoly returns.")

3. G. J. Stigler, The Organization of Industry 67 (1968). See also von Weizsacker: "A cost of producing which must be borne by a firm which seeks to enter an industry but is not borne by firms already in the industry and which implies a distortion in the allocation of resources from the social point of view." C. von Weizsacker, A Welfare Analysis of Barriers to Entry, 11 Bell J. Econ. 399, 400 (1980).

example, under the Bainian definition economies of scale is a qualifying barrier to entry. If scale economies are significant, then incumbent firms with established markets may have a large advantage over any new entrant, who will enter the market at a low rate of output. As a result, scale economies can permit incumbent firms to earn monopoly returns up to a certain point without encouraging new entry.

By contrast, scale economies are not a qualifying entry barrier under the Stiglerian definition. Both incumbent firms and new entrants had to deal with them at the time of entry; so scale economies are not a cost that applies only to new entrants.

The Stiglerian conception of entry barriers is based on a powerful analytic point: entry barrier analysis should distinguish desirable from undesirable entry. If prospective entrants face precisely the same costs that incumbents faced but still find entry unprofitable, then this market has probably already attained the appropriate number of players, even though monopoly profits are being earned. For example, suppose that minimum efficient scale (MES) in a market requires a 30% market share. Such a market has room for only three MES firms—and a three-firm market is quite likely to perform oligopolistically or else be conducive to collusion. The Stiglerian approach to entry barriers would say that, although monopoly profits are being earned in the industry, entry barriers should not be counted as high because entry by a fourth firm is not socially desirable. Additional entry would force at least one firm to be of suboptimal size, and eventually one of the four would probably exit the market.[4] The socially desirable solution to the problem of oligopoly performance in this market is *not* to force entry of a fourth, inefficiently small firm; but rather to look for alternative measures that make collusion more difficult.

Nevertheless, antitrust analysis has mainly used the Bainian rather than the Stiglerian definition of entry barriers. The Bainian definition is written into the 1992 Horizontal Merger Guidelines promulgated by the Justice Department's Antitrust Division and the Federal Trade Commission (FTC).[5] In all antitrust decisions except for a few in the FTC, tribunals have relied on the Bainian definition.[6]

Although the Stiglerian approach to entry barriers offers a useful insight into the relationship between market structure and socially desirable entry, there are nevertheless good reasons for antitrust policy to prefer the Bainian approach. In particular, the Bainian definition is free of the value judgment of what constitutes socially desirable entry. This is important because the existence of entry barriers is not itself an antitrust violation. The antitrust policy maker does not use entry barrier analysis in order to consider whether further entry into a market is socially desirable; the market itself will take care of that question. Rather, the question is whether a particular practice is plausibly anticompetitive. This distinction is critically important because we know so little about the minimum efficient scale of operation in any given market.

For example, suppose the relevant question is whether a market structure is sufficiently conducive to oligopoly behavior that we should be concerned about a merger that further reduces the number of firms in the market. The Stiglerian approach provides no basis for distinguishing markets in which oligopoly behavior is likely to be successful from those in which it is not. Markets that have high entry barriers in the Bainian sense but not the Stiglerian sense—for example, those with substantial scale economies—could nevertheless be quite susceptible to coordination of prices. The Bainian approach goes straight to the question whether attempts to raise price above the competitive level will be disciplined by new entry into the market. If the answer is no, the merger is a matter for antitrust scrutiny. Of course, we may still wish to conclude that the merger is necessary to enable the firms in-

4. See H. Demsetz, Barriers to Entry, 72 Am. Econ. Rev. 47 (Mar. 1982); H. Demsetz, Industry Structure, Market Rivalry, and Public Policy, 16 J.L. & Econ. 1 (1973).

5. On entry barriers under the 1992 Merger Guidelines, see § 12.6d.

6. For more detail, see § 12.6.

volved to achieve scale economies, but that is a different matter.

Numerous things have been suggested as entry barriers in antitrust cases. Among these are scale economies, product differentiation, high initial investment, risk, cost of capital, advertising, extent of vertical integration or vertical contracting, and government regulation. The case for treating each of these as a qualifying barrier to entry is considered later.[7]

Barriers to entry can also be classified by their height and source. On the question of height, "blockaded" entry occurs when the firm or firms in a market are able to charge their short-run profit-maximizing price without concern about new entry. Suppose an incumbent monopolist has marginal costs of $1.00, a profit-maximizing price of $1.50, and that new entry will not occur unless the entrant anticipates post-entry prices of $1.55 or higher. In that case the monopolist could freely charge $1.50 without concern about new entry. Since post-entry prices will be lower than current prices, the prospective entrant will see that entry is unprofitable.

As the illustration suggests, firms contemplating entry must base their calculations on *post*-entry rather than *pre*-entry prices. The firm needs to know whether it will make a profit after its own output has been added to the output of firms already in the market, taking into account any adjustments in output that incumbent firms might make in response to entry.

The difference between pre-entry and post-entry prices varies from the trivial to the substantial, depending on the size of the market, the degree of market concentration, the extent of scale economies, and the market's elasticity of demand. To take one extreme example, if the market for egg production contains 10,000 farmers, Farmer Brown, who is contemplating entering egg production, can safely assume that the market price after her entry will be the same as it is before. The entry by a single firm in an unconcentrated market will generally have no measurable impact on price. By contrast, assume that a market has three MES firms and a demand elasticity of one. Assuming that the new firm enters at the efficient rate of output, total market output will increase by one-third. The price will fall by one-third. Entry that appears quite profitable at pre-entry prices may prove unprofitable at post-entry prices.

This analysis suggests that entry will not necessarily occur in a market where the incumbent monopolist (or cartel) is charging its short-run profit-maximizing price *even* if that price is higher than the new entrant's costs. To return to the previous example, suppose that a monopolist has marginal costs of $1.00 and a profit-maximizing price of $1.50. The new firm can earn a profit at a price of $1.00, but the firm predicts that in response to its entry the incumbent will increase output to the competitive level, and the entrant's own output must then be added, yielding a market price of 90¢. Entry would not be profitable.

In other situations, entry may be profitable when the monopolist is charging its short-run profit-maximizing price. The monopolist may have to engage in "limit" pricing. For example, suppose the monopolist's marginal costs are $1.00, its short-run profit-maximizing price is $1.50, but a prospective entrant has costs of $1.20. Further, the entrant's output will reduce the market price by about 20¢. In this case, the incumbent firm would invite new entry if it charged a price of $1.50. But it could deter the prospective entrant indefinitely at a price of $1.35.

Finally, the optimal strategy in some markets may be for firms to permit a certain amount of entry to occur. This is likely to be the case when prospective entrants have upward sloping cost curves. That is, the new entrants can get into the market and produce on a small scale rather cheaply, but entry at a larger scale very quickly becomes more expensive.[8] In that case the dominant firm will compute its profit-maximizing price by determin-

7. See § 12.6.

8. Alternatively, there may be pockets of customers who can be served by fringe sellers, but these sellers could not expand their sales without incurring substantially higher costs.

ing its "residual" demand, or demand after the fringe firms have served a small portion of the market. The most profitable strategy may be to permit a small amount of entry.[9]

As noted previously, entry barriers can be classified by their source as well as their height. Here antitrust policy makers distinguish between natural and artificial entry barriers. Once again, the distinction is driven less by considerations of economic theory than by the conduct-driven requirements of the antitrust laws. An entry barrier is "natural" if it is simply an inherent condition of operation in a market. An entry barrier is "artificial" if it is strategically erected by incumbent firms in order to make entry more difficult. As a basic matter, economies of scale are natural, although in some instances they can be strategically manipulated. For example, firms might lobby the government for regulatory provisions that large firms can satisfy more easily than small firms.[10] Likewise, such practices as patent accumulation, limit pricing, solicitation of government regulation, and (in a few instances) vertical integration or contracting can be designed to deter entry.

The distinction between natural and artificial barriers is important because, although the existence of entry barriers is not illegal, the strategic creation of entry barriers in order to facilitate monopoly pricing may be. For example, a dominant firm may pursue a practice of buying up and then refusing to use every patent developed in its industry. The result is that prospective entrants must use obsolete technologies, invent around the patents, or risk patent litigation with the dominant firm. In such cases a market that could be made competitive fails to become so because of the incumbent firm's strategic practices. A great deal of the law of monopolization deals with the strategic construction of barriers to entry.[11]

§ 1.7. The Troubled Life of the Structure–Conduct–Performance Paradigm

Beginning already in the 1930's economists such as Edward Chamberlin and Edward S. Mason began to identify the threat of anticompetitive conduct with particular industry structures.[1] Joe S. Bain, perhaps the most important economist contributor to antitrust policy in the 1950's, developed this "structure-conduct-performance" (S–C–P) paradigm to its fullest.[2]

The S–C–P paradigm argued that certain industry structures, particularly high concentration accompanied by high entry barriers, dictate that the firms in that industry will engage in certain kinds of conduct, such as oligopoly behavior. This behavior would then lead to poor economic performance, namely, reduced output and monopoly prices.

An important and widely accepted corollary of the S–C–P paradigm was that one could improve performance by regulating structure. Trying to regulate conduct directly is fruitless,

9. See § 3.5a, which diagrams this problem in the context of the domestic firm's decision whether to exclude or permit foreign imports.

10. For example, see P. Pashigian, The Effect of Environmental Regulation on Optimal Plant Size and Factor Shares, 27 J.L. & Econ. 1 (1984); G. Neumann & J. Nelson, Safety Regulation and Firm Size: Effects of the Coal Mine Health and Safety Act of 1969, 25 J.L. & Econ. 183 (1982).

11. See chs. 6–8; and see 3/3A Antitrust Law (rev. ed. 1996).

§ 1.7

1. See E. S. Mason, Economic Concentration and the Monopoly Problem (1964) (reprinting earlier articles); E. Chamberlin, The Theory of Monopolistic Competition. For even earlier work on the relation between structure and conduct, see H. Hovenkamp, Enterprise and American Law, 1836–1937 (1991), at ch. 22.

2. See J. S. Bain, Barriers to New Competition (1956); Industrial Organization (1959; 2d ed. 1968); Relation of Profit Rate to Industry Concentration: American Manufacturing, 1936–1940, 65 Q.J.Econ. 293 (1951). Other important work includes H. M. Mann, Seller Concentration, Barriers to Entry, and Rates of Return in Thirty Industries, 1950–1960, 48 Rev. Econ. & Stat. 296 (1966).

For incisive and divergent perspectives on the paradigm, see R. A. Posner, The Chicago School of Antitrust Analysis, 127 Univ. of Pennsylvania L. Rev. 925 (1979); Industrial Concentration: the New Learning (H. J. Goldschmid, H. M. Mann, & J. F. Weston, eds. Boston: Little, Brown, 1974). For good historical perspective, see M. S. Jacobs, An Essay on the Normative Foundations of Antitrust Economics, 74 N.C. L. Rev. 219 (1995); L. W. Weiss, The Structure–Conduct–Performance Paradigm and Antitrust, 127 U. Pa. L. Rev. 1104, 1105 (1979).

because the underlying structure dictates the conduct. But regulating the structure directly makes regulation of the conduct unnecessary. In sum, the S–C–P paradigm represents the extreme in antitrust *structuralism*. As a matter of logic, if S entails C and C entails P, then S entails P and C drops out. One can infer the quality of performance from the structure alone.

Some of the roots of the S–C–P theory are very old. For example, the Cournot theory of oligopoly pricing, first developed in 1838, predicts an inverse relationship between the number of firms in the oligopolized market and the resulting price: the fewer the firms that must coordinate their behavior, the closer they will come to mimicking the price and output of a single-firm monopolist.[3] Most defenders of the S–C–P paradigm relied on relatively orthodox formulations of Cournot oligopoly where the number of players in the market was the main factor that determined the market's competitiveness. As illustrated later, however, oligopoly markets are far more complex than the simple Cournot model suggests, and structure is only a small part of the story.[4]

Defenders of the S–C–P paradigm generally attempted to prove its claims empirically by showing that accounting rates of return in highly concentrated industries exceed those in competitive industries.[5] These studies generally found positive correlations between profit rates and concentration levels, with profits seeming to be particularly high in industries that Bain had classified as having high entry barriers. Following the strongly structural impulse that the S–C–P paradigm suggests, these studies generally did not test for conduct, the middle term of the paradigm. They simply correlated high accounting returns with highly concentrated industries. As Bain noted, identifying specific elements of conduct in each industry could prove extraordinarily difficult, while determining its structure was relatively simple and generally possible from public data.

Those advocating the S–C–P paradigm then made the important suggestion to antitrust policy makers that the emphasis on anticompetitive conduct should be minimized; rather, antitrust should go after monopoly performance by altering industry structures.[6] Judicial and agency focus on conduct should be turned mainly to low concentration industries where more extreme forms of conduct, such as explicit price fixing, were needed to enable participants to achieve monopoly returns.

An even more important conclusion of the S–C–P paradigm was that antitrust remedies directed at conduct would generally not work in highly concentrated industries, for the tendency to engage in the conduct was inherent in the industry. For example, it would be futile for a court to order the only three firms in a capital intensive, specialized industry to "behave competitively." The very nature of the industry required such firms to monitor one another's price and output decisions.[7]

In practice, the S–C–P paradigm has had broad implications for antitrust policy. Most specifically, in merger policy it has meant that mergers can be challenged *strictly* on the basis of market structure. That is, one need not show explicitly that certain kinds of conduct, such as collusion or predatory pricing, would be more likely to occur after the merger was consummated. The merger's impact on structure was thought to speak for itself.[8] This set

3. See Augustin Cournot, Researches in the Mathematical Principles of the Theory of Wealth [1838] (N. T. Bacon, trans. 1971); for a fuller explanation of the theory see § 4.2a. For a more technical description, see F.M. Scherer & D. Ross, Industrial Market Structure and Economic Performance, ch. 6 (3d ed. 1990).

4. See §§ 4.4–4.6.

5. E.g., Bain, *Barriers*, note 2; Bain, 1951 article, note 2; Mann, note 2.

6. See J. W. Meehan, Jr. and R. J. Larner, "The Structural School, Its Critics, and its Progeny: An Assessment," in *Economics and Antitrust Policy* (R. J. Larner & J. W. Meehan, Jr., eds. 1989), at 182. For a defense of the paradigm, arguing for a less economic approach to antitrust, see W. Adams and J. Brock, Antitrust, Ideology and the Arabesques of Economic Theory, 66 U. Colo. L. Rev. 257 (1995).

7. D. F. Turner, The Definition of Agreement Under the Sherman Act: Conscious Parallelism and Refusals to Deal, 75 Harv.L.Rev. 655 (1962). The merits of Turner's position are discussed more fully in § 4.4a.

8. E.g., United States v. Philadelphia Nat. Bank., 374 U.S. 321, 83 S.Ct. 1715 (1963); Brown Shoe Co. v. United States, 370 U.S. 294, 82 S.Ct. 1502 (1962). See generally C. Kaysen & D. F. Turner, Antitrust Policy (1959).

of principles was effectively read into the highly influential merger guidelines promulgated by the Justice Department's Antitrust Division in 1968.[9] In monopolization cases the effect of the S–C–P paradigm was to turn courts to increased (but often misguided) analysis of a defendant's market power, but reduced analysis of conduct. That is, once the market power requirements were met, liability could be based on much weaker forms of anticompetitive conduct than courts had previously required. Indeed, although courts formally insisted on a showing of exclusionary practices in monopolization cases, some decisions came close to giving defendants the burden of showing that persistently high profits in an industry were not the result of exclusionary practices. Some prominent commentators argued that certain monopolies could be condemned without any specific judicial finding of fault.[10]

Even as the S–C–P paradigm was maturing in the economic literature, it came under relentless attack, primarily by economists from the University of Chicago. Critics of the S–C–P paradigm raised several important arguments: (1) the accounting rates of return that Bain and others used did not reliably establish that monopoly profits were higher in highly concentrated industries than in less concentrated ones; (2) high industry concentration is generally the result of scale economies or other types of efficiency, and the efficiency costs of breaking up such industries could exceed any gains that might be achieved from more competitive performance; (3) even firms in highly concentrated industries should ordinarily be expected to behave competitively, particularly if entry is unrestrained, although the nature of the competition might be more complex; (4) many of the rather moderate practices identified by S–C–P advocates as anticompetitive were really not anticompetitive at all.

These four arguments are closely interrelated, and one cannot be developed without reference to the other. First, many S–C–P critics argued that accounting rates of return are very different from monopoly profits. For example, such rates of return say nothing about risk, and we should expect higher profits in riskier industries. Further, accountants frequently make divisions between fixed costs (capital investments) and variable costs (expenses) that might make sense from an accounting perspective but not to an economist.[11] In addition, the way accountants depreciate and value assets is driven by a host of considerations, including tax consequences, that make the true basis upon which returns are to be calculated extremely difficult to identify. Finally, when accountants deal with multiproduct firms they often allocate costs over the various products in ways that, from an economic perspective, seem completely arbitrary. For these reasons and perhaps others, accounting rates of return seem to be completely unreliable indicators of monopoly profits.[12]

A second, closely related argument is that even if firms in highly concentrated markets earn higher returns, these returns are justified by the increased efficiency of the firms. Harold Demsetz showed that although there was a correlation between industry concentration and firm profits, the correlation existed only for the larger firms in the market. Fringe firms tended to earn only competitive rates of return. That is, over time, some firms prove to be more efficient than others. These firms tend to grow and earn higher profits; other firms earn lower profits, fail to grow, or perhaps even drop out of the market altogether. The more pronounced this movement, the more tendency toward concentration the market will exhibit *and* the higher will be the returns of the successful firms.[13] Demsetz ar-

9. 1968 Merger Guidelines, 33 Fed. Reg. 23,442, reprinted in 4 Trade Reg. Rep. (CCH) ¶ 13,101. See § 12.1.

10. The proposals are discussed in § 6.3.

11. For example, accountants generally treat advertising as a current expense, not as a long-term investment. The result is that the investment base for the accountant is smaller, and relative profits, as a percentage of this base, seem to be higher. See Franklin M. Fisher & John J. McGowan, On the Misuse of Accounting Rates of Return to Infer Monopoly Profits, 73 Am. Econ. Rev. 82 (Mar. 1983); H. Demsetz, Accounting for Advertising as a Barrier to Entry, 55 J.Business 345 (1977).

12. These problems are discussed more fully in § 3.9c.

13. See H. Demsetz, Industry Structure, Market Rivalry, and Public Policy, 16 J.L. & Econ. 351 (1971); H. Demsetz, "Two Systems of Belief about Monopoly," in Industrial Concentration: the New Learning, note 2 at 164–184.

gued that this trend is exhibited even when entry barriers are low—that is, the more efficient firms in the industry could exhibit returns substantially higher than marginal firms. However, as long as entry is unrestricted, these higher returns must be classified as "competitive."

Third, Demsetz and others argued that firms will behave competitively as long as entry is easy, even if the number of firms producing in the market is very small. That is, the competitive price is determined not only by who is already producing in the market, but who could easily come in if the price were increased. A high rate of return in such a market cannot be characterized as monopolistic, because if it were additional firms would come in and drive prices down.[14]

Finally, the critique of the S–C–P paradigm aimed most directly at judicially created antitrust rules concerned the supposedly anticompetitive effects of various business practices, such as resale price maintenance, nonprice restraints, tying arrangements, predatory pricing, patent procurement policies, and the like. This literature, which is discussed throughout this book, has had an enormous influence on antitrust policy, particularly since the late 1970's.[15] The thrust of this critique was that defenders of the S–C–P paradigm, but especially courts and the government enforcement divisions, had been much too quick to condemn ambiguous practices as exclusionary. Often the courts had identified conduct as anticompetitive simply because it appeared to injure rivals or vertically related firms. However, aggressive competition always injures rivals, and firms are generally better off if other firms with whom they deal (vertically related firms) are forced to behave competitively as well.

These attacks notwithstanding, the S–C–P paradigm has proven hard to kill. It continues to play a role, although greatly attenuated, in antitrust analysis. Occasionally Chicago School scholars write as if the S–C–P paradigm has been thoroughly discredited, or has no place in antitrust law. But that overstates the case. The structural emphasis of the S–C–P paradigm remains, but today structure no longer appears to dictate performance; rather, we think of structure as a *prerequisite* to anticompetitive performance. Structure has become a necessary but not a sufficient cause. Within this substantially revised paradigm, conduct has acquired considerable independent significance.

The S–C–P paradigm left certain marks that seem all but indelible—for example, the greatly increased attention to market definition, barriers to entry, and proof of market power that even the most convinced members of the Chicago School acknowledge to be important. Antitrust without structural analysis has become impossible, thanks largely to the S–C–P writers. To be sure, they may have gone too far in emphasizing structure over conduct, but that is a question of balance, not of basic legitimacy. Not even S–C–P's most vehement critics would roll the clock back completely.

Overall, the literature attacking the S–C–P paradigm creates an imposing argument that industry concentration is not a bad thing in and of itself. At the same time, concentration seems to be a prerequisite for the existence of market power, and market power is not always a good thing. Further, certain industry structures seem peculiarly conducive to various anticompetitive strategies, and if these strategies are profitable, a profit-maximizing firm can be expected to carry them out.[16]

The most significant development in industrial organization since the Chicago School attacks on the S–C–P paradigm has been a much increased interest in strategic behavior by business firms. This new strategic school of

14. H. Demsetz, Barriers to Entry, 72 Am. Econ. Rev. 47 (Mar. 1982). As noted earlier, Demsetz classified barriers to entry as any phenomenon (such as a government regulation) that restricts socially desirable entry. Scale economies did not qualify, for they restricted only entry that would not be socially desirable in any event. See § 1.6.

15. Some important examples include J. McGee, Predatory Price Cutting: the Standard Oil (N.J.) Case, 1 J.L. & Econ. 137 (1958); W. Bowman, Tying Arrangements and the Leverage Problem, 67 Yale L.J. 19 (1957).

16. See, e.g., E. Granitz & B. Klein, Monopolization by "Raising Rivals' Costs": The Standard Oil Case, 39 J.L. & Econ. 1 (1996).

industrial organization shares some important things in common with the S–C–P paradigm, but is also characterized by some pronounced differences. In general, the new strategies fall into such categories as strategic entry deterrence by dominant firms, through the making of credible threats to impose losses on anyone contemplating entry. A firm can do this through such devices as over-investing in excess capacity which will be very expensive to carry in the event of new entry, but also will enable the firm to increase output and drop its prices immediately if entry occurs.[17] Likewise, a firm might be able to deter entry by raising its rivals' costs. For example, a dominant firm having many patents might threaten every new entrant with litigation alleging infringement. If the costs of litigation are the same for both parties, the *per unit* costs could be much smaller for the dominant firm than for the relatively small new entrant.[18] Firms in product differentiated markets might use proliferation of brands, or the ability to vary their products on short notice to make new entry relatively unattractive.[19] These strategies and others are considered more fully in chapters 6 and 7. What all of them have in common is that they rely on game theory, which is simply another way of saying that people bent on maximizing profits plot strategies that consider (1) the structure of the market as well as (2) the reasonably anticipated responses of other participants in the market, including consumers, suppliers, rivals, and potential rivals.[20]

What the new strategic literature shares in common with the S–C–P paradigm is the notion that market structure, entry barriers, and the market position of the strategizing firms are all important in determining whether a particular anticompetitive strategy is plausible. But the new literature and the S–C–P paradigm depart company in their treatment of conduct. The new literature is far more rigorous about defining the circumstances under which anticompetitive conduct is plausible; further, the anticompetitive effects are generally not considered to be *inherent* in the structure of the market—so that one can ignore or minimize conduct evidence. A better way to state the proposition is that certain market structures make certain anticompetitive strategies plausible, and in that case the antitrust enforcer had better be on the lookout for them. In this highly modified form, the S–C–P paradigm continues to have importance for antitrust.

Finally, there is one area where the orthodox form of the S–C–P paradigm continues to have force, and that is merger policy. The "may * * * substantially * * * lessen competition" standard of § 7 of the Clayton Act[21] invites courts to consider whether a merger may be anticompetitive after it has occurred. In order to make that decision the judge need not observe actual non-competitive conduct, but must ascertain only that market conditions are conducive to such conduct, and that the merger changes the structure in a way that increases the likelihood of such conduct. This analysis remains mainly, although not exclusively, structural.[22]

17. See, for example, M. Spence, Entry, Investment and Oligopolistic Pricing, 8 Bell J. Econ. 534 (1977); A. Dixit, The Role of Investment in Entry Deterrence, 90 Econ. J. 95 (1980); O. Williamson, "Antitrust Enforcement: Where Has It Been; Where is it Going," in Industrial Organization, Antitrust, and Public Policy (J. Craven, 1983), 41–68.

18. See S. Salop and D. Scheffman, Raising Rivals' Costs, 73 Am. Econ. Rev. 267 (May, 1983); T. Krattenmaker & S. Salop, Antitrust Analysis and Anticompetitive Exclusion: Raising Rivals' Costs to Achieve Power over Price, 96 Yale L.J. 209 (1986); T. Krattenmaker & S. Salop, Analyzing Anticompetitive Exclusion, 56 Antitrust L.J. 71 (1987); H. Hovenkamp, Antitrust Policy, Restricted Distribution, and the Market for Exclusionary Rights, 71 Minn.L.Rev. 1293—1318 (1987).

19. On brand proliferation, see R. Schmalensee, Entry Deterrence in the Ready–to–Eat Breakfast Cereal Industry, 9 Bell J. Econ. 305 (1976); on product variation, see T. Campbell, Predation and Competition in Antitrust: the Case of Nonfungible Goods, 87 Col. L. Rev. 1624 (1987).

20. See C. Holt and D. Scheffman, "Strategic Business Behavior and Antitrust," in Economics and Antitrust Policy (R. Larner & J. Meehan, Jr., eds. 1989), at 39.

21. 15 U.S.C.A. § 18.

22. See ch. 12.

Chapter 2

HISTORY AND IDEOLOGY IN ANTITRUST POLICY

Table of Sections

---

§ 2.1 The Development of American Antitrust Policy

2.1a. The Goals of the Sherman Act: Efficiency and Interest Group Explanations

Few elements of statutory interpretation are more frustrating than the study of legislative history to determine a statute's meaning. The debates and compromises leading to a statute's passage often contain conflicting statements, made by persons who were elected by disparate interest groups, who had different motives and different perceptions about what a statute would do. Sometimes legislative committees achieve compromises by making statutory language intentionally ambiguous, leaving to the courts to decide later which interpretation should prevail.

One solution to this problem is to ignore legislative history and look only to the plain language of the statute.[1] But the antitrust laws are not conducive to such an approach because their language is so vague and malleable. For example, the Sherman Act condemns "every contract, combination * * * or conspiracy in restraint of trade," or every person who shall "monopolize," without giving a clue about what those phrases mean.[2] The meaning must be discerned from collateral sources.

§ 2.1

1. See, for example, Blanchard v. Bergeron, 489 U.S. 87, 98, 109 S.Ct. 939, 946 (1989), on remand, 893 F.2d 87 (5th Cir.1990) (statutory language trumps legislative history, particularly when latter is simply a report of single committee of single House of Congress); Public Citizen v. U.S. Dep't of Justice, 491 U.S. 440, 479, 109 S.Ct. 2558, 2579 (1989) (same). See also EEOC v. Arabian American Oil Co., 499 U.S. 244, 247, 111 S.Ct. 1227, 1230 (1991) (construing plain language of statute rather than its legislative history).

2. 15 U.S.C.A. §§ 1, 2.

Unfortunately, the legislative histories of the federal antitrust laws are not always that helpful either. Their ambiguous language has produced considerable scholarly dispute over Congressional intent. This is particularly true of the Sherman Act, whose expansive text has always been the driving force in American antitrust policy. Some scholars have argued that the framers of the Sherman Act were concerned almost exclusively with allocative efficiency as measured by modern neoclassical economics.[3] Others have concluded that Congress has often expressed concern with "justice" or fairness in business behavior, but has never articulated any concept of efficiency as such, not even in the antitrust laws.[4] Still others have argued that Congress' chief concern was to arrest wealth transfers away from consumers and toward price fixers or monopolists.[5] Finally, others have argued that the Sherman Act was passed at the behest of particular non-consumer interests groups, such as small firms[6] or farmers.[7] These divergent, conflicting theories of the Sherman Act reflect underlying ideologies about the nature of legislation generally, or the nature of the relationship between the Sherman Act and the common law.[8]

At one point the Chicago School of antitrust analysis[9] was dominated by a belief that preserving economic efficiency was the guiding concern of those who drafted the Sherman Act. This Congressional concern was said to have been undermined, however, by judicial interpretations and subsequent legislation, particularly the Robinson–Patman Act and the Celler–Kefauver amendments to the merger law.[10] The Chicago School scholars who did this writing were generally uninformed or uninterested in Public Choice theory, something that later members of the School embraced with considerably more enthusiasm.[11] Under Public Choice theory, or interest group analysis, the efficiency position gave way to the idea that the legislative intent of those passing the antitrust laws has never been economic efficiency. Rather, the Sherman Act was special interest legislation, and the principal protected class was small business.[12]

Clearly, the framers of the Sherman Act did not have Pareto-efficiency in mind when they drafted the statute, for Pareto had not yet developed it at the time the Sherman Act was passed.[13] The concepts of allocative efficiency and deadweight loss from monopoly were almost certainly not known to the framers of the Sherman Act.[14] Most of the modern welfare economics of competition and monopoly was developed during the 1930's and after.

Of course, the Sherman Act's framers could have had a less technical conception of efficiency in mind. A great deal of writing in the classical economic tradition defended competitive markets on what we today would call "efficiency" grounds. However, only a few statements in the debates leading up to the Sherman Act sound even remotely like efficiency arguments, and even these are ambiguous. Most of these statements concern the impact of monopoly on consumer prices, or a

3. For example, R. Bork, Legislative Intent and the Policy of the Sherman Act, 9 J.L. & Econ. (1966).

4. For example, L. Schwartz, "Justice" and other Non–Economic Goals of Antitrust, 127 U.Pa.L.Rev. 1076 (1979).

5. R. Lande, Wealth Transfers as the Original and Primary Concern of Antitrust: the Efficiency Interpretation Challenged, 34 Hastings L.J. 65 (1982).

6. See G. Stigler, The Origin of the Sherman Act, 14 J. Legal Stud. 1 (1985); T.J. DiLorenzo, The Origins of Antitrust: An Interest–Group Perspective, 5 Int'l. Rev. L. & Econ. 73 (1985).

7. See W. Shughart, Antitrust Policy and Interest Group Politics 11–12 (1990); and for a critique of this view generally, see Stigler, note 6; and The Causes and Consequences of Antitrust: the Public Choice Perspective (F. McChesney & W. Shughart, eds. 1994).

8. For the great ideological diversity, both at the time the Sherman Act was passed and during its first century of enforcement, see the essays collected in The Political Economy of the Sherman Act: the First Hundred Years (E. T. Sullivan, ed., 1991).

9. See § 2.2b.

10. For example, R. Bork, The Antitrust Paradox: A Policy at War With Itself (1978; rev. ed. 1993).

11. On public choice theory and antitrust, see § 2.2c.

12. See Stigler, note 6.

13. V. Pareto, Manual D' Economie Politique (1909).

14. They were developed mainly in Cambridge University economist Alfred Marshall's Principles of Economics, which was published in 1890. See H. Hovenkamp, The Marginalist Revolution in Legal Thought, 46 Vand.L.Rev. 305 (1993).

desire to protect consumers from high prices. As a result, the statements may suggest that the primary intent of the Sherman Act's framer was not economic efficiency at all, but rather the distributive goal of preventing monopolists from transferring wealth away from consumers.[15]

To characterize the concerns of the framers as "distributive," however, is just as anachronistic as to believe that the framers adopted a theory of allocative efficiency that had not yet been invented. All policies, including those motivated solely by concerns for efficiency, affect the distribution of wealth. An antitrust policy based exclusively on allocative efficiency, for example, may make consumers or large, low-cost businesses richer at the expense of small businesses.

The fact that a policy has certain distributive consequences does not mean that it is "distributive." A policy is purposefully distributive only if it is adopted instead of a policy believed to be more efficient, because the adopted policy distributes wealth in a way the policy maker finds more appealing. The fact that the framers of the antitrust laws had no articulated theory of allocative efficiency suggests that they did not articulate a theory of distributive justice either. As a result it is unrealistic to look at a particular concern expressed in the legislative history—such as the concern that monopolies might impoverish consumers—and pronounce it either "efficient" or "distributive." The framers of the antitrust laws did not perceive economic policies within such a framework, not even after these terms became an accepted part of economic literature.[16]

The argument that the passage of the antitrust laws was driven by efficiency concerns has one additional problem: even as the conceptions of allocative efficiency and the social cost of monopoly became articulated in the economics literature, Congress appeared to become less and less concerned with efficiency and more and more preoccupied with protecting small businesses from larger, more efficient competitors.

Most of the substantive federal antitrust laws were passed in four years: 1890, 1914, 1936, and 1950.[17] The legislative history of the Sherman Act of 1890 contains the best case for the "efficiency" view: that Congress intended the antitrust laws to protect consumers from the high prices and reduced output caused by monopolies and cartels. The legislative history of the Federal Trade Commission Act and Clayton Act of 1914 is somewhat more concerned with the protection of small businesses from the unfair or "exclusionary" practices of bigger firms.[18] The legislative history of the Robinson–Patman Act in 1936,[19] and the Celler–Kefauver Amendments to the antimerger provisions of the Clayton Act in 1950,[20] depart much more decisively from any consumer welfare model. In both 1936 and 1950 Congress was concerned chiefly with protecting small businesses from larger competitors who faced lower costs, even though the result of such protection would be lower total output and higher consumer prices.

The trend in the legislative history does not necessarily undermine a general antitrust goal of improving allocative efficiency, however. The legislative history of the Robinson–Patman Act is relevant only in Robinson–Patman Act cases, and the legislative history of the Celler–Kefauver Act is relevant only in merger cases. Cases involving cartels, monopolization and attempts to monopolize are still decided under the 1890 Sherman Act. Nevertheless, Congress' "regression" on the matter of efficiency and consumer welfare is hard to ignore.

15. Lande, note 5.

16. See H. Hovenkamp, Distributive Justice and the Antitrust Laws, 51 Geo.Wash.L.Rev. 1 (1982).

17. 1890: Sherman Act; 1914: Clayton and Federal Trade Commission Acts; 1936: Robinson–Patman Act; 1950: Cellar–Kefauver Amendments to Clayton Act.

18. See E. Fox, The Modernization of Antitrust: A New Equilibrium, 66 Cornell L.Rev. 1140, 1144 (1981); Hovenkamp, *Distributive Justice*, note 16, at 19.

19. See 14 Antitrust Law ¶ 2303 (1999); H. Hansen, Robinson–Patman Law: A Review and Analysis, 51 Fordham L.Rev. 1113 (1983). See § 14.6a.

20. See 4 Antitrust Law ¶ ¶ 901–904 (rev. ed. 1998); D. Bok, Section 7 of the Clayton Act and the Merging of Law and Economics, 74 Harv.L.Rev. 226 (1960); H. Hovenkamp, Derek Bok and the Merger of Law and Economics, 21 J. L. Reform 515 (1988). See § 12.2.

Further, both the allocative efficiency theory and the consumer wealth transfer theory of the Sherman Act seem inconsistent with other historical facts. *First*, the same Congress that passed the Sherman Act also passed the McKinley Tariff, one of the largest and most anticonsumer tariffs in United States history. Senator Sherman himself was a fierce protectionist.[21] *Second*, the decade before 1890 was generally a period of declining rather than increasing prices. Indeed, by some measures the rate and extensiveness of price declines was unprecedented—a general 7% decline in the consumer price index, as output expanded dramatically.[22] Although much of the wrath of the Sherman Act's framers was directed at two targets, the Standard Oil Company and the sugar trust, the price of the products produced by those firms had declined precipitously during the preceding decade.[23] From 1880 through 1890 the price of refined petroleum had fallen by 61% and output had increased four-fold. Refined sugar prices fell by more than eighteen percent between 1880 and 1889.[24] The iron and steel industry, another target of the Sherman Act's proponents, had witnessed declines of about twenty percent. *Third*, railroad rates were also in rapid decline.[25] *Fourth*, the decade preceding the passage of the Sherman Act was one of rapid economic growth, with the real gross national product increasing by about 24%.[26] Points two, three and four make it unlikely that a Congress concerned about allocative efficiency would suddenly want federal legislation to intervene in markets and make them work better. Points one, two and three make it unlikely that Congress was really very concerned about consumers' having to pay high prices.

The allocative efficiency theory and the consumer wealth transfer theories are also called into question by the fact that the vast majority of economists were opposed to the statute.[27] They generally believed that the emergent "trust," or large business firm was efficient and would result in higher output and lower consumer prices. Indeed, the notion that the Sherman Act was pure protectionism for the benefit of small business appears to have been widespread.

A theory with more explanatory power is that the Sherman Act was passed at the behest of small businesses who had been injured by the formation of larger, more efficient firms. This was the one group of people who were injured, were well organized, and had long been effective in making their case to legislative bodies. Among the most effective lobbying organizations of the day were various associations of independent and small businesses, whose positions were threatened by large vertically integrated firms. Senator Sherman himself may have been acting at the behest of independent oil producers in Ohio, who wanted protection from the Standard Oil Company and the railroads. Various labor organizations also lobbied Congress, but their principal concern seems to have been that new technology would steal jobs.[28] Although the Sherman Act included provisions for private lawsuits, nearly everyone who spoke on the issue believed that *consumer* lawsuits would be ineffectual. When the Congressmen spoke of private lawsuits, they were thinking of competitor suits.[29]

An alternative explanation that is less consistent with the interest group theory of politics but perhaps more consistent with nineteenth century American ideology generally, is

21. See T. Hazlett, The Legislative History of the Sherman Act Re–Examined, 30 Econ. Inquiry 263, 267 (1992).

22. See Hazlett, id. at 273; DiLorenzo, note 6 at 79–81.

23. See Hovenkamp, Antitrust's Protected Classes, 88 Mich.L.Rev. 1, 28 (1989); G. Gunton, The Economic and Social Aspect of Trusts, 3 Pol.Sci.Q. 385, 394 (1888); J. Jenks & W. Clark, The Trust Problem 108 (1929).

24. See L. Telser, A Theory of Efficient Cooperation and Competition 28–29 (1987); J. Jenks & W. Clark, note 23 at 82.

25. Hovenkamp, note 23 at 29; Telser, note 24 at 30–31.

26. Shughart, note 7 at 13.

27. See H. Hovenkamp, Enterprise and American Law: 1836–1937 at 308–315 (1991); T. DiLorenzo & J. High, Antitrust and Competition, Historically Considered, 26 Econ. Inquiry 423 (1988); Gordon, Attitudes Toward Trusts Prior to the Sherman Act, 30 S. Econ. J. 156 (1963).

28. See H. Hovenkamp, *Enterprise*, note 27 at 246–247; J. Blicksilver, Defenders and Defense of Big Business in the United States, 1880–1900 at 122–128 (1985).

29. See H. Hovenkamp, Antitrust's Protected Classes, 88 Mich. L. Rev. 1, 25–27 (1989).

that the antitrust laws were passed out of a pervasive fear of private "bigness" and the political power that it engendered. The nineteenth century American rhetoric on monopoly is concerned at least as much with bigness *per se* as it is with monopoly prices. Further, the American ideal was a market economy into which any entrepreneur could enter and compete on the merits—that was the American worker's escape from the sweatshop. Big firms such as Standard Oil or Carnegie Steel threatened that ideal by signalling that only big firms could survive. If one looks at the ideology of nineteenth century Americans, rather than at the interest groups that may have contributed to the Sherman Act's formation, the anti-bigness rationale seems to be very important.

Ironically, however, if the Sherman Act was directed at bigness, it had precisely the opposite consequence that its framers had in mind. The period 1895–1905 witnessed the largest wave of mergers (measured as a percentage of the economy) in American history. Most likely the mergers occurred because the Sherman Act made looser forms of organization such as joint ventures illegal. Firms were forced to do by merger what they could not longer accomplish by contract.[30]

2.1b. The Common Law and the Federal Antitrust Laws

One solution to the problem of ambiguous statutory language and legislative history is to assume that antitrust violations are a kind of "common law" offense, where judicial precedent defines the substance of the legal rules to be applied. Most of the practices challenged under the Sherman Act had previously been addressed under common law rules.[31] The framers of the Sherman Act believed that they were simply "federalizing" the common law of trade restraints, making the common law more effective by creating a forum with jurisdiction over monopolies or cartels that operated in more than a single state.[32] The earliest Sherman Act decisions construed the statute in that way: they generally decided cases by reference to common law precedents.[33]

The federal antitrust laws differed from the common law in at least one important respect, however. At common law most of the agreements addressed under § 1 of the Sherman Act were unenforceable but not affirmatively illegal. For example, contracts in restraint of trade could not be enforced by one participant against another. However, a consumer or competitor of the contracting parties was generally not permitted either to enjoin the contract or to obtain damages for injuries.[34] By contrast, § 7 of the original Sherman Act (and later §§ 4 and 16 of the Clayton Act) gave *non*participants in Sherman Act contracts, combinations or conspiracies a right to challenge such practices and obtain either damages or an injunction. The importance of this expansion

30. See Hovenkamp, *Enterprise*, note 27 at Ch. 20; G. Bittlingmayer, Did Antitrust Policy Cause the Great Merger Wave?, 28 J.L. & Econ. 77 (1985). For a contemporary view, see G. Canfield, Is a Large Corporation an Illegal Combination or Monopoly under the Sherman Anti–Trust Act?, 9 Col. L. Rev. 95, 113 & n. 27 (1909), arguing that the Sherman Act "fosters the very thing it was designed to check.". England was much more tolerant of cartels, with the result that British firms lacked the same incentive to merge and remained inefficiently small. See T. Freyer, Regulating Big Business: Antitrust in Great Britain and America, 1880–1990 (1992).

31. For a survey of the nineteenth century common law decisions, see 1 Antitrust Law ¶ 104 (rev. ed. 1997); H. Hovenkamp, The Sherman Act and the Classical Theory of Competition, 74 Iowa L. Rev. 1019 (1989). On the common law nature of antitrust rules, see A. Director and E. Levi, Law and the Future: Trade Regulation, 51 Nw. U. L. Rev. 281 (1956), the symposium in 17 Miss. Col. L. Rev. 1 (1996); and W. Page, Legal Realism and the Shaping of Modern Antitrust, 44 Emory L.J. 1 (1995).

32. Senator Sherman described his bill as setting "out in the most specific language the rule of the common law which prevails in England and this country * * *." 20 Cong.Rec. 1167 (1889); see D. Dewey, The Common–Law Background of Antitrust Policy, 41 Va.L.Rev. 759 (1955); Hovenkamp, *Sherman Act*, note 31, 74 Iowa L. Rev. 1029 et seq.

33. For example, United States v. Addyston Pipe & Steel Co., 85 Fed. 271, 278–291 (6th Cir.1898), affirmed, 175 U.S. 211, 20 S.Ct. 96 (1899); see W. Baxter, Separation of Powers, Prosecutorial Discretion, and the "Common Law" Nature of Antitrust Law, 60 Tex.L.Rev. 661 (1982).

34. See Central Shade–Roller Co. v. Cushman, 143 Mass. 353, 363–364, 9 N.E. 629, 631 (1887); Perkin v. Lyman, 9 Mass. 522, 530 (1813); and see A. Stickney, State Control of Trade and Commerce by National or State Authority 157 (1897); Hovenkamp, *Sherman Act*, note 31, 74 Iowa L. Rev. at 1026–1027.

should not be overlooked, for it effectively carried the doctrine of contracts in restraint of trade out of the realm of "private" law and into the realm of "public" law.

The idea that antitrust violations are a special kind of common law offense makes statutory language and legislative history less important than the language and legislative history of other statutes. Furthermore, the stated intention was not to "freeze" the common law as it existed in 1890, but rather to regard the common law as an ongoing, ever changing body of rules. As Sherman Act precedent began to accumulate, the courts began to diverge from the nineteenth century common law. The federal antitrust laws took on a life of their own. In short, the Sherman Act can be regarded as "enabling" legislation—an invitation to the federal courts to learn how businesses and markets work and formulate a set of rules that will make them work in socially efficient ways. The standards to be applied always have and probably always will shift as ideology, technology and the American economy changes.[35]

Federal courts have always interpreted the antitrust statutes in a common law fashion,[36] and the result is a substantial divergence between statutory language and judicial decision. For example, the language of the antitrust statutes does not contain anything resembling the distinction between the *per se* rule and the rule of reason, the market power requirement for monopolization cases, the "potential entrant" doctrine of conglomerate mergers, the "shared monopoly" theory, or the "indirect purchaser" rule.

The common law approach to antitrust analysis is implicit in Congress' use of statutory language. Section 1 of the Clayton Act, like the opening sections of many federal statutes, defines the terms used later in the Act.[37] These words include "antitrust laws," "commerce," and "person." Amazingly, the list does not also include "competition," "monopoly," or "restraint of trade." Congress expressly told the courts what kind of "person" could sue or be sued under the statute but it did not define "competition" or "restraint of trade" or even "monopoly"—effectively yielding the meaning of the most essential terms to the courts.[38]

But the fact that the Sherman Act authorized a common law approach to antitrust analysis in no way entails that courts interpreting the Sherman Act would be tied to state court judicial precedents of the nineteenth century and earlier. The record is quite to the contrary. Only the earliest Sherman Act decisions paid very much attention to actual common law decisions, and federal courts very quickly deviated from the common law as it existed when the Sherman Act was passed.[39] Thus the "common law" approach of the federal antitrust laws refers to a precedent-oriented manner of interpretation, not a set of substantive doctrines.

Indeed, the most famous "common law" interpretation of the Sherman Act actually distorted the common law so badly that it effectively cut the knot between common law and antitrust approaches to combinations in restraint of trade. Judge Taft's opinion in United States v. Addyston Pipe & Steel Co.[40] has often been praised for its expression of the relationship between the Sherman Act and the common law. The great brilliance of the opinion, its admirers have argued, is that Taft was able to show that the common law had always condemned anticompetitive price fixing agreements, while it had approved efficiency creat-

35. See W. Page, Ideological Conflict and the Origins of Antitrust Policy, 66 Tul.L.Rev. 1, 36 (1991).

36. For example, see the discussion in Apex Hosiery Co. v. Leader, 310 U.S. 469, 497–99, 60 S.Ct. 982, 994–996 (1940).

37. 15 U.S.C.A. § 12.

38. Judicial definitions of words such as "competition" have gone through quite an evolution in federal antitrust decisions. See H. Hovenkamp, Book Review, 33 Hastings L.J. 755, 762 (1982). Judge Bork has identified five distinct meanings of "competition." See R. Bork, The Antitrust Paradox: A Policy at War With Itself 58–61 (1978; rev. ed. 1993). On changing meanings in antitrust litigation, see D. Gifford, The Jurisprudence of Antitrust, 48 SMU L. Rev. 1677 (1995).

39. See generally Hovenkamp, *Sherman Act*, note 31; 1 Antitrust Law ¶ 104 (rev. ed. 1997).

40. 85 Fed. 271 (6th Cir.1898), affirmed, 175 U.S. 211, 20 S.Ct. 96 (1899).

ing joint ventures.[41] Under Taft's rule, "naked" restraints such as price fixing were condemned automatically, under a *per se* analysis, while restraints that were legitimately "ancillary" to an efficiency creating joint venture were approved.[42]

In fact, Judge Taft's vision was much narrower and was based on a deeply flawed view of the common law.[43] The cases that Judge Taft cited for the reasonableness of ancillary restraints actually involved covenants not to compete contained in employment agreements or agreements for the sale of property. Although they were subject to a rule of reason, the content of the rule was generally nothing more than consideration of whether the noncompetition agreement was limited in duration and confined to a fairly narrow geographic area. The relationship between approval of such agreements and their underlying efficiency is no more than haphazard. Judge Taft's list of rule of reason restraints did not include any production enhancing or transaction cost reducing joint ventures. The ancillary restraints that courts generally upheld, Taft said, were:

> (1) by the seller of property or business not to compete with the buyer in such a way as to derogate from the value of the property or business sold; (2) by a retiring partner not to compete with the firm; (3) by a partner pending the partnership not to do anything to interfere, by competition or otherwise, with the business of the firm; (4) by the buyer of property not to use the same in competition with the business retained by the seller; and (5) by an assistant, servant or agent not to compete with his master or employer after the expiration of his time of service.[44]

Today very few of the restraints characterized by courts as ancillary and efficiency enhancing, such as production joint ventures, fall within one of Taft's examples. Taft gave these examples because they were the only ones he could find in the law of trade restraints up to that time. In sum, Taft's interpretation of common law decisions to distinguish between "naked" and "ancillary" restraints was nothing more than an indication that covenants not to compete should continue to be analyzed by a rule of reason under the federal antitrust laws.[45]

At the same time, Taft painted an impressionistic, noninterpretivist picture of the law of cartels and contracts in restraint of Trade. His *Addyston Pipe* opinion was as important for its disingenuousness as for its brilliance. He ignored or misconstrued common law and even Sherman Act decisions that had unambiguously approved naked price-fixing.[46] He cited half the opinions in order to explain why they were wrong.[47] Some of the cases he cited for the common law position on trade restraints actually relied on statutes that deviated from the common law.[48] Some of the opinions he cited as condemning "naked" restraints in fact condemned joint ventures with

41. See, for example, R. Bork, The Antitrust Paradox: a Policy at War With Itself 26–30 (1978; rev. ed. 1993).

42. On cartels, joint ventures, and the rule of reason, see Chs. 4 & 5.

43. See 1 Antitrust Law, id. at ¶ 104d; Hovenkamp, *Sherman Act* note 31 at 1041–1044; M. Grady, Toward A Positive Economic Theory of Antitrust, 30 Econ. Inquiry 224, 229–232 (1992).

44. *Addyston Pipe*, 85 Fed. at 281.

45. On the narrow conception of ancillary restraints doctrine contained in the *Addyston Pipe* decision, see H. Hovenkamp, 11 Antitrust Law ¶ 1905 (1998).

46. For example, United States v. Nelson, 52 Fed. 646, 647 (D.Minn.1892) (upholding collusion under Sherman Act); Dolph v. Troy Laundry Mach. Co., 28 Fed. 553, 555–556 (C.C.N.Y.1886), rev'd, 138 U.S. 617, 11 S.Ct. 412 (1891) (upholding price fixing under common law); Pierce v. Fuller, 8 Mass. 223 (1811) (upholding naked noncompetition agreement—basically, a horizontal service division agreement); Clark v. Frank, 17 Mo.App. 602 (1885) (same); Skrainka v. Scharringhausen, 8 Mo.App. 522, 527 (1880) (upholding price fixing limited to time and place).

47. For example, Gloucester Isinglass & Glue Co. v. Russia Cement Co., 154 Mass. 92, 27 N.E. 1005 (1891) (upholding combination in restraint of trade because it did not involve a necessity of life); Leslie v. Lorillard, 110 N.Y. 519, 18 N.E. 363 (1888) (upholding naked noncompetition agreement). Other cases are discussed in Hovenkamp, *Sherman Act*, note 31, 74 Iowa L. Rev. at 1043.

48. Gibbs v. Consolidated Gas Co of Baltimore., 130 U.S. 396, 9 S.Ct. 553 (1889) (relying on statute that prohibited a gas company from combining with another gas company); Ford v. Chicago Milk Shippers' Ass'n., 155 Ill. 166, 39 N.E. 651 (1895) (relying on statute forbidding combinations by trust); People v. Sheldon, 139 N.Y. 251, 34 N.E. 785 (1893) (same); Morris Run Coal Co. v. Barclay Coal Co., 68 Pa. 173 (1871) (same).

great efficiency-creating potential. For example, People v. Sheldon[49] involved a joint venture that established a uniform grading system for coal and a common sales agency, but also facilitated the fixing of prices. The *Morris Run Coal* case[50] rejected the defense that the coal grading and selling joint venture at issue was designed in part "to lessen expenses," because the resulting restraint was "too general" for that end. In other words, the court applied the traditional common law rule that the restraint could not be broader than necessary to protect the parties' business. In addition, Taft failed to acknowledge that the restraint at issue in the *Trans–Missouri* case, where the Supreme Court had applied the Sherman Act to a railroad joint venture, was ancillary—an efficiency creating cargo-transfer, scheduling, and freight rate division agreement among unregulated railroads.[51]

Disingenuous or not, all of this was immensely valuable to emergent federal antitrust policy. One of the great accomplishments of Taft's *Addyston Pipe* opinion was to fuse the emerging economic model of competition with the traditional legal doctrine of combinations in restraint of trade. In the process Judge Taft created the illusion that the law of combinations in restraint of trade had always been concerned with competition as defined in neoclassical economics. The result was a Sherman Act whose ideology was much more economic than that reflected in either the common law or the Congressional history. Congress' own notion that the Sherman Act simply federalized the common law cut the courts free from the Act's legislative history, but Taft's *Addyston Pipe* decision effectively freed the courts from the substance of the historical common law. From that point on, federal courts forged their own set of antitrust rules through an essentially common law process in which only Sherman (and later Clayton) Act precedents counted. Common law precedents were mainly, although not entirely, ignored.

Does the nonspecific language of the Sherman Act entitle the judiciary to engage in such usurpation? When the courts interpret the antitrust laws, they are interpreting federal statutes, and Congress can always respond to an unpopular or ill-conceived decision by amending the statute. Congress has frequently done so, in both liability expanding and liability contracting directions. For example, in 1912 the Supreme Court concluded that the Sherman Act did not condemn tying arrangements.[52] Congress responded in 1914 with § 3 of the Clayton Act,[53] which condemns them if they are anticompetitive (without defining that word). In 1911 the Supreme Court suggested that resale price maintenance was illegal under the Sherman Act,[54] and in 1937 Congress responded by giving the states the right to authorize resale price maintenance for sales within their borders. Forty years later, Congress changed its mind.[55] On many other occasions Congress has either passed or considered legislation that would overrule unpopular antitrust decisions.

Ideology, politics and theory have always changed and undoubtedly always will. American economic and business policy invariably changes with them. The federal antitrust laws were designed in a way that will enable courts to respond to those changes. Congress, if it wants, may rejoin. Perhaps the most isolationistic and regressive of views is that in 1890 or today we have all the right answers. We did not and we do not. The common law nature of antitrust policy permits us to make the best of what we have.

49. Note 48.

50. 68 Pa. 173, 184 (1871) (decided by a Pennsylvania court applying New York law).

51. United States v. Trans–Missouri Freight Assn., 166 U.S. 290, 17 S.Ct. 540 (1897). See the lower court's opinion, 58 Fed. 58, 67–80 (8th Cir.1893); H. Hovenkamp, *Enterprise*, note 27 at 144–148. The efficiency of the *Trans–Missouri* joint venture is discussed in § 5.2a.

52. Henry v. A.B. Dick Co., 224 U.S. 1, 32 S.Ct. 364 (1912).

53. 15 U.S.C.A. § 14.

54. Dr. Miles Medical Co. v. John D. Park & Sons Co., 220 U.S. 373, 31 S.Ct. 376 (1911).

55. The Miller–Tydings Act of 1937, 50 Stat. 693, permitted states to authorize resale price maintenance. The authorization was withdrawn and the *per se* rule restored for all states by the Consumer Goods Pricing Act of 1975, 89 Stat. 801. See § 11.5a.

2.1c. A Thumbnail History of Federal Antitrust Policy

The history of American antitrust policy has been told many times, at varying levels of detail and sophistication. The following is an extremely brief overview, with citations to other historical works.[56] The review concludes with the 1960's.

Most early enforcement of the Sherman Act was by the federal government, and its main target was cartels and the array of tighter combinations then known as "trusts." Many of the earliest attempts foundered, because the federal courts interpreted the Act under the general common law rules that (1) agreements to increase price not accompanied by any coercive actions against third parties were not illegal; and (2) cartels were generally not illegal unless they controlled virtually all of the affected market.[57] Equally pessimistic was the first Supreme Court decision interpreting the Sherman Act, the *E. C. Knight* case of 1895, which held that the Act did not reach a combination of sugar producers because the combination mainly affected manufacturing, and manufacturing itself was not interstate commerce. As a result, the indictment was outside the federal government's jurisdictional reach under the commerce clause.[58]

Blame for the early failures of the Sherman Act is sometimes laid at the feet of Richard Olney, President Cleveland's Attorney General, who was not an enthusiastic trustbuster. But an alternative view of Olney is that he was highly restrained because he predicted—correctly, it turned out—that the courts were unlikely to cooperate in any attempt to use the Sherman Act expansively.[59] The one place the Sherman Act did find aggressive use, much to the horror of some of its early supporters, was as a tool against labor union organizing. Indeed, twelve out of the first thirteen Sherman Act convictions, obtained between 1890 and 1897, were against labor unions.[60] Congress eventually responded to labor's concerns by exempting most labor organizing from the antitrust laws, first in § 6 of the Clayton Act,[61] and later in the Norris–LaGuardia Act.[62]

The federal government's first major Sherman Act successes were against railroad cartels operating mainly in the midwest,[63] and in 1904 against a railroad merger.[64] By the turn of the century the government's win record in cases against capitalists rather than labor began to improve, with victories against cartels,[65] and major convictions against the Standard Oil Company and the tobacco trust in 1911 for monopolization, allegedly by predatory practices and merger to monopoly.[66]

The period 1895–1905 witnessed an enormous wave of mergers, caused in part by the Sherman Act itself. Many entrepreneurs be-

56. The classic, highly factual account is Hans B. Thorelli, The Federal Antitrust Policy: Origination of an American Tradition (1955). A few of the others are R. Peritz, Competition Policy in America, 1888–1992: History, Rhetoric, Law (1996); W. Letwin, Law and Economic Policy in America: the Evolution of the Sherman Antitrust Act (1981); M. M. Sklar, The Corporate Reconstruction of American Capitalism, 1890–1916: the Market, the Law, and Politics (1988); H. Hovenkamp, Enterprise and American Law: 1836–1937 (1991); T. Freyer, Regulating Big Business: Antitrust in Great Britain and America, 1880–1990 (1992). The legislative history of the antitrust laws is collected in E. Kintner, The Legislative History of the Antitrust Laws (1978).

57. See for example In re Greene, 52 Fed. 104, 114 (C.C.Ohio 1892) (merger of distillers intending to control entire market not illegal where the acquisition agreements did not prevent sellers from re-entering); United States v. Nelson, 52 Fed. 646, 647 (D.Minn.1892) (lumber producer cartel not illegal unless the companies controlled or intended to control entire market); United States v. Greenhut, 50 Fed. 469, 470 (D.Mass.1892) (liquor producers; same).

58. United States v. E.C. Knight Co., 156 U.S. 1, 15 S.Ct. 249 (1895). See H. Hovenkamp, *Enterprise*, note 56 at 241–245.

59. Letwin, note 56 at 117–118.

60. H. Hovenkamp, *Enterprise*, note 56 at 229.

61. 15 U.S.C.A. § 16, passed in 1914.

62. 29 U.S.C.A. §§ 101–110, 113–115, passed in 1932. On antitrust's labor exemption today, see § 19.7b, infra; and 1A Antitrust Law ¶¶ 255–257 (rev. ed. 1997).

63. United States v. Trans–Missouri Freight Assn., 166 U.S. 290, 17 S.Ct. 540 (1897); United States v. Joint–Traffic Assn., 171 U.S. 505, 19 S.Ct. 25 (1898).

64. Northern Securities Co. v. U.S., 193 U.S. 197, 24 S.Ct. 436 (1904).

65. For example, United States v. Addyston Pipe & Steel Co., 85 Fed. 271, 278–291 (6th Cir.1898), affirmed, 175 U.S. 211, 20 S.Ct. 96 (1899).

66. Standard Oil Co. (N.J.) v. United States, 221 U.S. 1, 31 S.Ct. 502 (1911); United States v. American Tobacco Co., 221 U.S. 106, 31 S.Ct. 632 (1911).

lieved that the Act would prohibit cartels but be quite tolerant of tighter combinations involving asset acquisitions or holding companies.[67] At any rate, following the great merger wave, the United States became deeply involved in merger policy—a concern that has not subsided to the present day.

Two things account for the great interest in antitrust during the 1912 Presidential election. One was the great merger wave noted above. The other was the development of the "rule of reason" in the *Standard Oil* and *American Tobacco* decisions of 1911.[68] Notwithstanding the convictions in those cases, many Progressive Era liberals believed that the rule of reason would greatly weaken the Sherman Act, a position reinforced by rulings such as Henry v. A.B. Dick & Co.[69] that tying arrangements should be considered reasonable under the Sherman Act. The new Wilson administration responded with the Clayton Act[70] and the Federal Trade Commission Act.[71] The Clayton Act explicitly condemned anticompetitive price discrimination, tying and exclusive dealing, expanded private enforcement, created an early but rather ineffectual exemption for labor organizing,[72] and condemned mergers on a far more aggressive standard than the Sherman Act had done. The FTC Act created the Federal Trade Commission, an administrative body that could summon expertise unavailable to the courts,[73] and also created a more expansive basis for liability, namely § 5 of the FTC Act, which condemned unfair methods of competition. Under that statute, as eventually interpreted, the FTC could go after practices it deemed anticompetitive, but which did not violate one of the other antitrust laws.[74]

The period from the end of the Progressive Era, through World War One and up to the New Deal is generally characterized by a very moderate merger policy[75] and greatly increased attention to joint ventures and trade associations.[76] The government also became heavily involved in enforcing the law against resale price maintenance, which had been condemned by the Supreme Court in 1911,[77] and of exclusive dealing, which was condemned when anticompetitive by the Clayton Act.[78]

The 1930's was a highly ambiguous, turbulent and contradictory period for both economic theory and antitrust policy. On one side were those who believed that price competition was unworkable and inefficient, and who advocated broad freedom from antitrust prosecution for joint ventures, trade associations or other group activities thought to increase efficiency.[79] On the other were those who insisted on aggressive antitrust enforcement against all combinations. The first group temporarily won

67. See H. Hovenkamp, *Enterprise*, note 56, ch. 20; R. Nelson, Merger Movements in American Industry, 1895–1956 (1959); S. Bruchey, Enterprise: the Dynamic Economy of a Free People (1990); N. Lamoreaux, The Great Merger Movement in American Business, 1895–1904 (1985).

68. See note 66.

69. 224 U.S. 1, 32 S.Ct. 364 (1912).

70. 15 U.S.C.A. § 12 et seq.

71. 15 U.S.C.A. § 41 et seq.

72. See Hovenkamp, *Enterprise*, note 56 at Ch. 19.

73. The best detailed history remains Gerard C. Henderson, The Federal Trade Commission: A Study in Administrative Law and Procedure (1924).

74. See FTC v. Brown Shoe Co., 384 U.S. 316, 86 S.Ct. 1501 (1966); FTC v. Sperry & Hutchinson Co., 405 U.S. 233, 92 S.Ct. 898 (1972).

75. For example, United States v. United Shoe Machinery Co., 247 U.S. 32, 38 S.Ct. 473 (1918); United States v. United States Steel Corp., 251 U.S. 417, 40 S.Ct. 293 (1920); United States v. Southern Pacific Co., 259 U.S. 214, 42 S.Ct. 496 (1922).

76. For example, Board of Trade of City of Chicago v. United States, 246 U.S. 231, 38 S.Ct. 242 (1918); American Column & Lumber Co. v. United States, 257 U.S. 377, 42 S.Ct. 114 (1921); Maple Flooring Mfrs'. Ass'n v. United States, 268 U.S. 563, 45 S.Ct. 578 (1925).

77. Dr. Miles Medical Co. v. John D. Park & Sons Co., 220 U.S. 373, 31 S.Ct. 376 (1911). United States v. Colgate & Co., 250 U.S. 300, 39 S.Ct. 465 (1919); United States v. A. Schrader's Son, Inc., 252 U.S. 85, 40 S.Ct. 251 (1920); FTC v. Beech–Nut Packing Co., 257 U.S. 441, 42 S.Ct. 150 (1922); and numerous others.

78. For example, FTC v. Sinclair Refining Co., 261 U.S. 463, 43 S.Ct. 450 (1923). On other early decisions, see 11 H. Hovenkamp, Antitrust Law ¶ 1801 (1998).

79. See generally E. Hawley, The New Deal and the Problem of Monopoly (1974); E. Hawley, Herbert Hoover and the Sherman Act, 1921–1933: an Early Phase of a Continuing Issue, 74 Iowa L. Rev. 1067 (1989); R. Himmelberg, The Origins of the National Recovery Administration, Business, Government, and the Trade Association Issue, 1921–1933 (1976).

out during the New Deal, when Roosevelt's "Codes of Fair Competition" virtually legalized various forms of collusion. But after the National Recovery Administration was struck down by the Supreme Court, Roosevelt changed course. He made Thurman Arnold head of the antitrust division. Until World War II intervened, Arnold pursued vertical integration,[80] collusion and, for the first time, oligopoly aggressively, going after obvious collusion facilitators such as price-posting as well as tacit agreements.[81] He also greatly expanded the use of antitrust consent decrees as a mechanism for obtaining government relief faster and more predictably than more protracted litigation would produce. At the same time, Congress expanded § 2 of the Clayton Act by passing the Robinson–Patman Act,[82] which greatly limited the ability of firms to charge lower prices to large customers than they did to smaller ones. With that statute, the government enforcement agencies embarked on the highly anticompetitive policy of trying to protect small business from more efficient, larger firms.[83]

Undoubtedly the most lasting legacy of the problems attending the New Deal and the recovery was the increasing attempt by antitrust policy makers after World War II to take efficiency concerns more seriously, and to recognize that bigness and even a certain amount of oligopoly were a fact of life.[84] This required a more sophisticated dialogue between antitrust and economic theory.[85] The economic theory of the day placed a heavy emphasis on structural issues. Concern for concentration, entry barriers, and the linkage between structure and oligopoly dominated the post-war period.[86] At the same time American enforcement agencies became highly concerned—in fact, almost paranoid—about vertical practices that were thought to increase entry barriers, facilitate collusion, or enable firms to leverage additional monopoly profits out of secondary markets. The result was continued aggressive enforcement of the laws against resale price maintenance, new attention to vertical nonprice restraints, and numerous challenges to tying arrangements, exclusive dealing and vertical mergers.[87]

The most prominent antitrust policy document of the period was the Report of the Attorney General's National Committee to Study the Antitrust Laws (1955), which was mildly expansionary by the standards of that time. The report advocated stricter merger standards that relied heavily on structural factors but generally disregarded the efficiencies that could result from mergers. Even Carl Kaysen's and Donald F. Turner's *Antitrust Policy*,[88] which was more rigorous economically, identified the promotion of "fair" conduct and the limiting of growth of big business as desirable antitrust goals.[89] Indeed, they even suggested that a legitimate goal of antitrust policy is the equitable distribution of income.[90] Much of the foundational analysis for this thinking, but without the explicit normative concerns, was contained in Harvard economist

80. For example, United States v. Paramount Pictures, Inc., 334 U.S. 131, 68 S.Ct. 915 (1948); United States v. Pullman Co., 330 U.S. 806, 67 S.Ct. 1078 (1947).

81. For example, American Tobacco Co. v. United States, 328 U.S. 781, 66 S.Ct. 1125 (1946); United States v. Socony–Vacuum Oil Co., 310 U.S. 150, 60 S.Ct. 811 (1940). See also Sugar Institute v. United States, 297 U.S. 553, 56 S.Ct. 629 (1936); Interstate Circuit, Inc. v. United States, 306 U.S. 208, 59 S.Ct. 467 (1939).

82. See ch. 14.

83. See § 14.6; and F.M. Rowe, Price Discrimination Under the Robinson–Patman Act (1962).

84. For example, J. Clark, Toward a Concept of Workable Competition, 30 Am. Econ. Rev. 243 (1940).

85. See Thurman Arnold's call for more economics in antitrust. Arnold, Antitrust Law Enforcement, Past and Future, 7 L. & Contemp. Prob. 10 (1940); and see generally W. Kovacic, Failed Expectations: the Troubled Past and Uncertain Future of the Sherman Act as a Tool for Deconcentration, 74 Iowa L. Rev. 1105 (1989).

86. For example United States v. Aluminum Co. of America, 148 F.2d 416 (2d Cir.1945); United States v. Columbia Steel Co., 334 U.S. 495, 68 S.Ct. 1107 (1948).

87. Among the long list of examples are United States v. Yellow Cab Co., 332 U.S. 218, 67 S.Ct. 1560 (1947); International Salt Co. v. United States, 332 U.S. 392, 68 S.Ct. 12 (1947); United States v. Griffith, 334 U.S. 100, 68 S.Ct. 941 (1948); Standard Oil Co. of California v. United States, 337 U.S. 293, 69 S.Ct. 1051 (1949).

88. C. Kaysen & D. Turner, Antitrust Policy: An Economic and Legal Analysis (1959).

89. Id. at 11–17.

90. Id. at 11: ("[E]quitable distribution of income" is a "desirable economic result," against which antitrust policy should be tested.).

Joe S. Bain's 1950's work on barriers to entry, industry structure, and oligopoly.[91]

By 1950, when the Celler–Kefauver amendments to § 7 of the Clayton Act were passed, concern with market imperfections had become the most pronounced feature of antitrust policy. Economists' concerns about oligopoly and concentration were translated and greatly exaggerated in Congressional policies that were suspicious of business expansion and even hostile toward efficiency. At the same time, Congress may have been overly responsive to lobbying organizations of small businesses who were injured by the efficient practices of larger firms. The culmination of this thinking was a 1960's antitrust policy that was openly hostile toward innovation[92] and large scale development, and a zealous protector of the right of small business to operate independently.[93]

The literature criticizing 1960's antitrust policy for its numerous excesses routinely blames the Warren Court. But the first party to blame is the enforcement agencies of the government, particularly the Federal Trade Commission. The great majority of Warren era decisions that are characterized today as overly aggressive came in suits brought by the government, in which the Court did precisely what the government asked it to do.[94] For this reason arguments such as those analyzed in § 2.2c below that competitors are inferior plaintiffs, or that most antitrust litigation should be pursued by the government, must be seen in historical perspective. Over the one hundred year history of the antitrust laws most of the zealotry and expansiveness in doctrine has been requested by the government itself. The aggressive private plaintiff has done no more than pick up where the government left off. Today the tables are turned, and the private plaintiff is generally viewed as the enforcer who pushes antitrust to its limits. But these are contingent rather than eternal positions, and they could change once again.

This brief history concludes here, with the end of the Warren Era. The Chicago School, which was in large part energized by the expansive antitrust policy of the 1950's and 1960's, is discussed in § 2.2b. From that point on, we are speaking not of history but of current policy, and that is the subject of the rest of this book.

§ 2.2 On the Role of Economics in Antitrust

2.2a. Antitrust and Economics Before 1960

As noted in § 2.1b, great early antitrust opinions such as Taft's *Addyston Pipe* decision effectively freed the antitrust laws from both Congressional intent and the substantive rules of the common law. From that point the federal courts forged their own antitrust policy, taking advantage of the best applied economics of the day. One of the great myths about American antitrust policy is that courts first began to adopt an "economic approach" to antitrust problems in the relatively recent past.[1] This belief has led some to argue that antitrust could escape from ever-changing, in-

91. See, for example, J. Bain, Barriers to New Competition: the Character and Consequences in Manufacturing Industries (1956).

92. It was particularly hostile toward innovations in distribution systems that tended to replace small, independent entrepreneurs.

93. For example, Brown Shoe Co. v. United States, 370 U.S. 294, 82 S.Ct. 1502 (1962). For an evaluation of the period that is more optimistic than the one given here, see T. Kovaleff, Business and Government During the Eisenhower Administration: A Study of the Antitrust Policy of the Antitrust Division of the Justice Department (1980); and see Peritz, note 56.

94. For example, *Brown Shoe*, note 93; United States v. Von's Grocery Co., 384 U.S. 270, 86 S.Ct. 1478 (1966); FTC v. Procter & Gamble Co., 386 U.S. 568, 87 S.Ct. 1224 (1967); United States v. Arnold, Schwinn & Co., 388 U.S. 365, 87 S.Ct. 1856 (1967); FTC v. Consolidated Foods Corp., 380 U.S. 592, 85 S.Ct. 1220 (1965).

§ 2.2

1. See, for example, P. Gerhart, The Supreme Court and Antitrust Analysis: the (Near) Triumph of the Chicago School, 1982 Sup. Ct. Rev. 319; R. Posner, The Rule of Reason and the Economic Approach: Reflections on the Sylvania Decision, 45 U. Chi. L. Rev. 1, 5, 12–13 (1977). But the view is not limited to members of the Chicago School. See, e.g., R. Peritz, Competition Policy in America, 1888–1992: History, Rhetoric, Law (1996), which proceeds as if pre-New Deal antitrust policy was largely ignorant of economics. See Hovenkamp, Book Review, 28 J. Interdisciplinary History 156 (1997).

determinate economic theories by looking to its common law heritage.[2]

Antitrust has always been closely tied to prevailing economic doctrine. To be sure, antitrust policy makers sometimes applied economics ineptly, sometimes gravitated toward the fringes of economic theory rather than the center, and sometimes pushed good points too far. But even the common law was driven largely by the then-prevailing rules of classical political economy concerning the nature of competition and the efficiency consequences of various anticompetitive practices.[3] The older common law was quite tolerant of collusion and most vertical practices simply because classical political economy had an extremely robust view of the market, particularly of the role of potential competition and easy entry in disciplining any attempt to raise prices above the competitive level.[4] With the rise of neoclassicism in the 1870's and 1880's (best identified with the development of the marginal cost and marginal revenue curves), the analysis became more subtle and economists became increasingly aware of market imperfections that might allow various anticompetitive practices.[5] Antitrust policy was not far behind.

One of the great difficulties in defining the role of economics in early judicial interpretations of the Sherman Act, is that the neoclassical revolution in economics was occurring at the very time that statute was passed. During the period from 1890 to 1920, economics was unsettled, with numerous battles between old-line classicists and emergent neoclassicism, and a great variety of views about the harmfulness of various practices.

If a case can be made that antitrust was ever out of touch with prevailing economic theory, it would have to be made about the earliest period of Sherman Act enforcement. At that time most traditional economists condemned the statute as at best irrelevant and at worst harmful, since it would likely challenge the ability of large business firms to achieve lower prices through economies of scale.[6] But many of the new breed of economists, those most heavily infected by the neoclassical revolution, were more suspicious of big business and inclined to see the antitrust laws as a good thing.[7] The best explanation of antitrust enforcement during this period is that it gradually came to reflect the views of a younger generation of post-classicist economists, rather than the more established classicists.

As noted in § 2.1c, the New Deal period saw substantial inroads of economic theory into antitrust policy. But at that time the dominant economic ideology was also quite suspicious of unregulated markets and inclined to believe that government regulation would work better. Beginning after 1935 or so, American antitrust policy became increasingly aggressive against mergers and various vertical practices. Once again, the change did not occur in spite of prevailing economic doctrine. On the contrary, it was driven by economic theories such as those developed in Edward Chamberlin's theory of monopolistic competition, a New Deal classic that emphasized the role of imperfections such as product differentiation in American markets.[8] Within this framework competition was regarded as a fragile state of affairs that could be maintained only by constant antitrust supervision. The reaction to this New Deal ideology led directly to the concept of "workable competition," which was

2. For example, T. Arthur, Farewell to the Sea of Doubt: Jettisoning the Constitutional Sherman Act, 74 Calif. L. Rev. 263 (1986).

3. See H. Hovenkamp, The Sherman Act and the Classical Theory of Competition, 74 Iowa L. Rev. 1019 (1989).

4. See H. Hovenkamp, The Antitrust Movement and the Rise of Industrial Organization, 68 Texas L. Rev. 105 (1989).

5. In addition to the articles cited at notes 3 & 4, see H. Hovenkamp, The Marginalist Revolution in Legal Thought, 46 Vand. L. Rev. 305 (1993).

6. See Hatfield, The Chicago Trust Conference, 8 J. Pol. Econ. 1, 6 (1899) (noting that most economists of the day believed that large firms were efficient, and the "outgrowth of natural industrial evolution," and that the Sherman Act would be positively harmful).

7. For example, H. C. Adams, Relation of the State to Industrial Action, 1 Pub., Am. Econ. Assn. 465 (1887) (arguing for more aggressive intervention against monopolies); R. Ely, Monopolies and Trusts (1900); C. Van Hise, Concentration and Control: A Solution to the Trust Problem in the United States 76–87, 255–256 (1912).

8. E. Chamberlin, The Theory of Monopolistic Competition (1933).

extremely influential on American antitrust policy in the 1940's and 1950's.[9] That theory was incorporated in the 1955 Report of the Attorney General on antitrust policy, which attempted to develop an antitrust policy based on then prevailing industrial organization theory.[10] Competition was seen not as something inherent in many American industries, but rather as something that could be made workable, even in highly imperfect markets, provided that the government was willing to intervene and challenge anticompetitive practices.

Even the relative aggressiveness of the Warren Court era was grounded in economic theory, although antitrusters often pushed it too far. The economic theory that prevailed in the 1960's was quite different from the economics of the 1980's, and economists of the earlier period were much more suspicious of the unregulated market. For example, Joe S. Bain, probably the most influential antitrust economist of the day, based his relatively interventionist theories on three important economic premises. The first was that economies of scale were not substantial in most markets and dictated truly anticompetitive concentration levels in only a small number of industries.[11] As a result, many industries contained larger firms and were more concentrated than necessary to achieve optimal productive efficiency.[12] The second theory was that barriers to entry by new firms were very high and could easily be manipulated by dominant firms.[13] The third was that the noncompetitive performance (monopoly pricing) associated with oligopoly began to occur at relatively low concentration levels.[14] The combination of these views created an antitrust policy that was quite concerned with deconcentrating oligopolistic markets and, to a degree, with protecting small firms from larger rivals.[15] The underlying theory was generally that a large number of small firms would yield lower prices than a relatively small number of larger firms.[16] Although Warren Era antitrust enforcement policy may seem excessive even in light of these economic views, government enforcement policy was largely defined by them. For example, the 1968 Justice Department Merger Guidelines, while far more aggressive than the Guidelines of the 1980's and 1990's, were based squarely on Bainian views about the relation between competition and market concentration.[17]

2.2b. The Chicago School and its Aftermath

The revolution in market economics that took place at the University of Chicago in the 1950's and after was a full assault on the New Deal/Chamberlain/Bain conception of the frailty of markets and the appropriate scope of antitrust intervention.[18]

Very briefly (and thus at some risk of misstatement) the Chicago School stands for the following ten propositions:

(1) Economic efficiency, the pursuit of which should be the exclusive goal of the antitrust laws, consists of two relevant parts: productive efficiency and allocative efficiency. *Productive* efficiency is a fraction in which the value of a firm's output is the numerator and the value of its inputs is the denominator; the higher this ratio, the more efficient the firm. Gains in productive

9. See J. Clark, Toward a Concept of Workable Competition, 30 Am. Econ. Rev. 241 (1940).

10. Report of the Attorney General's National Committee to Study the Antitrust Laws (1955).

11. See J. Bain, Economies of Scale, Concentration, and the Condition of Entry in Twenty Manufacturing Industries, 44 Am. Econ. Rev. 15, 38 (1954).

12. J. Bain, Barriers to New Competition: their Character and Consequences in Manufacturing Industries 53–113 (1956); J. Bain, Relation of Profit Rate to Industry Concentration: American Manufacturing, 1936–1940, 65 Q.J.Econ. 293 (1951).

13. J. Bain, *Barriers*, note 12 at 1–42, 114–43.

14. Ibid. On oligopoly, see ch. 4.

15. The concerns were exacerbated by the fact that the first post-war census appeared to show rapidly increasing industrial concentration. The data are discussed in the second edition of F.M. Scherer, Industrial Market Structure and Economic Performance, ch. 3 (2d ed. 1980).

16. See C. Kaysen & D. Turner, Antitrust Policy: An Economic and Legal Analysis (1959), discussed in § 2.1c.

17. On the Merger Guidelines, see § 12.1.

18. On the development of the Chicago School generally and in antitrust see E. Kitch, The Fire of Truth: A Remembrance of Law and Economics at Chicago, 1932–70, 26 J.L. & Econ. 163 (1983); R. Posner, The Chicago School of Antitrust Analysis, 127 U.Pa.L.Rev. 925 (1979).

efficiency come about mainly by research and development. Allocative efficiency refers to the general efficiency of markets, generally measured by the Pareto criterion.[19] As a general matter, markets attain optimal allocative efficiency when they are competitive—that is, when price equals marginal cost. Because monopoly profits provide an important incentive to research and development, however, increases in productive efficiency often operate to reduce the market's allocative efficiency. For example, construction of a large plant and acquisition of a large market share may increase a firm's productive efficiency by enabling it to achieve economies of scale; however, these actions may simultaneously reduce allocative efficiency by facilitating monopoly pricing. A properly defined antitrust policy will attempt to maximize *net* efficiency gains.[20]

(2) Most markets are competitive, even if they contain relatively few sellers. Even if firms in concentrated markets are able to coordinate prices, they will continue to compete in other ways, such as by increasing customer services. It is very difficult for oligopolies or cartels to close off every possible avenue of competition. Further, product differentiation tends to undermine competition far less than was formerly presumed. and it makes collusion far more difficult to maintain. As a result, neither high market concentration nor product differentiation are the anticompetitive problems earlier oligopoly theorists believed them to be.[21]

(3) Monopoly, when it exists, tends to be self-correcting; that is, the monopolist's higher profits generally attract new entry into the monopolist's market with the result that the monopolist's position is quickly eroded. About the best that the judicial process can do is hasten the correction process.[22]

(4) "Natural" barriers to entry are more imagined than real. As a general rule, investment will flow into any market where the rate of return is high. The one significant exception consists of barriers to entry that are not natural—that is, barriers that are created by government itself. In most markets society would be best off if the government left entry and exit unregulated.[23]

(5) Economies of scale are far more pervasive than economists once believed, largely because earlier economists looked only at intra-plant or production economies, and neglected economies of distribution.[24]

(6) A firm generally maximizes its own profits when downstream and upstream firms behave competitively; so it has no incentive to facilitate monopoly in vertically related markets. Further, a monopolist cannot possibly "leverage" additional monopoly profits by using its monopoly position in one market to foreclose access to a vertically related market.[25] As a result, virtually all instances of vertical integration, including resale price maintenance and vertical nonprice restraints, are efficient.[26]

19. A situation is Pareto optimal when no person can be made better off without making someone else worse off.

20. For example, R. Bork, The Antitrust Paradox: A Policy at War with Itself 91 (1978; rev. ed. 1993): "[t]he whole task of antitrust can be summed up as the effort to improve allocative efficiency without impairing productive efficiency so greatly as to produce either no gain or a net loss in consumer welfare."

21. See, for example, Y. Brozen, Concentration, Mergers and Public Policy (1982); J. McGee, In Defense of Industrial Concentration (1971).

22. For example, F. Easterbrook, The Limits of Antitrust, 63 Texas L. Rev. 1, 2 (1984) (in the long-run markets become competitive; the goal of antitrust is merely to "speed up the arrival of the long run.")

23. For example, H. Demsetz, Barriers to Entry, 72 Am. Econ. Rev. 47 (1982).

24. See the debate between John McGee (Chicago School) and F.M. Scherer (critic), in Industrial Concentration: the New Learning 15–113 (H. Goldschmid, H. Mann & J. Weston, eds. 1974).

25. E.g., W. Bowman, Tying Arrangements and the Leverage Problem, 67 Yale L.J. 19 (1957).

26. L. Telser, Why Should Manufacturers Want Fair Trade? 3 J.L. & Econ. 86 (1960); R. Bork, The Rule of Reason and the Per Se Concept: Price Fixing and Market Division (part 2), 75 Yale L.J. 373 (1966); R. Posner, The Rule of Reason and the Economic Approach: Reflections on The *Sylvania* Decision, 45 U.Chi.L.Rev. 1 (1977).

(7) Business firms are profit maximizers. That is, their managers generally make decisions that they anticipate will make the firm more profitable than any alternative. The model would not be undermined, however, if it should turn out that many firms are not profit maximizers but are motivated by some alternative goal, such as revenue maximization, sales maximization, or "satisficing."[27] The integrity of the market efficiency model requires only that a few firms be profit-maximizers. In that case, the profits and market shares of these firms will grow at the expense of the non-profit-maximizers.[28]

(8) Antitrust enforcement should be designed in such a way as to penalize conduct precisely to the point that it is inefficient, but to tolerate or encourage it when it is efficient.[29] Further, competitors in a market are generally benefitted by collusive practices and injured by efficient practices; as a result, they have precisely the wrong set of incentives to sue. Most competitor lawsuits for alleged antitrust violations should be thrown out, and private enforcement limited to consumers.

(9) Even if markets are imperfect and prone to anticompetitive outcomes, government intervention is justified only if the result is an improvement, taking the costs of intervention into account. As a general matter, claims that government intervention is better should be treated skeptically. We probably know very little about the optimal structure of markets or firms, and the complexity of some models of industry behavior tend to strengthen this view. In that case it is highly presumptuous to think that State-administered relief will yield more efficient outcomes than natural market processes.[30]

(10) The decision to make this market efficiency model the exclusive guide for antitrust policy is nonpolitical. That is, it is adopted without regard for the way that wealth or entitlements are distributed in society, but only so as to maximize society's overall wealth.[31] Thus if a practice produces greater gains to business than losses to consumers, it is efficient and should not be illegal under the antitrust laws. But the same should be said about practices that produce larger gains to consumers than losses to business. The member of the Chicago School can thus argue that he is not taking sides in any political dispute about how wealth or entitlements ought to be distributed among conflicting interest groups. Such things should always go where they do the most net good.

Some of these principles are empirically robust and have become all but uncontroversial in antitrust writing. Others have no more than ideology to support them and must be characterized as acts of faith. The substance of each is taken up at various points in this book, but two deserve particular mention here.

2.2c. Skepticism; Competitor v. Consumer Suits; Private v. Public Suits

On point (9), to be skeptical about the appropriateness of government intervention in the market means that we do not trust our

27. A firm "satisfices" when its management adopts a certain goal for profits, sales, or market share and then tries to meet the goal but not necessarily to exceed it. Under the theory, management will not be inclined to set an extremely high goal, because they do not want to be viewed later as failing. The theory of satisficing is part of a more general theory of the firm, emphasizing the separation of ownership and control, suggesting that managers and stock holders often have different motives, and that these interfere with profit maximization. See, for example, A. Berle, Jr., and G. Means, The Modern Corporation and Private Property (1932). For a firm rejection, see F. Easterbrook & D. Fischel, The Economic Structure of Corporate Law (1991).

28. See R. Posner & F. Easterbrook, Antitrust: Cases, Economic Notes and Other Materials 855–857 (2d ed. 1981).

29. W. Landes, Optimal Sanctions for Antitrust Violations, 50 U.Chi.L.Rev. 652 (1983). On the "optimal deterrence model," see §§ 17.1–17.2.

30. See, for example, F. Easterbrook, Ignorance and Antitrust 119, in Antitrust, Innovation, and Competitiveness (T. Jorde & D. Teece, eds., 1992); F. Easterbrook, Workable Antitrust Policy, 84 Mich. L. Rev. 1696 (1986).

31. For example, R. Bork, note 20 at 90: "Antitrust * * * has nothing to say about the ways prosperity is distributed or used." For a critique, see H. Hovenkamp, Distributive Justice and the Antitrust Laws, 51 Geo. Wash. L. Rev. 1, 16–26 (1982).

judgment about which theory explains the particular situation in front of us or about government's ability to make things better. For example, we have theories showing resale price maintenance to be competitive under certain circumstances, and other theories showing it to be anticompetitive. But which theory explains the defendant's actions in the case before us?[32] A commonly given Chicago School answer is that unless we are extremely sure about a monopoly explanation, we are obliged to assume a competitive explanation and should refrain from intervening.

Skepticism goes only so far. For example, within the classical competition model, entry by new firms in response to monopoly prices was presumed to be easy and instantaneous. Several conclusions might flow from this assumption:[33] (a) predatory pricing is irrational because as soon as the predator drives out a rival and increases price, competitors will flood the market and prices will return to competitive levels;[34] (b) the law against horizontal mergers is unnecessary, for new entrants will always discipline any attempt by the postmerger firm to charge monopoly prices;[35] and (c) even the law against price-fixing is unnecessary, for any attempt to fix prices will be met with new entrants who will undermine the cartel.[36]

Few scholars, Chicago School or otherwise, accept all three of these propositions. At the risk of some overgeneralization, the Chicago School position is that (a) is correct, (b) must be modified at least to permit condemnation of horizontal mergers that create dominant firms or that obviously facilitate collusion, and (c) is false. The question is not whether intervention is *ever* appropriate, for nearly everybody believes it is appropriate sometimes. The question is when. Within the Chicago School model, the economic case for condemning naked price fixing is generally regarded as very strong; the economic case for condemning alleged predatory pricing is regarded as weak to nonexistent.

The rhetoric of skepticism in Chicago School analysis is based on numerous economic studies during the 1960's which found that practices once thought to be anticompetitive were really not so.[37] But many of those studies are now dated, and some of their assumptions have been called into question. One detects a certain resistance among Chicago School antitrust scholars to new developments in economic theory that undermine favorite Chicago School ideas. Chicagoans themselves have attacked the idea that there should be a "ratchet" in antitrust law—that is, that antitrust can appropriately proceed in the direction of increasing liability, but it may not go "backward" and approve some practices that were previously condemned.[38] But the same argument applies to economics. Chicagoans are quick to cite voluminous Chicago school scholarship that laid older anticompetitive theories to rest by substituting entirely competitive explanations. This writing revolutionized antitrust theory in such areas as resale price maintenance, tying arrangements, and predatory pricing. But the last two decades have produced a mountain of post-Chicago scholarship that has substantially changed the landscape once again.[39] The "free rider" explanation of resale price maintenance was a good one, but it probably applies to only a small percentage of RPM situations.[40] The Chicago models showing vertical integration to be invariably efficient rested on assumptions that firms could not vary the proportions of the inputs that they use; when that assumption is relaxed the conclusion is much more ambiguous.[41]

32. On the manifold theories of resale price maintenance, see §§ 11.2, 11.4.

33. See H. Hovenkamp, The Antitrust Movement and the Rise of Industrial Organization, 68 Texas L. Rev. 105 (1989).

34. On predatory pricing, see ch. 8.

35. On horizontal mergers, see ch. 12.

36. On price-fixing, see ch. 4.

37. See, for example, the citations in notes 21–26 above.

38. F. Easterbrook, Is There a Ratchet in Antitrust Law?, 60 Texas L. Rev. 705 (1982).

39. A good summary is M. Jacobs, An Essay on the Normative Foundations of Antitrust Economics, 74 N.C. L. Rev. 219 (1995).

40. See §§ 11.2–11.3.

41. See §§ 9.2–9.3.

Strategic behavior, which appears in a variety of disguises, is both plausible and anticompetitive under a host of situations that standard Chicago scholarship failed to recognize.[42] Finally, the Chicago theory that market power is a relative rarity has given way to numerous econometric procedures for measuring market power with greater precision than we have had in the past. These procedures indicate that significant market power is not all that rare, even in markets that do not have dominant firms.[43] Just as there is no ratchet in antitrust law, so too there is no ratchet in antitrust economics.

Like the Chicago School scholar, the antitrust moderate also believes in markets, and even believes that the self-interest of business firms most often works to the benefit of consumers and the economy. But the antitrust moderate is more likely to believe that (a) business firms act only in their self-interest; and (b) markets contain imperfections that permit self-interest and the public interest to diverge. In robustly competitive markets, the presumption that a challenged practice is simply a "way of competing" should be very strong. In more concentrated markets where the exercise of market power is possible, that presumption should simply disappear. Both the Chicagoan and the moderate draw a line in the sand, trust competition to take care of things on one side, but warn business firms not to step across. However, they draw the line in different places.

The Chicago School antitrust scholar is likely to believe that courts should not intervene unless the economic case against a practice is so strong that all reasonable dissenting voices have been squelched. When in doubt, let the market take care of itself. By contrast, the antitrust moderate is more willing to weigh conflicting economic theories and decide which one, competitive or anticompetitive, is a better fit for the case at hand. This process admittedly involves some trial and error. Mistakes of overdeterrence may occur. Whether they occur more often than Chicago School mistakes of underdeterrence is an empirical question, and so far no one has been able to answer it.

The process by which courts decide antitrust cases is much like the common law process generally. Overall, the process is arguably efficient. If a common law rule is inefficient, the losses it produces are greater than the gains. In that case the rule will be challenged relatively more times, because the challengers have more to gain. As a result, the common law process gradually gravitates toward efficient rules,[44] or at least toward rules that are efficient most of the time.[45]

Notwithstanding antitrust's common law nature, one can doubt whether this process occurs in antitrust litigation. Competitive markets have many of the characteristics of a public good. The beneficiaries of competition tend to be scattered widely across a large group of consumers, each of whom experiences relatively small gains. By contrast, those who benefit from anticompetitive practices are few and individual benefits are quite large. For example, the victims of anticompetitive resale price maintenance in the market for blue jeans may be 10,000,000 consumers, each of whom pays $5 or perhaps $10 more per year. The beneficiaries may be a small group of manufacturers or retailers, each of whom gains several million dollars annually. The major players in resale price maintenance litigation may both have the wrong incentives. Those wishing to impose it may be facilitating collusion. Dealers who challenge it may be wishing to take a free ride on the efforts of other dealers.[46] The group whose interests are most closely aligned

42. See generally J. Tirole, The Theory of Industrial Organization (1988).

43. See Ch. 3, and see, e.g., J. Baker & T. Bresnahan, Empirical Methods of Identifying and Measuring Market Power, 61 Antitrust L.J. 3 (1992); J. Kattan, Market Power in the Presence of an Installed Base, 62 Antitrust L.J. 1 (1993).

44. G. Priest, The Common Law Process and the Selection of Efficient Rules, 6 J. Legal Stud. 65 (1977); G. Priest & B. Klein, The Selection of Disputes for Litigation, 13 J.Legal Stud. 1 (1984).

45. On this point, see R. Cooter & L. Kornhauser, Can Litigation Improve the Law Without the Help of Judges? 9 J. Legal Stud. 139 (1980).

46. On these aspects of resale price maintenance, see §§ 11.2–11.3.

with the competitive outcome, consumers, may lack either the organization or the awareness of injury that would make them effective plaintiffs.

In the field of economics called "public choice," which studies the workings of democratic government, this kind of structure works to the advantage of special interest groups, who are generally producers, at the expense of consumers.[47] Producer groups are small and their interests are unified. Consumer groups are large, and the individuals differ greatly from one another. The tendency to shirk is large, because each consumer is motivated to take a free ride on the work of others. As a result, government regulation is often inefficient, benefitting small special interest groups at the expense of the public at large.

The theory of public choice suggests serious difficulties with the Chicago School position, outlined in (8) above, that competitor standing to bring antitrust actions should be greatly restricted or perhaps eliminated.[48] According to this position, consumers have the correct incentives while competitors do not. Consumers are injured by monopoly overcharges, but competitors are injured most often by the increased efficiency of the firms whose conduct is being challenged.

Competitors are simultaneously the worst and best of antitrust plaintiffs. First, their incentives are almost always questionable. Although competitors are injured by monopolistic exclusionary practices, they are also injured by increased efficiency. Since competitors, just as any private party, sue to vindicate private rights they cannot be expected to distinguish efficient from inefficient practices. They will sue if they have a cause of action and the value of the expected remedy exceeds the cost of suit.

But competitors are also the best antitrust plaintiffs. Competitors are knowledgeable participants in a market, who generally know about an anticompetitive practice long before consumers do, assuming that consumers find out at all. Competitors are well placed to pursue an antitrust violation before it produces monopoly, or at a much earlier stage. Remember, the social cost of monopoly is a function not only of its size but also of its duration.[49] Likewise, competitors generally feel the injury in much more perceptible ways. An exclusionary practice may create a monopoly that raises the price of photocopying by one cent per page. But the same practice may drive a rival out of business. This gives the rival an incentive to sue that consumers often lack.

For some of the same reasons, the value of consumer suits has been greatly exaggerated. First of all, just as both efficient and inefficient exclusionary practices injure competitors, efficient and inefficient practices also give a firm power to raise price above marginal cost or to limit consumer choice. In the consumer suit, the plaintiffs must run the same set of gauntlets to prove an anticompetitive exclusionary practice that competitors must prove.

Consider predatory pricing, a favorite for Chicago School critiques of competitor lawsuits. When a competitor complains of predatory pricing, the basis could be either that the defendant is pricing predatorily, or else that the defendant has lower costs than the plaintiff or is undercutting the plaintiff's comfortable monopoly profits. If the law against predatory pricing is applied in the latter situations, competitor suits challenging predation themselves become a powerful anticompetitive weapon.

The solution proposed by some members of the Chicago School is to give the predatory pricing lawsuit only to consumers.[50] The classic theory of predatory pricing is that the predator uses a temporary period of below cost

47. See D. Farber & P. Frickey, Law and Public Choice: A Critical Introduction (1991); H. Hovenkamp, Legislation, Well-Being and Public Choice, 57 Univ.Chi. L.Rev. 63 (1990).

48. For a summary of the position, see E. Snyder & T. Kauper, Misuse of the Antitrust Laws: the competitor Plaintiff, 90 Mich. L. Rev. 551 (1991); for a response, see W. Page & R. Blair, Controlling the Competitor Plaintiff in Antitrust Litigation, 91 Mich. L.Rev. 111 (1992).

49. See § 1.3.

50. F. Easterbrook, Predatory Strategies and Counterstrategies, 48 Univ.Chi.L.Rev. 263 (1981); R. Bork, The Antitrust Paradox: A Policy at War With Itself 144–55 (1978; rev. ed. 1993).

pricing to discipline rivals or drive them from the market so that it can charge monopoly prices later.[51] Are consumers really better placed than rivals to prove such claims? First, we must trust that consumers are as aware of what has been going on in the market as competitors were, that the consumers can organize themselves, and that their suit will be cost effective. Second, one must identify whether there has been a post-predation price hike to monopoly levels. The fact that a market experienced a period of low prices, one or more bankruptcies or shutdowns by established firms, and then a period of higher prices could describe a competitive situation as well as a monopoly situation. For example, when a market is subject to excess capacity, prices will be low. Later, when some firms have exited from the market, prices could rise considerably. How do we distinguish whether the earlier low price was competitive or predatory? A court would have to use a set of screening devices in consumer brought predatory pricing cases, just as they use in competitor suits. The court would insist on a market structure conducive to predatory pricing, and on evidence that the prices charged by the dominant firm were below some measure of cost.[52] But the consumers are in no better a position to do this, and they may be in a far worse position, particularly if the consumer suit comes later than the competitor suit. Further, basic consumer incentives are no more righteous than competitor incentives. The consumer's main interest is in the anticipated recovery, not in the more abstract question whether a price hike was caused by predation or something else. Incidentally, it is no answer that devices such as class actions can unify consumers and permit them to pursue antitrust cases effectively. Although class actions have been effective against cartels and some tying arrangements, they have not been very successful in challenges to exclusionary practices.[53] In any event, the class action solves only the organizational problem; it does nothing to change basic incentives or standards of proof.

In sum, we can concede that competitors have the wrong set of incentives. However, consumers do not automatically have the correct set. They sue to reap private benefits, and their incentives will be driven by anticipated gains. In order for consumer suits to be superior to competitor suits we must be confident that consumer suits are better mechanisms for showing that (1) alleged high prices are in fact monopoly prices; and (2) the mechanism that gave the firm the market power to charge high prices was anticompetitive rather than efficient.

To be sure, limiting standing to consumers would reduce the *number* of antitrust suits. But there is no good reason for thinking that those eliminated would be the nonmeritorious suits, while the meritorious suits would survive. Rather, the number of suits would be reduced simply because information costs are much higher for consumer groups, because consumer groups are much less well organized than competitors are, and because individual consumer injuries tend to be much smaller. These reasons presumably cut across all antitrust challenges, both meritorious and nonmeritorious.

This author believes that a far better way to reduce the number of nonmeritorious antitrust suits is to develop substantive and procedural rules that distinguish good lawsuits from bad. For example, the cure for excessive predatory pricing suits is not the elimination of the competitor plaintiff, whose early challenge can be far more effective than the later challenge of any consumer group. The cure is rigorous use of market structure and market share thresholds that will enable us to determine whether predatory pricing is a plausible monopolistic strategy;[54] and close attention to price-cost relationships to help us determine whether prices were indeed predatory. The law has been moving in that direction, although it

51. See ch. 8.

52. See § 8.4.

53. On antitrust class actions, see 2 Antitrust Law ¶ 356 (rev. ed. 1995).

54. As, for example, in Brooke Group Ltd. v. Brown & Williamson Tobacco Corp., 509 U.S. 209, 113 S.Ct. 2578 (1993). See § 8.8.

still has some distance to go.[55] More generally, the law must continue to develop a rigorous conception of "antitrust injury" to enable it to distinguish competitive from anticompetitive uses of the antitrust laws.[56]

Finally, any argument that private antitrust enforcement should generally yield to public enforcement aborts in the face of one powerful historical fact: over time, the government has not done much better. The truly scandalous decisions in the Chicago School lexicon are cases such as *Brown Shoe*, *Von's Grocery*, *Procter & Gamble*, and *Schwinn*.[57] But only antitrust scholars with the shortest of memories believe that the plaintiff in *Von's Grocery* was Sally's Family Foods, or in *Schwinn* was Pop's Bike & Trike. Most of the overdeterrent antitrust law based on innovative or even crackpot economic theories was made in cases brought by the United States Department of Justice and the Federal Trade Commission. At least private plaintiffs are consistent about one thing: they sue in order to further their own interests. Courts can began with that premise and limit standing or remedies accordingly. When the government sues, it may be difficult to tell what interest is being vindicated. To be sure, the record of government enforcement in the 1980's and 1990's is considerably different than the record in the 1960's, but the historical record is there just the same, and the fault cannot be lain entirely at the feet of a liberal judiciary unable to understand economics. To be sure, the Warren Court decided the four antitrust decisions listed above. But they did no more than give the executive branch what it asked for. If history has taught us anything, it is that government plaintiffs are not invariably better than private parties in identifying meritorious suits.

2.2d. Politics and Democratic Policy

On point (10) in the above list of Chicago School principles, the claim that a particular policy has managed to transcend politics is both appealing and dangerous. Its appeal is that it permits the creation of a stable policy that will not change with every change in political leadership. Antitrust policy has been particularly vulnerable to such political changes. The danger, on the other hand, is that the assertion takes a particular policy out of the political process altogether—which means, in the case of a democracy, that it is taken out of the democratic process. At the extreme, Chicago School antitrust policy may even permit the antitrust policy maker to ignore Congressional intent in passing the antitrust laws. For example, the legislative history of some antitrust statutes reveals that Congress was hostile to efficiency concerns.[58] Both Chicago School scholarship and the courts themselves have deviated substantially from Congress' original concern.

This book takes a manifestly economic approach to antitrust analysis. But the author's position differs from that of the Chicago School in two important ways. First, the range of relevant economic theories is more catholic, and takes seriously at least some economic theories that question Chicago School theories. The problem, of course, is to separate the plausible from the implausible, and the workable from the purely theoretical. These are fundamentally exercises in judgment.

Second, this book tries to preserve a perspective in which economics is dominant but not necessarily exclusive. Much Chicago School analysis is written as if there were only one antitrust statute and it read "Promote business efficiency." But that is not the antitrust statute that we have. The antitrust student

55. See § 8.4.

56. On antitrust injury, see § 16.3. For a critique of this view, see E. Snyder & T. Kauper, Misuse of the Antitrust Laws: the Competitor Plaintiff, 90 Mich. L. Rev. 551 (1991) (concluding that the "antitrust injury" doctrine has done little to deter inefficient competitor suits).

57. Brown Shoe Co. v. United States, 370 U.S. 294, 344, 82 S.Ct. 1502, 1534 (1962); United States v. Von's Grocery Co., 384 U.S. 270, 86 S.Ct. 1478 (1966); FTC v. Procter & Gamble Co., 386 U.S. 568, 579, 87 S.Ct. 1224, 1230 (1967); United States v. Arnold, Schwinn & Co., 388 U.S. 365, 87 S.Ct. 1856 (1967).

58. For example, the Celler–Kefauver amendments to § 7 of the Clayton Act, governing mergers. See §§ 12.1–12.2. See also D. Bok, Section 7 of the Clayton Act and the Merging of law and Economics, 74 Harv. L. Rev. 226, 233–238 (1960) (criticizing Congressional concern with protecting small business); H. Hovenkamp, Derek Bok and the Merger of Law and Economics, 21 J. L. Reform 515 (1988).

begins with a body of statutes in which economic efficiency plays a disturbingly small part. The relative weight given to efficiency concerns in this book already exceeds by a wide margin the proportion justified by the legislative history of the major antitrust statutes. But competing concerns, such as those for protecting consumers from wealth transfers (whether caused by efficient or inefficient practices), and even more unholy concerns, such as protecting other interest groups that Congress was determined to protect, simply cannot be ignored. If they are, then we are not living in a democratic society.

2.2e. Antitrust Policy in the Wake of the Chicago School

As noted previously, antitrust policy has always tracked prevailing economic theory to one degree or another. Problematically, economic theory has not been much more stable than legal theory. The revision of antitrust policy that occurred during the 1970's and 1980's and is closely associated with the Chicago School should not be viewed as antitrust's "discovery" of economics. Rather, it was simply a change in the prevailing economic model. Of course, one might characterize the change differently, perhaps by saying that during the 1970's and 1980's the courts and perhaps the Reagan Era antitrust division first recognized economic efficiency as the *exclusive* goal of antitrust policy. In that case, one could say with some meaning that the rise of the Chicago School represented the triumph of an "economic approach" to antitrust analysis.

But such a characterization considerably overstates the case. To this day, the Supreme Court has not come close to saying that economic efficiency is the exclusive concern of the antitrust laws, and many recent decisions are extraordinarily hard to rationalize if one considers only economics.[59]

Chicago School arguments notwithstanding, federal courts deciding antitrust cases have not eliminated noneconomic concerns from antitrust policy. Indeed, one must doubt whether such concerns can ever be eliminated from policy making in a democratic society. The public purpose of economics is not to eliminate political concerns from policy making. Rather, it is to enable policy makers to make judgments about the costs or effectiveness of a particular policy. The relative weight to be given to efficiency concerns varies with the ability of the relevant economic model to identify efficient policies in the real world. If the efficient solution is clear, and the degree to which alternative solutions deviate from the efficient solution is also quite clear, then policy makers are likely to weigh efficiency concerns heavily.

By contrast, if economics' relevance to some problem is not particularly clear, or if the economic model is complex, then the efficient solution will not necessarily emerge as obvious. In that case, distributive or political concerns, which are always present, will weigh much more heavily. For example, if the relevant economic model does not reveal unambiguously that big business is more efficient than small business, but the small business lobby is powerful or democracy's other participants value small businesses for reasons unrelated to cost, small business welfare is likely to be present as a legislative concern. The antitrust policy maker may not ignore it.

One important difference between the Chicago School market efficiency model and earlier economic models is that the Chicago model claims a much larger domain for efficient practices, and a correspondingly smaller domain for inefficient ones. Further, the model itself is both simple and elegant. The monopolistic competition model that drove post-New Deal policy was far more complex and made it far more difficult to examine a particular business practice and proclaim it efficient or inefficient.

59. For example, Eastman Kodak Co. v. Image Technical Services, 504 U.S. 451, 112 S.Ct. 2072 (1992); Texaco, Inc. v. Hasbrouck, 496 U.S. 543, 548, 110 S.Ct. 2535, 2538 (1990); Aspen Skiing Co. v. Aspen Highlands Skiing Corp., 472 U.S. 585, 105 S.Ct. 2847 (1985); Monsanto Co. v. Spray–Rite Serv. Corp., 465 U.S. 752, 104 S.Ct. 1464 (1984). For the principal discussions of these cases, see chs. 7, 10, 11 & 14. See also L. Kaplow, Antitrust, Economics, and the Courts 50 L. & Contemp. Prob. 181 (1987) (arguing that federal judges have been driven more by political ideology than by Chicago School economics).

For example, within that model product differentiation could increase consumer choice or encourage innovation; however, it could also be a mechanism by which large firms in concentrated industries avoided price competition. Likewise, Joe S. Bain's complicated notion of entry barriers appeared simultaneously to praise and condemn economies of scale in the production process. On the one hand, economies of scale reduced costs and facilitated lower consumer prices. On the other, they made it more difficult for new firms to enter the market and, at least in concentrated industries, facilitated oligopoly behavior.[60] Within the Chicago School model, by contrast, both of these problems have unambiguous solutions. Product differentiation is almost always a blessing for consumers. When it is not, the firms participating in the differentiation will be injured rather than benefitted, for customers will refuse to buy.[61] Likewise, economies of scale are an unmixed blessing in all but extremely concentrated markets.[62]

The same thing can be said of modern game theory in industrial organization. The theories are complex and many of them may not even be testable.[63] As the present time the principal impact of game theory is negative rather than positive—it serves to undermine our confidence that the market is always as efficient as traditional Chicago economics implied, but we don't really know very much about the nature or extent of the deviations. When the democratic policy maker acts under this kind of uncertainty about the efficacy of the unregulated market, then noneconomic justifications for intervention begin to carry more weight.

Increasingly, antitrust economics is being driven by "post-Chicago" theories that are both more complex and more ambiguous than Chicago orthodoxy. For example, modern theories of industrial organization give much wider play to the possibilities of strategic behavior that can facilitate noncompetitive results.[64] This new complexity makes it much more difficult for enforcement agencies and courts to make judgments about whether a particular practice is competitive or anticompetitive. Supreme Court decisions such as *Kodak*, while seemingly quite unsophisticated in their economics, clearly reflect some of these doubts.[65]

The Horizontal Merger Guidelines adopted by the Antitrust Division and the Federal Trade Commission in 1992 reflect some of this complexity as well. Earlier Guidelines issued in 1982 and 1984 had followed the dominant Chicago School line of regarding product differentiation as a mitigating factor in merger analysis. When products in a market are not identical, firms have a harder time achieving consensus on price and output; as a result, collusion is harder to sustain. But the 1992 Guidelines once again recognize, as economists from the 1930's through the 1970's had often noted, that product differentiation can facilitate unilateral price increases under the right set of circumstances.[66] Further, the Guidelines at least implicitly make room for game theoretic considerations that seem to make anticompetitive behavior more likely.

When markets are both concentrated and complex, characterized by product differentiation, relatively high fixed costs, and aftermarkets closely tied to primary markets, the current economic literature is less helpful in providing robust and unambiguous answers. This has several implications for antitrust policy. *First*, as the *Kodak* case held, simple

60. On Bain's work, see § 2.2a.

61. See, for example, R. Bork, note 20 at 312–313.

62. Id. at 312–329.

63. See B. Kobayashi, Game Theory and Antitrust: a Post–Mortem, 5 Geo. Mason L. Rev. 411 (1997); S. Peltzman, The Handbook of Industrial Organization: a Review Article, 99 J.Pol.Econ. 201 (1991).

64. For example, O. Williamson, Predatory Pricing: A Strategic and Welfare Analysis 87 Yale L.J. 284 (1977); S. Salop & D. Scheffman, Raising Rivals' Costs, 73 Amer. Econ.Rev. 267 (1983); J. Tirole, The Theory of Industrial Organization (1988). For readable surveys of developments, see Jacobs, note 39; and J. B. Baker, Recent Developments in Economics that Challenge Chicago School Views, 58 Antitrust L.J. 645 (1989).

65. Eastman Kodak Co. v. Image Technical Services, 504 U.S. 451, 112 S.Ct. 2072 (1992). The decision denied summary judgment against a plaintiff's claim that a nondominant firm in the primary market for photocopiers could manipulate the aftermarket for its replacement parts in an anticompetitive manner.

66. These concerns are developed in § 12.3.

answers are not likely to work, and more information must be gathered. This may make early grants of summary judgment less likely. *Second,*—another implication of *Kodak*—judges are going to be less likely to find certain practices to be harmless as a matter of law; more is going to go to juries. The outcomes will certainly not be more coherent, but the noneconomic (and constitutionally mandated) values of the jury will receive relatively greater weight as economics is increasingly characterized by internal conflict and indeterminacy.

These results are disturbing. The Chicago School offers simplicity, elegance and often relatively easy answers to antitrust questions. The alternatives are almost always messier, more expensive, and less determinate. But policy has to reflect the world we live in, and the world is a messy place.

§ 2.3 On the Need for Economics in Antitrust

2.3a. The Domain of Antitrust Economics

The economic model of markets and industry structure outlined briefly in Chapter one is rigorous, elegant and intuitively appealing. But using the model to guide legal policy is invariably more difficult and involves many softer questions of policy and judgment. First of all, fact finders are never able to collect all relevant information. Invariably they must fill in gaps, resolve inconsistencies, or deal with facts that do not fit a given paradigm. Sometimes the litigation process yields facts that appear inconsistent with the predictions offered by the economic model.[1] This may be because the process has not generated enough facts, or because one or more of the facts is inaccurate. It may also be because the model itself needs some adjusting to account for "anomalies"—things that the model in its current form is unable to explain.[2]

The antitrust policy maker also faces a second, more pervasive problem. The model may work perfectly, and the fact finder may be amply supplied with the information necessary for a prediction. However, some value that the model does not take into account may force a different decision than the model suggests. The perfect competition model does one thing quite well: given sufficient data it can predict whether a certain practice is efficient or inefficient, by a given definition of efficiency. What the model cannot do is tell us whether efficiency is the only thing that counts.

The issue of economics' appropriate role in antitrust actually evokes two questions. *First,* should economic efficiency be the only goal of antitrust policy, or should it share that role with other values or perhaps even other disciplines? *Second,* what kind of economics should antitrust policy use?

For decades antitrust writers have debated whether economic efficiency should be the exclusive goal of antitrust policy, or whether antitrust should incorporate a broader set of noneconomic as well as economic values. As § 2.1 notes, the legislative history of most of the antitrust statutes fails to reveal that efficiency concerns dominated. Indeed, Congress was generally willing to tolerate a great deal of allocative *in*efficiency in order to protect certain classes of people, such as small business. Does this mean that merger law today (which is still governed by the same, anticompetitively motivated statute as amended by Congress in 1950) should ignore economics? Conversely, does it mean that courts should ignore the legislative history of federal merger legislation and read economic efficiency into the statute? Section 7 of the Clayton Act, after all, is a democratically passed statute. The United States Code is full of inefficient, democratically

§ 2.3

1. As in Eastman Kodak Co. v. Image Technical Services, 504 U.S. 451, 112 S.Ct. 2072 (1992), where the model said that a firm that lacked market power in its primary market must also lack market power in the markets for replacement parts. Nevertheless, the facts suggested little market power in the former, but substantial market power in the latter. See §§ 3.3a, 10.3b; H. Hovenkamp, Market Power in Aftermarkets: Antitrust Policy and the *Kodak* Case, 40 UCLA L. Rev. 1447 (1993).

2. For one view of the relationship between scientific models, anomalies, and scientific progress, see T. Kuhn, The Structure of Scientific Revolutions (2d ed. 1970).

passed statutes, many of which are regularly enforced.

There is a principled and viable position that antitrust policy must admit certain noneconomic values.[3] At the same time, no one believes that efficiency concerns are irrelevant to antitrust policy. Today the most important debate about basic principles in antitrust is between those who believe that allocative efficiency should be the exclusive goal of the antitrust laws,[4] and those who believe that antitrust policy should consider certain "competing" values—that is, values that either cannot be accounted for within the economic model, or values that can be asserted only at the cost of a certain amount of efficiency. These competing values include maximization of consumer wealth, protection of small businesses from larger competitors, protection of easy entry into business, concern about large accumulations of economic or political power, prevention of the impersonality or "facelessness" of giant corporations, encouragement of morality or "fairness" in business practice, and perhaps some others.

All these alternative goals can be inconsistent with the economic goals of maximizing allocative and productive efficiency. In addition, many are inconsistent with each other. If courts adopt any mixture of goals, antitrust is likely to be guided by conflicting policies which must then be balanced against each other.[5] To be sure, this is not a unique phenomenon. Constitutional law is filled with decisions that balance conflicting policies. Antitrust could reasonably be expected to balance a policy of low consumer prices against a policy of protecting small businesses from larger competitors, and choose different policies to win in different cases.

By contrast, those who believe that antitrust should be concerned exclusively with efficiency can offer a relatively consistent policy, provided there is consensus about the relevant elements of the economic model. If vertical integration is efficient, then the "efficiency only" advocate believes it should be legal, even if it injures small businesses, makes big businesses even bigger, and makes it more difficult for newcomers to enter a particular field. She will not attempt to balance these "competing" concerns against economic efficiency, because she does not see them as competing. They are simply ignored.

Before someone can "balance" competing values, however, he must have a fairly good idea about what is being thrown into the scales. This means that the multi-valued policy maker, who believes that antitrust should consider small business welfare as well as economic efficiency, must have a good basic knowledge of prices, markets and industrial organization. There is no basis for the view that the adoption of some "competing" noneconomic policy for antitrust, such as the protection of small business welfare, permits one to do antitrust without knowing economics. Even the multi-valued policy maker needs economics to help her estimate the relative costs of protecting certain noneconomic values and determine whether society is willing to pay the price. Presumably, it is not worth *any* price to protect small businesses. If that were the policy, even price fixing by small businesses would be legal.

Further, economic theory will often help the multi-valued policy maker determine whether a particular legal rule will effectively protect the interest she wants to protect. The history of American antitrust is strewn with the corpses of small businesses who fell victim to antitrust rules designed to protect them. In a dissenting opinion in Standard Oil Co. of

3. See H. Hovenkamp, Distributive Justice and the Antitrust Laws, 51 Geo.Wash.L.Rev. 1 (1982); H. Hovenkamp, Antitrust Policy After Chicago, 84 Mich. L. Rev. 213 (1985); L. Schwartz, "Justice" and Other Non–Economic Goals of Antitrust, 127 U.Pa.L.Rev. 1076 (1979); R. Pitofsky, The Political Content of Antitrust, 127 U.Pa.L.Rev. 1051 (1979); L. Sullivan, Book Review, 75 Colum.L.Rev. 1214 (1975).

4. The best statements of this position are R. Posner, The Chicago School of Antitrust Analysis, 127 U.Pa.L.Rev. 925 (1979); and R. Bork, The Antitrust Paradox: A Policy at War With Itself (1978; rev. ed. 1993).

5. For development of this point, see 1 Antitrust Law ¶¶ 111–112 (rev. ed. 1997).

California v. United States.[6] Justice Douglas, who placed a high value on the protection of small business, chastised the Court for undermining its own policy. The majority had condemned an exclusive dealing contract imposed by a major oil refiner on its independent retail dealers. The restrictions reduced Standard's distribution costs, but they also restricted the freedom of dealers to make independent choices and made it more difficult for new, independent dealers to enter the market. Justice Douglas accurately predicted the effects of the decision: the need to reduce costs would force Standard to eliminate independent dealers and open its own, company-owned retail outlets. The result would be far more harmful to the independent gasoline station owners than the cost-reducing restrictions struck down by the Court.

The same phenomenon has occurred often in merger law. In the 1950's and 1960's the Supreme Court and the lower courts struck down a number of mergers between major brewers and small regional brewers, generally on the ground that the mergers were destroying the small, locally owned brewery. The major brewers then entered the new markets not by merger, but by building their own competing plants. These new plants were more efficient than those operated by the local brewers, and the national brewers had the advantage of large, well established distribution systems. Many of the local brewers were forced out of business and could not legally sell out to the larger firms. The economics of beer production had determined their fate. The Supreme Court's decisions simply made their painful exit from the market even more painful and expensive than it need have been.[7]

The robustness of economics as problem solver is easily exaggerated. Nonetheless, the notion that a nonarbitrary antitrust policy can be crafted without a coherent economic model is absolutely untenable. Absent the model antitrust will fall much too easily to constantly fluctuating interest group politics. Worse yet, there will be a very poor fit between the articulated goals of an adopted antitrust rule and its success in achieving these goals. A good example is the lower court's disposition of the *Kodak* case after remand from the Supreme Court.[8] The Supreme Court paved the way for the lower court to find a relevant market for Kodak brand photocopier parts, but the lower court went a big step further and found a *single* relevant market for all Kodak brand photocopier parts, even though the parts are complements rather than substitutes. The court reasoned:

> The "commercial reality" faced by service providers and equipment owners is that a service provider must have ready access to all parts to compete in the service market. As the relevant market for service "from the Kodak equipment owner's perspective is composed of only those companies that service Kodak machines," id., the relevant market for parts from the equipment owners' and service providers' perspective is composed of "all parts" that are designed to meet Kodak photocopier and micrographics equipment specifications.[9]

To be sure, it is a "commercial reality" that one using or fixing a photocopier must have "all" the parts, just as someone who wishes to drive needs both a car and gasoline; and one wishing to make toast needs both bread and a toaster. But that fact hardly justifies the existence of a "car/gasoline" market or a "toaster/bread" market. Further, the idea that a "market" consists of goods that are substitutes, not complements, is hardly a proposition that divides Chicago and post-Chicago economists. Rather, it is a proposition that divides people who know something about economics and people who do not. By defining the market as it did, the court lost any possible hope of assessing the defendant's market power.[10]

6. 337 U.S. 293, 69 S.Ct. 1051 (1949). See § 10.9.

7. See Y. Brozen, Concentration, Mergers, and Public Policy 366–67 (1982); FTC, The Brewing Industry 64–65 (1978).

8. Eastman Kodak Co. v. Image Technical Services, Inc., 504 U.S. 451, 462, 112 S.Ct. 2072, 2079 (1992), on remand, 125 F.3d 1195 (9th Cir.1997), cert. denied, ___ U.S. ___, 118 S.Ct. 1560 (1998),

9. 125 F.3d at 1203.

10. For more on the *Kodak* market power decision and the importance of grouping complements, and the consequences of not doing so, are developed further in § 3.3b.

Critics of economic analysis in antitrust sometimes argue that the economic approach to antitrust is a function of economists' myopia—their inability to see all the manifold issues that make up value systems in the real world. Economists, it is alleged, are uncomfortable with such competing values, so they create models that purport to account for everything. Nothing is left to chance, philosophy, or humanitarianism.[11]

Perhaps the world is overrun by myopic economists. However, in this particular instance a far better case can be made for the converse of the above argument: antitrust writers who are untrained in economics rely heavily on noneconomic values because this enables them to have an antitrust policy without undertaking the (sometimes difficult) task of learning how the market system works. That approach may be easier in the short run, but it is calculated to have painful consequences in the long run.

2.3b. The Substance of Antitrust Economics

Antitrust policy has changed dramatically over the century since the Sherman Act was passed, but changes in economic theory have been equally dramatic. In 1890 the marginalist revolution in economics was just taking hold. Alfred Marshall's great *Principles of Economics*, which did much to formalize our modern conceptions of marginal cost, marginal revenue, the demand curve, consumers' surplus and allocative efficiency, was published the same year as the Sherman Act.[12] Most likely, none of the framers of the Sherman Act knew anything about marginalism. During the first four decades of the twentieth century the economic study of markets was dominated by two groups of liberals, Progressives and New Dealers, who had relatively little faith in markets, a great deal of faith in regulation, and believed that a wide variety of business practices were harmful to both competitors and consumers.[13] But the 1960's and after witnessed a great revitalization of Anglo–American economics' traditional commitment to the market, and a concurrent distrust of government regulation or other forms of market intervention. Today, thanks largely to the incursions of game theory into industrial organization, a stronger case is beginning to re-emerge that many business practices are inefficient and that stronger forms of government intervention may be appropriate.[14]

One distressing part of this century long debate is that it does not seem to be heading toward an equilibrium. Relatively few of the important questions are permanently settled. Further, the debate is increasingly buried in technical mathematics known only to practitioners of the discipline. Marshall intimidated other economists in 1890 with his mathematics, but they are child's play compared to the mathematics almost any graduate student in economics knows today. Finally, notwithstanding increasingly technical notation, it is becoming clear that many of economics' most relevant conclusions cannot be verified in the strict sense. Rather, many economic conclusions should be described as stories that explain certain behavior and tend to be confirmed by the available data. But the lack of finality suggests that today's story will be replaced by a different one tomorrow.

What is the student of antitrust to make of this inconsistency and complexity in economic analysis? Two extremes seem particularly ill-advised. The first is to throw up one's hands and simply abandon any effort to develop a coherent antitrust policy driven by economic assumptions. The second is to leap at every new economic theory that sounds plausible and attempt to incorporate it into antitrust policy analysis.

Any consideration of the kind of economics antitrust should use must begin with this premise: the primary purpose of economics is

11. For example, E. Fox, The Modernization of Antitrust: A New Equilibrium, 66 Cornell L.Rev. 1140, 1156 (1981).

12. A. Marshall, Principles of Economics (1890).

13. See H. Hovenkamp, Enterprise and American Law, 1836–1937, esp. chs. 22–25 (1991).

14. See R. Pindyck & D. Rubinfeld , Microeconomics 453–90 (3d ed. 1995); D. Baird, R. Picker, & R. Gertner, Game Theory and the Law (1994).

rhetorical: we use it to tell consistent and relevant stories that make sense out of the world we face. In order to be helpful, the story must be understood by those who make policy. Of course, policy makers have an obligation to learn the tools of their trade, but economists also have an obligation to make their theories meaningful to a large audience. This is particularly true in a democracy, where excessive reliance on technical expertise can easily yield a kind of totalitarianism.

The best economics for antitrust is generally that which is relatively uncontroversial and well established in the literature. More complex theories certainly have policy implications, and someday they may become economic orthodoxy. But until that time occurs, they are best left to academics, who often write for the future rather than the present.

2.3c. The Meaning of "Efficiency" and "Consumer Welfare" in Antitrust Economics

The two kinds of efficiency relevant to antitrust analysis are *productive* efficiency and *allocative* efficiency. Productive efficiency is most simply understood as a ratio of a firm's output to its inputs. A firm that produces a product valued at $100 and requires inputs valued at $80 is more efficient than a firm that produces a product valued at $100 but requires inputs valued at $90. Firms achieve higher levels of productive efficiency by building efficient plants, developing cost-saving procedures, using employees more effectively, and a host of other ways. Many acts that arguably violate the antitrust laws are mechanisms by which firms increase their productive efficiency. These include mergers, vertical integration, exclusive dealing or tying arrangements, and even certain agreements among competitors.

The attitude of the antitrust laws toward productive efficiency is affirmative but passive. On the one hand, antitrust policy generally permits activities that increase a firm's productive efficiency, unless the activity also enhances the firm's market power. On the other hand, a firm does not generally violate the antitrust laws simply by being inefficient. For example, although vertical integration may reduce a firm's costs and permit it to produce and deliver a product at a lower price, failure to integrate is not illegal under the antitrust laws. The market itself disciplines inefficient firms.

Allocative efficiency is a more theoretical and controversial concept than productive efficiency. Allocative efficiency refers to the welfare of society as a whole. Given a certain amount of inputs or resources, what use and assignment of these resources will make society best off, economically measured? The concept of allocative efficiency is not self-defining, and different economists and philosophers prefer different definitions. The most influential definition was given by Vilfredo Pareto early in the twentieth century: a given assignment of resources is most efficient ("Pareto-optimal") if no alternative assignment will make at least one person better off without making at least one person worse off as well.[15] If one begins with an imperfect economy, a change is "Pareto-superior" if it makes at least one person better off and makes no one worse off.

The concept of Pareto-superiority is so rigorous that it would be satisfied by only the most trivial of social changes. A change in a social policy is Pareto-superior only if no one objects. All legal changes—even outrageously good ones—have adverse affects on at least one person. The adoption of a rule condemning robbery, for example, makes robbers worse off. Likewise, the adoption of a legal rule against monopolization or price fixing is not Pareto-superior for the same reason: it makes monopolists and price fixers worse off than they were before the rule was adopted.

For this reason antitrust economists sometimes use a variation of Pareto-efficiency called "potential" Pareto-efficiency. A change is efficient under the potential Pareto measure if the gainers from the change gain enough so that they can fully compensate all losers out of their gains—that is, if the total value placed on the gains exceeds the total value placed on the losses. If those who are made better off by

15. V. Pareto, Manual D' Economie Politique (1909).

the adoption of a rule against price fixing gain more than those who are made worse off lose, then the rule is efficient under the potential Pareto criterion even though its adoption produces some losers. Whether the gainers *actually* compensate the losers out of their gains is irrelevant to the determination of efficiency. For example, it is unlikely that potential price fixers would be compensated for any losses they suffer from the adoption of a rule that makes price fixing illegal.

Figure 1 suggests why the adoption of a rule against monopolization or price fixing is efficient under the potential Pareto criterion. In a competitive market, with price at marginal cost, consumers' surplus would equal triangle 1–3–6 in the figure. The monopolist or cartel will reduce output to Q_m and raise price to P_m. Consumers' surplus will be reduced to triangle 1–2–4, and the loss to consumers that results from the monopoly pricing will equal quadrilateral 2–3–6–4.

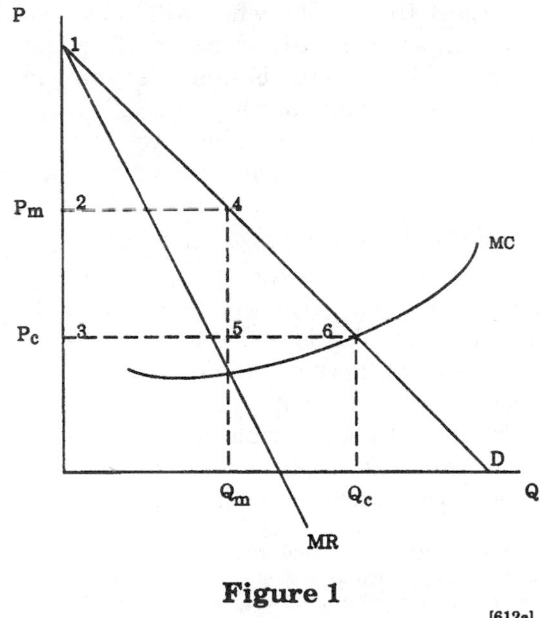

Figure 1

[612a]

The gain to the monopolist, however, is only rectangle 2–3–5–4.[16] The other part of the consumer loss, triangle 4–5–6, is lost to both the consumers and the monopolist. This is the traditional deadweight loss that is caused by monopoly. Although monopolists are richer as a result of monopolization, consumers are poorer by an even greater amount. For that reason a move from monopoly to competition is efficient by the potential Pareto measure.

The same thing is generally true of actions that increase a firm's productive efficiency without increasing its market power. Cost-reducing vertical integration, for example, makes both consumers and the vertically integrating firm better off, while it makes the firm's competitors worse off. But the integrating firm and its customers gain more than the injured competitors lose.

Potential–Pareto efficiency can be a useful guide for antitrust policy, but it is subject to two important qualifications. First, as with other economic measures of allocative efficiency, potential Pareto analysis is indifferent to how resources are distributed in society. If it could be shown that a certain practice made monopolists richer by exactly the same amount that it made consumers poorer, and no one else was affected, the practice would be judged "neutral" under potential Pareto criteria.[17] However, the legislative history of the Sherman Act shows a great deal of concern for the fact that monopolists transfer wealth away from consumers, but no concern at all for any articulated concept of efficiency.[18]

Second, although the change from orthodox Pareto-efficiency to potential Pareto-efficiency makes an antitrust policy based on efficiency theoretically possible, the change comes with one enormous cost. The efficiency of a social change is relatively easy to measure by the traditional Pareto criterion: if the change produces one identifiable loser, it is inefficient. The potential Pareto criterion, however, requires someone to discover all persons benefitted by the change and sum the value of their benefits, and then to identify all losers and sum their losses. The identity of all such people and the amount of their relative gains and losses is often neither obvious nor easy to

16. Even this rectangle probably overstates the gain to the monopolist. See the discussion of the social cost of monopoly in § 1.3.

17. Perfect price discrimination is such a practice. See § 14.3.

18. See § 2.1.

calculate. Even the above demonstration that monopoly is inefficient is necessarily valid only if one considers the single market depicted in the figure. But the destruction of monopoly in this market may create monopoly power in other markets. The total allocative losses in those other markets might exceed the gains in the market at hand.[19]

These criticisms aside, the potential Pareto criterion can help us obtain some idea whether the net effect of a practice is a social gain or a social loss. It may help us estimate the gain or loss, even though we likely cannot quantify it precisely. Furthermore, the ambiguities in the potential Pareto criterion are a disabling factor only in relatively close cases. Many cases are not close, and it is easier to predict that the social gains outweigh the social losses, or vice-versa.

Although economists often advocate potential Pareto-superiority or some variation of it as the guiding policy for antitrust, you will look a long time to find a judicial opinion articulating antitrust policy in such terms. The term "potential Pareto-efficiency" is an imposing one, carrying with it many implications of technical economic rules and quantification that makes lawyers uncomfortable. Antitrust analysts commonly use a substitute, the "consumer welfare" principle. Many people who probably believe that maximizing allocative efficiency should be the exclusive goal of antitrust, *state* that the goal of antitrust should be to maximize the welfare of consumers. Spoken in such terms, the goal sounds very attractive and certainly less technical than "potential Pareto efficiency."

Although "maximizing consumer welfare" is an appealing term, its content is ambiguous. To say that antitrust should maximize consumer welfare is one thing; to discern an antitrust policy that will do it is quite different. In fact, the consumer welfare principle is predicated on the observation that *everyone* is a consumer. An antitrust policy of maximizing small business welfare would have to be regarded as distributive, because it would force transfer payments from one group of people (consumers or large businesses) to another group of people (small businesses) even though such a transfer might not make society as a whole better off. Since all of us are consumers, however, an antitrust policy of maximizing consumer welfare is really a policy of maximizing everyone's welfare, at least in their capacity as consumers.[20]

But this observation about the consumer welfare principle brings us right back where we started. *All* definitions of allocative efficiency purport to describe what will make society better off, economically speaking. If "maximizing consumer welfare" is simply a synonym for "maximizing everybody's welfare," then we still do not have a useable prescription for antitrust policy, but only a homily that the best antitrust policy is one that makes everyone better off.

The consumer welfare principle in use has become identical with the principle that the antitrust laws should strive for optimal allocative efficiency. Perhaps an only slightly cruder alternative is that antitrust policy under the consumer welfare principle chooses that option which leads to highest output and lowest prices in the market in question.

19. On these "second best" problems, see § 1.5e.

20. There is one important difference between maximum consumer welfare and maximum allocative efficiency. Allocative efficiency is maximized when the *sum* of consumers' surplus and producers' surplus is maximized. See Figure One in § 1.1. By contrast, consumer welfare is presumably maximized when the consumers' surplus triangle is maximized. A situation in which the area of the consumers' surplus triangle was ten units and the area of the producers' surplus triangle was five units would be more efficient than a situation in which consumers' surplus was twelve units and producers' surplus was one unit. The latter alternative, however, would maximize the welfare of consumers.

Chapter 3

MARKET POWER AND MARKET DEFINITION

Table of Sections

---

§ 3.1 Introduction

Market power is the ability of a firm to increase its profits by reducing output and charging more than a competitive price for its product. In the *du Pont* (cellophane) case the Supreme Court defined market power as "the power to control prices or exclude competition."[1] But that definition is not very descriptive and is partly misleading. Market power itself is not an "exclusionary" practice: in fact, the exercise of market power—the sale of products at a supracompetitive price—generally attracts new sellers into the market. While exclusion of competitors is not market power, it is an important mechanism by which a firm obtains or maintains market power. Further, the power to hold market power for a significant period of time is always important to antitrust policy makers, who must weigh the costs of limiting market power against the potential for gain. The more durable market power appears to be, the greater its social cost, and thus the greater the gains from getting rid of it.

Likewise, to say that market power is the power to "control" prices is not particularly descriptive. Any firm will begin to lose sales when it raises the price of a product. More appropriately, market power is the power to raise prices above competitive levels without losing so many sales that the price increase is unprofitable.[2] A firm that can make more money by selling its output at a higher-than-competitive price has a certain amount of market power.

Many antitrust violations require the plaintiff to show that the defendant[3] has some market power. For example, illegal monopolization under § 2 of the Sherman Act requires that the defendant have monopoly power, which is a high degree of market power.[4] The offense of attempt to monopolize has a somewhat more ambiguous market power requirement depending on the nature of the activity that is alleged to be an illegal attempt.[5] At the very least, however, the defendant must be shown to have a dangerous probability of acquiring market power in a properly defined relevant market.[6] Establishment of an illegal

§ 3.1

1. United States v. E.I. du Pont de Nemours & Co., 351 U.S. 377, 391–92, 76 S.Ct. 994, 1005 (1956).

2. Rebel Oil Co., Inc. v. Atlantic Richfield Co., 51 F.3d 1421, 1434 (9th Cir.), cert. denied, 516 U.S. 987, 116 S.Ct. 515 (1995); Graphic Products Dist., Inc. v. Itek Corp. 717 F.2d 1560, 1570 (11th Cir.1983); Valley Liquors, Inc. v. Renfield Importers, Ltd., 678 F.2d 742, 745 (7th Cir.1982); FTC v. Staples, 970 F.Supp. 1066, 1076–1078 (D.D.C. 1997). See W. Landes & R. Posner, Market Power in Antitrust Cases, 94 Harv.L.Rev. 937 (1981); W. Krattenmaker, R. Lande & S. Salop, Monopoly Power and Market Power in Antitrust Law, 76 Geo. L.J. 241 (1987).

3. Or group of defendants acting in concert. The term "defendant" is often used in this book to describe the firm whose activity is being evaluated, even though it has not been sued or is purely hypothetical.

4. 15 U.S.C.A. § 2; see chs. 6–8.

5. See § 6.5.

6. Spectrum Sports v. McQuillan, 506 U.S. 447, 455–6, 113 S.Ct. 884, 892 (1993), on remand, 23 F.3d 1531 (9th Cir.1994); Tops Markets, Inc. v. Quality Markets, Inc., 142 F.3d 90, 100 (2d Cir.1998). When predatory pricing is challenged as a so-called "primary line" violation of the Robinson–Patman Act, 15 U.S.C.A. § 13, a relevant mar-

tying arrangement under § 1 of the Sherman Act and generally under § 3 of the Clayton Act[7] requires a showing that the defendant has a certain amount of market power in the market for the tying product.[8] Today most courts require a showing of market power in cases alleging unlawful vertical restrictions or dealer terminations.[9] The law of mergers under § 7 of the Clayton Act[10] does not generally require a showing that either of the merging firms has present market power. Mergers are condemned in part, however, because of their propensity to create market power. As a result, market power and market definition analysis is essential in merger cases. Finally, although market power is not a requirement in most *per se* cases, such as price fixing, a consumer plaintiff seeking damages must generally show that there has been an "overcharge." There will not be an overcharge unless the cartel members collectively wield some market power.[11]

The discussion in chapter one suggested four rationales for our social policies disfavoring monopoly. 1) The monopolist's price increase and output reduction transfer wealth away from consumers and to the monopolist. 2) Monopoly produces a "deadweight" loss, or value that is lost to consumers but is not regained by the monopolist or anyone else. 3) The monopolist may spend resources inefficiently in acquiring or maintaining its monopoly position. 4) The putative monopolist's exclusionary practices may destroy investments made by victims, mainly the monopolist's competitors.

Creating a deductive model that describes the consequences of market power and monopoly is relatively easy. As the discussion in §§ 1.1–1.2 shows, a competitor charges a price which tends toward its marginal cost. By contrast, the monopolist charges a price determined by the intersection of its marginal cost and marginal revenue curves, and this price is often much higher than marginal cost. Output is correspondingly smaller. But these deductive models have a simplicity that belies the difficulty of measuring market power empirically. Identifying market power in the markets encountered in litigation is often difficult, and *quantifying* market power with anything approaching precision is frequently impossible.

3.1a. Market Power Technically Defined

Market power is a firm's ability to deviate profitably from marginal cost pricing. Further, marginal cost, or competitive, pricing is an important goal of the antitrust laws. Marginal cost is therefore a useful base from which to measure market power: the greater the ratio of a firm's profit-maximizing price to its marginal cost, the more market power the firm has. The Lerner Index is one attempt to quantify market power in terms of marginal cost. Its simplest formulation is:[12]

$$\frac{P - MC}{P}$$

Where,

P = the firm's price at its profit-maximizing level of output; and

MC = the firm's marginal cost at the profit-maximizing level of output.

Under perfect competition, where price equals marginal cost, the index gives a reading of zero. As P approaches infinity, or as marginal cost approaches zero, the Index value approaches one. If a firm maximizes its profits at a price double its marginal cost, its market power measured by the Lerner Index would be

ket must be defined as well. Henry v. Chloride, 809 F.2d 1334, 1347 (8th Cir.1987). See § 8.8.

7. 15 U.S.C.A. §§ 1, 14.

8. See ch. 10. On whether a tying arrangement can be condemned under the Clayton Act without market power in the tying product, see § 10.3

9. For example, *Graphic Products*, note 2. See ch. 11.

10. 15 U.S.C.A. § 18. See chs. 9, 12 & 13.

11. See ch. 17.

12. For more technical variations, see Landes & Posner, note 2, at 940–941. The formula measures the profit-maximizing price accurately only if the firm's marginal costs are the same at all output levels. If marginal cost rises with output, the formula will overstate the difference between the competitive and monopoly prices, because the monopolist will have a lower marginal cost at its monopoly price than at the competitive price. See A. Lerner, The Concept of Monopoly and the Measurement of Monopoly Power, 1 Rev.Econ.Stud. 157, 169 (1934).

(2X − X)/2X, or .5. If a firm maximizes its profits at a price 20% above its marginal cost, its Lerner Index number would be (1.2X − X)/1.2X, or .167.

The Lerner Index can also be shown to equal the reciprocal of the elasticity of demand facing the firm.[13] For example, if the elasticity of demand facing a firm is 3, then the Lerner Index reading is 1/3; or,

$$\frac{P - MC}{P} = 1/3$$

Solving this,

$$3P - 3MC = P$$

$$2P = 3MC$$

or P/MC=1.5

In that case a firm with marginal costs (the competitive price) of $1.00 would have a profit-maximizing price of $1.50.[14]

The simplicity of Lerner's formula is misleading. If we knew the elasticity of demand facing any firm we could plug it into the formula and immediately know the ratio of that firm's monopoly price to its competitive price. The higher the ratio, the more market power the firm has. Likewise, if we knew any firm's marginal costs, we could compare marginal cost with the firm's current price and we would also have an immediate, simple "reading" of the firm's market power. From such data we could develop some presumptive legal rules about how high a reading would be necessary to make a merger illegal, or to establish one of the requirements for illegal monopolization.

3.1b. Market Share as a Surrogate for Market Power

Marginal cost and firm elasticity of demand are extraordinarily difficult to measure. For most markets, they cannot realistically be measured in the courtroom. Courts rely instead on the fact that there is a positive correlation between market *share* and market power. Suppose that the market for widgets is shared by 10 firms, each with 10% of the market. The marginal cost (and competitive price) of widgets is $1.00. If firm A attempts to raise its price to $1.25, A's customers will look to A's competitors for widgets at the old price. If each of the other nine firms can increase its own output by a little over 10%, A will lose all of its sales.

By contrast, if A has 90% of the market for widgets, A's price increase is much more likely to be profitable. A's customers will still look to A's rivals for lower-priced widgets, but now the rivals will have to increase their own output substantially in order to steal a large percentage of A's customers. For example, suppose that A reduces its output from 90 units to 80 units in order to raise the price from $1.00 to $1.25. If A's competitors, who make the remaining 10 units, are to raise output back to the competitive level, each will have to double its output. To be sure, over the long run A's monopoly profits will encourage the existing rivals to increase their production and new firms to enter the widget market. Eventually A's market share will erode, unless A devises some scheme for excluding its rivals.

13. Recall from Chapter one that marginal revenue can be expressed as follows:

$$MR = P + Q(\delta P/\delta Q)$$

Since the monopolist equates marginal cost and marginal revenue at its profit maximizing price, we can substitute:

$$MC = P + Q(\delta P/\delta Q)$$

subtracting P from both sides, we get

$$MC - P = Q(\delta P/\delta Q)$$

dividing by P yields

$$\frac{MC - P}{P} = \frac{Q(\delta P/\delta Q)}{P}$$

or, $$\frac{MC - P}{P} = \frac{Q\delta P}{P\delta Q}$$

Since the elasticity of demand is a negative number, we can rewrite the left side as:

$$\frac{P - MC}{P}$$

The right side is then the reciprocal of the elasticity of demand which, as you recall from § 1.1, equals:

$$\frac{P\delta Q}{Q\delta p}.$$

Thus,

$$\frac{P - MC}{P} = 1/e$$

14. A firm has no market power when the elasticity of demand facing it is infinite. In that case the ratio of Pm to Pc approaches 1.

All other things being equal, a firm with a large market share has a greater ability to increase price profitably than a firm with a smaller share. When A's market share is 10%, the effect of A's unilateral price increase would likely be the *immediate* loss of most sales. When A's market share is 80%, however, A may be able to make sales at the higher price for quite some time. This correlation of market power and market share has permitted courts to use market share as a qualified proxy for market power in antitrust cases.

The word "qualified" is important. Market share is an incomplete proxy for market power. The correlation between market share and market power can be rigorously expressed in a formula.[15] However, the formula contains *three* variables: market share, market demand elasticity, and the elasticity of supply of competing and fringe firms. If the two elasticity variables remain constant, then market power would be proportional to market share. In the real world, however, market elasticities vary from one market to another. Thus in order to estimate a firm's market power we must gather some information not only about a firm's market share, but also about the demand and supply conditions that it faces.[16]

3.1c. Market Share as More Than a Surrogate; Independent Relevance of Market Share

So far the discussion suggests that market share of a defined relevant market is a "surrogate" for market power. Since we cannot measure market power directly, we look at the next best thing. But the power questions that antitrust litigation presents are more complex than this statement suggests. Often the thing that the antitrust tribunal really seeks to measure is market share itself. In such cases market share would have to be determined even if market power could be measured by alternative means.

The underlying evil that antitrust addresses is the power to raise price profitably above marginal cost. But antitrust itself is concerned with the *process* by which market power is created. This process question forces the tribunal to consider whether some practice is likely to be anticompetitive. The answer often depends, not on the firm's abstract ability to raise price above marginal cost, but on its ability to "dominate" a market.

For example, many monopolization cases involve "exclusionary" practices that are plausible only because the defendant occupies a large portion of the relevant market in question. This is certainly true of predatory pricing, where the relative costs of predation are a function of the predator's market share. But the same thing is true of the various "foreclosure" offenses, whether under § 2 of the Sherman Act (monopolization and attempt), § 1 of that statute (vertical agreements), § 3 of the Clayton Act (tying and exclusive dealing), or Clayton Act § 7 (vertical and some other mergers). In each of these cases the claimed harm to competition results, not from the defendant's ability to raise price above marginal cost, but rather from its ability to cut rivals off from sources of supply, distribution outlets and the like. The real "power" basis of the offense, then, is market share, not market power as such. To be sure, antitrust's central concern is increased market power. But when we consider the threat and basic plausibility of

15. The formula is:

$$(P_m - P_c) / P_m = S_i / (\epsilon_m^d + \epsilon_j^s (1 - S_i)).$$

Where:

P_m = the monopoly price

P_c = the competitive price (marginal cost)

S_i = the firm's market share

ϵ_m^d = the market elasticity of demand

ϵ_j^s = the elasticity of supply of competing or fringe firms

See Landes & Posner, note 2 at 945.

16. See the discussion of elasticities of supply and

the alleged offense we are examining means, not ends.

3.1d. The Relevant Antitrust Market

In antitrust cases that require proof of market power the court generally determines whether some "relevant market" exists in which the legally necessary market power requirement can be inferred. In order to do this, the court usually 1) determines a relevant product market, 2) determines a relevant geographic market, and 3) computes the defendant's percentage of the output in the relevant market thus defined. Section 2 of the Sherman Act and § 7 of the Clayton Act, the two statutes that most often require analysis of market power, both suggest this approach. Section 2 of the Sherman Act condemns monopolization of "any part of * * * trade or commerce * * *."[17] Section 7 of the Clayton Act makes mergers illegal if they tend to lessen competition "in any line of commerce in any section of the country."[18] The court must identify some part or "line" of commerce in which injury to competition is threatened.

§ 3.2 Estimating the Relevant Market

A firm with a large share of a properly defined relevant market likely has market power. Markets do not define themselves, however. The passenger car division of Ford Motor Company makes "Ford cars," "American passenger cars," "passenger cars," "passenger vehicles," and "vehicles." Which of these is a relevant market for antitrust purposes? If the first, Ford Motor Company's share of the relevant market is 100%. If the last, it is trivial, perhaps less than 1%.

A relevant market is the smallest grouping of sales for which the elasticity of demand and supply are sufficiently low that a firm with 100% of that grouping could profitably reduce output and increase price substantially above marginal cost. Consider first the possibility that the relevant market is "Ford cars." What would happen if Ford raised the price of its cars by, say, $1,000 each. Customers would turn away from Ford cars in droves and go to General Motors, Chrysler, Toyota or some other automobile manufacturer instead. The likely result of Ford's unilateral $1,000 price increase would be that Ford would lose much of its business. In that case "Ford cars" is not a relevant antitrust market.

Consider next the market for "American passenger cars." Suppose that a single firm made 100% of American passenger cars, and increased the price by $1,000. Once again, many customers would probably attempt to buy Japanese, German or other foreign cars instead. However, this time we cannot be so certain that these firms will be able to increase their output or imports enough to satisfy this new demand. If they can, however, our "market" is still too small to be a relevant antitrust market.

Now consider the market for "passenger cars." Suppose that a single firm manufactured all the world's passenger cars and increased the price by $1,000. This time it would seem that the elasticity of the market on the *demand* side is rather low. Many automobile customers would probably switch from American to foreign cars if the price difference were great enough. But if the price of *all* passenger cars went up, they would have to switch to trucks, bicycles, horses, or simply do without cars. A far higher percentage of consumers would simply pay the higher price.

How about the supply side? If the passenger car monopolist raised its price by $1,000, the passenger car market would become very attractive to firms in related industries, such as tractor manufacturers, and they might switch to production of cars. Eventually enough new firms would enter the passenger car industry to deprive the monopolist of its monopoly profits. However, switching takes

demand in § 1.1.

17. 15 U.S.C.A. § 2. See Standard Oil Co. v. United States, 221 U.S. 1, 61, 31 S.Ct. 502, 516 (1911): "The commerce referred to by the words 'any part' construed in the light of the manifest purpose of the statute * * * includes any portion of the United States and any one of the classes of things forming a part of interstate or foreign commerce."

18. 15 U.S.C.A. § 18.

time, depending on how specialized the tractor producing equipment and plants are, and how long it takes tractor manufacturers to develop a system for distributing their new automobiles. This could be three or four years or even more. During that time the $1,000 price increase might be very profitable. "Passenger cars" is probably a relevant market.

Having determined the smallest relevant market, now we must calculate Ford's share of it.[1] In this case it appears that Ford is not a monopolist. Its share of the world passenger car market is less than 10%.

As the above illustration indicates, a grouping of sales is not a relevant market unless *both* the elasticity of demand and the elasticity of supply are sufficiently low. This is simply another way of saying that (1) customers must not be able to find adequate substitutes easily in response to the price increase; and (2) other firms must not be able to enter the market in question or change their own production so as to compete with the price increaser's sales.

For example, suppose that an area contained one printer of recipe books and 25 printers of mystery novels. The recipe book printer has 100% of the "recipe book printing" market. Furthermore, the demand for recipe books may be quite inelastic. Many people need them in order to cook, and mystery novels are poor substitutes. But suppose that mystery novel printers can switch production to recipe books very quickly and at almost no cost. The incremental cost of setting type for a recipe book is no greater than the cost of setting type for a new mystery novel. The price of mystery novels is currently competitive, and printers of mystery novels are making only a competitive rate of return. As long as the profitability of mystery books and recipe books is identical and a printer can sell as much as he wants of each, any cost of switching will prevent a change. When the recipe book monopolist attempts to reduce output and obtain monopoly profits, however, the high returns will immediately attract the mystery novel printers, who will switch part or all of their capacity from mystery novels to recipe books.[2]

If a firm can costlessly switch from making product A to product B, then as soon as product B is more profitable the firm will switch production to B. In the real world such production changes are seldom costless, but they can be relatively inexpensive. A farmer with standard, unspecialized equipment and 100 acres of tillable soil will decide each spring whether to plant barley or oats. She will plant the one that she predicts will be more profitable. Likewise, a book printer, whose equipment is generally unspecialized, can easily switch from mystery novels to recipe books. By contrast, it might be quite expensive and time-consuming for a plant currently manufacturing tractors to switch to passenger cars. As a result, a firm that acquired 100% of the market for passenger cars might get away with monopoly pricing for a time, while tractor manufacturers retooled their plants to enter the passenger car market. The 1992 Government Horizontal Merger Guidelines, of which more will be said later,[3] make this distinction by speaking of "uncommitted" and "committed" entrants. The mystery novel printer is an "uncommitted" entrant into the recipe book market because it can switch from one to the other with very little commitment of new resources. By contrast, the tractor manufacture must make a major commitment to the expense of retooling, setting up a new distribution network, and so on, in order to begin selling automobiles. It is a "committed" entrant.

An existing producer of a similar product can generally switch to a more profitable alternative much more easily than a new firm can enter the field. The latter are treated under

§ 3.2

1. On calculating market share, see § 3.7.

2. See Brown Shoe Co. v. United States, 370 U.S. 294, 325 n. 42, 326, 82 S.Ct. 1502 (1962) ("cross-elasticity of production facilities may ... be an important factor in defining a product market"); Rebel Oil Co., Inc. v. Atlantic Richfield Co., 51 F.3d 1421, 1436 (9th Cir.), cert. denied, 516 U.S. 987, 116 S.Ct. 515 (1995) (full-service and self-service gasoline retailing a single market, for supplier of one could readily switch to the other); Telex Corp. v. IBM, 510 F.2d 894 (10th Cir.), cert. dismissed, 423 U.S. 802, 96 S.Ct. 8 (1975) (suppliers could easily substitutes plugs to make non-compatible computer equipment compatible).

3. § 3.8a.

the concept of "barriers to entry."[4] Moreover, elasticity of supply is higher in those industries where plants and equipment are relatively unspecialized. Thus elasticity of supply in the market for recipe books may be very high; elasticity of supply in the market for passenger cars, much lower.

While market elasticities of demand and supply are frequently difficult to calculate,[5] both can be estimated more accurately than marginal cost or firm elasticity of demand can be. In litigation a court generally tries to identify some grouping of sales in which there are no close substitutes on the demand side (that is, where elasticity of demand is low) and for which entry on the supply side is either expensive or time-consuming (that is, where elasticity of supply is also low). Having identified this relevant market, the court then computes the defendant's share of it, to see if the market share will support an inference that the defendant has the necessary amount of market power. However, one of the prominent features of recent economic analysis, as seen below, is significant improvement in our ability to calculate the relevant elasticities directly.[6]

The basic framework for delineating markets outlined above suggests a few additional issues, to which we now turn.

3.2a. Size of Hypothesized Price Increase

In the example concerning Ford automobiles we spoke of estimating the supply and demand responses to a hypothesized price increase of $1000. Clearly, however, if the hypothesized price increase had been only $1.00, the supply and demand shifts would have been far less dramatic. By contrast, if the increase had been $10,000 they would have been more dramatic. Which number should we use?

The size of the price increase presents a question of policy, not one of economics *per se.* It all depends on how much market power we want to squeeze out of markets, given our capabilities and the costs of antitrust enforcement. A few considerations must be kept in mind:

First, in a world of differentiated and branded goods many manufacturers have at least a small ability to profit by raising price above marginal cost. Other imperfections in markets, such as information failures, transaction costs, and small geographic market size, or high transportation costs, imply the same result. Market power giving profit-maximizing prices somewhat above marginal cost seems to be ubiquitous[7] and may even be desirable. After all, markets are differentiated because customers want them that way, and these small monopoly profits are often nothing more than the consequences of a firm's differentiating itself sufficiently from rivals to make its output more attractive to consumers. Likewise, firms innovate in order to capture returns above the competitive level and the incentive to innovate disappears when firms are permitted to earn only competitive returns.

Second, the institutional costs of reducing market power are high. First, market power is difficult to measure. Second, when courts do measure it, they are prone to make errors, and as they try to make increasingly fine judgments the error rate will rise. Third, if numerous sellers have sufficient market power, then the volume of litigation would be extremely large. Finally, even when it is properly identified, correcting it may be costly.

Third, the size of the *optimal* price increase to use for antitrust enforcement purposes is not necessarily the same for all markets. For example, if a market is very large (such as passenger cars) the social loss caused by pricing at 10% above marginal cost could be quite large as well. By contrast, if a market is quite small (such as navigational systems for space shuttles), then the social loss could be corre-

4. Entry barriers are discussed generally in § 1.6, and with respect to mergers in § 12.6.

5. For some attempts at calculating elasticities of demand for a variety of products see H. Houthakker & L. Taylor, Consumer Demand in the United States (1970); W. Baumol, The Empirical Determination of Demand Relationships, in E. Mansfield, Microeconomics: Selected Readings 55–72 (4th ed. 1982).

6. See § 3.9a.

7. See D. Hall, The Relation Between Price and Marginal Cost in U.S. Industry, 96 J.Pol. Econ. 921, 940–948, 949 (1988).

spondingly smaller. However, enforcement costs do not vary in proportion. It may cost as much to eliminate market power in the small market as the large one. Finally, some price increases of a given magnitude produce a relatively small output reduction while others produce a much larger one; both the social cost of the monopoly and the resulting wealth transfer vary accordingly. Unfortunately, *implementing* this third factor is not easy, for we do not know where to draw the lines. We simply do not have enough data to go from one market to another and compute the tolerable amount of market power in each.[8]

At least presumptively, it seems that 10% above the competitive level (generally marginal cost) is about the correct hypothesized price increase for antitrust market delineation.[9] A smaller number encourages us to pursue market power that is not worth the costs of correction. A larger number might seem in order, particularly in product differentiated markets. But there are some reasons for adhering to a 10% figure. First of all, the ability to set price at 10% above marginal cost could represent the ability to earn *double* the competitive profit rate in a particular industry. Suppose that when a particular market is behaving competitively, it produces 8% in accounting profits—a typical number. For example, the firm might earn 8¢ in accounting profits on an item priced at $1.00. In this case, a 10% price increase above marginal cost represents an accounting profit increase from 8¢ to 18¢ per unit; however, one would have to subtract from this the monopoly output reduction, on which the monopolist earns no profits at all. The net increase could quite easily double the monopolist's profits.[10] Of course, eliminating high profits is not a goal of the antitrust laws, but exclusionary practices and cartelization are profitable precisely to the extent that they increase profits. The chance to double one's profits could represent a major incentive to engage in anticompetitive practices. We do not abhor the profits, but we do abhor the exclusionary practices that the opportunity to earn them invites.

The approach suggested here is that the fact finder hypothesize a price increase of ten percent above the *competitive* level, and consider the impact of such a price increase on customer demand, competitor supply and entry. Importantly, the hypothesized price increase must be computed from the *competitive* level, which is not necessarily the current level.[11]

3.2b. The "Profit-maximizing" Increase

Given our decision to hypothesize price increases in the range of 10% above the competitive level, the question that we ask is whether the profit-maximizing price increase is *10% or more*. We do *not* ask whether a 10% price increase would be profitable. This difference may seem subtle, but it can be very important.

Suppose firms A, B & C make widgets. Another group of firms, D, E & F, make gidgets, which are an imperfect substitute for widgets. Customers are grouped into two classes. One is a "low elasticity" class which must have widgets and are willing to pay much more than the competitive price for them. The other is a "high elasticity" class which is quite sensitive to price and will quickly substitute to gidgets if the widget price goes up. The first class collectively purchases 80 units and the second class collectively pur-

8. But see J. Morris & G. Mosteller, Defining Markets for Merger Analysis, 36 Antitrust Bull. 599, 630 (1991), who argue that varying the increase would confuse the fact of consumer injury with amount or level, and injury occurs in small markets as well as large. However, their observation ignores the relationship between enforcement costs and offsetting benefits. We cannot afford to eliminate all exercises of market power, so we must pick those that are most serious. See §§ 17.1–17.2.

9. Also advocating a 10% rule is L. White, Antitrust and Merger Policy: Review and Critique, 1 J.Econ. Perspectives 13, 15 (1987).

10. For example, suppose that at a marginal cost price of $1.00 accounting profits are 8¢ per unit and output is 100. Accounting profits would be $8.00. In response to a 10% price increase, demand falls by 5% to 95 (a not atypical elasticity of demand in markets for which an additional price increase would be profitable). At the new price and output the firm will earn 18¢ multiplied by 95 units, or $17.10. Even if the elasticity of demand were one, post-increase profits would be 18¢ multiplied by 90 units, or $16.20.

11. This problem is discussed in § 3.4.

chases 20 units, for a total of 100 units. The current price of widgets is $1.00. We also assume that costs are zero.[12]

Suppose that the firm raises its price from $1.00 to $1.10 and the high elasticity class immediately substitutes to gidgets. The result is that the firm sells 80 units at 1.10, for revenues of $88. Since revenues before the price increase were $100, the 10% price increase is unprofitable. That would suggest that the market for "widgets" is too small, and should be drawn larger to include at least "widgets plus gidgets."

But now suppose that in response to a 60% price increase precisely the same thing happens—that is, the 20 high elasticity sales are lost, but the 80 low elasticity sales are maintained. In that case total revenue is $1.60 multiplied by 80 units, or $128. This price increase is highly profitable and suggests that the market should be drawn as widgets alone.

The second answer is the correct one. It would be anomalous to draw a market in such a fashion that a 10% price increase were unprofitable but a price increase by some greater amount were profitable. So the relevant question is whether the profit-maximizing price increase would be 10% *or more*. A profit-maximizing firm in the above market would charge at least $160, and it might charge more.

By the same token, we do not ask whether a 10% price increase would be profitable. In some circumstances a 10% price increase might be profitable, but a 4% price increase would be more profitable.[13] In that case, the profit-maximizing firm (or cartel) will increase price by only 4%, and this would not meet our market definition test. In sum, the relevant question is whether the *profit-maximizing* price increase is 10% or more.

3.2c. Broader and Narrower Markets; General Irrelevance of Submarkets[14]

The existence of a relatively large relevant market does not preclude the existence of smaller relevant markets within it. For example, we might rationally conclude that "motor vehicles" constitutes a relevant market. On the demand side, most purchasers of motor vehicles value them by much more than alternatives, such as horse-drawn vehicles. On the supply side, the amount of durable specialized equipment and investment that one needs to manufacture motor vehicles is substantial, suggesting that entry or transfer of productive assets would not occur readily in response to a monopoly price increase.

But clearly the fact that "motor vehicles" is a relevant market does not entail that a sub-grouping such as "four-wheel-drive motor vehicles" or "diesel fueled vehicles" could not be a relevant market as well. Further, we would employ *precisely the same criteria* in determining whether one of these sub-groupings is a relevant market. That is, we would ask whether on the demand side consumers would be willing to pay an above-cost price before they would switch—for example, from four-wheel-drive to two-wheel-drive vehicles; or from diesel to gasoline powered vehicles. Maybe they would or maybe they would not, but one could certainly surmise that customers who buy four-wheel-drive or diesel fueled vehicles value these alternatives highly. On the supply side, one would ask whether people who do not make four-wheel-drive vehicles or diesel fueled vehicles could readily do so in response to a non-cost-justified price increase.

12. Alternative cost assumptions will not change the analysis, but they will make it more complex.

13. For example, a firm might lose almost no sales in response to a 4% price increase, but 20% of its sales in response to a 10% price increase. In that case the smaller increase is probably more profitable.

14. On submarkets, see 2A Antitrust Law ¶ 533 (2d ed. 1995).

As a result, this grouping of markets might look like this:

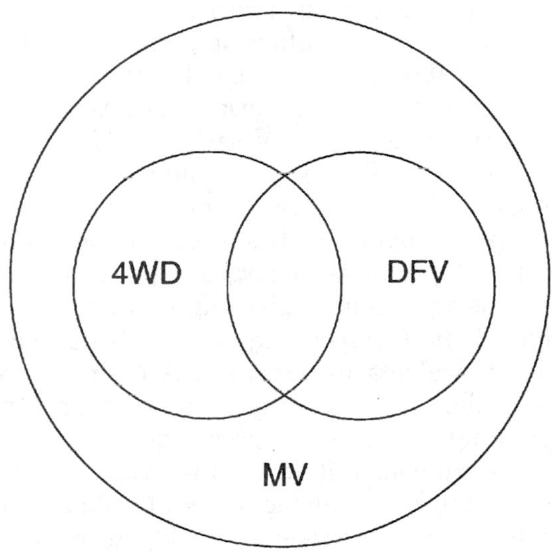

The large circle represents the market for motor vehicles (MV) generally. The two smaller circles indicate relevant markets for four-wheel-drive (4WD) and diesel fueled vehicles (DFV), and the overlap indicates that there may be some vehicles that are both four-wheel-drive and diesel fueled.

If an antitrust enforcer were to consider a merger or claims of monopolization in a motor vehicle market, clearly any one of these circles could be a relevant market—*provided* that it met the usual criteria for market definition. For example, if the Antitrust Division feared that a merger threatened higher prices in the market for "four-wheel-drive" vehicles, it would have to show that this particular grouping of sales constituted a relevant market.

This reasoning illustrates the general uselessness of the term "*sub*market." Since the 1950's, the Supreme Court has held that relevant antitrust markets might contain one or more "submarkets" in which the challenged practice should be analyzed. The Supreme Court noted in *Brown Shoe*:

> The outer boundaries of a product market are determined by the reasonable interchangeability of use or the cross-elasticity of demand between the product itself and substitutes for it. However, within this broad market, well-defined submarkets may exist which, in themselves, constitute product markets for antitrust purposes. The boundaries of such a submarket may be determined by examining such practical indicia as industry or public recognition of the submarket as a separate economic entity, the product's peculiar characteristics and uses, unique production facilities, distinct customers, distinct prices, sensitivity to price changes, and specialized vendors.[15]

The Court then added that § 7's language, which prohibited mergers "in any line of commerce" made it

> necessary to examine the effects of a merger in each such economically significant submarket to determine if there is a reasonable probability that the merger will substantially lessen competition. If such a probability is found to exist, the merger is proscribed.[16]

This language, which has since been used by courts in market power analysis under both the Sherman and Clayton Acts,[17] often suggests things that make little sense. Did the Supreme Court mean to say that one uses ordinary economic criteria in defining a market, but then uses something other than economic criteria in defining a submarket?[18] If so,

15. Brown Shoe Co. v. United States, 370 U.S. 294, 325, 82 S.Ct. 1502, 1524 (1962).

16. Ibid.

17. See SuperTurf v. Monsanto Co., 660 F.2d 1275 (8th Cir.1981) (§ 2 case; finding relevant market for athletic playing turf, but relevant submarket for artificial turf); Grumman Corp. v. LTV Corp., 527 F.Supp. 86 (E.D.N.Y.), affirmed, 665 F.2d 10 (2d Cir.1981) (merger case; relevant market for military aircraft; relevant submarket of carrier based military aircraft). Dicta in the Supreme Court's decision in United States v. Grinnell Corp., 384 U.S. 563, 572, 86 S.Ct. 1698, 1704 (1966), suggested the use of submarkets in a monopolization case. The term "submarket" was first used by Judge Wyzanski in a monopolization case: United States v. United Shoe Machinery, 110 F.Supp. 295, 302 (D.Mass.1953), affirmed per curiam, 347 U.S. 521, 74 S.Ct. 699 (1954).

18. The court in Image Technical Services, Inc. v. Eastman Kodak Co., 125 F.3d 1195 (9th Cir.1997), cert. denied, ___ U.S. ___, 118 S.Ct. 1560 (1998), apparently thought so, and used the term in a way not even contemplated by the Supreme Court. It held that the term "sub-

then the purpose of submarkets is not to identify groupings of transactions where there is a genuine possibility of monopoly. They must be for some other, unarticulated purpose.

But if submarkets are to be defined under the same criteria as are applied to markets, then the concept of the submarket serves no purpose. For example, suppose we should decide that "latex paint" defines a relevant market on the basis of evidence that the sole manufacturer of such paint could profitably raise price 10% above competitive levels. What if we also conclude that "latex barn paint," which differs in certain respects from other latex paints, satisfied the same test. That is, the only manufacturer of latex barn paint could profitably raise prices 10% above competitive levels, and would not face excessive demand or supply substitution. In that case either of these groupings of sales could be a relevant market. However, if we were concerned about the impact on competition of a merger between two latex barn paint manufacturers, it would be quite irrelevant that "latex paint" also defines a relevant market. Alternatively, if we were concerned about the horizontal effects of a merger between two general manufacturers of latex paint we might examine the impact in the latex paint market generally and, if both made latex barn paint, in that market as well. But the two groupings of sales would simply be separate, properly defined relevant markets.[19]

Why, then, the concept of submarkets? In general, submarkets have been used to take several possibilities into account. Among them are product differentiation, price discrimination, differences in physical characteristics, manufacturing in different plants, and different distribution networks. In some of these cases, the term "submarket" states only that the smaller grouping of sales is in fact a relevant market. For example, suppose a seller of widgets discriminates in price among three groups of buyers, A, B and C. Further, buyers in the A group are charged a price that is at least ten percent higher in relation to costs than B and C buyers pay. This tells us that the sale of widgets to buyers in A defines a relevant market. With respect to that particular grouping of sales, a price increase to 10% above the competitive level is profitable. If we then analyze the impact of an alleged antitrust violation in a market of "widgets sold to A buyers," it becomes totally irrelevant that there might be a larger grouping of sales that is also a relevant market. That is, the A grouping is not a "submarket," but a market.[20]

The same thing can be said of product differentiation among various sellers. When products are differentiated, each seller faces a downward sloping demand curve and may maximize its profits at a price higher than marginal cost.[21] If a particular seller is sufficiently isolated from other sellers and has an attractive product, that seller's output might constitute a relevant market unto itself. But in

market" could be used to link together goods that were not even within the same market—in this case, the various parts in a photocopier, which are complements rather than substitutes. Id. at 1204. Under the court's analysis, for example, the flat glass plate on a photocopier and the castors on which it rolls were in the same "submarket" because they were used by the same class of customers, namely those who used or service photocopy machines. Unfortunately, such a usage provides no information whatsoever about whether a price increase in one will result in a price increase in the other as well. For example, the glass plate might be made in any machine shop while the castors are patented and impossible to copy.

19. Several courts have used the term "submarket" but made clear that they were using it in the same way as the term "market," thus making the former term superfluous. See, e.g., Forsyth v. Humana, 99 F.3d 1504, 1513 (9th Cir.1996), vacated in part on other grounds, 114 F.3d 1467 (9th Cir.1997) (submarket exists "if it is sufficiently insulated from the larger market so that supply and demand are inelastic with the larger market"—that is, precisely the same criteria one uses to define "market"); FTC v. Staples, 970 F.Supp. 1066 (D.D.C.1997) (same); FTC v. Cardinal Health, 12 F.Supp.2d 34 (D.D.C.1998) (same).

20. See Owens–Illinois, 5 Trade Reg.Rep. ¶ 23162 (FTC, 1992), which refused to hold that the fact that different buyers of glass bottles had differing abilities to substitute justified placing these different groups in submarkets:

> [I]f in fact price could be raised above competitive levels for the glass containers sold in these end-use segments, those segments would be proper topics of antitrust concern not because they are submarkets, but because they would be relevant product markets in their own right. At least in theory, each end-use segment could stand as a grouping of sales for which a hypothetical monopolist might be able to impose a significant price increase.

21. See § 1.2.

that case it would make no sense to say that the general product is a market and that particular brands are "submarkets." If we are examining claimed monopolization by a firm capable of raising price 10% above costs in its own brand, then that brand is a relevant market and it would not matter that the product as a whole was a relevant market as well. By contrast, if an individual seller in a product differentiated market is *not* able to raise its price 10% above its costs, then its own output is not a relevant market, notwithstanding physical differences between its own offering and that of others making the same product.[22]

The evils of submarket analysis is well illustrated by the lower court's jury instructions in the *Aspen Skiing* case.[23] The trial court found a relevant product market of downhill skiing services and a relevant geographic market of North America, but a relevant geographic submarket of Aspen, Colorado, and a relevant product submarket of "downhill skiing services in the Aspen area." The judge instructed the jury:

> *Submarkets* : * * *. Even though a group of products are sufficiently interchangeable to be grouped in one product market, there may be within that group a smaller group of products that compete so directly with each other as to constitute a submarket within the larger market; or the products or services of a particular seller may have such particular characteristics and such particular consumer appeal and are sufficiently insensitive to price variations of other products that they constitute a relevant submarket all by themselves.
>
> There can be both a relevant market and a relevant submarket or just a relevant market without any relevant submarket. Thus, if you decide that the relevant product market is downhill skiing at destination ski resorts, you must still determine whether downhill skiing services in Aspen, including multi-area, multi-day lift tickets is a submarket within the larger market.[24]

The instruction simply evaded the basic issue that the jury was being asked: could a skiing company that controlled most of the slopes in Aspen, Colorado, charge monopoly prices, or would competition from other areas restrain its power? In order to answer that question we need to know only one thing: whether *Aspen* was the relevant market. Whether someone who owned all the skiing facilities in North America might also have the power to charge monopoly prices might also be an interesting question, but it was not relevant to that litigation.[25] The judge would have offered far less confusion if she had simply instructed the jury to consider whether downhill skiing in Aspen was a relevant market.

§ 3.3 The Product Market; General Considerations

This Section offers some introductory analysis of the problem of product market definition, and then examines the product market mainly from the demand side. Section 3.4 then looks at one particularly vexing problem of product market definition, the so-called *Cellophane* fallacy. Finally, § 3.5 examines product market definition from the supply side. Importantly, no grouping of sales is a relevant market unless *both* the elasticity of demand and the elasticity of supply are sufficiently low to warrant a conclusion that the sole seller of that grouping could profitably raise price substantially above the competitive level.

In one sense the problem of product market definition is less tractable than that of geographic market definition. Often geograph-

22. Several courts agree. For example, Domed Stadium Hotel v. Holiday Inns, 732 F.2d 480 (5th Cir.1984) (defendant's own hotel rooms not distinct submarket); Nifty Foods Corp. v. Great Atl. & Pac. Tea Co., 614 F.2d 832 (2d Cir.1980) (private label frozen waffles not distinct submarket within frozen waffle market).

23. Aspen Highlands Skiing Corp. v. Aspen Skiing Co., 738 F.2d 1509 (10th Cir.1984), aff'd on other grounds, 472 U.S. 585, 105 S.Ct. 2847 (1985). See § 7.5.

24. Id. at 1528–1529.

25. Compare Montvale Mgmt. Group v. Snowshoe Co., 1984–1 Trade Cas. (CCH) ¶ 65,990 at 68,373, 1984 WL 2949 (N.D.W.Va.1984) (geographic market for ski resort included not only the local area but the entire Mid–Atlantic area and perhaps even more remote ski resorts. This result is not necessarily inconsistent with *Aspen*. This may have been a disadvantaged or poorly placed resort, while Aspen had significant market advantages.).

ic market definition is a function of cost of transportation, and this is an objective number that can be measured. By contrast, product market definition is often a function of consumer taste, and taste cannot be measured so easily. To be sure, there are exceptions on both sides. In some geographic markets, such as the market for movie exhibition, consumers go to the theater, and consumer willingness to travel is a function of taste or preference as well as objectively measurable cost. Likewise, many products are used by businesses as intermediate inputs, and substitutability is largely a function of technology and cost.

But over a broad range of cases, product definition depends on substitutability in consumers' eyes, and since consumer utility cannot be measured by some easily identified criterion, such as cost of transportation, the market definition question can become very difficult. Theoretically, we can measure consumer responses directly by looking at substitution rates, or elasticities. For example, if 50% of consumers are observed to shift from widgets to gidgets in response to a 10% widget price increase, that may give us enough information to conclude that widget sales do not define a relevant market. But such methodologies depend on the existence of good data, and these are not always available.

Even if we cannot measure consumer response directly, however, we can still employ certain assumptions about consumer behavior that generate fairly safe conclusions. For example, we generally assume that consumers "maximize," in the sense that they are constantly on the lookout for the product that best meets their needs at the lowest possible price. This rationality assumption may yield plausible market definitions, even if the assumption cannot be empirically verified. Suppose that "regular latex house paint" currently lasts seven years and costs $5 per gallon to produce. Now someone develops "modified latex house paint" that lasts ten years and costs $4 per gallon to produce. Further, there are no known disadvantages of the latter product. In a case such as this we probably do not need to observe consumer behavior directly in order to conclude two things: *First*, the modified paint does not face substantial competition from the regular paint. As a result, if the modified paint producer is accused of monopolization, the regular paint should not be added to the market. *Second*, the regular paint *does* face substantial competition from the modified. As a result, if two regular paint producers should merge, the modified paint should be included in the market.

We can draw these conclusions about market definition simply because our basic assumptions about consumer rationality tell us that (1) consumers prefer paint that lasts 10 years to paint that last 7 years; and (2) consumers prefer to pay less rather than more.[1] Unfortunately, many cases are not this simple. For example, the modified paint may last longer but cost more to produce as well. Then we must decide how the rational consumer will trade off increased wear against increased cost. Very likely, one set of customers will prefer the increased wear while another set will prefer the lower price. There may be no substitute for direct observation of consumer response to the new paint.

In all events, we should never group two things into the same market simply because the same customers buy both. The Supreme Court made this error in *Alcoa (Rome Cable)*, which involved a merger between Alcoa, which made bare and insulated aluminum electric conductor, and Rome, which made bare and insulated conductor of both aluminum and copper.[2] The Supreme Court concluded that a single market existed for bare and insulated

§ 3.3

1. For example, see National Bancard Corp. (NaBanco) v. VISA U.S.A., 779 F.2d 592 (11th Cir.), cert. denied, 479 U.S. 923, 107 S.Ct. 329 (1986), which concluded that Visa credit card transactions did not define a relevant market, because rational consumers were interested in little more than the cost of the transactions, and there were numerous alternative credit cards as well as other media, such as cash and checks. Of course, merchants are a different story; if transaction fees are low in relation to the total profit, they might be willing to pay a monopoly transaction fee before losing business by not accepting a card.

2. United States v. Aluminum Co. (Rome Cable), 377 U.S. 271, 84 S.Ct. 1283 (1964), rehearing denied 377 U.S. 1010, 84 S.Ct. 1903 (1964).

aluminum conductor, but cited only the fact that both were used for the same purpose (conducting electricity) and sold to the same customers.[3] Whether or not the Court was correct, those facts alone were insufficient to establish a single market. One could say the same thing about electric dish washers and dish cloths. The fact that they are used for the same purpose and that the same customers buy both does not establish a relevant "dish washer/dish cloth" market.

As the illustration suggests, problems of product market definition become most difficult when things that meet the same need are produced by different technologies, or are composed of different materials. Further, although they meet the same generalized need, customers are not indifferent among them. For example, should cable television and rental videos be included in the same market? The two products may be partly, but not completely, interchangeable in consumers' eyes. The consumer who watches two or three movies a month and nothing else will probably prefer to rent videocassettes. The consumer who watches a great deal of television but has no videotape player will prefer cable television. Once again, we may be able to observe consumer choices directly—but often this approach commits the *Cellophane* fallacy of finding high cross-elasticity of demand at current prices because the seller of one of the technologies (say, the local cable television company) is already a monopolist.[4]

When there are no obvious differences in the cost of production[5] and consumer substitutability is high, the inference is strong that the two alternatives should be in the same relevant product market.[6] By contrast, products that do not compete in the eyes of consumers should not be regarded as in the same market on the basis of demand analysis.[7] For example, in *NCAA* the Supreme Court concluded that the audience for televised NCAA football games was sufficiently differentiated from the television audience for other sporting events. Indeed, advertisers were willing to pay a premium for spots on college football games. As a result, televised college football was a relevant market.[8]

Measuring customer response as between two products often requires tracking of prices over time. If the price of two products move with no apparent correlation, then the two should ordinarily be placed in separate markets. Closely parallel prices both upward and downward may suggest that two products are in the same relevant market, but one must be cautious. If one of the products is already monopolized, its price will move up and down in accordance with the price of the closest rivals. In that case the monopolized product

3. Id. at 277, 84 S.Ct. at 1287.

4. See § 3.4.

5. Even complete functional substitutability does not indicate a relevant market when production costs differences are substantial. For example, see Consolidated Gas Co. v. City Gas Co., 665 F.Supp. 1493, 1517 (S.D.Fla.1987), affirmed, 880 F.2d 297 (11th Cir.1989), reinstated on rehearing, 912 F.2d 1262 (11th Cir.1990), vacated as moot, 499 U.S. 915, 111 S.Ct. 1300 (1991). The court correctly refused to place natural gas and propane (LP gas) in the same relevant market because, although they performed the same functions, the cost of producing the latter was far higher than the cost of producing the former. Propane was generally purchased by rural customers who were out of reach of a natural gas utility. Given the production cost differential, buyers of natural gas would pay a large monopoly markup before they would substitute to propane.

6. For example, Morgan, Strand, Wheeler & Biggs v. Radiology, Ltd., 924 F.2d 1484, 1489 (9th Cir.1991) (grouping university and osteopathic radiologists into the same market as radiologists in private practice).

7. Omni Outdoor Advertising, Inc. v. Columbia Outdoor Advertising, Inc., 891 F.2d 1127 (4th Cir.1989), reversed on other grounds, 499 U.S. 365, 111 S.Ct. 1344 (1991) (billboard advertising and advertising in newspapers or radio not in the same product market, because customers did not view them as substitutes); Ad-Vantage Tel. Directory Consultants v. GTE Directories Corp., 849 F.2d 1336 (11th Cir.1987), appeal after remand 37 F.2d 1460 (1994) (state law; since consumers did not view yellow pages advertising and other forms of advertising as interchangeable, they were not in a single relevant market); United States v. Rockford Memorial Corp., 717 F.Supp. 1251 (N.D.Ill.1989), affirmed, 898 F.2d 1278 (7th Cir.), cert. denied, 498 U.S. 920, 111 S.Ct. 295 (1990) (inpatient and outpatient care in separate markets where patients and their physicians did not regard them as good substitutes).

However, supply side analysis might indicate a single market even though customers do not find alternative goods to be good substitutes. See § 3.5.

8. Board of Regents of the Univ. of Okla. v. NCAA, 546 F.Supp. 1276 (W.D.Okl.1982), affirmed in part, reversed in part, and remanded, 707 F.2d 1147 (10th Cir.1983), affirmed, 468 U.S. 85, 111–112, 104 S.Ct. 2948 (1984).

defines a relevant market.[9] By contrast, actual customer shifts back and forth when the market seems to be competitive tend to show a common market.

3.3a. Markets and Brands; "Lock-in"

3.3a1. Single Brand Ordinarily Not a Relevant Market; Kodak

Suppose the biggest difference between alternative products is not technological. Rather, the offerings are distinct brands, which may or may not exhibit significant technological differences as well. For example, Maytag washing machines may be technologically different from General Electric washing machines; however, the differences are likely to be small in relation to the total cost of producing the product. In such cases most courts refuse to find single brand relevant markets,[10] although a few disagree.[11]

Our analysis should start with a few premises. *First*, patents, trademarks and copyrights standing alone very rarely confer substantial market power.[12] *Second*, sometimes brand differences reflect very substantial technological differences, or differences in both cost of production and consumer appeal, and sometimes they do not. The case for narrower markets becomes stronger as these differences become more pronounced. For example, the case for placing aspartame ("Nutrasweet"), an artificial sweetener greatly superior to commercial alternatives, in a distinct market is much stronger than the case for placing Band–Aid plastic bandages and Buy–Rite plastic bandages in separate markets. *Third*, in a few extreme cases customers may become "locked in" to a particular brand, and this fact may justify a narrower market definition.

The lock-in problem arises this way. Although Chrysler automobiles are sold in competition with Chevrolets, Fords, Toyotas and many others, many of the repair parts for Chryslers are unique. For example, when the Chrysler owner's transmission fails, she will not be able to purchase a Ford or Toyota transmission as a substitute. So the person who has made a relatively major investment in a Chrysler automobile has been "locked in" to Chrysler repair parts. The relevant antitrust question is whether this lock-in enables Chrysler to somehow take advantage of its own automobile owners, and if any such advantage amounts to "monopoly."

If the firm in question is already a monopolist in the primary product (the automobile), the question of ability to monopolize replacement parts is relevant for reasons discussed elsewhere.[13] The more interesting issue arises when the primary market is competitive but the seller is thought to be taking advantage of locked-in previous customers by charging monopoly prices for replacement parts or service. This case will arise only where the primary good is durable, its replacement parts or service unique, and the customer's cost of extracting itself from a previous purchase are substantial. For example, the customer who rents a durable good under a short-term lease may be easily able to extract himself simply by abandoning the lease. Finally, there must be some element of "surprise," in the sense that the consumer could not reasonably have known when making the initial purchase that aftermarket parts or servicing would be very costly.

In a well functioning market where customers have adequate information, such lock-

9. See § 3.4.

10. See Tunis Bros. Co. v. Ford Motor Co., 952 F.2d 715 (3d Cir.1991), cert. denied 505 U.S. 1221, 112 S.Ct. 3034 (1992) (plaintiff did not meet burden of showing that Ford tractors were distinct market from tractors in general); Town Sound & Custom Tops v. Chrysler Motors Corp., 959 F.2d 468 (3d Cir.), cert. denied, 506 U.S. 868, 113 S.Ct. 196 (1992) (relevant market was automobiles, not Chrysler automobiles); International Logistics Group v. Chrysler Corp., 884 F.2d 904 (6th Cir.1989), cert. denied, 494 U.S. 1066, 110 S.Ct. 1783 (1990) (same); Key Financial Planning Corp. v. ITT Life Ins. Corp., 828 F.2d 635, 643 (10th Cir.1987) (ITT life insurance not distinct market from life insurance generally).

11. For example, National Assn. of Pharmaceutical Mfrs. v. Ayerst Laboratories, 850 F.2d 904 (2d Cir.1988) (a branded drug, Inderal, could be a relevant market); Parts and Elec. Motors v. Sterling Elec., 866 F.2d 228 (7th Cir.1988), cert. denied, 493 U.S. 847, 110 S.Ct. 141 (1989) (defendant's brand of electric motors a relevant market).

12. See § 3.9d.

13. The claim raises concerns that generally go under the rubrics of "leverage" or foreclosure. See §§ 7.6, 9.2–9.3.

in cannot occur. Suppose that automobiles last ten years but their transmissions last only two years. Further, automobiles are sold in a competitive market, where costs for new automobiles are $10,000 and for replacement transmissions are $1000. Consumers generally know these facts. Can Chrysler seriously "monopolize" this market by selling automobiles for the going price of $10,000, but then charge buyers $3000 for subsequent transmission replacements? Almost certainly not. The customer is interested in the package of automobile-plus-subsequent-maintenance, and the overcharge for subsequent transmissions will show up in her calculus as nothing other than an increase in the price of the package. She will go to another seller who behaves competitively.

But the real world is a less tidy place where the initial competition is imperfect, costs of subsequent repairs are uncertain (some Chryslers need a new transmission after two years; others never need one) and are probably unknown to the consumer. Presumably the customer who knows the current price and is highly uncertain about the price of future repairs discounts the latter and considers mainly the former. Further, sometimes anticipated repairs will be only a small fraction of the original package price. Finally, some sellers may find it advantageous to change their policies when they withdraw from a market. For example, suppose Maytag has decided to abandon the washing machine business (or has already abandoned it). Now it can double the price of replacement parts, knowing that previous customers have no alternative. It does not have to worry about the impact on future sales, for there will not be any.

This range of concerns quickly shades from "antitrust" to "consumer protection." As a general premise, the goal of the antitrust laws is competitive pricing and output consistent with the nature and (legal) structure of the market at hand. Competition in concentrated markets for durable goods is inherently imperfect, however, and so the policy question becomes one of degree: how many and what kinds of deviations should be tolerated?

In Eastman Kodak Co. v. Image Technical Services, Inc.,[14] the Supreme Court held that a manufacturer of photocopiers might have substantial market power in the market for its own replacement parts, notwithstanding that it lacked market power in the market for the photocopiers themselves. Kodak sold photocopiers in competition with several other firms, and had a market share of about 20 to 23 percent.[15] Most courts require market shares far larger than this to support market power claims of any sort, including tying claims.[16] Although Kodak repaired many of its own machines, numerous independent service organizations (ISOs) repaired them as well. The antitrust dispute arose when Kodak refused to sell parts to Kodak machine users unless they had their machines serviced with Kodak as well. This effectively denied several ISOs an opportunity to service Kodak's machines.[17] They alleged that Kodak had illegally tied Kodak service to the replacement parts for Kodak machines, and that Kodak was attempting to monopolize the market for its own replacement parts, as well as service.

Both the tying claim and the attempt claim required a showing of at least some market power in the market for Kodak replacement parts. Kodak's defense was that, given its competitive position in the primary market, it followed as a matter of law that Kodak could not have market power in the market for its own replacement parts. To hold to the contrary would make every manufacturer of durable equipment with brand-specific replacement parts into a monopolist for antitrust purposes.

The policy problem of such single brand "relevant markets" is very real, because such findings have the potential to make a wide range of single firm distribution decisions subject to challenge. For example, suppose Chrys-

14. 504 U.S. 451, 112 S.Ct. 2072 (1992).

15. See the Ninth Circuit's opinion. 903 F.2d 612, 616 & n. 3 (9th Cir.1990).

16. For example, Jefferson Parish Hospital Dist. No. 2. v. Hyde, 466 U.S. 2, 104 S.Ct. 1551 (1984) (tying; 30% insufficient). See generally §§ 6.2, 6.5b, & 10.3; and 10 Antitrust Law ¶ 1740 (1996)

17. 504 U.S. at 451, 112 S.Ct. at 2078.

ler is thought to be a "monopolist" in the market for "Chrysler transmissions," simply because these transmissions have different specifications than the transmissions of other automakers. At that point Chrysler is no longer free to streamline its auto service business, thus displacing some independent service providers, without antitrust challenge. The threat of overdeterrence is particularly severe in concentrated markets because the focus of competition in such markets is often on factors other than price. Firms try to capture customers by having the best or the most responsive service networks, the best warranty protection, the most reliable equipment, and the like. Excessive antitrust scrutiny could penalize firms for engaging in the kind of competition that is often most robust in concentrated markets for durable technical equipment.

Courts viewing the manufacturers of differentiated products as monopolists tend to give great weight to superficial indicia of market power—such as the "uniqueness" of the replacement parts, and the "dominance" of the primary manufacturer over the parts for its own equipment. But we can presume that every manufacturer of sophisticated durable equipment has such control over its own replacement parts, unless it is merely an assembler of off-the-shelf parts produced by others. In the process of looking at these irrelevant factors, such courts ignore the real meaning of market power, which is the power to earn profits by reducing output in a properly defined relevant market. The facts that Chrysler is the only producer of "Chrysler transmissions," and that only Chrysler transmissions will fit into Chrysler automobiles, provide absolutely no useful information about the degree of Chrysler's market power in either its automobiles or its transmissions. Further, any conclusion that it is a monopolist is belied by the firm's own historical position as a bare survivor in the automobile market.

The contrary position, summarized in Justice Scalia's *Kodak* dissent, is based on the perfect competition/perfect information model described above. He concluded that a manufacturer of a durable good sold in a competitive primary market *never* has substantial market power in the market for its own replacement parts.[18] A customer asked to pay a monopoly price for replacement parts will shop elsewhere, just as surely as a customer asked to pay a monopoly price for the original product itself.[19]

Both the proposition that market power in aftermarkets can be inferred from uniqueness and control, and the Scalia proposition that competition in the primary market entails competition in the aftermarket, are often wrong. The former proposition is nearly always wrong, but the latter is sometimes wrong as well. In fact, each of the markets must be evaluated separately, and market power in one might exist quite independently of market power in the other.

Consider this example. BMW has developed and patented an effective antilock brake device. The system can be produced at a marginal cost of $50, but BMW's profit-maximizing price for the system is $75, suggesting that BMW has substantial market power in the device. Suppose in addition that BMW installs the device in a luxury car sold in a competitive market, and produced at a marginal cost of $50,000, including the antilock brake device. Assuming that BMW lacks market power in any portion of its production except the antilock brake device, the profit-maximizing price for this automobile is $50,025—that is, BMW reaps $25 in monopoly profits from its position in the antilock brake device market, but it earns only competitive profits on the balance of the car.[20]

The above figures are consistent with the propositions that (1) BMW lacks market power

18. *Kodak*, 504 U.S. at 451–453, 112 S.Ct. at 2095–2097.

19. *Kodak*, 504 U.S. at 493–494, 112 S.Ct. at 2097 (J. Scalia, dissenting). See also *Parts & Elec.* Motors, note 11, 866 F.2d at 236 (Posner, J., dissenting).

20. See H. Hovenkamp, Market Power in Aftermarkets: Antitrust Policy and the *Kodak* Case, 40 UCLA L. Rev. 1447 (1993); and see B. Klein, Market Power in Antitrust: Economic Analysis After Kodak, 3 Sup. Ct. Econ. Rev. 43 (1993); C. Shapiro, Aftermarkets and Consumer Welfare: Making Sense of Kodak, 63 Antitrust L.J. 483 (1995).

in the primary market for its automobiles, but it (2) has substantial market power in one of the aftermarkets—namely, the market for its antilock brake device. For example, employing the kind of analysis suggested by the 1992 Horizontal Merger Guidelines,[21] BMW can profitably raise the price of the antilock device by 50% above marginal cost—clearly a sign that the device defines a relevant antitrust market. However, its profit maximizing price for the automobile as a whole is only one-twentieth of one percent above the competitive price, suggesting nearly perfect competition.

Clearly, one cannot *infer* lack of market power in aftermarkets from lack of market power in primary markets. Rather one must look at the various components in the aftermarkets individually. For this reason the *Kodak* decision was probably correct on its bare holding: further discovery was necessary on the market power question.

Evidence that (a) a manufacturer in a primary market is the only manufacturer of its own replacement parts; or (b) that the replacement parts are unique, or that (c) no substitute replacement parts will work in the manufacturer's product are, by themselves, absolutely irrelevant to the manufacturer's market power in aftermarkets.[22] Such evidence did not show "market power" at all, but only that Kodak, like most other manufacturers of durable goods subject to repair, has a great deal of control over the manufacturing of its own repair parts, and that its own repair parts are the only ones that will fit in its machines.[23] These things are generally true in product differentiated markets for durable goods, regardless of the amount of competition in the market.

However, two pieces of evidence in the *Kodak* decision did raise substantial questions about Kodak's market power. First, when Kodak maintained its own machines it charged higher prices than the ISOs had charged for maintaining the same machines.[24] Second, Kodak was able to engage in price discrimination in providing service to various groups of its photocopier customers.[25]

The higher prices are evidence of market power, if we can assume that Kodak and the ISOs had identical costs and that the ISOs were earning a profit.[26] In that case, at least part of Kodak's service prices were supracompetitive. For largely the same reason, price discrimination is pretty good evidence of market power. If a firm has two groups of customers that cost the same amount to service, but charges them two different prices, then one of two things must be true. Either the lower price is below cost or the higher price is producing monopoly profits.[27] There was no evidence of the former; so we can conclude that Kodak was earning some monopoly returns from at least some of its repair customers.

But how should evidence of price discrimination be considered? An observation reflected in Justice Scalia's dissent becomes relevant, although perhaps not with the same weight that he attached to it: customers purchase a package of photocopying services that includes both the original machine and subsequent maintenance. In an imperfectly competitive market, pricing imperfections might show up in *any* part of the package—that is, they are as likely to show up in the price of maintenance as in the original price of the primary equipment. The important observation is not that competition in the primary market entails competition in the aftermarket. It is that consumers' measure of relevant costs aggregates all the costs of the entire package: original equipment, supplies, and subsequent repair and service.

Often evidence of higher prices or price discrimination will emerge in the aftermar-

21. See § 3.8.

22. A decision relying exclusively on such a litany is *Parts and Electric Motors,* note 11, 866 F.2d at 232–233.

23. *Kodak,* 504 U.S. at 463–464, 112 S.Ct. at 2081.

24. Ibid.

25. Id. at 457–458, 112 S.Ct. at 2077.

26. Kodak argued that the ISOs in fact had lower costs than Kodak because they were free-riding on Kodak's investment. If true, Kodak's higher price could have been competitive, reflecting its own higher costs. However, the Supreme Court found little evidence supporting Kodak's argument. *Kodak,* 504 U.S. at 482–484, 112 S.Ct. at 2091–2092.

27. See § 14.1.

kets. But upon inspection, such evidence does not reflect any more market power than the manufacturer has in the primary machine itself. Indeed, evidence suggesting large amounts of market power in aftermarkets is most likely to be an artifact, reflecting the fact that we have used the wrong denominator in our market power fraction.

Consider this example. Suppose that a photocopier costs $3000 and has a life expectancy of five years. Thus the costs of the photocopier are $600 per year, disregarding the time value of money. In addition, suppose that the copier has a one year unlimited warranty. Thereafter, providing repair parts costs $100 per year. Suppose further that by use of tying arrangements or similar practices by which the manufacturer restricts subsequent service, the manufacturer is able to increase the price of repair services to $125 per year—a 25% "monopoly" price increase, which appears to be a sign of substantial monopoly power in the aftermarket.

But note further that this $25 yearly increase for four years adds only $100 to the total cost of owning a photocopier. At the competitive price, ownership of the photocopier over its five year lifetime costs $3400. At the "monopoly" price for replacement parts, ownership costs $3500, which is a little less than a 3% price increase above the competitive level. In the case finding a 25% price increase, the denominator in the market power fraction is the cost of the repair parts alone, while in the case finding a 3% increase the denominator is the total cost of the photocopier. Importantly, the photocopier *package* is the only thing that the end use customer regards as relevant; so in this case an apparent 25% monopoly overcharge (when considering repairs alone) is really nothing more than an effective 3% overcharge. Evidence of price discrimination or of higher prices in repair contracts, or in the purchase price of replacement parts, should count as evidence of substantial market power only if the evidence would count in that fashion when the total cost of owning a photocopier is taken into account.

The same analysis applies to Kodak's ability to engage in price discrimination.[28] Using the same numbers, what appears to be price discrimination of 25% between the most favored (competitive) and most disfavored (monopoly) purchasers, when looking only at the price of repair services, is really only 3% price discrimination when we view the entire market for the photocopier package.

Suppose the defendant is alleged to have little or no market power in the primary market, but substantial, independent market power in an aftermarket—as in the BMW antilock brake illustration given above. That allegation makes little sense when the *only* function of the aftermarket product or service is to support the same manufacturer's primary product. For example, Chrysler may develop a superior transmission that makes its automobile's more desirable and permits Chrysler to raise its price well above its costs. But in that case we would speak of the market power as being in the automobile, not in the transmission. Indeed, most decisions that a firm has market power in a particular product reduce to the conclusion that the firm has a competitive advantage in some particular process or component that goes into that product. For example, du Pont had a patented process for making cellophane, but it was alleged to monopolize the market for cellophane itself.[29] Likewise, Aspen Skiing Company controlled some vertically inclined real estate in Aspen, Colorado, but it was alleged to have monopolized a relevant market of "downhill skiing," of which that real estate was only a component.[30]

It makes sense to speak of market power in an aftermarket distinctly only if the product or service at issue is traded in some market other than the aftermarket for the primary firm. For example, once it has developed and patented its antilock brake device, BMW might sell the device to other automobile manufacturers for

28. *Kodak*, 504 U.S. at 457–458, 112 S.Ct. at 2077.

29. United States v. E.I. du Pont de Nemours & Co., 351 U.S. 377, 76 S.Ct. 994 (1956).

30. Aspen Skiing Co. v. Aspen Highlands Skiing Corp., 472 U.S. 585, 105 S.Ct. 2847 (1985).

installation in *their* (non-BMW) automobiles. In *that* market, we can speak of BMW as having market power quite independent of its market power in the market for the automobiles that it manufactures.

In sum, in a product differentiated market firms have the ability to exploit small amounts of market power. One can expect that this exploitation will occur in those parts of the market where comparison shopping is most difficult and isolation of customers is easiest. For example, if photocopiers are sold in multi-brand stores permitting close price comparison, initial prices will be closely comparable. Exploitation is more likely to occur in markets for servicing and replacement parts, where comparison shopping is far more difficult.

Perhaps manufacturers should not be encouraged to enlarge their market power by channeling their noncompetitive pricing into those areas where price comparison is most difficult. But absent market power, antitrust concerns are generally misplaced. The fact that aftermarkets become the locus for the gains available from product differentiation does not establish that such gains are substantial. Further, when such exploitation is measured, it must be measured against the package price of the whole, for that is what the customer is purchasing. What may appear to be significant power over price when one looks only at the aftermarket may be nothing more than the price discretion that exists in a moderately competitive, product differentiated market.

3.3a2. Lower Court Decisions Limiting Kodak

The scholarship and lower court decisions on *Kodak* have been somewhat mixed but mainly quite critical. The courts have found various ways of limiting *Kodak*'s lock-in theory so as not to make monopoly power so easy to prove that almost every seller in a moderately concentrated market is found to have it. The first significant limitation is that relevant lock-in can occur only if the "locked-in" product is purchased at a significantly later period than the primary product. Suppose, for example, that a firm with a nondominant share of the computer market sells a computer and requires buyers to take its operating system as well. We cannot say that buyers are "locked-in" to the defendant's operating system, thus justifying a smaller relevant market limited to that seller's brand, because the buyer makes the decision to purchase the computer and the operating system at the same time. The *PSI* decision so held, distinguishing the *Kodak* situation where the defendant supposedly changed its policy "after its customers were 'locked-in,'" thus taking advantage "of the fact that its customers lacked the information to anticipate this change."[31]

By the same token, even if the aftermarket parts are sold in a latter transaction, the courts have required plaintiffs to be able to point to a *change* in the defendant's policy respecting tied aftermarket parts.[32] A customer can legitimately be said to be "locked in" if aftermarket parts were one price when she purchased the machine, but were increased afterward. Further, the change must be one that adversely affected consumers. For that reason one court denied relief when the plaintiff repair organization complained that the defendant prospectively changed its warranty from one year to three.[33] The court noted that pre-existing customers were not affected at all by the change, and new customers knew of the extended warranty when they first bought their computer. Suppose, however, that the defendant had retroactively extended its warranty to three years. This change would un-

31. PSI Repair Servs. v. Honeywell, 104 F.3d 811, 821 (6th Cir.), cert. denied, 520 U.S. 1265, 117 S.Ct. 2434 (1997). Accord Digital Equip. Corp. v. Uniq Digital Techs., 73 F.3d 756, 763 (7th Cir.1996); Lee v. Life Ins. Co. of N. Am., 23 F.3d 14, 20 (1st Cir.), cert. denied, 513 U.S. 964, 115 S.Ct. 427 (1994).

32. See Metzler v. Bear Automotive Service Equip. Co., 19 F.Supp.2d 1345 (S.D.Fla.1998)) (granting summary judgment: defendant refused to sell certain internal parts for its diagnostic equipment, but had never changed its parts policy vis-a-vis already existing customers; thus no "lock-in" justifying a finding of single-brand power).

33. SMS Systems Maintenance Services v. Digital Equipment Corp., ___ F.3d ___, 1999 WL 618046 (1st Cir.1999). On this problem, see S. Kumar, Comment, Parts and Service Included: an Information–Centered Approach to *Kodak* and the Problem of Aftermarket Monopolies, 62 U. Chi. L. Rev. 1521 (1995).

doubtedly injure independent service organizations who would be denied lucrative repair work—but it would also benefit pre-existing customers, who are getting something for free. It would be hard to find antitrust injury in such a claim.

Finally, no one is locked in if other companies make equally suitable repair parts. For example, while Chrysler makes gaskets or axle joints that fit only Chrysler automobiles, no one could be locked in if several other firms are also in the business of making parts that, while not bearing Chrysler's brand, fit and work just as well.[34]

3.3a3. Contract "Lock-in;" Franchisor Brand as Market

Suppose that a utility enters into a ten year requirements contract with a mining company to purchase all its coal needs at $100 per ton. At the time the contract is negotiated that seems like a good deal to the utility, but a year or two later the coal market drops. The utility could purchase coal on the open market for $75 per ton, but is forced by the contract to pay $100 to the mining company. It then files an antitrust suit, alleging that the mining company is monopolizing a "relevant market" for the coal covered by the long term contract.

In fact, there are some similarities between the general concept of a relevant market and the grouping of coal sales covered by a long term requirements contract. Most important is lack of buyer or seller substitutability: under the terms of the contract (1) the buyer cannot buy elsewhere and (2) no alternative coal mining company can sell to this buyer. Indeed, many if not most contracts have the property that they oblige the buyer to buy the goods covered by the contract from the contracting seller. At the same time, to conclude that these criteria are sufficient to create a "relevant market" for antitrust purposes would effectively turn antitrust into a device for "repairing" contracts that seem less wise after the fact than they were when first entered. Indeed, the repair would be performed on what we must presume is a legally valid and binding contract as far as contract law is concerned; otherwise the antitrust relief would be unnecessary.[35]

Most courts have adopted this reasoning. In the leading *Queen City* decision the plaintiffs were Domino's pizza franchisees and the defendant was their franchisor.[36] The franchisees claimed that their franchise contract required them to purchase pizza dough mix from their franchisor at above-market prices. Pizza dough is made from common ingredients such as flour, water and salt, however, and not even a big franchisor such as Domino's has anything approaching a monopoly share of it. But in this case the franchisees alleged that there was a relevant market for Domino's own pizza dough, even though that dough was identical to the dough of others. Since the contract required them to purchase Domino's dough, they reasoned, they could not substitute away and this turned Domino's own brand into a relevant market. The Third Circuit responded by distinguishing between "pre-contract" and "post-contract" market power. After a contract is negotiated, a contracting party is typi-

34. Tarrant Service Agency v. American Standard, 12 F.3d 609 (6th Cir.1993), cert. denied, 512 U.S. 1221, 114 S.Ct. 2709 (1994) (several firms made "generic" parts that fit defendants equipment; judgment as a matter of law); Godix Equipment Export Corp. v. Caterpillar, 948 F.Supp. 1570 (S.D.Fla.1996) (similar; other firms made parts that fit Caterpillar tractors).

35. See Antitrust Law ¶ 510' (current Supplement). Other literature addressing the issue includes W. Grimes, When do Franchisors have Market Power? Antitrust Remedies for Franchisor Opportunism, 65 Antitrust L.J. 105 (1995) (arguing that franchise contract lock-in can create antitrust market power); J.H. Beales & T. Muris, The Foundations of Franchise Regulation, 2 J. Corp. Fin. 157 (1995) (disagreeing); P. Kaufmann & F. Lafontaine, Costs of Control: the Source of Economic Rents for McDonald's Franchises, 37 J.L. & Econ. 417 (1994) (similar); G. Hadfield, Problematic Relations: Franchising and the Law of Incomplete Contracts, 42 Stan. L. Rev. 927 (1990) (similar). Important seminal pieces are B. Klein & L. Saft, The Law and Economics of Franchise Tying Contracts, 28 J.L. & Econ. 345 (1985); P. Rubin, The Theory of the Firm and the Structure of the Franchise Contract, 21 J.L. & Econ. 223 (1978).

36. Queen City Pizza v. Domino's Pizza, 922 F.Supp. 1055, 1061 (E.D.Pa.1996), aff'd, 124 F.3d 430 (3d Cir.), rehearing denied, 129 F.3d 724 (3d Cir.1997), cert. denied, ___ U.S. ___, 118 S.Ct. 1385 (1998). The Third Circuit divided 8 to 5 on the denial of rehearing and there was a lengthy dissent. See also E. Dunham, D. Kaufmann & E. Lokker, Kodak's Reach Uncertain, 17 Franchise L. J. 101 (1998) (summarizing the cases).

cally locked in to buy what the contract specifies. However, prior to contract formation Domino's was only one of many franchisors and the putative franchisee could choose from a variety of business opportunities.[37] In any event, there are other problems with the claim the franchisees were making. First, while they were claiming a "relevant market" of Domino's brand pizza dough, the requested relief was that they be permitted to purchase equally good pizza dough elsewhere. This acknowledgement that non-Domino's pizza dough was in fact a suitable substitute was inconsistent with the pleading that Domino's own dough constitutes a relevant market. Second, the reason that the franchisees were locked in to Domino's dough was a provision in their contract requiring them to purchase it, but they knew about this provision at the time they initially signed up. This fact places the contract lock-in cases into the § 3.3a2 classification of situations where the primary and "aftermarket" purchases occur at the same time, and lock-in is impossible for a contracting party who takes the time to read the franchise agreement. Third, and most importantly, there is no relevant market in which output is being reduced. To be sure, one consequence of the high prices that Domino's supposedly charges for its pizza dough is that Domino's franchisees sell less pizza. But pizza *consumers* are not locked in to anything, and the underlying pizza market is presumably quite competitive. In that case, any output reduction in Domino's pizza is offset by output increases by Pizza Hut, Godfather's, and thousands of other pizza sellers.

Finally, a short-term contract that imposes no or only nominal switching costs cannot create market power in any event. So *Brokerage Concepts* held that HMO members who were free to switch to a different HMO at any time could not be locked in.[38]

3.3b. Substitutes v. Complements; Cluster Markets

3.3b1. Relevant Market Consists of Substitutes

A relevant market consists of goods that are effective *substitutes* for each other. For example, we place all canned tomatoes in a single relevant market because the Del Monte brand competes with the General Foods brand, which in turn competes with A & P's house brand, and so on.[39] This definition of a market is so fundamental that few courts get it wrong, but there have been some exceptions. In the *Kodak* case after remand from the Supreme Court, for example, the Ninth Circuit confused substitutes and complements, concluding that there was a single relevant market for all Kodak photocopier parts because a machine user or repairer needs "all the parts" in order

37. Accord Tominaga v. Shepherd, 682 F.Supp. 1489, 1494 (C.D.Cal.1988) ("the analysis must take place at the 'pre-contract' stage"); and compare Mozart Co. v. Mercedes–Benz of N. Am., 833 F.2d 1342, 1346–1347 (9th Cir.1987), cert. denied, 488 U.S. 870, 109 S.Ct. 179 (1988) ("obviously there are costs in surrendering one franchise and acquiring another, but these are costs unrelated to the 'market power' of a unique automobile."); see also Valley Products Co. v. Landmark, 128 F.3d 398 (6th Cir.1997) (similar). Or, as another decision put it:

> Economic power derived from contractual arrangements such as franchises or in this case, the agents' contract with Farmers', has nothing to do with market power, ultimate consumers' welfare, or antitrust."

United Farmers Agents Ass'n v. Farmers Ins. Exchange, 89 F.3d 233 (5th Cir.1996), cert. denied, 519 U.S. 1116, 117 S.Ct. 960 (1997).

The one dissenting decision at this writing is Collins v. International Dairy Queen, 939 F.Supp. 875 (M.D.Ga. 1996), 980 F.Supp. 1252 (M.D.Ga.1997), which permitted the plaintiffs to proceed with both a tying claim and a monopolization claim on charges that DQ required its franchisees to use only Nabisco brand Oreo cookies in making its blizzards, as well as tying other common items.

38. Brokerage Concepts v. U.S. Healthcare, 140 F.3d 494, 513–516 (3d Cir.1998).

39. See, e.g., Levine v. Central Florida Medical Affiliates, 72 F.3d 1538, 1552 (11th Cir.), cert. denied, 519 U.S. 820, 117 S.Ct. 75 (1996) (relevant market must be limited to services that are reasonably interchangeable with one another); Rebel Oil Co., Inc. v. Atlantic Richfield Co., 51 F.3d 1421, 1434 (9th Cir.), cert. denied, 516 U.S. 987, 116 S.Ct. 515 (1995) (in order to be in the same "market" sellers must have the "actual or potential ability to deprive each other of significant levels of business."—"If consumers view the products as substitutes, the products are part of the same market." Id. at 1435.); Thurman Indus. v. Pay 'N Pak Stores, 875 F.2d 1369, 1374 (9th Cir.1989) ("product market is typically defined to include the pool of goods or services that qualify as economic substitutes because they enjoy reasonable interchangeability of use and cross-elasticity of demand.").

to make the machine function properly.[40] The court cited a "commercial reality" that a service provider "must have ready access to all parts."

While true, that is hardly the rationale for placing goods in the same relevant market. People need both cars and gas to operate an automobile, both a toaster and bread to make toast, or both a racket and a ball to play tennis. But these facts hardly establish a single "car/gas," "toaster/bread," or "racket/ball" market. The relationship that exists between these pairings is that they are complements, not substitutes. Placing complements into a "relevant market" ignores the fact that a market must be a set of sales that *compete* with each other. For example, when we place the four gasoline stations at the same intersection into a single relevant market, it is manifestly not because a customer needs to go to all of them—the rationale that the Ninth Circuit used in *Kodak*. Quite the contrary. The four stations are in the same relevant market because the customer does *not* need to go to all of them; as a result, the firms must compete with one another for sales.

One critical reason for not placing complements in the same relevant market is that the price of complements in demand actually move in *opposite* directions. By contrast, the price of goods in the same market tends to be uniform. To illustrate, if gasoline prices rise significantly people will respond by driving less, thus reducing the demand for cars. Another reason for not placing complements in the same market is that the extent of monopoly in one typically provides no useful information about the other. For example, it is quite plausible that toasters are made by a toaster monopolist, while bread is sold in a fiercely competitive market. The list of 5000 parts that went into a Kodak photocopier included a patented image loop and several other patented parts in which Kodak may have had some power. But it also included thousands of nuts, bolts, screws, belts, springs and switches that were sold off-the-shelf by numerous manufacturers; and things such as a flat glass plate and metal doors that could readily be made to size specifications by any glass cutter or machine shop. Once the court grouped all of these things into a single "relevant market" it lost control of the power issue altogether, for there is no way of looking at this grouping in the aggregate and saying that Kodak did or did not have market power in any relevant grouping of sales.

Even when goods are complements in production, market power in one seldom establishes market power in the other. Consider the slaughterhouse, whose production process yields both beef and cowhide. These two goods are said to be complements in production, because one cannot readily produce one without producing the other. In this case the proportions of the two goods are fixed by nature, so a firm that was the only slaughterer of cattle would have 100% of both beef and hides. But the relevant antitrust market question would consider whether there is monopoly power in beef by looking at substitutes for it—pork, lamb, chicken, and the like. It would consider monopoly power in cowhides by looking at a completely different set of substitutes—vinyl, cloth fabrics, and so on. It is quite plausible that the slaughterhouse has significant market power in a market for meat used for human consumption, but little market power in a market for fabrics. This all depends on the effectiveness with which meat competes in one market and leather in the other.

There are a few cases in which goods can function as both substitutes and complements. Computer hardware and software is a good example. For most purposes the two are complements. But in some circumstances a customer might be able to improve performance by purchasing *either* additional software or additional hardware.[41] However, to place them in the same market requires not merely a

40. Eastman Kodak Co. v. Image Technical Services, Inc., 504 U.S. 451, 462, 112 S.Ct. 2072 (1992), on remand, 125 F.3d 1195, 1203 (9th Cir.1997), cert. denied, ___ U.S. ___, 118 S.Ct. 1560 (1998). See also Coast Cities Truck Sales v. Navistar Intl. Transp., 912 F.Supp. 747 (D.N.J. 1995).

41. See Allen–Myland v. IBM, 33 F.3d 194 (3d Cir.), cert. denied, 513 U.S. 1066, 115 S.Ct. 684 (1994) (hardware and software were substitutes as well as complements, and thus could be in same market).

showing that the goods are substitutes, but that they are sufficiently close substitutes so that one good holds the other to its costs. For example, if the hardware fix for a computer problem is very costly, and does not become a viable alternative for the software fix until the software is sold at a price equal to double its costs, then there is still a relevant market for the software alone. A firm that controlled the relevant software could charge nearly double its costs without incurring competition from the hardware supplier.

3.3b2. The Limited Rationale for Finding "Cluster" Markets

Sometimes courts must consider whether a grouping of products is a relevant market even though each individual product or service in the group might not be. For example, in the *Philadelphia Bank* case the court found a "cluster" of commercial banking services to be a relevant market.[42] For some of these services, such as business checking accounts, the banks had few competitors. For others, such as savings deposits and small loans, banks faced competition from savings and loan associations and small loan companies. Problematically, checking accounts and consumer loans are not *competing* products at all. By contrast, the court in *Thurman* refused to accept a relevant market of "home centers," which offered electrical, plumbing and building supplies under one roof. Although numerous stores in the area sold electrical, plumbing or building supplies alone, few offered all three.[43] Further, electrical supplies and plumbing supplies did not compete, nor did electrical supplies and building supplies.

Clusters of complementary products are sometimes grouped into a relevant market if there are substantial economies of joint provision, sometimes called economies of scope.[44] While an economy of scale is an economy that results from doing more of one thing, an economy of scope results from doing two things together more cheaply than each can be done separately.[45] One likely example of a cluster market is the central station protective services at issue in *Grinnell*.[46] The defendant's central station system simultaneously offered burglary protection, fire protection, and well as other services. Since burglary protection and fire protection do not compete with each other, they cannot be grouped together on the basis of high cross-elasticity of demand. But providing the services jointly is likely much cheaper than providing them separately. For example, much of the wiring of the system could be used for both services. Likewise, the system set off alarms by placing calls to an attended central station, and the same station agents could take fire calls and burglar calls.

Likewise, suppose the cost of providing checking account services alone is $1.50 per $1000 of activity and the cost of providing small loans alone is $3.00 per $1000. However, a bank that does both of these things simultaneously eliminates the transaction costs and risks of borrowing and lending money on the third-party market, for it can use its checking account deposits to make the loans. Suppose this bank can reduce the aggregate cost of supplying checking account and small loan services to $3.50. It could then price the checking account services at $1.00 and the small loan services at $2.50. Clearly, this cost advantage could enable the only bank in town to compete with single service institutions while charging a price substantially above its marginal costs—50% more in the case of checking and 20% more in the case of small loans. Further, any firm that entered only one part of this business would be at a cost disadvantage. Defining a relevant "cluster" market makes sense.

42. United States v. Philadelphia National Bank, 374 U.S. 321, 356–357, 83 S.Ct. 1715, 1737–1738 (1963). See also Brown Shoe Co. v. United States, 370 U.S. 294, 327–328, 82 S.Ct. 1502 (1962) (clustering men's, women's and children's shoes).

43. *Thurman*, note 39, 875 F.2d at 1374.

44. See generally I. Ayres, Rationalizing Antitrust Cluster Markets, 95 Yale L.J. 109 (1985).

45. See A. Chandler, Scale and Scope: Dynamics of Industrial Capitalism, chs. 5 & 6 (1990), who offers a rich history of the way American firms achieved economies of scope through diversification.

46. United States v. Grinnell Corp., 236 F.Supp. 244 (D.R.I.1964), affirmed except as to decree, 384 U.S. 563, 86 S.Ct. 1698 (1966).

By contrast, suppose that the cost savings that result from offering electric, plumbing and building supplies under one roof are trivial. To be sure, renting a larger building to house all three types of merchandise costs less, but the savings amount to less than 1% of the seller's overall costs. In that case the economies of scope do not justify finding a cluster market.

In most cases, a cluster market based on economies of scope is nothing more than a way of identifying a particular facility or a particular productive system as a relevant market even though it produces goods that, strictly speaking do not compete with each other. For example, consider a hospital operating room. It can be used for heart transplants, tonsillectomies, and delivering babies. None of these procedures is a good substitute for the others; yet it might make sense to speak of a monopoly hospital as having a monopoly in "surgical services" in a given community, and then estimating market share by counting the number of operations performed there in comparison to the number performed elsewhere. It might seem that we are counting heart transplants and tonsillectomies and placing them in the same "relevant market." But in fact we are attributing the power to the durable and specialized piece of hardware—the hospital room—in which these various types of surgery are performed.

One word of warning: an economy of scope does not justify a cluster market definition unless other firms face barriers to attaining the same economies of joint provision. Suppose the first retailer to cluster electrical, plumbing and building supplies under one roof discovers substantial cost savings. But existing plumbing stores, electric supply stores and lumberyards can easily expand and do exactly the same thing. In this case, the only entry requirement might be the construction or enlargement of a cheaply built, general purpose building. In that case any monopoly pricing in the clustered "market" will not last long.

Finally, there may be a few cases in which cluster markets are justified by administrative convenience—but as long as there is no compelling reason for thinking that the firm has differential amounts of market power in the different products in the grouping. For example, in *Alliant Techsystems* the court approved the FTC's finding of a relevant market for tank ammunition, even though different tanks used different sizes and types of rounds, and they were not interchangeable.[47] One rationale for the conclusion is that the real source of the power was the production facility, as in the hospital operating room example. Another, however, is that the defendant had the same market share in all, the same competitors, that barriers to entry were the same for all, and so on. As a result, grouping the different types together saved the tribunal costly, repetitive work of going through the same process for each type of ammunition. Of course, as soon as the rationale for grouping disappears, then such a cluster must be abandoned. For example, suppose that Alliant made 100% of the tank ammunition for tank types A, B, and C, but there was a significant rival who made 40% of the ammunition for D types tanks, while Alliant made the remaining 60%. In that case the only thing the court can do is group types A, B and C together, and consider power in type D separately.[48]

The government's Horizontal Merger Guidelines generally avoid clustering. When assessing a merger the government agencies "will first define the relevant product market with respect to *each* of the products of *each* of the merging firms...."[49]

§ 3.4 "Cross-Elasticity of Demand:" the "Cellophane" Fallacy and Its Consequences

3.4a. Cross-Price Elasticities and Their Meaning

When the price of a product rises, some buyers substitute away. A cross-elasticity (or

47. FTC v. Alliant Techsystems, 808 F.Supp. 9, 20 (D.D.C.1992).

48. See, e.g., *Brown Shoe*, note 42, 370 U.S. at 327–328 (clustering men's, women's and children's shoes, but only after concluding that the defendants' market shares were about the same in all).

49. 1992 Horizontal Merger Guidelines § 1.1. For further discussion of market definition under the Merger Guidelines, see § 3.8. See, e.g., Fruehauf Corp. v. FTC, 603 F.2d 345 (2d Cir.1979) (considering separately the markets for shock absorbers, wheels and brakes, in which the merging firms operated).

cross-price elasticity, in economic jargon) is a measure of the rate at which buyers substitute to some product B in response to a price increase in product A. For example, if wheat and corn are close substitutes for many uses when both are sold at a competitive price, a small increase in the price of wheat will encourage many wheat customers to buy corn instead.[1] In that case we would say that the cross-elasticity of demand between wheat and corn is quite high. For antitrust purposes the two may be in the same relevant market.

Judges are more comfortable estimating cross-elasticity of demand than attempting to quantify elasticity of demand directly. The reason is clear. The concept of "cross-elasticity" enables the fact-finder to compare two relatively tangible "products" against each other and determine whether one is a good substitute for the other. Even though I may know nothing about economics, my common sense tells me that Fords and Chryslers are often good substitutes for each other. By contrast, recipe books and mystery novels are not.

Used properly, cross-elasticity measures should help the fact-finder assemble into a single relevant market products that are close substitutes when each is sold at a competitive price. For example, if Ford Motor Company was accused of monopolizing the market for Ford automobiles, the fact-finder should consider whether Chevrolet automobiles, Chrysler automobiles or others ought to be included in the relevant product market. The fact-finder would probably decide that when Fords, Chevrolets and Chryslers are sold at cost many customers regard them as competitive with each other. If the price of Fords increased, these customers would switch to Chevrolets or Chryslers. As a result the relevant product market is "automobiles" and not "Fords."

What if the fact-finder were asked to include bicycles and horses in this same relevant market? The effect would be to reduce Ford's share of the "market" even further. In that case the fact-finder would have to make some estimate about the degree to which the demand for horses and bicycles would change in response to a price change in the automobile market. When automobiles and bicycles or horses are all being sold at the competitive price, the cross-elasticity of demand between them is probably not very high. Not many prospective automobile purchasers would regard a horse or bicycle as a good substitute unless the price of automobiles increased by a very large amount. The fact-finder would probably conclude that bicycles or horses should not be included in the relevant market.

3.4b. Cross-elasticity of Demand in the du Pont (Cellophane) Case

Judges have often misused the concept of cross-elasticity of demand because they have not understood its limitations. Markets can then be defined too broadly. In United States v. E.I. du Pont de Nemours & Co.[2] the defendant was alleged to have monopolized the market for cellophane. du Pont produced about 75% of the cellophane sold in the United States. du Pont argued that the relevant

§ 3.4

1. If the cross-price elasticity between wheat and corn is three, then customers will respond to a ten percent price increase in wheat by buying thirty percent more corn. If corn is the only substitute for wheat, if one unit of corn precisely replaces one unit of wheat, and the two are perfect substitutes, customers will buy thirty percent less wheat as well. But if some customers respond to the price increase by simply buying less wheat, without buying corn; or if there are two substitutes for wheat—say, corn and rice—then the customers will reduce their wheat purchases by more than thirty percent. This is simply saying that the own-price elasticity of demand for a product is generally as high or higher than the cross-price elasticity as between that product and some other product.

Economists commonly express cross price elasticity of demand as follows:

$P_{xy} = \delta Q_x / \delta P_y$

Where P_{xy} is the cross price elasticity as between product x and product y;

δQ_x = the change in the quantity demanded of x; and

δP_y = the change in the price of y.

If the goods are substitutes, this number will be positive—that is in response to a 10 percent increase in the price of wheat, customers will buy thirty percent more corn. If the goods are complements (such as computers and software), then it will be negative—for example, a 10% rise in computer prices (which yields a decrease in computer consumption), produces a 30% decrease in software consumption. We would say the cross-price elasticity is –3.

2. 351 U.S. 377, 76 S.Ct. 994 (1956).

market was not cellophane, but "flexible packaging materials," which included not only cellophane but also aluminum foil, glassine, pliofilm, greaseproof paper and waxed paper.

Some forms of flexible packaging materials, such as glassine, were cheaper than cellophane. Others, such as polyethylene, were much more expensive. Different wrapping materials had various degrees of acceptance among different buyers, and some buyers were far more cost-conscious than others. For example, virtually all grocery store meats and vegetables had to be wrapped in transparent materials in order to attract grocery consumers. Cellophane occupied about 35% of the market for retail meat wrapping and about half of the market for retail vegetable wrapping. By contrast, bread was commonly wrapped in opaque paper, and cellophane furnished only 7% of the bakery products market. When a product was expensive in proportion to the amount of wrapping material it needed, cellophane obtained an advantage over cheaper, less transparent packaging materials. For example, 75%–80% of all cigarettes were wrapped in cellophane.[3] However, the court refused to hold that "cellophane for cigarettes" constituted a relevant market, even though cigarette manufacturers would have been willing to pay a monopoly price before substituting to an alternative flexible wrap. That aspect of the decision is discussed in § 3.9b.

The Supreme Court concluded that the relevant market must include "products that have reasonable interchangeability for the purposes for which they are produced. That was the entire market for flexible packaging materials.[4]

The court's definition of the relevant market was probably wrong. A simple example will illustrate. Suppose that widgets are sold in a competitive market for $1.00, which is also their marginal cost of production. Suppose that A invents the gizmo, which performs the same functions as a widget but can be manufactured for 80¢. A is the only producer of gizmos. At what price will A sell them?

We would need to know more facts to be sure about A's price. For example, if there were no consumers who preferred gizmos to widgets, then A would be unable to charge more than $1.00 for gizmos. Customers would buy widgets instead. Whether A would sell gizmos at a much lower price—say 90¢—depends on the elasticity of demand. If there is a very large group of potential customers who will buy gizmos at 90¢ but not at $1.00, then A might be better off selling gizmos at 90¢ and attracting that group of marginal customers. If the elasticity of demand in the gizmo market is rather low, however, then A will worry only about competition from widgets and will set the price of gizmos slightly under the widget price. At a price of 99¢ A will sell all the gizmos A can produce to customers who would otherwise buy widgets.[5]

Now suppose A is charged with illegal monopolization. A defends by arguing that he has no market power because the relevant market is not gizmos (in which A's market share is 100%) but rather gizmos plus widgets (in which A's market share is lower). A supports this market definition by providing evidence that the current market price of gizmos is 99¢, while the market price of widgets is $1.00. At those prices there is a high cross-elasticity of demand between gizmos and widgets. In fact, if A attempts to raise his price by as little as 1% (1 cent), A will lose large numbers of customers to widgets. If A raises his price by 2%, he may lose all his customers.

Is A's defense good? Clearly not. To be sure, cross-elasticity of demand between gizmos and widgets at the *current price* is very high. It is not high because A lacks market power in gizmos, however, but because A has market power in widgets *and is already exercising that power.* Every seller, whether monopolist or competitor, sells its output in the high elasticity region of its demand curve. That is to say, every seller sets as high a price

3. Id. at 399–400, 76 S.Ct. at 1009–10.

4. Id. at 404, 76 S.Ct. at 1012. The decision is criticized in D. Turner, Antitrust Policy and the *Cellophane* Case, 70 Harv.L.Rev. 281 (1956).

5. This discussion assumes that A is not able to price discriminate. See ch. 14.

as it can without losing so many customers that the price increase is unprofitable. To say it another way, the monopolist that is not pricing at a level where the elasticity of demand is high is probably not maximizing its profits, and we would ordinarily regard such behavior as irrational. High cross-elasticity of demand at the current market price is simply evidence that the seller could not profitably charge an even higher price.[6]

The 1992 Horizontal Merger Guidelines also commit a version of the Cellophane fallacy by defining markets in terms of current prices. The result may be that some markets are defined too broadly for government merger analysis.[7]

3.4c. Correcting for the "Cellophane" Fallacy

The Cellophane analysis exposes a dilemma for antitrust market definition. If the concept of cross-elasticity of demand serves a useful function in antitrust analysis, it is to establish whether two products are close substitutes when both are sold at the *competitive* price. If two things appear to be close substitutes when both are sold at marginal cost, then the two should be included in the same product market. But how do we know if the current price is competitive? Normally we identify the competitive price in terms of marginal cost. But if we could measure marginal cost directly, then market definition might be unnecessary.

The impact of the *Cellophane* fallacy depends on the question one is asking. Suppose that a manufacturer of paper cartons wants to acquire a manufacturer of plastic cartons. A merger between two firms selling in the same relevant market is termed "horizontal" and is subject to a rather strict legal standard. A merger between two firms selling in different markets, however, is a "conglomerate" or "potential competition" merger, and is subject to a much more lenient standard.[8]

Suppose that the paper carton manufacturer is in competition with five other carton manufacturers, and that its own share of those sales is 20%. The plastic carton manufacturer is in competition with eight other plastic carton manufacturers, and its share of plastic carton sales is 10%. For nearly all uses plastic cartons and paper cartons compete intensely with each other. In the past customers of paper cartons have responded to a small price increase by switching in large numbers to plastic cartons, and vice-versa.

In this case the high cross-elasticity of demand at current market prices tells us quite reliably that paper and plastic cartons ought to be included in the same product market. The small market shares and relatively large numbers of firms *within* each fungible product category suggest that both kinds of cartons are currently being sold at a competitive price. The sensitivity of each to a price change in the other indicates that cross-elasticity of demand between the two is high even at this price. As a result, the presence of the plastic carton manufacturers tends to hold paper carton manufacturers to the competitive price, and vice-versa. The merger should be treated as horizontal.[9]

Much more difficult is the monopolization case such as *du Pont*. When the defendant is accused of being a monopolist, we must assume that its current price is *not* the competitive price, and we would ordinarily expect cross-elasticity of demand to be high at current prices. As a general rule, computing the defendant's marginal cost and determining

6. In spite of the substantial, convincing criticism of *du Pont's* analysis, some courts continue to apply it. See, e.g., Satellite Television & Associated Resources, Inc. v. Continental Cablevision of Virginia, Inc., 714 F.2d 351, 355 (4th Cir.1983), cert. denied, 465 U.S. 1027, 104 S.Ct. 1285 (1984), holding, without cost analysis, that a relevant market was not cable television, but "cinema, broadcast television, video disks and cassettes and other types of leisure and entertainment-related business * * *."; Cable Holdings of Ga. v. Home Video, 825 F.2d 1559, 1563 (11th Cir.1987) (same); United States v. Syufy Enters., 712 F.Supp. 1386 (N.D.Cal.1989), affirmed, 903 F.2d 659 (9th Cir.1990) (district court holding that first-run movies, subsequent-run movies, video rentals, and cable television movies were in the same market). Other cases are discussed in 2A Antitrust law ¶ 539 (rev. ed. 1995).

7. See § 3.8e.

8. See chs. 12 & 13.

9. See United States v. Aluminum Co. of America, 377 U.S. 271, 84 S.Ct. 1283 (1964); United States v. Continental Can Co., 378 U.S. 441, 84 S.Ct. 1738 (1964).

what the cross-elasticity of demand would be at the competitive price is impossible. Nevertheless, there might be some clues to look for.

First, if the monopolist's product and the products of other firms are so similar in design, technology and inputs that we can infer that their production costs are about the same, then the products should be grouped in the same relevant market. For example, suppose a firm is accused of monopolizing the market for three-hole buttons. At current prices the cross-elasticity of demand between three-hole buttons and four-hole buttons is very high. Furthermore, the firms making four-hole buttons use precisely the same materials and machinery as the three-hole button maker. If the grouping of firms making both kinds of buttons seems to be competitively structured, the relevant market should include both. Of course, if the grouping of firms is fixing prices or behaving oligopolistically, then collectively they still may be able to exercise market power, but that fact would not justify placing the three-hole button maker into a market by itself.[10]

Even when technologies are similar, however, a finding of a single product might not be warranted if (1) the fringe firms are licensees of the dominant firm; and (2) the license royalty is sufficiently high to permit the dominant firm to charge monopoly prices. For example, du Pont was not the only manufacturer of cellophane in the *du Pont* case. Sylvania also manufactured cellophane under a patent license from du Pont. Suppose the following facts, which are not true of the *du Pont* case: (a) du Pont manufactured 60% of the cellophane and Sylvania 40%; (b) the cost of manufacturing cellophane was $1.00 per unit; and (c) Sylvania paid *du Pont* a royalty of 15% of its revenues.[11] In this case Sylvania might be charging a price of $1.18 and paying du Pont a royalty of 17.7¢ (15% of $1.18), leaving it with competitive profits. *du Pont* could very likely maximize its profits at a price of $1.18 as well, reflecting 18% monopoly profits.

In deciding whether a grouping of truly *diverse* products, such as cellophane, foil and waxed paper, belong in the same relevant market one should always consider looking for cost shocks that affected the defendant but not other firms alleged to be in the same market.[12] Here the same technological differences that make the Cellophane fallacy problematic may actually help us out. Suppose that an ingredient called "plioclear" is used in cellophane, but not in either wax paper or aluminum foil. The defendant purchases plioclear from upstream suppliers. Several months ago the price of plioclear increased by 20%, and the defendant immediately raised cellophane's price by 18%. Assuming we can control for other factors in the market, the inference is strong that the defendant had market power, at least at the time the plioclear price increase took effect. A true competitor, who faces a horizontal demand curve, would be unable to respond to a firm specific cost increase by raising price. But a firm with a downward sloping demand curve would calculate a new price that equated its marginal cost and marginal revenues.

The fact finder might also look for evidence of monopoly profits. As noted later, however, the enterprise of inferring monopoly power from high accounting profits is fraught with difficulties.[13]

Finally, one might wish to look at past price movements as between the defendant and the firms alleged to be its competitors. Suppose cellophane prices have been declining over recent years and output has been increasing. By contrast, the price of wax paper has held steady. This evidence suggests that cellophane and wax paper are in different product markets, since cellophane appears to have a cost advantage. Likewise, if the price of wax paper has declined while the price of cello-

10. As the example suggests, use of similar technologies and inputs often justifies grouping two things into a single relevant market on the basis of supply considerations. See § 3.5.

11. In the actual case Sylvania's market share was 25% and the royalty rate was 2%. *du Pont*, 351 U.S. at 384–385, 76 S.Ct. at 1001–1002.

12. Use of cost shocks to estimate residual demand curves is discussed in § 3.9a. Using them effectively requires an expert economist.

13. See § 3.9c.

phane remained constant, cellophane's pricing is probably not constrained by the price of wax paper; the two should be placed in separate markets. What if the price of wax paper has been declining steadily while the price of cellophane has also declined? To conclude that cellophane and wax paper are in the same market could once again invoke the Cellophane fallacy. As the monopolist's nearest rivals innovate in ways that reduce their costs, the monopolist's profit-maximizing price may decline as well.[14]

§ 3.5 Supply Elasticities; Foreign Imports

Elasticity of supply has been an implicit part of judicial market definition for many years, although courts have begun to recognize it explicitly only recently.[1] A firm with a large share of a proposed market will have little power to increase prices if other firms can immediately flood this market with their own output. Courts often refer to this as supply "substitutability."

Existing firms already manufacturing a similar product in the same region, or manufacturing the same product some distance away, will often be able to respond to a dominant firm's price increase far more quickly than firms that do not yet exist when the price increase occurs. Often existing firms need merely to increase their output, frequently out of existing capacity. By contrast, new firms must still raise capital, build a plant and develop a distribution network. As a result, the best initial question to ask when measuring supply elasticity is whether the defendant's current competitors can increase their own output in response to the defendant's price increase; or alternatively, whether firms making products similar to the defendant's can easily switch to the defendant's product and ship them into the defendant's sales area if the profits are attractive.

One significant source of high supply elasticity is the divertible production or excess capacity of competing firms. Divertible production refers to the output of rivals or potential rivals that is currently not sold in the defendant's geographic market, but could come in if the price rose. Excess capacity generally refers to unused plant capacity that can be brought into production at a cost no higher than current production costs.

3.5a. Foreign Imports and the Alcoa Case

Historically, judges were rarely attentive to divertible production or excess capacity in measuring market power. For example, in *Alcoa*[2] Judge Learned Hand attempted to determine whether Alcoa had a monopoly in the production of aluminum. Alcoa's market share of virgin aluminum produced in the United States was 100%. Its market share dropped to 90% when Judge Hand included aluminum that was manufactured abroad but imported into the United States. Judge Hand refused to include either (1) foreign aluminum sold elsewhere or (2) the additional plant capacity of the foreign aluminum producers. Clearly, how-

14. Another complicating factor in identifying product markets on the basis of price movements is government intervention, which can sometimes place technologically identical products in separate markets. See United States v. Archer–Daniels–Midland Co., 866 F.2d 242 (8th Cir. 1988), cert. denied, 493 U.S. 809, 110 S.Ct. 51 (1989), which defined a market for "high fructose corn syrup" notwithstanding that numerous other corn sweeteners were close substitutes. However, government price supports effectively maintained the price of these substitutes at a level 10 to 30 percent above the cost of product of the high fructose product. In that case, a purchase of the latter could raise price slightly less than 10 to 30 percent above the competitive level without losing sales. On the general problem of market power measurement in regulated industries, see § 19.5.

§ 3.5

1. However, see United States v. Columbia Steel Co., 334 U.S. 495, 510, 68 S.Ct. 1107, 1116 (1948), a merger case in which one issue was whether steel plates and shapes should be included in the same product market as other rolled steel products. The Court concluded that if

> rolled steel producers can make other products as easily as plates and shapes, then the effect of the removal of Consolidated's demand for plates and shapes must be measured not against the market for plates and shapes alone, but for all comparable rolled products. The record suggests * * * that rolled steel producers can make other products interchangeably with shapes and plates * * *.

The Court therefore included both in the relevant market.

2. United States v. Aluminum Co. of America, 148 F.2d 416, 424 (2d Cir.1945).

ever, the fact that some aluminum was coming into the United States indicated that foreign aluminum could be sold profitably here. What would have happened if Alcoa had attempted to raise the price of aluminum? The foreign producers could have diverted some aluminum destined for other markets into the now more profitable American market. Alternatively, they could have produced more aluminum and shipped it into the United States.[3] Assuming that foreign aluminum shipped into the United States and Alcoa's aluminum were price competitive, Judge Hand was wrong to include only foreign aluminum actually imported into the United States in the relevant market.

Does this analysis ignore the error that the Supreme Court made in the *Cellophane* case?[4] Perhaps foreign aluminum was entering the United States market because Alcoa was already charging a monopoly price. However, the fact that *some* aluminum was coming into the United States suggests that Alcoa was unable to exclude the foreign production. Suppose, for example, that Alcoa's costs are $1.00 per unit. It is the only producer of domestic aluminum. Foreign competitors also have costs of $1.00 per unit, but they additionally have 30¢ in transportation costs. In that case Alcoa would be able to charge $1.29 for its aluminum in the United States and exclude all the foreign competition. By contrast, if it charged $1.31 for aluminum it would have no way of limiting the amount of foreign aluminum that came in. The fact that *some* foreign aluminum was coming in at Alcoa's current market prices suggests that Alcoa did not have sufficiently low costs to exclude these importers. The full output or perhaps even the capacity of the importers who were actually importing some aluminum into the United States should have been included in the relevant market.[5]

The "foreign" producer problem is pervasive. Most of the analysis applies not only to the imports of foreign firms, but also to imports from remote geographic areas domestically. For example, if a firm were accused of monopolizing the retail market for gasoline in Washington County, one should consider the actual imports, divertible output and excess capacity of firms in other counties that could ship into Washington County. The analysis would not be materially different than that in the *Alcoa* case.

In addition, the *Alcoa* analysis is subject to several complicating factors. *First*, the fact that some aluminum was coming into the market does not entail that either world production or world capacity should be included. Suppose that the only foreign aluminum actually sold in the United States came from all parts of Canada and Mexico, but no aluminum was coming in from Europe, even though many plants were located there. We would infer that the Mexican and Canadian plants have lower transportation or production costs, and can compete with Alcoa in the United States market, but that the European producers cannot. In that case the divertible output of the Mexican and Canadian plants, but not of the European plants, should be included in the relevant market.[6]

Second, this analysis applies when the foreign firms' supply curve (industry cost curve) is flat, but it does not necessarily apply when the foreign firms face increasing costs. In that case the profit-maximizing strategy for Alcoa might be to set a price that permitted some of

3. Judge Hand supposed as much:

> While the record is silent, we may therefore assume—the plaintiff having the burden—that, had "Alcoa" raised its prices, more ingot would have been imported. Thus there is a distinction between domestic and foreign competition: the first is limited in quantity, and can increase only by an increase in plant and personnel; the second is of producers who, we must assume, produce much more than they import and whom a rise in price will presumably induce immediately to divert to the American market what they had been selling elsewhere.

148 F.2d at 426.

4. See § 3.4b.

5. See 2A Antitrust Law ¶ 561 (rev. ed. 1995); W. Landes & R. Posner, Market Power in Antitrust Cases, 94 Harv.L.Rev. 937, 966–967 (1981). If there were an absolute quota, however—a legal maximum amount of aluminum that could be imported into the United States in any given year—then only the legal limit should be included in the relevant market.

6. The approach taken by the Supreme Court in Tampa Electric Co. v. Nashville Coal Co., 365 U.S. 320, 81 S.Ct. 623 (1961), which looked at those suppliers willing to ship at the prevailing price, is more accurate. *Tampa* may have overruled *Alcoa sub silentio* on this point. See § 3.6c.

the relatively low cost foreign aluminum to come into the market, but excluded all the aluminum produced at a higher cost.[7] If the foreign firms are operating in a competitive market and there are no bottlenecks in input markets,[8] we can assume that foreign supply costs are about constant. By contrast, if there were only a single foreign producer, it might face rising costs and Alcoa might decide to permit some, but not all, of its input to enter the market.

Third, basing market power/market share estimates on the divertible output or excess capacity of the foreign firms is accurate only when the product is fungible. Any product differentiation will tend to understate the domestic defendant's market power. Although this limitation can be expressed mathematically,[9] one can also understand it intuitively. Suppose that a domestic manufacturer is making 40,000 units per year and a group of importers are bringing in an additional 10,000; however, the total output of the foreign firms is 40,000 and their total capacity is 80,000. Under these numbers the market share of the domestic firm is 80% if we count only foreign imports, 50% if we count total foreign production, and 33.3% if we count total foreign capacity. If the product is perfectly fungible, we can assume that those firms already shipping the 10,000 units into the United States and easily able to shift additional production or increase their output would do so in response to any price increase above their costs. For example, suppose the domestic firm had costs of $10 per unit, while the foreign firms had constant costs (including the additional transportation costs) of $12 per unit. In that case the domestic firm could set price at $11.99 and keep out *all* foreign imports, but as soon as its price hit $12 the floodgates would be opened and it would have no way of limiting the amount of foreign imports. That suggests that if any amount of foreign aluminum is coming in *and* the product is fungible, the domestic firm is behaving competitively.

But suppose the product is differentiated. Now there may be American customers who prefer the foreign product over the American product. For example, suppose the domestic

7. Figure One illustrates.

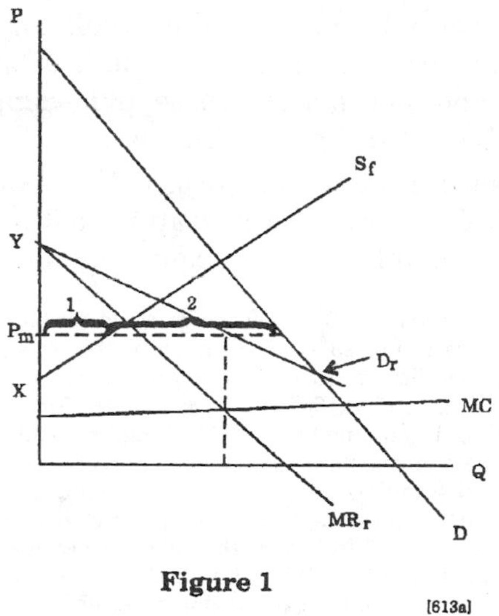

Figure 1

Suppose that Alcoa had marginal cost curve MC and the market demand curve was D. The foreign suppliers had a supply curve (the sum of their individual marginal cost curves) S_f. In that case we can draw a "residual" demand curve D_r, which represents the demand curve that Alcoa faces after the fringe has been able to sell all it can at its costs.

The concept of the residual demand curve is intuitively explained as follows. Point x in Figure One, where the foreign supply curve originates, is the lowest possible price at which any foreign firm can profitably make a sale in the United States. At any price below that level, Alcoa faces the entire market demand curve. At any price higher than x, the fringe will start making sales; so at point D_r, which is horizontally opposite x, the demand curve that Alcoa faces will begin to deviate from the market demand curve. If the price is only slightly above x, the deviation will be small, for only a few units of foreign aluminum will be sold. But the deviation will increase as the price goes up, since increasing amounts of foreign aluminum will come into the market. Finally, when Alcoa's price hits y, the foreign suppliers will be able to match Alcoa's price and saturate the entire demand for aluminum at that price. At any price higher than y, Alcoa will make no sales and the foreign firms will have 100% of the market.

Under these conditions, Alcoa would maximize its profits by equating marginal cost and its *residual* marginal revenue curve MR_r. This would yield price P_m. At that price, the foreign firm's output would be equal to {1 along the horizontal line measured from P_m, and Alcoa's output would be {2.

8. For example, even if aluminum production was competitive, a foreign monopolist of bauxite, an essential input into aluminum, might cause rising supply prices.

9. See L. Kaplow, The Accuracy of Traditional Market Power Analysis and a Direct Adjustment Alternative, 95 Harv. L. Rev. 1817, 1836–1837 (1982).

firm has costs of $10.00, while the foreign firms have total costs, including transportation, of $12.00. When the domestic firm charges a price of $11.90, a small group of customers prefer the foreign product at $12.00, and import it. The balance of the customers do not have this preference and they purchase the domestic firm's $11.90 aluminum. In this case the domestic firm is already charging a price nearly 20% above its cost. Including either total foreign output or foreign capacity (with the attendant conclusion that the domestic firm is not a monopolist) would be a serious mistake.[10]

Fourth, foreign output sold elsewhere should be included only if it is "divertible." Output that is subject to long term contracts, or required by law to be sold domestically should not be included.

Finally, the question whether a competing firm's output or capacity should be used to measure the defendant's market share is reserved for § 3.7, on market share measurement.

3.5b. Other Decisions Addressing (or Failing to Address) Supply Issues

When judges measure market power, they often ignore elasticity of supply[11] or else they have difficulty in stating the relevant concerns. For example, in Telex Corp. v. IBM Corp.,[12] the issue was whether IBM had monopolized the market for "plug-compatible peripherals." A peripheral is a unit such as a printer, monitor, or disk drive, that is attached to the central data processing part of a computer. Historically, peripherals were designed to work with a particular central processing unit (CPU). An IBM "plug-compatible" peripheral is one that is capable of easy attachment and use with an IBM CPU. Telex and other plaintiffs alleged that IBM monopolized the market for peripherals that were plug-compatible with its own CPUs. IBM's share of the market for IBM plug-compatible peripherals was quite large. But if *all* peripherals were included in the market, IBM's share was fairly small.

The district judge found that IBM plug-compatible peripherals were a relevant market because the elasticity of demand was low: customers who already owned IBM CPUs could not use peripherals unless they were compatible.[13] In reversing, the circuit court noted two things: first, a producer of IBM non-plug-compatible peripherals could easily and cheaply switch to producing plug-compatible peripherals; secondly, by the use of an "interface," which cost as little as $100, a non-compatible peripheral could often be made compatible with the IBM. This degree of "substitutability of production" convinced the circuit court that the relevant market should include all peripherals, and not merely those plug-compatible with IBM central processing units.[14]

Likewise, Calnetics Corp. v. Volkswagen of America[15] involved an allegation that an automobile manufacturer's acquisition of a firm

10. An important difference between aluminum and the "flexible packaging material" presumed to be the relevant product in the *Cellophane* case is that aluminum is fungible while the packaging material is not. Different types of materials, such as cellophane and grease paper, appealed to different users. As a result du Pont could price its product in such a way as to include one set of buyers (such as retail butchers, who were willing to pay a premium for a transparent wrap) but exclude another set (bakers, who were very price conscious and did not value transparency as highly). The producer of a fungible product does not have that choice.

11. For example, see Fineman v. Armstrong World Industries, 980 F.2d 171 (3d Cir.1992), cert. denied, 507 U.S. 921, 113 S.Ct. 1285 (1993), concluding that video tape "magazines" of floor coverings were a relevant market because linoleum sellers wishing to purchase such videos would not find other kinds of videos a substitute; but totally ignoring the fact that someone with the equipment needed to videotape floor coverings could probably videotape refrigerators, sofas or farm animals, or vice-versa, with little additional investment. See also Kaiser Alum. & Chem. Corp. v. FTC, 652 F.2d 1324, 1330 (7th Cir.1981), which placed two kinds of brick-making material in different markets on the basis of lack of customer substitutability, notwithstanding almost perfect interchangeability in production on the supply side. The court conceded that "economic theory" indicated the relevance of supply elasticities but found that that court had adhered to the view that such considerations were "not meaningful."

12. 510 F.2d 894 (10th Cir.), cert. dismissed, 423 U.S. 802, 96 S.Ct. 8 (1975).

13. 367 F.Supp. at 280–82.

14. 510 F.2d at 919.

15. 348 F.Supp. 606 (C.D.Cal.1972), reversed on this issue, 532 F.2d 674 (9th Cir.1976), cert. denied, 429 U.S. 940, 97 S.Ct. 355 (1976).

that produced automobile air conditioners was an illegal vertical merger under § 7 of the Clayton Act. If the relevant product market was "Volkswagen air conditioners," then the percentage of the relevant market "foreclosed" by the vertical merger was large enough to be illegal under the standard established for vertical acquisitions.[16] By contrast, if the relevant market was air conditioners for all compact automobiles, then the percentage of the market foreclosed by the merger was not very high. The district judge held that the relevant market was Volkswagen air conditioners and condemned the merger.[17] The circuit court reversed, holding that the lower court had refused to consider "production cross elasticity * * *."[18] Although a Volkswagen air conditioner, once built, would fit only Volkswagens, a plant capable of manufacturing automobile air conditioners could easily shift its production to air conditioners for any model automobile. And *Rebel Oil* concluded that there was no relevant market for self-service gasoline; if the price of self-service gas rose to monopoly levels, providers of full-service gas could almost instantaneously switch to self-service.[19]

A recurring problem in addressing supply concerns is the relevant weight that should be given to technological as opposed to behavioral considerations. For example, suppose the evidence in the *Telex*[20] case, discussed above, revealed (1) that non-IBM plug compatible peripherals could be redesigned so as to be plug compatible for a cost as little as 1% of their value; but (2) customers greatly preferred to purchase CPUs and peripherals from the same seller. For example, if something went wrong with the computer, the customer did not want to get involved in a finger-pointing game where the CPU seller blamed the disk drive seller and the disk drive seller blamed the problem on the CPU. Clearly, *relevant* elasticity of supply is the rate at which potential competitors will actually steal sales from the price-increasing monopolist, and this question is not fully addressed by considering only the costs of developing the necessary technology or building the plant.

Where the technological cost of redesigning is indeed very low, the best rule seems to be a presumptive conclusion that the firm capable of doing the redesigning should be included in the market; but this evidence could then be rebutted by evidence that consumer resistance to the redesigned product would be substantial. As the *Telex* and *Calnetics* decisions suggest, this will depend largely on the nature and sophistication of the customers. The circuit court in *Telex* may have been wrong to assume that low technological cost of redesigning established that customers for IBM CPUs would readily switch to non-IBM peripherals. In this case, the customer is likely to be highly dependent on the technological sophistication of the seller. By contrast, Volkswagen and its dealers are sophisticated buyers of automobile

16. See § 9.4.

17. 348 F.Supp. at 618. On single brand market definitions, see § 3.3a.

18. 532 F.2d at 691. In Heatransfer Corp. v. Volkswagenwerk, A.G., 553 F.2d 964 (5th Cir.1977), cert. denied, 434 U.S. 1087, 98 S.Ct. 1282 (1978), the Fifth Circuit decided that Volkswagen air conditioners was a relevant market. See also Twin City Sportservice, Inc. v. Charles O. Finley & Co., 512 F.2d 1264 (9th Cir.1975), appeal after remand, 676 F.2d 1291 (9th Cir.1982), cert. denied, 459 U.S. 1009, 103 S.Ct. 364 (1982), in which the court refused to hold that the defendant possessed market power in the provision of concession services at major league baseball stadiums. "Many aspects of the concession services provided at major league baseball games were identical to the services provided at other public events. The same concessionaires often covered a variety of events and used the same equipment and employees for all of them." The court concluded that the relevant market was concession services for all leisure time activities. A hot dog is a hot dog, even at the opera. See also FTC v. Owens–Illinois, 681 F.Supp. 27 (D.D.C.), vacated as moot, 850 F.2d 694 (D.C.Cir.1988) (glass and plastic containers comprise single market because many assembly lines used to make former could readily make latter); FTC v. Illinois Cereal Mills, 691 F.Supp. 1131 (N.D.Ill.1988), affirmed sub nom. FTC v. Elders Grain, 868 F.2d 901 (7th Cir.1989) (market includes all food products made by a group of dry corn millers; although each miller did not currently make identical products, their mills could easily be reconfigured to produce one another's products).

19. Rebel Oil Co. v. Atlantic Richfield Co., 51 F.3d 1421 (9th Cir.), cert. denied, 516 U.S. 987, 116 S.Ct. 515 (1995). See also Israel Travel Advisory Serv. v. Israel Identity Tours, 61 F.3d 1250, 1255 (7th Cir.1995), cert. denied, 517 U.S. 1220, 116 S.Ct. 1847 (1996) ("Bar mitzvah tours of Israel by families who live in N.J. or near Chicago or Boston" characterized as an "absurd" market definition; any travel agent could assemble the tours from existing air carriers, hotels, and the like).

20. Note 12.

air conditioners and are probably in a position to take competitive bids from suppliers. In that case, the fact that a manufacturer currently making air conditioners for Toyota can readily and cheaply redesign for the Volkswagen market bears considerable weight.

3.5c. Accounting for Elasticity of Supply: Market Inclusion or Low Barriers to Entry?

Antitrust market analysis accounts for high supply elasticity in two different ways. *First*, it can include in the market definition those firms easily able to switch to the defendant's market in response to the principal firm's price increase. *Second*, it can define the market more narrowly, but conclude that entry barriers are low. If supply elasticities are high under either measure, the defendant lacks substantial market power, so in this sense the two alternatives can be regarded as interchangeable. Nevertheless, there are differences in the relevant evidence and perhaps the degree of confidence we can have in our judgment.

If the entire output increase by competitors will come from firms that are unidentified or do not even exist at the time of analysis, then including them in the relevant market is impossible. For example, suppose a local retailer of wood stoves is accused of monopolization. No one else currently sells wood stoves but it seems clear that (1) entry into wood stove retailing requires no specialized investment and is quite easy; and (2) numerous furniture stores, hardware stores, discount department stores as well as other retailers could add wood stoves to their product lines at little cost. In this case it would hardly make sense to include the potential competition in the relevant market. The "output" of the nonexistent firms cannot be included in the denominator of the market share equation at all, and it might be impossible to predict which of the existing businesses would start selling wood stoves, how many they would sell, etc. The appropriate method of analysis is to conclude that entry barriers are very low, whatever the defendant's market share happens to be.

By contrast, suppose that manufacturing of cars and pickup trucks requires a great deal of sophisticated and specialized machinery, but that the two products generally use the same machinery and the cost of switching over from cars to pickups is relatively small. In this case, barriers to entry from outside could in fact be very high. Now the appropriate alternative is to include the divertible production of one in the relevant market of the other. For example, if we were examining a merger by automobile companies we would include in the denominator of the fraction (a) all automobile production plus (b) all pickup production or capacity[21] that could easily be diverted into automobile production in response to a monopoly price increase.

In close cases, evidence that existing suppliers can switch production is usually more convincing than evidence that entry barriers are low. Firms with existing productive assets that do not need substantial modification are generally more likely "entrants" than firms that do not even exist or firms who can move into the principal firm's market only by substantial modification of production facilities. In the former case, we have real actors that we can look at, and perhaps make historical judgments about whether they have been quick to enter in the past. In the latter case the new entrants may be hypothetical, and we can only make judgments about what a profit-maximizing actor would do under the circumstances.

§ 3.6 The Geographic Market

Someone who has market power does not generally have it everywhere. A relevant market for antitrust purposes includes both a product market and a geographic market.[1]

21. On use of capacity measures, see § 3.7b.

§ 3.6

1. Determination of a relevant product market and of a relevant geographic market both address the same question: is there a grouping of sales in which the defendant has market power? As a result the distinction made between the two markets in antitrust case law is exaggerated. Economists often note that "From the standpoint of economic analysis the distinction between product and geographic markets is not particularly useful." J. Ordover & R. Willig, The 1982 Department of Justice Merger

Firms that produce different products are considered not to compete with each other. Neither do firms that sell the same product in mutually exclusive geographic areas. The size of the geographic market depends on the nature of the product and of the people who buy and sell it. The relevant geographic market for Alcoa's aluminum, for example, was the entire United States. By contrast, the owner of the only movie theater in Ozona, Texas, may have substantial market power in Ozona, but virtually none 50 miles away.

Elasticity of demand and supply are important to determining the proper geographic market, and the discussion in the preceding sections applies as much to geographic markets as to product markets. For example, assume that widgets are manufactured in Chicago and St. Louis. The owner of Chicago's only widget factory may have no market power if all its customers can costlessly shift their purchases to the St. Louis manufacturers. Likewise, the Chicago widget manufacturer will have no market power in Chicago if the St. Louis manufacturers can flood the Chicago outlets at a price close to the Chicago manufacturer's costs.

The relevant geographic market for antitrust purposes is some geographic area in which a firm can increase its price without 1) large numbers of its customers quickly turning to alternative supply sources outside the area; or 2) producers outside the area quickly flooding the area with substitute products.[2] In the first case elasticity of demand is high; in the second elasticity of supply is high. If either of these things happens when the firm attempts to charge a supracompetitive price, then the estimated geographic market has been drawn too narrowly and a larger market must be drawn to include these outside suppliers.[3]

A final introductory warning is that the "*Cellophane*" fallacy, discussed in § 3.4 applies as much to geographic market definition as it does to product market definition. For example, suppose that the only movie theater in a small town charges $7.00 per seat, and many local residents travel to the movies in towns ten or fifteen miles away. Including the theaters in these other towns in the geographic market may overstate the market's size if these customers are traveling in order to avoid the monopoly prices that the local theater is already charging. Likewise, if the only plumber in town is currently charging monopoly prices, it may be profitable for plumbing companies from more remote towns to perform services in that town as well. However, if the local town had competitive plumbing prices the more remote companies would find it unprofitable to send their plumbers such long distances. In that case, drawing a larger market to include the remote companies, on the basis of observed competition at current prices, would serve to understate the market power of the local firm.

3.6a. Shipped Goods; Minimum Geographic Market

For many manufactured products the size of the geographic market boils down to transportation costs. For example, the facts that automobile plants are scattered about the country and most of these plants ship automobiles nationwide suggest at least a national market. In general, the size of the geographic market for shipped products is a function of three things: (a) shipping costs, (b) the value

Guidelines: An Economic Assessment, 71 Calif.L.Rev. 535, 543 (1983).

2. If it is obvious that the plaintiff's alleged geographic market is too small, the court may dismiss the complaint on a Rule 12(b)(6) motion. This might seem peculiar, for a motion on the pleadings is supposed to look only at the pleadings and not at empirical data; but what if plain common sense tells the judge that there is no way the plaintiff has properly alleged a geographic market. See, e.g., Double D Spotting Service v. Supervalu, 136 F.3d 554 (8th Cir.1998) (approving 12(b)(6) dismissal of complaint alleging that the right to load trucks at one warehouse in a Des Moines suburb was a relevant market); Elliott v. United Center, 126 F.3d 1003 (7th Cir.1997), cert. denied, ___ U.S. ___, 118 S.Ct. 1302 (1998) (approving 12(b)(6) dismissal because "food sales within United Center," a sports complex in the middle of Chicago, could not be a relevant market).

3. See 2A Antitrust Law, Ch. 5C–2 (rev. ed. 1995); W. Landes & R. Posner, Market Power in Antitrust Cases, 94 Harv.L.Rev. 937, 963–972 (1981); and see Baxley–DeLamar v. American Cemetery Assn., 938 F.2d 846, 850 (8th Cir.1991) (geographic market consists of "the geographic area in which the defendant faces competition and to which consumers can practically turn for alternative sources of the product.").

of the product, and (c) the size of the hypothesized price increase that expresses our degree of concern about monopoly power. Suppose the production cost of a product is $50, shipping costs are $1 per one hundred miles, and we hypothesize a 10% price increase above the competitive level for purposes of market delineation. These numbers suggest that the *minimum* geographic market is a circle with a radius of 500 miles. That is, any firm within 500 miles, or $5 in transportation costs, would be able to respond to a 10% price increase by shipping its own product to the same customer at a profitable price.

As a result, the *minimum* geographic market for a delivered product or a product shipped under uniform transportation costs can always be given by the formula

$M_r = IC/T$

where

M_r = the radius of the minimum geographic market, expressed in miles, drawn as a circle with its center at the plant producing the product under consideration.

I = the percentage price increase supposed by the policy maker to warrant antitrust concern.

C = the cost of producing the product; or its price in a competitive market, expressed in dollars.

T = transport costs by the cheapest practicable method, expressed as dollars per mile, where such transportation costs are constant and are the same for all firms.

Note that the formula gives the size of the minimum geographic market. Basically, it determines the range over which a competitor can get the product to the primary firm's doorstep in response to the primary firm's price increase of a given magnitude. Depending on where the customer is located, firms much further away may be able to do the same thing.[4] The principal advantage of the formula is that by using it one can quickly compute a minimum geographic market without reference to the location of customers. If that market is sufficiently large to eliminate antitrust concerns, or if it is substantially nationwide and foreign trade is not at issue, then the formula may be sufficient to settle the antitrust issue. If the formula does not indicate a large enough market to warrant dismissal of the complaint, then there may be no substitute for plotting the location of actual customers and alternate sellers, and trying to determine how many sales would be lost.

The formula also assumes constant transportation costs. When transportation costs are not constant, long hauls are typically cheaper than short hauls. This tends to increase the size of the geographic market even more. In a few cases the firm under consideration may have lower transport costs than rivals, but these would be exceptional. For many manufactured commodities transportation costs per mile average about one ten-thousandth of the manufactured cost of the product, or less.[5] Assuming a 10% price increase, this suggests a radius of at least 1000 miles, and that many markets for common manufactured and nonperishable commodities are probably nationwide.

Finally, as in the case of foreign imports,[6] product differentiation upsets the calculus. Here, however, the effects are less predictable and generally not as pronounced unless the product differentiation is very substantial. There may be some customers in the primary firm's sales area who prefer that firm's product and will pay a certain overcharge before substituting a rival's product; this tends to make the geographic market smaller. By con-

4. For example, if the customer lies *between* the primary firm and the competitor, then the range would be tripled. Using the above numbers as an example, suppose the product costs $50, transportation costs are $1 per 100 miles, and the firm imposes a 10% price increase; but the customer is located on a line drawn from the primary firm to the competitor. If the customer were 500 miles from the primary firm the delivered price would be $60 ($50 cost, plus $5 markup plus $5 transportation costs). But a competitor an additional 1000 miles away could match that by bidding the competitive price, $50, plus $10 in transportation costs. See 2A Antitrust Law ¶ 552 (rev. ed. 1995).

5. See F. M. Scherer, A. Beckenstein, E. Kaufer & R. D. Murphy, The Economics of Multi–Plant Operations: an International Comparisons Study 429–433 (1975).

6. See § 3.5a.

trast, there may be customers who, although they are in the primary firm's area, actually prefer the output of a rival and will substitute more readily in response to the primary firm's price increase; these would tend to make the geographic market larger.

3.6b. Stationary Goods and Services

Geographic markets may be smaller and also more difficult to measure if the customers, rather than the goods or the suppliers, do the traveling. This is particularly true if the customers are end use consumers rather than business firms.[7] As a result some goods are quite mobile in the wholesale market but stationary in the retail market. For example, although grocery items are wholesaled in large, often national or even international markets, they are retailed over a much smaller geographic range. The average grocery store customer may not want to drive more than 12 or 15 miles to buy groceries.[8] On the supply side, however, competition might cover a wider region than customer willingness to travel suggests, particularly if the competitors are chains that operate in several states. For example, if grocery chains A & B both operate in California and chain A has a store in Sacramento which is earning monopoly profits, chain B will likely regard the Sacramento market as attractive for entry. Ordinarily, we would not take this fact into account by placing the entire area where the two chains operate in the same geographic market. Rather, we would say that entry barriers in Sacramento are low, given the likelihood that chain B will enter.

The Supreme Court must have had such considerations in mind when it decided that the merger in United States v. Von's Grocery Co.,[9] was a merger between competitors, and therefore should be treated as horizontal. The merger united two grocery store chains, Von's, Inc. and Shopping Bag, Inc., that operated in the Los Angeles area. The Von's stores were located in the southwest part of the city, however, and the Shopping Bag stores were located in the northeast part.[10] Except for a few pairs of stores in the middle of the city, the Von's stores did not compete on the demand side with the Shopping Bag stores. Few consumers would drive half way across Los Angeles to buy groceries. By contrast, analysis of supply elasticities might indicate that the market was indeed citywide. Von's could probably supply any location in the city from its existing warehouses. As a result, if there were supracompetitive profits to be earned in the northeast part of the city, Von's could easily have responded by building its own stores there.[11]

The geographic market definition in United States v. Grinnell Corp.,[12] was more problematic. The Supreme Court decided that the defendant had monopolized the business of providing accredited central station protective services, and that the relevant market was the entire United States. An accredited central

7. One reason for the difference is that business firms have cost functions—they will presumably do things the cheapest way, and costs can be measured objectively. By contrast, customers have *utility* functions that are much harder to measure. So, for example, the distance that a grocery shopper will travel to the store, or a theater patron to a musical, cannot easily be rationalized on the basis of transportation costs. See Houser v. Fox Theatres Mgmt. Corp., 845 F.2d 1225, 1230 & n. 10 (3d Cir.1988) (relevant market is a single municipality because most (but not all) theater goers were local and limited their patronage to theaters there.). Of course, for some kinds of services, such as necessary medical services, customers may be willing to travel a considerable distance. Thus Morgan, Strand, Wheeler & Biggs v. Radiology, Ltd., 924 F.2d 1484, 1490 (9th Cir.1991), refused to limit the market for radiology services to a single city; Accord: FTC v. Tenet Health Care Corp., ___ F.3d ___, 1999 WL 512108 (8th Cir.1999); and United States v. Mercy Health Services, 902 F.sup. 968 (N.D.Iowa 1995), vacated as moot, 107 F.3d 632 (8th Cir.1997), concluded that the relevant geographic market was of at least 70 mile radius because some firms in the defendant hospital's town (Dubuque, Iowa) travelled to a hospital 70 miles away (in Cedar Rapids, Iowa) for cosmetic surgery. But query: do people having heart attacks, women going into labor, or highway accident victims also travel 70 miles when there is another hospital in their own town? Cf. Brader v. Allegheny General Hospital, 64 F.3d 869 (3d Cir.1995) (defining local geographic market for vascular and traumatic care services); see 2A Antitrust law ¶ 550 (rev. ed. 1995).

8. See United States v. Von's Grocery Co., 384 U.S. 270, 296, 86 S.Ct. 1478, 1492 (1966).

9. Id.

10. Id. at 295, 86 S.Ct. at 1492 (J. Stewart, dissenting).

11. In merger cases courts have generally regarded high elasticity of supply as evidence of "potential" rather than actual competition. See ch. 13.

12. 384 U.S. 563, 86 S.Ct. 1698 (1966). Product market definition in this case is discussed in § 3.3b.

station protective service involved an electronic hook-up between a building to be protected and a central station that monitored the building for break-ins, fires, or other threatening events. "Accredited" services were approved by insurers and qualified the subscriber for lower premiums. The nature of the central station system meant that people who owned buildings in Chicago had to purchase their services from the Chicago station, people in St. Louis from the St. Louis station, etc. On the demand side the market was quite clearly local, since the service itself could be transmitted only a relatively small distance. Of course, the defendant could build additional central stations in new areas.

In explaining why it accepted a nationwide market, rather than a set of individual markets, the Supreme Court observed that the defendant had a "national schedule of prices, rates, and terms, though the rates may be varied to meet local conditions."[13] This is merely another way of saying that the defendant charged its profit-maximizing price in each city. Where it faced competition that price was generally lower than it was in cities where it had a monopoly. But these facts tend to establish that the local areas rather than the entire nation were the correct geographic markets.

On the supply side, however, ADT may have been able to exercise market power on a nationwide basis. For example, it might have used below-cost pricing in one city to "signal" its willingness to engage in predatory pricing to competitors located in many cities.[14] However, the court did not cite any evidence that the defendant was actually engaged in such practices, or even that it was capable of doing so. Even if it were, that would not justify the creation of a larger geographic market. There was also some evidence that ADT faced intense competition from local companies,[15] and this suggests a local rather than national market. For example, Pizza Hut operates pizza restaurants nationwide, but in many towns it faces competition from single store pizza operations. It this competition is effective in keeping Pizza Hut's prices at the competitive level, then its relevant market must be considered as local even if prices are set by a central office.

The Court ordered Grinnell to divest its stations in some cities.[16] This order is consistent with the decision that the market was nationwide and not citywide. But if the Court's market definition was incorrect and the defendant really had a large number of citywide monopolies, then the only effect of the divestiture was to give the defendant a smaller number of monopolies than it had before, and to transfer the other monopolies to one or more additional firms. Consumers may have been no better off.

But perhaps the Court thought that if there were two or more nationwide companies competing for the business of providing central station protective services, then any attempt by one to charge monopoly prices in a certain city would invite entry by the competitor. On that basis, the court's decision that the market was nationwide may have been correct. By increasing the number of firms supplying central station services, the court increased the elasticity of supply in the market. The effect would be to reduce the defendant's market power even if the market were completely local on the demand side.

As a general proposition, the relevant geographic market for "hard wired" services of the public utility type is the actual service area of the utility.[17] This may not be the case of ordinary competitive firms, as § 3.6d shows.

13. 384 U.S. at 575, 86 S.Ct. at 1706. The district court had found that customers of a particular station were located within 25 miles of the station. It nevertheless concluded that the relevant market was national because "financing, selling, advertising, purchasing of equipment, process of management, and over-all planning" were conducted by central company headquarters on a national scale. 236 F.Supp. at 253.

14. See S. Salop, Strategic Entry Deterrence, 69 Amer. Econ.Rev. 335 (1979).

15. See 384 U.S. at 575, 86 S.Ct. at 1706 (Fortas, J., dissenting).

16. 384 U.S. at 577–79, 86 S.Ct. at 1707–08.

17. See, for example, Anaheim v. Southern Cal. Edison Co., 1990–2 Trade Cas. (CCH) ¶ 69,246 at 64,899, 1990 WL 209261 (C.D.Cal.1990) (geographic market is electric utility's service area); Town of Concord v. Boston Edison Co., 721 F.Supp. 1456, 1459–1460 (D.Mass.1989), reversed on other grounds, 915 F.2d 17 (1st Cir.1990), cert. denied, 499 U.S. 931, 111 S.Ct. 1337 (1991) (same); TV Signal Co.

3.6c. Price Movements and Shipping Patterns

3.6c1. Price movements generally; asymmetry.

A study of price movements in two different areas will often help a court determine whether they should be included in the same geographic market. For example, if over a certain period a price decrease in area A is always followed by a price decrease in area B, and vice-versa, A and B are likely to be in the same geographic market. Likewise, if producers in A make sales in both areas A and B, the two are likely a single geographic market.[18] Thus in Tampa Electric Co. v. Nashville Coal Co.,[19] the Supreme Court decided that the petitioner did not have monopsony power in the market for coal sold in Florida, because coal producers as far away as western Kentucky were eager to sell coal at the competitive price in the Florida market. This suggested to the court that not only the Kentucky producers of coal, but all coal producers closer to Florida than the Kentucky producers should be included in the relevant geographic market.

Once we have determined that a remote plant in Kentucky can provide coal to the Florida market at the competitive price, we should include the entire divertible output of the Kentucky plant, and not merely the amount that it is currently shipping into the Florida market. If the Kentucky plant can profitably sell *any* of its coal into the Florida market, then it will probably be able to respond to a price increase in the Florida market by selling even more coal there.[20]

Determining a relevant geographic market means identifying some area such that the firm or firms inside the area have a cost advantage over firms not inside the area. In that case the favored firms will be able to raise the price as much as the cost advantage permits. Frequently the local firms' cost advantage results from transportation costs. For example, if Dallas and Denver firms can both make widgets at a cost of $1.00, but it costs 25¢ to ship widgets from Dallas to Denver, then a Denver monopolist could charge any price up to $1.25 in the Denver market without worrying about competition from Dallas. The size of the geographic market depends heavily on the relationship between the value of the product and the costs of shipping. Certain products such as cement and gravel have very high transportation costs in proportion to their value. A Denver producer of cement would probably not worry about competition from Dallas producers. By contrast, the transportation costs of mink coats may be trivial in comparison to their value, and a Dallas manufacturer could respond quickly to a price increase in the Denver market.

A good illustration of use of shipping information is the Seventh Circuit's *A.A. Poultry* decision.[21] The court held that the state of Indiana could not be a relevant market for eggs. The defendant itself shipped eggs more than 500 miles to Buffalo, N.Y., and there was ample evidence that egg processors turned to suppliers over a 500 mile radius.

Suppose that there were no actual 500 mile shipments to observe. Would a 500 mile market still be a possibility? Yes, if the markets were competitive on both the selling and buying side and there was a local equilibrium, then any shipping costs proportional to distance would tend to confine transactions over a small range. Shipments would extend over a larger range only if an area produced more than was locally consumed. In that case one should look at the formula for minimum geographic markets outlined in § 3.6a to determine whether a larger geographic market is warranted.[22]

v. AT & T, 1981–1 Trade Cas. (CCH) ¶ 63,944 at 75,862, 1981 WL 2049 (D.S.D. 1981) (relevant market for cable television services is town served by the CATV company).

18. See 2A Antitrust Law ¶ ¶ 550–552 (rev. ed. 1995).

19. 365 U.S. 320, 81 S.Ct. 623 (1961), on remand, 214 F.Supp. 647 (M.D.Tenn.1963).

20. See § 3.5a.

21. A. A. Poultry Farms v. Rose Acre Farms, 881 F.2d 1396 (7th Cir.1989), cert. denied, 494 U.S. 1019, 110 S.Ct. 1326 (1990).

22. See Baxley–DeLamar v. American Cemetery Assn., 938 F.2d 846, 851 (8th Cir.1991) ("[T]he fact that a party does all its business in a certain geographic area does not necessarily mean that that area constitutes the relevant geographic market.").

Geographic markets are often asymmetrical. Suppose that A Co. and B Co., which make chocolate cream pies in Manhattan, plan to merge. Each company sells 15% of the pies sold in Manhattan. There are 15 producers of pies in Manhattan, and there is no evidence that they are colluding. However, there are a large number of pie makers in nearby Brooklyn, who have lower labor costs and can produce equally good pies at a lower price. Currently many of the pies retailed in Manhattan are baked and shipped from the Brooklyn companies.

In this case the Manhattan pie makers operate at a cost disadvantage with respect to the Brooklyn companies. Any attempt by the Manhattan pie makers to charge a supracompetitive price will flood the market with Brooklyn pies. Therefore the divertible output of the Brooklyn pie makers must be included in the relevant market. The market shares of A Co. and B Co. may be substantially lower as a result.

It would not follow, however, that Manhattan must be included in the relevant market if two Brooklyn companies planned to merge. In fact, on the above facts it is clear that the Manhattan pie makers will not be able to compete effectively with the Brooklyn pie makers in Brooklyn unless the Brooklyn price rises substantially above the competitive level. In a merger case involving two Brooklyn pie makers, Manhattan should not be included in the relevant geographic market.

3.6c2. The Elzinga–Hogarty Test

In 1973[23] Elzinga and Hogarty proposed that an area could not be a well defined market if (1) more than 25% of the product produced in the area was sold outside,[24] or (2) if buyers inside purchased more than 25% from outside.[25] In a later article the authors revised their proposal and suggested that an area was a relevant geographic market if the average of production inside the area shipped outside, and of production outside the area consumed inside, was less than 10%.[26] Today some courts speak of the 25% rule as defining a "weak" market, and the 10% rule as defining a "strong" market.[27] Numerous decisions have cited this test for geographic markets.[28] But many have also been critical. As the cited cases indicated, the Elzinga–Hogarty test has had its biggest impact in health care markets, particular in challenges to hospital mergers.

One complaint about the Elzinga–Hogarty formulation is that it provides an instantaneous snapshot of what buyers and sellers are doing in the current situation; but it does not address the question that is more relevant in antitrust: what *would* buyers and sellers do in response to a future price increase.[29] While true, this criticism may go too far. *All* of our data about markets is historical, in the sense that it measures what was happening at the time the measurement was taken. A rule that firmly required "evidence" of what people would do in response to a price increase that has not been experienced would make relevant markets virtually impossible to prove.

The possibility of price discrimination or differential buyer preference must also be considered, or else the Elzinga–Hogarty test may define markets too broadly. To illustrate, suppose that patient data show that 20% of the people in a town go elsewhere for surgery, and this number is sufficient to suggest that the

23. K. Elzinga & T. Hogarty, The Problem of Geographic Market Delineation in Antimerger Suits, 18 Antitrust Bull. 45 (1973).

24. This is sometimes called "little out from inside," or LOFI.

25. This is sometimes called "little in from outside," or LIFO.

26. K. Elzinga & T. Hogarty, The Problem of Geographic Market Delineation Revisited: the Case of Coal, 23 Antitrust Bull. 1 (1978).

27. See FTC v. Freeman Hospital, 911 F.Supp. 1213 (W.D.Mo.1995), aff'd 69 F.3d 260 (8th Cir.1995); FTC v. Butterworth Health Corp., 946 F.Supp. 1285 (W.D.Mi. 1996), aff'd, 121 F.3d 708 (6th Cir.1997).

28. United States v. Rockford Memorial Corp., 717 F.Supp. 1251, 1266–75 (N.D.Ill.1989), aff'd, 898 F.2d 1278 (7th Cir.), cert. denied, 498 U.S. 920, 111 S.Ct. 295 (1990); United States v. Country Lake Foods, 754 F.Supp. 669 (D.Minn.1990); Hospital Corp. of Am., 106 F.T.C. 207, 396–402 (1985). On use of the tests in cases involving hospitals and other health care facilities, see G. Werden, The Limited Relevance of Patient Migration Data in Market Delineation for Hospital Merger Cases, 8 J. Health Econ. 363 (1989).

29. See *Freeman Hospital*, note 27, 69 F.3d at 269.

local municipality is not a geographic market. However, further inquiry reveals that all of these 20% are patients who need cosmetic or other elective surgery that can be scheduled in advance. In this case a local hospital might very well have the power to charge monopoly prices for people who are not getting elective surgery, because they are not in as good a position to travel or shop for alternatives.[30]

3.6d. Trade Area; Non-competition Covenants

A relevant geographic market, it should be recalled, is an area within which customers are constrained. They cannot reasonably turn elsewhere in response to a non-cost-justified price increase. This definition indicates that a seller's "trade area," or the area from which it currently draws its customers, is not the same thing as a relevant antitrust market. In fact, the "trade area" and the "relevant market" are precisely reverse concepts.

Consider the following illustration. Fifteen miles outside of City A is a small town, Town B, which contains a single shoe store, Smith's Clothing. The only people who ever shop in Smith's Clothing are residents of Town B. When Smith's is accused of monopolization, the plaintiffs argue that Town B defines the relevant geographic market, since all of the store's customers come from there. In that case, Smith's market share is 100%.

But further inquiry shows the following. Last year 800 residents of Town B purchased shoes. 400 of them purchased from Smith's Clothing, and the other 400 purchased from the numerous shoe stores in City A. Note that this conclusion is absolutely consistent with the proposition that Smith's "trade area" is Town B. The *only* customers Smith's had were from Town B, assuming no one drove from City A to buy shoes at Smith's. In fact, Smith's is probably in close competition with the City A shoe stores.[31] To the extent Town B residents go into City A to work or to shop, they regard the City shoe stores as interchangeable, and would respond to any local price increase by purchasing even more of their shoes in City A.[32]

In sum, "trade area" considers the extent to which customers will travel in order to do business at Smith's. "Relevant market" considers the extent to which customers will travel in order to *avoid* doing business at Smith's. Unfortunately, this means that using discovery to obtain the addresses of a seller's customers seldom provides us with useful information about geographic market. What we really need to know is the extent to which people from the immediate area can readily turn to *alternative* sellers, and the defendant is far less likely to have such information.

In making empirical judgments about the willingness of customers to travel in such cases, one must consider not only the maxi-

30. See Santa Cruz Med. Clinic and Derjjan Assoc. v. Dominican Santa Cruz Hosp., 1995–2 Trade Cas. ¶ 71,254, 1995 WL 853037 (N.D.Cal.1995) ("those patients with strong preferences for obtaining services at distant hospitals such as many tertiary care patients ... may be willing to travel ... even if most patients are unwilling to travel.")

31. For example, see Falls City Indus., Inc. v. Vanco Beverage, Inc., 460 U.S. 428, 433, 103 S.Ct. 1282, 1287 (1983), a Robinson–Patman case which relied on a district court finding that two counties in different states were in the same relevant geographic market for retail beer purchases; residents of one county were quite willing to drive into the other county in order to obtain lower beer prices. In that case, a store in the high priced county would likely have a "trade area" that included only people from its own county.

32. See Bathke v. Casey's General Stores, 64 F.3d 340 (8th Cir.1995), which relied on this reasoning; accord: *Tenet Health Care*, note 7; and see Baxley–DeLamar v. American Cemetery Assn., 938 F.2d 846, 850–1 (8th Cir. 1991), which held that expert testimony that the geographic market was "the primary area in which Baxley [the defendant] did business" provided "no evidentiary basis for defining the geographic area." See also L.A. Draper & Son v. Wheelabrator–Frye, Inc., 735 F.2d 414, 424 (11th Cir.1984) (fact that plaintiff made nearly all of its sales within a four state area did not create a jury issue on whether that area constituted a relevant antitrust market. "For proof of sales patterns to support a geographic market definition, we would have to know that consumers could not realistically turn to outside distributors should prices rise within the four-state area."); T. Harris Young & Assocs. v. Marquette Electronics, 931 F.2d 816 (11th Cir.1991), cert. denied, 502 U.S. 1013, 112 S.Ct. 658 (1991) (fact that most customers purchased within a nine-state area where plaintiff did business did not create jury issue on whether that area was a geographic market, because there was no evidence "that consumers within the nine-state area could not turn to outside sellers if the prices increases within the nine-state area.").

mum travel distances observed, but the relevant proportion willing to travel such a distance. For example, suppose that in a competitive market 95% of customers travel within twenty miles or less, but the remaining 5% are willing to travel further, say, fifty miles. The loss of sales from this 5% may not be sufficient to restrain monopoly pricing.[33]

The previous analysis also tells us that noncompetition covenants or clauses seldom tell us anything useful about the size of a geographic market. For example, numerous lessees in shopping centers are subject to lease covenants that prohibit them from selling certain items. The beneficiaries of those covenants are other stores in the same shopping center. Likewise, some businesses require employees to sign covenants agreeing that they will not compete in a specified geographic area for a certain time after the employment relationship is terminated. Although such covenants may arguably be part of a monopolization scheme, in the vast majority of cases they are devices for ensuring the protected seller of a sufficient volume of business or protection of goodwill *within* its trade area. For example, small town Smith's Clothing in the previous example might very well ask its employee manager to sign a restrictive covenant promising that she will not sell shoes in the same town for several years after quitting her job with Smith's. Otherwise the manager could force Smith's to share the customers it already has, and could take advantage of everything she had learned at her old job. But Smith's and the former manager would still be in close competition with the nearby big city shoe stores. The geographic scope of the restrictive covenant fails to identify the extent of the relevant geographic market.[34]

3.6e. Price Discrimination[35]

True geographic price discrimination occurs when differences in a firm's prices as between two areas do not reflect differences in costs. Price discrimination indicates that the firm has market power in at least some geographic areas.[36] For example, if a firm charges $4.00 in Milwaukee and St. Paul, and $3.00 in Dubuque, while its costs appear to be the same, then presumptively it has a certain amount of market power in Milwaukee and St. Paul, assuming the price in Dubuque is competitive. If a relevant market is defined in terms of ability to raise price 10% above cost, the area including Milwaukee and St. Paul over which prices are $4.00 would appear to be a relevant market.[37]

Used in this fashion, price discrimination really operates as a limited surrogate for the defendant's marginal cost. That is, assuming we can measure the price discrimination, which requires us to observe both prices and cost differentials, then the percentage amount of price discrimination provides us a minimum percentage of the defendant's ability to raise price above marginal cost in the high priced area. Of course, the low priced area might already be priced above marginal cost, so the price in the high priced area reflects even greater market power than the price difference

33. However, in most situations the fact that 10% of customers purchase outside of a defined region in which they are located indicates that the defined region is too small to be the relevant geographic market. See Elzinga & Hogarty, note 26; M. Vita, J. Langenfeld, P. Pautler & L. Miller, Economic Analysis in Health Care Antitrust, 7 J. Contemp. Health L. & Policy 73 (1991).

34. See Polk Bros. v. Forest City Enterprises, 776 F.2d 185 (7th Cir.1985) (it could not be assumed that noncompetition covenants covering a single shopping area defined a relevant geographic market); Jetro Cash & Carry Enterprises v. Food Distribution Center, 569 F.Supp. 1404, 1409, 1412 (E.D.Pa.1983) (noncompetition covenant covers 400 acres, but court rejects plaintiff's argument that geographic market covers same area; rather it extends 100 to 150 miles); Caremark Homecare, Inc. v. New England Critical Care, Inc., 700 F.Supp. 1033, 1036–1037 (D.Minn. 1988) (allegation that covenant not to compete violates § 2 requires plaintiff to give independent proof of relevant geographic market).

35. See 2A Antitrust Law ¶ 522 (rev. ed. 1995).

36. Technically, a firm price discriminates when it has different ratios of price to marginal cost. If the price to "favored" purchasers is equal to marginal cost, then the price to "disfavored" purchasers must reflect a certain amount of market power. See § 14.1.

37. See In re Midcon, 5 Trade Reg. Rep. ¶ 22,707 (FTC 1989) (noting that price discrimination justifies the definition of smaller markets. "If a hypothetical monopolist could impose a discriminatory increase at isolated locations within a larger market, then it is appropriate to collect those locations into a separate market for assessing competitive effects." Id. at 22,383.).

suggests. The only exception to this rule would be where the price in the low priced area is less than marginal cost—as, for example, if the defendant were practicing predatory pricing in that area. But predatory pricing can never be assumed and is presumably rare.[38]

Price discrimination devices such as delivered or basing point pricing systems should also be considered in geographic market definition. Basing-point and delivered pricing systems frequently enable sellers to obtain monopoly returns from nearby "captive" customers, while competing for more remote customers who may be equally close to alternative suppliers. Thus the seller may "compete" in a relatively large geographic area, while continuing to earn significant monopoly profits in a smaller area.[39] Improved competition in the smaller area should be an important concern of the antitrust laws. Accordingly, the smaller area should be considered a relevant geographic market.[40]

§ 3.7 Computation and Interpretation of Market Shares

After a relevant product and geographic market have been delineated, the market share must be computed. Monopolization, attempt, tying, exclusive dealing and vertical restraints cases ordinarily require computation of the market share of the defendant.[1] Merger cases analyzed under the Herfindahl theoretically require one to compute the market share of every firm in the market.[2] Restraints analyzed under the rule of reason may require computation of the market share of the collected participants in the restraint.[3]

Conceptually, computing market share seems easy. The fact finder sums total market output and places it in the denominator of the fraction, with the output of the firm under consideration in the numerator. The resulting fraction, expressed as a percentage, gives the firm's market share. But the difficult issue is deciding which numbers to use in the fraction: revenue, units of output manufactured, units of output sold, capacity, or perhaps some other number reflecting an amalgam of these.

The easiest case for computing market share involves the group of firms selling a fungible product at the same price and operating at full capacity. In that case measures based on revenue, units produced or capacity will all give the same percentage. But product differentiation accompanied by price differences complicates the problem. Suppose we conclude that Marantz stereos and Panasonic stereos are in the same relevant product, but the typical Marantz sells for $1200, while the typical Panasonic with the same features sells for $600. During the period in question each company has produced 10,000 units. Market share numbers based on units produced give us a 50% share for each firm; market share numbers based on revenue suggest that Marantz's share is 66.7%, while Panasonic's is 33.3%. Using the first number, Marantz is probably not capable of being charged with monopolization. Using the second number, it probably is.

Further, would we want to use a different measure, depending on whether the question was (1) Marantz's ability to monopolize; or (2) the likelihood that Marantz and Panasonic will collude? In the first case, we are considering Panasonic's ability to increase its own presence in the market in response to Marantz's price increase; so the market positions of the two firms are being used against each other. By contrast, in the second case we are considering the joint presence of Marantz and Panasonic in the market, effectively treating them as a single entity.

3.7a. Revenue v. Units

In most cases, market share is based on either revenue or the number of units pro-

38. See Ch. 8.

39. See D. Haddock, Basing–Point Pricing: Competitive vs. Collusive Theories, 72 Amer.Econ.Rev. 289 (1982). Basing point pricing is discussed in § 4.6c.

40. See J. Ordover & R. Willig, The 1982 Dept. of Justice Merger Guidelines: An Economic Assessment, 71 Calif.L.Rev. 535, 548 (1983).

§ 3.7

1. See Chs. 6 & 10.

2. See § 12.4a.

3. See § 5.2.

duced. One clear advantage of these numbers is that they are readily available in many markets. As noted above, when products are fungible, the two numbers tend to be the same. That is also true of products that are only modestly differentiated, or where the differentiations are purely cosmetic. For example, the ready-to-eat breakfast cereal industry exhibits an enormous amount of product differentiation (Wheaties, Trix, Captain Crunch, raisin bran, and hundreds of others) but a relatively small amount of price difference among offerings. The market shares of the producers probably would not vary much if we moved from computations based on revenue to computations based on units produced.

Even when products are differentiated substantially, it is important not to exaggerate the impact of differentiation on market share measurements. The Marantz/Panasonic example given above assumed that one firm's product sold for double the price of the other firm's. But such extreme price variations usually indicate that the two brands are not in the same relevant market at all. Where the price differences range over, say, 10%, the impact on market share measurement is much less. For example, assume one firm produced 100 widgets per year that are sold at $1.00, while another produced 100 slightly higher quality widgets sold at $1.10. Market share measurements based on units produced suggest 50% for each firm. Measurements based on revenue suggest about 52.4% for the higher priced firm and 47.6% for the smaller firm. These variations should ordinarily be considered inside the "margin of error" for market share measurement, given the imprecision in our underlying assumptions about market delineation.[4]

Technically speaking, units rather than revenue seems to be the best measure of market share for most, but not all, purposes. For example, if Marantz is accused of monopolization, the relevant question is to what extent Panasonic, its rival, will be able to satisfy customers when Marantz reduces its output. Presumably, the customer will purchase either *one* $1200 Marantz or *one* $600 Panasonic. The substitution takes place unit-by-unit rather than dollar-by-dollar. The person who switches to Panasonic steals one sale from Marantz for each unit of Panasonic.

The important exception to this rule is where the customer typically uses *more* of the lower priced good—that is, the lower priced good is cheaper, in part, because one needs more of it than of the higher priced substitute. House paint might be a good example. Cheap paint costs $10 per gallon but gives poor coverage. One needs 30 gallons to paint a typical house. "Premium" paint costs $20 per gallon but one needs only 15 gallons to paint the same house. In this case the consumer responding to a price increase in the market for premium paint must substitute at a ratio of two gallons of cheap paint for each one gallon of premium paint. Market shares based on units tend to understate the market power of the premium paint manufacturer, and revenue might be a better measure of the cheap paint manufacturer's ability to steal sales from the premium manufacturer. To be sure, a more technically accurate measure would be a unit measure that took the substitution rate into account—in this case, by counting two gallons of cheap paint as one gallon of premium paint. Unfortunately, substitution rates in the real world are not that easy to compute. That is, the rate will vary depending on the surface to be painted, the tastes of the individual consumer, and the like.

When units are used, is the correct number units manufactured or units sold? Once again, large differences between these two numbers should not be common. Most often, an observed difference is a function of the fact that we have looked at too short a time period.[5] In a given three month period a firm might pro-

4. When the Herfindahl is used to measure market concentration for merger analysis, *squaring* of the numbers tends to exaggerate large market shares. In that case, the difference between units and revenue may be more substantial—for example, if the largest firms in the industry also sell the highest priced product. On the Herfindahl and its use, see § 12.4a.

5. See, for example, Associated Radio Serv. Co. v. Page Airways, 624 F.2d 1342, 1352 (5th Cir.1980), cert. denied, 450 U.S. 1030, 101 S.Ct. 1740 (1981), where the relevant market, avionics systems in a particular brand of aircraft, had produced only 20 sales over a nine or ten year period.

duce much more or much less than it sells during that same period, but very few firms would do this over a time period of, say, two or three years. In all events, the *ability to produce* is most generally the best estimate of a rival's ability to steal customers from a price-increasing firm. A firm with an accumulated inventory of non-perishable goods may have even a greater ability and desire to steal sales than does a firm that is currently selling all it produces. As a general matter, production figures are better than sales figures.

3.7b. Output v. Capacity

A theoretical case can easily be made that the denominator of the market share fraction should include (1) the output of the firm or firms whose market power is being assessed; and (2) the capacity of rival firms.[6] The argument is simply that, when the ability of a firm to increase price above the competitive level is assessed, we wish to know the ability of rivals to fill in the gap by increasing their own output. A rival with excess capacity can increase its output without making an expensive and perhaps irreversible investment in additional productive capacity. Indeed, the rival with substantial excess capacity might be able to increase output on very short notice and deprive the putative monopolist from any possible gains.

But the theoretical case for capacity measures of rival firms runs into numerous practical problems that generally preclude its use in all but the most obvious cases.[7] *First*, almost any firm can increase its output if cost of production is not a factor. Properly measured excess capacity includes capacity where average variable cost of production does not exceed current costs. But this constraint makes excess capacity very difficult to measure in most situations.[8] *Second*, properly defined capacity must include not only the capacity to produce an extra unit, but also the capacity to distribute it to the consumer. In some cases distribution of additional output is easy, but in others it may be very difficult. *Third*, even the capacity to produce an extra unit depends on more than the existence of unused equipment in a plant. For example, new personnel may have to be brought in and trained, and this itself could be an irreversible investment and a time-consuming activity. *Fourth*, use of capacity measures may greatly increase the cost of litigation since production and revenue figures are readily available, while capacity figures often are not.

Finally, the defendant or defendants may already be charging a monopoly price. This would certainly be the premise in a monopolization case, but it could also be true in a merger or horizontal restraint case. Although the excess capacity of rivals might restrain a yet further price increase, clearly it is not restraining the monopoly pricing that is already occurring. In such cases observed excess capacity must be available only at higher cost, is subject to bottlenecks in distribution, or is not being used with sufficient aggressiveness by rival firms.[9] Indeed, the excess capacity in this case may be the result of express or tacit collusion on the part of the rival firms themselves, who would prefer to restrain their own output and keep prices high rather than compete too aggressively with the dominant firm.

In most cases, therefore, the output rather than the capacity of rivals is the better measure, although there are some exceptions.[10] If

6. We use the output of the firm or firms under investigation because their *own* excess capacity cannot be used to defeat their price increase.

As an illustration: suppose a market contained firms A, B, C, D & E. Each currently produces 10 widgets, but each has 5 units of excess capacity. A's market share as measured by capacity would be its own output divided by the sum of its own output plus the capacity of B—E. This would be 10/70, or about 14%. A's market share based strictly on output would be 20%.

7. W. Landes & R. Posner, Market Power in Antitrust Cases, 94 Harv. L.Rev. 937, 949–950 (1981), generally prefer capacity measures in all cases.

8. See generally G. Stigler, The Theory of Price 156–158 (3d ed. 1966).

9. See 2A Antitrust Law ¶ 535c (rev. ed. 1995).

10. A few courts have used capacity measures. See FTC v. Bass Bros. Enters., 1984–1 Trade Cas. (CCH) ¶ 66041 at 68, 610, 1984 WL 355 (N.D.Ohio 1984) (suggesting that capacity is better measure of future competition); Gearhart Indus. v. Smith Int'l, Inc., 592 F.Supp. 203, 213 (N.D.Tex.), affirmed in part, modified in part, 741 F.2d 707 (5th Cir.1984) (stating capacity as best measure, but using revenue, since capacity information was not available, given that market was new and utilization rates varied between regions); Monfort of Colo., Inc. v. Cargill,

there is excess capacity that can obviously be brought into a market at very low additional cost, it should be counted. For example, suppose an airline's rival is flying the same route with a 200 seat airplane currently carrying only 50 passengers. The marginal cost of adding additional passengers is extremely low, and the distribution network for tickets is presumably already in place. The 200 figure seems a much better estimate than the 50 figure of the rival's ability to restrain future monopoly pricing. Likewise, suppose an intersection contains four gasoline stations. Each has four hoses for gasoline, and each hose is capable of serving 100 customers per day. But currently each station serves only 250 customers. Once again, the distribution network is fully in place and the cost of serving additional customers is little more than the price of the additional gasoline itself. Presumably, if one of the firms attempted to charge monopoly prices each of the three rivals could immediately absorb up to 150 customers at no greater cost per customer than at the current level. The capacity measure is superior.

3.7c. The Impact of Product Durability

Product durability affects market power in two ways: (1) a market for second-hand versions of the product might compete with the market for the new good; and (2) the original customer might respond to a price increase by keeping the product longer. The effect may be either to reduce the significance of the defendant's market share or to change the way in which we want to measure it. For example, suppose purchasers respond to a price increase in automobiles by (1) purchasing a second hand car instead of a new one, or (2) keeping their original car longer. The effect is that the new car manufacturer faces a higher elasticity of demand and its ability to charge a monopoly price is correspondingly reduced.

When market power is assessed in the traditional antitrust way of computing market share of a relevant antitrust market, the durability problem is not easily addressed. One partial solution is to include any second-hand product in the market definition and count its sales as competing with sales of the new good. In the case of the "perfectly durable" good—where customers are indifferent as between the new and the used good—this is a good solution. For example, the owner of the only 100 residential lots on an island faces immediate loss of market share as soon as he begins to sell. By the time he has sold his fiftieth lot, his market share has dropped to as little as 50%, depending on how many of the "used" lots are on the market.

When the good is only imperfectly durable, as most are, the problem is more difficult. Although there is a market for used aluminum, used cars, used tires, and used clothing, customers readily distinguish the two and the amount of competition between the new good and the second hand good can range from quite substantial to barely discernible.[11] In *Alcoa*, Judge Hand refused to include secondary aluminum, or aluminum made from reclaimed aluminum products that had been discarded, in the same market as virgin, or new aluminum.[12] The impact of this decision was significant. Excluding secondary aluminum gave Alcoa a market share of about 90%; including it would have dropped Alcoa's market share to about 64%.

Judge Hand reasoned that Alcoa effectively controlled the market for secondary just as much as the market for virgin, since its output decision respecting virgin determined the future output of secondary. Even assuming that Alcoa actually considered the supply of secondary aluminum ten or fifteen years down the road, however, that does not suggest that sec-

Inc., 591 F.Supp. 683, 706 (D.Colo.1983), affirmed, 761 F.2d 570 (10th Cir.1985), reversed on other grounds, 479 U.S. 104, 107 S.Ct. 484 (1986) (attempting to calculate market shares on the basis of the capacities of all efficient firms).

11. See D. Carlton & R. Gertner, Market Power and Mergers in Durable–Good Industries, 32 J.L. & Econ. S203 (1989) (arguing that mergers should be of much less concern in durable goods industries); Foreb, Evaluating Mergers in Durable Goods Industries, 34 Antitrust Bull. 99 (1989) (in many markets durability limits market power).

12. United States v. Aluminum Co. of America (Alcoa), 148 F.2d 416 (2d Cir.1945).

ondary should be excluded from the market. On the contrary, it suggests that secondary in fact competes and should be counted in the market in some fashion.

Nonetheless, it seems clear that the 64% figure noted above would exaggerate the impact of secondary aluminum on Alcoa's market power. First is the high probability of a *Cellophane* fallacy; the high observed cross-elasticity of demand between virgin and secondary was probably a function of the fact that virgin was already being sold at a monopoly price.[13] In that case, the production of secondary would almost certainly have been less had virgin been priced competitively. Second, the market contained numerous "low elasticity" buyers who were willing to pay a high premium for virgin aluminum and found secondary unacceptable at virtually any price.[14]

One admittedly rough way to take product durability into account is to include the durable good in the market but measure shares by revenue rather than units sold. For example, suppose that each year 1000 new cameras and 1000 used cameras of a given type are sold. However, the price of a new camera averages $200, while the price of a used camera averages $75. In this case the new camera manufacturers' market share would be reckoned at 50% on the basis of units sold, but as approximately 73% on the basis of revenue. The 50% figure probably understates the manufacturer's power. Further, the price difference between the new good and the used one indicates something about the degree to which customers differentiate the two, and the extent to which some customers find the used good not to be a good competitor at all. For example, a new suit might cost $400 but end up on the rack in a used clothing store for $15. This indicates very little competition between the new and the used good, and the revenue measure would reflect that fact.

One way the durable goods monopolist can reduce the impact of competition from used goods is to lease, but not sell, its durable product.[15] Before such a scheme will work, the extra profits must outweigh the transaction costs of the leasing system itself. For example, Alcoa could probably not lease aluminum cookware, automobile parts or electric wire to the exclusion of sales. But other durable goods monopolists such as United Shoe Machinery and IBM have pursued highly restrictive lease only policies.[16] In such cases the lease only policy itself may be evidence of market power, although it may be justified by other factors, such as the lessor's wish to protect its goodwill by controlling the maintenance of its equipment. In any event, price discrimination in the offering of leases is evidence of at least some market power.[17]

The other problem of product durability—that some customers will simply use the primary product longer—is even less tractable when market power is estimated from market share. In this case there is no alternative market for second-hand goods that can be thrown into the calculus. Likewise, we cannot consider this a problem of cross-elasticity of demand generally, since there is no alternative product to which the customer turns. Mainly, the problem serves to remind us that, once we have defined a relevant market and computed market share, those numbers have little *inherent* meaning. In the case of the product that can be used a longer time, we would simply say that the elasticity of demand is higher than when the product is used once and discarded. As a result, any given market share should be

13. See § 3.4b.

14. *Aluminum Co.*, 148 F.2d at 425.

15. See, for example, R. Coase, Durability and Monopoly, 15 J. L. & Econ. 143 (1972); J. Wiley, E. Rasmusen, & J. Ramseyer, The Leasing Monopolist, 37 U.C.L.A. L. Rev. 693 (1990); J. Tirole, The Theory of Industrial Organization 72–92 (1988).

16. United States v. United Shoe Machinery Corp., 110 F.Supp. 295, 348–351 (D.Mass.1953), affirmed, 347 U.S. 521, 74 S.Ct. 699 (1954); IBM Corp. v. United States, 298 U.S. 131, 134–135, 56 S.Ct. 701, 703 (1936) (condemning IBM's lease only policy); In re Xerox Corp., 86 FTC 364, 367–368 (1975) (consent decree limiting lease only policy). Compare Williamsburg Wax Museum v. Historic Figures, Inc., 810 F.2d 243, 253 (D.C.Cir.1987) (permitting leasing arrangement where defendant also occasionally sold and there was no "panoply of practices" as in *United Shoe Machinery*); Souza v. Estate of Bishop, 821 F.2d 1332 (9th Cir.1987) (permitting lease only policy where defendants were competitors, not monopolists, and there was no evidence of an agreement between them not to sell).

17. See § 3.9b.

accorded somewhat less weight. There is probably no substitute for getting an expert economist to estimate the residual demand elasticity facing the firm.[18]

§ 3.7d. Interpreting Market Share Data; Questions of Fact or Law

In *Alcoa*, Judge Hand concluded that a market share of 90% is enough to make a monopoly. He added that "it is doubtful whether sixty or sixty-four percent would be enough; and certainly thirty-three percent is not."[19] From that time on, market share has become decisive in most antitrust cases where market power must be estimated.

The market share requirements for particular antitrust offenses are discussed in the Sections of this book pertaining to those offenses. Here we note the problem of determining the weight that should be given to market share data, particularly since such data are not the only way that market power can be measured.[20] In fact, however, a dominant share of a properly defined relevant market has been a requirement in monopolization cases ever since *Alcoa*. Structural issues have predominated in merger analysis ever since the 1960's, particularly since the Supreme Court's *Philadelphia Bank* decision.[21] Tying Arrangement and exclusive dealing analysis seems to be gravitating toward a requirement of a 30% share or greater of a properly defined relevant market.[22] In its *Spectrum Sports* decision the Supreme Court insisted that a relevant market be defined in an attempt to monopolize case, although the market share requirements are unclear and undoubtedly vary with the offense.[23] To be sure, defendants increasingly use non-market-share evidence to *defeat* assertions of market power—for example, courts sometimes cite low barriers to entry as evidence that the defendant lacks market power no matter what its market share.[24] But in order to establish market power, a plaintiff cannot rely exclusively on high profits, the ability to exclude competition or to discriminate in price. These alternative measures generally serve to confirm or to undermine evidence of market power based on market share.

The significance of market share data often reduces to one question: does failure to meet a certain market share threshold establish the defendant's innocence as a matter of law, or may the jury infer market power from alternative forms of evidence? The dominant approach is illustrated by the Fifth Circuit's *Dimmitt* decision.[25] The court refused to condemn a firm of monopolization when its own market share hovered around 25% and where the top five firms controlled over 70% of the market.[26] The record showed that the defendant was a clear price leader in a tightly knit oligopoly, and its internal memoranda suggested its ability to control rivals by disciplinary price cutting.[27] Further, the industry was characterized by high entry barriers and a low elasticity of demand, because corn sweeteners

18. See § 3.9a. Since residual elasticity measures are based on consumers' actual substitution behavior, they presumably take durability considerations into account.

19. United States v. Aluminum Co. of America (Alcoa), 148 F.2d 416, 424 (2d Cir.1945). In the *du Pont* (Cellophane) case the Supreme Court indicated that a 75% market share, if proven, would be sufficient. United States v. E.I. du Pont de Nemours & Co., 351 U.S. 377, 404, 76 S.Ct. 994, 1012 (1956).

20. See § 3.9.

21. United States v. Philadelphia National Bank, 374 U.S. 321, 83 S.Ct. 1715 (1963). See § 12.4.

22. See §§ 10.3–10.9e.

23. Spectrum Sports v. McQuillan, 506 U.S. 447, 458–459, 113 S.Ct. 884, 892 (1993), on remand, 23 F.2d 1531 (9th Cir.1994). See § 6.5.

24. For example, United States v. Syufy Enters., 903 F.2d 659, 664–669 (9th Cir.1990); see §§ 8.4b, 12.6.

25. Dimmitt Agri Industries, Inc. v. CPC International, Inc., 679 F.2d 516 (5th Cir.1982), cert. denied, 460 U.S. 1082, 103 S.Ct. 1770 (1983). Accord Morgenstern v. Wilson, 29 F.3d 1291 (8th Cir.1994), cert. denied, 513 U.S. 1150, 115 S.Ct. 1100 (1995); Valley Liquors v. Renfield Importers, 822 F.2d 656 (7th Cir.), cert. denied, 484 U.S. 977, 108 S.Ct. 488 (1987). Compare Arthur S. Langenderfer v. S. E Johnson Co., 917 F.2d 1413, 1432 (6th Cir. 1990), cert. denied, 502 U.S. 899, 112 S.Ct. 274 (1991) ("it would be rare indeed to find that a firm with only 25 percent or 50 percent of the market could control price over any significant period.").

26. *Dimmitt*, 679 F.2d at 527 & n. 9.

27. As quoted in defendant's memoranda: "[W]e must realize we can go into a negative profit situation for an extended period of time. * * * I am sure that all competition will announce new market policies within a few hours after our announcement * * * [W]e are determined to be the price leader." 679 F.2d at 522–523.

generally make up a small percentage of the product costs of most buyers, such as soft drink manufacturers. Nonetheless, the court concluded, an individual market share of 50% was insufficient to condemn single firm monopolization.

By contrast to *Dimmitt*, consider the Second Circuit's decision in *Broadway Delivery*,[28] which represents a distinctly minority tradition of letting the jury decide market power questions even on low market shares. The jury had been instructed that they could not find monopoly power on market shares less than 50%, and the defendant's market share never exceeded 50%. But the appellate court found this instruction to be an error:

> [W]hen the evidence presents a fair jury issue of monopoly power, the jury should not be told that it must find monopoly power lacking below a specified share or existing above a specified share. * * * However the instruction is phrased, it should not deflect the jury's attention from indicia of monopoly power other than market share.[29]

However, the court also warned that when market shares were this low there must be "other evidence * * * of the power to control prices or exclude competition."[30] Further, the jury could properly be instructed that monopoly on market shares lower than 50% is rare.[31]

Which approach is better? First, didn't the court in *Dimmitt* place the cart before the horse? In order to violate § 2 someone must have sufficient market *power*, and the most common way courts measure market power is by market share. But market share measures are not the only way power is measured, and power can sometimes be inferred from other kinds of conduct.[32] So the real question is Does a firm with the self-proclaimed ability to control market prices in a highly concentrated industry have market power? The principal difference between the *Dimmitt* defendant and the ordinary monopolist is that the latter raises price by reducing its output unilaterally. The oligopoly price leader, by contrast, reduces output and raises price by coaxing or coercing smaller rivals into doing the same thing. But if the firm has achieved the ability to do this effectively, does it not have market power?

Of course, there are competing concerns. A court decision permitting "monopolization" against a 25% firm might invite a host of lawsuits against nondominant firms generally considered to fall below § 2's market power threshold. But that problem can be addressed by articulating in advance the requirements for a violation on small market shares: high industry concentration, high entry barriers, a history of poor industry performance and price leadership by the defendant.

Finally, the difference between *Dimmitt* and *Broadway Delivery* may go more to the substance of the antitrust laws than to the market power question itself. The *Dimmitt* court interpreted the evidence as showing that the defendant did not have the power to reduce output and increase price on its own; it had to rely on a certain level of cooperation by rivals. Thus the issue was not whether § 2's monopoly power requirement could be met on the basis of a 25% market share, but whether it could be established on the basis of evidence tending to show price leadership and oligopoly rather than monopoly.

For the present time, at least, market share of a relevant market is the predominant, if not

28. Broadway Delivery Corp. v. United Parcel Serv., 651 F.2d 122 (2d Cir.), cert. denied, 454 U.S. 968, 102 S.Ct. 512 (1981). A more recent, but unconvincing decision in the Second Circuit may call Broadway Delivery into question. See Glendora v. Gannett Co., 858 F.Supp. 369, 371 (S.D.N.Y.), aff'd mem., 40 F.3d 1238 (2d Cir.1994), cert. denied, 514 U.S. 1054, 115 S.Ct. 1435 (1995). The court granted a motion to dismiss a monopolization claim on an alleged market share of 50%, but incorrectly held that a market share of a given magnitude counts for purposes of § 2 only if it was unlawfully acquired. The measurement of power is not a question of innocence of guilt. Of course, the plaintiff would have to establish separately the conduct elements of the offense. The *Glendora* court did not cite the Second Circuit's previous *Broadway Delivery* opinion.

29. *Broadway Delivery*, 651 F.2d at 129–130.

30. 651 F.2d at 129.

31. Ibid. The court elaborated:

> Sometimes, but not inevitably, it will be useful to suggest that a market share below 50% is rarely evidence of monopoly power, a share between 50% and 70% can occasionally show monopoly power, and a share above 70% is usually strong evidence of monopoly power.

32. On alternative measures of market power, see § 3.9.

the decisive, mechanism by which court's measure market power. Numerous economists object to this, believing that alternative methods, such as direct estimates of residual demand curves,[33] provide more accurate measures, particularly in product differentiated markets. But acceptance of such methods is still on the margins of antitrust. They appear to have more influence on enforcement decisions within the Antitrust Division and the FTC than on the courts themselves.

§ 3.8 Market Definition in the Justice Department Merger Guidelines

The 1992 Horizontal Merger Guidelines issued by the United States Justice Department's Antitrust Division (Division) and the Federal Trade Commission[1] state the criteria that these Agencies[2] will use to determine whether it will challenge a particular merger. The Guidelines also describe how the Agency will determine the relevant market in merger cases. The Guidelines define markets exclusively for the purpose of analyzing horizontal mergers, in which the chief concern is not exercises of market power by a single firm, but rather increased likelihood of collusion.[3] However, many of the economic principles of market delineation developed in the guidelines serve equally well in other antitrust contexts.

3.8a. Product Market Delineation in the Guidelines

The Guidelines define a relevant market as:

> a product or group of products and a geographic area in which it is produced or sold such that a hypothetical profit-maximizing firm, not subject to price regulation, that was the only present and future producer or seller of those products in that area likely would impose at least a "small but significant and nontransitory"[4] increase in price, assuming the terms of sale of all other products are held constant. A relevant market is a group of products and a geographic area that is no bigger than necessary to satisfy this test.[5]

The Agency's analysis begins "with each product (narrowly defined) produced or sold by each merging firm and asks what would happen if a hypothetical monopolist of that product imposed at least a 'small but significant and nontransitory' increase in price," which will usually be assumed to be 5% for one year, although different assumptions may be used, depending upon the nature of the industry.[6] Then,

> If, in response to the price increase, the reduction in sales of the product would be large enough that a hypothetical monopolist would not find it profitable to impose such an increase in price, then the Agency will add to the product group the product that is the next-best substitute for the merging firm's product.

The relevant product market is generally the smallest group of products that satisfies this test. The same methodology is used to define

33. See § 3.9a.

§ 3.8

1. 1992 Horizontal Merger Guidelines, 57 Fed. Reg. 41552 (Sep. 10, 1992); 4 Trade Reg. Rep. (CCH) ¶ 13,104. The 1992 Guidelines can be found reprinted in numerous other places, including many antitrust casebooks, as well as in P. Areeda & H. Hovenkamp, Antitrust Law (current Supplement). The 1992 Guidelines are a substantial revision of Guidelines that originally appeared in 1982 and were revised in 1984. Some of the law review commentary in this section refers to the 1982 or 1984 Guidelines, but is still relevant to the 1992 Guidelines.

2. The term "Agency" hereafter refers to either the Antitrust Division or the Federal Trade Commission, depending on which is analyzing the merger in question. The 1992 Guidelines are the first to be issued jointly by the two Agencies.

3. See G. Werden, Market Delineation and the Justice Department's Merger Guidelines, 1983 Duke L.J. 514, which gives step-by-step instructions for defining a market under the 1982 guidelines. In most respects the procedure in the 1992 Guidelines is the same.

4. In the 1984 Guidelines the suggested price increase was five percent and the minimum duration of this price increase was one year. 1984 Guidelines § 2.11 & n.7. In the 1992 Guidelines the presumptive five percent figure is maintained but the duration of the price increase is stated to be "the foreseeable future." 1992 Guidelines § 1.11.

5. 1992 guidelines, § 1.0.

6. The Guidelines make clear that the relevant test is whether the *profit-maximizing* price increase will be 5% or more, not whether a 5% price increase would be profitable. See Guidelines, § 1.0. On the importance of the distinction, see § 3.2b of this book.

geographic markets.[7] The guidelines do not speak of "submarkets."[8]

The Guidelines then give a rather explicit list of evidentiary criteria that the Agency will look for in seeking to determine whether buyers will substitute elsewhere in response to the unjustified price increase:

(1) evidence that buyers have shifted or have considered shifting purchases between products in response to relative changes in price or other competitive variables;

(2) evidence that sellers base business decisions on the prospect of buyer substitution between products in response to relative changes in price or other competitive variables;

(3) the influence of downstream competition faced by buyers in their output markets; and

(4) the timing and costs of switching products.[9]

On the supply side, the Agency seeks to know which firms could easily compete with the firm in question in response to the latter's "small but significant and nontransitory" increase in price." In making this determination, the Agency distinguishes between "committed" and "uncommitted" entrants. A committed entrant is a firm that must make a substantial, irreversible ("sunk") expenditure of resources in order to enter a market. Such entrants are treated under the concept of barriers to entry.[10] By contrast, an uncommitted entrant is a firm that can enter or divert output into the subject firm's market without making significant irreversible investments.[11] When such firms are identified, the Guidelines include the output or capacity of these firms in the relevant market.

Under this analysis, *customer* substitution (elasticity of demand) defines the product, while *producer* substitution identifies the firms that are capable of producing the product. For example, suppose that two makers of kitchen stoves planned to merge. On the demand side, customers find gas stoves not to be good substitutes for electric stoves and would not substitute in large numbers in response to a 5% price increase. On the supply side, however, assume that makers of gas stoves are "uncommitted entrants," in that they could easily switch to production of electric stoves. In this case the Agency would define the market as "electric stoves" but include the gas stove makers among the firms operating within the market.[12]

7. 1992 horizontal merger guidelines, § 1.2.

8. However, the agencies have continued to use "submarkets" in litigation, even since the 1982/84 Guidelines apparently abandoned them. See United States v. Archer–Daniels–Midland Co., 695 F.Supp. 1000 (S.D.Iowa 1987), reversed on other grounds, 866 F.2d 242 (8th Cir.1988), cert. denied, 493 U.S. 809, 110 S.Ct. 51 (1989); United States v. Gillette Co., 828 F.Supp. 78 (D.D.C.1993). See also FTC v. Staples, 970 F.Supp. 1066 (D.D.C.1997) (using "submarket" in FTC case); Olin Corp. v. FTC, 986 F.2d 1295 (9th Cir.1993) (same), cert. denied, 510 U.S. 1110, 114 S.Ct. 1051 (1994). On submarkets, see § 3.2c.

9. 1992 Guidelines § 1.11.

10. See § 12.4d in this volume.

11. In distinguishing committed from uncommitted entrants on the basis of sunk costs, the Agency will look at the following:

> the acquisition costs of tangible and intangible assets that cannot be recovered through the redeployment of these assets outside the relevant market, i.e., costs uniquely incurred to supply the relevant product and geographic market. Examples of sunk costs may include market-specific investments in production facilities, technologies, marketing (including product acceptance), research and development, regulatory approvals, and testing. A significant sunk cost is one which would not be recouped within one year of the commencement of the supply response, assuming a "small but significant and nontransitory" price increase in the relevant market. In this context, a "small but significant and nontransitory" price increase will be determined in the same way in which it is determined in product market definition, except the price increase will be assumed to last one year. In some instances, it may be difficult to calculate sunk costs with precision. Accordingly, when necessary, the Agency will make an overall assessment of the extent of sunk costs for firms likely to participate through supply responses.

1992 Guidelines, § 1.32.

12. See Owens–Illinois, 5 Trade Reg.Rep. ¶ 23162 (FTC, 1992):

> * * * [T]he presence of supply-side substitutability means only that if an end-use segment otherwise qualifies as a market, we should evaluate concentration and likely competitive effects by treating as participants in the market producers that are both (1) easily and economically able and (2) likely to shift production into the market in response to a small but significant price increase. * * * In essence, the scope of the market is defined on the basis of demand-side substitution. The *participants* in that market are identified on the basis of supply-side substitution.

3.8b. Geographic Markets Under the Guidelines

Respecting geographic markets, the Agency seeks to identify a region such that, in the absence of price discrimination, "a hypothetical monopolist that was the only present or future producer of the relevant product at locations in that region would profitably impose at least a 'small but significant and nontransitory' increase in price, holding constant the terms of sale for all products produced elsewhere."[13]

Beginning with the location of each merging firm or relevant plant, the guidelines consider:

> what would happen if a hypothetical monopolist of the relevant product at that point imposed at least a "small but significant and nontransitory" increase in price, but the terms of sale at all other locations remained constant. If, in response to the price increase, the reduction in sales of the product at that location would be large enough that a hypothetical monopolist producing or selling the relevant product at the merging firm's location would not find it profitable to impose such an increase in price, then the Agency will add the location from which production is the next-best substitute for production at the merging firm's location.[14]

The Guidelines then note the following as relevant to its determination of whether and to what extent buyers will shift the purchases in response to price increases of the hypothesized magnitude:

> (1) evidence that buyers have shifted or have considered shifting purchases between different geographic locations in response to relative changes in price or other competitive variables;
>
> (2) evidence that sellers base business decisions on the prospect of buyer substitution between geographic locations in response to relative changes in price or other competitive variables;
>
> (3) the influence of downstream competition faced by buyers in their output markets; and
>
> (4) the timing and costs of switching suppliers.[15]

The Guidelines observe that these general standards apply to foreign as well as to domestic competition. They do not specify whether they will use total foreign output or only that part of foreign output actually shipped into the United States in calculating market share.[16] However, they use total output as a general matter, and note that "[m]arket shares will be assigned to foreign competitors in the same way in which they are assigned to domestic competitors."[17] The Guidelines also add that if foreign imports are subject to a quota, "the market shares assigned to firms in that country will not exceed the amount of shipments by such firms allowed under the quota."[18]

3.8c. Significance of Price Discrimination

If the sellers practice price discrimination the Agency may define smaller geographic or product markets:

> [W]here a hypothetical monopolist likely would discriminate in prices charged to different groups of buyers, distinguished, for example, by their uses or locations, the Agency may delineate different relevant markets corresponding to each such buyer

Id. at 22,815.

13. Guidelines, § 1.21. See generally D. Scheffman & P. Spiller, Geographic Market Definition Under the U.S. Dept. of Justice Merger Guidelines, 30 J.L. & Econ. 123 (1987).

14. Ibid.

15. Ibid.

16. On this problem, see § 3.5a.

17. Guidelines, § 1.43.

18. Id. at § 1.43. The Guidelines also note,

> In the case of restraints that limit imports to some percentage of the total amount of the product sold in the United States (i.e., percentage quotas), a domestic price increase that reduced domestic consumption also would reduce the volume of imports into the United States. Accordingly, actual import sales and capacity data will be reduced for purposes of calculating market shares. Finally, a single market share may be assigned to a country or group of countries if firms in that country or group of countries act in coordination.

Ibid.

> group. Competition for sales to each such group may be affected differently by a particular merger and markets are delineated by evaluating the demand response of each such buyer group. A relevant market of this kind is described by a collection of products for sale to a given group of buyers.[19]

In the context of product markets, the Guidelines then explain as follows:

> A different analysis applies where price discrimination would be profitable for a hypothetical monopolist. Existing buyers sometimes will differ significantly in their likelihood of switching to other products in response to a "small but significant and nontransitory" price increase. If a hypothetical monopolist can identify and price differently to those buyers ("targeted buyers") who would not defeat the targeted price increase by substituting to other products in response to a "small but significant and nontransitory" price increase for the relevant product, and if other buyers likely would not purchase the relevant product and resell to targeted buyers, then a hypothetical monopolist would profitably impose a discriminatory price increase on sales to targeted buyers. This is true regardless of whether a general increase in price would cause such significant substitution that the price increase would not be profitable. The Agency will consider additional relevant product markets consisting of a particular use or uses by groups of buyers of the product for which a hypothetical monopolist would profitably and separately impose at least a "small but significant and nontransitory" increase in price.[20]

The intuition behind these sections is clear enough. Suppose that a seller is able to sell its product to group A at a price 10% higher than the price to group B, while costs appear to be the same. If the relevant standard for delineating a market is a profit-maximizing price at least 10% above costs,[21] *and* we can assume that the lower price sales to group B are profitable, then we can conclude that the sales to group A constitute a relevant market.[22]

3.8d. Calculation of Market Shares

The Guidelines statement about how market shares will be calculated adds some clarity to the case law, but not very much:

> The Agency normally will calculate market shares for all firms (or plants) identified as market participants * * * based on the total sales or capacity currently devoted to the relevant market together with that which likely would be devoted to the relevant market in response to a "small but significant and nontransitory" price increase. Market shares can be expressed either in dollar terms through measurement of sales, shipments, or production, or in physical terms through measurement of sales, shipments, production, capacity, or reserves.

The Guidelines then observe that

> Dollar sales or shipments generally will be used if firms are distinguished primarily by differentiation of their products. Unit sales generally will be used if firms are distinguished primarily on the basis of their relative advantages in serving different buyers or groups of buyers. Physical capacity or reserves generally will be used if it is these measures that most effectively distinguish firms.

The Guidelines also state that they will not include total output in the market unless that output is actually capable of being diverted—that is, it is not tied up through long-term contracts and the like.[23]

19. Guidelines, § 1.0.

20. Guidelines, § 1.12. Respecting geographic markets, the Guidelines employ analogous reasoning:

> [I]f a hypothetical monopolist can identify and price differently to buyers in certain areas ("targeted buyers") * * * [t]he Agency will consider additional geographic markets consisting of particular locations of buyers for which a hypothetical monopolist would profitably and separately impose at least a "small but significant and nontransitory" increase in price.

Guidelines, § 1.22.

21. See § 3.2b.

22. See § 3.9b2.

23. Guidelines, § 1.41.

3.8e. The "Cellophane" Fallacy in the Merger Guidelines

The Horizontal Merger Guidelines begin their analysis of mergers by estimating cross-elasticity of demand at current market prices, just as the Supreme Court did in the *du Pont* (Cellophane) decision.[24] The result, as in *du Pont*, is that markets may be defined too broadly if the firms under analysis are *already* charging a monopoly price.

For example, suppose that the provisional market for cellophane includes four firms, A, B, C & D, who are currently charging $3.00 per unit for cellophane. The evidence reveals that in response to a 5% price increase, to $3.15, numerous customers would substitute to wax paper, which is manufactured by 30 firms. As a result, the Agency includes the 30 firms in the relevant market, overall market concentration and the market shares of A, B, C & D drop precipitously, and a merger between A and B is approved.

But a closer look reveals that A, B, C & D are currently charging $3.00 because they are fixing prices or they have already attained a high degree of oligopoly coordination. In fact, the competitive price of cellophane is $2.00, and at that price its cross-elasticity of demand with wax paper is very low. The consequence of reliance on current prices as a base point from which to measure the effects of an additional price increase is to permit mergers precisely in those markets where mergers seem most harmful: in markets already subject to coordination of prices.

Initially the Justice Department, author of the 1982/1984 Guidelines where this methodology first appeared, responded to this criticism by noting two things. First, the administrative burdens of hypothesizing a price increase from competitive levels, rather than from the actually observed price level, would be very large. Second, the Clayton Act standard actually authorizes this approach. Section 7 condemns only those mergers that may "lessen" competition.[25] If a market is already subject to collusion or oligopoly, competition has *already* been "lessened" and the merger will not make the situation worse.[26]

But is this second defense correct as a factual matter? In most cases the answer is no. As Chapter 4 notes, the stability of cartels and oligopoly, as well as the likely price increase, is related inversely to the number of firms in the market. If a market is already subject to collusion or oligopoly, almost any horizontal merger within that market is likely to make a bad situation worse by making a cartel more stable or by increasing the oligopoly price.

The other defense of using current prices—that they are readily available while the competitive price is difficult to determine—has considerably more weight. In order to correct for the Cellophane fallacy, the Agency must do two things. First, it must identify situations where the current price is not the competitive price. Second, it must identify what the competitive price would be in these situations.

The drafters of the 1992 Guidelines have acknowledged the problem. They have added the following qualifier to previous versions of the Guidelines: if coordinated interaction among the firms in the provisional market is observed already to be occurring, the Agency will not use the current price as a starting point, but rather "a price more reflective of the competitive price."[27] The Guidelines themselves say nothing about how the Agency will determine whether the current price is noncompetitive and, when it makes that determi-

24. See § 3.4b.

25. See § 12.1 of this book.

26. See W. Baxter, Responding to the Reaction: The Draftsman's View, 71 Calif. L. Rev. 618 (1983); G. Werden, A Closer Analysis of Antitrust Markets, 62 Wash. L. Rev. 647, 652 (1984). The late Mr. Baxter, who was head of the Antitrust Division when the 1982 Guidelines were drafted, noted that basing market definition on current prices:

> can lead to erroneous analysis under § 2 of the Sherman Act because in such a case it is necessary to determine whether a firm is presently exercising power in order to determine whether corrective action is necessary to reduce that power. On the other hand, horizontal merger analysis under § 7 of the Clayton Act is concerned with the probability that a merger will decrease competition in the future.

Baxter, Id. at 623 n.35.

27. 1992 Guidelines § 1.11.

nation, how it will identify the competitive price.

Determining whether tacit or express collusion is already occurring is not always difficult. Oligopoly can often be identified by structure plus certain kinds of conduct such as price leadership, price posting practices, use of other facilitating devices, and the like.[28] A truly well-designed secret cartel might be difficult to detect, however.

One question worth considering is whether the Agency should simply stop the inquiry and challenge the merger when collusive practices are found. Suppose, drawing from the previous example, the Antitrust Division observes that coordinated interaction (oligopoly or collusion) is already occurring among A, B, C & D, the four makers of cellophane. The question is whether to permit a merger among two of these firms. Need the Division bother to guess at the competitive price and then estimate the cross-elasticity of demand with wax paper at that price? If the merger standard condemns mergers that may substantially lessen competition, then the existence of the coordinated interaction itself tells us that the market is *already* performing poorly. A horizontal merger will only make things worse.[29]

3.8f. Conclusion; the Guidelines as a Policy Statement

The Horizontal Merger Guidelines convey an impression of considerable precision in market definition. Nevertheless, the degree of uncertainty remains large. "Hypothesizing" a "small but significant" price increase in a fluctuating market, and then considering how neighboring firms will respond, requires predictive abilities not demanded by the old analysis of current prices and shipments. Furthermore, the predictions must be made in situations where the variables are manifold and complex. Even after a decade of use, it is by no means clear that the Guidelines' approach simplifies litigation or produces more consistent, judicially administrable rules.[30]

§ 3.9 Alternative Methods of Establishing Market Power

As previous sections of this chapter indicate, computation of a firm's market share involves a plethora of uncertainties. Often market share analysis fails to produce a reliable measure of a firm's market power. The exercise of the power to raise prices by reducing output leaves other traces, however, and these can sometimes be used as evidence of market power. Courts have not used the following methods exclusively to determine market power; rather, they have been used to supplement market share data and give greater strength to an inference that a firm has or does not have market power.

3.9a. Measuring Residual Demand Directly

"Residual" demand, or residual demand elasticity, refers to the demand for a particular firm's product after the sales of competitors have been taken into account. Thus we can say that a true monopolist's residual demand curve is equal to the market demand curve. By contrast, a perfect competitor's residual demand curve is horizontal, reflecting the fact that the competitor will lose all sales if it attempts to charge more than the going price.[1]

The Lerner Index is one measure of a firm's residual demand.[2] Using empirical data about the firm's marginal cost and its current

28. See §§ 4.4–4.6.

29. See § 12.8, which develops this idea further; and see 4 Antitrust Law ¶ 917 (rev. ed. 1998).

30. For criticism of the 1982 Guidelines' approach to market definition, see J. Shenefield, Market Definition and Horizontal Restraints: A Response to Professor Areeda, 52 A.B.A. Antitrust L.J. 587, 597 (1983); R. Harris & T. Jorde, Antitrust Market Definition: An Integrated Approach, 72 Calif.L.Rev. 1 (1984); R. Harris & T. Jorde, Market Definition in the Merger Guidelines: Implications for Antitrust Enforcement, 71 Calif.L.Rev. 464 (1983); J. Ordover & R. Willig, The 1982 Dep't of Justice Merger Guidelines: An Economic Assessment, 71 Calif.L.Rev. 535, 543–552 (1983).

§ 3.9

1. See § 1.1. If a perfect competitor chose to charge less than the market price it could sell all it pleased (assuming other firms maintained their price), and would thus face the entire market demand curve. See W. Landes & R. Posner, Market Power in Antitrust Cases, 94 Harv. L.Rev. 937, 945 (1981).

2. See § 3.1a.

price, the Index measures the demand elasticity facing a firm; but the Index is difficult to use because marginal cost is so difficult to measure.

Residual demand can also be measured directly if one knows the market share, the market elasticity of demand, and the elasticity of supply of competing firms.[3] But market elasticity of demand and the elasticity of supply of competing firms are not always easy to compute either. Further, this method requires defining a market and computing a market share. Thus, although it is useful for clarifying the meaning of market shares once a market share of a properly defined relevant market is known, it cannot be used as an alternative to market definition.

It would be far more useful to estimate residual demand directly without the need of market definition.[4] This is particularly true in product differentiated markets, where some competitors compete with the principal firm much more strenuously than others, but classical market definition does not generally permit us to take these differences into account. That is, we have the choice of defining the other firms as inside or outside the market, but not as something in between. For example, suppose we found an area where medium priced Buick and high priced BMW were the principal car sellers, and we want to estimate BMW's market power. Simply including Buick's output in the market understates BMWs power, because there may be many people with strong preferences for BMW, and who are willing to pay a monopoly price. By contrast, excluding Buick's output altogether exaggerates BMW's power, because Buick does in fact provide substantial competition.

The most promising approach is to measure the response of the firm to "cost shocks." A "cost shock" occurs when a firm faces a cost increase (or decrease) that does not affect other firms in the market.[5] When a perfect competitor experiences a unique cost increase it has no choice but to absorb the loss in net revenue. For example, if bolts are produced in a perfectly competitive market and one particular firm experiences labor problems that increase its labor costs above those of rivals, the firm does not have the option of raising price.[6]

3. Expressing the demand elasticities as positive numbers, where ε_d^r denotes the elasticity of the dominant firm's residual demand curve, ε^d denotes the elasticity of demand for the good, ε_f^s denotes the elasticity of the competitive fringe's supply curve, and S_d denotes the dominant firm's share of total production. Let $Q_d^r(P)$ denote residual demand for the dominant firm, $Q^d(P)$ denote demand for the homogeneous good, and $Q_f^s(P)$ denote the supply of the competitive fringe. Then $Q_d^r = Q^d - Q_f^s$; differentiating with respect to price and multiplying through by $(-P/Q_d^r)$ yields:

$$\varepsilon_d^r = -\frac{P}{Q_r}\frac{\partial Q^d}{\partial P} + \frac{P}{Q_r}\frac{\partial Q_f^s}{\partial P},$$

Where ε denotes the elasticity of the respective function. Multiplying the first term on the right hand side by Q^d/Q^d and the second term by Q_f^s/Q_f^s, and letting $S_d = Q_d^r/Q^d$ denote the share of the dominant firm, we have;

$$\varepsilon_d^r = \frac{\varepsilon^d + (1-S_d)\,\varepsilon_f^s}{S_d}.$$

[621a]

4. *Drawing* a residual demand curve on the basis of assumptions about the market demand curve, the principal firm's marginal cost curve, and the supply curve facing competitors, is relatively easy. See Figure 1 and the accompanying discussion in § 3.5a of this chapter.

The demand curve for a proposed antitrust market is nothing more than the residual demand curve facing a defined group of producers. Indeed, the "price increase" methodology of the Merger Guidelines is nothing more than a mechanism for measuring the residual demand elasticity of the grouping of firms under consideration. See D. Scheffman & P. Spiller, Geographic Market Definition Under the Department of Justice Merger Guidelines, 30 J.L. & Econ. 123 (1987).

5. One particular value of the cost shock approach is that firm specific cost shocks are more readily found in product differentiated markets, where market share information is least useful. For example, given the different technologies used to produce cellophane and other flexible wrapping materials, it would be easier to find a cost change that affected the cellophane producers but not the producers of waxed paper, aluminum foil and so on.

6. As Figure 2 on the next page shows, the perfect competitor faces a horizontal demand curve. When its marginal costs rise from MC to MC′ it reduces output, but if it attempted to raise price it would lose all sales. The profit maximizing strategy for the firm is to continue to equate price and marginal cost, thus reducing output from Q to Q′ but leaving Price the same.

By contrast, when the firm with substantial market power experiences an increase in costs, it simultaneously reduces output and raises price.[7] By observing the price increase that results from a particular cost increase that is unique to that firm, an economics expert can measure the degree of market power that the firm had at the time the cost shock occurred.[8] Doing this does not require a market definition. As noted previously, however antitrust policy may require a market definition for other reasons.[9] In all events, using the method requires a trained expert economist.[10]

3.9b. Persistent Price Discrimination[11]

Not all purchasers of widgets place the same value on them. Suppose that the marginal cost of producing a widget is $1.00. Some buyers will be willing to pay exactly $1.00 for them, others $1.25, others $1.50. A seller can maximize its profits by selling every widget to a customer for the largest price that particular customer is willing to pay. Competition prevents such persistent price discrimination from occurring, however. Even though a particular customer is willing to pay $1.50 for a widget, the customer would prefer to pay $1.00 and will do so if it can find a willing seller. Competition tends to drive all sales to the competitive price.

The monopolist has the power to discriminate, however, provided that it can identify and segregate groups of customers who place different values on the monopolist's product. Not all sellers with market power can engage in price discrimination. For example, arbitrage occurs when the buyers who pay a low price resell the product to buyers asked to pay a high price. If the monopolist cannot prevent arbitrage, then price discrimination may not work. So the absence of price discrimination

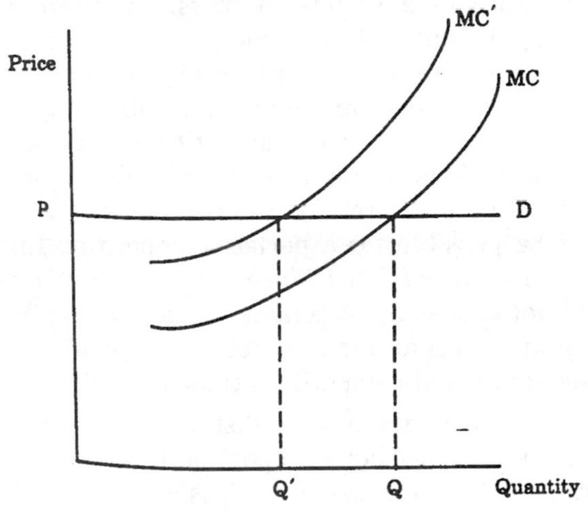

Figure 2

[614a]

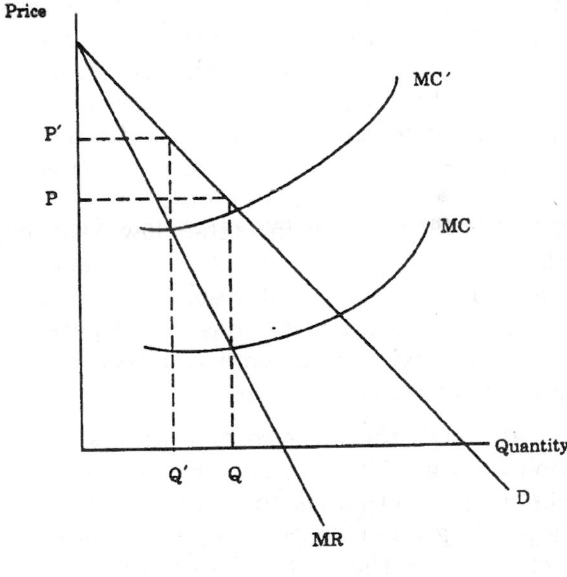

Figure 3

[615a]

7. As Figure 3 illustrates, the firm with market power responds to a cost increase from MC to MC′ by doing two things: (1) reducing output from Q to Q′; and (2) raising price from P to P′. The ratio of the quantity change to the price change expresses the residual demand that the firm faces at the time the cost increase occurs. For a firm's profit-maximizing markup to be at least 10% of its price, its residual demand elasticity must be no greater than 10.

8. The technical methodology is described in more detail in 2A Antitrust Law ¶ 525 (rev. ed.); J. Baker & T. Bresnahan, The Gains from Merger or Collusion in Product–Differentiated Industries, 33 J. Indus. Econ. 427 (June 1985); Baker & Bresnahan, Estimating the Residual Demand Curve Facing a Single Firm, 6 Int'l J. Indus. Org. 283 (1988). For a less technical summary, see J. Baker & T. Bresnahan, Empirical Methods of Identifying and Measuring Market Power, 61 Antitrust L.J. 3 (1992).

9. See § 3.1c.

10. For application to geographic market delineation, see Scheffman & Spiller, note 4.

11. For a more complete discussion of price discrimination, see ch. 14.

does not necessarily show the absence of market power. A corollary is that the mere fact that some customers are willing to pay a higher price is not evidence of market power unless the higher price is actually charged. In the *du Pont* (Cellophane) decision the Supreme Court refused to conclude that cellophane was a relevant market from the fact that certain buyers, such as cigarette manufacturers, were willing to pay a very high price for cellophane before switching to other wrapping materials.[12] By contrast, in *Grinnell* the Court found that central station alarm systems were a relevant antitrust market because customers strongly preferred them to alternative systems and would apparently pay a monopoly price before switching.[13] The decisions are not inconsistent. In *du Pont* an attempt at price discrimination would have been defeated by arbitrage. For example, if *du Pont* had attempted to charge the low elasticity cigarette manufacturers $3.00 per unit, while it charged the high elasticity bakers only $1.00, bakers would resell the cellophane to cigarette manufacturers and the price discrimination would not work. This suggests that in the *absence* of observed price discrimination there is little justification for dividing up customers into classes based on willingness to pay, and finding smaller relevant markets covering the low elasticity classes. By contrast, in *Grinnell* customers could not purchase and resell the accredited central station alarm systems, which were subscription services that required direct, ongoing provision from the seller to the buyer.

Although the absence of price discrimination does not show absence of market power, the presence of persistent price discrimination is pretty good evidence that a seller has market power in the high priced markets.[14] Further, it is often much easier to measure price discrimination empirically than it is to determine the difference between a seller's prices and its marginal costs. For example, if we see widely different prices being charged to two groups of customers for whom the cost of service seems to be about the same, we suspect price discrimination and may be able to measure it, even though we know nothing about the seller's marginal costs.

Only "persistent" price discrimination is evidence of market power. Price discrimination is a common occurrence, even in the most competitive of markets. Prices fluctuate daily as markets are continually shocked by new information and changing supply and demand conditions. Price discrimination is good evidence of market power only when a particular seller has been able systematically to achieve a higher rate of return from one group of customers than it does from another.[15]

A seller with market power can price discriminate in a variety of ways. In *Alcoa*, for example, Judge Hand noted that Alcoa had different rates of return for aluminum ingot, aluminum sheet, and aluminum cable, depending on the amount of competition it faced in the particular section of the aluminum market.[16] Such differential rates of return would not be possible for a perfect competitor. Likewise in *United Shoe Machinery* Judge Wyzanski noted that the defendant leased its machinery at different rates of return, depending on the amount of competition that it faced.[17]

A very common price discrimination mechanism is the variable proportion tying arrangement.[18] Often a seller or lessor will grant a customer one product only on the condition that it take another. In the 1936 IBM case, for example, IBM was accused of leasing comput-

12. United States v. E.I. du Pont de Nemours & Co., 351 U.S. 377, 399, 76 S.Ct. 994, 1009 (1956).

13. United States v. Grinnell Corp., 384 U.S. 563, 566–567, 86 S.Ct. 1698, 1701–1702 (1966).

14. Or alternatively, the markets where the cost of providing the product or service is smallest.

15. Price discrimination may sometimes be evidence that the market contains one or more powerful, monopsony *buyers*, rather than a monopoly seller. A monopsonist may be able to reduce its demand for a product and buy at a lower price. A seller who deals with the monopsonist as well as other buyers may be price discriminating even though it has no market power. See 12 Antitrust Law ¶ 2011 (1999).

16. United States v. Aluminum Co. of America, 148 F.2d 416, 438 (2d Cir.1945).

17. United States v. United Shoe Machinery, 110 F.Supp. 295, 297 (D.Mass.1953), affirmed, 347 U.S. 521, 74 S.Ct. 699 (1954).

18. See § 10.6e.

ing machines only to lessees who also agreed to purchase paper computing cards from IBM. Assuming that IBM's rate of return on paper cards was higher than its rate of return on the machine itself, IBM was in fact price discriminating against lessees who were heavy users.[19] A lessee who made, say, 1000 computations daily requiring one card each, placed a higher value on the machine itself than a lessee who made only 10 computations per day. By charging the same, fairly low rate for the machine to all lessees (say, a 5% rate of return) and a higher rate for the cards (say, 25%) IBM could effectively receive a much higher overall rate of return from high volume users of the machine.

IBM's price discrimination scheme could be successful, however, only if IBM had market power in the market for the computing machines. If there had been significant competition in the computing machine market, then the high volume purchasers—those asked to pay the supracompetitive overall price—would have leased or purchased their computing machines from someone willing to give them a more competitive rate. The law of tie-ins generally requires a plaintiff to show that the defendant has market power in the tying product. Often, however, that market power can be inferred from the mere existence of the variable proportion tying arrangement.[20]

Persistent price discrimination is fairly good evidence that a seller has *some* market power. But quantifying market power on the basis of price discrimination is difficult. The success of a price discrimination scheme depends on the seller's market power *and* on its ability to segregate customers and prevent arbitrage. The fact that a seller discriminates in a relatively narrow range may indicate that the seller cannot segregate customers very effectively, not that it has only a small amount of market power. Another seller with far less market power may be much more successful at price discrimination if buyers in its market can more easily be segregated and arbitrage prevented, perhaps because the buyers are not as well informed. As a result evidence of price discrimination may be fairly useful in tying arrangement cases, where the market power requirements are relatively small. It may also be useful in a cartel case to prove that the defendants are colluding. It is somewhat less useful in a monopolization case, where proof of "monopoly power" is necessary.

3.9b1. Price Discrimination and Intellectual Property

In markets where variable costs are extremely low, the antitrust fact finder must be particularly wary of price discrimination evidence. Markets for intellectual property are a good example. The licensing fees for patents, copyrights, performance rights, or trademarks are largely a return on prior investments. The cost that the licensor currently incurs is often little more than the transaction costs of negotiating the agreement. Further, such licensing arrangements often base payment (royalties) on usage or profitability to the licensee. Since the licensor's costs do not vary with the licensee's use, these are clear price discrimination devices.

For example, suppose that White Castle, a fast food franchisor, licenses its White Castle trademark and various copyrights to individual franchisees. The cost of negotiating these licensing arrangements is the only cost that the franchisor incurs, which is $100 per contract, and the contracts are redone each year. Royalties under the arrangement are 1% of sales; so the franchisee who sells $10,000 annually pays White Castle $100, or the competitive (marginal cost) price. But the franchisee who does $30,000 of business annually pays White Castle $300, and the franchisee who does $100,000 of business pays $1000. In this case, both the Lerner Index and direct measurements of price discrimination suggest that White Castle has a very large amount of market power. With respect to the largest buyers

19. IBM Corp. v. United States, 298 U.S. 131, 136, 56 S.Ct. 701, 704 (1936).

20. The existence of a variable proportion tie-in is not necessarily evidence of market power, however. The tie could be a nondiscriminatory metering device that simply measures the wear and tear on the machine. See § 10.6e.

(franchisees) it is obtaining a price ten times its marginal costs.

In fact, White Castle could be a struggling competitor among fast food chains, with franchisees barely surviving and its own returns barely enough to cover its prior investment. The reason is that in this particular market a true marginal cost price is never enough to enable the firm to recover its fixed cost investment. As a result, marginal cost does not determine the price, and the presence of price discrimination (technically, the ratio of price to marginal cost) tells us little about the firm's monopoly power. That is to say, White Castle may have absolutely no power to increase the price of fast food franchises generally by reducing its output of such franchises; nevertheless, its franchise arrangements reflect a great deal of price discrimination.

3.9b2. Price Discrimination and Market Definition

Price discrimination evidence is useful not only as an *alternative* mechanism for measuring market power, but also as a mechanism for helping us define the traditional antitrust market. For example, suppose we have established the threshold of our market power concern as the ability to raise price above cost by 10%. We now observe that a seller of widgets has segregated two groups of buyers, whether by geography or by configuration of the product. Costs of serving the buyers appear to be the same, but one group of buyers pays $1.00 per widget while the other group pays $1.15.

We do not know the seller's marginal cost, but we assume that the $1.00 price is equal to marginal cost. It might exceed marginal cost, but that only increases the seller's total market power. Assuming the low price equals marginal cost, the high priced sales must be 15% higher than marginal cost. With this information we can conclude either (a) that the grouping of sales to the high priced buyers constitutes a relevant market; or (b) that with respect to the high priced buyers the market power requirement has been met, without the need to define a relevant market.

3.9c. Persistent Monopoly Profits

Courts have frequently acknowledged high profits as evidence that a firm has market power, or absence of high profits as evidence that it does not.[21] Such evidence comes with enormous, potentially disabling qualifications, however. First, accounting profits are not the same thing as economic profits. Second, the fact-finder must be able to distinguish between monopoly profits and "rents."

3.9c1. Monopoly Profits v. Accounting Profits

Economic profits are profits in excess of the amount that is necessary to sustain investment in the industry. Thus a firm that is earning "zero profits" may still be paying its expenses and providing a dividend to its shareholders. It will simply be earning a competitive return. By contrast, "accounting profits" refers to a collection of conventions used by accountants for reporting the difference between a firm's revenues and its expenses during a given time period. The differences between the two concepts of profit are significant. Indeed, some people believe they are so significant that monopoly power simply cannot be inferred from the data produced by accountants.[22]

The difference between economic profit, which is the true measure of market power, and accounting profit, is not merely a question of data. There are important conceptual differences. Accountants generally divide the world into finite time periods, such as years or quar-

21. In *du Pont* (cellophane), 351 U.S. 377, 76 S.Ct. 994 (1956), discussed in § 3.4b, the evidence indicated that du Pont had an extraordinarily high rate of return on cellophane: 31% before taxes. 351 U.S. at 420, 76 S.Ct. at 1020 (Chief Justice Warren, dissenting). In other markets, such as rayon, du Pont's rate of return was much lower. Id. at 420–421 n. 15, 76 S.Ct. at 1020. See also Borden, Inc. v. FTC, 674 F.2d 498, 512 (6th Cir.1982), vacated on other grounds, 461 U.S. 940, 103 S.Ct. 2115 (1983) (high profits supported other findings that Borden had monopoly power). See R. Pitofsky, New Definitions of Relevant Market and the Assault on Antitrust, 90 Col.L.Rev. 1805, 1846–1847 (1990).

22. For example, F. Fisher & J. McGowan, On the Misuse of Accounting Rates of Return to Infer Monopoly Profits, 73 Am. Econ. Rev. 82 (March 1983); 74 Am. Econ. Rev. 492 (June 1984).

ters, and consider "profits" earned over those periods. By contrast, the economist's measure of profits looks at an investment over its lifetime, from development, through marketing and sales, until it is closed out. Second, accounting profits reflect the way durable equipment is depreciated, and the rate of depreciation may bear little relation to the useful life of the asset—as, for example, when depreciation at a certain rate is required by the tax laws. Third, accounting data is generally aggregated over a firm, a plant or a division. By contrast, economists generally consider the profitability of each product separately.

Perhaps most importantly, economic profits include the opportunity costs of capital, while accounting profits do not. This has various implications. First, the opportunity cost of capital itself shows up as a profit in the accountant's ledger. For the economist, by contrast, capital that is earning only its opportunity cost, or a "reasonable" rate of return, is not earning profits at all; economic profits are only those profits earned *in excess of* the opportunity cost of the capital supplied. So a firm earning zero in economic profits is nevertheless paying its investors the opportunity cost of their capital—or the same rate that they could get in an alternative competitive investment of equivalent risk.

In other ways, accounting data considers opportunity costs only sporadically. For example, suppose a firm needs a large building for storage purposes. If the firm rents the building for $5000 monthly, the accountant will carry the building as a cost. By contrast, if the building is owned and has already been depreciated, the accountant will likely attribute no cost to the building itself, other than maintenance, taxes and the like. But the value of the building is an opportunity cost of capital whether or not the building is owned. That is, the firm could either sell the building or rent it to someone else for $5000 a month, if it were not using the building itself. By not showing this opportunity cost, accounting data tends to show a "profit" rate higher than true economic profits.

Does all of this mean that accounting data is worthless? Not necessarily. For example, suppose we had identical firms whose accountants use precisely the same techniques to measure accounting profits. Over an extended period, say ten years or more, the first firms shows returns of 10% and the second shows returns of 30%. The second firm's ability to earn revenues substantially above economic costs must account for the difference. Importantly, this observation tells us little about how much market power the second firm has. For example, we still know nothing about price/marginal cost ratios. But perhaps we could confirm a finding of market power based on other methods of analysis.

Secondly, useful conclusions can be drawn from accounting data if we can adjust them to consider the true cost of a firm's capital, including the opportunity costs, or estimated market value, of owned assets that are fully depreciated.[23]

In all events, the time period over which accounting profits are examined must generally be much longer than the time period for determining market share. Market share data based on one or two years of sales usually gives a fairly good reading, although particularly volatile or "lumpy" markets may require a longer period. By contrast, evidence taken from profits should ordinarily involve a period of at least five years or so. High profits may be a sign that a market is expanding, that a particular firm has fully depreciated major capital components, is in the "return" rather than "development" stage of numerous projects, that the economy is in a robust phase where the firm is operating at full capacity, or other things, none of which necessarily suggests a high degree of market power.

3.9c2. *Absence of High Accounting Profits*

Relying on the absence of high accounting profits to infer lack of power is just as unreliable as the converse. First, as § 1.3c shows, "rent-seeking" behavior by the monopolist may swallow up most or even all of its monop-

23. See 2A Antitrust Law ¶ 520 (rev. ed. 1995). Likewise, market power can also be proven from price-cost margins, although the technique is rarely used. Id. at ¶ 521.

oly profits, giving it a competitive rate of return. Second, if the firm, or some of its assets, already had monopoly power the last time they were sold, the current owners may have paid a purchase price that included the capitalized value of future monopoly profits. In that case, the firm will earn a competitive rate of return on the current owners' actual investment. A good example is the New York City taxicab medallion. Because of entry restrictions and price regulation, a New York City taxicab earns substantially more than the competitive rate of return for one car and one driver. Does this mean that the current owners of taxicabs are making monopoly profits? Not necessarily. They may have paid $300,000 each for the medallion that each cab needs. Once the opportunity cost of the additional $300,000 is factored in, the current owners are probably obtaining only a competitive rate of return.

This phenomenon is particularly true of publicly traded stocks where the price is typically determined by such things as price/earnings (P/E) ratios, which assess value on the basis of current earnings. For example, if Alcoa is currently a monopolist earning monopoly profits, stock purchasers will bid its price up to the point that its P/E is about the same as for other firms in its class. At that point, the firm is earning only a competitive return on the price that the new shareholders paid. The monopoly profits have gone to the selling shareholders.

3.9c3. *The Problem of "Rents."*

Not all firms in a competitive market have identical costs. First-comers, for example, are likely to take advantage of the best sites and leave increasingly marginal sites for those who come later.

Figure 4 illustrates the problem in a competitive market, in which each firm faces a horizontal demand curve. The industry supply curve, however, rises to competitive equilibrium at its intersection with the demand curve. If the price at that point (the competitive market price) is $20, then we know that the least efficient firm (the marginal firm) capable of sustaining itself in the market is a firm whose costs are $20. The market may contain other firms whose costs are much less than $20. These firms may make high profits even though they are not monopolists—that is, they may have a trivial share of the market and no power to charge a higher price by reducing their output.

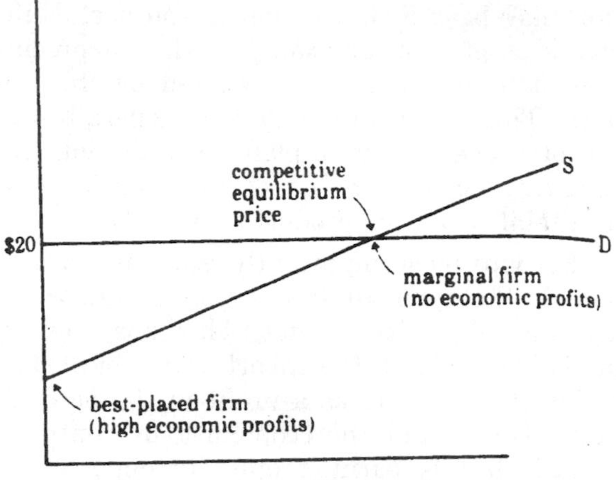

Figure 4

For example, in the 30 years from 1950 to 1980 real estate prices in San Francisco increased as much as twentyfold. San Francisco has approximately 100 Continental restaurants. Some of those restaurants have been in business for more than 20 years, and their owners bought their locations when both real estate prices and interest rates were low. Today those restaurants have mortgage payments of $200 per month, or perhaps no mortgage payments at all. At the other extreme are new entrants who must pay rentals on the order of $4000 per month. No restaurant is a monopolist. Further, the old restaurants generally do not have the power to increase their seating capacity at their original costs—any new space they acquire will be at the same high rate as their newer competitors. However, if the cost of restaurant space is a substantial part of the cost of operating a restaurant, the old restaurants with the low costs will earn higher profits than the new restaurants which have much higher space costs. Furthermore, the best-placed restaurants' low cost space is protected from new entry: any newcomer will have to pay the higher rental rate. These rents, unlike monopoly profits, are not likely to be consumed by the best-placed restaurants' efforts to retain their monopoly position.

Rents are commonplace in most competitive businesses. Some farmers have fertile soil or ample irrigation supplies, or both; some have neither. Some miners have rich reserves, others marginal.

Perhaps the most important difference between rents and monopoly profits is that the firm that operates in a competitive market but that has a low cost asset prices its output at marginal cost, just as other competitors. It has no power to raise the market price by reducing its own output, so it faces the same horizontal demand curve as everyone else. It is simply making a higher rate of return on its sales. For this additional reason one must not infer monopoly power too quickly from accounting data showing a high rate of return.

The technically correct treatment of rents, if they can be identified as such, is to treat them as part of cost. So for purposes of measuring market power, the San Francisco rental house should be valued at its current market value, not its historical value. Current market value reflects the true opportunity cost of the capital that the building's owner is supplying. The relevant question is not the amount of her original investment, but the amount that she could earn if she sold the house. Likewise, the superior farmland should be valued at its current fair market value; if that land were sold today at its market price, the new owner would probably earn zero returns on his investment. Of course, this suggests the importance of distinguishing clearly between rents and monopoly profits. The monopoly asset will also claim a price calculated to give its new buyer a merely competitive return.[24]

3.9d. Market Power and Intellectual Property.

For many years courts in tying arrangement cases have indulged a presumption that market power in the tying product can be presumed if the tying product is patented.[25] Other courts have extended the presumption to copyrights and occasionally even to trademarks.[26] As a general matter these presumptions have not been extended to other antitrust violations, such as monopolization or attempt. Indeed, in *Walker Process*, an attempt to monopolize case, the Supreme Court agreed in principle that fraudulent procurement of a patent could be a violation, but it remanded for a determination whether the patent created any market power.[27] At least for attempt cases, the presumption seems not to apply.[28]

The entire notion that an intellectual property right creates market power is belied by one simple fact: such rights are very easy to obtain. In the case of a copyright, one need only write down a few words and mail a copy with the required fee to the copyright office. Getting a trademark is not much more difficult. Obtaining a patent is a little harder, because the patent application must provide evidence that the device or process for which a patent is sought is new, useful and nonobvious. Once again, however, patents are rather easily granted, and most of them have no commercial value.

24. One final possibility for using price-cost data to estimate market power is direct measurement: For example, many firms have average variable costs that are relatively constant over a wide range of output choices. When the bottom of the average variable cost curve is flat, marginal cost and average variable cost are identical through that range. This suggest that there are circumstances where average variable cost can be used as a surrogate for marginal cost in measuring market power. Once again, however, the method must be used with great care. The firm that is recovering only its average variable costs is not earning the opportunity cost of its capital, for its fixed costs are not covered. As a result, depreciation values must be factored in. Further, allocation of expenses for such things as advertising and research as fixed or variable may present large areas for discretion. See 2A Antitrust Law ¶ 521 (rev. ed. 1995).

25. For example, see the dicta in Jefferson Parish Hosp. Dist. No. 2 v. Hyde, 466 U.S. 2, 16–17, 104 S.Ct. 1551, 1560–1561 (1984). See § 10.3c; and 2A Antitrust Law ¶ 523 (rev. ed. 1995).

26. See generally, § 10.3c, which summarizes the case law.

27. Walker Process Equipment, Inc. v. Food Machinery & Chemical Corp., 382 U.S. 172, 86 S.Ct. 347 (1965).

28. See also Abbott Labs. v. Brennan, 952 F.2d 1346 (Fed.Cir.1991), cert. denied, 505 U.S. 1205, 112 S.Ct. 2993 (1992) (patent creates no presumption of market power in a monopolization case).

Intellectual property rights are a fact of life in modern markets, where each firm seeks product differentiation in the eyes of consumers. Toasters, cameras, small computers, lamps and laundry detergents are all protected by patent rights, but all are sold in markets that range from moderately to robustly competitive. Likewise, fast food restaurants, grocery stores, clothing stores and banks have copyrights or trademarks protecting their various products, slogans, symbols, or advertisements. All of these markets are competitive—some, such as grocery stores, are intensely competitive. In many, entry is quite easy and the market shares of most individual firms quite small. Putting it bluntly, to presume market power in a product simply because it is protected by intellectual property is nonsense.[29]

Does this mean that the presence of intellectual property rights is absolutely irrelevant to market power questions? Not entirely. On the demand side, one can seldom infer that an intellectual property right so strengthens customer appeal that they are willing to pay a monopoly price rather than substitute. But on the supply side, intellectual property rights can restrict entry. This is particularly true of patents.

For example, suppose a paint manufacturer develops a process that makes its paint more durable than the paint of competitors, without increasing the cost. Customers prefer this 12–year paint to the 8–year paint offered by rivals, and they are willing to pay more if no one else manufacturers the superior paint as well. Now the scope of the patent right may be able to tell us something about the nature and duration of the monopoly in question. If the patented process is really needed to make the better paint, then the patent operates as an entry deterrence device. If, as a result, the paint manufacturer can reduce the output of the better paint and raise its price for a substantial length of time, the better paint defines a relevant market.

Note that the existence of the patent is only one element in this analysis. Every major paint manufacturer probably has patents covering its products. But most patents cover fairly idiosyncratic differences in manufacturing process or product. They serve to keep the processes or products of rivals from being absolutely identical—that is, they facilitate product differentiation. But just as the various products in a product differentiated market are not ordinarily relevant markets unto themselves, so to the intellectual property rights themselves do not serve to turn competitors into monopolists.

The case for inferring market power from copyrights or trademarks is even weaker. Often the debate reduces to no more than the question whether advertising has a durable, or capital, value. If brand name advertising is merely a variable cost investment that informs current customers but has little or no accumulated value, then brand names themselves confer no market power. By contrast, if advertising has a significant durable component, then built-up advertising may serve as a barrier to entry.[30] Once again, however, the presence of a copyright or trademark is only one, fairly small factor in the analysis. Further, the relevance of copyrights or trademarks pertains to entry barriers as such, not to market power. A market may be quite competitive notwithstanding high entry barriers. For example, entry barriers into automobile manufacturing are quite high, and all manufacturer use an array of trademarks and copyrights as well as patents to protect their products. But the market is presumably quite competitive already. It would be quite far fetched to conclude that any particular model's distinctive, copyrighted advertisement or trademarked insignia conferred any substantial degree of market power.

29. In 1988 the Patent Act was amended to provide that tying of unpatented to patented products does not qualify as "patent misuse," with this qualifier: "unless, in view of the circumstances, the patent owner has market power in the relevant market for the patented product."35 U.S.C.A. § 271(d)(5). This is tantamount to Congressional recognition that market power in a patented product is something that must be proven separately.

30. See § 12.6b. Advertising is generally a sunk cost, which cannot be recovered in the event of failure; so the need to engage in substantial advertising at entry time can make entry less attractive.

Part II

THE SUBSTANCE OF ANTITRUST

Chapter 4

ANTITRUST POLICY TOWARD COLLUSION AND OLIGOPOLY

Table of Sections

---

§ 4.1 Introduction: The Basic Economics of Price Fixing

A cartel is an agreement among otherwise competing firms to reduce their output to agreed upon levels, or sell at an agreed upon price. The firms acting in concert can earn monopoly profits just as a single-firm monopolist.[1] Price fixing is said to be "naked" when it involves no more than an agreement to restrict output or raise price, with no collateral agreements organizing production or distribution.[2] In that case, the agreement is profitable only if the firms jointly have the power to raise market prices by reducing output.[3] Naked price

§ 4.1

1. On price and output of the monopolist, see § 1.2. According to the Coase theorem two or more firms bargaining together will maximize joint profits, which in the case of a perfect cartel occurs when its price and output are equal to that of a monopolist. See 12 Antitrust Law ¶ 2002b (1999); R. Coase, The Problem of Social Cost, 3 J.L. & Econ. 1 (1960).

2. In fact, however, almost any output restriction agreement "allocates" output and creates at least the potential for realizing some production efficiencies.

3. On this definition of "naked" restraints, see § 5.1; for elaboration, see 11 Antitrust Law ¶ 1906 (1998).

fixing is not only illegal *per se*, it is also a felony.[4]

In general, joint conduct of competitors warrants closer antitrust scrutiny and more severe rules than those that apply to single firm conduct.[5] This is true even though cartels are inherently more volatile than single-firm monopolists. First, they can come into existence far more easily. The formation of a monopoly may take many years of mergers, superior research and development, marketing, predation or simply good luck. By contrast, a cartel theoretically can be created overnight.

At the same time, however, the cartel is inherently more fragile than the monopolist. The interests of the cartel as a whole often diverge substantially from the interests of individual members. The nature of a cartel is to invite cheating by members. Often cleverly disguised cheating can impose rather small losses on the cartel as a whole, but give large gains to the individual cheater. If enough cartel members cheat, however, the cartel will fall apart. As a result, many cartels go to extraordinary lengths to reduce the opportunities for cheating.

In order for a cartel to succeed for any length of time, six conditions must exist:

(1) The product or service to be cartelized must define a relevant market with sufficiently high barriers to entry that newcomers cannot undermine the cartel's pricing decisions.[6]

(2) The cartel members must produce a sufficiently large share of the product or service that their decisions are not undermined by producers who are not cartel members; further, these nonmembers must be unable or unwilling to expand their own output rapidly.

(3) The cartel members must be able to arrive at an agreement about the output that each cartel member will produce—in most cases the important decision variable is *output*, not price.

(4) The cartel must be able to detect cheating on the cartel by cartel members.

(5) The cartel must be able to punish cheating effectively when it is detected.

(6) The cartel must be able to do all these things without being detected from the outside.[7]

The perfect cartel would contain relatively few members who collectively account for 100% of production in a relevant market. All members would be the same size and equally efficient, and they would produce identical products. The product would be sold by sealed auction bids made by the sellers in a market containing many, relatively small purchasers, and the winning bids publicly announced.

The cartel would have the most success in raising price by reducing output if its members controlled 100% of the market. If they were equally efficient and produced identical products, they would all have the same profit-maximizing price and would agree quite easily about a cartel price. If they were the same size they would have little trouble allocating the output reduction among members. If the cartel had relatively few members, made its sales by sealed auction bids with publicly announced results, and sold to a large number of small buyers, there would be little opportunity for cheating.[8]

The real world contains few such markets. The products of different competing firms often differ from each other, and the firms vary even more. Few markets make their sales by simple auction bidding. The variations from one market to another are considerable. As a

4. See § 15.1a.

5. On the rationale for treating multilateral conduct more severely than unilateral conduct, see § 5.1b.

6. On market definition and entry barriers, see ch. 3 and §§ 1.6, 12.6.

7. The stability of cartels varies widely, and in one study of immune cartels a quarter of them were found to have lasted fifteen years or more. See A. Dick, When Are Cartels Stable Contracts?, 39 J. L. & Econ. 241, 242 (1996).

8. For evidence that cartels are most successful in such situations see Hay & Kelley, An Empirical Survey of Price Fixing Conspiracies, 17 J.L. & Econ. 13 (1974). See also A. Dick, Identifying Contracts, Combinations and Conspiracies in Restraint of Trade, 17 Managerial & Decision Econ. (1996).

result, some markets are more conducive to cartelization than others, and in some markets effective cartelization is impossible.

Theoretically, the cartel would determine its profit-maximizing price just as a single-firm monopoly does. For example, if the cartel controlled 100% of the market and new entry was blockaded or relatively slow,[9] the cartel price would be determined by the intersection of the market's marginal revenue curve with the cartel's supply curve—effectively, the marginal cost curve of the cartel as a whole.[10] The cartel faces problems that the monopolist does not, however, because individual members of the cartel generally have different costs: some are more efficient than others; different firms may operate on different portions of their average cost curves (for example, some may have excess capacity while others do not); some may produce slightly different products, which cost either a little less or a little more than the product sold by other cartel members.

Figure 1 illustrates some of these difficulties. Assume for simplicity's sake that three firms are the same size. Operating at optimum capacity, each would produce the same number of widgets. Firms 1 and 2 produce identical widgets, but firm 1 is more efficient. Firm 1's marginal costs are MC_1 while firm 2's marginal costs are MC_2. Firm 3 has still higher marginal costs, MC_3 but it also produces a higher quality widget that commands a higher price. As a result firm 3 operates on demand curve D′, which is to the right of demand curve D, the curve that firms 1 and 2 face in a cartelized market. At any given price, demand for firm 3's widgets is greater than the demand for widgets produced by firms 1 or 2. Likewise, at any given output level, firm 3's widgets will clear the market at a higher price. Because firm 3 faces a different demand curve, it also has a different marginal revenue curve. The marginal revenue curve for firms 1 and 2 is MR, while the marginal revenue curve for firm 3 is MR′.

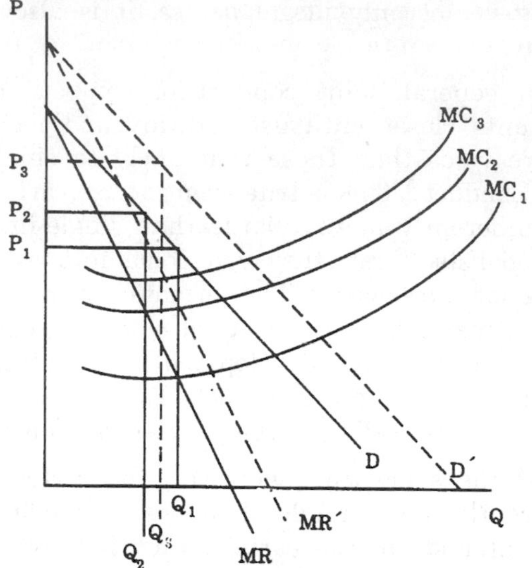

Figure 1

[616a]

Will the three firms agree about a cartel price? Firm 1 will maximize its profits at a price of P_1, firm 2 at a price of P_2, and firm 3 at a price of P_3. Any cartel price reached by the three firms will be a compromise. A firm whose individual profit-maximizing price deviates substantially from the compromise price is likely to feel cheated, and may be more likely to cheat on the cartel. The wider the variations in the marginal costs or the products produced by the individual cartel members, the less stable the cartel will be.[11] One commonly held theory is that when individual firms' profit-maximizing prices differ, the firm with the lowest profit-maximizing price will be likely to prevail in any dispute about the price the cartel should charge, because the low cost firm can steal sales from the others simply by charging its profit-maximizing price—that is, if every firm charged its profit-maximizing price, the firm with the lowest price would gain market share at the expense of others.

The three firms in the above illustration would probably not agree on a single price at

9. On entry barriers and "blockaded" entry, see § 1.6.

10. If the monopolist or cartel controlled less than 100% of the market, or if entry at the monopoly price was likely, the profit-maximizing price would be lower, lest market share would erode too quickly. See § 1.2c.

11. For a more technical discussion, see R. Schmalensee, Competitive Advantage and Collusive Optima, 5 Int'l. J. Ind. Org. 351 (1987).

all. Since Firm 3 produces a superior product, under single price collusion customers would buy all of Firm 3's output first. The only solution may be a price schedule, or an agreement on one cartel price for Firms 1 and 2, and a higher price for 3.

4.1a. The (Virtual) Universality of Cartel Cheating

Incentives to cheat are present even in the most homogeneous of cartels. They are merely exacerbated by heterogeneity. If the cartel is successful each member will be selling its output at a price such that its own individual marginal revenues exceed its marginal costs. If a member can secretly make sales at a lower price, it can enlarge its own profits, either by attracting buyers unwilling to pay the cartel price but willing to pay the "shaved" price, or else by stealing buyers from other cartel members.

4.1a1. Divergence Between Cartel and Single Firm Profit Maximization

The optimal cartel sets output the way a monopolist would, which is to equate *cartel-wide* marginal revenue with marginal cost. But for each individual cartel member, the marginal revenue obtained from a sale is significantly higher than the firm's marginal cost because the cartel member absorbs only a fraction of the price reduction that accompanies an output increase. For example, when a monopolist increases output from 100 units to 101 units, it must consider that the price for all 101 units will be lower as a result of the output increase.[12] When one member of an identical-firm ten-member cartel increases output by one unit, the market price of all units drops by the same amount, but the cartel member experiences these losses only for the ten units that it is producing.

Consider this example. The monopolist sells widgets at a price of $10.00, and demand is 100. For simplicity, marginal cost is presumed to be constant at $5. If the monopolist increases output to 101, the price will drop to $9.90. Total revenue at output of 100 is $1000. Total revenue at output of 101 is $999.90. The monopolist will not increase output. It would lose $5.10.[13]

By contrast, if a cartel of ten identical firms operated in this same market, an individual cartel member would face this calculation. Its current output is 10 units at a price of $10.00, for total revenue of $100. If the cartel member increases output by one (and no one else increases as well), then total market output will be 101 and the market price will drop to $9.90, as in the case of the monopolist. The cheater's total revenue at output of 11 will be $108.90 ($9.90 X 11), and the output increase will yield profits of $8.90 less $5 in increased costs, or $3.90. The cartel member will increase output unless it is restrained.[14]

12. See § 1.2a.

13. When the firm increases output from 100 to 101, total revenue will go down by ten cents, and total costs will increase by $5.00.

14. Figure 2 (following page) illustrates an alternative way to consider the issue: what is the individual cartel member's profit-maximizing price, assuming that other cartel members adhere to the cartel agreement? Assuming demand curve D and constant marginal costs MC, which are identical for all cartel members, the cartel as a whole will maximize profits by equating marginal cost and marginal revenue, yielding a price of P_m. But each *individual* cartel member faces residual demand curve D_r. A residual demand curve is the demand faced by a firm, taking into account the sales made by all the other firms in the market. Note that the portion of the demand curve identified by the bracket lettered A is the demand curve that remains in the market after all sales have been made at price = P_m. That is, if everyone else held price at P_m, a seller who was not so restrained would maximize its revenue by taking the bracketed part of the demand curve as given, and equating its own marginal cost and marginal revenue. For ease of analysis, we slide this remaining demand curve to the left until its top touches the vertical axis; so it appears in the figure as D_r. The residual demand curve produces residual marginal revenue curve MR_r, and by equating residual marginal revenue for the single firm with its marginal cost we arrive at P_{cheat}, which is the price that would maximize the individual cartel member's profits, assuming no one else cheated.

Note that the cheater's decision described above is unprofitable for the remaining non-cheaters. Their output remains constant at ten units, but their price drops to $9.90. So the cheating costs each of them a dollar. Furthermore, the cheating injures the cartel as a group. It results in $9 in total losses to the nine non-cheaters, but only $3.90 in gains to the cheater. Finally, note that this incentive to cheat is totally independent of entry barriers, product differentiation, differences in levels of efficiency, in firm size and so on. Thus even the "perfect" cartel must regard cheating as a problem.

Cheating is particularly profitable in industries that have relatively high fixed costs. In the railroad industry, for example, short-run marginal costs (the costs of shipping one extra package on a partially loaded train that is already scheduled) are quite small in comparison with the total costs of operating a railroad. As a result the cartel price, which covers total costs plus monopoly profits, will be much higher than the lowest price that is profitable to the railroad. The railroad could give a substantial secret price reduction and still make large profits from the transaction.[15]

4.1a2. Cartel Cheating Strategies

A cartel member would not likely be able to make all its sales at a price less than the agreed cartel price. Such pervasive cheating would be quickly detected. Often it is more profitable and less risky for the cartel member to honor the cartel price as a general rule, but look for opportunities to make large, secret sales at a lower price.

Cheating by secret price discrimination has been rampant in many cartels, particularly secret cartels that cannot be enforced by law (such as those within the jurisdiction of the American antitrust laws).[16] The chance of detection increases with the number of sales, so it is important that the sales be large. The terms of the sale will usually be disguised in some way. For example, in the 1911 *Standard Oil* case the defendant was accused of monopolizing the oil market by obtaining "secret rebates" from railroads in exchange for its trade. The secret rebates were used to explain how Standard could undersell its competitors and drive them out of business. In fact, the railroads were engaged in price fixing, and the secret rebates enabled a cheating railroad to make a large sale to Standard at a profitable price. If two or more cartelized railroads had secretly competed for Standard's business, they would have bid the rebates up to the point that the net price equaled their marginal cost. If Standard's competitors made smaller purchases of the railroads' services, however, the railroads' incentive to give them rebates would be much less. The smaller competitor

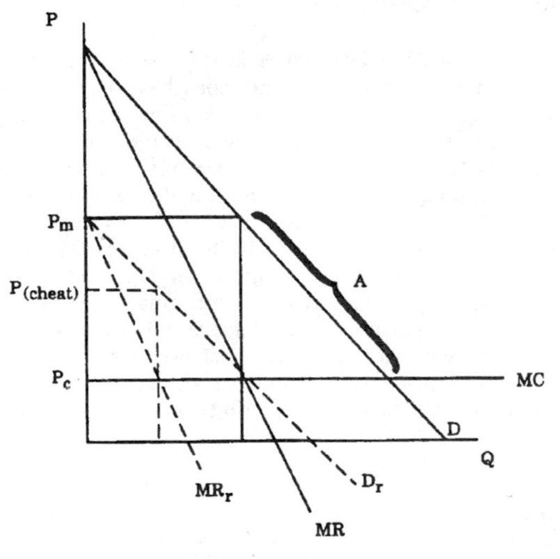

Figure 2 [617a]

Suppose a second firm wished to cheat. Given that the first firm's cheating has lowered the market price, the second cheater faces an even lower residual demand curve, and its profit-maximizing cheating price would be lower than that of the first firm. If all ten of the firms cheated, the market would stabilize at the ten-firm oligopoly level, which would yield a price only slightly above marginal cost.

15. See H. Hovenkamp, Enterprise and American Law, 1836–1937, at chs. 12 & 13 (1991).

16. For example, see the discussion of the *Addyston Pipe* cartel in 2 S. Whitney, Antitrust Policies: American Experience in 20 Industries 5 (1958); U.S. v. Addyston Pipe & Steel Co., 85 Fed. 271 (6th Cir.1898), modified and affirmed, 175 U.S. 211, 20 S.Ct. 96 (1899). If the cartel is legal, it might enlist the help of the government in prosecuting cheating. For an analysis of cheating in legal cartels, see J. McGee, Ocean Freight Rate Conferences and the American Merchant Marine, 27 U.Chi.L.Rev. 191 (1960). See also Dick article, note 7.

would end up with higher freight costs than Standard had.[17]

Cartel members have become ingenious at cheating by this kind of price discrimination. For example, a cartel member may price discriminate by designating or labeling a product in such a way that it falls out of the cartel agreement. Suppose that manufacturers of bathroom fixtures have a significant percentage of "seconds"—fixtures that are usable but have slight defects and normally command a lower price. The cartel agrees about price and output of perfect fixtures, but neglects to include seconds in the agreement. If the seconds command a price higher than the cost of producing them,[18] individual cartel members will make money by selling fixtures as seconds, even though they are perfect. The market will then become flooded with these "seconds". As soon as consumers discover this, demand for the cartelized product, designated first quality, will drop. At least one famous cartel was able to solve this problem only by an agreement that all members would destroy their seconds or ship them abroad, so that none would be sold on the domestic market.[19]

A cartel member can cheat on the cartel price in a number of ways. These include secret rebates, reciprocity agreements in which the cartel member buys something back from the customer at a supracompetitive price,[20] and increased services. In fact, often the effect of a price fixing agreement is merely to change the nature of the competition among the cartel members. Before the cartel was formed they competed in price. After they compete by throwing more and more services into the bargain until their marginal costs rise to the cartel price.[21] The cartel members then end up with no more than a competitive return. Customers take the services whether or not they would have been willing to pay their market value in a competitive market. Several empirical studies of unlawful cartels conclude that their members earn no more than the competitive rate of return, and some earn even less.[22]

The cartel might also cheat by enlisting the aid of the government. For example, the Interstate Commerce Act of 1887 condemned various kinds of price discrimination among interstate railroads. The effect of the statute may have been to facilitate collusion in the railroad industry, by prohibiting individual cartel members from making discriminatory sales.[23]

4.1a3. Detecting and Punishing Cheating

Often cartels take elaborate measures to prevent cheating. Some cartels have developed sophisticated bookkeeping, reporting or accounting methods so that each member can check the price and output of other members. Of course, such methods are useless if each member doubts that other members are providing honest disclosure. Most cartels have tried to produce alternative methods of verification—for example, by agreeing on a standard product and the services that can be provided with it, by agreeing to destroy all imperfect merchandise that would be discounted in a competitive market, by making all pricing public, or sometimes by vertically integrating into retailing so that all final output sales are small and public.

17. See Standard Oil Co. v. United States, 221 U.S. 1, 32–33, 31 S.Ct. 502, 505 (1911), charging Standard with obtaining "large preferential rates and rebates in many and devious ways over [its] competitors from various railroad companies, and * * * by means of the advantage thus obtained many, if not virtually all, competitors were forced either to become members of the combination or were driven out of business * * *." See E. Granitz & B. Klein, Monopolization by "Raising Rivals' Costs:" the Standard Oil Case, 39 J. L. & Econ. 1 (1996); and R. Chernow, *Titan: the Life of John D. Rockefeller, Sr.* 113–117, 144–147, 443–444 and *passim* (1998).

18. The cartel's price increase in perfect units will increase demand for the seconds, and their price will rise.

19. See United States v. Trenton Potteries Co., 273 U.S. 392, 405, 47 S.Ct. 377, 382 (1927). In spite of the agreement, cheating was widespread; 20 out of 24 companies were found to have done it. See 12 Antitrust Law ¶ 2003d (1999).

20. On reciprocity and collusion, see § 10.8.

21. See D. Ginsberg, Nonprice Competition, 38 Antitrust Bull. 83 (1993).

22. See P. Asch & J. Seneca, Is Collusion Profitable?, 58 Rev. Econ. & Stat. 1 (1976). However, see Dick, Stable Contracts, note 7, 39 J. L. & Econ. at 243–244, who argues that such studies skew the data by looking at condemned or challenged cartels, in which cartel enforcement costs are presumably higher because the cartel is illegal and the risk of detection requires elaborate precautions.

23. See Hovenkamp, *Enterprise*, note 15 at ch. 13.

The ease of cheating varies considerably with the type of market. Cheating is most difficult (and cartels therefore most successful) in auction markets where sales are large, relatively infrequent, and determined by secret bids with publicly announced results.[24] In such a market the cartel members will merely pick the "winning" bidder for each prospective sale and determine the bid price. All other members agree to bid a higher price. If a different member wins the bid, the cartel members will know immediately.[25] A famous cartel involving 29 American companies in the market for large electrical equipment used such schemes.[26]

By contrast, if sales are individually negotiated with specifications and terms that vary from one transaction to the next and not publicly disclosed, cheating will be far more difficult to detect. Cheating is also easy to conceal if buyers and the cartel members deal with each other outside the cartelized market. For example, if a manufacturer of widgets and gidgets is involved in a widget cartel, it might cheat by selling widgets to a firm at the cartel price but giving a compensating price reduction in gidgets. Conversely, if a cartel member sells widgets but purchases gidgets from a customer, it might sell the customer widgets at the cartel price, but pay a premium price for gidgets that it buys in return.[27]

Sometimes cartels can reduce cheating by using alternatives to the simple fixing of prices. For example, some industries may be more conducive to output restriction agreements, in which the members decide how much each should produce and sell. The market itself determines the price. This kind of agreement generally works well in industries where the government requires detailed reporting of output, or where output or number of units sold is easy to verify.

An alternative to the output reduction agreement is the agreement on market share, with penalties for firms that exceed their assigned shares.[28] Under such an agreement, each member promises to reduce its output by a certain, agreed-upon percentage. The result is that the market shares of the respective firms remain constant, although each produces less than it would under competition. Price will rise to reach a new equilibrium with output. Such an agreement can be far more flexible than a strict output reduction agreement, because it enables the parties to deal with sudden changes in demand for the product without consulting each other. In general, market share agreements discourage firms from bidding aggressively for new customers, or from trying to use low bids to steal customers away from other cartel members.

Horizontal market division can be an effective method of cartelization, although it may not work in as many markets.[29] Naked market division agreements come in three general kinds. Under horizontal territorial division, firms divide the map and agree that each one will obtain exclusive sale rights in a designated area. In a horizontal product division agreement the firms agree that each will avoid

24. See 12 Antitrust Law ¶ 2005 (1999); and United States v. Romer, 148 F.3d 359 (4th Cir.1998), cert. denied, ___ U.S. ___, 119 S.Ct. 1032 (1999) (buyer's cartel; defendant buyers of foreclosed real property at auction selected winning bidder in advance and other refrained from bidding against him); United States v. Heffernan, 43 F.3d 1144 (7th Cir.1994) (suggesting that bid-rigging should be treated more harshly than ordinarily price fixing); and see United States Sentencing Guidelines § 2R1.1 (Nov. 1, 1997) (harsher penalty for bid-rigging than ordinary price-fixing).

25. As a result, statutes regulating government procurement which require secret competitive bidding and public announcement of the winning bid can actually facilitate cartelization. See J. Joyce, The Effect of Firm Organizational Structures on the Incentives to Engage in Price Fixing, 7 Contemp. Policy Issues 19 (1989) (importance of auction markets as facilitating collusion).

26. See R. Smith, The Incredible Electrical Conspiracy, *Fortune* 224 (May 1961); F.M. Scherer & D. Ross, Industrial Market Structure and Economic Performance 236–237 (3d ed. 1990).

27. See § 10.8.

28. See G. Stigler, The Organization of Industry 42–43 (1983). E.g., United States v. Andreas, 39 F.Supp.2d 1048 (N.D.Ill.1998) (cartel assigned market share to each member).

29. Cartelization by territorial division works only if the members are able to divide a relevant market into sections such that each is a monopolist in its own section. An alternative is horizontal customer division, in which the firms agree that each will deal exclusively with certain groups of customers.

production of a designated product produced by a rival.[30] In a customer division agreement the firms agree not to compete for one another's pre-assigned customers.[31]

For example, four widget manufacturers may divide the country into exclusive zones. The effect of successful horizontal territorial division is to give each cartel member a monopoly in its territory, with a promise of no competitive entry from other members. Once each firm has an exclusive territory it is free to estimate its own profit-maximizing price and make its own output decisions. As a result the cartel may circumvent many of the problems attending a compromise agreement on price and output. Horizontal market division robs the firms of an opportunity to cheat simply by cutting price. Indeed, one important difference between price fixing and territorial division is that within a territory each firm equates its own marginal cost and marginal revenue, and thus has no incentive to cheat.[32] However, firms can still cheat by making secret sales to customers in the territory of another cartel member. This kind of cheating may be easier to detect, particularly if the firms are fully integrated to the retail level. One problem with such territorial division is that outsiders can often see what is happening. Firms who deal with the cartel members may learn quickly that each member is a monopolist in its own territory. This may invite prosecution or new entry by firms looking for an opportunity to make monopoly profits.

Detecting cheating by cartel members is one thing. Punishing it is quite another. Most importantly, cartels are illegal, and the members of a cartel cannot take cheaters to court. They must devise ways to punish cheaters that simultaneously (a) make cheating unprofitable without (b) causing public discovery of the cartel. Even if cheating can be punished, the punishment will not be effective unless its expected costs exceed the value of cheating. As a result, it is also important that cheating be detected quickly.

Among the most successful and credible punishments for cheating is for the non-cheating cartel members to lower their price to the competitive level.[33] If cheating could be detected immediately and punished without exception, it would become unprofitable. For example, if each cartel member knew that in response to a single cheating sale it would earn only competitive returns for a subsequent month, no one would cheat. In order for such a strategy to work perfectly, however, the cheating would have to be detected almost immediately. If a firm can cheat for an extensive period of time without detection, then it will trade the gains from cheating against the costs of punishment and the cheating may be profitable.[34]

Another problem with using price reductions to the competitive level to discipline cheating is that it costs the other cartel members more than it costs the cheater.[35] Nevertheless, there is good reason to think that competitive pricing is one of the most common mechanisms by which cartels discipline cheaters. One reason is that it is natural and may

30. For example, Microsoft allegedly proposed to Netscape that Microsoft would design and sell its web browser, Internet Explorer, only for Windows machines, and Netscape would service only non-Windows machines. See United States v. Microsoft Corp., 1998 WL 614485 (D.D.C. 1998) (denying summary judgment).

31. On the three types of market division, see 12 Antitrust Law ¶¶ 2030–2033 (1999). See also Palmer v. BRG of Georgia, 498 U.S. 46, 111 S.Ct. 401 (1990) (per curiam; condemning horizontal territorial division under per se rule); United States v. Brown, 936 F.2d 1042 (9th Cir.1991) (rivals divide market for billboard sites and agree not to compete for one another's cites; affirming criminal conviction); United States v. Suntar Roofing, 897 F.2d 469 (10th Cir.1990) (horizontal customer allocation among roofers; unlawful per se; criminal conviction upheld).

32. On this problem under price fixing, see § 4.1a1.

33. See M. Osborne & C. Pitchik, Cartels, Profits and Excess Capacity, 28 Int'l Econ. Rev. 413 (1987).

34. As a result, such punishment is credible only if cartel members maintain sufficient excess capacity that they can easily and quickly increase their output in response to the cheater's additional sales. For an argument focusing on the single dominant firm rather than the cartel, see G. Saloner, Excess Capacity as a Policing Device, 18 Econ. Letters 83 (1985).

35. It costs the other members *more* than the cheater because the cheater was able to take advantage of at least one cheating sale. So the cheater is worse off by the cost of the period of competitive pricing, less the gains from cheating. By contrast, non-cheating members are worse off by the entire cost of the period of competitive pricing.

happen without any communication among the cartel members. When one firm increases output, each of the others naturally responds by increasing its own output because it does not want to lose market share to the cheater. However, the output increases naturally stop at the point that price equals marginal cost, for the firms do not wish to lose money either. The result is that price and output move closer to the competitive level without the need of a specific agreement to discipline cheaters in this fashion.[36]

It is sometimes thought that cartel members will discipline a cheater by charging a below cost, or predatory, price.[37] But there are good reasons for thinking that this form of discipline is not common, unless perhaps the cartel wishes to drive the cheater out of business altogether, which is a sure way to provoke a lawsuit and risk exposure of the cartel. Predatory pricing is costly to predators, and the target of predatory pricing can minimize its consequences by reducing its own output. As a result, predation calculated to discipline, rather than destroy, cartel cheaters generally costs more to the predators than it does to the target.[38]

Nonetheless, the fact that punishment by cutting price is so expensive to the non-cheating cartel members inclines them to look for cheaper, and thus more credible, mechanisms for disciplining cheaters. A punishment becomes more credible, and thus deters cheaters better, if it imposes higher costs on the cheater than it does on the punishers. Punishing becomes even more credible if punishing costs the punishers less than not punishing, or if customers can be counted on to aid in the punishment effort.

Cartels have used a variety of punishment schemes. For example, if they share a common distribution network, or common access to some other input, they might deny the cheater access. This seems to be the underlying complaint in many antitrust cases alleging that hospital boards have denied staff privileges to physicians.[39] If the board contains five obstetricians and one persistently charges a lower price than the others, the four (together with other board members) might find an excuse to revoke the price-cutter's right to admit patients into the hospital. Such a strategy may be particularly good for a market that is subject to product differentiation. For example, suppose that M.D. physicians' collective efforts to keep their prices up are undermined by chiropractors, who charge lower prices. Even if the physicians cut their prices to cost, the chiropractors could continue to earn a profit. In a product differentiated market customers have preferences for a particular variation of the product, so price cuts to the competitive level do not necessarily have to be perfectly matched. It would be far better if the physicians could punish the price-cutting chiropractors in a way that imposed higher costs on the latter than it did on the physicians—for example, by passing an "ethical" rule that denies chiropractors shared access to certain hospital facilities, such as X-ray laboratories.[40] These strategies work equally well against cartel cheaters or "fringe" competitors who were never part of the cartel in the first place.

Finally, the cartel may employ various facilitating practices, many of which operate to raise the costs of cheating or make it more easily detected. These are discussed in § 4.6.

4.1b. Competitive Fringe Firms

The thorn in every cartel's flesh is the firm that refuses to participate. Conversely, the outsider in a cartelized market has the best of

36. However, in the absence of a pre-existing agreement the firms may raise output to the Cournot oligopoly level rather than the competitive level. See § 4.2a.

37. On predatory pricing, see ch. 8.

38. See I. Ayres, How Cartels Punish: A Structural Theory of Self–Enforcing Collusion, 87 Col.L.Rev. 295, 302 (1987); D.K. Osborne, Cartel Problems, 66 Am.Econ.Rev. 835 (1976). One decision addressing the problem is Brooke Group Ltd. v. Brown & Williamson Tobacco Corp., 509 U.S. 209, 113 S.Ct. 2578 (1993), discussed in § 8.8.

39. For example, Summit Health v. Pinhas, 500 U.S. 322, 111 S.Ct. 1842 (1991), where the plaintiff physician alleged that the defendant physicians denied him hospital staff privileges because he refused to duplicate their costly procedures.

40. See Wilk v. AMA, 895 F.2d 352 (7th Cir.), cert. denied, 498 U.S. 982, 111 S.Ct. 513 (1990).

all possible situations. First, it suffers no risk of antitrust liability. Second, it can ride on the cartel's price increases without reducing its own output. In fact, it can increase output and sell all it wishes at a large profit by charging only slightly less than the cartelized price.[41]

A nonmember who increases output substantially can destroy a cartel by depriving it of sufficient demand to obtain supracompetitive returns.[42] Cartel members often find it necessary to put various forms of pressure on competitors who refuse to join. Many private actions alleging illegal predatory pricing, concerted refusals to deal or a variety of business torts have been based on the theory that the defendants were attempting to cartelize the market, and that the plaintiff was a competitor who refused to participate.[43] While predatory pricing to discipline a cartel cheater may not seem very plausible, predatory pricing or concerted refusals to deal may be an effective way of dealing with fringe competitors, depending on the underlying market structure.

41. A few plaintiffs have attempted to obtain damages from an illegal cartel for overcharges they paid in purchases from a nonmember. See § 16.6e.

42. As Figure 3 (following page) illustrates, even high cost fringe producers can rob cartels of significant profits and lower the market price. The two panels show the same market except that the panel on the right contains one or more high cost fringe producers. In the panel on the left, a cartel with marginal cost MC, demand D and marginal revenue MR maximizes profits at PM_1. In the panel on the right we include a fringe whose marginal costs, MC_f, are higher at every point than the cartel's marginal costs. But the effect of the fringe is to give the cartel a "residual" demand curve which runs from A to D′ to D. That is, at all cartel prices below D′, the fringe will make no sales, and at all cartel prices higher than A, the fringe will capture the entire market. MR_r is the marginal revenue curve that the cartel has in the presence of the fringe. The cartel will now maximize its profits by equating residual marginal revenue with marginal cost, given the residual demand curve. The profit-maximizing price, PM_2, is significantly lower than PM_1, and total market output (the sum of cartel output plus fringe output) is higher. In general, the higher the fringe's elasticity of supply—that is, the greater the extent to which it can respond to a price increase by increasing output—the less will be the market power of the cartel.

For variations of the argument, see Note, Standing at the Fringe: Antitrust Damage and the Fringe Producers, 35 Stan.L.Rev. 763, 770 (1983); W. Page, Optimal Antitrust Penalties and Competitors' Injury, 88 Mich.L.Rev. 2151, 2155 (1990). For further exploration of the mathematics, see J. M. Perloff, Microeconomics 410–412 (1999); R. Pindyck & D. Rubinfeld, Microeconomics 462–465 (4th ed. 1998).

4.1c. *Internal Efficiencies of the Cartel*

Cheating and the fringe producer are not the only problems that the cartel faces. Cartels often encounter the problem that individual members have few incentives for reducing overall costs. The single-firm monopolist generally has such incentives: it must bear the full costs of its own internal inefficiency. By contrast, each cartel member would prefer to have a certain sale itself, even though it is not the most efficient seller in the cartel. This problem is particularly serious in markets where individual firms have natural advantages with respect to a particular customer—for example, where transportation costs are high.

Suppose that a half dozen manufacturers of heavy pipe are involved in price fixing. The firms generally deliver the pipe to construction sites, and contractors generally select a seller by taking competitive bids. Different cartel members will be located different distances from any particular construction site, and a competitive market would naturally favor the closest firm. If the firms have equal production costs, the closest firm to the site can deliver the pipe for the lowest total price for pipe plus freight. Even a monopolist who owned all six plants would, other things being equal, deliver the pipe from the plant closest to the delivery point.

A simple price fixing agreement among the pipe manufacturers would destroy the natural advantage of the closest firm. For example, if the contractor received six identical bids for delivered pipe he would have little incentive to select the closest firm. He might choose a firm he has dealt with before, or one that a different contractor has reported to be good. If transportation costs are a high percentage of total costs, a substantial part of the monopoly overcharge would go, not to the cartel members, but to the railroad or trucking company that delivered the order.

The cartel is best off if each particular sale is made by the cartel member who can make

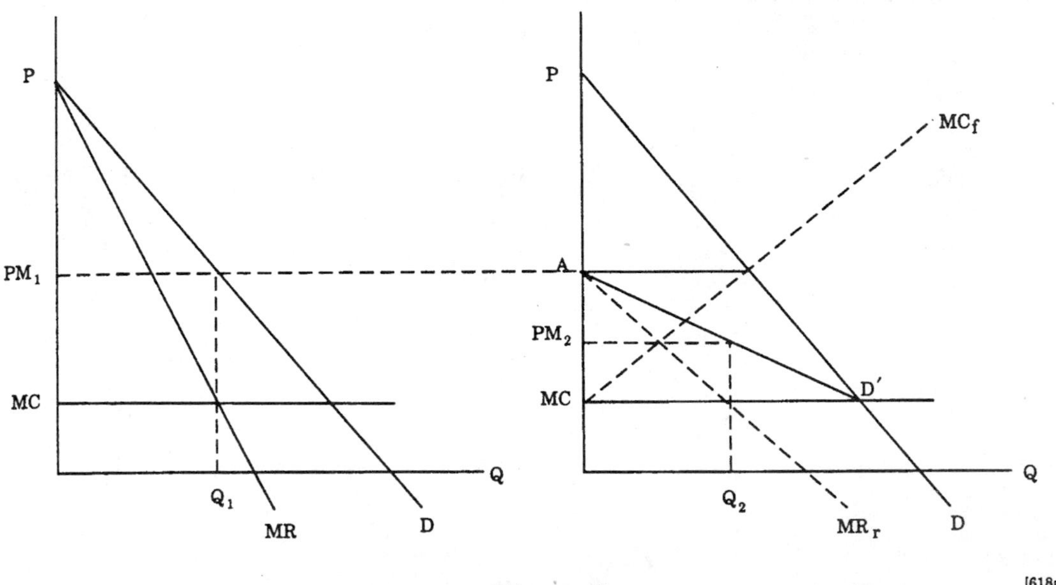

Figure 3

43. For example, Utah Pie Co. v. Continental Baking Co., 386 U.S. 685, 87 S.Ct. 1326, rehearing denied, 387 U.S. 949, 87 S.Ct. 2071 (1967) (allegations of collusive predatory pricing); and see Matsushita Elec. Indus. Co. v. Zenith Radio Corp., 475 U.S. 574, 106 S.Ct. 1348 (1986) (alleged predatory pricing by cartel); Eastern States Retail Lumber Dealers' Ass'n. v. United States, 234 U.S. 600, 34 S.Ct. 951 (1914) (boycott orchestrated by lumber dealers against "obnoxious" lumber wholesalers who had entered retailing themselves).

the sale most efficiently—that is, by the firm that would have been most likely to make the sale in a competitive market. Given a fixed price, any reduction in the costs of manufacture and delivery will go to the cartel's members. Sometimes cartels preserve this efficiency by holding out a fixed price to customers but engaging in internal competition for the right to make the sale. For example, the cartel condemned by the Supreme Court in U.S. v. Addyston Pipe & Steel Co.[44] used a complex internal bidding arrangement to award the right to sell. First the companies agreed about a bid price that would be presented to the customer as the competitive bid. Then the cartel members bid against each other to see who would transfer the largest amount of the bid price as a "bonus" to the cartel as a whole. Presumably, that would be the firm capable of performing the job at the lowest cost. The winning member would keep the bid price less the bonus; the bonus would be divided among the cartel members in proportion to size.[45]

In spite of all these efforts, naked cartels are generally not able to operate as efficiently as single-firm monopolists. First of all, the cartel must sustain the transaction costs of bargaining, coordinating activities, and investigating and punishing cheating among its own members. To be sure, the monopolist must coordinate as well. However, the costs of such coordination are higher for the cartel, because each member's interests are different. The primary interest of each member is to maximize its own, not the cartel's, profit. Since each member knows that the other members have monopoly profits to look forward to, they will probably be willing to spend much time and resources in bargaining. This generally means a great deal of posturing—threats to pull out of the cartel, to report it to the Justice Department, to exceed quotas, etc. Some public cartels that are not reachable by the antitrust laws, such as OPEC, have been unable to arrive at agreements that the members can accept and live with for prolonged periods. For illegal cartels, whose negotiations must be secret and infrequent, the problems are even greater.

Cartels may also have less flexibility than monopolists in coordinating overall production. For example, the monopolist who has five plants and wishes to cut production to 80% of capacity has the option of closing the least efficient plant and running the other four at optimal capacity. A cartel of five firms, each having one plant, may not have that option. The cartel will probably have to settle on some compromise scheme for allocating production among the members, even though the result is not optimal.[46]

44. Note 16 above.

45. The internal bidding scheme created certain frictions among members. Sometimes firms bid up the bonus so their own share would be larger, even though they did not want the job themselves. See G. Stigler, The Theory of Price 230–231 (3d Ed. 1966). An alternative to the internal bidding scheme is "pooling," in which each cartel member's revenues are divided among the members, usually in proportion to their market share. See McGee, Ocean Freight Rates, note 16 above, at 229–230.

See also *United States v. Romer*, 148 F.3d 359 (4th Cir.1998), cert. denied, ___ U.S. ___, 119 S.Ct. 1032 (1999), which involved bid rigging by buyers at foreclosure auctions of real property. The conspirators selected a winner in advance, and others refrained from bidding. Then, as in *Addyston Pipe*:

> Following the auction, members of the conspiracy would hold a private auction amongst themselves, at which point they would discuss the price they each would have bid for the property. The person with the highest bid would be given the deed, and the conspirators would divide amongst themselves the money saved by artificially holding down the price of the property.

Id. at 363.

46. Cartels may try to improve productive efficiency by giving members transferable production quotas. A firm with lower costs can then "purchase" the right to produce more from a firm with higher costs. For example, if the cartel price is $5.00, one cartel member has costs of $4.00 and another costs of $3.00, the latter firm will purchase production quotas from the former, at a price somewhere between $1.00 and $2.00.

Theoretically, an inefficient firm could sell *all* its production quotas to more efficient firms and cease production. For example, law reformer Henry Carter Adams noted already in the 1880's that Buffalo, New York, had thirty-four grain elevators located in an area where only twelve were needed to handle the traffic. But all divided the pool's profits. "One of these has not been used in twenty years, and many of them * * * were built for the sole purpose of coming into and receiving a share in the pool." H.C. Adams, Relation of the State to Industrial Action, 1 Pub. Am.Econ.Assn. 472 (1887). However, a cartel member would be willing to shut down and accept side payments only if it had a great deal of confidence in the durability and profitability of the cartel.

As a result of all these difficulties, cartels often do not last long, and often their members make little or no monopoly profits. Nevertheless, as § 4.3 below suggests, there is good reason for thinking that the social cost of cartels is quite high, notwithstanding the inability of many of them to lower market output substantially or earn supracompetitive returns for lengthy periods of time. As long as firms are tempted to fix prices, the strong policy against cartels in the American antitrust laws is a good one.

Not all cartels are inefficient, however. They may reduce costs if they can organize production or distribution in ways that are not available to individual members acting alone. As soon as a cartel does this, it is no longer involved in naked price fixing, but rather in a joint venture. These are taken up in chapter 5.

4.1d. Cartels of Buyers

A cartel of buyers operates by suppressing the buying price, which they do by purchasing less than the competitive amount. Buyers' cartels are fairly common, and price-fixing by buyers can be a felony, just as price-fixing by sellers.[47] The social losses caused by buyers' cartels are equivalent to those caused by sellers' cartels, and also resemble the social losses caused by monopsony.[48]

Nonetheless, courts have not always treated purchasing cartels with the same level of hostility as they have treated cartels of sellers. This appears to be true for two reasons. First, many joint buying agreements are efficient because they reduce transaction costs and enable smaller purchasers to obtain some of the buying advantage that accrue to larger buyers. Indeed, bona fide joint purchasing is looked on with favor by the antitrust laws.[49]

Second, even when buying cartels are "naked," in the sense that they do not represent joint purchasing, they result in lower input prices, and some courts have expressed reluctance to use the antitrust laws to challenge lower prices. But as noted in the discussion of monopsony, anticompetitive buying can actually produce *higher* output prices even as it is producing infracompetitive input prices. Whether this happens depends on whether the cartel also has market power in the market in which it sells.[50] Indeed, if the buying cartel has market power on the selling side as well, higher output prices will follow from the purchase agreement even if the cartel members do not also fix the resale price.[51] As a result, it was incorrect for the Sixth Circuit to conclude in *Balmoral* that agreements among theaters not to bid against each other for films may have served rather than injured consumer welfare, because the result was that the theaters paid less for films.[52] To be sure, in the short run such an agreement may have resulted in theaters paying less money for films. But this would entail that fewer films (or lower quality

47. E.g., *Romer*, note 45 (criminal conviction of cartel of buyers at real estate foreclosure auctions). See also Mandeville Island Farms v. American Crystal Sugar Co., 334 U.S. 219, 68 S.Ct. 996 (1948) (sugar beet processors fix price at which they will purchase beets); United States v. Brown University, 5 F.3d 658, 668 (3d Cir.1993) (Ivy League colleges agree on maximum amount of financial aid they will pay to students admitted to two or more colleges); Beef Industry Antitrust Litigation, 907 F.2d 510 (5th Cir.1990) (meat packers allegedly fix maximum price they will pay for beef cattle); Quality Auto Body v. Allstate Insurance Company, 660 F.2d 1195 (7th Cir.1981), cert. denied, 455 U.S. 1020, 102 S.Ct. 1717 (1982) (automobile insurers allegedly agree on maximum amount they will pay for covered automobile body repairs).

48. On monopsony, see § 1.2b. On the basic economics of buyers' cartels, see 12 Antitrust Law ¶ 2011 (1999).

49. See, e.g., Northwest Wholesale Stationers v. Pacific Stationery and Printing Co., 472 U.S. 284, 105 S.Ct. 2613 (1985) (speaking of efficiencies of cooperative buying); United States v. Topco Assocs., 405 U.S. 596, 92 S.Ct. 1126 (1972) (condemning grocery cooperative's territorial division requirements, but not its joint buying in order to obtain lower prices); All Care Nursing Svces. v. High Tech Staffing Svces., 135 F.3d 740 (11th Cir.1998), cert denied., ___ U.S. ___, 119 S.Ct. 1250 (1999) (approving joint venture among hospitals to take bids from nursing service providers).

50. See § 1.2b.

51. To illustrate, suppose that a buying cartel in widgets resells them in a market in which the same firms collectively have market power. The cartel reduces its buying price by suppressing its purchases from the competitive level of 100 widgets to the cartel level of 70 widgets. In that case, the output of widgets will also necessarily decline from 100 to 70, and the resale market will clear at a higher price whether or not the cartel members have also agreed on their selling price.

52. Balmoral Cinema v. Allied Artists Pictures Corp., 885 F.2d 313, 317 (6th Cir.1989); see 12 Antitrust Law ¶ 2013c (1999).

films) would be produced, which is not in consumers' interest. Further, if the participants in such a scheme also had market power in the resale market, the result would have been higher prices or reduced output there. Most courts today take the correct view that such "split" agreements among motion picture operators are unlawful per se.[53]

§ 4.2 Oligopoly, Cooperative and Non-cooperative

Section 1 of the Sherman Act is addressed to "contracts," "combinations," or "conspiracies" in restraint of trade. This language requires the plaintiff or prosecutor to prove an "agreement" among two or more firms to fix prices or reduce output. In determining whether such an agreement exists, courts have relied heavily on common law contract formulations, such as "meeting of the minds" or "mutual assent."

By contrast, § 2 of the Sherman Act generally applies to conduct by the single firm acting alone.[1] Concerted conduct is inherently suspicious; single-firm conduct is not. As a result the law of § 2 applies to a relatively narrow range of circumstances. For example, § 2 generally requires a showing either that the defendant is a monopolist, or else that there is a dangerous probability it will become one.

Some conduct falls through a fairly wide crack in the Sherman Act. Although anticompetitive, there is no evidence that it resulted from explicit agreement among competitors. Nor is it the unilateral conduct of a firm that has or threatens to have monopoly power. Since early in the nineteenth century economists have argued that firms in concentrated markets can increase their prices above the competitive level without expressly communicating with one another, and certainly without the need for anything resembling a "conspiracy" or agreement among the parties. Today the theoretical and empirical literature on oligopoly is enormous and complex.[2] Although wide disagreement exists about details, as well as the ubiquity and extent of oligopoly behavior in the American economy, there is general agreement that it exists. Further, the resulting social loss (as compared to competitive behavior by firms with the same costs) seems to be quite substantial.

One disconcerting conclusion for antitrust policy is that oligopoly strategies can be more stable and free from incentives to cheat than are cartel strategies. Further, the more stable strategies are often those that come furthest from satisfying the agreement requirement of § 1 of the Sherman Act, because in such markets the firms do not *need* to engage in the kinds of explicit communication that the law tends to regard as a "contract" or agreement. A related, equally disturbing conclusion is that the agreement requirement obliges antitrust enforcers to put their limited resources in the wrong place. Since the antitrust laws require "agreement," enforcement money is generally spent in areas where an agreement can be proven. But only the least stable situations require a qualifying antitrust agreement. In those areas where cooperative interaction among firms is likely to do the most damage, no "agreement" is required.[3]

4.2a. Non-Cooperative Cournot Oligopoly

The most important historical model of non-cooperative oligopoly came from Augustin Cournot and is more than 150 years old.[4] In

53. See 12 Antitrust Law ¶ 2013c.

§ 4.2

1. See chs. 6–8.

2. § 4.2 For a survey, see F. M. Scherer & D. Ross, Industrial Market Structure and Economic Performance, chs. 6–8 (3d ed. 1990). Good introductions to the issue are contained in J. M. Perloff, Microeconomics ch. 12 (1999); R. Pindyck & D. Rubinfeld, Microeconomics ch. 12 (4th ed. 1998).

3. See H. Marvel, J. Netter & A. Robinson, Price Fixing and Civil Damages: an Economic Analysis, 40 Stan. L. Rev. 561 (1988), noting that many criminal price fixing cases fail to produce subsequent private damages actions, presumably because the defendants—although they "fixed" prices—were unable to sustain supracompetitive prices for any length of time.

4. A. Cournot, Studies in the Mathematical Principles of the Theory of Wealth (1838; English translation by N. Bacon, 1897).

some ways the model seems quite crude and counter-intuitive. Nonetheless, it remains highly influential and forms the basis of many more complex variations. Furthermore, its simplicity may not be crudeness at all, but an important insight into the kinds of simplifying assumptions that firms make when the information they have is imperfect.

Cournot assumed that firms in concentrated markets choose output rather than price as the relevant decision variable; that is, they select an output, and then attempt to sell that output at whatever price the market will bear. In case that strategy strikes you as unrealistic, keep in mind that it is the same as the choice made by the perfect competitor, who has no control over price but can produce as much or as little as it pleases. The farmer planting corn at the beginning of the season asks "How much shall I plant?" not "What price shall I charge?" Second, Cournot presumed that each firm would set its output on the assumption that others would hold their output constant; that is, they would not respond to the actor's output decision by adjusting their own output. Once again, the competitor makes the same assumption.

The process by which a Cournot equilibrium is reached goes like this. We begin with a market with two firms, called a duopoly. The first firm sets its output as if it were a monopolist, by equating its marginal cost and marginal revenue. That is, it simply assumes that the other firm will produce zero. The second firm then takes the *residual* demand—the demand that is left over after the first firm has set its price and output[5]—and equates its own marginal cost and marginal revenue. The first firm will then need to revise its price downward, or it will lose too many sales to the second firm; so it will equate its marginal cost and marginal revenue once again, using the residual demand curve left by the output of the second firm. The second firm will respond to this revised output by the first firm, and so on. They will finally reach an equilibrium point where each is equalizing its own marginal cost and marginal revenue. If the two firms are the same size and have identical marginal cost curves, they will end up with the same output as well. Each will produce two-thirds of the monopoly output; so total output will be 1.333 times the monopoly output.[6]

As the number of firms in a Cournot oligopoly increases, total market output increases as well, and the price is correspondingly lower. In a market with N identical firms and market elasticity of demand *e*, the amount of market power exercised by the firms will be determined by the Lerner Index:

$$\frac{P - MC}{P} = \frac{1}{N_e}$$

So, for example, assuming an elasticity of demand of 1, if the market has two firms the Lerner Index would have a reading of 1/2, which would occur when the price was double marginal cost. If there were three firms in the market the Lerner Index would read 1/3, which would occur when price was 1.5 times marginal cost. If there were four firms in the market, the price would be 1.33 times marginal cost, and so on.[7]

A critical distinction between the Cournot equilibrium and the cartel equilibrium is that in the former each member equates its own marginal cost and marginal revenue.[8] Once the

5. On the residual demand curve, see Figures 2 and 3 above.

6. For simple explications, see Perloff, note 2 at 430–439, particularly the table on p. 439; R. Blair & D. Kaserman, Antitrust Economics 193–195 (1985); S. Martin, Industrial Economics: Economic Analysis and Public Policy (2d ed. 1994).

7. For derivation of the formula, see C. Shapiro, Theories of Oligopoly Behavior 329, 331–337, in 1 Handbook of Industrial Organization (R. Schmalensee & R. Willig, eds. 1989). One can also relate the oligopoly output to the competitive output by the following formula:

$$Q_n = (1 - 1/(N + 1))Q_c$$

Where,

Q_n = total oligopoly output of an oligopoly of N identical firms.

Q_c = the competitive output.

For example, a two-identical-firm Cournot oligopoly would produce two thirds the competitive output; an ten-identical-firm Cournot oligopoly would produce 10/11, or about 91% of the competitive output. A fifty-firm market produces about 98% of the competitive output. See Perloff, note 2 at 439.

8. Figure 4 (on the following page) illustrates, for two identical firms. For simplicity, the market demand curve D and marginal revenue curve MR are linear, and the two

equilibrium is reached, any across the board price cut will reduce the cutter's profits, assuming the other firms keep their output constant. The cut will reduce profits even more if the other firms reduce their price as well. Further, as a general rule the most rational response by other firms to one firm's price cut will be to reduce price. Otherwise they will lose even more money.

One reason antitrust needs to take game theoretic solutions such as Cournot's more seriously is that the resulting arrangements can be more stable than cartel solutions. Under collusion each firm has marginal revenues that greatly exceed marginal costs. This makes cheating highly profitable.[9] By contrast, in the Cournot equilibrium each firm is maximizing its profits, and no one has an incentive to deviate. For this reason Cournot-style oligopolies may be a much more substantial competitive problem in concentrated markets than are classic cartels.[10]

However, Cournot stability is ensured only if price cuts must be made across the board. If firm's are able to make customer-specific, secret price cuts it becomes very difficult to predict what the resulting equilibrium will be, and prices may even be driven to the competitive level.[11] This situation may require the firms to take corrective actions designed to make selective price cuts more readily detectable; however, the actions themselves, which we sometimes term "tacit" collusion, may come closer to satisfying Sherman § 1's "agreement" requirement.[12]

The basic Cournot theory seems to be an oversimplification of reality. But just as the theory of perfect competition, it seems quite vigorous and one would be hard pressed to find a book on industrial organization that did not develop it at considerable length. Alternatives and more sophisticated approaches designed to take market complexities into account have been developed as well.[13] These alternatives consider markets where there is a threat of entry, markets where firms are of different sizes or are not equally efficient, firms that produce differentiated products, and firms that are presumed to be capable of more complex strategic behavior. The models generally try to identify a "Cournot–Nash equilibrium,"[14] which is a situation in which no firm

firms have constant marginal costs. If the first firm sets price at P_m, the second firm faces a residual demand curve equal to the market demand curve below point X on the figure. We slide that portion of the curve leftward to the vertical axis, where it becomes the residual demand curve facing the second firm, or $D_{Cournot}$. This curve yields $MR_{Cournot}$ as the marginal revenue curve facing the second firm. The second firm then equates its marginal cost and its own marginal revenue, yielding price $P_{Cournot}$. That price is lower than the monopoly price, P_m, but nevertheless significantly higher than the competitive price, P_c. Any across-the-board deviation from that price would be unprofitable for the oligopolist, unless the rival actually reduced its output to compensate.

At this point, however, the second firm's output is too high. It will take the first firm's output as given and equate its own residual marginal revenue and marginal cost. This process will be repeated until an equilibrium is reached where the two firms have equal output, and each is equating marginal revenue and marginal cost.

9. See § 4.1a1.

10. Another disconcerting implication of Cournot oligopoly is that inefficient firms will be able to survive, although their market shares will be smaller than those of lower cost firms. See Shapiro note 7 at 336.

11. See G. Stigler, The Organization of Industry 39–63 (1983).

12. See §§ 4.4, 4.6.

13. For surveys and critiques, see Shapiro, note 7, id.; and F. M. Scherer & D. Ross, note 2; and see generally J. Tirole, The Theory of Industrial Organization (1988).

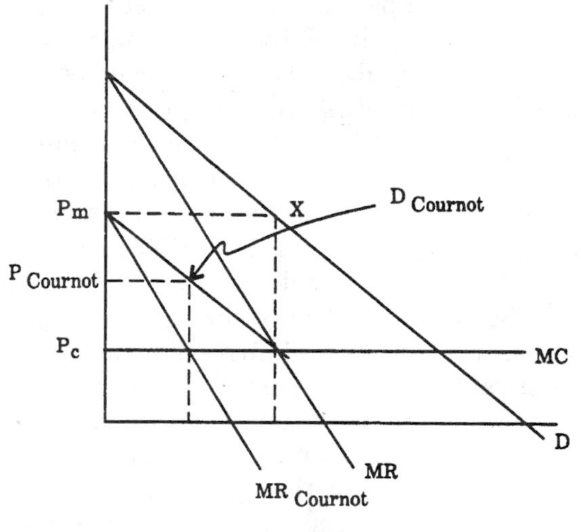

Figure 4

[619a]

14. Named after Cournot and John F. Nash, Jr. who formalized the concept. See J. Nash, Noncooperative Games, 54 Annals of Mathematics 286 (1951).

can profit from deviating (such as by price cutting), provided the other firms stay put as well. Importantly, in the absence of effective punishment of violators, a classic cartel may not be a Cournot–Nash equilibrium. Each firm can profit by charging a lower price than the cartel has set.

4.2b. Cooperative v. Non-cooperative Oligopoly Strategies

Cooperative theories of oligopoly are best analyzed as a species of *collusion* rather than as a species of oligopoly behavior. For antitrust purposes they have generally been grouped with the latter, however, because they may not involve a classic "agreement" of the kind that § 1 of the Sherman Act requires.[15]

Cooperative strategies are devices that enable firms to reach the same levels of price and output that would be produced by a profit-maximizing monopolist or a perfectly functioning explicit cartel. Presumably, cooperative strategies will be employed by firms who believe they can obtain higher returns than non-cooperative, Cournot behavior will yield. As the previous section notes, although Cournot strategies may theoretically be more stable than cartel strategies, they are also less profitable. For example, in the simplest Cournot model, an oligopoly of five equal sized firms has an output of about 83% of the competitive output. This would likely yield price increases in the range of 10% to 30% above the competitive level, depending on the market elasticity of demand. A perfect cartel could do much better, perhaps achieving prices 50% or more above the competitive level. In the Cournot oligopoly, the profit-maximizing price goes down as the number of firms increases. But theoretically, the 10–member explicit cartel has the same profit-maximizing price as the 2–member cartel—that is, the monopoly price. As a result, cooperative strategies may be more likely to emerge in markets that have more members.

The explicit cartel can be viewed as simply one variation of the cooperative strategy. Cooperative game theories are nothing other than a variety of cartel theories in which agreements or understandings are communicated among the parties implicitly rather than explicitly. To the extent that the strategies work imperfectly, we would expect the market price to hover between the Cournot price and the cartel price.

Those involved in cooperative strategies generally face the same set of problems that explicit cartels face: most importantly, cheating is profitable. As a result, some mechanism must be developed for detecting it and making it unprofitable. For example, suppose that two firms occupy a market in which the total competitive output would be 300, the monopoly output 150, and the Cournot output 200. At joint output of 200, neither firm would have an incentive to cheat, for each would be equating marginal cost and marginal revenue. The firms could earn more, however, if they restricted market output to 150, or 75 each. At that level, however, each firm individually would have an incentive to cheat: if it increased output by a few units while the other held output constant, the price increase could be profitable. For example, suppose that the market clearing price at an output of 150 is $1.00, while the market clearing price at an output of 165 is 90 cents. In that case a monopolist would not increase the price because at 150 revenues would be $150, while at 165 revenues would be $148.50. However, the duopolist might be tempted to do so. It would sell 75 units at the $1.00 price, for $75 in revenue; or 90 units at the 90 cent price, for $81 in revenue. If marginal costs were 40 cents or less, the output increase would be profitable for the duopolist. This is simply another illustration of the fact that each member of a classic cartel has higher marginal revenues than marginal costs.[16]

15. For a good discussion of the difference between non-cooperative and cooperative game theory, and its relevance to antitrust policy, see D. Yao & S. DeSanti, Game Theory and the Legal Analysis of Tacit Collusion, 38 Antitrust Bull. 113, esp. at 122–126 (1993).

16. See § 4.1a1.

But suppose that in response to firm A's output increase from 75 to 90, firm B immediately increased its own output from 75 to 90. If the demand curve were linear, price would drop to 80 cents rather than 90 cents. Now the price increase would be unprofitable for firm A. That is, at a price of 80 cents its revenues would be $72 rather than 75. Further, and importantly, firm B's revenues would also drop from $75 to $72; *however, this would be a smaller drop then if firm B did nothing*. That is, if firm B simply held its output at 75 while firm A went to 90, then firm B would end up earning 90 cents times 75 units, or $67.50 in revenues. So it is more profitable for firm B to match A's output expansion then it is to keep output constant. To say this another way, the possibility that B will retaliate against cheating is *credible*, because retaliating is more profitable (or less costly) than not retaliating. Of course, this depends on B's ability to detect A's cheating promptly and react quickly.

After a few iterations of such cheating, followed by a swift and sure response, firm A would discover that the cheating is unprofitable. It would then conclude that the profit-maximizing strategy would be for it to hold output at 75.[17] Such a market may go through a price war or two, but eventually each firm will realize that profits for the group will be maximized when total market output is held at the same level that a single-firm monopolist would produce, and neither firm could permit the other to produce more without responding in kind.[18]

There is good reason to believe that some markets will be characterized by non-cooperative oligopoly, while others will be cooperative. In the abstract, firms would naturally prefer the cooperative solution, for it yields the higher monopoly profits rather than the relatively lower Cournot profits. If a market is structured in such a way that cheating can be quickly detected and effectively punished, firms may be able to settle upon a cooperative equilibrium. In general, non-cooperative, Cournot outcomes are most likely where an explicit agreement cannot be enforced or would create too large a risk of detection and prosecution, but secret, discriminatory price cuts are also impossible—that is the price must be announced and given to everyone. In that case, the profit-maximizing strategy will likely be for each firm to set its own output by equating its marginal cost and marginal revenue, given the situation in which it finds itself.

The preference for non-cooperative over cooperative solutions seems to be quite strong in markets where cartel-like agreements cannot readily be reached or, if reached, cannot easily be enforced. For example, cheating may be difficult to detect. This is easily illustrated with a pair of prisoners' dilemma games. In the classic prisoners' dilemma, two criminals acting together are caught and subjected to questioning separately. Each is the only good witness to the others' criminal acts. If neither talks, both will likely be tried for a much less serious offense. Each is told that if he talks and implicates the other he will receive a lighter sentence but the other will receive the full weight of the law. Neither prisoner can speak with the other before being put to this choice, and now each must decide whether to confess or to stay silent. For each prisoner not talking is the best solution if the other prisoner keeps silent as well, but it is the worst solution if the other prisoner talks.

Figures 5 & 6 below illustrate two different prisoners' dilemma games. The first games is between two people (duopolists) who have agreed to fix prices but are tempted to raise output to the Cournot, or noncooperative oli-

17. See E. Chamberlin, The Theory of Monopolistic Competition (1933); see also, W. Fellner, Competition Among the Few (1950).

18. The agreement is more likely to be facilitated by the availability of "cheap talk"—or the ready ability of firms to communicate with one another about price without explicitly agreeing or even making commitments. This readily occurs in network industry where firms have to talk to one another or have immediate access to one another's prices in order to do business. See J. Baker, Identifying Horizontal Price Fixing in the Electronic Marketplace, 65 Antitrust L.J. 41 (1996), which discusses at length the use of signals in communication among airlines and internet firms. "The airlines probably conveyed more information through their computers than the prototypical conspirators meeting in a hotel room ever would." Id. at 52. See also W. Evans & I. Kessides, Living by the "Golden Rule": Multimarket Contact in the U.S. Airline Industry, 109 Q. J. Econ. 341 (1994).

gopoly level. The second game is between two people who have not agreed about anything, and who are considering the option of producing at the Cournot level of output or at some higher level. Assume that the competitive output in this market is 12 units per firm, the Cournot output is 8 units per firm, the monopoly output is 6. Suppose also that 9 is the output that results if someone tries to "cheat" on the Cournot equilibrium.

In each case the participants, A and B, have two choices about what to do in a particular situation. Their individual payoffs depend not only on their individual choices, however, but also on how their choice pairs off with the choice made by the other. The pairings are given in each quadrant, with the profit consequences of A's choice being the first and B's the second. For example, if A chooses output 6 and B chooses output 6, they will each earn $60. However, if A chooses output 6 and B chooses output 8, A will earn $30 and B will earn $80.

The first prisoners' dilemma shows the relation between Cournot oligopoly and collusion:

Figure 5

		B: 6	B: 8
A	6	60, 60	30, 80
	8	80, 30	40, 40

Assuming that neither side knows what the other side will do, the way to maximize one's individual returns is to select a "dominant" strategy, if there is one. The dominant strategy is the one that works best for a particular player no matter what the opposing side chooses. In Figure 5, A's dominant strategy is to select output 8, which is the Cournot output. That output will make A better off no matter which choice B makes. That is, assuming B selects output 6, a selection of output 8 will give A $80 rather than $60. Assuming B selects output 8, a selection of output 8 will give A $40 rather than $30. B is in the same position. B will also select output 8.[19]

Even if the firm's agree on the cartel output of 6, which will maximize their total profits and will give each of them more (60) than the Cournot strategy does (40), they will not actually adhere to the cartel output unless they can rest assured that the other side will adhere to it as well. Since cartel agreements are not enforceable legally, and there may be no reasonable means to punish cheating, each firm planning on its own will have a strong incentive to go for the Cournot output rather than the cartel output. We would expect prices to drop from the cartel level to the Cournot level. But this is precisely the output that they would go for in the total absence of any agreement.[20]

This particular prisoners' dilemma game is then said to have a Cournot–Nash equilibrium solution in which both players select their second alternatives, which give them the Cournot output and profits of 40 each. As noted above, in a Cournot–Nash equilibrium no player has any incentive to deviate from the present situation, given the options available to the opponent. Note, however, that the Cournot–Nash equilibrium solution to the prisoners' dilemma game in Figure 5 is not the joint maximizing solution. Indeed it is the joint *minimizing* solution. Its net value is 80 (A's profit plus B's profit), while the other three alternatives yield joint profits of 110 or 120.

The second game, by contrast to the first, shows the relationship between Cournot equilibrium and a higher output, 9, that would result if a firm in a Cournot equilibrium "cheats" by increasing output:

Figure 6

		B: 8	B: 9
A	8	40, 40	25, 35
	9	30, 25	10, 10

19. That is, if A selects output 6, B's profits will be 80 if B selects output 8 but only 60 if she selected output 6. If A selects output 8, B's profits will be 40 if she selects output 8 but only 30 if she selects output 6.

20. This may also suggest why price cuts to the competitive level will sometimes work to discipline the rivals in a cartel: that is, they give the firms *less* than Cournot profits and thus force it to choose between competitive profits, which are zero, and cartel profits, which are high. See § 4.1a3.

Once again, Cournot is the dominant strategy. If A assumes that B selects an output of 8, A will make 40 if it selects output 8 as well, but only 30 if it selects output 9. That is, in Cournot A is already equating marginal cost and marginal revenue and an output increase beyond that point would result in lower profits for A, assuming that B holds output constant. (B's profits will go down even more because B is now obtaining the lower price, but against only 8 units of output). If A increases to 9 and B also increases to 9, then both of them will earn profits of only ten. (Since the competitive output is 10 apiece, their profits would drop to zero at that point). So the dominant strategy is for A to produce 8. B is in precisely the same position. B makes $5 more (40–35) by producing 8 if A stays at 8, and $15 more (25–10) by producing 8 if A moves to 9. The two firms will once again set output at the Cournot level.[21]

The pair of prisoners' dilemma games is a considerable oversimplification of realty (most economic models are). Perhaps most importantly, they are "single shot" games, where each firm selects its dominant strategy, if there is one, only once. The unrealistic element in the prisoners' dilemma is that each makes a single choice and that is the end of the game. But oligopolies are relatively durable situations where firms continually revise their own output decisions in response to the decisions of others. It would be more appropriate to think of the oligopoly as a kind of game in which A choose; then B chooses; then A is entitled to change his mind in response to B's choice; then B may change her mind in response to A's revision. If the same game is repeated in this fashion, the players may readily learn to adopt the joint maximizing solution rather than the solution that is dominant for the single shot.

Consider the dilemma illustrated in Figure 5, above. A might choose first, selecting output of 6. B would then choose 8, giving A 30 and B 80. A would then immediately revise to 8, giving A 40 and B 40. B might now sense what A had in mind and choose 6 again, and this time A would chose 6 as well, giving each participant 60. At that point, each would realize that no deviation is profitable, given how the other will respond. *Whether* they will do this is difficult to say, and presents a problem in psychology as much as economics.[22]

Have A and B agreed? Perhaps, but the judicial record finding agreement in such situations is frustrating. First, when we say that Cournot is the dominant strategy for the single shot game, or that the strategy yields a Cournot–Nash equilibrium, we mean that it is the best strategy for each individual firm *regardless* of what the other firm does. This robs such strategies of the essential element of an agreement—namely, that an action be profit-maximizing only on the assumption that other firms will follow suit. Second, although repeated games look a little more like an agreement, the courts have generally insisted on formulations of the agreement requirement that are too traditional to take repeated games into account. In any event, it is difficult for courts to identify the kind of game that oligopolists are playing.

§ 4.3 The Social Cost of Collusion

As § 1.3 noted, the social cost of monopoly consists of three parts: (1) WL1, which is the "deadweight" loss, or the loss that results from inefficient allocation of resources resulting from inefficient consumer substitutions; (2) WL2, which is the resources that the monopolist spends inefficiently in acquiring or maintaining its monopoly position; and (3) WL3 which are certain losses that the monopolist's anticompetitive exclusionary practices impose on others, principally competitors and potential competitors.

By design, a cartel behaves like a monopolist and one might expect its social costs to be approximately the same. But the real picture

21. Indeed, A's output increase beyond 8 would be profitable only on the assumption that B *decreased* its output in response—effectively giving A a larger share of the market at the oligopoly price. But this response would be irrational, given B's general goal of maximizing its own profits.

22. See R. Axelrod, The Evolution of Cooperation 33–36 (1984), arguing that when games are repeated the participants are more likely to arrive at the cooperative, or joint maximizing, solution.

is rather different. First, WL1 losses may actually be lower when the monopolist is a cartel. As § 4.1 notes, cartels have extraordinary problems in agreeing on price and output, disciplining cheaters, and preventing defections. As a result, they are generally thought to be less successful in identifying the profit-maximizing price and in restraining their joint output to keep prices at that level.

By contrast, the WL2 losses that result from collusion are generally higher than those that result from monopoly. For the very same set of reasons, cartels often spend much of their anticipated profits in efforts to come to agreement about price and output. Individual members also take elaborate steps to cheat in secret, and the cartel takes equally elaborate steps to detect cheating and then to punish it. Finally, the cartel must exclude rivals just as the monopolist must, but exclusion may be much more difficult and expensive when it must be orchestrated by a group of firms rather than by a single dominant firm. Most important of all, truly naked cartels are formed by simple agreement, not by innovation; so there are few offsetting dynamic efficiency gains. All of these factors make generalizing about the social cost of collusion even more difficult than generalizing about the social cost of monopoly; but the total social cost of the former is likely to be as large or larger.

The social cost of non-cooperative oligopoly is probably less than the social cost of monopoly. First of all, WL1 losses are less to the extent that the Cournot output reduction is not as great as the monopoly output reduction. Further, WL2 loss may be less to the extent that the firms have no incentive to cheat, under the ordinary assumptions. However, if secret, *discriminatory* price cuts are available,[1] firms may still make them and other firms may try to detect them and discipline them. So WL2 losses could be significant as well. WL3 losses are likely to be less because it is much more difficult for firms not acting in concert to strategize exclusionary practices than for single firm monopolists. Of course, few Cournot oligopolies have an even distribution of firm sizes. Many have dominant firms that may have almost as much power to exclude as a single firm monopolist has.

While we can generalize about the *types* of welfare losses that result from monopolization, cartelization, and cooperative and noncooperative oligopoly, measuring the social cost in a particular instance is extremely difficult and (to this writer's knowledge) there have been no complete attempts to do so.

One important caveat even increases our uncertainty. When the policy maker measures social cost, she must always ask "relative to what?" The goal of the antitrust policy maker is generally to find the solution that produces the largest net social gains. As the discussion in the next section indicates, the social cost of certain kinds of remedies, such as the forced breakup of large firms to achieve more competition, may be larger than the social cost of simply leaving the oligopoly industry as it lies.

§ 4.4 Antitrust Policy Toward Oligopoly and Tacit Collusion

One reason antitrust law has had so little success with oligopoly is its continued adherence to a common law concept of "agreement" that makes little sense in the context of strategic behavior among competing firms. This agreement requirement frequently targets the wrong set of practices. *Non-cooperative* oligopoly situations are often more stable, and thus more easily sustained, than cooperative ones. For example, in the Cournot oligopoly described in § 4.2a, each firm charges its own profit-maximizing price, determined by equating its own marginal cost and marginal revenue on the assumption that other firms will hold their output constant. Adhering to the oligopoly price is profit-maximizing behavior, given the status quo. As a result, nothing resembling a common law contract or conspiracy will be found in the orthodox noncooperative oligopoly.

By contrast, in a cartel or cooperative setting, price cuts may be *individually* profitable, at least if cheating cannot be effectively punished. Cooperative arrangements are therefore

§ 4.3

1. See § 4.4a.

less stable. Their success depends on mutual forbearance or "understandings" among the parties, or at least on repeated plays of the same game. However, even when § 1 is directed at cooperative oligopoly, it often fails to find a qualifying agreement under traditional common law principles.

Under Sherman Act analysis, the collusion question has generally reduced to consideration of whether there is sufficient agreement-like behavior that one can say a "contract," "combination" or "conspiracy" existed among the parties. Historically, this kind of question caused a great deal of difficulty in the common law of contracts. By its language, Sherman § 1 invited the same problems into antitrust analysis of concerted behavior. Many Sherman § 1 decisions hold that the statute requires an explicit agreement, although evidence of the agreement may sometimes be circumstantial.[1] Much § 1 case law is preoccupied, not with the defendant's conduct as such, but with whether that conduct was undertaken pursuant to such an agreement. This unfortunate bit of formalism has been the major impediment to effective antitrust action against poor economic performance in oligopoly markets. In such cases the market structure itself produces a "consensus" about how each firm can maximize its own profits by tacitly participating in a strategy to maximize the joint profits of the group.

4.4a. Attacking Oligopoly; the Turner–Posner Debate

The emphasis of Sherman § 1 case law on "agreement" has led many commentators to think that price fixing and oligopoly are two quite different things, and that oligopoly is effectively out of reach of the antitrust laws. In an important article written in 1962, Professor Donald Turner argued that such behavior was beyond the reach of the Sherman Act for an additional reason: it is rational and virtually inevitable, given the structure of the market.[2] Each firm in an oligopoly market is forced by circumstance to consider its own profit-maximizing rate of output, given the output of rivals and their anticipated responses to its own price and output decisions. To ignore these issues would be completely irrational. Furthermore, no court could draft a decree that would force the firms to "ignore" each other in their market decision-making. The only solution, Turner concluded, was structural relief: persistent, poor economic performance in highly concentrated markets should warrant a court decree breaking the firms into smaller units that would give the market a more competitive structure. Turner believed that such an approach would require new legislation.

Turner's argument made the most sense in the context of the traditional non-cooperative Cournot oligopoly. In that case, a rational profit-maximizing firm would set a price by equating marginal cost and marginal revenue under its residual demand curve.[3] But this would yield the Cournot price without requiring any communication with other firms, any "understanding" with respect to their behavior, or anything else resembling a Sherman Act agreement. Indeed, under the Cournot assumption each firm totally ignored the possible strategic choices that other firms could make. It would simply fill orders up to the point that marginal revenues fell to marginal cost.

Turner's critics emphasized that the term "agreement" makes more sense when one thinks of oligopoly as a kind of "tacit" collusion. In a response to Turner, Professor (now Judge) Posner emphasized the similarities rather than the differences between cartel and oligopoly behavior.[4] Whether firms in a con-

§ 4.4

1. See First Natl. Bank of Arizona v. Cities Serv. Co., 391 U.S. 253, 88 S.Ct. 1575 (1968) (conspiracy could be inferred from fact that conduct was parallel, and that an agreement would have been beneficial to the defendants by giving them higher prices); Theatre Enterprises, Inc. v. Paramount Film Distributing Corp., 346 U.S. 537, 74 S.Ct. 257 (1954) (discussed in § 4.5); and see 6 Antitrust Law ¶ 1400 (1986).

2. D. Turner, The Definition of Agreement Under the Sherman Act: Conscious Parallelism and Refusals to Deal, 75 Harv.L.Rev. 655 (1962); see also C. Kaysen & D. Turner, Antitrust Policy 110–119, 266–272 (1959).

3. See § 4.2a.

4. R. Posner, Oligopoly and the Antitrust Laws: A Suggested Approach, 21 Stan.L.Rev. 1562 (1969). Posner's theory was heavily influenced by a pathbreaking article in the theory of oligopoly authored by George Stigler: G.

centrated market act in response to an express agreement or simply have read the market's clear signals in the same way should be a mere detail. Under this approach to oligopoly analysis, explicit cartel agreements are referred to as "express collusion," while oligopolistic, interdependent behavior is called "tacit collusion." This term is designed to draw attention to the fact that there is a certain "meeting of minds" of competitors in at least some oligopolistic markets, even though the firms do not formally communicate with each other.

Posner argued that one could not assume that an oligopolist acting individually would be reluctant to initiate price cuts, for fear that rivals would retaliate. That depends on numerous factors, such as whether the price cut is known to rivals, and whether the price cutter's additional business is taken from rivals or comes from outside the market. Clearly, Posner was not talking about the textbook Cournot oligopoly, where firms have an additional incentive for not wishing to cut price: they are already equating their marginal cost and marginal revenue. In that case a further price cut would be unprofitable as long as rivals hold their output constant. It would be even more unprofitable if rivals cut their price, as they likely would.

But when we relax the Cournot assumptions, Posner's critique becomes more forceful. The simple Cournot model, just as the simple monopoly model,[5] assumes that the seller cannot engage in price discrimination. The only way that it can cut price to the nth customer is to cut the price to all other customers as well. In that case the market reaches the Cournot equilibrium as described in § 4.2a, at price levels between the competitive and monopoly level. From that point, the oligopolist has no incentive to cut price further, because it would earn less money, assuming that rivals did nothing.

But suppose that each customer negotiates its own price, and these prices are not known to other persons than the seller and the particular buyer. For example, suppose that one seller in a three-seller market must bid for a sale, but the price for this next sale will have no impact at all on the price given to earlier customers. What will the price be? At the margin, it will very likely be marginal cost. That is, if the firm can bid for each new customer without concern about the impact of the current transaction on prices charged to other customers, then it will make money at any price above marginal cost. Of course, the three firms may come to an understanding that they will not bid against each other—but this understanding may be difficult to enforce if prices are negotiated in secret. In any case, it would be an "understanding," and that would move the situation from the realm of the non-cooperative into that of the cooperative. A finding of Sherman Act "agreement" might follow, provided the concept was suitably defined.[6]

In short, often highly concentrated markets will not produce the classic Cournot equilibrium at all, but may actually yield competitive pricing. In that case, the firms may have to reach collateral agreements or understandings if they are to maintain prices at supracompetitive levels. For example, they may agree with each other that they will post sales prices publicly and at regular intervals, or that all transaction terms will be publicly announced. Or to state it another way, Cournot behavior cannot be inferred from number of market participants alone; it also depends on the way prices are disseminated and transactions are structured. Some highly concentrated markets

Stigler, A Theory of Oligopoly 72 J. Pol. Econ. 44 (1964). Stigler introduced the problems of game theory to oligopoly and revised the basic Cournot model to include situations in which selective and secret cheating sales were possible. A critique of both Turner's and Posner's proposal is summarized in R. Posner, Oligopolistic Pricing Suits, the Sherman Act, and Economic Welfare, 28 Stan.L.Rev. 903 (1976); and R. Markovits, A Response to Professor Posner, 28 Stan.L.Rev. 919 (1976).

5. See § 1.2.

6. See D. Ginsberg, Nonprice Competition, 38 Antitrust Bull. 83 (1993), arguing that effective collusion will not be profitable in markets where nonprice competition is possible. However, the more important question, not inconsistent with Judge Ginsberg's argument, is whether the nonprice competition must be announced publicly, in which case collusion could be quite effective, or whether it can be conducted secretly on a customer-by-customer basis. See G. Stigler, A Theory of Oligopoly, 72 J.Pol.Econ. 44, 56 (1964).

may in fact perform very competitively, unless the participants go the extra step of restructuring transactions or changing the way pricing information is disseminated. If they engage in these "facilitating practices," the antitrust enforcer may be able to go after the practices directly.

A subsequent criticism of the Stigler–Posner position, noted in § 4.2, is that firms learn from reiteration. In a set of repeated games they will soon learn that cheating is unprofitable, even if they have incomplete information about one another's prices. Importantly, even secret and discriminatory price cuts generally send *some* kind of signal to rivals. Perhaps the cheater's output increases; perhaps customers report the lower prices charged by a rival; perhaps demand in the market is much less than expected, from the noncheater's viewpoint. If non-cheaters merely *suspect* that cheating is occurring, their best strategy is often to cut the price to competitive levels themselves. If the market is simply weak, a price cut is rational. But if a firm is cheating, the fellow oligopolist that fails to cut price will be hurt even worse than the one that cuts; so cutting price is rational as well. That is, cutting price is the rational response to suspected cheating, whether or not cheating is actually occurring.

The result is that the cheater quickly faces a competitive market that makes the cheating unprofitable. There will be a few price "wars" until firms discover that most cheating is unprofitable. Soon firms will learn that any cut threatens collapse of the oligopoly, followed by an indefinite period of competitive prices. So the dominant strategy for each firm is not to cheat.[7] Thus if we think of oligopoly games as capable of being repeated, and of firms as learning from bad experiences, then oligopoly outcomes may be quite robust. Importantly, nothing about these stories requires an "agreement" as the antitrust laws use that term.

To summarize, whether the (1) competitive, (2) Cournot, or (3) cartel equilibrium emerges in a concentrated market is a function not only of the number of firms in the market, but also of the way transactions are structured, the degree to which prices must be disclosed, and the ability of firms to charge different prices to different customers. In some cases the firms will be unable to reach any result other than the competitive one without coming to certain kinds of agreements, but that condition cannot be presumed. To the extent that the sale to any particular customer affects the price given to other customers, marginal revenue must be considered with respect to the entire group of affected customers. This situation makes the oligopoly equilibrium more likely to emerge, without anything resembling a Sherman Act "agreement."

All of this leaves us where we started, with a Sherman Act that is ineffective to remedy many situations that we think are anticompetitive. This makes merger policy all the more important as a device for limiting the damage.[8]

4.4b. Identifying Tacit Collusion and Facilitators; Policy Options

As noted previously, the term "tacit collusion" does not seem to fit very well with the traditional Cournot model of oligopoly, which is not cooperative at all. However, the term does fit quite well with two situations: (1) price fixing, where the terms of agreement are communicated by informal or non-verbal means; (2) cooperative oligopoly that consists in a serious of repeated actions and reactions until the parties settle upon an equilibrium price or output level. Most importantly, firms may be able to facilitate the Cournot or cartel outcome by changing the way information is communicated in the market, the way that transactions take place, or the terms of those transactions. This raises some possibilities for antitrust policy. We must be able to identify oligopoly performance when we see it. Then, however, we may be able to direct antitrust at

7. J. Baker, Two Sherman Act Section 1 Dilemmas: Parallel Pricing, the Oligopoly Problem, and Contemporary Economic Theory, 38 Antitrust Bull. 143, 150–169 (1993).

8. See Chapter 12.

market conditions or practices that make oligopoly outcomes more likely. The principal weapon here is merger policy, but it is preventive rather than corrective.[9] Alternatively, we may challenge various facilitating practices themselves.[10]

Oligopoly pricing is aided by a market that is highly concentrated on the selling side, but it should also be rather diffuse on the buying side. If the market contains a small number of large and knowledgeable firms on the buying side, they may be able to force the sellers to bid against each other and offer concessions, particularly if the terms of individual sales are kept secret. If the market contains numerous small buyers, then prices may have to be advertised or publicly posted in a way that makes them apply equally to all customers. In that case, the oligopolist may be able to cut price substantially only by giving all buyers the same cut. The Cournot oligopolist will have no incentive to cut prices, assuming it was equating marginal cost and marginal revenue to begin with.

Likewise, oligopoly pricing just as much as express price fixing can be frustrated by easy entry or output increases from fringe firms. The lower the market share of fringe firms on the "edge" of the market, and the more difficult and time-consuming entry is, the greater will be the returns from tacit collusion.

Both oligopoly pricing and collusion are less successful if the firms in the market are not equally efficient or produce distinguishable products. In addition, however, as the number of firms in a market increases, or if one of the above impediments to collusion exists, tacit collusion becomes ineffectual more quickly than express collusion. In the case of non-cooperative Cournot models, this is true simply because the individually profit-maximizing decision yields higher marketwide outputs as the number of firms increases. In the case of cooperative strategies, it is so because tacit collusion relies on more primitive forms of communication, such as price or output signaling by means of public announcements. Although such signaling may enable firms to reach a tacit meeting of minds about price and output, it is less likely to produce detailed agreements covering many variables. Thus fifteen firms might conceivably manage an explicit cartel. Cooperative oligopoly pricing in a market containing fifteen firms is implausible, however, unless one or two firms were extremely large and able effectively to dominate the others. Even a market containing five or six firms will find tacit collusion difficult if there are significant disparities in firm size or efficiency, a substantial amount of product differentiation or customizing, or if most transactions are confidential.

Firms in oligopoly markets often develop certain "facilitating devices" that make tacit collusion easier by reducing the benefits of cheating, making price discrimination more difficult, or by increasing the likelihood of detection or the costs of punishment. For example, if all firms produce uniform products, offer similar terms or conditions of sale, and make all transactions public, they can make the market more conducive to oligopoly or collusive results. If the facilitating device results from an express agreement, it may receive rule of reason treatment under the antitrust laws, because it does not explicitly affect price. For example, an agreement that all firms will produce "standardized" products may appear to be efficiency creating if it lowers customer search costs.[11] Further, the facilitating devices themselves often result from tacit agreement. The firms never formally communicate with each other but simply reach a shared perception about how to maximize joint monopoly profits.

Some of these facilitating devices increase the profitability of *both* non-cooperative and cooperative oligopoly. For example, the ability of firms to make secret price concessions on a discriminatory basis makes non-cooperative, Cournot-style oligopoly less stable, since price cutting becomes profitable. The same ability gives those involved in cooperative arrange-

9. See § 12.1b.

10. See § 4.6; and G. Hay, Oligopoly, Shared Monopoly, and Antitrust Law, 67 Cornell L. Rev. 439 (1982).

11. See 12 Antitrust Law ¶ 2136 (1999).

ments an enhanced opportunity to cheat. By contrast, product differentiation seems to undermine cooperative strategies more than noncooperative ones.[12]

One of the most controversial questions in antitrust policy is how courts and enforcers should deal with the problem of poor economic performance in concentrated markets when there is no evidence of express collusion. The Turner proposal favoring structural relief[13] (that is, judicially mandated dissolution of the firms in the market) was predicated on the premise that monopoly pricing was inevitable in oligopoly markets. The poor performance was perfectly rational, profit-maximizing behavior dictated by the environment in which the oligopoly firm found itself. Marginal cost pricing, by contrast, was irrational.

Even if courts could administer the restructuring of an entire industry, however, it is by no means clear that consumers would benefit. Absent unusual deterrents to competitive entry, markets are generally concentrated because operation at minimum efficient scale (MES) requires a firm with a relatively large share of the market.[14] For example, if MES in the widget industry requires an output level equal to 30% of market demand at the competitive price, the market in equilibrium is likely to have three or fewer firms. Smaller firms would either combine by merger, increase their own market share by driving other firms out of business, or else go out of business themselves. A program of combatting oligopoly by breaking the market into a dozen firms would deprive all or most of MES, and the costs of the loss in productive efficiency might well exceed the social loss caused by oligopoly performance. Indeed, the fact that the firms are inefficiently small would likely lead to a further round of cartels, bankruptcies or mergers until the industry once again hit an equilibrium in which the firms operated efficiently. *Maintaining* such an industry at inefficient output levels would require the ongoing, intervening hand of the State.

One might qualify the basic rule by recommending breakup only to the point that the resulting firms operated at MES, but that rule would probably not work either. Most economists are not confident about their ability to measure minimum efficient scale, except perhaps by a rule of survival: inefficiently small firms must either grow or die.[15] It is very difficult to compute MES of, say, an automobile producer. If one considered production economies alone, she might conclude that a plant with 5% of national output is efficient. But the production and distribution of automobiles includes advertising, a retail network, post-sale services, and a host of things that may give a larger firm a cost advantage over small firms.[16] Furthermore, MES is a function of constantly changing technology and demand. In the 1950's computers filled giant warehouses and cost millions of dollars to produce. As a result production required enormous plants and market demand was relatively small. Minimum optimal scale under such circumstances may have been 30% to 40% of market demand, and the market would have room for only two or three firms. Today, a computer of the same capacity might be the size of a large book and cost less than $1000.

12. Product differentiation undermines cooperative strategies and explicit-price fixing for the simple reason that it makes agreeing on a single price far more difficult. Theoretically, product differentiation has little effect on Cournot oligopoly because each firm simply looks at its own residual demand curve on the assumption that the other firm will continue to do what it is already doing. The computation of one's own residual demand curve already takes the product differentiation into account. But more complex models of Cournot behavior involve price leadership and repeated rounds of following or refusing to follow, and product differentiation may make these games more difficult for the oligopolists to manage.

On oligopoly pricing under product differentiation, see J. M. Perloff, Microeconomics 464–469 (1999); R. Pindyck & D. Rubinfeld, Microeconomics 450–453 (4th ed. 1998).

13. Note 2 above.

14. See § 1.4a.

15. For a somewhat inconclusive attempt to do this, see G. Stigler, The Organization of Industry 71–89 (1983).

16. See Y. Brozen, Concentration, Mergers and Public Policy 56–127 (1983). For one attempt to determine the minimum optimal plant size in several American industries see F. Scherer, A. Beckenstein, E. Kaufer, & R. Murphy, The Economics of Multiplant Operations (1975). On the relation between scale economies and industrial concentration, see W. Viscusi, J. Vernon & J. Harrington, Jr., Economics of Regulation and Antitrust 152–155 (2d ed. 1995).

The result is that smaller firms can manufacture them and the total market is many times larger. Today a firm might achieve MES with a market share of 2%–3%, and the market could have room for 30 or 40 efficient firms. Over American economic history such changes in technology and market demand have undoubtedly contributed far more than the antitrust laws to the destruction of monopolies.

The problem of scale economies and concentrated markets leaves the antitrust policy maker in a quandary. An oligopoly is an oligopoly, whether or not the high concentration results from economies of scale. Indeed, an oligopoly market in which MES is very high is likely to perform more poorly than an oligopoly in which MES is low. The firms in the latter oligopoly have to worry about new entry. When they measure price and output, they must consider not only how the other firms in the market will respond, but also the possibility that new equally efficient firms will enter if the price rises too much. By contrast, if there are three firms in a market in which MES exceeds a 30% market share, the firms have less reason to fear new entry. Any new entrant whose market share is less than 30% will have a cost disadvantage. The greater that disadvantage, the more room there will be for supracompetitive pricing by the firms already in the market.

So the consequences of severe structural change in most industries are difficult to predict, and the litigation process is certainly not well designed to make such predictions. Break-up of oligopoly firms will certainly yield an industry with more firms, and they will likely price their output closer to their costs, but their costs could be higher. *Ex ante*, it may be difficult to say whether the structural change will yield a price increase or a price decrease.[17] Once we include the large administrative costs of predicting when such relief would be appropriate, and the costs of administering such relief, it is doubtful that the result of structural reorganization of oligopoly industries would be efficient.

There are some reasons for believing that the social costs of oligopoly behavior, at least of the noncooperative kind, are small compared to the costs of denying firms the chance to achieve their most efficient rate of output.[18] If that is the case, consumers may be best off if firms are permitted to attain minimum optimal scale, even at the expense of some high concentration, with the antitrust laws used to make both non-cooperative and cooperative price coordination as difficult as possible.

In practice, this has meant that plaintiffs and prosecutors hobbled by § 1's "agreement" requirement have attempted to do three different things. First, they have tried to loosen up the evidentiary standards for proving a combination or conspiracy, or to convince courts that certain kinds of understandings should be interpreted as "agreements" for antitrust purposes, even though they do not seem to fit the common law understanding. This effort is directed largely at cooperative forms of oligopoly behavior, or at explicit price-fixing for which there is insufficient direct evidence of a classical "agreement."

Second, antitrust enforcers have tried to convince the courts that certain kinds of conspicuously parallel behavior should be condemned whether or not there is an underlying agreement about price or output. In particular,

17. However, industry performance may provide some hints as to the significance of both scale economies and collusion in concentrated industries. Consider highly concentrated industries that contain a few giant firms and some tiny fringe firms. If both the giant firms and the fringe firms earn supranormal profits, that would indicate that economies of scale are not substantial and that collusion is occurring. By contrast, if the large firms are earning supracompetitive profits while the fringe firms are earning only competitive returns, that suggests that economies of scale account for the concentration, and that there is some collusion or oligopoly behavior among the larger firms. Several studies have suggested that in concentrated industries very large firms consistently show higher profits than very small firms. Very likely such industries are concentrated because of economies of scale. Breaking the firms up could produce higher prices, lower profits, or both. For diverse views, see L. Weiss, The Structure–Conduct–Performance Paradigm and Antitrust, 127 U.Pa.L.Rev. 1104, 1115–19 (1979); J.R. Carter, Collusion, Efficiency and Antitrust, 21 J.L. & Econ. 435 (1978); H. Demsetz, Industry Structure, Market Rivalry, and Public Policy, 16 J.L. & Econ. 1 (1973).

18. See S. Peltzman, The Gains and Losses from Industrial Concentration, 20 J.L. & Econ. 229 (1977); J. McGee, In Defense of Industrial Concentration (1971).

the Federal Trade Commission has tried to employ § 5 of the FTC Act, which does not require proof of an agreement. Unfortunately, its record is not particularly promising.[19]

Finally, those bringing antitrust cases have challenged certain "facilitating" practices because they tend to make both cooperative and non-cooperative behavior more likely. In some cases these practices result from agreement among firms; in other cases they appear to be unilateral but widespread across the industry. These facilitating practices are treated mainly in § 4.6, although we return to the issue in the next chapter, since the presence of such practices plays an important role in determining the legality of joint ventures.

§ 4.5 Proving a Price or Output "Agreement" From Indirect or Circumstantial Evidence

Occasionally the Supreme Court has condemned practices as collusive without direct evidence of explicit collusion. In Interstate Circuit, Inc. v. United States,[1] the defendants were a group of eight distributors and several exhibitors of motion pictures. The distributors controlled about 75% of "first-class feature films exhibited in the United States." One of the largest exhibitors sent a letter to the eight distributors suggesting that each insert two clauses in future exhibition contracts with theaters: 1) a clause requiring the theatre to charge at least 40¢ admission for first-run films, and 25¢ admission for subsequent-run films; 2) a clause prohibiting the theaters from exhibiting first-run films with other films as double features. Subsequently the eight distributors incorporated these clauses into many of their contracts. There was no evidence, other than the fact that all eight had received the letter, that the distributors had agreed among themselves.

It is easy to see why an exhibitor would want such clauses in its contracts and those of other exhibitors: the "price maintenance" clause effectively prevented the theaters served by these distributors from price competition with each other. Likewise, the clause restricting double features prevented the theaters from competing by increasing the amount of entertainment they would provide at the maintained price.

If each of these restrictions had been imposed unilaterally by a distributor on an exhibitor, they would probably have been legal. They were not illegal vertical price maintenance because the films were not sold to the exhibitors, but merely licensed to them. The Supreme Court had not yet dealt with vertically imposed nonprice restraints, so the status of the clause against double features was uncertain.[2]

The use of the clauses was clearly illegal, however, if the eight distributors had agreed *among themselves* to place them in every exhibitor's license agreements. In that case there would have been an agreement among competitors which effectively reduced output: fewer people would have attended movies because the price was higher, and those who did attend would have seen fewer movies for their admission price. Often the best way for a cartel to enforce its terms is to find a vertically related firm to do it for them, since such a firm deals with all of them directly. Further, the vertically related firm can sometimes force unwilling competitors to participate. In effect, Interstate Circuit was asking the distributors to make exhibitor collusion enforceable by means of vertical contracts.

The Supreme Court held that the offer given to the eight distributors, plus their nearly unanimous acceptance, was sufficient evidence from which the district court could infer the existence of an agreement among them. As the Court noted:

> Each [distributor] was aware that all were in active competition and that without substantially unanimous action with respect to the restrictions * * * there was risk of a substantial loss of the business and good

19. See § 4.6d.

§ 4.5

1. 306 U.S. 208, 59 S.Ct. 467 (1939).

2. On such restrictions, see ch. 11.

will of the * * * exhibitors, but that with it there was the prospect of increased profits.[3]

In other words, each distributor's apparently unilateral decision to impose resale price and double feature restrictions was irrational given the presumption of competition: a theatre that did not wish to be bound by the restrictions would have sought out a different distributor. In a competitive market, a distributor that could profitably increase its market share by eliminating the restrictions would do so.

The Court characterized the case not as using the antitrust laws to reach tacit collusion, but as using circumstantial evidence to infer the existence of express collusion. There was an explicit "offer." Although there may not have been an explicit "acceptance," acceptance could nonetheless be inferred from the evidence.

A rigorous use of such an approach suggests the following: (1) because the proof is not available, many antitrust conspiracies cannot be established by "direct" evidence, such as written agreements, tape recordings, or testimony of offer and acceptance.[4] As a result, *some* kind of circumstantial proof must be accepted. However, (2) the mere fact that the firms had an opportunity to collude, or that collusion would appear to be profitable to them, is not sufficient to prove collusion;[5] and (3) the plaintiff relying on circumstantial evidence must show in addition to (2) that the defendants' actions were rational (with rational generally meaning profit-increasing) only if they were undertaken with the understanding that other firms would modify their behavior in a similar fashion.[6]

The fact that defendants had the opportunity to conspire is particularly unhelpful if regular meetings are part of the ordinary business of the firms at issue. For example, one should not infer price fixing merely from the fact that competitors had an opportunity to meet at trade association conventions, and that one of the items on the agenda was declining market conditions.[7] Likewise, the fact that competitors occasionally socialize is clearly insufficient.[8] Of course, if there is some evidence that these meetings included discus-

3. 306 U.S. at 222, 59 S.Ct. at 472.

4. See Todorov v. DCH Healthcare Authority, 921 F.2d 1438, 1456 (11th Cir.1991) (evidence of explicit agreements found "only in rare cases"); accord Petroleum Products Antitrust Litigation, 906 F.2d 432, 439 (9th Cir.1990).

5. See, e.g., United States v. General Electric Co., 869 F.Supp. 1285 (S.D.Ohio 1994) (granting motion for acquittal in criminal case; meeting creating opportunity to conspire plus fact that conspiracy would have been profitable insufficient). Cf. the following: Pacific Gas and Elec. Co. v. Howard P. Foley Co., 79 F.3d 1154, 1996–1 Trade Cas. ¶ 71,340 (9th Cir., unpub.), cert. denied, 519 U.S. 1056, 117 S.Ct. 685 (1997) (bid-rigging conspiracy among contractors could have been inferred from evidence that contractors met together, that a manager of one admitted that on other occasions he had submitted bids on behalf of other contractors, and that a witness testified that allocation of bids had been discussed in at least one meeting); Medical X–Ray Film Antitrust Litig., 946 F.Supp. 209 (E.D.N.Y.1996) (following was sufficient to defeat motion to dismiss: (1) manufacturers increased prices by comparable amounts each January; (2) sales representatives met and exchanged information on planned price increases before they were announced, and supplied this information to their own sales representatives; (3) managers requested representatives to seek out information about rivals' planned price increases; (4) at least one manufacturer obtained internal documents from another manufacturer concerning prospective price increases).

6. See, e.g., Toys "R" Us, 5 Trade Reg. Rptr. ¶ 24516 (F.F.C. 1998), which found a horizontal conspiracy among toy manufacturers to refuse to sell same toys to discount warehouses (Sam's, Costco, etc.) as they were selling to plaintiff on the following facts: Toys "R" Us (TRU) was the largest single customer of the major toy manufacturers, and they regarded its business as highly valuable; TRU communicated with each manufacturer that it would purchase toys from them only if they discriminated against discount warehouses; each manufacturer knew that the same communications were sent to others; the manufacturers were in fact looking for new outlets for their toys; each would have lost business to the warehouses if other manufacturers refused TRU's threat and agreed to sell to them. But query, if each toy manufacturer really "needed" TRU's business, could it not make a unilateral decision to favor TRU and disfavor the warehouses?

7. See Weit v. Continental Illinois Nat. Bank, 641 F.2d 457 (7th Cir.1981), cert. denied, 455 U.S. 988, 102 S.Ct. 1610 (1982) (interest rate fixing on credit cards could not be inferred from similarity of actual rates, plus the fact that rates had been discussed at meetings on one or two occasions, and then only with reference to usury laws); accord Seagood Trading Corp. v. Jerrico, Inc., 924 F.2d 1555, 1574–1575 (11th Cir.1991).

8. Souza v. Estate of Bishop, 821 F.2d 1332 (9th Cir. 1987) (extensive social contacts among land owning families insufficient to establish agreement to restrict output, particularly where the lease-only land policies being challenged seemed to be independently rational).

sions of price fixing, or the carrying out of plans to exclude a rival, the evidence is ordinarily admissible and may establish a qualifying agreement, but then we would be back in the territory of establishing an agreement by explicit evidence.[9] Likewise the mere fact that competitors express a common dislike for others and even discuss the problem does not establish a conspiracy if their actions are in their individual self-interest. For example, in *Alvord–Polk* the Third Circuit found sufficient inference of a conspiracy among full service wallpaper sellers in their trade association's opposition to the activities of "800–number" sellers.[10] The latter stocked no wallpaper and advertised in various home improvement magazines that customers should go to the local wallpaper store, identify the wallpaper that they wished to purchase by manufacturer and pattern number, and then order it by the 800 number at a substantial discount. The court concluded that if the trade association served as a "mere conduit" through which the full service sellers could express their frustration to the manufacturers, then no conspiracy could be inferred. However, if the effect of the discussions was associational pressure on the manufacturers to cut of the 800–number sellers, then the trade association discussions amounted to a conspiracy.

As a general proposition, decisions made by trade associations must be regarded as an "agreement" of their members. At the same time, of course, the mere fact that participants in a trade association discuss price or output does not mean that they are agreeing to fix price or reduce marketwide output.

Most forms of parallel behavior, standing alone, establish an agreement only infrequently. Indeed, both competition and oligopoly price leadership induce firms to behave like one another.[11] If all are setting their prices at cost and costs rise, prices will likely go up in tandem.[12] In the *American Tobacco* case the Supreme Court identified consciously parallel behavior that seemed irrational—parallel price increases notwithstanding the arrival of the Great Depression and apparently declining costs.[13] But such conclusions are risky unless a great deal is known about the market. A cartel, just as much as a group of competitors, would ordinarily decrease price in response to falling demand and falling costs; so what the Court discovered may have been as consistent with competition as with cartelization.[14] Courts often say that parallel behavior alone does not establish an agreement unless the plaintiff can also show the presence of certain "plus factors" making the inference of agreement stronger. Relevant plus factors include such things as an oligopolistic market structure, advance posting of parallel prices, a history of price fixing or exchange of price information.[15] Alternatively, as in *Interstate Circuit*,[16] the plaintiff must show that the actions were contrary to the individual self-interest of the actors, and can be explained as rational behavior only on the premise that they were undertaken in con-

9. ES Development v. RWM Enterp., 939 F.2d 547 (8th Cir.1991), cert. denied, 502 U.S. 1097, 112 S.Ct. 1176 (1992) (meeting to discuss tactics for excluding a rival tended to establish a conspiracy).

10. Alvord–Polk v. F. Schumacher & Co., 37 F.3d 996 (3d Cir.1994), cert. denied, 514 U.S. 1063, 115 S.Ct. 1691 (1995).

11. See Reserve Supply Corp. v. Owens–Corning Fiberglas Corp., 971 F.2d 37, 50 (7th Cir.1992) (parallel behavior in oligopoly fails to establish agreement); Market Force Inc. v. Wauwatosa Realty Co., 906 F.2d 1167, 1172–1173 (7th Cir.1990) (same); Clamp–All Corp. v. Cast Iron Soil Pipe Inst., 851 F.2d 478, 484 (1st Cir.1988), cert. denied, 488 U.S. 1007, 109 S.Ct. 789 (1989) (identical price list showed only "that each firm, acting individually, copied the price list of the industry leader * * * "; no agreement).

12. For example, Wilcox v. First Interstate Bank of Or., 815 F.2d 522 (9th Cir.1987) (no conspiracy could be inferred from fact that banks' lending rates changed in tandem); *Petroleum Products*, note 4 (same; petroleum prices).

13. American Tobacco Co. v. U.S., 328 U.S. 781, 803, 66 S.Ct. 1125, 1136 (1946).

14. The Court was obviously influenced by the fact that the defendants had appeared not only to fix prices at high levels for a time, but then to engage jointly in predatory pricing against lower priced firms. See Id. at 797–798, 805.

15. For a more detailed account, see W. Kovacic, The Identification and Proof of Horizontal Agreements under the Antitrust Laws, 38 Antitrust Bull. 5 (1993).

16. Note 1.

cert.[17]

The Ninth Circuit reached quite far in Long Beach v. Standard Oil,[18] concluding that an agreement could be inferred from evidence that firms in a concentrated market simultaneously refused to pay more for petroleum, when each knew that prices would rise if any one of them began paying more. That behavior is as consistent with noncooperative oligopoly as with an agreement, but the court held that it was sufficient evidence to prove an agreement.[19] For example, considering the selling side, oligopolists in a Cournot equilibrium would ordinarily refuse to cut their price to marginal cost. But that conclusion does not establish an agreement among the parties to fix prices.[20] In a Cournot equilibrium a firm is *already* maximizing its profits (by equating marginal cost and marginal revenue), given the output of other firms. One cannot infer that because a firm refuses to cut price to a level closer to marginal cost that the firms have agreed to refuse such cuts.

As a result the conclusion in the *Petroleum Products* decision that "parallel pricing alone" may be sufficient to establish agreement in a highly concentrated market seems incorrect.[21] One would ordinarily expect parallel pricing in such a market, particularly if it is sequential—that is, if each firm is able to observe the prices of others before setting its own price. Of course, if prices are publicized simultaneously, as in a sealed bid auction, then identical prices become far more suspicious, depending on the circumstances. For example, a court should have little difficulty inferring an agreement in the circumstances of the *Cement Institute* decision, in which ten of the Institute's members once bid $3.286854 per barrel of cement—that is, the ten bids were identical to the 1/10,000 of one cent.[22]

In sum, parallel behavior in a concentrated market may establish an agreement, depending on how transactions in the market are designed and information is ordered. If the nature of the market requires all prices and terms to be publicized, then no agreement can be inferred. For example, in the passenger airline industry we can assume that (1) price and service information is communicated to customers through shared computer reservation systems, the internet, and public advertising; and (2) large numbers of customers are indifferent to which carrier they choose, provided that price is the same. The same assumptions would generally apply to, say, the retail sale of gasoline. In such cases a firm that fails to follow a price cutter will face immedi-

17. For example, see In re Beef Indus. Antitrust Litig., 713 F.Supp. 971, 974 (N.D.Tex.1988), affirmed, 907 F.2d 510 (5th Cir.1990):

> [a] plaintiff relying on a theory of conscious parallelism must show two things: (1) that the defendants engaged in consciously parallel action, and (2) that this parallel action was contrary to their economic self-interest so as not to amount to a good-faith business judgment. To avoid summary judgment under this theory, Plaintiffs cannot rely on proof of parallel behavior alone. Significant probative evidence of conscious parallelism is required, with some "plus factor" tending to exclude the possibility that the packers' behavior was unilateral.

Compare Petruzzi's IGA Supermarkets v. Darling–Delaware Co., 998 F.2d 1224 (3d Cir.), cert. denied, 510 U.S. 994, 114 S.Ct. 554 (1993), which concluded that a customer allocation conspiracy among buyers of meat by-products could be inferred from this evidence: (1) The alleged conspirators made various statements about their unwillingness to steal existing accounts from one another, and in fact never attempted to do so ("It is one thing for competitors all to charge the same price, as a perfectly competitive market could lead them to do so. It is quite another for competitors all to refrain from soliciting each other's accounts.") (2) The defendants purchased from new sellers at higher prices than they offered to existing sellers, thus suggesting a customer allocation agreement as to the existing sellers, but free bidding as to new sellers. (3) The defendants each engaged in predatory bidding against allegedly non-conspiring buyers who offered to pay higher prices.

18. City of Long Beach v. Standard Oil Co. of Cal., 872 F.2d 1401, 1409 (9th Cir.1989), amended, 886 F.2d 246 (9th Cir.1989), cert. denied, 493 U.S. 1076, 110 S.Ct. 1126 (1990).

19. Problematically, the court concluded that the oligopolistic market structure entailed that each firm knew that cooperation was essential to making the plan working. Id. at 1407. But this seems precisely wrong. If a market were sufficiently oligopolistic and price could be observed, each firm could reach an individually profit-maximizing decision *without* relying on the cooperation of others. As the market became less oligopolistic, more cooperation would be necessary to make the plan work.

20. See § 4.2a.

21. *Petroleum Products*, note 4, 906 F.2d at 445 n. 9.

22. FTC v. Cement Institute, 333 U.S. 683, 713 & n. 15, 68 S.Ct. 793 (1948). All the bids also offered a 10¢ per barrel discount for payment within 15 days. The Court noted that there were many such situations.

ate loss of market share. As a result, mere parallel behavior does not create an inference of agreement.[23]

By contrast, if one or more important terms of sale are negotiated individually and not publicly disclosed, then parallel behavior in the oligopolistic market creates a much stronger presumption of mutual forbearance, from which an "agreement" can be inferred without stretching § 1 requirements unreasonably far.

Finally, even invited common action fails to establish an agreement if the actors had perfectly rational reasons for engaging in the practice, whether or not they had agreed with others. The relevant question is whether for each individual a particular act would be profit-maximizing whether or not others did the same thing. For example, in *Interstate Circuit* the distributors were invited to adopt uniform contracts forbidding double features of first run films. An affirmative response would be proof of agreement if it would have been foolish for a distributor to do so unilaterally. For example, if the structure and nature of the market made clear that any distributor who unilaterally restricted double features would simply lose market share to other distributors who did not, then the conduct was rational only in the presence of an agreement. The affirmative responses themselves indicate an understanding that all would do the same thing.

By contrast, assume that a credit agency reports that Smith is not paying his bills and a half dozen sellers who receive the support immediately stop doing business with Smith. The half dozen sellers all received the same communication. But on this evidence alone, Smith has no claim of a concerted refusal to deal. Each firm could quite independently decide that it would be profit-maximizing not to deal with Smith. Indeed, firms that continued to deal with Smith might be worse off.[24] Thus, for example, the Supreme Court found no agreement when several film distributors followed the same policy of issuing exclusive first runs only to larger downtown theaters. To be sure, the firms behaved uniformly in denying the plaintiff's request for exclusive first run films at its suburban theaters. But the suburban theatre would probably produce a smaller audience, and each distributor acting in its own interest would ordinarily give an exclusive right only to theaters predicted to have the largest audiences.[25] Applying this form of analysis courts have had little difficulty in holding, for example, that record companies did not necessarily "agree" with each other to adopt policies forbidding stores from renting their records; record rental results in lost sales, and each firm acting unilaterally could quite easily conclude that it was bad business.[26] Likewise, tax consequences that made the sale of land very unattractive justified the conclusion that land owners' acted unilaterally when they all refused to sell their land, but only rented it.[27]

Numerous antitrust cases have challenged competitors' practices of simply publishing manuals that suggest common transaction terms, freight rates, or product quality standards.[28] The problem most of the cases run

23. For example, see Reserve Supply Corp. v. Owens–Corning Fiberglas Corp., 971 F.2d 37 (7th Cir.1992), granting the defendants summary judgment under Sherman § 1 where the principal evidence of agreement was advance posting of identical prices. Although the market was highly concentrated, the product was fungible. The court also noted, however, that discounting from the posted price was common, with different customers obtaining different discounts. Id. at 50.

24. See Richards v. Neilsen Freight Lines, 810 F.2d 898 (9th Cir.1987) (four long distance trucking companies did not necessarily conspire with each other to refuse to deal with the plaintiff local trucker; any long distance trucker who permitted the plaintiff to carry its freight locally risked the possibility that the plaintiff would have taken over the long distance business as well).

25. Theatre Enterprises, Inc. v. Paramount Film Distrib. Corp., 346 U.S. 537, 74 S.Ct. 257 (1954). See also Houser v. Fox Theatres Management Corp., 845 F.2d 1225 (3d Cir.1988) (same). See 6 Antitrust Law ¶ 1415 (1986).

26. A & M Records v. A.L.W., 855 F.2d 368 (7th Cir.1988).

27. Souza v. Estate of Bishop, 821 F.2d 1332 (9th Cir.1987).

28. For example, Jays Foods v. National Classification Comm., 646 F.Supp. 604 (E.D.Va.1985), affirmed mem., 801 F.2d 394 (4th Cir.1986), refusing to condemn truckers' joint use of a classification manual, that enabled truckers to compute relatively complex freight rates for agricultural products; no evidence of either purpose or effect of fixing price. See In re Beef Indus. Antitrust Litig., 713 F.Supp. 971 (N.D.Tex.1988), affirmed, 907 F.2d 510

into is that such manuals seem to be efficiency enhancing.[29] Indeed, many of them provide basic information for compliance with state and federal regulation.[30] To the extent that use of the manual is efficient, a firm will use it whether or not other firms agree to use it as well. As a result, no agreement can be inferred from the use itself.

Often parallel behavior is vertically imposed by contract, and then no necessary conclusion of collusion can be drawn. For example, in *Barry* the Ninth Circuit refused to find horizontal price fixing among physicians in the fact that they had signed identical contracts for reimbursement with a single insurer, Blue Cross.[31] To be sure, uniformity of vertical contracts could conceivably be used to facilitate collusion—but uniformity alone hardly establishes collusion. Many sellers offer standardized terms, with the result that all their buyers, acting quite independently of one another, end up dealing under the same terms. Likewise, one cannot infer horizontal territorial division merely from the fact that individual firms have vertical contracts assigning them exclusive territories, and effectively eliminating competition among them across territorial lines.[32]

The complex issues raised in cases where agreement must be proven by circumstantial evidence has invited the Supreme Court to consider an expanded role for summary judgment—that is, for narrowing the range of circumstances in which conspiracy claims can be given to the jury. These matters are taken up in § 16.8b.

§ 4.6 Reaching Oligopoly Behavior Without Proof of an Agreement on Price or Output

This section deals with two different issues that are directed at the same result. The first is the use of the antitrust laws to go after conspicuously parallel and apparently anticompetitive behavior in the absence of any agreement among the firms in question. The second is antitrust's success in going after "facilitating" practices, that may or may not be the product of an agreement among firms, but which are believed to make collusion or oligopoly behavior more likely to occur. Although the questions are analytically distinct, most decisions that deal with either issue at any length involve both, and their discussion often mixes the two.

4.6a. Introduction; Supreme Court Sherman Act Decisions

In *Interstate Circuit*, discussed in the previous section,[1] the Supreme Court relied on circumstantial evidence that the distributor's responses were inconsistent with profit-maximization unless there had been an understanding, or agreement, among the firms. However, in often-quoted dicta the Supreme Court added the following:

> While the District Court's finding of an agreement of the distributors among themselves is supported by the evidence, we think that in the circumstances of this case such agreement * * * was not a prerequisite to an unlawful conspiracy. It was

(5th Cir.1990) (refusing to condemn use of a sheet showing cattle prices; no evidence of agreement).

29. One good example is the Relative value scales (RVS), which is a published list of the *relative* values, or time consumed, by individual services delivered by doctors, dentists, auto mechanics, etc. By using such a published book competing professionals can arrive at substantial price uniformity simply by matching each other's hourly fees. But the RVS may simply be a form of information exchange designed to tell a professional whether the amount of time and attention she devotes to a certain procedure is in line with that of others in her field, or to enable her to bill rationally without measuring actual time at all. For example, if a physician see three patients at once, measuring actual time serving each one may be costly. See United States v. American Soc. of Anesthesiologists, 473 F.Supp. 147 (S.D.N.Y.1979); and 13 Antitrust Law ¶ 2112d (1999).

30. Several of these practices are discussed in the section on information changes in the next chapter. See § 5.3.

31. Barry v. Blue Cross of Cal., 805 F.2d 866 (9th Cir.1986).

32. See Package Shop v. Anheuser–Busch, 675 F.Supp. 894 (D.N.J.1987) (evidence of conduct by wholesale beer distributor which was equally consistent with brewer initiated vertical restraints and possible horizontal restraints insufficient to defeat a motion for summary judgment).

§ 4.6

1. Interstate Circuit, Inc. v. United States, 306 U.S. 208, 59 S.Ct. 467 (1939).

> enough that, knowing that concerted action was contemplated and invited, the distributors gave their adherence to the scheme and participated in it.[2]

Whether the Court really meant that an agreement was not required seems unclear. The statement that an "agreement * * * was not a prerequisite to an unlawful conspiracy" seems to be a contradiction in terms. The most reasonable meaning is that a "conspiracy" for antitrust purposes need not contain a classically defined "agreement" as the common law of contracts uses that term.

The closest the Supreme Court has come to dispensing with the traditional agreement requirement is American Tobacco Co. v. United States,[3] where it condemned sudden, simultaneous, and fairly radical price movements among three major manufacturers of tobacco products who collectively controlled 90% of the market. Based on the evidence of the price movements, the jury found that a conspiracy existed and the Court concluded that the "record of price changes is circumstantial evidence of the existence of a conspiracy * * *." However, the court then added, in words recalling *Interstate Circuit* :

> No formal agreement is necessary to constitute an unlawful conspiracy. Often crimes are a matter of inference deduced from the acts of the person accused and done in pursuance of a criminal purpose. Where the conspiracy is proved, as here, from the evidence of the action taken in concert by the parties to it, it is all the more convincing proof of an intent to exercise the power of exclusion acquired through that conspiracy. The essential combination or conspiracy in violation of the Sherman Act may be found in a course of dealings or other circumstances as well as in any exchange of words. Where the circumstances are such as to warrant a jury in finding that the conspirators had a unity of purpose or a common design and understanding, or a meeting of minds in an unlawful arrangement, the conclusion that a conspiracy is established is justified.[4]

This statement, just as the one in *Interstate Circuit*, is hardly a model of clarity. But it appears not to mean that a Sherman Act conspiracy can be established without any agreement whatsoever. The intended meaning seems to be that Sherman Act agreements can be established by circumstantial, or indirect, evidence. Further, the agreement need not be "formal," in the sense of involving discrete, identifiable acts of offer and acceptance.

Beginning with these relatively unhelpful statements from the Supreme Court, the lower courts have repeatedly wrestled with the claim that certain kinds of parallel activity deserve antitrust condemnation even though there is not convincing evidence, whether direct or circumstantial, of an agreement.

The problem is not so much that we do not know how to recognize the signs of collusion or oligopoly, or the kinds of markets in which they are likely to occur. Although there is plenty of disagreement at the margins, there is broad agreement in the middle. Factors such as high concentration on the seller's side and diffusion on the buyer's side, significant economies of scale, a standardized product and publicly announced prices and terms, are generally believed to suggest that a market is conducive to express or tacit collusion, as well as noncooperative oligopoly.[5] Some additional factors can help a law enforcer determine the degree to which such collusion is actually occurring. These include: 1) stable market shares; 2) a rigid price structure that seems unresponsive to changes in demand; 3) industry-wide use of facilitating devices that make tacit collusion easier. Important among these devices are exchanges of price or output information among competitors, standardization of products or terms of sale, and market-wide vertical integration or resale price maintenance. Facilitating devices are especially suspect if they are the product of explicit agreement among the competing firms, or if they result in systematic, market-wide price discrimination.

2. 306 U.S. at 226, 59 S.Ct. at 474.

3. 328 U.S. 781, 66 S.Ct. 1125 (1946). See § 4.5.

4. 328 U.S. at 809–810, 66 S.Ct. at 1139.

5. See § 4.4.

Both stable market shares and prices that fail to fluctuate with demand are good indicators that a market is not performing competitively. In a competitive market, the relative positions of individual firms usually changes. The market shares of the most efficient firms are likely to grow, while those of the least efficient become smaller. Prices generally decline in times of falling demand, as firms try to clear inventories and cut losses. In a cartelized market, however, these things will happen far more slowly. As market demand declines the monopoly profit-maximizing price will decline, but it will not decline as fast. Furthermore, in a cartel it will not decline at all until the cartel members decide to lower it—which they generally will do only in response to widespread cheating or defection, a sure sign that the market as a whole is deteriorating.

4.6b. Challenging Facilitators Established by Agreement

Firms may agree among themselves, either explicitly or tacitly, to engage in certain practices that will make collusion easier. In all such cases it is important to distinguish the agreement to engage in the practice from the agreement to fix prices.[6] Agreements to exchange price information or to standardize products are clearly agreements, and they may facilitate the maintenance of prices at supracompetitive levels. But in and of themselves such agreements are not price-fixing and may be quite pro-competitive.

One of the most obvious of these facilitating agreements is exchanges of price information. Nothing makes monitoring of market prices easier than an agreement that every firm will disclose its sale prices to competitors. Like many suspicious nonprice agreements, however, information exchanges can also make a market perform more competitively. Their relative merits are discussed in the next chapter.

Agreements among competitors to standardize products or terms of sale fall into the same ambiguous category. Such standardization can substantially reduce customer information costs and make the market operate more efficiently; if "number two plywood" or "grade A eggs" mean exactly the same thing to all sellers and buyers in a market, customers can determine what they are buying far more easily and the market will perform more efficiently. However, in a concentrated industry, product standardization can facilitate express or tacit collusion because it enables each firm more effectively to monitor the pricing of another firm. It may make noncooperative oligopoly behavior more successful as well.[7]

Courts have seldom condemned simple product standardization by agreement among competitors.[8] However, they have been very strict about any agreed standardization of price or other transaction terms. For example, in Sugar Institute, Inc. v. United States[9] the Supreme Court condemned a trade association rule that required the Institute members to publicize their prices in advance and forbad deviation from those prices, price discrimination, or giving secret discounts or other price concessions. The industry was highly concentrated, and the rules may have permitted sugar manufacturers to achieve cartel-like prices.[10] In *Catalano*,[11] the Supreme Court

6. See 6 Antitrust Law ¶ 1409 (1986).

7. Standardization agreements can sometimes be input restriction agreements. If the firms have monopsony power in some product that they buy, an agreement to "standardize" the product may be no more than an explicit agreement to fix the purchase price. For example, see National Macaroni Manufacturers v. FTC, 65 F.T.C. 583 (1964), affirmed, 345 F.2d 421 (7th Cir.1965), condemning an agreement among macaroni manufacturers to "standardize" the contents of macaroni products at 50% semolina (hard wheat) and 50% farina (soft wheat). Since the macaroni producers used most of the nation's semolina, they were in a position to depress its price by reducing the proportion of semolina in their products. By contrast, an agreement among bolt manufacturers to standardize a metal alloy for bolts at 50% steel could not plausibly be calculated to depress the market price of steel, for the steel used in bolts is only a tiny part of the steel market. See 12 Antitrust Law ¶ 2136 (1999).

8. But see § 5.4c, on standard setting coupled with refusals to deal; and *C-O-Two Fire Equip. Co. v. United States*, 197 F.2d 489 (9th Cir.), cert. denied, 344 U.S. 892, 73 S.Ct. 211 (1952) (condemning collusion facilitated by an agreement to manufacture standardized fire extinguishers); see 12 Antitrust Law ¶ 2136b (1999).

9. 297 U.S. 553, 56 S.Ct. 629 (1936).

10. The *Sugar Institute* case revealed a pattern of price leadership much like that used in the airline industry today. A dominant firm in one area would announce a

condemned an agreement among beer wholesalers to eliminate a short term trade credit that many of them had formerly given to retailers. Under the agreement the wholesalers would sell only if the buyer paid before or at delivery. The effect of the agreement was to standardize the price terms and make a firm's sale prices easier to monitor. For example, a price of $6.00 per case, payable 180 days after delivery is lower than a price of $6.00 per case payable immediately upon delivery. The Supreme Court treated the agreement as little more than a variant of price fixing and condemned it under the *per se* rule.[12]

The problem with so many facilitators established by agreement is that, while they may facilitate collusion, they may also make production or distribution work more efficiently. Information exchanges, product standardization and testing, agreements creating markets, regulating them, and standardizing transactions all fall within this category. They are treated in the subsequent chapter on joint ventures.

4.6c. "Unilateral" Facilitators; Basing–Point Pricing Schemes

The case for bringing facilitating practices within § 1 of the Sherman Act becomes much more strained when the facilitators themselves seem to be unilateral—that is, when there is inadequate evidence that the firms agreed among each other to use them.

A variety of practices can facilitate collusion, even though the practices themselves are unilateral. Some of the practices may be independently efficient, and thus firms may employ them without regard for their ability to facilitate collusion. For example, industry-wide vertical integration and resale price maintenance can facilitate cartel behavior even as they improve the efficiency of a firm's distribution network.[13] At the same time, they can enable firms to monitor one another's final output prices. If manufacturers deal with large distributors, their sales are likely to be infrequent, covering large amounts of merchandise, and having individually and privately negotiated terms. In such cases both express and tacit collusion will be difficult to maintain. However, if all sales are small, with publicly announced prices and terms, then price cutting will be detected far more quickly.[14] But in any event, today it seems clear that only a small percentage of RPM or vertical nonprice restraints are in fact used to facilitate horizontal conclusion.[15] As a result, proving the vertical restraint in no way establishes a horizontal agreement.

Facilitators of price discrimination are particularly interesting. Price discrimination occurs whenever a seller has two different rates of return on different sales of the same product.[16] Assuming that the lower price sale is competitive, the higher price sale must give the seller some monopoly profits. Persistent price discrimination is inconsistent with competition: customers asked to pay the discriminatorily high price will seek out a different seller, and in a competitive market there will always be a seller willing to make the sale at marginal cost. The existence of persistent price discrimination is therefore evidence that the market is not performing competitively.

price increase well in advance of the effective date. If other firms went along, the increase would stick. If the other firms did not, it would be rescinded. The Court noted that a "move," or price increase "takes place only if all refiners follow a similar course. If any one fails to follow with a like announcement, the others must withdraw their advance, since sugar is a completely standardized commodity." 297 U.S. at 580, 56 S.Ct. at 634. "Often, too, the advance [that is, price increase] would be withdrawn because one refiner would refrain from following the announcement. Except in a few instances, a decline announcement was followed by all." Ibid.

11. Catalano, Inc. v. Target Sales, Inc., 446 U.S. 643, 100 S.Ct. 1925 (1980). See 12 Antitrust Law ¶ 2022 (1999).

12. See also *Int'l. Assn. of Conference Interpreters*, 5 Trade Reg. Rep. ¶ 24235 (FTC, 1997) (condemning agreement among interpreters regulating the prices and reimbursement they would receive for off-days, travel, and other collateral expenses, as well as the number of interpreters that must be employed at a conference of a particular size).

13. See generally ch. 11.

14. Likewise, vertical integration by price or territorial restrictions may facilitate cartelization at the *retail* level. See § 11.2b.

15. See P. Ippolito, Resale Price Maintenance: Empirical Evidence from Litigation, 34 J. L. & Econ. 263 (1991).

16. See § 14.1.

Among the most revealing collusion cases involving price discrimination are the delivered pricing cases, particularly those involving basing point pricing. Delivered pricing schemes have been common in industries in which transportation costs are high in proportion to the value of the commodity sold. Such schemes involve a certain amount of price discrimination. As a result, their existence alone may be enough to create an inference of express or tacit collusion. Like information exchanges, agreements to standardize products and terms, or vertical integration, delivered pricing schemes can enable firms to monitor each other's prices and respond to changes more effectively.[17]

Suppose that a single firm sells to three customers located 10, 100 and 400 miles away from the seller. All three buyers place the same value on the product, $100, and the seller sells the product to each of them at that price, which includes delivery. If delivery costs are proportional to distance and the sale to the most remote buyer is profitable, the sales to the closer buyers will give the seller a monopoly profit. In this case the seller clearly is engaging in price discrimination.

In a perfectly competitive market, the two buyers who were 10 and 100 miles from the seller would have found a seller willing to charge a lower delivered price. Competition tends to drive prices to actual costs and favors the "best placed" or closest seller to any particular buyer, particularly if transportation costs are substantial in relation to the value of the product.

A cartel will often want to eliminate this "placement" competition. If price fixers merely set a price, to which actual freight costs are added, the firms may continue to compete by establishing a proliferation of "shipping points" close to customers. The firms can then cheat on the cartel by billing a lower freight rate from one of these shipping points, even though the shipment actually originated somewhere else. Further, demand in the industry may shift geographically from one period to the next, and the current sales of individual sellers in a competitive market will reflect these cycles. By contrast, most cartels would prefer that market shares of their members be relatively stable from one period to the next.[18]

Finally, complicated shipping tariffs make policing of the cartel very difficult.[19] If every member of a cartel adds actual freight costs to the cartel price in order to produce a delivered price, final output prices will vary considerably from one transaction to the next. For one firm to monitor the prices of other firms in the cartel would be very difficult.

In order to solve all these problems many cartels have not only fixed the price of the commodity itself, but they have also "fixed" the freight rates. One of the most effective mechanisms for eliminating all placement competition and producing uniform delivered prices across the entire cartel is basing point pricing. In basing point pricing systems the sellers identify some central point as the "basing point." All quoted prices then add freight charges measured from the basing point to the buyer's delivery point, even though the product was in fact shipped from somewhere else. For example, under the "Pittsburgh Plus" formula once used in the steel industry, steel mills located across the northeastern and north central United States billed all customers for freight computed from Pittsburgh to the delivery destination.[20] If the price of the

17. See 12 Antitrust Law ¶ 2025 (1999).

18. Stable market shares can increase the cartel's overall profitability by permitting individual members to operate with smaller plants. For example, a firm that sells 6,000 units per year will sell 12,000 in a two year period. A firm that sells 10,000 units one year and 2,000 units the next also sells 12,000 units in a two year period. However the first firm needs to carry enough capacity to produce 6,000 units per year. The second must carry enough capacity to produce 10,000 units per year and perhaps operate at far less than the optimal rate of output during the second year. The firm whose output is constant from one year to the next is likely to have lower costs.

19. This appears to be the explanation for delivered pricing in the *du Pont (Ethyl)* case, 101 FTC 425 (1983), reversed sub nom. E.I. du Pont De Nemours & Co. v. FTC, 729 F.2d 128 (2d Cir.1984). The Commission noted the great difficulty that the participants would have had tracking each other's prices in the absence of such a scheme. 101 FTC at 637.

20. See United States Steel, 8 F.T.C. 1 (1924); FTC v. Cement Institute, 333 U.S. 683, 714, 68 S.Ct. 793 (1948). For a more detailed economic analysis of basing point

steel were fixed, the buyer would receive identical bids for delivered steel. In this way the basing point system facilitates collusion, for each firm finds it fairly easy to track the actual price of steel in the market.[21]

Basing point pricing systems can increase the social costs of the cartel. As a general rule even the monopolist or cartel has an incentive to reduce costs: the sellers will be able to keep more profits for themselves. Basing point pricing, however, can destroy any incentive for either buyer or seller to reduce transportation costs. If buyers 10 miles and 500 miles from a seller use a basing point formula they will add in the same freight charges, even though the charges incurred by the closer seller are far lower. As a result the buyer has no cost incentive to select the closer seller.

Courts have consistently condemned basing point pricing under § 5 of the Federal Trade Commission Act, when the evidence indicated an agreement among competitors to engage in basing point pricing.[22] More controversial, however, has been judicial treatment of industry-wide basing point pricing when there is no evidence that the sellers agreed to engage in the practice. In Triangle Conduit and Cable Co. v. FTC[23] the Court upheld the FTC's condemnation of market-wide basing point pricing on two different theories: first, that the firms had agreed with each other to engage in basing point pricing; second, that the mere "concurrent use of a formula" in making delivered price bids, with the knowledge that other firms did the same thing, violated § 5 of the FTC Act. The Court affirmed the FTC's finding of a conspiracy, but also approved the second theory, noting that even absent express agreement,

> each conduit seller knows that each of the other sellers is using the basing point formula; each knows that by using it he will be able to quote identical delivered prices and thus present a condition of matched prices under which purchasers are isolated and deprived of choice among sellers so far as price advantage is concerned * * *. [W]e cannot say that the Commission was wrong in concluding that the individual use of the basing point method as here used does constitute an unfair method of competition.

In Boise Cascade Corp. v. FTC[24] the Ninth Circuit called the *Triangle Conduit* decision into question, refusing to condemn industry-wide basing point pricing when there was no evidence of an agreement among the firms to engage in the practice. The Court concluded that § 5 of the Federal Trade Commission Act requires the Commission to show *either* an "overt agreement" among the firms to engage in basing point pricing or else that the practice "actually had the effect of fixing or stabilizing prices." The Fifth Circuit condemned the same practice under § 1 of the Sherman Act, however, by affirming a jury verdict that the practice did have an effect on prices and that the plaintiffs had been injured as a result. There was also evidence of communication among the parties from which the jury could have inferred an explicit agreement.[25]

There is some merit to the Ninth Circuit's requirement that, absent sufficient evidence of a horizontal conspiracy, the plaintiff must show that basing point pricing had an anticompetitive effect. Although basing point pricing is a form of price discrimination, and price

pricing see G. Stigler, The Organization of Industry 147–164 (1983).

21. Lastly, basing point pricing schemes can give cartels a mechanism for punishing cheaters: they can make the cheaters' location an involuntary basing point for a fixed period of time. During that period the cheater can compete for sales only by cutting its sale prices or absorbing some of its actual freight costs. See *Cement Institute*, note 20, which describes use of this method of discipline.

22. *Cement Institute*, note 20, condemned basing point pricing under § 5 of the FTC Act. There was no direct evidence of explicit agreement among the firms; however, firms in the industry were notorious for submitting identical competitive bids for projects. The Court held that the Commission could infer a conspiracy, whether "express or implied," from these facts. Basing point pricing has also been condemned as illegal price discrimination under the Robinson–Patman Act. Corn Prod. Ref. Co. v. FTC, 324 U.S. 726, 65 S.Ct. 961 (1945). See 14 Antitrust Law ¶ 2321 (1999).

23. 168 F.2d 175 (7th Cir.1948), affirmed sub nom. Clayton Mark & Co. v. FTC, 336 U.S. 956, 69 S.Ct. 888 (1949). Quotation at 181.

24. 637 F.2d 573 (9th Cir.1980).

25. In re Plywood Antitrust Litigation, 655 F.2d 627, 634 (5th Cir.1981), cert. dismissed, 462 U.S. 1125, 103 S.Ct. 3100 (1983).

discrimination is inconsistent with perfect competition, in the real world competition is never perfect. Many sellers, even in multi-seller markets, have substantial market power over certain classes of customers. In such markets price discrimination sometimes can increase competition. This is particularly true of markets in which sellers are dispersed and freight costs are high in relation to the value of the product. In that case a seller may have a great deal of market power over buyers that are near to it but far from any other seller. At some distance away, however—midway between the firm and a competitor—there will be other buyers who have a choice between two firms that could sell the product at the same delivered price. If a firm wants to make sales at this fringe of its own dominant territory, it will have to compete for them. If it competes by lowering its sale price, however, it must lower the price to all customers, even to those "captive" customers which are nearby and from whom it would otherwise obtain monopoly profits.

Instead, the firm would like to find some mechanism for price discriminating: for selling to nearby "captive" purchasers at a monopoly price but to more remote purchasers at a more competitive price. The seller can do this by establishing a basing point in the direction of the firms on the fringe of the market whose business it would like to obtain. It will bid for sales to those firms, not by lowering its price, but by absorbing part of the freight costs.

For example, firms A and B in Figure 7 manufacture cement, in which transportation costs are high. They are located 100 miles apart. Each firm has a natural advantage with respect to buyers located within a 40 mile (solid) circle from its plant. That is, before B could make sales in A's circle, B's delivered price would have to be less than B's marginal costs. However, buyers located in the area between the two solid circles, such as X, are roughly equidistant from A and B. If A wants to obtain X's trade, A will have to compete with B. One way A can compete is by lowering the price of cement. In that case, however, A will have to lower the price to all buyers and A will lose the monopoly profits from customers within his own circle. The alternative is for A to engage in multiple basing point pricing. A sets up a basing point, A.′ If the buyer is located within A's solid circle, A can keep the buyer's trade by charging actual freight costs from its plant. A can effectively give X a lower price, however, by billing X for freight from point A′ even though the cement was probably shipped from point A.[26] In the absence of explicit agreement among competitors, therefore, a court must make some kind of determination whether a basing point pricing scheme is competitive or collusive.

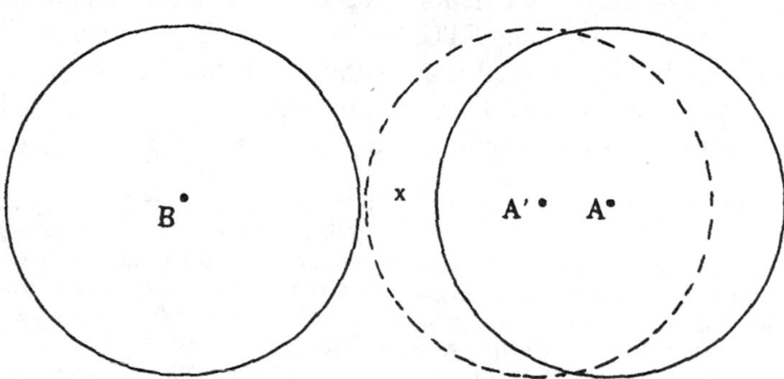

Figure 7

26. See D. Haddock, Basing–Point Pricing: Competitive vs. Collusive Theories, 72 Amer.Econ.Rev. 289 (1982); D. Carlton, A Reexamination of Delivered Pricing Systems, 22 J.L. & Econ. 51 (1983); S.J. DeCanio, Delivered Pricing and Multiple Basing Point Equilibria, 99 Q.J.Econ. 329 (1984). On the use of basing-point pricing by fringe firms, see I. Ayres & J. Braithwaite, Partial–Industry Regulation: A Monopsony Standard for Consumer Protection, 80 Calif. L. Rev. 13, 53 (1992).

Under the Ninth Circuit's analysis, the relevant question is how much evidence of anticompetitive effect is needed to warrant condemnation of basing point pricing under § 5 of the FTC Act when there is no proof of a horizontal agreement. The evidence in *Boise Cascade* and the Fifth Circuit *Plywood* litigation seems much more consistent with collusive rather than competitive use of basing points. For example, the defendants all used exactly the same set of multiple basing points. If the basing points were created unilaterally by firms to enable them to compete at the fringes of their markets, different firms would probably establish different basing points.[27]

4.6d. Other Facilitators; § 5 of Federal Trade Commission Act

The "contract," "combination" or "conspiracy" requirement has frustrated judicial efforts to use § 1 of the Sherman Act to reach poor performance in concentrated markets without some evidence of express collusion. The Federal Trade Commission has tried repeatedly to take advantage of the broader language of § 5 of the FTC Act, which condemns "unfair methods of competition," to attack apparent tacit collusion. That statute's language does not explicitly require an agreement. Further, the courts have held that in enforcing § 5, the FTC may condemn practices that would not constitute violations of the Sherman Act.[28] Cases like *Triangle Conduit*, discussed in § 4.6c, essentially dispensed with any agreement requirement in order to reach parallel uses of basing point pricing under the FTC Act.[29]

Nevertheless, the Commission's efforts to use the FTC Act to attack collusion or oligopoly facilitators in the absence of agreement have not been encouraging. In Ethyl Corp.[30] the FTC relied on § 5 to condemn several sales practices of the four firms that manufactured gasoline antiknock compounds. The practices, all undertaken uniformly but without apparent agreement among the four firms, included 1) a policy of announcing price changes 30 days in advance; 2) "most favored nation" clauses in sales contracts, which promised that the buyer would receive the full benefit of any subsequent price reduction for a certain specified period; and 3) uniform delivered prices.

The Commission placed great emphasis on the fact that FTCA § 5, unlike § 1 of the Sherman Act, does not require proof of agreement among the firms. If a practice both affects competition adversely *and* violates the "basic legislative goals of the Sherman Act," then it could be reached under § 5 even though it might fall outside the Sherman Act. The Commission evaluated the market and found all the indicators of tacit collusion: very high concentration and firms with roughly equal costs; high entry barriers compounded by extensive government regulations; inelastic demand; a generally homogenous and undifferentiated product; and finally, a net rate of return 50% higher than the rate earned by most producers of chemicals.[31]

In such a market any of the alleged practices could have facilitated tacit collusion. The policy of announcing price changes 30 days in advance would enable firms to monitor and respond to the price decisions of the other firms. In this case, two smaller firms in the market generally followed the price leadership of the two larger firms.

Price protection clauses, sometimes called "most favored nation" clauses, and price matching guarantees are somewhat more ambiguous. In the first of these, the seller retroactively promises the buyer that it will match a competitor's lower price. By contrast, matching price guarantees are a promise usually made by a retailer that it will match any advertised price offered by a competitor.

27. Probably, but not necessarily. A firm might compete with a rival by duplicating its basing points, particularly if the latter firm had lower costs and wanted to invite customers to make price comparisons that were uncomplicated by differential freight rates. Whether such competition would result in a multi-firm system of identical basing points across an entire market is a different matter.

28. See § 15.2.

29. See also National Lead Co., 49 F.T.C. 791, 876 (1953), affirmed on other grounds, 352 U.S. 419, 77 S.Ct. 502 (1957) (ambiguously suggesting that conspiracy could be proven without agreement).

30. Note 19.

31. On the use of accounting data to infer monopoly profits, see § 3.9c.

Buyers may think price protection clauses protect *them* from subsequent price reductions that might be given to other firms. If A buys today at a price of $50, and tomorrow the seller sells to B at a price of $45, A will be entitled to a refund of $5. Nonetheless, such clauses are often a sign not of hard customer bargaining but of tacit seller collusion. Price protection clauses tend to make oligopolies perform more like the Cournot model in which secret price cuts, which are profitable at any price above marginal cost, are impossible.[32] The clauses effectively make discriminatory price reductions very expensive and easy to detect, and give the cartel a new set of policemen: customers. If the seller attempts to cheat by giving B a $5 reduction in price, A will demand similar treatment under its price protection clause.[33]

Indeed, one way of looking at both price protection clauses and price matching guarantees is as price fixing agreements with customer-victims. If A and B agreed that each would match the other's prices, we would have a cartel. But if A and B individually agree with customers that each will match the other's prices, we have two vertical agreements that look superficially pro-competitive, but could have precisely the same anticompetitive result.[34] We sometimes think that the Wal–Marts of the world are doing us a favor by advertising that they will match any competitors' price. In fact, they could simply be making advertised low prices less attractive to competitors. As low price advertising becomes less attractive, it will also become less frequent and the result could be an oligopoly structure with the large "discount" store as price leader.[35]

The Second Circuit was not impressed by any of the Commission's theories of tacit collusion. The court vacated the Commission's decision, expressly refusing to hold that § 5 could be "violated by non-collusive, non-predatory and independent conduct of a non-artificial nature," even when the conduct *results* in a substantial lessening of competition. Rather, the Commission would have to show either "1) evidence of anticompetitive intent or purpose on the part of the producer charged, or (2) the absence of an independent legitimate business reason for its conduct."[36] The court opined that oligopoly is a market "condition," not a "method" of avoiding competition. This characterization would appear to be a reference to Professor Turner's observation that poor economic performance is inherent in oligopoly, and marginal cost pricing would be irrational.[37] But as § 4.4a notes, the observation ignores the fact that *discriminatory* price cuts, given to some buyers but not others, can undermine oligopoly and restore competitive prices. Practices that make discriminatory price cuts expensive or impossible are not a natural condition in the market; they must be interposed.

32. See § 4.4a. That is, since the price protection clauses make price discrimination difficult, each firm will equate its own marginal cost and marginal revenue in the Cournot style.

33. For further explication, see A. Edlin, Do Guaranteed–Low–Price Policies Guarantee High Prices, and Can Antitrust Rise to the Challenge, 111 Harv. L. Rev. 528 (1997); J. Baker, Vertical Restraints with Horizontal Consequences: Competitive Effects of "Most–Favored-Customer" Clauses, 64 Antitrust L.J. 517 (1996); G. Hay, Oligopoly, Shared Monopoly, and Antitrust Law, 67 Cornell L. Rev. 439, 455 (1982); G. Hay, Facilitating Practices: the *Ethyl* Case 182, in The Antitrust Revolution (3d ed.; J. Kwoka & L. White eds. 1999); M. Sargent, Economics Upside–Down: Low–Price Guarantees as Mechanisms for Facilitating Tacit Collusion, 141 Univ. Pa. L. Rev. 2055 (1993).

34. See J. Simons, Fixing Price With Your Victim: Efficiency and Collusion with Competitor–Based Formula Pricing Clauses, 17 Hofstra L. Rev. 599 (1989).

35. See 6 Antitrust Law ¶ 1435 (1986).

36. *du Pont*, note 19, 729 F.2d at 139.

37. The court did note one thing that the Commission failed to account for adequately. The buyers in the additive market were the "large, aggressive and sophisticated" major oil companies. If profits in the antiknock compound market were high, "nothing would prevent them from integrating backwards into the antiknock industry," thereby transferring these monopoly profits to themselves. 729 F.2d at 131. The fact that they had not integrated backward suggests either that they could not produce the compound at minimum efficient scale, or else that the ethyl market was not performing as anticompetitively as the Commission suggested.

There is an alternative explanation for the oil companies' failure to integrate vertically, however. For environmental reasons, lead antiknock compounds were being phased out; as a result, the industry at issue had a short life expectancy, perhaps not justifying the entry costs of vertical integration. See ibid.

The court did not rule out any possibility that § 5 could be used in the future to pursue facilitating devices in oligopoly markets. However, it held that the FTC "owes a duty to define the conditions under which conduct claimed to facilitate price uniformity would be unfair," so that firms would be able to predict what they could legally do and what they could not.

A troublesome part of the Second Circuit's reversal is that it fails to consider the limited remedies available to the FTC, which make the social cost of overdeterrence in FTC actions smaller than it would be in cases brought by the Justice Department or private plaintiffs under the Sherman Act. The FTC could not imprison the defendants' officers or make them pay damages. It merely issued a prospective cease and desist order forbidding them from communicating price changes in advance or using delivered pricing, and forbidding the largest two defendants from using price protection clauses.

The fact that FTC remedies are both prospective and limited to injunctive relief justifies broader standards of liability under the FTC Act than under the Sherman Act. In this particular case, even if the FTC were wrong and the practices at issue were not intended to facilitate tacit collusion, the social cost of enjoining the practices would not be high, for there was no convincing evidence that the practices were efficiency creating either. In a concentrated market, easily conducive to collusion, a little overdeterrence in cases involving ambiguous practices can be a good thing, at least if the practices have little obvious social value.

Equally troublesome is the high standard that the court created for proving oligopoly. For example, the court noted that the facilitating practices that the FTC challenged were not used uniformly, discounts were frequently given, and there was a certain amount of non-price competition.[38] But no oligopoly is perfect. Indeed, the most likely effect of oligopoly is price discrimination. Large, well-informed buyers receive discounts or other amenities that tend to drive the price/cost relationship toward the competitive level. Smaller, more isolated buyers pay full price. One would have to search a long time for an oligopoly where discounting or non-price competition were completely absent.

An FTC proceeding against the manufacturers of ready-to-eat breakfast cereals fared no better than the *Ethyl* case.[39] The allegations were that the four national manufacturers of breakfast cereal violated § 5 of the FTC Act by agreeing, either implicitly or explicitly, to monopolize the market. Since there was no worthwhile evidence of conspiracy, the action proceeded on a theory that the FTC characterized initially not as tacit collusion, but as "shared monopoly." This oxymoron has been used to suggest that oligopoly firms might tacitly collude not only in maintaining supracompetitive prices, but also in excluding other firms from the market. The FTC alleged that the cereal manufacturers simultaneously avoided competition with each other and made entry of new firms more difficult by engaging in excessive product differentiation. Under the theory the firms "made it extremely difficult for new firms to enter, since an entrant would have to offer several brands to achieve minimal scale economies." The Commission noted, however, that consumer demand appeared to support the multiplicity of offerings.

The relation between product differentiation and competition or collusion is very complex. The proliferation of cereal offerings probably deterred new entry by denying to any prospective entrant a market niche large enough to establish itself.[40] Further, under traditionally accepted models of product differentiation, the exclusiveness of trademarked names and styles create at least modest consumer preferences that are unrelated to price. (Only Kellogg's, for example, manufactures Rice Krispies, and some people prefer them strongly enough to pay a little more). As a

38. *du Pont*, 729 F.2d at 141.

39. In re Kellogg Co., 99 F.T.C. 8 (1982).

40. See R. Schmalensee, Entry Deterrence in the Ready–to–East Breakfast Cereal Industry, 9 Bell J.Econ. 305 (1978).

result each manufacturer probably has at least a small amount of market power.

By contrast, product differentiation often complicates tacit collusion by making it more difficult for firms to arrive at consensus about price, output, and quality.[41] However, one must not push this point too far. Not all forms of product differentiation represent substantial differences in firm technology or costs, or even significant differences in consumer preferences. For example, ready-to-eat breakfast cereals generally use commonly known recipes and standard agricultural products. The real differences are confined to copyrighted names and labeling, and perhaps to the shape of the extruder that is used to produce each particle. You may make a cereal containing 45% wheat and 55% sugar, run it through a duck shaped extruder and call it "Ducks." I may make a cereal in a similar machine, with 55% corn and 45% sugar, put it through a rabbit shaped extruder and call it "Rabbits." You might sell your cereal in a red box, while I choose green. We have now achieved a degree of product differentiation that may be significant in the eyes of a four year old child, but have we really undermined the possibilities of collusion? Probably not very much. Our costs are very likely much the same and the demand curves we face are probably close to identical.

In all cases involving ambiguous practices—that is, practices that are plausibly either competitive or anti-competitive—it is wise to look first at structural evidence. Sifting through numerous theories about whether product differentiation, publication of freight books, or most favored nation clauses promote or undermine competition is frequently a frustrating task. In such cases the ambiguity of the practice precludes automatic application of the per se rule.[42] At least a quick look at market structure can help a court weed out those practices for which further inquiry is unnecessary, because there is little chance that the practice could facilitate effective collusion. For example, the publication of a freight rate book in a market that contains dozens of trucking firms where entry is easy suggests that, whatever the intent, effective collusion is not likely. This conclusion could be bolstered by some evidence that competition in the market is in fact quite vigorous. By contrast, the same practice in a highly concentrated industry, with high entry barriers and a fungible product or service, suggests a danger of collusion. In that case the burden should shift to the defendants to show that the practice is calculated to result in higher output.

But such screening by structural evidence does not enable us to deal with troubling cases such as *Kellogg*, where the market is concentrated, entry barriers are high, product differentiation seems to be desired by consumers (at least to a point), and there is no agreement among the firms to differentiate or to engage in other practices. In such cases, the only viable decision may be to let the practice alone for the time being but to scrutinize mergers within the industry very closely. We simply do not know enough to make a judgment one way or another, and in antitrust that conclusion generally entails nonliability.

§ 4.7 Intraenterprise Conspiracy

For a half century the courts were plagued by questions about whether firms related by ownership, such as a parent and its wholly owned subsidiary, can "conspire" within the meaning of the Sherman Act.[1] In Copperweld Corp. v. Independence Tube Corp. the Supreme Court gave a definite answer, at least with respect to one version of the question: a parent and its wholly owned but separately incorporated subsidiary should be treated as a single firm; they cannot be considered "con-

41. See § 12.5, on the relationship between tacit collusion and product differentiation for merger analysis.

42. On the per se rule, see § 5.6.

§ 4.7

1. For example, United States v. Yellow Cab Co., 332 U.S. 218, 67 S.Ct. 1560 (1947); Kiefer-Stewart Co. v. Joseph E. Seagram & Sons, 340 U.S. 211, 71 S.Ct. 259 (1951); Timken Roller Bearing Co. v. United States, 341 U.S. 593, 71 S.Ct. 971 (1951); Perma Life Mufflers v. International Parts Corp., 392 U.S. 134, 88 S.Ct. 1981 (1968). In each case, the Court used broad dicta stating approval of an intra-enterprise conspiracy doctrine, but in each there were alternate grounds for the decision. See 6 Antitrust Law ¶ 1463 (1986).

spiring entities" for the purposes of § 1.[2] The Court concluded that just as the "officers of a single firm" are not separate economic actors for the purposes of § 1 of the Sherman Act, so too a parent and its wholly owned subsidiary "have a complete unity of interest."[3] A corporation's decision whether to create an unincorporated division or an incorporated subsidiary turns almost entirely on tax consequences or questions of law unrelated to competition. A firm cannot enhance its market power simply by separately incorporating a division.

The basic question exposes a tension between the law of § 1 conspiracies and the law of monopolization under § 2. Antitrust is generally more hostile to inter-firm agreements than to alleged exclusionary practices by the single firm. But this extra deterrence gives plaintiffs an incentive to try to turn single-firm conduct into a conspiracy or combination. If Kodak's practice can be characterized as a conspiracy between its president and vice president; or if General Motors' policies can be characterized as a conspiracy among Pontiac and Buick (its wholly owned subsidiaries), then the plaintiff can take advantage of § 1's more expansive reach. He might even be able to turn price setting by the single firm, a completely legal act, into a *per se* illegal price fixing conspiracy.

In light of these possibilities, the *Copperweld* doctrine is clearly important to the rational administration of the antitrust laws. The question is how far to push the point. When the firm is unmistakably a single profit-maximizing entity and has always been so, it makes no sense to find a Sherman Act "conspiracy" among any of its personnel, divisions, subsidiaries or other subordinate organizations. But the rationale of *Copperweld* becomes more strained in two different circumstances: (a) where ownership is less than completely unified; and (b) where one or more agents of the firm has a separate profit-making interest that is different than the interests of the principal firm.

Suppose that a parent company has an ownership interest in two subsidiaries, but the interest is less than 100%. The two extremes seem rather easy. If the parent owns a controlling interest in each subsidiary and effectively makes all of their decisions, then the firms should be treated as part of a single entity and *Copperweld* should apply. By contrast, if the "parent" owns a trivially small share in one or both subsidiaries, and has little legal or practical influence on their decision-making, then the subsidiaries are separate profit-maximizing entities, responsible to largely different sets of stockholders. *Copperweld* should not apply.

The question may be seen as reducing to what constitutes a "firm" for the purposes of antitrust policy. Within economics, the individual maximizing entity is generally thought of as being either an individual or a firm. The firm is more relevant than the individual to most antitrust questions, since the firm maximizes profits while individuals maximize utility. Agreements within the firm are to be treated as the conduct of a single actor, on the presumption that such a firm is a single profit-maximizer. The question of what is a *legal* actor is not particularly helpful to this analysis. Corporations are "persons" under the law, but so are biological persons. Just as the multiplicity of biological persons is not decisive for establishing whether a single company with many employees is a firm, so to the multiplicity of incorporated entities within a single orga-

2. 467 U.S. 752, 104 S.Ct. 2731 (1984).

3. 467 U.S. at 771, 104 at 2741–42. See also Zachair v. Driggs, 141 F.3d 1162, 1998–1 Trade Cases ¶ 72,139 (4th Cir.1998, unpublished) (complaint alleging a conspiracy between one individual and numerous corporations that he "controlled" failed to state § 1 conspiracy claim); Advanced Health–Care Servs. v. Radford Community Hosp., 910 F.2d 139 (4th Cir.1990), on remand, 846 F.Supp. 488 (D.Va.1994) (wholly owned subsidiaries of same parent cannot conspire). Other significant decisions include Century Oil Tool v. Production Specialties, 737 F.2d 1316 (5th Cir.1984) (two corporations who had identical stockholders lacked conspiratorial conspiracy); Guzowski v. Hartman, 969 F.2d 211 (6th Cir.1992), cert. denied, 506 U.S. 1053, 113 S.Ct. 978 (1993) (same); and Fishman v. Wirtz, 807 F.2d 520, 542 & n. 19 (7th Cir.1986), which found conspiratorial capacity where some, but not all, of the owners of two corporations were the same persons. Williams v. I.B. Fischer Nevada, 999 F.2d 445 (9th Cir.1993) held that a fast food franchisor and franchisee were a single entity and lacked conspiratorial capacity with respect to a vertical agreement; but that seems quite wrong.

nization—such as a parent plus numerous subsidiaries—tells us nothing about whether the organization should be treated as one firm or as many.

One helpful way to think about the problem is to look back at the analysis of cartel cheating, discussed in § 4.1. Cartels fail to behave like single profit-maximizing entities, because individual members have both the inclination and the power to cheat on the agreement by making secret price concessions. Although cheating benefits the cheater, it injures the cartel as a whole. If these same incentives to cheat remain when a parent and, say, a partially owned subsidiary jointly commit themselves to a policy, then presumptively they are independent actors with conspiratorial capacity. In the case of a wholly owned subsidiary such an incentive to cheat should ordinarily not be present, for the subsidiary's ledger sheet is simply a page of the parent's ledger; any additional profits that the subsidiary makes by cheating would be more than offset by losses that accrued to the parent, and *all* relevant owners would treat that as a loss.[4]

By contrast, when the subsidiary is only partially owned there may be a divergence of interest among the owners. Those owners who are able to control the decisions of one subsidiary may be able to profit by cheating on the agreement. This analysis suggests that legal control should be decisive against conspiratorial capacity. If a controlling interest of alleged cartel members is held by common owners, then the firm will already behave as a single profit-maximizing entity absent the challenged agreement. Conspiratorial capacity is lacking. The court's have been moving to a position relatively close to this one.[5]

The previous analysis of the *Copperweld* problem might be seen as *structural*, in that it focuses on the permanent, or at least quasi-permanent, relationship that exists between two firms alleged to be conspiring entities. But *Copperweld* also has a more transaction-specific manifestation. In such cases the focus is not on the structural relationship between the two entities, but rather on the interests that were at play in the course of one particular decision. This second *Copperweld* question arises when agents of the same firm have independent economic interests. They effectively wear two hats. Most of the cases have involved physicians who simultaneously act as the administration or peer review board of a hospital, while having their own separate practices. Suppose that a general hospital has a peer review staff containing three anesthesiologists, each of whom has an independent practice from which he earns substantial profits. The three use their peer review powers to deny staff privileges, or the privilege of having one's patients admitted, to a fourth anesthesiologist. The fourth anesthesiologist believes she was dismissed because she charged a lower price than the other three. However, the decision to deny admission was made by the three anesthesiologists in the course of a peer review meeting in which they were acting officially as agents or perhaps even as employees of the incorporated hospital.

In a case like this, if the hospital and its agents are to be regarded as a single entity, the plaintiff must prove single-firm monopolization in a vertical setting: that is, the hospital itself stands in a vertical relationship with its anesthesiologists. The courts have not generally been kind to plaintiffs making such claims.[6] By contrast, if the plaintiff can treat the three anesthesiologists as distinct entities, she has a

4. However, the suggestion may not work if the managers of individual subsidiaries are not profit-maximizers. For example, if they are awarded on the basis of sales or output, they may do things that increase the sale or output of their own subsidiary while injuring the firm as a whole. Likewise, if their actions are evaluated only with respect to their effect on the subsidiary's profits, rather than the profits of the parent, the subsidiary's actions may be inconsistent with the parent's interests.

5. For example, Rohlfing v. Manor Care, 172 F.R.D. 330 (N.D.Il.1997) (one firm, its wholly owned subsidiary, and another 82%-owned subsidiary lacked conspiratorial capacity); Bell Atlantic Business Sys. Servs. v. Hitachi Data Sys. Corp., 849 F.Supp. 702 (N.D.Cal.1994) (firm could not conspire with 80%-owned subsidiary); Novatel Communications, Inc. v. Cellular Tel. Supply, Inc., 1986–2 Trade Cas. (CCH) ¶ 67,412, 1986 WL 15507 (N.D.Ga.1986) (no conspiratorial capacity where parent owned 51 percent of subsidiaries).

6. See § 7.6.

decidedly better claim of concerted boycott against a competitor by a group of price fixers. Furthermore, the latter claim seems inherently more plausible. Physicians with an established niche have good reason to wish to exclude an interloper threatening their profits with lower prices.[7]

In general the courts have been receptive of this argument, although many have been reluctant to include the hospital as a defendant. Once again, the whole question of conspiratorial capacity derives from the fact that the individual physician can profit by making a decision that injures the hospital, or the group as a whole. The hospital stands in a vertical relationship with its physicians. It profits from filling its capacity, which it generally does by granting staff privileges to every competent physician likely to admit patients. By contrast, the anesthesiologists' cartel, if there is one, monopolizes by reducing output and this will injure the hospital as well as the excluded anesthesiologist. As a result, for some courts the logic of this particular exception to *Copperweld* suggests that the physicians' competitors may be included in the conspiracy, but not the hospital.[8]

Finally, in its controversial *Chicago Professional Sports* decision the Seventh Circuit concluded that the National Basketball Assn. (NBA) should be treated as a single entity for the purpose of considering an agreement among the member teams limiting the televising of NBA basketball games on "superstations" such as WGN of Chicago.[9] The court reasoned that, although the teams were separately incorporated, had different owners, and maximized profits individually, they had been formed only for the purpose of participating in the NBA and were not even permitted to engage in significant outside business.[10] As a result, they should be treated as a single entity. The single entity conclusion suggested to the court that the output restriction would be treated under the rule of reason rather than the per se rule. In fact, however, a unilateral

7. The same argument can come up in the context of trade associations, professional boards, and the like. E.g., California Dental Assn. v. FTC, 128 F.3d 720, 728 (9th Cir.1997), vacated on other grds., ___ U.S. ___, 119 S.Ct. 1604 (1999) ("Professional associations are routinely treated as continuing conspiracies of their members"); Bankers Ins. Co. v. Florida Residential Property and Casualty Assn., 137 F.3d 1293 (11th Cir.1998) (officers of an insurance trade association lacked conspiratorial capacity); Massachusetts Board of Registration in Optometry, 5 Trade Reg. Rep. ¶ 22,555 (FTC 1988) (board members with independent optometry practices could "conspire" while acting as agents for the Board to promulgate rules restricting advertising). See also Hahn v. Oregon Physicians' Serv., 868 F.2d 1022 (9th Cir.1988), cert. denied, 493 U.S. 846, 110 S.Ct. 140 (1989) (considering whether the board members of a prepaid health insurance plan, who were also independent practitioners, had conspiratorial capacity with respect to allegedly unfavorable treatment directed at podiatrists: "The proper inquiry is not whether individual board members *themselves* were in actual competition with the complaining nonmembers [podiatrists]. Rather, the proper inquiry is whether practitioners sharing substantially similar economic interests collectively exercised control of a plan under whose auspices they have reached agreement which works to the detriment of competitors." Id. at 1029).

8. For example, Oksanen v. Page Memorial Hosp., 945 F.2d 696, 704 (4th Cir.1991), cert. denied, 502 U.S. 1074, 112 S.Ct. 973 (1992):

> Given that hospitals compete for the admission of patients, they have an incentive to maximize the number of physicians to whom they grant admitting and staff privileges. If a physician is qualified and does not disrupt the hospital's operations, it is in the hospital's interest to include, not exclude, that physician.

Accord: Rea v. Hospital Corp. of Am., 892 F.Supp. 821 (N.D.Tex.1993), aff'd in relevant part, 95 F.3d 383 (5th Cir.1996) (hospital could not conspire with staff to dismiss physician, since it benefitted from competent physician's presence); Nanavati v. Burdette Tomlin Memorial Hosp., 857 F.2d 96, 118 (3d Cir.1988), cert. denied, 489 U.S. 1078, 109 S.Ct. 1528 (1989); Nurse Midwifery Assocs. v. Hibbett, 918 F.2d 605 (6th Cir.1990), modified, 927 F.2d 904 (6th Cir.), cert. denied, 502 U.S. 952, 112 S.Ct. 406 (1991). Other courts permit the hospital to be included in the conspiracy as well. For example, Bolt v. Halifax Medical Center, 891 F.2d 810 (11th Cir.), cert. denied, 495 U.S. 924, 110 S.Ct. 1960 (1990). See also Boczar v. Manatee Hospitals & Health Systems, 993 F.2d 1514 (11th Cir. 1993), concluding that the hospital could be a conspirator because the disciplined physician had uncovered numerous hospital deficiencies which, if exposed, would cost the hospital much money to correct. As a result, "the hospital * * * came to view Dr. Boczar's practice * * * as inconsistent with its interests." But to infer conspiratorial capacity from such evidence seems precisely wrong. The evidence indicates that the hospital, acting unilaterally, wished to dismiss Dr. Boczar. In that case the hospital's action was perhaps ill-motivated and even illegal under another body of law; but it was not an antitrust conspiracy. See generally 7 Antitrust Law ¶ 1471 (1986 & Supp.).

9. Chicago Professional Sports Ltd. Partnership v. NBA, 95 F.3d 593, 597 (7th Cir.1996).

10. See id. at 599, noting that the NBA "has no existence independent of sports" and its only product is "NBA basketball."

output restriction, even by a monopolist, is legal. Just as the monopolist is free to set its price, it must also be free to adjust output accordingly. Indeed, even express collusion, such as the fixing of player salaries, would have to be considered as a lawful unilateral act under the Seventh Circuit's expansion of *Copperweld*.[11]

11. Contrast Brown v. Pro Football, 518 U.S. 231, 116 S.Ct. 2116 (1996), discussed at § 19.7b (upholding agreement among NFL teams fixing maximum salaries of certain players, but only because agreement was undertaken as part of collective bargaining process).

Chapter 5

JOINT VENTURES OF COMPETITORS, CONCERTED REFUSALS, PATENT LICENSING, AND THE RULE OF REASON

Table of Sections

---

§ 5.1 Introduction: Naked and Ancillary Agreements Among Competitors

Agreements among competitors are not necessarily monopolistic or harmful to consumers, although the legal presumption against them is sometimes thought to be strong. An agreement can enable a group of firms to carry on an activity at a more efficient scale, reduce information or transaction costs, or eliminate free rider problems. A primary task of antitrust policy is to distinguish those agreements that pose significant anticompetitive threats from those that do not. If an agreement cannot facilitate collusive pricing or output reductions, then its purpose must be the reduction of costs or the improvement of a product or service.

One of antitrust's more difficult tasks is to evaluate the relevant social costs and benefits of the wide variety of agreements among competitors. Further, antitrust must be able to do this by means that are both relatively inexpensive and tolerably accurate. In a world of perfect and costless information, we could learn everything there is to know about a restraint before deciding whether to condemn it. But the actual world is characterized by ignorance and ambiguity, and obtaining reliable information is costly. Antitrust has had to devise shortcuts for evaluating business practices. Because of their complexity, their great potential for harm, but the offsetting potential for considerable good, horizontal restraints is an area where the use of these shortcuts is particularly prominent.

The most important shortcut is the (rough) tripartite classification of restraints that determines the kind and amount of proof that is necessary for illegality, and the kinds of defenses that are permitted.[1] At one extreme, a "naked" restraint is one that is thought to have little potential for social benefit, and thus that can be condemned under a "*per se*" rule, which requires little or no inquiry into market power or actual anticompetitive effects. At the other extreme, an "ancillary" restraint is one that arguably serves a legitimate and socially beneficial purpose. Such restraints are analyzed under a "rule of reason," which means that they can be condemned only after a relatively elaborate inquiry into power and likely anticompetitive effects. Further, a broader range of defenses are considered. Finally, in the middle are a group of restraints that we call "nearly naked" because at first glance they seem highly suspicious but we are not quite sure. Perhaps judicial experience with them is insufficient to warrant a confident conclusion, or perhaps they present some unique attribute not formerly encountered. In such cases we at least give the defendants an opportunity to formulate an argument that they are, on balance, procompetitive. However, if that argument fails, then summary condemnation may be appropriate.

The widespread application of the *per se* rule to price-fixing agreements has often obscured the underlying complexities of joint arrangements involving competitors and their great potential for efficiency. For example, it is not generally a defense to a price fixing charge that the cartel members did not hold enough market power to reduce output profitably. If a town contains ten similar grocers, and three of

§ 5.1

1. See 11 Antitrust Law ¶ ¶ 1910–1912 (1998).

them jointly run a newspaper advertisement quoting retail prices, the arrangement would reduce advertising costs for each of the three. Furthermore, three grocers out of ten could not plausibly fix prices. Customers would buy from the other 7. The inference that the arrangement reduces costs is strong, while the inference of anticompetitive price fixing seems weak. Nevertheless, a court is likely to hold that the *per se* rule prevents it from considering both the argument that the defendants had no market power and that their agreement produced cost reductions that benefit consumers.[2]

Whether this outcome is wrong depends on a variety of factors. One is the cost of making the additional market power inquiry in this particular case. But another is the cost of making the similar additional inquiries in an entire class of cases where the same defense will be raised, or in producing some rules for distinguishing when the defense of lack of market power can be raised and when it cannot be.

5.1a. Distinguishing Naked from Ancillary Restraints; Question of Law

We sometimes say that an agreement among competitors is "naked" if it is unrelated to any organization of production or distribution. But that expresses an empirical conclusion about what the participants are doing. In the litigation context it is better to ask the defendants to justify their arrangement. The proffered justification, assuming it is provable, may suggest the rule to be applied. This definition seems better: a restraint is "naked" if it is formed with the objectively intended purpose or likely effect of increasing price or decreasing output in the short run, with output measured by quantity or quality.[3] By contrast, a restraint is ancillary if its objectively intended purpose or likely effect is lower prices or increased output.[4] Importantly, under this definition a naked restraint is a rational act only if the actors collectively have sufficient power to affect marketwide output and price. By contrast, an ancillary restraint can be profitable, and thus rational, whether or not the participants collectively control the market. Thus the antitrust decision maker must consider the provable explanation of the restraint. If the explanation makes sense even in the absence of any market power, then the restraint is at least presumptively ancillary. That does not necessarily save the restraint; rather, it means that the rule of reason is to be applied.

A useful way to determine whether a restraint is naked or ancillary is to listen to the proffered explanation and then ask Would this restraint work if the participants collectively held a nondominant position in the market? For example, suppose that the only five physicians in town jointly purchase expensive radiological equipment and operate it as a joint venture. When this basic venture is challenged as facilitating price fixing, they answer that the fixed costs of this equipment is very high and one set of it is sufficient for all five physicians. At that point, the antitrust decision maker might consider whether this explanation would work if the market contained 100 physicians and these five had purchased the same equipment. The answer is clearly yes. Cost reduction is profitable even in a highly competitive market, and these five physicians could profitably share such equipment in the same way that two farmers might share an infrequently used combine or several firms might jointly set up a specialized firm to dispose of their hazardous waste. To be sure, the physicians might be lying about their reasons, or we might ultimately conclude that the

2. See, for example, United States v. Pittsburgh Area Pontiac Dealers, 1978–2 Trade Cas. ¶ 62,233, 1978 WL 1398 (W.D.Pa.1978) (consent decree prohibiting defendants from "adopting, participating in or adhering to any plan, practice or program, the purpose or effect of which is to advertise the sale price of a Pontiac automobile or fix the advertised price of a Pontiac automobile. . . .").

3. On the meaning of relevant "output," see 11 Antitrust Law ¶ 1901d (1998).

4. See Polk Brothers v. Forest City Enters., 776 F.2d 185, 190 (7th Cir.1985) ("The reason for distinguishing between 'ancillary' and 'naked' restraints is to determine whether the agreement is part of a cooperative venture with prospects for increasing output. If it is, it should not be condemned per se.").

threat of price fixing outweighed any efficiency gains from joint provision. But prima facie, at least, the physicians have made a claim for rule of reason treatment.

By contrast, consider the agreement at issue in the *Engineers* case, where members of a professional association of consulting engineers agreed not to bid competitively for jobs and would not even discuss fees until after they had been selected.[5] Their offered rationale was that competitive bidding would force engineers to cut corners because the resulting prices would be too low to enable them to do an adequate job. Now ask yourself, suppose that five New York City engineers refused to take competitive bids while NYC's remaining 2000 engineers did. Clearly, the restraint would not work. The agreement was necessary in the first place only because a significant number of customers *wanted* engineers to bid competitively. Further, the proffered justification admitted that prices would be higher under the rule than without it. If the participants in the restraint who collectively refused competitive bidding amounted to a small percentage of the market, prospective customers would turn away from them and go to other engineers who were willing to bid competitively. Thus the engineers' restraint was naked.

The agreement in *California Dental* is somewhat more complex.[6] A dental association defended its limitations on dentists' advertising by arguing that they were necessary to prevent misleading or deceptive claims. But the limitations were so severe that they effectively prohibited almost any price advertising at all, and virtually all quality claims. The claim that advertising restrictions reduce deception suggests rule of reason treatment, because even a trade association without market power could profit by guaranteeing nondeceptive advertising, thus raising consumer confidence. By contrast, the four dissenters saw the restraint as likely to eliminate all or most price advertising altogether. *That* restraint would be naked: a group of firms lacking power could not profit by agreeing not to advertise their prices or services, assuming that their rivals did advertise and consumers valued advertising.

While the question whether a restraint is naked or ancillary is a mixed one of law and fact, the question whether the per se rule or the rule of reason applies is clearly one of law.[7] The premise of the per se rule is that *judicial* experience with a certain class of restraints justifies more expedited treatment.[8] Jurors lack not only judicial experience, but have no experience at all in the matter. Further, the source material to which a court looks in determining the rule to be applied is prior opinions, mainly from the Supreme Court but also from the lower federal courts, making the question inappropriate for the jury.

5.1b. Why Multilateral Activity Deserves Closer Antitrust Scrutiny.[9]

Under the antitrust laws unilateral conduct receives the lowest level of antitrust scrutiny. Purely unilateral actions are unlawful only if they fall into the general classifications of monopolization or attempt to monopolize, and both the conduct and the power requirements are quite severe.[10] Occasionally someone argues that the level of antitrust scrutiny given to joint ventures should be no higher than that

5. National Society of Professional Engineers v. United States, 435 U.S. 679, 98 S.Ct. 1355 (1978).

6. California Dental Assn. v. FTC, ___ U.S. ___, 119 S.Ct. 1604 (1999).

7. See Arizona v. Maricopa County Medical Society, 457 U.S. 332, 337 n. 3, 102 S.Ct. 2466 (1982).

8. See National Collegiate Athletic Association v. Board of Regents (*NCAA*), 468 U.S. 85, 100–101, 104 S.Ct. 2948 (1984). ("judicial experience" determines when per se rule should be applied). See also FTC v. Superior Court Trial Lawyers Assn., 493 U.S. 411, 433, 110 S.Ct. 768 (1990) ("Once experience with a particular kind of restraint enables the Court to predict with confidence that the rule of reason will condemn it, it has applied a conclusive presumption that the restraint is unreasonable,") quoting *Maricopa*, note 7, 457 U.S. at 344; Broadcast Music v. Columbia Broadcasting System, 441 U.S. 1, 2, 99 S.Ct. 1551 (1979) ("It is only after considerable experience with certain business relationships that courts classify them as per se violations of the Sherman Act,") quoting United States v. Topco Associates, 405 U.S. 596, 607–608, 92 S.Ct. 1126 (1972).

9. See 11 Antitrust Law ¶ ¶ 1902b, 1903 (1998); and 13 id. at ¶ 2221d (1999).

10. See generally chs. 6–8.

given to single firms.[11] According to this argument, stricter scrutiny will condemn or at least put a chill on joint activity that is on balance procompetitive but that an antitrust court might not sufficiently understand.

But there are many good reasons for closer antitrust scrutiny of joint activity. *First*, of course, is the structure of the Sherman Act. Section 1 condemns any agreement of competitors that is in "restraint of trade," while § 2 condemns unilateral conduct only when it "monopolizes" or threatens to do so. While these statutory terms are hardly self-defining, a restraint of trade both historically and in the modern era can amount to very much less than a monopoly. Indeed, antitrust has and continues to condemn many restraints such as price fixing or resale price maintenance that occur in quite competitive markets. While this is a very powerful legal argument, however, it is not a particularly appealing economic argument.

But the economic arguments for closer scrutiny of joint activity are overwhelming. The *second* argument for such scrutiny is that the participants in joint ventures are private actors seeking private gains. The gains from joint ventures come from two sources: efficiency gains, which result from reduced costs or improved products; and market power gains, which result from the fact that the venture has sufficient power to cause marketwide output reductions and price increases. One important reason for looking more closely at joint activity is that agreements creating significant market power can be formed very quickly. Most firms do not become monopolists overnight. For a single firm to acquire monopoly power ordinarily takes many years of innovation and aggressive production and marketing. Rivals can generally be expected to resist a single firm's attempts to dominate its market. Although monopolies can be created by anticompetitive acts, most such attempts are unsuccessful. It is usually very difficult for a nondominant firm to become dominant *simply* by doing anticompetitive things. In most cases such firms also have superior products or lower costs than their rivals, at least during the period when their monopoly is developing.

In sharp contrast, monopoly power can be created by agreement in a very short time and with little resistance. All it takes is firms who collectively dominate a market and agree to do something jointly. The acquisition of a dominant market share is easy because the joint venture acquires the sum of the market shares of its participants. Resistance is much less because the agreement creates market power by bringing firms *into* the venture rather than excluding them from the market. As a result, *either* the opportunity to reduce costs or the opportunity to exercise market power can explain the formation of a joint venture. Without conducting any analysis it is hard to say which reason dominates.

A *third* reason for applying a more aggressive antitrust standard to joint activity than unilateral conduct harkens back to the "restraint of trade" standard stated in § 1 of the Sherman Act. Conduct restrains trade when it results in lower market output—measured by quantity or quality—and thus higher prices than competition would produce. By contrast, efficient conduct results in higher output and thus lower prices. Antitrust tries to determine the classification in which a particular venture rule belongs. By contrast, the antitrust laws do not recognize an offense of merely "being a monopoly." A firm with monopoly power is free to set its monopoly price, and is thus also free to reduce its output accordingly. Because most dominant firms are the result of either historical accident or a long period of growth resulting from efficiency, we ordinarily leave the dominant firm alone as long as it does not engage in anticompetitive exclusionary practices designed to perpetuate or strengthen its monopoly position. But the joint venture enjoys no such presumption. We permit competitors to join together *only* because we expect the result to be a better product, higher output, or lower prices. If they cannot produce these results then there is little reason to

11. See, e.g., H. Chang, D. Evans & R. Schmalensee, Some Economic Principles for Guiding Antitrust Policy Towards Joint Ventures, 1998 Colum. Bus. L. Rev. 223; D. Baker, Compulsory Access to Network Joint Ventures Under the Sherman Act: Rules or Roulette, 1993 Utah L. Rev. 999, 1025.

tolerate them as long as the threat to competition is significant. In sum, the mere exercise of market power by means of an output reduction or price increase is lawful for the monopolist, but appropriately unlawful for the joint venture.

A *fourth* reason for applying a different standard to joint ventures has to do with courts' ability to fashion appropriate relief.[12] Judicial relief ordering a monopolist to behave competitively generally turns that firm into a regulated utility. By contrast, judicial relief against a joint venture typically involves little more than an injunction against the harmful conduct. Consider a single pair of examples in two different contexts, price fixing and refusal to deal. American Express is a single firm that issues a "unitary" general purpose credit card. By contrast, Visa, Inc., which issues a competing general purpose credit card, is a joint venture of some 6000 banks and other financial institutions. Suppose that in different courts these two organizations are accused of two different things and found guilty: (1) fixing supracompetitive consumer interest rates and (2) refusing to share their card processing facilities with a rival card issuer.

On the interest rate claim, an injunction against American Express would not be able simply to order AmEx to set a "competitive" interest rate. Rather, it would have to develop some criteria by which the competitive interest rate is determined, and this rate might change as the inflation rate changes. An interest rate order directed against a single firm effectively regulates its prices—an activity for which federal courts are not well suited and which in any event seems quite contrary to the general antitrust goal of facilitating competition rather than regulation. By contrast, an interest rate injunction against the Visa venture requires no more than is required in any cartel case: an order prohibiting the Visa members from fixing an interest rate. After that, competition among the 6000 Visa issuing banks would probably produce the appropriate rate. Thus, for example, a court order forbidding the NCAA from fixing the maximum price of basketball coaches need do no more than enjoin the fix, letting competition determine the proper salaries.[13] By contrast, assuming that General Motors had market power in the hiring of automotive engineers, an antitrust decree against allegedly low salaries would have to substitute the judgment of the court for the judgment of the market about what appropriate salaries should be.

Largely the same thing applies to the refusal to deal claim. Suppose that a court were to order AmEx to share its card processing facilities with a rival. Whatever one thinks of the wisdom of such relief, granting it requires a significant regulatory effort. The price of sharing and all of the numerous terms will have to be set, just as they would be for a regulated utility required to interconnect with a rival. By contrast, the refusal-to-deal claim in the Visa case arises from a joint venture rule forbidding member banks from issuing a competing card.[14] A judicial decree need not "force" sharing at all; it need only enjoin enforcement of the rule. After that, competition among the 6000 banks, who are now free to issue a competitor's card if they wish, will determine whether and how many rivals' cards will be distributed through banks.

In sum, antitrust relief against multilateral activity is or can be made to be consistent with the general antitrust goal of permitting competitive markets. This does not mean that such relief is always appropriate, but it does suggest that antitrust solutions can be brought to bear more effectively against multilateral than unilateral conduct.

5.1c. Partial condemnation; less restrictive alternatives

Some so-called "joint ventures" are nothing more than fronts for naked restraints.[15] In

12. See 11 Antitrust Law ¶ 1903 (1998).

13. Law v. NCAA, 134 F.3d 1010 (10th Cir.), cert. denied, ___ U.S. ___, 119 S.Ct. 65 (1998).

14. See SCFC ILC v. Visa USA., 36 F.3d 958, 961 (10th Cir.1994), cert. denied, 515 U.S. 1152, 115 S.Ct. 2600 (1995).

15. See, e.g., United States v. Romer 148 F.3d 359 (4th Cir.1998), cert. denied, ___ U.S. ___, 119 S.Ct. 1032 (re-such cases the courts can condemn them with confidence that they are not disturbing socially valuable relationships. But often the defendants' overall arrangement or venture is clearly efficient or harmless and only one particular rule seems offensive. Further, a court order forbidding enforcement of the anticompetitive rule will not necessarily impair the operation of the venture. For example, courts have condemned NCAA rules that both limited the number of times an NCAA football team could have its games televised[16] and that fixed the maximum salaries of certain basketball coaches.[17] However, no one suggested that the antitrust laws required that the NCAA athletic joint venture of more than 1000 colleges be dissolved. Likewise, although courts have condemned the engineers' ban on competitive bidding,[18] the AMA's professional rules excluding chiropractors,[19] and the Indiana Federation of Dentists' collective refusal to submit x-ray data to an insurer,[20] none of these actions dissolved the trade associations that made these anticompetitive rules.

Indeed, many restraints are "naked" even though contained in elaborate joint ventures that were not being challenged and were almost certainly socially beneficial. For example, while the NCAA is a socially beneficial athletic venture involving colleges and universities, both its rule limiting televised football games and the rule fixing maximum coaching salaries were properly characterized by the courts as "naked" restraints on price or output.[21]

When an efficient joint venture employs an anticompetitive restraint the court must disaggregate the restraint from the venture's overall activities. It then asks whether the restraint serves an important, socially beneficial purpose. If the answer is yes, then the plaintiff still has a chance to show that the beneficial purpose could be achieved by a less restrictive alternative.[22] If the answer is no, then the inquiry into less restrictive alternatives is unnecessary.[23]

§ 5.2. Joint Ventures as Market Facilitators

Agreements among competitors that include some coordination of research, production, promotion or distribution are commonly referred to as "joint ventures." A joint venture is any association of two or more firms for carrying on some activity that each firm might otherwise perform alone. Some joint ventures require the parties to agree about price or output, although many do not. Likewise, the participants in some joint ventures are competitors, while in others they are firms at different levels in a distribution chain, firms producing related products, or the same product in different geographic markets. As a result, to characterize something as a "joint venture" is to say nothing about its effect on

jecting argument that bid-rigging agreement was in fact a "joint venture").

16. National Collegiate Athletic Ass'n (NCAA) v. Board of Regents of the Univ. of Oklahoma, 468 U.S. 85, 104 S.Ct. 2948 (1984).

17. *Law* case, note 13.

18. *Engineers* case, note 5.

19. Wilk v. American Medical Association, 671 F.Supp. 1465 (N.D.Ill.1987), aff'd, 895 F.2d 352 (7th Cir.), cert. denied, 496 U.S. 927, 110 S.Ct. 2621 (1990).

20. FTC v. Indiana Federation of Dentists, 476 U.S. 447, 106 S.Ct. 2009 (1986).

21. On the definition of "naked" restraint, see § 5.1a.

22. The courts are divided on the question whether the burden of proof in showing a less restrictive alternative is on the plaintiff or the defendants. See Hairston v. Pacific 10 Conference, 101 F.3d 1315, 1319 (9th Cir.1996) (burden of showing less restrictive alternative on the plaintiff); United States v. Brown University, 5 F.3d 658, 668–668 (3d Cir.1993) (burden on plaintiff); Capital Imaging v. Mohawk Valley Medical Associates, 996 F.2d 537, 541, 543 (2d Cir.), cert. denied, 510 U.S. 947, 114 S.Ct. 388 (1993) (burden on plaintiff); Bhan v. NME Hospitals, 929 F.2d 1404, 1413 (9th Cir.1991), cert. denied, 502 U.S. 994, 112 S.Ct. 617 (1991) (burden on plaintiff); Kreuzer v. American Acad. of Periodontology, 735 F.2d 1479, 1495 (D.C.Cir. 1984) (burden on the defendant); North Am. Soccer League v. NFL, 670 F.2d 1249, 1259 (2d Cir.), cert. denied, 459 U.S. 1074, 103 S.Ct. 499 (1982) (burden on defendant "to come forward with proof that any legitimate purposes could not be achieved through less restrictive means"). See 11 Antitrust Law ¶ 1914 (1998).

23. See *Law*, note 13, 134 F.3d at 1024 n. 16 ("Because we hold that the NCAA did not establish evidence of sufficient procompetitive benefits, we need not address the question of whether the plaintiffs were able to show that comparable procompetitive benefits could be achieved through viable, less anticompetitive means."). On less restrictive alternatives, see § 5.6c. See also 11 Antitrust Law ¶ 1913 (1998).

competition or its legality under the antitrust laws.

Concerns about how innovation should be encouraged in a capitalistic economy lie at the heart of American antitrust policy toward joint ventures, other market facilitating agreements, and agreements respecting the use of intellectual property. Today there is a broad consensus that the social gains from innovation are substantial—even substantial enough to warrant a certain toleration of monopoly.

To state this another way, the *dynamic* efficiency gains that accrue from innovation very likely exceed the *static* efficiency gains that accrue from a policy of ensuring that all prices be competitive. Static concepts of efficiency look at the relationship between price and marginal cost under a stationary market demand curve, and generally consider monopoly to be bad. The various figures in Chapter 1 illustrate static conceptions of the market. By contrast, dynamic concepts of efficiency consider the impact of market growth or the creation of new markets. For example, American patent policy permits the creation of short-run monopolies. But if the policy is well-conceived, the welfare gains that accrue from the innovation will exceed the welfare losses that result from the monopoly pricing during the time that the patent is used.[1] Antitrust has the rather difficult job of accommodating our traditional short-run concerns with monopoly with another set of concerns for long-run progress, many of which are reflected in other legislative policies.

Antitrust policy toward joint ventures is central to this concern. However, antitrust analysis has not generally discriminated between joint ventures expressly concerned with research and development and joint ventures designed to achieve other, less dazzling gains. For purposes of antitrust analysis, the joint venture of four computer firms to develop a new memory device, and of a collegiate football conference to structure its playing schedule and rules, are treated in a surprisingly similar fashion. But there is some wisdom in that approach. The question whether a joint activity constitutes "innovation" is not answered by counting transistors or Ph.D's in the sciences. *Market* facilitators can also be innovative and productive of dynamic efficiency gains.[2] The very low tech blanket licensing agreement in the *BMI* case,[3] for example, produced gains from transaction cost reduction that certainly rivaled the gains from many research joint ventures in technical fields.

§ 5.2a. Joint Ventures: an Overview

5.2a1. Potential Harms and Benefits

Firms enter into joint ventures for many reasons. If they are competitors or potential competitors, one reason that cannot be overlooked is price fixing or marketwide output restrictions. If the venturers dominate a market they may attempt to earn monopoly profits by reducing output and raising price, dividing markets, or by refusing to compete in innovation or some avenue other than price. They may also try to protect their own competitive positions by excluding price cutters or firms that are more innovative than themselves.

But price fixing, output restriction or monopoly-creating market division explain only a small percentage of joint venture agreements. Most are created to enable the participants to achieve certain economies, either by allowing them to do something at a lower cost, or else by permitting them to do something for themselves that they would otherwise purchase on the marketplace or do without. The benefits generally accrue to consumers.

A joint venture of competitors reached the Supreme Court in the very first antitrust case the Court decided on the merits, United States

§ 5.2

1. For good discussions of these issues, see T. Jorde & D. Teece, Rule of Reason Analysis of Horizontal Arrangements: Agreements Designed to Advance Innovation and Commercialize Technology, 61 Antitrust L.J. 579 (1993); P. Stoneman, The Economic Analysis of Technological Change (1983); J. Ordover & R. Willig, Antitrust for High Technology Industries: Assessing Research Joint Ventures and Mergers, 28 J.L. & Econ. 311 (1985).

2. On this point, see G. Calabresi, The Pointlessness of Pareto: Carrying Coase Further, 100 Yale L.J. 1211 (1991).

3. Broadcast Music, Inc. v. Columbia Broadcasting System, Inc., 441 U.S. 1, 99 S.Ct. 1551 (1979). See § 5.2c.

v. Trans–Missouri Freight Ass'n.[4] The Association was a consortium of eighteen railroad companies that formed a joint running agreement. Under the agreement the members coordinated schedules, transfer of cargo, and freight rates. Both the trial court and the federal court of appeals upheld the arrangement, emphasizing its efficiency-creating potential. As the circuit court observed,

> The fact that the business of railway companies is irretrievably interwoven, that they interchange cars and traffic, that they act as agents for each other in the delivery and receipt of freight and in paying and collecting freight charges, and that commodities received for transportation generally pass through the hands of several carriers, renders it of vital importance to the public that uniform rules and regulations governing railway traffic should be framed by those who have a practical acquaintance with the subject * * *.[5]

In the 1890's most railroads were small, located entirely within a single state. The Supreme Court had held that states had no power to regulate interstate railway traffic,[6] and it had substantially denied such regulatory power to the Interstate Commerce Commission.[7] Railroads are generally thought to be natural monopolies, however, and they perform poorly under unregulated competition. The circuit court noted that a package shipped several hundred miles would probably be handled by several different railroads. Absent rulemaking by a government agency, the railroads needed an agreement among themselves concerning how such packages or cars should be transferred from one line to the next. Such transfers would naturally be facilitated by coordinated scheduling. The freight bill had to be collected either by the railroad that started the package on its route, or else by the railroad that delivered it to its final destination. The money must then be divided up among the participating railroads according to some formula—perhaps in proportion to the number of miles that each line carried the package.

The railroad industry may be unique, but the joint venture at issue in the *Trans–Missouri* case shares two common elements with many such agreements. First, it permitted the participants to operate more efficiently by eliminating much of the chaos that would exist in a market full of small, unregulated railroads. Second, the Association gave the member railroads the power to agree about freight rates.

An often given traditional justification for joint ventures is that they can enable two or more firms working together to perform an activity at minimum efficient scale (MES), while a single firm acting alone could not. For example, suppose that three firms use a particular, specialized metal alloy in the production of certain parts. Efficient production requires a plant capable of producing 100,000 tons per year, but the three firms each require only 40,000 tons per year in their production processes. If the three firms together build the plant, they will be able to maintain output at an efficient rate. In this case the three firms need not be competitors in the market in which they sell, although they must all be consumers of the same alloy. If the alloy is specialized, however the three firms will likely be competitors in the output market as well.

This joint venture can save the participating firms (and eventually their customers) a great deal. First, the joint venture permits them to produce the alloy at an efficient rate. Second, it enables them to avoid the costs of using the market, and those costs can be rather high, particularly if alternative producers have substantial market power, or if the alloy is specialized and must be made according to individualized specifications, necessitating ex-

4. 166 U.S. 290, 17 S.Ct. 540 (1897).

5. United States v. Trans–Missouri Freight Ass'n., 58 Fed. 58, 79–80 (8th Cir.1893), reversed, 166 U.S. 290, 17 S.Ct. 540 (1897).

6. Wabash, St. Louis & Pac. Rwy. Co. v. Illinois, 118 U.S. 557, 7 S.Ct. 4 (1886).

7. Cincinnati, New Orleans & Tex. Pac. Ry. Co. v. I.C.C., 162 U.S. 184, 16 S.Ct. 700 (1896). The Interstate Commerce Commission apparently approved of the joint running agreement at issue in the *Trans–Missouri* case. See 12 ICC Ann.Rep. 10–16 (1898); and H. Hovenkamp, Enterprise and American Law, 1836–1937, chs. 12, 13 (1991).

pensive negotiations with an independent supplier.[8]

Joint ventures can also reduce a firm's marketing costs, or enable it to take advantage of new marketing opportunities. Suppose that three growers of California kiwi berries want to introduce their relatively unfamiliar product to New York. None of the three has output large enough to justify paying a full-time sales agent, but the three operating together could send an agent, each paying one third of the cost. If the product is fungible—that is, if customers cannot distinguish A's kiwi berries from B's kiwi berries—the agent will probably have to charge the same price for all berries of a certain grade or size.[9] So the use of the joint selling agency for fungible products may require a certain amount of "price fixing." However, that information alone does not suggest that the growers are reducing output or charging a supracompetitive price for their product. It merely suggests that a common price may be a necessary element of some market facilitating joint ventures.[10]

The Supreme Court approved such a joint sales agency agreement in Appalachian Coals, Inc. v. United States.[11] The defendants were 137 coal producers who created an exclusive joint selling agency that classified the coal, marketed it, and distributed the proceeds to the participants. Since coal is fungible, the agent had to sell all coal of a certain grade and size at the same price. The Court's decision upholding the agency agreement has been criticized by some commentators as a relic of the New Deal's distrust of competition and the antitrust laws. At the very least, however, the decision deserves further study, particularly in light of modern rules for measuring market power.[12] The defendants collectively controlled about 12% of coal production east of the Mississippi River, or about 55% of relevant production in the greater Appalachian region, which was not the region in which the coal was marketed. The market contained a great deal of excess capacity, however, and even these figures seriously overstated the agency's market power.[13]

Courts have generally approved joint sales agreements, provided they found at least some integration of promotion, advertising or other activities among the participants.[14] A few exclusive joint sales arrangements have been condemned.[15] Joint purchasing agreements have been treated with even greater tolerance.[16] Most recently, in *All Care Nursing* the Eleventh Circuit approved an arrangement under which a group of hospitals took bids for nursing services to be their preferred providers.[17] The court held that the rule of reason must be employed, and dismissed the plaintiff's case for failing to show market power.

In buying cases one can often determine whether the arrangement is anticompetitive

8. See § 9.2b.

9. If the product of the three farmers was perfectly fungible but the agent charged different prices for the output of the three farmers, buyers would buy all the lowest priced berries first, then all the next lowest, and finally the highest. If the product were not fungible but brand specific, such as televisions, automobiles, or personal computers, then the three producers could each set their own price and customers buying through the agent could compare the merits of each brand, including price.

10. See 13 Antitrust Law ¶ 2132 (1999).

11. 288 U.S. 344, 53 S.Ct. 471 (1933).

12. See Ch. 3.

13. The joint venture was defended as designed to *increase* coal sales through "better methods of distribution, intensive advertising and research, and the achievement of economies of marketing," as the Court restated the defendant's arguments. 288 U.S. at 359, 53 S.Ct. at 473. These claims, if proven, indicate an ancillary rather than naked restraint. See § 5.1.

14. E.g., *Broadcast Music*, note 3; Ohio–Sealy Mattress Mfg. Co. v. Sealy, 585 F.2d 821, 837–838 (7th Cir.1978), 440 U.S. 930, 99 S.Ct. 1267 (1979) (applying rule of reason and approving nonexclusive joint sales agreement, while applying per se rule to horizontal territorial division scheme); Association of Indep. Television Stations v. College Football Ass'n, 637 F.Supp. 1289 (W.D.Okla.1986) (upholding athletic associations' joint sales of televised football games); Hudson's Bay Co. Fur Sales v. American Legend Coop., 651 F.Supp. 819, 839 (D.N.J.1986) (joint auctioning upheld).

15. Virginia Excelsior Mills v. FTC, 256 F.2d 538 (4th Cir.1958) (applying per se rule to joint selling of shredded wood packing material). Other decisions are discussed in 13 Antitrust Law ¶ 2137 (1999).

16. See id. at ¶ 2135; and Northwest Wholesale Stationers v. Pacific Stationery & Printing Co., 472 U.S. 284, 295, 105 S.Ct. 2613 (1985) (dicta approving of joint purchasing cooperatives).

17. All Care Nursing Service v. High Tech Staffing Services, 135 F.3d 740 (11th Cir.1998), cert. denied, ___ U.S. ___, 119 S.Ct. 1250 (1999).

by querying whether the venturers made any attempt to suppress the volume of their purchases. As § 1.2b noted, a monopsonist, or monopoly buyer, suppresses the competitive price by purchasing less. A buying cartel must do the same thing, thus requiring a purchasing reduction equivalent to the ordinary cartel's reduction of sales. By contrast, a buying cooperative whose purpose is to reduce the costs of using the market is typically not concerned with limiting the amount that its participants purchase. To the contrary, the more they buy the lower market costs become.

5.2a2. The Two Sides of the Exclusivity Problem

Every joint venture is "exclusive" in the sense that it cannot offer an infinite number of products. But many joint ventures are also exclusive in two other important senses that may have antitrust significance: *first*, they may limit the joint venture's membership, thus excluding others who might wish to join; *second*, they might limit the right of existing members to engage in certain non-venture business, particularly if that business competes with the venture.

Limitations on joint venture membership are generally thought necessary to keep the transaction costs of operating the venture manageable. It is one thing for two firms to join together to manufacture a product; it is quite another for twenty firms to do so, particularly if they have unique interests. Then the costs of negotiating product design, settling on the appropriate size plant, its location, and so on, can become quite unmanageable. Or in a different context, a sports league of ten or even twenty teams might readily manage a season schedule and conduct playoffs to pick a champion. But management would become far more difficult if the league had 1000 members or even 100. Thus all sports leagues have rules that limit the number of teams that can participate or place stringent limitations on new entry. As we shall see later, these problems are more significant in some joint ventures than others, and many ventures become more profitable as their membership increases. Such ventures have open membership policies.[18]

The two types of exclusion noted above may both be necessary to help the venture avoid free-rider problems, which make it impossible for the venture to capitalize on its own investment and risk-taking. For example, most joint ventures are closed to new members because the risk-to-reward ratio changes as the venture progresses. When a research joint venture is first formed the potential for success may be rather limited while the risks attached to the upfront investment are substantial. Three years later, however, when the venture has made important breakthroughs, it may be a much more attractive proposition and others might wish to join in. But a rule permitting them to join would encourage people to wait rather than invest up front.

Limitations on non-venture business may also be necessary to prevent free rider problems. For example, consider the law firm rule forbidding partners from practicing law outside the partnership. Within the firm, each partner probably contributes a percentage of her receipts to the firm to account for operating costs and the payments of non-partners. But if the partner engages in "outside" practice she may be able to keep 100% of what she earns and may even be able to draw on the law firm's reputation, library, office equipment and the like. As a result, partners would be tempted to practice outside more and more, for their individual earnings would be higher. In the process they would cannibalize the firm.

Unfortunately, exclusivity has a serious downside as well: in the presence of market power, it makes anticompetitive results much more likely. Recall from Chapters One and Four that a monopoly or cartel succeeds only by reducing market output. When a joint venture comes to dominate a relevant market, we have the makings of the threat of a market-wide output reduction. However, output will not be reduced as long as the venture is unable to exclude. Further, exclusion entails two quite different things. First, the venture must be able to succeed in reducing output within the

18. See § 5.4b2.

venture, with output measured by either quantity or quality. Second, the venture must be able to reduce non-venture output in the same market.[19]

For example, suppose a group of physicians organize a health maintenance organization (HMO) and agree to cover all of a patient's medical needs for a fixed fee per month. Currently 90% of the community's physicians are in this venture, but (1) the venture permits any new physician who wishes to join in, provided his credentials are in order; and (2) physicians are permitted to engage in unlimited fee-for-service practice outside the venture, or even participate in other HMOs. While the 90% market share is a danger signal suggesting possible collusion, the non-exclusivity of the venture pretty much ensures that price-fixing will not occur. The rule permitting new members means that in response to any non-cost-justified price increase more and more physicians will join. The rule permitting non-venture business means that the venture will always be competing with its own members. As a result, it is highly unlikely that this venture would ever succeed in reducing market output below the competitive level, unless secret pressures are brought to bear.

Thus non-exclusivity often serves to mitigate our fears about joint venture exercises of market power. By contrast, exclusivity may be necessary to create the proper incentives to make a joint venture run properly, but if the venture has a dominant position in its market, then exclusivity rules have to be justified. The combination of market power and exclusivity rules makes anticompetitive outcomes plausible.

This is not to say, however, that market dominating joint ventures cannot have exclusivity limitations. Even if the NFL dominates a properly defined market for "professional football," it still has very good administrative reasons for limiting the number of teams. It undoubtedly has equally good reasons for prohibiting its team members from playing for competing teams outside the NFL. The point is not that ventures with market power cannot have exclusivity rules; it is only that antitrust scrutiny is most justified in such circumstances, and firms must be ready to explain exclusivity rules that seem particularly likely to facilitate marketwide output reductions.

§ 5.2b. Ventures Facilitating R & D, Advertising and Promotion; Ancillary Market Divisions

§ 5.2b1. Joint Ventures and Free Rider Problems

A free rider is a firm who takes free advantage of a service or product that is valued by customers but provided by a different firm. If free riding is widespread the valued service or product may disappear.[20]

Research and development (R & D) and advertising are two areas in which free rider problems are significant. For example, many of the results of expensive R & D cannot be patented or, even if patented, cannot effectively be excluded from appropriation by others. If one firm spends vast sums in R & D, a competing firm might be able to reap the benefits without having to pay the high costs. A firm in competition, facing the likelihood that a particular research project will cost a substantial amount but will benefit all firms in the market, will forego the project. It cannot afford to subsidize its competitors. A research joint venture will benefit all the firms in the market, however, and force all to share in the costs. Such joint ventures are relatively common in certain industries.[21]

§ 5.2b2. National Cooperative Research Act

In 1984 Congress responded to widespread belief that § 1 as then interpreted acted as a

19. See 11 Antitrust Law ¶ 1908h (1998); and 13 id. ¶ 2104 (1999).

20. Free riding is discussed more fully in § 11.3a.

21. See E. Kitch, The Law & Economics of Rights in Valuable Information, 9 J.Leg.Stud. 683 (1980); and J. Brodley, Joint Ventures and Antitrust Policy, 95 Harv. L.Rev. 1523 (1982). Research joint ventures have rarely been condemned under the antitrust laws. But see Berkey Photo, Inc. v. Eastman Kodak Co., 603 F.2d 263, 299–304 (2d Cir.1979), cert. denied, 444 U.S. 1093, 100 S.Ct. 1061 (1980). Kodak, Sylvania and General Electric formed a research joint venture to develop the "Magicube," a flash attachment for cameras. The activity was condemned not for the research, but for the firms' agreement not to disclose the results of their efforts to outsiders.

deterrent to efficient joint ventures. It enacted the National Cooperative Research Act.[22] The statute provides that properly constructed research joint ventures should be evaluated under the rule of reason rather than the *per se* rule—thus resolving any possible lingering doubt about whether they might receive the same treatment as cartels or naked refusals to deal. The statute contains a procedure for filing with the Justice Department and Federal Trade Commission a notice of any venture, stating its nature, its objectives, and the identities of the parties. If a registered venture should be challenged under the antitrust laws, prevailing plaintiffs receive single rather than treble damages, and defendants, if successful, recover reasonable attorney's fees. Importantly, the statute excludes from its definition of research joint ventures any venture that involves (1) the exchanging of information among competitors relative to prices, costs, sales, profitability, marketing or distribution; (2) agreements restricting output of products, although the venture may limit the output of trade secrets or intellectual property that is produced by the venture itself; (3) agreements governing the sale of goods or sharing of technology with respect to things not within the scope of the venture itself.[23]

§ 5.2b3. Ancillary and Naked Agreements Pertaining to Advertising[24]

Joint advertising agreements pose some of the same concerns as joint research agreements, although there is some justification for treating them more harshly. First, joint advertising is much more explicitly involved with "sales" than is joint research and development, and quite naturally steps into the area of price setting. Second, scale economies and free rider problems may not loom as large in advertising as in R & D.

Nevertheless, joint advertising arrangements are often efficient, depending on the circumstance. Interbrand arrangements[25] covering differentiated products are the hardest to justify. For example, if a Sylvania television dealer advertises the qualities of Sylvania televisions, potential television customers will attribute the information only to Sylvanias. The advertising is not likely to benefit dealers in Sonys or Zeniths; on the contrary, it is calculated to attract to Sylvania customers that might otherwise go to a competitor. By contrast, if products are fungible, advertising will benefit all local producers of the product, whether or not they paid for the advertising. For example, if Farmer Brown advertises the merits of Farmer Brown's Potatoes, she might be horrified to discover that many customers think potatoes are potatoes. Farmer Brown's advertisement may increase potato sales, but they will be distributed over all potato producers in the advertising market.

In a competitive market Farmer Brown cannot afford to pay for advertising that benefits all local producers of potatoes. She will not advertise at all, even though the effect of the advertising would be to give consumers better information. However, the farmers collectively could increase their joint welfare, as well as that of consumers, if they organized a potato growers association, and each paid a proportionate share of the costs of the advertising. In that case both the benefit and the cost would be shared by all growers.

Most of the decisions condemning joint advertising involve not merely the agreement to advertise jointly, but also some other restraint. For example, in *Serta* the defendants not only

22. 15 U.S.C.A. §§ 4301–4304. See J. Ordover & R. Willig, Antitrust for High–Technology Industries: Assessing Research Joint Ventures and Mergers, 28 J.L. & Econ. 311 (1985); and see T. Piraino, Reconciling Competition and Cooperation: A new Antitrust Standard for Joint Ventures, 35 Wm. & Mary L.Rev. 871 (1994); T. Jorde & D. Teece, Acceptable Cooperation Among Competitors in the Face of Growing International Competition, 58 Antitrust L.J. 529 (1989).

23. For criticism of the statute, see T. Jorde & D. Teece, "Innovation, Cooperation, and Antitrust" 47, in Antitrust, Innovation, and Competitiveness (T. Jorde & D. Teece, eds. 1992). The authors note that, although the statute applies a rule of reason to joint ventures, little is said about its content, and it provides no "safe harbor" for ventures falling below a specified market share.

24. See 12 Antitrust Law ¶ 2023 (1999).

25. An "interbrand" agreement is one among the manufacturers or dealers in different brands—for example, Fords, Chevrolets, and Chryslers. An "intrabrand" agreement is one among the distributors or dealers of a single brand, such as an agreement among Ford dealers.

advertised jointly, they also agreed not to engage in comparative advertising with other firms in the venture.[26] And in *Detroit Auto Dealers* the defendants jointly advertised that all their showrooms would be closing at 6 P.M.[27] In that case the restraint was not the joint advertising, but rather the agreement to shorten business hours, which was an output reduction.

Also suspicious are agreements *not* to advertise. Advertising is a valuable way of communicating information to consumers, and price advertising is particularly valuable because it is often costly for consumers to compare prices.[28] To be sure, advertising is often misleading or even fraudulent, and consumer confidence in a market might be strengthened if advertising were policed more rigorously. But the sellers themselves are generally the wrong policemen, for they are injured not only by the misleading advertising of their rivals but also by rivals' aggressive but essentially truthful advertising. Nonetheless, in its *California Dental* decision the Supreme Court concluded that a professional association's advertising restraints must be addressed under the rule of reason.[29] The five-member majority, led by Justice Souter, saw a sufficient potential that the restraints were sufficiently well designed to prohibit only deceptive advertising, and thus might increase consumer confidence in dental services. Justice Breyer wrote for four dissenters who emphasized the apparently excessive nature of the restrictions, which often operated to prohibit all advertising whatsoever.[30]

When deception or fraud are not in issue, competitor initiated restraints on advertising are highly dubious. They have been used to facilitate market divisions,[31] to make it more difficult for consumers to engage in price comparison,[32] or to ward off the threat posed by lower cost distribution methods or more aggressive rivals.[33]

Numerous decisions have attacked agreements among cigarette manufacturers to withhold information about the health effects of cigarettes, or to advertise that their cigarettes were less unhealthful than those of rivals. While these would seem to be easy cases, the plaintiffs have often been denied standing to sue.[34] When a product poses health risks we

26. United States v. Serta Assocs., 296 F.Supp. 1121, 1125–26 (N.D.Ill.1968), aff'd per curiam, 393 U.S. 534, 89 S.Ct. 870 (1969) (joint price advertising and agreement to limit comparative advertising among Serta mattress dealers unlawful per se).

27. Detroit Auto Dealers Assn., 111 F.T.C. 417 (1989), aff'd, 955 F.2d 457 (6th Cir.), cert. denied, 506 U.S. 973, 113 S.Ct. 461 (1992).

28. Cf. Bates v. State Bar of Arizona, 433 U.S. 350, 377–378, 97 S.Ct. 2691 (1977) (limits on price advertising increase consumer search costs); Virginia State Board of Pharmacy v. Virginia Citizens Consumer Council, 425 U.S. 748, 765, 96 S.Ct. 1817 (1976) (truthful advertising informs consumers about "who is producing and selling what product, for what reason, and at what price.")

29. California Dental Assn. v. FTC, ___ U.S. ___, 119 S.Ct. 1604 (1999).

30. The dissent noted that while nominally designed to prevent deceptive advertising, "[a]s implemented, the ethical rule reached beyond its nominal target, to prevent truthful and nondeceptive advertising." Id. at 1618.

31. Blackburn v. Sweeney, 53 F.3d 825, 827 (7th Cir. 1995) (agreement between lawyers that they would not advertise in one another's territories illegal per se).

32. E.g., Massachusetts Board of Registration in Optometry, 110 F.T.C. 549, 605 (1988) (striking down ban on all advertising, even if truthful). See also the following consent decrees: American Inst. of Certified Public Accountants, 113 F.T.C. 698 (1990) (prohibiting ban on truthful advertising); United States v. Gasoline Retailers Ass'n, 285 F.2d 688, 691 (7th Cir.1961) (criminal case; per se unlawful for gasoline retailers to agree not to advertise their gasoline prices except by posting it directly on the pump).

33. See, e.g., Federal Prescription Serv. v. American Pharm. Assn., 484 F.Supp. 1195, 1207 (D.D.C.1980), aff'd in part and rev'd in part, 663 F.2d 253 (D.C.Cir.1981), cert. denied, 455 U.S. 928, 102 S.Ct. 1293 (1982) (condemning pharmacy association's efforts to limit mail order pharmaceutical companies by banning advertising). Cf. Denny's Marina v. Renfro Productions, 8 F.3d 1217, 1219 (7th Cir.1993) (marine dealers' exclusion of dealer from trade show because of its "meet or beat" any price advertising illegal per se). However, joint advertising for the same purpose may be lawful. See, e.g., Greene County Memorial Park v. Behm Funeral Homes, 797 F.Supp. 1276 (W.D.Pa.1992) (refusing to apply per se rule to funeral homes' group advertising warning local public against out-of-town sellers of caskets; no violation).

34. Many of the cases have been undermined by denials of standing. See, e.g., Laborers Local 17 Health and Benefit Fund v. Philip Morris, 172 F.3d 223 (2d Cir.1999) (withdrawn) (labor union health fund lacked standing to sue for health related injuries caused by its members from alleged tobacco conspiracy); Texas v. American Tobacco Co., 14 F.Supp.2d 956, 1998–1 Trade Cas. ¶ 72205 (E.D.Tex.1997) (state not victim of antitrust injury from alleged conspiracy of tobacco companies to deceive public concerning quality of its cigarettes; increased medical

would expect firms to compete by innovating so as to reduce those risks and then announcing their success via advertising. An agreement among rivals not to advertise in this fashion reduces the innovation incentive.

Closely related to joint advertising is joint development of trademarks or other intellectual property. The promotion of brand names may require more advertising resources than a single small firm can command. But a group of firms may develop and promote a trademark jointly and thus compete more effectively with larger firms. Alternatively, joint promotion may enable small firms to compete in a wider market. For example, restauranteurs scattered across a wide area might develop joint menus, building plans, and methods of doing business, and then promote their "chain" nationally. This national name recognition will enable them to reach traveling customers that might otherwise avoid a local restaurant about which they know nothing. The *Topco* case, discussed below, involved such a venture.[35]

§ 5.2b4. Ancillary Market Divisions and Noncompetition Agreements

A market division is an agreement among two firms that each will stay out of some portion of the market occupied by the other. Markets can be divided by *geography* (I'll sell only west of the Mississippi and you only east); by *product* (I'll sell only the electric version of this appliance and you agree to sell only the gas version), or by *customer* (I'll sell only to restaurants and you only to hospitals). A naked market division is simply a form of collusion,[36] is illegal per se,[37] and can be a criminal offense.[38]

But market division agreements ancillary to other joint activity can increase output by reducing free rider problems, thus giving each firm an incentive to promote more aggressively. Nevertheless, the Supreme Court has been intolerant of horizontal agreements to use territorial division to overcome free rider problems. In the leading case, United States v. Topco Associates, Inc.,[39] the Court condemned an arrangement involving about 25 small grocery chains. Under the agreement the stores marketed their products separately and did not set or advertise prices jointly or pool earnings. The association created by the agreement bought grocery items in large quantities and redistributed them to members. Its most distinctive contribution was a jointly held "Topco" trademark that appeared on many of its grocery products, and which had acquired large consumer appeal. Under the agreement, each member promised to sell Topco brand merchandise only in its own assigned marketing territory. The member was free to open stores in another territory, but these stores could not display or sell the Topco brand. Thus each member had an exclusive area in which it could market Topco brand products.

costs paid for Medicaid recipients not the type of injury that antitrust laws contemplated).

35. See also Rothery Storage & Van Co. v. Atlas Van Lines, 792 F.2d 210, 214 (D.C.Cir.1986), cert. denied, 479 U.S. 1033, 107 S.Ct. 880 (1987) (approving agreement among moving firms jointly using "Atlas" name that they would not employ that name in advertising their separate operations).

36. See, e.g., Blue Cross & Blue Shield United of Wisconsin v. Marshfield Clinic, 65 F.3d 1406, 1415 (7th Cir.1995), cert. denied, 516 U.S. 1184, 116 S.Ct. 1288 (1996):

> the analogy between price fixing and division of markets is compelling. It would be a strange interpretation of antitrust law that forbade competitors to agree on what price to charge, thus eliminating price competition among them but allowed them to divide markets, thus eliminating all competition among them.

37. E.g., Palmer v. BRG of Georgia, 498 U.S. 46, 111 S.Ct. 401 (1990) (per curiam) (geographic market division of bar review offers unlawful per se); Blackburn v. Sweeney, 53 F.3d 825 (7th Cir.1995) (agreement among lawyers not to advertise in one another's cities unlawful per se). Cf. Timken Roller Bearing Co. v. United States, 341 U.S. 593, 71 S.Ct. 971 (1951) (finding naked territorial division and applying per se rule, notwithstanding an argument that the three firms used the same trademark and would be subject to free riding if they sold in the same territory).

38. United States v. Brown, 936 F.2d 1042 (9th Cir. 1991) (affirming criminal conviction of rivals who divided market for billboard sites); United States v. Suntar Roofing, 897 F.2d 469 (10th Cir.1990) (horizontal customer allocation among roofers; unlawful per se; criminal conviction).

39. 405 U.S. 596, 92 S.Ct. 1126 (1972). See also United States v. Sealy, Inc., 388 U.S. 350, 87 S.Ct. 1847 (1967), which struck down a territorial division agreement among mattress manufacturers that owned the Sealy trademark in common.

The government challenged the market division scheme as a cartel, claiming that it operated "to prohibit competition in Topco-brand products among grocery chains engaged in retail operations." But the record revealed that each member's share of the grocery market within its assigned territory averaged about 6%. Further, entry into the retail grocery business was quite easy. The market division in the *Topco* case could not plausibly have turned the defendants into monopolists.

Why would a group of grocery chains divide territories if they could not earn monopoly profits as a result? In *Topco*, the defendants were trying to compete more effectively against larger grocery chains. A nationally recognized "Topco" brand could be created only by advertising. If two or more competing chains sold Topco brands in the same market area, however, all chains would benefit from the brand advertising of one. As a result, none of the stores would advertise. The territorial division scheme gave each member the exclusive right to sell the Topco brand in a territory, and thus the incentive to advertise the brand there. As the Supreme Court would recognize five years later in a vertical restraints case,[40] the territorial division arguably lessened "intrabrand" competition—that is, competition among different stores selling Topco brand products.[41] However, it very likely increased "interbrand" competition—competition between stores selling Topco brand products and those selling other brands of the same products. The territorial division scheme enabled the consortium of small chain stores to compete more effectively with the large chain groceries that could afford to produce and advertise their own exclusive labels.

Topco has been widely criticized for ignoring the distinction between naked and ancillary horizontal market division schemes. While some market division is nothing more than a form of price fixing, the *Topco* arrangement was almost certainly efficient. In that case we must consider whether the division agreement reduced costs or gave the participants an incentive to invest that they would not otherwise have had. If so, rule of reason application would be called for. At that point the defendants' small market shares should have been decisive.[42]

Although *Topco* has never been overruled,[43] it is widely criticized and not infrequently honored in the breach. In *General Leaseways* the Seventh Circuit analyzed an agreement among two companies that leased and maintained trucks.[44] Under the venture the companies divided their operating territories,[45] but also agreed to perform emergency repairs on trucks owned by the other company that happened to break down in the repairer's territory. Judge Posner criticized *Topco* for ignoring the threat of free riding that the Topco arrangement had been designed to solve. In the present case, by contrast, the two parties had agreed to reimburse each other for repairs made; so free riding seemed not to be a threat. He concluded that the territorial arrangement was illegal *per se*.

Noncompetition covenants are ubiquitous in both employment agreements and deeds, leases, or other agreements covering business property. They generally have the same economic effect as ancillary market division agreements. For example, one physician may sell her pediatrics practice in Bryan, Texas, to another physician and promise not to practice

40. Continental T.V., Inc. v. GTE Sylvania, Inc., 433 U.S. 36, 97 S.Ct. 2549 (1977), on remand, 461 F.Supp. 1046 (N.D.Cal.1978), affirmed, 694 F.2d 1132 (9th Cir. 1982). See § 11.6. Some have speculated that *Sylvania* overruled *Topco*. See R. Posner, The Next Step in the Antitrust Treatment of Restricted Distribution: Per Se Legality, 48 U.Chi.L.Rev. 6, 25 (1981). However, the Supreme Court's heavy reliance on *Topco* in *Palmer*, note 37, indicates the contrary.

41. However, for a critique of the concept of "lessening" intrabrand competition, see § 11.6a.

42. See § 5.6.

43. And indeed, some courts still follow it to the letter. See Bascom Food Prods. Corp. v. Reese Finer Foods, Inc., 715 F.Supp. 616, 632 (D.N.J.1989) (applying per se rule to territorial division agreement in grocery industry).

44. General Leaseways v. National Truck Leasing Assn., 744 F.2d 588 (7th Cir.1984).

45. The agreement prohibited the parties from doing business at any location other than those established by agreement and spaced competing franchisees at least twenty miles apart. Id. at 540.

pediatrics in Bryan for five years following the sale.

Noncompetition agreements are sometimes challenged as concerted refusals to deal—most typically, when they deny market access to some person who was not a party to the original agreement.[46] For example, in order to attract a high quality shoe store into its shopping mall, lessor A may provide in its lease to shoe retailer B that A will not permit another store in the mall to sell shoes. Sometimes such covenants are challenged by customers who believe they have paid a higher price as a result of an anticompetitive agreement. Often they are challenged by one of the original parties seeking to escape from its own agreement. In other cases they are challenged by firms who have been excluded from the market by the noncompetition covenant. The legal analysis applied is generally the same.[47]

Noncompetition covenants are typically regarded as "ancillary" restraints because they usually are contained in agreements providing for the sale of a business, the start of employment, or perhaps the beginning of a broader ongoing contractual relationship. They may be collateral to ongoing joint-venture agreements but they need not be. For example, the owner of a shoe store on Blackacre may sell Whiteacre across the street subject to a covenant that no shoes be sold on Whiteacre. In that case there is no obvious integration of entrepreneurial activities by the parties. Nonetheless, the trend is to treat such covenants under the rule of reason.

As the Supreme Court made clear in *Palmer*, however, not all noncompetition covenants are to be analyzed under the rule of reason.[48] That decision applied the *per se* rule to a horizontal territorial division scheme created when one offeror of a bar review course in Athens, Georgia, sold another firm the right to use its materials in Athens and promised not to offer a competing course in the Athens market. In return, the licensee of the materials promised not to offer bar review courses anywhere else in the United States. The immediate result was a dramatic increase in bar review fees for University of Georgia Law School graduates. The Supreme Court treated the case as nothing more than a naked territorial division scheme. But noncompetition covenants attending the sale of businesses are both common and not typically suspect unless the acquiring firm ends up with significant market power.[49] In *Palmer* the licensee's promise not to offer bar review courses in the rest of the United States was clearly excessive, but that was not the covenant that caused the Athens price to rise. The price increase was a consequence of the licensor's promise to stay out of Athens—a quite common form of ancillary

46. On concerted refusals to deal, see § 5.4.

47. The substantive legal analysis is the same, but *in Pari Delicto* may apply when a noncompete covenant is challenged by a person who was also a party to the agreement. The doctrine of *in Pari Delicto* prevents a plaintiff from recovering damages if he was "at equal fault" in the violation. In Perma Life Mufflers, Inc. v. International Parts Corp., 392 U.S. 134, 88 S.Ct. 1981 (1968), the Supreme Court rejected a general *in Pari Delicto* defense and permitted a franchisee to challenge several provisions in his own franchise agreement. The Court held that the relevant question was whether the plaintiff had been a willing participant in the conspiracy, or was merely one of its victims, in the sense that the agreement was foisted on him unwillingly. See THI–Hawaii, Inc. v. First Commerce Financial Corp., 627 F.2d 991 (9th Cir.1980), holding that the plaintiff could not recover damages from an allegedly illegal restrictive covenant contained in its lease agreement. In this case, the lease was the result of an "arm's length bargaining process," so the antitrust plaintiff was at equal fault. Bateman Eichler, Hill Richards, Inc. v. Berner, 472 U.S. 299, 105 S.Ct. 2622 (1985), held that a plaintiff in a securities case would be barred from recovering damages:

> where (1) as a direct result of his own actions, the plaintiff bears at least substantially equal responsibility for the violations he seeks to redress, and (2) preclusion of suit would not significantly interfere with the effective enforcement of the securities laws and protection of the investing public.

In General Leaseways v. National Truck Leasing Assn., 830 F.2d 716 (7th Cir.1987), the court applied *in Pari Delicto* to defeat an antitrust claim where the plaintiff had in fact solicited the contract he later attacked as an antitrust violation. See 2 P. Areeda & H. Hovenkamp, Antitrust Law ¶ 390 (rev. ed. 1995).

48. Palmer v. BRG of Georgia, 498 U.S. 46, 111 S.Ct. 401 (1990), on remand, 928 F.2d 1097 (11th Cir.1991).

49. See 13 Antitrust Law ¶ 2134d (1999); and see LDDS Communs. v. Automated Communs., 35 F.3d 198, 199 (5th Cir.1994) (approving noncompetition covenant attending sale of business assets between providers of long distance telephone service); R.W. Int'l v. Borden Interamerica, 673 F.Supp. 654, 656 (D.P.R.1987) (product division agreement attending transfer of food distribution business; no antitrust violation).

noncompetition agreement. The arrangement should probably have been treated as a merger to monopoly, but that analysis would have required that a relevant market be determined.[50]

If a horizontal territorial or customer division is found to be reasonably ancillary to a joint venture, several circuit courts have applied the rule of reason, notwithstanding *Topco*. For example, in *Polk* the Seventh Circuit upheld a lease covenant between two stores occupying the same building that one would not sell appliances in competition with the other.[51] In approving this agreement, Judge Easterbrook observed that it was ancillary to the lease and that a noncompetition agreement covering a single building in an urban area lacked anything resembling market power.

Likewise, in *Rothery* the court refused to condemn an agreement among independent moving firms operated as franchisees to Atlas, a national branded moving company. The firms agreed not to use Atlas' name, goodwill or other services for any form of carriage made outside of the franchise arrangement, for which Atlas as franchisor was not compensated. As the court put it,

> A carrier agent can attract customers because of Atlas' "national image" and can use Atlas' equipment and order forms when undertaking carriage for its own account. To the degree that a carrier agent uses Atlas' reputation, equipment, facilities,and services in conducting business for its own profit, the agent enjoys a free ride at Atlas' expense. The problem is that the van line's incentive to spend for reputation, equipment, facilities and services declines as it receives less of the benefit from them. * * *[52]

The free-rider argument used to defend horizontal market divisions is dangerous, however, and should ordinarily not absolve division agreements that do not accompany significant integration of production or distribution. Consider the *Metro Industries* case, in which the Ninth Circuit held that a "design registration" system among competing manufacturers of kitchenware should be accorded rule of reason treatment, for the system gave firms an incentive to invest in new designs without fear of copying.[53] Under the agreement, when a member firm designed a qualifying piece of kitchenware (such as a stainless steel vegetable steamer), that design was registered. For a three year period, renewable for three additional years, no other member could copy the design for export purposes. As the court paraphrased a defendant's free rider defense:

> [T]ooling and production of a new product takes several years. Thus, the limited protection could encourage manufacturers to develop and produce new products, knowing that they would have the exclusive right to export a particular design for a limited period of time.[54]

This fact gave the registration system "output increasing potential."

To be sure, that argument may be factually true. For example, my expansion of paintball dealerships in New Jersey will be much more attractive if all other paintball equipment manufacturers agree to stay out; so an agreement giving me exclusive rights to New Jersey and someone else exclusive rights to New York operates as an incentive to invest. The problem with the Ninth Circuit's argument, howev-

50. On mergers to monopoly, see § 12.3b.

51. Polk Brothers, Inc. v. Forest City Enterprises, Inc., 776 F.2d 185 (7th Cir.1985). See also St. Louis Convention & Visitors Comm'n v. NFL, 154 F.3d 851 (8th Cir.1998) (NFL relocation rule limiting teams' ability to move addressed under rule of reason); Northrop Corp. v. McDonnell Douglas Corp., 705 F.2d 1030, 1050–1053 (9th Cir. 1983), cert. denied, 464 U.S. 849, 104 S.Ct. 156 (1983) (upholding production agreement entered by parties at government's request, and restricting one firm to selling land-based aircraft, and another to selling aircraft for aircraft carriers); Van Dyk Research Corp. v. Xerox Corp., 478 F.Supp. 1268, 1304 (D.N.J.1979), affirmed, 631 F.2d 251 (3d Cir.1980), cert. denied, 452 U.S. 905, 101 S.Ct. 3029 (1981) (approving joint venture dividing world market geographically; firms not competitors at time venture was created).

52. Rothery Storage & Van Co. v. Atlas Van Lines, 792 F.2d 210, 221 (D.C.Cir.1986), cert. denied, 479 U.S. 1033, 107 S.Ct. 880 (1987).

53. Metro Industries v. Sammi Corp., 82 F.3d 839 (9th Cir.), cert. denied, 519 U.S. 868, 117 S.Ct. 181 (1996).

54. Id. at 844.

er, is that the incentive operates only to the point that the investor achieves the monopoly rate of output. Assume that the competitive sales of paintball in New Jersey would be 100 units per month while monopoly sales would be 70 units. A territorial division agreement might get me to invest faster, but only up to a production level of 70 units per month.[55] At that point, I would have a monopoly for the duration of the agreement. By contrast, unrestrained entry ordinarily produces investment up to the competitive amount.[56]

Notwithstanding *Palmer*, if a non-competition covenant is truly ancillary to the sale of a business or other productive assets, then it is generally treated under the rule of reason.[57] In that case it is generally legal if it does not eliminate too much competition within a properly defined relevant market. Most such covenants restrict competition within a single shopping center or perhaps on a single piece of property. Courts also purport to consider such questions as whether the covenant is necessary to protect the promisee's legitimate business interests.[58] Some courts have done this even when the restrictive covenant at issue included a price term. For example, in *Drury Inn* the court applied the rule of reason and then approved a covenant that provided that land adjacent to a hotel operator's land would not be used by a hotel whose room rates were within twenty percent of the former's room rates.[59]

§ 5.2c. Transactional Efficiencies Justifying Joint Venture Price Setting

Certain joint ventures of competitors are valuable because they reduce transaction costs so substantially that they virtually create a new market or make a market much larger than it had been before. Justice Brandeis characterized the agreement in Chicago Board of Trade v. United States[60] this way. At issue was the "call" rule adopted by the Board, which was the world's leading market for grain. During regular trading sessions from 9:30 a.m. to 1:15 p.m. the Board operated as one of the most perfect markets that can be found: hundreds of buyers and sellers of grain met on the floor and made transactions by public bids. Current price information was made available to both buyers and sellers, as fast as it could be displayed on the chalk boards. Under the "call" rule, Board members were permitted to trade after the close of the regular session only at the session's closing price. For example, if wheat closed at $1.00 per bushel at the end of the regular Wednesday session, all transactions by Board members after closing until the opening of the Thursday session had to be made at that price. A new price would be established competitively when the Thursday session opened.

In challenging the call rule, the government made no attempt to show that it generated an output restriction or enabled the Board members to increase price. They argued simply that the rule "fixed" prices and was therefore illegal. In rejecting that proposition, Justice Brandeis noted that the call rule "created" a public market for grain scheduled to arrive. The market, after all, is not where the transaction is consummated but where the price is determined. Under the "call" rule all price determination was made under the most public and competitive of circumstances, with no buyer or seller in a position to take advan-

55. And in any event, the fact that I invest more slowly under competition does not mean that the *aggregate* of investors would invest more slowly.

56. See 12 Antitrust Law ¶ 2032 (1999).

57. See 13 Antitrust Law ¶ 2134 (1999).

58. For example, Lektro–Vend Corp. v. Vendo Co., 660 F.2d 255, 265 (7th Cir.1981), cert. denied, 455 U.S. 921, 102 S.Ct. 1277 (1982); Verson Wilkins Ltd. v. Allied Prods. Corp., 723 F.Supp. 1, 12–13 (N.D.Ill.1989) (striking down covenant whose territorial range was greater than necessary to protect business).

59. Drury Inn–Colorado Springs v. Olive Co., 878 F.2d 340 (10th Cir.1989). The court also noted that the covenant could not be anticompetitive in the absence of market power, and power could not be inferred from the covenant alone.

60. 246 U.S. 231, 38 S.Ct. 242 (1918). For a fuller treatment of the facts, see S. Pirrong, The Efficient Scope of Private Transactions–Cost–Reducing Institutions: the Successes and Failures of Commodity Exchanges, 24 J. Legal Stud. 229 (1995); P. Carstensen, The Content of the Hollow Core of Antitrust: The Chicago Board of Trade Case and the Meaning of the "Rule of Reason" in Restraint of Trade Analysis, 13 Res. in L. & Econ. 1 (1991); and see 11 Antitrust law ¶ 1912b (1998).

tage of another party's ignorance. Finding no plausible way that the rule could disguise price fixing, the Court unanimously ordered the complaint dismissed.

Although the Court may have overlooked some important facts,[61] the rationale was obvious enough: markets are often created by sellers. A competitive market usually requires multiple sellers; as a result, the creation of a market may involve a certain amount of joint activity. Some of the most successful and competitive of markets, such as the Board of Trade, the stock exchanges, and many farmers' cooperatives, are created by joint venture of competing firms. The result can be a substantial reduction in transaction costs.

Often a consumer's highest cost of using a market is search costs. The reasonable consumer will search for the best bargain until the marginal cost of one additional inquiry exceeds its expected utility.[62] The lower the search costs relative to the value of the product, the more searching the consumer will do before he purchases, and the more likely he will obtain a competitive price. Search costs would be very low if all sellers were gathered together at one place and time so that the consumer could survey their offerings. If consumer search costs were zero then we would expect the market price to be uniform. No consumer would buy from any seller who charged more than other sellers. However, when consumer search costs are relatively high there will be wider variations in the market price. The market in *Chicago Board of Trade* forced all transactions into an environment in which consumer search costs were very low.

A dramatic example of a market facilitating agreement was the blanket licensing arrangement at issue in Broadcast Music, Inc. v. Columbia Broadcasting System, Inc. (BMI).[63] BMI was an association made up of thousands of composers, publishers and others who owned the performance rights to musical compositions. A performance right gives its holder the exclusive right to perform a composition or license the right of performance to others. The market for such performance rights is vast: tens of thousands of radio stations, television stations, movie producers, and high school drama clubs may need to purchase a performance right before they can perform a musical composition publicly for profit. Theft can be a substantial problem for the owners of intellectual property. If someone 1000 miles away performs a song to which you have the exclusive right, you will not notice that any of it is missing; nevertheless you have been robbed.[64]

BMI sold "blanket licenses," which permitted the licensee to perform everything in BMI's library. The library consisted of performance rights to compositions owned by its members. The licensees paid a charge that varied with their revenues. The performance right holder received income that varied with the amount that his compositions were used. BMI also enforced its members' rights by the relatively inexpensive process of listening for the broadcasting of anything in its library by someone who had not purchased a blanket license.

The blanket license arrangement saved untold millions of dollars in transactions costs. Few radio stations could afford to negotiate individually for the right to perform every piece of music they played on the air. If they

61. Brokers on the Board had fixed commission rates which were added to the transaction price. As a result there was no price competition among brokers for sales made during the regular session. A broker might be tempted to "cheat" on post-session sales, however, and steal customers away from another broker. He would do this, not by shaving his commission, which would violate exchange rules, but by shaving the market price. For example, suppose a broker could buy wheat at $1.00 and had a buyer willing to pay $1.05, but the fixed commission rate was 10¢. The broker could make the sale by paying $1.00 for wheat, reselling it at 95¢, and adding in the 10¢ commission. The "call" rule required the broker to resell the wheat at $1.00. Together, the fixed commission rate plus the call rule effectively prevented brokers from price competing in post-session trades. Whether this fact should have changed the Court's decision is unclear. Price competition among brokers in post-session trades would have moved sales out of the regular session and into the post-session, perhaps undermining the open market. See generally R. Zerbe, The Chicago Board of Trade Case, 1918, 5 Research in L. & Econ. 17 (1983).

62. See G. Stigler, The Theory of Price 2 (3d ed. 1966).

63. 441 U.S. 1, 99 S.Ct. 1551 (1979).

64. See Kitch, note 21 above.

did, advertising costs would soar and the amount of music played would drop. In fact, if the market had operated on an individual contract per performance basis, the costs of the transactions would often have dwarfed the price of the performance right itself. Furthermore, the "shelf life" of many popular songs is rather short. The performance right might become worthless while the station was negotiating for the right to play it. The single blanket license, however, substituted for thousands of individual transactions and gave licensees immediate access to anything in BMI's library.[65]

BMI differs from *Chicago Board* in one important way: the blanket licensing agreement fundamentally altered the price structure of the market. The "product" that would exist in an uncontrolled market—the right to a single performance of a single composition—all but disappeared, and its price disappeared at the same time. The blanket licensing arrangement certainly seemed to run afoul of the Supreme Court's conclusion that agreements among competitors that tamper with a market's price structure are illegal *per se.*[66] In addition, the agreement completely eliminated price competition among artists. Once a radio station had purchased its blanket license it could perform any composition by any artist in the BMI library at no additional cost.

Furthermore, the blanket licensing agreement was price discriminatory. The price of the blanket license varied with the buyer's revenues; however, this formula bore no relationship to the cost that the blanket licenses imposed on either BMI or the performance right holders. They simply made more money from large purchasers than they did from small ones. This kind of persistent price discrimination can exist only if the seller (or group of sellers) has some market power.[67]

All this evidence of price fixing and monopoly power notwithstanding, the Court refused to apply the *per se* rule to blanket licensing. The efficiency-creating potential of the arrangement was too obvious. Moreover, the licenses that the performance right owners conferred on BMI were non-exclusive: any owner could continue to sell the right to perform a single composition or group of compositions on an individual transaction basis. The fact that the blanket licensing arrangement could coexist with a market in which thousands of individual performance right holders were free to negotiate individual transactions (but few did), suggests that buyers obtained a lower price through blanket licensing than they would have through individual transactions.[68]

The *BMI* case may be regarded as *sui generis*. The product that the defendants sold and the nature of their property rights in it were different than the commodities involved in most cartel cases. It is also unclear that *BMI* involved price fixing by "competitors." To say that the thousands of owners of performance rights were competitors implies that "Heartbreak Hotel" and the "Moonlight Sonata" are fungible, which means that radio listeners are indifferent to whether they hear one or the other. If "Heartbreak Hotel" and the "Moonlight Sonata" each occupies its own relevant market, then the owner of the exclusive right to perform one of them is a monopolist.[69] Perhaps the blanket licensing arrangement should more accurately be characterized as an association of monopolists than an agreement among competitors.

The economics of the market for musical compositions suggests that the owner of the

65. See 13 Antitrust Law ¶ 2132 (1999).

66. See United States v. Socony–Vacuum Oil Co., 310 U.S. 150, 223–224, 60 S.Ct. 811, 844 (1940), rehearing denied, 310 U.S. 658, 60 S.Ct. 1091 (1940).

67. See § 14.3.

68. Compare CBS v. ASCAP, 620 F.2d 930, 932, 936–939 (2d Cir.1980), cert. denied, 450 U.S. 970, 101 S.Ct. 1491 (1981) (upholding blanket licensing, emphasizing that composers retained the right to sell their rights outside of the blanket licensing arrangement).

69. The district court in Buffalo Broadcasting Co., Inc. v. American Soc. of Composers, 744 F.2d 917 (2d Cir. 1984), cert. denied, 469 U.S. 1211, 105 S.Ct. 1181 (1985) found that a very small percentage of composers obtained a very large percentage of the blanket license revenues, which were paid in proportion to the number of times a composition was played by a licensee. In 1979 less than .8% of the composers received 75% of all television royalties. 546 F.Supp. at 284. If compositions were fungible the royalties would end up being about evenly distributed among performance right owners.

exclusive right to perform a particular composition may have substantial market power. Virtually all the costs of producing a musical composition are fixed. Once it has been recorded or printed, the costs of licensing it to someone are virtually zero, disregarding transaction costs. In a competitive market, in which price is driven to marginal cost, individual composers would license their compositions for a net price near zero. In that case, of course, the market price would not cover the total costs and many composers—at least those who made their living from composing—would exit the market.

But a radio station might be quite willing to pay far more than marginal cost to perform a popular piece of music, even though it could obtain another piece of music more cheaply (or even free). Radio listeners, and therefore radio stations, do distinguish one composition from another, often with great enthusiasm. As a result the holder of the exclusive right to perform a particular, successful composition faces a downward sloping demand curve. The aggregation of all these little monopolists into BMI's library may have given BMI no more market power than its individual, more successful artists had alone.[70]

§ 5.2d. The Relation Between Joint Venture Analysis and Merger Analysis

Virtually any efficiency that firms can achieve through a joint venture could also be achieved by a merger. This has suggested different things to different courts. In *Addyston Pipe* Judge Taft noted that a merger of the firms accused of fixing prices would probably have been legal; the "price fixing" that resulted would be an essential consequence of the union of firms.[71] However, the price fixing agreement in the actual case before the court was not ancillary to anything, and thus deserved to be condemned.[72] By contrast, in *Appalachian Coals*, which upheld a joint sales venture, Chief Justice Hughes reasoned that the coal companies involved in the venture could lawfully have merged; so why shouldn't they be able to accomplish the same goal by agreement?[73]

The problem is more complicated than either Judge Taft or Chief Justice Hughes suggested. In one set of cases, Judge Taft appears to have the better of the argument. The integration of production and distribution is a natural consequence of a merger. The same integration may result from a simple agreement among competitors, but it may not. Simple agreements are more quickly reached and more quickly abandoned than mergers are, and the firms do not have as much at stake. The "easy in/easy out" nature of cartels contributes to their perniciousness. As a result, we do not engage in a detailed "structural analysis" of most price-fixing agreements, and many cartels are illegal even though a merger among the same firms would be approved.

But the reverse is sometimes true as well. If an agreement among competitors has no obvious impact on price or output it will be approved even though every seller in the market participates in the agreement. A merger

70. For example, if a monopoly manufacturer of toasters and a monopoly manufacturer of televisions were to merge, the post-merger firm would not likely have increased market power. The new firm might find that the profit-maximizing price and output for televisions and toasters were exactly the same as they had been before the merger.

71. United States v. Addyston Pipe & Steel Co., 85 Fed. 271, 280 (6th Cir.1898), modified and affirmed, 175 U.S. 211, 20 S.Ct. 96 (1899) ("* * * [W]hen two men become partners in a business, although their union might reduce competition, this effect was only an incident to the main purpose of a union of their capital enterprise * * * and * * * useful to the community."). Indeed, after the price-fixing agreement was condemned the defendants merged and the government did not object. See 2 S. Whitney, Antitrust Policies: American Experience in Twenty Industries 7 (1958).

72. On *Addyston Pipe*, see §§ 2.1b, 4.1.

73. *Appalachian Coals*, note 11, 288 U.S. at 376, 53 S.Ct. at 480:

> Defendants insist that * * * no valid objection could have been interposed under the Sherman Act if [they] had eliminated competition between themselves by a complete integration of their mining properties in a single ownership. * * * We agree that there is no ground for holding defendants plan illegal merely because they have not integrated their properties and have chosen to maintain their independent plants, seeking not to limit but rather to facilitate production. We know of no public policy * * * that in order to comply with the law those engaged in industry should be driven to unify their properties and business in order to correct abuses which may be corrected by less drastic measures.

among the same group of firms would almost certainly be unlawful.

One might therefore be tempted to conclude that asking whether a merger among the same firms would be lawful is simply irrelevant to the legality of a venture. But that would also be a mistake. When a joint venture simultaneously permits the parties to coordinate price or output *and* has the clear potential to produce substantial economies, then we must consider further whether the competitive risks outweigh the potential rewards. In that case a structural analysis similar to that undertaken in mergers is wholly appropriate.

For example, suppose that two firms undertake a production joint venture that involves the joint construction of a new plant and development of a product. The firms must necessarily agree about the quality of the product and the amount that will be produced in this plant; so competitive concerns are raised. At the same time, the efficiency potential is obvious. In this case the court undertakes a structural analysis similar to that applied to mergers.[74] It determines the market share of the proposed venture, the market share of the two firm's non-venture production, the overall structure of the market, barriers to entry, and the like. The joint venture should be evaluated under standards similar to those applied to horizontal or potential competition mergers.[75] Indeed, some joint ventures are themselves "mergers," directly implicating the standards of § 7 of the Clayton Act. This can happen if a firm purchases, say, a 50% share in another firm's existing plant, in order to create a joint venture in production; or alternatively, if the two firms create a new subsidiary and become its joint shareholders.[76]

Nevertheless, the analysis is very different to the extent that the joint venture (1) does not restrain the firms' non-merger output; and (2) actually expands production. To illustrate, consider the joint venture between GM and Toyota to build a new plant to produce small cars in Freemont, California.[77] Assume at the time that GM and Toyota each accounted for 20% of automobile production in the relevant market. A merger between the two firms would almost certainly be challenged. Significantly, however, the venture places no restraint whatsoever on the two firms' ability to produce cars at all of their other plants around the world and in competition with each other. Further, assuming they have not agreed to shut other plants down, the venture actually expands market capacity by resulting in the creation of a new plant. Clearly the anticompetitive potential of this joint venture is far less than the anticompetitive potential of a merger between the same two firms.[78]

Finally, a joint venture itself may be a merger, but the joint venture agreement may contain collateral agreements that affect price or output. For example, one firm may purchase half of another firm's plant for joint operation. This transaction would be analyzed under merger principles. In the same agreement, however, the firms may do such things as 1) agree on the price or output of products produced by separately held plants; 2) divide sales territories; or 3) agree to exchange information about various subjects. These agreements would all be evaluated under § 1 of the Sherman Act.

§ 5.3 Competitor Exchanges of Price or Output Information; Posting Agreements

The nature and extent of price information available to buyers and sellers varies consider-

74. For example, United States v. Ivaco, Inc., 704 F.Supp. 1409, 1426–1427 (W.D.Mich.1989) (enjoining venture under merger standards where venture's market share was high, competitive justifications were not deemed sufficient, and a less anticompetitive alternative was available). Accord, General Motors Corp., 103 F.T.C. 374, 376–385 (1984) (approving production joint venture between GM and Toyota, applying merger-like standards and requiring the firms to hold the venture separate from their other business activities).

75. See §§ 12.3–12.4 (horizontal mergers); § 13.4 (potential competition mergers). See United States v. Penn–Olin Chem. Co., 378 U.S. 158, 170, 84 S.Ct. 1710, 1716 (1964) (applying merger analysis to joint venture).

76. E.g., *Penn–Olin Chem.*, note 75; Yamaha Motor Co. v. FTC, 657 F.2d 971 (8th Cir.1981), cert. denied, 456 U.S. 915, 102 S.Ct. 1768 (1982). In each case the venturing firms became the shareholders of an incorporated production firm.

77. See *General Motors Corp.*, note 74.

78. See 13 Antitrust Law ¶ 2121c (1999).

ably from one market to another. For example, current prices of every stock listed by the major stock exchanges are printed in daily newspapers. By contrast, in markets for rare works of art prices are often kept secret from everyone except the parties to the transaction.

If neither buyer nor seller has information about the market price, the market will probably not function very well. The seller can never be sure that he is asking the most the buyer will pay, and the customer can never be sure that she is paying the least the seller will take. The seller will probably begin negotiations by asking an inflated price, and the buyer is sure to respond by making a counteroffer. Each party has an incentive to negotiate as long as he perceives that the other party's position is "soft"—that further negotiations will yield a change in the price. It is not uncommon for the sale of a unique, expensive piece of property, such as a mansion or rare painting, to be negotiated for weeks or even months before the sale is made. It is also common that, after a substantial investment in negotiation, the parties finally decide that they cannot agree on a price.

At the other extreme is a market with a large number of buyers and sellers with full knowledge about current prices. In such a market price negotiations are extremely limited. Every seller knows that if he asks more than the prevailing price the buyer will not even bother with a counteroffer, but will go to a competitor. Every buyer knows that the price is competitive and that each seller can clear the market at the current price. Transactions will take place at the published market price and someone unwilling to pay that price will never enter the market.

The two extremes are easy to characterize: markets in which information is very bad function poorly; markets in which information is perfect on all sides function well. Unfortunately, there is not a smooth continuum in between. It does not follow that the more information that exists, the more efficiently and competitively the market will perform. Indeed, sometimes exchanges of price information among competing sellers can facilitate collusion.[1]

5.3a. Industry-Wide Dissemination of Price and Output Information

The Supreme Court's approach to industry wide exchanges of price information was first developed in two cases decided during the 1920's, involving trade associations in the hardwood industry. In American Column & Lumber Co. v. United States[2] the Supreme Court condemned a price information exchange program under which each member manufacturer furnished the trade association with detailed reports showing the price of each sale and the purchaser's name, the member's rate of production and inventory on hand, plus an estimate of future production. This information was organized around uniform classifications of hardwood sizes and types adopted by the association. The association was clearly concerned about "overproduction," and the members occasionally met to urge members to hold back on output. These discussions convinced the Court that the information exchange was really a plan to raise prices.

However, the association contained 365 producers who collectively controlled only one-third of American hardwood production. Even assuming an explicit price fixing agreement, it is difficult to see how a cartel with that many members, controlling only one-third of the market, could have a substantial effect on prices.[3] Indeed, one frequently overlooked but very important issue in data dissemination cases is the relationship between the domain over which information is exchanged and the scope of the relevant market. For example, the Johnson County Pork Producers Association may collect information from its members about their output and pricing of hogs. But if hogs are sold in a nationwide market, one county's collection of such data is not likely to facilitate price-fixing.

§ 5.3

1. See 13 Antitrust Law ¶ 2111 (1999).

2. 257 U.S. 377, 42 S.Ct. 114 (1921).

3. See R. Posner, Antitrust Law: An Economic Perspective 135–44 (1976).

If collusion was not the motive, why did the hardwood producers exchange such detailed information? Justice Brandeis's dissent suggested some reasons: the hardwood manufacturers were small, generally isolated, located in the forests that provided their essential material. No public agency gathered data about production in the industry,[4] and the isolated producers knew very little about market conditions. Furthermore, many of the direct purchasers were very large and presumably had good information about their demand. The result in such a situation could be overproduction, particularly if the marginal cost of producing wood from established trees is very low, but the cost of replacing the wood—for example, planting an oak tree and cultivating it for fifty years—is high. For a producer with large investments in an established hardwood forest, overproduction would drive prices to a level sufficient to cover the cost of cutting, sawing and planing the lumber, but insufficient to replace the trees.

The more realistic competitive threat posed by the *American Column* data dissemination scheme was probably not its publication of marketwide output and price data, but the detailed production, inventory and pricing information concerning individual members of the Association.[5] The Court offered almost no analysis of the relevant market other than to assume that it was hardwood and apparently nationwide. But hardwood was shipped mainly by rail and transportation costs were undoubtedly a significant factor in determining value. Each hardwood mill competed mostly with fairly nearby mills and much less intensely with more remote mills.[6] As a result, a particular mill desiring to win the bid of a customer was concerned mainly with the inventory, output and pricing policies of a few nearby mills. The detailed data probably permitted such a firm to bid aggressively when it knew that its rivals had ample stock or excess production, but to bid far more conservatively if it thought its rivals were already producing and selling all they could handle.[7]

Four years later, in Maple Flooring Mfrs' Ass'n. v. United States[8] the Court approved a program for the exchange of price information among the producers of hardwood flooring, again undertaken through a trade association. The Court distinguished *American Column* by emphasizing that the flooring manufacturers did not give the names of customers and that they reported only completed, past transactions instead of current prices. Why these differences made cartelization less likely the Court did not explain. The Court all but overlooked other facts that distinguished *Maple Flooring*: this time there were only 22 producers instead of 365, and they collectively controlled 70% of the market. Further, the information items that the Court stressed were relatively inconsequential: average figures will do as well as specific individual prices for establishing a cartel price, and the names of buyers are not essential. Most likely the Association distributed the information as it did because it had been organized about the time of the Supreme Court's *American Column* decision. It tailored its information exchanges around the language of that opinion.

One incriminating part of the case against the Maple Flooring Association was evidence that the members disseminated a book giving freight rates from Cadillac, Michigan, to various delivery points in the United States.[9] The defendants may have been engaging in basing

4. Justice Brandeis's dissent noted, however, that all information gathered by the defendants was public and open to everyone, and copies of all reports were filed with the Department of Justice and the Federal Trade Commission. 257 U.S. at 414–15, 42 S.Ct. at 122.

5. See *American Column*, note 2, 257 U.S. at 396 (detailed reporting requirements included size and price of specific transactions).

6. See 257 U.S. at 415–416 (Brandeis, J., dissenting).

7. See also United States v. American Linseed Oil Co., 262 U.S. 371, 43 S.Ct. 607 (1923), an unilluminating opinion condemning an arrangement under which manufacturers in an industry subscribed to an independent publication from the Armstrong Bureau of Related Industries, which published detailed reports on the markets and activities of its subscribers and disseminated the reports to others in the same market. See 13 Antitrust Law ¶ 2112c2 (1999).

8. 268 U.S. 563, 45 S.Ct. 578 (1925).

9. 268 U.S. at 570–72, 45 S.Ct. at 580–581.

point pricing.[10] However, the Supreme Court noted that most of the mills were located in northern Michigan and Wisconsin, relatively close to Cadillac, and that for most mills the differences between actual freight costs and costs from Cadillac were trivial. Furthermore, computation of actual freight rates was time consuming, and it was important to the sellers to be able to quote promptly a delivered price. Dissemination of the freight rate book was only ambiguous evidence of collusion.[11]

5.3b. Direct Competitor Exchange of Price Information

In United States v. Container Corp. of America[12] the Supreme Court faced an entirely different type of information exchange. The defendant manufacturers of pasteboard boxes agreed that one could call another and obtain price information for some upcoming transaction. For example, Firm A, preparing a bid for a buyer, might call Firm B to ask what B charged for the same product to the same customer. While there was an industry wide understanding that firms would supply each other with the requested information,[13] that fact would not serve to make the case resemble the industry wide dissemination cases. Direct competitor exchange of price information offers none of the informational benefits of industry wide promulgation. Indeed, its most likely and in most cases only reasonable purpose is the fixing of prices. Nevertheless, Justice Douglas opinion regarded the *Container* agreement as "analogous" to the one *American Column*,[14] and the two types of cases have largely been lumped together ever since.

Container Corp. concluded that direct competitor exchanges of price information are likely to be harmless in competitive markets. However, if concentration is high the exchange is more likely to affect price, and any interference "with the setting of price by free market forces" is illegal. The Court concluded that the information exchange in this case caused prices to "stabilize * * *, though at a downward level." The practical effect of the exchanges was that a prospective seller who knew a competitor's price would try to match it. However, these observations are as consistent with healthy competition in a properly informed market as they are with collusion. Given the tenuousness of any empirical conclusion about the reason for changes in price, the Court would have done well to avoid a rule that required a trial court to determine how a particular information exchange program affected the market price.

Further, the focus on overall industry concentration probably missed the real competitive danger of direct exchanges.[15] Even in relatively unconcentrated markets, product or spatial differentiation may give some firms advantages over others in bidding for a particular customer. For example, even if the container market has 100 sellers, high transportation costs may give sellers A and B a price advantage vis-a-vis customer X. A rule permitting a direct exchange of information between A and B can operate to create a kind of "mini-cartel" with respect to that particular customer.[16]

Under the rule of reason applied in *Container*, if the market in which the price information exchange occurred is concentrated, if the product is fungible so that price is the predominant element in competition, and if demand at the competitive price is inelastic, the exchange is virtually certain to be condemned, particularly if the court finds *any* relationship, downward or upward, between

10. See § 4.6c.

11. See also Cement Manufacturers' Protective Assn. v. United States, 268 U.S. 588, 45 S.Ct. 586 (1925), which approved a cement producers' exchange of information about contractors who were overbuying cement by ordering from multiple firms to ensure delivery, and then cancelling unneeded orders at the last minute. The Court also rejected the government's claim of price-fixing, finding insufficient evidence of agreement.

12. 393 U.S. 333, 89 S.Ct. 510 (1969).

13. See *Container*, note 12 at 335.

14. *Container*, note 12, 393 U.S. at 337, citing *American Column*, note 2; and *Linseed*, note 7.

15. See 13 Antitrust Law ¶ 2113 (1999).

16. The impact is not unlike that of a merger between adjacent or similar firms in a product differentiated market, thus facilitating a unilateral price increase. See § 12.3d.

the information exchange and the market price.[17]

One problem with the rule developed in *Container* is that *every* exchange of price information has some effect on price, or else the exchange is of no value. One effect of a published price of $200 for IBM stock is that there will be fewer uninformed buyers paying $2000 for shares, or uninformed sellers parting with their shares for $2.00. All market prices fluctuate, but those in which information is readily available tend to fluctuate within a narrower range than those in which information is scarce.[18]

Exchanges of price information continue to be risky for participants for one additional reason: many courts hold that the exchanges create a fact issue as to whether the firms were really fixing prices, particularly if they are accompanied by any other suspicious circumstances, such as mutually expressed concerns about output or the direction of market prices.[19] Nevertheless, if the parties adhere strictly to the rules, do nothing more than exchange information, and if there are no other "plus factors" that appear to be collusion facilitators, courts continue to apply the rule of reason.[20] However, the Supreme Court's *Gypsum* decision signalled much greater hostility toward direct competitor exchange of price information,[21] noting that such exchanges have "the greatest potential for generating anti-competitive effects and although not *per se* unlawful have consistently been held to violate the Sherman Act."[22] In fact, the only defense that the *Gypsum* defendants could muster was that they needed to verify prices in order to avoid engaging in unlawful price discrimination, which might occur if the relied on customer information to meet a presumably lower bid but the customer was lying.[23]

In general, there seem to be no efficiency rationales for direct exchange of price information of the type going on in *Container* and *Gypsum*. The one possible exception is the product sold at a publicly announced market price and the occasional seller who lacks access to public information about that price. For example, isolated Farmer Brown, who does not get the *Wall Street Journal*, may call her neighbor to determine the price of hogs before making a sale. But this is not the type of case in which direct seller verification of prices has been challenged.[24]

As the subject of the exchanged information wanders further from price and output, courts are less likely to condemn the exchange. For example, exchanges of credit information on customers, or the histories of customer dealings, are generally legal.[25] Such information is itself valuable intellectual property and expensive to produce; significant economies could result from joint provision. Exchanges of

17. 393 U.S. at 337, 89 S.Ct. at 512. The Supreme Court did not clearly characterize *Container* as a rule of reason decision until United States v. Citizens & Southern Nat. Bank, 422 U.S. 86, 113, 95 S.Ct. 2099, 2115 (1975). Although the Supreme Court did not know it in 1969, the *Container* defendants were probably engaged in explicit price fixing. In 1978 many of the same defendants were indicted for price fixing during the period 1960–1974. After that followed one of the largest private antitrust damages actions in antitrust history. See In re Corrugated Container Antitrust Litigation, 643 F.2d 195 (5th Cir. 1981).

For an argument that information exchanges are generally harmless even in concentrated markets, see R. Posner, Information and Antitrust: Reflections on the *Gypsum* and *Engineers* Decisions, 67 Geo.L.J. 1187 (1979).

18. See G. Stigler, The Organization of Industry 171–190 (1983).

19. For example, In re Coordinated Pretrial Proceedings in Petroleum Prods. Antitrust Litig., 906 F.2d 432, 446–447, 462 (9th Cir.1990) (information exchanges accompanied by evidence of interdependent, lock-step pricing; advance posting of prices; and numerous contacts among competitors); accord King & King Enters. v. Champlin Petroleum Co., 657 F.2d 1147, 1151–1152 (10th Cir.1981), cert. denied, 454 U.S. 1164, 102 S.Ct. 1038 (1982).

20. Supermarket of Homes, Inc. v. San Fernando Valley Bd. of Realtors, 786 F.2d 1400, 1407 (9th Cir.1986); Amey, Inc. v. Gulf Abstract & Title, Inc., 758 F.2d 1486, 1505 (11th Cir.1985), cert. denied, 475 U.S. 1107, 106 S.Ct. 1513 (1986).

21. United States v. United States Gypsum Co., 438 U.S. 422, 98 S.Ct. 2864 (1978).

22. Id. at 440 n. 16, 98 S.Ct. at 2875.

23. For an explanation of price discrimination and the "lying buyer" problem, see § 14.6f2.

24. See 13 Antitrust Law ¶ 2113c (1999).

25. Zoslaw v. MCA Distrib. Corp., 693 F.2d 870 (9th Cir.1982), cert. denied, 460 U.S. 1085, 103 S.Ct. 1777 (1983) (approving exchanges of credit histories and information on credit balances).

information totally unrelated to price or output generally raise no antitrust issues.

§ 5.3c. Agreements to Post, or to Post and Adhere

Many firms post their prices periodically, perhaps by faxing or sending a price list to their regular accounts. Such price lists are valuable because buyers can compute their own costs readily without having to call for a quote. A firm's unilateral decision to post its price is legal. However, there is little competitive justification for competitors to agree with *each other* to post their prices. If posting is valuable to buyers, each firm has an incentive to do it unilaterally. Agreed posting, as the previous Chapter indicates, is a strong inducement to price fixing.[26] Even more suspicious is an agreement among firms that they will post their prices monthly and then adhere to the posted prices during that month. In *Sugar Institute* the Supreme Court rejected the defense that an agreement to post and adhere to the posted prices was necessary to prevent secret discounts, which the participants regarded as "unethical."[27] But ethical or not, secret discounting is the means by which a cartel or oligopoly can be undermined. The courts generally conclude that such agreements are unlawful *per se*.[28]

§ 5.4 Concerted Refusals to Deal

§ 5.4a. Harms and Benefits; Appropriate Antitrust Standard

The "concerted" refusal to deal, or agreement of two or more persons not to deal with a third, has traditionally been characterized as *per se* illegal under the antitrust laws.[1] Today only a small minority of concerted refusals fall into that category.

In most antitrust litigation involving refusals to deal the refusal itself is not the violation. Many antitrust complaints brought by victims of refusals to deal allege that the defendants were involved in illegal monopolization, tying, price fixing, resale price maintenance or vertical nonprice restraints, or an illegal merger. Other complaints do not explicitly allege a secondary violation, but the theory of the complaint makes sense only on the premise that the defendant was committing a secondary violation. If this "supporting" antitrust violation is not apparent, often the plaintiff is unable to offer any explanation why the refusal to deal is anticompetitive.

So the refusal to deal might more appropriately be considered a type of antitrust harm rather than a substantive violation. For example, if a firm engaging in resale price maintenance refuses to sell to a noncomplying retailer, the alleged antitrust violation is the attempt to control resale prices.[2] If the plaintiff's theory of injury is that the defendant refused to deal because the plaintiff was a price cutter, then the plaintiff must prove illegal resale price maintenance in order to recover.

The refusal to deal can perform two important functions in antitrust law, even when it is not a separate violation. First, it gives a cause of action to a set of plaintiffs who have good knowledge about a market and are highly motivated to sue. A high percentage of private antitrust filings come from people who have been excluded from a market by the collective decisions of others.

Second, the presence or absence of a refusal to deal often helps a court evaluate activities such as joint ventures, that are arguably both efficient and anticompetitive. No court can quantify efficiency and injury to competition and balance one against the other, particularly in close cases. This complicates legal analysis of joint ventures that have a potential to be

26. See § 4.4; and see 12 Antitrust Law ¶ 2024 (1999).

27. Sugar Institute v. United States, 297 U.S. 553, 56 S.Ct. 629 (1936).

28. E.g., Miller v. Hedlund, 813 F.2d 1344 (9th Cir. 1987), cert. denied, 484 U.S. 1061, 108 S.Ct. 1018 (1988) (per se). See also United States v. United Liquors Corp., 149 F.Supp. 609 (W.D.Tenn.1956), aff'd per curiam, 352 U.S. 991, 77 S.Ct. 557 (1957) (condemning detailed agreement requiring posting of liquor prices and elimination of quantity discounts).

§ 5.4

1. For example, Klor's, Inc. v. Broadway–Hale Stores, Inc., 359 U.S. 207, 79 S.Ct. 705 (1959).

2. See § 11.5.

both anticompetitive and efficient. But often all the efficiencies could be attained without the refusal to deal. That is, although the joint venture might be competitive, an anticompetitive motive best explains the refusal to deal. For example, Appalachian Coals, Inc. v. United States[3] involved a joint selling agency created by a group of competing coal producers. The agency almost certainly marketed coal more efficiently than the members did separately. Because coal is fungible, however, the agency charged the same price for all deliveries of a particular grade of coal. Therefore producers had to agree about price or the mechanism by which the price was to be set. But members were required to sell their coal exclusively through the agency. A member of the venture would have refused to deal with anyone who tried to buy coal from it directly. Even assuming that the sales agency was efficient, no reasonable explanation was offered why the agreement required exclusivity. One explanation is that the defendants were fixing prices and wanted to prevent members from making noncartel sales.

§ 5.4a1. A Rule of Reason, With a Few Exceptions

It was once commonly said that concerted refusals to deal were illegal *per se*, but this rule is subject to so many exceptions that the presumption must be turned around. Today, most concerted refusals to deal, even those involving competitors, are evaluated under a rule of reason. As a general matter, concerted refusals should be treated as devices for making joint ventures or other associations of competitors operate more efficiently. This does not make them legal, but it means that most of the time *per se* analysis is inappropriate. The *per se* rule is reserved for so-called *naked* boycotts—that is concerted refusals of competitors to deal with another competitor, customer or supplier when no case can be made that the refusal is ancillary to any legitimate joint activity.

To be sure, naked boycotts abound in antitrust history. In W.W. Montague & Co. v. Lowry the Supreme Court first held that a competitors' concerted refusal was illegal.[4] The defendants, who were members of a trade association, agreed with each other not to sell their products to non-member dealers. The Court condemned the refusal using common law restraint of trade language, but nothing approaching the modern *per se* rule. A more categorical *per se* approach had to wait another decade. In Eastern States Retail Lumber Dealers' Ass'n v. United States[5] the Supreme Court decided that, although a firm acting alone may refuse to deal with anyone, an agreement among competitors not to deal with certain persons acts as a clog on the market and hinders competition. *Eastern States* involved an agreement among lumber retailers to identify lumber wholesalers who were dealing directly with consumers. If a wholesaler was found to be retailing directly, the wholesaler's name was put on a "blacklist" and the retailers refused to purchase at wholesale from him.[6]

The lumber retailers might have wanted wholesalers to stay out of retailing for two reasons. First, by eliminating one firm in the distribution chain, the wholesalers may have been more efficient retailers than the unintegrated retailers themselves.[7] By refusing to deal with wholesalers engaged in such vertical integration, the independent retailers may have tried to prevent the wholesalers' entry into retail markets. If vertical integration to retailing reduced the lumber wholesalers' costs, however, the boycott by the independent retailers would probably only delay, not prevent, the vertical integration. Some wholesalers would establish retail outlets and retail *all* their lumber through them. Then they would be immune from the boycott.

3. 288 U.S. 344, 53 S.Ct. 471 (1933). See § 5.2a.

4. 193 U.S. 38, 24 S.Ct. 307 (1904).

5. 234 U.S. 600, 34 S.Ct. 951 (1914).

6. Accord *Re/Max Intl. v. Realty One*, 173 F.3d 995, (6th Cir.1999) (denying summary judgment on claim that dominant realtors conspired to impose punitive commission splits on plaintiff because of plaintiff's way of compensating agents, which induced the better agents to transfer to it).

7. See the discussion of vertical integration in § 9.2.

The second possibility is that the lumber retailers were fixing prices. The retailers' mark-up is the wholesalers' cost of distribution, and the wholesalers would naturally prefer to keep that cost as low as possible. If the retailers were engaged in price fixing the wholesalers would lose volume to the cartel's output reduction, but all the monopoly profits would go to the retailers. The wholesalers might try to protect their own interests by finding retailers who were not members of the cartel or else by retailing the lumber themselves. The concerted refusal to deal may have been a cartel's effort to prevent loss of sales because of competitive entry by the wholesalers.[8]

As recently as 1990, the Supreme Court reaffirmed that concerted refusals are illegal *per se* when their only purpose is to facilitate collusion. *Superior Court Trial Lawyers* condemned a boycott organized by trial lawyers against the City of Washington, D.C.[9] The lawyers were in the business of representing indigent criminal defendants, and received payment directly from the government. They believed that the rates the government paid were too low, and collectively withheld their services until the government agreed to pay more. The Court rejected, as it always has, the argument that the boycott should be legal because the old rates were too low; unrestrained markets should determine the rates. Perhaps the buyer could be seen as a monopsonist, setting an anticompetitively low price; but even a monopsonist is generally entitled to pay what the market will bear.[10] Further, the facts in this case probably would not support the proposition that the buyer was a monopsonist. Representation of indigent criminals represents only part of the practice of criminal law, and a much smaller part of law practice as a whole. The Court noted that "[t]he city competes with other purchasers of legal services to obtain an adequate supply of lawyers, and the city's offering price is an element of that competition."[11]

Beginning in the late 1960's, the Supreme Court began to clarify that only a limited subset of concerted refusals should be considered illegal *per se*.[12] In *Northwest Wholesale Stationers*, discussed below, the Court suggested that the *per se* rule be reserved for "joint efforts by a firm or firms to disadvantage competitors by 'either directly denying or persuading or coercing suppliers or customers to deny relationships the competitors need in the competitive struggle.' "Such activities would have to fall into the set of practices "likely to have predominantly anticompetitive effects."[13] A year later in the *Indiana Dentists* decision, also discussed below, the Court limited the *per se* classification to "cases in which firms with market power boycott suppliers or customers in order to discourage them from doing business with a competitor."[14] Or as the Seventh Circuit has put it, "boycotts are illegal per se only if used to enforce agreements that are

8. A third possibility is that there were large retail buyers who did not require the special services provided by the retailers. The wholesalers could enlarge their profits by making these large sales directly to the retail buyers, and eliminating an additional market transaction, transportation, storage, etc. See also Engine Specialties, Inc. v. Bombardier Ltd., 605 F.2d 1 (1st Cir.1979), on rehearing, 615 F.2d 575 (1st Cir.1980), cert. denied, 446 U.S. 983, 100 S.Ct. 2964 (1980), where the refusal to deal was probably part of a horizontal territorial division scheme.

9. FTC v. Superior Ct. Trial Lawyers Assn., 493 U.S. 411, 110 S.Ct. 768 (1990). The decision is discussed more fully in § 18.2b. See also Rossi v. Standard Roofing, 156 F.3d 452 (3d Cir.1998) (finding sufficient evidence that defendant roofing materials sellers boycotted the plaintiff, a rival, to entitle him to a trial).

10. "If the offering price had not attracted a sufficient supply of qualified lawyers willing to accept [indigent criminal] assignments for the city to fulfill its constitutional obligation [to provide representation for such defendants], then presumably the city would have increased its offering price or otherwise sought to make its offer more attractive." 493 U.S. at 423 n.9, 110 S.Ct. at 775 n.9.

11. Id. at 423 n.9, 110 S.Ct. at 775 n. 9.

12. See FMC v. Aktiebolaget Svenska Amerika Linien, 390 U.S. 238, 250, 88 S.Ct. 1005, 1012 (1968) (under "the Sherman Act, any agreement by a group of *competitors* to boycott a particular buyer or group of buyers is illegal *per se*.") The Court later applied this rule in St. Paul Fire & Marine Ins. Co. v. Barry, 438 U.S. 531, 98 S.Ct. 2923 (1978).

13. Northwest Wholesale Stationers v. Pacific Stationery & Printing Co., 472 U.S. 284, 298, 105 S.Ct. 2613, 2621 (1985).

14. FTC v. Indiana Federation of Dentists, 476 U.S. 447, 458, 106 S.Ct. 2009, 2018 (1986).

themselves illegal per se—for example price fixing agreements."[15]

Even the Supreme Court's earlier and expansive application of the *per se* rule in Klor's, Inc. v. Broadway–Hale Stores, Inc.[16] is consistent with the proposition that only concerted refusals facilitating collusion or collusion-like behavior are illegal *per se*. The allegations in *Klor's* were somewhat dubious. The plaintiff was a retailer in kitchen appliances. One defendant, Broadway–Hale, was a competing, although larger, retailer. The other defendants were major manufacturers and distributors of kitchen appliances. Klor's claimed that Broadway–Hale conspired with these distributors and manufacturers to refuse to supply Klor's with appliances, or else to supply them only at discriminatorily high prices and unfavorable terms.

Assuming that Broadway–Hale had a motive for driving its competitor out of business, why would the major appliance manufacturers agree with *each other* to participate in this scheme? The plaintiff alleged that Broadway–Hale used its "monopolistic" buying power to force manufacturer agreement. That allegation is plausible only on the assumption that Broadway–Hale had market power in its local retail market, and Klor's was underselling its monopoly price. However, the large appliance manufacturers would be best off if their retailers were behaving as competitively as possible, and Broadway–Hale's monopoly mark-up would make them worse off.

There is a more plausible explanation: Klor's was a free rider and Broadway–Hale complained to the manufacturers. The manufacturers wanted their retailers to spend substantial resources displaying and servicing their merchandise and providing information to customers. If Broadway–Hale performed these services but Klor's did not, Klor's would be able to charge a lower price. Furthermore, customers would be tempted to take a free ride on Broadway–Hale's services. They might go to Broadway–Hale and obtain all essential information about appliances, but then purchase at Klor's. A manufacturer might eliminate free riding either by giving its retailers exclusive territories, or else by resale price maintenance.[17] When *Klor's* was decided, the status of the first practice was undetermined, but the second was *per se* illegal.

Klor's stands only for the proposition that the plaintiff should have been entitled to prove its case of conspiracy. The court adopted a *per se* rule by concluding that the plaintiff's simple allegation of a concerted refusal involving competing manufacturers was sufficient to withstand a motion for summary judgment, even though the plaintiff had not alleged any injury to the "public," in the form of reduced output or higher prices.[18] Today, more expansive use of summary judgment in agreement cases suggests dismissal of Klor's complaint, unless fairly probative evidence of a horizontal agreement or a vertical price agreement were found.[19] As developed later, the Supreme Court has also made clear that if the horizontal agreement does not exist, the individual agreements between the larger retailer and individual suppliers must be governed by the rule of reason.[20]

Somewhat more difficult to characterize than *Klor's* is Fashion Originators' Guild of Amer. v. FTC[21] (FOGA). Garment designers and manufacturers agreed not to sell their "original creations" to retailers who also purchased garments from "pirates"—manufacturers who allegedly copied the designs of FOGA members and sold the garments at a lower

15. Collins v. Associated Pathologists, 844 F.2d 473 (7th Cir.1988), cert. denied, 488 U.S. 852, 109 S.Ct. 137 (1988).

16. 359 U.S. 207, 79 S.Ct. 705 (1959).

17. See §§ 11.5–11.6.

18. See also Malley–Duff & Assoc., Inc. v. Crown Life Ins. Co., 734 F.2d 133 (3d Cir.1984), which adopted the entire line of reasoning in *Klor's*. The court reversed a district court decision holding that a plaintiff must show that the concerted refusal had an adverse impact on consumers. See J. Bauer, Per Se Illegality of Concerted Refusals to Deal: A Rule Ripe for Reexamination, 79 Col. L. Rev. 685 (1979), which summarizes other decisions and scholarly writings.

19. See § 16.8b.

20. NYNEX Corp. v. Discon, Inc., 525 U.S. 128, 119 S.Ct. 493 (1998), on remand, 184 F.3d 111 (2d Cir.1999); see § 5.4d.

21. 312 U.S. 457, 61 S.Ct. 703 (1941).

price. As a defense, the FOGA members offered to show that the boycott was reasonable because manufacturers, laborers, retailers and consumers needed protection from the pirates. However, the garment designs could not themselves be copyrighted or patented. Two decades earlier, in International News Service v. Associated Press[22], the Supreme Court had decided that Associated Press had a property right in its uncopyrighted news stories and could enjoin a competitor from paraphrasing them. However, in Cheney Bros. v. Doris Silk Corp.[23] Judge Learned Hand decided that the *International News* protection did not extend to clothing design piracy.

The patent and copyright laws encourage innovation by giving a limited legal monopoly to the developer of a new invention, composition or design. The kind of innovation that qualifies for such protection has always been a subject of intensive legislative and judicial regulation. Both Congress and the courts had agreed that clothing designers did not merit such monopoly protection. The members of FOGA were effectively trying to give themselves the monopoly protection that the legislative and judicial branches had denied them. Justice Black concluded that it was not error for the FTC to refuse to consider FOGA's defense that many constituents needed protection from style pirates.[24]

The "piracy" claim makes *FOGA* difficult to characterize. Lack of copyright or patent protection notwithstanding, the members of FOGA had a substantial free rider problem. If one group of manufacturers spends money developing new fashion designs, but another group is entitled to copy the designs at no charge, the result might be that creating original designs will become unprofitable and no one will do it.[25] In that case the Guild was correct and consumers are better off if the free riders can be controlled. Nevertheless, the concerted refusal to deal employed by the defendants has a large potential to cover price fixing. If the free rider problem in this instance is serious enough to have a solution, it should come from Congress.

In *Hartford* the Supreme Court gave the term "boycott" a narrow definition that may exclude at least some of the previously discussed cases.[26] Five members of the Court distinguished "concerted agreements on contract terms" from "boycotts." If a group of firms simply refuses to sell except at an agreed upon price, their action is not a boycott but merely a cartel.[27] Likewise, if a group of firms agree to sell only a particular quality of product—as for example, if insurers should agree only to offer certain kinds of coverage—their agreement is a cartel but not a boycott. The latter term applies only when those negotiating a contract with another make concerted demands that are unrelated to the subject matter of that particular contract. For example, in the labor context a "boycott" is not merely an agreement by workers to withhold their labor, it occurs only when the workers make collateral demands unrelated to the labor contract at issue. For example, in the great Pullman railroad car strike, the strikers were employees of Pullman refusing to work unless they received higher wages. But other employ-

22. 248 U.S. 215, 39 S.Ct. 68 (1918).

23. 35 F.2d 279 (2d Cir.1929), cert. denied, 281 U.S. 728, 50 S.Ct. 245 (1930). See D. Baird, Common Law Intellectual Property and the Legacy of International News Service v. Assoc. Press, 50 U.Chi.L.Rev. 411 (1983).

24. 312 U.S. at 468, 61 S.Ct. at 708. Some states have tried to give designs greater protection than is offered by federal law. In Sears, Roebuck & Co. v. Stiffel Co., 376 U.S. 225, 84 S.Ct. 784 (1964), the Supreme Court declared one such attempt to be preempted by federal patent and antitrust law.

25. For discussion of free rider problems see § 5.2b1 above, and § 11.3a. Presumably, the members of FOGA had labels, which were trademarked. Although a pirate might be entitled to copy an Yves St. Laurent design, he would not be entitled to copy the Yves St. Laurent label affixed to the article of clothing. Many customers might value the label as much as the design itself. This explains the proliferation of "designer" clothing in which the designer's label appears prominently on the article of clothing itself, while the *design* is quite undistinctive.

26. Hartford Fire Ins. Co. v. California, 509 U.S. 764, 113 S.Ct. 2891 (1993).

27. In the ordinary Sherman Act case this distinction would be irrelevant, for both the cartel and the boycott would be illegal. But in *Hartford* the court was interpreting the boycott exception to the McCarran–Ferguson Act, a statute that permits insurance cartels but condemns "boycotts." For further discussion, see § 19.7c. The term "boycott," however, presumably had the same meaning under McCarran as under the antitrust laws generally.

ees in the same union also refused to work for any railroad carrying Pullman cars. The first agreement was not a "boycott," but the second was.[28]

But this distinction is formalistic, finely drawn, and often impossible to apply. For example, in *FOGA* the defendants refused to sell clothing to retailers who also dealt with design pirates. The Court used the term "boycott" to describe this agreement,[29] and it certainly seems apt. But the *Hartford* opinion apparently (but ambiguously) refused to permit the term "boycott" to be applied to an agreement among reinsurers[30] and the defendant group of primary insurers that the reinsurers would not sell insurance to a second group of primary insurers unless the latter eliminated certain forms of coverage from their policies.[31] Clearly, the defendant primary insurers could negotiate any contract they pleased with the reinsurers with respect to their own reinsurance coverage. But could they negotiate the reinsurers' refusal to deal with the non-conspiring primary insurers as well? How this case should be distinguished from *FOGA*, which the Court appeared to approve, is difficult to say. The Court seemed to assume that because both primary insurers and reinsurers are inside the insurance industry, the agreement was simply one about the terms of coverage.[32] But this ignores the facts (a) that the relationship between reinsurers and primary insurers is vertical, not horizontal, and (b) that the challenged agreement affected the contracts between the reinsurers and the non-conspiring insurers as well.

By the Court's analysis, since both fashion designers and fashion retailers are in the "fashion industry," the agreement among them should be treated simply as an agreement that no one would sell "pirated" designs. This would then, under the Court's definition, be a simple cartel, or output restriction agreement, rather than a boycott.[33]

§ 5.4a2. Special Treatment for the Learned Professions?

As recently as 1986 the Supreme Court purported to apply the rule of reason to a boycott if the boycotters were members of the learned professions. In *Indiana Dentists* it considered an agreement among dentists to withhold X-Rays from a health insurer, who was purchasing dental services in behalf of its insureds.[34] The Court used the same kinds of sweeping statements that it would have applied in a *per se* decision—for example,

> "[a] concerted and effective effort to withhold (or make more costly) information desired by consumers for the purpose of determining whether a particular purchase is cost justified is likely enough to disrupt the proper function of the price-setting mechanism of the market that it may be condemned even absent proof that it resulted in higher prices. * * * "[35]

However, the Court then observed that it had always been reluctant to apply the *per se* rule to the collective decisions of professional associations.[36] Nonetheless, the Court condemned the agreement, noting that determination of a

28. *Hartford*, 504 U.S. at 805, 113 S.Ct. at 2913 ("A refusal to work changes from strike to boycott only when it seeks to obtain action from the employer unrelated to the employment contract.").

29. See *FOGA*, 312 U.S. at 461, 465, 467, 61 S.Ct. at 337–338.

30. Reinsurers are companies that sell insurance to primary insurance companies, permitting the latter to reduce the risk of catastrophic losses.

31. For more details, see § 19.7c.

32. See *Hartford*, 504 U.S. at 805–808, 113 S.Ct. at 2914–2915.

33. The Court may have viewed the facts of the insurance complaint as suggesting that the defendant primary insurers merely asked the reinsurers not to reinsure the broader policies offered by other primary reinsurers. See 509 U.S. at 809–810, 113 S.Ct. at 2916. That is to say, suppose that the defendant designers in *FOGA* simply agreed with each other that they would request that stores selling their designs not deal with design pirates. In that case, there would be no qualifying boycott because there was no vertical agreement. But this distinction places courts in the impossible position of distinguishing unilateral from agreed upon activities in the context of underlying actions that are clearly collusive.

34. FTC v. Indiana Federation of Dentists, 476 U.S. 447, 106 S.Ct. 2009 (1986).

35. Id. at 461, 106 S.Ct. at 2019.

36. Id. at 458, 106 S.Ct. at 2018, citing National Society of Professional Engineers v. United States, 435 U.S. 679, 98 S.Ct. 1355 (1978). An earlier decision containing similar statements is Goldfarb v. Virginia State Bar, 421 U.S. 773, 778 & n. 17, 95 S.Ct. 2004, 2008 & n. 17 (1975).

relevant market and a comprehensive market analysis were not necessary where there was clear evidence of actual anticompetitive effects.[37] Four years later in the *Trial Lawyers'* decision the Court seemed quite willing to apply the *per se* rule.

Although the Court claimed to be applying a rule of reason in *Indiana Dentists*, the analysis in fact looked *per se*. *Trial Lawyers'* failure even to discuss the topic suggests that any notion that there is a substantial difference in the treatment of restraints among the learned professions has been abandoned.

A better way to view the whole problem is to begin with the premise that the learned professions trade heavily in information and expertise, areas prone to free-riding as well as other kinds of abuse. As a result, the scope of efficiency-creating joint practices may be somewhat larger in the learned professions than it is in, say, ordinary manufacturing. But the issues raised by *Indiana Dentists* and *Trial Lawyers* are in substance no different than those raised in many ordinary cases involving cartels and boycotts designed to facilitate collusion. Respecting such refusals to deal, the learned professions need be treated no differently.

The Supreme Court implicitly returned to the issue in the *California Dental* case, which involved a professional association's restraints on advertising rather than a concerted refusal to deal.[38] However, that distinction is largely semantic: if the plaintiff had been a dentist expelled for violating the advertising rules rather than the FTC, the complaint would have sounded in boycott. The challenged rules purported to control deceptive advertising, but in fact were so broad that they served to restrain much non-deceptive advertising as well. Nevertheless, the five-member majority insisted that the rule of reason be applied, emphasizing imperfections in the market for professional services:

> In a market for professional services, in which advertising is relatively rare and the comparability of service packages not easily established, the difficulty for customers or potential competitors to get and verify information about the price and availability of services magnifies the dangers to competition associated with misleading advertising. What is more, the quality of professional services tends to resist either calibration or monitoring by individual patients or clients, partly because of the specialized knowledge required to evaluate the services, and partly because of the difficulty in determining whether, and the degree to which, an outcome is attributable to the quality of services (like a poor job of tooth-filling) or to something else (like a very tough walnut).[39]

Thus *California Dental* may stand for the relatively narrow conclusion that more suspicious restraints will be tolerated in complex markets where consumers are more likely to be misled. That is a troublesome proposition, for collusion is likely to be more effective in such markets. Because cartels can be profitable even in the absence of durable market power, the result of rule of reason treatment requiring proof of significant power may be to legalize effective cartelization of complex markets. In any event, the limitation to complex markets is important. An association of gasoline retailers could still presumably not defend an agreement not to advertise their prices by simply noting that some gasoline price advertising is deceptive.

One area where rule of reason treatment is clearly appropriate is professional peer review, which often involves concerted exclusion of a professional from the market. That subject is taken up in § 5.4c.

§ 5.4b. *Efficient Joint Ventures and Refusals to Deal*

5.4b1. *Closed–Membership and Other Traditional Joint Ventures*

An antitrust policy based on efficiency would try to condemn inefficient concerted

37. Id. at 457, 106 S.Ct. at 2017. Accord Wilk v. AMA, 895 F.2d 352 (7th Cir.1990), cert. denied, 496 U.S. 927, 110 S.Ct. 2621 (1990) (applying rule of reason to physician agreement excluding chiropractors, but finding actual competitive effects sufficient to justify condemnation).

38. California Dental Assn. v. FTC, ___ U.S. ___, 119 S.Ct. 1604 (1999).

39. Id. at 1613.

refusals and approve efficient ones. A court would apply the *per se* rule if a practice was highly likely to be inefficient, but the cost of full economic inquiry was very large when balanced against the likelihood that the inquiry would produce a substantially more accurate result.[40]

Many joint ventures involving refusals to deal are efficient—they enable the participating firms to operate at lower cost. As a result, a court evaluating a refusal to deal that accompanies a joint venture must ask two questions. First, is the joint venture itself competitive or anticompetitive? Second, if the venture is competitive, what policy is furthered by the refusal to deal? A refusal to deal might injure competition even if it is attached to a joint venture which is, on balance, socially beneficial.

The clearly anticompetitive joint venture presents the simplest case. If the only plausible motive for the joint activity is price fixing or delay of competitive entry, as it was in the *Eastern States* case,[41] both the joint venture and the refusal to deal are illegal.

At the other extreme is the joint venture whose capacity for efficiency is large and whose danger to competition is very small. Consider a decision by three small firms in an unconcentrated market to undertake jointly a risky, expensive, but potentially profitable project. For any firm acting alone, the risk in proportion to the cost would make the venture unpromising. For three working together, however, the investment is far more attractive.[42] A fourth firm in the market is invited to participate but refuses. The project is developed, succeeds, and the new product or process is profitable. Now the fourth firm changes its mind and asks to "buy in." The three participants refuse.[43]

In this example any question about the competitive effects of the joint venture can be answered by looking at one fact: the participants collectively appear to have no market power. Three firms in an unconcentrated market could not likely reduce output or injure competition in some other way. They did not combine to fix prices but to reduce their costs.[44]

Given that the venture itself appears to be both harmless and efficient, should the antitrust laws require the three defendants to admit the fourth firm? Once again, the answer is a relatively easy no: the fourth firm is attempting to take a free ride on the participants' willingness to take a risk. If any firm could refuse to participate in a high risk project today, knowing that later when the project has become a success it will have a legal right to enter, the result would be that no firms would join immediately, but all would wait and see.

This particular free rider problem applies to the traditional "closed membership" joint venture, whose membership is determined when the joint venture is created. As developed in the next sub-section, it does not generally apply—and thus closer antitrust scrutiny is often warranted—in the open ended joint venture that continues to accept members on an ongoing basis.

The problem of evaluation is much more difficult when the overall impact of the joint venture is ambiguous—for example, when the joint venture has the potential to create substantial efficiency but the participants collectively have substantial market power. In evaluating the claim of an excluded rival a court might be asked to balance the injury to competition that results from the exclusion, against the inefficiency of a rule that permits all latecomers to join. Courts are not capable of quantifying these two things and measuring them against each other.

40. On the *per se* rule, see § 5.6.

41. See § 5.4a1.

42. This is particularly true of research and development joint ventures. A three-way joint venture to develop a patentable product or process will cost each firm one-third as much as individual development would. However, the process, once developed, can be duplicated by all three firms. Each one will receive as great a benefit as if it had developed the patented product or process alone (ignoring monopoly profits that might be obtained by an individual developer but not by each of three competing developers).

43. See 13 Antitrust Law ¶ ¶ 2200–2213 (1999).

44. See *Northwest Wholesale Stationers*, note 13 (joint venture's expulsion of member not illegal per se in absence of market power).

5.4b2. Open–Membership Ventures; Positive Network Externalities

The traditional joint venture is "closed" in the sense that its membership is determined when it is first created and no one else is subsequently invited to join. For example, when Toyota and General Motors decided to join in the production of subcompact cars in Freemont, California, they probably never intended to invite Ford or Chrysler to join later. Further, as the previous section notes, there are good reasons why antitrust would not want to force Toyota/GM to open the venture to latecomers.

But many joint ventures are designed at the outset to take new members on an ongoing basis. For example, real estate multiple listing services, which permit competing brokers to sell one another's properties or split transactions, generally accept any licensed real estate broker.[45] Likewise, any new bank that qualifies for federal deposit insurance may become a participant in joint ventures that issue general purpose charge cards such as Visa or MasterCard, or that facilitate electronic fund transfers through ATM machines.[46] Or any newly licensed lawyer or physician may join the ABA or the AMA.

Depending on the advantages they confer,[47] open membership ventures can readily take up the entire relevant market. This places them in a position to use their membership rules anticompetitively. Furthermore, the latecomer argument for limiting free riders does not apply—everyone except the original members is a latecomer to one degree or another. To the extent that the original owners have intellectual property rights or are otherwise entitled to compensation for their risk, they generally do so through membership fees.

Open membership joint ventures have important interests in intellectual property rights that may be subject to free riding, and this entitles the venture to make rules about how members might compete with the venture. For example, the Atlas moving joint venture at issue in the *Rothery* case enabled numerous local moving companies to participate in a nationwide joint venture facilitating the loading and shipment of goods across the country.[48] However, the Atlas members also engaged in local moving, which the joint venture permitted, but only on the condition that the member not use the Atlas name for business in which other joint venture members did not participate in the profits. This rule seems well designed both to protect the joint venture's intellectual property interests while minimizing the impact of any market power that the venture members might have.

By contrast, in the *Visa* case the Tenth Circuit upheld a rule that prohibited the 6000 banks that issued a Visa or MasterCard from issuing any competitors' charge card.[49] The Visa and MasterCard ventures are open to any bank qualifying for federal deposit insurance, and new members are accepted on an ongoing basis. Further, every significant bank in the country issues Visa and MasterCard, thus effectively denying bank access to any competing charge card issuer, such as American Express, Discover, or a new entrant. In such a case intellectual property rights developed by the original members can be compensated for through license fees for all members. Beyond that, there may of course be other free rider problems. For example, the Tenth Circuit not-

45. See, e.g., United States v. Realty Multi–List, Inc., 629 F.2d 1351 (5th Cir.1980) (condemning restrictive membership rules established by a multiple-listing service for real estate brokers).

46. SCFC ILC v. Visa U.S.A., 36 F.3d 958, 961 (10th Cir.1994), cert. denied, 515 U.S. 1152, 115 S.Ct. 2600 (1995) (any financial institution qualified for federal deposit insurance may be Visa member).

47. A venture that confers few competitive advantages ordinarily raises little anticompetitive potential. For example, the National Lawyers Guild is a professional association open to any licensed lawyer, but only a small percentage of lawyers join, thus making it a poor price-fixing facilitator. Cf. Sanjuan v. American Bd. of Psychiatry and Neurology, 40 F.3d 247, 249–250 (7th Cir.), cert. denied, 516 U.S. 1159, 116 S.Ct. 1044 (1996), which noted that a psychiatrist or neurologist could practice his profession without membership in the defendant Board and membership appeared to confer few advantages; as a result, exclusion from the Board was unlikely to be anticompetitive.

48. Rothery Storage & Van Co. v. Atlas Van Lines, 792 F.2d 210, 214–16 (D.C.Cir.1986), cert. denied, 479 U.S. 1033, 107 S.Ct. 880 (1987).

49. *SCFC ILC* case, note 46.

ed that if a Visa issuer became sufficiently large it was entitled to membership on the Visa Board, and this would give it access to secret information that would be valuable to a rival.[50] But in that case the free rider problem should have been addressed by the less restrictive alternative of re-defining the entitlement to sit on the Visa Board—not by justifying a rule that permitted a market dominating joint venture to close the nation's entire network of banks to competing issuers. The Tenth Circuit appeared to believe that any articulation of a free rider problem was sufficient to support a rule denying bank access to rivals, with not even minimal exploration of less restrictive alternatives.[51]

While free-rider claims must always be taken seriously, the concept of free riding has been overused as a defense. A free rider is someone who is able to take advantage of another firm's investment in such a way that the first firm cannot appropriate the value of the investment to itself. For example, suppose Beltone expends considerable expense effort obtaining customer lists for its hear aid dealers. If the dealers sell both Beltone and a cheaper Brand X hearing aid, they would be tempted to use Beltone's customer list to sell Brand X hearing aids. Beltone may be able to capture the market returns to its investment in the customer list only by exclusive dealing—that is, by prohibiting the dealer's to sell any other brand.

Properly defined free riding is always an output reducing strategy. That is, it undermines the primary firm's incentive to invest in a valuable asset, with the result that less of the asset is produced. But free rider problems do not exist every time they are asserted. *First*, not every instance of one firm's trading on another firm's investment is the kind of free riding that presents a policy concern. Many instances are simply product complementarity. For example, Ford profits greatly from the fact that Standard Oil, Exxon, and numerous others have developed a convenient network for the distribution of gasoline. If gasoline were hard to find, automobiles would be much less attractive. In this case, however, automobile makers and gasoline producers are "free riding" on each other, in a sense—that is, each profits because the other exists. For example, a bank that currently issued a Visa but wished to add American Express might be able to develop a Visa/AmEx package that is particularly valuable to consumers. But the result would be that *both* the Visa card and the American Express card would be sold in larger numbers.

Second, free riding is not a problem if the investor can capture the return on its investment by other means, such as an admission charge. Often the founding members in an open membership joint venture such as FTD, a joint venture of florists who will deliver flowers across the country, have intellectual property rights such as trademarks. But the value of these is readily captured by a membership or user fee.[52]

Third, anticompetitive rules designed to solve free rider problems can often be addressed by less restrictive alternatives. In the Visa case, for example, if the feared danger was that one of the dozen or so Visa board member that issued a competing card might be able to engage in unauthorized transfers of trade secrets, the appropriate rule would be one prohibiting Visa board members from issu-

50. See *Visa*, 819 F.Supp. at 995; and see 13 Antitrust Law ¶ 2222 (1999).

51. On free rider defenses of rules excluding firms from open membership ventures, see 13 Antitrust Law ¶ 2223 (1999). For conflicting views of the Visa case, see D. Evans & R. Schmalensee, Economic Aspects of Payment Card Systems and Antitrust Policy Toward Joint Ventures, 63 Antitrust L.J. 861, 882 (1995); D. Carlton & A. Frankel, The Antitrust Economics of Credit Card Networks, 63 Antitrust L.J. 643 (1995); H. Hovenkamp, Exclusive Joint Ventures and Antitrust Policy, 1995 Columbia Bus. L. Rev. 1.

52. See, e.g., Chicago Professional Sports Limited Partnership & WGN v. National Basketball Assn., 961 F.2d 667, 675 (7th Cir.), cert. denied, 506 U.S. 954, 113 S.Ct. 409 (1992) (NBA could capture value of its name and other intellectual property by charging a fee when its games were televised). Cf. United States v. Associated Press, 52 F.Supp. 362, 365 (S.D.N.Y.1943), aff'd, 326 U.S. 1, 65 S.Ct. 1416 (1945) (use of new member entry fees to compensate existing members for previous investments); General Leaseways v. National Truck Leasing Ass'n., 744 F.2d 588 (7th Cir.1984) (rejecting free rider claims involving members' repairs of each other's trucks when they charged for the service).

ing a competing card, not a rule prohibiting any one of the 6000 member banks from issuing such a card.[53]

The dangers imposed by market dominating open membership ventures are twofold—facilitating of collusion and limitations on innovation. As an example of the first, if the ABA can effectively require every lawyer to be a member *and* enforce a rule setting minimum fees, it has created a market dominating cartel. Importantly, such a cartel can work quite effectively even if it has thousands of members, because enforcement is done through the joint venture's disciplinary machinery.[54]

But even if price fixing is unlikely, open membership joint ventures can engage in anticompetitive exclusion of innovators that threaten the market share of the venture's existing members. The *Allied Tube* decision involved a standard setting joint venture that was open to a wide variety of manufacturers, insurers and other firms involved in the design, manufacturing and evaluation of electrical components used in buildings.[55] Approval by the venture was essential to market success, because the venture's proposals were typically incorporated without change into local building codes. The defendants were firms that manufactured metal electrical conduit and felt their market shares threatened by the plaintiff, whose plastic conduit was cheaper, easier to install, and safer than metal. The defendants then "packed" a standard setting meeting and managed to get a rule adopted that disapproved the plastic conduit and effectively kept it off the market for several years.

In such a case the competitive harm does not result from the fixing of prices, but rather from the restraint on innovation. Even if the steel conduit makers were competing vigorously with one another and earning only competitive returns, they would still be severely injured by an innovation that threatened to make their own product obsolete and idle their capacity. The result of the exclusion, however, was to deny consumers the benefit of a product that they would have preferred and that a competitive market would have given them.

In sum, once a joint venture opens itself to all firms in the market as a general matter and confers a significant advantage, such that all or most firms feel obliged to join, then rules that selectively deny access to new members, that forbid members from making competing products, or that restrain firms' ability to innovate in ways that compete with existing members' technology, must be examined carefully. The problem is closely akin to that of standard setting by market dominating professional organizations.[56] On the one hand, consumers benefit from standards set by qualified professionals and have an interest in seeing that unqualified people are disciplined or removed. On the other hand, once the association has acquired control of the profession, it is in a position to use standard setting for anticompetitive purposes. This does not entail that all or even most standards are anticompetitive. But it does mean that when the venture or professional association wields market power, rules that exclude people, products or techniques that seem desirable and marketable must have a satisfactory explanation. Further, less restrictive alternatives to outright exclusion must always be examined.

The same analysis generally applies to industries subject to positive network externalities. In such industries being connected to or compatible with the network is valuable in and of itself, without regard to the absolute quality of the plaintiff's product.[57] For example, the

53. See also National Bancard Corp. (NaBanco) v. VISA U.S.A., 779 F.2d 592 (11th Cir.), cert. denied, 479 U.S. 923, 107 S.Ct. 329 (1986) (upholding fixing of bank interchange fees without serious inquiry into whether there were alternative methods of communicating the fees, such as printing them on the back of the card).

54. See, e.g., *Goldfarb*, note 36, which noted that there was no deviation in the prices quoted by lawyers under the mandatory fee rule in question.

55. Allied Tube & Conduit Corp. v. Indian Head, 486 U.S. 492, 108 S.Ct. 1931 (1988); see 13 Antitrust Law ¶ 2220b (1999).

56. See § 5.4c.

57. See 13 Antitrust Law ¶ 2220 (1998). See also M. Lemley & D. McGowan, Legal Implications of Network Economic Effects, 86 Calif. L. Rev. 479 (1998); M. L. Katz & C. Shapiro, Product Introduction with Network Externalities, 11 J. Indus. Econ. 55 (1992); J. Farrell & G. Saloner, Installed Base and Compatibility: Innovation,

best telephone in the world isn't worth much if it cannot be connected into the telephone system. Those controlling the system are likely to have significant market power, but they also have a significant investment in their own technologies. As a result, a joint venture rule excluding a telephone instrument, switching device, or other component that seems to be superior and might threaten the investments of incumbents would have to be justified, and less restrictive alternatives examined.

Refusals to deal in open membership ventures have come to the Supreme court several times. The *Allied Tube* case just discussed is one of them. In two others the Supreme Court condemned a refusal to deal under § 1 of the Sherman Act. The first case, United States v. Terminal R.R. Ass'n. of St. Louis,[58] involved an association of several railroad companies and bridge companies into a giant railroad terminal and transfer system in St. Louis, Missouri, where the Mississippi River and several railroad lines came together. The system greatly facilitated transfers of cargo and coordination of traffic and was obviously efficient; in fact, it was almost certainly a natural monopoly. The system was initiated by six of the railroads, however, and latecomers were admitted to joint ownership only upon a unanimous vote of all existing owners. A nonowner could use the system only by unanimous consent of existing owners.

The Supreme Court held that the efficiency-creating potential of the system, plus the fact that outsider railroads could not effectively compete with it, gave the owners a duty to admit "any existing or future railroad to joint ownership and control of the combined terminal properties, upon such just and reasonable terms as shall place such applying company upon a plane of equality" with the existing owners. Secondly, the terminal operators must make the system available on nondiscriminatory terms to any railroad who wished to use it but elected not to become an owner.[59]

Because the joint venture in *Terminal Railroad* was a natural monopoly, anyone denied access would face higher costs. As a result, member firms might be able to reduce output and charge a price significantly above their costs without worrying about competition. When a natural monopoly market contains a single firm, the State may have to decide whether to permit the natural monopolist to charge a monopoly price, force divestiture even though multiple firms would have higher costs, or impose statutory price regulation.

In the case of a natural monopoly joint venture such as *Terminal Railroad*, however, the court may force competition *within* the joint venture. If the giant railroad transfer system were operated by a single firm, the opportunity for monopoly profits would be substantial. In fact, such systems are generally either publicly owned or price regulated. But the Supreme Court used the Sherman Act to produce an alternative: common ownership and control of the system by a large number of competing railroads. Assuming that the railroads continued to compete with each other, the jointly operated transfer system would be unable to earn monopoly profits.

Perhaps the leading case involving a refusal to deal by an open membership joint venture is Associated Press v. United States.[60] Associated Press (AP) was a joint venture whose members were about 1,200 newspapers. AP gathered, drafted and disseminated news. Part of the work was done by employees who worked for AP, and part by reporters that AP borrowed from member newspapers. When the AP correspondent gathered news and wrote a news story in, say, Washington, D.C., all member newspapers were entitled to a copy of the story. In effect, AP enabled a single reporter to

Product Preannouncements, and Predation, 76 Amer. Econ. Rev. 940 (1986); M. L. Katz & C. Shapiro, Technology Adoption in the Presence of Network Externalities, 94 J. Pol. Econ. 822, 824 (1986).

58. 224 U.S. 383, 32 S.Ct. 507 (1912).

59. Id. at 411–12, 32 S.Ct. at 516. The court was in fact applying a set of rules that were frequently applied to monopoly utilities: they must serve all paying customers on a nondiscriminatory basis. See H. Hovenkamp, Enterprise and American Law, 1836–1937 (1991), Part III, "The Rise of Regulated Industry."

60. 326 U.S. 1, 65 S.Ct. 1416 (1945).

gather news that would be reported by each of the 1,200 member newspapers.

The joint venture itself was conceded to be very efficient. But the government challenged various by-laws adopted for AP by its members. The members were prohibited from selling news to non-members, and AP took several steps to insure that non-AP newspapers had no access to AP-gathered news until after it was published. AP's board of directors could freely elect new members unless the applicant competed with a newspaper that was already an AP member. In that case, if the competing member objected the new member had to pay a large fee and receive a majority vote of existing AP members. The Supreme Court held that these provisions on their face violated the Sherman Act.

Associated Press's organization and its by-laws are relatively easy to understand. Assuming that news stories are fungible—that one reporter's coverage of the San Francisco Earthquake is as good as another's—the creation of news is a natural monopoly. The costs of producing a news story are largely the costs of sending a reporter to the scene to collect the information and write the story. Once the story is finished, it can be transmitted to another newspaper for little more than the costs of the wire service. If ten daily newspapers want to gather news from San Francisco, the cheapest method would be for the ten newspapers to have a single news staff in San Francisco, which would compose the stories and send copies simultaneously to all ten.

Assume that the world contains ten cities and that each city has one or two newspapers. One reporter is sufficient to cover one city's news, and the costs of maintaining one reporter are $100 per week. Absent news sharing, each newspaper would face total news gathering costs of $1,000—$100 for each reporter in each of the ten cities. Suppose that eight of the newspapers agree that the home reporter for each of them will distribute the news to the other seven. Assuming that transmission of the story is costless, each of these eight newspapers will now be able to gather news at a cost of $300 per week: $100 for its own home reporter, who will also supply news to the other seven joint venturers, and $200 in order to maintain reporters in each of the two cities not having a participating newspaper.

Suppose now that a newspaper in city #9 wants to join the news-sharing venture. The existing members will likely agree. News gathering costs will drop by another $100, for there will be joint venture members in nine cities instead of eight. No newspaper will be injured by the "competition" of the newcomer, for newspapers compete with each other only in their own circulation market. Everyone will be better off if the newspaper in the ninth city is permitted to join.

But what will happen if a *second* newspaper in city #1 wants to join? The members are already being provided with news from city #1, through its first member newspaper. As a result, entry by the second newspaper in city #1 will not lower the costs of the incumbent newspapers—it will not add anything to the efficiency of the organization, assuming that news stories are fungible and that the incumbent newspaper in city #1 is doing its job well. However, entry by the second newspaper in city #1 may injure the first member newspaper in city #1 substantially. Before entry, the first newspaper in city #1 had a $700 cost advantage over the second newspaper in city #1. After the second newspaper's entry the first newspaper will face much stiffer competition. The cost savings produced by membership in the joint venture will accrue not to the member newspaper, but to the newspaper's subscribers or advertisers.

This analysis suggests that although the joint venture in the *Associated Press* case was efficient, the by-laws that permitted competitors to object to new applicants were anticompetitive. Furthermore, AP could maintain all the efficiencies created by the venture without the anticompetitive by-laws. Finally, AP seemed not to be concerned about latecomers wishing to take a free ride on its earlier risk taking, for the organization was willing to admit latecomers who did not compete with existing members.[61]

§ 5.4c. *Standard Setting and Rule Enforcement in Private Entrepreneurial and Professional Associations*

Concerted refusals are an important mechanism by which trade associations, privately run markets, cooperatives and professional associations enforce rules and standards governing product or service quality. Disciplining violators most generally takes the form of excluding a firm from membership or penalizing it in some way that restricts its access to the market. Overwhelmingly, challenges to such discipline are evaluated as concerted refusals to deal under the rule of reason.

Both standard setting and rule making are generally in the best interests of consumers, because they substantially reduce information costs, and therefore consumer search costs.[62] The labels "approved by united testing laboratories," "number two plywood," or "board certified operator" all convey information to a consumer about the product or service that he is purchasing.

An inevitable result of any meaningful standard-setting procedure is that some do not meet the standard and are excluded from the business association or even the market. This becomes an antitrust problem when the persons making and enforcing the standards are competitors of the person or firm who is excluded by them. At the same time, the providers of certain products or services are experts, and often are in a better position than anyone else to evaluate the quality of a competitor's product. For example, a patient would have a difficult time determining whether a particular surgeon is competent, unless perhaps she knows several people who have been under the surgeon's scalpel. Those in the best position to make this judgment are fellow surgeons familiar with the same area of practice. For this reason most medical institutions have peer review boards, composed largely of doctors, which evaluate the performance of other doctors. If the board members act in good faith, consumers are better off. If they act in bad faith, consumers suffer.

Although professionals generally review others in good faith, the contrary may sometimes by true. For example, the reviewers may believe that the surgeon being evaluated is cutting prices, perhaps by eliminating certain pre-surgical services that she regards as optional. Alternatively, the peer review board may believe that the hospital already has "too many" surgeons. Rather than reducing fees to attract more patients to the hospital, they would prefer to reduce the supply.[63] Or a group of firms that both manufacturer and evaluate products may be committed to an existing technology or method of doing business. When a new technology or business method comes along that threatens their investment in the status quo they may respond, not by competing with the

61. Using largely the same reasoning, the Ninth Circuit condemned a rule adopted by the National Football League forbidding a team from changing locations unless 3/4 of the league's teams approved the change. Los Angeles Memorial Coliseum Commn. v. NFL, 726 F.2d 1381, 1396 (9th Cir.), cert. denied, 469 U.S. 990, 105 S.Ct. 397 (1984). Although creation of the league by mutual agreement was obviously efficient, the rule made it quite easy for a team to prevent another team from moving so close by as to become a competitor for ticket sales. That restriction was not essential to the efficient operation of the League.

62. See D. W. Carlton & J.M. Klamer, The Need For Coordination Among Firms, With Special Reference to Network Industries, 50 U.Chi.L.Rev. 446 (1983).

63. See generally, Symposium on Antitrust and Health Care, 51 L. & Contemp. Prob. 1 (1988); for the historical development, see P. Starr, The Social Transformation of American Medicine 164–169 (1982).

Similar problems have arisen in professional sports. For example, see Weight–Rite Golf Corp., v. United States Golf Ass'n, 766 F.Supp. 1104 (M.D.Fla.1991), aff'd mem., 953 F.2d 651 (11th Cir.1992) (rejecting challenge by manufacturer whose golf shoes were disapproved by golfers association); Eleven Line v. North Texas State Soccer Ass'n, 1998 WL 574893 (N.D.Tex., 1998) (Sherman Act condemned dominant indoor soccer league's attempt to disqualify stadiums of competing soccer league); Blalock v. Ladies Professional Golf Assn., 359 F.Supp. 1260 (N.D.Ga. 1973), declaring *per se* unlawful a rule suspending the plaintiff for alleged cheating. The makers and enforcers of the rule were the plaintiff's competitors, and the rule gave them "unfettered, subjective discretion;" Molinas v. National Basketball Assn., 190 F.Supp. 241 (S.D.N.Y.1961) upholding a rule formulated by agreement among professional basketball teams requiring the suspension of a player who placed bets on his own team.

In other contexts, see United States v. ABA, 60 Fed. Reg. 39,421 (1995) (consent decree forbidding ABA from tying law school accreditation to faculty compensation).

new method, but rather by using the standard setting process to keep it off of the market.

Standard setting can be just as important in products as it is in professional services, particularly if the product is complex or likely to be dangerous. In some cases public agencies such as the Food and Drug Administration evaluate and approve products. In other cases, evaluation is performed by private laboratories, often operated by associations composed of sellers and related firms. Antitrust is relevant mainly to the latter.

The problem of professional and product standard setting by private organizations is closely akin to that of refusals to deal by open membership joint ventures.[64] The fact that membership is desirable or even legally essential for market access effectively turns these organizations into market gatekeepers. While such organizations have the capacity to do much good, we cannot ignore the potential for competitive harm.

Radiant Burners, Inc. v. Peoples Gas Light & Coke Co.[65] involved an association of gas heater manufacturers, pipeline companies and utilities which evaluated products that burned natural gas and placed a "seal of approval" on products judged to be safe. If a product was judged unsafe, the association not only refused its seal of approval, but the utility companies in the association refused to provide gas to a home or business containing the disapproved product. The plaintiff manufacturer claimed that its Radiant Burner had been disapproved by the association, and that the standards used to evaluate the Burner were arbitrary and capricious, largely because the burner was evaluated by the manufacturers of competing gas burners. In a *per curiam* opinion the Supreme Court concluded that the allegations stated a cause of action for a *per se* violation of the Sherman Act, citing Klor's, Inc. v. Broadway–Hale Stores.[66]

The plaintiff's complaint in *Radiant Burner* contained two important allegations, both of which may be necessary to bring the concerted refusal by competitors under the *per se* rule: 1) that the plaintiff's product was not evaluated objectively, but in a capricious way by competitors who had a vested interest in disapproving the product; 2) that the defendants actually forced customers not to buy the disapproved product, or in some way prevented it from entering the market. Courts have been reluctant to apply the *per se* rule when one of these elements was present but not the other. They have usually approved the activity when neither was present.

For example, in Eliason Corp. v. National Sanitation Foundation[67] the plaintiff, who manufactured commercial refrigerators, accused the defendant testing association of refusing to approve one of its designs. The standards were drawn up by a large group of manufacturers and users of commercial refrigerators. There was no evidence that the testing laboratory itself was "controlled" by competing refrigerator manufacturers, or that the plaintiff's equipment was treated any differently than the equipment of competitors. Furthermore, several other manufacturers had also received disapprovals and were forced to make design changes. Finally, approved products received the testing laboratory's seal of approval. The consequence of disapproval was merely that the seal was withdrawn. The defendants made no effort to prevent anyone from purchasing a refrigerator that did not have the seal.

In refusing to apply the *per se* rule, the Sixth Circuit held that if the alleged boycott resulted from industry self-regulation or standard making, the plaintiff "must show either

64. See § 5.4b2.

65. 364 U.S. 656, 81 S.Ct. 365 (1961).

66. 359 U.S. 207, 79 S.Ct. 705 (1959), discussed earlier. See also American Medical Association v. United States, 317 U.S. 519, 63 S.Ct. 326 (1943) which held that an accreditation or standard-setting association may not dismiss or discipline a member simply because she is a price cutter.

67. 614 F.2d 126 (6th Cir.1980), cert. denied, 449 U.S. 826, 101 S.Ct. 89 (1980); see also Structural Laminates, Inc. v. Douglas Fir Plywood Assoc., 261 F.Supp. 154 (D.Or. 1966), affirmed, 399 F.2d 155 (9th Cir.1968), cert. denied, 393 U.S. 1024, 89 S.Ct. 636 (1969) (approving joint establishment of independent testing laboratory and seal of approval, even though unapproved products may have been excluded from the market).

that it was barred from obtaining approval of its products on a discriminatory basis from its competitors, or that the conduct as a whole was manifestly unreasonable." Finding no such evidence, the court affirmed dismissal of the complaint.

If the purpose of testing and approval is to provide buyers with needed information, then the forced exclusion of the unapproved product from the market, as was alleged in *Radiant Burners*, is suspicious.[68] The presence or absence of the "seal of approval" will provide the consumer with information about whether a product is safe. Forcing the product off the market is competitive only on the theory that consumers will not be able to respond rationally to the information that the seal (or its absence) provides, perhaps on the assumption that consumers do not know about the seal's existence or meaning.

Even a coercive refusal is unlikely to be anticompetitive if those making the adverse decision are not in competition with the firm whose product or service is rejected. For example, in *Radiant Burners* the defendant gas utilities might have justified their refusal to provide gas to installations using the Radiant Burner on the grounds that the product could injure the utility companies' lines or increase their insurance risks.[69] Often standard setting claims can be dismissed by the simple observation that those setting the standards are not in competition with the firm or person who is excluded. For example, if an anesthesiologist is denied staff privileges at a hospital by a board composed of rival anesthesiologists, an anticompetitive explanation is plausible. But the hospital itself, its surgeons, and physicians in non-competing areas of practice generally cannot profit by excluding a price-cutting or unusually innovative anesthesiologist. In fact, many of them would be benefitted. For example, both the hospital and its surgeons would be better off if the anesthesiologist charged lower prices or used an innovative procedure that had positive results.[70]

A requirement that the standards by which a product is evaluated be reasonable and applied in a nondiscriminatory way is important if a court is to avoid considering subjective intent.[71] To be sure, the protection offered by

68. See *Allied*, note 55, 486 U.S. at 501 n. 6, 108 S.Ct. at 1937 (1988): "Concerted efforts to enforce (rather than just agree upon) private product standards face more rigorous antitrust scrutiny."

69. The gas companies were not required to justify their refusal because the district court dismissed the complaint for failure to state a claim, and the Seventh Circuit affirmed. Radiant Burners, Inc. v. Peoples Gas, Light & Coke Co., 273 F.2d 196 (7th Cir.1959).

70. See Super Sulky v. United States Trotting Assn., 174 F.3d 733 (6th Cir.1999) (association of drivers and race associations would not have incentive to disapprove plaintiff's racing sulky design if it really were superior); Moore v. Boating Industry Assoc., 819 F.2d 693 (7th Cir.), cert. denied, 484 U.S. 854, 108 S.Ct. 160 (1987) (association of boat trailer manufacturers did not violate antitrust laws by disapproving plaintiff's trailer light; they would stand to benefit from low cost high quality lights); M & H Tire Co. v. Hoosier Racing Tire Corp., 733 F.2d 973, 980 (1st Cir.1984) (auto racing association, with no interest in tire production, approves a single tire design and manufacturer for each season); ECOS Elecs. Corp. v. Underwriters Labs., 743 F.2d 498, 500 (7th Cir.1984), cert. denied, 469 U.S. 1210, 105 S.Ct. 1178 (1985) (Underwriters Laboratories could not restrain trade by approving the product of the plaintiff's rival; it was an independent organization and none of its managers could "be associated with a manufacturer or vendor of products investigated by UL."). See 13 Antitrust Law ¶ 2232d (1998).

In the health care industry, see Marin v. Citizens Memorial Hospital, 700 F.Supp. 354 (S.D.Tex.1988) (antitrust complaint dismissed where most of hospital's review committee not rivals with the plaintiff). Cf. Miller v. Indiana Hosp., 843 F.2d 139 (3d Cir.), cert. denied, 488 U.S. 870, 109 S.Ct. 178 (1988) (reversing district court grant of summary judgment against surgeon who claimed that his hospital staff privileges were denied because he built a lower cost clinical facility in competition with the hospital; most of relevant decision makers were plaintiff's competitors). To be sure, the hospital may be nothing more than the pawn of the peer review panel or the hospital administration, but that fact cannot be presumed. As to the hospital itself, rule of reason treatment is virtually always appropriate. Other hospital cases include Mathews v. Lancaster Gen. Hosp., 883 F.Supp. 1016, 1044 (E.D.Pa.1995), aff'd, 87 F.3d 624 (3d Cir.1996); Oksanen v. Page Memorial Hosp., 945 F.2d 696 (4th Cir.1991), cert. denied, 502 U.S. 1074, 112 S.Ct. 973 (1992); Nurse Midwifery Assocs. v. Hibbett, 918 F.2d 605 (6th Cir.1990); Weiss v. York Hosp., 745 F.2d 786 (3d Cir.1984), cert. denied, 470 U.S. 1060, 105 S.Ct. 1777 (1985). See generally Havighurst, Doctors and Hospitals, 1984 Duke L.J. 1071.

71. Simple statements of disapproval, with no attempt at forced removal from the market, are typically approved. See 13 Antitrust Law ¶ 2232e (1999); and Schachar v. American Academy of Ophthalmology, 870 F.2d 397 (7th Cir.1989) (no violation where defendant Academy had simply labeled plaintiff's procedure "experimental"); Clamp–All Corp. v. Cast Iron Soil Pipe Inst., 851 F.2d 478 (1st Cir.1988), cert. denied, 488 U.S. 1007, 109 S.Ct. 789 (1989) (simple declaration of approval or disapproval un-such a legal requirement is not perfect. Often, however, it is the only means by which an outsider can assess the true effect of what purports to be a disciplinary act.

For example, in Silver v. New York Stock Exchange (NYSE)[72] a stockbroker complained that the Exchange members denied him access to the private telephone connections necessary to monitor and execute stock transactions on the exchange. Without such lines a stockbroker is generally unable to carry on its business. The NYSE refused to provide any explanation why Silver's communication was cut off, telling him only that "it was the policy of the Exchange not to disclose the reasons for such action." When Silver charged the Exchange members with violating the Sherman Act, they answered that under the Securities Exchange Act of 1934 the members were authorized to pass and enforce their own rules and regulations governing broker activity. As a result the termination was exempt from antitrust scrutiny.

The Supreme Court did not deny that the Securities Exchange Act gave members the authority to make and enforce their own business rules. However, "nothing built into the regulatory scheme * * * performs the antitrust function of insuring that an exchange will not in some cases apply its rules so as to do injury to competition which cannot be justified as furthering legitimate self-regulative ends." At the time *Silver* was decided, brokerage commissions on the NYSE were fixed. The purpose of fixed commissions was arguably to force brokers to provide the optimal number of customer services. However, the members may have reached an "understanding" about the number of services they would give. A disruptive broker who provided more services could do substantial damage to such a service cartel. The defense asserted in *Silver* would effectively have given the NYSE members the power to cartelize all aspects of the stock brokerage market.[73]

The Supreme Court took a step back from *Silver* in the *Northwest Wholesale Stationers* decision.[74] The plaintiff stationery retailer had been expelled from a cooperative that wholesaled products to member retailers. Further, the record (of both the cooperative proceedings and the subsequent litigation) gave no explanation why the plaintiff had been expelled. The Supreme Court held that the lower court had incorrectly applied the *per se* rule. The activities of a wholesale cooperative that bought stationery supplies and resold them to members clearly represented substantial integration of the distribution process; so this was not a "naked" refusal to deal. As a result, the expulsion could not be condemned without a showing that the cooperative had "market power or unique access to a business element necessary for effective competition."[75]

Northwest substantially increases the plaintiff's burden in cases involving an association's refusal to deal. Under *Silver* the defendants had to provide minimal due process and an explanation for the discipline. Under *Northwest*, the defendant apparently need provide nothing at all unless the plaintiff shows market power. Or to say it another way, the mere fact that an expulsion from a joint venture is unexplained does not mean that it is unreasonable in the antitrust sense. The plaintiff has the initial obligation to allege and show that an expulsion *either* (1) facilitates a naked restraint such as price-fixing; or (2) is "unreasonable," with reasonableness measured in the antitrust sense of facilitating the exercise of market power, and not in the lay person's more general sense which might conclude that any unexplained or certainly any arbitrary expulsion is "unreasonable." Of course, once power is found, the defendant's failure to provide an explanation may be highly relevant to the determination whether the expulsion was competitively reasonable or whether less restrictive alternatives were available. Unex-

likely to cause competitive harm when buyers are sophisticated and can make their own choices).

72. 373 U.S. 341, 83 S.Ct. 1246 (1963).

73. There was some history of the NYSE warning or disciplining members for competing too intensely. Brief for United States as Amicus Curiae 37–41, Silver v. NYSE, Oct. Term 1962.

74. Note 13, 472 U.S. 284, 105 S.Ct. 2613 (1985).

75. Id. at 298, 105 S.Ct. at 2621.

plained exclusions are more likely to raise the fact finder's suspicions.[76]

Allegations of concerted refusals by entrepreneurial or professional associations often arise in complex areas where the court has little competence to determine whether the standard setting is really "objective" or reasonable. In such circumstances the court is often forced to look at other factors. Of these objective structural criteria such as lack of market power or lack of competitive relationship between the plaintiff and the defendant generally provide reliable evidence. Subjective intent is often unreliable but may be necessary.

Thus, for example, suppose that an automobile racing association sets standards for tires that exclude those manufactured by the plaintiff.[77] The first step in the antitrust analysis might be to ask whether the defendant association and the plaintiff compete with each other. If the association is dominated by firms that also manufacture or sell tires, and anticompetitive explanation is plausible. But if the association is made up entirely of race track owners or racing drivers who have no interest in tire sales, the complaint should probably be dismissed. Second, the fact finder should look at power. If the restraint at issue injures competition, it will presumably be in the tire market, or perhaps a market for racing tires. If the association's rule covers only a small percentage of a properly defined relevant market, then anticompetitive effects are also unlikely. Only after these structural hurdles have been jumped should subjective intent become relevant.

But there are areas where examination of intent is necessary. Medical association review of areas of practice or of individual care givers has probably provoked the largest amount of antitrust litigation. For example, Wilk v. AMA[78] involved "Principle 3" of the AMA Principles of Medical Ethics, which states that "a physician should practice a method of healing founded on a scientific basis; and he should not voluntarily professionally associate with anyone who violates this principle." Wilk was a chiropractor who claimed that physicians, acting under Principle 3, concertedly refused to give chiropractors access to medical educational facilities and hospitals, and refused to refer patients to them. The Seventh Circuit applied the rule of reason but minimized any inquiry into whether the physicians' disapproval of chiropractors was well-founded. Rather, it held that the plaintiff should have the initial burden of showing that Principle 3 restricted competition. If so, then the defendant physicians would have to show:

> (1) that they genuinely entertained a concern for what they perceive as scientific method in the care of each person with whom they have entered a doctor-patient relationship; (2) that this concern is objectively reasonable; (3) that this concern has been the dominant motivating factor in defendants' promulgation of Principle 3 and in the conduct intended to implement it; and (4) that this concern for scientific method in patient care could not have been adequately satisfied in a manner less restrictive of competition.

The factor that ultimately seemed to be most relevant to condemnation was the presence of less restrictive alternatives. In other areas the AMA had authorized the use of informational pamphlets warning patients about certain practices or procedures. Alternatively, it had communicated its concerns to physicians and permitted them to make up their own minds. But in the case of chiropractic it had forbidden physicians from referring patients to chiropractors or accepting referrals from chiropractors, denied chiropractors access to hospital facilities, and prevented physicians from teaching at schools of chiropractic—all of

76. See 13 Antitrust Law ¶ 2214 (1998).

77. Cf. *M & H Tire* case, note 70.

78. 719 F.2d 207, 213, 227 (7th Cir.1983), cert. denied, 467 U.S. 1210, 104 S.Ct. 2398 (1984). The court eventually condemned the arrangement. 895 F.2d 352 (7th Cir.), cert. denied, 498 U.S. 982, 111 S.Ct. 513 (1990). Accord Kreuzer v. American Academy of Periodontology, 735 F.2d 1479 (D.C.Cir.1984). For an argument that professional licensing and regulation is efficient because it reduces customer search costs, see H. Leland, Quacks, Lemons, and Licensing: A Theory of Minimum Quality Standards, 87 J.Pol.Econ. 1328 (1979).

this in spite of the fact that chiropractic was licensed in every state.[79]

Nonetheless, physicians and other highly specialized professionals must set their own standards if the standards are to be rational at all. Not every exclusion can be turned into an antitrust boycott.[80] So, for example, in its *Bhan* decision the Ninth Circuit applied the rule of reason to a hospital's policy of requiring that those practicing anesthesiology be physicians.[81] The policy excluded nurse anesthesiologists who, by some arguments, were equally qualified for most of the tasks. Quite simply, only the hospital or similarly qualified health care professionals were in a position to make daily judgments about the types of qualifications needed to perform certain tasks.

Since *Northwest*, the rule of reason in ancillary exclusion cases has become quite burdensome to plaintiffs, particularly if the hospital or other facility or association does not have a dominant position in its relevant market. But liability is sometimes still found if the abuses are clear. For example, in *Allied Tube* the Supreme Court condemned a member of a trade association for corrupting a standard setting meeting in order to have the plaintiffs' competing product disapproved.[82] Likewise, standards that the court finds excessive or irrational can invite condemnation.[83]

In sum, an associational exclusion violates the antitrust laws if the association has market power and the decision is both anticompetitive and irrational or unjustified. Alternatively, and rarely, a violation can be established without a market power requirement if the plaintiff can show that the challenged action was nothing more than a naked, anticompetitive exclusion disguised as an associational rule. *Allied Tube* belongs in this latter category. On the one hand, the Court indicated that it was applying the rule of reason to the substantive restraint;[84] on the other, it was willing to condemn corruption of the standard setting process that was plainly anticompetitive, with no apparent showing of market power.[85]

5.4d. Agreements Involving Non–Competitors

The *Klor's* case,[86] you might recall, involved allegations that a group of appliance manufacturers conspired with each other and a competing appliance store to boycott the plaintiff's store. Whatever one might think of the factual plausibility of that claim, the allegation that a group of competing appliance sellers conspired with *each other* was essential to the Supreme Court's conclusion that the complaint alleged a per se violation. The Court made this clear in its *NYNEX* decision, which involved an agreement not to deal between a

79. *Wilk*, 895 F.2d at 356. See 13 Antitrust Law ¶ 2235d (1999).

80. Apparently beginning with this proposition, in 1986 Congress passed the Health Care Quality Improvement Act, 42 U.S.C.A. §§ 11,101—11,152, which creates an antitrust immunity for peer review actions undertaken "in the reasonable belief that [the action] was in the furtherance of quality health care." The Supreme Court noted that "[i]n enacting this measure, Congress clearly noted and responded to the concern that the possibility of antitrust liability will discourage effective peer review." Patrick v. Burget, 486 U.S. 94, 105 n. 8, 108 S.Ct. 1658, 1666 n. 8 (1988). See Austin v. McNamara, 731 F.Supp. 934 (C.D.Cal.1990), affirmed, 979 F.2d 728 (9th Cir.1992), which exempted a peer review disciplinary proceeding under the Act. The HCQIA is discussed more fully 1A Antitrust Law ¶ 250 (rev. ed. 1997).

81. Bhan v. NME Hospitals, 929 F.2d 1404 (9th Cir. 1991), cert. denied, 502 U.S. 994, 112 S.Ct. 617 (1991). Compare Hahn v. Oregon Physicians' Serv., 868 F.2d 1022, 1030 (9th Cir.1988), cert. denied, 493 U.S. 846, 110 S.Ct. 140 (1989) (arrangement excluding podiatrists from prepaid health care plan; per se analysis appropriate only if either (a) the boycott denies the victim access to an essential facility or other essential source of supply; or (b) if the boycotters have a dominant market position and there no efficiencies are created by the arrangement.).

82. Allied Tube & Conduit Corp. v. Indian Head, Inc., 486 U.S. 492, 108 S.Ct. 1931 (1988). See also American Society of Mechanical Engineers v. Hydrolevel Corp., 456 U.S. 556, 102 S.Ct. 1935 (1982) (association liable for the anticompetitive acts of agents acting with apparent authority, when they applied the association's safety standards in a corrupt manner at the behest of the plaintiff's competitor).

83. For example, Thompson v. Metropolitan Multi–List, Inc., 934 F.2d 1566, 1581–1582 (11th Cir.1991) (condemning standard requiring broker to be a member of real estate association in order to use multi-list system).

84. *Allied Tube*, note 55, 486 U.S. at 501, 108 S.Ct. at 1937.

85. See 635 F.2d at 118.

86. See note 1.

single purchaser and a single seller.[87] The plaintiff Discon sold removal services of obsolete telephone equipment. Defendant NYNEX, the local phone company for New York, entered into an agreement with a rival under which (1) the rival agreed to supply all of NYNEX's removal services; (2) the "public" price of these services would be inflated, thus going into NYNEX's regulated rate base and producing higher telephone rates; but (3) the rival would pay NYNEX a secret year-end rebate for this right.

This was clearly a scheme to defraud purchasers of price regulated local telephone services. But was it also a per se unlawful concerted refusal to deal? The Second Circuit thought so, concluding that a concerted refusal to deal involving only non-competitors could be unlawful per se under the antitrust laws if there was no reasonable business justification for the agreement. In reversing, the Supreme Court was willing to concede the plaintiff's claim:

> that the petitioners' behavior hurt consumers by raising telephone service rates. But that consumer injury naturally flowed not so much from a less competitive market for removal services, as from the exercise of market power that is lawfully in the hands of a monopolist, namely, New York Telephone, combined with a deception worked upon the regulatory agency that prevented the agency from controlling New York Telephone's exercise of its monopoly power.[88]

Applying the per se rule in such a case:

> would transform cases involving business behavior that is improper for various reasons, say, cases involving nepotism or personal pique, into treble-damages antitrust cases. And that per se rule would discourage firms from changing suppliers—even where the competitive process itself does not suffer harm.[89]

NYNEX makes clear that when vertically related firms refuse to deal that refusal must be treated as a type of vertical restraint, so far as antitrust is concerned. To be sure, it could also be fraud or some other legal violation. But antitrust treats vertical agreements not to deal under highly focused inquiries that generally prevent any broad per se rule even when the restraint is harmful on its face. The two possibilities for per se analysis are resale price maintenance and tying. A terminated dealer might be able to allege that it was excluded as a result of supplier enforcement of an unlawful RPM agreement.[90] But no such agreement was at issue in *NYNEX*, as the Supreme Court noted.[91] Likewise, a foreclosed rival in a tying arrangement case might claim the benefits of tying law's rather idiosyncratic per se rule, but there was no tying claim in *NYNEX* either.[92] The antitrust violation that most closely resembled the allegations in NYNEX was exclusive dealing, where one firm promises to deal exclusively with another, but exclusively dealing is a rule of reason violation requiring proof of a relevant market and anticompetitive effects.[93]

It follows as a matter of course that legitimately ancillary agreements between vertically related firms not to deal with a rival must be treated under the rule of reason. In fact, after *NYNEX* the "boycott" label seems quite inappropriate. In Berkey Photo, Inc. v. Eastman Kodak Co.[94] the Second Circuit applied the rule of reason to a concerted refusal that accompanied a research and development joint venture of noncompetitors. Kodak and General Electric jointly developed a flash attachment to go with a new line of cameras developed by Kodak. The parties also agreed not to predisclose details of the new technology to competing camera and flash manufacturers, one of

87. *NYNEX v. Discon, Inc.*, 525 U.S. 128, 119 S.Ct. 493 (1998), on remand, 184 F.3d 111 (2d Cir.1999).

88. 119 S.Ct. at 498.

89. Ibid.

90. See § 11.5.

91. See NYNEX, 119 S.Ct. at 498, discussing Business Electronics Corp. v. Sharp Electronics Corp., 485 U.S. 717, 734, 108 S.Ct. 1515 (1988); see § 11.5d.

92. On tying, see Ch. 10.

93. On exclusive dealing, see § 10.9.

94. 603 F.2d 263 (2d Cir.1979), cert. denied, 444 U.S. 1093, 100 S.Ct. 1061 (1980).

which was the plaintiff. As a result, Berkey could not quickly enter the market for either the new camera or the new flash equipment. The court held that a joint agreement between "a monopolist [Kodak] and a firm in a complementary market" necessarily qualified for rule of reason treatment, because the parties to the agreement did not eliminate competition between themselves. But the court went on to find the agreement unreasonable. Kodak's monopoly position was essential to that determination. As a result the refusal to predisclose might more appropriately be treated as an exclusionary practice by a monopolist, rather than a "concerted" refusal to deal.[95]

5.4e. Expressive and Noncommercial Boycotts

A properly defined noncommercial boycott is generally exempt from antitrust liability, even though the boycott is anticompetitive. The exemption rests on two different theories. One is that the boycotters are protected by Constitutional rights that "trump" the antitrust laws, such as the First Amendment or Equal Protection clause.[96] The other theory, which generally makes litigation of constitutional issues unnecessary, is that the Sherman and Clayton Acts were not designed to be applied to noncommercial activities.[97] For example, in Missouri v. NOW, the Eighth Circuit held that the Sherman Act did not reach a boycott organized by the National Organization for Women and others directed against states that had failed to ratify the federal Equal Rights Amendment.[98] Likewise, concerted attempts by antiabortion demonstrators to interfere with the operation of clinics offering abortion services might be "boycotts," but they are not the sort of boycotts that concern the Sherman Act.[99]

Claiborne Hardware was an antitrust action brought against civil rights groups for boycotting merchants who had allegedly discriminated on the basis of race. The Supreme Court found the boycott to be a form of Constitutionally protected speech, thus making it unreachable under the Sherman Act.[100] But the line between "commercial" and "political" boycotts is not self-defining, and the Supreme Court rejected a similar defense in the *Trial Lawyers* case, involving a boycott by lawyers wishing higher fees from the government purchaser of legal services.[101] As the Supreme Court noted, nearly every boycott has a certain "expressive component"—that is, it operates as a statement to its victims that the boycotters want something. Indeed, "[t]he most blatant, naked price-fixing agreement is a product of communication, but that is surely not a reason for viewing it with special solicitude."[102] The Court then held that the "expressive" content of the lawyers' boycott was not sufficient to save it from *per se* condemnation.

Locating the line between *Claiborne Hardware* and *Trial Lawyers* is not easy. The fact that the lawyers' principal goal was to earn higher fees, while the civil rights boycotters' principal goal was the noncommercial one of obtaining racial justice, might be decisive.[103] As the Court characterized the difference, the civil rights boycotters "sought no special advantage for themselves," but "only the equal

95. The evidence indicated that the agreement not to predisclose was initiated by Kodak, and General Electric went along only reluctantly. 603 F.2d at 300.

96. For example, NAACP v. Claiborne Hardware Co., 458 U.S. 886, 102 S.Ct. 3409 (1982), rehearing denied, 459 U.S. 898, 103 S.Ct. 199 (1982). See E.T. Sullivan, First Amendment Defenses in Antitrust Litigation, 46 Mis. L.Rev. 517 (1981).

97. See 1A Antitrust Law ¶ 262 (rev. ed. 1997).

98. Missouri v. National Organization for Women, Inc., 620 F.2d 1301, 1309 (8th Cir.1980), cert. denied, 449 U.S. 842, 101 S.Ct. 122 (1980).

99. National Organization for Women v. Scheidler, 968 F.2d 612 (7th Cir.1992), rev'd on non-antitrust issue, 510 U.S. 249, 114 S.Ct. 798 (1994).

100. *Claiborne*, note 96, 458 U.S. at 907, 914, 102 S.Ct. at 3422, 3426.

101. FTC v. Superior Ct. Trial Lawyers Assn., 493 U.S. 411, 110 S.Ct. 768 (1990). For more on this decision, see § 18.2b.

102. Id. at 433, 110 S.Ct. at 780.

103. In *Trial Lawyers*, the Court also rejected the claim that the lawyers were vindicating a constitutional right—namely that of the indigent defendants who were receiving inadequate representation under the low fees. 110 S.Ct. at 777 n. 11.

respect and equal treatment to which they were constitutionally entitled. By contrast, the lawyers stood to profit directly and immediately from the success of their boycott.[104] More to the point, the Trial Lawyers' boycott was organized in order to cartelize a product that the lawyers themselves sold, namely, their own legal services. That could not be said of the antitrust defendants in the *Claiborne Hardware* and *NOW* cases.

§ 5.5 Agreements Governing the Licensing and Use of Patents and Other Intellectual Property

§ 5.5a. Introduction; Basic Issues

Two facts complicate antitrust analysis of agreements governing the use of patents and other intellectual property. First, problems of free-riding and economies of scale are substantial, thus suggesting greater leniency toward such arrangements. The free rider problem derives from the fact that intellectual property rights can easily be appropriated if they are not given greater legal protection than is given to more tangible property rights. If the innovator cannot effectively exclude others from copying the innovation, then many of the returns to innovation will be lost and we can expect less innovation to occur.

Economies of scale exist because the costs of *duplicating* products or processes protected by intellectual property are so much lower than the cost of developing them in the first place. For example, if Chrysler develops a better airbag to protect automobile passengers and uses the patent only on its own automobiles, the development costs must be divided over its own limited output. But if Chrysler can license the patents to all other interested automobile manufacturers, the development costs can be spread over a much larger output. Of course, the licensing agreement would be a contract among competitors, and it may affect the price or output of automobiles—in sum, it may raise some of the flags that usually signal antitrust concern.

The second complicating factor is that patents, as well as copyrights and trademarks, are governed by detailed federal statutes that create numerous potential conflicts with antitrust policy.[1] As a result, the antitrust laws and the federal intellectual property laws must be interpreted so as to accommodate one another. Importantly, the United States has both a patent policy and an antitrust policy, and neither should be interpreted in such a way as to disregard the other. One may therefore dispute the *SCM Corp.* conclusion that if a "patent has been lawfully acquired, subsequent conduct permissible under the patent laws cannot trigger any liability under the antitrust laws."[2] Simple legality under the patent laws cannot be decisive of an antitrust question, although *clear authorization* under the patent laws generally is decisive.

This section deals with agreements between competitors or other firms respecting the use of patents. But the issue of patent abuse and antitrust policy comes up in two other places: the abuse of the patent system as an exclusionary practice by a dominant firm,[3] and the right of every person to petition the government, in this case by filing patent or copyright infringement lawsuits that may be improperly brought.[4] Also treated separately is the question whether the owner of a patent can be presumed to have significant market power in the product or process covered by the patent.[5] Most of the discussion that follows is directed at the problem of patents. Although copyrights and trademarks raise similar con-

104. *Trial Lawyers*, 493 U.S. at 426, 110 S.Ct. at 777: "No matter how altruistic the motives of respondents may have been, it is undisputed that their immediate objective was to increase the price that they would be paid for their services. Such an economic boycott is well within the category that was expressly distinguished in * * * *Claiborne Hardware.* * * *"

§ 5.5

1. A good discussion of the conflict is L. Kaplow, The Patent–Antitrust Intersection: A Reappraisal, 97 Harv. L.Rev. 1813 (1984).

2. SCM Corp. v. Xerox Corp., 645 F.2d 1195, 1206 (2d Cir.1981), cert. denied, 455 U.S. 1016, 102 S.Ct. 1708 (1982).

3. See § 7.11.

4. See §§ 18.2–18.3.

5. See § 3.9d.

cerns, these are not as well developed in the antitrust literature or the case law. They are treated briefly in § 5.5d.[6]

In 1995 the Antitrust Division of the Department of Justice and Federal Trade Commission jointly issued Antitrust Guidelines for the Licensing of Intellectual Property. These Guidelines state the enforcement policies of the two antitrust agencies and also serve as a useful summary of the applicable law.[7]

§ 5.5b. The Scope of the Patent Misuse Doctrine

Article I, Section 8, clause 8 of the Constitution grants Congress the power to "promote the Progress of Science and useful Arts" by "securing for limited Times to Authors and Inventors the exclusive Right to their respective Writings and Discoveries." This authorization is not limited by the commerce clause or other considerations of federalism, and thus gives Congress full authority over patents and copyrights.

Antitrust policy in patent licensing schemes has always been closely tied to the patent law's doctrine of "misuse." The concept of patent misuse is broad, and misuse can be found not only in licensing agreements, but also in the patentee's infringement suits directed at non-licensees (so-called contributory infringement).[8] The misuse claim typically arises when the patent holder sues another firm, claiming that its patent rights or contract rights under a licensing agreement have been violated. The defense raised is that the patent has been "misused," which is tantamount to a defense that the way the patent's owner used the patent violates patent law, antitrust law, or perhaps some less clearly articulated legal policy. If the misuse defense prevails, the patent is generally held to be unenforceable.[9]

"Misuse" arises because, in the court's view, the patent is being used *anticompetitively* in some sense. This fact is important because the question it invites is whether allegations of anticompetitive use of a patent should be addressed under antitrust principles, or some other set of principles that are presumably to be found in patent policy, even though they are not articulated in the Patent Act.[10] Many, but not all,[11] instances of patent misuse are practices analogous to unlawful tying arrangements, which are taken up in chapter 10. Clayton Act § 2, which was intended to be applied to tying and exclusive dealing, applies its proscriptions to all goods and commodities, "whether patented or unpatented."[12] In general, a "tie" of two products, or refusal to sell separately, is unlawful only if the seller has market power in the tying product or substantial anticompetitive effects result from the requirement. Indirectly, by admitting various de-

6. For fuller treatment, see 10 Antitrust Law, Ch. 17G (1995) (vertical arrangements likened to tying); and 12 id. Ch. 20E (1999) (horizontal arrangements).

7. These Guidelines are printed as Appendix C in the Annual Supplement to Antitrust Law. They can also be found reprinted in a wide variety of treatises and casebooks, or viewed in Westlaw by using "find" and 68 ATRR S–1.

8. Contributory infringement occurs when someone does not duplicate the entire patent without permission, but rather duplicates some unpatented part and places it on the market in such a fashion that purchasers, in order to make the marketed part useful, will have to commit infringement. The doctrine, which is judge made, originated in Wallace v. Holmes, 29 F.Cas. 74 (#17,100) (C.C.Conn. 1871), a generation before the Sherman Act was passed.

9. See Mercoid Corp. v. Mid–Continent Investment Co., 320 U.S. 661, 64 S.Ct. 268 (1944) (*Mercoid I*) (applying the doctrine); Morton Salt Co. v. G.S. Suppiger Co., 314 U.S. 488, 62 S.Ct. 402 (1942) (same; patentee who was engaged in unlawful tying could not bring infringement claim against rival). See generally Myers, Tying Arrangements and the Computer Industry: Digidyne Corp. v. Data General Corp., 1985 Duke L.J. 1027 (considering parallel doctrine of copyright misuse; objecting to application of misuse doctrine in the absence of a market power finding).

10. 35 U.S.C.A.

11. Cases finding "misuse" in contexts other than tying include United States v. Line Material Co., 333 U.S. 287, 68 S.Ct. 550 (1948) (price fixing in patent cross licensing); Cummer–Graham Co. v. Straight Side Basket Corp., 142 F.2d 646 (5th Cir.1944), cert. denied, 323 U.S. 726, 65 S.Ct. 60 (1944) (resale price maintenance of patented good); Compton v. Metal Prod., 453 F.2d 38 (4th Cir.1971), cert. denied, 406 U.S. 968, 92 S.Ct. 2414 (1972) (noncompetition covenants covering competing goods). See also General Talking Pictures Corp. v. Western Elec. Co., 304 U.S. 175, 58 S.Ct. 849 (1938), which found misuse in field-of-use restrictions, which limit the purpose for which a patent may be used, if they are imposed after the first sale.

12. 15 U.S.C.A. § 14.

fenses, many courts effectively assess both of these requirements.[13] By contrast, ties have often been found to be patent misuse even though neither requirement was shown.

In *Motion Picture Patents* the court invalidated a license restriction printed on a motion picture projector that only movies leased from the patent owner could be shown with the projector. The patentee had brought an infringement action against film distributors that violated the restriction by supplying films not leased by the patentee itself. In invalidating this restriction, the Court did not rely on the antitrust laws, but rather a general patent policy against using tying requirements such as this one to extend the scope of the patent monopoly.[14]

Likewise, in *Morton Salt* the patent holder had tied the lease of its patented salt injecting machines to the purchase of unpatented salt tablets.[15] The Court held that this tying arrangement constituted misuse of the patent and refused to enforce the patent against an admitted infringer. In the process, the Court held that it was "unnecessary to decide whether [the patent owner] has violated the Clayton Act," because enforcement of the tying arrangement under these circumstances was "contrary to public policy."[16] This holding suggested that the patent misuse defense permitted the alleged infringer to raise "antitrust-like" defenses and prevail even though the challenged practice was not literally an antitrust violation.[17]

The high point of this reasoning was the Supreme Court's two decisions in *Mercoid*, where the Court held that a patentee could not prevent another firm from making an unpatented switch used in a patented combination, even if the only use of such a switch would be to infringe the patentee's patent.[18] The Court analogized this to "tying" of the unpatented switch to the patented combination, but it made no mention of the defendant's market power or of any lessening of competition in the tied product market—both requirements under the antitrust law of tying arrangements generally. Nevertheless, *Mercoid II* suggested that such "tying" in the patent context could constitute an antitrust violation and perhaps even yield treble damages. Forty years later *Mercoid*'s basic holding was overruled by *Dawson Chemical*, which permitted a patentee to tie "nonstaple" goods whose only use by outsiders would be to infringe the patent.[19]

Dawson did not undermine the basic proposition that patent misuse could be found even though there was no antitrust violation. Nonetheless, a few lower courts have held that the patent misuse defense should be defined by antitrust principles. That is, if the alleged infringer is arguing that the patent holder's enforcement policy or licensing agreement is anticompetitive, that defense will prevail only if the policy or licensing agreement violates the Sherman or Clayton Acts. In *Windsurfing* the court held that the misuse defense must either (a) identify a practice by the patent owner that is illegal *per se* or else must show "that the overall effect of the [patent licensing agreement] tends to restrain competition unlawfully in an appropriately defined relevant market."[20] The Seventh Circuit, which first articulated the requirement, observed that "[o]ne still finds plenty of statements in judi-

13. See §§ 10.3–10.5.

14. "[T]o enforce [this monopoly] would be to create a monopoly in the manufacture and use of moving picture films, wholly outside of the patent in suit and of the patent law as we have interpreted it." Id. at 518. For an extensive discussion of the case and its economic background, see 9 Antitrust Law ¶ 1701b (1991).

15. Morton Salt v. Suppiger, note 9.

16. Id. at 494, 62 S.Ct. at 406.

17. Accord Leitch Mfg. Co. v. Barber Co., 302 U.S. 458, 463, 58 S.Ct. 288, 291 (1938) ("every use of a patent as a means of obtaining a limited monopoly of unpatented material is prohibited.").

18. Mercoid Corp. v. Mid–Continent Inv. Co., 320 U.S. 661, 64 S.Ct. 268 (1944), rehearing denied, 321 U.S. 802, 64 S.Ct. 525 (1944) (*Mercoid I*); Mercoid Corp. v. Minneapolis–Honeywell Regulator Co., 320 U.S. 680, 64 S.Ct. 278 (1944) (*Mercoid II*). The patented combination was for a heating system, including a stoker to supply fuel. The unpatented switch regulated the stoker.

19. Dawson Chemical Co. v. Rohm & Haas, 448 U.S. 176, 213, 100 S.Ct. 2601, 2622 (1980), rehearing denied, 448 U.S. 917, 101 S.Ct. 40 (1980) interpreting 35 U.S.C.A. § 271(c), (d), which had been amended in the interim.

20. Windsurfing International, Inc. v. AMF, Inc., 782 F.2d 995 (Fed.Cir.), cert. denied, 477 U.S. 905, 106 S.Ct. 3275 (1986).

cial opinions that less evidence of anticompetitive effect is required in a misuse case than in an antitrust case." But the court could find no case where broader standards were in fact applied.[21] The court then noted that the most likely reason a patent holder would tie unpatented products is to engage in price discrimination. But nothing in patent or antitrust policy forbad price discrimination as such.[22] Other recent decisions continue to find patent "misuse" even when there is no antitrust violation.[23]

Legislation passed in 1988 addresses, but does not resolve, the question whether a patent can be "misused" when there is no antitrust violation. The Patent Misuse Reform Act[24] provides that a claim of patent infringement cannot be resisted simply because the patentee tied patented and unpatented goods unless the patent owner has market power "in the relevant market for the patent or patented product on which the license or sale is conditioned." This provision does not require that patent misuse and unlawful tying be identical—but it does add to the patent misuse doctrine the economically reasonable requirement applied in the law of tying arrangements—namely, market power in the market for the tying product.[25]

As historically stated in *Morton Salt*, the patent misuse doctrine seems precisely wrong. The clear implication was that patents were a kind of "suspect class," and that arrangements involving patents were to be treated with greater hostility than would be applied to similar practices not involving patents. In fact, the opposite is generally true. Patent licensing is most generally efficient and should be encouraged. Concerns that the patent holder could "leverage" additional monopoly profits by combining its rights under the patent with contract requirements governing unpatented goods are either fanciful or greatly exaggerated.[26]

In all events, claims of anticompetitive patent misuse are best tested by the antitrust laws. The existing regime implies that there are two standards for identifying "anticompetitive" acts, one embodied in the antitrust laws and another (tacitly) embodied in the Patent Act. But such a distinction makes no sense, particularly when Congress has never articulated it. Unless legislation tells us otherwise, we identify practices as anticompetitive by applying antitrust principles.

§ 5.5c. *Patent Licensing*

The statutory patent scheme contemplates that patentees will license to others the right to manufacture or use a patented product or process. Such agreements are ubiquitous in American industry, and one of the greatest incentives toward research and development is the profit one can earn by licensing the result-

21. USM Corp. v. SPS Technologies, Inc., 694 F.2d 505, 511–512 (7th Cir.1982), cert. denied, 462 U.S. 1107, 103 S.Ct. 2455 (1983).

22. Id. at 511.

23. For example, Senza–Gel Corp. v. Seiffhart, 803 F.2d 661 (Fed.Cir.1986). See also Transitron Electronic Corp. v. Hughes Aircraft Co., 487 F.Supp. 885, 892–893 (D.Mass.1980), affirmed, 649 F.2d 871 (1st Cir.1981) (stating that less evidence of an "anticompetitive effect" is required to show patent misuse than to show an antitrust violation). Compare Practice Management Information Corp. v. AMA, 121 F.3d 516 (9th Cir.), cert. denied, ___ U.S. ___, 118 S.Ct. 339 (1997) (licensing copyrighted coding system on licensee's promise not to use a competing coding system constituted copyright misuse, whether or not it was an antitrust violation); Lasercomb Am., Inc. v. Reynolds, 911 F.2d 970 (4th Cir.1990) (copyright case; effectiveness of copyright misuse defense does not require a showing of antitrust violation). See 10 Antitrust Law ¶ 1781 (1996).

24. 35 U.S.C.A. § 271(d):

(d) No patent owner otherwise entitled to relief for infringement or contributory infringement of a patent shall be denied relief or deemed guilty of misuse or illegal extension of the patent right by reason of his having done one or more of the following: ... (3) sought to enforce his patent rights against infringement or contributory infringement; (4) refused to license or use any rights to the patent; or (5) conditioned the license of any rights to the patent or the sale of the patented product on the acquisition of a license to rights in another patent or purchase of a separate product, unless, in view of the circumstances, the patent owner has market power in the relevant market for the patent or patented product on which the license or sale is conditioned.

. . .

25. See § 10.3.

26. On the "leverage" theory, see §§ 7.9, 10.6a, 13.3b. In the patent context, see W. Baxter, Legal Restrictions on Exploitation of the Patent Monopoly: an Economic Analysis, 76 Yale L.J. 267 (1966).

ing patents to other firms. Historically, the government was quite hostile toward a variety of patent licensing practices.[27] Today most of these practices are treated under the rule of reason and are legal most of the time. The following list and discussion of patent licensing practices is not exhaustive, but it covers the most significant ones and the relevant antitrust rules.

§ 5.5c1. Price Fixing; Output Restrictions; Royalty Rates; Exclusivity

In *General Electric* the Supreme Court held that a firm could license technology to a competitor with the provision that the product manufactured by the licensee be sold at a price stipulated by the licensor.[28] The Court reasoned that (1) General Electric could have kept the right to manufacture its lightbulbs to itself, in which case it would have charged the monopoly price. As a result, (2) it should be able to license to others on the condition that they charge its monopoly price as well, or else the right created under the patent monopoly would not be recognized. The Court might also have noted that General Electric could have reached the same result, at least approximately, by setting a license fee equal to the monopoly markup. That is, if the patented lamps cost $1.00 to make but General Electric maximized its profits at a price of $1.50, it could have charged Westinghouse, the licensee, a 50¢ per lamp license fee.[29] The courts have also generally found that the licensor of a patent may limit the quantity of the patented product produced by the licensee.[30]

General Electric remains good law,[31] but is subject to some exceptions. First, the price fixing provision may not be extended to unpatented goods or processes.[32] Second, the *General Electric* doctrine extends to the price initially charged by the licensee, but not to the resale price: that is, the licensor may not engage in a form of resale price maintenance in which it regulates the price charged at resale by those who purchase from the licensee.[33] This rule flows not from any articulated patent policy, but simply from the fact that resale price maintenance is illegal *per se*.[34] Third, if patents are "cross-licensed"—that is, re-licensed from the original licensee to a second, or sub-licensee, the latter licensing agreement may not fix the price.[35] Finally, several decisions have suggested that while *GE* permits a single patentee to fix the price with a single licensee, it does not apply to agreements involving multiple patentees or a patentee and several licensees.[36]

27. The forbidden practices were popularly referred to as the "Nine No Nos." They included:

1. Tying the purchase of unpatented materials as a condition of the license;
2. Grantbacks.
3. Restricting the right of the purchaser of the product in the resale of the product.
4. Restricting the licensee's ability to deal in products outside the scope of the patent.
5. A licensor's agreement not to grant further licenses.
6. Mandatory package licenses.
7. Royalty provisions not reasonably related to the licensee's sales.
8. Restrictions on a licensee's use of a product made by a patented process.
9. Minimum resale price provisions for the licensed products.

28. United States v. General Electric Co., 272 U.S. 476, 47 S.Ct. 192 (1926). The doctrine originated in E. Bement & Sons v. National Harrow Co., 186 U.S. 70, 22 S.Ct. 747 (1902); see 12 Antitrust Law ¶ 2041 (1999).

29. For criticism of the decision, see Kaplow, note 1 at 1846, 1855–1862.

30. United States v. Parker–Rust–Proof Co., 61 F.Supp. 805 (E.D.Mich.1945). The licensor may also limit the quantity of an unpatented product that is produced by a patented process. Ethyl Corp. v. Hercules Powder Co., 232 F.Supp. 453, 460 (D.Del.1963).

31. In 1965 a divided Supreme Court declined to overrule it. United States v. Huck Manufacturing Co., 382 U.S. 197, 86 S.Ct. 385 (1965).

32. Cummer–Graham Co. v. Straight Side Basket Corp., 142 F.2d 646, 647 (5th Cir.1944), cert. denied, 323 U.S. 726, 65 S.Ct. 60 (1944).

33. United States v. Univis Lens Co., 316 U.S. 241, 243–251, 62 S.Ct. 1088, 1090–1094 (1942); Ethyl Gasoline Corp. v. United States, 309 U.S. 436, 446–457, 60 S.Ct. 618, 620–626 (1940).

34. On resale price maintenance, see § 11.5. Maximum RPM is governed by the rule of reason; presumably, a maximum price agreement in a patent license would receive the same treatment. See § 11.5c.

35. United States v. Line Material Co., 333 U.S. 287, 293–315, 68 S.Ct. 550, 553–564 (1948).

36. *Line Material*, id. at 314–315. See also United States v. United States Gypsum Co., 333 U.S. 364, 68 S.Ct. 525 (1948) (no immunity for licensing arrangement fixing

The government has never concealed its hostility for the *GE* rule and has attempted repeatedly to have it overruled.[37] Its 1995 Antitrust Guidelines never discuss the rule and take the position that horizontal price restraints with efficiency prospects will be evaluated under the rule of reason, while the per se rule will be applied to naked restraints.[38] That approach is clearly preferable to the *GE* rule, which is not an antitrust rule of reason at all but rather a blanket immunity for price-fixing that falls within its realm.

The royalty rate charged by the patent owner may generally be whatever the market will bear.[39] Royalties are generally based on the number of units manufactured under the licensee, or on the revenues obtained from sale of goods manufactured under the license. Courts have found antitrust violations only where they have perceived the patent holder to be using royalties as a device for leveraging additional profits from unlicensed products. For example, in *Zenith Radio* the Supreme Court held that the patent owner could not require the payment of royalties on goods that were not manufactured under the patent as well as goods that were.[40] Its argument was yet another version of the leverage theory

> [J]ust as the patent's leverage may not be used to extract from the licensee a commitment to purchase, use, or sell other products according to the desires of the patentee, neither can that leverage be used to garner as royalties a percentage share of the licensee's receipts from sales of other products; in either case, the patentee seeks to extend the monopoly of his patent to derive a benefit not attributable to use of the patent's teachings.

However, if the "convenience of the parties rather than patent power"[41] dictates that royalties be based on the output of an unpatented good, the agreement is legal. For example, suppose the licensee has licensed a patented production process, which it then uses to make an unpatented good more efficiently. The royalty could lawfully be based on the number of units of the unpatented good that are produced under the patented process.[42] Likewise, the licensee may manufacture some units that use the patented process and others that do not, but it might be difficult for the licensor to determine after the fact the number of units that employ the patent. In order to solve this problem the parties might simply agree that the licensee will pay a royalty on all units, whether or not they use the patent. The licensee is then free to determine the extent to which it wishes to use the patent in each unit. The Supreme Court approved such a contract in the *Automatic Radio* case.[43] However, a 1995 consent decree forbad Microsoft from using "per processor" licensing of its Windows software—or an arrangement under which computer manufacturer's paid Microsoft a royalty for each computer they manufactured, whether or not that computer actually used Windows.[44] Under the arrangement, if a com-

prices industry wide; *GE* "gives no support for a patentee, acting in concert with all members of an industry, to issue substantially identical licenses to all members of the industry under the terms of which the industry is completely regimented"); accord United States v. New Wrinkle, 342 U.S. 371, 72 S.Ct. 350 (1952). The most restrictive reading of *GE* is Newburgh Moire Co. v. Superior Moire Co., 237 F.2d 283, 291–294 (3d Cir.1956), which limits that decision to an agreement between a single patentee and a single licensee. See 12 Antitrust Law ¶ 2041b (1999).

37. For a list of the decisions, see 12 Antitrust Law ¶ 2041d (1999).

38. See Antitrust Guidelines for the Licensing of Intellectual Property, note 7, at § 5.1.

39. Brulotte v. Thys Co., 379 U.S. 29, 33, 85 S.Ct. 176, 179 (1964). See generally H. See & F. Caprio, The Trouble with *Brulotte* : the Patent Royalty Term and Patent Monopoly Extension, 1990 Utah L. Rev. 813.

40. Zenith Radio Corp. v. Hazeltine Research, Inc., 395 U.S. 100, 89 S.Ct. 1562 (1969). Quote at 135. See also *United States Gypsum*, note 35, 333 U.S. at 385–386, 68 S.Ct. at 537–538 (royalty provision requiring payment of royalties for both patented and unpatented product unlawful).

41. *Zenith Radio*, 395 U.S. at 138, 89 S.Ct. at 1584.

42. See Western Electric Co. v. Stewart–Warner Corp., 631 F.2d 333, 339 (4th Cir.1980), cert. denied, 450 U.S. 971, 101 S.Ct. 1492 (1981).

43. Automatic Radio Mfg. Co. v. Hazeltine Research Inc., 339 U.S. 827, 70 S.Ct. 894 (1950), rehearing denied, 340 U.S. 846, 71 S.Ct. 13 (1950).

44. United States v. Microsoft Corp., 1995 WL 505998 (D.D.C., Aug. 21, 1995). Other parts of the decree are interpreted in United States v. Microsoft Corp., 980 F.Supp. 537 (D.D.C.1997), rev'd, 147 F.3d 935 (D.C.Cir. 1998).

puter manufacturer wanted to sell a computer with a non-Microsoft operating system two royalty fees would have to be paid, one to the owner of the rival system and another to Microsoft even though the computer contained no Windows software. In this case, detection of computers with Windows operating systems would appear not to be a problem. Anyone who knew very much about computers could readily make that determination.

A few courts have condemned discriminatory royalty rates under a variety of theories.[45] In the *Shrimp Peelers* cases, several lower courts condemned a patent holder for licensing patented shrimp cleaning equipment at different royalty rates in different geographic areas.[46] But it is hard to see how discriminatory royalty rates can be any more anticompetitive than price discrimination by the monopolist generally.[47] Price discrimination of this kind usually results in higher output. The patent monopolist constrained to charge the same royalty rate to all would determine its profit-maximizing price, thus foregoing those potential licensees unwilling to pay that amount. This is particularly likely to be true of intellectual property, where marginal costs are extremely low. Further, nearly all patent licensing provisions with royalties based on quantity produced or revenue yield substantial price discrimination.[48]

Several courts have condemned license agreements that require the licensee to continue to pay royalties after the patent has expired.[49] The given rationale is another variation of the leverage theory used to condemn ties of patented and unpatented products—in this case, that the patent holder is trying to take advantage of its monopoly power in the patented product to leverage additional monopoly profits from post-expiration sales.

Finally, a patent licensing agreement is lawful even if it is exclusive. In an exclusive patent license, the patent holder promises not to license the patent to others. Often the licensor promises not to practice the patent itself as well. Even the latter agreement is no more than a transfer of the right to use a patent from one firm to another, something that does not ordinarily raise competitive concerns. Section two of the Sherman Act may be implicated, however, if a firm has a practice of acquiring exclusive licenses in an area and then not practicing the patents under these licenses.[50] Likewise, competitors may not lawfully agree with each other not to license their patents.[51]

§ 5.5c2. Territorial and Other Restrictions

The Patent Act expressly permits the patentee to grant exclusive rights "to the whole or any specified part of the United States."[52]

45. Licensing agreements containing discriminatory rates do not violate the Robinson–Patman Act, which applies only to "commodities." See Ch. 14.

46. See Peelers Co. v. Wendt, 260 F.Supp. 193 (W.D.Wash.1966); Laitram Corp. v. King Crab, Inc., 244 F.Supp. 9 (D.Alaska), modified, 245 F.Supp. 1019 (D.Alaska 1965).

47. See § 14.3; and see W. Bowman, Patent and Antitrust Law 105–110 (1973).

48. For example, suppose a patent holder licenses the patent to two different licensees at a royalty rate of 2% of revenues from sale of the product, or alternatively, at $1.00 per unit produced. The first licensee produces 1000 units per week while the second produces 100 units per week. The costs of negotiating the license agreements are probably the same for both licensees; in any event, these costs are not a function of the licensees' subsequent output. Further, the cost to the licensor of units produced under the license agreement are zero. As a result, the licensor makes substantially more from the high volume licensee than from the low volume licensee. Indeed, so-called "discriminatory" royalty rates are often designed to offset this price discrimination. For example, the licensor may charge a higher royalty per unit from the licensee who produces only a few units than from the licensee who produces many. See *USM Corp.*, note 21, 694 F.2d at 513 (making similar criticisms).

49. See *Brulotte*, note 39, 379 U.S. at 30–33, 85 S.Ct. at 178–180; Meehan v. PPG Indus., 802 F.2d 881 (7th Cir.1986), cert. denied, 479 U.S. 1091, 107 S.Ct. 1301 (1987); Pitney Bowes v. Mestre, 701 F.2d 1365, 1372 (11th Cir.), cert. denied, 464 U.S. 893, 104 S.Ct. 239 (1983). Both of the latter cases held that if the license agreement covers both patents and trade secrets, and the royalty rate is not reduced when the last patent expires, then the agreement unlawfully requires royalties on expired patents.

50. See § 7.11.

51. Blount Mfg. Co. v. Yale & Towne Mfg. Co., 166 Fed. 555 (C.C.Mass.1909).

52. 35 U.S.C. § 261. See E. Bement & Sons v. National Harrow Co., 186 U.S. 70, 92–93, 22 S.Ct. 747 (1902) (upholding territorial restrictions in license agreement to make agricultural harrows); Brownell v. Ketcham Wire &

Thus a patent holder may legally restrict its licensee's sales to a given territory, even if the patent holder and the licensee are competitors.[53] A naked territorial division agreement between competitors is ordinarily illegal *per se*.[54]

Patent licensing arrangements between competitors are often a form of joint venture in which multiple firms share a technology. The patent owner has every right to manufacture the product itself without licensing to anyone. But it may wish to grant others the right to produce in a given geographic area because barriers to new entry in that area are high, the market already has sufficient basic capacity, or the licensee has goodwill or intellectual property that can be used to advantage. In such cases the effect of the geographically restricted licensing agreement is to *increase* total output under the patent. That is, the patented product will be produced in the new area under the arrangement, while it would probably not be produced there at all, or at least in a smaller amount, if the arrangement were unlawful. By the same reasoning, courts generally uphold patent licensing agreements that restrict sales to specified classes of customers.[55]

An important exception to this rule is that the "licensing agreement" may not be merely a sham to cover naked territorial division. For example, firms cartelizing a market may agree to use a licensing agreement to give effect to a territorial division scheme, with the agreement covering a patent of dubious validity or a patent whose role in the production process is trivial.[56] Palmer v. BRG of Georgia,[57] condemned such an agreement under the *per se* rule even though the territorial division at issue involved a licensing agreement for copyrighted materials.

Also generally legal under the antitrust laws are so-called "field of use" restrictions, under which the patentee restricts the range of products or uses to which a patent license can be applied. The field of use restriction can thus operate as a kind of product division scheme. For example, in *General Talking Pictures* the Court approved an arrangement under which the patent owner used the licensed patent in manufacturing amplifiers for theaters, but authorized a licensee to use the same patent for making radio receivers.[58] The same arguments for the efficiency of territorial restrictions generally apply to field of use restrictions. For example, suppose a manufacturer of airplanes patents a navigation device that is useful in both aircraft and boats. The patent owner does not wish to license another aircraft manufacturer to use the patented device, and the law does not require it to do so. But boats do not compete with aircraft, and the world would be a better place if boats as well as aircraft could take advantage of the new device. The owner of the patent could enter the boat manufacturing market itself, but it could also license existing boat manufacturers, restricting them to making the device only for boats and not for aircraft.[59]

Mfg. Co., 211 F.2d 121, 128 (9th Cir.1954) ("owner of a patent may license another and prescribe territorial limitations.").

53. Ethyl Gasoline Corp. v. United States, 309 U.S. 436, 456, 60 S.Ct. 618, 625 (1940).

54. See § 5.2.

55. See In re Yarn Processing Patent Validity Litig., 541 F.2d 1127, 1135 (5th Cir.1976), cert. denied, 433 U.S. 910, 97 S.Ct. 2976 (1977) (upholding agreement restricting sales to other licensees of patentee).

56. See Timken Roller Bearing Co. v. United States, 341 U.S. 593, 598–599, 71 S.Ct. 971, 975 (1951) (court believed that intellectual property license was simply a device for suppressing competition, notwithstanding common ownership of participants); United States v. Crown Zellerbach Corp., 141 F.Supp. 118, 126 (N.D.Ill.1956).

57. 498 U.S. 46, 111 S.Ct. 401 (1990), on remand, 928 F.2d 1097 (11th Cir.1991).

58. General Talking Pictures Corp. v. Western Electric Co., 304 U.S. 175, 58 S.Ct. 849, on rehearing, 305 U.S. 124, 59 S.Ct. 116 (1938). Accord Benger Laboratories v. R.K. Laros Co., 209 F.Supp. 639 (E.D.Pa.1962), affirmed per curiam, 317 F.2d 455 (3d Cir.), cert. denied, 375 U.S. 833, 84 S.Ct. 69 (1963). If a field of use restriction conditions the patent license on limitations on the use of *un*patented products, the restriction may be illegal. See Robintech, Inc. v. Chemidus Wavin, Ltd., 628 F.2d 142, 146–149 (D.C.Cir.1980).

59. See *Benger Lab. v. R.K. Laros Co.*, 209 F.Supp. 639 (E.D.Pa.1962), aff'd per curiam, 317 F.2d 455 (3d Cir.), cert. denied, 375 U.S. 833, 84 S.Ct. 69 (1963) (approving arrangement in which one licensee could manufacture patented drug for vetinary use and another for human use). The government's Antitrust Guidelines for the Licensing of Intellectual Property, note 7, § 2.3 & Example 1 (1995) recognize the procompetitive potential of field of use restrictions.

§ 5.5c3. Package Licenses

A package license covers more than one patent. Package licenses are ubiquitous and reduce transaction costs substantially if a single process is covered by many patents, each of which covers a small part of the process. For example, the old fashioned stapler sitting on the author's desk—hardly a piece of high technology—is covered by seven listed patents. Were the owner of these patents to license another firm to manufacture the stapler, it would likely draft a single licensing agreement covering all. Package licensing of patents reduces the transaction costs of individual negotiations much like blanket licensing of numerous copyrights reduced transaction costs in the *Broadcast Music* case.[60]

Package licensing is generally legal,[61] although it is sometimes thought to be anticompetitive when a patent holder with market power in one patent conditions its license on the licensee's acceptance of a package of patents.[62] In this case the underlying concerns of tying law as well as patent misuse are implicated. The 1988 Patent Misuse Reform Act discussed previously covers package licensing as well as tying, approving it unless the patentee has market power in the market for the desired patent.[63] However, the Copyright Act contains no such provision, and one recent decision has condemned "block-booking"—a form of package licensing—of television shows.[64] The court reasoned that by licensing shows in blocks the defendant licensor was foreclosing rival program producers from access to the licensee station's time slots. However, the court appears to have erred on the foreclosure issue; tying nearly always forecloses rivals from the particular buyer upon whom a tying arrangement is imposed. But the relevant foreclosure issue is whether the *market* is foreclosed. For example, if the market contained ten television stations, block-booking that entirely filled the programming slots of one station would nevertheless leave the other nine to receive the programming of rivals.[65]

§ 5.5c4. Patent Pools

A patent pool occurs when a group of firms license their individually held patents to one another, or sometimes exchange licenses. The metaphor of the pool is taken from the oil industry, where multiple surface owners might have an interest in the same subterranean pool of oil. They could then profit and minimize conflict by drilling a single well and sharing the operating expenses and revenues.

In general, patent pools are treated under the rule of reason, and most are legal.[66] In *Zenith Radio*, however, the Supreme Court approved a lower court finding that an *exclusive* patent pool was illegal *per se*.[67] The court interpreted the agreement at issue as one among competitors that they would not license their patents to others. Such an agreement could be an effective collusion facilitator, in that it could permit the firms to fix prices while deterring new entry.[68] The Intellectual Property Guidelines note that pools:

> may provide procompetitive benefits by integrating complementary technologies, reducing transaction costs, clearing blocking

60. Broadcast Music v. CBS, 441 U.S. 1, 99 S.Ct. 1551 (1979). See § 5.2c.

61. Automatic Radio Manufacturing Co. v. Hazeltine Research, 339 U.S. 827, 70 S.Ct. 894 (1950).

62. Hazeltine Research v. Zenith Radio, note 40, 388 F.2d at 33–35. The patents at issue covered devices for color televisions. See also Rocform Corp. v. Acitelli–Standard Concrete Wall, 367 F.2d 678 (6th Cir.1966) (finding patent misuse where patentee used a highly desired patent that was about to expire to leverage a package license containing many longer lived patents).

63. The Act makes it lawful to "condition * * * the license of any rights to the patent * * * on the acquisition of a license to rights in another patent * * * unless * * * the patent owner has market power in the relevant market for the patent or patented product on which the license or sale is conditioned." 35 U.S.C.A. § 271(d). The government's Antitrust Guidelines for the Licensing of Intellectual Property, note 7, § 5.3, state that the agencies will evaluate package licensing under the same criteria as are applied to tying arrangements.

64. *MCA Television Limited v. Public Interest Corp.*, 171 F.3d 1265 (11th Cir.1999).

65. See § 10.6b2.

66. For example, Standard Oil Co. v. United States, 283 U.S. 163, 51 S.Ct. 421 (1931).

67. Note 40, 395 U.S. at 113 n. 8, 89 S.Ct. at 1571 n.8.

68. See G. Priest, Cartels and Patent License Arrangements, 20 J.L. & Econ. 309, 376–377 (1977).

> positions, and avoiding costly infringement litigation. By promoting the dissemination of technology, cross-licensing and pooling arrangements are often procompetitive.

However,

> collective price or output restraints in pooling arrangements, such as the joint marketing of pooled intellectual property rights with collective price setting or coordinated output restrictions, may be deemed unlawful if they do not contribute to an efficiency-enhancing integration of economic activity among the participants.

The Guidelines would then apply the per se rule to patent pools involving naked price fixing or market division.[69]

One type of patent pool that is typically approved involves so-called "blocking patents," which are patents that cannot be practiced without infringing one another. As a result, protected use of either patent requires licensing of both. As one court noted, if patents are blocking, then "no third party would want just one license, and each party [licensor] is effectively precluded from licensing its own patent unless the other party agrees to licensing of its patent as well."[70]

§ 5.5c5. Grantbacks

A grantback is an agreement requiring the licensee to license back to the licensor any patented improvements that the licensee makes on the licensed technology.[71] The Supreme Court has addressed grantbacks under the rule of reason, and most are legal.[72] The great majority of grantbacks should be regarded as devices by which firms share the costs and rewards of joint research, and few seem anticompetitive. Competitive concerns are raised, however, when the grantback operates so as to reduce the licensee's incentives to engage in research and development on its own. For example, if the grantback requires the licensee to give the licensor the *exclusive* right to practice the patent on the improvement, the licensee's incentive to improve the process may be greatly reduced or effectively destroyed.[73] The 1988 Patent Misuse Reform Act[74] appears to apply to grantbacks as well as package licensing—that is, they can never be illegal unless the patentee has market power in the market for the primary patent.

The 1995 government Guidelines on intellectual property licensing observe that exclusive grantbacks pack more anticompetitive potential than non-exclusive ones. However, even exclusive grantbacks will be evaluated under a rule of reason analysis that requires that the primary licensor have market power in its market. After that:

> If the Agencies determine that a particular grantback provision is likely to reduce significantly licensees' incentives to invest in improving the licensed technology, the Agencies will consider the extent to which the grantback provision has offsetting procompetitive effects, such as (1) promoting dissemination of licensees' improvements to the licensed technology, (2) increasing the licensors' incentives to disseminate the licensed technology, or (3) otherwise increasing competition and output in a relevant technology or innovation market.... In addition, the Agencies will consider the extent to which grantback provisions in the relevant markets generally increase licensors' incentives to innovate in the first place.[75]

69. Antitrust Guidelines for the Licensing of Intellectual Property, note 7, § 5.5. On patent and other intellectual property pools, see 12 Antitrust Law ¶ 2043 (1999).

70. *Boston Scientific Corp. v. Schneider*, 983 F.Supp. 245, 271 (D.Mass.1997), dism'd by consent, 152 F.3d 947 (Fed.Cir.1998) (alleged patent pool lawful when patents were found to be blocking).

71. See generally 10 Antitrust Law ¶ 1782e (1996).

72. See Transparent–Wrap Machine Corp. v. Stokes & Smith Co., 329 U.S. 637, 67 S.Ct. 610, rehearing denied, 330 U.S. 854, 67 S.Ct. 859 (1947).

73. See T. Lipsky, Current Antitrust Division Views on Patent Licensing Practices, 50 Antitrust L.J. 515, 520 (1981).

74. Quoted above in note 63.

75. Antitrust Guidelines for the Licensing of Intellectual Property, note 7 at § 5.6.

§ 5.5d. Agreements Concerning Intellectual Property Other Than Patents[76]

Economically speaking, the competitive concerns with copyrights, trademarks or other forms of intellectual property are about the same as those applying to patents. Many of the underlying practices are the same. For example, the *Broadcast Music* case discussed in § 5.2c really involved nothing more than package licensing of a product that was copyrighted rather than patented.[77] The important difference that made this particular package license problematic was that the blanket licensing arrangement was the result of an agreement *among competitors* to engage in blanket licensing. If a single actor unilaterally requires package licensing of copyrights—for example, if Willie Nelson licenses all of his performances in a single package on a take-it-or-leave-it basis—competitive concerns are not readily apparent.[78] Nevertheless, certain practices such as the "block booking" of films have been condemned under just such circumstances. For example, in *Paramount Pictures* the Supreme Court condemned a film producer's policy of licensing its films only in blocks.[79]

The Court in *Paramount Pictures* also extended the patent "misuse" doctrine[80] to copyrights. In *Lasercomb*, the Fourth Circuit found copyright misuse in the licensor's insistence that licensee's of its software refrain from developing competing software for ninety-nine years.[81] The court expressly held that the defendant could show anticompetitive copyright misuse without proving that the restraint constituted an antitrust violation in its own right. As a result, *Lasercomb* suggests a broader range for the "copyright misuse" defense than courts are currently recognizing for the "patent misuse" defense.[82] This distinction seems poorly conceived, since a copyright is much more easily created than a patent. As the Supreme Court has noted, nothing more than "some minimal level of creativity" entitles one to a copyright.[83] As a result, the presumption that the copyright holder has market power is substantially weaker than the already weak presumption in the case of patents.[84] Accordingly, the presumption that licensing restrictions can be anticompetitive should be weaker as well.[85]

§ 5.6 Characterization and Evaluation: The Per Se Rule and the Rule of Reason

§ 5.6a. The Supreme Court and the Per Se Rule

Consider the following statements, all from the Supreme Court:

> The true test of legality is whether the restraint imposed is such as merely regulates and perhaps thereby promotes competition or whether it is such as may suppress or even destroy competition. To determine that question the court must ordinarily consider the facts peculiar to the business

76. See generally 12 Antitrust Law ¶ 2041e (1999) (*GE* rule and price-fixing of non-patent intellectual property), ¶ 2043c (pooling), 2044e (horizontal market divisions of non-patent intellectual property).

77. On package licensing of patents, see § 5.5c3.

78. For a suggestion to the contrary, see CBS v. American Society of Composers, Authors & Publishers, 562 F.2d 130, 140–141 & n. 29 (2d Cir.1977), reversed and remanded sub nom. Broadcast Music, Inc. v. CBS, 441 U.S. 1, 99 S.Ct. 1551 (1979).

79. United States v. Paramount Pictures, 334 U.S. 131, 68 S.Ct. 915 (1948). Accord United States v. Loew's, Inc., 371 U.S. 38, 83 S.Ct. 97 (1962). *Loew's* held that block booking was illegal only if the seller had market power, but then held that the copyright in the motion picture created a presumption of market power. Id. at 45. But see American Manufacturers Mutual Ins. Co. v. American Broadcasting–Paramount Theatres, Inc., 270 F.Supp. 619 (S.D.N.Y.1967), reversed on other grounds, 388 F.2d 272 (2d Cir.1967), finding that selling of television advertising only for blocks of channels was legal. On block booking generally, see § 10.6e and the brief discussion of *MCA*, note 64, supra.

80. See § 5.5b.

81. See Lasercomb America, Inc. v. Reynolds, 911 F.2d 970 (4th Cir.1990). See also Practice Management Information Corp. v. AMA, 121 F.3d 516 (9th Cir.), cert. denied, ___ U.S. ___, 118 S.Ct. 339 (1997) (similar).

82. See § 5.5b.

83. Feist Pub., Inc. v. Rural Tel. Serv. Co., 499 U.S. 340, 357, 111 S.Ct. 1282, 1294 (1991).

84. See § 3.9d. But see *MCA*, note 64, which also indulged the presumption that a copyright confers power.

85. The misuse doctrine has also been applied to trademarks. For example, Phi Delta Theta Fraternity v. J.A. Buchroeder & Co., 251 F.Supp. 968 (W.D.Mo.1966) (applying the doctrine to an agreement among college fraternities, sororities and jewelry manufacturers to manufacture trademarked jewelry).

to which the restraint is applied; its condition before and after the restraint was imposed; the nature of the restraint and its effect, actual or probable.

Justice Brandeis, in Board of Trade of City of Chicago v. United States, 246 U.S. 231, 238, 38 S.Ct. 242, 244 (1918).

Under the Sherman Act a combination formed for the purpose and with the effect of raising, depressing, fixing, pegging, or stabilizing the price of a commodity * * * is illegal *per se.*

Justice Douglas, in United States v. Socony–Vacuum Oil Co., 310 U.S. 150, 223, 60 S.Ct. 811, 844 (1940).

Whether or not we would decide this case the same way under the rule of reason used by the District Court is irrelevant.

Justice Marshall, in United States v. Topco Associates Inc., 405 U.S. 596, 609, 92 S.Ct. 1126, 1134 (1972).

[P]er se rules * * * are * * * directed to the protection of the public welfare; they are complementary to, and in no way inconsistent with, the rule of reason.

Chief Justice Berger, dissenting, in United States v. Topco Associates, 405 U.S. at 621, 92 S.Ct. at 1140.

Contrary to its name, the Rule [of Reason] does not open the field of antitrust inquiry to any argument in favor of a challenged restraint that may fall within the realm of reason. Instead, it focuses directly on the challenged restraint's impact on competitive conditions. * * *

There are * * * two complementary categories of antitrust analysis. In the first category are agreements whose nature and necessary effect are so plainly anticompetitive that no elaborate study of the industry is needed to establish their illegality—they are "illegal per se;" in the second category are agreements whose competitive effect can only be evaluated by analyzing the facts peculiar to the business, the history of the restraint, and the reasons why it was imposed. In either event, the purpose of the analysis is to form a judgment about the competitive significance of the restraint; it is not to decide whether a policy favoring competition is in the public interest, or in the interest of the members of an industry.

J. Stevens, in National Society of Professional Engineers v. United States, 435 U.S. 679, 688–692, 98 S.Ct. 1355, 1363–65 (1978).

[The] *per se* rule is a valid and useful tool of antitrust policy and enforcement. And agreements among competitors to fix prices on their individual goods or services are among those concerted activities that the Court has held to be within the *per se* category. But easy labels do not always supply ready answers. * * *

[The defendants] have joined together into an organization that sets its price for the blanket license it sells. But this is not a question simply of determining whether two or more potential competitors have literally "fixed" a "price." As generally used in the antitrust field, "price fixing" is a shorthand way of describing certain categories of business behavior to which the *per se* rule has been held applicable. [However, when] two partners set the price of their goods or services they are literally "price fixing," but they are not *per se* in violation of the Sherman Act. * * * Thus, it is necessary to characterize the challenged conduct as falling within or without that category of behavior to which we apply the label "*per se* price fixing." That will often, but not always, be a simple matter.

J. White, in Broadcast Music, Inc. v. CBS, Inc., 441 U.S. 1, 8–9, 99 S.Ct. 1551, 1556–57 (1979).

The costs of judging business practices under the rule of reason * * * have been reduced by the recognition of *per se* rules. Once experience with a particular kind of restraint enables the Court to predict with confidence that the rule of reason will condemn it, it has applied a conclusive presumption that the restraint is unreasonable.

J. Stevens, in Arizona v. Maricopa Cty. Med. Society, 457 U.S. 332, 343–44, 102 S.Ct. 2466, 2473 (1982).

The rationale for *per se* rules *in part* is to avoid a burdensome inquiry into actual

> market conditions in situations where the likelihood of anticompetitive conduct is so great as to render unjustified the costs of determining whether the particular case at bar involves anticompetitive conduct. (emphasis added)

J. Stevens, in Jefferson Parish Hospital District No. 2 v. Hyde, 466 U.S. 2, 16 n. 25, 104 S.Ct. 1551, 1560 n. 25 (1984), on remand, 764 F.2d 1139 (5th Cir.1985).

> In its opinion, the Court of Appeals assumed that the antitrust laws permit, but do not require, the condemnation of price fixing and boycotts without proof of market power. The opinion further assumed that the *per se* rule prohibiting such activity "is only a rule of 'administrative convenience and efficiency," not a statutory command. * * * This statement contains two errors. The *per se* rules are, of course, the product of judicial interpretations of the Sherman Act, but the rules nevertheless have the same force and effect as any other statutory commands. Moreover, while the *per se* rule against price fixing and boycotts is indeed justified in part by "administrative convenience," the Court of Appeals erred in describing the prohibition as justified only by such concerns. The *per se* rules also reflect a long-standing judgment that the prohibited practices by their nature have "a substantial potential for impact on competition." [citing *Jefferson Parish*]

J. Stevens, in FTC v. Superior Ct. Trial Lawyers Assn., 493 U.S. 411, 432, 110 S.Ct. 768, 780 (1990).

5.6b. The Exaggerated Distinction Between Rule of Reason and Per Se Treatment

Courts and commentators often say that most practices analyzed as antitrust violations are considered under a "rule of reason," while the *per se* rule applies only to a limited number—perhaps price fixing, horizontal territorial or customer division, naked concerted refusals to deal, resale price maintenance and some tying arrangements.

In fact, all legal analysis is "*per se*" to one degree or another.[1] The *per se* rule says that once we know a certain amount about a practice we can pass judgment on its legality without further inquiry. The difference between a "*per se*" and a "rule of reason" standard lies in how much we need to know before we can make that decision. A rational decision maker will collect information, beginning with that which is most relevant and easiest to gather, until he reaches a point at which the marginal cost of acquiring more exceeds its expected marginal return. In this case the "marginal return" is the increased accuracy of the final decision. If the cost of obtaining certain information is very high, and the chance is small that it will make the final decision more accurate, the rational decision maker will not seek the additional information.[2] For this reason Justice Marshall was wrong in *Topco*, quoted in § 5.6a, when he said it was "irrelevant" whether a *per se* case would come out the same way under the rule of reason. Given some final, accurate decision, O, the *per se* rule rests on a judicial judgment that the court can approximate O with sufficient accuracy once it knows a few specific things. Further, learning more things is likely to be very expensive and unlikely to bring the court substantially closer to O. The *per se* rule manifestly does not rest on a judgment that the two antitrust rules are calculated *ex ante* to yield different decisions.

Even in a so-called rule of reason case, however, the parties will not produce *all* the marginally relevant information. They will produce sufficient information to satisfy some judicially created presumptions—for example,

§ 5.6

1. See R. Posner, The Rule of Reason and the Economic Approach: Reflections on the *Sylvania* Decision, 45 U. Chi.L.Rev. 1, 14–15 (1977); See the debate between professors Easterbrook and Markovits. F. Easterbrook, The Limits of Antitrust, 63 Tex.L.Rev. (1984); R. Markovits, The Limits to Simplifying Antitrust: A Reply to Professor Easterbrook, 63 Tex.L.Rev. (1984).

2. See Justice Stevens' statement in the *Maricopa County* case, § 5.6a. See also W. Landes, Sequential Versus Unitary Trials: an Economic Analysis, 12 J. Legal Stud. 99 (1993); R. Posner, an Economic Approach to Legal Procedure and Judicial Administration, 2 J.Legal Std. 399 (1973); J. Kaplan, Decision theory and the Fact Finding Process, 20 Stan.L.Rev. 1065 (1968).

that a defendant with 90% of a well defined market has monopoly power, or that a merger between the two largest firms in a concentrated market is anticompetitive. In sum, every inquiry is cut off at some point; the label "*per se*" simply refers to a class of situations where we find it appropriate to cut the inquiry off at a relatively early stage. In order to be useful, of course, the label *per se* must also tell the court *how* the inquiry is to be truncated. Even under *per se* rules, some facts are relevant while others are not.

To this end, Justice Brandeis' statement of the rule of reason in *Chicago Board of Trade*, quoted in § 5.6a, has been one of the most damaging in the annals of antitrust. The statement has suggested to many courts that, if the analysis is under the rule of reason, then nearly everything is relevant. We need to know about the history of the business, its condition before the restraint was imposed, its condition after, peculiarities of the business that might make the restraint permissible here but not elsewhere, and so on. Taken individually, each element of Justice Brandeis' summary of the rule of reason is accurate, and may apply in at least some circumstances. The problem with the statement is that it identifies the haystack but not the needle. It never tells us what facts are decisive for determining whether a practice merely "regulates" and thus "promotes" competition, or whether it may "suppress" or even "destroy" competition. Under the rule of reason, relevant facts are those that tend to establish whether a restraint increases or decreases output, or decreases or increases prices. Most other facts are irrelevant.[3]

If one examines two kinds of cases at opposite ends of the spectrum, the distinction between "rule of reason" and "*per se*" analysis is clear enough. Suppose that on the left side of our spectrum we place alleged monopolization involving the innovation policies of a single firm. On the right side we place naked price fixing. In the first case we insist on a well-developed inquiry into the defendant's market power and the competitive effects of its practices. In the second we require little more than proof of the price fixing agreement. We can quite easily conclude that the first practice requires rule of reason analysis while the second is illegal *per se*. The great majority of innovation, even by dominant firms, is competitive; indeed, provable anticompetitive innovation is extremely rare, and should be condemned only in the case of an unambiguously anticompetitive abuse by an unambiguously dominant firm. By contrast, naked price fixing rarely or never has anything to be said in its behalf.

But as soon as we begin to fill in the space between these two practices we see that the gray area is rather large, filling perhaps three-quarters of the space in the middle. Resale price maintenance and tying arrangement are both illegal *per se*, but the basic inquiries are much more complicated, and the tying analysis even requires some proof of market power.[4] By contrast, vertical nonprice restraints are said to involve a rule of reason, but more than 90% of the cases are disposed of quite easily after a quick look at market structure. A difficult "*per se* "tying arrangement case can involve an inquiry that is far more elaborate than an easy rule of reason vertical restraints case.

The *per se* rule, incidentally, is a two-edged sword. Granted that a small number of practices are classified as *per se* illegal under the antitrust laws, a giant host are *per se* legal. For example, a record alleging illegal monopolization but showing that the defendant controls only 10% of its market will probably be dismissed on the pleadings. Even though monopolization is a "rule of reason" offense, once it has been determined that a firm's market share is small, further inquiry into whether the defendant monopolized the market is not likely to yield a different decision.

The *per se* rule is an empirical rule. To be sure, the legal jargon requires a judge to hold certain conduct illegal *per se* as a "matter of law" rather than fact. But the judge arrives at that conclusion only because courts have had sufficient experience with a certain kind of

3. See 11 Antitrust Law ¶ 1912b (1998).

4. On RPM, see § 11.5; on tying, see § 10.3f.

practice that they can comfortably pigeon-hole it into the *per se* box.[5]

Like all empirical rules the *per se* rule is not based on logical necessity but on accumulated observation. Its applications are subject to continual testing, falsification, and modification. Further, when judges attempt to clarify the *per se* rule, the clarifications are subject to the same limitations. In United States v. Socony–Vacuum Oil Co.,[6] the Supreme Court was faced with a public (not surreptitious) agreement among oil and gasoline producers to "allocate" the supply of gasoline. Prices were not fixed, but under the allocation agreement each major oil producer was assigned to independent oil producers who had no marketing outlets. The major producers agreed to buy up the independent producers' output, and in the process each major producer had an opportunity to reduce its own production. As a result, total output in the market may have decreased. Prices did move up somewhat, but that change could have been attributed to factors other than the alleged conspiracy.

Whether these practices fell under the *per se* rule against "price fixing" troubled Justice Douglas only as long as it took him to "clarify" the *per se* rule adopted in earlier, more explicit price fixing cases such as United States v. Trenton Potteries Co.[7] "Any combination which tampers with price structures is engaged in unlawful activity," he concluded, whether or not the practice fit the pre-*Socony* meaning of "price fixing."

But wasn't Justice Douglas wrong? The combination in *Chicago Board of Trade*[8] clearly "tampered" with the price at which wheat could be sold by a Board member outside the regular trading session. The combination at issue sixty years later in *Broadcast Music*[9] "tampered" with the price structure so much that nothing approximating an "unrestrained" market continued to exist. The Supreme Court refused to apply the *per se* rule in either case.

As this development of cases suggests, the most difficult aspect of the jurisprudence of the *per se* rule is determining when it should be followed. Sometimes this is called the problem of "characterization." Once a court has properly characterized a practice as price fixing, it is *per se* illegal. However, determining *when* a practice should be so characterized can be difficult, and may involve a fair amount of sophisticated economic inquiry. In *Chicago Board of Trade* and *Broadcast Music* the Court was willing to consider arguments that agreements among competitors, conceded to "fix" prices, were not "price fixing" and did not warrant *per se* treatment. By contrast, *Socony–Vacuum* and National Society of Professional Engineers v. United States[10] involved arrangements that less obviously "fixed" prices; nevertheless, the Court characterized the arrangements as "price fixing." It then applied the *per se* rule in the first, and a very truncated rule of reason inquiry in the second.

Because *per se* rules are empirical judgments, their fate is to go through a continual evolutionary process. In 1918 the "price fixing agreement" at issue in *Chicago Board of Trade* was sufficiently novel that the Court was forced to distinguish it from earlier cartel cases. Likewise, the blanket licensing agreement in *Broadcast Music* presented the Court with a very Pickwickian sort of price fixing.

So what is the use of a "*per se*" label? As a practical matter, to label something illegal *per se* is simply a shorthand form for expressing one of two different concepts, or perhaps both together. The first concept is that we can determine the legality of a practice without inquiring into the market structure or the market power of those engaged in the practice. The *per se* rule against tying arrangements is

5. On the status of the per se rule as one of law, see § 5.1a.

6. 310 U.S. 150, 60 S.Ct. 811 (1940). See 12 Antitrust Law ¶ 2003e (1999); D.B. Johnsen, Property Rights to Cartel Rents: The *Socony–Vacuum* Story, 34 J. L. & Econ. 177, esp. at 202–203 (1991).

7. 273 U.S. 392, 47 S.Ct. 377 (1927). See 12 Antitrust Law ¶ 2003d.

8. Chicago Board of Trade v. United States, 246 U.S. 231, 38 S.Ct. 242 (1918). See § 5.2c.

9. Broadcast Music, Inc. v. Columbia Broadcasting, 441 U.S. 1, 99 S.Ct. 1551 (1979). See § 5.2c.

10. 435 U.S. 679, 98 S.Ct. 1355 (1978).

clearly an exception to this rule, but that simply reflects the fact that the *per se* label for tie-ins was ill conceived from the beginning.[11] At least two-thirds of the time, a statement that a practice is illegal per se is simply shorthand for the conclusion that we can condemn this practice without defining a relevant market or measuring the defendant's market share.[12]

The second concept, far more difficult to manage, is that the label "illegal *per se*" entails that certain justifications or defenses will not be permitted.[13] But even under the *per se* rule some justifications can be considered. More importantly, the court must consider claimed justifications in determining whether the conduct falls inside or outside the *per se* rule.

Consider the arguments offered by the defendants in these cases. In *Socony* the defendants argued that overproduction of oil had led to a glut on the market which was driving prices so low that producers would go bankrupt but for an agreement among themselves to allocate production. In *Engineers* a professional association of engineers defended a canon that prohibited members from bidding competitively for jobs. The defense was that unrestrained competitive bidding would motivate engineers to cut corners in an effort to produce the lowest bid. As a result they might produce unsafe projects that would injure the public. The Court responded that "the Rule of Reason does not support a defense based on the assumption that competition itself is unreasonable."[14]

The Court's response is ambiguous, because over the years "competition" has been used in antitrust cases to mean several different things.[15] However, Congress passed the antitrust laws in order to give courts a basic presumption that "competition" is the preferred state of affairs in any market. Courts are entitled to presume the contrary only when Congress or another appropriate sovereign has passed a law regulating price or entry into some market. When no such law has been passed, the courts simply are not entitled to listen to a plea that "competition" is not working well in a market and needs a hand from the participants.

Within this paradigm "competition" solves the problem of excess capacity in the same way that nature solves the problem of excess population—by starvation and death. That takes care of the argument in *Socony–Vacuum*. The argument raised by *Engineers* is only a little more difficult: "competition" evidently refers to a state of affairs in which consumers are presumed to know what they want and what they are willing to pay for. The engineer who produces a well-publicized defective product once is not likely to do it twice. Within the competition model that alone should create sufficient incentive not to cut corners unreasonably.

The Court elaborated on this conception of consumer sovereignty in the *Indiana Dentists* case.[16] The dentists had argued that it was in the best interest of patients that they collectively refuse to submit X-rays to Blue Cross, the patients' insurer, so that Blue Cross could make its own decisions about the nature and appropriateness of the dentists' care. The dentists' basic argument was that "X-rays, standing alone, are not adequate bases for diagnosis of dental problems or for the formulation of

11. See § 10.3f.

12. See, e.g., All Care Nursing Service v. High Tech Staffing Services, 135 F.3d 740 (11th Cir.1998), cert. denied, ___ U.S. ___, 119 S.Ct. 1250 (1999) (claim proceeded under per se theory, so relevant market was never alleged or proven; dismissed when court applied rule of reason).

13. See 7 Antitrust Law ¶ 1510 (1986) and 11 id. ¶ 1907. Compare General Leaseways v. National Truck Leasing Assn., 744 F.2d 588, 593 (7th Cir.1984):

> The per se rule would collapse if every claim of economies from restricting competition, however implausible, could be used to move a horizontal agreement not to compete from the per se to the Rule of Reason category. We are told, therefore, to apply the per se rule when "the practice facially appears to be one that would always or almost always tend to restrict competition and decrease output" [quoting *Broadcast Music*]. In other words, if the elimination of competition is apparent on a quick look, without undertaking the kind of searching inquiry that would make the case a Rule of Reason case in fact if not in name, the practice is illegal per se.

14. Id. at 697, 98 S.Ct. at 1368 (1978).

15. See Hovenkamp, Book Review, 33 Hastings L.J. 755, 762 (1982).

16. FTC v. Indiana Federation of Dentists, 476 U.S. 447, 106 S.Ct. 2009 (1986). See § 5.4a2.

an acceptable course of treatment." The Court characterized this argument as "in essence, that an unrestrained market in which consumers are given access to the information they believe to be relevant to their choices will lead them to make unwise and even dangerous choices."[17] The Court rejected the argument as inconsistent with the proposition that consumers are presumed to know their own best interests. By contrast, in its more recent *California Dental* decision the Court seemed to regard consumers of dental services as poorly informed and easily manipulated, thus possibly justifying competitor-enforced restraints on price and quality advertising.[18] One possible difference is that the relevant consumer decision maker in *Indiana Dentists* was an expert insurer seeking to minimize its insureds' costs; by contrast, in *California Dental* the relevant advertising guided the choices of dental patients themselves.

As the Supreme Court suggested in *Engineers*, an agreement among competitors that arguably affects price will not be saved from the *per se* rule by an argument that "competition" is bad for a particular industry. This is talking in circles, however, unless "competition" has a meaning. The Supreme Court seems to be tending in this direction: "competition" is that state of affairs in which output is maximized, price is minimized, and consumers are entitled to make their own choices. Naked agreements among competitors likely to affect price are presumed illegal without further inquiry into the market conditions or the nature of the restraint. The presumption can be defeated and the defendant permitted to offer further evidence under the rule of reason only if it can provide a plausible argument and evidence that the agreement is efficient—that is, not "naked" at all—and the injury to competition minimal.

Alternatively, and much less workable, the defendant may have to show that the output increasing or price reducing consequences of the venture greatly outweigh anticompetitive consequences. This alternative is clearly less attractive for the simple reason that attaching numbers to these consequences is far beyond the court's capability as a general matter. When one expected consequence is zero and the other positive, the court may reach a reasoned decision. But if both consequences are positive, the court is unlikely to be able to assign weights that will permit balancing. We sometime hear the deceptively simple proposition that all the court needs to do is balance efficiency effects against anticompetitive effects and see which way the scale tips. But courts are not capable of measuring either efficiency or power over price with anything approaching scientific accuracy. Most such judicial measurements are simply hunches, based on several presumptions about the nature and effects of certain practices.

This reasoning process explains why the Court was forced to listen to the defendant's answering argument in *BMI*. Blanket licensing surely involved an agreement among competitors that affected price. However the non-exclusive nature of the agreement and the fact that there were thousands of participants made collusion impossible. Further, the defendants produced a plausible argument that the agreement resulted in substantially larger output and lower prices. By contrast, the arrangement in *Engineers* was exclusive; it forbad the engineers from competing on price. Further, their argument that "excessive" price competition would force engineers to cut corners was impermissible, for it was an argument that the public had an interest in higher bid prices. That argument may or may not be sound, but it must be settled by legislation. The defendant will not be permitted to avoid condemnation by showing that low prices or high output are not in the best interest of consumers in the particular case.

Finally, the "*per se*" analysis given in this section applies to most, but not all, of the practices said to be "illegal *per se*" under the antitrust laws. One important exception is the rule against resale price maintenance.[19] Although that rule may once have rested on a

17. Id. at 463, 106 S.Ct. at 2020.

18. California Dental Assn. v. FTC, ___ U.S. ___, 119 S.Ct. 1604 (1999).

19. See § 11.5.

judgment that RPM was virtually always anticompetitive, today it no longer does. The Supreme Court has conceded as much.[20] Today the *per se* rule for RPM rests on the proposition that Congress wishes it that way, and that judicial precedent is too strong to warrant a change without statutory intervention.

The *per se* rule against tying arrangements rests largely on the same footing. For that reason the Supreme Court refused to jettison it in the *Jefferson Parish* case.[21] This is what Justice Stevens apparently meant in the previously quoted statements in *Maricopa* and *Trial Lawyers* when he said that the *per se* rule is driven only "in part" by administrative convenience. In part, it is also a substantive policy choice, driven by legislative judgment, stare decisis, or inertia.

§ 5.6c. Identifying Anticompetitive Conduct: A Tentative Road Map and Some Concluding Illustrations

Characterizing agreements among competitors as competitive or anticompetitive is not easy, and the following guide is not foolproof. Further, even this "road map" leaves some avenues uncharted.

The Road Map is as follows:

1. Does the agreement arguably threaten either to reduce output or raise price in some nontrivial way?[22] If not, it should generally be declared legal. If yes, go to step two.

2. Is the agreement naked or ancillary to some other joint venture or agreement that is itself plausibly efficiency creating or otherwise beneficial to consumers?[23] An agreement is naked if it is formed with the objectively intended purpose or likely effect of increasing price or decreasing output in the short run. As a result, a naked agreement is rational only on the premise that the participants have market power. By contrast, an ancillary agreement reduces cost or improves the product and can be profitable whether or not the firms have any market power. If the agreement is naked, it is illegal,[24] although we may pause briefly for "nearly naked" restraints, as discussed below. If the arrangement is ancillary, continue on.

3. Look at the market power held by the parties to the challenged restraint. How numerous are they? How concentrated is the market? Is there a substantial competitive market outside the venture? Are entry barriers high or low? Is the venture nonexclusive—that is, are participants to the venture free to offer the covered product or service outside the restraints imposed upon the venture? If this quick analysis suggests that the exercise of market power is not plausible, the challenged practice is legal. Proof of actual anticompetitive effects, properly defined, can be used as a substitute for formal market analysis.[25] If the

20. See Business Electronics Corp. v. Sharp Electronics Corp., 485 U.S. 717, 724, 108 S.Ct. 1515, 1519 (1988) ("Although vertical agreements on resale prices have been illegal per se, * * * we have recognized that the scope of per se illegality should be narrow. * * * ").

21. Jefferson Parish Hospital District No. 2 v. Hyde, 466 U.S. 2, 8, 104 S.Ct. 1551, 1556 (1984), on remand, 764 F.2d 1139 (5th Cir.1985) ("It is far too late in the history of our antitrust jurisprudence to question the proposition that certain tying arrangements pose an unacceptable risk of stifling competition and therefore are unreasonable 'per se.' ").

22. In the case of monopsony, or joint ventures among buyers, the query is whether the venture threatens to lower the buying price or reduce the quantity of the input. On monopsony, see § 1.2b.

23. "Efficiency creating" refers to agreements that coordinate production or distribution in order to increase productive efficiency by improving quality or lowering costs; agreements that solve nontrivial free rider problems, including agreements to share intellectual property; market facilitators; and perhaps others. That is, the step 2 inquiry should give broad scope to the *domain* of efficiency-creating agreements.

24. As the Supreme Court has noted, as "a matter of law, the absence of proof of market power does not justify a naked restriction on price or output. * * * " The latter "requires some competitive justification even in the absence of detailed market analysis." FTC v. Indiana Federation of Dentists, 476 U.S. 447, 457, 106 S.Ct. 2009, 2017 (1986).

25. Since market definition and analysis is a surrogate for the plausibility of anticompetitive effects, obvious and actual anticompetitive effects might serve as a substitute. See *Indiana Dentists*, note 16 at 457, holding that "proof of actual detrimental effects, such as a reduction of output can obviate the need for an inquiry into market power, which is but a surrogate for detrimental effects." Quoting 7 *Antitrust Law* ¶ 1511. Detrimental effects include observed decreases in output, an observed increase in price

exercise of market power *is* plausible, go to step four.[26]

4. Is there strong evidence that the challenged practice creates substantial efficiencies by reducing participants' costs or improving product or service quality? If not, the practice is illegal. If yes, go to step 5.

5. Can the same efficiencies be achieved by reasonably available alternatives that have less potential to harm competition? If yes, the practice in its present form is illegal, although the injunctive remedy should be limited to condemning the current form or ordering the alternative. If no less restrictive alternative is available, go to step 6.

6. Balancing. Hopefully, few cases require real balancing; but if a challenged restraint simultaneously produces opportunities for both anticompetitive practices and substantial efficiencies, a court must have a guide one way or the other. The best guide seems to be that if the threat to competition is real, and if the defendants cannot come up with a way of restructuring their venture so that this threat is substantially dissipated, the court's only conclusion must be to condemn the arrangement. At this point, intent and good faith may become relevant, particularly in cases where the defendants have technical expertise and their professional judgment must have a certain amount of deference if their market is to function properly. Nevertheless, any court faced with the prospect of balancing must go back to step 5 and look hard for workable less restrictive alternatives.

The map treats the distinction between the *per se* rule and the rule of reason as soft rather than hard. In order to determine the likely effects of a horizontal agreement or other restraint as efficiently as possible, courts go through a series of steps. Cases that require a small number of steps are the ones we generally call "*per se*." Those that require more steps fall into the rule of reason category. As a purely linguistic convention, the most likely breaking point in the road map is step 3. If the inquiry must proceed to a market analysis, the complexity rises and it becomes appropriate to speak of a "rule of reason." Inquiries that end at step 2 fall into the domain of *per se*. That conclusion is generally consistent with the case law. Subjective intent is generally regarded as irrelevant until one reaches step 6, and we hope that not many cases will.[27]

Critically, the inquiries are stated in a sequence which is logical and typical, but there may be alternative sequences that work equally well and are more cost-effective. The best way to think of this process is as a decision-tree rather than a purely sequential trail.[28] Once a question is answered in a particular way, the answer may either stop the litigation or involve a new set of questions. Further, sometimes the answer to a preceding question will determine that, if the claim is to proceed, affirmative answers are necessary to two or three new questions. If the answer to any one of them is negative, then the litigation stops. In that case the parties have an incentive to provide answers that (1) are most likely to resolve the litigation in their favor; (2) that are least ambiguous (most convincing) and least costly to produce.

This makes staged inquiries particularly conducive to summary judgment motions, or sometimes even motions on the pleadings. For example, if the complaint alleges that surgeons in a town have fixed prices and the answer

coordination, or exclusion from the market of firms that seem to be competitive entrants.

26. On the importance of market power in queries involving joint ventures, see F. Easterbrook, The Limits of Antitrust, 63 Tex. 1, 19–23 (1984).

27. The modes of inquiry are elaborated in 7 Antitrust Law Ch. 15 (rule of reason generally), and 11 id. at ¶¶ 1909–1914 (horizontal restraints).

28. See, e.g., C.F. Beckner III & S.C. Salop, Decision Theory and Antitrust Rules, 67 Antitrust L.J. 41 (1999). See also the series of questions suggested by Justice Breyer in his *California Dental* dissent, note 18, 119 S.Ct. at 1618: "(1) What is the specific restraint at issue? (2) What are its likely anticompetitive effects? (3) Are there offsetting procompetitive justifications? (4) Do the parties have sufficient market power to make a difference?" Significantly, Justice Breyer was querying only whether there was substantial evidence in the record justifying the FTC's decision; as a result the list does not purport to be a complete set of rules for horizontal restraints; for example, it does not discuss less restrictive alternatives.

replies that price fixing is necessary in this market in order to maintain the quality of surgery, then the plaintiff is entitled to an immediate judgment on the merits (although perhaps not the remedy). No discovery is necessary. By contrast, the litigation must be terminated in the defendant's favor any time it becomes clear that an essential element of the plaintiff's case will fail. The defendant need not go through the elements sequentially or even pursue other elements at all. As a result, there are short cuts and detours that the road map does not show. Short cuts occur when a step further down the line seems decisive; so one can skip earlier steps. A detour is needed when the answer to one question is inconclusive. Then the question becomes whether the issue can be resolved by skipping a step. Often the answer is yes. For example, if one is unsure about whether an agreement affects price or output (step 1), a step 3 conclusion that the defendants could not exert market power will settle the issue.[29] A slightly more difficult detour occurs if step 3, market power, is inconclusive, because it is so late in the inquiry. But the existence of an obviously less anticompetitive alternative (step 5) may convince the court to condemn the arrangement in its current form.

Consider the following hypothetical and real situations on the list.

First, suppose the only three grocers in a rural community place a joint advertisement in a newspaper, advertising tomatoes at $1.19 per pound. The nearest grocer not a party to this agreement is 50 miles away. When a grocery customer sues the three stores for price fixing they offer to show that the cost of the newspaper advertisement was $150. By advertising jointly, at a cost of $50 each, the stores were able to save $100 apiece on advertising costs. They claim that these costs were passed along to consumers in the form of lower prices.

On its face the grocers' argument is plausible, and it is an argument that the agreement yields higher output and lower prices. But should a court listen to the grocers' evidence? Probably not. First, the stores obviously agreed about a price before they ran the advertisement. Their agreement affects price; so we go to step 2. In this case the price agreement is ancillary to a joint advertising venture and the defendants have made a plausible claim that it reduces costs, and thus is profitable without regard to any market power they might have. So we go to step 3, where a quick examination of the market shows that the firms appear to control 100% of it. Entry barriers are likely low, but there are good reasons for not making that fact alone decisive, particularly when the advertising involves one product of a multi-product store and single product stores are not feasible. Even if entry into the grocery market is easy, it will not necessarily result from monopoly pricing at retail of tomatoes alone. Further, such cartel agreements can be made and broken on a moment's notice. Entry that is profitable at cartel prices may not be profitable at competitive prices. On step 4, there does in fact seem to be strong evidence that the challenged practice created substantial efficiencies, which showed up in reduced advertising costs.

Step 5 instructs us to consider less restrictive alternatives. Could the grocers advertise tomatoes without agreeing on or posting a price?[30] Could they advertise that tomatoes are at "very low prices," or that they are "1/3

29. For example, suppose the complaint alleged that adjacent Iowa corn farmers agreed jointly to build an irrigation lake that straddled their farms. The arrangement arguably reduces the farmers' output of corn, since the lake is built on tillable land. But immediately upon reading the complaint one would likely know that such an agreement among two out of 7,000,000 farmers could not conceivably have any effect on corn output or prices. The agreement is competitive and the complaint should be dismissed. See, e.g., *Elliott v. United Center*, 126 F.3d 1003 (7th Cir.1997), cert. denied, ___ U.S. ___, 118 S.Ct. 1302 (1998) (granting 12(b)(6) motion to dismiss because peanut vending in an athletic stadium in Chicago could not be a relevant geographic market).

30. See *Broadcast Music*, 441 U.S. at 23, 99 S.Ct. at 1564: "Joint ventures and other cooperative arrangements are * * * not [unlawful] as price fixing schemes, where the agreement on price is necessary to market the product at all." This effectively distinguished the agreement in *NCAA*, where the output restriction was not essential to the marketing of the product. See National Collegiate Athletic Ass'n (NCAA) v. Board of Regents of the Univ. of Oklahoma, 468 U.S. 85, 104 S.Ct. 2948 (1984), on remand, 601 F.Supp. 307 (W.D.Okl.1984), discussed below.

off," without agreeing upon or publishing the base from which the 1/3 deduction was taken? As a general matter, an agreement among firms to fix the terms of a sale is illegal, but some price-affecting agreements are less troublesome than others.

If we can find a less restrictive alternative that satisfies our objection, then the restraint may be condemned, or the defendants ordered to modify the venture so as to take the less restrictive alternative into account. If no workable, unobjectionable alternative can be found, the court probably has no choice but to condemn the arrangement. As should be clear, the inquiry into less restrictive alternatives is necessary only if (a) a substantial anticompetitive threat is found and (b) efficiency justifications are also found. If the threat is lacking, then it does not matter that the defendants might have done what they did in a less restrictive manner.[31] By contrast, if there are no offsetting social benefits to the restraint in the first place, then we need not search for a less restrictive means of achieving whatever the restraint intended.[32]

Conceding that the tomato advertisement lowered each store's costs by $100.00, we might want to say that the relevant question is whether the cost reduction was large enough to offset any price increase that might result from the grocer's exercise of monopoly power. However, courts are poorly equipped to answer such questions. Further, the court will have to make an important policy judgment: what if the defendants actually did set a higher price for tomatoes, but the advertising costs saved them $100 each? As a result the efficiency gain may have outweighed the monopoly deadweight loss, but the entire efficiency gain accrued to the price fixers.

Further, balancing would require information about the stores' marginal costs, the market elasticity of demand for tomatoes, and the ease and rapidity with which additional tomato retailers could supply the market. This inquiry would cost a great deal and the information would be sufficiently unreliable that the court would not likely make a better decision. The risk that the agreement will produce anticompetitive consequences is substantial, and the extent of compensating efficiencies is very difficult to measure.

By contrast, analysis of a case such as *Detroit Auto Dealers* should be easy, notwithstanding the court's efforts to make it difficult.[33] Automobile dealers in Detroit, Michigan, agreed with each other to close their showrooms early rather than leave them open into the evening. The Federal Trade Commission had applied the *per se* rule to the agreement. The Sixth Circuit ended up condemning it as well, but it said the rule of reason was necessary because the agreement did not obviously reduce the number of cars that were sold. But the Sixth Circuit overlooked the fact that automobile dealers do not sell "cars." They sell a package of goods and services of which the car is a part. An agreement to reduce showroom hours was an agreement to reduce the quality of the offered product, just as much as an agreement among automobile manufacturers to use plastic rather than leather for their seatcovers.[34] Since the agreement

31. See, e.g., Buffalo Broadcasting Co. v. American Soc'y of Composers, Authors & Publishers, 744 F.2d 917, 933 (2d Cir.1984), cert. denied, 469 U.S. 1211, 105 S.Ct. 1181 (1985) (once the restraint was found not to have any anticompetitive effects it is not even "amenable to scrutiny" under the Sherman Act, and no inquiry into less restrictive alternatives is necessary); American Motor Inns v. Holiday Inns, 521 F.2d 1230, 1249 (3d Cir.1975) (once market power found to be lacking, no inquiry into less restrictive alternatives was needed). *Accord* Rothery Storage & Van Co. v. Atlas Van Lines, 792 F.2d 210, 227 (D.C.Cir.1986), cert. denied, 479 U.S. 1033, 107 S.Ct. 880 (1987). See 11 Antitrust Law ¶ 1913c (1998).

32. See *Law v. NCAA*, 134 F.3d 1010, 1024 n. 16 (10th Cir.1998), cert. denied, ___ U.S. ___, 119 S.Ct. 65 (1998):

> Because we hold that the NCAA did not establish evidence of sufficient procompetitive benefits, we need not address the question of whether the plaintiffs were able to show that comparable procompetitive benefits could be achieved through viable, less anticompetitive means.

33. In re Detroit Auto Dealers Ass'n, 955 F.2d 457 (6th Cir.), cert. denied, 506 U.S. 973, 113 S.Ct. 461 (1992).

34. By the same token, an agreement among cigarette manufacturers to withhold information about the health effects of smoking is a naked restraint. The buyer of a "cigarette" purchases a package of physical cigarette, a great deal of intellectual property, advertising, and information. See Laborers Local 17 Health & Ben. Fund v. Philip Morris, 7 F.Supp.2d 277, 290 n. 9 (S.D.N.Y.1998), rev'd on other grds., 172 F.3d 223 (2d Cir.1999) (withdrawn), which incorrectly concluded that an agreement to suppress information about health effects was not a trade restraint because it led to greater rather than less output

involved no other efforts by the dealers to integrate their activities, it should have been condemned under Step 2 as a naked cartel. The FTC was correct to apply the *per se* rule.

Evaluation of a case like United States v. Topco Associates, Inc.,[35] falls somewhere between the above two extremes. The joint venture among Topco brand grocers, which included territorial division, flunks step 1 because in the absence of any information about the market the agreement arguably decreases output. It passes step 2, because the Topco stores are involved in considerable integration of their businesses, including joint production of Topco branded goods and joint advertising. Further, the joint venture solved "free rider" problems by ensuring that a Topco grocer's promotion efforts in its own territory accrued entirely to its own store. Step 3 should end the inquiry. The low market shares of the individual members—about 6% each in their respective territories—indicates that there is almost no chance that the defendants can profitably reduce output and charge monopoly prices.

The blanket licensing arrangement at issue in the *Broadcast Music* case is more difficult. Once again, the blanket licensing arrangement flunks step 1, since it clearly affected price or output. The arrangement passes the step 2 inquiry, but it then (at first glance) produces ambiguous results at the step 3 (market power) inquiry. The venture covers a large share of the relevant market and as a practical matter it is very difficult for an artist to market her work outside the venture. At the same time, however, the venture includes thousands of artists and it is non-exclusive: any artist is free to sell her work outside the venture. A careful examination of the venture in its market setting should convince a court that there is no reasonable way the blanket licensing agreement is going to lead to a marketwide output reduction. When thousands of cartel members are given absolutely unrestrained freedom to make unlimited non-cartel sales, the cartel is virtually guaranteeing that its prices can never be higher than they would have been in a market in which the cartel did not exist. In sum, in this case there was no reasonable prospect that the venture could be a socially harmful exercise of market power, notwithstanding its high market share.

If that analysis leaves some discomfort, the step 4 inquiry should settle the matter. The transactional efficiencies achieved by blanket licensing were truly extraordinary: many radio stations would have been unable to function if they had to purchase all their performance rights one at a time.[36] Further, this efficiency was present and manifest, not merely plausible. Even the plaintiff did not want to abolish blanket licensing; it merely wanted the defendants to subdivide the blanket licenses into categories.

In Arizona v. Maricopa County Medical Society,[37] the Supreme Court applied the *per se* rule to an agreement among physicians to set the *maximum* fee they would charge for services. The 1750 doctors involved represented about 70% of the medical practitioners in Maricopa County. If Maricopa County was a relevant geographic market the participants probably had some market power.

The maximum fee agreement in *Maricopa* was ostensibly designed to contain medical costs. The third party health insurance programs that most Americans use to finance health coverage yields little face-to-face accountability for prices. The doctor's fee, or most of it, is paid directly by the health insurer. The fee shows up, of course, in health insurance premiums—but these are either paid by the patient at a different time or paid substantially by the patient's employer. The lack of accountability in the system contributes to rapidly increasing health care costs.

of cigarettes. That might be true, for the same reason that an agreement among automobile manufacturers not to install antilock brakes would result in more car sales by keeping prices lower. But that is not the point; rather, it is that consumers are entitled to the mixture of product + information + other collateral benefits that a competitive market would produce.

35. 405 U.S. 596, 92 S.Ct. 1126 (1972). See § 5.2b.

36. See § 5.2c.

37. 457 U.S. 332, 102 S.Ct. 2466 (1982).

Under the Maricopa Plan, a group of doctors agreed not to charge more than a certain price for specified services. Insurance companies in return agreed to pay the full cost of these services if they were provided by a participating doctor.[38] The list of participating doctors was made available to consumers. As a result, purchasers of medical services had information readily available about the price of medical services and an incentive—total coverage—to seek out a doctor who agreed to be bound by the maximum fees. If this argument were sound, the result of the Plan was lower consumer prices.[39] On the other side of the scale was the argument that "maximum" price fixing is really nothing more than disguised minimum price fixing, since most participating doctors charged the full maximum price.

No court could balance the savings from reduced consumer information costs against the monopoly loss that might have accrued from doctor price fixing. However, several aspects of the case suggest that the court was wrong to apply the *per se* rule. For example, if the "maximum" price fixing agreement was really a disguised minimum price fixing agreement why did the insurance companies agree to participate? The doctors and the health insurers stand in a *vertical* relationship. As a general rule an insurer is injured by a price increase that increases the amount of its insured risk. Just as automobile insurance companies are better off in a world of safe drivers and cheap auto body repair shops, health insurers are better off in a world of healthy people and inexpensive doctors.[40]

Because it applied the *per se* rule the Court failed to analyze some additional evidence mentioned in its opinion. For example, it noted that 85%–95% of all physicians in Maricopa County charged rates "at or above" those stipulated in the defendants' program. Since the program involved about 70% of the physicians in the county, this suggests that at least half and perhaps all of the nonparticipating physicians were charging as much as or more than the participants. It would have been worthwhile for a court to compare the rates charged by the participants with those charged by nonparticipants. If the participants had been engaged in ordinary price fixing and charging their profit-maximizing prices, equally efficient nonparticipating physicians would have maximized their own profits by billing at or slightly less than the cartel price: they could then have obtained all the customers they wanted. However, if all nonparticipating physicians charged *more* than the fees charged by the participating physicians, then either the cartel had miscalculated its profit-maximizing prices, or—more likely—the nonparticipating doctors were the true monopolists, taking advantage of high consumer search costs in health care. Evidence that nonparticipating doctors charged more than participants would have suggested that the agreement was doing exactly what the defendants argued it was doing: reducing health care prices.

Finally, as Justice Powell noted in his dissent, doctors were free to join or leave the Plan at will, and participating doctors were free to deal with patients outside the Plan on any basis they pleased. These facts are quite inconsistent with the economics of cartelization: no cartel could restrict its output and raise price if it permitted its members freely to come and go, or to make unlimited "noncartel" sales, especially if the cartel's members numbered in the thousands.

Under the road map given above, the *Maricopa* joint venture at least arguably threatens to raise prices or reduce output, if we accept the claim that maximum price fixing can be disguised minimum price fixing. It flunks step

38. Under most private insurance plans the patient must produce some form of "copayment" at the time the services are delivered. The copayment may reflect the difference between the doctor's actual fee and maximum policy coverage, or it may simply be a percentage of the total fee, or a combination of the two.

39. See F. Easterbrook, Maximum Price Fixing, 48 U.Chi.L.Rev. 886 (1981); K.B. Leffler, Arizona v. Maricopa County Medical Society: Maximum–Price Agreements in Markets with Insured Buyers, 2 Sup.Ct.Econ.Rev. 187 (1984).

40. This is simply a variation of the vertical integration argument presented in § 9.2. In *Maricopa* two of the employers were self-insurers: the State of Arizona, and Motorola Corp. A self-insurer certainly stands to gain from an action that reduces the amount of expected claims against it.

1. Step 2 required much more analysis than the Supreme Court was willing to give. The *Maricopa* agreement was a joint venture producing transactional efficiencies—in this instance, reducing customer search costs for a variety of medical services. Effectively, the *Maricopa* health consumer was given a list that said "The doctors on the enclosed list have agreed to charge no more than the stated prices for the enclosed list of services." At that point the customer could still make a choice between buying inside the venture or buying outside. The Supreme Court was wrong to end the inquiry at step 1.

An equally difficult decision is *NCAA*, where the Supreme Court condemned an agreement among NCAA football colleges to restrict the number of times that each team's football games could be televised.[41] The Court of Appeals had held that the NCAA television restriction was illegal *per se* as an output-restricting agreement among competitors in the market for televised college football. The Court of Appeals rejected the NCAA's defense that the arrangement actually promoted competition in a different market—the market for live attendance at football games. That argument was well rejected. *All* output restrictions in one market tend to increase the demand in markets for substitute products. For example, price fixing in the beef industry will drive up the price of pork and lamb.

The Supreme Court affirmed the lower court's judgment, but held that the conduct at issue must be evaluated under the rule of reason. The NCAA is a special "network" industry in which "horizontal restraints on competition are essential if the product [NCAA football games] is to be available at all." As the Court noted, NCAA football teams simply cannot produce their product without agreeing with each other about certain things, such as a playing schedule, the size and shape of the football field and the rules of the game, and on rules determining player eligibility.

Further, some of these agreements clearly have an effect on price or "output." For example, the teams must agree with one another whether there should be ten games or twenty games in a football season. They might also have to agree about how gate receipts are to be divided among home and away teams. Other agreements, such as one concerning the size of the playing field, may have little or no effect on output. The Supreme Court effectively held that since the delivery of the product at issue *forced* the NCAA members to agree about certain things, and since some of these things necessarily affected output, all agreements among the teams should be subject to the rule of reason.[42]

The Court then went on to condemn the television restriction under the rule of reason. Faced with substantial evidence that the agreement made televised NCAA football less available, that some schools wanted to televise more football games than the rule permitted, and that no plausible procompetitive justifications for the rule had been offered, the rule seemed anticompetitive.

Using our road map, the NCAA agreement restricting televised games flunks step 1. While the NCAA joint venture generally is efficient, thus passing step 2, the agreement limiting television output seems to be naked: its only purpose was to reduce the output of televised games. The inquiry could properly have ended there, once the defendant failed to assert any procompetitive benefit from the output restriction.[43]

Step 3, the market power inquiry, was difficult and the resolution still indeterminate. The Court's quick definition of the market as college football games may have been too narrow. But in this case the uncertainties about the market can be set aside if we continue down the road map. At first glance, step 4 may not seem dispositive either. On the one hand, the venture overall seems to create substantial

41. Note 30.

42. *NCAA*, 468 U.S. at 100, 104 S.Ct. at 2959. But doesn't this go too far? Suppose another provision of the venture agreement fixed the price of sweatshirts bearing team logos. Is a full rule of reason inquiry necessary? For my criticism of the NCAA conclusion, see 11 Antitrust Law ¶ 1910d (1998).

43. See, e.g., *Law v. NCAA*, note 32, 134 F.3d 1010, 1020 (dispensing with power requirement in challenge to NCAA fix of maximum coaching salaries).

efficiencies. On the other, the court is not in a very good position to quantify these efficiencies and balance them against the costs of any reduction in television output. But more decisively, the plaintiff's challenge was not to the overall venture, but only to the restriction on televised games; that restriction was not shown to produce any acceptable consumer benefits. Notwithstanding all the good things to be said about the NCAA venture overall, the restriction on the number of games was simply not essential to the economic success of the basic venture itself. NCAA football will not work without an agreement regulating the number of games that the teams will play, but it probably does not require an agreement fixing the price of hot dogs sold in the stadium or fixing the number of games that can be televised. The correct remedy, however, is not to condemn the entire venture but rather to condemn that part of the venture restricting the number of televised games.

Finally, the road map provides some hints about why the Supreme Court does what it does in certain classes of cases. For example, in *Goldfarb* it rejected the argument that agreements within the learned professions should be either exempt from the antitrust laws or else given an extraordinary amount of deference.[44] Later, in *Indiana Dentists*, it adhered to this position generally but held that such agreements should generally be considered under the rule of reason, even if their form and nature would ordinarily make them subject to *per se* analysis.[45]

Certain kinds of agreements among professionals may have to be characterized as "joint ventures" simply because professionals are their own best police officers, notwithstanding a substantial threat to competition. Who but an anesthesiologist is really in a position to pass judgment on the competence of another anesthesiologist? For this reason the Supreme Court has always been somewhat deferential to professional agreements, at least when they have been developed through so-called ethical canons. In *California Dental*,[46] its most recent decision involving the learned professions, the Supreme Court accorded a degree of deference that would be quite imprudent if applied to a more ordinary market. It held that a full rule of reason inquiry must be applied to an agreement among dentists limiting price and quality advertising in order to control deception. The Court noted complexities in health care markets that seemed to make consumers particularly vulnerable to exaggerated advertising claims. As a result, it was at least possible that even overly broad restraints stated to reach deceptive advertising would actually make the market work better and more competitively. But deference is not the same thing as exemption; it means simply that such agreements need a little closer look.[47]

Production joint ventures involving competitors also pose unique problems. Joint production seems efficient under the circumstances, but the venturers must decide how much to produce and at what price to sell the venture-produced product; so the venture itself is directly involved in determination of price and output. A good example is *General Motors Corp.*, where the Federal Trade Commission decided not to pursue an investigation of a joint venture between General Motors and Toyota to manufacture subcompact automobiles.[48] General Motors was the largest seller of automobiles in both the United States and the world. Toyota was the fourth largest seller in the U.S. and the third largest in the world.

The venture itself involves integration of production, so it survives a step 2 inquiry. But the market power inquiry increases our concern, so we have to go through step 4 and then Step 5. We insist on a showing that the venture produce substantial economies that could not be achieved by alternative means. In this case the FTC found that the venture would result in larger numbers of low-priced cars in

44. Goldfarb v. Virginia State Bar, 421 U.S. 773, 95 S.Ct. 2004, rehearing denied, 423 U.S. 886, 96 S.Ct. 162 (1975).

45. FTC v. Indiana Federation of Dentists, 476 U.S. 447, 106 S.Ct. 2009 (1986). See § 5.4a2.

46. See note 18.

47. On special treatment of the learned professions, see § 5.4a2, which also discusses the *California Dental* decision in more detail.

48. General Motors Corp., 103 F.T.C. 374 (1984).

the United States,[49] and an educational opportunity for General Motors personnel to learn about Japanese manufacturing methods.[50] Significantly, it also seemed to increase output because (a) it resulted in the creation of a new plant; and (b) it imposed no limits on the production of the joint venture participants in their separate, individually owned plants.

The courts have always realized that the line between the *per se* rule and the rule of reason is not as hard or as easy to locate as we might wish. But beginning with the *NCAA* decision in 1984 and the *Indiana Dentists* decision in 1986, the courts have begun to take more seriously an intermediate form of inquiry that generally falls under the rubric of "nearly naked" or "facially unreasonable" restraints, the "quick look," or the "abbreviated" or "bobtailed" rule of reason. Typically, we say that a restraint falls within this classification if it is highly suspicious, almost to the point of deserving *per se* condemnation. Nevertheless, some doubts remain, perhaps resulting from the fact that our experience with the restraint is so limited.[51] At the very least, we want to listen to the defendant's justification for its restraint. If that justification seems both plausible and sufficient to suggest that the restraint is profitable without regard to any power that the defendants might have, then a full rule of reason inquiry will be necessary. By contrast, if the justification indicates that the restraint is naked, at that point we can apply the per se rule.

The truncated inquiry is usually best reserved for circumstances where the restraint is sufficiently threatening to place it presumptively in the per se class,[52] but lack of judicial experience requires at least some consideration of proffered defenses or justifications. Further, the only justifications that are acceptable are those tending to show that the challenged restraint really does tend to increase output, and thus decrease price. The purpose is *not* to broaden the range of defenses for a restraint that is conceded to reduce output or increase price.

The Supreme Court has not been entirely clear on the methodology for analyzing nearly naked restraints. The *Indiana Dentists* case had begun with the premise that an alleged "boycott" carried out by members of a learned profession was not a clear per se offense, largely because of the Court's history of deference to professional organizations.[53] However, it then found that the dentists' collective refusal to supply x-ray data to an insurer was a "naked" restraint on output *and* that the dentists on a relatively quick look appeared to have significant market power.[54]

Later decisions have found the market power inquiry unnecessary. For example, in *Law v. NCAA* the Tenth Circuit began with the Supreme Court's *NCAA* premise that all restraints involving a network joint venture such as intercollegiate athletics merit rule of reason treatment.[55] But then it condemned an agreement among NCAA members fixing maximum coaches' salaries without any power inquiry:

> No "proof of market power" is required where the very purpose and effect of a horizontal agreement is to fix prices so as to make them unresponsive to a competitive marketplace. Thus, where a practice has obvious anticompetitive effects—as does price-fixing—there is no need to prove that the defendant possesses market power. Rather, the court is justified in proceeding directly to the question of whether the procompetitive justifications advanced for the restraint outweigh the anticompetitive effects under a "quick look" rule of reason.

49. Import restrictions prevented Toyota from simply increasing its sales into the United States.

50. Id. at 384.

51. See 11 Antitrust Law ¶ 1911 (1998).

52. Thus, for example, vertical nonprice restraints are never subjected to "quick look" analysis. See, e.g., *Orson v. Miramax Film Corp.*, 79 F.3d 1358, 1367 (3d Cir.1996), on remand, 983 F.Supp. 624 (D.Pa.1997) (refusing to apply "quick look" to movie distributor's exclusivity policy—essentially, an output contract); *Holmes Products Corp. v. Dana Lighting*, 958 F.Supp. 27, 33–34 (D.Mass.1997) (same—output contract); *U.S. Healthcare v. Healthsource*, 986 F.2d 589, 594 (1st Cir.1993) (exclusive dealing not subject to "quick look").

53. See *Indiana Dentists*, note 16, 476 U.S. at 459.

54. See 11 Antitrust Law ¶ 1911b.

55. See note 30.

> ... Under a quick look rule of reason analysis, anticompetitive effect is established, even without a determination of the relevant market, where the plaintiff shows that a horizontal agreement to fix prices exists, that the agreement is effective, and that the price set by such an agreement is more favorable to the defendant than otherwise would have resulted from the operation of market forces.[56]

But there is no real inconsistency between the *Law* and *Indiana Dentists* decisions. The point is that the "quick look" cannot readily be pigeonholed into a single set of inquiries. As noted previously, all antitrust analysis proceeds on the premise that the fact finder collects information up to the point that its incremental value is no longer worth the costs of obtaining it. The price-fixing agreement in *Law* presented a much less ambiguous case for competitive harm than did the concerted refusal to deal arrangement in *Indiana Dentists*, particularly given the tendency of the courts to apply a rule of reason in concerted refusal cases.[57] Once the Tenth Circuit had listened to the NCAA's defense of price-fixing of coaches salaries, they new with sufficient assurance that they were looking at a naked restraint whose *only* possible impact was almost certain to be anticompetitive. That made the further, expensive inquiry into market power unnecessary.[58]

At this writing, the most recent Supreme Court discussion of truncated approaches is its *California Dental* decision.[59] A five-member majority held that an agreement among dentists restricting price and quality advertising could not be assessed on a quick look, but required full rule of reason treatment. The defendant's restraints were stated to be efforts to prevent deceptive advertising, but they were so aggressive that they virtually prohibited all price or quality advertising of any sort.[60] The Court rejected the abbreviated inquiry that the Ninth Circuit had approved, noting that the health care market was particularly vulnerable to unsubstantiated and difficult-to-verify claims.[61] Perhaps most significantly, the Court noted that the literature and economic theory had suggested the "plausibility of competing claims about the effects of the professional advertising restrictions. . . ."[62] This suggested at least some possibility that restrictions appearing to be overly broad on their face might end up being reasonable in the unusually complex market for dental services. While the Court did not state it, a complex market with poorly informed buyers also suggests vulnerability to collusion. But in any event, assessing overall competitive effects, the majority concluded, would require a full rule of reason query.

The Court then remanded to the lower court to make that determination. As the dissent pointed out, the record seemed to be quite full of evidence about market power and anticompetitive effects that might be sufficient to support the FTC's conclusion even under a full rule of reason, and the majority did not disagree. Thus the narrowly focused decision may serve mainly as a warning to the FTC that if it has sufficient evidence to condemn a restraint under the rule of reason, there is no point in using "quick look" language suggesting that anything less has been undertaken. The majority did not state how harmful effects on com-

56. *Law*, note 32, 134 F.3d at 1020, citing G. Roberts, The NCAA, Antitrust, and Consumer Welfare, 70 Tul. L.Rev. 2631, 2636–39 (1996).

57. See § 5.4.

58. Accord *Barnett Pontiac–Datsun v. FTC*, 955 F.2d 457, 475 (6th Cir.), cert. denied, 506 U.S. 973, 113 S.Ct. 461 (1992) (Ryan, J., concurring and dissenting) (nearly naked price fixing and market division arrangements can ordinarily be condemned on quick look without power inquiry).

59. See note 18.

60. See Justice Breyer's dissent:

> As implemented, the ethical rule reached beyond its nominal target, to prevent truthful and nondeceptive advertising. In particular, the Commission determined that the rule, in practice:
>
> (1) "precluded advertising that characterized a dentist's fees as being low, reasonable, or affordable," [121 F.T.C. 190, 301 (1996)]
>
> (2) "precluded advertising ... of across the board discounts," ibid.; and
>
> (3) "prohibit[ed] all quality claims," id., at 308.

California Dental, 119 S.Ct. at 1618.

61. 119 S.Ct. at 1619–1621.

62. Id. at 1616.

petition were to be assessed, but they would clearly be established by evidence that truthful claims about lower prices were unnecessarily suppressed, thus denying their benefit to consumers.[63]

In such a case, if the evidence of power and anticompetitive effects seems sufficient, the weight of a full rule of reason analysis would then fall on an inquiry into less restrictive alternatives, which the Court did not discuss. The Dental Association would have to explain why its concern for deceptive claims could not be satisfied by more finely crafted rules designed to distinguish that which is deceptive in fact from that which is not.

63. See also Justice Breyer's dissent, 119 S.Ct. at 1620, speaking of quality claims:

> An agreement not to advertise, say, "gentle care" is anticompetitive because it imposes an artificial barrier against each dentist's independent decision to advertise gentle care. That barrier, in turn, tends to inhibit those dentists who want to supply gentle care from getting together with those customers who want to buy gentle care.

Chapter 6

EXCLUSIONARY PRACTICES AND THE DOMINANT FIRM: THE BASIC DOCTRINE OF MONOPOLIZATION AND ATTEMPT

Table of Sections

§ 6.1 The Monopolization Offense

Section 2 of the Sherman Act, 15 U.S.C.A. § 2, condemns "every person who shall monopolize * * *." Today "monopolization" refers to a number of activities that may be illegal when performed by the dominant firm in a properly defined relevant market.[1]

In one sense the law of monopolization is concerned with what Louis D. Brandeis once called "The Curse of Bigness."[2] Today even more than in Brandeis's time, Americans are dominated by giant firms.[3] But big business and Americans always have had a love-hate relationship. Big corporations employ more Americans and pay them higher salaries than small businesses do. They do most of our research and development, introduce most of our new products, defend us, entertain and inform us, and pay most of our taxes.

Notwithstanding these bounties, Americans have always mistrusted big business. We have written and read about the "organization man" who has ceded his freedom and identity to his employer.[4] We believe that big business homogenizes us, over-standardizes us, and—worst of all—makes us pay high prices for

§ 6.1

1. On market definition, see Chap. 3.

2. L. Brandeis, The Curse of Bigness (1934).

3. However, some writers dispute the common assertion that industrial concentration in America has risen throughout the last half century. See Y. Brozen, Concentration, Mergers, and Public Policy 119–55 (1982).

4. W. H. Whyte, Jr., The Organization Man (1956).

shoddy products or poor service. Antitrust is properly concerned only with the last of these sins.

In United States v. Grinnell Corp.[5] the Supreme Court defined illegal monopolization to include two elements: "(1) the possession of monopoly power in the relevant market and (2) the willful acquisition or maintenance of that power as distinguished from growth or development as a consequence of a superior product, business acumen, or historic accident." Both of these elements must be established before the defendant is guilty of monopolization.

During the first half of the twentieth century the judicial definition of the monopolization offense experienced considerable flux. Courts generally agreed that the offense required a showing of the defendant's substantial market power. In the earliest cases, however, the defendant's market power was obvious, and courts spent little time discussing it.[6] Today the market power requirement is clearly established, although courts still have difficulty measuring market power and are not entirely clear about how much market power a defendant must have to be guilty of illegal monopolization.

Over the years courts have had broad disagreements about the offense's bad conduct requirements. In United States v. United Shoe Machinery Corp. (*USM*)[7] Judge Wyzanski examined the monopolization case law and found three approaches to the monopolization offense. Before Judge Learned Hand's famous decision in *Alcoa*[8] the prevailing view was that "[a]n enterprise has monopolized * * * if it has acquired or maintained a power to exclude others as a result of using an unreasonable 'restraint of trade' in violation of § 1 of the Sherman Act."[9] This definition implied that a firm could not violate § 2 unless it had also violated § 1. However, already in the 1911 *American Tobacco* case, Chief Justice White suggested that conduct that would violate § 1 of the Sherman Act when performed by agreement with another firm, would violate § 2 when performed unilaterally by a firm with monopoly power, or perhaps with the intent to monopolize.[10]

Next Judge Wyzanski described a "more inclusive approach" that Justice Douglas had developed in United States v. Griffith.[11] Under that rule a firm monopolizes illegally when "it (a) has the power to exclude competition, and (b) has exercised it, or has the power to exercise it." Judge Wyzanski interpreted this to mean that "it is a violation of § 2 for one having effective control of the market to use, or plan to use, any exclusionary practice, even though it is not a technical restraint of trade" in violation of § 1.

Finally, the third and broadest approach came from Judge Hand in the *Alcoa* case, although Justice Douglas endorsed it in *Griffith* as well. Under this approach "one who has acquired an overwhelming share of the market 'monopolizes' whenever he does business * * * apparently even if there is no showing that his business involves any exclusionary practices." Judge Hand had softened this rule, however. A defendant could escape liability by showing that it had acquired its monopoly exclusively by its own

> superior skill, superior products, natural advantages, (including accessibility to raw materials or markets), economic or technological efficiency, (including scientific research), low margins of profit maintained permanently and without discrimination, or [legally used patents].[12]

5. 384 U.S. 563, 570–71, 86 S.Ct. 1698, 1704 (1966).

6. For example, Standard Oil Co. of N.J. v. United States, 221 U.S. 1, 31 S.Ct. 502 (1911) (defendant controlled 90% of business of producing, shipping, refining and selling petroleum); United States v. American Tobacco Co., 221 U.S. 106, 31 S.Ct. 632 (1911) (86%); United States v. American Can Co., 230 Fed. 859 (D.Md.1916), appeal dismissed, 256 U.S. 706, 41 S.Ct. 624 (1921) (at least at one time, over 90% of can producing plants).

7. 110 F.Supp. 295 (D.Mass.1953), affirmed per curiam, 347 U.S. 521, 74 S.Ct. 699 (1954).

8. United States v. Aluminum Co. of America, 148 F.2d 416 (2d Cir.1945).

9. *USM*, 110 F.Supp. at 342.

10. *American Tobacco*, 221 U.S. at 181–184, 31 S.Ct. at 648–650.

11. 334 U.S. 100, 107, 68 S.Ct. 941, 945 (1948).

12. *USM*, 110 F.Supp. at 342.

Today courts clearly have reached beyond Judge Wyzanski's first, most narrow definition of illegal monopolization. Although violation of § 1 of the Sherman Act is often used to satisfy the conduct element of illegal monopolization, it is not necessary; firms innocent of § 1 violations are frequently condemned under § 2.

However, there is little precedent for Judge Wyzanski's third, most expansive rule: that a firm with monopoly power violates the Sherman Act whenever it "does business." Over the years legal scholars and several members of Congress have recommended at least a limited law against so-called "no fault" monopolization, but those debates remain academic. The merits of such proposals are addressed in § 6.3.

Today the prevailing legal rule closely resembles Judge Wyzanski's second proposal: illegal monopolization requires a showing that the defendant (a) has "monopoly power", which is substantial market power; and (b) has "exercised" that power.

What it means to "exercise" monopoly power is ambiguous. The sale of products at a monopoly price is certainly an "exercise" of monopoly power—however, courts have consistently held that even the monopolist may legally sell its product at its profit-maximizing price and reduce output to a level capable of clearing the market at that price.[13] Judge Wyzanski wisely defined the "exercise" of monopoly power as an "exclusionary" practice—that is, a practice that deters potential rivals from entering the monopolist's market, or existing rivals from increasing their output in response to the monopolist's price increase. The monopolist's sale of its product at a monopolistic price is not an "exclusionary" practice. Far from it, monopoly profits attract investors and new entry into the market, and the resulting increased output drives the price back to the competitive level. The monopolist, however, would prefer that these investors place their money somewhere else. "Exclusionary practices" are acts by the monopolist designed to discourage potential competitors from entering the field, or to prevent competitors from increasing output.

Even here some qualification is in order. Not all exclusionary practices merit condemnation. Many of them make consumers better off: for example, research and development, or the production of a better product at a lower price. To say that illegal monopolization consists of monopoly power plus *any* exclusionary practice would cut far too broadly. A great deal of case law has been concerned with distinguishing the monopolist's "exclusionary" practices worthy of condemnation from those practices which, although exclusionary, should be tolerated or even encouraged.

§ 6.2 Monopoly Power and Illegal Monopolization

Chapter three defines market power and describes how courts attempt to measure it. "Monopoly power," the requirement assessed for illegal monopolization, is a large amount of market power.

If the law of monopolization were directed exclusively at the "curse of bigness," or at vast private concentrations of wealth or political power, then the market power requirement assessed by the courts would be inappropriate to the offense. Chrysler Corp., for example, is among the largest manufacturing corporations in the United States, but no court would hold Chrysler capable of monopolizing the market for American passenger cars. Its output is smaller than that of General Motors or Toyota. By contrast, the owner of the only movie theater in Ozona, Texas, may well be guilty of illegal monopolization, even though his company is tiny by American corporate standards,

13. See Berkey Photo, Inc. v. Eastman Kodak Co., 603 F.2d 263, 275 (2d Cir.1979), cert. denied, 444 U.S. 1093, 100 S.Ct. 1061 (1980) (monopoly seller):

> The mere possession of monopoly power does not *ipso facto* condemn a market participant. But, to avoid the proscriptions of § 2, the firm must refrain at all times from conduct directed at smothering competition. This doctrine has two branches. Unlawfully acquired power remains anathema even when kept dormant. And it is not less true that a firm with a legitimately achieved monopoly may not wield the resulting power to tighten its hold on the market.

Accord Kartell v. Blue Shield, 749 F.2d 922 (1st Cir.1984), cert. denied, 471 U.S. 1029, 105 S.Ct. 2040 (1985) (monopsony buyer); 3 Antitrust Law ¶ 720 (rev. ed. 1996).

and his theater only one-fourth the size of movie theaters in New York or Chicago.

The notion that the antitrust laws should be used to stop giant accumulations of wealth or influence is directed at absolute size. By contrast, the law of monopolization is directed at relative size in relation to some properly defined market.

6.2a. Monopolization's Market Power Requirement

The monopoly power requirement in monopolization cases helps courts to characterize a firm's conduct and predict its consequences. Much of the "exclusionary" conduct at issue in litigated monopolization cases is ambiguous when considered alone. For example, in a competitive market a refusal to deal, a sudden price reduction, a policy of leasing and not selling a product, or of keeping research secret are absolutely consistent with competition on the merits.

If a firm already has significant market power, however, courts have found these practices to be more threatening to the competitive process, and more likely to result in reduced output and higher prices. In general, the more market power a firm has, the more damaging its exclusionary practices might be.[1] For this reason some commentators have suggested a "sliding scale" relationship between the amount of a defendant's monopoly power and the bad conduct requirements. If the defendant has enormous monopoly power, relatively minor exclusionary conduct may be condemned as anticompetitive. If the defendant's market power is smaller, however, the amount of bad conduct should be proportionately larger.

Courts generally have not adopted this approach. The whole notion of a "sliding scale" implies that courts are able to measure market power or the effect of alleged exclusionary practices much more accurately than they really can.[2] Rather, courts have developed a compromise. If the evidence suggests a high degree of monopoly power, then the courts have identified a certain set of practices that will condemn the defendant of illegal monopolization. If the evidence suggests a smaller amount of market power, then courts have used the law of attempt to monopolize, which carries stricter and more explicit conduct requirements.

Before a firm can be guilty of illegal monopolization it must be the dominant firm in the relevant market. Courts usually rely on market share data to determine whether the plaintiff has enough market power to be guilty of illegal monopolization. They fairly consistently hold that a 90% market share is enough to support the necessary inference of market power. Several courts have found a market share on the order of 75% to be sufficient,[3] but if the share is lower than 70% courts become much more reluctant to find monopoly power.[4] Some courts hold as a matter of law that a share of less than 50% is insufficient, even if the defendant clearly had the power to raise its price by reducing output.[5]

§ 6.2

1. As Justice Scalia noted in his *Kodak* dissent:

> Where a defendant maintains substantial market power, his activities are examined through a special lens: Behavior that might otherwise not be of concern to the antitrust laws—or that might even be viewed as procompetitive—can take on exclusionary connotations when practiced by a monopolist.

Eastman Kodak Co. v. Image Technical Services, Inc., 504 U.S. 451, 488, 112 S.Ct. 2072, 2093 (1992) (Scalia, J., dissenting).

2. See 3A Antitrust Law ¶ 802 (rev. ed. 1996).

3. See United States v. Grinnell Corp., 384 U.S. 563, 571, 86 S.Ct. 1698, 1704 (1966) (87% sufficient); United States v. Paramount Pictures, Inc., 334 U.S. 131, 68 S.Ct. 915 (1948) (suggesting that 70% is sufficient).

4. See Moore v. Jas. H. Matthews & Co., 473 F.2d 328, 332 (9th Cir.1972), appeal after remand, 550 F.2d 1207 (9th Cir.1977) (market share of 65%–70% raised a fact question).

5. See Valley Liquors v. Renfield Importers, 822 F.2d 656 (7th Cir.), cert. denied, 484 U.S. 977, 108 S.Ct. 488 (1987) (50% insufficient as a matter of law for monopolization); Dimmitt Agri Indus., Inc. v. CPC Int'l Inc., 679 F.2d 516 (5th Cir.1982), cert. denied, 460 U.S. 1082, 103 S.Ct. 1770 (1983) (same); Arthur S. Langenderfer v. S.E. Johnson Co., 917 F.2d 1413, 1432 (6th Cir.1990), cert. denied, 502 U.S. 899, 112 S.Ct. 274 (1991) ("rare indeed" for firm with market share under 50% to have sufficient market power for either monopolization or attempt); United Air Lines v. Austin Travel Corp., 867 F.2d 737, 742 (2d Cir.1989) (31% insufficient). But see Broadway Delivery Corp. v. United Parcel Service of Amer., Inc., 651 F.2d 122 (2d Cir.), cert. denied, 454 U.S. 968, 102 S.Ct. 512 (1981), suggesting that 50% is "rarely" sufficient, but holding that the jury may nevertheless consider the issue of monopoly power even if the defendant's market share is

In any event, if the court has a high degree of confidence in its market definition, then sufficient power can be found along the minima of the above ranges. By contrast, if a market is poorly defined, our confidence level in the definition is not particularly high, or entry barriers seem to be only marginal, then it should insist on a higher market share. Unfortunately, the fact finding process sometimes encourages courts to compartmentalize the two different issues. Once a market is defined, no matter how tenuously, they examine market share on the assumption that all market definitions are alike. A particularly egregious example of this is the Ninth Circuit's Kodak decision after remand from the Supreme Court.[6] First the court found a relevant market for "Kodak parts" on the highly controversial "lock-in" theory approved by the Supreme Court in its 1992 *Kodak* decision.[7] Then it erroneously confused complements and substitutes, grouping into a single "relevant market" parts that were not substitutable for one another and that included both technically complex patented parts and off-the-shelf hardware parts anyone could buy.[8] By this time the market was so poorly defined that not even a 100% share of the resultant "all parts" market would have indicated whether Kodak had any power to exclude anyone from any particular part. In fact, Kodak made only some 30% of its own parts. But the court permitted the plaintiff to include an additional 20–25% made by other firms under contracts that forbad these firms from using dies supplied by Kodak to make parts for third parties, as well as Kodak's "discouragement" of parts sales by owners of Kodak copiers who were entitled to buy parts for their own machines.[9] The latter accounted for an unspecified percentage.

Even this meaningless aggregation led to a "market share" of something on the order of 55%, at or below the bottom margin necessary for the monopolization offense. But in finding that percentage adequate, the court paid no attention to the series of hoops through which it had jumped in getting to that number. Other decisions have been more circumspect, however, and have insisted on higher market shares to offset doubts about a market definition, the availability of substitutes, or the height of entry barriers.[10]

6.2b. The Relation Between Market Power and Market Share

As chapter three develops, market share percentages are imperfect surrogates for market power. Indeed, even when markets are defined with great care a significant amount of approximation is usually involved. *First*, our data are incomplete and often imperfect. *Second*, traditional market share measurements require the court to include differentiated or geographically dispersed substitute products as either completely inside or completely outside the market. Inclusion understates the defendant's market power while exclusion overstates it, and our traditional market definition criteria do not readily permit compromise positions.[11]

As a result, it would be unwise to attempt to establish a "sliding scale" relationship between the egregiousness of the conduct and

established to be less than 50%. Accord Baxley–DeLamar Monuments v. American Cemetery Assn., 843 F.2d 1154 (8th Cir.1988), on remand, 938 F.2d 846 (8th Cir.1991) (57% share created jury issue for attempt)

6. Image Technical Services v. Eastman Kodak Co., 125 F.3d 1195 (9th Cir.1997), cert. denied, ___ U.S. ___, 118 S.Ct. 1560 (1998).

7. See note 6; and see the discussion of market power created by lock-in in § 3.3a.

8. On the difference between substitutes and complements, see § 3.3b.

9. *Kodak*, 125 F.3d at 1206.

10. See, e.g., Ford v. Stroup, 113 F.3d 1234, 1997–1 Trade Cas. ¶ 71838 (6th Cir. 1997, unpublished) (radiologist group's market share of 50–55 percent insufficient for attempted monopolization claim when where entry barriers not affirmatively shown to be high). See also Tops Markets v. Quality Markets, 142 F.3d 90 (2d Cir.1998) (79% share insufficient for monopolization claim in presence of doubts about market definition and easy entry, but could support attempt claim). Other courts have held that the presence of high entry barriers might justify a finding of monopoly power on somewhat lower market shares than normal. See Syufy Enters. v. American Multicinema, Inc., 793 F.2d 990, 995–996 (9th Cir.1986), cert. denied, 479 U.S. 1031, 107 S.Ct. 876 (1987). But stated in that fashion the conclusion is incorrect. A well defined market *requires* high entry barriers.

11. On the problem of imperfect substitutes, see § 3.3a.

the required amount of market power. Our measures are not sufficiently calibrated. At the same time, however, some kinds of conduct are plausibly anticompetitive on smaller market shares than other kinds. For example, predatory pricing is reasonable strategic behavior only for firms with extremely large market shares. Although it is formally treated as part of the law of attempt, it should be treated as part of the law of substantive monopolization.[12] Likewise, various vertical contracting arrangements by which a firm seeks to "foreclose" rivals from the market could effectively be anticompetitive only on large market shares. For example, if Kodak uses long-term contracts with its photocopier purchasers to force them to purchase Kodak's maintenance service, independent service organizations (ISOs) would not be able to maintain Kodak's machines. But these contracts would drive the ISOs out of the maintenance market generally only if (a) Kodak controlled all, or nearly all, of the photocopier market; or (b) other photocopier makers used similar vertical contracts. Otherwise there would be plenty of photocopiers left for the ISOs to maintain.

By contrast, monopolization through abuse of government process might be reasonable anticompetitive conduct on a much lower share. For example, a firm with a 50% market share and numerous small rivals of 5% or 10% each might use vexatious litigation or abusive processes before an administrative agency to restrain its rivals' expansion or increase their costs.[13] In sum, one must examine the logic of the alleged exclusionary practice in order to determine the minimum requisite market share to make the practice anticompetitive. Courts often fail to do this.

As the previous paragraphs suggest, market share can have independent relevance in monopolization cases. Some writers have suggested that if we could measure market power directly, through an economic device such as the Lerner Index,[14] definition of a relevant market and computation of a market share would be unnecessary.[15] But most often that is not the case: the "lever" that the dominant firm needs in order to make its exclusionary practice work is not the present ability to raise price above marginal cost (economic market power), but rather its ability to dominate a market in a way that forecloses access to rivals. Courts have rightfully insisted that relevant markets and market shares be determined in monopolization cases, even if market power could be assessed by mechanisms that make market definition unnecessary.[16]

Equally important is the relationship between market power and entry barriers. If entry is easy, even a very large market share fails to establish the defendant's market power. As soon as it raises its price to monopoly levels new competitors will appear and the price increaser's market share will drop rapidly until it lowers its price once again.[17] Although courts in monopolization cases have not always taken ease of entry as seriously as they should, several have noted that entry is easy and then concluded that the defendant lacked substantial market power.[18]

§ 6.3 Conduct Requirements—Is Bad Conduct Necessary?

Judge Wyzanski's third, most expansive definition of illegal monopolization was that a

12. See § 8.4a.

13. See § 7.12.

14. See § 3.1. Since the Lerner Index measures market power on the basis of price-marginal cost relationships, it does not require definition of a relevant market or computation of a market share.

15. W. Landes & R. Posner, Market Power in Antitrust Cases, 94 Harv.L.Rev. 937 (1981).

16. See Spectrum Sports v. McQuillan, 506 U.S. 447, 458–459, 113 S.Ct. 884, 892 (1993), requiring market definition in an attempt to monopolize case.

17. See e.g., *Tops Markets*, note 10; on entry barriers, see § 1.6.

18. *Tops Markets*, note 10; United States v. Syufy Enterp., 903 F.2d 659, 664–669 (9th Cir.1990) (no entry barriers to exhibiting of films); Ball Memorial Hosp. v. Mutual Hosp. Ins., 784 F.2d 1325, 1335–1336 (7th Cir.), rehearing denied, 788 F.2d 1223 (7th Cir.1986) (insurance business requires cash and risk management, for which there are ample supplies and markets).

With *Ball Memorial*, compare Reazin v. Blue Cross & Blue Shield, 899 F.2d 951, 971 (10th Cir.), cert. denied, 497 U.S. 1005, 110 S.Ct. 3241 (1990) (finding monopolization; although health insurance requires only capital and licensing, other firms were extremely small by comparison, and defendant had historically enjoyed some advantages given by state legislation).

firm with sufficient monopoly power monopolizes whenever it "does business." No court has ever explicitly adopted such a rule, although a few have inadvertently come close.[1] Today illegal monopolization still requires monopoly power *plus* some form of anticompetitive conduct. The sale of output at a monopoly price is itself not sufficient to brand someone an illegal monopolist.[2]

Over the years, however, both Congress and antitrust scholars have proposed a variety of "no fault" monopoly statutes that would condemn a firm with persistent, substantial market power without evidence of impermissible exclusionary conduct. The idea is worth brief discussion because it helps illustrate the ambiguity of conduct requirements in monopolization cases.

The framers of the Sherman Act did not intend to condemn someone "who merely by superior skill and intelligence * * * got the whole business because nobody could do it as well as he could * * *."[3] Such "monopolization" and the monopoly profits that may result are essential to economic development. Firms innovate because they expect their successes to produce economic returns. Eventually the high profits will attract other producers into the market. Collectively these producers will increase output and prices will be driven to the competitive level. A rule that condemned all prices higher than, say, average cost could stop innovation dead. The continual creation of monopoly, and its eventual correction by competitive entry is part of a never-ending process that explains most of the technical achievements of modern industry in market economies.[4]

There are other reasons for not condemning mere monopoly. Many markets are large enough to support only one or two firms efficiently. In a natural monopoly market a single incumbent would have lower costs than two or more equally efficient incumbents. Some natural monopoly markets are recognized as such and price regulated by the State, but many are not.[5]

Courts are generally unable to identify natural monopoly markets except in relatively obvious cases. The court would have to decide whether two or more firms operating in the market could reach minimum efficient scale (MES) of output. However, even economists can do little more than guess the minimum efficient level of output for a particular firm. The most reliable way of measuring MES is to watch markets for long periods of time and measure the size of the successful firms.[6] The fact that for many years Ozona, Texas, contained only one movie theater may indicate that Ozona is big enough to support only one theater. To condemn the theater's owner of monopolization on the basis of large market share alone might well result in Ozona's not having any theater at all.

Most advocates of no fault monopolization rules rely on the fact that exclusionary conduct is often difficult to discover and, when discovered, difficult to interpret. We expect persistent, long-term monopoly profits to invite entry. When entry has not occurred, perhaps we should infer the existence of exclusionary practices even though we do not have

§ 6.3

1. For example, in United States v. Aluminum Co. of America, 148 F.2d 416, 431 (2d Cir.1945) Judge Hand suggested that mere expansion of capacity by a dominant firm could constitute illegal monopolization. See also Judge Wyzanski's invitation to the Supreme Court in *Grinnell* to decide that "where one or more persons * * * had acquired so clear a dominance in a market as to have the power to exclude competition therefrom, there was a *rebuttable* presumption that such power had been criminally acquired and was * * * punishable under § 2." The Supreme Court responded with a rule that where a "consciously acquired" monopoly is shown, "the burden is on the defendant to show that [its] dominance is due to skill, acumen, and the like." United States v. Grinnell Corp., 236 F.Supp. 244, 248 (D.R.I.1964), affirmed except as to decree, 384 U.S. 563, 577, n. 7, 86 S.Ct. 1698, at 1707 (1966).

2. See § 6.1.

3. 21 Cong.Rec. 3151–52 (1890).

4. See F.M. Scherer, Innovation and Growth: Schumpeterian Perspectives (Cambridge: MIT Press 1984).

5. For a monopolization case in a market that was probably a natural monopoly, see Union Leader Corp. v. Newspapers of New England, Inc., 284 F.2d 582 (1st Cir.1960), cert. denied, 365 U.S. 833, 81 S.Ct. 747 (1961); see also, H. Hovenkamp, Vertical Integration by the Newspaper Monopolist, 69 Iowa L.Rev. 451 (1984).

6. See § 1.4.

convincing evidence of them. Such a rule is not so much a "no fault" monopolization doctrine as a rule that fault can be inferred from the existence of persistent monopoly power and profits.

In the first edition of their antitrust treatise, Areeda and Turner argued that a legal rule against "mere monopoly" should be adopted for those monopolies that are both "substantial" and "persistent," and where competitive entry is not otherwise restricted by means outside of the monopolist's control. They would generally require evidence of "substantial market power that has persisted 10 years or more" before intervention would be appropriate.[7] They would never permit intervention where the monopoly power has persisted less than five years, and they would permit intervention against a monopoly between 5 and 10 years old only "on a convincing showing of likely persistency * * *." Finally, Areeda & Turner would have permitted attacks on monopoly without fault only in equitable proceedings brought by the government and normally seeking divestiture.[8]

The Areeda & Turner proposal presumes that courts have a significant ability to measure relevant efficiencies in litigation. If the MES firm in a certain market must be large enough to satisfy the entire market demand at a price equal to marginal cost—that is, if the market is a natural monopoly—then persistent monopoly can be easily explained: no new entrant will be able to match the incumbent's costs. A rule that permits a court to break up a monopoly without evidence of inefficient, exclusionary conduct greatly increases the risk that the defendant merely has the advantage of economies of scale that are not available to a new entrant.[9] In such cases the efficiency losses that result from divestiture could outweigh any efficiency gains that might result from the competition of incumbents.[10]

Finally, because mergers can violate § 2,[11] a no fault monopolization proceeding would very likely be brought only against firms that have developed by internal growth. This means that there are unlikely to be obvious "fault lines," such as those created by a very recent merger, along which a firm can be broken up. To say that courts are not good at breaking up monopoly firms into competitive constituents is a gross understatement.

§ 6.4 Defining and Identifying Monopolizing Conduct

6.4a. The Rule of Reason in Sherman § 2 Cases

The law of monopolization requires a showing that the defendant has monopoly power and has engaged in impermissible "exclusionary" practices with the design or effect of protecting or enhancing its monopoly position. The rule of reason was originally formulated by the Supreme Court in a monopoly case as a means of distinguishing permissible from impermissible exclusionary practices.[1]

The meaning and scope of the rule of reason in monopolization cases are nevertheless ambiguous. Most recent Supreme Court analysis of the rule of reason appears not in monopolization cases but in cases involving agreements among competitors. These are discussed in chapter 5.

In antitrust litigation most practices are considered to be analyzed under a rule of reason. A *per se* rule is generally appropriate only after judges have had long experience with a certain practice, and have concluded that the practice produces many pernicious

7. 3 P. Areeda & D. Turner, Antitrust Law ¶ 623d (1978). The current edition, written by this author, largely rejects the proposal. See 3 Antitrust Law ¶ 630a (rev. ed. 1996).

8. This limitation may be inherent in the "antitrust injury" requirement, which applies to private plaintiffs seeking damages, at least if they are competitors of the defendant. See § 16.3.

9. For some of the problems of measuring scale economies see J. McGee, Efficiency and Economies of Size, in H. Goldschmid, H. Mann & J. Weston, eds., Industrial Concentration: the New Learning 55–96 (1974).

10. Furthermore, even a natural monopolist can face substantial competition—not from incumbents, but from potential entrants. See § 1.4b.

11. See § 7.2

§ 6.4

1. Standard Oil Co. of N.J. v. United States, 221 U.S. 1, 31 S.Ct. 502 (1911).

results and almost no beneficial ones. Some forms of unilateral conduct by dominant firms might fall into the *per se* category—for example, if the sole incumbent in a market dynamites the newly constructed plant of a prospective entrant. However, such cases seldom end up as monopolization cases. Single firm exclusionary practices are generally analyzed under the rule of reason.

As several decisions state the exclusionary practices test, if conduct is rational (that is, profit-maximizing) only on the premise that it will destroy competition, then it should be condemned.[2] This best explains the supreme Court's decision in *Aspen* that a dominant ski company's refusal to continue a joint venture with a rival was anticompetitive.[3] The joint venture in marketing ski packages was mutually beneficial to both firms and increased total market output; however, it was much more essential for the smaller plaintiff than the larger defendant. The defendant could thus profit from terminating the venture only on the premise that the plaintiff would suffer a sharp decline in sales at the defendant's expense. Significantly, the product that the defendant sold after its refusal to deal was less attractive to consumers than the product when the two were cooperating.

Many monopolization cases involve fairly ambiguous conduct. The problem is that most efficient practices are "exclusionary" in the sense that they injure rivals or make entry more difficult. If a firm continually innovates, expands its output and reduces its price, one likely result will be its perpetuation of a large market share. Should simple expansion of capacity or output ever be the basis for illegal monopolization? Judge Hand thought so in the *Alcoa* case.[4] In 1980, in *du Pont* (Titanium Dioxide), however, the Federal Trade Commission disagreed.[5]

No court has articulated a general theory of what the rule of reason in monopolization cases is, or how it should function. Justice Brandeis's simple conclusion in *Chicago Board of Trade*, a § 1 case, that practices which "promote" competition should be approved,[6] while practices that "destroy" competition should be condemned, is not very helpful.

The scope of the rule of reason can vary considerably with changes in antitrust ideology. If the goal of the antitrust laws is to prohibit bigness or to facilitate ease of entry for small business, for example, then expansion of capacity might be considered an unjustifiable exclusionary practice. However if the goal of the antitrust laws is the maximization of consumer welfare, and if consumers are benefitted by low prices, then expansion of capacity should generally not be illegal, because increased output results in lower prices. One important difference between the *Alcoa* case in 1945 and the *du Pont* case in 1980 is that the prevailing ideology had changed.

6.4b. Unnecessarily Harmful Conduct; Public and Private Suits Distinguished

The emergence of new methodologies in industrial economics, including a revolution in game theory, has given economists a new appreciation for strategic anticompetitive behavior by dominant firms. The result has been a moderate amount of expansiveness in our defi-

2. For example, Advanced Health–Care Servs. v. Radford Community Hosp., 910 F.2d 139, 148 (4th Cir.1990) (if defendant makes a "short-term sacrifice" in order to further "exclusive, anticompetitive objectives," it has monopolized); Instructional Sys. Dev. Corp. v. Aetna Casualty and Sur. Co., 817 F.2d 639, 649 (10th Cir.1987) ("abnormal" business conduct).

3. Aspen Skiing Co. v. Aspen Highlands Skiing Corp., 472 U.S. 585, 105 S.Ct. 2847 (1985). The decision is discussed more fully in § 7.5.

4. United States v. Aluminum Co. of America, 148 F.2d 416, 431 (2d Cir.1945):

> It was not inevitable that [the defendant] should always anticipate increases in * * * demand * * * and be prepared to supply them. Nothing compelled it to keep doubling and redoubling its capacity before others entered the field. It insists that it never excluded competitors; but we can think of no more effective exclusion than progressively to embrace each new opportunity as it opened, and to face every newcomer with new capacity already geared into a great organization, having the advantage of experience, trade connections and the elite of personnel.

5. E. I. du Pont de Nemours & Co., 96 F.T.C. 653, 747 (1980). For further discussion, see § 7.3.

6. Board of Trade v. United States, 246 U.S. 231, 238, 38 S.Ct. 242, 244 (1918). The decision is discussed in § 5.6.

nition of unreasonable exclusionary conduct. Unfortunately, however, at this writing the courts have still not developed very useful tools for distinguishing anticompetitive behavior that should be condemned from aggressively competitive behavior that would better be left alone. Errors have been made in both directions.

Significantly, nondominant firms acting unilaterally typically lack the market position to make certain kinds of strategic conduct work. Consider the *Microsoft* litigation.[7] A nondominant seller of computer operating systems would have every incentive to maximize compatibility with other types of software, such as internet browsers or word processors, even if it sold these applications itself. After all, it would be competing in the market with sellers of other operating systems, and customer choice would be heavily driven by compatibility concerns. But a market dominating seller of operating systems stands in a very different position: by limiting compatibility with rivals' software applications it can force buyers to switch to its own applications. Changing operating systems in response to lack of compatibility is not a realistic possibility. The same phenomenon explains why the antitrust consent decree that broke up the telephone company[8] separated local telephone service from long distance, and why the FCC acting under the 1996 Telecommunications Act[9] has been slow to permit the local operating companies to enter into long distance markets.[10] As long as those companies hold dominant positions in the local market they have every incentive to degrade the long distance systems of rivals in order to switch customers to their own long distance offerings. By contrast, once meaningful competition exists in local service, each local firm will profit only by maximizing its compatibility with long distance providers.

But even traditional case law is helpful with this problem. For example, if skiing in Aspen, Colorado, had been competitive and a jointly issued ticket increasing the number of slopes that a skier could use was attractive to customers, firms would have every incentive to engage in such ventures.[11] The defendant could profit by walking away from a profitable joint venture that was pleasing to customers only because, as far as the plaintiff was concerned, the defendant was the only game in town.

It should be clear by now that a great deal of strategic behavior is concerned with the "maintenance" rather than the acquisition of monopoly power. That is, the conduct is rational behavior only on the premise that the firm is already a monopolist, and frequently the conduct is designed not to much to create monopoly in a secondary market as to maintain the dominant firm's position in the primary market. Here too, the traditional case law makes clear that the monopolist acts unlawfully when it uses unreasonably exclusionary conduct to "maintain" rather than create monopoly power. For example, Grinnell spoke of the offense as "the willful acquisition *or maintenance* of [monopoly] power as distinguished from growth or development as a consequence of a superior product, business acumen, or historic accident."[12]

7. See United States v. Microsoft Corp., 1995 WL 505998 (D.D.C., Aug.21, 1995) (consent decree), interpreted by United States v. Microsoft, 147 F.3d 935 (D.C.Cir. 1998).

8. United States v. AT & T, 552 F.Supp. 131 (D.D.C. 1982), aff'd mem. sub. nom. Maryland v. United States, 460 U.S. 1001, 103 S.Ct. 1240 (1983).

9. Telecommunications Act of 1996, PL 104–104, 110 Stat. 56 (1996), codified at scattered sections of 47 U.S.C.A.; see 3A Antitrust Law ¶ ¶ 785–787 (rev. ed.); and P. Huber, M. Kellogg, & J. Thorne, The Telecommunications Act of 1996 (1996). See also H. Hovenkamp, The Takings Clause and Improvident Regulatory Bargains, 108 Yale L.J. 801 (1999).

10. See BellSouth v. FCC, 162 F.3d 678 (D.C.Cir.1998); SBC Communic. v. FCC, 154 F.3d 226 (5th Cir.1998), cert. denied, ___ U.S. ___, 119 S.Ct. 889 (1999).

11. See *Aspen*, note 3.

12. United States v. Grinnell Corp., 384 U.S. 563, 570–571, 86 S.Ct. 1698, 1703–1704 (1966). See also *Aspen*, note 3, 472 U.S. at 602 (speaking of the "purpose to create or maintain a monopoly," quoting United States v. Colgate & Co., 250 U.S. 300, 307, 39 S.Ct. 465, 468 (1919)). These formulations are widely quoted or paraphrased. See, e.g., Eastman Kodak Co. v. Image Technical Services, Inc., 504 U.S. 451, 483, 112 S.Ct. 2072, 2090 (1992) (§ 2 violated by wilful actions designed to maintain defendant's monopoly position when not supported by valid business justifications); Christianson v. Colt Industries, 486 U.S. 800, 810,

Of course, most innovations and expansions by dominant firms that injure rivals are not § 2 violations, even though they do have the effect of expanding or maintaining monopoly power. Furthermore, even a dominant firm cannot be required to expand or innovate at its peril. This suggests two things: first, *ex ante* rather than *ex post* analysis is the most helpful. Second, considerations of subjective intent are sometimes essential.

Consider, for example, the *C.R.Bard* case, which raises issues similar to those in *Aspen*, *Microsoft*, or *AT & T*. Bard owned and had a monopoly position in a patented "gun" for taking tissue samples from patients. While the gun itself was durable hardware, it used disposable, one-use needles, and these were originally supplied by both Bard and others, including the plaintiff. Bard then modified the gun so that it would take only proprietary needles manufactured by Bard. This exclusion of rival needle makers was the basis of the § 2 claim, in which a divided panel of the Federal Circuit affirmed liability.

The following observations are important. *First*, a *non*dominant maker of biopsy guns would have no incentive to make a gun incompatible with others' needles unless the gun/needle combination were a significant improvement over prior technology. The nondominant firm maximizes its profits, *ceteris paribus*, by maximizing compatibility. As a result, a finding of strong dominance of a properly defined relevant market is essential.

Second, both the patent laws and the general policy of the antitrust laws would permit Bard to innovate to make a better gun, even if the result were a re-designed needle that was incompatible with the needles of rivals. Further, innovation is risky and undertaken under great uncertainty. Many planned innovations do not meet with market success. As a result, one cannot look *ex post*, proclaim that the innovated gun is no better than the earlier gun, and conclude from that fact that the innovation is anticompetitive. The real question is what the innovator had in mind. If Bard's intent was to develop a superior gun, but this required a unique needle, then Bard should not be penalized because its new gun/needle combination ended up working no better than the old combination did. Thus, for example, in the *Aspen* case the Supreme Court emphasized that the defendant did not refuse to participate in the skiing joint venture because it could offer a better product on its own or because customers had rejected the joint venture's offerings. To the contrary, customers preferred the joint venture. Ski Co. did what it did *only* in order to injure a rival.[13]

Formulating an administrable test that takes these competing considerations into account has not been easy. On the one hand, we do not want to hamper the monopolist's ability to innovate, even if the result is exclusion of competitors. On the other hand, the record of strategic behavior by dominant firms makes clear that dominant firms often select technologies or other methods of doing business simply because of the adverse impact on rivals.

The resulting formulation is similar to the one contained in a jury instruction that the Supreme Court approved in *Aspen*: exclusionary conduct by a dominant firm is unlawful when it "unnecessarily excludes or handicaps competitors."[14] This includes "conduct which does not benefit consumers by making a better product or service available—or in other ways—and instead has the effect of impairing competition."[15] The courts often say that such conduct lacks a "legitimate business pur-

108 S.Ct. 2166, 2174 (1988) (§ 2 violated by wilful maintenance of monopoly power as opposed to growth or development that results from a superior product, business acumen, or historic accident); Hanover Shoe v. United Shoe Machinery Corp., 392 U.S. 481, 486, 88 S.Ct. 2224, 2228 (1968) (noting and approving lower court's conclusion that restrictive lease policies were designed to maintain defendant's monopoly); C.R. Bard, Inc. v. M3 Sys., Inc., 157 F.3d 1340, 1371 (Fed.Cir.) (similar), rehearing denied, 161 F.3d 1380 (Fed. Cir.1998).

13. See § 7.5.

14. *Aspen*, note 3, 472 U.S. at 597, 105 S.Ct. at 2854.

15. See, e.g., Advanced Health–Care Servs. v. Radford Community Hosp., 910 F.2d 139, 148 (4th Cir.1990); Instructional Sys. Dev. Corp. v. Aetna Cas. & Sur. Co., 817 F.2d 639, 649 (10th Cir.1987).

pose."[16] What this means is that if the dominant firm marketed or structured its product in a way that made it more difficult for rivals or potential rivals to sell their product, and if this marketing or restructuring was not reasonably necessary to improve the defendant's own product, then it has violated § 2.[17]

Further, it is critically important to distinguish the private plaintiff's burden of proof in an action for damages or an injunction from the government's burden in an enforcement action. As Chapter 16 develops, the private plaintiff seeking damages must show causation and quantifiable injury. The private plaintiff seeking an injunction has a slightly smaller burden: it must show threatened injury, and the amount need not be quantified provided that it is substantial. The government acting as enforcer, however, has the power to enjoin violations, and a violation can be inferred if the natural and likely consequences of an act are injury to competition. When conduct (1) by a firm with monopoly power is (2) clearly harmful to competitors; and (3) not supported by a reasonable business justification or more harmful than necessary given the justification that is offered, then the inference is strong that the challenged act is anticompetitive. This proof is sufficient to support the government's suit in equity, although not the private plaintiff's action.

6.4c. Intent.

The case law of monopolization contains categorical statements that subjective intent is not an element of illegal monopolization, and categorical statements that it is. In *Alcoa* Judge Hand purported to "disregard any question of 'intent,' "concluding that "no monopolist monopolizes unconscious of what he is doing."[18] In *Grinnell,* however, the Supreme Court defined the offense of monopolization to include "the willful acquisition or maintenance of [monopoly] power * * *."[19]

Historically the intent requirement in monopolization cases has followed the formula of the criminal law. In *attempt* cases, the law may require a specific intent to achieve the prohibited result. That requirement is elaborated in § 6.5. In the case of the completed offense, however, courts either dispense with an intent requirement, or else infer intent from evidence of monopoly power plus exclusionary practices.

Evidence of intent comes in two kinds, objective and subjective. Objective evidence of intent is evidence inferred from the defendant's conduct. Subjective evidence of intent is evidence such as statements that indicate that the defendant consciously had a certain end in mind. A general requirement of subjective intent in monopolization cases vastly complicates discovery, and protects those companies who carefully and systematically destroy any paper trail of monopolistic purpose. The result is a great deal of arbitrariness.

Most courts have at least tacitly agreed with Justice Hand that, since no monopolist is unconscious of what it is doing, clear evidence of an impermissible exclusionary practice by a firm with monopoly power is the only proof of intent required. That is virtually the same thing as saying that the law of monopolization does not contain a separate intent require-

16. *Aspen*, 472 U.S. at 597; Multistate Legal Studies, Inc. v. Harcourt Brace Jovanovich, 63 F.3d 1540, 1550 (10th Cir.1995) (conduct not unlawful unless it lacks a "legitimate business justification"); General Indus. Corp. v. Hartz Mountain Corp., 810 F.2d 795, 804 (8th Cir.1987) (equating conduct "without a legitimate business purpose" with conduct "that makes sense only because it eliminates competition").

Other courts sometimes distinguish conduct that merely injures competitors from conduct that harms the "competitive process." Town of Concord v. Boston Edison Co., 915 F.2d 17, 21 (1st Cir.1990), cert. denied, 499 U.S. 931, 111 S.Ct. 1337 (1991).

17. See, e.g., *Multistate Legal Studies*, 63 F.3d at 1550, where the defendant offered both a general bar review course, in which it had a dominant position, and a complementary professional responsibility (PR) course, while the plaintiff offered only the latter. The court denied summary judgment on evidence that the defendant intentionally scheduled sessions of its general bar review course so as to conflict with the only times that the plaintiff's PR course could be offered, thus forcing students to take the defendant's PR course. See 3 Antitrust Law ¶ 658f1 (rev. ed. 1996).

18. United States v. Aluminum Co. of America, 148 F.2d 416, 431–32 (2d Cir.1945). See also Ball Memorial Hospital v. Mutual Hospital Insurance, 784 F.2d 1325, 1338 (7th Cir.1986) ("intent to harm rivals is not a useful standard in antitrust").

19. United States v. Grinnell Corp., 384 U.S. 563, 570–71, 86 S.Ct. 1698, 1704 (1966).

ment. Nevertheless, in *Aspen* the Supreme Court found intent to be relevant to both attempt and substantive monopolization. In monopolization, "evidence of intent is merely relevant to the question whether the challenged conduct is fairly characterized as 'exclusionary' or 'anticompetitive. * * * ' "[20]

On its face the *Aspen* statement is not very helpful, but it contains the germ of an important observation. Many kinds of conduct, such as the refusal to deal with a competitor in *Aspen*, is extremely difficult for courts to characterize. In such cases evidence of intent can aid courts in the characterization problem. However, evidence such as this should then be confined to those situations where (1) the defendant clearly has sufficient market power to justify the conclusion that it is capable of monopolization; and (2) the challenged conduct is sufficiently threatening that evidence of intent will lead the court in one direction or the other. In all other cases, this observation of the Seventh Circuit is apt:

> * * * [I]n the context of a monopolization case "intent" is an elusive concept. The "intent" to achieve or maintain a monopoly is no more unlawful than the possession of a monopoly. Indeed, the goal of any profit-maximizing firm *is* to obtain a monopoly by capturing an ever increasing share of the market. * * * Monopolies achieved through superior skill are no less intentional than those achieved by anticompetitive means * * *, so the intent relevant to a § 2 Sherman Act claim is only the intent to maintain or achieve monopoly power by *anticompetitive means*. Section 2 forbids not the intentional pursuit of monopoly power but the employment of unjustifiable means to gain that power.[21]

To return to the *C.R. Bard* illustration discussed previously,[22] once we know that the defendant's modified gun that accepts only its own needles really is a significant improvement over prior technology, it really does not matter whether Bard did this intending to injure rival needle makers. The right to innovate better products in good faith must be protected, even for dominant firms. Only after we conclude that the "innovation" is no better or that the improvements are nominal should we even consider examining what Bard's intentions were.

§ 6.5 The Offense of Attempt to Monopolize

The offense of attempt to monopolize is one of the most complex of federal antitrust violations. On the one hand, many acts alleged to be illegal attempts may also be illegal monopolization or violations of another antitrust law. In such cases a separate "attempt" offense is superfluous. On the other, expansive use of the attempt offense to reach conduct not condemned by the other antitrust laws may do more harm than good to the competitive process. If attempt analysis focuses too heavily on unfair conduct and too little on market power the offense can operate to protect inefficient businesses from their more efficient rivals.[1] In the great majority of cases, a firm that is nondominant to begin with cannot create a dominant position by purely unilateral conduct.

Nonetheless, § 2 of the Sherman Act condemns every "person who shall monopolize or attempt to monopolize * * *."[2] Congress clearly recognized a distinct attempt offense, and the offense itself is statutory. At common law the attempt to commit a crime could be illegal even though the language of the relevant criminal statute condemned only the completed act. One of the great architects of the modern American common law, Justice Oliver Wendell

20. Aspen Skiing Co. v. Aspen Highlands Skiing Corp., 472 U.S. 585, 105 S.Ct. 2847 (1985). Likewise, Spectrum Sports v. McQuillan, 506 U.S. 447, 113 S.Ct. 884 (1993), on remand, 23 F.3d 1531 (9th Cir. 1994) suggests that intent remains important in an attempt case. See § 6.5.

21. Illinois ex rel. Burris v. Panhandle E. Pipe Line Co., 935 F.2d 1469, 1481 (7th Cir.1991), cert. denied, 502 U.S. 1094, 112 S.Ct. 1169 (1992).

22. See note 12.

§ 6.5

1. See generally, E. Cooper, Attempts and Monopolization: A Mildly Expansionary Answer to the Prophylactic Riddle of Section Two, 72 Mich.L.Rev. 375 (1974).

2. 15 U.S.C.A. § 2.

Holmes, Jr.,[3] read the common law formulation of attempt into the Sherman Act in 1905. In Swift & Co. v. United States the defendants were accused of attempting "to obtain a monopoly of the supply and distribution of fresh meats throughout the United States * * *."[4] Their defense was that the indictment failed to allege specific acts that were themselves illegal. To this Justice Holmes responded:

> * * * Where acts are not sufficient in themselves to produce a result which the law seeks to prevent,—for instance, the monopoly—but require further acts in addition to the mere forces of nature to bring that result to pass, an intent to bring it to pass is necessary in order to produce a dangerous probability that it will happen. * * * But when that intent and the consequent dangerous probability exist, this statute, like many others and like the common law in some cases, directs itself against that dangerous probability as well as against the completed result.[5]

The three elements of the attempt offense today are taken directly from Holmes's formulation. The plaintiff must establish the defendant's: 1) specific intent to control prices or destroy competition in some part of commerce; 2) predatory or anticompetitive conduct directed to accomplishing the unlawful purpose; and 3) a dangerous probability of success.[6]

Courts generally agree that the offense includes these three elements,.[7] and the Supreme Court has cited their use with apparent approval.[8] When the lower courts interpret these elements, however, all agreement stops. The discussion that follows will address the element of specific intent first, and then dangerous probability of success. The attempt offense's conduct requirements, and how these compare with the conduct requirements for monopolization, are taken up in the following chapter.

6.5a. The Attempt Law's Specific Intent Requirement

Intent has often been antitrust's ghost in the machine. Courts use it to help them make sense of conduct that they do not fully understand. Problematically, however, the essence of competition is the intent to triumph over one's rivals. One of the most perplexing problems in antitrust policy is discerning between illegitimate and legitimate intent—a problem that looms distressingly large if intent is the only thing we have to help us characterize ambiguous conduct.

The most commonly stated position is that specific intent is an established element of the attempt offense, approved by the Supreme Court, and cannot be considered irrelevant.[9]

3. See O.W. Holmes, The Common Law 65 (1881).

4. 196 U.S. 375, 393, 25 S.Ct. 276, 278 (1905).

5. Id. at 396, 25 S.Ct. at 279. See also American Tobacco Co. v. United States, 328 U.S. 781, 785, 66 S.Ct. 1125, 1127 (1946), which defined attempt to monopolize as the "employment of methods, means and practices which would, if successful, accomplish monopolization, and which, though falling short, nevertheless approach so close as to create a dangerous probability of it * * *."

6. See 3A Antitrust Law Ch. 8B (rev. ed. 1996); and International Distribution Centers v. Walsh Trucking Co., 812 F.2d 786, 790 (2d Cir.), cert. denied, 482 U.S. 915, 107 S.Ct. 3188 (1987); H.J. v. IT & T Corp., 867 F.2d 1531, 1541–1543 (8th Cir.1989), rehearing denied 876 F.2d 59 (8th Cir.1989); William Inglis v. ITT Continental Baking Co., 668 F.2d 1014, 1027 (9th Cir.1981), cert. denied, 459 U.S. 825, 103 S.Ct. 57 (1982). This three-part test is sometimes called the "classic" formulation of the attempt offense.

7. Some decisions add "antitrust injury" as a fourth requirement. See California Computer Products, Inc. v. IBM Corp., 613 F.2d 727, 736 (9th Cir.1979). The antitrust injury requirement is not part of the substantive law of attempt to monopolize, however, but rather a requirement that private antitrust plaintiffs must meet. See § 16.3.

8. Spectrum Sports, Inc. v. McQuillan, 506 U.S. 447, 454–455, 113 S.Ct. 884, 890–891 (1993), on remand, 23 F.3d 1531 (9th Cir. 1994):

> Courts of Appeals * * * have generally required a plaintiff in an attempted monopolization case to prove that (1) the defendant has engaged in predatory or anticompetitive conduct with (2) a specific intent to monopolize and (3) a dangerous probability of achieving monopoly power. Unfair or predatory conduct may be sufficient to prove the necessary intent to monopolize.

9. See Times–Picayune Pub. Co. v. United States, 345 U.S. 594, 626, 73 S.Ct. 872, 890 (1953): "While the completed offense of monopolization under § 2 demands only a general intent to do the act, 'for no monopolist monopolizes unconscious of what he is doing,' a specific intent to destroy competition or build monopoly is essential to guilt for the mere attempt * * *." See also, United States v. Aluminum Co. of America, 148 F.2d 416, 432 (2d Cir. 1945), in which Judge Hand held that the attempt offense required "specific intent," which was "an intent which goes beyond the mere intent to do the act." Accord Multi-

No one has ever developed a general rule for identifying illegitimate intent. To be sure, evidence in extreme cases can be more-or-less conclusive. The fact that a firm planned to dynamite its competitor's plant shows illegitimate specific intent. By contrast, evidence that a firm planned to produce a better product that could be sold at a lower price almost certainly reveals legitimate intent, even though the purpose and clear result may be to injure rivals.

In between are a host of phenomena that must be characterized as ambiguous: evidence that a firm dropped its price, knowing that a less efficient rival would go out of business;[10] that a firm initiated unsuccessful litigation, knowing the effect would be to delay or prevent a competitor's entry into a market;[11] that a firm knew that its failure to predisclose a product innovation would injure competitors in a complementary product.[12]

Further, business firms are not monoliths: thinking and decision making are the product of many minds. Memoranda are written by careless people, and they often contain puffing about competitive prowess that far exceeds a firm's actual planning and policy. The unexpurgated paperwork of every large corporation probably includes memoranda that could appear incriminating to a jury, because they manifest an intent to defeat, abuse or even destroy rivals. Many jurors, who may be inexperienced in business, simply do not know this.[13] Some firms do a better job than others of systematically destroying or suppressing such evidence—but there is no positive correlation between the firms that are good at suppressing suspicious memoranda and the firms that are innocent of antitrust violations. The well-publicized years-long discovery search through corporate documents for evidence of specific intent is a turkey shoot.

An overinclusive rule that finds specific anticompetitive intent readily and relies on it heavily may frequently end up condemning competition on the merits. The result will be higher prices for consumers. This is particularly true when the attempt allegations involve highly ambiguous conduct, such as predatory pricing. An overinclusive rule can actually force some firms to sell at prices higher than their costs in order to avoid antitrust liability. For this reason the Supreme Court has held that evidence of (1) a price cut below cost; and (2) intent to injure or destroy a rival are, standing alone, insufficient to produce an antitrust violation.[14] However, an underinclusive rule may result in the creation of a certain amount of market power, and in injury to competitors who would not have been injured in a competitive market. These problems are taken up in Chapter 8.

The problem goes much deeper than mere identification of evidence of intent. Intent, once determined, must be evaluated. Most courts agree that mere intent to do better than or to vanquish one's rivals is insufficient to warrant condemnation. Intent of the following kinds, however, has been found sufficient: 1) intent to achieve monopoly power, or to acquire sufficient power to control price;[15] 2)

state Legal Studies v. Harcourt Brace Jovanovich, 63 F.3d 1540, 1549 (10th Cir.1995), cert. denied, 516 U.S. 1044, 116 S.Ct. 702 (1996); Rebel Oil Co. v. Atlantic Richfield Co., 51 F.3d 1421, 1432 (9th Cir.1995), cert. denied, 516 U.S. 987, 116 S.Ct. 515 (1995); Glaverbel Societe Anonyme v. Northlake Marketing & Supply, 45 F.3d 1550, 1559 (Fed.Cir.1995); Roy B. Taylor Sales v. Hollymatic Corp., 28 F.3d 1379, 1388 (5th Cir.1994), cert. denied, 513 U.S. 1103, 115 S.Ct. 779 (1995).

10. See ch. 8.

11. See Professional Real Estate Investors, Inc. v. Columbia Pictures Industries, Inc., 508 U.S. 49, 113 S.Ct. 1920 (1993); and see §§ 7.12, 18.3.

12. See Berkey Photo, Inc. v. Eastman Kodak Co., 603 F.2d 263 (2d Cir.1979), cert. denied, 444 U.S. 1093, 100 S.Ct. 1061 (1980). See § 7.8.

13. See Morgan v. Ponder, 892 F.2d 1355, 1359 (8th Cir.1989) (statements such as "we will not be underbid," or "we'll do whatever it takes" are "prime examples of remarks which, if portrayed by plaintiffs' attorneys as damning evidence of predatory intent, may lead juries to erroneously condemn competitive behavior. * * * These are phrases often legitimately used by business people in the heat of competition.") Accord, Abcor Corp. v. AM Int'l, 916 F.2d 924, 927 (4th Cir.1990).

14. Brooke Group Limited v. Brown & Williamson Tobacco Corp., 509 U.S. 209, 113 S.Ct. 2578 (1993). See § 8.8.

15. See Photovest Corp. v. Fotomat Corp., 606 F.2d 704, 711 (7th Cir.1979), cert. denied, 445 U.S. 917, 100 S.Ct. 1278 (1980); FLM Collision Parts, Inc. v. Ford Motor Co., 543 F.2d 1019, 1030 (2d Cir.1976), cert. denied, 429 U.S. 1097, 97 S.Ct. 1116 (1977).

intent to exclude competition;[16] or 3) intent to perform the specific act fulfilling the conduct requirement of the attempt offense.

None of these descriptions adequately distinguishes harmful from competitive intent. Intent to "exclude" is consistent with both efficient practices (research and development) and inefficient ones (predatory pricing). The last alternative—intent to engage in the specific act that satisfies the conduct requirement of the attempt offense—is inadvertently used by courts who hold that the requisite intent can be inferred from the conduct itself. This standard can become dangerously overdeterrent bootstrapping unless courts put strict limits on the kind of conduct that satisfies the requirement, and insist upon a meaningful showing of dangerous probability that the conduct is both anticompetitive (inefficient) and reasonably calculated to yield a monopoly. If these restrictions are followed, however, the intent requirement becomes superfluous.[17]

Today many economists and some legal commentators believe that subjective intent should either be irrelevant, or else should be used only to help a court characterize ambiguous conduct. Economists would prefer to analyze the structure of a market and determine from objective evidence whether (1) conduct is anticompetitive or efficient, (2) whether the danger of monopoly is real, and (3) whether the conduct at issue was reasonably calculated to create a monopoly. Judges are often less sanguine about their ability to evaluate conduct exclusively on objective evidence, against the background of a particular market structure. They are particularly skeptical when the analysis requires a fair amount of economic sophistication. Predatory pricing is one example. Finally, judges are inclined to let ambiguous evidence go to the jury and to regard intent, conduct and dangerous probability as three elements that must be established separately.[18]

One effect of economic thinking on attempt jurisprudence has been to restore the specific intent element to its historical position in common law attempt analysis. Historically, the specific intent requirement was designed "to *confine* the reach of an attempt claim * * *."[19] The specific intent requirement acted as a limiting device to help a court decide whether conduct that met the other requirements for an attempt offense should nevertheless be held lawful because the defendant had no evil design. But in the 1950's and 1960's the specific intent element in attempt cases came to perform an expansionary rather than limiting role. In some cases evidence of bad intentions created a presumption of illegal attempt, and could be used to condemn conduct which itself was not clearly calculated to create a monopoly, or under market circumstances where monopoly was improbable.[20]

The trend in most courts is to use the intent requirement as a liability-restricting rather than liability-expanding device. Some courts use specific intent as an aid in characterizing ambiguous conduct. If the conduct is sufficiently close to the line that it could go

16. See United States v. Empire Gas Corp., 537 F.2d 296, 302 (8th Cir.1976), cert. denied, 429 U.S. 1122, 97 S.Ct. 1158 (1977); but see, Blair Foods, Inc. v. Ranchers Cotton Oil, 610 F.2d 665, 670 (9th Cir.1980): "The mere intention * * * to exclude competition * * * is insufficient to establish specific intent to monopolize by some illegal means. * * * To conclude otherwise would contravene the very essence of a competitive marketplace which is to prevail against all competitors."

17. For example, General Indus. Corp. v. Hartz Mount. Corp., 810 F.2d 795, 802 (8th Cir.1987) ("specific intent need not be proven by direct evidence but can be inferred from the defendant's anticompetitive practices or other proof of unlawful conduct.").

18. For example U.S. Philips Corp. v. Windmere Corp., 861 F.2d 695, 698–703 (Fed.Cir.1988), cert. denied, 490 U.S. 1068, 109 S.Ct. 2070 (1989) (letting the jury decide whether defendant's internal memoranda statements such as "let's pound them [our competitors] into the sand" were simply sales talk or sufficient evidence of anticompetitive intent.).

19. William Inglis & Sons Baking Co., Inc. v. ITT Continental Baking Co., 668 F.2d 1014, 1027 (9th Cir. 1981), cert. denied, 459 U.S. 825, 103 S.Ct. 57 (1982) (emphasis added).

20. See Union Leader Corp. v. Newspapers of New England, Inc., 180 F.Supp. 125, 140 (D.Mass.1959), modified, 284 F.2d 582 (1st Cir.1960), cert. denied, 365 U.S. 833, 81 S.Ct. 747 (1961), where Judge Wyzanski described an attempt offense as prohibiting "a person (a) who has an intent to exclude competition (b) from using not merely technical restraints of trade, but even predatory practices, unfair methods of competition, or business patterns not honestly industrial—in short, what may loosely be called unfair means."

either way, knowledge of specific intent or its absence can help the court decide whether to condemn it.[21] In such cases of ambiguous conduct, specific intent generally becomes an additional requirement that the plaintiff must establish. However, if conduct considered alone clearly offers "the basis for a substantial claim of restraint of trade,"[22] most courts are far more willing to dispense with a separate showing of specific intent. They either ignore the intent requirement or else hold that the particular conduct alleged is sufficiently clear that evil intent can be inferred. In *Spectrum Sports*, the Supreme Court approved a formulation of the attempt offense that permits intent to be proven from objective evidence. "Unfair or predatory conduct may be sufficient to prove the necessary intent to monopolize."[23] However, the Court also held that intent could not be inferred from dangerous probability of success alone.[24] So specific intent may be inferred, but only from conduct.[25]

6.5b. "Dangerous Probability of Success"

Often the circumstances surrounding an alleged attempt to monopolize indicate clearly the potential harm to competition. If there are only two firms in a relevant market and one dynamites the other's plant the danger to competition is clear. In most cases, however, the danger is difficult to evaluate. The purpose of the "dangerous probability" requirement is to avoid overdeterrence in situations when the defendant's conduct is difficult to assess or the market in which the conduct occurred is not clearly conducive to monopoly.

The "dangerous probability" requirement was traditionally controversial. For example, the Ninth Circuit found the requirement unnecessary if the conduct that formed the basis of the attempt claim was also a per se violation of the antitrust laws.[26] But in *Spectrum Sports* the Supreme Court made clear that (1) "dangerous probability of success" is a required showing in any attempt case, (2) that dangerous probability of success cannot be inferred from intent alone but must be proven separately;[27] and (3) that the dangerous probability requirement in turn requires the plaintiff to define and prove a relevant market which is threatened with monopolization.[28]

Spectrum Sports also holds that the dangerous probability requirement cannot be met merely by showing that conduct alleged to be an attempt violates a different antitrust law. For example, tying arrangements, mergers and certain refusals to deal have all been treated

21. For example, several courts have taken this approach in predatory pricing cases, where the conduct is almost always ambiguous. See § 8.5.

22. See *Inglis*, note 19 at 1028.

23. *Spectrum Sports*, note 8, 506 U.S. at 459, 113 S.Ct. at 892.

24. Ibid. ("We hold that petitioners may not be liable for attempted monopolization * * * absent proof of a dangerous probability that they would monopolize a particular market and specific intent to monopolize.").

25. See, e.g., Tops Markets, Inc. v. Quality Markets, Inc., 142 F.3d 90 101 (2d Cir.1998) (specific intent could be inferred from dominant grocer's statements that it did not want a rival grocer to use a certain parcel of land; preemptive contract with landowner was "strong evidence" of exclusionary intent).

26. Lessig v. Tidewater Oil Co., 327 F.2d 459, 474 (9th Cir.1964), cert. denied, 377 U.S. 993, 84 S.Ct. 1920 (1964). The Supreme Court's *Spectrum Sports* decision expressly overruled *Lessig*. *Spectrum Sports*, note 8, 506 U.S. at 891–892.

27. Clearly, *Spectrum Sports* overrules such decisions as Mt. Lebanon Motors, Inc. v. Chrysler Corp., 283 F.Supp. 453 (W.D.Pa.1968), affirmed on other grounds, 417 F.2d 622 (3d Cir.1969), which approved a jury verdict of attempted monopolization. The court directed a verdict for the defendant on the plaintiff's monopolization claim because Chrysler faced substantial competition from other automobile manufacturers, but held that the attempt to monopolize could be inferred from the intent alone. The conduct complained of was that Chrysler ended its franchise agreement with the plaintiff and began selling its cars directly through a factory owned outlet. Query: what market was Chrysler monopolizing?

28. *Spectrum Sports*, note 8, 506 U.S. at 892 (intent alone insufficient to establish dangerous probability of success; the claim also "requires inquiry into the relevant product and geographic market and the defendant's economic power in that market."). In fact, the Supreme Court had assessed the requirement earlier. See Walker Process Equip., Inc. v. Food Machinery & Chem. Corp., 382 U.S. 172, 177, 86 S.Ct. 347, 350 (1965): "To establish monopolization or attempt to monopolize * * * it would then be necessary to appraise the exclusionary power of the illegal * * * claim in terms of the relevant market for the product involved. Without a definition of that market there is no way to measure * * * ability to lessen or destroy competition."

as illegal attempts.[29] In any event, in such cases the violation of § 2 is usually inconsequential: a plaintiff's remedy is usually not greater when the same activity violates two statutes instead of one.

6.5b1. The "Dangerous Probability" Requirement as a Screening Device

Reliable evidence of specific intent can be difficult to find and inconclusive when it is found. Conduct can be equally ambiguous. Often the simplest way to assess the danger a defendant's conduct poses is to examine the market in which the alleged attempt occurred. If the defendant's conduct is ambiguous, arguably consistent with both monopolization and competition on the merits, examination of the market will help a court determine whether a dangerous probability of monopoly existed. If the answer is no, the court need study the conduct no further.

More importantly, since evaluation of conduct is imprecise, examination of the market's proclivity to monopolization will reduce the rate and costs of error. The possibility for error is two-fold. First, a legal rule that is too harsh on defendants will tend toward overinclusiveness or overdeterrence: that is, it may recognize all (or most) true instances of conduct likely to cause monopoly, but it will sometimes condemn competition on the merits as well. Secondly, a legal rule that is too harsh on plaintiffs will tend toward underinclusiveness or underdeterrence: it may recognize most instances when monopolization is unlikely, but in the process may overlook some instances when monopoly is a real threat.[30]

Both kinds of errors can impose economic costs on society. Overinclusive rules are inefficient when they brand efficiency as monopolistic. The result is that firms charge higher prices than necessary in order to avoid legal liability, and they refrain from doing things that benefit consumers but that may harm competitors. Furthermore, to the extent that the more efficient firms refrain from exploiting their efficiencies to the full extent, the market becomes attractive to other, less efficient firms. The result will be higher costs and prices.

Underinclusive rules are also inefficient. A rule that fails to recognize incipient monopolization will permit the growth of some monopolies. Both the monopolist's reduced output and its anticompetitive efforts to maintain its monopoly position are socially costly. A perfect legal rule would avoid both overdeterrence and underdeterrence. Unfortunately, when conduct is ambiguous, the legal rule is necessarily an oversimplification of reality. For example, no comprehensible legal rule can weigh all the relevant variables in a predatory pricing case.[31] Recognizing that the rule will sometimes miss the mark, courts must nevertheless strive to minimize the costs of such errors.

When a market is already highly concentrated and has a dominant firm with substantial market power, then the cost of overdeterrence is relatively low, while the cost of underdeterrence is high. The effect of overdeterrence may be to force the monopolist to create a safe harbor for itself by pricing at above its marginal cost, or by avoiding aggressive developmental or marketing techniques that are ambiguous but might be characterized as exclusionary. However, the market power of such a firm would encourage it to price at above marginal cost anyway. Furthermore, an overdeterrent attempt rule in such a market would tend to protect new entrants—both those that are equally efficient with the dominant firm and those that may be somewhat less efficient. Even a market with one dominant, efficient firm and two or three less efficient ones likely will have higher total output and lower prices than a

29. See Kearney & Trecker Corp. v. Giddings & Lewis, Inc., 452 F.2d 579, 598 (7th Cir.1971), cert. denied, 405 U.S. 1066, 92 S.Ct. 1500 (1972) (tying arrangement); Knutson v. Daily Review, Inc., 548 F.2d 795 (9th Cir. 1976), cert. denied, 433 U.S. 910, 97 S.Ct. 2977 (1977), on remand, 468 F.Supp. 226 (1979), affirmed, 664 F.2d 1120 (9th Cir.1981) (acquisition of competitors).

30. See P. Joskow & A. Klevorick, A Framework for Analyzing Predatory Pricing Policy, 89 Yale L.J. 213, 222–39 (1979).

31. See Ch. 8.

market containing only the larger firm.[32] The general effect of such protection will be to erode the dominant firm's status. Eventually competition will drive prices, output and innovation to the competitive level.

However, in competitive markets the cost of overdeterrence is high, and of underdeterrence quite low. Predatory conduct is much more expensive in competitive markets, where the expected benefits must be discounted by the decreased likelihood of success. This is particularly true, as we shall see, of predatory pricing. In a competitive market an aspiring monopolist has a relatively small percentage of the market, and it shares the market with many other firms. As a result, even if it succeeds in driving one firm out of business, it will be unable to reap monopoly profits afterwards. An underdeterrent rule in a competitive market will seldom create a monopoly. By contrast, an overdeterrent rule may force firms to avoid hard competition, even though the market is conducive to competition. In competitive markets the best attempt rule is no rule at all.

6.5b2. Dangerous Probability and Market Power

Although the *Spectrum Sports* decision[33] required the plaintiff to define a relevant market in an attempt case, it said little about the kind of proof of market power or market share necessary to support the claim. Courts have expressed concern that the attempt offense can be used anticompetitively to condemn "unfair" business conduct when there is little likelihood of monopoly. This has generally led to the requirement that the plaintiff in an attempt case must show that the defendant has a certain minimum market share. The Fourth Circuit has articulated the market share requirements for attempt cases this way:

> (1) claims of less than 30% market shares should presumptively be rejected; (2) claims involving between 30% and 50% shares should usually be rejected, except when conduct is very likely to achieve monopoly of when conduct is invidious, but not so much so as to make the defendant per se liable; (3) claims involving greater than 50% share should be treated as attempts at monopolization when the other elements for attempted monopolization are also satisfied.[34]

Most other courts use numbers in the same range,[35] with a few indicating that a rising market share is a stronger indicator of sufficient power.[36]

32. See § 4.1b.

33. Note 8.

34. M & M Medical Supplies and Service v. Pleasant Valley Hospital, 981 F.2d 160, 168 (4th Cir.1992) (en banc).

35. See, e.g., Springfield Terminal Rwy. Co. v. Canadian Pacific Limited, 133 F.3d 103 (1st Cir.1997) (ten percent insufficient for attempt); Ford v. Stroup, 113 F.3d 1234, 1997-1 Trade Cas. ¶ 71838 (6th Cir. 1997, unpublished) (radiologist group's market share of 50–55 percent insufficient for attempted monopolization claim when where entry barriers not affirmatively shown to be high); Arthur S. Langenderfer, Inc. v. S.E. Johnson Co., 917 F.2d 1413, 1432, 1443 (6th Cir.1990), cert. denied 502 U.S. 899, 112 S.Ct. 274 (1991) (58% market share sufficient; 35% share insufficient); Bacchus Indus. v. Arvin Indus., 939 F.2d 887 (10th Cir.1991) (45% to 60% not sufficient to support "dangerous probability" requirement); Kelco Disposal v. Browning-Ferris Indus., 845 F.2d 404, 409 (2d Cir.1988), affirmed on nonantitrust grounds, 492 U.S. 257, 109 S.Ct. 2909 (1989) (55% sufficient); McGahee v. Northern Propane Gas Co., 858 F.2d 1487, 1506 (11th Cir.1988), cert. denied, 490 U.S. 1084, 109 S.Ct. 2110 (1989) (60% or 65% sufficient); Indiana Grocery v. Super Valu Stores, 864 F.2d 1409, 1415 (7th Cir.1989) (50% insufficient); Barr Laboratories v. Abbott Laboratories, 978 F.2d 98, 113 (3d Cir.1992) (50% insufficient when new entry had occurred during alleged predation period); White & White, Inc. v. American Hosp. Supply Corp., 723 F.2d 495, 508 (6th Cir.1983) (25% insufficient); H.L. Hayden Co. of N.Y. v. Siemens Medical Sys., 879 F.2d 1005 (2d Cir.1989) (20% market share too small); International Logistics Group v. Chrysler Corp., 1988-2 Trade Cas. ¶ 68127 (E.D.Mich. 1988), affirmed, 884 F.2d 904 (6th Cir.1989), cert. denied, 494 U.S. 1066, 110 S.Ct. 1783 (1990) (20% too small); FMC Corp. v. Manitowoc Co., 654 F.Supp. 915, 936 (N.D.Ill.), affirmed, 835 F.2d 1411 (Fed.Cir.1987) (fraudulent patent procurement claim could not be illegal attempt unless the patents "dominate a real market"). See 3A Antitrust Law ¶ 807d (rev. ed. 1996).

36. See 3A Antitrust Law ¶ 807e2 ("A rising market share is more likely to suggest a dangerous probability of success than a falling share."); Fiberglass Insulators v. Dupuy, 856 F.2d 652 (4th Cir.1988) (correct to focus on resulting market share of 51% rather than initial market share of 5%). The inference to be drawn from a specific market share is also significantly stronger when the defendant also controls collateral markets that operate as limiters or gateways to the market at issue. See, e.g., Virgin Atlantic Airways Limited v. British Airways, 872 F.Supp. 52 (S.D.N.Y.1994) (airline's passenger shares of 40% and 31% sufficient where defendant also controlled ground

But generalizing about market share requirements in this fashion is problematic. The plausibility of an attempt to monopolize depends on a host of factors, of which market share is only one. Further, the market power requirements in attempt cases vary with the conduct alleged to be an attempt. A firm that seeks to create a monopoly by dynamiting its competitor's plants does not need market power—only a saboteur and a match. The same thing generally applies to other kinds of conduct that have been held to be an attempt to monopolize, such as bad faith litigation or patent fraud. However, in Lorain Journal Co. v. United States[37] the defendant was accused of refusing to sell newspaper advertising to any purchaser who also purchased advertising on a nearby radio station. Lorain Journal's scheme could not have been successful unless it held a dominant market share. If there were competing daily newspapers in the relevant area, anyone who wanted to advertise in both a newspaper and the radio station would have purchased its newspaper advertising from a newspaper that did not assess the restriction.

Thus it is impossible to generalize: some attempts to monopolize require the defendant to have significant market power while others do not. Further, the success of a particular attempt scheme often depends not on the defendant's market power, but on its relatively large market share. Predatory pricing is such an offense: the act of predatory pricing does not require a defendant to have the ability to sell its output at a price higher than marginal cost. On the contrary, the offense itself involves selling at a price often lower than short-run marginal cost. However, predatory pricing is prohibitively expensive and unlikely to yield a monopoly unless the predator has a fairly large market share to begin with.[38]

In all cases it is important to remember that the attempt offense is designed to reach conduct likely to create a monopoly. The attempt offense was not designed to condemn the exercise of present market power. Nor was it designed, however, to condemn conduct unlikely to give the defendant a monopoly. At the very least a plaintiff should be required to identify some market in which the defendant's activities, if allowed to run their course, plausibly would have generated a monopoly.

One corollary of this proposition is that the grouping of sales identified as a relevant market in an attempt claim must be capable of being monopolized. For example, in the *Tops Markets* case the defendant was accused of monopolizing the market for large grocery stores. But entry into the grocery business was easy and numerous sites were available, as was evidenced by recent entry. As a result, the evidence "refute[d] any inference of the existence of monopoly power that might be drawn from [the defendant's] market share," found to be 79 percent. However, then the court went on to find that the defendant could have been guilty of an unlawful attempt to monopolize, for attempt could be established with a "less degree of market power.".[39]

But the court's analysis of the substantive monopolization claim did not identify a nondominant firm that threatened to acquire monopoly power. Rather, it had held that a high market share did not establish monopolization because entry was very easy. Significantly, however, this established that the grocery business was simply not a grouping of sales that was capable of being monopolized. Dismissal of the monopolization claim on that ground should have entailed dismissal of the attempt claim as well.[40] That is so say, the purpose of *Spectrum Sports* was not to require a relevant market definition for its own sake, but to identify groupings of sales in which monopolization was a serious possibility—thus giving meaning to the "dangerous probability of success" requirement.

§ 6.6 Conspiracy to Monopolize[1]

Although § 2 of the Sherman Act expressly condemns conspiracies to monopolize, conspir-

services, gates, ticket counters, baggage handling facilities, and connecting carriers).

37. 342 U.S. 143, 72 S.Ct. 181 (1951).

38. See § 8.4.

39. *Tops Markets*, note 25, 142 F.3d at 101.

40. See also *Mt. Lebanon Motors*, discussed in note 27, which made a similar error.

§ 6.6

1. See 3A Antitrust Law ¶ 809 (rev. ed. 1996).

acy has never enjoyed the distinctive status held by monopolization and attempt. In part this is so because a conspiracy to monopolize is virtually always a § 1 violation, except that the conspiracy allegation is harder to prove because it requires a showing of specific intent[2] and—following after the common law—at least one overt act in furtherance of the conspiracy. Further, allegations of conspiracy to monopolize can be undermined by the failure to prove a qualifying "agreement" in just the way that § 1 allegations are often upset.[3]

Courts generally agree that the "dangerous probability of success" requirement that applies in attempt cases does not apply to conspiracy claims.[4] As a result, it is generally unnecessary for the plaintiff to define a relevant market where the monopoly would be created.[5]

This last proposition may be defensible when the conspiracy involves an agreement that would be illegal *per se*, for in such a case the Sherman § 1 violation can be established without proof of market power. But it makes little sense when the underlying agreement would be analyzed under the rule of reason for § 1 purposes, and proof of market power would be required. In that case the requirement of an overt act adds nothing, because the agreement must still be shown to be anticompetitive.

Finally, at least one decision has found liability for a conspiracy, or at least an invitation to conspire, to attempt to monopolize. In 1982 American Airlines President Robert Crandall phoned Braniff President Howard Putnam and suggested that the two jointly increase fares by 20%. Instead of raising fares, Putnam gave a tape of the telephone conversation to the government, who brought suit.[6] The defense argued that this was in fact an attempt to fix prices, not an attempt to monopolize, and "attempts" to fix prices are not specifically condemned by the Sherman Act. But as the court properly pointed out, a successful cartel acts as a single entity and controls the market, thus "monopolizing" it in the truest sense of the word.[7]

2. The cases generally speak of specific intent as absolutely essential to a conspiracy claim: Todorov v. DCH Healthcare Authority, 921 F.2d 1438, 1460 n. 35 (11th Cir.1991); Murrow Furniture Galleries v. Thomasville Furn. Indus., 889 F.2d 524, 529 (4th Cir.1989) ("vital element"); International Distrib. Centers v. Walsh Trucking Co., 812 F.2d 786 (2d Cir.), cert. denied, 482 U.S. 915, 107 S.Ct. 3188 (1987); Belfiore v. New York Times Co., 826 F.2d 177 (2d Cir.1987), cert. denied, 484 U.S. 1067, 108 S.Ct. 1030 (1988) (specific intent is "essence" of conspiracy offense).

3. For example, Seagood Trading Corp. v. Jerrico, Inc., 924 F.2d 1555 (11th Cir.1991) (summary judgment for defendant on plaintiff's conspiracy to monopolize claim where there was insufficient evidence of agreement). On proof of agreement, see § 4.5. Likewise, the *Copperweld* doctrine holding that subsidiaries of the same firm cannot "conspire" applies equally to conspiracy to monopolize claims. Advanced Health–Care Servs. v. Radford Community Hosp., 910 F.2d 139, 146 (4th Cir.1990), on remand, 846 F.Supp. 488 (D.Va.1994) (subsidiaries of the same parent could not conspire to monopolize); Directory Sales Mgmt. Corp. v. Ohio Bell Tel. Co., 833 F.2d 606, 611 (6th Cir.1987) (same). On *Copperweld* and the intra-enterprise conspiracy doctrine, see § 4.7.

4. See American Tobacco Co. v. United States, 328 U.S. 781, 789, 66 S.Ct. 1125, 1129 (1946) (defendants could be condemned even though they never "acquired the power to carry out the object of the conspiracy. * * * "); H.L. Hayden Co. v. Siemens Medical Sys., 879 F.2d 1005, 1019 (2d Cir.1989) (dangerous probability "need not be proven").

5. For example, Key Enters. v. Venice Hosp., 919 F.2d 1550, 1564 (11th Cir.1990), vacated and rehearing granted, 979 F.2d 806 (11th Cir.1992); Monument Builders v. American Cemetery Ass'n., 891 F.2d 1473, 1484 (10th Cir.1989)., cert. denied, 495 U.S. 930, 110 S.Ct. 2168 (1990).

6. United States v. American Airlines, Inc., 743 F.2d 1114 (5th Cir.1984), cert. dismissed, 474 U.S. 1001, 106 S.Ct. 420 (1985).

7. 743 F.2d at 1122. As the court noted, "Under [the defendant's] construction of the Act, an individual is given a strong incentive to propose the formation of cartels. If the proposal is accepted, monopoly power is achieved; if the proposal is declined, no antitrust liability attaches." Ibid. But on use of § 5 of the FTC Act to condemn unaccepted solicitations to fix price, see Antitrust Law ¶ 1419.1 (current Supp.). Cf. United States v. Microsoft, 1998 WL 614485 (D.D.C.1998) (denying summary judgment and noting allegations that Microsoft attempted to divide markets with Netscape and Apple Computer).

Chapter 7

EXCLUSIONARY PRACTICES IN MONOPOLIZATION AND ATTEMPT CASES

Table of Sections

§ 7.1 Introduction

The chapter discusses various practices that have been branded by courts or plaintiffs as monopolistic. Before these practices can be condemned under § 2 of the Sherman Act, the defendant's product must be found to dominate a properly defined relevant market,[1] and the general considerations and definitions given in the previous chapter apply. The same conduct may also constitute an "attempt" to monopolize if the firm is currently not a monopolist in the market at issue, but threatens to become one. The "power" showing in attempt cases is less, but the conduct requirements are stricter.[2] By contrast, any practice that will support a charge of attempt will also support a charge of illegal monopolization, provided that the higher market power requirements of the latter offense are met.

Since the Sherman Act was passed, many practices have been condemned as illegal monopolization if the firm that carried them out had sufficient market power. These include:

espionage or sabotage

mergers

reduction of output

expansion of capacity or output

price discrimination

refusals to deal

vertical integration

tying arrangements

supply or price "squeezes"

predatory or "manipulative" research and development; altered complementary products

failure to predisclose research and development

attempts to "leverage" a monopoly in one area or market into an unfair advantage in a second area or market

raising rivals' costs

patent abuses, including improperly brought infringement suits, patent acquisitions and "accumulation," and refusal to license

abuse of government process through vexatious litigation or administrative claims

predatory pricing

Predatory pricing and a few related practices are considered in Chapter 8. But, as § 6.1 notes, the mere buying and selling of goods at the monopoly price is not a qualifying exclusionary practice.

§ 7.2 Merger and Monopoly

The first wave of monopolization cases to reach the Supreme Court involved defendants who had reached a monopoly position by merger, allegedly by weakening their rivals and then buying them out. A merger is not an "exclusionary" practice, however. The knowledge that a prospective entrant might be bought up would encourage it to enter a market. A merger or acquisition could "exclude" or discourage someone from entering a market only if the merger created a new firm that had lower costs and was harder to compete with

§ 7.1

1. See Ch. 3.

2. See § 6.5.

than the two firms had been before the merger.

Nonetheless, a merger *can* create a firm with monopoly power, and this firm could then reduce output and raise prices. Further, it might be tempted to engage in exclusionary practices in order to entrench its position. Courts have fairly consistently held that the Sherman Act condemns mergers to monopoly.[1] The most notable exception was the 1920 U.S. Steel case. United States Steel Company had been formed in 1901 by the merger of some 180 firms controlling around 90% of the market.[2] But by 1920 its market share had declined to 50%, largely because it pursued a strategy of setting high prices that encouraged entry.[3] A divided Supreme Court refused to condemn the conduct as monopolization, noting (a) that the firm was no longer a monopoly, given the new entry; (b) that the government had waited about a decade before bringing suit; (c) that the merger seemed to be a consequence of natural developments in the industry, such as economies of scale caused by new technology.

Several early monopolization cases, particularly the *American Can* decision, involved allegations that a dominant firm bought its rivals' plants and shut them down in order to keep market output low. Such a tactic also seems calculated to invite new entry rather than deter it. Any new entrant could use the dominant firm's monopoly price as an umbrella that would permit it to price monopolistically as well. Further, it would have a profitable means of bailing out of the market: it could sell its plant or its output to the dominant firm.[4]

The § 2 prohibition reaches not only the acquisition of an actual rival, but also of a likely entrant or a nascent firm. Indeed, one of the most effective ways for a dominant firm to maintain its monopoly position[5] is to acquire incipient rivals as they appear on the horizon.[6] This is particularly true of intellectual property acquisitions—for example, a firm whose monopoly depends on patented technology might acquire an exclusive right in potentially competing patents developed by others, thus staving off a competitive uprising.[7] Section 2 is presumptively violated by the monopolist's acquisition of an exclusive right in a patent or other intellectual property right at the heart of its monopoly power, although acquisitions of non-exclusive rights are generally lawful.[8]

Today § 7 of the Clayton Act condemns most horizontal mergers involving firms with sufficient market power to be found guilty of illegal monopolization.[9] As a result Sherman Act treatment of mergers to monopoly has become all but superfluous.

§ 7.3 Output Expansion; Strategic Capacity Construction

In *Alcoa* Judge Hand held that Aluminum Company's continual expansion of capacity to meet anticipated market demand was "exclu-

§ 7.2

1. Northern Securities Co. v. United States, 193 U.S. 197, 24 S.Ct. 436 (1904); Standard Oil Co. of N.J. v. United States, 221 U.S. 1, 31 S.Ct. 502 (1911); United States v. First Nat'l Bank & Trust Co. of Lexington, 376 U.S. 665, 84 S.Ct. 1033 (1964). See also 3 Antitrust Law ¶ 701 (rev. ed. 1996); and 4 id. ¶ 911–912 (rev. ed. 1998).

2. United States v. United States Steel Corp., 251 U.S. 417, 40 S.Ct. 293 (1920).

3. See A. Chandler, Scale and Scope: Dynamics of Industrial Capitalism 126–129 (1990).

4. See United States v. American Can Co., 230 Fed. 859 (D.Md.1916), appeal dismissed, 256 U.S. 706, 41 S.Ct. 624 (1921). The district court found that the defendant had acquired its rivals by buying them at inflated prices. It then became short of capital and raised the price of cans dramatically. The result was a flood of new entry. The defendant's prices

> were put up to a point which made it apparently profitable for outsiders to start making cans with any antiquated or crude machinery they could find in old lumber rooms * * * or even to resume can making by hand * * *.

In order to keep the price up, the defendant found it necessary to buy "some millions of cans" from these new rivals. 230 Fed. at 879–880.

5. On maintenance of monopoly power as a § 2 offense, see § 6.4b.

6. See 3 Antitrust Law ¶ 701d (rev. ed. 1996).

7. See, e.g., United States v. Baroid Corp. 59 Fed. Reg. 2610 (1994) (consent decree conditioning acquisition by large firm of competing technology on the granting of licenses to others); Westinghouse Elect. Corp., 54 Fed. Reg. 8839 (1989) (similar).

8. See 4 Antitrust Law ¶ 912d (rev. ed. 1998).

9. See § 12.1.

sionary" because it denied potential competitors a fair share of the market.[1] But expansion of capacity will exclude an *equally efficient* rival only if the monopolist increases output to the point that it must sell at marginal cost. That is, if a firm builds a plant so large that it can service all the output demanded at a competitive price, there will be no economic profits to attract equally efficient competitors into the market. If the monopolist produces less than that, however, the monopoly profits will attract any rival capable of producing at the same costs. Thus expansion of capacity is exclusionary only at the expense of the monopolist's monopoly profits, which are lost when output is increased to the competitive level.

The foregoing may not apply, however, when economies of scale are significant. In that case, the established firm might take strategic measures designed to deprive potential rivals of the opportunity to enter at the efficient scale.[2] For example, it might build a very large plant, but operate it at only half capacity. The low output serves to keep prices high, but the excess capacity, seen by prospective rivals, serves to deter new entrants.

But even assuming that expansion of capacity can sometimes be anticompetitive, antitrust policy cannot condemn it unless it is able to separate efficient from anti-competitive expansions. In the *du Pont* (titanium dioxide) case, the Federal Trade Commission virtually concluded that this was impossible, and criticized Judge Hand for jumping too quickly to the conclusion that Alcoa's output expansion was anticompetitive. Du Pont had developed a new method for producing titanium dioxide, and then built a plant large enough to supply foreseeable demand for the entire market, thus depriving other firms of access. The Commission faulted *Alcoa* for saying "nothing about the scale economies inherent in Alcoa's expansion" or addressing whether "Alcoa's additional output conformed to demand estimates or resulted in excess capacity." The Commission then concluded:

> DuPont's pricing strategy stemmed from its clear cost advantage over competitors and occurred in conjunction with its long-term plan to capture future market growth. * * *
>
> [T]he essence of competitive process is to induce firms to become more efficient and to pass the benefits of the efficiency along to consumers. That process would be ill-served by using antitrust to block hard, aggressive competition that is solidly based on efficiencies and growth opportunities, even if monopoly is a possible result.[3]

Since *du Pont*, output or capacity expansion has not been condemned under § 2 unless it resulted in predatory prices, which must be lower than the relevant measure of cost.

§ 7.4 Price Discrimination; Leasing Practices

Price discrimination occurs when a seller obtains different rates of return from the same product from different groups of customers. Some courts have considered price discrimination by the monopolist to be an exclusionary practice warranting condemnation. In United States v. United Shoe Machinery Co. (USM), Judge Wyzanski condemned the defendant for obtaining a high rate of return from leases of machines in which it had no competitors, and a much lower rate of return from leases of machines in which competition was greater.[1] In this case leasing may have facilitated price discrimination by preventing arbitrage. That is, if USM had simply sold its machines, those charged a relatively low price would have resold to those asked to pay a higher price. Leasing enabled USM to keep the machines from being transferred and also to monitor use, with lease rates tied to intensity of use.

§ 7.3

1. United States v. Aluminum Co. of America, 148 F.2d 416, 431 (2d Cir.1945).

2. See § 8.3b, on strategic pricing behavior.

3. E. I. du Pont de Nemours & Co., 96 F.T.C. 653, 747 (1980).

§ 7.4

1. 110 F.Supp. 295, 340, 341 (D.Mass.1953), affirmed per curiam, 347 U.S. 521, 74 S.Ct. 699 (1954).

The ability to engage in persistent price discrimination is evidence that a seller has market power.[2] But is price discrimination itself an exclusionary practice? Suppose that a monopolist has costs of $1.00 per widget. It identifies two sets of customers who are willing to pay different prices, selling to one set at $1.00 per widget (a competitive but nevertheless profitable price), and to the other set at $1.50 per widget. Now a court forbids it to price discriminate. The firm will either sell to both sets of customers at $1.00, or else it will sell only to the high preference customers at a price of $1.50. Which price maximizes the seller's profits will vary from one situation to another.[3]

Clearly, if the monopolist's non-discriminatory profit-maximizing price is $1.00, its earlier price discrimination was not "exclusionary." On the contrary, the sales at a price of $1.50 to the high preference purchasers would attract new competitors into at least that part of the market. However, if the monopolist's non-discriminatory profit-maximizing price is $1.50, then its price discrimination was exclusionary. If forbidden to price discriminate the monopolist would charge $1.50 for all units, and those customers willing to pay only $1.00 would not be served. They would be available for any new entrant who was willing to serve them at a price of $1.00. By price discriminating, however, the monopolist made the sales to the low preference customers, and competitors were less likely to enter that market.

However, the price discrimination in the above example is exclusionary because it *increases* the monopolist's total output. Price discrimination in the real world sometimes results in larger output than non-discriminatory pricing, and sometimes it does not. When the price discrimination results in a larger output, then the practice also has the effect of excluding competitors. When it does not result in a larger output, it excludes no one. On the contrary, the higher profits that accrue from price discrimination will invite new entry.

So-called price "discrimination" under the Robinson–Patman Act has also been analyzed as a monopolistic predatory pricing strategy. The theory is that the antitrust defendant charges customers in one area a high price in order to subsidize predatory, below-cost sales in another area. This theory and the case law applying it are discussed below in § 8.8.

Although leasing of durable equipment such as shoe machinery may be an effective price discrimination device, it can perform other functions as well. First, as § 3.7c noted, it can enable the monopolist of a durable good to enlarge the returns to its monopoly by protecting itself from competition with its own second hand goods. As the Court noted in the *United Shoe Machinery* case, one impact of USM's restrictive policy of leasing but not selling certain machines was that no second hand market came into existence.[4] Likewise, lessees faced substantial penalties if they terminated their leases prematurely in order to switch to a competitor's machines.[5] In sum, the leases could have acted as an entry deterrence device.[6]

But there is ample evidence that USM's lease policy was also efficient, designed to maximize the reliability of its technically complex machines. The leases gave USM an ongoing interest in the maintenance of its machines and removed from lessees the temptation to look for cheaper fixes elsewhere. In sum, the lease transformed the transaction from one whose subject was a machine, to one that involved a machine-plus-service, and that apparently left the great majority of customers satisfied, although it made life more difficult for independent service providers who wanted part of the market for the repair of USM's machines.[7] Further, many of the

2. See § 3.9b.

3. See 3 Antitrust Law ¶ 721 (rev. ed. 1996).

4. *United Shoe Machinery*, note 1, 110 F.Supp. at 348–351.

5. Ibid., and C. Kaysen, *United States v. United Shoe Machinery Corporation* : an Economic Analysis of an Antitrust Case 13–16, 75–76 (1956).

6. On the general theory, see P. Aghion & P. Bolton, Contracts as a Barrier to Entry, 77 Am.Econ.Rev. 388 (1987).

7. See S. Masten & E. Snyder, United States versus United Shoe Machinery Corp.: on the Merits, 36 J.L. & Econ. 33 (1993).

ongoing improvements that USM made on its machines were small and not capable of being patented. USM apparently had a legitimate concern, which the court acknowledged, that easy access to its machines by competitors would enable them to reverse engineer.[8] The USM decree requiring USM to sell as well as lease may have made the shoe machinery market more competitive. But it probably did so by denying to USM the benefits of its own innovations and by making USM a less effective supplier of well-serviced equipment than it had been previously. Under the decree, rivals naturally did better than they had before, but consumers were not obviously so well served.

§ 7.5 Unilateral Refusals to Deal I: General Doctrine

7.5a. Refusals Directed at Competitors

In United States v. Colgate & Co.[1] the Supreme Court reiterated the ancient common law doctrine that "[i]n the absence of any purpose to create or maintain a monopoly" a private trader may freely "exercise his own independent discretion as to parties with whom he will deal." The rule remains good law.[2]

The *Colgate* doctrine of refusal to deal contains two explicit exceptions. First, the decision not to deal must be "independent." The per se legality rule does not apply to concerted refusals, which are discussed in chapter 5. Second, the refusal must occur "[i]n the absence of any purpose to create or maintain a monopoly."[3] If a unilateral refusal to deal is ever illegal, it is when the refusal is undertaken by a monopolist, or by someone who hopes by the refusal to become one.

For example, in the 1927 *Kodak* case, a monopoly manufacturer of camera film and other photographic supplies attempted to integrate forward into retail sales of those supplies. Accordingly, it refused to wholesale its supplies to an independent retailer.[4] The Court condemned the refusal on the now dubious theory that Kodak was attempting to leverage a second monopoly out of the first. Likewise, in Lorain Journal Co. v. United States[5] the Supreme Court condemned a monopoly newspaper's refusal to sell newspaper advertising to customers who also purchased advertising on a nearby radio station. Although the Court characterized this as an "attempt" to monopolize, the scheme required that *Lorain Journal* be a monopolist to begin with, or else anyone who wanted to buy both radio and newspaper advertising would have bought the newspaper advertising from a competitor. More properly, *Lorain Journal* was trying to force the radio station out of business in order to protect its local advertising monopoly from erosion.[6]

In its more recent *Aspen* decision, the Supreme Court relied heavily on *Lorain Journal* in deciding that a larger skiing company (Ski Co.) violated the antitrust laws when it refused to cooperate in a joint venture with a smaller company (Highlands), the plaintiff.[7] Assuming that the market was properly defined as downhill skiing in Aspen, Colorado,[8] the two firms shared the market, but the defendant was roughly three times as big as

8. See 110 F.Supp. at 350, noting that USM's loss of power to exclude would "confer upon United's competitors the unearned opportunity to copy the unpatented features of United's Machines. These competitors get a free ride." C. Kaysen, note 5 at 76.

§ 7.5

1. 250 U.S. 300, 307, 39 S.Ct. 465, 468 (1919).

2. Reeves, Inc. v. Stake, 447 U.S. 429, 100 S.Ct. 2271 (1980); accord Official Airline Guides, Inc. v. FTC, 630 F.2d 920 (2d Cir.1980), cert. denied, 450 U.S. 917, 101 S.Ct. 1362 (1981).

3. 250 U.S. at 307, 39 S.Ct. at 468. At the time of this writing the FTC has filed a closely watched complaint against Intel Corporation, accusing it of violating § 2 by selectively refusing to license its technology to firms with whom it had intellectual property disputes. See In re Intel Corp., Docket #9288 (FTC, June 8, 1998).

4. Eastman Kodak Co. v. Southern Photo Materials Co., 273 U.S. 359, 47 S.Ct. 400 (1927).

5. 342 U.S. 143, 72 S.Ct. 181 (1951).

6. See also Otter Tail Power Co. v. United States, 410 U.S. 366, 93 S.Ct. 1022 (1973), where the Court applied similar analysis to a statutory monopolist.

7. Aspen Skiing Co. v. Aspen Highlands Skiing Corp., 472 U.S. 585, 105 S.Ct. 2847 (1985).

8. For doubts about this proposition, see § 3.2c.

the plaintiff and controlled three mountains to the plaintiff's one.

The situation seemed highly conducive to a joint venture in marketing. For some time, Ski Co. and Highlands had participated in various ventures to market "All Aspen" tickets that would permit skiers to ski all four mountains at their will. Actual use was monitored and the two firms split revenues in proportion to actual use. Of course, price or output affecting agreements among competitors are suspect under § 1 of the Sherman Act, particularly when they involve the only two firms in the market. In the 1970's the Colorado Attorney General's office had challenged the joint venture and obtained a consent decree permitting the venture to continue, provided that the firms set ticket prices unilaterally.[9]

In the late 1970's Ski Co. became unhappy about the venture arrangement and began to insist on larger divisions of the revenues. The arrangement fell apart when Ski Co. insisted on a formula giving Highlands only 12.5% of the revenue, even though historical usage suggested its percentage should be 14% or 15%. Ski Co. then offered its own three mountain ticket, and refused to cooperate with Highlands' efforts to give its own customers access to Ski Co.'s mountains. For example, Ski Co. refused to sell Highlands lift tickets to Ski Co.'s mountains, so that Highlands could include the tickets in its ski packages. This repeated refusal to continue participation in the joint venture was challenged by the plaintiff under § 2.

In affirming lower court findings of monopolization, the Supreme Court asserted two propositions: first, a monopolist does not have a general obligation to cooperate with rivals; but second, some refusals to deal may have "evidentiary significance" and may produce liability in certain occasions. In this instance, the important factor was that Ski Co. *had* participated in the joint venture for many years, and then refused to do so without a good business justification for the change. Indeed, Ski Co. had failed to offer "any efficiency justification whatever for its pattern of conduct."[10]

The Court concluded that mere failure to provide a sensible business explanation for the change was insufficient for condemnation. The plaintiff also had to show that the refusal to deal had a negative impact on consumers as well as on the plaintiff itself. In this case the evidence was clear that skiers preferred the combined four mountain ticket, and that Ski Co's refusal deprived them of that choice.[11]

Aspen can be criticized in two ways. First, the Court may have erred in concluding that a monopolist *ever* has a duty to cooperate with a rival. Second, it may have been right on the basic principle but located the line in the wrong place.

The first criticism makes sense if we believe that monopolist's refusals to deal with competitors are never harmful to competition, or that courts are ill equipped to recognize the relatively small number of such refusals that are harmful. The facts of *Aspen* appear to belie the first point. Customers were better off to be able to purchase the four-mountain package. To be sure, this could have been accomplished through a merger, but it would have been a merger to monopoly. The refusal to deal robbed consumers of a package that the market had provided in the past and apparently could have provided in the future had the defendant cooperated.

Given that conclusion, the Court's rules for recognizing an inefficient unilateral refusal to deal seem to be quite conservative—not likely calculated to condemn many efficient refusals. First, there must have been a pre-existing dealing relationship. Second, the refusal to continue in this relationship must be shown to harm consumers, as well as the plaintiff. Third, the defendant must be unable to produce a legitimate business justification for the refusal.

The part of the decision that seems most troublesome is Ski Co,'s failure to come forward with any justification. The one that

9. Id. at 591 & n.9, 105 S.Ct. at 2851 & n.9.

10. Id. at 608, 105 S.Ct. at 2860.

11. Id. at 606, 105 S.Ct. at 2859.

seems most obvious is that, when revenue was divided according to actual use, the joint venture agreement permitted single-mountain Highlands to take a free ride on Ski Co.'s stronger market position. As the record in the case bore out, once Highlands no longer participated in the venture, its market share dwindled to as low as 11%.[12] That was so for the same reason that the Court noted in recognizing the consumer value of the venture: customers almost invariably preferred a four mountain ticket to a three mountain ticket, but they also preferred a three mountain ticket to a one mountain ticket. In that case, the venture permitted Highlands to leverage itself from a one mountain offering to shared participation in the four mountain offering.

The real problem with the venture as it was originally conceived is that it gave too high a share of the revenue to Highlands. When division of revenue was based strictly on use, the venture reduced Ski Co.'s share of total market revenue. Assume, for example, that in a market where the venture did not exist Highland claims 10% of the revenues and Ski Co. 90%. This is because skiers have a choice between three mountains only or one mountain only, and nearly all prefer the former, even if they like the four mountains equally well. Under the venture, however, skiers can buy a four-mountain ticket and apply it to the mountains interchangeably. Now, assuming that they like the mountains equally well, we would expect 25% of the use to go to Highlands. Ski Co.'s defense should have been that it was quite correct to insist on a higher share of the total revenue from the joint venture than actual use under the venture suggested. The optimal division would have been for the firms to share the revenue in the same proportion as the market should have produced without the joint venture. In that case the venture would increase *total* sales, and both companies would be better off in the same proportion.

The difficult question for those supporting *Aspen* is finding a way of applying its principle, without losing control of it. The most sensible way is to restrict its application to pre-existing joint ventures or other arrangements: *Aspen* prevents a firm from canceling its participation in a previously created joint arrangement with a competitor, in which the competitor has made a substantial investment, where customers prefer the venture's product and there is no good reason business reason for the termination.

Reading *Aspen* to create a *new* obligation to deal where no arrangement had existed before is a significant extension of its holding. It is one thing to condemn a dominant firm's withdrawal from a venture that the parties had previously developed by negotiation, and one upon which the lesser firm has come to rely. It is quite another to ask a court to create a joint venture for two firms that have not cooperated in the past.[13] For example, suppose that Berkey Photo came to Kodak, proposing a joint venture for the development of a new camera.[14] Should the antitrust laws ever impose upon Kodak an obligation to join such a venture? If so, Berkey (and other small firms) have effectively acquired the right to a say in Kodak's decisions about product or process development. Even the Supreme Court's aggressive 1992 *Kodak* decision, should be read subject to this limitation.[15] The antitrust dispute arose when Kodak adopted a more restrictive policy that made it difficult for independent service organizations to obtain repair parts for Kodak photocopiers. Kodak changed a business relationship that already existed. *Kodak* should not be read for the considerably broader proposition that a firm that develops a new product has a duty from the onset to

12. Id. at 595, 105 S.Ct. at 2853.

13. See 3A Antitrust Law ¶ 772c3 (rev. ed. 1996); and SmileCare Dental Group v. Delta Dental Plan, 88 F.3d 780 (9th Cir.), cert. denied, 519 U.S. 1028, 117 S.Ct. 583 (1996) (dominant dental insurer had no duty under *Aspen* to enter new joint arrangement with supplementary insurer; limiting *Aspen* to refusal to continue in previously created joint venture).

14. The facts are borrowed from Berkey Photo, Inc. v. Eastman Kodak Co., 603 F.2d 263 (2d Cir.1979), cert. denied, 444 U.S. 1093, 100 S.Ct. 1061 (1980), which is discussed in § 7.8.

15. Eastman Kodak Co. v. Image Technical Services, 504 U.S. 451, 112 S.Ct. 2072 (1992). See § 7.6a.

supply parts to independent service firms wishing to repair it.

In all events, a firm's unilateral refusal to deal is monopolistic only if it leads to domination of a market capable of being monopolized. For that reason the Seventh Circuit held that a firm's decision to sell its old inventory in order to exit from the market could not be monopolistic, even if the firm used its own sales personnel to clear out the inventory and terminated its relationship with an independent reseller.[16] One could view the result in two ways: first, the conduct could not be monopolistic because the firm was exiting from the market. Second, a firm's decision to exit from a market should always be regarded as a sufficient business justification for a refusal to deal. Just as the antitrust laws do not impose upon dominant firms a general duty to cooperate with competitors, so to they do not impose an obligation upon them to remain in business forever.

7.5b. Scope of Duty to Deal

The antitrust law requiring a dominant firm to deal with its rivals must be regarded as a severe exception to the general, and quite competitive rule, that firms are supposed to develop their own inputs and expertise and conduct their own innovation. Indeed, forced sharing is inimical to general antitrust goals: it undermines the competitive market process of forcing firms to develop their own sources of supply. Once we have ordered Kodak to sell its film and camera supplies to rival camera supply stores, these stores have lost their main incentive to develop alternative sources for these supplies. That remedy should *never* be offered where the development of alternative sources is feasible; in that case we have used the antitrust laws to undermine rather than foster competition.

Second, as we shall develop in § 7.7, ordering a firm to deal invariably involves the court in setting the terms of sale, including but not limited to price. In the process we will have turned the defendant into a virtual public utility. Antitrust, it should be recalled, is designed to be a *market alternative* to price regulation, not merely price regulation by another name.

For these reasons, if antitrust is going to impose a duty to deal on dominant firms, the obligation must be limited to inputs that the competitive market is not realistically capable of producing. The Ninth Circuit lost sight of these concerns in its *Kodak* decision after remand from the Supreme Court.[17] It concluded that once a relevant market was defined for all Kodak parts,[18] Kodak had a duty to sell every part in that market whether or not the part could readily be produced or obtained from alternate sources.[19] To put this into context with earlier decisions, in *Aspen* the relevant market had been defined as "downhill skiing in Aspen, Colorado." In order to sell in such a market one would need some ski slopes in Aspen, a ski lodge and restaurant, equipment for rental or sale, perhaps a ski lift, and numerous other pieces of equipment. Of course, the *Aspen* plaintiff was not asking that the defendant be required to supply it with all these things; it wanted only continued participation in a joint marketing venture. Under the Ninth Circuit's *Kodak* decision, however, a firm that wished to fix Kodak photocopiers need supply only its labor, office, telephones and trucks; Kodak was required to supply all the rest. Further, while a few of the 5000 parts in a Kodak photocopier were patented and very difficult to duplicate, most were not. Many were common, readily fabricated items

16. Olympia Equip. Leasing v. Western Union Tel. Co., 797 F.2d 370 (7th Cir.1986), cert. denied, 480 U.S. 934, 107 S.Ct. 1574 (1987). Compare Abcor Corp. v. AM Int'l, Inc., 916 F.2d 924, 929 (4th Cir.1990) (firm had no duty to sell repair parts to competitor, particularly where competitor was free riding on defendant's investment in inventory); Oahu Gas Serv. v. Pacific Resources, Inc., 838 F.2d 360 (9th Cir.), cert. denied, 488 U.S. 870, 109 S.Ct. 180 (1988) (firm had no duty to deal with rival when dealing would cost it market share).

17. Image Technical Services, Inc. v. Eastman Kodak Co., 125 F.3d 1195 (9th Cir.1997), cert. denied, ___ U.S. ___, 118 S.Ct. 1560 (1998).

18. For the problems with this market definition, see § 3.3b.

19. See 3A Antitrust Law ¶ 765 (rev. ed. 1996). Disagreeing with *Kodak*: Godix Equip. Export Corp., 948 F.Supp. 1570 (S.D.Fla.1996), aff'd mem. 144 F.3d 55 (11th Cir.1998).

such as cabinet doors, braces, casters, and a flat glass panel. Others were off-the-shelf items such as bolts, nuts, washers, springs, and electrical connectors readily available from numerous sources. By requiring Kodak to supply all these things the court reduced the likelihood that the plaintiffs would develop alternative sources of their own. As a result, the market for fixing Kodak copy machines became less rather than more competitive.

§ 7.6 Unilateral Refusal to Deal II: Vertical Integration, Price Squeezes, Tying and Exclusive Dealing[1]

Cooperative arrangements with competitors are somewhat suspicious, particularly in highly concentrated markets. By contrast, vertically related firms deal with each other all the time. Perhaps for this reason, courts have been more willing to characterize a monopolist's refusal to deal with a vertically related firm as anti-competitive than its refusal to deal with a competitor.

Nevertheless, a broad rule condemning refusals to deal by the monopolist would prevent a dominant firm from achieving cost savings through vertical integration. More fundamentally, a monopolist's simple refusal to deal is only rarely the kind of "exclusionary practice" that warrants condemnation under § 2 of the Sherman Act. For example, if a monopoly manufacturer sells to 50 retailers, and then arbitrarily cuts one of them off, the retail market will remain competitive. Such a refusal cannot result in lower output or higher prices. Absent any showing that the refusal will create a second monopoly in the retail market, it should be legal. Even when the refusal does create a second monopoly, the argument that the refusal will result in lower output and higher prices is weak.[2]

Refusals to deal are a common consequence of vertical integration. The integrated firm begins to deal only with its newly-developed (or newly-acquired) suppliers or outlets, and terminates its relationship with independent firms.[3] Private plaintiffs as well as the government have frequently alleged that vertical integration by a monopolist is an exclusionary practice warranting § 2 treatment.

7.6a. Kodak and its Aftermath

The Supreme Court's 1992 *Kodak* decision denied the defendant's motion for summary judgment and indicated that if a photocopier manufacturer controlled 100% of a properly defined market for its own replacement parts, its refusal to deal with an independent firm that serviced such photocopiers could be monopolistic.[4] The Court briefly considered whether a firm can have substantial market power in a market for its own replacement parts.[5] More problematically, it suggested that a firm could monopolize by refusing to deal with others in markets for its own replacement parts if the firm was engaged in a program of "willful acquisition" of a monopoly—the monopoly, once again, being defined in terms of its own brand of parts and the servicing of its own equipment.

Kodak was only the second largest seller of photocopies, and its share of the general photocopy market (some 23%) was too small to support any § 2 claim. However, the theory of the complaint was that Kodak was taking advantage of "locked in" customers who had already purchased a Kodak photocopier by forcing them to purchase their subsequent repair service from Kodak as well.[6] To be sure, someone who already owns a Chrysler that

§ 7.6

1. Vertical integration by the monopolist is explored more fully in §§ 9.2–9.3.

2. See § 9.2; and 3A Antitrust Law ¶¶ 770–774 (rev. ed. 1996).

3. If the monopolist's vertical integration is by merger, exclusive dealing contract, or tying arrangement, they may be analyzed under both the Clayton Act and the Sherman Act. These are considered at greater length in chs. 9 & 10.

4. Eastman Kodak Co. v. Image Technical Services, 504 U.S. 451, 112 S.Ct. 2072 (1992).

5. On this question, see § 3.3a.

6. The economic literature does contain several models of profit-maximization in markets where existing customers have switching costs—that is, they are locked in to their past seller's particular brand. See R. Gilbert, Mobility Barriers and the Value of Incumbency, in 1 Handbook of Industrial organization 475, 506–508 (R. Schmalensee & R. Willig, eds. 1989).

For example, a firm whose product is nearing the end of its lifecycle will have a relatively large base of past customers and a rather small set of prospective customers. In

needs a new transmission may be stuck, for only a Chrysler transmission will fit into a Chrysler automobile. But customers purchasing goods in a competitive market will generally regard monopoly prices for services and replacement parts as a higher price for the original good, and normally they will buy elsewhere.[7]

However, (1) some customers may not be well informed and Chrysler might be able to charge a higher-than-market price as a result; or (2) Chrysler might change its pricing policy or its policy of dealing with third party suppliers after a significant number of customers are already locked-in to Chrysler automobiles.

Whether or not these propositions are ever factually true, it is hard to see how the truth of either can lead to monopolization of a properly defined relevant market. As § 10.6a elaborates, a firm that controls a monopoly at one stage of a distribution process can seldom enlarge its monopoly profits by monopolizing one or more additional stages as well. From any given firm's perspective, there is a single profit-maximizing price that stays the same as the firm moves into additional vertically related markets. As a result, claims that a firm "monopolizes" simply by controlling the distribution of its own product, replacement parts, or service should be viewed with deep suspicion. Nevertheless, *Kodak* contains a troubling aspect: the defendant had actually raised its repair prices considerably above that charged by the independents, once the independents were denied access to replacement parts, and there was no adequate explanation for this increase. In sum, the case seems to stand for the proposition that when the economic theory is belied by the facts, the plaintiff is entitled to take the facts to the jury.[8]

Unfortunately, the *Kodak* opinion has ensured that the issue rises frequently in markets characterized by complex durable goods that need continual maintenance, servicing, or updating. In such markets ongoing relationships between the manufacturer and those who service its equipment are essential, for the latter must have access to newly acquired information and procedures. In cases where the durable goods themselves are sold in a competitive market, the best approach would be to presume that the manufacturer is in the best position to determine the optimal mechanisms for maintaining its own equipment, even if that involves a strict policy of manufacturer-supplied maintenance. Fortunately, the great majority of courts have confined the damage by construing *Kodak* narrowly, in the following ways:[9]

7.6a1. "Lock-in" Requires Initial Purchase and Subsequent Change of Policy

Suppose that Apex computer company, with 10% of the computer market, bundles its computer with its own unique operating system, thus refusing to permit rival firms to

that case the firm may maximize its profits by raising the price of replacement parts even though the price increase will decrease the amount of profits earned from new sales, either because the firm sells less or else because it has to lower the price of future units in order to offset the higher maintenance costs. In deciding whether such a practice violates § 2, consider the firm that has stopped manufacturing the primary product and now sells *only* the replacement parts. In that case it could set prices above marginal cost to the extent the customers faced switching costs that were even higher. But the monopoly would come to an end when the last copy of the primary product wore out.

7. See § 3.3a; Parts & Elec. Motors, Inc. v. Sterling Elec., 866 F.2d 228, 234–236 (7th Cir.1988), cert. denied, 493 U.S. 847, 110 S.Ct. 141 (1989) (Posner, J., dissenting; purchaser of original motor would consider cost of replacement parts when making initial decision).

8. See § 16.8b, discussing summary judgment aspects of the decision.

High repair prices may be a way of engaging in price discrimination, assuming that those who use photocopiers relatively more require more repairs, and that these place a higher value on the copier. The price discrimination strategy in that case would be to charge relatively less for the fixed cost item (the copier), but charge relatively more for the variable cost items (whether paper and ink, or parts and labor). Such a price discrimination strategy is not anticompetitive, however, and usually results in higher output. For more on this type of price discrimination, see § 10.6e; 9 Antitrust Law ¶ 1711 (1991); and 10 id. ¶ 1769d (1996).

9. For a view permitting liability under broader circumstances than those acknowledged here, see W. S. Grimes, Antitrust Tie–In Analysis After *Kodak*: Understanding the Role of Market Imperfections, 62 Antitrust L.J. 263 (1994). For some economic theory supporting *Kodak* style lock-in under at least a few narrowly defined circumstances, see J. MacKie–Mason & J. Metzler, Links Between Vertically Related Markets: *Kodak* (1992) 386–408 in The Antitrust Revolution: Economics, Competition and Policy (J. Kwoka & L. White, eds. 3d ed. 1999); and see C. Shapiro, Aftermarkets and Consumer Welfare: Making Sense of *Kodak*, 63 Antitrust L.J. 495 (1995).

supply operating systems. A rival operating system manufacturer complains that this is unlawful tying by a monopolist. While Apex has only 10% of the computer market, its customers are "locked in" to the Apex operating system, thus making Apex's own product the relevant market, just like the "Kodak parts" in the *Kodak* case.

But in our Apex case there is no lock-in of underinformed customers, because they buy the hardware and the operating system at the same time, and presumably evaluate the entire package against the offerings of those selling the other 90% of the market for computers. The lower courts interpreting *Kodak* have consistently held that a *Kodak*-style lock-in claim can be made only when the underinformed customer purchase at time T1, and then some change of policy occurs creating a lock-in that the customer could not reasonably have anticipated at time T2 when she has already made her purchase commitment.[10] A corollary of this proposition is that the "lock-in" cannot occur as a result of a contract. For example, a pizza franchisee whose contract requires it to take the franchisor's pizza dough cannot complain of monopolization of the market for "Domino's Pizza Dough" by virtue of lock in. If the contract requires the franchisee to take the franchisor's dough, then the franchisee knew or should have known that fact at the time he originally signed it. At that point in time, Domino's competed with all other franchisor's for this franchisee's account.[11]

7.6a2 "Average" Customer Must be Poorly Informed; or Price Discrimination Must be Possible

One reason that nonmonopolist Chrysler cannot get away with charging $5,000 for its aftermarket transmission is that most customers are sufficiently knowledgeable about aftermarket prices that they will attribute the monopoly transmission price to the cost of the basic automobile. But suppose that there are a few customers who are extremely poorly informed. Couldn't Chrysler then profit by charging monopoly prices. Probably not. While Chrysler might get away with charging the poorly informed customers monopoly prices, it would lose thousands of sales to well-informed customers, who would buy a car whose manufacturer did not charge exorbitant aftermarket prices.[12] The other possibility would be if Chrysler could somehow identify the badly informed customers and price discriminate by charging them a higher price than the well informed customers pay.[13]

7.6a3. Summary: Taking Advantage of Market Imperfections not Within § 2's Purview

It is in fact possible for most firms to charge above cost prices for aftermarket replacement parts, notwithstanding a modest market share of the foremarket. For example, if one adds up all of the off-the-shelf prices for the parts needed to reconstruct an automobile, the price is far higher than if the automobile were purchased in one piece from a car dealer. Much of the excess is a function of the fact that distribution and inventorying of aftermarket parts is costly. Part of it is a result of attempts to engage in price discrimination.[14]

But part of the problem is precisely the one that the Supreme Court's *Kodak* decision confronted: even well-informed customers lack perfect information; they tend to overempha-

10. See PSI Repair Servs., Inc. v. Honeywell, Inc., 104 F.3d 811 (6th Cir.), cert. denied, 520 U.S. 1265, 117 S.Ct. 2434 (1997) (requiring subsequent change in policy); Digital Equip. Corp. v. Uniq Digital Tech., Inc., 73 F.3d 756, 763 (7th Cir.1996) (similar); Lee v. Life Ins. Co. of N. Am., 23 F.3d 14 (1st Cir.) (similar) cert. denied, 513 U.S. 964, 115 S.Ct. 427 (1994); Metzler v. Bear Automotive Service Equip. Co., 19 F.Supp.2d 1345 (S.D.Fla.1998): summary judgment: defendant refused to sell certain internal parts for its diagnostic equipment, but had never changed its parts policy vis-a-vis already existing customers; thus no "lock-in" justifying a finding of single-brand power); SMS Systems Maintenance Services v. Digital Equipment Corp., ___ F.3d ___, 1999 WL 618046 (1st Cir.1999) (similar).

11. See Queen City Pizza, Inc. v. Domino's Pizza, Inc., 124 F.3d 430 (3d Cir.1997), cert. denied, ___ U.S. ___, 118 S.Ct. 1385 (1998); accord Little Caesar Enterp. v. Smith, 34 F.Supp.2d 459 (E.D.Mich.1998).

12. See 10 Antitrust Law ¶ 1740 (1996). For the mathematics of the text proposition, see MacKie–Mason and Metzler, note 9.

13. See *Kodak*, 504 U.S. at 475; *Little Caesar*'s, note 11, 34 F.Supp.2d at 483 n. 38.

14. See note 13.

size the immediate price of original equipment, and to discount the price of subsequent repair. As a result, even a seller with a 5% market share can probably charge high prices for aftermarket parts.

But not every market imperfection is an antitrust problem—and certainly not a § 2 problem, which requires a dominant firm. The real problem of *Kodak* is that if it is taken seriously there is no good means of stopping it short of being willing to call hundreds of nondominant manufacturers and other sellers "monopolists."

As the subsequent chapter on pricing practices reveals, antitrust is not the easy answer to every competitive problem. There are many pricing strategies that are admittedly anticompetitive but that are lawful because they are beyond the judiciary's capacity to identify and regulate with tolerable accuracy. The same is very largely the case in *Kodak* situations. Making the general observation that market imperfections permit manufacturers to charge high aftermarket prices is one thing. Quantifying the amount or the domain of such high prices or the anticompetitive effects of a particular restricted distribution policy is quite another. Applying antitrust sanctions can be much more anticompetitive than the practice itself—particularly if the sanction forces the defendant to supply goods that could be obtained elsewhere.

The complexity problem becomes even more severe when one considers relief. Once we have found that Kodak has an antitrust duty to sell parts to independent service organizations, then we must identify and administer the terms of the sale. The Ninth Circuit did this by identifying a large customer to whom Kodak was selling parts and ordering it to charge others the same price as it charged this customer.[15] But nondiscriminatory pricing is hardly an efficient solution in a world in which some repairers use hundreds of parts every day while other use only one or two per year.

Further, a simple order forbidding price discrimination does not address the problem of aftermarket monopoly. The fundamental problem, it should be recalled, is that the manufacturer has the power to charge monopoly prices to locked-in buyers. Kodak chose to do this by providing the parts only to its own technicians and building the higher parts price into the total service bill. But if forbidden from doing this, the rational strategy would be to charge the monopoly price for the parts themselves. That is, a simple nondiscrimination order may permit other firms to fix Kodak photocopiers, but if Kodak has market power in its aftermarket parts, its nondiscriminatory price will continue to be a monopoly price. Consumers are no better off. The only way to address that problem is through detailed price regulation.

7.6b. The Price or Supply "Squeeze;" Vertical Integration

The price or supply "squeeze" is a variation of the refusal to deal. Suppose that a monopolist at the manufacturing level owns some of its retail outlets and also sells its product to independent retailers. The independent retailers have a difficult time competing with the retailers owned by the monopolist, however. They allege that the monopolist always favors its own outlets in times of short supply, and sometimes refuses to sell to independents altogether. Further, the monopolist either charges the independents a higher price for the product than it charges its own dealers, or else the outlets owned by the monopolist resell the product at a price that the independents are unable to match. The first of these practices is sometimes referred to as a "supply squeeze," and the second as a "price squeeze". In principle they are identical: the integrated monopolist allegedly manipulates the market price in order to injure the unintegrated rivals. The independent retailers are squeezed both by short supply and by their own high costs relative to those of the monopoly-owned outlets.[16]

15. *Kodak*, 125 F.3d at 1225–1226 & n. 19.

16. In *Alcoa* Judge Hand discussed the supply and price squeeze at some length. Alcoa allegedly used the squeeze against independent fabricators of its ingot. United States v. Aluminum Co. of America, 148 F.2d 416, 436–438 (2d Cir.1945).

Most alleged price and supply "squeezes" result because vertically integrated firms have lower costs than do independent firms who must rely on the market. The monopolist who reduces its costs by vertical integration will sell to the consumer at a lower price, and independent dealers will be unable to compete. Any "squeeze" that results from the monopolist's reduced costs should not be an antitrust violation.[17]

But this analysis presents one problem: although vertical integration can create substantial efficiencies, these efficiencies are almost impossible to measure. Further, an overdeterrent rule (for example, refusals to deal by monopolists are illegal *per se*) is bound to cause injury to consumers in the form of higher prices. As a result, courts must have some reliable mechanism for distinguishing efficient refusals to deal or "squeezes" from harmful ones. When might a refusal to deal or squeeze be harmful? Three explanations have been offered. One is the leverage theory, that the monopolist is trying to turn one monopoly into two. However, a monopolist at any single level of a distribution chain can recover all monopoly profits available in that chain. As a result a monopolist of two successive links will not make more monopoly profits than a monopolist of only one.[18]

The two remaining explanations are that vertical integration by the monopolist raises barriers to entry or facilitates price discrimination. Vertical integration by the monopolist allegedly creates a barrier to entry in the monopolist's market because any prospective entrant must come in at two levels instead of one. For example, if a monopolist aluminum manufacturer did all its own fabricating there would be no independent market for fabricators. Anyone who wanted to enter aluminum manufacturing might also have to enter aluminum fabricating.

There are two economic objections to this rationale for condemning vertical integration by the monopolist. First, vertical integration by the monopolist will force a new entrant to integrate as well only if the vertical integration lowers the monopolist's costs. Suppose that the cost of manufacturing aluminum to the independent manufacturer is 10¢ per unit, and the cost of fabricating to the independent fabricator is 5¢ per unit. If the monopolist can reduce the total cost to 14¢ per unit by doing its own fabricating, then a new entrant will have to do the same thing or else be at a cost disadvantage. However, if the vertical integration produces no cost savings, then the market can continue to accommodate independent manufacturers and independent fabricators. If the vertical integration is *in*efficient—that is, if the integrated firm has costs higher than 15¢ per unit—independent firms will actually be encouraged to come into the market, for they will have the cost advantage. The example simply illustrates that many so-called "barriers to entry" are nothing more than the efficiency of the firms already in the market. Few things deter entry more effectively than an efficient firm, whose low costs will be difficult to match.

The second objection to the entry barrier theory of vertical integration by the monopolist is that the theory does not explain why vertical integration is a "barrier" in any useful sense. To be sure, two-level entry may require a firm to raise more capital than one-

17. One possible exception arises when the dominant firm takes advantage of a vertically related firm's specialized investment and effectively transfers the latter's revenues above variable costs to itself. In Bonjorno v. Kaiser Aluminum & Chemical Corp., 752 F.2d 802 (3d Cir.1984), cert. denied, 477 U.S. 908, 106 S.Ct. 3284 (1986), the court found liability where Kaiser was found to have used a price squeeze to drive fabricator Bonjorno's revenue down to a level just sufficient to cover its average variable costs, but insufficient to enable it to earn a profit. See H. Hovenkamp, Antitrust Policy After Chicago, 84 Mich. L.Rev. 213, 270–271 (1985). Of course, as a general matter a firm does not have an obligation to enable other firms to earn profits. But in the absence of vertical integration firms may be in a position to take anticompetitive advantage of the irreversible, or "sunk" investments of others. See generally B. Klein, R.J. Crawford & A. Alchian, Vertical Integration, Appropriable Rents, and the Competitive Contracting Process, 21 J.L. & Econ. 297 (1978); O. Williamson, Credible Commitments: Using Hostages to Support Exchange, 73 Am.Econ.Rev. 519 (1983).

18. See the discussion of the economics of vertical integration in § 9.2. In the context of the price squeeze, see Town of Concord v. Boston Edison Co., 915 F.2d 17, 24 (1st Cir.1990), cert. denied, 499 U.S. 931, 111 S.Ct. 1337 (1991).

level entry requires. But if profits can be made in the market, the capital will generally follow. Vertical integration by the monopolist can create real barriers to entry only when the monopolist buys up all sources of supply of a scarce natural resource or integrates into an area in which entry is restricted by the government and acquires all the available licenses.

The creation of entry barriers, or at least barriers to mobility, may be more plausible if the two levels achieve minimum efficient scale (MES) at widely different outputs. In that case, a firm seeking to enter at the level with fewer scale economies would not be able to compete unless it also entered at the other level, produced at a much higher rate there, and then had to seek a market for the excess production. For example, if efficient production of bicycles requires an output of 10,000 per month, but efficient retailing requires a single-store output of only 100 per month, widespread vertical integration may force those wishing to retail bicycles to manufacture them as well. Even in that case, however, vertical integration could be branded as anticompetitive only under strictly defined conditions. For example, perhaps bicycle production is subject to oligopoly, but large bicycle retailers have been effective at forcing the manufacturers to compete with one another. By integrating into retailing, the manufacturers could make their oligopoly (or cartel) scheme more effective.

Vertical integration by the monopolist may also facilitate price discrimination. Suppose a monopolist manufactures widgets which are retailed in two kinds of stores, boutiques and discount stores. The stores serve different groups of customers who are willing to pay different prices for widgets. The monopolist believes it could wholesale widgets to the boutiques for $4.00 and to the discount stores for $3.00.

However, the monopolist's attempt to price discriminate between the boutiques and discount stores would be frustrated by two things: 1) arbitrage: the discount stores would resell to the boutiques at a price of $3.50, and deprive the seller of its monopoly profits; 2) the boutique owners would file a secondary-line Robinson–Patman action against the monopolist.[19]

The monopolist can avoid both problems by acquiring its own set of either boutiques or department stores. If it owned its own boutiques, for example, it could sell to the boutiques' retail customers directly at a higher price. On the wholesale market it would sell only to discount stores at the lower price. It could achieve the same result by buying or building its own discount stores. In any case, the same argument applies to price discrimination by vertical integration that applies to other forms of price discrimination: it is not "exclusionary." The higher price charged to customers of the boutiques will, if anything, encourage new entry into the boutique business.[20]

7.6c. Tying and Exclusive Dealing—Technical Requirements not Met

Tying and exclusive dealing are most commonly addressed under § 3 of the Clayton Act or § 1 of the Sherman Act. The Clayton Act was designed to go after certain anticompetitive practices under a more aggressive standard than the Sherman Act encompassed. At least in tying cases, however, the Sherman Act test has evolved so as to be largely the same as the Clayton Act test.[21] In any event, the law of both tying and exclusive dealing was intended to apply to firms falling short of the § 2 market share requirements for monopolization. Indeed, only recently have the courts put real teeth into the market power requirements for exclusive dealing and tying, and even today the minimum market share hovers in the range of 30%–40%, which is little more than half of the amount needed for a § 2 violation.[22]

19. On the Robinson–Patman Act, see Ch. 14.

20. See § 7.4.

21. See § 10.3. Several decisions continue to state that in exclusive dealing cases the Clayton Act test is more aggressive than the Sherman Act test. See 11 Antitrust Law ¶ 1800c4 (1998).

22. On the market share requirements for unlawful tying and exclusive dealing, see §§ 10.3, 10.9e.

Thus it makes sense to relax the technical requirements of the tests for tying and exclusive dealing tests when we are dealing with a monopolist rather than a firm with a 30% or 40% market share. In any event, the general test for monopolization would require that. A § 2 offense requires an exclusionary practice which harms rivals unnecessarily,[23] whether or not the technical tying requirements have been met.

The most obvious difference between the § 2 tying or exclusive dealing offense and the traditional § 1 or Clayton § 3 offenses is the lack of any agreement requirement in the former. Monopolization is a unilateral practice. So when a dominant firm unilaterally imposes tying or exclusive dealing under circumstances where a qualifying agreement cannot be proven, the practice may still constitute an antitrust violation.

The § 2 decisions on forced bundling generally do not discuss the "separate product" requirement in tying cases, because they do not follow the tying logic at all; rather they go straight to the question whether the practice is exclusionary under the circumstances.[24] This is simply another way of saying that a monopolist's unilateral "ties" can be unlawful under the general § 2 test whether or not they involve the "separate products" that tying law requires.

Likewise, while the Supreme Court never used the term "exclusive dealing" in the *Lorain Journal* case, the practice condemned under § 2 was in fact exclusive dealing.[25] The defendant newspaper forbad its purchasers of advertising from buying advertising time from a competitor. The Supreme Court never considered what percentage of the market was foreclosed by Lorain Journal's practices—an essential requirement in exclusive dealing cases.[26] Once again, the question in the § 2 case is whether the practice injures rivals unnecessarily and without business justification, and the technical requirements for exclusive dealing by nondominant firms are not the only way of approaching this problem.

7.6d. Use of Vertical Refusals by Private Antitrust Plaintiffs

Vertical integration is a commonly alleged exclusionary practice in monopolization cases, largely because it creates an immediate set of victims who are not injured by anything as subtle as a monopoly overcharge—namely, terminated dealers and retailers.[27] In Paschall v. Kansas City Star Co.[28] a sharply divided Eighth Circuit held that a daily newspaper did not violate § 2 of the Sherman Act by terminating all its independent delivery agents and shifting to self-distribution. The defendant occupied 100% of the Kansas City market for daily newspapers, so its refusal to deal with independent carriers effectively destroyed the secondary market. However, the court could find no injury to competition. It noted that vertical integration by a monopolist could have three anticompetitive effects: it might 1) facilitate price discrimination; 2) increase barriers

23. See § 6.4b.

24. On tying law's "separate products" requirement, see § 10.5. And see Eastman Kodak Co. v. Image Technical Services, Inc., 504 U.S. 451, 462, 112 S.Ct. 2072 (1992), on remand, 125 F.3d 1195 (9th Cir.1997), cert. denied, ___ U.S. ___, 118 S.Ct. 1560 (1998) (conditional refusal to sell parts without service treated as tying arrangement by Supreme Court, but found to be § 2 violation on remand after tying claim had dropped out for failure of agreement; no "separate products" requirement). See also C.R. Bard, Inc. v. M3 Sys., Inc., 157 F.3d 1340, 1379 (Fed.Cir.), rehearing and suggestion for rehearing en banc denied, 161 F.3d 1380 (Fed.Cir.1998) (unlawful under Sherman Act § 2 for firm to reconfigure its patented biopsy machine so that it would accept only its own disposable needles rather than those of rivals; plaintiff chose not to bring tying claim; no separate product requirement assessed). See also 10 Antitrust Law ¶ 1752g at 289 n. 46 (1995).

25. Lorain Journal Co. v. United States, 342 U.S. 143, 72 S.Ct. 181 (1951).

26. On the foreclosure requirement in exclusive dealing, see § 10.9e. In *Lorain Journal*, by contrast, the only evidence of foreclosure was that "[n]umerous Lorain County merchants testified that, as a result of the publisher's policy, they either ceased or abandoned their plans to advertise over WEOL." 342 U.S. at 149.

27. The law of monopolization and the law of vertical nonprice restraints are converging on this point. A unilateral dealer termination is lawful unless the defendant has substantial market power or is attempting to enforce resale price maintenance. See § 11.6.

28. 727 F.2d 692 (8th Cir.), *en banc*, cert. denied, 469 U.S. 872, 105 S.Ct. 222 (1984).

to entry in the primary market; 3) enable a rate-regulated monopolist to evade the regulated price.

The third effect was dismissed as inapplicable. Likewise, the court discounted the entry barriers argument: the absence of independent carriers would not likely deter a second daily newspaper from entering the market, particularly since independent carriers routinely carried periodicals for more than one supplier.

The court believed that the *Kansas City Star* did not integrate vertically in order to price discriminate, because after integration it charged a uniform price to all newspaper subscribers. Before, independent carriers had set their own prices, which varied considerably from route to route. The court appears to have confused price discrimination with price difference, however. Some routes were more costly to serve than others—for example, a sparsely populated rural route likely cost more per newspaper in time and gasoline than a dense apartment route. The different prices charged by the independent carriers probably reflected these cost differences. By switching to a uniform delivery price the *Star* was probably *increasing* the amount of price discrimination; however, the effect was probably to increase the *Star's* circulation. Had it charged rural customers a rate that reflected fully the cost of serving them, it would have had fewer subscribers in rural markets. This conclusion must be read in light of the fact that a daily newspaper makes only a small percentage of its revenue from subscriptions. Most of its income comes from advertising, and advertising rates vary with circulation. Although the *Star* was a "monopoly" daily newspaper, it was almost certainly not in a position to increase profits by reducing its circulation.

Furthermore, *both* the *Star* and its independent carriers were monopolists. The carriers had been given exclusive territories, probably because such territories are natural monopolies. The result was a classic bilateral monopoly, in which the second level monopolist could maximize its profits by reducing output at the expense of the first level monopolist. By eliminating the second level monopoly the *Star* could reduce its own costs, increase its circulation and in the process increase its advertising revenues. Nothing in the case suggested that the termination would enable the *Star* to make more money by reducing its output of newspapers.[29]

The downstream monopoly problem suggests an additional reason for concluding that vertical integration by the monopolist might be efficient and in consumers' best interest. The monopolist, just as consumers or any other firm, is better off if those with whom it deals behave competitively. The monopolist might integrate vertically in order to eliminate a downstream firm's market power. In that case the result could be lower prices and higher output. In *Concord* the First Circuit relied on this theory in refusing to condemn an alleged price "squeeze" by an electric utility. The court used this example:

> If * * * ingot costs $40, the fabricating process costs $35, and the profit-maximizing price for sheet is $100, an ingot monopolist will charge $65 for the ingot, hoping that competition at the fabricating level will keep the total price at $100. If a different, independent monopolist dominates the fabricating level, however, that independent monopolist buying ingot at $65 will mark up the price by more than $35, because he wants to earn monopoly profits as well. The result will be a market price of more than $100, resulting in smaller monopoly profits overall (for the final price is too high), but greater profits for the second monopolist than if he sold sheet for only $100. * * * Under these circumstances, entry by the ingot monopolist into the sheet-fabrication level—even by means of a price squeeze—will help the consumer by limiting the final price of sheet to $100.[30]

29. See generally H. Hovenkamp, Vertical Integration by the Newspaper Monopolist, 69 Iowa L.Rev. 451 (1984).

30. *Concord*, note 18 at 24.

The court's analysis is incomplete in one sense: it is inconsistent with the Coase Theorem, which predicts that successive monopolists in a distribution chain will not woodenly set their individual monopoly prices without regard for the other. Rather, they will bargain their way to a solution that maximizes their joint profits. See R. Coase, The Problem of Social Cost, 3 J. L. & Econ. 1 (1960); H.

7.6e. *Legitimate Business Purpose*

In many cases involving refusals to deal,[31] the court cites the presence or absence of a legitimate business purpose as a controlling factor. The term "legitimate business purpose" in this context is ambiguous and easily misused. Presumably, any act that is lawful and tends to increase the profits of the firm is the product of a "legitimate business purpose." But that, of course, begs the question. One might be tempted to say that an act results from a legitimate business purpose when it is profitable without regard to its tendency to increase the actor's market power or injure competitors. But such a definition cuts much too broadly. For example, research and development would have to be counted as acts not performed for a legitimate business purpose, because they may increase the actor's market power.

Rather, the term "legitimate business purpose" seems to be used in two ways by the courts. First it may mean simply that the defendant had no anticompetitive animus, either generally or directed at the private plaintiff. Second, and more appropriately, the term means that the challenged practice is efficient. For example, a monopolist who integrates vertically in order to reduce its own costs, is acting legitimately, even though cost reductions produce market power and may injure rivals. The better rule seems to be that a defendant who can show that its action produces identifiable efficiencies has presumptively acted for a legitimate business purpose, and further inquiry concerning subjective intent is inappropriate. The defendant's problem in *Aspen* was that it was unable to point to an efficiency rationale for its decision to stop dealing with its rival.

7.6f. *Unilateral Refusal by Nonmonopolist*

In all events, a practice that is legal for the monopolist is also legal for the nonmonopolist. Unilateral refusals to deal by the nonmonopolist are illegal, if at all, because they are part of some other antitrust violation. In many of the important antitrust cases discussed elsewhere in this book, the plaintiff's claimed injury resulted from the defendant's unilateral refusal to deal. For example, in Continental T.V., Inc. v. GTE Sylvania Inc.,[32] which established that vertically imposed territorial restrictions are governed by a rule of reason, the plaintiff was a terminated retailer. Likewise, in many cases alleging illegal tying,[33] exclusive dealing,[34] or mergers[35] the plaintiff claims that, as a result of an antitrust violation, the defendant refused to deal with it, or forced others to do so. In such cases the refusal to deal is generally a mere detail in the court's evaluation of the substantive offense, although it may be important in the determination of the plaintiff's standing or the computation of damages.[36]

§ 7.7 Refusal to Deal III: the "Essential Facility" Doctrine

The so-called "essential facility" doctrine is one of the most troublesome, incoherent and unmanageable of bases for Sherman § 2 liability. The antitrust world would almost certainly be a better place if it were jettisoned, with a little fine tuning of the general doctrine of the monopolist's refusal to deal to fill in the resulting gaps.

Hovenkamp, Mergers and Buyers, 77 Va. L. Rev. 1369 (1991). So the story that firms use vertical integration to eliminate second level monopolists must be reserved for those situations where bargaining between the monopolists is not working well for some reason, perhaps because they are bilateral monopolists and the Coase theorem exaggerates the ability of bilateral monopolists to achieve joint-maximizing solutions. On this point, see H. Hovenkamp, Rationality in Law & Economics, 60 Geo. Wash. L. Rev. 293 (1992).

31. The issue is relevant to both horizontal and vertical refusals to deal. On the former, see Aspen Skiing Co. v. Aspen Highlands Skiing Corp., 472 U.S. 585, 105 S.Ct. 2847 (1985). See § 7.5.

32. 433 U.S. 36, 97 S.Ct. 2549 (1977), on remand, 461 F.Supp. 1046 (N.D.Cal.1978), affirmed, 694 F.2d 1132 (9th Cir.1982). See § 11.6.

33. E.g., Heatransfer Corp. v. Volkswagenwerk, A.G., 553 F.2d 964 (5th Cir.1977), cert. denied, 434 U.S. 1087, 98 S.Ct. 1282 (1978). See §§ 10.3–10.4.

34. E.g., Barnosky Oils, Inc. v. Union Oil Co., 665 F.2d 74 (6th Cir.1981), on remand, 582 F.Supp. 1332 (E.D.Mich.1984). See § 10.9.

35. E.g., *Heatransfer*, note 33.

36. See Ch. 16–17.

In general terms, the essential facility doctrine proclaims that the owner of a properly defined "essential facility" has a duty to share it with others, and that a refusal to do so violates § 2 of the Sherman Act. But this definition leaves numerous questions unanswered, among them: 1) what is a qualifying "essential facility"? 2) does the duty to deal extend only to rivals, or also to vertically related firms or others? 3) when is the refusal to deal unjustified?

The essential facility doctrine is said to have originated in the Supreme Court's *Terminal Railroad* decision,[1] which required a group of firms controlling a railroad bridge and transfer and storage facilities at the Mississippi River to share these facilities with other railroad lines. But the case makes a poor ancestor for the essential facility doctrine, because it was a § 1 case, involving an agreement among multiple firms who controlled the facility. Other decisions sometimes identified with the origins of the essential facility doctrine, such as the *Associated Press* case discussed elsewhere,[2] also involved concerted activities.

Today the essential facility doctrine is concerned mainly with unilateral refusals to deal. Of course, once a properly defined "essential facility" is at issue, it really should not matter whether the facility is controlled by a single firm or a group of firms acting in concert. But if someone is dubious about the essential facility doctrine as a distinct principle of antitrust liability, then the difference between concerted and unilateral action becomes quite important. Concerted refusals to deal are condemned more easily than unilateral refusals, with less elaborate proofs of actual competitive effects.[3] For this reason, the new focus on unilateral conduct has made it critical that "essential facility" be defined with rigor.

The first Supreme Court decision that looks like a modern essential facility case is *Otter Tail Power*, which used § 2 to condemn a public utility's refusal to "wheel" or distribute power for municipal utility companies that wished to supply their own electricity by purchasing it elsewhere.[4] Otter Tail's apparent purpose was to force the municipalities to become its own customers. Most of the Court's analysis was not very helpful, but some important factors that became important in later decisions do stand out. First, Otter Tail may have controlled a natural monopoly, depending on how one views the market for "wholesale" as opposed to retail electric power. Second, Otter Tail was at least partially regulated.

The next Supreme Court case contributing substantially to the "essential facility" doctrine is the *Aspen* decision, discussed previously.[5] The Supreme Court did not decide the case on essential facility grounds, but a great deal of *Aspen*'s language has been incorporated into more recent essential facility cases. Ironically, the Supreme Court's approval of liability in *Aspen* without invoking the essential facility doctrine itself suggests that an essential facility doctrine is unnecessary. One need only look at the market power of the defendant, the rationale for the refusal to deal, and the competitive harm that results. Unfortunately, courts have not followed that route.

In *MCI*, the Seventh Circuit stated the essential facility doctrine in a way that has influenced numerous subsequent decisions. The doctrine has four elements:

> (1) control of the essential facility by a monopolist; (2) a competitor's inability practically or reasonably to duplicate the essential facility; (3) the denial of the use of the facility to a competitor; and (4) the feasibility of providing the facility.[6]

§ 7.7

1. United States v. Terminal R.R. Assn., 224 U.S. 383, 32 S.Ct. 507 (1912). See 3A Antitrust Law ¶ 772b1 (rev. ed. 1996).

2. Associated Press v. United States, 326 U.S. 1, 65 S.Ct. 1416 (1945). See § 5.4b.

3. See § 5.4a.

4. Otter Tail Power Co. v. United States, 410 U.S. 366, 93 S.Ct. 1022 (1973).

5. Aspen Skiing Co. v. Aspen Highlands Skiing Corp., 472 U.S. 585, 105 S.Ct. 2847 (1985); see § 7.5.

6. MCI Communic. Corp. v. AT & T, 708 F.2d 1081, 1132–1133 (7th Cir.), cert. denied, 464 U.S. 891, 104 S.Ct. 234 (1983).

7.7a. What Is a Qualifying "Essential Facility"?

Most of the things found by courts to be essential facilities have fallen into one of three classifications: (1) natural monopolies or joint venture arrangements subject to significant economies of scale;[7] (2) structures, plants or other valuable productive assets[8] that were created as part of a regulatory regime, whether or not they are properly natural monopolies;[9] or (3) structures that are owned by the government and whose creation or maintenance is subsidized.[10] What all these structures have in common is that those who have control over or access to them may have significant cost advantages over those who do not.

Since monopolization is a market power offense, a properly defined essential facility must define a relevant market or a substantial portion of one; alternatively, it must serve as a bottleneck that permits market power to be exercised in a properly defined relevant market. This proposition seems beyond dispute, although not all courts have required that an essential facility define a relevant market.[11] But if the alleged facility does not constitute or control a relevant market, then competitive alternatives are available and the facility can hardly be characterized as "essential."[12]

At bottom, an essential facility is nothing more than a relevant market for some input that is crucial to the production of some secondary product. The fact that an essential facility is nothing other than a relevant market is often disguised from courts by virtue of the fact that the essential facility is generally an upstream input into a production process, rather than a final output product. If one takes the more economic definition of a relevant market as any "grouping of sales" for which substitution is sufficiently difficult to make supracompetitive pricing profitable,[13] then it is hard to find a meaningful distinction between an essential facility and a properly defined relevant market, howbeit, one with no good substitutes.

Of course, one might insist that a qualifying essential facility be *more* than merely a relevant market. This would be quite appropriate if the law imposed more expansive duties to deal on the controllers of essential facilities than on monopolist's generally. But the defendant's duty to deal in the essential facility cases appears to have about the same scope as the defendant's duty to deal in the *Aspen* case, where the Court did not rely on the essential facility doctrine. If the essential facility duty to deal is regarded as broader than the monopolist's duty generally, then the essential facility must be more narrowly defined than the relevant market is. One notable difference is that in an appropriate essential facility case, the defendant's market share is ordinarily 100% and entry barriers are high. That is, the if the essential facility defines a relevant market and a single firm controls the facility, then there are no competitors. If entry is easy, then the facility can readily be duplicated, so it is not essential. Thus essential facility cases could be

7. E.g., *Terminal Railroad* case, note 1; *Associated Press* case, note 2; Consolidated Gas Co. of Fla. v. City Gas Co. of Fla., 665 F.Supp. 1493 (S.D.Fla.1987), affirmed, 880 F.2d 297 (11th Cir.1989), on rehearing, 912 F.2d 1262 (11th Cir.1990), vacated and dismissed on nonantitrust grounds, 499 U.S. 915, 111 S.Ct. 1300 (1991) (gas pipeline). Perhaps in this category fall such cases as Bellsouth Advertising v. Donnelley Inf. Pub., 719 F.Supp. 1551 (S.D.Fla.1988), reversed on other grounds, 999 F.2d 1436 (11th Cir.1993), holding that a telephone company's subscriber list could be an essential facility; the plaintiff wished to publish a competing telephone directory.

8. An "essential facility" need not be a tangible asset. See *Bellsouth*, id., holding that a customer list could be an essential facility. The plaintiff ultimately lost because the defendant was willing to give the substance of the list, but not the format in which it was contained.

9. For example, *Otter Tail*, note 4.

10. For example, Hecht v. Pro–Football, 570 F.2d 982 (D.C.Cir.1977), cert. denied, 436 U.S. 956, 98 S.Ct. 3069 (1978) (public athletic stadium).

11. For example, Helix Milling Co. v. Terminal Flour Mills Co., 523 F.2d 1317 (9th Cir.1975), cert. denied, 423 U.S. 1053, 96 S.Ct. 782 (1976).

12. For example, Castelli v. Meadville Medical Center, 702 F.Supp. 1201 (W.D.Pa.1988), affirmed, 872 F.2d 411 (3d Cir.1989) (hospital not essential facility, since there were several others within the geographic market); Illinois Bell Tel. Co. v. Haines & Co., 905 F.2d 1081 (7th Cir. 1990), cert. granted and judgment vacated, 499 U.S. 944, 111 S.Ct. 1408 (1991), on remand, 932 F.2d 610 (7th Cir.1991) (alleged essential facility must dominate properly defined relevant market); City of Malden v. Union Elec. Co., 887 F.2d 157 (8th Cir.1989) (same; jury instruction).

13. See Ch. 3.

addressed as cases of *extreme* amounts of monopoly.

Most cases finding an essential facility have required more than mere dominance of a relevant market. For example, several essential facility cases have arisen in regulated industries, where the defendant's facility enjoyed legal protection from new entry or was perhaps subsidized by the government. The essential facility doctrine was relied on in the antitrust suit that forced AT & T to divest the local operating telephone companies.[14] The gist of this suit as well as several private suits[15] was that AT & T controlled a monopoly network of telephone lines and had made it difficult for both rival manufacturers of terminal equipment and rival long distance carriers to attach to its network, an essential facility. One might wish to say, for example, that a regulated firm who operates in adjacent competitively structured markets has a duty to give others equal access to its regulated facilities.

In one important respect, the definition of an essential facility is narrower than the definition of a relevant market, and this may justify a somewhat broader duty to deal. A relevant market is a grouping of sales for which the supplier has a cost *advantage* over rivals. For example, suppose that hospital A can treat patients of a certain kind at a cost of $100, but hospital B, which is further away, faces cost of $120. In that case, if our market definition proceeds by hypothesizing a price increase of 10% above the competitive level,[16] we might well conclude that hospital A defines a relevant market, because its managers could increase price by more than 10% above the competitive level without losing sales to hospital B. However, hospital A might not constitute an essential facility, for hospital B is in fact an available alternative. The courts have generally interpreted the essential facility doctrine to require a showing that no practical alternatives are available, including alternatives that face cost disadvantages.[17]

7.7b. The Extent of the Duty to Deal

The trend in judicial decisions is to limit the essential facility doctrine to refusals to deal with firms that compete with the defendant in some market.[18] This conclusion seems appropriate as a general matter, although there are some qualifications. First, although public utilities may have a duty to serve all paying customers, that duty is generally imposed by legislation, and it is not the province of an antitrust court to decide when the duty should be imposed in the absence of a statute requiring it. Second, a refusal to deal with a firm that does not compete at any level with the defendant rarely has anticompetitive consequences. Of course, one must distinguish the situation where the vertically related firm is also an actual or potential rival of the defendant. For example, in *Fishman* the defendant controller of Chicago Stadium was also an intending purchaser of the Chicago Bulls, as was the plaintiff.[19] As a result, the defendant stood simultaneously in a vertical (lessor-lessee) and competitive relationship with the defendant, and the refusal should be regarded as directed against a competitor.

14. United States v. AT & T, 552 F.Supp. 131 (D.D.C. 1982), affirmed mem. sub nom. Maryland v. United States, 460 U.S. 1001, 103 S.Ct. 1240 (1983); United States v. AT & T, 524 F.Supp. 1336 (D.D.C.1981).

15. For example, *MCI* case, note 6 at 1133. See also United States v. Western Electric Co., 900 F.2d 283, 296 (D.C.Cir.1990) (local telephone exchange characterized as essential facility); Southern Pacific Communications Co. v. AT & T, 740 F.2d 980, 1007 (D.C.Cir.1984), cert. denied, 470 U.S. 1005, 105 S.Ct. 1359 (1985) (same); Litton Sys. v. AT & T, 700 F.2d 785, 811 (2d Cir.1983) (same). Cf. AT & T Corp. v. Iowa Utilities Board, ___ U.S. ___, 119 S.Ct. 721 (1999), a nonantitrust case in which the Supreme Court majority said that the antitrust essential facility doctrine might define a dominant local telephone company's duty to share its facilities with rival local carriers, but refused to decide the issue (id. at 734); and Justice Breyer's concurrence arguing more forcefully for that result (id. at 753).

16. See § 3.2.

17. See McKenzie v. Mercy Hospital, 854 F.2d 365 (10th Cir.1988) (hospital not an essential facility when doctor could treat patients in his office); Alaska Airlines v. United Airlines, 948 F.2d 536, 544–546 (9th Cir.1991), cert. denied, 503 U.S. 977, 112 S.Ct. 1603 (1992) (computer reservation system not essential facility, where denial would merely impose higher costs on rivals).

18. For example, Interface Group v. Massachusetts Port Authority, 816 F.2d 9 (1st Cir.1987); Garshman v. Universal Resources Holding, 824 F.2d 223 (3d Cir.1987).

19. Fishman v. Estate of Wirtz, 807 F.2d 520 (7th Cir.1986).

As a general matter a firm is best off when it serves every customer able to pay;[20] so a refusal to deal with a customer who is not a competitor is generally explained by reasons that have nothing to do with competition—for example, the customer may have a bad record paying its bills or getting along with others; or perhaps the facility is already at capacity.

One possible exception to a rule limiting protection to competitors occurs when the current users of the essential facility are engaged in cartel or oligopoly behavior and using the facility as a device for restricting entry. Suppose a pipeline company ships no natural gas itself, but leases space to four customers. The four customers are fixing or tacitly coordinating gas prices. They now convince the pipeline company to refuse to lease space to a fifth or subsequent shipper, even though space is available. As a starting premise, it would be in the pipeline company's best interest to lease the line to as many customers as it can, right up to the line's full capacity. But the four current lessees may be in a position to share their cartel profits with the pipeline company.[21] In that case, the pipeline's refusal to lease space to additional lessees would be anticompetitive. Once again, however, the story describes a *concerted*, rather than unilateral, refusal to deal; the "essential facility" analysis is unnecessary to justify condemning the refusal.

7.7c. Reasonableness of Refusal to Deal

The question of justifiable refusals reduces to two issues. *First*, must an anticompetitive motive or effect be shown, or is the mere refusal to share an essential facility sufficient to establish liability? *Second*, can the controller of an essential facility defend by showing that the refusal was for a legitimate business purpose?

As a premise, Sherman § 2 should be applied only to refusals to deal that threaten higher prices or reduced output in some relevant market, or that threaten to perpetuate monopoly power already owned. As a result, the plaintiff must show that the refusal to deal is exclusionary, or anticompetitive in the economic sense. With respect to private plaintiffs, the "antitrust injury" doctrine confirms this requirement, and there is no reason for thinking that doctrine does not apply in essential facility cases.[22]

Nevertheless, some courts have applied the essential facility doctrine even when it seemed quite clear that competition was largely unaffected by the defendant's refusal to deal. For example, in Fishman v. Wirtz the defendant refused to make the Chicago Stadium available to the plaintiff, who consequently lost the opportunity to purchase the Chicago Bulls professional basketball team.[23] But the Bulls were already playing at Chicago Stadium, and it was not clear that there would be more competition in any market as a result of the defendant's refusal to deal. The dispute at hand was about ownership of the Bulls, not about the insertion of competition via a second team into a monopolized market.[24]

To view the problem in another way, if the controller of an essential facility—say, a natural gas pipeline—is already leasing space to a dozen shippers of natural gas, competition may not be affected by the controller's refusal to lease the line to yet another shipper. That decision may harm the shipper, but it does not appear to make any market less competitive. Alternatively, if two firms vie to ship in a

20. As a result, courts have been skeptical about claims that hospital refusals to grant certain doctors staff privileges are anticompetitive under the essential facility doctrine. Since hospitals make money by admitting patients up to their full capacity, and since doctors admit patients, a hospital would presumably wish to approve every competent doctor that met its needs. See, for example, Weiss v. York Hosp., 745 F.2d 786 (3d Cir.1984), cert. denied, 470 U.S. 1060, 105 S.Ct. 1777 (1985).

21. This would likely be true only if they, but not the plaintiff, are in a position to build a competing line or seek alternative arrangements. In that case the pipeline company would be better off sharing the monopoly profits that result from the current situation than earning only a competitive rate of return otherwise.

22. See § 16.3. See also Flip Side Productions, Inc. v. Jam Productions, Ltd., 843 F.2d 1024 (7th Cir.), cert. denied, 488 U.S. 909, 109 S.Ct. 261 (1988) (applying antitrust injury doctrine to essential facility claim).

23. Note 19.

24. See Judge Easterbrook's dissent, 807 F.2d 520 at 563–564.

natural monopoly pipeline, and one wins by unfair means, the unfairness goes to the *identity* of the monopolist, not to the question whether the market will be monopolized or competitive. In the first of these cases the antitrust injury requirement is not met; in the second, it may or may not be met depending on the nature of the dispute. If the low price bidder for a natural gas contract was ousted by unfair means, then its replacement by a higher price bidder could be anticompetitive even though at any given time the essential facility could be occupied by only one firm.

Most courts also hold that, even if there might be anticompetitive effects, the controller of an essential facility need not compromise or impair its own business in order to accommodate others. For example, if the owner of a natural gas pipeline is using it to full capacity to carry its own gas, for which it has a ready market, it has no duty to lease space in the line to a competitor.[25]

7.7d. Essential Facility Doctrine Inconsistent with General Antitrust Goals

One problem with the logic of the "essential facility" doctrine is that, if the doctrine is restricted to refusals calculated to create or perpetuate monopoly power, then the more general antitrust rules respecting refusals to deal seem quite adequate to do the job.[26] But if the limitation is not imposed, then the essential facility doctrine loses its mooring in § 2 of the Sherman Act. It begins to operate as a "fair access" statute that forces one set of private firms to accommodate another set even when competition is not improved. As a result, the doctrine is either superfluous or else inconsistent with basic antitrust principles.

7.7d1. Forced Sharing Requires Price Administration

As noted in § 7.6, compelling a single firm to deal requires a court to set terms and conditions of the sale, thus turning it into a kind of regulatory agency. To illustrate, suppose that the defendant owns a gas pipeline from origin point X to market point Y. The cost of gas at point X is $10.00 per unit, and the cost of pipeline shipment to point Y is $2.00 per unit. But X is a monopolist and charges a delivered price of $15.00 per unit, thus capturing $3.00 in excess profits per unit shipped. Now a gas producer at point X, wishing to ship to point Y itself, uses the essential facility doctrine to obtain a judicial injunction ordering the defendant to lease space on its pipeline. What price will the defendant charge?

Unless constrained by the court's order the defendant will charge its profit-maximizing price of $5.00 per unit shipped, reducing its own shipments accordingly. The result is that the amount of gas shipped through the pipeline will remain unchanged and the price will not budge. The pipeline owner simply obtains its monopoly overcharge through the lease of the pipeline rather than as a markup on the shipped gas.

As the illustration suggests, the essential facility doctrine does nothing to improve consumer welfare.[27] When forced to share, the monopolist owner of an essential facility will charge the plaintiff the same monopoly price that it would otherwise charge to customers. The only way that the court can avoid this result is by ordering sharing *and* regulating the price. At that point the pipeline has become, for all practical purposes, a public utility.[28]

7.7d2. Forced Sharing Undercuts Incentives to Develop Alternative Sources of Supply

The impact of the observation in § 7.7d1 becomes even more severe when we consider a

25. Illinois, ex rel. Burris v. Panhandle Eastern Pipe Line Co., 935 F.2d 1469 (7th Cir.1991), cert. denied, 502 U.S. 1094, 112 S.Ct. 1169 (1992); City of Chanute v. Williams Natural Gas Co., 955 F.2d 641 (10th Cir.), cert. denied, 506 U.S. 831, 113 S.Ct. 96 (1992).

26. See §§ 7.6–7.7. See generally P. Areeda, Essential Facilities: an Epithet in Need of Limiting Principles, 58 Antitrust L.J. 841 (1989).

27. See Blue Cross & Blue Shield United of Wisconsin v. Marshfield Clinic, 65 F.3d 1406, 1413 (7th Cir.1995), cert. denied, 516 U.S. 1184, 116 S.Ct. 1288 (1996) (essential facility doctrine has "nothing to do with antitrust principles," for "consumers are not better off if the natural monopolist is forced to share some of his profits with potential competitors. . . .").

28. See 3A Antitrust Law ¶ 771b (rev. ed. 1996).

second consequence of forced sharing: once the plaintiff has been given the right to share the defendant's pipeline, it loses its incentive to build its own pipeline. In this sense, the essential facility doctrine is manifestly hostile toward the general goal of the antitrust laws. It serves to undermine rather than encourage rivals to develop alternative inputs of their own. In the pipeline situation, real competition occurs when a second or third pipeline are built, and they are most likely to be built when rivals are forced to build them, rather than obtaining judicially mandated access to the defendant's pipeline.

§ 7.8 "Predatory" Product Design and Development; Failure to Predisclose; Altered Complementary Products

Many private plaintiffs have alleged that the defendant was a monopolist and that it "manipulated" the product or the market in such a way as to prevent the plaintiff from competing. These manipulatory practices have included physical bundling or other strategic selection of technologies, "predatory" research and development, failure to predisclose certain technical or design innovations, and strategic use of brand name advertising. The 1970's and early 1980's witnessed a wave of such cases, but they began to subside in the late 1980's.

Courts have generally presumed that an attempt by a monopolist to use a tie-in or similar arrangement to extend its monopoly power into a second market is illegal. Suppose, for example, that a monopolist in the film market includes processing in the sale price of its film, and refuses to sell film without the processing. In 1954 the Eastman Kodak Co. agreed in a consent decree not to engage in mandatory package pricing of this sort.[1] The government's theory was that Kodak was attempting to use its monopoly in one market (film) to obtain a second monopoly in another market (processing). Alternatively, the film-processing tie could be seen as raising barriers to entry in the markets for both film and processing. Once Kodak had succeeded in monopolizing both markets, no one could enter at either level without entering both levels simultaneously.[2] Today most commentators and many courts are skeptical about such claims. They note that if monopoly profits are available in any market, the absolute cost of capital will not deter entry or even delay it significantly.[3] Nevertheless, the entry barrier theory in the *Kodak* case makes sense if economies of scale are far more substantial at one level than they are at the other. If a small, local firm can efficiently process film but only a large national firm with a significant share of the market can manufacture it, Kodak's film-processing tie would effectively retard entry into the processing market.[4]

7.8a. Predatory Product or Process Innovation

A somewhat different claim of monopolization by bundling was raised in several cases brought against IBM, such as *California Computer Products*.[5] The defendant manufactured central processing computer units and various "peripherals" such as memory devices, monitors, and controllers. The plaintiff manufactured only disk drives, a type of memory device. The defendant introduced a new line of computers in which the memory and central processing units were assembled in the same box and sold as a single product. The defendant was generally able to show that the new units performed faster and were less expensive than their predecessors. However, the plaintiffs characterized the new line of computers as "technological manipulation" designed only to eliminate the independent market for separate memory units. The court refused to condemn such innovation.

§ 7.8

1. United States v. Eastman Kodak Co., Civ. #6450, 1954 Trade Cas. ¶ 67920 (W.D.N.Y. Dec. 21, 1954).

2. See J. Bain, Barriers to New Competition 1–41 (1956).

3. See R. Bork, The Antitrust Paradox: A Policy at War With Itself 310–29 (1978; rev. ed. 1993); H. Demsetz, Barriers to Entry, 72 Amer.Econ.Rev. 47 (1982).

4. For more on tying arrangements, see ch. 10.

5. California Computer Products, Inc. v. IBM Corp., 613 F.2d 727 (9th Cir.1979).

Should the development of a new product that reduces or eliminates the market for some existing product manufactured by a competitor ever be illegal monopolization?[6] Two possibilities come to mind: 1) if it is undisputed that the new product is not superior to the old product, but is perhaps even inferior; 2) if there is clear evidence that the defendant's intent in developing the new product was to destroy the independent market for the competitor's product.

Both situations raise significant problems of administration. First, whether a new product is "superior" or "inferior" to an old product is entirely a matter of consumer preference, not of judicial decision.[7] If IBM's new computer system with the built-in memory was inferior to the old system in the eyes of consumers, they would refuse to buy the new system.

The question of bad intent is even clearer: every inventor "intends" his invention to injure the competing products of close competitors, for that is the only way his own invention is likely to find a market. Suppose that Henry Ford knew absolutely that production of the Model T would destroy the business of a carriage maker across the street. Should its development be illegal? Certainly not. Suppose that Henry Ford developed the Model T for no other reason than to ruin the business of the carriage maker, whom he disliked intensely? We might wish to condemn such behavior, but there is simply no way to distinguish between "legitimate" and "illegitimate" manifestations of intent. Intent is merged into the completed result, in this case a new product whose development injures or destroys certain competitors. No reasonable basis exists for concluding that the development of a new product or group of products is illegal monopolization. Such a rule would certainly do far more harm to the innovative processes in a market economy than it would promote competitive efficiency.[8] *Ex ante*, it would entitle firms injured by the technological development of another to a discovery trip through their records in search of anything that might be construed as bad intent. Better to start at the onset by making intent irrelevant.

This rule probably requires a single, cautiously stated exception: inquiries into intent may be permissible when the new technology clearly raises a rivals costs *and* appears to render no improvement in product. As a general matter, rivals need not be worried about products that are not improvements, because the improver will not be able to sell more. But one situation is troublesome. To borrow a few facts from *Automatic Radio*,[9] suppose a monopoly automobile manufacturer has always placed a "standard" 2 by 6 inch opening on the dashboard for a car radio. The auto maker will sell a radio, but a large industry has come into existence of firms that sell car radios as well, and the customer has quite a set of choices. Without warning, when the new automobile models come out the shape and size of the opening has been changed to 2.5 by 5 inches, and the automaker has a redesigned radio to match. The radio is not technically superior to the old radio. Whether it is an aesthetic improvement is a matter of opinion. Further, the prospect exists that the automaker will frequently change the shape of the radio, and the smaller radio makers will require at least a year to redesign their own competing radios.[10]

6. The Ninth Circuit thought not. See Id. at 744:

> IBM, assuming it was a monopolist, had the right to redesign its products to make them more attractive to buyers—whether by reason of lower manufacturing cost and price or improved performance. It was under no duty to help Cal Comp or other peripheral equipment manufacturers survive or expand. * * * The reasonableness of IBM's conduct in this regard did not present a jury issue.

7. See Automatic Radio Mfg. Co. v. Ford Motor Co., 272 F.Supp. 744 (D.Mass.1967), affirmed, 390 F.2d 113 (1st Cir.1968), cert. denied, 391 U.S. 914, 88 S.Ct. 1807 (1968), where the innovation may have been an aesthetic improvement, but not a technical one.

8. For a contrary view see J. Ordover & R. Willig, An Economic Definition of Predation: Pricing and Product Innovation, 91 Yale L.J. 8 (1981). For a response, see J. G. Sidak, Debunking Predatory Innovation, 83 Col.L.Rev. 1121 (1983).

9. Note 7.

10. See J. Farrell & G. Saloner, Installed Base and Compatibility: Innovation, Product Pre–Announcements and Predation, 76 Am. Econ. Rev. 940 (1986).

Cases like this are dangerous for antitrust policy makers. The story is barely different from *Berkey Photo*, discussed below, but it does expose a problem. The world is full of complementary products. Indeed, almost every product is complementary to something else. Two conclusions follow. First, the label "free riding" is not very helpful. One can easily conclude that the small radio manufacturers are "free riding" on the automaker, or that Berkey Photo was "free riding" on Kodak. In each case, the smaller firm was building a product designed to take advantage of what had gone into the development of the other's product. The implication, of course, is that neither plaintiff deserves relief.

But how far is the free rider point to be pushed? Are butter makers "free riding" on bakers, simply because butter takes advantage of customer's taste for good bread? Technically speaking, the answer may be yes. Indeed, butter makers even profit from advertising in bread: if bread sales increase, butter increases will follow. But this tells us only that the concept of "free riding" is often not very useful for distinguishing between worthy and unworthy sellers of complementary goods.

Second, whether this is a monopoly problem depends on our assumptions about how imperfect markets are. Ford probably cannot leverage additional monopoly profits in automobiles by monopolizing the markets for car radios as well. But serious damage to Automatic Radio in the market for car radios may also damage its incipient developments in the market for household radios, and Ford may be a player there as well.

But, to repeat, the exception must be stated very narrowly. When the claim of monopolization or attempt rests on an innovation in product or process, inquiries into the innovator's intent should generally be dismissed as irrelevant. The inquiry should be permitted only where both of the following conditions are met: (1) the innovation at issue clearly raises the rivals, or plaintiffs, costs or excludes it from a properly defined relevant market; and (2) there is no basis for believing that the challenged innovation is or could reasonably have been intended to be an improvement. It goes without saying that the defendant firm must also have substantial market power in a properly defined relevant market.[11]

In the *C.R. Bard* case the Federal Circuit believed it had found such a situation.[12] Bard produced a patented gun that took tissue samples by injecting a small disposable needle beneath the surface of the skin. Formerly the needles had been sold by multiple firms, one of which was the plaintiff. However, *Bard* redesigned the gun so as to accept only its own needles. There was some evidence that the redesigned gun was not an improvement over the earlier version and that Bard's only purpose in redesigning it was to make rivals' needles incompatible. The plaintiff could probably have manufactured the redesigned needle but for the fact that the new needle was itself patented.[13] The court permitted a jury to find unlawful monopolization on these facts. It affirmed a jury instruction that "conduct that involves the introduction of superior products" is not exclusionary, but that if the "conduct is ambiguous, direct evidence of a specific intent to monopolize may lead you to conclude that the conduct was intended to be and was in fact exclusionary or restrictive."[14]

7.8b. Failure to Predisclose New Technology

In *Berkey Photo* a rival claimed that Kodak, a camera and film monopolist, violated § 2 by failing to predisclose information about a new product package. The facts were roughly these: Kodak developed a revolutionary new camera that pleased consumers and may have performed better than equivalently priced cameras. The camera also used a new type of film in a patented cartridge that was difficult for rivals to duplicate. Kodak then introduced the new camera and film cartridge simultaneously. Within a few months competing manufactur-

11. See Ch. 3. On problem with *Automatic Radio*, note 7, is Ford's apparent lack of market power in the automobile market.

12. C.R. Bard, Inc. v. M3 Sys., Inc., 157 F.3d 1340, 1371 (Fed.Cir.1998). The case is also discussed in § 6.4b.

13. See *C.R. Bard*, note 12 at 1370.

14. Ibid.

ers would very likely be able to copy both the camera and the film and bring them to market themselves. During the interval, however, the camera monopolist would enjoy not only the monopoly profits in its new camera, but would also be the only provider of the new film.[15]

Competing film manufacturers are undoubtedly injured by this failure to predisclose. They would have been better off if they also could have had film on the market the day the new camera was introduced. Is competition injured? Kodak could probably make all available monopoly profits by selling the camera at its profit-maximizing price. It would then have to charge a competitive price for the film anyway. In this case, however, Kodak very likely used its domination of both camera and film to price discriminate. The high use photographer who shoots 20 rolls of film per day may value the new camera much more highly than the person who shoots 3 rolls per year. By transferring part of the available monopoly profits from the camera to the film, Kodak may have been able to obtain a higher overall rate of return from the higher intensity users.[16]

While Kodak's failure to predisclose may have facilitated price discrimination, such discrimination is generally not socially harmful. Indeed, it probably permitted the monopolist to sell more cameras than it would have otherwise. That will generally benefit consumers, and in the long run it may even mean a larger market for the competing film manufacturers. In *Berkey* the Second Circuit refused to require a monopolist to predisclose new technology, and no court since has assessed that requirement.

7.8c. Strategic Entry Deterrence; Predatory Advertising, Excessive Product Differentiation

The economic literature contains numerous other discussions of anticompetitive strategies that rely on innovation or manipulation of product design to facilitate monopoly pricing. Such strategies may impose higher costs on rivals or prospective entrants than they do on the strategizing firm. For example, a firm in a product differentiated market might respond to new entry by redesigning its product (or introducing an additional product variation) that resembles the design of the newcomer's product closely. The result is that the new firm's entry is less profitable, since it was counting on its separation from other firms in product space. Such a move could make the new entrant's entry unprofitable and may deter future entrants from planning the same thing.[17]

It is often important to distinguish whether such practices are directed at firms that are already in the market, or whether they are designed to deter new entrants. The firm already in the market generally faces a quite different set of calculations than the firm contemplating entry. For example, the outsider will not enter unless it calculates that its own entry will be profitable even after its anticipated output is added to current market output. Likewise, the firm contemplating entry will very likely also be looking at alternative uses for its capital. If one market looks a little less profitable, it may respond by investing elsewhere. By contrast, the firm already in the market is much more tenacious, and will likely continue producing even if it is not earning a profit. The greater its irreversible, or "sunk" commitment, the less likely it will be willing to leave.

These facts suggest that many exclusionary practices are more effective at *deterring* entry than at forcing the exit of a firm who is already in the market. Unfortunately, howev-

15. Berkey Photo, Inc. v. Eastman Kodak Co., 603 F.2d 263 (2d Cir.1979), cert. denied, 444 U.S. 1093, 100 S.Ct. 1061 (1980); see also Foremost Pro Color, Inc. v. Eastman Kodak Co., 703 F.2d 534 (9th Cir.1983), cert. denied, 465 U.S. 1038, 104 S.Ct. 1315 (1984).

16. In this case the failure to predisclose operates in the same way as a variable proportion tying arrangement. See § 10.6e. Price discrimination is less likely in a case like *Automatic Radio*, note 7, where one product was an automobile and the other product a car radio. Most purchasers of one car will buy only one car radio.

17. Strategies such as these were at issue in the Supreme Court's decision in Brooke Group Ltd. v. Brown & Williamson Tobacco Corp., 509 U.S. 209, 113 S.Ct. 2578 (1993), but the Court did not deal with them at any length. See § 8.8. See also T. Campbell, Predation and Competition in Antitrust: the Case of Nonfungible Goods, 87 Col. L.Rev. 1625 (1987).

er, firms who merely contemplate entry and are then deterred from doing so have a particularly bad record as antitrust plaintiffs. Most are denied standing.[18] The practices are also generally subtle and hard to identify, and the public enforcement agencies are generally reluctant to spend vast amounts of money in litigating them. Further, their own record has not been very good. For example, after many resources spent, the FTC abandoned its claim that the ready-to-eat breakfast cereal industry was using product differentiation as an entry deterrence device.[19]

Nevertheless, entry deterrence strategies play an important role in antitrust litigation. Often the role has been negative. For example, in both predatory pricing and merger cases it is commonly said that the threat of monopoly pricing need not detain us if entry is easy.[20] As noted previously, a firm with monopoly power may lawfully charge a monopoly price, even if the firm enjoys the protection of unusually high entry barriers.[21] However, if a firm goes out of its way to erect "artificial" entry barriers—that is, entry barriers that would not exist but for the firm's conscious choice—then antitrust liability may be appropriate. One of these strategies, so-called "limit" pricing, is taken up in the following chapter.[22] Other strategies discussed elsewhere in this chapter, such as fraudulent patent litigation,[23] petitions to the government,[24] and refusal to share an "essential facility"[25] fall into the same category. Often they are used more effectively against incipient rivals than well established ones.

One of the practices often cited as an entry barrier in the 1950's and 1960's was brand name advertising.[26] The effect of brand advertising to deter entry is hotly contested, and the question generally depends on whether advertising can be "banked," in the sense that past advertising expenditures create consumer brand loyalty that persists even after the advertising has come to an end. In that case, brand advertising which must be met by a new entrant becomes an irreversible, or "sunk" component that considerably raises the stakes of new entry. For example, if the new entrant knows it must spend $10,000,000 in advertising in order to raise sufficient consumer appreciation of its product even before the first sale is made, and if this total expenditure will be lost in the event of failure, then entry will be much less attractive than if advertising is simply something that must be matched dollar for dollar against the ongoing advertising of an incumbent. The incumbent's ongoing advertising is a cost it must still incur, and an equally efficient new entrant can match it. The "banked" advertising is a cost that the incumbent has already incurred, and this cost will not affect its current pricing decisions. Unfortunately, we know little about advertising and its effects as a general matter, and it is generally impossible for a court to deter anticompetitive truthful advertising without deterring beneficial advertising as well.[27]

The problem of advertising suggests some of the considerable difficulties that courts have had in recognizing dominant firms' subtle entry deterrence strategies. Strategic product differentiation provides another example. The key to successful entry in a product differentiated market (assuming the new firm does not have some new technology or product superiority not claimed by incumbents) is to discover a niche that is large enough to enable the newcomer to establish a toehold in the market. In such markets entry deterrence may take the form of responding to new entry by imme-

18. See § 16.5a.

19. In re Kellogg Co., 99 F.T.C. 8, 269 (1982). See R. Schmalensee, Entry Deterrence in the Ready-to-Eat Breakfast Cereal Industry, 9 Bell J. Econ. 305 (1976).

20. On barriers to entry generally, see § 1.6.

21. See § 6.1.

22. See § 8.3b; and see 1 Handbook of Industrial organization, ch. 8 (R. Schmalensee & R. Willig, eds. 1989).

23. See § 7.11.

24. See § 7.12.

25. See § 7.7.

26. The literature is discussed in R. Gilbert, Mobility Barriers and the Value of Incumbency, in 1 Handbook of Industrial organization 475, 504–505 (R. Schmalensee & R. Willig, eds. 1989).

27. The FTC's *General Foods* case dealt with some of these problems, ultimately concluding that investment in promotion is no more likely to be anticompetitive than is investment in new equipment. 103 F.T.C. 204, 354 (1984).

diately developing a product as similar as possible to the newcomer's product, and selling it at a barely profitable or perhaps even unprofitable price.[28] If the incumbent firm does this, the new entry will be unprofitable. Importantly, however, development of the new variation is not a profitable strategy for the incumbent *unless* new entry is threatened. That is, as long as the product space that would be occupied by the new entrant is vacant, most of those customers go to the incumbent anyway and its sales would not be noticeably enlarged by developing the new product.[29] When new entry is not on the horizon, development of the new product is not cost justified.

In this situation, the trick for the incumbent is to make prospective rivals see a dilemma that looks something like this:

Incumbent (first number)		Rival: (second number)
	Enter	Don't Enter
Don't Develop	4, 5	8, 0
Develop	6,–2	7, 0

The little game diagrammed here is not an orthodox prisoners' dilemma, because the incumbent's strategy is based on knowledge about the new entrant's strategy. In a prisoners' dilemma, each side must make a decision not knowing what the other is doing. But in this sequential game the rival moves first, by deciding whether or not to enter.[30] Then the incumbent responds, knowing what the rival has done, by deciding whether or not to develop a closely matching product. In the illustrated situation, it is unprofitable for the incumbent to develop the product that resembles the new entrant's product, as long as the new entrant doesn't enter. If the rival enters, then the incumbent still earns less after developing the new product than if neither entry nor development had occurred; but it earns more than it would if entry occurred and it did not develop. The equilibrium solution in the above game is the one in the upper right hand corner, under which the rival does not enter and the incumbent does not develop the new product.[31] The *efficient* solution, however, is very likely the one in the upper left hand corner, which maximizes the joint profits of the two firms *and* presumably results in the highest total output, measured by the sum of the two firms' outputs.

Game theory such as this (although generally far more technical and complex) has been applied to numerous presumed entry deterrence strategies,[32] and there is ample empirical evidence to establish that such strategies form an important component of the marketing policy of incumbent firms. Unfortunately, we have not developed techniques for identifying such strategies and branding them as anticompetitive in antitrust litigation. Further, as noted above, most frequently the immediate "victims" of the strategies tend to be firms that make a relatively brief study of a market from the outside, decide that entry would be unprofitable, and then go elsewhere. This is precisely what the incumbent has in mind. In that case, no set of plaintiffs except perhaps consumers, who are a highly diffuse and poorly informed group, have standing to sue.

This analysis does suggest that an agency such as the Federal Trade Commission could be given more leeway in applying § 5 of the Federal Trade Commission Act to strategic anticompetitive behavior. The Commission commands the expertise to evaluate such problems, and its relatively modest remedy (most commonly a "cease and desist" order) minimizes inefficient overdeterrence. Unfortunately, as noted in the earlier discussion of oligopo-

28. As in the Supreme Court's *Brooke* decision, note 17.

29. The facts of *Brooke* indicated as much. Among the six cigarette manufacturers, the defendant, Brown & Williamson, made the largest number of cigarettes sold to price conscious buyers. As a result it suffered disproportionately when plaintiff Liggett began selling "generics" at very large discounts. See *Brooke*, note 17, 509 U.S. at 212, 113 S.Ct. at 2582. Brown & Williamson responded by duplicating Liggett's generic and engaging in an aggressive price war. For more on the case, see § 8.8.

30. On the prisoners' dilemma, see § 4.2b.

31. This solution is generally called the Nash–Cournot equilibrium, and it represents a position such that neither firm has any incentive to change, given its anticipation of how the other firm will respond.

32. For a summary of the literature, see F.M. Scherer & D. Ross, Industrial Market Structure and Economic Performance, ch. 6 (3d ed. 1990).

ly,[33] the record of the FTC in pursuing subtler, more ambiguous forms of strategic anticompetitive behavior has not been particularly promising.[34]

§ 7.9 The Troublesome "Leverage" Theory; Nonmonopolistic Advantage in Second Market

Already in the 1940's the Supreme Court declared that a firm was forbidden to use monopoly power in one market to acquire a competitive advantage in a second market.[1] The meaning and scope of these decisions has remained ambiguous ever since,[2] but in its broadest form the rule has been read to prevent a monopolist from obtaining a competitive advantage in a second market "even if there has not been an attempt to monopolize the second market."[3] The liability comes from the "abuse" of economic power already held in the first market; not from any threat that monopoly will be created in the second market.

This leverage theory has been applied most frequently to claims that a monopolist used restrictive agreements or vertical integration to obtain an unfair advantage over rivals in the secondary market. For example, in *Kerasotes* the defendant was charged with taking advantage of its monopoly position as a movie exhibitor in some cities to negotiate exclusive contracts that covered other cities where it had no monopoly.[4]

As a general principle, even vertical integration by a monopolist that creates a second level monopoly will not result in higher prices or lower output.[5] The same thing applies to markets that are not vertically related. For example, if I am a monopoly seller of sewing machines and a competitive seller of toasters I might be able to use my monopoly position to force you to buy my toasters—for example, I would agree to sell my sewing machines only to retailers who agreed to deal in my toasters exclusively. But any monopoly markup I might receive from toaster sales in this fashion would have to be offset by a reduction in the price of sewing machines. In virtually all such cases, the same analysis of leveraging applies as that used to explode the leverage theory of tying arrangements, discussed in § 10.6a.

In sum, "leveraging" that creates a second level monopoly generally does not result in higher market prices or lower output. Leverage that fails to create a second level monopoly can do no worse. To be sure, it might make life less pleasant for other firms selling in the secondary market, but to that extent it should be analyzed as a business tort rather than an antitrust violation.

Although some recent decisions have recognized the leverage theory as plausible, others have either rejected it outright or expressed broad skepticism.[6] As the Ninth Circuit noted in its *Alaska Airlines* decision,

> leveraging activity may tend to *undermine* monopoly power, just like monopoly pric-

33. See § 4.6d.

34. In a case such as *Brooke*, note 17, the FTC might be able to insist that for, say, five years after a small firm developed a new product variation it would be illegal for an established rival to copy the variation or make an extremely close substitute and sell it at less than average variable cost. But even such a solution would be economically wasteful, depending on the circumstances.

§ 7.9

1. United States v. Griffith, 334 U.S. 100, 107–109, 68 S.Ct. 941, 945–947 (1948) (firm used dominant position in some theaters to obtain a competitive advantage in other locations); United States v. Paramount Pictures, 334 U.S. 131, 174, 68 S.Ct. 915, 937 (1948) (similar).

2. See 3 Antitrust Law ¶ 652 (rev. ed. 1996).

3. Berkey Photo v. Eastman Kodak Co., 603 F.2d 263, 276 (2d Cir.1979), cert. denied, 444 U.S. 1093, 100 S.Ct. 1061 (1980) (ultimately not finding liability on this theory); Kerasotes Mich. Theatres v. National Amusements, 854 F.2d 135, 138 (6th Cir.1988), cert. dismissed, 490 U.S. 1087, 109 S.Ct. 2461 (1989) (reversing dismissal of leverage claim); Advanced Health–Care Servs. v. Radford Community Hosp., 910 F.2d 139 (4th Cir.1990), on remand, 846 F.Supp. 488 (D.Va.1994) (accepting leverage theory in principle); see also Fineman v. Armstrong World Industries, 980 F.2d 171 (3d Cir.1992), cert. denied, 507 U.S. 921, 113 S.Ct. 1285 (1993) (ultimately approving dismissal of complaint).

4. Note 3.

5. See § 9.2c.

6. For example, Catlin v. Washington Energy Co., 791 F.2d 1343 (9th Cir.1986) (expressing extreme doubts about the viability of such a theory). Accord Aquatherm Indus. v. Florida Power & Light Co., 971 F.Supp. 1419 (M.D.Fla. 1997), aff'd, 145 F.3d 1258 (11th Cir.1998).

ing. Every time the monopolist asserts its market dominance on a firm in the leveraged market, the leveraged firm has more incentive to find an alternative supplier, which in turn gives alternate suppliers more reason to think that they can compete with the monopolist.[7]

In a footnote in its 1992 *Kodak* decision, the Supreme Court seemed to breathe new life into the leverage theory:

> The Court has held many times that power gained through some natural and legal advantage such as a patent, copyright, or business acumen can give rise to liability if "a seller exploits his dominant position in one market to expand his empire into the next."[8]

That statement seemed calculated to resurrect a dubious theory whose main effect had been to preserve the Sherman Act as a small business protection statute. However, less than a year later, in *Spectrum Sports*, the Court seemed to reject the theory altogether.

> § 2 [of the Sherman Act] makes the conduct of a single firm unlawful only when it actually monopolizes or dangerously threatens to do so. The concern that § 2 might be applied so as to further anticompetitive ends is plainly not met by inquiring only whether the defendant has engaged in "unfair" or "predatory" tactics.[9]

The statements in *Kodak* and *Spectrum Sports* were both dicta, and neither case involved a leverage claim as such.[10] But read together, the statements give more reason for doubting the continued viability of the leverage theory than for supporting it.[11] First, the *Kodak* statement did *not* add the dubious additional proposition that the monopolist in one market violates the Sherman Act by abusing its power in a second market "even if there has not been an attempt to monopolize the second market."[12] Second, the *Spectrum Sports* decision seems quite categorical in its insistence that the threat of monopoly in a properly defined relevant market is the Sherman Act's only true concern.[13] As a result, several decisions accept only a narrow version of the leverage theory that involves using monopoly power in one market to create a second monopoly in a related market. In the process, however, they generally hold that all the elements of an attempt to monopolize offense must be met for the second market. This effectively robs the leverage theory of its distinctiveness.[14]

§ 7.10 Raising Rivals' Costs (RRC)

A monopolist may be able to create or secure its own position by raising its rivals' costs relative to its own.[1] As a monopolistic strategy, RRC has some attractions over alter-

7. Alaska Airlines v. United Airlines, 948 F.2d 536, 549 (9th Cir.1991), cert. denied, 503 U.S. 977, 112 S.Ct. 1603 (1992).

8. Eastman Kodak Co. v. Image Technical Services, 504 U.S. 451, 479 n. 29 112 S.Ct. 2072, 2089 n. 29 (1992).

9. Spectrum Sports v. McQuillan, 506 U.S. 447, 459, 113 S.Ct. 884, 892 (1993), on remand, 23 F.3d 1531 (9th Cir.1994).

10. The decisions interpreting *Spectrum Sports* are not uniform. See Davis v. Southern Bell Tel. & Tel. Co., 1994–1 Trade Cas. ¶ 70510, 1994 WL 912242 (S.D.Fla.1994) (nonmonopolistic leveraging claims do not survive *Spectrum Sports*) with Ortho Diagnostic Sys. v. Abbott Laboratories, 822 F.Supp. 145, 153 (S.D.N.Y.1993) (some "leveraging" claims might survive).

11. See, for example, the decision on summary judgment in United States v. Microsoft, 1998 WL 614485 (D.D.C. 1998, unreported), (dismissed the state's separate claim of "monopoly leveraging" as "inconsistent with both the Sherman Act's plain text and with Supreme Court pronouncements on the general limitations of its reach....").

12. The quote is from *Berkey Photo*, note 3, 603 F.2d at 276.

13. For a view more sympathetic to leveraging claims, see L. Kaplow, Extension of Monopoly Power Through Leverage, 85 Col. L. Rev. 515, esp. at 543–545 (1985).

14. See, e.g, Cost Management Services v. Washington Natural Gas, 99 F.3d 937, 952 (9th Cir.1996) (accepting as "viable" a revised theory of leveraging as "an attempt to use monopoly power in one market to monopolize another market," but "under this theory [the plaintiff] must establish each of the elements normally required to prove an attempted monopolization claim....").

§ 7.10

1. See generally S. Salop & D. Scheffman, Raising Rivals' Costs, 73 Amer.Econ.Rev. 267 (1983); T. Krattenmaker & S. Salop, Competition and Cooperation in the Market for Exclusionary Rights, 76 Am.Econ.Rev. 109 (1986); E.T. Sullivan, On Nonprice Competition: an Economic and Marketing Analysis, 45 U.Pitt.L.Rev. 771, 776–785 (1984).

natives such as predatory pricing.[2] The predator must forego immediate substantial losses from price cutting in the hope that it will be able to charge monopoly prices later, after rivals have been forced out of the market. By contrast, RRC produces profits to the strategizer immediately, and nothing so catastrophic as a firm's forced exit from the market need happen.

Writers have offered a variety of theories explaining how a firm might raise its rivals' costs. Many of them involve concerted action by numerous firms, and are included in the general discussion of concerted refusals to deal.[3] Strategies that could involve only a single firm, and are thus reachable only under § 2, include the following:

1) A large firm might petition the government for regulations that have a more severe impact on smaller firms. For example, a regulation requiring airplanes to use three-person flight crews might cost much more for a small airline flying tiny planes than a large airline flying mainly large planes over long routes.[4] Such conduct is probably protected activity under the *Noerr–Pennington* doctrine, if it is directed at a government agency, although it may not be if it is directed at a private standard-setting association.[5]

2) A dominant firm engages in litigation against the smaller firm. Assume that litigation costs the same amount for both parties—perhaps $100,000 per year. The established incumbent who files the action has an output of 100,000 units per year, while the recent entrant who is the defendant has an output of 10,000 units per year. In this case the litigation costs the established firm $1.00 per unit, and the new entrant $10.00 per unit. If the new entrant has not yet begun to produce, the costs will be felt even more strongly. The costs of litigation in this instance must be considered as fixed costs—that is, they do not vary with the output of either firm. The difference between $1.00 in additional costs per unit and $10.00 in additional costs could easily be the difference between profit and loss selling.

3) A large capital intensive firm may bargain with a union in such a way as to cause marketwide wage increases, knowing that the impact of the increase will be felt much more heavily by smaller, labor-intensive firms.[6]

4) A dominant firm leading the race in research and development intentionally selects a technology for which scale economies are substantial, knowing that the fringe firms will have to follow along. Alternatively, a firm may create an array of patents on marginal or even nonexistent innovations, knowing that other firms will either have to invent around the patents or else litigate their validity.[7]

7.10a. The Pedigree and Judicial Development of RRC

Many antitrust violations previously analyzed under other rubrics could be considered

2. On predatory pricing, see Ch. 8.

3. See § 5.4. For an extensive development of concerted activities that can raise rivals' costs, see T. Krattenmaker & S. Salop, Anticompetitive Exclusion: Raising Rivals' Costs to Achieve Power over Price, 96 Yale L.J. 209 (1986) (evaluating many strategies); and H. Hovenkamp, Antitrust Policy, Restricted Distribution, and the Market for Exclusionary Rights, 71 Minn.L.Rev. 1293 (1987) (evaluating and expressing doubts about many proffered strategies).

4. There is an extensive literature on economies of scale in regulatory compliance. See M. Maloney & R. McCormick, A Positive Theory of Environmental Quality Regulation, 25 J.L. & Econ. 99 (1982); G. Neumann & J. Nelson, Safety Regulation and Firm Size: Effects of the Coal Mine Health and Safety Act of 1969, 25 J.L. & Econ. 183 (1982); B. P. Pashigian, The Effect of Environmental Regulation on Optimal Plant Size and Factor Shares, 27 J.L. & Econ. 1 (1984). Others are discussed in H. Hovenkamp, Antitrust Policy After Chicago, 84 Mich.L.Rev. 213, 277 (1985).

5. See generally ch. 18; and see S. Salop, D. Scheffman & W. Schwartz, "A Bidding Analysis of Special Interest Legislation: Raising Rivals' Costs in a Rent Seeking Society," in Federal Trade Commission, Political Economy of Regulation: Private Interests in the Regulatory Process 103 (1984).

6. See O. Williamson, Wage Rates as a Barrier to Entry: the Pennington Case in Perspective, 82 Q.J.Econ. 85 (1968).

7. See R. Gilbert & D. Newbery, Preemptive Patenting and the Persistence of Monopoly, 72 Am.Econ. Rev. 514 (1982).

as strategies for RRC. Tying arrangements, concerted refusals to deal, exclusive dealing, and solicitation of discriminatory prices could all fall into this category. At this writing, however, RRC has been discovered in the economic and legal literature much more often than it has been explicitly acknowledged in the antitrust case law.

Nevertheless, telling examples can be found in antitrust history, instructing that antitrust has always recognized that some practices may inefficiently raise rivals' costs. For example, in W.W. Montague & Co. v. Lowry,[8] the defendant trade association was accused of requiring its members to sell to non-members at full list price, while permitting them to negotiate any price in sales to members. If entry into the association was also restricted, it was very likely a device for keeping outsiders' costs up. Today it would be actionable as price fixing under § 1 of the Sherman Act. Likewise, Alcoa was once accused of purchasing "naked" exclusionary rights from electric utilities—in this case, contractual promises that the utilities would not sell electricity to Alcoa's rivals. Since the manufacture of aluminum required a great deal of electricity, such a restriction could have substantial cost-raising effects. The restriction is characterized as "naked" because Alcoa itself did not purchase any electricity from these particular utilities for its own use; it merely contracted that the utilities would not sell to others.[9] The *Aspen* case, discussed previously,[10] may also have involved a defendant's strategy of raising its rivals costs. By refusing to participate in a joint venture, the defendant may have forced the plaintiff to match its advertising and promotional expenses, even though the defendant could spread these costs over its three mountain resort, while the plaintiff had only one mountain.[11] Finally, although covenants not to compete are often efficient,[12] they can also be used to raise the costs of rivals or potential rivals by making it more difficult to find suitable employees, sites, or other productive assets.

Only a few judicial decisions have explicitly invoked the literature on RRC in condemning alleged monopolization.[13] One district court decision approved a jury verdict on the theory that Blue Cross used cost-cutting techniques with respect to its own customers to raise the costs of others.[14] However, in *Ball Memorial Hospital*, the Seventh Circuit found an alleged strategy of RRC to be implausible.[15] The theory was that Blue Cross forced hospitals to accept extra low rates for its own subscribers, thus requiring them to charge the patients of other insurance companies (or those without insurance) extra high rates. But Blue Cross

8. 193 U.S. 38, 24 S.Ct. 307 (1904).

9. See United States v. Aluminum Co. of Am., 44 F.Supp. 97, 121, 144 (S.D.N.Y.1941), reversed in part, 148 F.2d 416 (2d Cir.1945).

10. Aspen Skiing Co. v. Aspen Highlands Skiing Corp., 472 U.S. 585, 105 S.Ct. 2847 (1985). See § 7.5.

11. The case could also be viewed as strategic shifting of a rivals' demand curve—that is, making the rivals' product less attractive, with the result that more customers substitute to one's own product.

12. See § 5.2b4.

13. See National Org. for Women v. Scheidler, 968 F.2d 612 (7th Cir.1992), reversed on nonantitrust grounds, 510 U.S. 249, 114 S.Ct. 798 (1994) (rejecting claim that anti-abortion picketers violated antitrust laws by raising costs of abortion clinics; Query: are anti-abortion picketers and abortion clinics "rivals" for Sherman Act purposes?); Premier Electrical Constr. Co. v. National Electrical Contractors Assoc., 814 F.2d 358, 368 (7th Cir.1987) (finding that agreement to make businesses contribute money to collective bargaining process could operate to raise rivals' costs); Ball Memorial Hosp., Inc. v. Mutual Hosp. Ins., Inc., 784 F.2d 1325, 1339–1340 (7th Cir.), rehearing denied, 788 F.2d 1223 (7th Cir.1986) (rejecting RRC claim). Cf. In re Brand Name Prescription Drugs Antitrust Litigation, 123 F.3d 599 (7th Cir.1997), cert. denied, ___ U.S. ___, 118 S.Ct. 1178 (1998), cert. denied, 516 U.S. 1044, 116 S.Ct. 702 (1996) (denying summary judgment on a § 1 RRC claim); Multistate Legal Studies, Inc. v. Harcourt Brace Jovanovich Legal and Professional Publications, Inc., 63 F.3d 1540, 1553 (10th Cir.1995), cert. denied, 516 U.S. 1044, 116 S.Ct. 702 (1996) (denying summary judgment on claim that dominant bar review course offeror raised rivals' costs by imposing unnecessary scheduling conflicts); accord Forsyth v. Humana, Inc., 114 F.3d 1467 (9th Cir.1997), cert. granted on nonantitrust issue, ___ U.S. ___, 118 S.Ct. 2339 (1998) (reversing district court's grant of summary judgment against defendant hospital accused of raising rivals' costs by, inter alia, referring indigent and critical care patients to other hospitals and forcing its own physicians to discriminate in offering their services to rival hospitals).

14. Reazin v. Blue Cross & Blue Shield of Kan., 635 F.Supp. 1287 (D.Kan.1986), affirmed, 899 F.2d 951 (10th Cir.), cert. denied, 497 U.S. 1005, 110 S.Ct. 3241 (1990).

15. Ball Memorial Hospital v. Mutual Hospital Insurance, Inc., 784 F.2d 1325 (7th Cir.), rehearing denied, 788 F.2d 1223 (7th Cir.1986).

was found not to have market power, and the court was hard pressed to see how such a strategy could be pursued by a competitive firm.

7.10b. Pre-emption of Markets or Customers as RRC

Under this heading we note several practices, many of which can be addressed under other antitrust statutes, such as Sherman § 1 or Clayton § 3, as well as § 2 of the Sherman Act. The basic claim is that the defendant took an action that deprived its competitor of access to a needed input or a channel of distribution, and thus raised its costs.

In *Syufy Enterprises* the defendant was condemned under § 2 for purchasing exclusive licenses to exhibit motion pictures over a larger geographic area than the court thought justified, given that the area was significantly larger than the area from which the defendant actually drew viewing customers.[16] Such a strategy could raise the costs of rivals, by making it more difficult for them to acquire suitable licenses themselves. The court did not explain why motion picture producers would acquiesce in such contracts, which presumably injured them as much as they injured competitors. Other firms have also been accused of monopolization by "overbuying" or stealing essential inputs from competitors. For example, in *Potters Medical Center* the court denied summary judgment on the plaintiff hospital's claim that the defendant hospital stole local physicians by using bonuses to get them to send their patients exclusively to the defendant's hospital.[17]

However, in *Midwest Radio* the Eighth Circuit held that it was not illegal for one firm to steal another's employees as long as the defendant firm actually used the employees to improve its own production or distribution processes.[18] Employee theft could be a form of monopolization by raising rivals' costs, but the employment market at issue would have to be one in which providers were scarce and difficult to replace. Suppose that a skilled engineer could be hired for $100,000 per year. Her value to a small firm earning competitive returns is $100,000 per year. But to a dominant firm fearing the loss of its monopoly if the engineer goes elsewhere, the engineer is worth the present value of the monopoly profits that would otherwise be lost, *plus* whatever amount the engineer would contribute to the dominant firm's productivity. *Midwest Radio* effectively held that if the only value of the engineer to the defendant is the perpetuation of its monopoly (for example, if the engineer were hired to play solitaire or do whatever she pleased, as long as she did not work for the rival), then such "predatory hiring" might be an antitrust violation. But if the engineer actually performs services for the antitrust defendant, then the court would not interfere. Technically speaking, that rule seems underdeterrent. For example, the defendant may have hired the engineer even though she would contribute only $20,000 in increased productivity to the firm, but her real value lay in the injury to the rival denied her services. However, there are few cases in which a court would be able to second guess the motives behind a hiring decision where the employee was qualified to do the job and she was actually employed.

In most cases of this sort, the courts recognize that the challenged practice can have both efficiency producing and efficiency reducing consequences. They seem willing to condemn the practice only where (1) the other prerequisites for monopolization have been met, (2) the practice appeared not to improve the defendant's own productivity, and (3) the defendant engaged in the practice only to harm a rival. Theoretically, a court would have

16. Syufy Enters. v. American Multicinema, 793 F.2d 990 (9th Cir.1986), cert. denied, 479 U.S. 1031, 107 S.Ct. 876 (1987).

17. Potters Med. Center v. City Hosp. Assn., 800 F.2d 568 (6th Cir.1986).

18. Midwest Radio Co. v. Forum Pub. Co., 942 F.2d 1294 (8th Cir.1991); accord Universal Analytics v. MacNeal–Schwendler Corp., 707 F.Supp. 1170 (C.D.Cal.1989), affirmed, 914 F.2d 1256 (9th Cir.1990) (competitor did not engage in employee raiding, since employees had been dissatisfied with their jobs; no antitrust violation unless there is no legitimate business reason for the hiring). Other decisions are discussed in 3 Antitrust Law ¶ 702 (rev. ed. 1996).

to inquire into intent only if the practice flunked both steps (1) and (2). In practice, inquiries into intent are far more frequent.

Customer pre-emption occurs when a dominant firm purchases from its own customers or others the right that they not purchase from a competitor. Such cases have always been difficult to analyze. First, they must be classified. Some are no more than exclusive dealing or tying arrangements, and these may be quite efficient even when the upstream party is a monopolist.[19]

The more problematic exclusionary contracts are those where the contract (1) excludes a specific named competitor; or (2) where the contract is "naked"—that is, it is not attached to the sale of any other product or service at all. An example of the first is *Lorain Journal*, where the defendant refused to sell advertising to buyers who also purchased advertising from nearby radio station WEOL.[20] An example of the second is the allegation in *Alcoa* that the defendant once purchased from utilities a promise that they would not provide electricity to Alcoa's competitors or potential competitors.[21] Alcoa purchased no electricity itself from these utilities; so the only apparent purpose of the contract was to exclude the rivals.

Are contracts of these two kinds viable anticompetitive strategies? A traditionally given answer is that the monopolist could not pay enough to make the contract profitable to all contracting parties; so the contract would never be formed. Recalling the discussion in §§ 1.2–1.3, monopoly produces three dislocations in wealth: it (1) transfers wealth to the monopolist; (2) transfers wealth away from the consumers; and (3) produces a deadweight loss. Given a positive deadweight loss, the amount by which the monopolist is enriched is always less than the amount by which customers are impoverished. That is, the wealth transfers cancel one another out, but customers are additionally injured by the deadweight loss.

So, the argument goes, a monopolist would never be able to pay customers enough to make them agree to maintain the monopoly. As long as the monopolist paid customers less than the sum of the wealth transfer plus the deadweight loss, there would be at least one customer who would find it profitable to deal with the rival; but the monopolist would never pay more than the wealth transfer alone, because that represents its entire profits from the monopoly.[22] Exclusionary contracts must therefore have an efficiency explanation, not a monopoly explanation.

But the story is seldom this simple, and there may be instances when exclusionary conduct is both monopolistic and profitable to all contracting parties. First of all, the monopolist may not need to purchase the right from every customer, but from only enough customers to prevent the rival from becoming a viable competitor. If economies of scale are substantial, the purchases would have to be sufficient to prevent the rival from attaining an efficient rate of output; but they may not have to be much more than that. If the monopolist were already using exclusive dealing or another "legitimate" exclusionary contracts with one set of customers, the naked exclusionary contracts would need to cover only enough of the remaining customers to deny the rival a sufficient rate of output.

Even if there were scale economies, however, the strategy would not work if the customers were able to organize. In the aggregate, they would benefit from having two rivals and a competitive market by more than the monopolist gains from the monopoly. For example, in *Belcher*[23] fuel customers believed their monopoly supplier was charging too high a

19. See generally ch. 10.

20. Lorain Journal Co. v. United States, 342 U.S. 143, 72 S.Ct. 181 (1951).

21. See note 9.

22. See R. Posner, Antitrust Law: an Economic Perspective 212 (1976); R. Bork, The Antitrust Paradox: A Policy at War with Itself 309 (1978).

23. Belcher Oil Co. v. Florida Fuels, 749 F.Supp. 1104 (S.D.Fla.1990). The antitrust plaintiff was, of all persons, the monopolist. The court held he was not a victim of "antitrust injury," since he was complaining about more rather than less competition in the market. On antitrust injury, see § 16.3.

price. They organized, and collectively asked a rival to enter the market. When the rival hesitated, the customers promised the rival the minimum volume of purchases necessary to make entry profitable. But if the customers are not able to organize, then anticompetitive exclusion may be quite possible.[24]

Another form of customer pre-emption is the contract penalty. The dominant firm may enter into a long-term lease with its customers, and charge a substantial penalty for early termination. If the penalty is sufficiently large and covers enough customers, a prospective rival may not be able to attain a scale sufficient to make entry profitable.[25] If the customers have perfect information and know that the impact of signing such an agreement is continuation of the monopoly, they may refuse to sign. But in the usual case the customers' information will be imperfect and the prospects of new entry uncertain.[26] Several cases have involved such clauses, although in most the judicial analysis has not been all that helpful.[27]

Modeling situations in which exclusionary contracts such as these might be anticompetitive is relatively easy. Problematically, however, the antitrust tribunal must run the process *backwards*. That is, it begins with the contract containing the allegedly anticompetitive provision, and must then determine whether the provision is anticompetitive or competitive. The great majority of contract penalty clauses are nothing more than devices to make contract participants perform, and that purpose is undoubtedly competitive.[28]

§ 7.11 Abuse of Patents or Other Intellectual Property

Monopolists have also been condemned under the antitrust laws for abusing rights created under the patent laws. A patent itself implies a property right to prevent others from duplicating a certain product or process. But this power to exclude is not unlimited, and courts have often found patentees guilty of exclusionary practices, particularly if they have tied some unpatented article to the patented one, accumulated patents in order to make entry into the monopolized market difficult, or in a few situations if they have refused to license the patent to others. In addition, the Supreme Court has stated obtaining a patent monopoly by fraud may violate § 2 of the Sherman Act,[1] as can attempts to enforce a patent known by the holder to be invalid or unenforceable. Several of these practices are discussed elsewhere.[2]

One word of caution in patent/monopoly cases. The "monopoly" that is sometimes said to result from an enforceable patent is not the same thing as the "monopoly" or monopoly

24. On this point, see E. Rasmusen, J.M. Ramseyer, & J. Wiley, Naked Exclusion, 81 Am.Econ.Rev. 1137 (1991).

25. See P. Aghion & P. Bolton, Contracts as a Barrier to Entry, 77 Am. Econ. Rev. 388 (1987); J. Brodley & C.A. Ma, Contract Penalties, Monopolizing Strategies, and Antitrust Policy, 45 Stan. L. Rev. 1161 (1993).

26. Even if entry is likely, each customer knows that the prospective entrant needs only a portion of the customer base in order to enter. Suppose that the dominant firm offers a high lease price without the penalty clause, but a lower price with the penalty clause. Each customer will likely pay the lower price and take the penalty clause, hoping that enough other customers will pay the higher price to make the new entry profitable. See S. Salop, Practices that (Credibly) Facilitate Oligopoly Coordination, in New Developments in the Analysis of Market Structure 265, 272–273, 278–284 (J. Stiglitz & F. Mathewson eds. 1986).

27. Telex Corp. v. IBM, 510 F.2d 894 (10th Cir.), cert. dismissed, 423 U.S. 802, 96 S.Ct. 8 (1975) (upholding lease cancellation penalties where rival lessors used them too); United Air Lines v. Austin Travel Corp., 681 F.Supp. 176 (S.D.N.Y.1988), affirmed, 867 F.2d 737 (2d Cir.1989) (upholding penalty clause where lessor lacked monopoly power). Compare Automatic Radio Mfg. Co. v. Hazeltine Research, 339 U.S. 827, 70 S.Ct. 894 (1950) (upholding package license of patents requiring licensee to pay royalties whether or not patents were used, effectively requiring licensee to pay two sets of royalties if it switched to other patent licensor); Zenith Radio Corp. v. Hazeltine Research, 395 U.S. 100, 89 S.Ct. 1562 (1969) (striking down similar agreement). See Brodley & Ma, note 25 at 1184–1194.

28. For one evaluation of RRC in a famous antitrust case, see E. Granitz & B. Klein, "Monopolization by 'Raising Rivals' Costs': The Standard Oil Case," 39 J.Law & Econ. 1 (1996).

§ 7.11

1. Walker Process Equip., Inc. v. Food Machinery & Chemical Corp., 382 U.S. 172, 86 S.Ct. 347 (1965).

2. Improprieties in patent licensing and the complex relationship between antitrust policy and patent "misuse" are taken up in § 5.5. Tying arrangements involving patented articles are discussed further in ch. 10.

power which is a predicate for illegal monopolization. Indeed, it would be better not to speak of a patent "monopoly" at all; a patent is a right in intellectual property limited to the article or process described in the patent application. A patented product may compete intensely with similar products which are either unpatented or covered by different patents.[3] As a result, a single patent seldom defines the scope of a relevant market for antitrust purposes. The Supreme Court made this position clear already in its *Walker Process* decision, where it required an antitrust plaintiff claiming patent abuses to allege and prove a relevant market.[4] Recently, in *Spectrum Sports*, the Court reiterated in dicta that one cannot presume that a patent itself defines a relevant market.[5] In tying arrangement cases and occasionally elsewhere courts formerly indulged a presumption that a seller has market power if its good is patented.[6] But this presumption makes little sense in that context, and it certainly makes no sense in a § 2 case.[7]

Procedurally, the antitrust claim of patent abuse most often appears as a counterclaim brought by the defendant in an infringement suit. The patentee sues, charging infringement. The defendant denies that the patent is valid because of the claimed fraud on the patent office, and then counterclaims that the infringement action violates the antitrust laws. This creates the confusing situation that the antitrust plaintiff is the defendant in the underlying infringement action, and the antitrust defendant the plaintiff in the underlying action. The discussion that follows uses the terms "antitrust plaintiff" and "antitrust defendant" to speak of the parties to the antitrust claim; we are not generally concerned with the original alignment of the parties.

§ 7.11a. Walker Process: "Obtaining" Patent by Fraud

In *Walker Process*[8] the patentee brought an infringement suit against a rival. The rival counterclaimed that (1) the patentee had obtained the patent by committing a fraud on the patent office; and (2) its enforcement action under such a patent was an attempt to monopolize. The Supreme Court agreed, but Justice Clark's opinion for the Court presented the question as "whether the maintenance and enforcement of a patent obtained by fraud on the Patent Office[9] may be the basis of an action under § 2 of the Sherman Act...."[10] As a result, the so-called *Walker Process* doctrine is sometimes described as stating that "obtaining" a patent by fraud can violate § 2. But *Walker Process* itself was a patent infringement action with an antitrust counterclaim and thus holds only that the enforcement attempt could violate the antitrust laws.

Fraud on the PTO is not itself an antitrust violation. However, if a patentee obtains a patent fraudulently (usually by giving false information in a patent application), the patent itself becomes unenforceable. In that case, under *Walker Process* the attempt to enforce a fraudulently obtained patent may violate either § 2 of the Sherman Act or § 5 of the FTC Act.[11] In *Walker Process* itself the patentee Food Machinery had filed a sworn statement in the PTO that it neither knew nor believed that its invention had already been used in the United States for more than one year prior to the filing of the patent application.[12] In fact,

3. On the relation between patents and market power, see § 3.9d.

4. *Walker Process*, note 1 at 177. See § 6.5b.

5. Spectrum Sports v. McQuillan, 506 U.S. 447, 455, 113 S.Ct. 884, 890 (1993), on remand, 23 F.3d 1531 (9th Cir.1994).

6. See § 3.9d. Today, the presumptions is routinely rejected.

7. See Abbott Laboratories v. Brennan, 952 F.2d 1346 (Fed.Cir.1991), cert. denied, 505 U.S. 1205, 112 S.Ct. 2993 (1992) (presumption that patent confers market power not warranted in monopolization case).

8. Note 1.

9. Referring to the United States Patent and Trademark Office, or PTO.

10. *Walker Process*, note 1, 382 U.S. at 173.

11. On the latter, see Charles Pfizer & Co. v. FTC, 401 F.2d 574, 579 (6th Cir.1968), cert. denied, 394 U.S. 920, 89 S.Ct. 1195 (1969) (false statements to patent office in order to procure monopoly of potent drug violated § 5 of FTC Act).

12. The Patent Act provides that "[a] person shall be entitled to a patent unless * * * [the] invention was patented or * * * in public use or on sale in this country, more than one year prior to the date of application for patent in the United States. * * *" 35 U.S.C.A. § 102(b).

Food Machinery itself had been involved in such use, and the use invalidated the patent.

Today the courts generally hold that merely obtaining a patent by fraud, however unlawful under the Patent Act, is not an antitrust violation until the patentee actually tries to enforce the patent against someone else or use it in some other anticompetitive manner.[13] However, the *Walker Process* language has provoked a great deal of confusion, as the following section develops.

The Supreme Court also, and unfortunately, spoke of the fraud in the patent application as "strip[ping] Food Machinery of its exemption from the antitrust laws."[14] The implication was that a patent monopoly was a kind of antitrust "exemption," when in fact it is not in any technical sense. What the Court really meant was that the use of litigation to exclude rivals from copying one's invention is legal if the invention is protected by a valid patent and the rival is really infringing. Such suits can create antitrust liability, however, if the patentee knows that the patent is unenforceable but pursues litigation anyway.

§ 7.11b. Enforcement of Patent Known to Be Invalid or Unenforceable; Noerr Issues

Courts have often found that an established firm's improper litigation or appeals to an administrative agency can be an illegal exclusionary practice. Although firms have a First Amendment right to petition the government for redress of their grievances, this right does not extend to baseless claims filed against a rival or prospective entrant for the purpose of excluding the rival from a certain market.[15]

The question often arises when a firm brings patent infringement suits against rivals even though (a) the firm procured its own patent fraudulently; or (b) it knows that its own patent is unenforceable, invalid or expired, or that the rival's product or process does not infringe its patent. Whether such a lawsuit is used to raise a rivals' costs[16] or simply as an entry deterrence device, it can be a § 2 violation if the plaintiff in the patent suit either has or threatens to acquire substantial market power.

At the same time, however, courts are quite sensitive to the fact that patent holders, even if they are dominant firms, have constitutionally protected legal rights to enforce their claims in court. For this reason they have been reluctant to accept too readily the argument that such suits are improperly brought. They have assessed such requirements as proof of "knowing and willful patent fraud," apparently meaning that the antitrust plaintiff must produce evidence that the antitrust defendant actually knew that the patent it was enforcing was invalid or not infringed.[17] Other courts have held that such misuse must be established by clear and convincing evidence.[18]

In the *Handgards* litigation the patentee had a patent that was invalid because the patented product had been on sale in the United States for more than one year preceding the patent application. In this case, however, the patentee had not known of this fact at the time the application was filed. But it did find out subsequently, before it brought the infringement action.[19] The court held that, whether or not the patent was *obtained* in bad faith, a subsequent suit by a patentee who

13. FMC Corp. v. Manitowoc Co., 835 F.2d 1411, 1418 & n. 16 (Fed.Cir.1987) ("Mere procurement of a patent, whatever the conduct of the applicant in the procurement, cannot without more affect the welfare of the consumer and cannot in itself violate the antitrust laws."). Accord Cygnus Therapeutics Sys. v. ALZA Corp., 92 F.3d 1153 (Fed.Cir.1996); K–Lath v. Davis Wire Corp., 15 F.Supp.2d 952, 1998–2 Trade Cas. ¶ 72276 (C.D.Cal.1998) (whether or not patentee's patent was fraudulently or improperly procured, patentee had not attempted to enforce it against declaratory judgment plaintiff nor threatened to do so).

14. *Walker Process*, 382 U.S. at 177, 86 S.Ct. at 350.

15. See § 18.3.

16. See § 7.10.

17. Argus Chem. Corp. v. Fibre Glass–Evercoat Co., 812 F.2d 1381, 1385 (Fed.Cir.1987).

18. For example, Loctite Corp. v. Ultraseal Ltd., 781 F.2d 861 (Fed.Cir.1985); SmithKline Diagnostics, Inc. v. Helena Labs., 859 F.2d 878, 891 (Fed.Cir.1988); FMC Corp. v. Manitowoc Co., 835 F.2d 1411, 1415 (Fed.Cir. 1987).

19. See Handgards, Inc. v. Ethicon, Inc., 601 F.2d 986 (9th Cir.1979) (*Handgards I*); Handgards, Inc. v. Ethicon, Inc., 743 F.2d 1282 (9th Cir.1984), cert. denied, 469 U.S. 1190, 105 S.Ct. 963 (1985) (*Handgards II*).

knew at the time the suit was filed that the patent was invalid could also create antitrust liability. By the same token, an infringement suit on a presumably valid patent against someone known by the patentee not to be an infringer can give rise to § 2 liability.[20]

The *Walker Process* suggestion[21] that merely obtaining a patent by fraud can be an antitrust violation has led many courts to seek out differential standards for infringement lawsuits based on patents obtained by fraud and patents that, while unenforceable, were not fraudulently obtained. Some have indicated that where there is not intentional fraud, but merely negligence or even gross negligence, there cannot be a *Walker Process* claim under § 2.[22] The courts have also distinguished between "fraud" and "inequitable conduct" in the procurement of patents. Under the patent laws the applicant has "an uncompromising duty" to report any irregularities in the patent application.[23] Irregularities that fall short of fraud may nevertheless constitute "inequitable conduct." The important difference between the two, it was said, is that while both fraud and inequitable conduct can be asserted as defenses in a patent infringement action, enabling the infringement defendant to avoid enforcement of the patent, only fraud can form the independent basis for a § 2 counterclaim.[24] The *factual* differences between fraud and inequitable conduct are generally easy to identify. A merely negligent misrepresentation is generally inequitable conduct. For example, in *Argus* the patent application neglected to report that the patented good had been on sale in the United States for more than one year prior to the application. Although this was the same defect as the one at issue in *Walker Process*, discussed above, Argus had apparently acted in good faith, and at least the attorney who had filed the application was unaware of the prior sales.[25] By contrast, in *Karody–Colyer* the antitrust plaintiff submitted evidence that General Motors submitted a patent application even though it knew of several earlier patents and existing technology that made the technology described in the current application "obvious." Things that are "obvious," because they have already been developed by others, are generally not patentable. This constituted fraud, not simply inequitable conduct.[26]

Both the cases involving patents obtained by fraud and those involving bad faith infringement actions implicate *Noerr–Pennington* concerns with every person's constitutional right to seek redress in court. In general, a lawsuit brought to enforce intellectual property rights cannot constitute a § 2 violation unless it is a "sham"—brought in bad faith and not in order to obtain a particular judicial result, but rather to harass a rival. Although these concerns are discussed elsewhere,[27] a brief summary of the Supreme Court's *Professional Real Estate* (*PRE*) decision is necessary here.[28] The Court held that a copyright owner's enforcement suit on a novel question of law could not be deemed a "sham" where there were no important factual issues in dispute, the infringement suit was intended by the copyright owner to bring the requested relief, and there was a plausible legal basis for the claim. In a very brief footnote, the Court stated that it was not deciding the extent to which a litigant's "fraud or other misrepresen-

20. United States v. Besser Mfg. Co., 96 F.Supp. 304, 312 (E.D.Mich.1951), affirmed, 343 U.S. 444, 72 S.Ct. 838 (1952).

21. See § 7.11a.

22. See Argus Chemical Corp. v. Fibre Glass–Evercoat Co., 812 F.2d 1381 (Fed.Cir.1987) (nonfraudulent failure to disclose prior sales insufficient); American Hoist & Derrick Co. v. Sowa & Sons, 725 F.2d 1350, 1368 (Fed. Cir.), cert. denied, 469 U.S. 821, 105 S.Ct. 95 (1984) (must be intentional fraud, not merely gross negligence).

23. See Precision Instrument Manufacturing Co. v. Automotive Maintenance Machinery Co., 324 U.S. 806, 65 S.Ct. 993 (1945).

24. Korody–Colyer Corp. v. General Motors Corp., 828 F.2d 1572, 1578 (Fed.Cir.1987) (there is an important "difference between inequitable conduct that may render a patent unenforceable and intentional fraud that may lead to antitrust liability.").

25. Argus Chem. Corp. v. Fibre Glass–Evercoat Co., 812 F.2d 1381, 1385 (Fed.Cir.1987).

26. Korody–Colyer Corp. v. General Motors Corp., 828 F.2d 1572, 1578 (Fed.Cir.1987).

27. See § 18.3.

28. Professional Real Estate Investors v. Columbia Pictures Industries, 508 U.S. 49, 113 S.Ct. 1920 (1993). For a fuller discussion see § 18.3.

tations" before a court might constitute sham.[29]

PRE is thus a fairly narrow decision, not dispositive of the great majority of claims based on bad faith patent infringement actions. The questions in these cases do not typically concern the technical interpretation of a term in the statute about which reasonable people could differ, as *PRE* did.[30] Rather, they concern allegations that the plaintiff in the infringement action (the antitrust defendant) had in its possession facts showing that the patent application process was corrupted, that the patent was invalid or that the defendant in the infringement action was not an infringer. *Professional Real Estate* requires the antitrust plaintiff to show that the infringement action was "objectively baseless." If it is not, then the suit cannot form the basis for an antitrust violation. If it is, then further discovery into the antitrust defendant's intent in bringing the suit is appropriate.[31] But *all* suits that fit into the *Walker Process* definition of attempts to enforce patents obtained by fraud, or the *Handgards* definition of attempts to enforce patents known to be invalid, are "objectively baseless" in this sense. That is, someone knowing all the facts would also know that the suit had no merit.

PRE thus reduces the significance that the previously cited decisions drew between patents obtained by fraud and patents wrongly obtained by error or by lesser degrees of improper activity. Rather, one must focus on the validity of the subsequent infringement suit. If the patentee knew or should have known that the patent was unenforceable under the circumstances of this particular suit, then the conduct requirement of a § 2 violation has been established. It does not matter so much whether the lack of enforceability arises from fraud, inequitable conduct, expiration,[32] or knowledge that the infringement defendant was not an infringer. What matters is whether the patentee knew or should have known this when the suit was brought. Of course, outright fraud can create a stronger presumption of scienter than lesser types of conduct. But that is largely a fact question.

Nevertheless, in its important *NobelPharma* decision,[33] the Federal Circuit continued to find two possible routes to antitrust liability for improperly brought patent infringement suits. First, if the fraud elements of the *Walker Process* claim could be made out, as well as the "other criteria" for antitrust liability, "such liability can be imposed without the additional sham inquiry required under *PRE*."[34] Second,

> [o]n the other hand, irrespective of the patent applicant's conduct before the PTO, an antitrust claim can also be based on a *PRE* allegation that a suit is baseless; in order to prove that a suit was within *Noerr*'s "sham" exception to immunity, an antitrust plaintiff must prove that the suit was both objectively baseless and subjectively motivated by a desire to impose collateral, anti-competitive injury rather than to obtain a justifiable legal remedy.[35]

As the court explained:

> Thus, under *PRE*, a sham suit must be both subjectively brought in bad faith and based on a theory of either infringement or validity that is objectively baseless. Accordingly, if a suit is not objectively baseless, an antitrust defendant's subjective motivation is immaterial. In contrast with a *Walker Process* claim, a patentee's activities in procuring the patent are not necessarily at issue. It is the bringing of the lawsuit that is subjectively and objectively baseless that

29. *Professional Real Estate*, 508 U.S. at 61 n. 6, 113 S.Ct. at 1929 n. 6., citing *Walker Process*.

30. See § 18.3b.

31. *Professional Real Estate*, 508 U.S. at 60, 113 S.Ct. at 1928.

32. See, e.g., International Technologies Consultants v. Pilkington PLC, 137 F.3d 1382 (9th Cir.1998) (infringement suit based on expired patents a possible antitrust violation; but query, if the infringement defendant can readily determine that the asserted patent has expired, how significant a monopoly could such a lawsuit create?).

33. Nobelpharma v. Implant Innovations, 141 F.3d 1059 (Fed.Cir.), cert. denied, ___ U.S. ___, 119 S.Ct. 178 (1998).

34. *Nobelpharma*, note 33 at 1071.

35. *Nobelpharma*, id. at 1071, citing *PRE*, 508 U.S. at 60–61.

must be proved.[36]

Of course, if the patent had been obtained by fraud, then *objective* baselessness would be clear: a patent obtained by fraud is clearly unenforceable. But the Federal Circuit seemed to be leaving open the possibility that a patentee might have obtained a patent by fraud but not have the anticompetitive state of mind necessary to support an antitrust claim under *PRE*. Alternatively, the court may have been preserving the possibility that where a patent has been obtained by fraud, actions falling short of an infringement suit might still constitute an antitrust violation. Neither possibility was clearly articulated. Clearly, however, certain actions falling short of an infringement suit can be anticompetitive. For example, suppose that a patentee acquires its patent by fraud, misstating facts that are exclusively within its control. It then refuses to license the patent to another firm, and this firm, assuming the patent's validity, chooses not to enter the market. In that case the patent obtained by fraud has been used anticompetitively by conduct falling short of an infringement suit. Of course, the same story might apply to cases where the patent is invalid for reasons falling short of fraud.

At least one court has held that the improper appropriation of a *valid* patent from someone else is not an antitrust violation, because the "theft" creates no monopoly. It merely transfers the monopoly from one person to another.[37] That analysis may be true as a general matter, but there might be cases where the amount of market power conferred by a patent depends on the identity of its holder. For example, suppose firm *X* has patented process *A*, which gives it a cost advantage over rivals and permits it to charge supracompetitive prices. Now firm *Y* develops patented process *B*, which is as efficient or perhaps even a little better than *B*. *Y* intends to use process *B* itself, or perhaps license it to others; but *X* obtains the patent through fraud, and then sits on the new technology. In this case the mere "transfer" of a patent from one firm to another could perpetuate *X*'s monopoly and deprive consumers of competition between firms using the alternative processes. To state this another way, when competitive technologies are owned by competing firms, the result is likely to be competitive. But when competitive technologies are owned and controlled by a single firm, a monopoly result is still possible.

Several courts have extended the baseless litigation and improper use rules to other forms of intellectual property. For example, in *CVD* the court held that trade secret litigation pursued by a dominant firm in bad faith could constitute an antitrust violation.[38] In *Lasercomb* the court stated in dicta that copyright litigation brought in bad faith could constitute an antitrust violation as well.[39]

Finally, note that an improperly brought infringement action satisfies the *conduct* portion of a monopolization or attempt to monopolize claim. It does not satisfy any structural requirements pertaining to relevant market definition, market share, or dangerous probability of success in creating a monopoly. Each

36. *Nobelpharma*, note 33 at 1072.

37. Brunswick Corp. v. Riegel Textile Corp., 752 F.2d 261 (7th Cir.1984), cert. denied, 472 U.S. 1018, 105 S.Ct. 3480 (1985). The antitrust plaintiff had disclosed its invention in confidence to the defendant, which promised to keep it secret. Then, while the PTO searched for the plaintiff's misplaced patent application, the defendant filed its own patent application, which was granted.

38. CVD v. Raytheon Co., 769 F.2d 842, 851 (1st Cir.1985), cert. denied, 475 U.S. 1016, 106 S.Ct. 1198 (1986) (in this case the alleged facts were not trade secrets at all; the antitrust defendant "regularly published * * * detailed information related to the [technology] in periodic reports. * * * ").

39. Lasercomb America v. Reynolds, 911 F.2d 970, 977 (4th Cir.1990); accord DSC Communications Corp. v. DGI Techs., Inc., 81 F.3d 597, 601 (5th Cir.1996) (possible copyright misuse to prevent competitor from designing a competing switch); Data General Corp. v. Grumman Sys. Supp. Corp., 36 F.3d 1147, 1185 n. 63 (1st Cir.1994) ("well settled that concerted and contractual behavior that threatens competition is not immune from antitrust inquiry simply because it involves the exercise of copyright privileges."). Contrast Bellsouth Advertising v. Donnelley Information Pub., 933 F.2d 952 (11th Cir.1991), vacated and rehearing *en banc* granted, 977 F.2d 1435 (11th Cir. 1992) (refusing to apply broad patent misuse principles to copyright; restricting *Lasercomb*). See Note, Clarifying the Copyright Misuse Defense: the Role of Antitrust Standards and First Amendment Values, 104 Harv. L. Rev. 1289 (1991).

of those elements must be established by separate proof.[40]

§ 7.11c. *Accumulation; Nonuse*

Suppose that firm A owns the patents and exclusive right to manufacture a sophisticated machine. A's research laboratory continually improves the machine in various ways, and each significant new improvement is patented. The result may be that the machine will never completely enter the public domain. By the time the patent on any particular component expires it will be obsolete and will have been replaced with a new patented component. By trailing out its patents in this way, the innovator effectively acquires a permanent monopoly, or at least a monopoly of far longer duration than the Patent Act contemplates.

The continuing development and actual use of new patented devices should ordinarily not be treated as an illegal exclusionary practice. The disincentive created to research and development would far outweigh any injury to the competitive process that might result. In some high technology fields the commercial life expectancy of some components is only a fraction of the legal life of the patents that protect them. In any field where technology changes at a rapid rate, research and development is likely to render components or processes obsolete long before their patents expire.[41]

A more difficult question arises when the monopolist acquires or becomes the exclusive licensee of related patents and refuses to use them or relicense them to others. Suppose that Firm A has developed patented process X, and uses it to manufacture widgets. Under both the patent and antitrust laws A may use process X exclusively; it need not license the process to any competitor.[42] Now, however, an inventor develops process Y, which will manufacture widgets at about the same price as process X. The inventor does not want to manufacture widgets herself, but proposes instead to license the process to anyone who wants it. Firm A then pays the inventor a high price for the exclusive license to use process Y. However, firm A never employs process Y. It continues to manufacture widgets using process X, and continues to have a monopoly in the widget market.

In this case the chance of injury to competition is more substantial. Firm A has its monopoly profits in widgets to protect. Any new entrant into the widget market, using process Y, will face competition from A as well as from other possible licensees of process Y. As a result, firm A may be willing to pay more for the exclusive right to use (or in this case to prevent the use of) process Y than any potential competitor would. The systematic acquisition and non-use of patents licensed from others should therefore be an antitrust concern, in appropriate cases.[43]

For these reasons, it would be wise do distinguish between internally developed and acquired patents. Acquisition from others and nonuse of patents could be an antitrust violation, even though nonuse of one's internally developed patents is not.[44] The courts have generally not followed the distinction.

7.11d. *Refusal to License, Simple and Conditional*

7.11d1. Absolute refusal to license

A 1988 amendment to the Patent Act provides:

40. See § 7.12; 1 Antitrust Law ¶ 208 (rev. ed. 1997).

41. See Automatic Radio Mfg. Co. v. Hazeltine Research, Inc., 339 U.S. 827, 834, 70 S.Ct. 894, 898 (1950): "The mere accumulation of patents, no matter how many, is not in and of itself illegal." Accord SCM Corp. v. Xerox Corp., 645 F.2d 1195 (2d Cir.1981), cert. denied, 455 U.S. 1016, 102 S.Ct. 1708 (1982), rehearing denied, 456 U.S. 985, 102 S.Ct. 2260 (1982).

42. In the *SCM* case, Id., the district court held that creating antitrust liability "for a monopolist's unilateral refusal to license patents" would pose "a threat to the progress of science and the useful arts not warranted by a reasonable accommodation of the patent and antitrust laws." 463 F.Supp. at 1014.

43. See Kobe, Inc. v. Dempsey Pump Co., 198 F.2d 416, 423–424 (10th Cir.), cert. denied, 344 U.S. 837, 73 S.Ct. 46 (1952) (finding that the systematic licensing, nonuse and enforcement of every patent in the relevant technology could be an attempt to monopolize). The prevailing case law, however, is that mere nonuse of a patent is not an antitrust violation. See Continental Paper Bag Co. v. Eastern Paper Bag Co., 210 U.S. 405, 28 S.Ct. 748 (1908). A good discussion of these issues is contained in L. Kaplow, The Patent–Antitrust Intersection: A Reappraisal, 97 Harv.L.Rev. 1813 (1984).

44. See 3 Antitrust Law ¶ ¶ 705, 707 (rev. ed. 1996).

> (d) No patent owner ... shall be ... deemed guilty of misuse or illegal extension of the patent right by reason of his having done one or more of the following: ... (3) sought to enforce his patent rights against infringement or contributory infringement; (4) refused to license or use any rights to the patent; or (5) conditioned the license of any rights to the patent or the sale of the patented product on the acquisition of a license to rights in another patent or purchase of a separate product, unless, in view of the circumstances, the patent owner has market power in the relevant market for the patent or patented product on which the license or sale is conditioned.[45]

This provision makes clear that under the Patent Act a simple refusal to license a patent cannot be "misuse" of a patent, and thus cannot violate the antitrust laws.[46] It is also consistent with an unbroken line of decisions holding that the owner of a patent has no antitrust duty to license its patent to others.[47]

The one outlying case is the Ninth Circuit's *Kodak* decision, which held that a firm had a duty to sell its patented parts and share its copyrighted diagnostics software with rivals.[48] First, looking at the statute quoted above, the court concluded that it did no more than state pre-existing law.[49] That was true in the sense that no case had ever condemned a simple refusal to license, and the statute simply declared the legality of such refusals. Indeed, the court acknowledged that it could "find no reported case in which a court has imposed antitrust liability for a unilateral refusal to sell or license a patent or copyright."[50] But at that point there was a logical disconnect with the court's conclusion that the defendant did have such a duty. It reasoned that because the statute declared existing law it was not entitled to be taken seriously and thus left room for a decision manifestly inconsistent with its words.

Further, the duty that the *Kodak* decision declared was a very broad one. The court reasoned that a patent rightfully creates a power to exclude from one market, not more. In the case at hand, a refusal to license a part excluded rivals from parts but also disabled them from servicing Kodak photocopiers. As the court reasoned, the patent entitled Kodak to protect its parts monopoly but not its service monopoly. As a result, it was for the jury to decide whether Kodak's intended merely to protect the former, or to create or maintain monopoly power in the latter.

But this reasoning rests on a flawed understanding of a patent. A patent describes an invention, not a market. Many patents, particularly for intermediate goods, might be used in final products or processes that operate in a wide variety of markets. For example, a patented mixing process might be applied to paint, peanut butter, and prescription drugs. A patented microprocessor circuit might be used in personal computers, navigation systems, or bread machines.[51]

45. 35 U.S.C.A. § 271(d).

46. On the concept of patent "misuse," see § 5.5.

47. The decisions include Cygnus Therapeutics Sys. v. ALZA Corp., 92 F.3d 1153, 1160 (Fed.Cir.1996) (patentee "under no obligation to license;" antitrust claim dismissed); Genentech v. Eli Lilly & Co., 998 F.2d 931, 949 (Fed.Cir.1993), cert. denied, 510 U.S. 1140, 114 S.Ct. 1126 (1994) (same; patentee's "right to select its licensees, to grant exclusive or non-exclusive licenses or to sue for infringement and the pursuit of optimum royalty income, are not of themselves acts in restraint of trade"); Data General Corp. v. Grumman Systems Support Corp., 36 F.3d 1147 (1st Cir.1994); USM Corp. v. SPS Techs., 694 F.2d 505, 513 (7th Cir. 1982), cert. denied, 462 U.S. 1107, 103 S.Ct. 2455 (1983) (may license "only on such terms as [the patentee] sees fit"); United States v. Studiengesellschaft Kohle, m.b.H., 670 F.2d 1122, 1131 (D.C.Cir.1981) (finding no cases imposing a duty to license, and refusing to create one). The copyright cases are similar: Tricom v. Electronic Data Systems Corp., 902 F.Supp. 741, 743 (E.D.Mi.1995) (owner of copyrighted software may not be compelled to license); Advanced Computer Services v. MAI Sys. Corp., 845 F.Supp. 356 (E.D.Va.1994) (unilateral copyright licensing policies cannot be antitrust violation); Corsearch v. Thomson & Thomson, 792 F.Supp. 305, 322 (S.D.N.Y.1992) ("Under the copyright laws, the copyright owner has a right to license the use of its intellectual property and to terminate or limit that use in such manner as it deems appropriate...."). Other decisions are discussed in Antitrust Law ¶ 704.1 (current Supplement).

48. Image Technical Services v. Eastman Kodak Co., 125 F.3d 1195 (9th Cir.1997), cert. denied, ___ U.S. ___, 118 S.Ct. 1560 (1998).

49. 125 F.3d at 1215.

50. *Kodak*, 125 F.3d at 1216.

51. A district court in similar litigation involving Xerox understood this. See Independent Service Organizations Antitrust Litigation, 964 F.Supp. 1454 (D.Kan.1997), 964 F.Supp. 1479, and 989 F.Supp. 1131 (D.Kan.1997):

Further, the Ninth's Circuit's rule emphasizing the defendant's *intent* to create a monopoly in a second market is inconsistent with the Supreme Court's *Professional Real Estate* (*PRE*) decision.[52] In that case the Supreme Court held that the owner of intellectual property had a right to exclude others by filing an infringement action without regard to any anticompetitive intent it might have. The *Kodak* rule thus creates the anomalous situation that under *PRE* a patentee who files an infringement action intending to exclude the alleged infringer from some market may have its infringement claim resolved on the patent law merits without regard to its intent. By contrast, the patentee who merely refuses to license its patent is subject to antitrust scrutiny depending on whether its intent was anticompetitive.[53]

At this writing, no other circuit has followed the *Kodak* line of reasoning,[54] and the law should be regarded as doing what § 271(d) of the Patent Act states: it is not an antitrust violation for a firm acting unilaterally and without condition to refuse to license its patented process or article to another person.

7.11d2. Conditional Refusals to License

Conditional refusals to license rest on a different footing than simple refusals. A conditional refusal might be one of the following: (1) I will license you my patented photocopier only if you agree to purchase my paper and ink; (2) I will license you my patented photocopier only if you agree not to obtain photocopiers from anyone else; or (3) I will license you my patented photocopier only if you agree to give me a royalty free license for your paper collating attachment. The first of these is a tying arrangement, the second exclusive dealing, and the third a reciprocity agreement.

Significantly, § 3 of the Clayton Act makes its prohibitions of tying and exclusive dealing apply to goods "whether patented or unpatented."[55] Further, § 271(d) of the Patent Act as quoted above expressly permits simple refusals to license, but also indicates in § 271(d) that tying can still be unlawful if the patentee "has market power in the relevant market for the patent or patented product...."[56]

These statutes indicate that basic antitrust principles govern the use of tying arrangements, exclusive dealing, or reciprocity in the licensing of patented processes or products. In each case, condemnation requires an agreement, market power or significant market foreclosure, and some assessment of anticom-

The scope of a "patent monopoly" is defined by the claims of the patent, not by the limits of what a court determines is the most analogous antitrust market. ...

We believe that the Ninth Circuit in *Kodak*, in reaching its conclusion, implicitly assumed that a single patent can create at most a single "inherent" economic monopoly. The Supreme Court in *Kodak* certainly did not reach this issue....

Patents only claim inventions. Because each use of that invention may be prevented by the patent holder, the patent may have some anticompetitive effect in each market in which it is used or not used. The patent statute expressly grants patent holders the right to exclude others from manufacturing, selling, or using their inventions. Manufacturing, retail, and service markets all fall within this statutory grant of power to patent holders. Thus, Congress, by enacting the patent statute, apparently contemplated that a single patent could implicate more than one market. ...

The reward for a patented invention is the right to exploit the entire field of the "invention," not the right to exploit the single most analogous antitrust market.

52. Professional Real Estate Investors v. Columbia Pictures Indus., 508 U.S. 49, 113 S.Ct. 1920 (1993). See § 18.3b.

53. The *Kodak* rule is also difficult to harmonize with the doctrine of contributory infringement as developed by the Supreme Court in Dawson Chemical Co. v. Rohm & Haas Co., 448 U.S. 176, 100 S.Ct. 2601 (1980). Contributory infringement occurs when someone makes a good knowing that the only way the good can be used is by infringing another's patent. In *Dawson* the patentee produced an unpatented chemical, Propanil, but owned a patent on the only known process for applying it. The defendant manufactured the chemical in competition with the patentee, knowing that the only way the chemical could be applied was by infringing the patentee's patented application process. The Supreme Court approved a contributory infringement claim. Under the *Kodak* reasoning, the patentee was presumably entitled to a patent covering the application process, but no to exclude others from making the chemical.

54. The one exception, which is on appeal to the Federal Circuit at the time of this writing, is Intergraph Corp. v. Intel Corp., 3 F.Supp.2d 1255 (N.D.Ala.1998). The district court never cited the Patent Act provision but held that Intel's microprocessor patents could be an "essential facility," thus imposing a duty of license.

55. 15 U.S.C.A. § 14.

56. 35 U.S.C.A. § 271(d)(5).

petitive effects.[57]

§ 7.12 Abuse of Government Process

Economists have often remarked that the best way to create or sustain monopoly is by soliciting the help of the government. Literally hundreds of antitrust cases involving exclusionary franchises, licensing restrictions, or other kinds of favorable treatment have alleged precisely this. In most cases the conduct is immune from antitrust liability for the simple reason that every citizen has a constitutionally protected right to petition her government for whatever she wants, even if what she wants is anticompetitive. The general problem of anticompetitive petitions to the government is considered in Chapter 18.

As a general principle, a petition to the government can be a § 2 violation only if it creates or threatens to create or perpetuate monopoly power. For this reason it is inaccurate to think of the petitioning conduct itself as the antitrust violation. Rather, the petitioning constitutes the conduct component of the violation.[1] Other components, such as the defendant's substantial market power in a monopolization case, or the "dangerous probability of success" in an attempt case,[2] must also be established. Likewise, the plaintiff must be able to point to a relevant market in which the defendant's market power will be exercised. Most, but not all, courts agree, and require the plaintiff to prove all the traditional elements of its case, even if the challenged conduct is a petition to the government.[3]

§ 7.13 Conduct Requirements in Attempt Cases

Any principled rule for determining the kinds of conduct that will support an attempt offense must recognize the following limitations: 1) the conduct, or planned or threatened conduct, must be capable of giving the defendant substantial and durable market power; 2) conduct that is legal for someone who is already a monopolist cannot be illegal for someone who is not a monopolist; 3) sometimes socially beneficial conduct can create substantial market power. Conduct in this last class should not be illegal.

A plaintiff cannot make out an attempt offense if the alleged conduct could not have given the defendant a monopoly. This may be the primary distinction between the offense of attempt to monopolize and the law of so-called business torts or unfair practices. False advertising, misrepresentation, certain refusals to deal, fraudulent inducement, and various dirty tricks may be illegal under the law of many states. They are not attempts to monopolize, however, unless there is a substantial likelihood that they will give the actor market power.

Often we can analyze such conduct by determining whether there was a "dangerous probability of success" that it would yield monopoly power.[1] For example, in some cases the market may be robustly competitive, with numerous firms, and the threat to competition (rather than to a particular competitor) seems fanciful. But in other situations determining "dangerous probability" may require a court to make an expensive economic analysis of the market in which the alleged illegal conduct

57. See § 10.6 (tying), § 10.9 (exclusive dealing), and § 10.8 (reciprocity).

§ 7.12

1. See 1 Antitrust Law ¶ 208 (rev. ed. 1997). The Supreme Court made this clear in Professional Real Estate Investors v. Columbia Pictures Industries, 508 U.S. 49, 61, 113 S.Ct. 1920, 1928 (1993), where it stated in dicta:

> Of course, even a plaintiff who defeats the defendant's claim to *Noerr* immunity by demonstrating both the objective and the subjective components of a sham [that is, litigation filed in bad faith] must still prove a substantive antitrust violation. Proof of a sham merely deprives the defendant of immunity; it does not relieve the plaintiff of the obligation to establish all other elements of his claim.

2. See § 6.5b.

3. See Neumann v. Reinforced Earth Co., 786 F.2d 424 (D.C.Cir.), cert. denied, 479 U.S. 851, 107 S.Ct. 181 (1986); compare Rickards v. Canine Eye Registration Foundation, 783 F.2d 1329 (9th Cir.), cert. denied, 479 U.S. 851, 107 S.Ct. 180 (1986) (finding a violation on the basis of the conduct alone, in the apparent absence of market power). On this point, *Rickards* is probably overruled sub silentio by *Professional Real Estate*.

§ 7.13

1. See § 6.5b.

took place. Sometimes one can infer from the conduct itself that monopoly power was not a likely result. For example, a mere claim of false advertising or refusal to deal unaccompanied by allegations that the market is already noncompetitive should be dismissed on its face.

Any act that is legal for a monopolist in the market in which it has monopoly power should be legal for a nonmonopolist: the conduct requirements for attempt should be substantially stricter than the requirements for illegal monopolization.[2] This means that activities that are only "marginally" illegal for monopolists are almost certainly legal for nonmonopolists. Price discrimination,[3] failure to predisclose new technology,[4] aggressive research and development,[5] expansion of capacity,[6] acquisition of or refusal to license patents,[7] and some dealer terminations and exclusive dealing contracts[8] may be legal when they are performed by a monopolist. They are then necessarily legal when they are performed by a nonmonopolist.[9]

Finally, some conduct should not be the basis for an attempt offense even though it threatens to create market power. This is particularly true of practices such as research and development and many instances of vertical integration. Further, such practices should be legal for the nonmonopolist even though they might be illegal for the monopolist. For example, there is economically dubious but nevertheless well established case authority that vertical integration by a monopolist can be illegal, particularly when it results in the termination of dealers or firms at a different distributional level than the one in which the defendant has a monopoly, or when it effectively gives the defendant a monopoly in two markets instead of one.[10]

Firms integrate vertically in order to reduce costs. One result of such cost reduction is that the integrated firm may be able to price its output above its new marginal cost or to steal part of the market away from competitors. This procurement of a "competitive advantage" has occasionally been characterized by courts as an illegal attempt to monopolize the primary market.[11]

Condemning such efficiency creating practices would undermine the entire competitive process, however. The nature of competition is to encourage competing firms to increase their own efficiency, necessarily at the expense of competitors. Any principled theory of attempt must condemn only inefficient, socially injurious conduct. This suggests that unilateral vertical integration by the nonmonopolist should be legal *per se*.[12]

Several courts agree that before the conduct requirements for an unlawful attempt are met, the conduct must be sufficiently hostile

2. Transamerica Computer Co. v. IBM Corp., 698 F.2d 1377, 1382 (9th Cir.), cert. denied, 464 U.S. 955, 104 S.Ct. 370 (1983) (if conduct is not monopolization, it is not attempt either).

3. See Pacific Eng. & Prod. Co. v. Kerr–McGee Corp., 551 F.2d 790 (10th Cir.1977), cert. denied, 434 U.S. 879, 98 S.Ct. 234 (1977), rehearing denied, 434 U.S. 977, 98 S.Ct. 543 (1977). But see, United States v. United Shoe Machinery Corp., 110 F.Supp. 295, 297 (D.Mass.1953) affirmed, 347 U.S. 521, 74 S.Ct. 699 (1954), where Judge Wyzanski included price discrimination among the exclusionary practices that made the defendant an illegal monopolist.

4. Berkey Photo, Inc. v. Eastman Kodak Co., 603 F.2d 263 (2d Cir.1979), cert. denied, 444 U.S. 1093, 100 S.Ct. 1061 (1980).

5. California Computer Products v. IBM Corp., 613 F.2d 727, 744 (9th Cir.1979).

6. E.I. du Pont de Nemours & Co., 96 F.T.C. 653 (1980).

7. See SCM Corp. v. Xerox Corp., 645 F.2d 1195 (2d Cir.1981), cert. denied, 455 U.S. 1016, 102 S.Ct. 1708 (1982).

8. Paschall v. Kansas City Star Co., 727 F.2d 692 (8th Cir.1984) (*en banc*), cert. denied, 469 U.S. 872, 105 S.Ct. 222 (1984).

9. See 3 Antitrust Law ¶ 806 (rev. ed. 1996).

10. See § 7.6.

11. For example, Industrial Building Materials v. Interchemical Corp., 437 F.2d 1336, 1344 (9th Cir.1970).

12. See 3A Antitrust Law ¶ 756 (rev. ed. 1996).

toward competition so as to be branded "predatory."[13] The meaning of "predatory," particularly of predatory pricing practices, is taken up in the following chapter.

13. For example, Neumann v. Reinforced Earth Co., 786 F.2d 424, 427 (D.C.Cir.), cert. denied, 479 U.S. 851, 107 S.Ct. 181 (1986) (attempt generally refers to predation, which means driving rivals from market or deterring their entry); Universal Analytics, Inc. v. MacNeal–Schwendler Corp., 707 F.Supp. 1170, 1178 (C.D.Cal.1989), affirmed, 914 F.2d 1256 (9th Cir.1990).

Chapter 8

PREDATORY AND OTHER EXCLUSIONARY PRICING

Table of Sections

---

§ 8.1 Introduction

In its most orthodox form, "predatory pricing" refers to a practice of driving rivals out of business by selling at a price below cost. The predator's intent—and the only intent that can make predatory pricing rational, profit-maximizing behavior—is to charge monopoly prices after rivals have been dispatched or disciplined. Predatory pricing is analyzed under the antitrust laws as illegal monopolization or attempt to monopolize under § 2 of the Sherman Act, or sometimes as a violation of Clayton Act § 2, generally called the Robinson–Patman Act. One of the arguments made in this chapter[1] is that predatory pricing should not generally be viewed as an "attempt" to monopolize. The market share requirements are so substantial that the offense

§ 8.1

1. See § 8.4.

is best viewed as part of the substantive law of monopolization. Nevertheless, many courts have considered predatory pricing to be part of the law of attempt, and many have not taken the structural requirements as seriously as they should.

Courts once believed that predatory pricing was easy for a well-financed firm to accomplish, and that it was a common means by which monopolies came into existence.[2] In the last generation, however, many economists, legal writers and courts have concluded otherwise: predatory pricing is in fact very expensive, most often likely to fail, and not plausible in the vast majority of markets in which it has been alleged to occur.[3] A few legal scholars believe that anticompetitive predatory pricing in any market is irrational and virtually never happens.[4]

The legal tests for predatory pricing have changed with judicial attitudes about how frequently it occurs. When courts believed predatory pricing was common, plaintiffs could sometimes establish it by showing that the defendant firm was large, the victim small, that prices in the predated area went down, and the defendant intended to harm its rivals.[5] Today, increased skepticism about the frequency of predatory pricing has led courts to develop much stricter tests. Since 1975 when the Areeda–Turner test was introduced,[6] only a small number of plaintiffs have prevailed in predatory pricing actions.[7] But no circuit has held that pricing at below cost is *per se* legal. The Supreme Court has not considered the appropriate price test for predatory pricing since the Areeda–Turner test was first developed.

Few antitrust allegations are more sensitive or difficult for courts to assess than predatory pricing claims. Low prices are a principle if not the primary goal of antitrust policy. In a predatory pricing case, however, a court must consider a charge that a price is unlawful because it is too low. Further, the relationship between any firm's prices and its costs is ambiguous and difficult to compute. If the judge uses an overdeterrent rule the result will be inefficiently high prices. This in turn will permit less efficient firms to stay in the market. Small wonder that some commentators argue that courts should dismiss all predatory pricing complaints, at least when the plaintiff and the defendant are competitors.[8]

Predatory pricing is not condemned because it results in current lower prices. It is condemned because, if successful, it will eventually result in reduced output and higher prices. A price is predatory if it is reasonably calculated to drive rivals from the market today or else discipline them so that the predator can enjoy profitable monopoly pricing in the post-predation period.

In order for such a scheme to be successful, several things must be true. First, the victims must be sufficiently weak or have sufficiently

2. For example, in the early twentieth century it was widely believed that the Standard Oil monopoly was created this way. See J. McGee, Predatory Price Cutting: the Standard Oil (N.J.) Case, 1 J. L. & Econ. 137 (1958) (debunking predatory pricing theory); and E. Granitz & B. Klein, "Monopolization by 'Raising Rivals' Costs': The Standard Oil Case," 39 J.Law & Econ. 1 (1996) (arguing that Standard mainly acquired its dominant position by agreements with railroads and others imposing higher costs on rivals).

3. See 3 Antitrust Law, Ch. 7C (rev. ed. 1996); R. Posner, Antitrust Law: An Economic Perspective 184–192 (1976).

4. For example, R. Bork, The Antitrust Paradox: A Policy at War With Itself 144–55 (1978; rev. ed. 1993); F. Easterbrook, Predatory Strategies and Counterstrategies, 48 Univ.Chi.L.Rev. 263 (1981).

5. E.g., Utah Pie Co. v. Continental Baking Co., 386 U.S. 685, 87 S.Ct. 1326, rehearing denied, 387 U.S. 949, 87 S.Ct. 2071 (1967).

6. P. Areeda & D. Turner, Predatory Pricing and Related Practices Under Section 2 of the Sherman Act, 88 Harv.L.Rev. 697 (1975). See § 8.2.

7. But there have been some. See U.S. Philips Corp. v. Windmere Corp., 1992–1 Trade Cas. ¶ 69,778, 1991 WL 338258 (S.D.Fla.1991) (evidence of drastic price reductions by a firm threatened by new entrant and holding 90% of a market characterized by substantial barriers to entry was sufficient to show monopolization under the Sherman Act); William Inglis & Sons Baking Co. v. Continental Baking Co., 942 F.2d 1332 (9th Cir.1991) (state law), vacated in part on rehearing, 981 F.2d 1023 (9th Cir. 1992); D & S Redi–Mix v. Sierra Redi–Mix and Contracting Co., 692 F.2d 1245 (9th Cir.1982).

8. However, Easterbrook, note 4, at 331–333, would permit suits by consumers forced to pay a higher price after the predation was successful.

high costs that the predator can drive them from business or make them obey. Second, the market must be structured in such a way that the predator can predict a profitable period of monopoly pricing. Third, the discounted present value of the future period of monopoly pricing must be greater than the present losses that the predator incurs during the predatory period. The following sections analyze these requirements and describe some of the difficulties that courts have encountered in evaluating predatory pricing claims.

§ 8.2 When Is a Price Predatory? The Areeda–Turner Test

Competition drives prices to marginal cost.[1] When a firm considers whether to produce one additional unit, it weighs the added revenues the additional sale will generate against the added costs of production and sale. Two things are generally true: 1) prices in competitive markets tend toward marginal costs; 2) dropping a price below short-run marginal cost is not reasonable profit-maximizing behavior, unless the resulting losses are more than offset by future monopoly profits.

Marginal cost pricing is consistent with competition; supramarginal cost pricing is consistent with monopoly.[2] But prices lower than marginal cost are consistent with neither. In an influential article published in 1975, Professors Areeda and Turner argued that a price lower than reasonably anticipated short-run marginal cost is predatory, while a price equal to or higher than reasonably anticipated short-run marginal cost is nonpredatory.[3]

Areeda and Turner argued further that use of short-run marginal cost as a benchmark for predation is impractical, because marginal cost is extraordinarily difficult to compute.[4] The primary value of marginal cost to economists is conceptual. The question it asks—what is the additional cost incurred in producing one more unit of output—is extremely difficult to answer when one studies a firm's history over perhaps two years and inquires as to its marginal costs during that period. Marginal cost generally cannot be computed in litigation when the relevant question is whether over some past, extended period of time a seller's prices were lower than its marginal costs, unless the disparity between the two is large.

Therefore Areeda and Turner proposed a surrogate: average variable cost (AVC).[5] A firm's total production costs can be divided into two kinds, fixed and variable. A fixed cost is one that does not change with variations in output over a given time period; a variable cost

§ 8.2

1. See F. Scherer & D. Ross, Industrial Market Structure and Economic Performance 20 (3d ed. 1990); and see § 1.1.

2. See § 1.2.

3. P. Areeda & D. Turner, Predatory Pricing and Related Practices Under Section 2 of the Sherman Act, 88 Harv.L.Rev. 697 (1975). The current formulation of the Areeda–Turner test is contained in 3 Antitrust Law Ch. 7C–3 (rev. ed. 1996). "Short-run" marginal cost is the appropriate standard because the evaluation of a firm's pricing behavior must be based on its existing plant and durable equipment, not on the most efficient possible plant and equipment. Long-run marginal cost, just as long-run average cost, measures a firm's costs when it is in a position to choose plant size as well as rate of output. See § 1.4 above.

We speak of "reasonably anticipated" marginal cost because a price that *ex ante* seems to be competitive may turn out later to be too high or too low. For example, a firm should not be condemned for predatory pricing if it made a $5.00 winning bid and the bid seemed reasonable when it was made. In fact, the firm may encounter unexpected difficulties and its true costs could eventually be above $5.00. Likewise, since the firm is presumed to be a profit-maximizer, "reasonably anticipated" is generally measured by an objective test, which involves looking at all relevant costs.

4. While marginal cost is difficult to compute, it may not always be difficult to determine that a price is below marginal cost. For example, suppose that a gasoline retailer pays a wholesale price of $1.00, including taxes, and sells the same gasoline at a price of 90¢. In that case we do not need to know precisely what marginal cost is in order to know that the price is below it. Any price per unit that is lower than the per unit cost of a basic input has to be lower than marginal cost. See 3 Antitrust Law ¶ 740a (rev. ed. 1996); and Rebel Oil Co. v. Atlantic Richfield Co *(Rebel Oil II)*., 146 F.3d 1088, 1094 & n. 1 (9th Cir.1998), cert. denied, ___ U.S. ___, 119 S.Ct. 541 (1998).

5. See 3 Antitrust Law ¶ 740 (rev. ed. 1996). AVC is discussed more fully in § 1.1b.

One place where neither the marginal cost nor the AVC rule for predatory pricing will work is in markets for intellectual property—patent licensing, licensing of films, performance rights, computer software, etc. In many such cases short-run marginal cost or AVC is very close to zero. A rule that permitted the licensor of, say, performance rights to cut price to AVC would be a virtual nonliability rule.

is one that does. For example, over a one-year period the capital cost of the plant itself is a fixed cost: it will have to be paid whether or not the firm produces, and the amount of the payment will not change as output varies. However, most labor costs, the costs of basic raw material or ingredients, and utility costs are generally variable. A bakery that increases its bread production by 100 loaves per day for three weeks likely will not enlarge its plant. However it will spend more money on flour, salt, and probably electricity and labor.

Although marginal cost is virtually impossible to compute in litigation, AVC is not—at least theoretically. One must identify which costs are variable, add them up, and divide by the number of units produced. Under the Areeda–Turner test, a price above AVC is presumed to be lawful. A price below AVC, if other prerequisites are met, is conclusively presumed to be illegal.[6]

Distinguishing fixed from variable costs can itself be difficult. The categories change from one industry to another and they vary depending on the time period being considered. Further, there is not complete agreement about how certain costs, such as advertising, whose effects can last a long time, should be counted. Distinguishing fixed from variable costs in litigation can add serious complexities to a fact finder's already difficult task. Areeda and Turner therefore proposed a "more categorical" laundry list of costs that should always be considered fixed. These include interest on debt, all taxes that do not vary with output, such as property taxes, and depreciation on the plant. Under the Areeda–Turner test all other costs are considered as part of marginal costs, or as part of AVC when it is used as a surrogate.[7]

§ 8.3 Predatory Pricing: Application and Criticism of the Areeda–Turner Test

Many courts initially adopted the Areeda–Turner test with little qualification.[1] Academics were more critical, and a lively scholarly debate ensued about the proper legal standards for predatory pricing.[2] Eventually this debate influenced courts as well, and some circuits that initially embraced the Areeda–Turner test had second thoughts.[3] Although the debate continues, today nearly all circuits adopt a version of the test. However, several deviate in some respects from Areeda and Turner's original formulation.[4]

6. Id. at ¶ 711d. A price above average total cost (the sum of fixed and variable costs divided by the number of units of output) is *per se* legal under the Areeda–Turner test.

7. Id. at ¶ 715c.

§ 8.3

1. For example, Janich Bros., Inc. v. American Distilling Co., 570 F.2d 848, 858 (9th Cir.1977), cert. denied, 439 U.S. 829, 99 S.Ct. 103 (1978); Pacific Eng'r. & Prod. Co. v. Kerr–McGee Corp., 551 F.2d 790, 797 (10th Cir.1977), cert. denied, 434 U.S. 879, 98 S.Ct. 234 (1977); International Air Indus., Inc. v. American Excelsior Co., 517 F.2d 714, 724 (5th Cir.1975), cert. denied, 424 U.S. 943, 96 S.Ct. 1411 (1976).

2. The debate is summarized in J. Hurwitz & W. Kovacic, Judicial Analysis of Predation: the Emerging Trends, 35 Vand.L.Rev. 63 (1982); J. Brodley & G. Hay, Predatory Pricing: Competing Economic Theories and the Evolution of Legal Standards, 66 Cornell L.Rev. 738 (1981).

3. However, there is little basis for the Eleventh Circuit's suggestion that "The Areeda and Turner test is like the Venus de Milo: it is much admired and often discussed, but rarely embraced." McGahee v. Northern Propane Gas Co., 858 F.2d 1487, 1495 (11th Cir.1988), cert. denied, 490 U.S. 1084, 109 S.Ct. 2110 (1989). As judges have become increasingly sophisticated in their economics, they have become more acceptant of the Areeda–Turner test.

4. Among the most orthodox are Kelco Disposal, Inc. v. Browning–Ferris Indus., 845 F.2d 404 (2d Cir.1988), affirmed on nonantitrust grounds, 492 U.S. 257, 109 S.Ct. 2909 (1989); Barry Wright Corp. v. ITT Grinnell Corp., 724 F.2d 227 (1st Cir.1983). The Federal Trade Commission also follows a fairly orthodox Areeda–Turner test under which prices higher than average total cost are conclusively legal; prices between average total and average variable cost have a strong presumption of legality; and prices below average variable cost are presumptively predatory. In re ITT, 104 F.T.C. 280, 403–404 (1984). Accord Stearns Airport Equip. Co. v. FMC Corp., 170 F.3d 518 (5th Cir.1999) (suggesting use of average variable cost test).

The Ninth Circuit once permitted prices above average total cost to be found predatory, but only on "clear and convincing evidence." Transamerica Computer Co. v. IBM, 698 F.2d 1377 (9th Cir.), cert. denied, 464 U.S. 955, 104 S.Ct. 370 (1983). Virtually all other courts that have addressed the issue have concluded that prices above average total cost are lawful. See, for example, *McGahee*, note 3, 858 F.2d at 1503 (11th Cir.); *Barry Wright*, id. at 235–236 (1st Cir.); Henry v. Chloride, 809 F.2d 1334, 1346 (8th Cir.1987) (interpreting Robinson–Patman Act). The

The Areeda–Turner test has been subjected to two broad classes of criticism: 1) Even assuming marginal cost is the proper benchmark for predation, AVC is often a poor surrogate; 2) short-run marginal cost is not an appropriate benchmark for identifying predation: although few prices below short-run marginal cost are nonpredatory, a price higher than short-run marginal cost can also be "predatory."

8.3a. The Average Variable Cost (AVC) Surrogate

Figure 1 illustrates some of the problems of the AVC test. The figure shows the cost functions of a plant of roughly optimal size. Its competitive rate of output is Q_c, which is at the intersection of the demand curve and the firm's marginal cost curve.[5] At this rate of output and with a market price of P_c, the firm is earning enough to cover its average total costs (AC), and more than AVC.

At the competitive rate of output, marginal costs are higher than AVC. More importantly, the two are diverging: if the firm increases its output, marginal costs and AVC will be even further apart. Under the Areeda–Turner rule, however, the firm legally would be able to increase its output all the way to Q_p and drop its price to P_p. At levels of output higher than optimum capacity (where predation can be expected to occur),[6] marginal cost and AVC tend to be quite far apart, with marginal cost higher than AVC. The result is that the Areeda–Turner test can give the predator considerable room for maneuvering. In fact, under the Areeda–Turner rule a firm could compute its AVC and legally sell at a price one cent higher, all the while imposing significant losses on its victim. One answer, of course, is that when AVC and marginal cost diverge substantially, a price below marginal cost will generally be easier to recognize and the AVC surrogate may be unnecessary.[7]

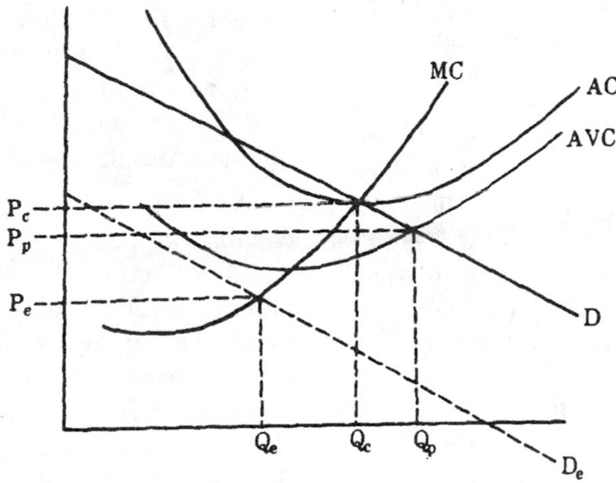

Figure 1

Precisely the opposite happens in a sick industry, plagued with excess capacity. As § 8.4b below shows, an industry with substantial excess capacity is not a plausible candidate for predatory pricing because the predator cannot reasonably look forward to a period of monopoly pricing. Shifted demand curve D_e in Figure 1 shows the consequences of excess capacity. Price will drop to P_e and output to Q_e, less than the optimal rate of output for the

Supreme Court's decision in Brooke Group Limited v. Brown & Williamson Tobacco Corp., 509 U.S. 209, 113 S.Ct. 2578 (1993), probably overruled the Ninth Circuit on this point. See § 8.3b.

5. The demand curve slopes downward because, although the firm may not have market power, it will make more sales if it lowers its price.

6. Since predatory pricing is a short-run phenomenon, the predator would ordinarily wish to do it without constructing an additional plant, even though during the predatory period output must be very high. As a result, we anticipate that predation will occur most often at inefficiently high levels of output.

7. See 3 Antitrust Law ¶ 740c (rev. ed.).

plant. Marginal cost and AVC also diverge, but this time AVC is higher. Under the Areeda–Turner test a firm pricing its output at marginal cost could nevertheless be guilty of predatory pricing.[8]

In short, the Areeda–Turner test makes predatory pricing easy to "prove" in markets where it is almost certain not to occur, but more difficult to prove in markets that are conducive to predation.

8.3b. The Problem of Long–Run, Strategic Behavior; "Predatory" Prices Above Cost; Multiple–Benefit Predation

Other criticisms of the Areeda–Turner test are more complex. Although there are numerous variations, the academic literature has suggested two variations on the predatory pricing story that the Areeda–Turner test fails to consider.[9] First is "limit pricing." That is, the predator directs its pricing activities, not against rivals already in the market, but against those contemplating entry. Second is what we call multiple-benefit predation: the predator that operates in numerous markets engages in well publicized price cutting in one as a threat, with the result that oligopoly prices are maintained elsewhere. A variation on this story is that one or more oligopolists respond to a price cutter (or other kind of innovator) with predation in order to send a message to other oligopolists that such competitive excursions will not be tolerated.

8.3b1. Limit Pricing and Strategic Entry Deterrence

Critics have argued that the Areeda–Turner test ignores the possibility of "strategic entry deterrence." For example, sometimes dominant firms intentionally create excess capacity and use it to deter potential entrants, without ever lowering their price below marginal cost or even average total cost. To the extent this is true, the Areeda–Turner conclusion that short-run marginal cost is the proper benchmark for predation is flawed. Most people agree that a price below short-run marginal cost is likely to be predatory. Several of Areeda's and Turner's critics have argued, however, that often a price higher than short-run marginal cost can be predatory as well—that is, it can be calculated to exclude an equally efficient rival or to permit the predator to engage in prolonged periods of monopolistic pricing.[10]

Suppose, for example, that an industry operating at optimal efficiency can produce widgets at $1.00 each. Demand at that price is 1000 per year. The minimum efficient scale (MES) for a widget plant is 250 widgets per year. Such a market has room for three or four efficient firms. However, a firm could construct a single efficient plant producing 1000 widgets annually and satisfy the entire market. Several industries probably have structural characteristics similar to this.[11]

A single dominant firm that built a plant capable of producing 1000 widgets per year could effectively deter future competitors. Having built a 1000–widget plant, the dominant firm could actually produce widgets at a rate of perhaps 700 per year and sell them at a monopoly price of $1.50. Any time a prospective entrant appeared, however, the dominant firm could increase its output to, say, 900 widgets per year and drop its price to slightly more than $1.00. Even though the current

8. In the short-run a firm would ordinarily cease production if the price dropped to a level below its average variable costs—that is, it could then minimize losses by producing nothing at all. However, the firm must consider the cost of ceasing production and restarting it. If it intends to stay in business and wants to retain certain customers or contracts, short periods of producing at a price lower than AVC may be more profitable than ceasing production. In any case, prolonged periods of pricing below AVC are not likely to occur in an industry with excess capacity. See P. Joskow & A. Klevorick, A Framework for Analyzing Predatory Pricing Policy, 89 Yale L.J. 213, 251 n. 77 (1979).

9. For these variations and some others, see J. Ordover & G. Saloner, Predation, Monopolization, and Antitrust, in 1 Handbook of Industrial Organization 537 (R. Schmalensee & R. Willig eds. 1989).

10. See F.M. Scherer, Predatory Pricing and the Sherman Act: A Comment, 89 Harv.L.Rev. 869 (1976); O. Williamson, Predatory Pricing: A Strategic and Welfare Analysis, 87 Yale L.J. 284 (1977); W. Sharkey, The Theory of Natural Monopoly 159–164 (1982).

11. See F.M. Scherer & D. Ross, Industrial Market Structure and Economic Performance 97–151 (3d ed. 1990).

price is highly profitable and the prospective entrant has access to the same technology, it would see that post-entry prices will probably be unprofitable. In particular, if demand is not sufficient to enable the firm to achieve MES *after* entry occurs, the new entrant will face higher costs than the incumbent. The post-entry price might then be too low to enable the entrant to earn a profit, even though that price is above the incumbent's marginal costs and average variable costs.[12]

In this way the excess capacity of the dominant firm can always stand ready as a weapon in its hands: prospective entrants know that the incumbent can easily increase output and reduce price in response to any attempt at entry or output expansion. Such a strategy will work best in an industry where assets are specialized and a great deal of the investment required for entry is "sunk"—that is, the new entrant will not be able to recover these costs in the event of failure.[13]

Economists have suggested a number of legal approaches to the problem of "limit" pricing. For example, Oliver Williamson proposed a rule that would make it illegal for a dominant firm to increase its output in response to entry by a competitor.[14] William Baumol suggested that if a competing firm is driven from business by a dominant firm's price reduction, the dominant firm should be prohibited from increasing its price for several years thereafter.[15] Finally, Paul Joskow and Alvin Klevorick proposed a more complex test that includes elements of the Areeda–Turner AVC test: 1) a price below AVC is predatory; 2) a price between AVC and average total cost is presumed predatory, but the defendant can rebut by showing that it has excess capacity that was not caused by its own exclusionary policy; 3) a price increase following a price reduction within two years is presumptive evidence of predation, even if the lower price was above average total cost.[16] So far no court has adopted any of these proposed alternative tests. Indeed, Professor Baumol appears to have changed his mind and now regards the AVC test as correct in principle, provided that AVC is defined in terms of average avoidable costs.[17] That proposal is discussed infra in § 8.3c.

For the courts, dealing with the limit pricing problem has generally boiled down to a consideration of whether prices above average total cost can ever be deemed "predatory." Once a court ventures into this territory, the rationale for antitrust intervention changes. A price above average total cost is "sustainable," in the sense that a firm charging such a price is earning a profit and will likely be able to stay in business indefinitely. Further, the entry deterrence strategy is one that the firm may very well pursue indefinitely, because it maximizes *current* profits, when both the size and the duration of profits are taken into account. By contrast, all prices below average total cost are non-sustainable in the long run. That is, the firm must eventually either get its prices above average total cost or else go out of business.

The difference between sustainable and non-sustainable pricing strategies is conceptually immense, and courts have not yet begun to appreciate it. For example, when one is examining a sustainable strategy the relevant question is generally whether the defendant has intentionally built a plant much too large for its reasonably anticipated needs. Unfortunately, the courts that have accepted in principle that prices higher than average total cost can be predatory, have tended to treat sustainable strategies in the same way they treat orthodox predation. They have tended to look at whether the defendant had a certain kind of "intent" to harm rivals.

12. The illustration is a simplification of Williamson, note 10, at 292–301. It is simply explained in G. Hay, A Confused Lawyer's Guide to the Predatory Pricing Literature 155–202, in Strategy, Predation, and Antitrust Analysis (S. Salop, ed. 1981).

13. See § 1.6 on sunk costs as barriers to entry.

14. Id. at 331–337.

15. W. Baumol, Quasi–Permanence of Price Reductions: A Policy for Prevention of Predatory Pricing, 89 Yale L.J. 1, 5 (1979).

16. Joskow & Klevorick, note 8 at 255.

17. W. Baumol, Predation and the Logic of the Average Variable Cost Test, 39 J. L. & Econ. 49 (1996).

Another feature of sustainable strategies is that, since they are long run, they are directed principally at *prospective* entrants rather than firms that are already established in the market. A few cases may involve situations where a firm sends implied threats to incumbents: either keep your prices up or else I will dump price dramatically. But in general, "limit" pricing strategies such as these are designed to force potential entrants to measure the relevant costs of entry vs. non-entry.

In a market where sunk costs are significant,[18] a firm contemplating entry may be easily deterred; but a firm already in the market will prove to be quite tenacious. It has more to lose in the event of failure. By contrast, in a market where sunk costs are trivial, entry barriers are likely not high enough to make predation a plausible strategy to begin with. For these reasons, courts should be deeply suspicious of claims by *incumbent* firms that a larger competitor's fully profitable prices should nevertheless be counted as "predatory." Indeed, the Fifth Circuit has suggested that allegations of limit pricing should not be made by an incumbent firm, if the limit prices are shown to be profitable to the defendant.[19]

The real justification for the Areeda–Turner rule is administrability.[20] Most economists acknowledge that strategies such as limit pricing occur and can be anticompetitive. The fundamental problem is that no one has developed the tools for evaluating such claims and determining appropriate relief. In general, the fact that an anticompetitive pricing strategy is sustainable entails that it is "above cost" in the short run, and this makes evaluation far more difficult. Further, it typically forces the court to look at the one thing—subjective intent—that has proved consistently to be the undoing of a rational predatory pricing policy. The worst of all possible rules would be one that (1) permitted prices to be proved predatory even when they exceed average total cost; and (2) permitted plaintiffs to establish (1) on the basis of evidence drawn from intent.

Finally is the almost insurmountable problem of administering relief. A dominant firm's "limit" price is very likely a price that is well above the competitive level. If it is below cost, then it is a predatory price in the orthodox sense; if it is at the competitive level, then the firm is "excluding" simply by charging a competitive price—something that the antitrust laws seek to encourage. A firm will rationally pursue limit pricing because it has a monopoly position to protect, and limit pricing produces both immediate monopoly profits and a long duration to its monopoly power. Consumers are of course benefitted by competitive prices, but a court order forcing a firm to charge the competitive price will do a competitor plaintiff no good.

For example, consider the Fifth Circuit's rule in *International Air* that predatory pricing can be shown by evidence that a "competitor is charging a price below its short-run profit-maximizing price and barriers to entry are great enough to enable the discriminator to reap the benefits of predation before new entry is possible."[21] The *potential* competitor plaintiff in such a case needs relief that forces the defendant to *increase* its price, perhaps to the short-run profit-maximizing level, so that the plaintiff can enter. The *actual* competitor plaintiff (who in this case must have higher costs than the "predator") is effectively asking the court to force the dominant firm to set price at its short-run monopoly level so that the plaintiff can survive. In each case, the plaintiff ends up making the peculiar claim that, although a competitive price (say, $1.00) and a short-run profit maximizing price (say, $2.00) would both be legal, an intermediate "limit" price (say, $1.50) is not. Such a plaintiff probably cannot establish either causation or antitrust injury.[22] At the very least, claims

18. That is, where many of the costs of entry cannot be recovered. See § 1.6.

19. Phototron Corp. v. Eastman Kodak Co., 842 F.2d 95, 101 (5th Cir.), cert. denied, 486 U.S. 1023, 108 S.Ct. 1996 (1988).

20. For elaboration, see 3 Antitrust Law ¶ ¶ 735a, 736 (rev. ed. 1996).

21. International Air Indus. v. American Excelsior Co., 517 F.2d 714, 724 (5th Cir.1975), cert. denied, 424 U.S. 943, 96 S.Ct. 1411 (1976).

22. See § 16.3.

of limit pricing should be limited to the public enforcement agencies and perhaps consumers.

In any event, the Supreme Court's *Brooke* decision[23] appears to have limited predation claims to those where prices are below average total cost. To be sure, price-cost relationships were not at issue and the Court refused to decide the proper cost test for predatory pricing. Further, the case was brought under the Robinson–Patman Act rather than the Sherman Act. However, since the Robinson–Patman Act is more expansive than the Sherman Act,[24] any restriction that applies to Robinson–Patman Act predation must apply to Sherman Act predation as well.

Speaking of price-cost relationships, the Supreme Court said this:

> [W]hether the claim alleges predatory pricing under § 2 of the Sherman Act or primary-line price discrimination under the Robinson–Patman Act, two prerequisites to recovery remain the same. First, a plaintiff seeking to establish competitive injury resulting from a rival's low prices must prove that the prices complained of are below an appropriate measure of its rival's costs. * * *[25]

And:

> Although *Cargill* and *Matsushita* reserved as a formal matter the question "whether recovery should ever be available * * * when the pricing in question is above some measure of incremental cost,"[26] the reasoning in both opinions suggests that only below-cost prices should suffice, and we have rejected elsewhere the notion that above-cost prices that are below general market levels or the costs of a firm's competitors inflict injury to competition cognizable under the antitrust laws.[27]

8.3b2. Multiple–Benefit Predation

Multiple-benefit predation occurs when the predator predates in one situation, but stands to benefit in several. If multiple-benefit predation is widespread, then Areeda and Turner may have underestimated predation's frequency. Accordingly, their test may be too rigorous.[28]

Multiple–Benefit predation theoretically occurs in two classes of cases. In the first, the dominant firm operates in many geographic areas. It responds to an aggressive rival in one area by engaging in predatory pricing that is quite obvious to rivals operating in the other areas. As a result of the predation, rivals in the other areas are intimidated and decline to cut price. If such possibilities exist they may make predatory pricing more profitable, since the post-predation "recoupment" is spread across several markets rather than one. The Robinson–Patman Act may have been drafted with this form of predation in mind, although the Act addresses the relevant issues rather poorly.[29]

A variation, which seems more plausible, is that an oligopolist uses predatory pricing in order to discipline a smaller price cutter, in the process sending a message to others contemplating similar cuts. In that case, the post-predation benefits, or recoupment, include not only the benefits of getting the first price cutter to behave, but also the clear message sent to future price cutters. The Supreme Court's narrow definition of "recoupment" in the *Brooke* case, discussed above, was not well calculated to inquire whether this strategy is possible. The Court held that the plaintiff must show that a particular instance of predatory pricing was reasonably calculated to produce sufficient post-predation profits to pay the predation's costs.[30] Further, in this case

23. See note 4.

24. See § 8.8.

25. 509 U.S. at 222, 113 S.Ct. at 2587.

26. Referring to Cargill v. Monfort of Colorado, 479 U.S. 104, 117–118 & n. 12, 107 S.Ct. 484, 493–494 & n. 12 (1986); Matsushita Electric Industrial Co. v. Zenith Radio Corp., 475 U.S. 574, 585, n. 9, 106 S.Ct. 1348, 1355 n. 9 (1986).

27. 509 U.S. at 223, 113 S.Ct. at 2588, citing Atlantic Richfield Co. v. USA Petroleum Co., 495 U.S. 328, 340, 110 S.Ct. 1884, 1892 (1990).

28. See 3 Antitrust Law ¶ 727g (rev. ed.).

29. See § 8.8.

30. *Brooke*, note 4, 509 U.S. at 223–226, 113 S.Ct. at 2587–2588.

the oligopoly was imperfect, with numerous discounts and promotions, so such recoupment seemed unlikely.[31]

But no oligopoly is perfect. Suppose that one or more dominant oligopolists have decided that *X* constitutes an acceptable amount of variation in prices, terms of sale, or product innovation in their market. When an aggressive competitor does more, say 1.5*X*, the dominant oligopolist responds with predation that is costly to everyone in the market. The result is that the oligopoly balance is restored *and* other firms who may have been thinking about stepping beyond *X* reconsider and decide not to. In such a case, the oligopoly would appear quite imperfect, but the predation could keep its imperfections within boundaries set by the dominant firm. Further, a single act of predation may have substantial "general deterrence" effects that last far into the future. *Brooke* did not consider these possibilities.

8.3c. AVC Measured as Average Avoidable Cost

An important variation on the Areeda–Turner formulation of the average variable cost test considers which costs can be *avoided* if the predator reduces its output or ceases production. For example, suppose a truck depreciates with use and lasts precisely 100,000 miles. Someone engaged in predatory pricing of delivery services (or of a good that is subject to seller-provided delivery) can avoid using the truck, or can use it less by selling less.[32] That makes it a variable cost for predatory pricing purposes. Indeed, some goods generally characterized as fixed costs should be considered as variable if the predator can avoid their use by raising its price and selling less. Suppose, for example, that the predator rents additional warehouse space during the predation period. Ordinarily the extra land and building would probably be considered a fixed cost; but in this case the relevant asset is the *rental* of the extra facilities—a cost that can be avoided if the seller produces less. The rental and additional maintenance expense should thus be included in average variable cost.[33]

Now consider a claim that an airline which has an established position in a certain hub airport has reduced its price dramatically in response to entry by a new carrier.[34] In speaking of predatory pricing in air passenger services, many of the cases have referred to the incremental cost of supplying a single seat on an already scheduled airline.[35] But in those

31. For further analysis, see § 8.8.

32. On use depreciation as a variable cost, see 3 Antitrust Law ¶ 735c (rev. ed.).

33. See W. Baumol, Predation and the Logic of the Average Variable Cost Test, 39 J. L. & Econ. 49 (1996) (defending average variable cost test but arguing that AVC should be understood as average avoidable cost). See id. at 58–59:

> RULE 2. The proper AVC figure to be used in the Areeda–Turner test to determine whether some price constitutes a threat to an efficient rival is the average avoidable cost of the pertinent output increment (decrement). If the average incremental cost is used instead, and the price nevertheless passes the test, one can be confident that the price is not predatory, because in general AIC >= AAC. The AAC figure must, however, include all pertinent portions of the product-specific fixed but avoidable costs, that is, all portions of such costs that can be escaped in the pertinent period of time.

34. The Department of Transportation has produced draft rules that are more aggressive, but that seem much more difficult to administer. In any event, these rules are not proposed Sherman Act tests. Rather, they are intended to establish whether a carrier is engaged in unfair exclusionary practices as defined under 49 U.S.C. § 41712. That provision is not enforceable by private parties. See Dept of Transportation, Enforcement Policy Regarding Unfair Exclusionary Conduct in the Air Transportation Industry (April 10, 1998), 63 Fed. Reg. 17919, 17920 (1998), which suggests that the Department will conclude that a carrier is engaged in unfair exclusionary practices as defined under 49 U.S.C. § 41712, if its pricing policy:

> . . . (1) causes [the major carrier] to forego more revenue than all of the new entrant's capacity could have diverted from it or (2) results in substantially lower operating profits—or greater losses—in the short run than would a reasonable alternative strategy for competing with the new entrant.

On such proposals, see Baumol, op. cit. at 68–69:

> There is absolutely nothing predatory about a price decision by a firm that fails to maximize the profits it can expect to earn during some brief proximate time period, provided that this price passes the (average variable cost) Areeda–Turner test and that this act can be expected to yield returns in the future that make up for whatever has been sacrificed in this way.

35. E.g., International Travel Arrangers v. NWA (Northwest Airlines), 991 F.2d 1389 (8th Cir.), cert. denied, 510 U.S. 932, 114 S.Ct. 345 (1993).

cases the claim was that the airline was selling individual discounted seats at below relevant costs, while presumably continuing to earn positive returns overall. When the question is whether the airline's rate structure as a whole is below relevant costs, then the airplane itself must be considered a variable cost item. First, it is subject to use depreciation in proportion to the number of hours it flies. Second, its cost is avoidable because it can readily be transferred to another market if not needed in the market in question. Of course, to the extent the aircraft is a variable cost, all expenses for servicing, operating and storing it are variable as well.

The same thing can generally be said of airport gate space rental. On the one hand, gate space is a piece of real estate, which is ordinarily a fixed cost. But while an airline needs gates to operate, it does not need as many gates as it has. Even long term gate space leases can be assigned or sublet to other tenants. If that is so, then an airline can avoid at least some gate space costs by producing less and transferring the residual leasehold to others. If that is so, the cost of gate space is variable.[36]

In sum, a business firm always tries to put its assets to their best use. The concept of average avoidable cost asks What is the cost of this asset in the actual use as compared with some alternative use to which it could have been placed. Thus even a fully depreciated warehouse has a cost, which is the foregone revenue that the predator could have obtained by renting it to others instead of using it store additional inventory during a predatory pricing campaign.

§ 8.4 Structural Issues: When Is Predatory Pricing Plausible?

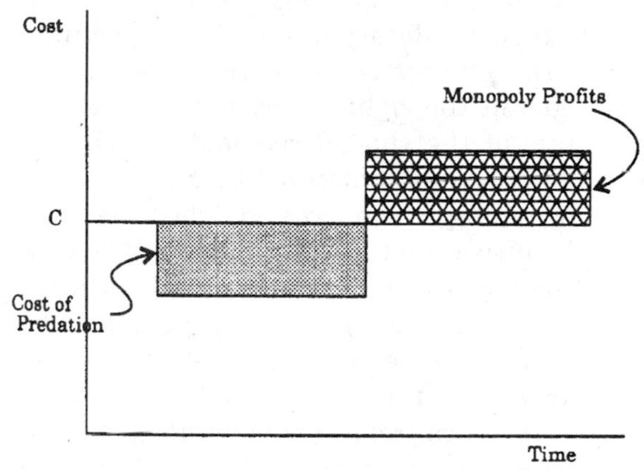

Figure 2

[622A]

Figure 2 illustrates some of the problems facing the putative predator. The central line labelled C measures the predator's costs, which formally are its total costs. This line represents a finite time period sufficiently long to cover both the predation period and the period of post-predation monopoly pricing. The shaded rectangle on the left, which hangs below line C, represents the costs of predatory pricing, which consists of two elements: the duration of the pricing scheme and the extent of loss per unit sold. The first of these is measured by the horizontal length of the rectangle, and the second is measured by its height. The cross-hatched rectangle on the right, which sits atop line C, represents the monopoly returns from predatory pricing. The size of these returns depends on their duration, measured by the horizontal length of the cross-hatched rectangle, and also the amount of monopoly profit per unit sold, measured by the cross-hatched rectangle's height.

36. See Baumol, note 33 at 62:

RULE 5. The time horizon pertinent for the calculation of the AAC for an Areeda–Turner test is the time period over which the price in question prevailed or could reasonably have been expected to prevail. Where a sequence of prices is alleged to be predatory in combination the pertinent horizon is the end of all the time periods during which those prices prevailed, and the test should require that the present value of the incremental revenues for this extended period equal or exceed the present value of the avoidable costs. Once again, it should be the obligation of the plaintiff to specify in advance what pertinent time period or sequence of time periods it is challenging.

Predatory pricing is not a profitable strategy unless the cross-hatched rectangle on the right is larger than the shaded rectangle on the left. Indeed, that does not quite tell the whole story: predatory pricing is not profitable unless the *present value* of the cross-hatched rectangle on the right is larger than the present value of the shaded rectangle on the left, when one is contemplating the scheme at the very beginning. The cross-hatched rectangle must be discounted in two quite distinct ways. *First*, money to be received in the future is worth less than money in my pocket today. Indeed, if the underlying interest rate is 10%, a dollar a year from now is worth only ninety cents, two years from now is worth eighty-one cents, and so on.[1] *Second*, the cross-hatched rectangle must be reduced if the probability that the predatory pricing scheme will succeed is anything less than one hundred percent, taking into account several possibilities: (1) the rivals will prove tenacious and stay in the market, so the monopoly period will never materialize; (2) the rivals will be driven from the market, but shortly after the monopoly price increase new entrants will appear, driving prices back to the competitive level; (3) the predator will be caught, convicted of a Sherman Act violation, enjoined and assessed damages. If a predator believes there is only a 50–50 chance of success, the size of anticipated profits must be cut in half.

The discussion in §§ 8.2–8.3 dealt only with how to identify a *price* as predatory. Even if it were legal, predatory pricing is risky and expensive and is plausible only in markets conducive to monopolization. Often a court can evaluate the market much more easily than it can determine whether a defendant's particular price level was predatory.

As a general matter, a claim of predatory pricing is implausible unless two things are true: 1) the market must be susceptible of monopolization; and 2) the defendant must be a dominant firm within that market. Virtually all the proposed predatory pricing tests discussed in the preceding section apply only to dominant firms.[2]

8.4a. The Predator's Market Position

As a matter of legal theory, courts have traditionally dealt with predatory pricing claims as attempts to monopolize. As a matter of economics, this seems wrong. Predatory pricing and other pricing strategies are generally plausible only for firms that are *already* dominant in their markets. Indeed, predatory pricing may require a higher market share than other practices (such as baseless patent litigation) that are generally condemned as substantive monopolization. For many years courts largely ignored structural issues in predatory pricing cases and focused instead on price/cost relationships. More recently, however, some have discovered that the quickest road to a resolution may be to look at structure first. If structural analysis indicates that predatory pricing simply cannot be a profitable strategy in a particular market, then further inquiry need not be made into price/cost relationships. As the discussion in § 8.7 shows, many courts recognize this.[3] The Supreme Court's *Brooke* decision, discussed at some length in § 8.8, is a bold turn in this direction. There the court assumed that (1) prices were below average variable cost and (2) the defendant's anticompetitive intent was clear. However, it dismissed the complaint because an analysis of market structure convinced it that "recoupment" was not likely. That is, the market structure did not indicate that the defendant could have anticipated that its current below cost prices would yield sufficiently large future monopoly gains.

One objection to this focus on structure is that if the goal of antitrust law is deterrence,

§ 8.4

1. See Brooke Group Ltd. v. Brown & Williamson Tobacco Corp., 509 U.S. 209, 210 113 S.Ct. 2578, 2581 (1993): "The plaintiff must demonstrate that there is a likelihood that the predatory scheme alleged would cause a rise in prices above a competitive level that would be sufficient to compensate for the amounts expended on the predation, including the time value of the money invested in it."

2. See 3 Antitrust Law ¶ ¶ 728–729 (rev. ed. 1996).

3. For example, American Academic Suppliers v. Beckley–Cardy, 922 F.2d 1317, 1319 (7th Cir.1991) ("Firms found guilty of attempting to monopolize are typically, and in predatory pricing cases must always be, monopolists.").

then the law should look at conduct rather than results. Refusing to find predatory pricing in competitive markets sounds a little like failing to find attempts generally. The common law offense of "attempt," after all, is directed toward *failures*. Someone who points a gun at someone and pulls the trigger may be convicted of an attempt even though the powder is wet or the firing pin defective. *He* thought the gun would work, and if we want to deter murders, that should be the thing that counts. So, the argument goes, if the goal of antitrust law is deterrence, then we want to deter people from attempting antitrust violations, even those where the likelihood of success is small. Indeed, the attempt itself can be socially costly. Failed predation has been described as a "gift" to consumers, because it produces low prices today and no subsequent monopoly prices later.[4] But it is hardly a gift to competitors, and it may impose costs on others, such as those from whom the competitor purchases its inputs. Indeed, it may even hurt some consumers to the extent that the "false" signalling about price leads them to make investments or alter their activities in some other fashion.[5]

This approach to the attempt offense makes considerable sense when the conduct under examination is unambiguous. The pointing of a gun at someone's head is a fairly unambiguous act, and it generally remains unambiguous even after it turns out that the gun is defective or the powder wet. Not so with predatory pricing. By all odds, we do a very poor job of identifying the line between predatory and non-predatory prices. Conceptually, our scheme for measuring price/cost relationships is full of holes, as the discussion in the first three sections of this chapter reveals. Questions about how costs should be classified, what cost level is predatory, and under what circumstances, all yield highly disputed and variant answers.[6] Further, even if we all agreed about the basic concepts, we haven't done well enough in *measuring* the appropriate costs to make the scheme workable with tolerable accuracy.

So we take a rational actor approach.[7] We presume that firms are profit maximizers, and that their managers have at least an intuitive knowledge of the kinds of strategies that will and will not work in their respective areas. Then we ask ourselves "Could a manager who knows these things about the market she works in believe that her firm could profitably drop price today, dispatch rivals, and charge monopoly prices later?" If our economic answer to that question is no, it helps us characterize the ambiguous conduct. No, a rational person would not have done this. So assuming this particular defendant's manager is rational, that must not be what happened.

Suppose that a market contains five firms of the following size: A has 30% of the market, B, C & D each have 20%, and E has 10% of the market. B attempts predatory pricing and drops its price from a competitive level of $1.00 to a predatory level of 80¢.

Assume for the sake of convenience that the market has an elasticity of demand of 1. The 20% price reduction will cause a 20% general increase in market demand. The predator will have to pick up all these sales. Assuming that total market demand before predation was 1000 units per year, and that B's output had been 200 units, B will now have to increase its output to 400 units just to take care of new customers who have entered the market at the predatory price: B has dou-

4. See Judge Easterbrook's opinion in A.A. Poultry Farms v. Rose Acre Farms, 881 F.2d 1396, 1401 (7th Cir.1989), cert. denied, 494 U.S. 1019, 110 S.Ct. 1326 (1990) ("Price less than cost today, followed by the competitive price tomorrow, bestows a gift on consumers. * * * Because antitrust laws are designed for the benefit of consumers, not competitors, a gift of this kind is not actionable.").

See also *Brooke* decision, note 1: "Although unsuccessful predatory pricing may encourage some inefficient substitution toward the product being sold at less than its cost, unsuccessful predation is in general a boon to consumers. * * * " 509 U.S. at 224, 113 S.Ct. at 2588.

5. For example, predatory pricing in product A may encourage a customer of product A, who uses A as an input into product B, to enter the market for B or expand her capacity there, since the market appears quite profitable. But once the A price is increased to the competitive level, that entry or expansion may turn out to be unprofitable.

6. See §§ 8.5–8.6, infra.

7. See 3 Antitrust Law ¶ 725a (rev. ed.).

bled its output without stealing a single customer from a competitor!

If B triples its output to 600 units, it will presumably steal 200 sales from competitors. These will not come from any single firm, however, but from each of the other firms, perhaps equally, or perhaps in proportion to their market share. Assuming the latter, each firm will lose about 25% of its business. Now the predator has increased its output threefold—accruing 20¢ in losses on each sale—and has caused a mere 25% loss of sales to its competitors.

Suppose that one firm is so weak that B actually manages to drive it from the market. If firm C leaves the market, its market share will be divided among each of the four surviving firms in proportion to their market shares, with perhaps a somewhat larger percentage going to the predator because of its large current output. At most, however, firm B can expect to end up with a market share on the order of 30%—hardly enough to engage in prolonged monopoly pricing.

Worse yet, what will become of victim C's plant? More often than not, when a firm goes out of business its plant passes into the hands of a successor.[8] Further, the successor will probably buy the bankrupt firm's plant at a bargain price and as a result will have lower fixed costs than its predecessor. Firm B's predation could well end up giving B a stronger rival than it had before.

By contrast, if a predator has a 90% market share and its only rival 10%, the picture is quite different. In that case a 10% price reduction in a market with demand elasticity of 1 would require a 10% output increase to take care of new customers. A 20% output increase would virtually wipe out the rival. Once the rival was eliminated, no one would be left to restrain the predator's ability to raise prices. A market with two competitors, one of which is very large, is far more conducive to predatory pricing than a market with several relatively small competitors. Predatory pricing is simply implausible in competitive markets. In such situations a court would do well to dismiss a predatory pricing complaint without analyzing the relationship between the defendant's prices and its costs.[9] One way courts could achieve this is by characterizing predatory pricing as monopolization, requiring a showing of a large market share, rather than as an attempt to monopolize. In Robinson–Patman Act cases, this would require the alternative showing that anticipated post-predation gains would be insufficient to make predation profitable.[10]

One effect of this analysis is that predatory pricing analysis simply cannot proceed without a market definition and a computation of market share. The Supreme Court has required the former in attempt cases generally,[11] although it has said little about specific market share requirements.[12] The same rules should apply to predatory pricing under the Robinson–Patman Act, and some circuit courts have required plaintiffs under that statute to define a relevant market.[13] Although the Supreme Court did not address the issue in the *Brooke* case, it spoke of the ability to "control * * * prices in the relevant market" as if a market definition was required. It also spoke of the need for plaintiffs to prove the plausibility of predation from evidence concerning "the structure and conditions of the relevant market."[14]

8. Unless the market contains a large amount of excess capacity.

9. See H. Hovenkamp & A. Silver–Westrick, Predatory Pricing and the Ninth Circuit, 1983 Arizona St.L.J. 443, 460–64.

10. As in the *Brooke* decision, note 1. See § 8.8.

11. Spectrum Sports v. McQuillan, 506 U.S. 447, 459, 113 S.Ct. 884, 892 (1993), on remand, 23 F.3d 1531 (9th Cir.1994). See § 6.5b.

12. See § 8.7. However, the Supreme Court has suggested that predatory pricing is not plausible on market shares of less than 20%. Cargill v. Monfort of Colo., 479 U.S. 104, 106 n. 2, 107 S.Ct. 484, 487 n. 2 (1986).

13. On predatory pricing and the Robinson–Patman Act, see § 8.8. See also Henry v. Chloride, 809 F.2d 1334, 1347 (8th Cir.1987) (requiring market definition in Robinson–Patman Act predatory pricing case).

14. *Brooke*, 509 U.S. at 209, 226, 113 S.Ct. at 2587, 2589. The Court also spoke of the predation inquiry as addressing "whether it would likely injure competition in the relevant market." Id. at 225, 113 S.Ct. at 2589.

When a court evaluates a predatory pricing claim, it should consider several additional structural features of the relevant market:

8.4b. Barriers to Entry

The rationale for predatory pricing is the sustaining of losses today that will give a firm monopoly profits in the future. The monopoly profits will never materialize, however, if new entrants appear soon after the successful predator attempts to raise its price. Predatory pricing will be profitable only if the market contains significant barriers to new entry. The relevant barriers are Bainian, not Stiglerian: that is, one must ask whether post-predation monopoly profits will be disciplined by new entry.[15]

There is one important difference between entry analysis in predatory pricing cases and, say, merger cases. In the latter, the only relevant question is whether entry is likely to occur in response to collusion or monopoly pricing.[16] In predatory pricing cases, that question is certainly central, but one must also consider whether predatory pricing occurred in the first place. In answering this question, historical evidence of entry can prove quite helpful.

In a merger case, evidence of recent entry is not necessarily good proof that entry barriers are low. Each new entrant adds to total market output and drops the market price, and entry is not attractive unless the prospective entrant predicts that the market will be profitable *after* its own output is added to that of others in the market. As a result, a market that was conducive to entry before firm A entered, may not be conducive after A is already there and producing. For this reason, the federal government's Merger Guidelines play down the significance of historical evidence of entry in merger analysis.[17]

By contrast, the claim in a predatory pricing case must be that the market was *already* unprofitable during the predation period—that is, output was already higher and prices lower than required for profitability. This claim is directly contradicted by the fact that one or more firms entered *during* the predatory period. Such entry entails that the entering firm believed prices were sufficiently high that it could make a profit. Any price low enough to impose losses on established rivals is necessarily low enough to make entry by an equally efficient firm unprofitable.[18]

8.4c. Excess Capacity

Excess capacity is the capacity of the firms in a market to produce more than the market demands at a competitive price. Excess capacity is generally inefficient unless the market is volatile and subject to indefinite but dramatic spurts in demand. Indeed, capacity reasonably calculated to take such spurts into account should not be considered "excess" at all.

Excess capacity can exist for a number of reasons, and can be distributed in a corresponding number of ways. Excess capacity sometimes exists because the industry itself is in decline. The invention of the electronic calculator, for example, created excess capacity in the market for slide rules. In such cases excess capacity is ordinarily distributed among the firms in the market in rough proportion to their market shares.

Excess capacity can also exist because a new entrant has appeared, and its additional plant creates more productive capacity than the market is able to absorb in a short period of time. In this case the new entrant is likely to have more excess capacity than the incumbents, whose markets are already established.

Finally, as § 8.3b indicates, excess capacity can be part of the entry deterrence strategy of a dominant firm. The dominant firm can hold its excess capacity, plus the threat of future output increases, over the heads of smaller firms thinking about enlarging output or entering the market. In this case the dominant

15. On the differences between "Bainian" and "Stiglerian" barriers, see §§ 1.6, 12.6. See also 3 Antitrust Law ¶ 729 (rev. ed.).

16. On entry barriers and merger policy, see § 12.6.

17. See § 12.6d of this book.

18. See, e.g., Stearns Airport Equip. Co. v. FMC Corp., 170 F.3d 518 (5th Cir.1999) (large number of foreign firms coming into market indicated entry barriers to low to support predatory pricing claim).

firm is likely to have more excess capacity than its competitors.

Excess capacity can distort analysis of predatory pricing in several ways. First, it can affect the definition of which costs are fixed and which are variable. A variable cost is a cost that varies with changes in output as measured over some given period. A fixed cost is one that does not respond to changes in output. Because of measurement difficulties, the Areeda–Turner test for predatory pricing uses a pre-established "laundry list" of fixed and variable costs.[19] Some courts have rejected this approach, however, as too arbitrary. They hold that the pricing period alleged to be predatory ought to determine variable costs. For example, the Ninth Circuit's definition of variable costs in predatory pricing cases is "those expenses that increased as a result of the output expansion attributable to the price reduction" alleged to be predatory.[20]

If a firm is already operating at full capacity, any enlargement of output may require additional capacity, which would then have to be considered a variable cost. However, a firm that operates at far less than full capacity may be able to increase output substantially at relatively low cost. For example, in *Inglis* the district court determined that the defendant's excess capacity was so large that the ovens could accommodate more bread at no additional cost, that delivery trucks were running half empty, and that wages were being paid to people who were working only part of the time. The court concluded that the only variable costs that the firm would incur in increasing its output of bread were "ingredients, wrappers, fuel and commission."[21]

The effect of excess capacity in the hands of the defendant can therefore reduce the number of costs considered variable and increase the proportionate amount of costs considered fixed. The result is to make it more difficult for the plaintiff to prove predatory pricing under the Areeda–Turner test.

Whether such a result is good depends on the reasons for the excess capacity in the market. If the excess capacity is the result of a sick industry, the effect is good. Competition in a declining industry drives prices below average total costs, because the capacity exceeds the demand in the market, but the capacity must be paid for. Eventually the firms in the market will either retire some of their plants as they wear out, or else exit the market. Sales at below average total cost in such a sick industry do not represent predatory pricing, but rather the market's natural correcting processes.

However, if the excess capacity is a result of the dominant firm's strategic entry deterrence scheme, the lowered estimate of AVC plays into the firm's hands. In such a situation the excess capacity was designed by the defendant to enable it to deter prospective entry without reducing its price below AVC. Any rule that defines variable costs as those costs a defendant incurs as part of an allegedly predatory output expansion gives the firm even more room for strategic maneuvering. If the defendant's excess capacity was strategically planned the court would be better off to use Areeda's and Turner's laundry list of fixed and variable costs.

This coin has another side, however. If the defendant has always operated at near capacity, then predation is unlikely for the simple reason that it will be unable to absorb the market shares of its rivals. For example, suppose that a dominant firm has generally operated at capacity and that during a slack period it chooses to cut price rather than output. Less efficient rivals will be injured but predation is unlikely unless the decline is permanent. The firm will be unable to steal its rivals' market share. In *Brooke*, the Supreme Court suggested in dicta that the defendant's lack of excess

19. See § 8.2; and 3 Antitrust Law ¶ 740b,d (rev. ed.).

20. William Inglis & Sons Baking Co. v. ITT Continental Baking Co., Inc., 668 F.2d 1014, 1037 (9th Cir.1981), cert. denied, 459 U.S. 825, 103 S.Ct. 57 (1982).

21. Id. 461 F.Supp. 410, 418 (N.D.Cal.1978), affirmed in part, reversed in part, 668 F.2d 1014 (9th Cir.1981), cert. denied, 459 U.S. 825, 103 S.Ct. 57 (1982). In *Brooke*, the Supreme Court also noted that the market was subject to substantial excess capacity. *Brooke*, note 1, 113 S.Ct. at 2583.

capacity was so important as to justify dismissal of a predatory pricing complaint.[22]

Finally, excess capacity held by a firm's competitors can frustrate any predatory pricing scheme. The success of predatory pricing depends on the predator's ability eventually to reduce output and charge a monopoly price. If competitors have excess capacity, however, they will be able to respond quickly to the predator's output reduction with an offsetting output increase, and the predator's monopoly profits will never be realized. If such industry-wide excess capacity not in the defendant's control will likely remain in the post-predation market, the claim should generally be dismissed without inquiry into the defendant's prices.[23]

8.4d. Disposition of Productive Assets

Predatory pricing is a profitable strategy only if the victim's productive assets are removed from the market. The predator's worst nightmare goes like this: after a long, expensive period of predation the victim files for bankruptcy and its plant and equipment are auctioned off to a prospective rival who intends to stay in the market; further, the bid price is only 10 cents on the dollar, thus giving the rival substantially lower fixed costs and perhaps even some lower variable costs (such as use depreciation)[24] than the predation victim had.

Perhaps the predator could purchase the victim's plant itself and then dismantle it. Precisely this happened in a few early antitrust cases.[25] But today, if the market meets the structural requirements for predatory pricing the predator will probably not be able to acquire the victim's assets. The market would be so concentrated and entry barriers so high that any such merger would be challenged under § 7 of the Clayton Act. To be sure, merger law has a defense for the acquisition of failing firms—but the defense rarely succeeds, and a predator could certainly not count on being able to use it successfully.[26]

In order for its predation to succeed, the predator must be fairly secure, then, that the victim's productive assets will be removed from the market, thus permitting the predator to raise prices to monopoly levels. To be sure, certain conditions will facilitate this. If the victim's assets are generalized rather than specialized, the likelihood is great that they will be re-deployed in a different market. For example, if the victim's assets consisted mainly of general purpose delivery trucks, the trucks could easily be transferred to a different geographic area or used to deliver a different product. Alternatively, the market could have so much excess capacity, or be in such a weakened condition, that there will likely not be any takers for the victim's old plant; it will be shut down. If the predator can predict with some confidence that this will happen, it will not have to worry about redeployment.

But these very considerations that make continued use of the victim's productive assets in the same market less likely also make predatory pricing less plausible. Markets where assets are generalized are rarely conducive to

22. *Brooke*, 509 U.S. at 226, 113 S.Ct. at 2589. "In certain situations—for example, where * * * defendant lacks adequate excess capacity to absorb the market shares of his rivals and cannot quickly create or purchase new capacity—summary disposition of the case is appropriate." See also *Cargill*, note 12, 479 U.S. at 119–120 n. 15, 107 S.Ct. at 494–495 n.15.

23. In Zoslaw v. MCA Distrib. Corp., 693 F.2d 870, 888 (9th Cir.1982), cert. denied, 460 U.S. 1085, 103 S.Ct. 1777 (1983), the court dismissed a predatory pricing claim without inquiring into price, because the record demonstrated that the defendant's market share was only 10%.

24. Depreciation caused by *use* of a machine, as opposed to depreciation that results simply from age, can be considered a variable cost if the rate of depreciation varies with the amount of use. For example, if a truck has a useful life of 200,000 miles, then a pro rata share of its costs should be assigned to each mile driven, even though the truck itself is ordinarily regarded as a fixed cost asset. In that case, if the truck were purchased for a small fraction of its replacement value, its owner would have lower variable costs. See Kelco Disposal v. Browning–Ferris Indus. of Vt., 845 F.2d 404, 408 (2d Cir.1988), affirmed on nonantitrust grounds, 492 U.S. 257, 109 S.Ct. 2909 (1989) (depreciation resulting from use is a variable cost, while that resulting from obsolescence is a fixed cost; then holding that depreciation of defendant's trucks and other heavy equipment could be counted as a variable cost). See 3 Antitrust Law ¶¶ 735c2, 740d5 (rev. ed. 1996).

25. For example, United States v. American Can Co., 230 Fed. 859, 867–868 (D.Md.1916), appeal dismissed, 256 U.S. 706, 41 S.Ct. 624 (1921).

26. See § 12.9.

predatory pricing, because entry into such markets is usually quite easy. The same factors that make the assets easily redeployable in a different market also reduce the amount of "sunk," or nonrecoverable costs that generally act as the most substantial barrier to entry in real world markets. Likewise, the conclusion that a market is so weakened that purchase of a victim's plant is unlikely also suggests that any below cost pricing that may have occurred was a result of general market conditions rather than predation. Such a market is not likely to produce a future period of monopoly profits.

Are there situations when the predator can have confidence that productive assets will be taken off the market *and* the predation itself will be a profitable strategy? Perhaps some. The victim may be a multi-product firm, and the predation may work to force the victim to stay in business but stop handling the predated product. In that case, third firms are less likely to pick up the product. But the problem with that strategy is, what is to prevent the victim from adding the predated product back to its line once the period of post-predation monopoly pricing begins? The victim does not have to re-enter the market; it needs only to re-introduce the missing product.

8.4e. Should Competitor Predatory Pricing Suits Be Abolished?

The problems noted in this section have led some people to conclude that predatory pricing virtually never occurs. Further, competitors are the worst possible people to complain about it. Upon inspection, they are almost always complaining about efficient, competitive behavior rather than inefficient, predatory conduct.

Judge Easterbrook has proposed that only consumers be permitted to bring predatory pricing claims.[27] Consumers, the argument goes, have no general incentive to complain about *low* prices; they will complain only about the high prices that occur during the post-predation period. As a result, when they complain, we can assume that they are complaining about the real thing.

But restricting suits to consumers hardly solves many of the problems of identifying predation. First are the innumerable problems of informing and organizing consumers. Consumers are numerous, and typically quite badly informed about the underlying conditions in a certain market. Typically they have no knowledge of the defendants' costs, certainly not the kind of knowledge that a competitor has. Second, not every sudden price increase is the result of predatory pricing. Some are a function of increased costs; some a result of monopoly power created by lawful means. A consumer would still have to prove predatory pricing by some cost-based test—perhaps the Areeda–Turner test or a fairly close equivalent. In the typical predatory pricing case, the plaintiff is a firm that has been driven from business and the defendant dominates the remaining market. The plaintiff must then show that it was driven out by predation, and not by the defendant's greater efficiency or the plaintiff's own ineptness. A consumer would have to make the same showing, perhaps without access to evidence controlled by the victim, who is not a party.

So all the numerous difficulties attending conceptualization and proof of the basic offense would still be with us. In the case of consumer suits, however, the evidence would not be as fresh, for the suit would not come until well after the predation period, when the predator increased its prices. In addition, restricting suits to consumers denies society the advantage of the "early warning system" that competitor suits give us. In spite of their often improper motives, competitors often feel the injury caused by monopolistic exclusionary practices long before consumers do, and the injuries are more concentrated and less subtle. This makes competitors particularly well placed to attack antitrust violations at a relatively early stage, when their social cost is still minimal. For these reasons the competitor lawsuit challenging predatory pricing should not be jettisoned so quickly.[28]

27. F. Easterbrook, Predatory Strategies and Counterstrategies, 48 Univ.Chi.L.Rev. 263, 331–333 (1981).

28. See § 2.2c; and see H. Hovenkamp, Antitrust's Protected Classes, 88 Mich. L. Rev. 1 (1989).

§ 8.5 Judicial Adaption of the Areeda–Turner Test: Price/Cost Relationships and Intent

Courts initially embraced the Areeda–Turner test for predatory pricing with enthusiasm.[1] Eventually, however, the excitement waned and courts began to create various exceptions and qualifications to the test. No court has completely rejected every aspect of the test, however, and the basic Areeda–Turner AVC paradigm continues to influence every circuit that has considered a predatory pricing case since 1975.

8.5a. Price/Cost Relationships

The original promise of the Areeda–Turner average variable cost test lay in its simplicity. AVC seemed much easier to calculate than marginal cost, and the test itself greatly simplified judicial analysis of the structural features of the markets in which predatory pricing occurred. Much of the subsequent disaffection with the test has resulted from two phenomena: 1) the AVC test is more difficult to apply than its proponents suggested; and 2) sometimes the test fails to consider all relevant variables.

The Areeda–Turner test *sounds* simple: a price lower than AVC is illegal, and the court can refer to a "laundry list" describing which costs should be considered fixed and which variable. An accountant using this formulation would find it rather easy to testify about the relationship between a defendant's prices and its costs.

As some courts discovered, however, computing variable costs is not always as easy as first appeared.[2] Second, the presumption that the average variable cost surrogate should be used only when AVC is relatively close to marginal cost was unworkable. Third, the proposed "laundry list" of fixed and variable costs did not account for the wide variety of industries in which predatory pricing might occur—concrete and college textbooks, bakery bread, industrial chemicals, and so on. Fourth, the test seemed unable to take strategic long-term behavior into account, particularly because it disavowed any attempt to measure the defendant's subjective intent. Finally, at high output levels the test was a paradise for defendants, and virtually none lost a case.[3]

The AVC paradigm itself has also provoked some controversy. A very few courts have rejected it altogether. For example, the Eleventh Circuit has held that average *total* cost is the measure that Congress apparently intended when it passed the Sherman Act.[4] But nothing in the legislative history of the antitrust laws distinguishes which costs are relevant, or even suggests that the members of Congress knew the difference between marginal, variable and total costs. Indeed, the famous economics textbook that formalized these concepts in price theory was not published until 1890, the year the Sherman Act was passed, and not a shred of evidence suggests that any member of Congress new about it.[5]

Certainly Congress would not have intended a rule that would prevent a firm such as Chrysler Motor Corp to temporarily cut prices below average total cost in order to minimize losses. In any industry with nontrivial fixed costs, the loss-minimizing price over periods of weak demand may be a price too low to cover fixed as well as variable costs.[6] On this question, the legislative history is simply not help-

§ 8.5

1. See § 8.2.

2. For some of the difficulties, see Weber v. Wynne, 431 F.Supp. 1048, 1059 (D.N.J.1977); William Inglis & Sons Baking Co. v. ITT Continental Baking Co., 461 F.Supp. 410, 418 (N.D.Cal.1978), affirmed in part, reversed in part, 668 F.2d 1014 (9th Cir.1981), cert. denied, 459 U.S. 825, 103 S.Ct. 57 (1982).

3. This, of course, is consistent with Areeda's and Turner's premise that bona fide predatory pricing occurs only rarely. See J. Brodley & G. Hay, Predatory Pricing: Competing Economic Theories and the Evolution of Legal Standards, 66 Cornell L.Rev. 738, 768–89 (1981).

4. McGahee v. Northern Propane Gas Co., 858 F.2d 1487, 1500 (11th Cir.1988), cert. denied, 490 U.S. 1084, 109 S.Ct. 2110 (1989).

5. See A. Marshall, Principles of Economics (1890); and see H. Hovenkamp, The Marginalist Revolution in Legal Thought, 46 Vand. L. Rev. 305 (1993).

6. Building a new plant is profitable if its costs are recovered over its *lifetime*—say, thirty years. But this does not mean that the plant will be profitable every quarter or even every year.

ful. Most importantly—and here Congressional intent is clear—the Sherman Act is concerned with activity that is reasonably likely to create a monopoly, and pricing below average total cost is simply not that kind of activity as a general matter.

A few courts have suggested that strategic entry deterrence or "limit pricing" at prices above average total cost could violate § 2 of the Sherman Act.[7] But they simply have not worked out the implications of this conclusion for their basic theory of the case in front of them. For example, if the defendant was engaged in "limit" pricing at prices above average total cost, why should a competitor who had been in the market but been unable to compete have a damages action, as opposed to prospective entrants who found entry unprofitable?[8] Extending the protection of a rule prohibiting prices above average total cost to *incumbent* rivals is guaranteed to force dominant firms to set high prices lest smaller, less efficient rivals be driven from the market. In any event, the Supreme Court's *Brooke* decision rules out claims of predation based on prices higher than average total cost.[9]

8.5b. Intent

Many courts have been uncomfortable with Areeda's and Turner's refusal to consider the defendant's intent. They have responded by "softening" the rule. The Ninth Circuit, for example, holds that a price below AVC creates a rebuttable presumption of predation.[10] A price above AVC but below average total cost creates a rebuttable presumption of nonpredation.[11] Prior to *Brooke* that court also held that a price above average total cost is not conclusively legal, as it would be under the Areeda–Turner formulation, but created a strong presumption of legality.[12] Other circuits have also expressed their willingness to soften the hard presumptions of the Areeda–Turner test.[13]

The relevance and meaning of the defendant's intent continues to be a fiercely debated issue. Invariably, when courts admit evidence of intent, they find it difficult to distinguish between predatory and competitive acts. A good example is U.S. Philips Corp. v. Windmere Corp., where the court found predatory pricing on evidence that an incumbent firm cut its prices by 40% in response to a new entrant, but raised prices again when the entrant left the market.[14] Coupled with this was some evidence that the defendant had an "intent" to exclude rivals. The problem with the price evidence of this sort is that it is perfectly consistent with competition as well as predation. Any time a firm enters a market, total market output will rise. The amount of the

7. For example, California Computer Products v. IBM Corp., 613 F.2d 727, 743 (9th Cir.1979): "[L]imit pricing by a monopolist might, on a record which presented the issue, be held an impermissible predatory practice. * * * And we do not foreclose the possibility that a monopolist who reduces prices to some point above marginal or average variable costs might still be held to have engaged in a predatory act because of other aspects of its conduct." Likewise in Transamerica Computer Co. v. IBM, 698 F.2d 1377, 1388 (9th Cir.1983), cert. denied, 464 U.S. 955, 104 S.Ct. 370 (1983), the Ninth Circuit held that a price above average total cost created a presumption of legality that could be defeated by clear and convincing evidence of predatory design. The First and Sixth Circuits expressly disagree and hold prices above average total cost to be legal. Barry Wright Corp. v. ITT Grinnell Corp., 724 F.2d 227, 231–34 (1st Cir.1983); Arthur S. Langenderfer, Inc. v. S.E. Johnson Co., 729 F.2d 1050 (6th Cir.1984).

8. See § 8.3b.

9. Brooke Group Ltd. v. Brown & Williamson Tobacco Corp., 509 U.S. 209, 113 S.Ct. 2578 (1993). See § 8.3b.

But see Cost Management Services v. Washington Natural Gas, 99 F.3d 937 (9th Cir.1996), which accepted a claim that a public utility engaged in "predatory pricing" by charging a price that was above cost but less than its filed tariff. The theory was that the rivals were forced either to comply with their own tariffs and lose sales, or else match the price and risk legal sanctions. This confuses violation of the regulatory regime with predatory pricing.

10. William Inglis & Sons Baking Co. v. ITT Continental Baking Co., Inc., 668 F.2d 1014, 1036 (9th Cir.1981), cert. denied, 459 U.S. 825, 103 S.Ct. 57 (1982).

11. Id. at 1035–36.

12. Transamerica Computer Co. v. IBM Corp., 698 F.2d 1377, 1388 (9th Cir.), cert. denied, 464 U.S. 955, 104 S.Ct. 370 (1983). The First and Sixth Circuits hold that a price above average total cost is lawful. *Barry Wright,* note 7; *Arthur S. Langenderfer,* note 7.

13. For example, D.E. Rogers Assoc., Inc. v. Gardner–Denver Co., 718 F.2d 1431, 1437 (6th Cir.1983), cert. denied, 467 U.S. 1242, 104 S.Ct. 3513 (1984); Adjusters Replace–A–Car, Inc. v. Agency Rent–A–Car, Inc., 735 F.2d 884, 890–91 (5th Cir.1984). See 3 Antitrust Law ¶ 728c (rev. ed. 1996).

14. U.S. Philips Corp. v. Windmere Corp., 1992–1 Trade Cas. ¶ 69778, 1991 WL 338258 (S.D.Fla.1991).

increase depends on the ratio of the entrant's added output to that of the market as a whole. In response to the output increase, the price will decline, with the amount depending on the percentage of output increase and the market's elasticity of demand. In a highly competitive market the entry of a single firm (such as an additional farmer into the market for soy beans) may have no measurable effect on post-entry prices. By contrast, in a concentrated market—the kind where predation is plausible—a single firm's entry can have a rather dramatic impact on post-entry prices. For example, if the new entrant added twenty percent to total market output and the elasticity of demand were one, post-entry prices would drop by roughly twenty percent, assuming that incumbents simply kept output constant. The Philips court's rule may actually encourage firms to *reduce* their own output in response to entry in order to keep post-entry prices up—hardly a competitive result. A better rule than the one adopted in *Philips* is that a dominant firm's increase of *output* in response to entry by a competitor is suspicious, and could be predatory if the resulting prices fell below the dominant firm's average variable or avoidable costs.

A few courts have followed the Areeda–Turner paradigm and concluded that intent should not generally be relevant.[15] As the First Circuit put it,

> * * * "[I]ntent to harm" without more offers too vague a standard in a world where executives may think no further than "Let's get more business," and long-term effects on consumers depend in large measure on competitors' responses. * * *

Thus, most courts now find their standard, not in intent, but in the relation of the suspect price to the firm's costs.[16]

The Supreme Court's *Brooke* decision[17] goes very far in the direction of making intent evidence irrelevant—or at least, making it a limiting rather than expanding factor. That is, absence of anticompetitive intent may still disprove predation, but its presence will not establish it unless structural factors are also present. Although *Brooke* was brought under the Robinson–Patman Act,[18] everything the Supreme Court said about intent applies with equal force to Sherman Act predation claims, since the latter statute requires even stronger proof. In *Brooke*, the evidence of the defendant's anticompetitive intent was "more voluminous and detailed than in any other reported case."[19] Nevertheless, the Court dismissed the complaint because its structural analysis demonstrated that predatory pricing was not a profitable strategy.

§ 8.6 Judicial Adaption of Areeda–Turner: Identifying Relevant Costs; Multi-product Firms; Customer–Specific Pricing

Suppose that an established firm selling 100 products is accused of predatory pricing in one of them. How should the relevant costs be calculated? When a firm decides whether the

15. For example, A.A. Poultry Farms v. Rose Acre Farms, 881 F.2d 1396, 1401–1402 (7th Cir.1989), cert. denied, 494 U.S. 1019, 110 S.Ct. 1326 (1990):

> Reference to intent could not help the court determine whether recoupment is possible, and unless recoupment lies in store even the most vicious intent is harmless to the competitive system. * * * Intent does not help to separate competition from attempted monopolization and invites juries to penalize hard competition. It also complicates litigation. * * * Stripping intent away brings the real economic questions to the fore at the same time as it streamlines antitrust litigation. Although reference to intent in principle could help dambiguate bits of economic evidence in rare cases * * *, the cost (in money and error) of searching for these rare cases is too high—in large measure because the evidence offered to prove intent will be even more ambiguous than the economic data it seeks to illuminate.

See also Morgan v. Ponder, 892 F.2d 1355, 1359 (8th Cir.1989) (statements suggesting predatory intent "provide no help in deciding whether a defendant has crossed the elusive line separating aggressive competition from unfair competition."); Barry Wright Corp. v. ITT Grinnell Corp., 724 F.2d 227 (1st Cir.1983) (same).

16. *Barry Wright*, note 7, 724 F.2d at 232; see also Henry v. Chloride, 809 F.2d 1334, 1345 (8th Cir.1987) (if on the basis of structural evidence one concludes that "the defendant could not have captured the market, its conduct cannot be predatory, no matter what its 'intent.' "). Accord, Abcor Corp. v. AM Int'l, 916 F.2d 924, 927 (4th Cir.1990).

17. See note 9.

18. The decision is discussed at some length in § 8.8.

19. *Brooke*, 509 U.S. at 248, 113 S.Ct. at 2601.

addition of a new product is profitable, it compares *incremental* costs and gains, rather than total averages. For example, suppose the addition of a new product is being considered by a ninety-nine item grocery store. The store, which is very small, generally has only one employee on duty at a time, and the single employee can quite easily handle the new item in addition to the previous ninety-nine. In that case, incremental labor costs are zero, even though labor is a variable cost as a general matter. The same thing could be said of utilities, another variable cost item. It probably costs no more to heat and light the store with the one hundred items than with the ninety-nine, so utilities contribute little or nothing to *incremental* variable costs. At the margin, the cost of selling an additional item may be no more than the wholesale price of the item itself. If that is the case, then the wholesale price should be the only relevant variable cost for purposes of analyzing alleged predation in that item.[1]

An alternative rule requiring that costs be averaged operates as a deterrent to firms to do efficient things, such as add products where the cost of adding them is less than the additional revenue they produce. That is to say, the alternative rule prevents firms from achieving available economies of *scope*, which are economies that result from a firm's ability to do two things at once. It should not be the policy of the antitrust laws to prevent firms from adding products when the incremental cost of their doing so is less than the revenue they produce.[2] For example, in *International Travel*[3] a major airlines was accused of predatory pricing in its cut rate, or "supersaver" fares. However, the airline's overall fare structure was profitable and the alternative to supersaver fares would have been empty seats, which produced no revenue at all. If an airline can fill an additional seat on an already scheduled airline for $100, the antitrust laws should not prevent it from doing so, provided that the *incremental* cost of servicing that passenger is less than $100. The court correctly held that price-cost relationships should be determined from the airline's overall fare structure, not simply by looking at its lowest fares.

Closely related to the above problem is the allocation of variable costs when a firm is alleged to engage in predatory pricing in one of its many products, but the products are more or less interchangeable parts of the seller's inventory and most of their cost demands are non-unique. Consider once again the grocer who sells ninety-nine items but is accused by a rival of predatorily pricing only one, milk. Allocation of variable costs in such situations can impose enormous, probably insurmountable measurement problems. For example, one would have to figure out how much of the employees' time was spent stocking and selling milk as opposed to other items, how much of the utility bill went to taking care of the space occupied by the milk in the refrigerated case, and so on. By the same token, on the demand side multiple products are often used to "subsidize" one another. For example, the small grocery store may sell gasoline in order to attract customers inside the store where they are likely to purchase additional grocery items as well. In that case, any analysis of price/cost relationships must look at the impact that gasoline has on the revenue of the store as a whole.[4] If gasoline is sold "at cost" but each

§ 8.6

1. The Supreme Court's opinion in Brooke Group Ltd. v. Brown & Williamson Tobacco Corp., 509 U.S. 209, 113 S.Ct. 2578 (1993), does not discuss this issue, although it was almost certainly relevant to cost determination. B & W was accused of predatory pricing in "generic" cigarettes. But generic cigarettes were probably nothing more than ordinary cigarettes, manufactured in the same production facilities, perhaps with lower quality tobaccos, wrappers, and so on. If there were excess capacity to begin with, then relevant variable costs should include only the *incremental* costs of making the generics. For further discussion of the decision, see § 8.3b.

2. Compare William Inglis & Sons Baking Co. v. Continental Baking Co., 942 F.2d 1332, 1336 & n. 6 (9th Cir.1991), vacated in part 981 F.2d 1023 (1992) (predatory pricing should be limited to costs "uniquely incurred" in making an additional sale).

3. International Travel Arrangers v. NWA (Northwest Airlines), 991 F.2d 1389 (8th Cir.), cert. denied, 510 U.S. 932, 114 S.Ct. 345 (1993).

4. See Lomar Wholesale Grocery, Inc. v. Dieter's Gourmet Foods, Inc., 824 F.2d 582, 595 (8th Cir.1987), cert. denied, 484 U.S. 1010, 108 S.Ct. 707 (1988) (rejecting charge of predatory pricing on four out of 180 grocery items); Morgan v. Ponder, 892 F.2d 1355, 1362 (8th Cir. 1989) ("Courts have been wary of plaintiffs' attempts to

gallon sold generates 10 cents in grocery profits, then the gallon of gasoline makes a positive revenue contribution of 10 cents; it does not matter that the revenue takes the form of milk or bread sales rather than gasoline sales. So, for example, if a seller of telephone directories gives away the first listing in its yellow pages but charges for subsequent listings, it is using the first listing offer to attract customers. In determining the relevant prices and costs, one must consider the total revenue for all listings.[5]

This problem of separating out relevant costs and revenues becomes especially important in industries with substantial fixed costs, where pricing is based on competitive bids that may vary from one sale to the next. Suppose, for example, that the prevailing price of custom made machine parts has been $12.00, but the market has been somewhat soft. An opportunity for a large sale comes along, and the winner takes it with a bid of $9.00. A rival charges that this particular bid, although not the defendants other sales at the $12.00 price, is predatory. Once again, the relevant costs for determining predation are the *incremental* costs that the firm must incur in filling the order. For example, perhaps the firm already has workers who are underutilized, floor space in its shop that is heated and lit but is currently not being used, delivery trucks that are running with half loads, and so on. The incremental cost of producing the additional order should not include a pro rata share of the labor, utilities or gasoline for the trucks—these costs are already being incurred to support output at the current level. A predatory pricing rule that counts them tends to deter firms from using their productive assets efficiently.

The economic source of cost allocation problems such as these is rather easily identified. Variable costs are lumpy. One cannot generally buy a truck to deliver only one sack of peanuts per week, or hire a laborer to work only ten minutes per week. Even constituent parts come in large sizes. For example, if flour comes in fifty pound sacks, which will make 200 loaves of bread, the baker who makes 150 loaves may end up throwing one fourth of the sack away. In that case, it may be profitable for the baker to seek out a buyer for fifty additional loaves of bread, *even* if the buyer does not pay a price equal to the wholesale cost of the flour. For this reason, competition "on the margin" often occurs at prices that seem, at first glance, to be too low. A few courts recognize these propositions. For example, in Marsann Co. v. Brammall,[6] the court noted that the sales challenged by the plaintiff as predatory may have "used almost entirely the surplus capacity" of the defendant. In that case, incremental cost for the challenged sales was the appropriate predatory pricing standard. The court used this illustration:

> Assume a seller manufactures widgets, each of which is identical to every other. The selling price is $1.25. Dividing total costs by the number of widgets manufactured and sold yields a $1 cost per widget. If production declines because of reduced demand and costs remain substantially the same, two things occur: the total cost of each widget increases; and surplus capacity comes into existence. To use this capacity the seller-manufacturer may reduce his selling price to all customers in the hope that demand will increase and his excess capacity will again become productive. Alternatively, the seller-manufacturer may engage in differential pricing, as [the defendant] has done in this case. That is, it may

prove predatory pricing through evidence of a low price charged for a single product out of many, or to a single consumer."); and see Stitt Spark Plug Co. v. Champion Spark Plug Co., 840 F.2d 1253, 1256 (5th Cir.), cert. denied, 488 U.S. 890, 109 S.Ct. 224 (1988), holding that when a firm sold original equipment spark plugs and aftermarket spark plugs at two different prices, ("any meaningful comparison of price and cost must encompass * * * sales to both markets."); Liggett Group v. Brown & Williamson Tobacco Corp., 748 F.Supp. 344 (M.D.N.C. 1990), affirmed on other grounds, 964 F.2d 335 (4th Cir.1992), affirmed on other grounds, 509 U.S. 209, 113 S.Ct. 2578 (1993) (where generic and branded cigarettes were identical, allegation of predatory pricing of branded cigarettes had to consider the revenues that defendant earned on branded and generic cigarettes collectively).

5. Directory Sales Management Corp. v. Ohio Bell Tel. Co., 833 F.2d 606, 613 (6th Cir.1987).

6. 788 F.2d 611 (9th Cir.1986).

maintain the $1.25 price to all existing customers but offer widgets at 50¢ to X, Y, and Z, potentially new customers. Should X, Y, and Z agree to buy widgets at 50¢, at least a portion of the excess capacity will be put back into use. Also it is likely that some costs not related to the then existing surplus capacity will be incurred in servicing those three customers. These costs are a portion of the variable costs of the widgets sold to X, Y, and Z. Another portion will consist of the difference between the cost of "using" the surplus capacity and the cost of permitting that capacity to remain idle. But the costs, whatever their nature, incurred in servicing all customers other than X, Y, and Z are not a portion of these variable costs.[7]

When cost allocation problems are not relevant, then predation in one of a firm's numerous products may be appropriate. To take a clear example, suppose that a firm makes televisions, toasters and disposable diapers in three different plants and that there are very few common costs. In that case predation might be plausible in televisions alone. Important to that finding, however, is the premise that production of the three products does not involve significant common costs. If it does, then the fact finder must determine incremental, rather than averaged, costs.

§ 8.7 Judicial Adaption of Areeda–Turner: Structural Issues

The initial impact of the Areeda–Turner test on judicial decisions was to turn the attention of litigants to issues of price/cost relationships. Courts often paid scant attention to structural issues. This was both ironic and unfortunate, because often analysis of structural issues would take the court to a much easier and more certain decision than analysis of the complexities of the AVC test. For example, in the *Inglis* case the court barely acknowledged the fact that the bakery market contained several competitors, and the defendant was only the second largest. In addition, the industry had a large amount of excess capacity. Computation of the defendant's market share including the excess capacity of competitors indicates that the defendant had approximately 8% of the market.[1] Third, barriers to entry were quite low, and at least one new firm entered the market even as the alleged predation was occurring. The defendant could not reasonably have expected a future period of monopolistic pricing in such a market. The court would have done better to dismiss the complaint without considering the price evidence.

The Supreme Court has noted the importance of structural issues. In dicta in a merger decision it stated:

> In order to succeed in a sustained campaign of predatory pricing, a predator must be able to absorb the market shares of its rivals once prices have been cut. If it cannot do so, its attempt at predation will presumably fail, because there will remain in the market sufficient demand for the competitors' goods at a higher price, and the competitors will not be drawn out of business. In this case, [the defendant's] 20.4% market share after the merger suggests it would lack sufficient market power to engage in predatory pricing * * *. Courts should not find allegations of predatory pricing credible when the alleged predator is incapable of successfully pursuing a predatory scheme.[2]

Likewise, in its 1993 *Brooke* decision the Supreme Court dismissed a predation claim under the Robinson–Patman Act after its struc-

7. Id. at 614 n.2.

§ 8.7

1. William Inglis & Sons Baking Co. v. ITT Continental Baking Co., 461 F.Supp. 410 (N.D.Cal.1978), affirmed in part, reversed in part, 668 F.2d 1014 (9th Cir.1981), cert. denied, 459 U.S. 825, 103 S.Ct. 57 (1982). Even the plaintiff's plant was sold to a competitor who remained in business after the plaintiff went bankrupt. For an analysis of the market in the *Inglis* case, see H. Hovenkamp & A. Silver–Westrick, Predatory Pricing and the Ninth Circuit, 1983 Arizona State L.J. 443, 464–67.

2. Cargill v. Monfort of Colo., 479 U.S. 104, 119, 107 S.Ct. 484, 494 (1986). See also Matsushita Electric Indus. Co. v. Zenith Radio Corp., 475 U.S. 574, 585 n. 8, 106 S.Ct. 1348, 1355 n. 8 (1986) (defining predation as activity undertaken by a firm with "a dominant share of the relevant market").

tural analysis indicated that "recoupment"—or post-predation recovery of the expense of predatory pricing—was unlikely.[3]

In *A.A. Poultry* the Seventh Circuit held that if structural evidence indicated a healthy competitive market, with repeated entry and a likely market share under ten percent, then the complaint should be dismissed without inquiry into the relationship between the defendant's prices and costs.[4] The court concluded:

> It is much easier to determine from the structure of the market that recoupment is improbable than it is to find the cost a particular producer experiences in the short, middle, or long run (whichever proves pertinent). Market structure offers a way to cut the inquiry off at the pass * * *. Only if market structure makes recoupment feasible need a court inquire into the relation between price and cost.[5]

A later Seventh Circuit decision went even further, holding that predatory pricing claims should be regarded as implausible unless the defendant "already has monopoly power" at the time of the alleged predatory campaign.[6]

Likewise, several courts have concluded that predatory pricing is not possible unless entry barriers in the market are substantial.[7] Other courts have appeared to disregard ease of entry,[8] or else to find entry barriers to be high when in fact they appeared to be extremely low.[9]

Finally, the length of any claimed period of predatory pricing is relevant. Plaintiffs are quite naturally inclined to allege long periods of predation, because their damages are usually based on lost profits during the predatory period, up to the maximum permitted by the antitrust statute of limitation, which is four years. But the longer the period of alleged predation, the less plausible the basic claim, simply because predatory pricing is such an extraordinarily expensive strategy. Markets have so many uncertainties that it is generally difficult for firms to plan such things more than a few months in advance. Further, the longer the period of predation, the longer the required period of monopoly sales to make the predation profitable.[10] In the *Matsushita* case, the Supreme Court expressed disbelief that an alleged predatory pricing scheme could have lasted two decades.[11] As a general matter, the

3. Brooke Group Ltd. v. Brown & Williamson Tobacco Corp., 509 U.S. 209, 113 S.Ct. 2578 (1993). See § 8.8.

4. A.A. Poultry Farms v. Rose Acre Farms, 881 F.2d 1396 (7th Cir.1989), cert. denied, 494 U.S. 1019, 110 S.Ct. 1326 (1990). See also Dial A Car v. Transportation, Inc., 82 F.3d 484, 488 (D.C.Cir.1996) (easy entry and rapid expansion in limousine service industry made predation claim implausible); Indiana Grocery Co. v. Super Valu Stores, 684 F.Supp. 561 (S.D.Ind.1988), affirmed, 864 F.2d 1409 (7th Cir.1989) (even if prices were lower than AVC, the competitive nature of the market made predation implausible). Cf. National Parcel Services v. J.B. Hunt Logistics, 150 F.3d 970 (8th Cir.1998) (recoupment in niche market created by parties' availability to undercut the price difference between UPS delivery zones was unlikely because if defendant attempted to charge monopoly prices in that market, UPS could always move in by altering its pricing regulations).

5. Id. at 1401. Accord C.A.T. Indus. Disposal v. Browning–Ferris, 884 F.2d 209 (5th Cir.1989) (claim of predatory pricing implausible on market share less than 10%). But see Fiberglass Insulators v. Dupuy, 1986–2 Trade Cas. ¶ 67316, 1986 WL 13356 (D.S.C.1986), affirmed, 856 F.2d 652 (4th Cir.1988) (predation possible where defendant's market share was 5% at beginning of alleged predation period, but increased to 51%); H.J. v. ITT, 867 F.2d 1531, 1543 (8th Cir.1989) (predation as attempt to monopolize can be established even when defendant did not have dominant market share). The *H.J.* decision, which relied on Ninth Circuit decisions to the effect that an attempt to monopolize can be based on evidence of conduct alone, was very likely overruled by the Supreme Court in Spectrum Sports v. McQuillan, 506 U.S. 447, 459, 113 S.Ct. 884, 892 (1993), on remand, 23 F.3d 1531 (9th Cir.1994). See § 6.5b.

6. American Academic Suppliers v. Beckley–Cardy, 922 F.2d 1317, 1319 (7th Cir.1991) ("Firms found guilty of attempting to monopolize are typically, and in predatory pricing cases must always be, monopolists."). See also Morgan v. Ponder, 892 F.2d 1355, 1358 (8th Cir.1989) (defining predatory pricing as applying to a firm having "a dominant share of a relevant market.").

7. *A.A. Poultry*, note 4 at 1402; *American Academic Suppliers*, note 6, 922 F.2d at 1320; Lomar Wholesale Grocery, Inc. v. Dieter's Gourmet Foods, Inc., 824 F.2d 582, 596 (8th Cir.1987), cert. denied, 484 U.S. 1010, 108 S.Ct. 707 (1988).

8. E.g., *Inglis*, note 1.

9. For example, Kelco Disposal v. Browning–Ferris Indus. of Vt., 845 F.2d 404 (2d Cir.1988), affirmed on nonantitrust grounds, 492 U.S. 257, 109 S.Ct. 2909 (1989) (finding high entry barriers where entry costs were $300,000 and only two firms had entered in 11–year period).

10. See K. Elzinga & D. Mills, Testing for Predation: is Recoupment Feasible?, 34 Antitrust Bull. 869 (1989).

11. Matsushita Electric Indus. Co. v. Zenith Radio Corp., 475 U.S. 574, 591, 106 S.Ct. 1348, 1358 (1986). See

correct number should be much shorter. Considered *ex ante*, it seems quite inconceivable that a firm would embark on a strategy of loss selling for as much as two years, if it anticipates that this duration will be needed to dispatch the victim. In *Brooke* the Supreme Court noted the implausibility of claims of lengthy predation, but it did not indicate that the eighteen month predation period alleged in that case was too long.[12]

A few courts have not only taken structural issues seriously, they have used that information to simplify the litigation process. For example, in *Rebel Oil* the court held that discovery should be bifurcated, with the first round limited to structural issues.[13] When that round was completed, a defendant's motion for summary judgment might be appropriate. This would obviate the need for expensive additional discovery into the relationship between the defendant's costs and prices.

§ 8.8 Predatory Pricing and the Robinson–Patman Act

Predatory pricing can also violate § 2 of the Clayton Act, which was amended in 1936 by the Robinson–Patman Act. The Act forbids sales of the same product at two different prices under certain conditions. Robinson–Patman lawsuits brought by competitors alleging price predation are known as "primary-line" Robinson–Patman cases.[1] These applications are largely governed by the original language created in 1914 when the Clayton Act was passed, rather than the 1936 Robinson–Patman Act amendments.

The framers of the Clayton Act adhered to a peculiar "recoupment" theory of predatory pricing. They realized that extended periods of loss selling made predation costly. They concluded that a predator "must of necessity recoup its losses in the particular communities or sections where [its] commodities are sold below cost or without a fair profit by raising the price of this same class of commodities above their fair market value in other sections or communities * * *."[2]

In the view of the Robinson–Patman Act's framers, most predators were large firms that operated in several geographic markets. Their victims were small firms that operated in only one. Under this recoupment theory a predator could "subsidize" its below-cost sales in one market by raising its price in a different market. Predation would thereby be cost-free.

The most obvious criticism of this theory is that a reasonable profit-maximizing firm would *already* be charging its profit-maximizing price in each market in which it operated. In that case a price increase in any market would produce less, not more revenue.

The Robinson–Patman Act, however, may prevent a large firm from charging its profit-maximizing price in each market individually. The Act makes it illegal to sell products of like grade or quality at different prices. Assume, for example, that A sells in markets #1, #2, and #3. It has monopoly power in #1 and #2, but is in competition in #3. The profit-maximizing monopoly price in #1 and #2 considered separately would be $1.00. The market price in market #3, however, is 90¢.

also North Carolina Elect. Membership Corp. v. CP & L Co., 780 F.Supp. 322 (M.D.N.C.1991), holding that a claim of predatory pricing lasting several decades was implausible. And see F. Easterbrook, The Limits of Antitrust, 63 Tex. L. Rev. 1, 26–27 (1984).

On the implausibility of predatory pricing in *Matsushita*, see R. Blair, J. Fesmire & R. Romano, An Economic Analysis of Matsushita, 36 Antitrust Bull. 355, 363–365 (1991); K. Elzinga, "Collusive Predation: Matsushita v. Zenith," in The Antitrust Revolution 241 (Kwoka & White eds. 1989).

12. *Brooke*, note 3, 509 U.S. at 231, 113 S.Ct. at 2592.

13. Rebel Oil Co. v. ARCO, 133 F.R.D. 41 (D.Nev. 1990); compare Barr Laboratories v. Abbott Laboratories, 1991–2 Trade Cas. ¶ 69,674, 1991 WL 322977 (D.N.J.1991) (approving bifurcated trial to establish relevant geographic market). The appellate court later found that the "dangerous probability of success" requirement could not be met on a market share of about 50%. Barr Laboratories v. Abbott Laboratories, 978 F.2d 98, 112–116 (3d Cir.1992).

§ 8.8

1. 15 U.S.C.A. § 13(a): "It shall be unlawful for any person * * * to discriminate in price between different purchasers of commodities of like grade and quality * * * where the effect of such discrimination may be substantially to lessen competition or tend to create a monopoly * * *." For further discussion of price discrimination and the Robinson–Patman Act, see ch. 14.

2. Senate Report No. 698, 63d Cong., 2d Sess. 3 (1914). This "recoupment" theory of predatory pricing is at least a generation older than the Clayton Act. See H. Stimson, Trusts, 1 Harv.L.Rev. 132, 134 (1887).

The Robinson–Patman Act may require A to make a hard choice. It can sell in all three markets at 90¢, in which case it will make sales in all three markets but lose its monopoly profits in markets #1 and #2. Otherwise it can sell in all three markets at $1.00, retaining the monopoly profits in #1 and #2, but losing most or perhaps all its sales in market #3. The first choice certainly may be more profitable, particularly if market #3 is large. In that case the Robinson–Patman Act has increased competition. A may find it more profitable, however, to keep its monopoly returns in #1 and #2, and give up market #3. In that case, the Robinson–Patman Act will diminish competition.

Assume A decides to drop its price in market #3 to 80¢ and drive its rivals there out of business, so that it can have a monopoly in all three markets. Again it has two choices. First it can drop the price in market #3 to 80¢ and raise the price in markets #1 and #2 to their profit-maximizing level, $1.00. Then A would be violating the Robinson–Patman Act. Alternatively, A could drop its price in all three markets to 80¢. In that case A would not be violating the Robinson–Patman Act, but the predation scheme would be far more costly.

In short, the Robinson–Patman Act can make predatory pricing much more expensive for a seller who operates in many markets but wants to predate only in one. It must lower its price in all markets simultaneously. Further, predatory pricing is difficult to identify: it requires a sophisticated knowledge of cost figures that are generally in the exclusive control of the predator and may not become available until after an action has been filed. Price differences, however, are easily detectable: if A sells its output at 80¢ in market #3 and at $1.00 in markets #1 and #2, competitors will know almost immediately.[3]

Unfortunately, analysis of the effect of the Robinson–Patman Act is not quite this simple. Although the Act may make predatory pricing either more expensive or harder to conceal, it also makes competitive pricing more expensive, for precisely the same reason.

Assume A has had a monopoly in markets #1, #2, and #3 for some time and has charged a monopoly price of $1.00 in each market. Now B enters market #3 and begins price-cutting to a competitive price of 90¢. The Robinson–Patman Act may put A to the difficult choice of dropping its price to 90¢ in *all three markets* in order to compete with B in market #3, or else simply closing its outlets in #3, effectively conceding a monopoly to B. The latter option may be more attractive, particularly if market #3 is relatively small.

A statute preventing differential pricing is just as likely to prohibit competitive pricing as predatory pricing. Which of the two it does more often depends on which occurs more often. At the time the Robinson–Patman Act was passed many people thought that predatory pricing was inexpensive, easy to accomplish and relatively common. Today we are much more inclined to think it is rare. If that is true, then the Robinson–Patman Act probably condemns competition on the merits much more often than it reaches price predation.

Utah Pie Co. v. Continental Baking Co., one of the most criticized antitrust decisions of the Supreme Court, was such a case.[4] The defendants were three, independently-acting sellers of frozen pies, each of whom had less than 20% of the relevant market.[5] The plaintiff's market share was about 50%. The evidence showed a period of intense competition in which prices went down, although the plaintiff continued to show a profit throughout the complaint period.[6] The defendants actively competed for customers, not only with the

3. See H. Hovenkamp, Judicial Reconstruction of the Robinson–Patman Act: Predatory Differential Pricing, 17 U.C. Davis L.Rev. 309 (1983).

4. 386 U.S. 685, 87 S.Ct. 1326 (1967).

5. The relevant market was frozen dessert pies in Salt Lake City, Utah.

6. At the beginning of the complaint period the market share of plaintiff Utah Pie was 66.5%. The market shares of the defendants were: Carnation, 10.3%; Continental, 1.3%; Pet, 16.4%. By the end of the complaint period the plaintiff's share had dropped to 45.3%, but it was still making a profit. Pet's share had risen to 29.4%. 386 U.S. at 692, n. 7, 87 S.Ct. at 1330.

plaintiff, but also with each other.[7] The defendants' violation was to sell pies in the Salt Lake City market at a lower price than they sold them in other cities. The Court never explained what would have happened if the three defendants had driven the plaintiff out of business: they still would have been in competition with each other. Further, the court did not discuss the relationship between the defendants' prices and their costs, except to observe that some prices were "below cost."[8] In *Utah Pie* the Supreme Court almost certainly used the Robinson–Patman Act to condemn hard competition rather than predation. The result was to protect the plaintiff's monopoly position and force consumers to pay a higher price.[9]

One way to avoid the anticompetitive trap of *Utah Pie* is to interpret the Robinson–Patman Act to condemn differential pricing when it is predatory but tolerate or even encourage it when it is competitive. But how does a court tell the difference? By determining if the sales in the low-price market were made below cost and with the reasonable expectation that they would dispatch or discipline competitors in that market so that the predator could charge monopoly profits in the future.

This is precisely the determination that courts make in cases alleging predatory pricing under § 2 of the Sherman Act. The presence or absence of sales at a different price in a different geographic market is generally irrelevant to determining whether a seller is engaging in predatory pricing in a particular market. Although a law against differential pricing makes both predation and competition in a single market more expensive for a firm that sells in other markets as well, the presence of differential pricing does not help determine whether a low price sale in a particular market is predatory or competitive. Rather, we must determine the relationship between the seller's prices and costs in the market in which predation is alleged, just as in a Sherman Act predatory pricing case.

Since the late 1970's, several federal courts have imported the Areeda–Turner test, or their own variation of it, into primary-line Robinson–Patman Act cases. In these circuits a plaintiff must show not merely that the defendant made sales at two different prices in two different areas. The plaintiff must also show that the price in the low-price (allegedly predatory) market was lower than the defendant's average variable cost. The apparent result is to make the Robinson–Patman Act nearly superfluous in predatory pricing cases: a plaintiff must prove a nearly complete Sherman Act attempt case, but must make the additional, irrelevant showing that the defendant was selling the same product at a higher price in a different geographic market. The result has been that the Robinson–Patman Act has not brought success to many predatory pricing plaintiffs.[10]

As the Seventh Circuit noted, "if judges employ the best feasible test for predatory pricing in § 2 cases, it is mischievous to use a different (necessarily inferior) test under the Robinson–Patman Act."[11] However, other courts have regarded this outcome as an anomaly in statutory interpretation: a statute (the Robinson–Patman Act) that was designed to give broader coverage than an earlier statute (the Sherman Act) actually ends up being

7. Id. at 695, 87 S.Ct. at 1332.

8. Id. at 703 n. 14, 87 S.Ct. at 1336 n.14.

9. See W. Bowman, Restraint of Trade by the Supreme Court: the *Utah Pie* Case, 77 Yale L.J. 70 (1967); K. Elzinga & T. Hogarty, *Utah Pie* and the Consequences of Robinson–Patman, 21 J.L. & Econ. 427 (1978).

10. See, A.A. Poultry Farms v. Rose Acre Farms, 881 F.2d 1396, 1399 (7th Cir.1989), cert. denied, 494 U.S. 1019, 110 S.Ct. 1326 (1990) (adopting same test for predatory pricing under Robinson–Patman and Sherman Acts); D.E. Rogers Assoc., Inc. v. Gardner–Denver Co., 718 F.2d 1431, 1439 (6th Cir.1983), cert. denied, 467 U.S. 1242, 104 S.Ct. 3513 (1984); William Inglis & Sons Baking Co. v. ITT Continental Baking Co., 668 F.2d 1014, 1039–42 (9th Cir.1981), cert. denied, 459 U.S 825, 103 S.Ct. 57 (1982); Pacific Engineering & Prod. Co. v. Kerr–McGee Corp., 551 F.2d 790, 798 (10th Cir.), cert. denied, 434 U.S. 879, 98 S.Ct. 234 (1977), rehearing denied, 434 U.S. 977, 98 S.Ct. 543 (1977); International Air Industries, Inc. v. American Excelsior Co., 517 F.2d 714, 720 n. 10 (5th Cir.1975), cert. denied, 424 U.S. 943, 96 S.Ct. 1411 (1976). On use of the Robinson–Patman Act in predatory pricing cases, see 3 Antitrust Law ¶ 745 (rev. ed. 1996), which notes many of that statute's rather quirky jurisdictional requirements. See also 14 Antitrust law Ch. 23 (1999), which treats the Robinson–Patman Act comprehensively.

11. *A.A. Poultry*, note 10 at 1404.

narrower. For that reason, some have tried to give the Robinson–Patman Act a broader scope, mainly by re-opening the door to evidence of subjective intent. For example, a few Circuits held that in Robinson–Patman Act cases the plaintiff may show either that the alleged predation was likely to create a monopoly, or that the predatory price cuts injured a competitor and were accompanied by predatory intent. Even under this latter rubric, however, the plaintiff must show prices lower than average total cost.[12] Of course, intent is no easier to interpret when the legal claim is based on the Robinson–Patman Act than when it based on the Sherman Act.

In its important *Brooke* decision,[13] the Supreme Court responded to these developments in several ways: (1) it essentially (although not expressly) overruled *Utah Pie* ; (2) it held that the fundamental inquiry in primary-line Robinson–Patman cases was the same as in Sherman Act predatory pricing cases—namely, whether the plaintiff is charging below cost prices today in order to earn monopoly profits tomorrow; (3) however, it found one important difference between Sherman Act and Robinson–Patman Act predatory pricing—the former applies only to predatory pricing that facilitates single-firm monopoly, but the latter applies to predatory pricing that might facilitate oligopoly as well; (4) it emphasized the importance of structural issues; (5) it made pricing below cost dispositive, although it declined to identify the relevant measure of cost; and (6) it held that below cost prices (in this case, below AVC) plus the clearest possible manifestations of anticompetitive intent were not sufficient to trigger liability; the plaintiff must also show that post-predation monopoly profits made the predation profitable, or else that the predator could reasonably anticipate such profitability at the time it embarked on the predatory pricing scheme.

Importantly for the law of predatory pricing, the Robinson–Patman test is more aggressive than the Sherman Act test. As a result, most of the limitations the Court placed on predatory pricing claims brought under the Robinson–Patman Act apply *pro tanto* to Sherman Act predatory pricing claims.

The *Brooke* case arose in the highly concentrated cigarette industry, where six firms dominate the market. Philip Morris, the largest, commanded a 40% share, and R.J. Reynolds had about 28%. The defendant, Brown & Williamson (B & W) was the third largest firm, with a market share of about 12%. The plaintiff Liggett & Myers (Liggett), formerly the Brooke Group, was small and struggling with a market share of 2.3% at the beginning of the period. The industry was a "textbook" oligopoly, with prices moving in lockstep through twice yearly price increases.[14] However, overall demand for cigarettes was declining as a result of controversies about health, and the firms were developing substantial excess capacity.

In 1980 Liggett introduced a generic, unadvertised cigarette sold in a simple black and white box which it sold for some 30% less than the general price. The assertion of price competition into this tightly oligopolistic industry was unprecedented, and succeeded immediately. Other oligopolists felt obliged to respond in kind. First, R.J. Reynolds repackaged one of its brands as a generic and cut the price as well. Then the defendant B & W entered with a generic packaged in an identical box to Liggett's box and began to undercut Liggett's price. During an 18 month price war which ensued, B & W allegedly cut its prices substantially lower than average variable cost. The record was filled with memorandum evidence to the effect that B & W's purpose was to discipline Liggett and force it to get its price up to an oligopoly level. Eventually B & W

12. Henry v. Chloride, 809 F.2d 1334, 1338, 1344–1345 (8th Cir.1987); Lomar Wholesale Grocery v. Dieter's Gourmet Foods, 824 F.2d 582, 596 (8th Cir.1987), cert. denied, 484 U.S. 1010, 108 S.Ct. 707 (1988); Double H Plastics, Inc. v. Sonoco Products Co., 732 F.2d 351, 354(3d Cir.), cert. denied, 469 U.S. 900, 105 S.Ct. 275 (1984); D. E. Rogers Associates, Inc. v. Gardner–Denver Co., 718 F.2d 1431, 1439 (6th Cir.1983) (anticompetitive effect may be proven inferentially from anticompetitive intent), cert. denied, 467 U.S. 1242, 104 S.Ct. 3513 (1984).

13. Brooke Group Ltd. v. Brown & Williamson Tobacco Corp., 509 U.S. 209, 113 S.Ct. 2578 (1993).

14. See Id. at 2599 (Stevens, J., dissenting); see F.M. Scherer & D. Ross, Industrial Market Structure and Economic Performance 250 (3d ed. 1990), upon which the Court relied.

succeeded, since Liggett could not sustain the below cost pricing. The price of generic cigarettes rose and stabilized at oligopolistic levels, somewhat below the price of premium cigarettes but at a much smaller discount than previously.

Liggett sued under the Robinson–Patman Act, because B & W's price cuts were effectuated through promotional discounts that were given to different distributors in varying degrees; as a result there was price "discrimination," or two different prices, under that statute. Although it received a substantial damage award in the district court, the judge set the judgment aside and the Fourth Circuit affirmed, holding essentially that B & W's 12% market share made predation implausible.

The Supreme Court affirmed, although on different grounds. It began with the premise that the Robinson–Patman Act must be interpreted in a manner consistent with other antitrust statutes. As a result, the fundamental inquiry in Sherman Act and Robinson–Patman predatory pricing cases was the same: does the evidence indicate that the defendant engaged in predatory pricing with the reasonable expectation that present below-cost prices would be more than offset by future monopoly (or oligopoly) prices?[15] The one important difference was that the Sherman Act, which reaches "monopolizing" conduct, focuses on single firm conduct calculated to achieve monopoly profits. By contrast, the "substantially lessen competition" language of Robinson–Patman permits other kinds of anticompetitive results, such as predation that might facilitate or preserve oligopolistic price coordination.[16]

Under either statute, however, the plaintiff must show that prices were below cost:

> As a general rule, the exclusionary effect of prices above a relevant measure of cost either reflects the lower cost structure of the alleged predator, and so represents competition on the merits, or is beyond the practical ability of a judicial tribunal to control without courting intolerable risks of chilling legitimate price-cutting.[17]

The Court did not specify the appropriate measure of cost, but the parties had assumed that it was average variable cost.[18]

In addition to showing below cost prices, however, the plaintiff must also demonstrate "that the competitor had a reasonable prospect, or, under § 2 of the Sherman Act, a dangerous probability, of recouping its investment in below-cost prices."[19] As the Court noted:

> Recoupment is the ultimate object of an unlawful predatory pricing scheme; it is the means by which a predator profits from predation. Without it, predatory pricing produces lower aggregate prices in the market, and consumer welfare is enhanced. Although unsuccessful predatory pricing may encourage some inefficient substitution toward the product being sold at less than its cost, unsuccessful predation is in general a boon to consumers. * * *[20]

In the process of evaluating the prospects for recoupment, the Court effectively overruled circuit level decisions holding that Robinson–Patman predatory pricing can be established by showing prices below cost plus intent to harm a rival:[21]

> Even an act of pure malice by one business competitor against another does not, without more, state a claim under the federal antitrust laws; those laws do not create a federal law of unfair competition or "purport to afford remedies for all torts committed by or against persons engaged in interstate commerce."[22]
>
> For recoupment to occur, below-cost pricing must be capable, as a threshold matter, of producing the intended effects on the firm's rivals, whether driving them

15. *Brooke,* 509 U.S. at 222–223, 113 S.Ct. at 2587–2588.

16. Ibid.

17. Id. at 223, 113 S.Ct. at 2588.

18. Id. at 223 n. 1, 113 S.Ct. at 2588 n. 1.

19. Id. at 224, 113 S.Ct. at 2588.

20. Ibid.

21. For example, the *Henry*, *Lomar*, *Double H*, and *Rogers* cases cited in note 12.

22. 509 U.S. at 225, 113 S.Ct. at 2589, quoting Hunt v. Crumboch, 325 U.S. 821, 826, 65 S.Ct. 1545, 1548 (1945).

from the market, or, as was alleged to be the goal here, causing them to raise their prices to supracompetitive levels within a disciplined oligopoly.[23]

In order to determine whether such recoupment is possible, a court must evaluate "the extent and duration of the alleged predation, the relative financial strength of the predator and its intended victim, and their respective incentives and will."[24] In all cases, "[t]he inquiry is whether, given the aggregate losses caused by the below-cost pricing, the intended target would likely succumb."[25] Further, the plaintiff must show not only that the intended target of predatory pricing would give in and either exit the market or raise prices; it must also show that "there is a likelihood that the predatory scheme alleged would cause a rise in prices above a competitive level that would be sufficient to compensate for the amounts expended on the predation, including the time value of the money invested in it."[26] This showing "requires an estimate of the cost of the alleged predation and a close analysis of both the scheme alleged by the plaintiff and the structure and conditions of the relevant market."[27] Further,

> If market circumstances or deficiencies in proof would bar a reasonable jury from finding that the scheme alleged would likely result in sustained supracompetitive pricing, the plaintiff's case has failed. In certain situations-for example, where the market is highly diffuse and competitive, or where new entry is easy, or the defendant lacks adequate excess capacity to absorb the market shares of his rivals and cannot quickly create or purchase new capacity-summary disposition of the case is appropriate.[28]

The Court then accepted in principle that predation in order to facilitate oligopoly could violate the Robinson–Patman Act, thus disagreeing with the Fourth Circuit.[29] However, it noted that predatory pricing in general is difficult to prove, and the claim becomes increasingly implausible as the market appears more competitive. Where the beneficiaries of predation are a group of firms rather than a single firm, the predators must "agree on how to allocate present losses and future gains among the firms involved, and each firm must resist powerful incentives to cheat on whatever agreement is reached."[30] In *Matsushita* the Court had rejected claims of predatory pricing by an organized cartel as implausible. Here there was not even an organized cartel, but only an oligopoly.

> Firms that seek to recoup predatory losses through the conscious parallelism of oligopoly must rely on uncertain and ambiguous signals to achieve concerted action. The signals are subject to misinterpretation and are a blunt and imprecise means of ensuring smooth cooperation, especially in the context of changing or unprecedented market circumstances. This anticompetitive minuet is most difficult to compose and to perform, even for a disciplined oligopoly.[31]

Further,

> In addition to the difficulty of achieving effective tacit coordination and the high likelihood that any attempt to discipline will produce an outbreak of competition, the predator's present losses in a case like this fall on it alone, while the later supracompetitive profits must be shared with every other oligopolist in proportion to its market share, including the intended victim. In this case, for example, Brown & Williamson, with its 11–12% share of the cigarette market, would have had to generate around $9 in supracompetitive profits for each $1 invested in predation; the re-

23. Id. at 225, 113 S.Ct. at 2589.

24. Ibid.

25. Ibid.

26. Ibid.

27. Ibid., citing K. Elzinga & D. Mills, Testing for Predation: Is Recoupment Feasible?, 34 Antitrust Bull. 869 (1989).

28. Id. at 226, 113 S.Ct. at 2589.

29. Id. at 228, 113 S.Ct. at 2591.

30. Id. at 227, 113 S.Ct. at 2590, citing Matsushita Electric Indus. Co. v. Zenith Radio Corp., 475 U.S. 574, 588–590, 106 S.Ct. 1348, 1356, 1358 (1986).

31. Id. at 227–228, 113 S.Ct. at 2590.

maining $8 would belong to its competitors, who had taken no risk.[32]

As a result, "on the whole, tacit cooperation among oligopolists must be considered the least likely means of recouping predatory losses."[33] The plaintiff must show that post-predation recoupment would be sufficient to make the predation scheme profitable. It could do this in one of two ways. First, it could show that during the post-predation period the price actually rose to supracompetitive levels. Alternatively, the plaintiff could show that the predator embarked on the predation scheme with a reasonable belief that prices would rise to such levels during the post-predation period.

But in this particular case, difficulties abounded. Although the evidence of oligopoly was strong, there was also considerable evidence of frequent discounting from list prices. Further, the oligopolists did not produce and promote generics in lock-step fashion; rather, some firms were more aggressive than others. In addition, the cigarette market as a whole was unstable because of its numerous outside critics and changes in people's smoking habits, and this fact was not conducive to predictable supracompetitive prices.

Brooke considerably increases the plaintiff's burden in a predatory pricing case, whether under the Sherman Act or the Robinson–Patman Act. If the plaintiff cannot show a substantial likelihood that the defendant would have enjoyed post-predation monopoly profits, then summary judgment is appropriate, notwithstanding prices lower than average variable cost and clear evidence of predatory intent. In this sense, *Brooke* is a "structural" case and carries predatory pricing analysis out of the area of price-cost relationships into the area of post-predation recoupment.

At the same time, the *Brooke* decision, just as the cases challenging tacit collusion directly,[34] underscores the absolute ineffectiveness of the antitrust laws in dealing with oligopoly. The judicial tendency is to "fly speck"—to look for deviations from perfect lock step pricing or other regimentation as indicating that the plaintiff's oligopoly theory cannot be proven. But no oligopoly is imperfect. Indeed, it is doubtful that an oligopoly exists that would satisfy the *Brooke* Court's standard for proving predatory pricing in an oligopolistic market. The defendant need only show that a nontrivial number of secret discounts occur, and that nonprice competition exists. But such evidence shows only that the essence of oligopoly is price discrimination. Only in textbooks do oligopolists succeed in charging everyone precisely the same supracompetitive price. In the real world, oligopoly serves as a device by which firms divide up customers, obtaining high prices from the small, poorly informed or previously committed. Others will negotiate more advantageous treatment. This does not mean that the oligopoly is performing badly. It simply means that oligopolists, just as anyone else, must maximize within their market situation.

§ 8.9 Miscellaneous Exclusionary Pricing Problems

This section briefly examines a few pricing practices that do not clearly fit within the traditional "predatory pricing" definition.

8.9a. Package Pricing

Suppose that Ford sells automobiles in an oligopolistic market. Its costs for a particular model are $15,000 and the market price is $17,000. During a period in which competition is intensifying Ford responds by including a car stereo system at no additional charge, even though the system costs $500. The result seriously injures a manufacturer of aftermarket car stereos, who can no longer profitably sell such stereos to purchasers of Ford automobiles. It claims predatory pricing. Has Ford made a sell at below cost?

If we look only at the price of the stereo system, Ford has clearly sold it at a price (zero) lower than any measure of cost. But if we look at the price of the car-plus-stereo, it is fully profitable. On these facts, Ford should not be convicted of predatory pricing. First,

32. Ibid.

33. Ibid.

34. See § 5.6.

oligopolists typically compete not by cutting price but by adding quality or product variety, and we do not want to undermine this avenue of competition. Second, a contrary rule would invite antitrust plaintiffs to break products down into their constituent parts, claiming that while the package as a whole was sold at a price above cost, this or that component was not. Third, the strategy of including the stereo is fully sustainable in the sense that even after the stereo is thrown in, the cost of the car (now $15,500) is still considerably less than the price. The courts are divided on the issue.[1]

8.9b. Quantity and Market Share Discounts, Bundled and Unbundled

Suppose the defendant offers buyers a discount that increases continuously as the firm's aggregate purchases increase over a one year period. Alternatively, suppose that the discount increases as the buyer's share of purchases from the defendant increases. For example, a buyer might get a 5% discount if it purchases 25% of its needs from the defendant, a 7% discount if it purchases 50% of its needs from the defendant, and so on.

Of course, these discounts could be predatory pricing if the discounted price satisfied the tests for prices below cost that the courts generally employ.[2] But let us suppose that even the price receiving the largest discount is fully profitable in the short run—that is, above the defendant's average total cost. Can the price nevertheless be anticompetitive and unlawful?

It is useful to distinguish two situations. First, suppose that the defendant makes a combination of products and aggregates the discount across all of them, while rivals make only one. For example, in *SmithKline* the defendant made three drugs and gave hospitals and other purchasers a discount that increased with purchases and was aggregated over all three drugs.[3] In that case the rival producing a single drug may be able to match the defendant's effective price only by offering a discount on its single drug that is equal to the discount given on *all three* of the defendant's drugs.[4] In this case the real gravamen of the offense is tying rather than predatory pricing: the defendant is bundling the three drugs together by using a discount rather than an absolute bundling requirement. Significantly, the tying prohibition contained in § 3 of the Clayton Act[5] applies not only to absolute ties, but also to offers of a "discount upon" the purchase price in exchange for a bundle. In sum, such cases should be addressed under the law of tying arrangements, not under the law of predatory pricing.[6]

The single product case is not an antitrust offense at all, unless the post-discount price meets the predatory pricing definition of prices below cost.[7] For example, suppose that Sylva-

§ 8.9

1. See Kentmaster Mfg. Co. v. Jarvis Products Corp., 146 F.3d 691 (9th Cir.1998) (lawful for defendant to give away primary cutting machine and make its money by selling replacement blades at high prices, provided that price of cutting machine plus blades was profitable; dissenter disagreed: defendant was "selling" primary product at a predatory price, and "recouping" by charging a monopoly price for the blades); Multistate Legal Studies v. Harcourt Brace Jovanovich, 63 F.3d 1540 (10th Cir.1995), cert. denied, 516 U.S. 1044, 116 S.Ct. 702 (1996) (defendant sold general bar review course and then added in free multistate course; permitting predatory pricing claim on theory that multistate course was added in at less than incremental cost, whether or not price of package was fully profitable). See 3 Antitrust Law ¶ 749 (rev. ed. 1996).

2. See § 8.5.

3. SmithKline Corp. v. Eli Lilly & Co., 427 F.Supp. 1089 (E.D.Pa.1976), aff'd, 575 F.2d 1056 (3d Cir.), cert. denied, 439 U.S. 838, 99 S.Ct. 123 (1978). See also LePage's Inc. v. 3M, 1997 WL 734005 (E.D.Pa.1997, unreported).

4. See *LePages*, id., describing *SmithKline*, id.:

In *SmithKline*, the defendant Eli Lilly & Co. ("Lilly") linked antibiotics Kellin and Keflex, products which faced no competition, with Kefzol, an antibiotic in another market that competed with Ancef, which was produced by SmithKline Corporation ("SmithKline"). Lilly offered rebates on the bundle of its three products. The Third Circuit reasoned that in order to compete, SmithKline would have had to offer on its one product the same rebate Lilly was offering on all three of its products bundled together. The court found that this use of "bundled rebates" to be anticompetitive and an "act of willful acquisition and maintenance of monopoly power" in violation of § 2 of the Sherman Act. *SmithKline*, 575 F.2d at 1065.

5. 15 U.S.C.A. § 14.

6. Tying law generally refers to these as package discounts. See 10 Antitrust Law ¶ 1758 (1996).

7. But see Concord Boat Corp. v. Brunswick Corp., 21 F.Supp.2d 923 (E.D.Ark.1998), appeal pending (finding a Sherman § 2 violation in defendant's market share dis-

nia offers television sets to dealers at a discount rate that progresses (1) as the absolute number of televisions per year that a dealer purchases increases; or (2) as the dealer's percentage of Sylvania as opposed to other televisions increases. Further, assume that even the price that reflects the largest discount is above all relevant measures of cost. In this case, an equally efficient rival will be able to steal the sales simply by matching the discount structure. Further, the price is fully sustainable in the sense that it is immediately profitable and does not depend on a later period of recoupment. One might liken the arrangement to exclusive dealing, but the exclusionary impact is clearly less, for a rival can steal the customer at any time simply by matching the discounted price.[8]

8.9c. Predatory Buying: Price Protection Provisions as Exclusionary Devices

A few courts have considered a dominant buyer's insistence that it obtain a price at least as low, or lower than, the price given to any rival. For example, Blue Cross as well as other insurers sometimes ask physicians or pharmacists to promise that they will charge BC patients no more than any other patient paid for the same good or service. As the Seventh Circuit noted in finding no antitrust violation, even a monopsonist is entitled to pay as little as it can.[9]

Should antitrust be more concerned when the monopsonist insists on paying *less* than any rival pays? Perhaps. If the seller, such as a hospital, has large fixed and joint costs, it may be in a position to shift these from one group of patients to another. For example, if the hospital's average fixed costs for a hospital stay are $100 per night but a dominant insurer insists on paying $90, the hospital might respond by making some set of more vulnerable patients pay $120. This may be a way of raising the costs of nondominant insurers.[10]

counts on a single product, notwithstanding that rival had equal or lower costs and thus could have stolen a customer simply by matching the discount).

8. Further, if the discounts are aggregated over a one year period, then the defendant must start over again each year, thus making the customer available for a new round of bidding. As a general matter, exclusive dealing contracts of one year or less are lawful. See § 10.9e. On quantity or market share discounts as exclusive dealing devices, see 11 Antitrust Law ¶ 1807 (1999).

9. See Blue Cross & Blue Shield United v. Marshfield Clinic, 65 F.3d 1406, 1415 (7th Cir.1995), cert. denied, 516 U.S. 1184, 116 S.Ct. 1288 (1996) (upholding such a contract). Contra, Blue Cross and Blue Shield of Ohio v. Bingaman, 1996–2 Trade Cas. ¶ 71600, 1996 WL 677094 (N.D.Ohio 1996) (similar situation; refusing to dismiss on the pleadings); United States v. Delta Dental of Rhode Island, 943 F.Supp. 172 (D.R.I.1996) (refusing to dismiss).

10. Cf. E. Granitz & B. Klein, "Monopolization by 'Raising Rivals' Costs': The Standard Oil Case," 39 J.Law & Econ. 1 (1996) (noting that Standard Oil required railroads to give it rebates that brought its transport rates below those of rival oil shippers).

Chapter 9

VERTICAL INTEGRATION AND VERTICAL MERGERS

Table of Sections

§ 9.1 Introduction

A firm is vertically integrated whenever it performs for itself some function that could otherwise be purchased on the market.[1] A lawyer who washes her own office windows and a pizza parlor that makes its own deliveries are both vertically integrated firms. The examples should illustrate that all firms are vertically integrated to some degree. A rule that prohibited firms from providing for themselves anything that could be procured on the market would impose unimaginable costs on society.

A firm can integrate vertically in three different ways. First, and most commonly, it can enter a new market on its own. The pizza parlor that purchases its own delivery car and the lawyer who washes her own windows in order to cut operating costs have integrated vertically by new entry.

Second, a firm can integrate vertically by acquiring another firm that is already operating in the secondary market. A lawyer who wanted to wash her own windows would be unlikely to acquire a window washing firm.[2]

§ 9.1

1. The economic and legal literature on vertical integration is particularly rich. Good discussions, from a variety of perspectives, can be found in F.M. Scherer & D. Ross, Industrial Market Structure and Economic Performance (3d ed. 1990); R. Blair & D. Kaserman, Law and Economics of Vertical Integration and Control (1983); R. Bork, The Antitrust Paradox: A Policy at War With Itself 225–245 (1978; rev. ed. 1993); O. Williamson, Markets and Hierarchies: Analysis and Antitrust Implications (1975); G. Stigler, The Organization of Industry (1983 ed.); much more technical are M. Perry, "Vertical Integration: Determinants and Effects," and M. Katz, "Vertical Contractual Relations," in Handbook of Industrial Organization, chs. 4 & 11 (R. Schmalensee & R. Willig, eds. 1989).

2. However, even the lawyer who purchased a bucket and a sponge would be engaging in a vertical acquisition of productive assets—strictly speaking, a vertical merger.

However, a gasoline refiner might acquire its own distributors or retail stations; a manufacturer might acquire its own retail outlets; or an electric utility might acquire its own coal or oil production company and its reserves.

Third, a firm might enter into a long-term contract with another firm under which the two firms coordinate certain aspects of their behavior. Although such long-term contracts are market exchanges, they can eliminate many of the uncertainties and risks that accompany frequent uses of the market.

Under a variety of theories, all three forms of vertical integration have been condemned under the antitrust laws. Vertical integration by new entry generally raises antitrust issues only when the integrating firm is a monopolist. It is analyzed under § 2 of the Sherman Act.[3] Vertical acquisitions are analyzed as mergers, most often under § 7 of the Clayton Act. Vertical integration by long-term contract is often condemned under § 1 of the Sherman Act if it is found to involve resale price maintenance or some other agreement in restraint of trade.[4] Vertical integration by contract can also be condemned as illegal tying or exclusive dealing under § 3 of the Clayton Act or § 1 of the Sherman Act.[5]

Some markets are more conducive to vertical integration by merger rather than by new entry. Vertical integration by new entry increases the capacity of the level into which the integration occurs. If a city has three movie theaters and a major film producer integrates vertically into the theater market by building a new theater, the city will have four. If the industry already has excess capacity, vertical integration by merger (in this case by acquisition of an existing theater) can be more efficient. As a general matter, the firm that wants to integrate by new entry must determine whether the new store or plant will be profitable at *post*-entry prices. If minimum efficient output by the new enterprise greatly increases total market output, post-entry prices could be much lower than current prices.[6] By contrast, if the firm integrates into the area by acquiring an existing plant or store, capacity in the area will remain the same and prices may not change.

A firm can integrate vertically in two different directions. If a firm integrates into a market from which it would otherwise obtain some needed raw material or service (such as the utility that purchases a coal production company or the lawyer who washes her own windows), the integration is said to be "backward," or "upstream." If a firm integrates in the direction of the end-use consumer (such as the oil refiner that acquires its own retail stations), the integration is said to be "forward," or "downstream."

§ 9.2 The Economics of Vertical Integration

9.2a. The Implications of Coase's Work

Many of our economic insights into vertical integration are a result of the important work of Ronald Coase. In "The Nature of the Firm," published in 1937, Coase laid the foundation for the modern neoclassical rationale for vertical integration.[1] Coase argued that use of markets is expensive, and a firm can avoid these costs by doing certain things for itself. With respect to any decision that the firm must make, it will generally compare the costs of using the market against the cost of internal production. The aggregation of such decisions determine the degree to which a firm is integrated vertically.

3. See § 7.6.

4. See Ch. 11.

5. See Ch. 10.

6. For example, suppose the market elasticity of demand is one, current market output is 1000 units, and a minimum efficient plant in the market needs to produce 400 units. Vertical integration into this market could result in a 40% decline in price—very likely unprofitable if the market were already behaving fairly competitively.

§ 9.2

1. R. Coase, The Nature of the Firm, 4 Economica (n.s.) 386 (1937). For more recent Coasian perspectives on the firm and vertical integration, see the other essays collected in R.H. Coase, The Firm, the Market, and the Law (1988); The Nature of the Firm: Origins, Evolution, and Development (O. Williamson & S. Winter, eds. 1991); and the *Symposium* on "The Nature of the Firm," 18 J.Corp.L. 173 (1993).

Coase's 1960 article on "The Problem of Social Cost," which developed the Coase Theorem, is almost as important for understanding vertical integration as is "The Nature of the Firm."[2] The Coase Theorem states that in the absence of transaction costs two bargainers over a legal entitlement or other property interest will arrive at an agreement that maximizes their joint wealth and will not depend on the legal assignment of the entitlement.

For example, a railroad and an adjacent farmer may have a dispute about sparks emitted by trains which burn the farmer's crops within 50 feet of the track. Suppose that the cost of effective spark arresters to the train is $100 per month, while the cost to the farmer of leaving 50 feet of land along the tracks unplanted is $70. Suppose also that the sparks constitute a nuisance or trespass, and that the farmer has the legal right to enjoin the train. Will the train install the spark arresters? The Coase theorem says no. Rather, the train will pay the farmer some amount between $70 and $100 not to plant in the first 50 feet along the track, and both the farmer and the railroad will be better off. If the underlying legal rule should change and the farmer had no cause of action against the railroad, the result would be the same except that no money would change hands. The farmer would not be willing to pay the railroad more than $70 to install the spark arresters, and the railroad would not accept less than $100.

Both the domain and the robustness of the Coase Theorem are rather controversial.[3] But the Theorem is highly relevant to the analysis of vertical integration, especially integration by contract. Two aspects of the theorem are particularly important. First, the Coase Theorem is concerned with short-run phenomena, just as the law of antitrust. In the long run, the farmer could relocate away from the tracks or the railroad could take competitive bids from farmers for the right to pass through their land free of liability. The context of the Coasian bargain is a situation where the two parties are stuck with each other.[4] Second, although the Coase Theorem is sometimes stated as showing that two parties will bargain their way to the "efficient" result, in the short run "efficient" really means *joint maximizing*. If there are imperfections in other markets, the joint maximizing result may in fact be a monopoly result. For example, the Coase Theorem predicts collusion even though it is inefficient: two firms occupying a single market and able to bargain freely will coordinate their output at the joint maximizing level.[5]

The Coase Theorem predicts that firms, whether they are competitors or vertically related, will generally bargain their way to results that maximize their joint wealth. Since vertical arrangements that preserve or create monopoly are generally more profitable than arrangements that produce the competitive result, an important corollary of the Coase Theorem is that vertical integration will be efficient only if the efficient result also is the joint maximizing result. Determining this is largely a problem in logic. It is virtually always true in situations where both firms operate in competitive markets. It may not be true where both firms are subject to monopoly or oligopoly.

For example, the discussion below notes that firms often integrate vertically in order to avoid monopoly at an adjacent market level. Eliminating such a monopoly benefits a firm, but participating in it and sharing its profits may benefit it even more. As a result, certain strategies may emerge. For example, suppose a monopoly upstream supplier sells to a monopoly downstream producer. Each firm has the resources to integrate into the market owned by the other. If that were to happen, both markets would become more competitive. But in that case the firms will likely find it even more profitable to share the monopoly profits currently available by preserving the monopoly

2. R. Coase, The Problem of Social Cost, 3 J. L. & Econ. 1 (1960).

3. See H. Hovenkamp, Marginal Utility and the Coase Theorem, 75 Cornell L. Rev. 783 (1990); H. Hovenkamp, The Nature of the Firm and the Efficiency of Coasian Markets, 18 J.Corp.L. 173 (1993).

4. See H. Hovenkamp, Rationality in Law & Economics, 60 Geo.Wash.L.Rev. 293 (1992).

5. On the economics of cartels, see § 4.1.

and producing at the joint profit-maximizing amount. They might do this through long-term exclusive dealing or vertical distribution contracts, or perhaps even through a vertical merger. The result could be a species of vertical integration that is both joint maximizing and economically inefficient.

9.2b. Cost Savings, Technological and Transactional

Notwithstanding the anticompetitive possibilities noted in § 9.2a, most vertical integration results from a firm's desire to reduce its costs. The lawyer washes her own windows because she "cannot afford" to have them done by an outside firm. More often than not, the same motivation impels the manufacturer to build or acquire its own retail stores, or the grocery chain to operate its own dairies or farms. Often little formal economic analysis goes into these decisions. A firm simply becomes dissatisfied with the way someone else is providing a service and believes it can do better itself.

Some cost savings from vertical integration are a result of technological economies. The classic example is the steel mill combined with a rolling mill. The steel mill produces steel in the form of ingots. The rolling mill presses very hot steel ingots into various shapes used in fabricating bridges, buildings, or other steel structures. If the steel mill sold the ingots on the open market they would have to be transported and reheated—two processes which are very expensive in proportion to the value of the steel. By contrast, the steel mill that operates its own rolling mill can produce ingots as they are needed and roll them in the same plant while they are still hot. Although steel mills and rolling mills are both large machines producing distinct products, most steel mills own and operate their own rolling mills.

Such economies in technology generally cannot be achieved by vertical merger, because they require new construction of fully integrated plants. However, this does not mean that vertical mergers contain little potential for producing efficiencies. Technological efficiencies are only a small proportion of the economies that can be achieved by vertical integration. Far more substantial are "transactional" efficiencies—economies that a firm achieves by avoiding the costs of using the marketplace.[6] In fact, there is no *technological* reason why the steel mill and the rolling mill could not be separate firms located in the same building and having a contractual relationship with each other. Such a relationship would be impractical for other reasons, however: two firms would be forced to deal with each other exclusively even though they likely would have inconsistent goals (each wants to maximize its own profits, and the two may have different profit-maximizing rates of output). The costs of writing a contract that would satisfy both firms and cover every contingency might be very high.[7]

Use of the market can be expensive. Negotiating costs money. Dealing with other persons involves risk, and the less information one firm has about the other, the greater the risk.[8] The two parties to a bargain almost

6. The classic statement of this theory is Coase, Nature of the Firm, note 1.

7. O. Williamson, Markets and Hierarchies: Analysis and Antitrust Implications 83–84 (1975). In this case the contracting costs would be even higher because the two firms are a "bilateral monopoly"—that is, a monopolist and a monopsonist forced to deal with each other. The technological efficiencies created by the presence of the steel mill and rolling mill in the same building give each of the two a cost advantage over competitors. For example, the steel mill might be able to supply the rolling mill in the same building with hot steel at a cost of $1.00 per unit. However, it would cost $1.50 for the rolling mill to purchase steel from the second closest steel mill and then transport and reheat it. Knowing this, the steel mill has a "captive" purchaser in the in-house rolling mill. It will not be content to charge $1.00 when it knows that it can charge any price up to $1.49. However, the rolling mill will be a monopsony buyer for the same reason. The result will be a great deal of wasteful negotiating. See G. Stigler, The Theory of Price 207–208 (3d ed. 1966); B. Klein, R. Crawford & A. Alchian, Vertical Integration, Appropriable Rents, and the Competitive Contracting Process, 21 J.L. & .Econ. 297 (1978). For an argument that the bilateral monopoly outcome will be efficient because even in a bilateral monopoly there is only one outcome that maximizes joint profits, see R. Blair, D. Kaserman, & R. Romano, A Pedagogical Treatment of Bilateral Monopoly, 55 S. Econ. J. 831 (1989).

8. On the relation between information and vertical integration, one of the classic studies is K. Arrow, Vertical Integration and Communication, 4 Collected Papers of Kenneth J. Arrow 185 ([1975] 1984).

always have different incentives. Suppose a manufacturer of aircraft agrees to buy its aircraft radios from another firm. Once the contract price has been established, the aircraft manufacturer wants the best radio it can get for the price, for that will increase the satisfaction of its aircraft customers at no additional costs to itself. The radio producer, by contrast, wants to produce as inexpensively as possible a radio that satisfies the specifications in the purchase agreement. The firms might try to outline in detail all the specifications of the radio. Many such contracts contain detailed specifications. However, such a contract may be negotiated several years before the radios are delivered. The aircraft itself is a developing and changing product, subject to new technology and unforeseen economic constraints. If the contract were drafted to anticipate every possible change, the contract negotiations would be prohibitively expensive. Sooner or later the radio manufacturer will have some discretion—perhaps in whether to use a more expensive component that clearly meets the specifications in the contract, or a cheaper component that is marginal. The radio manufacturer is likely to use the cheaper component if he predicts that it will meet the standard. If he miscalculates, or if the standard is ambiguous, there may be a dispute and perhaps costly litigation.

These problems multiply as the final cost of a product becomes more uncertain, as is frequently the case in construction projects, or with projects that need future research and development. If the aircraft manufacturer is not purchasing a radio "off the shelf" but is having a new type of radio designed, neither the aircraft producer nor the radio producer knows its final cost. If the aircraft manufacturer insists on a "firm" bid—i.e., if the radio manufacturer is asked to bear the risk of the uncertain final cost—the radio manufacturer will calculate the risk into its bid price. That risk premium may be very large. In sum, the cost of specifying everything in advance is often prohibitively high, because people do not have perfect foresight. But any shortfall makes the contractual arrangement incomplete, and may permit each of the parties to engage in strategic behavior that benefits itself at the expense of the other.[9]

The alternative is for the aircraft manufacturer to bear the risk. This can generally be done in two ways. First, the parties can enter a "cost-plus" contract, under which the radio manufacturer develops the radio and adds a specified mark-up to its costs. In that case, however, the radio manufacturer loses its incentive to reduce costs. In fact, the higher its costs, the higher the percentage mark-up will be.

The second alternative is for the radio manufacturer to submit an estimated bid that can be adjusted in the future for "overruns," or unanticipated cost increases. The United States Government, particularly the Department of Defense often purchases equipment under such contracts. Similar problems occur here, however. First, all the information about costs originates with the seller, and the buyer often cannot be sure that the seller is spending the money efficiently. Second, the transaction costs of accounting for and justifying cost overruns with respect to each component in a complex product can be very high, perhaps more than the cost of the components themselves.

The final and cheapest alternative may be for the aircraft manufacturer to produce its own aircraft radios.[10] To be sure, this is not always feasible. If minimum efficient scale (MES) of a radio plant is 1000 units per year, but the aircraft manufacturer produces only 40 aircraft per year, its production costs per radio might far exceed the uncertainty and

9. The literature on this subject is large and good. In addition to other works of Oliver Williamson cited throughout this chapter, see O. Williamson, Transaction–Cost Economics: the Governance of Contractual Relations, 22 J.L.Econ. 233 (1979); I. MacNeil, Contracts: Adjustment of Long–Term Economic Relations Under Classical, Neoclassical, and Relational Contract Law, 72 Nw. U.L.Rev. 854 (1978); D. Carlton, Vertical Integration in Competitive Markets Under Uncertainty, 27 J.Indus. Econ. 189 (1979).

10. For a real world application, see B. Klein, Vertical Integration as Organizational Ownership: the Fisher Body—General Motors Relationship Revisited 213, in *The Nature of the Firm* (Williamson & Winter eds. 1991), note 1.

transaction costs described above. Whether a particular instance of vertical integration will reduce a firm's costs is an empirical question—sometimes it will, and other times it will not, depending on the structure of the markets and the technology involved in the manufacturing process.[11] Since technology changes through time, incentives for vertical integration change as well.

Asset specificity often creates a motive for vertical integration. As a general proposition, the more specialized productive assets must be, the less satisfactory or competitive an independent market for them will be. The aircraft radio example given above in § 9.2b is apt. As long as the radio can be produced generically for a large number of aircraft, we can expect to see a large and perhaps robustly competitive market for it. But as soon as the radio becomes unique to one or a small number of specialized purchasers, then use of the market becomes more costly. First, the seller must invest in specialized productive facilities that will be used to satisfy only one or a small group of customers. Second, the buyer will probably have to rely on a small group of sellers.[12]

When a firm supplies a certain product or service for itself, the "price" it pays equals the cost of producing the product or service. As a result, *if* a firm can produce the product or service as cheaply as existing independent producers can, then any imperfection in the market for that product or service will make it more expensive to buy than to produce. All markets contain some imperfections. For example, a firm almost always has better information about itself than about other firms. Lack of information about an outside supplier or outlet increases a firm's risks, and therefore its costs. Firms transacting business in the market are inclined to overstate both their capacity and their financial stability. Often the true information is easy to disguise. On the other side, the firm negotiating a contract may often be asked to produce information that it would prefer to keep confidential. Vertical integration enables a firm substantially to solve both these problems of information "impactedness" and confidentiality.

Vertical integration can facilitate other efficiency savings by ensuring that the integrating firm's product will receive adequate promotion, distribution and sales services. For example, a refiner of gasoline might increase sales by assuring retail customers that the quality of its product and of the service given by retailers is uniformly high across the country. The refiner can make such an assurance, however, only if it has substantial control over the gasoline retailers themselves. One way the refiner can obtain such control is by building and operating its own retail stations. Another very common way is by means of elaborate franchise contracts that permit the retailers to retain their identity as separate firms while being substantially controlled by their larger supplier. Much of the law of tying arrangements and exclusive dealing is concerned with such vertical integration by contract.[13]

9.2c. Efficient Vertical Integration and the Monopolist; Eliminating Double Marginalization

Antitrust policy has traditionally been hostile toward vertical integration, particularly when one of the market levels involved is subject to monopoly.[14] But the relationship

11. See P. Joskow, Asset Specificity and the Structure of Vertical Relationships: Empirical Evidence, 4 J.L., Econ. & Org. 95 (1988); B. Klein, Vertical Integration as Organization Ownership, 4 J.L. Econ. & Org. 199 (1988).

12. The theory is summarized in P. Joskow, Asset Specificity and the Structure of Vertical Relationships: Empirical Evidence 117 in *The Nature of the Firm* (Williamson & Winter eds. 1991), note 1; O. Williamson, The Vertical Integration of Production: Market Failure Considerations 24, in O. Williamson, Antitrust Economics: Mergers, Contracting, and Strategic Behavior (1987).

13. See ch. 10.

14. On the law of vertical integration by the monopolist, see § 7.6. On the historical development of both the doctrine and the underlying economics, see H. Hovenkamp, Enterprise and American Law: 1836–1937, ch. 25 (1991). For an example of traditional hostility toward vertical integration, see Corwin D. Edwards, Vertical Integration and the Monopoly Problem, 17 J. Marketing 404 (1953). On the refusal of the Supreme Court to accept all of the implications of more benign attitudes toward vertical integration, see W. H. Page, Legal Realism and the Shaping of Modern Antitrust, 44 Emory L.J. 1 (1995).

between vertical integration and monopoly is complex, and vertical integration is probably used to reduce monopoly far more than to facilitate it.

One frequent motive for vertical integration is a firm's concern about known or presumed monopoly in a vertically related market.[15] Firms often know little about the costs of those with whom they deal. This is particularly true if the other firm produces or sells a variety of products. A high published rate of return may come from a different product than the one being purchased. Conversely, the seller's low rate of return may suggest that the buyer is obtaining a product at a competitive price, but it may also indicate that the selling firm is suffering losses in a different product. Every firm would like other firms in its distribution chain to charge the lowest possible price—but often a firm simply cannot be sure that this is really the case.

When vertical integration eliminates transactions with a monopolist, the result is higher profits for the integrating firm *and* lower prices for consumers, provided that the integrating firm can produce the product or service as efficiently as the monopolist did. A firm that suspects it is paying monopoly prices for a particular product or service will be highly motivated to provide that product or service for itself.

Vertical integration has been perceived as particularly pernicious when the integrating firm is itself a monopolist. However, the above rule holds true even for the monopolist: the monopolist that can eliminate another monopolist from its distribution chain will make more profits and will have a lower profit-maximizing price.

15. See generally O. Williamson, The Vertical Integration of Production: Market Failure Considerations, 61 Am. Econ. Rev. 61 (May 1971).

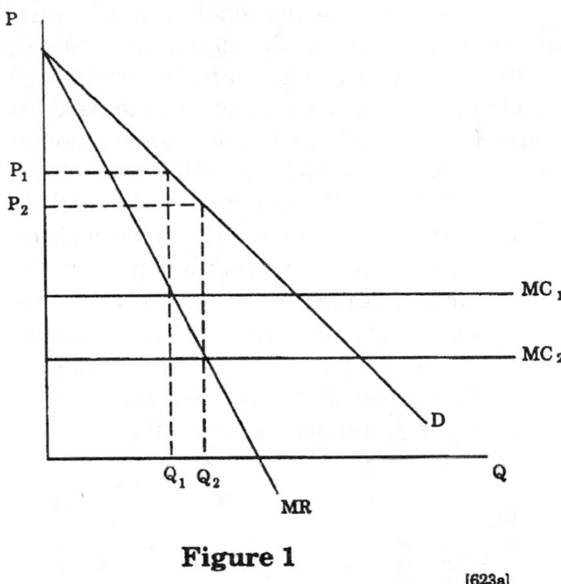

Figure 1

[623a]

Figures 1 (this page) and 2 (next page) illustrate the consequences of upstream and downstream vertical integration by a firm with substantial market power. Figure 1 shows what happens if a monopolist which has been purchasing some input from another monopolist begins to produce the input itself at a competitive price. The MC_1 curve represents the firm's marginal costs when it was paying a monopoly price, while the lower MC_2, curve represents its marginal costs after it provides the input for itself. The monopolist's profit-maximizing output and price, you will recall, are determined by the intersection of its marginal cost and marginal revenue (MR) curves. As the monopolist's marginal costs move downward from MC_1 to MC_2 that intersection moves downward and to the right. As a result of the cost reduction, the monopolist will increase its output from Q_1 to Q_2 and lower its price from P_1 to P_2.

Figure 2 illustrates the consequences of downstream vertical integration by the monopolist. Suppose that a monopoly manufacturer distributes its product through a retailer who is also a monopolist. The manufacturer's profit-maximizing price and output in Figure 2 are P_2 and Q_2, determined by the intersection of the manufacturer's MC and MR curves. Since P_2 is the final retail price, where demand for the product is determined, the manufacturer sells the product to the retailer at price P_3. The vertical distance from P_3 to P_2 is the retailer's costs. If the retailer behaved competitively, it would purchase at the wholesale price of P_3 and resell at price P_2, which would maximize the manufacturer's profits.

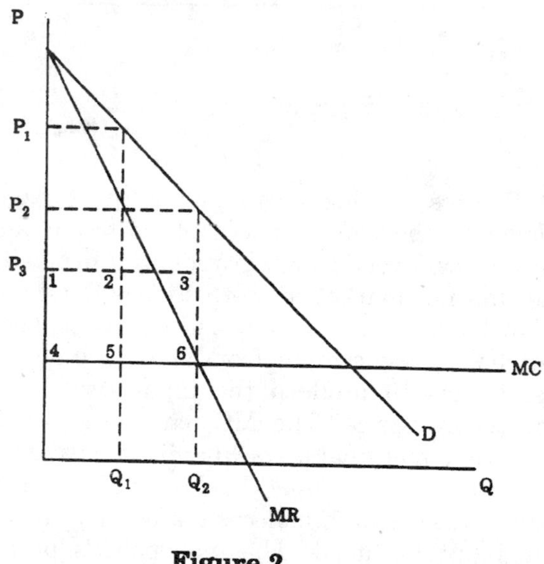

Figure 2

[624a]

However, if the retailer is also a monopolist it will determine its own profit-maximizing price by equating its own marginal cost and marginal revenue. This chain of monopolies is sometimes called "double marginalization." In this case the retailer's marginal costs are P_2 (the sum of the wholesale price plus its operating costs). Since the retail price determines demand, the retailer faces the same marginal revenue curve as the manufacturer. The retailer will maximize its profits by raising price to P_1 and reducing output to Q_1, making both the manufacturer and the retail customers worse off. The manufacturer's economic profits are reduced from rectangle 1–3–6–4 to rectangle 1–2–5–4. Customers are forced to pay P_1 for the product, rather than P_2.[16]

By building (or buying) its own retail outlets, however, the manufacturer will be able to maximize its own profits, which it will do when output is Q_2 and price is P_2. Both the manufacturer and consumers will be better off.

The economic effects of eliminating a monopolist from a distribution chain are generally the same, whether the vertical integration occurs by new entry or by merger. A law firm might eliminate the monopoly payout to a monopoly window washer simply by washing its own windows. Likewise, a shoe manufacturer might respond to price increases by a monopoly shoe store by opening its own shoe store in that area. An electric utility that buys its coal and suspects that the coal producers are engaged in price fixing, however, might respond by acquiring an existing coal producer.[17]

Sometimes vertical integration by contract is used by firms to control monopoly pricing by other firms in the distribution chain. For example, in Albrecht v. Herald Co.[18] The Supreme Court used the *per se* rule to condemn a maximum resale price maintenance agreement between a newspaper and its route carriers. Today most commentators believe that the case was wrongly decided and *Albrecht* has been overruled.[19] The route carriers were monopolists who could maximize their profits by reducing output and charging a higher price for delivering newspapers. The result, of course, was lower circulation and lower profits for the newspaper, as well as higher prices to the consumer. A firm forbidden by the antitrust laws to protect itself from monopoly pricing will likely choose the second-best alter-

16. Note, however, that the Coase Theorem predicts that this will not happen. The two firm's joint profits will be maximized at the single firm monopoly level, which is determined by taking the aggregate marginal cost curve and equating it with marginal revenue. The would occur at price P_2 and output Q_2.

17. On avoidance of double marginalization generally, see 3A Antitrust Law ¶ 758 (rev. ed. 1996).

18. 390 U.S. 145, 88 S.Ct. 869 (1968).

19. See § 11.5c, discussing State Oil Co. v. Khan, 522 U.S. 3, 118 S.Ct. 275 (1997), on remand, 143 F.3d 362 (7th Cir.1998).

native—perhaps outright termination of the independent carriers and their replacement by employees of the newspaper.[20]

§ 9.3 Plausible Anticompetitive Consequences of Vertical Integration

In most of the instances described above vertical integration enlarged a firm's profits but also benefitted consumers. Sometimes the value of vertical integration to consumers is not so clear, however, and some instances of vertical integration may be anticompetitive. If this were not the case there would be no need for antitrust laws against vertical practices.[1]

In a simple case involving an upstream monopolist and a downstream firm who uses the monopolist's product as its only input, a firm cannot increase its market power by vertical integration unless the integration also reduces costs.[2] This conclusion is probably true of most more complicated situations as well. The monopolist of a single distribution level can generally obtain all the available monopoly profits in that distribution chain. For example, a monopoly manufacturer of bicycles generally could not increase its monopoly profits by becoming a distributor or retailer of bicycles as well. The profit-maximizing price of bicycles is determined on the demand side by the amount that final consumers of bicycles are willing to pay. If the total cost of manufacturing a bicycle and distributing it to a cyclist is $70.00, but the profit-maximizing price is $90.00, the $20.00 in monopoly profits could be claimed by any single monopolist in the distribution chain, provided that the other links in the chain are competitive. If the monopoly manufacturer is already obtaining $20.00 in monopoly profits from sales to distributors, it will not be able to make more monopoly profits by acquiring its own distributor.

9.3a. Strategic Control of Inputs

A large, complex literature argues that certain instances of vertical integration in monopolized or imperfectly competitive markets permit firms to raise prices by manipulating inputs. This literature generally criticizes the strictly neoclassical ("Chicago School") analysis of vertical integration by the monopolist for considering only the two extremes of monopoly and perfect competition, and for disregarding the fact that inputs can often be substituted for one another.[3] In cases of oligopoly with differentiated products and inputs that can be used in variable proportions, the story is more complex.

For example, suppose an upstream bauxite monopolist charges a high price for bauxite that is converted into alumina, and then combined with tin to make various aluminum alloys. Importantly, the proportions of bauxite and tin can vary considerably, and many buyers do not care what the precise compound is. We assume tin is sold competitively. Downstream smelters will respond to the bauxite monopoly by using relatively less bauxite and relatively more tin to the degree that customers find the substitution acceptable. This substitution means that the demand for bauxite, and thus its price, tends to go down. By integrating vertically into smelting, the bauxite monopolist can restore the proportions to their

20. See Paschall v. Kansas City Star Co., 727 F.2d 692 (8th Cir.1984), cert. denied, 469 U.S. 872, 105 S.Ct. 222 (1984); Hovenkamp, Vertical Integration by the Newspaper Monopolist, 69 Iowa L.Rev. 451 (1984).

§ 9.3

1. For arguments that the preferred rule for most vertical practices should be legality, see R. Posner, The Next Step in the Antitrust Treatment of Restricted Distribution: Per Se Legality, 48 U.Chi.L.Rev. 6 (1981); F. Easterbrook, Vertical Arrangements and the Rule of Reason, 53 Antitrust L.J. 135 (1984). For an argument that all vertical mergers should be legal, see R. Bork, The Antitrust Paradox: A Policy At War With Itself 226 (1978; rev. ed. 1993).

2. Since market power is a function of the relationship between profit-maximizing price and marginal cost, a firm that reduces its marginal cost while competitors' costs remain the same will acquire additional market power. However, its output will be higher. Prices will be no higher and will usually be lower.

3. See F. M. Scherer & D. Ross, Industrial Market Structure and Economic Performance 522 (3d ed. 1990); R. Blair & D. Kaserman, Law and Economics of Vertical Integration and Control 48–50 (1983). See also W. Grimes, Spiff, Polish, and Consumer Demand Quality: Vertical Price Restraints Revisited, 80 Cal. L. Rev. 815 (1992).

previous level, and thus raise the demand for bauxite once again.

The economic effect of vertical integration in this case is twofold: (1) the mixture of inputs may be restored to the optimal, or competitive, level, thus increasing productive efficiency; but (2) the relative size of the monopolized market is enlarged, thus reducing allocative efficiency.[4]

The implications of these observations for antitrust policy are unclear. In the abstract, they may suggest increased concern about vertical integration in oligopolistic markets, but there is no easy way to generalize in a judicially administrable manner about the conditions that will make such vertical integration inefficient. Market power in at least one input is a prerequisite, but it is certainly not a sufficient condition for an economically harmful outcome. Scherer and Ross draw the following, rather pessimistic conclusion:

> Such explanations of the motives for vertical integration * * * are less elegant theoretically and messier empirically than the original Chicago propositions. Emphasizing oligopoly rather than pure monopoly and dynamics rather than statics, they are less easily hammered into a mathematically tractable mold. Because both benign and rapacious motives can seldom be ruled out conclusively and because the outcomes of strategic moves in oligopoly often diverge from what was originally intended, a good deal of skepticism is warranted in evaluating claims that monopoly power is being enhanced through vertical integration. Yet dogmatic insistence that it cannot happen is equally unwarranted.[5]

For the time being, it seems, the optimal antitrust response is to condemn vertical integration only where the firm or firms involved have substantial market power, where the integration results in significant foreclosure of a vertically related market, and only where the case for enhanced efficiencies is very weak. Substantial foreclosure is required to make the input substitution rationale plausible in the particular case. Lack of production efficiencies resulting from the vertical integration then suggests that input substitution is the probable function of the vertical integration, and that allocative efficiency losses predominate. Even this rule may exaggerate the ability of courts or other tribunals to measure efficiency gains and losses in a particular case.

9.3b. Price Discrimination

A firm with market power can sometimes increase its profits by practicing price discrimination, which vertical integration can facilitate. The economic consequences of price discrimination of this sort vary from situation to situation, and are often difficult to measure.[6]

Suppose that a monopoly manufacturer of Polish sausages discovers that it has two different groups of customers with different demands for sausages. One group purchases the sausages in grocery stores for home consumption. The profit-maximizing price for that group of customers is 25¢ per sausage. The other group of customers buys the sausages from concessionaires at public events such as baseball games. The profit-maximizing price for them is $1.00 per sausage.

If the firm must charge the same price to all buyers, its profit-maximizing price will depend on the circumstances. At one extreme it might charge 25¢ to all customers and make sales in both concessions and grocery stores. However, it might also charge $1.00 per sausage, in which case it will make higher profits from concession sales but lose most grocery store sales. Alternatively, it might find a profit-maximizing price somewhere between 25¢ and $1.00. Where that price lies depends on the marginal cost of the sausages and the relative size of the two groups of customers.

4. For technical, quite generalized treatments, see M. Salinger, Vertical Mergers and Market Foreclosure, 103 Q.J.Econ. 345 (May, 1988); M. Waterson, Vertical Integration, Variable Proportions and Oligopoly, 92 Econ. J. 129 (Mar. 1982).

5. F. M. Scherer & D. Ross, note 3 at 527.

6. On price discrimination generally, see §§ 14.1–14.2. See also W. Viscusi, J. Vernon, & J. Harrington, Economics of Regulation and Antitrust 295–296 (2d ed. 1995); J. Tirole, The Theory of Industrial Organization 142–149 (1992).

The firm might make substantially more money by price discriminating—by selling sausages for 25¢ each in grocery stores and for $1.00 each through concessionaires. Any attempt to price discriminate raises two problems, however. First is the Robinson–Patman Act, which might prevent the firm from selling the same product to two classes of buyers at two different prices.[7]

The second problem is arbitrage. If grocers were sold sausages for 25¢ each (less their mark-up), but concessionaires were charged $1.00 each (less their mark-up), the concessionaires would have a simple solution. They would go to grocery stores and fill their shopping carts with 25¢ Polish sausages. The sausage maker would end up making all his sales to grocery stores at the lower price.

The solution for the Polish sausage maker is to enter the concessions business itself, either by new entry or else by acquiring an existing concessionaire. Then the manufacturer will be able to retail its sausages directly to baseball fans at $1.00 each, while continuing to make 25¢ sales to grocery stores.

Vertical integration is a common way by which firms price discriminate.[8] Nevertheless, the proposition that vertical integration to achieve price discrimination should be condemned under the antitrust laws is questionable. On the one hand, price discrimination often results in higher output than a monopolist's nondiscriminatory pricing. For example, if the Polish sausage maker were forced to sell all sausages at the same price, it might decide to charge $1.00 and make only the concession sales. In that case many grocers and their customers would be impoverished. On the other hand, any imperfect price discrimination scheme produces a certain amount of inefficiency, both from less-than-competitive output and from the costs of operating the price discrimination scheme itself.

9.3c. *Foreclosure and Entry Barriers*

Other alleged injuries from vertical integration come not from vertical integration *per se*, but from the self-dealing that results from vertical integration. If a manufacturer of shoes acquires a chain of shoe stores it may sell its manufactured shoes only through its own stores, and the stores may stop buying shoes from other manufacturers. Before complete exclusivity would occur on both sides, however, the manufacturer's output and the shoe stores' demand must be roughly the same. If the manufacturer is large, it likely will continue to make some sales to other shoe stores as well. Ordinarily, however, if vertical integration produces lower costs, we would expect the integrated firm to take advantage of these economies by self-dealing up to its fullest available capacity.

By contrast, if vertical integration yields no economies, self-dealing ordinarily yields no advantages. In the *du Pont* (GM) case, for example, the record revealed that General Motors bought fabrics and finishes from the lowest bidder, and that the lowest bidder was not always du Pont, even though du Pont had a large ownership interest in General Motors and influenced its decisions.[9] The reason for this is clear. A profit-maximizing firm will purchase from its lowest-cost source of supply. If vertical integration yields measurable transaction savings, the lowest cost source of supply is likely to be the parent or controlled firm. If vertical integration yields no such savings,

7. See § 14.6.

8. George Stigler notes, for example, that Alcoa integrated into the aluminum cable business so that it could compete with copper cable, which drove the price of aluminum cable to less than the price of aluminum ingot sold in other markets. G. Stigler, The Organization of Industry 138 (1983 ed.). Price discrimination may also explain why Brown Shoe Company, which manufactured medium priced shoes, acquired the stores of Kinney, which specialized in lower priced shoes. If the lower priced shoes sold for more than Brown's costs, Brown would be able to label them Kinney's and sell them at a lower price. See Brown Shoe Co. v. United States, 370 U.S. 294, 326, 82 S.Ct. 1502, 1524 (1962).

9. See United States v. E.I. du Pont de Nemours & Co., 353 U.S. 586, 629–633, 77 S.Ct. 872, 896–98 (1957) (J. Burton, dissenting). Because of the absence of consistent self-dealing, at least one economist sees the *du Pont* (GM) cases as having no economic consequences whatsoever, except for breaking up "a corporate arrangement that makes many of us uneasy." See D. Dewey, The New Learning: One Man's View, in H. Goldschmid, H. Mann, & J. Weston, Industrial Concentration: The New Learning 12–13 (1974).

however, it may not be. In that case, the firm would lose money by dealing with its own subsidiary when it could buy more cheaply elsewhere.

In condemning specific instances of vertical integration, particularly by merger, courts have generally relied on two arguments. Both contain serious economic weaknesses and apply in a much narrower range of circumstances than courts have in fact applied them. One of these arguments is that vertical integration "forecloses" competitors from access to markets; the other is that vertical integration increases barriers to entry. The merits of these arguments are discussed in § 9.4 on the law of vertical mergers.

9.3d. Vertical Integration by Price Regulated Firms

Price-regulated firms have been known to integrate vertically in order to cheat on a regulatory statute. For example, a price-regulated electric utility might acquire its own coal producer and sell coal to itself at an inflated price. If it is clever it may convince the regulatory agency that the higher costs merit an increase in the regulated price. Whenever a price regulated natural monopoly integrates vertically with an input or output that is competitive, the regulated firm may have an opportunity to hide profits in the competitive product. The solution is to condemn the acquisition, or else to make sure that the regulatory agency scrutinizes carefully all markets in which the price regulated firm operates.[10] A recent example of vertical integration by contract in order to achieve a similar result is the *NYNEX* case.[11] The defendant telephone company contracted with an equipment removal firm to whom it paid a nominally high price for removal services, but then received a secret rebate at the end of the year. Since only the high price was reported, consumers were overcharged for telephone service. While this was regulatory fraud, the Supreme Court concluded that it was not an antitrust violation.[12]

A price-regulated utility might also integrate vertically into a competitive market and "cross-subsidize" the competitive subsidiary with revenues obtained in the regulated area. The danger of cross-subsidization was one of the principal justifications for the divestiture of American Telephone & Telegraph's local telephone exchanges from its long distance lines. Because of changes in technology long distance lines have become competitive, while local telephone services continue to be regulated natural monopolies. If AT & T operated both, it could drain funds off from the price regulated local exchanges and use them to engage in subsidized, below-cost pricing in the long distance lines. The effect would be to deter independent competitors in the otherwise competitive long distance market.[13]

One of the problems with cross-subsidization is that many of the costs of operating in vertically related markets are "joint costs," which means that there is no single correct way of allocating them as between the two markets. For example, when someone makes a long distance telephone call, it is virtually impossible to allocate the fixed costs that should be attributed to the local telephone exchange and those that should be attributed to the long distance transmission equipment. If too much is allocated to the natural monopoly local exchange, and too little to the otherwise competitive long distance equipment, then the regulated firm will charge a relatively high rate for local service and a relatively low rate for long distance service. Competing long distance providers who offer only the long distance service will not be able to match this subsidized rate.

10. See O. Williamson, Markets and Hierarchies 114 (1975). The use of tying arrangements to avoid regulated pricing is discussed in § 10.6c.

11. NYNEX Corp. v. Discon, Inc., 525 U.S. 128, 119 S.Ct. 493 (1998), on remand, 184 F.3d 111 (2d Cir.1999).

12. See § 5.4d, which discusses the decision further.

13. See United States v. AT & T, 552 F.Supp. 131 (D.D.C.1982), affirmed sub nom. Maryland v. U.S., 460 U.S. 1001, 103 S.Ct. 1240 (1983). A charge of cross-subsidization was made and rejected in MCI Commun. v. AT & T, 708 F.2d 1081, 1123–25 (7th Cir.1983), cert. denied, 464 U.S. 891, 104 S.Ct. 234 (1983). See M. Kellogg, J. Thorne, & P. Huber, Federal Telecommunications Law, esp. chs. 1, 9, & 10 (1992); L. Johnson, Competition and Cross–Subsidization in the Telephone Industry 42–49 (1982).

This problem has been the principal reason that the local Bell Telephone operating companies have been prevented from engaging in competitive enterprises. The antitrust laws, particularly the "essential facility" doctrine, have been used to effect these rules.[14] Today, these rules are written into the 1996 Telecommunications Act,[15] which will permit the local carriers to enter the long distance market, but only *after* the local markets become meaningfully competitive. Once the local markets are sufficiently competitive, the local carriers should lack the incentive to degrade long distance interconnection with others. Customers displeased with their long distance access will have an alternative local carrier to whom they can turn.[16]

9.3e. Vertical Integration and Cartels

Finally, vertical integration can be used by a cartel to discourage cheating by its members. Suppose that the market for televisions contains six firms who are fixing prices. As long as the firms deal with large distributors they will make sales in large quantities at terms which are individually negotiated and not disclosed to others. This combination of large sales and secret, negotiated contracts will invite members of the cartel to cheat by means of secret rebates, reciprocity[17] or other kinds of price concessions to the larger buyers.

If all the cartel members agree to sell exclusively through their own retail stores, however, cheating becomes much more difficult. As a general rule, concessions and special deals to retail customers must be advertised publicly. Furthermore, most retail customers purchase only one television at a time, so there is little incentive to offer a concession that violates the terms of the cartel.[18]

The most common form of vertical integration to facilitate collusion is very likely contractual—mainly, by vertical price and non-price restraints, exclusive dealing and perhaps tying. These cartel strategies and judicial responses are discussed in the following two chapters.

§ 9.4 Vertical Mergers and Antitrust Law

Notwithstanding extraordinary potential for creating efficiency and limited threat of economic harm, vertical mergers have historically not fared well under the antitrust laws. Most of the law of vertical mergers was written at a time when protection of small businesses rather than encouragement of efficiency was the underlying antitrust policy.[1] Efficiency-creating vertical mergers invariably injure smaller, unintegrated rivals. Decisions since the 1960s exhibit a dramatic shift in judicial policy.

Early vertical merger decisions drew from the common law of trade restraints, which placed heavy reliance on the defendant's intent. For example, in the 1911 *American Tobacco Co.* case the Supreme Court found that "the conclusion of wrongful purpose and illegal combination is overwhelmingly established" by the defendants' "gradual absorption of control over all the elements essential to the successful manufacture of tobacco products, and placing such control in the hands of seemingly independent corporations serving as perpetual barriers to the entry of others into the

14. See, for example, *MCI* case, note 13, 708 F.2d at 1133 (finding that interconnections were an essential facility that could reasonably have been provided); Southern Pacific Comm. Co. v. AT & T, 740 F.2d 980, 1009 (D.C.Cir. 1984), cert. denied, 470 U.S. 1005, 105 S.Ct. 1359 (1985) (same issue; opposite result); United States v. Western Electric Co., Inc., 673 F.Supp. 525 (D.D.C.1987). On the essential facility doctrine, see § 7.7.

15. Telecommunications Act of 1996, PL 104–104, 110 Stat. 56 (1996), codified at scattered sections of 47 U.S.C.A.

16. See 3A Antitrust Law ¶¶ 785–787 (rev. ed.); and see BellSouth v. FCC, 162 F.3d 678 (D.C.Cir.1998) (upholding interconnection denial); SBC Communic. v. FCC, 154 F.3d 226 (5th Cir.1998), cert. denied, ___ U.S. ___, 119 S.Ct. 889 (1999) (similar).

17. On the use of reciprocity to cheat on cartels or oligopolies, see § 10.8.

18. See §§ 4.1–4.2.

§ 9.4

1. For example, Brown Shoe Co. v. United States, 370 U.S. 294, 82 S.Ct. 1502 (1962), which condemned a vertical merger because it permitted the post-merger defendant to undersell its unintegrated rivals.

tobacco trade."[2]

This emphasis on evil intent prevailed for forty years. In United States v. Yellow Cab Co., the Supreme Court held that a manufacturer of taxicabs (Checker) violated § 1 of the Sherman Act[3] by acquiring cab operating companies in several large American cities, if it intended by the acquisition to suppress competition in the taxi operating market.[4] The Court found that as a result of the acquisition the operating companies might be forced to purchase their taxicabs exclusively from Checker, and other manufacturers of cabs would be excluded from competing for their business. The alleged result was that the cab companies "must pay more for cabs than they would otherwise pay, their other expenditures are increased unnecessarily, and the public is charged high rates for the transportation services rendered."

The Court's analysis is perplexing. No vice president has yet figured out how a vertically integrated firm can become rich by selling to itself at an inflated price. More likely, the cab companies (which already had monopolies in the individual cities) were buying taxicabs in a competitive market but charging monopoly prices to taxicab riders. By acquiring the cab companies, Checker was able to transfer these monopoly returns to itself. Alternatively, if the taxicab fares were price-regulated, then Checker could charge supracompetitive prices to its own operating companies, and the increased costs could be shown to the regulatory agency as justification for a fare increase.[5]

In any case, the Court's alternative argument against the merger became more prominent in the case law—namely, that Checker's acquisition of the operating companies excluded other cab manufacturers "from that part of the market represented by the cab companies under [its] control * * * "For many years vertical mergers were condemned under this "foreclosure" theory.

Foreclosure occurs when vertical integration by one firm denies another firm access to the market. Both vertical integration by new entry and vertical integration by merger can foreclose competitors. For example, if the only newspaper in a city terminates its contracts with independent carriers and switches to self-delivery, the result will be foreclosure of the independent carriers. They no longer have a newspaper to deliver.[6]

Foreclosure generally occurs only if one of the integrating firms is a monopolist or something close. Suppose that eight firms manufacture typewriters and fifty firms retail them. If a manufacturer acquires one retailer, the manufacturer likely will begin selling its typewriters through this retailer. This will force some realignment of buyers and sellers—firms that formerly dealt with one of the merging firms may have to find each other and enter new contracts. No one will be foreclosed, however.

After 1950 the Supreme Court condemned vertical mergers under the foreclosure theory, even when both merging levels were competitive.[7] In 1950 § 7 of the Clayton Act was amended, in part to clarify that the statute applied to vertical as well as horizontal merg-

2. United States v. American Tobacco Co., 221 U.S. 106, 182–83, 31 S.Ct. 632, 649 (1911). The *American Tobacco* trust included horizontal and conglomerate, as well as vertical acquisitions.

3. At the time § 7 of the Clayton Act, which covers most mergers today, did not apply to vertical acquisitions.

4. 332 U.S. 218, 67 S.Ct. 1560 (1947). The Court later affirmed a lower court finding that there was no such intent. United States v. Yellow Cab Co., 338 U.S. 338, 70 S.Ct. 177 (1949). See also United States v. Paramount Pictures, 334 U.S. 131, 174, 68 S.Ct. 915, 937 (1948), holding that a vertical merger "runs afoul of the Sherman Act if it was a calculated scheme to gain control over an appreciable segment of the market and to restrain or suppress competition, rather than an expansion to meet legitimate business needs * * *."

5. On vertical integration as a rate regulation avoidance device, see § 9.3d supra.

6. See Paschall v. Kansas City Star Co., 727 F.2d 692 (8th Cir.), *en banc*, cert. denied, 469 U.S. 872, 105 S.Ct. 222 (1984).

7. In 1948, however, the Supreme Court refused to condemn a vertical merger under the foreclosure theory when the vertical acquisition left several alternative buyers and sellers in the market, when one of the merging firms accounted for only 3% of the market for rolled steel, and that firm's previous suppliers could easily switch both their production and their business elsewhere. United States v. Columbia Steel Co., 334 U.S. 495, 507–510, 68 S.Ct. 1107, 1114–1115 (1948).

ers.[8] More importantly, the legislative history of amended § 7 reveals that Congress wanted stronger merger standards that would condemn acquisitions in their "incipiency," before they had a chance to work their full evil.

The Supreme Court's first big vertical merger case after § 7 was amended was United States v. E.I. du Pont de Nemours & Co.[9] The action had been filed in 1949 under original § 7, and the amendments did not apply to acquisitions that occurred before 1950. Nevertheless, the Court applied the "policy" of the Amendments. It found a violation in du Pont's 1917–19 acquisitions of a 23% stock interest in General Motors Co. Du Pont was a manufacturer of finishes and fabrics for automobiles. General Motors, a manufacturer of automobiles, purchased such finishes and fabrics for its manufactured cars. The primary issue, as the Court saw it, was

> whether du Pont's commanding position as General Motors' supplier of automotive finishes and fabrics was achieved on competitive merit alone, or because its acquisition of the General Motors' stock, and the consequent close intercompany relationship led to the insulation of most of the General Motors' market from free competition.[10]

As formulated, this question raised the specter of judicial inquiry into whether a firm's own dealings with upstream parents or downstream subsidiaries were on the competitive merits or simply a consequence of the ownership interest. Even more problematically, the inquiry suggested that a firm could somehow profit by making inefficient internal transfers of inputs rather than purchasing or selling them in a competitive market.

The Court held that the market should be evaluated as of the time of the trial, not the time of the acquisition. In the 1950's General Motors manufactured about 50% of the nation's automobiles, and du Pont supplied roughly 67% of GM's requirements for finishes.[11] This suggests foreclosure of the automobile finishes market on the order of 30%, provided that the relevant market was correctly defined as finishes for automobiles.[12] That is, 30% of automobile finishes were no longer sold on the open market, but passed from a supplier to a consumer which it substantially controlled.

The Court went much further in the first vertical merger decision under amended § 7. In Brown Shoe Co. v. United States,[13] it condemned a shoe manufacturer's acquisition of a shoe retailer when the manufacturer's market share was about 5% and the retailer's market share in the same market was about 1%. In justifying condemnation on such small market shares the Court cited a " 'definite trend' among shoe manufacturers to acquire retail outlets," followed by a " 'definite trend' for the parent-manufacturers to supply an ever increasing percentage of the retail outlets' needs, thereby foreclosing other manufacturers from effectively competing for retail accounts." The "necessary corollary" of these trends, concluded the Court, was "the foreclosure of independent manufacturers from markets otherwise open to them." The result was that other shoe manufacturers and retailers were forced to integrate vertically as well.

What did the Court mean by foreclosure "forcing" vertical integration in a market as atomized as the shoe industry? Clearly it could not mean that independent shoe retailers were unable to find independent manufacturers willing to sell them shoes. In 1963 less than 10% of American shoes were distributed

8. Before its 1950 amendments § 7 applied only to mergers that might lessen competition "between" the acquiring and acquired firms. A vertical merger involves firms that were not competitors before the merger. The legislative history of the 1950 Celler–Kefauver Amendments to § 7 is discussed in 4 Antitrust Law ¶¶ 902–903, 1002 (rev. ed. 1998); and in Brown Shoe Co. v. United States, 370 U.S. 294, 315–23, 82 S.Ct. 1502, 1518–23 (1962).

9. 353 U.S. 586, 77 S.Ct. 872 (1957).

10. Id. at 588–589, 77 S.Ct. at 875.

11. By contrast, at the time of the acquisition, General Motors market share was only 11%.

12. The market was probably defined too narrowly. Virtually all the "automobile finishes and fabrics" identified by the court were purchased by a wide variety of manufacturers, including clothing, furniture and luggage manufacturers. See J. Markham, The *DuPont–General Motors* Decision, 43 Va.L.Rev. 881, 887 (1957).

13. 370 U.S. 294, 82 S.Ct. 1502 (1962).

through manufacturer-owned or-operated stores.[14] The real cause of the "foreclosure" was the efficiency of the vertically integrated firms. By vertically integrating, firms were able to reduce their costs. Competition among vertically integrated firms drove prices below the costs of the unintegrated firms. They were forced to integrate not because outlets or sources of supply were unavailable, but because only vertical integration would enable them to compete with integrated firms.

Suppose that an independent shoe manufacturer has total production and wholesaling costs of $20.00 per pair. The independent shoe store, which buys them at wholesale and retails them to consumers, has additional costs of $10.00. If vertical integration reduces the combined costs to $28.00, the result will be a trend in the industry toward vertical integration—initially because of the extra $2.00 in profits; later, when competition among integrated firms drives the price to $28.00, because integration is essential to survival. If the vertical integration achieves no cost savings, however, then there will be no trend and independent firms at each level will continue to earn profits as before.

A related argument against vertical mergers is that they enhance the merging firm's market power by making entry into the industry more costly or more difficult. If incumbents are vertically integrated a prospective entrant may have to enter at two levels instead of one. The Supreme Court relied on this "barrier to entry" argument in Ford Motor Co. v. United States,[15] when it condemned Ford's acquisition of Autolite, a spark plug manufacturer.

The barriers to entry argument against vertical integration generally fares no better than the foreclosure argument. If vertical integration is efficient—if two processes that formerly cost $30 can be performed for $28.00 by a vertically integrated firm—then vertical integration is a "barrier to entry." *All* efficient practices are barriers to entry, because any new entrant must match the efficiency. However, vertical integration in a competitive market which produces no cost savings will not produce a barrier to entry either. If the vertically integrated firm still faces $30.00 in costs, as do its pairs of unintegrated rivals, then entry at each separate level will be as profitable as before.

The barriers to entry argument may have some force, however, when one of the integrating firms is a monopolist. If the world's only aluminum producer acquires an aluminum fabricator and refuses to sell to independent fabricators, the result will be complete foreclosure for existing fabricators and a substantial entry barrier for potential fabricators—neither will be able to obtain aluminum. There will also be a barrier to entry into the aluminum manufacturing industry: once all independent fabricators have disappeared, anyone who wants to enter the aluminum manufacturing industry will have to enter the fabricating industry at the same time.

Suppose that vertical integration by a monopolist can injure firms at the secondary level. For example, the aluminum monopolist's acquisition of a fabricator may destroy the business of rival fabricators. Does it follow that consumers have been injured? It does not, for two reasons. First, all the available efficiencies that can result from vertical integration may accrue to the monopolist as much as the competitor. Vertical integration by the monopolist may reduce its costs, and when its costs decrease its profit-maximizing price will decrease as well.[16] Second, assuming that the aluminum monopolist was charging its profit-maximizing price for raw aluminum, it will not be able to obtain higher monopoly profits by creating a second monopoly in the fabricating market (although it may be able to price discriminate).[17] In fact, if the independent fabricators had any market power at all, the newly-integrated monopolist's profit-maximizing

14. See J. Peterman, The *Brown Shoe* Case, 18 J.L. & Econ. 81, 117 (1975).

15. 405 U.S. 562, 92 S.Ct. 1142 (1972). For the same theory, see the quotation from *American Tobacco* (1911) at note 2 above.

16. See § 9.2c.

17. See § 9.3b.

price for fabricated aluminum will be lower than was the final output price of the independent firms before integration occurred. Although the monopolist's acquisition may injure independent fabricators, it is as likely to result in lower prices as higher ones. The one situation when vertical integration of this sort could be inefficient occurs when the monopolist is able to use vertical integration to vary the proportions of inputs that the fabricator employs. This may result in efficiency losses, depending on the circumstances.[18]

Vertical integration by the monopolist may sometimes preserve its monopoly position for a longer time. This will injure consumers even though it does not increase the monopolist's short-run profit-maximizing price. A monopoly that lasts ten years is more damaging to the economy than a monopoly that lasts two years, although both reduce annual output by the same amount.[19] The mere fact that it is more expensive for a potential rival to enter two markets instead of one, however, will not suffice to delay competitive entry significantly. The market for capital is quite competitive, and investors uniformly look for the highest rates of return. Money will flow toward a $10,000,000 project promising high profits more quickly than it will flow to a $10,000 project whose expected rate of return is low.

Vertical integration by the monopolist can effectively delay competitive entry when the monopolist integrates into a market containing *independent* entry barriers—that is, entry barriers which have nothing to do with the integration itself. Suppose, for example, that the aluminum monopolist fears competitive entry. Aluminum requires bauxite for its production, however, and the world contains only two known bauxite fields—Field A and Field B. The aluminum monopolist already owns Field A. By acquiring Field B and refusing to sell bauxite to any competitor, the aluminum monopolist could delay competitive entry into aluminum production indefinitely. This might not give the aluminum producer any immediate power to reduce output further.[20] It would, however, increase the time over which it could expect to earn monopoly profits.

The barriers to entry in such cases may be the result of legal restrictions. Returning to the *Yellow Cab* case, suppose that Checker was a monopolist in the manufacture of taxicabs but feared competitive entry by other automobile manufacturers. Suppose further that each of America's large cities licensed a legal maximum number of taxicabs and that all cities had reached the maximum. By acquiring the operating companies, Checker can effectively foreclose entry into those cities by competing manufacturers of taxicabs. Independent cab companies, even if they had a monopoly in their respective cities, would buy their cabs from the lowest bidder. By acquiring the cab companies, however, Checker perhaps did exactly what the court suggested—transferred cabs to its operating company subsidiaries at a supracompetitive price, which was reflected in the meter price paid by taxicab passengers.

The Supreme Court has not decided a vertical merger case since *Ford Motor* in 1972. During that time circuit courts have become increasingly critical of the foreclosure and entry barrier theories. For example, in Fruehauf Corp. v. FTC[21] the Second Circuit refused to enforce an FTC ruling condemning a vertical merger under § 7 and ordering divestiture. Fruehauf, the largest manufacturer of truck trailers in the United States, with about 25% of that market, acquired Kelsey–Hayes, which controlled about 15% of the market for heavy duty truck and trailer wheels. The FTC alleged that the acquisition foreclosed about 6% of the market for heavy duty wheels. However, the court was

> unwilling to assume that any vertical foreclosure lessens competition. Absent very high market concentration or some other factor threatening a tangible anticompeti-

18. See § 9.3a. See 4 Antitrust Law ¶ 1004 (rev. ed.).

19. See W. Wentz, Mobility Factors in Antitrust Cases: Assessing Market Power in Light of Conditions Affecting Entry and Fringe Expansion, 80 Mich.L.Rev. 1545 (1982).

20. If the aluminum manufacturer had been charging an entry deterring price before its acquisition of the second bauxite field, however, it might reduce output and raise price after the acquisition.

21. 603 F.2d 345 (2d Cir.1979). Quotation at 352 n. 9.

> tive effect, a vertical merger may simply realign sales patterns, for insofar as the merger forecloses some of the market from the merging firms' competitors, it may simply free up that much of the market * * * for new transactions * * *.

The Court then went on to require some showing of an anticompetitive effect, in addition to the mere fact of foreclosure. The FTC had alleged one anticompetitive effect: that in times of shortage Fruehauf would deny wheels to its competitors in the trailer market. The Court found no evidence that this would happen. It tentatively agreed with the FTC's finding that barriers to entry into the wheel market were high, based on evidence that entry required a minimum investment of $10–$20 million, and that minimum efficient scale for a new plant would be about 9% of the market. However, the Court found no evidence that these barriers would require any new entrant to come into the market at both levels, or would make entry at a single level more difficult.

Fruehauf is difficult to harmonize with the Supreme Court's decision in *Brown Shoe*. Other circuits have adhered more closely to the older standards. For example, in Ash Grove Cement Co. v. FTC[22] the Ninth Circuit enforced an FTC order condemning a cement manufacturer's acquisition of two companies that used the cement to manufacture ready-mix concrete for delivery to construction sites. The acquiring company controlled about 15% of the relevant market in raw cement. The larger acquired company purchased about 10% of the relevant market in cement, while the smaller company purchased about 3%.

The *Ash Grove Cement* case can be distinguished from *Fruehauf*. Most importantly, the foreclosure percentages in the cement case were higher. Under the foreclosure theory as it was accepted in the 1970's, a foreclosure of 5%–6% in the acquiring firm's market was marginal, but foreclosure of 15% was generally considered illegal. Further, in *Ash Grove Cement* the administrative law judge had found that entry into the ready-mix market alone was "virtually impossible" in view of the extent of vertical integration already apparent in the industry.[23] The ALJ's fact-findings suggested, however, that entry was difficult because the vertically integrated companies could undersell their unintegrated rivals.

Prevailing judicial opinion now seems to be that vertical mergers should be condemned only in the most extreme circumstances. For example, in Alberta Gas Chemicals Ltd. v. E.I. Du Pont De Nemours & Co.,[24] the court virtually rejected the "foreclosure" theory on principle, concluding that the self-dealing that results from a vertical acquisition is nearly always efficient. The *Reazin* district court held that vertical mergers are not even a "suspect category" of business practices and approved a hospital chain's acquisition of an HMO.[25]

Since the Supreme Court's decision in *Jefferson Parrish*, courts have tended to approve tying and exclusive dealing arrangements when the upstream firm's market share is less than 30%.[26] A slightly more aggressive stan-

22. 577 F.2d 1368 (9th Cir.1978), cert. denied, 439 U.S. 982, 99 S.Ct. 571 (1978), affirming 85 F.T.C. 1129 (1974). See also, Heatransfer Corp. v. Volkswagenwerk, A.G., 553 F.2d 964 (5th Cir.1977), cert. denied, 434 U.S. 1087, 98 S.Ct. 1282 (1978), where the Court condemned an automobile manufacturer's acquisition of a manufacturer of automobile air conditioners. A finding of very high foreclosure was guaranteed by the court's conclusion that the relevant market was "Volkswagen air conditioners," and not automobile air conditioners. This effectively made the defendant a monopsonist.

23. 85 F.T.C. at 1150. A third distinction, generally absent from the *Ash Grove Cement* opinion, is that there is a long history of price fixing in the cement manufacturing industry, and vertical integration was an important mechanism by which cartel members could police the cartel's output prices. See McBride, Spatial Competition and Vertical Integration: Cement and Concrete Revisited, 73 Amer. Econ.Rev. 1011 (1983); M.J. Peck & J.J. McGowan, Vertical Integration in Cement: A Critical Examination of the FTC Staff Report, 12 Antitrust Bull. 505 (1967).

24. 826 F.2d 1235 (3d Cir.1987), cert. denied, 486 U.S. 1059, 108 S.Ct. 2830 (1988).

25. Reazin v. Blue Cross & Blue Shield, 663 F.Supp. 1360, 1489 (D.Kan.1987), affirmed, 899 F.2d 951 (10th Cir.), cert. denied, 497 U.S. 1005, 110 S.Ct. 3241 (1990); accord United States v. Loew's, 882 F.2d 29, 33–34 (2d Cir.1989) (approving motion picture producer's acquisition of exhibitor); O'Neill v. Coca–Cola Co., 669 F.Supp. 217, 224 (N.D.Ill.1987) (consumers lacked standing to challenge soft drink producer's acquisition of bottler; no injury).

26. Jefferson Parish Hosp. Dist. No. 2 v. Hyde, 466 U.S. 2, 104 S.Ct. 1551 (1984). On the market share requirement for tying arrangements, see § 10.3a; for exclusive dealing, see § 10.9e.

dard seems appropriate for vertical mergers. To be sure, the similarities among these practices are substantial. Both are motivated mainly by efficiency concerns and are presumptively competitive. Both tying arrangements and vertical mergers are condemned under the same Clayton Act standard when they "may * * * substantially lessen competition," and the fundamental concerns are the same. However, there are important factual differences. The vertical merger is more permanent than either tying or exclusive dealing contracts, and this serves to eliminate the considerable competition that can occur when vertical contracts must be renewed. Secondly, when tying or exclusive dealing is used to facilitate collusion, downstream firms upon whom these arrangements are imposed can be expected to resist. When the integration occurs by merger, however, the downstream business becomes part of the colluding firm itself. As a result, condemnation on market shares of 25% or perhaps even 20% might be appropriate, provided that economies of scale are significant, entry barriers into both markets are high, and other market factors indicate that collusion or oligopoly is likely.

More recently, the attention in vertical merger cases has shifted away from simple foreclosure, or denial of access, and toward raising rivals' costs.[27] For example, a vertical merger might tie up so much of a market that a rival is denied sufficient output to attain scale economies. When that happens the rival's price will rise and the integrator can raise its price as well.

To illustrate, suppose that the relevant universe contains ten identical cable systems, six of which are owned by Firm X, while the others are independent. Further, there are two programmers who compete to supply programming to the ten systems. A program costs $10, and thus $10 must be recovered in licensing fees. If a programmer licenses to all ten systems, programming fees must be at least $1 per system; if each programmer licenses only half the systems, the fee must be at least $2 per system. Firm X now acquires (or is acquired by) one of the two programmers and the post-merger firm uses only its own programming in its cable systems. As a result, the rival programmer can no longer license to more than four stations, thus requiring it to charge license fees of at least $2.50. The dominant firm can then raise its own fees to these stations up to $2.50 as well.

This was basically the theory of the consent decree that the FTC obtained in the Time–Warner case in 1996.[28] The allegation was that a major cable television operator's (TW) acquisition of a major provider of cable television programming (Turner) threatened to prevent rivals in the programming market "from achieving sufficient distribution to realize economies of scale." The alleged result of the merger was that the remaining independent cable television systems were too few in number to enable rival programmers to recover the costs of producing programs without raising prices significantly. This would give TW the opportunity to raise its own programming prices, which were passed on to consumers in the form of higher cable rates.[29]

§ 9.5 Vertical Mergers and the Antitrust Division Merger Guidelines

In 1984 the Antitrust Division of the U.S. Department of Justice (Division) issued revised Guidelines describing its standards for approving mergers.[1] Although the Division and

27. On RRC as a monopolistic device, see § 7.10 See also M. H. Riordan & S. Salop, Evaluating Vertical Mergers: A Post–Chicago Approach, 63 Antitrust L.J. 513 (1995).

28. Time–Warner, 5 Trade Reg. Rep. ¶ 24,104 (consent decree, FTC, 1996).

29. See also Silicon Graphics, 5 Trade Reg Rep. ¶ 23,-838 (consent decree, FTC, 1995), which concerned the acquisition of computer workstation graphics software producers by a workstation manufacturer. The theory of the complaint was that the acquisition could deny remaining independent computer workstation manufacturers adequate access to graphics software, thus increasing their costs; and remaining independent software designers adequate access to workstation producers, thus increasing their costs.

Other decisions are discussed in 4 Antitrust Law ¶ 1008 (rev. ed. 1998).

§ 9.5

1. 49 Fed.Reg. 26,823 (1984). The earlier 1968 Guidelines relied heavily on the foreclosure and entry barrier

the FTC issued new Merger Guidelines in 1992, these Guidelines apply only to horizontal mergers.[2] However, the market definition section of the 1992 Merger Guidelines is quite general and theoretically covers all types of mergers. Vertical mergers are thus analyzed by the enforcement agencies under the market delineation and entry barrier criteria stated in the 1992 Guidelines, but under the substantive criteria given in the 1984 Guidelines.

The 1984 Guidelines abandoned the traditional three-part division of mergers into horizontal, vertical and conglomerate, and substituted instead two broad categories: horizontal and non-horizontal. The latter category includes what have traditionally been called vertical and conglomerate mergers. The new division is odd in at least one respect: conglomerate mergers are generally analyzed under the potential competition doctrine, which is concerned with competition *between* the merging firms. As a general rule potential competition mergers are more similar to horizontal mergers than to vertical mergers.[3] Horizontal mergers involve firms for whose output the cross-elasticity of demand is very high, while potential competition mergers involve firms for which the cross-elasticity of supply is high. The line between "actual" competition, the concern of horizontal mergers, and "potential" competition, the concern of conglomerate mergers, is often fuzzy. By contrast, mergers of vertically related firms raise quite distinct issues.

According to the 1984 Guidelines, the Division perceives three possible dangers to competition from vertical mergers: increased barriers to entry, facilitation of collusion, and avoidance of rate regulation. The "foreclosure" theory is generally ignored.

9.5a. Increased Barriers to Entry

The Guidelines state that three conditions are generally necessary (but not sufficient) for vertical mergers to raise anticompetitive entry barrier problems. First, vertical integration in the market must be so extensive that entrants must enter both markets simultaneously. The Division is "unlikely" to challenge a merger on the entry barrier theory if the market contains enough unintegrated firms that a new, unintegrated entrant could find its essential outlets or sources of supply. As a rule for guidance, the Division suggests that there must be sufficient unintegrated capacity at one level to service two minimum efficient scale plants at the other level involved in the merger.

The mere need for two-level entry is not sufficient to brand the merger anticompetitive, however. Second, the need for two-level entry must be shown to be a significant deterrent to new entry. If two-level entry into the market is so easy that existing competitors could not succeed in raising price for any significant period of time, the Division will probably not challenge the merger under the barriers to entry theory. The Division rejects any notion that the increased capital demands of two-level entry, standing alone, are a sufficient barrier. It acknowledges, however, that two-level entry by firms that are inexperienced at one level may increase the risk, and therefore the cost of capital. In this case the Division will treat the increased cost of capital as a barrier to entry.[4]

Third, the Division notes that economies of scale may constitute an entry barrier warranting challenge if the capacity of minimum efficient scale plants differs significantly at the two levels. Suppose that a widget manufacturer has 80% of the widget market. Widgets are an essential ingredient for the manufacture of gidgets. The minimum efficient scale (MES) of a widget plant, however, is 70% of the market, while MES for the gidget makers is not more than 2%–3% of the market. Now the widget

theories for vertical mergers. See 1 Trade Reg. Rep. (CCH) ¶ 4430 (1968).

2. See § 12.1.

3. On potential competition mergers under the 1984 Guidelines, see § 13.5.

4. 49 Fed.Reg. at 26,835–36. See O. Williamson, Vertical Merger Guidelines: Interpreting the 1982 Reforms, 71 Calif.L.Rev. 604, 606 (1983). Professor Williamson's article is a critique of an earlier version of the Division Guidelines published in 1982. The treatment of vertical mergers in the 1982 and 1984 Guidelines is almost identical. On entry barriers generally, see §§ 1.6 and 12.6 of this volume.

manufacturer begins acquiring its own gidget plants and selling only to them. If the number of uncommitted widgets available on the market declines substantially, any new entrant into the gidget market must either build a huge widget plant and look for a market for its excess widgets, or else build an inefficiently small widget plant and operate with higher costs. The Division notes that there would be no problem if a "significant outside market exists at the secondary level"—in this case, the market for widgets.[5]

Finally, the Division notes that barriers to entry have no effect on competitive markets—a market containing 100 perfect competitors will perform competitively in spite of insurmountable barriers against a potential 101st entrant. The Division is unlikely to challenge mergers on a barrier to entry theory unless overall concentration in one market is above 1800 as measured by the Herfindahl–Hirschman Index (HHI).[6]

9.5b. *Vertical Mergers That Facilitate Collusion*

The Division may also challenge vertical mergers that increase the likelihood of collusion.[7] The risk of collusion may be greater when manufacturers or distributors systematically acquire their own retail outlets. If the manufacturers or distributors are engaged in price fixing, they will find it easier to detect cheating by cartel members at the retail level, where prices and terms are generally made public. Vertical mergers are not likely to facilitate collusion, however, unless the manufacturer or distributor market is itself conducive to collusion. As a general rule, the Division will not challenge such mergers unless the HHI in the upstream market exceeds 1800.

The Division also notes that a vertical merger might facilitate collusion if it eliminates a large, particularly disruptive buyer which in the past had effectively forced sellers to compete with each other.[8] Once again, the disruptive buyer theory applies only when the upstream market is itself conducive to collusion. The Division is not likely to challenge a merger on this ground unless the upstream market's HHI exceeds 1800.

9.5c. *Avoidance of Rate Regulation*

Finally, the Division notes that vertical mergers may enable price-regulated utilities to circumvent rate regulation by inflating the costs of internal transactions with the unregulated subsidiary.[9] This could be particularly problematic if there is no independent market for the unregulated product or service, for the regulatory agency will have no basis for comparing prices. On the other hand, vertical integration by price-regulated firms can generate the same efficiencies that are available to competitive firms. Therefore the Division will challenge such mergers only if they produce "substantial opportunities for such abuses."

The impression created by the Antitrust Division's vertical merger Guidelines is that the Division does not put many resources into vertical merger enforcement. The FTC has done somewhat more. The Guidelines have all but abandoned several judicial theories of why vertical mergers should be condemned. Most of the factual predicates for the new theories occur only infrequently. This is consistent

5. This theory was first suggested by Areeda and Turner in 1980, who noted that no reported cases have relied on it. 4 P. Areeda & D. Turner, Antitrust Law ¶ 1008 (1980). The current version is at 4A Antitrust Law ¶ 1011 (rev. ed. 1998).

6. The Herfindahl–Hirschman Index (HHI) is discussed more fully below in § 12.4a. Briefly, the HHI is the sum of the squares of the market shares of all firms operating in the relevant market. A typical market with an HHI of 1800 would have one firm with a market share of 30%, one with 20%, and five firms with market shares of 10% each. ($30^2 + 20^2 + 10^2 + 10^2 + 10^2 + 10^2 + 10^2 = 1800$). A market with four 20% firms and two 10% firms also has an HHI of 1800.

7. See also 4 Antitrust Law ¶ 1005 (rev. ed. 1998).

8. 49 Fed.Reg. at 26,836. This theory was suggested by Areeda & Turner in 1980. 4 P. Areeda & D. Turner, Antitrust Law ¶ 1006 (1980). The authors cite no cases condemning vertical mergers under this theory, although they do note an "obscure passage" that may refer to it in an FTC decision: Union Carbide Corp., 59 F.T.C. 614 (1961). The current discussion is a 4 Antitrust Law ¶ 1006 (rev. ed. 1998).

9. 49 Fed.Reg. at 26,836. See § 9.3d above. Tying arrangements can be used by price-regulated firms for a similar purpose. See § 10.6c.

with the position that vertical mergers seldom injure competition.[10]

10. For criticism of the 1982 version of the Guidelines, see L. Schwartz, The New Merger Guidelines: Guide to Governmental Discretion and Private Counseling or Propaganda for Revision of the Antitrust Laws? 71 Calif.L.Rev. 575, 590–94 (1983); J. Ordover & R. Willig, The 1982 DOJ Merger Guidelines: An Economic Assessment, 71 Calif.L.Rev. 535, 571–73 (1983).

Chapter 10

TIE–INS, RECIPROCITY, EXCLUSIVE DEALING AND THE FRANCHISE CONTRACT

Table of Sections

§ 10.1 Introduction: The Judicial Test for Tie-Ins

A tie-in or tying arrangement is a sale or lease of one product or service on the condition that the buyer take a second product or service as well. Tie-ins may be illegal under § 1 of the Sherman Act or § 3 of the Clayton Act.[1] They have also been challenged under more aggressive standards under § 5 of the FTC Act.[2] Tying arrangements involving patent licenses or patented products may sometimes invoke the patent "misuse" doctrine; these and related patent issues are discussed in § 5.5.

The courts have developed an easily articulated test for so-called *per se* illegal tying arrangements, although the test varies from one circuit court to another. Some courts analyze tie-ins under a five-part test, others under a four-part test, and still others under a three-part test. In operation the tests are similar, and the three-part test combines elements that are separated in the tests of other circuits. For purpose of analysis we use this five-part test:[3] 1) There must be separate tying and tied products; 2) there must be "evidence of actual coercion by the seller that in fact forced the buyer to accept the tied product * * *"; 3) the seller must possess "sufficient economic power in the tying product market to coerce purchaser acceptance of the tied product * * *"; 4) there must be "anticompetitive effects in the tied market * * *"; and, 5) there must be "involvement of a 'not insubstantial' amount of interstate commerce in the tied product market * * *."

The Supreme Court has not approved all elements of this test, but neither has it articulated a complete test of its own.[4] The circuit courts have assembled their tests from various statements contained in different Supreme Court opinions. The circuits are close to unanimous in requiring elements 1, 3 and 5 of the test set forth above. Further, if the "coercion" requirement in element 2 means only that the seller must put pressure on a buyer to take a tied product as well as the tying product, courts agree that the plaintiff must show number 2 as well.

The fourth element, "anticompetitive effects," is the most ambiguous, with some courts permitting broad-based inquiries into the effect of the arrangement on competition. Others use the term as a synonym for coercion and still others as a synonym for antitrust injury. If a tying arrangement is really a *per se* violation of the antitrust laws, as the Supreme Court has often stated, then a separate analy-

§ 10.1

1. 15 U.S.C.A. § 14:

It shall be unlawful ... to lease or make a sale or contract for sale of goods, wares, merchandise, machinery, supplies, or other commodities, whether patented or unpatented ... or fix a price charged therefor, or discount from, or rebate upon, such price, on the condition, agreement, or understanding that the lessee or purchaser thereof shall not use or deal in the goods, wares, merchandise, machinery, supplies, or other commodities of a competitor or competitors of the lessor or seller, where the effect of such lease, sale, or contract for sale or such condition, agreement, or understanding may be to substantially lessen competition or tend to create a monopoly in any line of commerce.

2. See § 10.3e.

3. Yentsch v. Texaco, Inc., 630 F.2d 46, 56–57 (2d Cir.1980). The Fifth Circuit uses a four element test. Bob Maxfield, Inc. v. American Motors Corp., 637 F.2d 1033, 1037 (5th Cir.1981), cert. denied, 454 U.S. 860, 102 S.Ct. 315 (1981).

4. But see Justice O'Connor's concurring opinion in Jefferson Parish Hosp. Dist. No. 2 v. Hyde, 466 U.S. 2, 40, 104 S.Ct. 1551, 1573 (1984), advocating a universal rule of reason for tying arrangements, which would be invoked only if three "threshold" conditions were met—"market power in the tying product, a substantial threat of market power in the tied product, and a coherent economic basis for treating the products as distinct * * *." In addition, this rule of reason would require a showing of exclusionary or anticompetitive effect in the tied product market.

sis of anticompetitive effects is peculiar. The whole point of *per se* analysis is to avoid expensive individualized inquiries concerning competitive effects of particular arrangements. As a result, the use of an "anticompetitive effects" requirement probably reflects considerable doubt about the wisdom of the *per se* rule, although that rule is formally acknowledged in virtually every decision.

The fifth element of the test for *per se* illegality—a "not insubstantial" amount of commerce in the tied product market[5]—is pure formalism. The requirement is not jurisdictional, in the sense that there is a *de minimis* exception to the federal antitrust laws (perhaps there is such an exception, but it is not unique to tying arrangements).[6] To the extent that tying law is concerned with limits on competition facilitated by foreclosure or increased collusion,[7] the correct number should be some *percentage* of a relevant market foreclosed by the arrangement. The "quantitative substantiality" rule that tying law uses states a minimum dollar amount which generally does not vary with the size of the market.[8] No good reason for the "not insubstantial" rule has ever been articulated.

In any event, the *Jefferson Parish* decision[9] added a requirement of sufficient market foreclosure to warrant an inference of anticompetitive effects, and concluded that 30 percent was insufficient to meet this requirement on the facts of that case. Subsequent tying complaints have generally been dismissed when the foreclosure percentage fell below this number, the courts generally citing lack of anticompetitive effects.

Both courts and commentators have suggested several reasons why sellers impose tie-ins: 1) someone with a monopoly in the tying product can use a tie-in to create a second monopoly in the tied product and reap two sets of monopoly profits instead of one; 2) a monopolist can use a tie-in to raise barriers to entry and thereby protect its monopoly status; 3) tie-ins by a monopolist can cause inefficient market foreclosure, or tie-ins by a group of firms can facilitate oligopoly or collusion; 4) a tie-in can enable a price-regulated seller to avoid or conceal avoidance of price regulation; 5) tie-ins can facilitate or conceal predatory pricing; 6) tie-ins can permit monopoly sellers to engage in or conceal price discrimination without violating the Robinson–Patman Act; alternatively tie-ins can facilitate nondiscriminatory metering; 7) tie-ins may increase productive or transactional efficiency by improving the quality of a product, lowering its costs, or by facilitating its distribution. These varied explanations for tying arrangements, as well as

5. See Northern Pacific Rwy. v. United States, 356 U.S. 1, 6, 78 S.Ct. 514, 518, (1958) (tie-ins "are unreasonable in and of themselves whenever a party has sufficient economic power with respect to the tying product to appreciably restraint free competition in the market for the tied product and a 'not insubstantial' amount of interstate commerce is affected"); *Jefferson Parish*, note 4, 466 U.S. at 8 (quoting *Northern Pacific*).

6. Some courts treat the requirement as a kind of *de minimis* rule, notwithstanding that other antitrust violations are condemned without such a limit. See Fortner Enterprises v. U.S. Steel (Fortner I), 394 U.S. 495, 501, 89 S.Ct. 1252, 1258 (1969); Tic–X–Press, Inc. v. Omni Promotions Co., 815 F.2d 1407, 1419 (11th Cir.1987). The latter case decided that as little as $10,000 in sales of the tied product was a "not insubstantial" amount of commerce. The Supreme Court has found as little as $60,000 to be "not insubstantial." United States v. Loew's, Inc., 371 U.S. 38, 48, 83 S.Ct. 97, 103 (1962).

7. See § 10.6b.

8. See *Fortner I*, note 6, 394 U.S. at 502, 89 S.Ct. at 1258, articulating the requirement as "the total volume of sales tied in the sales policy under challenge, not the portion of this total accounted for by the particular plaintiff who brings suit." However, a few courts have acknowledged the relevance of the amount of commerce controlled by the defendant in relation to the overall market. M. Leff Radio Parts, Inc. v. Mattel, Inc., 706 F.Supp. 387, 399 (W.D.Pa.1988) ($12,000 not sufficiently substantial in multibillion dollar market); Hudson's Bay Co. Fur Sales, Inc. v. American Legend Co-op., 651 F.Supp. 819, 842 (D.N.J.1986) (looking at defendant's tied volume in relation to overall world market).

9. See note 4. However, not all courts have gotten the message. See, e.g., MCA Television Limited v. Public Interest Corp., 171 F.3d 1265 (11th Cir.1999), which condemned a television show licensor's "block-booking," or licensing of shows only in groups, by observing that such licensing "foreclosed" alternative programmers from access to *that station*. But many tying arrangements foreclose the firm upon whom tying is imposed. For example, Jefferson Parish hospital was completely foreclosed to alternate anesthesiologists. But the point of that decision was that the *market* was not foreclosed if it contained sufficient alternative hospitals or other buyers of anesthesiological services. The *MCA* court never inquired whether there were alternative television stations in the same relevant market.

their competitive consequences, are discussed mainly in §§ 10.6 & 10.7.

§ 10.2 Tying Arrangements and Consumer Welfare

Nearly every product or service sold can be divided into components or parts. A coat can be sold without its buttons, a desk without its drawers and a jar of pickles can probably be sold without its lid. The market would come to a standstill, however, if the antitrust laws gave every customer a legal right to atomize his purchases as much as he chose.

Why then a law of tying arrangements? Quite simply, some forced package sales have been perceived by both Congress and the courts as anticompetitive or injurious to the seller's customers or competitors. The law of tie-ins is concerned with identifying those forced combined sales that can credibly injure competition.

An antitrust policy maker might take a number of approaches to this problem. One would be to adopt a rule that maximized consumer welfare in the very short run. Such a rule might permit any consumer to subdivide any purchase to any extent. A store selling a coat would be required to snip off a single button for any customer who wanted to buy it. Such a rule would impose enormous costs on sellers, and consumers would end up paying higher prices for products. Looking at any range of transactions larger than the shortest run possible (a single purchase by a single consumer) such a rule clearly would not be in the best interest of consumers as a group.

This analysis raises an important issue, however. A legal policy designed to maximize the welfare of consumers will not necessarily make every single consumer better off in every situation.[1] Consider Captain Ahab, for example, who would greatly prefer to buy a single right shoe rather than a pair. Unfortunately for Ahab, most shoe stores sell shoes only in pairs, because the cost of stocking, returns, and record-keeping would soar if stores sold individual right shoes and were stuck with the remaining left shoes. These costs would be passed on to consumers, all of whom would pay a higher price for shoes. Although shoe sellers' (nearly) universal policy of selling shoes only in pairs makes most consumers better off, it injures a small number of consumers who would prefer a single shoe.[2]

A law of tying arrangements concerned with efficiency and competition must try to identify those forced combined sales that make most consumers better off, or that generate consumer gains that outweigh consumer losses. However, it is usually impossible to measure how all consumers are affected by a forced combined sale. Therefore a test must be designed to produce an inference that a particular tying arrangement injures consumers as a group. The judicial test described in the preceding section should be evaluated as an attempt to arrive at such an inference.

§ 10.3 Market Power and Per Se Unlawful Ties; Sherman v. Clayton Act Tests

In Times–Picayune Pub. Co. v. United States[1] Justice Clark tried to establish some differences between the law of tie-ins as considered under § 1 of the Sherman Act and § 3 of the Clayton Act. Justice Clark believed that the Clayton Act must have broader coverage than the Sherman Act. Otherwise § 3 of the Clayton Act would be superfluous.[2] The Sherman Act applied only to agreements actually "in restraint of trade," while the Clayton Act

§ 10.2

1. See H. Hovenkamp, Distributive Justice and the Antitrust Laws, 51 Geo. Wash.L.Rev. 1, 5 (1982).

2. The Supreme Court ignored this in Fortner Enter., Inc. v. United States Steel Corp., 394 U.S. 495, 503–504, 89 S.Ct. 1252, 1258–1260 (1969) (*Fortner I*), when it held that the tying arrangement could be condemned if it affected any "appreciable number of buyers."

§ 10.3

1. 345 U.S. 594, 73 S.Ct. 872 (1953). The alleged tie-in was that the defendant sold identical advertisements in its morning newspaper and evening newspaper as a package, and refused to sell advertising in either newspaper separately.

2. There is a better explanation: shortly before the Clayton Act was enacted the Supreme Court had suggested that the Sherman Act did not reach tie-ins at all. Henry v. A.B. Dick Co., 224 U.S. 1, 29–30, 32 S.Ct. 364, 372 (1912).

reached every agreement the effect of which "may be substantially to lessen competition."

Justice Clark concluded that a plaintiff can have the benefit of a *per se* rule under § 1 of the Sherman Act by showing *both* that the seller had sufficient market power in the tying product to restrain competition in the tied product *and* that the tie-in restrained a substantial volume of competition in the market for the tied product. If the plaintiff could show only one of these, however, the tie-in might still be a violation of § 3 of the Clayton Act under the rule of reason.[3]

Justice Clark's distinction made little sense in either law or economics, and it raised two unfortunate possibilities: 1) that some tie-ins could be found illegal even though the seller had no market power in the tying product market; 2) that if a seller had market power, its tie may be illegal *per se*: that is, evidence about the actual pro-competitive or efficiency effects of a particular arrangement would be irrelevant. Fortunately, subsequent case law has not followed Justice Clark's prescription very closely, and has softened both of these rules.

§ 10.3a. The Rationale and Development of Tying's Market Power Requirement[4]

Justice Clark's distinction suggested that a tying arrangement could be illegal even when the defendant had no market power in the tying product market. However, a seller in competition could not impose an unwanted second product on a buyer unless the seller compensated the buyer for taking the product. Suppose that a market contains 100 sellers of identical wheat, and one seller requires a buyer to purchase a chicken for $2.00 as a condition of taking the wheat. Some purchasers who want a chicken anyway might purchase the "package" from the farmer, if both the wheat and the chicken were competitively priced. Anyone who did not want a chicken, however, would treat the requirement as a $2.00 increase in the price of wheat and buy wheat from a competitor who did not impose a chicken tie. Anticompetitive tie-ins are implausible in perfectly competitive markets. Competition drives prices to marginal cost, and the forced purchase of an unwanted product will be treated by a purchaser as a price increase. Such an increase is possible only if the seller has some market power.

Today many courts ignore Justice Clark's two-fold standard for tie-ins permitting some to be condemned without a showing of market power. Several have adopted a single test under both the Clayton and Sherman acts that requires both market power and a significant amount of commerce in the tied product market. In 1977 the Ninth Circuit concluded that "[t]he practical difference between the two standards has eroded steadily since Justice Clark's attempt to draw a fine line" between the two.[5]

No recent decision has condemned a tie when there was an express finding that the defendant lacked market power in the tying product. Nevertheless, an occasional court acknowledges the possibility of a Clayton Act rule-of-reason violation without a power showing. In *Town Sound* the Third Circuit concluded that "even if [the defendant's] position is the sounder as a matter of economics, and even if [the defendant] accurately predicts the direction in which the Supreme Court is heading, still-binding precedent forecloses our adopting" a rule requiring the plaintiff to prove market power in the tying product.[6] Other courts have been willing to find market power on factors unrelated to market share,

3. *Times-Picayune*, 345 U.S. at 608–09, 73 S.Ct. at 880.

4. See 10 Antitrust Law ¶¶ 1731–1740 (1996).

5. Moore v. Jas. H. Matthews & Co., 550 F.2d 1207, 1214 (9th Cir.1977), appeal after remand, 682 F.2d 830 (9th Cir.1982). See also Jack Walters & Sons Corp. v. Morton Bldg., Inc., 737 F.2d 698, 702 (7th Cir.), cert. denied, 469 U.S. 1018, 105 S.Ct. 432 (1984) (tests are "similar, maybe identical").

6. Town Sound and Custom Tops v. Chrysler Motors Corp., 959 F.2d 468, 485 (3d Cir.), cert. denied, 506 U.S. 868, 113 S.Ct. 196 (1992). The statement was dicta, and the court went on to approve the arrangement. See also Ware v. Trailer Mart, Inc., 623 F.2d 1150, 1153 (6th Cir.1980) (market power in the tying product is "relevant only if [the plaintiff] intends to prove a *per se* violation of Section 1" of the Sherman Act, but not in a rule of reason case under § 3 of the Clayton Act.).

such as the uniqueness of the tying product offered by the defendant.[7]

The Supreme Court has never provided a useful rule for determining *how much* market power the seller must possess before the tying arrangement is illegal. Historically the Court did not take market power in tying cases very seriously. Many of the earliest cases involved patent "misuse" claims, where the Court found that the antitrust defendant improperly tied unpatented goods to the patented product or the patent license.[8] These decisions spoke generally of a patent "monopoly," but never considered whether the defendant actually had market power in any market. They are discussed further in § 5.5. Likewise, *International Salt* and *Paramount*, where the Supreme Court began to articulate the modern law of tie-ins, never required significant market power in the tying product.[9]

In *Times–Picayune* the Supreme Court appeared to require the seller's "dominance" in the tying product market.[10] By contrast, in the *Northern Pacific Rwy.* case a few years later, the Court assessed a much weaker requirement that the defendant control a "substantial" amount of the tying product and failed even to define a relevant market.[11] The Court interpreted *Times–Picayune* to require no more "than sufficient economic power to impose an appreciable restraint on free competition in the tied product. * * * "[12] In Fortner Enterprises, Inc. v. U.S. Steel Corp. (*Fortner I*) the Court not only found it unnecessary to define a relevant market for the tying product, but held that market power in the tying product could be inferred from the fact that the seller had "unique economic advantages over his competitors."[13]

But in the second *Fortner* case the Court greatly qualified this position and held that market power could not be inferred from the fact that the seller merely sold the tying product (credit) cheaper in order to obtain sales of a relatively high priced tied product (prefabricated houses).[14] More importantly, under *Fortner II* simple "uniqueness" of the tying product was not sufficient to meet the market power requirement unless there were a separate showing that the uniqueness at issue really created market power. The defendant's financing terms were said to be "unique" because it offered lower interest rates and was willing to take higher risks than competitors, but it made these loans only to purchasers of its rather overpriced houses. As the Court pointed out, this was not market power, but only "a willingness to provide cheap financing in order to sell expensive houses." If "the evidence merely shows that credit terms are unique because the seller is willing to accept a lesser profit—or to incur greater risks—than its competitors, that kind of uniqueness will not give rise to any inference of economic power."[15]

Fortner II was the Supreme Court's first signal that market power should be taken more seriously. The use of vague and diluted market power requirements was halted, at least for Sherman Act cases, in Jefferson Parish Hosp. Dist. No. 2 v. Hyde. The plaintiff anesthesiologist alleged that the hospital illegally tied the use of its operating rooms to a particular firm of anesthesiologists. The Court found that a market share of 30% in the tying product market was insufficient, because 70% of the market continued to be available to patients who wanted to use a different anesthesiologist than the one employed by the defendant. At the same time, the Court appeared to return to the "market dominance" test of

7. See § 10.3d; and see 10 Antitrust Law ¶¶ 1738–1739 (1996).

8. For example, Motion Picture Patents Co. v. Universal Film Mfg. Co., 243 U.S. 502, 37 S.Ct. 416 (1917); Carbice Corp. v. American Patents Development Corp., 283 U.S. 27, 51 S.Ct. 334 (1931).

9. International Salt Co. v. United States, 332 U.S. 392, 68 S.Ct. 12 (1947); United States v. Paramount Pictures, 334 U.S. 131, 68 S.Ct. 915 (1948).

10. *Times–Picayune*, note 1, 345 U.S. at 611, 73 S.Ct. at 882.

11. Northern Pacific Rwy. v. United States, 356 U.S. 1, 6–8, 78 S.Ct. 514, 518–519 (1958).

12. Id. at 11, 78 S.Ct. at 521.

13. 394 U.S. 495, 505, 89 S.Ct. 1252, 1259 (1969).

14. U.S. Steel Corp. v. Fortner Enterprises (Fortner II), 429 U.S. 610, 621–622, 97 S.Ct. 861, 868–869 (1977).

15. Id. at 622, 97 S.Ct. at 869.

Times–Picayune.[16] Finally, the Court appeared to require definition of a relevant market and computation of market share, at least if the tying product is not patented.[17]

The *Jefferson Parish* decision has had a large impact on the law of tying arrangements, reversing a trend in lower courts to condemn tying arrangements even when the defendant's market share of any properly defined relevant market for the tying product was very small.[18] Recent cases have generally refused to condemn tying arrangements on market shares smaller than 30% of the tying product market.[19] Likewise, the conclusion expressed in *Northern Pacific*[20] and *Fortner I*[21] that market power can be inferred from the mere fact that so many people accede to the tying arrangement, has been all but abandoned.[22]

§ 10.3b. Tying Arrangements in Imperfectly Competitive Markets; Locked–In Customers[23]

Could tie-ins be used in moderately competitive markets to exploit certain consumers? The Supreme Court thought so in the *Kodak* case, although it did not express its concern as whether tying arrangements might be harmful in competitive markets.[24] Kodak sold photocopy machines in a product differentiated market, where its market share was about 23%. Under the challenged policy, only those who purchased their repair service from Kodak could purchase Kodak's replacement parts, and Kodak effectively controlled the production of these parts. The tying challenge came from independent firms that serviced Kodak photocopiers and wanted to purchase repair parts from Kodak. The policy was alleged to be a tying arrangement in which the replacement parts were the tying product and the service was the tied product.[25]

The holding in *Kodak* was relatively narrow: lack of market power in a primary market need not entail, as a matter of law, lack of market power in aftermarkets. But the Court's opinion engaged in far-ranging speculation about how a manufacturer of a branded durable good could use tying arrangements to exploit "locked-in" customers—those who had already purchased a Kodak photocopier and could now be victimized by restrictive practices affecting aftermarkets for service and replacement parts.

Given that the market for photocopiers was competitive, could Kodak have the requisite market power in the market for replacement parts? A well informed consumer would treat high service prices as a price increase in the basic product, and purchase its photocopier from a rival.[26] However, the Court reasoned, in certain moderately competitive markets for durable goods, a seller could use a tie-in to take advantage of "locked in" customers who

16. Jefferson Parish Hosp. Dist. No. 2 v. Hyde, 466 U.S. 2, 7, 104 S.Ct. 1551, 1556 (1984).

17. The Court's dicta clung to the presumption that a *patented* tying product conferred market power. Id. at 16. Presumably, no relevant market need be defined in such a case. See § 10.3c.

18. See, e.g., Heatransfer Corp. v. Volkswagenwerk, A.G., 553 F.2d 964 (5th Cir.1977), cert. denied, 434 U.S. 1087, 98 S.Ct. 1282 (1978) (finding a large market share, but only because the market was defined as air conditioners for Volkswagens).

19. E.g., Marts v. Xerox, 77 F.3d 1109, 1113 n. 6 (9th Cir. 1996) (18% too small); Shafi v. St. Francis Hosp., 937 F.2d 603 (4th Cir.1991) (11% insufficient); Grappone, Inc. v. Subaru of New England, Inc., 858 F.2d 792, 797 (1st Cir.1988) (dicta requiring at least 30%); *Town Sound*, note 6 (10% insufficient). See also Technical Resource Services v. Dornier Medical Systems, 134 F.3d 1458 (11th Cir.1998) (affirming judgment on jury verdict that defendant lacked power in market for tying product).

20. Note 11.

21. Note 13.

22. See § 10.3d; and Grappone v. Subaru of New England, 858 F.2d 792, 796 (1st Cir.1988) (appreciable number not found). See 10 Antitrust Law ¶ 1738 (1996).

23. See also § 3.3a.

24. Eastman Kodak Co. v. Image Technical Services, Inc., 504 U.S. 451, 112 S.Ct. 2072 (1992).

25. After remand the tying claim dropped out for lack of any "agreement," but the Ninth Circuit affirmed liability under § 2 of the Sherman Act. See Image Technical Services, Inc. v. Eastman Kodak Co., 125 F.3d 1195 (9th Cir.1997), cert. denied, ___ U.S. ___, 118 S.Ct. 1560 (1998); and §§ 3.3a; 7.6, 7.11d1.

26. See Queen City Pizza, Inc. v. Domino's Pizza, Inc., 124 F.3d 430 (3d Cir.1997), cert. denied, ___ U.S. ___, 118 S.Ct. 1385 (1998); Digital Equip. Corp. v. Uniq Digital Tech., Inc., 73 F.3d 756 (7th Cir.1996); Lee v. Life Ins. Co. of N. Am., 23 F.3d 14 (1st.1994); Parts & Elec. Motors, Inc. v. Sterling Elec., Inc., 866 F.2d 228, 234–235 (7th Cir.), cert. denied, 493 U.S. 847, 110 S.Ct. 141 (1989) (Posner, J., dissenting).

had already purchased the defendant's durable good and now needed replacement parts and service that would fit.[27] The lock-in would make at least some customers willing to pay a higher price for Kodak's parts, given the costs of abandoning their existing machines and purchasing others. The Court reasoned that if the gains from high services prices were great enough to offset any lost sales to better informed customers who would forego the package, then the tie would be both profitable and injurious to consumer welfare, notwithstanding a competitive primary market for photocopiers.

The Court observed that consumers of durable goods needing frequent maintenance are not in an equally good position to engage in "lifecycle" pricing—that is, pricing that takes both the price of the original good and the cost of subsequent maintenance into account. For those whose purchase decision is driven mainly by the cost of the initial durable good (the photocopier itself), subsequent exploitation through high service prices might be possible, facilitated by arrangements mandating that only Kodak could repair its machines. Although some customers were sensitive to subsequent repair costs and presumably calculated them into the total cost of owning a photocopier, other customers operated on a much shorter horizon. For them the initial price was about all that mattered, and they did not look down the road to the price of future repairs. The Court then noted that if the costs of service are presumed to be small in relation to the total purchase price, and information about service costs is difficult and expensive to obtain, then one could not presume that consumers would gather the information. This might make anticompetitive practices in the aftermarket profitable, notwithstanding competition in the primary market.[28]

Even assuming that such exploitation is profitable, is it an antitrust concern? All imperfectly competitive markets contain some customers who do not inform themselves fully about what they are buying. Indeed, no customer acquires *all* the relevant information, but only as much information as seems cost justified in the circumstances. The consequence is to make certain kinds of customer exploitation possible. But this kind of exploitation is not monopoly unless it facilitates systematic supracompetitive returns in a properly defined relevant market.[29] At the same time, short run concerns are surely relevant to antitrust policy. For that reason, the fact that the primary market is competitive should not be absolutely dispositive. For example, suppose Kodak were contemplating exit from the photocopier market, but had an installed base of many thousands of existing customers. It might be able to exploit these customers by means of a tying arrangement, notwithstanding its lack of power in the primary market. The potential gains from customer exploitation could exceed the losses in sales in the competitive primary market, even if these sales dropped to zero.

The *Kodak* Court probably exaggerated the costs of obtaining information about aftermarket repairs. Information about repair costs is common to large classes of consumers; it does not have to be gathered individually for each. In a competitive primary market, rivals would be quick to point out comparisons between their own repair prices and the prices charged by Kodak. If a firm persistently charged more than other firms for aftermarket services, there is no obvious reason why this informa-

27. The Court relied on R. Craswell, Tying Requirements in Competitive Markets: The Consumer Protection Issues, 62 B. U. L. Rev. 661, 676 (1982); H. Beales, R. Craswell, & S. Salop, The Efficient Regulation of Consumer Information, 24 J. Law & Econ. 491, 509–511 (1981). *Kodak*, 504 U.S. at 473 n. 19, 112 S.Ct. at 2085 n. 19.

Craswell's argument rests on the proposition that in certain markets, such as health care, consumer search costs are very high. As a result, one seller can coerce acceptance of a tied product even in a multi-seller market, because the consumer is not in a good position to shop around. The Fifth Circuit relied on this argument to condemn a hospital's requirement that all patients operated on in its facilities use a particular anesthesiologist. The Supreme Court reversed. See Jefferson Parish Hosp. Dist. No. 2 v. Hyde, 686 F.2d at 290, reversed at 466 U.S. 2, 104 S.Ct. 1551 (1984).

28. *Kodak*, 504 U.S. at 473, 112 S.Ct. at 2085.

29. For the relevant concerns and some presumptions about the amount of monopoly profit that can be generated by such practices, see § 3.3a.

tion would not leak out to most consumers who are at least moderately attentive. One possibility that cannot be overlooked, however, is tacit or express collusion under which the hardware manufacturers concealed the price of post-purchase services. This was not alleged to be the case in *Kodak*.

Kodak also considered whether the manufacturer of durable, branded goods could be found to have market power in unique replacement parts.[30] Kodak's 23% market share in the photocopier market[31] was even less than the defendant had in the *Jefferson Parish* case, where the Supreme Court had refused to condemn a tie-in on a market share of around 30%.[32] However, the "aftermarket" for replacement parts included many items that would fit only on Kodak photocopiers, and a significant minority were manufactured by either Kodak or its licensees exclusively. Without addressing the uniqueness question at any length,[33] the Court suggested that there might be a relevant market for *Kodak-brand* parts and service.[34] In that case, of course, Kodak's market share might be 100%, at least if it and no one else manufactured all of its own parts.

Kodak should not be read for the proposition that sufficient market power in aftermarkets can be inferred merely from the fact that a manufacturer makes it own, unique replacement parts. That is, "Chrysler Transmissions" is not a relevant market merely because such transmissions will fit only on Chryslers. Rather, there must be independent evidence of market power in the aftermarket, evaluated by generally accepted antitrust criteria.[35] The main problem in *Kodak* was that the defendant's motion for summary judgment had come before discovery developed this issue.

The alternative implies that every manufacturer of product-differentiated durable goods has sufficient market power to subject its subsequent restrictions to antitrust challenge. Such an interpretation would be disastrous, not merely unfortunate, for consumers. When products are durable, differentiated by brand, and in need of regular servicing, manufacturer restrictions are most important. A Kodak photocopier technician probably needs to know things that a Xerox technician does not, and vice-versa. Further, independent technicians may be poorly trained, or may be in a position to blame difficulties on the manufacturer in order to absolve themselves. The ability of manufacturers to maintain a satisfied customer base may in fact depend on precisely the kind of restrictions that the *Kodak* decision cast into doubt.

Subsequent decisions have generally limited *Kodak* to situations where (1) the alleged tied product must be purchased *after* customers are "locked-in" by virtue of a previous purchase; and (2) where the defendant changed its aftermarket pricing policy after a significant number of customers had made their purchase, or a significant number of customers can actually show that they were misinformed about aftermarket prices.[36] On the first, customers are not locked in to anything if they purchase the primary and aftermarket good at the same time. For example, if a computer maker without a dominant market share bundles software with its computer, customers cannot be said to be locked in to the software, for they buy the hardware and software simultaneously, and thus at a time when they compare rival computer systems.[37] On the second, if there is no reason for thinking that customers as a group are not reasonably well informed, they can be locked in only if aftermarket policies change *after* they have made their purchase.[38]

30. The problem is analyzed in more detail in § 3.3.

31. See 903 F.2d, at 616, n. 3.

32. *Jefferson Parish*, note 27; see § 10.3a.

33. On "uniqueness" as conferring market power, see § 10.3d.

34. *Kodak*, 504 U.S. at 484, 112 S.Ct. at 2091 & n. 31. The issue is explored more fully in § 3.3a.

35. See § 3.3a, for a discussion of the evidence of market power that the Court cited, and its proper analysis; and see H. Hovenkamp, Market Power in Aftermarkets: Antitrust Policy and the *Kodak* Case, 40 UCLA L.Rev. 1447 (1993).

36. See generally 10 Antitrust Law ¶ 1740 (1996).

37. See *Digital Equipment*, note 26; *Queen City*, note 26; Little Caesar Enterp. v. Smith, 34 F.Supp.2d 459 (E.D.Mich.1998).

38. PSI Repair Services v. Honeywell, Inc., 104 F.3d 811, 817–818 (6th Cir.), cert. denied, 520 U.S. 1265, 117 S.Ct. 2434 (1997) (lock-in unlikely if policy respecting

For this reason, most courts agree that in tying claims brought by franchisees, market power must be established by looking at the franchisor's market position in the general market in which it sells. To be sure, after a franchisee has signed a contract requiring it to take all of its requirements of, say, pizza dough from the franchisor the franchisee is locked in and cannot buy cheaper dough elsewhere. But since the requirement is enforceable only if spelled out in the franchise contract, the franchisee already knew about the requirement at the time it decided to enter into the franchise arrangement in the first place.[39]

The result of the constraints noted above is that few plaintiffs have succeeded in *Kodak* style tying claims where the defendant has a nondominant share of the primary market.

§ 10.3c. Intellectual Property and the Presumption of Market Power

Courts have traditionally presumed a seller's market power in the tying product when the product is patented[40] or copyrighted.[41] A few courts give the same presumption when the tying product is trademarked.[42] In most cases courts regard the presumption as rebuttable,[43] and there is a strong recent trend away from the presumptions.[44]

As noted in Chapter 3, most patents confer absolutely no market power on their owners.[45] Often patented products are not even marketable at their cost of production. Likewise, any group of words or symbols can be copyrighted. The rules creating market power presumptions for patented, copyrighted or trademarked goods ignore the fact that in the world of brand-specific products almost everything is protected by intellectual property rights. These are the mechanisms by which consumers distinguish among brands. Automobiles, stereo equipment, home computers, watches, fast food franchises, clothing and canned food are all likely to be patented, trademarked or copyrighted, but most are sold in competitive markets.[46]

aftermarket parts was "consistently maintained and generally known"). See also id. at 821: "By changing its policy after its customers were" locked in, "Kodak took advantage of the fact that its customers lacked the information...." See also SMS Systems Maintenance Services v. Digital Equipment Corp., ___ F.3d ___, 1999 WL 618046 (1st Cir.1999) (no lock-in when defendant changed warranty on new computers from one year to three, thus locking out independent service organizations during that period; the change had absolutely no impact on customers who had previously purchased their computers, but applied only prospectively).

39. See *Queen City Pizza*, note 26; *Little Caesar*, note 37. At this writing, the only contrary decision is Collins v. Int'l Dairy Queen, 980 F.Supp. 1252, 1259 (M.D.Ga.1997). See Antitrust Law ¶ 510' (current Supplement).

40. See International Salt Co. v. United States, 332 U.S. 392, 68 S.Ct. 12 (1947), and see *Jefferson Parish*, note 27, 466 U.S. 2, 16, 104 S.Ct. 1551, 1560 (1984) (dictum).

41. United States v. Paramount Pictures, Inc., 334 U.S. 131, 158, 68 S.Ct. 915, 929 (1948); Digidyne Corp. v. Data General Corp., 734 F.2d 1336, 1341–42 (9th Cir. 1984).

42. Photovest Corp. v. Fotomat Corp., 606 F.2d 704 (7th Cir.1979), cert. denied, 445 U.S. 917, 100 S.Ct. 1278 (1980); Siegel v. Chicken Delight, Inc., 448 F.2d 43 (9th Cir.1971), cert. denied, 405 U.S. 955, 92 S.Ct. 1172 (1972). Other circuits reject the presumption for trademarks: Mozart Co. v. Mercedes-Benz of N.Am. 833 F.2d 1342 (9th Cir.1987), cert. denied, 488 U.S. 870, 109 S.Ct. 179 (1988) (no presumption for trademark); Tominaga v. Shepherd, 682 F.Supp. 1489 (C.D.Cal.1988) (same); Carpa, Inc. v. Ward Foods, Inc., 536 F.2d 39 (5th Cir.1976), appeal after remand, 567 F.2d 1316 (5th Cir.1978).

43. A few cases suggest a *conclusive* presumption of economic power when the tying product is patented. See United States Steel Corp. v. Fortner Enterprises (Fortner II), 429 U.S. 610, 619, 97 S.Ct. 861, 867 (1977); Fortner Enterprises v. United States Steel Corp. (Fortner I), 394 U.S. 495, 505 n. 2, 89 S.Ct. 1252, 1259 n. 2 (1969).

44. For example, Cassan Enterp. v. Chrysler Corp., 129 F.3d 124 (9th Cir.1997), cert. denied, ___ U.S. ___, 118 S.Ct. 1362 (1998) (market power would not be inferred from trademark); A.I. Root Co. v. Computer/Dynamics, Inc., 806 F.2d 673, 676–677 (6th Cir.1986) (refusing to find market power in copyrighted software); Allen-Myland, Inc. v. IBM, 693 F.Supp. 262, 281–282 (E.D.Pa.1988), vacated 33 F.3d 194 (3d Cir.1994) (no market power presumption with respect to freely licensed patent); Grappone v. Subaru of New England, 858 F.2d 792 (1st Cir. 1988) (brand name confers no market power). Cf. Abbott Labs. v. Brennan, 952 F.2d 1346 (Fed.Cir.1991) (patent creates no presumption of market power in Sherman § 2 monopolization case).

But see MCA Television Limited v. Public Interest Corp., 171 F.3d 1265 (11th Cir.1999), which concluded that each individual television program that the defendant licensor owned conferred sufficient power to make its package licensing of programs ("block-booking") per se unlawful.

45. See § 3.9d.

46. See Digidyne Corp. v. Data General Corp., 734 F.2d 1336, 1341–1345 (9th Cir.1984), in which the Court presumed that the defendant had market power in its computer software because the software was copyrighted.

One way to measure the market power created by intellectual property is to estimate the degree of difficulty the owner faced in acquiring these rights. If it is easy to create, then it probably confers little market power. Almost any original grouping of words can be copyrighted, and almost any unique symbol can be trademarked. If people could create monopoly power by simply doodling on a piece of paper for a few minutes or perhaps paying an advertising agency to develop a slogan, we would live in a world filled with monopolies. Patents, at least initially, are more difficult to acquire, but they are readily granted, and competitive markets are full of them.[47] The economic case for "presuming" sufficient market power to coerce consumer acceptance of an unwanted tied product simply because the tying product is patented, copyrighted, or trademarked is very weak.

This does not necessarily mean that the possession of intellectual property is totally irrelevant to the market power question. Occasionally a patent may in fact define a relevant market and confer substantial market power. For example, patents can serve to reduce the supply competition facing a firm by making its product harder to duplicate. If elasticity of demand is already low as well, the result of the patent may be to define a relevant market in which the patent holder's share is substantial. But the patent itself is only one piece of evidence in this inquiry into market power.

Finally, a 1988 amendment to the Patent Act makes the tying of patented products lawful "unless, in view of the circumstances, the patent owner has market power in the relevant market for the patent or patented product on which the license or sale is conditioned."[48] This appears to be Congressional recognition of the proposition that market power is not inherent in a patent grant, but must be separately proven.[49]

§ 10.3d. "Uniqueness" and Ubiquity as Market Power

During the expansive years when courts were highly suspicious of tying arrangements, the market power requirement was readily met. The Supreme Court concluded that sufficient market power could be inferred from the fact that the tying product was unique in some sense, or that its use was widespread.[50] Some lower courts continue to follow a similar formulation.[51]

Finding market power in the case of a "unique" good is sensible when the uniqueness question looks to the same criteria that governs market power queries generally. That is, the term "uniqueness" can be used to capture the set of surrogates for market power measurement that antitrust employs—namely, a large share of a properly defined relevant antitrust market.[52] But the term does positive harm when it permits a fact-finder simply to eyeball a product, note some differences that seem to make it attractive, and then proclaim the market power requirement to be met. Recent decisions exhibit a trend to merge the

Under that rationale *all* licensors of computer software have market power in their product. An additional problem with the presumption of market power is that the scope of the patent or copyright is frequently different than the scope of a relevant market for antitrust purposes. For example, the *Good Food Cookbook* is copyrighted. However, the relevant market for estimating market power is probably "cook books." Within that market, the *Good Food Cookbook* may be an intense competitor. The same analysis generally applies to patents. See § 3.9d.

47. See § 3.9d.

48. 371 U.S.C.A. § 271(d)(5).

49. See 10 Antitrust Law ¶ 1737c (1996).

50. See U.S. Steel Corp. v. Fortner Enters., 429 U.S. 610, 618–619 n. 10, 97 S.Ct. 861, 866–82 n. 10 (1977) (*Fortner II*) (noting that "the unique character of the tying product has provided critical support for the finding of illegality in prior cases," such as *Fortner I*, but then finding it insufficient); and Fortner Enters. v. U.S. Steel Corp., 394 U.S. 495, 505, 89 S.Ct. 1252, 1259 (1969) (*Fortner I*). In the latter case the Court did not accept the argument "that market power can be inferred simply because the [tying product is] 'unique and unusual.' " But it denied summary judgment, holding that the claims that market power was conferred by uniqueness should go to the jury.

51. For example, Thompson v. Metropolitan Multi–List, Inc., 934 F.2d 1566, 1576–78 (11th Cir.1991), cert. denied, 506 U.S. 903, 113 S.Ct. 295 (1992) (uniqueness of multiple listing service); Monument Builders v. American Cemetery Ass'n, 891 F.2d 1473, 1482–1483 (10th Cir.), cert. denied, 495 U.S. 930, 110 S.Ct. 2168 (1990) (uniqueness of cemetery lots); Tic–X–Press, Inc. v. Omni Promotions Co., 815 F.2d 1407, 1420 (11th Cir.1987) (uniqueness of indoor concert facility). Other decisions are discussed in 10 Antitrust Law ¶ 1739 (1996).

52. See generally Ch. 3.

"uniqueness" and the basic market power inquiries. For example, the Seventh Circuit has held that uniqueness creates an inference of market power only if the evidence suggests that rivals are unable to duplicate the particularly desirable characteristics of the defendant's tying product, and that this operates as a barrier to entry into the market.[53] Other courts have suggested that evidence of uniqueness must be combined with market share evidence, and the two together may suggest market power.[54] Anything less places the antitrust tribunal in the position of micro-managing distribution schemes in competitive but product differentiated markets.

An alternative route to a market power finding makes no sense at all—namely, the notion that market power can be inferred from the ubiquity of a tying arrangement, or the willingness of large numbers of customers to put up with it.[55] This argument stands the consumer welfare principle precisely on its head. What inference should be drawn from the fact that consumers have not revolted against automobile manufacturers' universal practice of selling cars with tires mounted, rather than permitting customers to shop around for their own? Most obviously, that the great majority of customers prefer it precisely that way. Most tying arrangements are efficient because they produce economies in production or distribution, but the economies will be lost unless the package is imposed on everyone. But if the arrangement *is* efficient, then we would also expect it to be ubiquitous.

Equally senseless is the notion that one can infer market power in the tying product from the fact that sales of the tied product increased when the arrangement was imposed.[56] Once again, that evidence is at least as consistent with the proposition that the arrangement is efficient: price cuts and improvements in product quality generally produce increased sales. A more sensible inquiry, relevant to the market power question, is whether output of the tying product *declined* when the tying arrangement was imposed.

§ 10.3e. Separate Sherman and Clayton Act Tests?

As noted earlier, in *Times–Picayune*[57] the Supreme Court suggested that a tying arrangement could be condemned under more aggressive standards under § 3 of the Clayton Act than under § 1 of the Sherman Act. In particular, the Clayton Act standard may not require proof of market power in the tying product. A few courts adhere to this formulation.[58] In general, however, the trend has been to apply a single test under both statutes and to require some kind of showing of market power in the tying product.[59] The four concurring Justices in the *Jefferson Parish* case believed that market power is required even in a rule of reason tying case.[60] Maintaining the illusion of separate Sherman and Clayton Act tests for tie-ins is senseless.

The Supreme Court has also approved broader standards under the Federal Trade Commission Act.[61] In FTC v. Brown Shoe Co.,[62] the Court upheld the FTC's condemna-

53. Will v. Comprehensive Accounting Corp., 776 F.2d 665, 672 (7th Cir.1985), cert. denied, 475 U.S. 1129, 106 S.Ct. 1659 (1986). Even *Fortner I*, note 50, spoke of the seller's "unique economic ability" to supply its variation of the tying product.

54. For example, Baxley–DeLamar Monuments, Inc. v. American Cemetery Ass'n., 843 F.2d 1154, 1157 (8th Cir. 1988), appeal after remand, 938 F.2d 846 (8th Cir.1991) (uniqueness plus 57% market share sufficient).

55. See *Fortner II*, note 50, 429 U.S. at 619 n. 10, 97 S.Ct. at 867 n. 10; Parts & Elec. Motors, Inc. v. Sterling Elec., Inc., 826 F.2d 712, 720 (7th Cir.1987) (buyer acceptance of tie evidences market power). See 10 Antitrust Law ¶ 1738 (1996).

56. For example, Barber & Ross Co. v. Lifetime Doors, Inc., 810 F.2d 1276, 1280 (4th Cir.), cert. denied, 484 U.S. 823, 108 S.Ct. 86 (1987).

57. Note 1.

58. For example, *Town Sound*, note 6.

59. For example, *Grappone*, note 44, 858 F.2d at 794 (same test "regardless of whether a plaintiff charges a violation of Sherman Act § 1 or Clayton Act § 3"); Mozart Co. v. Mercedes–Benz of N. Am., 833 F.2d 1342, 1352 (9th Cir.1987), cert. denied, 488 U.S. 870, 109 S.Ct. 179 (1988) (requirements under the two statutes are "virtually the same"). See 9 Antitrust Law ¶ 1719b (1991).

60. *Jefferson Parish*, note 27, 466 U.S. at 35, 104 S.Ct. at 1570 (J. O'Connor, concurring).

61. 15 U.S.C.A. § 45; see § 15.2 of this volume.

62. 384 U.S. 316, 86 S.Ct. 1501 (1966).

tion of a practice under which Brown provided special services[63] to franchisees in exchange for a promise that they would concentrate their sales efforts on Brown Shoes. The Court held that the practice could be condemned under § 5 of the FTC Act without the showing of anticompetitive effects ordinarily required in a Sherman or Clayton Act challenge.[64] Indeed, the stores upon which these requirements were imposed amounted to only 1% of the nation's shoe stores.

In backing up the Commission, the Supreme Court "reject[ed] the argument that proof" of anticompetitive effects was necessary, citing the FTC's power under § 5 of the FTC Act to "arrest trade restraints in their incipiency without proof that they amount to an outright violation of § 3 of the Clayton Act or other provisions of the antitrust laws."[65]

The Supreme Court's analysis stretched the already overdeterrent law of tie-ins much too far to serve any policy concerned with distinguishing the economically competitive from the anticompetitive. In other contexts, more recent courts have required the Commission to prove anticompetitive effects in cases applying § 5 directly. For example, the *Ethyl* case[66] involved oligopoly practices where the Sherman Act is ineffectual and the negative impact on competition fairly well supported. By contrast, tying arrangements are vertical arrangements, and the growing consensus today is that the vast majority are harmless to competition. This suggests that either the FTC or the courts apply a less expansive approach in future FTC tying arrangement challenges.

Perhaps more importantly, in oligopoly cases such as *Ethyl* the practices were challenged because they were believed to be anticompetitive. That is, the practices facilitated output reduction and pricing above the competitive level. By contrast, expansive applications such as *Brown Shoe* seem to serve no articulable economic policy at all, not even interests of consumer protection. Indeed, the FTC *Brown Shoe* decision operated as nothing other than a license to engage in free riding. Under the decision, independent retailers could take advantage of Brown's special retailing services while facing no obligation to deal exclusively or even predominantly in Brown's shoes. The retailers' natural response would be to stock up on lower priced shoes made by manufacturers that did not provide the services. The manufacturer's natural response would then be to stop providing the services.

The best approach would be to use a single test for tying arrangements under all statutes, generally including § 5 of the Federal Trade Commission Act. Market power should be required in all instances, and specific anticompetitive effects must be alleged and proven. This is the same as saying that tying arrangements should generally be addressed under the rule of reason.

§ 10.3f. The Rationale for Per Se Illegal Tie–Ins

The judicial test described in § 10.1 accounts poorly for the economic functions of tying arrangements in sellers' distribution schemes. The test is not well designed to enable a court to determine whether a particular tie-in is socially harmful. Whether it is used as a collusion facilitator, for price discrimination, metering, or rate regulation avoidance are all but irrelevant to the formal judicial analysis. At the same time, the test has mired countless courts in analysis of issues that are not central to the economic functions of tie-ins and their potential for injury.

Although courts commonly articulate a "*per se*" rule for tying arrangements, that usage is inappropriate and undermines effective analysis of the function of a tying arrangement in the defendant's distribution system. Even for the seller who has market power, tying arrangements are usually competitive; as a result, anticompetitive effects must be independently sought out.

63. The services included architectural plans for stores, group health insurance at reduced rate, and the aid of a Brown field representative. Id. at 322.

64. Id. at 321–322, 86 S.Ct. at 1504–1505.

65. Id. at 322, 86 S.Ct. at 1505.

66. In re Ethyl Corp., 101 F.T.C. 425 (1983), vacated sub nom. E.I. du Pont de Nemours & Co. v. FTC, 729 F.2d 128 (2d Cir.1984), discussed in § 4.6d.

As previously observed, a forced package sale by a seller without market power must be efficiency creating or else the seller could not successfully sell its product this way. "Efficiency-creating" means that the gains that accrue to customers who benefit from the combination are greater than the losses that accrue to those who are injured, and that the gains can be realized only if the combination is forced on everyone.

For example, a shoe store does not need market power to force all its customers to buy shoes in pairs. If it sold shoes singly it would face higher costs that would be passed on to customers. These costs would outweigh the benefit to the relatively small number of people who would be better off if they could buy a single shoe. Likewise, stores with no market power force customers to buy coats with their buttons, automobiles with their spare tires and dressed geese with their gizzards—even though there are people who would prefer all these "tying" products without their respective "tied" products. Often courts have addressed this consumer welfare problem by deciding that the two items were in fact a single legal "product."[67]

If a seller is a competitor, its forced combination sale is probably efficient. It does not follow, however, that if the seller has market power its forced combination sale is inefficient. One must therefore dispute Justice Clark's suggestion in *Times–Picayune*[68] that if a seller has market power, its tie-in involving a significant amount of interstate commerce is *per se* illegal—that is, illegal without regard to possible procompetitive effects. Even a monopoly seller of shoes would probably sell them in pairs. It would be efficient for the monopolist to do so, and both the monopolist and its customers are better off when the monopolist has lower costs.

The *per se* rule, as you may recall, is applied to certain practices after the court understands them sufficiently well to conclude that they are almost always harmful.[69] In that case the risk of overdeterrence is very low; that is, there is little chance that the court will end up condemning a practice that is really efficient. By contrast, the cost of litigating under the rule of reason is very high.

But are tie-ins even arguably within the category of practices, such as price fixing, that are almost always harmful? The Supreme Court concluded that they were in Northern Pacific Rwy. Co. v. United States[70] Justice Black wrote:

> Indeed, "tying agreements serve hardly any purpose beyond the suppression of competition * * *." They deny competitors free access to the market for the tied product, not because the party imposing the tying requirements has a better product or a lower price but because of his power or leverage in another market. At the same time buyers are forced to forego their free choice between competing products. For these reasons * * * [t]hey are unreasonable in and of themselves whenever a party has sufficient economic power with respect to the tying product to appreciably restrain free competition in the market for the tied product and a "not insubstantial" amount of interstate commerce is affected.

The result of *Northern Pacific* has been that often when the defendant has market power in the tying product the court has condemned its tie-in, even when the forced combined sale was probably in the best interest of consumers.[71] In the *Jefferson Parish* case, four concurring Justices were ready to jettison the *per se* rule for tying arrangements, but as of this writing it remains the law.[72] Although the 1992 *Kodak*

67. See § 10.5.

68. Times–Picayune Pub. Co. v. United States, 345 U.S. 594, 73 S.Ct. 872 (1953).

69. See § 5.6.

70. 356 U.S. 1, 6, 78 S.Ct. 514, 518 (1958). The Court was quoting Standard Oil Co. of Calif. v. United States, 337 U.S. 293, 305–306, 69 S.Ct. 1051, 1058 (1949).

71. See Hyde v. Jefferson Parish Hosp. Dist. No. 2, 686 F.2d 286, 294 (5th Cir.1982), reversed, 466 U.S. 2, 104 S.Ct. 1551 (1984). In reversing, however, the Supreme Court concluded that "It is far too late in the history of our antitrust jurisprudence to question the proposition that certain tying arrangements pose an unacceptable risk of stifling competition and therefore are unreasonable 'per se.' "466 U.S. at 8, 104 S.Ct. at 1556.

72. *Jefferson Parish*, note 71, 466 U.S. at 32, 104 S.Ct. at 1569.

decision is hardly explicit on the issue, the majority described the law of tying arrangements as if a *per se* rule were being applied.[73]

Even when the seller or sellers have substantial market power, their tying arrangement is not necessarily anticompetitive. Monopolists as well as competitors may find the selling of things in packages to be efficient. For this reason anticompetitive impact must be separately shown, and this fact makes the adjective "*per se*" inappropriate.

§ 10.4 When Are Products Tied Together?

Clearly, if a seller freely permits the buyer to take or decline a second product there is no tie. The buyer must somehow be forced, or coerced, into accepting the tied product. This coercion could result from (1) an absolute refusal to sell the tying product without the tied product; (2) a discount, rebate or other financial incentive given to buyers who also take the tied product; (3) technological design that makes it impossible to sell the tying product without the tied product.

§ 10.4a. Coercion by Contract, Condition, or Understanding

The term "coercion" seems clear enough. Coercion is at the heart of most exclusionary practices. As the Second Circuit stated most simply, "* * * there can be no illegal tie unless unlawful coercion by the seller influences the buyer's choice."[1] Nonetheless, the coercion doctrine has become beguiling in tie-in analysis.[2] The term "coercion" has been used by courts in tie-in cases to mean several things: 1) whether purchasers were actually forced to take the tied product as a condition of taking the tying product, or had the option of taking the tying product alone; 2) whether the defendant-seller had market power in the market for the tying product; 3) whether a particular purchaser would have taken the tied product anyway, and therefore was not injured by being "forced" to take it; 4) whether the tie-in foreclosed other options that the customer would have exercised but for the tying arrangement.

The first meaning of "coercion" is the correct one when we are considering whether two products are tied together. If a customer for item A is free to take or refuse item B as he pleases, there is no tie-in and there should be no liability. At the other extreme, if all purchasers of item A must also take item B there is coercion, or "conditioning," in this sense. In the middle are several possibilities. One, which arises often in class actions, concerns transactions that are individually negotiated by class members, some of whom received more pressure from the seller than others to take the tied product, depending on the economic position of each purchaser-class member. In such cases the fact of coercion must be established on an individual basis, and most courts have properly refused class action certification.[3]

Some courts infer coercion, or conditioning, from an explicit contractual provision requir-

73. See Eastman Kodak Co. v. Image Technical Services, Inc., 504 U.S. at 461, 112 S.Ct.at 2079 (1992):

> A tying arrangement is "an agreement by a party to sell one product but only on the condition that the buyer also purchases a different (or tied) product, or at least agrees that he will not purchase that product from any other supplier." [citation omitted] Such an arrangement violates § 1 of the Sherman Act if the seller has "appreciable economic power" in the tying product market and if the arrangement affects a substantial volume of commerce in the tied market.

Likewise, in his dissenting opinion Justice Scalia treated the issue as one of per se illegality. 504 U.S. at 486, 112 S.Ct. at 2092.

§ 10.4

1. American Mfrs. Mut. Ins. Co. v. American Broadcasting Paramount Theatres, Inc., 446 F.2d 1131, 1137 (2d Cir.1971), cert. denied, 404 U.S. 1063, 92 S.Ct. 737 (1972) (dismissing complaint; no pressure by defendant to take tied product). See 10 Antitrust Law ¶ 1753 (1996).

2. See J. Matheson, Class Action Tying Cases: A Framework for Certification Decisions, 76 Northwestern U.L.Rev. 855 (1982); D. Austin, The Individual Coercion Doctrine in Tie–In Analysis: Confusing and Irrelevant, 65 Calif.L.Rev. 1143 (1977).

3. Federal Rule of Civil Procedure 23(b)(3), which governs most class actions in antitrust cases, is generally interpreted to require that the "fact" of injury be established by common proof for all class members; otherwise certification is inappropriate. See 7A C. Wright, A. Miller, & M. K. Kane, Federal Practice and Procedure § 1778 (2d ed. 1986); Plekowski v. Ralston Purina Co., 68 F.R.D. 443, 449–51 (M.D.Ga.1975), appeal dismissed, 557 F.2d 1218 (5th Cir.1977); Matheson Id.; H. Hovenkamp, Tying Arrangements and Class Actions, 36 Vand.L.Rev. 213 (1983).

ing purchase of the tied product.[4] Other courts have refused to infer coercion if there is no such explicit contractual provision.[5] No basis exists in reason or economics, however, for the Sixth Circuit's broad rule that coercion, or conditioning is not "an element of an illegal tying arrangement" if the contract explicitly provides for the purchase of both tying and tied products. By that reasoning a contract to purchase "one thousand bolts and one thousand nuts" eliminates any need for the plaintiff to prove coercion, in spite of the fact that the plaintiff wanted to buy the nuts and bolts in the same transaction. The evidence in the Sixth Circuit case suggested as much.[6]

The second "coercion" question—whether the seller has market power in the tying product market—is a good one: a perfect competitor could not coerce any buyer into taking anything.[7] Although market power is a necessary condition for inefficient coercion, however, it is not a sufficient condition. A monopoly shoe seller who sells shoes only in pairs undoubtedly "coerces" the buyer of a right shoe to take a left shoe as well. That sale of shoes in pairs is not illegal for a monopolist, however, just as it is not illegal for a perfect competitor. Some courts have unwisely held that the seller's market power in the tying product creates a presumption of coercion.[8] In so doing they overlook the fact that even monopolists (and their customers) can profit from efficiency-creating package sales. Several courts have quite correctly held that market power in the tying product and "coercion" must be established separately.[9]

The third and fourth questions are closely related. They look at the tie-in from the buyer's side instead of from the seller's: conceding that the seller imposed the tie, must the buyer show that it was forced to take something it would not have taken anyway? Courts have disagreed about the need for such a showing. The Fifth Circuit has explicitly required it,[10] while the Sixth explicitly rejects the requirement.[11]

The Supreme Court probably put the issue to rest in Jefferson Parish Hosp. Dist. No. 2 v. Hyde, although its analysis is ambiguous.[12] The Court said that tying arrangements warrant condemnation when the seller has sufficient market power "to force a purchaser to do something that he would not do in a competitive market." Furthermore, condemnation would be warranted only if the tie restrains "competition on the merits by forcing purchases that would not otherwise be made." The Court then upheld the hospital-anesthesiologist tie, because there were several other hospitals in the market. As a result, a patient who wanted a different anesthesiologist than the one provided by the defendant could easily seek out an alternative. This analysis appears to preclude a tying claim when the plaintiff cannot show that at least some purchasers

4. Bogosian v. Gulf Oil Corp., 561 F.2d 434 (3d Cir. 1977), cert. denied, 434 U.S. 1086, 98 S.Ct. 1280 (1978) (if various station lessees can show similar lease provision that they must sell only defendant's gasoline, then coercion has been established.) Accord Little Caesar Enterp. v. Smith, 172 F.R.D. 236 (E.D.Mich.1997).

5. See CIA, Petrolera Caribe, Inc. v. Avis Rental Car Corp., 735 F.2d 636, 638 (1st Cir.1984); Moore v. Jas. H. Matthews & Co., 550 F.2d 1207, 1212 (9th Cir.1977), appeal after remand, 682 F.2d 830 (9th Cir.1982); Response of Carolina, Inc. v. Leasco Response, Inc., 537 F.2d 1307 (5th Cir.1976).

6. Bell v. Cherokee Aviation Corp., 660 F.2d 1123, 1131 (6th Cir.1981). See the well-reasoned dissent at pp. 1134–36, noting that nearly all customers preferred to purchase fuel and maintenance services from the company that stored their aircraft.

7. See § 10.3.

8. See Tire Sales Corp. v. Cities Serv. Oil Co., 410 F.Supp. 1222, 1227–29 (N.D.Ill.1976), reversed on other grounds, 637 F.2d 467 (7th Cir.1980), cert. denied, 451 U.S. 920, 101 S.Ct. 1999 (1981); Lessig v. Tidewater Oil Co., 327 F.2d 459, 469–70 (9th Cir.1964), cert. denied, 377 U.S. 993, 84 S.Ct. 1920 (1964). *Lessig* was overruled on other grounds by Spectrum Sports v. McQuillan, 506 U.S. 447, 113 S.Ct. 884, 892 (1993). See § 6.5.

9. Thompson v. Metropolitan Multi-List, Inc., 934 F.2d 1566, 1577 (11th Cir.1991), cert. denied, 506 U.S. 903, 113 S.Ct. 295 (1992) (separate proof of market power and coercion); Stephen Jay Photography, Ltd. v. Olan Mills, Inc., 903 F.2d 988, 991 (4th Cir.1990) (no coercion).

10. Response of Carolina, Inc. v. Leasco Response, Inc., 537 F.2d 1307, 1327 (5th Cir.1976); see also, Ungar v. Dunkin' Donuts of America, Inc., 531 F.2d 1211, 1218 (3d Cir.1976), cert. denied, 429 U.S. 823, 97 S.Ct. 74 (1976).

11. Bell v. Cherokee Aviation Corp., 660 F.2d 1123, 1131 (6th Cir.), cert. denied, 454 U.S. 860 (1981).

12. 466 U.S. 2, 12, 104 S.Ct. 1551, 1558–59 (1984).

took the tied product only because they were forced to.

Nevertheless, the *Jefferson Parish* suggestion that competition is restrained when a purchaser is forced to buy something he does not want is troublesome, and not well designed to identify truly anticompetitive arrangements. Production and distribution economies often dictate that at least some customers will have to purchase a package, whether they want it or not. For example, if 98% of all automobile purchasers want factory-installed car heaters while 2% do not, and the transaction costs of special treatment for 2% of the automobiles sold are high, the requirement is probably efficient. One way to get to this result is to conclude that the car and the heater are a single "product."[13] In this case a purchaser who would prefer not to have a heater certainly is being "coerced," but his loss is more than offset by the gains that accrue to other customers.

In addition to coercion, several courts require plaintiffs to show "anticompetitive effects" in the tied product market.[14] Once again, the precise meaning of "anticompetitive effects" is not always clear. Some cases suggest that there must be the threat that the seller will "acquire market power in the tied product market."[15] But such a requirement seems to be a castoff of the generally discredited "leverage" theory.[16] If the threat is the creation of market power in a second market, the law of attempt to monopolize would serve better.[17]

§ 10.4b. Proof of a Relevant Tying "Agreement;" Uncommunicated Conditions

Section 1 of the Sherman Act reaches tying arrangements only when there is a "contract," "combination," or "conspiracy."[18] Clayton Act § 3 requires a sale "on the condition, agreement, or understanding" that a tied product is required.[19] Suppose a seller simply refuses to sell to products separately, but will sell them together. Does the buy-sell agreement itself satisfy the requirement of a tying "agreement." Most courts say yes.[20] The act of coercion is not the agreement that results in an actual sale, but the refusal to sell one product without another.[21] The inference of a tie becomes even stronger if a buyer requested the tying good alone but was turned down, and later entered a contract covering both goods.[22]

A tie generally cannot be inferred from a completely uncommunicated condition if the seller sells to some buyers by contracts that include provision of the second product and by other contracts that do not so provide. The presumption of tying becomes stronger as the percentage of buyers who would prefer not to have the second product grows, and as the instance of contracts not covering the second product declines.[23] Likewise, courts often conclude that tying can be presumed when the defendant uses a form contract covering both products, particularly when it refuses to sell otherwise than by this form.[24] Significantly,

13. See § 10.5.

14. For example, Wells Real Estate, Inc. v. Greater Lowell Bd. of Realtors, 850 F.2d 803, 815 (1st Cir.), cert. denied, 488 U.S. 955, 109 S.Ct. 392 (1988); Hand v. Central Trans. Inc., 779 F.2d 8, 11 (6th Cir.1985), cert. denied, 475 U.S. 1129, 106 S.Ct. 1659 (1986).

15. Will v. Comprehensive Accounting Corp., 776 F.2d 665, 674 (7th Cir.1985), cert. denied, 475 U.S. 1129, 106 S.Ct. 1659 (1986). Some cases appear to assess the requirement only when the rule of reason is being applied. Grappone, Inc. v. Subaru of New England, Inc., 858 F.2d 792, 799 (1st Cir.1988); Parts & Elec. Motors, Inc. v. Sterling Elec., Inc., 826 F.2d 712, 720 (7th Cir.1987); Amey, Inc. v. Gulf Abstract & Title, Inc., 758 F.2d 1486, 1503 (11th Cir.1985), cert. denied, 475 U.S. 1107, 106 S.Ct. 1513 (1986).

16. See § 10.6a.

17. See Ch. 6.

18. 15 U.S.C.A. § 1.

19. 15 U.S.C.A. § 14.

20. E.g., Systemcare v. Wang Laboratories Corp., 117 F.3d 1137 (10th Cir.1997) (en banc) (overruling older Tenth Circuit decisions to the contrary).

21. See 10 Antitrust Law ¶ 1754 (1996).

22. See id. at ¶ 1756c.

23. See id., ¶ 1756.

24. See, e.g., IBM Corp. v. United States, 298 U.S. 131, 134, 56 S.Ct. 701 (1936) (apparent form contract requiring lessees of IBM's computers to use its tabulating cards); Photovest Corp. v. Fotomat Corp., 606 F.2d 704, 725 (7th Cir.1979), cert. denied, 445 U.S. 917, 100 S.Ct. 1278 (1980) ("express language in the [standard form] franchise agreement setting forth the condition constitutes a prima facie case" that the franchise was tied to the lease); Siegel v. Chicken Delight, 448 F.2d 43, 46 (9th Cir.1971), cert.

however, not even 100% bundling establishes tying conclusively. It may establish no more than that all customers want the two products together. For example, a shoe wholesaler may use a form contract that specifies "___ pairs of shoes," with the blank to be filled in for each purchase. As § 10.5 develops, universal bundling even in competitive markets generally indicates that the two goods are in fact a single product. Of course, a high bundling percentage has evidentiary significance because it shows that the seller is not making any sales except as a package. But the plaintiff would still have to show that at least some customers would have preferred the tying without the tied product.

§ 10.4c. *Package Discounts*

Another sort of conditioning occurs when the tie-in appears not as an absolute requirement, but as a discount or other favorable term to a customer who takes two products together. In such cases there is ample "coercion." If product A is $10.00 purchased alone but only $6.00 purchased with product B, coercion exists just as much as if all purchasers of A must also take B.[25] In any event, § 3 of the Clayton Act condemns tying not only when the defendant absolutely requires the purchaser to take the tied product, but also when it offers a "discount from, or rebate upon" the purchase price in exchange for tying.[26]

That rule is subject to one important qualification, however: if the discount is no greater than the additional cost of separate sales, then the discount itself must be regarded as noncoercive.[27] For example, buying an automobile as a "package" is much cheaper than buying individual parts and assembling them into an automobile, but the high price for the individual parts very likely reflects little more than the additional cost of inventorying, shipping and selling the parts one at a time rather than in a completed automobile.[28]

One important variation of the package discount is the "free" tied product. Suppose that a film manufacturer sells film with "free" mail-in processing, and refuses to sell at a lower price without the processing. This is simply a package discount in which the discount on the tied product is 100%—you can use the free processing envelope or throw it away, but the film price is the same. Such cases are properly analyzed as ties.[29]

§ 10.4d. *Coercion by Package Design; Technological Ties*

Forced package sales can also result from technological innovations that make joint production plus refusal to sell separately cheaper than separate production. The alleged tying arrangement in the *Times–Picayune* case is an early example.[30] The defendant was accused of refusing to sell classified advertising separately in its morning and evening newspapers. However, the record established that the newspaper set type once for the classified section of its morning and evening editions, thus

denied, 405 U.S. 955, 92 S.Ct. 1172 (1972) (standard form franchise agreement required that "franchises purchase [allegedly tied products] as a condition of obtaining a Chicken Delight trade-mark license [the allegedly tying product"); Aamco Automatic Transmissions v. Tayloe, 407 F.Supp. 430, 435 (E.D.Pa.1976) (stressing that required purchase of B was not subject of bargaining but was standard provision in form contract).

25. United States v. Loew's, Inc., 371 U.S. 38, 50, 83 S.Ct. 97, 104–105 (1962). See 10 Antitrust Law ¶ 1758 (1996).

26. 15 U.S.C.A. § 14.

27. However, not all courts recognize the qualification. For example Advance Business Sys. & Supply Co. v. SCM Corp., 415 F.2d 55, 62 (4th Cir.1969), cert. denied, 397 U.S. 920, 90 S.Ct. 928 (1970), appeared to assume that all package discounts are ties, whether or not cost savings were involved.

28. See 10 Antitrust Law ¶ 1758d (1996). See United States v. Loew's, Inc., 371 U.S. 38, 54–55, 83 S.Ct. 97 (1962) (modifying lower court's injunction to permit defendant to offer a package discount equal to the cost savings that bundling produced).

29. But see Marts v. Xerox, 77 F.3d 1109 (8th Cir. 1996), which incorrectly concluded that Xerox's requirement that its three-year photocopier warranty is valid only if the customer uses Xerox cartridges is not a tying arrangement because the customer can also get the maintenance service by simply paying for it. The service was free (under the terms of the warranty) only if the buyer accepted the tie. This is tantamount to saying that requirement that a customer take the seller's canary as a condition of buying its bird cage is not a tying arrangement because the buyer is free to let the canary go and purchase another.

30. Times–Picayune Pub. Co. v. United States, 345 U.S. 594, 73 S.Ct. 872 (1953).

saving considerable money. Further, once it did this the two sections were identical; so it could not offer some buyers the option of advertising in one edition but not the other.

For a long time the elements of electronic computers, such as central processing units and disk drives, were manufactured in separate boxes and connected to each other with cables. They could be sold separately, and were often sold by competing sellers. In the 1960's and 1970's IBM Corp. and others developed new computer technologies with more compact circuitry, combining the data processing unit, memory, and disk drives and their controllers in the same package. They necessarily were sold as a unit. The effect was to injure small companies that had been in the business of manufacturing only the peripheral devices for connection to IBM processing units.[31] In such cases the "tying arrangement" is not imposed contractually, but technologically. As a result, these arrangements have been dubbed "physical tie-ins." Courts have been skeptical about condemning such "tie-ins," noting that a rule prohibiting them could deter research and development.[32] No court could balance the social losses that a forced combination sale may impose against potential social gains. It must use short cuts and make inferences. Any demonstrated cost reduction that results from the way an arrangement of items is manufactured or sold should create an inference that the combination is a single product. Such "tie-ins" should generally be legal, even if the seller is a monopolist.[33]

True technological ties must be distinguished from assembled packages accompanied by contractual limitations on disassembly. The problem has arisen mainly in the computer software market. For example, Microsoft assembled its Windows 95/98 operating system and its Internet Explorer (IE) web browser into a single package and even interspersed the code so that the Windows operating system contains part of the browser code. However, a knowledgeable person could easily remove most of the IE code and files, as well as the IE browser icon from the Windows desktop, and then install a rival browser such as Netscape. The main objection to Microsoft's bundling of Windows and IE was not to the fact that Microsoft bundled them together in the first place, but rather that Microsoft had a contract with computer manufacturers that forbad them from de-installing IE and substituting a rival web browser. That requirement was a purely contractual tie, not a technological one.[34]

§ 10.5 The Requirement of Separate Tying and Tied Products

§ 10.5a. Introduction; Basic Competitive Market Test

A tying arrangement does not exist unless the defendant bundles "separate" tying and tied products, and generally refuses to sell the tying product without the tied product.[1] But

31. See ILC Peripherals Leasing Corp. v. IBM Corp., 448 F.Supp. 228 (N.D.Cal.1978), affirmed, 636 F.2d 1188 (9th Cir.1980), cert. denied, 452 U.S. 972, 101 S.Ct. 3126 (1981). Similar cases were brought as attempts to monopolize under § 2 of the Sherman Act, 15 U.S.C.A. § 2. See 3A Antitrust Law ¶ 776 (rev. ed. 1996).

32. See Foremost Pro Color v. Eastman Kodak Co., 703 F.2d 534 (9th Cir.1983), cert. denied, 465 U.S. 1038, 104 S.Ct. 1315 (1984), refusing to find an illegal tie-in in Kodak's introduction of a new camera and new film. Only the new Kodak film was compatible with the new camera, and the result was that purchasers of the new camera were required to use Kodak's film. However, purchasers of the new camera did not expressly "agree" to buy only Kodak film. The Ninth Circuit held that the law of tie-ins requires a sale of one product only on the contractual condition that the buyer take a second product as well. Further, it held that any rule condemning such "technological ties" could "unjustifiably deter the development and introduction of those new technologies so essential to the continued progress of our economy." Id. at 542–43. A technological tie-in could be used for price discrimination if the two goods were consumed in variable proportions. For example, if Kodak charged a monopoly price for the film, a serious photographer who used 10 rolls of film per week would be far more profitable to Kodak than a photographer who used only one roll per month. On tying and price discrimination, see § 10.6e. See also Note, An Economic and Legal Analysis of Physical Tie-ins, 89 Yale L.J. 769 (1980).

33. On technological ties and altered complementary products created by the monopolist, see § 7.8.

34. See United States v. Microsoft, 1998–2 Trade Cases ¶ 72,261, 1998 WL 614485 (D.D.C.1998) (denying defendant's motion for summary judgment).

§ 10.5

1. Or alternatively, charges a higher price when the tied product is not included. On package discounts, see § 10.4c.

determining when two products are "separate" has proven to be a vexing issue in hundreds of tying arrangement cases. Are a right shoe and a left shoe a single product or separate? what about a photocopier and its paper? A fountain pen and its ink? A computer and its hard drive? A Baskin–Robbins franchise contract and the ice cream that the franchisee sells?

Most forced package sales are the product of simple efficiency. For example, consumer retailing would come to a standstill if every purchaser were legally entitled to buy automobiles without tires or dressed geese without their gizzards. The competitive market is generally efficient in this manner; to the extent it is less costly to bundle things together under competitive conditions, competition forces them to be bundled together. For that reason shoes and gloves are sold almost exclusively in pairs, automobiles are universally sold with their tires, and personal computers are mainly sold with hard drives preinstalled. Importantly, there is no *technological* reason that these items cannot be packaged and sold separately; their combination is entirely a result of cost savings in the distribution or selling process.

Thus the basic test for tying: *the alleged tying and tied items are separate products if the tying item is commonly sold separately from the tied item in a well functioning market.*[2] Note that the relevant question is whether the tying product is commonly sold without the tied product under ordinary competitive conditions, not vice-versa. For example, one observing the automobile market generally sees that (1) automobiles are almost never sold without tires; but (2) tires are frequently sold without automobiles. The second statement is true because tires wear out more quickly than automobiles, and thus there is a significant aftermarket for replacement as well as some specialty tires. But under the basic test someone claiming that an automobile manufacturer or dealer unlawfully tied tires to cars would have to show that under ordinary competitive conditions cars are commonly sold without their tires. Failing this, there would be a single product and no tying arrangement.[3]

Thus *Jefferson Parish* concluded that whether "one or two products are involved" depends "on the character of the demand for the two items...."[4] And in *Kodak* the Supreme Court concluded that "for [photocopier] service and parts to be considered two distinct products, there must be sufficient consumer demand so that it is efficient for a firm to provide service separately from parts."[5]

The *Kodak* statement's inclusion of "efficiency" suggests a different type of analysis,

2. See 10 Antitrust Law ¶¶ 1744–1745 (1996). See also Multistate Legal Studies v. Harcourt Brace Jovanovich, 63 F.3d 1540, 1548 (10th Cir.1995), cert. denied, 516 U.S. 1044, 116 S.Ct. 702 (1996) (defendant tied multistate bar exam (MBE) course to its general bar review course; court finds question of fact "whether there is enough consumer demand in Colorado for full-service courses without supplemental MBE workshops to make it efficient to sell the two separately."); Souza v. Estate of Bishop, 821 F.2d 1332, 1335–(9th Cir.1987) (leased land and homes built on it a single product); Collins v. Associated Pathologists, Ltd., 844 F.2d 473 (7th Cir.), cert. denied, 488 U.S. 852, 109 S.Ct. 137 (1988) (hospital and pathologist a single product).

3. The contemporaneity of demand is therefore relevant. For example, since electric motors and replacement parts are required by customers at different times (the parts only after the motor breaks), courts find separate products for the two. Parts & Elec. Motors, Inc. v. Sterling, Inc., 826 F.2d 712, 720 (7th Cir.1987); Mozart Co. v. Mercedes–Benz of N. Am., 593 F.Supp. 1506, 1515 (N.D.Cal.1984), affirmed, 833 F.2d 1342 (9th Cir.1987), cert. denied, 488 U.S. 870, 109 S.Ct. 179 (1988).

4. Jefferson Parish Hosp. Dist. No. 2 v. Hyde, 466 U.S. 2, 19 104 S.Ct. 1551, 1562 (1984). The Court later explained that finding a tie of separate products in that case depended on "a sufficient demand for the purchase of anesthesiological services separate from hospital services to identify a distinct product market in which it is efficient to offer anesthesiological services separately from hospital services." But that seems to state the relationship incorrectly. The defendant hospital was accused of tying anesthesiological services (the tied product) to its hospital services. In that case, the relevant question should have been whether in a competitive market a hospital might offer surgical services without prepackaged anesthesia services. A yes answer would result if one could observe numerous situations in which hospitals simply gave anesthesiologists staff privileges, and permitted patients or their surgeons to select from alternative anesthesiologists. Accord SMS Sys. Maint. Svces. v. Digital Equip. Corp., ___ F.3d ___, 1999 WL 618046 (1st Cir.1999) (computers often sold separately from extended warranties).

5. Eastman Kodak Co. v. Image Technical Services, Inc., 504 U.S. 451, 462, 112 S.Ct. at 2072 (1992).

discussed infra in § 10.5e—namely, whether two things should be considered a single product when it is efficient to supply them together. But here, *Kodak* is using the term efficiency in a different way: the question is whether the market as a whole includes sufficient demand for parts without service that it is efficient for a firm to provide the parts separately. In the automobile example, the question would be whether there is sufficient demand for new automobiles without tires that it is efficient to provide them in that fashion. By contrast, the question in § 10.5e is whether a single product should be found when a particular firm finds a way to provide two products jointly at significantly lower cost (or with significantly higher quality) than under separate provision.[6]

The basic test of competitive market practices offers only one route to establishing that two items are in fact a single product. There are several others, as described next. Importantly, the defendant needs to establish that two items are a single product under only one of these separate products tests.

§ 10.5b. "New" Products

Often an innovation combines functions or features that had previously been sold separately. When this combination is the result of product design alone, the analysis for technological ties in § 10.4d applies. But in some cases the innovator will have to tie the innovated items by contract, presumably in order to ensure that they will work effectively together.

For example, in *Jerrold Electronics* the defendant had developed an early form of cable system using a large antenna, booster receivers, and cable connections going to numerous homes.[7] The items were physically separate, but the defendant would sell them only in complete installations. The court concluded that when this system was first introduced, knowledge about its assembly and operation was very limited, thus justifying Jerrold in insisting on package provision. For example, if the package contained items A, B, and C and pictures were fuzzy, the consumer might get lost in finger pointing, where the maker of A blamed the maker of B for the problem, and so on. The court concluded that during this early period the defendant could insist that it sell all the components, and not merely stipulate quality and specifications so that others could supply them as well.[8] However, once this introductory period was passed, this rationale no longer applied and the court found separate products.[9]

While the new product rationale makes sense, it invites two critical questions of fact: *first*, when is an amalgamation of formerly separate products really a "new" product, and when is it just plain tying? *second*, how long should a market dominating defendant be entitled to rely on the "new product" rationale for finding a single product?

On the first question, there has to be some reason for thinking that (a) the combination works better than separate provision; and (b) the consumer of the package cannot achieve the same result by combining the goods for him-or herself. That is to say, the combination works better when it is assembled by the seller than by the buyer.[10] The D.C. Circuit relied on this rationale in its 1998 *Microsoft* decision concluding that Windows 95 and Internet Explorer were a single product.[11] In that case Windows code and Internet Explorer code were interspersed in such a fashion that the same level of integration could not have been achieved either by computer manufacturers or by end users.[12] This fact is not particularly important in the software industry, however, where products can be reconfigured virtually any way the seller pleases. For example, Mi-

6. Lower court decisions are discussed in 10 Antitrust Law ¶ 1745 (1996).

7. United States v. Jerrold Electronics Corp., 187 F.Supp. 545 (E.D.Pa.1960), aff'd per curiam, 365 U.S. 567, 81 S.Ct. 755 (1961).

8. Id. at 559.

9. Id. at 560. See 10 Antitrust Law ¶ 1746 (1996).

10. See Id., ¶ 1746.

11. United States v. Microsoft, 147 F.3d 935, 953 (D.C.Cir.1998).

12. "Windows 95 is an example of what Professor Areeda calls" "physical or technological interlinkage that the customer cannot perform." Id. at 949, quoting 10 Antitrust Law ¶ 1746b.

crosoft can either offer Internet Explorer on a separate diskette, or else it can completely integrate the IE code into the Windows code in such a way that no one but a highly trained computer specialist could segregate the two. By contrast, in the *Jerrold* case the defendant could really show that the product package would not work as well if the consumer were permitted simply to substitute components and produce its own assemblage.

Second, how long should the new product rationale entitle a seller to insist that its formerly competing goods be sold as a package? *Jerrold* concluded only that bundling was acceptable during an "introductory" period in which market knowledge about the new assemblage was limited.[13] The court then concluded that this period had passed, and thereafter the arrangement was an unlawful tie. In *Microsoft* the D.C. Circuit ignored the issue, but since it found a single product on the "new product" rationale, it must havc assumed that the Windows/IE bundle was still in its "introductory" phase. In fact, however, the bundle had been on the market for several years, IE had attained a market share of the internet browser market on the order of 50 percent, and the evidence suggested that both computer manufacturers and end users could use alternative browsers such as Netscape without creating difficulties for the Windows system. This would suggest that the time period for asserting the "new product" rationale had expired.

§ 10.5c. Complete and Partial Substitutes as Separate Products

Unlawful tying has sometimes been alleged when the defendant offers quantity discounts. For example, in order to receive the lowest price the buyer must purchase at least 200 automobile engines.[14] The buyer then claims that the seller is unlawfully offering a discount[15] conditioned on the buyer's purchase of 199 unwanted engines (the tied product) in order to obtain the one that he wants (the tying product). But more of precisely the same thing has not been found to be a "separate" product.[16]

The problem is more complex when the two goods are imperfect substitutes. The tying of an established good to an emergent but potentially competing technology can enable a firm to move from one dominant market position to another. To illustrate, suppose that a firm has a dominant position in the market for CD–ROM drives for computers, but it has only a minor position in the emergent market for DVD drives, where there are several competitors. Although the market for DVD drives is new, it threatens to be a major rival for CD–ROM, in large part because a DVD disk holds about four times as much information as a CD–ROM disk. The dominant maker of CD–ROM drives then tells computer manufacturers that it will supply them with CD–ROM drives only if they agree to take its DVD drives exclusively. In this case the CD–ROM monopolist is trying to use the tying arrangement as a lever that will enable it to move from a dominant position in CD–ROM drives to a succeeding dominant position in DVD. That could undermine the chance for the new technology to be more competitive than the old technology. As a result, imperfect substitutes should be regarded as separate products, at least when there is a realistic threat that the dominant firm in product #1 can use its monopoly position to move into a dominant position in product #2.

Of course, not all tying of imperfect substitutes raises this problem. For example, a paint manufacturer might insist that its dealers handle both the manufacturer's latex (water-based) paints and its oil-based paints. The two paints are in fact imperfect substitutes, and there are some uses for which either will do. But if both types of paints are equally well established in the market, the manufacturer is probably doing no more than requiring its dealers to carry a full line.[17]

13. *Jerrold*, note 7 at 560.

14. See Reisner v. General Motors Corp., 671 F.2d 91, 100 (2d Cir.1982).

15. On discounts as tying, see § 10.4c.

16. See 10 Antitrust Law ¶ 1747b (1996).

17. On full-line forcing, see § 10.7b.

In its 1998 *Microsoft* decision,[18] the D.C. Circuit did not deal with the problem of imperfect substitutes. But the Internet Explorer browser may have been more than a complement to Windows; it may also have been a nascent substitute to the extent that a browser plus other software, such as JAVA, could lead to the creation of alternative operating systems that could compete with Windows. Or more likely, while Netscape plus JAVA did not themselves threaten to become a Windows substitute, they might serve as a link that would make other operating systems compatible with Windows. If the main reason that nearly all users of Intel-based computers use the Windows operating system is compatibility, an application that served to make rival operating systems compatible could turn Windows into one of many competing alternatives, thus upsetting its monopoly position. In that case, the court should find separate products.[19]

§ 10.5d. Intellectual Property and Labor as Separate Products

Several tying cases in franchise markets have alleged that the tying product was a trademark or copyright, and the tied product was various goods that the franchisee was required to sell. For example, a Baskin–Robbins franchisee is entitled to place trademarked Baskin–Robbins symbols on its store, but alleged tying may occur if it is required to purchase all of its ice cream from Baskin–Robbins as well. It might prefer to purchase significantly cheaper ice cream, while yet holding itself out as a Baskin–Robbins franchisee.[20]

If the trademark identifies the good itself as made by the manufacturer or made according to the manufacturer's specifications, then a single-product conclusion is required. For example, people may be willing to pay more for ice cream when they walk into a Baskin–Robbins ice cream store because they link the Baskin–Robbins name and symbols with the ice cream itself. In such cases, the franchisee is doing little more than asking the antitrust court to be a party to a kind of fraud, by permitting the franchisee to hold itself out as selling Baskin–Robbins when in fact it is not.[21]

A different outcome may seem appropriate when there is little or no connection between the trademark and the source or quality of the good to which it is attached. For example, a pizza franchisor may require the franchisee to take its pizza dough, even though the dough is completely indistinguishable from pizza dough generally and consumers did not attach any special value to the franchisor's particular dough.[22] In any event, the great majority of franchisors lack sufficient market power in the tying product to make their ties unlawful in the first place.[23]

The claim of labor as a tied product arises when a firm begins doing for itself something that it previously had purchased from others.[24] For example, suppose that a hospital formerly engaged an outside pathology group to perform its pathological services, but then hires its own pathologists and no longer permits any pathological services to be contracted out.[25] The now displaced external pathologists claim

18. See note 11.

19. See also 10 Antitrust Law ¶ 1747c. (1996).

20. See, e.g., Krehl v. Baskin–Robbins Ice Cream Co., 664 F.2d 1348 (9th Cir.1982) (trademark and ice cream a single product).

21. See 10 Antitrust Law ¶ 1749a1 (1996).

22. E.g., Siegel v. Chicken Delight, 448 F.2d 43, 51–52 (9th Cir.1971), cert. denied, 405 U.S. 955, 92 S.Ct. 1172 (1972) (generic herbs and paper products were separate product). See also Midwestern Waffles v. Waffle House, 734 F.2d 705, 712 (11th Cir.1984) (franchisor's vending machines that franchisee was required to use in restaurant lobby not integral part of franchisor's system and product; thus a separate product).

In a third type of franchise the *franchisee* produces the product, according to detailed specifications provided by the franchisor. Products as diverse as mattresses and soft drinks are manufactured under such arrangements. See United States v. Sealy, Inc., 388 U.S. 350, 87 S.Ct. 1847 (1967); Sulmeyer v. Coca Cola Co., 515 F.2d 835 (5th Cir.1975), cert. denied, 424 U.S. 934, 96 S.Ct. 1148 (1976).

23. See § 10.3b.

24. See § 9.2; and R. Coase, The Nature of the Firm, 4 Economica (n.s.) 386 (1937), which defines the firm in terms of what the firm does internally, as opposed to what it purchases from others.

25. Collins v. Associated Pathologists, 844 F.2d 473 (7th Cir.), cert. denied, 488 U.S. 852, 109 S.Ct. 137 (1988); Drs. Steuer & Lathan v. Natl. Medical Enterp., 672 F.Supp. 1489 (D.S.C.1987), aff'd mem., 846 F.2d 70 (4th Cir.1988).

that the hospital is "tying" its hospital services to its pathology services.[26] If *only* labor is involved, then a single product conclusion seems inescapable: the defendant is merely terminating a contract with an independent entity and substituting a contract with an employee. By contrast, if the new laborers are manufacturing a distinctive product that is tied as well, then traditional tying criteria would control. For example, the photocopier manufacturer might hire a group of employees for its new paper mill and thereafter require purchasers of the photocopier to take its paper, but this would not be a tie of the labor alone, but of a distinct physical product, the paper itself.

§ 10.5e. Efficiency—"Economies of Joint Provision"

One obvious defense to a tying arrangement is that joint provision is cheaper than separate provision. The efficiencies generated by forced combined sales can be broadly grouped into two kinds, transactional, and productive or technological.[27] The sale of shoes only in pairs is a good example of a transactional efficiency. Presumably shoes cannot be manufactured more cheaply in pairs than by the piece. However, they probably can be distributed and sold far more cheaply in pairs. If a store had to offer a solitary left shoe to the occasional customer who wanted one it would be stuck with the right shoe, and a very long wait until another customer came along who wanted only a right shoe of the same size and style. The shoe store would probably return it or order a new mate for it. If the additional costs generated by these extra maneuvers are greater than half the cost of a pair of shoes, it would be more efficient to force the one-legged purchaser to take a pair, even if he throws the left shoe away. If the purchaser were legally entitled to take a single left shoe at half the price of a pair, however, any added transaction costs would be shared by all other customers. Collectively they would be injured by a greater amount than the one-footed purchaser would be benefitted.

In *Times–Picayune* the Supreme Court permitted a newspaper to require advertisers to buy space in both its morning and evening newspapers simultaneously. Advertising in the two was found to be a single product, which Justice Clark identified as "readership."[28] While that conclusion was not particularly enlightening, Justice Clark also noted that when the sale of morning and evening advertising was combined into a single transaction, most of the costs of running an advertisement—soliciting, billing and setting type—were performed only once instead of twice. The newspaper could lower the cost of advertising by running identical advertising sections in its morning and evening newspapers.[29] In his dissenting opinion in *Fortner* fifteen years later, Justice White made a similar observation: "if the tied and tying products are functionally related, they may reduce costs through economies of joint production and distribution."[30] And in her *Jefferson Parish* concurrence, Justice O'Connor concluded that "When the economic advantages of joint packaging are substantial the package is not appropriately viewed as two products, and that should be the end of the tying inquiry."[31] Judge Posner has

26. See 10 Antitrust Law ¶ 1748c (1996).

27. Importantly, the Coase Theorem predicts that two firms will bargain their way to a joint-maximizing result, which means that they will minimize transaction costs as well as production costs. See R. Coase, The Problem of Social Cost, 3 J.L. & Econ. 1 (1960). See § 9.2. Bargained for ties that have no negative impact on third parties are probably efficient even if there are no obvious gains in productive efficiency.On this point, see G. Calabresi, The Pointlessness of Pareto: Carrying Coase Further, 100 Yale L.J. 1211 (1991).

28. Times–Picayune Pub. Co. v. United States, 345 U.S. 594, 613, 73 S.Ct. 872, 883 (1953).

29. Id.

30. Fortner Enter., Inc. v. United States Steel Corp., (Fortner I), 394 U.S. 495, 514 n. 9, 89 S.Ct. 1252, 1264 n. 9 (1969), (J. White, dissenting).

31. Jefferson Parish Hosp. Dist. No. 2 v. Hyde, 466 U.S. 2, 40–41, 104 S.Ct. 1551, 1573 (1984) (O'Connor, J., concurring). However, Justice O'Connor went on to conclude that "since anesthesia [the alleged tied product] is a service useful to consumers only when purchased in conjunction with hospital services [the tying product], the arrangement is not properly characterized as a tie between distinct products." But under this rule all package sales of complementary products (products that must be consumed together) would be viewed as sales of single products. Justice O'Connor's proposal would effectively wipe out three-fourths of the law of tying arrangements, for most

also concluded that two items should be considered a single product if there were "rather obvious economies of joint provision."[32]

Nevertheless, the five-Justice *Jefferson Parish* majority appeared to reject the idea that the efficiency of joint provision could justify finding a single product. It concluded that whether separate products exist depends "not on the functional relation between" the two items, but rather "on the character of the demand" for them.[33]

In defense of the majority's position, efficiency considerations can be dealt with by other means than the separate product test. Most obviously, one might find separate products by considering whether the items are sold separately in a competitive market, but then permit economies of joint provision to be shown as a defense. One would then have to balance the degree of competitive harm against the magnitude of any cost savings, but some kind of weight would have to be attached to efficiencies no matter what stage of the inquiry we consider them.

The O'Connor/Posner requirement of "rather obvious economies" seems to be a sensible single-product test, although one would want to interpret the phrase to mean "rather obvious and significant economies." That is to say, a provable and significant efficiency serves to undermine the plaintiff's prima facie case rather than merely warranting consideration as a defense to a presumptively unlawful arrangement. The law of monopolization under § 2 of the Sherman Act takes a similar approach, permitting even an absolute monopolist to create technological innovations that bundle formerly separate products, provided that there is a good business justification for the bundling.[34] An obvious and significant cost savings is clearly such a justification. There is no obvious reason that contractual ties should be treated any differently. If a defendant can point to obvious and significant economies of joint provision—such as the need to set type only once in the *Times-Picayune* case—then it should be unnecessary to complete the tying inquiry by defining a relevant market and proving market power in the tying product.

§ 10.6 Perceived Effects on Competition

As noted previously, the judicial test for the illegality of tying arrangements does not explain how ties affect competition. As a result, tie-ins have often been condemned by courts that apparently did not understand the economic function of the arrangement in the defendant's distribution scheme. Furthermore, judicial records were often developed without much concern for exploring actual economic effects. If tying doctrine is to be rationalized, however, economic effects must be explored. This Section looks at the major theories that have been presented to explain why firms use tying arrangements.

§ 10.6a. The Leverage Theory: Using Tie-Ins to Turn One Monopoly Into Two; Tipping

The leverage theory is the oldest theory under which tie-ins have been condemned. Under the theory, a seller who has a monopoly in one product, which is often patented, uses a tie-in to create a "limited" monopoly in a second product that is essential to the use of the tying product. Suppose that a seller has a patent monopoly in a freezer that preserves ice cream in transit better than any competing technology. The freezer requires solid carbon dioxide ("dry ice"), a common chemical, as a refrigerant. The seller requires all purchasers of its freezer to buy its carbon dioxide as well, and effectively corners the market for the carbon dioxide used in its freezers. In condemn-

involve complimentary products: for example, IBM v. United States, 298 U.S. 131, 56 S.Ct. 701 (1936) (computers and computer cards); International Salt Co. v. United States, 332 U.S. 392, 68 S.Ct. 12 (1947) (salt injecting machines and salt).

32. Jack Walters & Sons Corp. v. Morton Bldg., Inc., 737 F.2d 698, 703 (7th Cir.1984). The court concluded that a manufacturer's prefabricated building kits and its trademark were not separate products.

33. *Jefferson Parish*, note 31 at 19.

34. See §§ 7.5—7.6.

ing this arrangement Justice Brandeis wrote in 1931 that it permitted

> the patent-owner to "derive its profit, not from the invention on which the law gives it a monopoly, but from the unpatented supplies with which it is used" [and which are] "wholly without the scope of the patent monopoly" * * *. If a monopoly could be so expanded, the owner of a patent for a product might conceivably monopolize the commerce in a large part of the unpatented materials used in its manufacture. The owner of a patent for a machine might thereby secure a partial monopoly on the unpatented supplies consumed in its operation.[1]

The perceived evils of tie-ins under the leverage theory are twofold. First, the seller can make two monopoly profits and force consumers to pay even more for products than if there were only one monopoly. Second, by creating a monopoly in a second product, the monopolist in the tying product can drive other producers of the tied product out of business, or at least foreclose them from part of the market.

Such "leveraging" is not a plausible way to increase monopoly profits. Suppose that seller A has a monopoly in a patented glass jar. Each jar requires one lid, but the lids are not patented and are manufactured by many competitors. A produces jars for $1.00, but she sells them at $1.50, which is her profit-maximizing price. The competitive price of lids is 30¢.

A decides to manufacture lids herself and sell a jar and a lid as a package. What is A's profit-maximizing price for the package? The answer, quite clearly, is $1.80. A's computation of her profit-maximizing price for jars as $1.50 was *predicated* on the fact that lids were sold for 30¢. Since every jar must have a lid, buyers place a certain value on the package. Someone who buys a jar and a lid for $1.80 is generally indifferent whether the price is $1.00 for the jar and 80¢ for the lid, or $1.50 for the jar and 30¢ for a lid. As long as the proportion of jars to lids is constant the purchaser will attribute a price change in either to the price of the entire package. A monopolist of either jars or lids can extract all available monopoly profits from the sale of jars with lids. The jar monopolist cannot make any more monopoly profits by monopolizing the lid market as well.[2]

The leverage theory does not successfully explain how a seller can enlarge its monopoly profits by means of a tie-in. In fact, the jar monopolist is best off when lids are sold at the lowest price, for a lower lid price will increase the profit-maximizing price of the jars. If an efficient lid producer can sell lids for 28¢ the jarmaker will be better off: the profit-maximizing price of jars will rise by 2¢. Conversely, if the jarmaker made lids but was less efficient than its competitors, a tie-in would actually cost it money. Suppose that the jar monopolist makes lids, but because of an obsolete plant or other production inefficiencies its costs are 35¢. Most purchasers refuse to buy lids from the jar monopolist at 35¢ when they can obtain them elsewhere at 30¢. The jar monopolist hits

§ 10.6

1. Carbice Corp. of Amer. v. American Patents Development Corp., 283 U.S. 27, 31–32, 51 S.Ct. 334, 335–36 (1931). See also Fortner Enterprises v. U.S. Steel (*Fortner I*), 394 U.S. 495, 498–99, 89 S.Ct. 1252, 1256 (1969): "[tying arrangements] deny competitors free access to the market for the tied product, not because the party imposing the tying requirements has a better product or a lower price but because of his power or leverage in another market."; Motion Picture Patents Co. v. Universal Film Mfg. Co., 243 U.S. 502, 37 S.Ct. 416 (1917); International Salt Co. v. United States, 332 U.S. 392, 68 S.Ct. 12 (1947); IBM Corp. v. United States, 298 U.S. 131, 56 S.Ct. 701 (1936); and see Jefferson Parish Hosp. Dist. No. 2 v. Hyde, 466 U.S. 2, 36, 104 S.Ct. 1551, 1571 (1984): "Tying may be economically harmful primarily in the rare cases where power in the market for the tying product is used to create additional market power in the market for the tied product." (J. O'Connor, concurring). See generally W. Bowman, Jr., Patent and Antitrust Law—A Legal and Economic Appraisal 100–153 (1973).

2. This analysis assumes that the lids are being sold competitively. Suppose, however, that lids are sold by a monopolist or cartel for 50¢, 20¢ more than the competitive price. Since the profit-maximizing price of a jar-lid package is $1.80, the effect of the monopoly price in lids is to reduce the profit-maximizing price of jars. There are still 50¢ worth of monopoly profits in the market for jars with lids, but only 30¢ of those profits accrue to the jarmaker. By manufacturing lids and selling them herself the jar monopolist will be able to transfer this 20¢ in monopoly profits to herself.

upon a scheme, however: she will force purchasers of her jars to take her lids as well.

The scheme, far from being profitable, will reduce profits by 5¢ on each sale. Since the profit-maximizing price of a jar-with-a-lid remains constant, the jarmaker can force purchasers to take a 35¢ lid instead of a 30¢ lid and maintain her revenues only by reducing the price of jars by 5¢. The additional 5¢ in the lid price is not profit to the monopolist, however, because it is eaten up in the production inefficiencies. If the jar monopolist cannot manufacture lids as efficiently as its competitors, it would be better off to get rid of its lid factory and leave the lid market to more efficient producers.

The theory that a monopoly seller can use a tie-in to enlarge current monopoly profits has been condemned repeatedly by commentators for four decades.[3] In a few judicial opinions judges have also noted the implausibility of the leverage theory.[4] But a few court continue to rely on the theory to condemn a tying arrangement.[5]

Some variations on the leverage theory may be economically defensible. Fixed proportion ties (where the proportion of the tying and tied product are specified by the seller) may occasionally reduce the cross-elasticity of substitution for certain products. Suppose—to adapt a few facts from the *Kodak* case[6]—that a seller has monopoly power in various repair parts used in high-tech equipment. It sells these parts to equipment owners who combine them with technicians' service, which is principally labor. For the equipment owners, the repairs parts and the service labor are complementary products whose proportions can be varied up to a degree. That is, as parts become more expensive, it becomes cost effective for technicians to spend more time refurbishing or repairing the old parts. For example, if labor costs $20 per hour and a part is competitively priced at $100, a firm would not order a technician to repair the old part if the repair was estimated to take six hours. It would be cheaper to throw the old part away and buy a new one. But if the part price increased to a monopoly level of $130, the repair would be cost justified. In general, firms that are capable of varying the proportions of inputs can be expected to respond to monopoly pricing by using relatively less of the monopoly priced good and relatively more of some substitute. Photocopier users would therefore respond to Kodak's monopoly price in parts by using relatively more labor and relatively fewer parts.

Kodak can solve this problem by tying parts to labor and deciding the proportion for itself. That is, if it sells its parts only with its own labor, then it will restore the mixture to its profit-maximizing level. This is in fact a kind of leverage: Kodak is using its market power in parts to reduce the demand for labor, thus "monopolizing" the labor market.

Is this parts-labor tie economically inefficient? Not necessarily. The tie very likely restores the balance of parts and labor to the competitive balance—that is, since Kodak becomes the producer of both the parts and the labor, it maximizes its returns by using them in the optimal mixture. So on one view, the mixture of inputs that the equipment owner purchases is more efficient than it would be under monopoly without tying. But offsetting this is the fact that Kodak is increasing the amount of its monopoly power in parts by making it more difficult for machine owners to substitute service for parts. The restoration to the optimal mixture of parts and labor is a productive efficiency gain; but the enhancement of market power in parts is an allocative efficiency loss. The net efficiency of the practice depends on which efficiency effect is larg-

3. For example, see W. Bowman, Tying Arrangements and the Leverage Problem, 67 Yale L.J. 19 (1957); R. Markovits, Tie-ins, Leverage, and the American Antitrust Laws, 80 Yale L.J. 195 (1970).

4. For example, Hirsh v. Martindale–Hubbell, Inc., 674 F.2d 1343, 1349 n. 19 (9th Cir.1982), cert. denied, 459 U.S. 973, 103 S.Ct. 305 (1982).

5. For example, Smith Mach. Co. v. Hesston Corp., 1987–1 Trade Cas. (CCH) ¶ 67563 at 60,383, 1987 WL 14498 (D.N.M.1987), affirmed, 878 F.2d 1290 (10th Cir. 1989), cert. denied, 493 U.S. 1073, 110 S.Ct. 1119 (1990); Sandles v. Ruben, 89 F.R.D. 635 (S.D.Fla.1981); Martino v. McDonald's Sys., 86 F.R.D. 145 (N.D.Ill.1980).

6. Eastman Kodak Co. v. Image Technical Services, Inc., 504 U.S. 451, 112 S.Ct. 2072 (1992). See § 10.3b.

er.[7]

A much more plausible conception of leverage arises when the monopolies are consecutive rather than simultaneous. The previous discussion of imperfect substitutes as separate products[8] used the example of CD–ROM and DVD technology. The defendant has a monopoly position in the current technology, CD–ROM; but the incipient technology that will likely replace CD–ROM, is competitive. As a result, the defendant faces the prospect that its monopoly position will be lost. It then responds by attempting to "tip" the market in its favor. In this case, it ties its dominant CD–ROM technology to the incipient DVD technology by requiring computer manufacturers wishing to install its market dominating CD–ROMs to use its DVDs as well. The anticompetitive consequences of Microsoft's Windows/Internet Explorer (IE) tie vary depending on whether one regards IE as a complementary product or as a potentially rival technology. If the latter, then the tie could ensure that as computer users pass from Windows based systems to systems in which computer applications are delivered over the internet, Microsoft will retain its dominant position.[9] The reason such theories are plausible while the general leverage theory is not is that the monopolies are successive rather than simultaneous. First the defendant obtains a monopoly in the prior technology; then it uses the tie-in to leverage a second monopoly in the successor technology.

§ 10.6b. Entry Barriers, Foreclosure, and Collusion

§ 10.6b1. Entry Barriers and Tying Arrangements

Tying arrangements may raise entry barriers in the market for either the tying or the tied product. For example, suppose a newspaper company publishes both a morning newspaper and an evening newspaper. A second firm attempts to enter the market with an evening newspaper. The incumbent firm responds by engaging in "unit pricing": requiring all purchasers of advertising in its morning paper to buy an identical advertisement in the evening paper. The unit pricing scheme will foreclose the new entrant from advertisers who want to advertise in the morning, because they will be required to place their evening advertising in the incumbent's evening newspaper instead of the competitor's.[10]

Many tying arrangement cases in which the plaintiff and defendant are competitors are brought under a foreclosure theory like this one. In Heatransfer Corp. v. Volkswagenwerk, A.G.,[11] the Fifth Circuit condemned an arrangement under which an automobile manufacturer required its distributors and retail dealers to use their "best efforts" to sell Volkswagen's own air conditioners rather than those of competitors, which included the plaintiff. The Fifth Circuit decided that the plaintiff, which manufactured air conditioners suitable for installation in new Volkswagens, was unlawfully foreclosed from the market for "Volkswagen air conditioners."

The theory that tying arrangements raise barriers to entry is generally susceptible of the same criticisms that can be raised against all "entry barrier" arguments: namely, the fact that something is an entry barrier says nothing about whether it is socially harmful or beneficial.[12] Efficiency itself is a remarkably strong barrier to entry. Suppose the daily newspaper can show that by forcing all adver-

7. See R. Blair & D. Kaserman, Vertical Integration, Tying, and Alternative Vertical Control Mechanisms, 20 Conn. L.Rev. 523, 529–530, 538–540 (1988).

8. See § 10.5c.

9. At this writing, these possibilities have not been fully developed in the litigation, but they are considered in the secondary literature. See, e.g., M. A. Lemley & D. McGowan, Legal Implications of Network Economic Effects, 86 Calif. L. Rev. 479 (1998); M. L. Katz & C. Shapiro, Network Externalities, Competition, and Compatibility, 75 Am. Econ. Rev. 424 (1985).

10. See Times–Picayune Pub. Co. v. United States, 345 United States 594, 345 U.S. 594, 73 S.Ct. 872 (1953); Kansas City Star Co. v. United States, 240 F.2d 643 (8th Cir.1957), cert. denied, 354 U.S. 923, 77 S.Ct. 1381 (1957). See D. Turner, The Validity of Tying Arrangements Under the Antitrust Laws, 72 Harv.L.Rev. 50, 63 (1958).

11. 553 F.2d 964 (5th Cir.1977), cert. denied, 434 U.S. 1087, 98 S.Ct. 1282 (1978).

12. See H. Demsetz, Barriers to Entry, 72 Amer.Econ. Rev. 47 (1982); R. Schmalensee, Economies of Scale and Barriers to Entry, 89 J.Pol.Econ. 1228 (1981). And see § 1.6.

tisers to buy space in both morning and evening newspapers it can print identical advertising sections in the two newspapers and thereby set type once instead of twice. The largest cost of running an advertisement is the cost of setting the type. The cost saving can be realized, however, only if *all* purchasers of advertising advertise in both the morning and evening editions. Unit pricing may permit the incumbent to sell an advertisement in both newspapers together for $7.00, while the potential entrant must charge $5.00 for the evening advertising alone. The "barrier to entry" results from the lower cost of the unit pricing scheme.[13]

If the tie-in is inefficient, no barrier to entry will result. Suppose that a monopoly manufacturer of bolts requires customers to purchase one nut with each bolt. Bolts would sell in a competitive market for 25¢, and nuts for 10¢. Because of inefficiencies in production, however, the seller must charge 38¢ for the package. Entry barriers will not increase. An efficient bolt manufacturer can still enter the bolt market alone, as can an efficient nut manufacturer. If the bolt monopolist's tie reduces the cost of a bolt-nut package, then a single entrant will have to enter both the bolt market and nut market simultaneously in order to be competitive. But even here, the mere requirement of two-level entry is not a "barrier" unless economies of scale are substantially different at one level than at the other.[14]

The entry barrier argument may have force, however, when economies of scale or other impediments forbid entry or make it more difficult. The classic example is the seller who is a statutory monopolist and ties a product which does not have legal monopoly protection. For example, the telephone company, which has a legally protected monopoly in its lines, may require all lessees of its lines to rent a telephone instrument from the telephone company as well. The result will be to create an effective barrier to entry into the market for the tied product. Such a scheme will be profitable to the telephone company if it can use it to "cheat" on its regulated price.[15]

§ 10.6b2. Foreclosure; Market Share

Jefferson Parish shifted the emphasis in tying cases away from leverage and toward foreclosure, or the degree to which a tie-in denies market access to rivals.[16] This shift in emphasis also turns the appropriate market "power" inquiry into one concerning market *share*. That is, when the challenged anticompetitive effect is foreclosure we want to know something about the *coverage* of the restraint, not necessarily about the short-run ability of the seller to set prices above the competitive level. This entails that when the alleged harm is foreclosure, basing market share on a patent or trademark makes even less sense than it does in the more general run of tying cases.[17]

The foreclosure and entry barrier concerns are closely related, although foreclosure applies to existing firms as well as prospective entrants. The real foreclosure threat is that the tie might facilitate single firm dominance or oligopoly by denying market access to more aggressive competitors or potential entrants. As the previous examples suggest, entry barriers are not likely to arise in the ordinary case of tying. There must be some economy of scale or other impediment that prevents entry at one market level, and thus which could restrain competition at a second level if the two were joined by a tie. Foreclose occurs only under analogous circumstances; a tie that forecloses a large percentage of the market is not anticompetitive if entry into both the tying and tied product markets is easy. When entry is difficult, however, the concerns are real. For example, the patent monopolist of can-filling machinery might require lessees of its machinery to take its cans. In the process, rival can makers may be driven out of business or de-

13. See Record at 1127–29, *Times–Picayune*, note 10.

14. The tying arrangement in this case would have the same effect as vertical integration by the monopolist. See § 9.2c.

15. See § 10.6c.

16. Jefferson Parish Hosp. Dist. No. 2 v. Hyde, 466 U.S. 2, 41–42, 104 S.Ct. 1551, 1573 (1984).

17. See § 10.3c.

nied an opportunity to expand their sales.[18] Dominance in the can market could also retard innovation there. These threats may be measured most directly, first by ensuring that entry barriers into at least one of the tied levels are significant; and second by looking at the percentage of the can market that is foreclosed by the tie.

§ 10.6b3. Tie-Ins and Collusion

Tie-ins might make collusion or oligopoly pricing more stable or more likely to succeed.[19] For example, the tying arrangements in the *Northern Pacific*[20] and *International Salt*[21] cases required the purchaser to take the tied product or service only if no other seller was selling it cheaper. In such cases the seller could not have been attempting to leverage one monopoly into two, for the clause effectively required the tied product to be sold at the market price.

But what if the market price were not competitive. Suppose that in *Northern Pacific* the railroads were fixing freight rates and were concerned about cheating—a widespread phenomenon under railroad collusion.[22] Individual railroads then sell land and require land owners to use their own railroads for shipment if no one else undercuts the price. By this arrangement, the railroad can detect cartel cheating because it will be reported by the customer. If a customer goes elsewhere, he is either breaking the tying contract to no advantage of his own, or else another railroad is cheating on the cartel.[23]

Tying arrangements may also enable a cartel member to enlarge its market share at the cartel price. As § 4.1 notes, when a firm is fixing prices its marginal revenue is larger than its marginal costs. As a result, the cartel member has an incentive to find opportunities to make extra sales at the cartel price. If the cartel member operates in a vertically related market, it may use a tying arrangement. Once again, the railroads in *Northern Pacific* may have been fixing freight *rates*, but they were not taking any steps to limit individual cartel member output. In that case, a railroad that operates in a related market might be able to enlarge its own output at the cartel price, by requiring the purchaser in the related market—in this case, farm land—to take the cartelized product or service as well. The railroad would be selling the freight at what appears to be the going market price, and still be making excess profits. Customers, not knowing of the cartel, would presumably be indifferent between buying one railroad's freight or another's, assuming that the services are identical and the price is the same. This amounts to a version of the leverage theory that actually works, because the cartel member has marginal revenues larger than its marginal costs.[24]

Developing an antitrust policy for tie-ins that takes collusion into account is not easy, given that tie-ins can be efficient. Nevertheless, a few generalizations are possible. First of all, a horizontal agreement among competitors to use tie-ins is probably illegal *per se*, particularly if it appears to be a naked arrangement designed to bolster a price-fixing scheme.

If the antitrust enforcers cannot find the horizontal agreement to use the tying arrangement, then the arrangement might be considered in the same way as cartel facilitators generally, and certain questions emerge. Is the market concentrated and conducive to collusion? Is the arrangement being used by all (or at least most) of the firms in the market? Challenges to collusion facilitators in the absence of a horizontal agreement have not been particularly successful, under either the Sherman Act or the Federal Trade Commission

18. The illustration comes from 9 Antitrust Law ¶ 1700 at 7 (1991).

19. On collusion generally, see §§ 4.4–4.6.

20. Northern Pacific Rwy. v. United States, 356 U.S. 1, 6, 78 S.Ct. 514, 518 (1958).

21. International Salt Co. v. United States, 332 U.S. 392, 68 S.Ct. 12 (1947).

22. See H. Hovenkamp, Enterprise and American Law, 1836–1937 at 145–147 (1991).

23. See F.J. Cummings & W.E. Ruhter, The *Northern Pacific* Case, 22 J.L. & Econ. 329 (1979).

24. That is to say, since the cartel member's marginal revenue exceeds its marginal cost, additional sales at the cartelized price produces additional monopoly profits, until output increases so much that MR = MC.

Act.[25] The more aggressive language of § 3 of the Clayton Act, which condemns tying arrangements whose effect "may be to substantially lessen competition or tend to create a monopoly"[26] seems sufficient for this purpose. The same language operates in Clayton § 7's condemnation of mergers, and we regularly condemn mergers on the theory that they will facilitate collusion without requiring an actual horizontal agreement among market participants.[27]

But always lurking in the background should be our knowledge that most tying arrangements are competitive. Further, efficient practices tend to be copied by other firms in the market. As a result, widespread use of a tying arrangement in a concentrated market may tell us no more than that the arrangement was used by one firm, was thought by others to be a good idea and copied by them as well, lest they lose market share to the innovator. Use of § 3 to condemn arrangements such as these would be inefficient overreaching unless the court was quite sure that the arrangement was operating principally as a collusion facilitator.

§ 10.6c. *Evasion of Rate Regulation*

Many firms are required by law to sell their products or services at a specified price. The price is usually calculated by a public regulatory agency to give the firm a "fair" rate of return on the basis of information provided by the firm itself.[28]

Price-regulated firms generally have stockholders, pay dividends, and seek to maximize their profits. Sometimes they can increase their profits by avoiding the price regulation. If the regulated price is lower than the unregulated profit-maximizing price, as is often the case in public utilities, then the seller may tie an unregulated product or service to the regulated one. If the regulated price is higher than the unregulated profit-maximizing price, as was the case during price regulation of airline fares, then the seller may try to avoid the price regulation by throwing in some additional good or service at less than its market value.

Most litigated tie-in cases in price-regulated industries have been of the first sort: the tie-in acts as a "leverage" device to enable the seller to obtain more net profit than the price regulation would permit. For example, if the profit-maximizing price of a monthly telephone line subscription is $12.00, but a regulatory authority limits the phone company's price to $8.00, the telephone company might require all lessees of its lines to rent their equipment from the phone company as well, and build a $4.00 monopoly overcharge into the price of the equipment. In this case a version of the leverage theory works: the phone company makes more profits by adding an unregulated monopoly to a regulated monopoly and thereby evading the regulation.[29] Leveraging works in this situation because at the regulated price the firm's marginal costs are substantially less than its marginal revenue.

Public utilities are ideal candidates for such tying arrangements. First, most of them are natural monopolies, or are thought to be. Their monopoly status is often protected by statute. Second, most public utilities have very low marginal costs and very low elasticities of demand at a marginal cost price. Most people would be willing to pay considerably more for electricity and telephone service than the marginal cost of providing it. The result is that the profit-maximizing price for a telephone or electricity subscription is often much higher than the regulated price.

Tie-ins in price-regulated monopolies can injure two groups of people: competitors and

25. See § 4.6.

26. 15 U.S.C.A. § 14.

27. See § 12.1. Likewise, the Supreme Court has suggested that primary-line Robinson–Patman violations might be used to shore up an oligopoly. The Robinson–Patman Act uses about the same "lessen competition" language as § 3 of the Clayton Act. See Brooke Group Ltd. v. Brown & Williamson Tobacco Corp., 509 U.S. 209, 113 S.Ct. 2578 (1993), discussed at § 8.8.

28. See generally S. Breyer, Regulation and its Reform (1982).

29. See Litton Systems, Inc. v. American Tel. & Tel. Co., 700 F.2d 785, 790–91 (2d Cir.1983), cert. denied, 464 U.S. 1073, 104 S.Ct. 984 (1984); Cantor v. Detroit Edison Co., 428 U.S. 579, 96 S.Ct. 3110 (1976). See also O. Williamson, Markets and Hierarchies: Analysis and Antitrust Implications 113–15 (1975).

consumers. Competitors are injured because the tying product is a monopoly and the tie-in effectively turns the tied product into a monopoly as well. If a telephone line monopolist requires all subscribers to lease telephones from itself, then the market for competing sellers of telephones vanishes.[30]

Such tie-ins can also injure consumers, for the reasons outlined above. A few consumers are injured because the tie-in pushes the price of the service above their reservation price and they substitute away. The majority are injured, however, because they continue to buy the service, effectively paying more than the competitive price.

Tie-ins in price-regulated industries are not necessarily inefficient. First of all, marginal cost pricing is inappropriate in many natural monopolies because marginal costs are low in comparison with capital costs. Most regulated industries have legal rates that are substantially higher than short-run marginal cost. Resources are generally used most efficiently when they are priced at marginal cost. Once the telephone system is in place, for example, the marginal cost of serving one subscriber signals properly the resources that will be consumed in serving him. As a result, most utilities engage in various forms of price discrimination: people who will pay no more than marginal cost pay it, but people who place a higher value on the service are charged a higher price. One way to facilitate such price discrimination is through various tying arrangements. For example, some phone companies offer so-called "lifeline" service—a single black dial telephone and the right to make ten calls per month—at a very low monthly charge. More exotic service—voice mail, answering services, and call-forwarding services—cost more money, often much more than the additional cost of providing the service. Most price discrimination of this sort is explicitly sanctioned by the regulatory authority.[31]

A more benign version of the above story is that, if a price regulated seller has marginal revenues higher than marginal cost, it will be profitable for the seller to increase its sales at the regulated price. For example, the gas company may sell gas appliances, but only to its own customers, at highly favorable prices. The tying arrangement exists because only gas customers can buy the low priced appliances. The gas company makes up for lost profits on the appliance through increased sales of gas—for example, by bidding customers away from electric appliances. To illustrate, a $250 gas dryer might use $80 worth of gas annually, or $800 over its ten-year lifetime. If the marginal cost to the gas company of selling this customer an additional $800 in gas is only $300, the gas company could actually give the dryer away and earn a profit, assuming the customer would otherwise have purchased an electric dryer.

A variation of this occurred under airline price regulation. Many air fares were set so high that empty seats and excessive flights resulted. A firm might avoid the price regulation by selling the air ticket at the regulated price but throwing in a rental car at no additional cost. This scheme might actually benefit everyone except competitors: the airline makes an even higher profit, output is increased, and customers effectively pay a lower price.[32] The rental car in this case is the tying product and the airline ticket the tied product: presumably the airline will not give a free rental car to

30. See Phonetele, Inc. v. American Tel. & Tel. Co., 664 F.2d 716 (9th Cir.1981), cert. denied, 459 U.S. 1145, 103 S.Ct. 785 (1983). For a good discussion of the various tying arrangements once employed in the telephone industry, see J.P. Fuhr, Jr., Competition in the Terminal Equipment Market after *Carterfone*, 28 Antitrust Bull. 669 (1983). On the ability of price regulated firms to leverage additional revenues through such devices as tie-ins, see M. Kellogg, J. Thorne, & P. Huber, Federal Telecommunications Law, passim, but esp. at 140–143 (1992).

31. One type of price discrimination in basic utility rates, quite common in regulated utilities, is called "Ramsey pricing." See F. Ramsey, A Contribution to the Theory of Taxation, 37 Econ. Journal 47 (Mar., 1927); see also W.J. Baumol & D.F. Bradford, Optimal Departures from Marginal Cost Pricing, 60 Amer.Econ.Rev. 265 (1970); R. Schmalensee, The Control of Natural Monopolies 39–40 (1979). Ramsey pricing is generally efficient because it results in higher overall output, and thus reduces fixed costs per unit.

32. See Robert's Waikiki U-Drive, Inc. v. Budget Rent-A-Car Sys., 491 F.Supp. 1199 (D.Hawai'i 1980), aff'd, 732 F.2d 1403 (9th Cir.1984).

someone who does not purchase an airline ticket. Such tie-ins are also a kind of regulation avoidance.[33] The regulatory authority has established a fare under a policy given by some sovereign. However, it is difficult to fault on economic grounds a practice that increases output at the regulated price. In any event, the practice is best challenged under the law of the regulatory regime in question and not under the antitrust laws.

§ 10.6d. Predatory Pricing and Other Attempts to Monopolize

Dominant firms generally engage in predatory pricing by lowering the price of their product below its marginal cost.[34] They can accomplish the same purpose, however, by maintaining the price but providing an additional product or service at no additional charge or at some price less than cost. The price for the resulting combination is predatory under the Areeda–Turner test if it is less than average variable cost.[35] For example, a computer manufacturer might try to drive a competitor out of business by providing software with its computers at no additional charge.[36] In this case, the software is the tying product and the computer is the tied product: the predator will give free software only to someone who also buys its computer.

Competitors are injured by the package only if the net price is predatory, and they have a cause of action for predatory pricing, provided that the price of the package as a whole is less than the appropriate measure of cost.[37] Consumers are injured not by the attractively priced package but by the monopoly prices that will result after the rival has been driven out of business. They more appropriately have a cause of action for illegal attempt to monopolize.

§ 10.6e. Tie–Ins as Price Discrimination and Metering Devices; Franchise Agreements

Sellers often use tying arrangements to facilitate price discrimination.[38] Although courts sometimes acknowledge this fact,[39] the presence of price discrimination has generally been irrelevant to judicial analysis or determination of legality.

Although price discrimination can be very profitable, it is often difficult for sellers to accomplish for three reasons. First, certain forms of it are illegal under the Robinson–Patman Act,[40] which can prevent the sale of the same product at two different prices. Second, in order to price discriminate, a seller must identify and segregate different groups of customers for whom the elasticity of demand differs. That is, the seller must be able to distinguish in some relatively low-cost way buyers who place a high value on the seller's product from buyers who place a much lower value on it but are still willing to pay a price that is profitable to the seller. Finally, the seller must be able to prevent arbitrage, which occurs when favored purchasers (those charged a lower price) resell the product to disfavored purchasers (those charged a higher price).

A seller can solve all three problems by using a variable proportion tying arrangement,

33. In the *Robert's* case, id., 732 F.2d at 1406, the court noted that the Civil Aeronautics Board had found the defendant's activity to be improper rate regulation avoidance.

34. Or some other measure of cost. See §§ 8.3, 8.5.

35. See § 8.3.

36. See Symbolic Control, Inc. v. IBM Corp., 643 F.2d 1339, 1341 (9th Cir.1980).

37. For example, in *Symbolic Control*, id., the allegation was predatory pricing, not tying. Furthermore, there was neither allegation nor evidence that IBM had market power in the software, which would have constituted the tying product. On package pricing as predatory, see § 8.9a.

38. See W. Bowman, Tying Arrangements and the Leverage Problem, 67 Yale L.J. 19 (1957); R. Markovits, Tie-ins and Reciprocity: A Functional, Legal and Policy Analysis, 58 Tex.L.Rev. 1363, 1407–10 (1980); R. Posner, Exclusionary Practices and the Antitrust Laws, 41 U.Chi. L.Rev. 506, 506–15 (1974). Price discrimination is discussed in ch. 14.

39. See United States Steel Corp. v. Fortner Enter., 429 U.S. 610, 616 n. 7, 97 S.Ct. 861, 866 n. 7 (1977) (Fortner II); Fortner Enter., Inc. v. United States Steel Corp., 394 U.S. 495, 513, 89 S.Ct. 1252, 1264 (1969) (Fortner I) (White, J., dissenting); Hirsh v. Martindale–Hubbell, Inc., 674 F.2d 1343, 1349 (9th Cir.), cert. denied, 459 U.S. 973, 103 S.Ct. 305 (1982); Moore v. Jas. H. Matthews & Co., 550 F.2d 1207, 1213 (9th Cir.1977), appeal after remand, 682 F.2d 830 (9th Cir.1982).

40. 15 U.S.C.A. § 13. See § 14.6.

in which different customers use different amounts of the tied product.[41] For example, a monopoly seller of mimeograph machines might believe that a buyer planning to make 10,000 copies per week values the machine more highly than a buyer intending to make only 1,000 copies per week. The seller may sell the machine subject to a condition that all purchasers buy their mimeograph paper from the seller as well.[42] The seller prices the machine at the competitive level or perhaps even lower. However, the seller charges a high price for the paper. If the rate of return on the machine itself is 5% and the rate of return on the paper is 40%, the seller's net rate of return will be much higher from the 10,000 copy per week user than from the 1000 copy user.[43]

The variable proportion tying arrangement does not violate the Robinson–Patman Act, which applies only when the same product is sold to two different buyers at two different prices. Here, all machines are sold at the same price and all paper at the same price. Second, the tie-in makes identification of high demand and low demand customers easy: the variable use by the customers in practice tracks the value they place on the machine. Third, arbitrage will not work because there is no "spread" between the price of either machine or paper to favored and disfavored purchasers.

A seller must generally have market power in order to price discriminate. If the seller is a competitor, disfavored purchasers (those charged a supracompetitive price) will go to a different seller. In many variable proportion ties the fact of the tie establishes that the defendant has at least a small amount of market power.[44] However, the amount of market power that a seller needs to engage in price discrimination is small, and can result from no more than product differentiation in a relatively competitive market. As a result, the ability to engage in price discrimination does not establish that the seller has sufficient market power to make its tie anticompetitive.

Should tie-ins designed to achieve price discrimination be illegal? A monopolist may legally charge its nondiscriminatory profit-maximizing price. An antitrust policy based on economic efficiency would condemn such price discrimination only if its social costs are higher than the social cost of the single monopoly price. Many commentators argue that price discrimination is preferable because it results in higher output than nondiscriminatory monopoly pricing.[45] This argument applies unfailingly only to perfect price discrimination, however—that is, price discrimination in which every buyer pays its reservation price for the product. Imperfect price discrimination does not necessarily result in increased output, and sometimes the output may be even less than it is under nondiscriminatory monopoly pricing. The effect of imperfect price discrimination on output presents a fairly complex empirical

41. See 9 Antitrust Law ¶ 1711 (1991).

42. See Henry v. A.B. Dick Co., 224 U.S. 1, 32 S.Ct. 364 (1912).

43. Suppose the machine is priced at $1,000 and lasts one fifty-week year. Profits on the machine are $50.00, or $1.00 per week. Paper is priced at 1¢ per sheet, of which 40% is profit. The profits from the 1,000 sheet-per-week user will be $4.00 on paper and $1.00 on the machine, per week. The profits from the 10,000 sheet-per-week user will be $40.00 on paper and $1.00 on the machine, per week. The net rate of return on sales in the first case is about 17%, and in the second about 34%.

44. Not all variable proportion ties are price discrimination devices, however; so any presumption of market power ought to be rebuttable. One exception is when the tie-in is merely a metering device to measure the wear and tear imposed on the tying product. See the discussion infra. Sometimes variable proportion ties are used for efficiency reasons, such as protection of the seller's or lessor's equipment or goodwill. For example, in International Salt Co. v. United States, 332 U.S. 392, 68 S.Ct. 12 (1947) the defendants argued that the tying of salt to its patented salt injecting machines was designed to ensure that the machines functioned properly: they would break down if used with inferior grades of salt. The Supreme Court rejected the argument and condemned the arrangement. But the defendant's contract permitted lessees of the machine to purchase salt from a competitor if the competitor offered equally good salt at a lower price that the defendant would not match. 332 U.S. at 396–97, 68 S.Ct. at 15. Tie-ins work as price discrimination devices only if the seller or lessor charges a monopoly price in the tied product. See J. Peterman, The *International Salt* Case, 22 J.L. & Econ. 351 (1979). The efficiency or "goodwill" defense was also raised and rejected in IBM Corp. v. United States, 298 U.S. 131, 56 S.Ct. 701 (1936), where IBM was accused of tying paper tabulating cards to its patented computation machines.

45. See, e.g., 3 Antitrust Law ¶ 721 (rev. ed. 1996); R. Bork, The Antitrust Paradox: A Policy at War With Itself 394–98 (1978; rev. ed., 1993).

question.[46]

However, a variable proportion tie-in can come as close to perfect price discrimination as any business arrangement. Often the circumstances of a variable proportion tie-in suggest that it results in larger output than nondiscriminatory monopoly pricing would. In Siegel v. Chicken Delight, Inc., for example, the tying product, a license for the defendant's trademark and the right to use its method of doing business, was given to franchisees at no charge.[47] They paid a supracompetitive price, however, for the tied products: breading, spices, cooking equipment and other things necessary for running a fast-food fried chicken take-out.

Such an arrangement will result in more franchises, and thus larger output, than will result from nondiscriminatory pricing. Once the Chicken Delight trademark and method of doing business have been established, the marginal cost of licensing it to one additional franchisee is extremely low—perhaps zero, except for transaction costs. But the franchisor has significant sunk costs invested in developing its name and trademark. The franchisor's nondiscriminatory profit-maximizing price might well be $100,000 in fees per franchise. A franchise that did only enough business to be able to pay $10,000, however, would still be profitable to the franchisor. Even $10,000 in franchise fees would exceed the marginal cost of licensing the franchise.

Price discrimination by tie-in is common in franchise agreements.[48] By price discriminating the franchisor takes advantage of the fact that some franchise locations are far more profitable than others, but that almost any location profitable enough to keep the franchisee in business will also be profitable to the franchisor. The result of the variable proportion tie is that the $10,000 franchise, which would not exist at all if the franchisor charged each franchisee its nondiscriminatory profit-maximizing price, can be profitable to both franchisee and franchisor. Consumers will also be better off.[49] Those injured by such a scheme are the very successful franchisees who, because of the price discrimination, are forced to pay more than the franchisor's nondiscriminatory profit-maximizing price.

Not all variable proportion ties are used for price discrimination. The tie may simply be a metering device, designed to measure costs that vary with intensity of use. To use the mimeograph machine and paper as an example, if wear and tear on a lessor's machine varies directly with the number of copies, the lessor may tie paper to the machine in order to meter the costs that the lessee's use imposes on the lessor. There is no price discrimination if the price of the paper is calculated precisely to cover the wear and tear caused by each use.

Finally, some economists have argued that even fixed proportion tie-ins can serve as price discrimination devices. In a fixed proportion tie the ratio between the amount of the tied product and tying product is constant: a single left shoe with a single right shoe, one bolt with one nut, one grave site with one tombstone. Fixed proportion ties are not conducive to price discrimination in the way that variable proportion ties are; however, a kind of price discrimination can result when package sales are made to purchasers who place differential values on the components of the package.

The classic example is "block-booking" in the film rental industry. Suppose that television stations A and B want to rent Hollywood films from Q. Q's inventory includes *Casablanca* and *Robinson Crusoe on Mars*. Stations A and B have audiences with differing tastes in films. Station A values *Casablanca* at $7,000 and *Crusoe* at $3,000. Station B values

46. See § 14.4.

47. Siegel v. Chicken Delight, Inc., 448 F.2d 43, 46–47 (9th Cir.1971), cert. denied, 405 U.S. 955, 92 S.Ct. 1172 (1972).

48. For example, Queen City Pizza v. Domino's Pizza, 124 F.3d 430 (3d Cir.), cert. denied, ___ U.S. ___, 118 S.Ct. 1385 (1998); Kypta v. McDonald's Corp., 671 F.2d 1282 (11th Cir.1982), cert. denied, 459 U.S. 857, 103 S.Ct. 127 (1982) (tying the franchise license to a variable-rate rental of the franchise location); Krehl v. Baskin–Robbins Ice Cream Co., 664 F.2d 1348 (9th Cir.1982) (in which the tied product was ice cream).

49. See generally, H. Hovenkamp, Tying Arrangements and Class Actions, 36 Vand.L.Rev. 214 (1983); D. Rubin, The Theory of the Firm and the Structure of the Franchise Contract, 21 J.L. & Econ. 223 (1978).

Casablanca at $4,000 and *Crusoe* at $6,000. Q wants to maximize its profits.

Q can rent *Casablanca* once at $7,000 to A and *Crusoe* once at $6,000 to B, and its total revenues will be $13,000. Alternatively, Q can lower the price and rent both movies to both stations. It can rent *Casablanca* to both stations at $4,000 each and *Crusoe* to both stations at $3,000 each. In that case its total revenue will be $14,000.

Finally, Q can package, or "block" the two films and offer the package at $10,000. Since A is willing to pay $7,000 for *Casablanca* and $3,000 for *Crusoe*, A will buy the package. Since B is willing to pay $4,000 for *Casablanca* and $6,000 for *Crusoe*, B will also buy. Q's revenues now shoot up to $20,000. Whether or not this is "price discrimination" depends on one's definition. If one looks at the seller's rate of return on each sale there is no discrimination. The seller obtains $20,000 from each sale and presumably the cost of delivering the package to each of the two stations is the same. Nevertheless, the two stations will assign different values to each film in the package. From their viewpoint Q may be price discriminating. Economists have been content to call this "simulated price discrimination."[50]

Fixed proportion tying arrangements could be used to facilitate price discrimination in this fashion whenever two groups of customers place differential values on a product and the tying is used to reduce arbitrage—that is, the reselling of the product by low-cost buyers to high cost buyers. For example, suppose chemical X is valuable as both a veterinary medicine and a human medicine. In the first case it cures a common form of animal malady; in the second it slows or prevents a life threatening illness in humans. Customers for the first use value X at $1.00 per ounce, while customers of the second value X at $100.00 per ounce. If the manufacturer simply attempted to sell X at these differing prices, however, farmers (or veterinarians) would resell the product to pharmacists at some price between $1.00 and $100.00, and deny the manufacturer its monopoly returns on the latter. The manufacturer might solve this problem by selling X to the veterinarians only after it is mixed into animal feed. Assuming that the costs of extracting X from the feed and making it reusable as human medicine are very high, the manufacturer will have successfully prevented arbitrage in its product. In order for this strategy to succeed, the manufacturer need not be a monopolist in the market for animal feed—nor, for that matter, even a producer. It might simply buy various types of animal feed, treat it, and then sell the treated feed at the profit-maximizing price to the farmers and veterinarians.

§ 10.7 The Role of Efficiencies in Tying Analysis

§ *10.7a.* *Idiosyncratic Per Se Rule*

Although the judicial test for tie-ins does not expressly take efficiencies into account, they creep into the analysis in other ways. One is the "separate product" requirement, which may be interpreted to conclude that when bundling two items together reduces costs, the two are a single product.[1]

But the so-called per se rule applied to tying arrangements is idiosyncratic in two respects. One, it is unique in requiring proof of market power in the tying product, which usually entails a relevant market definition.[2] Second, even when market power is established courts ordinarily permit the defendant to offer various defenses. For example, in *Jerrold Electronics* the court recognized the defense that in a developing market for new technology, package sales might be necessary to encourage customer acceptance.[3] Other courts have held

50. See G. Stigler, United States v. Loew's, Inc.: A Note on Block–Booking, 1963 Sup.Ct.Rev. 152 (1963); R. Markovits, Tie-ins, Reciprocity, and the Leverage Theory, 76 Yale L.J. 1397, 1454–58 (1967). The classic block-booking case is United States v. Loew's, Inc., 371 U.S. 38, 83 S.Ct. 97 (1962), which condemned package licensing of films. More recently, see MCA Television Limited v. Public Interest Corp., 171 F.3d 1265 (11th Cir.1999), which applied the per se rule to condemn package licensing of television shows.

§ 10.7

1. See § 10.5e.

2. See § 10.3.

3. United States v. Jerrold Electronics Corp., 187 F.Supp. 545 (E.D.Pa.1960), affirmed per curiam, 365 U.S. 567, 81 S.Ct. 755 (1961).

that a history of customer unhappiness with their own pairings of complementary products justified a seller in bundling a pair together.[4] For example, a new type of computer may have to be bundled by the manufacturer with new operating software. If software manufactured by others is likely to perform poorly, customers may blame the performance on the computer.[5]

§ 10.7b. Distribution Economies; Full–Line Forcing; Lack of Consumer Injury

One particular type of tie-in that arises in the context of franchise or other authorized dealer contracts is so-called "full-line forcing." Full-line forcing occurs when a manufacturer insists that its dealer carry a full line of the manufacturer's product, rather than the models that the dealer finds most profitable. Most courts have found full-line forcing legal since the 1970's, sometimes by concluding that the manufacturer's "line" is a single product.[6]

An economic objection to full-line forcing is hard to find. Full line requirements help manufacturers achieve economies of scale or scope in distribution. Manufacturers use independent dealers as a substitute for self-distribution, and they can sell their products only if the dealers offer and promote them. If a manufacturer makes models A, B and C, and its authorized dealer refuses to sell C, then the manufacturer must find a second dealer to sell C, retail C itself, or drop C from that particular region. The better alternative is to dismiss the dealer and find one willing to sell the manufacturer's full line. Significantly, full-line forcing is an output-*increasing* activity; the manufacturer's only rationale for imposing it is to get all of its product variations before customers.

Further, in the absence of exclusive dealing no rival is foreclosed.[7] That is to say, unless the manufacturer also imposes exclusive dealing, other sellers are free to sell their product through this dealer as well.[8] The requirement is onerous only to the dealer itself, which must bear the costs of carrying a product that it does prefers not to have.

Finally, consumers are not injured by such an arrangement, for the tying requirement does not apply to them. While the dealer is required to carry a full line, the dealer's customer can pick and choose among the items as he or she pleases.[9]

§ 10.8 Reciprocity

Reciprocity, or reciprocal dealing, is the sale or lease of a product on the condition that the seller *purchase* a different product from the buyer. Reciprocity also occurs when a buyer conditions its purchase of one product on the sale of one of its own products to the

4. Dehydrating Process Co. v. A. O. Smith Corp., 292 F.2d 653 (1st Cir.), cert. denied, 368 U.S. 931, 82 S.Ct. 368 (1961). But see Metrix Warehouse, Inc. v. Daimler–Benz Aktiengesellschaft, 828 F.2d 1033, 1035 (4th Cir.1987), cert. denied, 486 U.S. 1017, 108 S.Ct. 1753 (1988) (seller's release of design specification for the tied product undermined claim that tying was necessary to facilitate reliable product design).

5. In addition, tying may permit the defendant to control free rider problems, monitor quality, or meter the use of the tying product. See 10 Antitrust Law ¶ ¶ 1760–1764 (1996).

6. For example, Southern Card & Novelty v. Lawson Mardon Label, 138 F.3d 869, (11th Cir.1998); Smith Mach. Co. v. Hesston Corp., 878 F.2d 1290, 1296–1298 (10th Cir.1989), cert. denied, 493 U.S. 1073, 110 S.Ct. 1119 (1990) (summary judgment for defendant); Famous Brands, Inc. v. David Sherman Corp., 814 F.2d 517, 523 (8th Cir.1987) (same); Southern Pines Chrysler–Plymouth, Inc. v. Chrysler Corp., 826 F.2d 1360, 1363 (4th Cir.1987) (no showing that line involved distinct products). But see Menominee Rubber Co. v. Gould, Inc., 657 F.2d 164 (7th Cir.1981) (approving preliminary injunction).

7. See 9 Antitrust Law ¶ 1724c (1991); and 10 Id. at ¶ 1747e2 (1996).

8. Exclusive dealing is covered in § 10.9.

9. See, e.g., Roy B. Taylor Sales v. Hollymatic Corp., 28 F.3d 1379 (5th Cir.1994), cert. denied, 513 U.S. 1103, 115 S.Ct. 779 (1995), which found no violation when the defendant required a dealer to carry the defendant's rather high priced hamburger patty paper as a condition of carrying its hamburger patty making machine. Customers, however, were free to buy the machine from the dealer and either make their own paper or buy it somewhere else. As a result, rival makers of patty paper were not foreclosed. Accord Queen City Pizza v. Domino's Pizza, 124 F.3d 430 (3d Cir.), cert. denied, ___ U.S. ___, 118 S.Ct. 1385 (1998) (requiring a Domino's franchisee to use its franchisor's dough exclusively limits the franchisee's choice, but customers remain free to purchase their pizza and underlying dough from numerous sources).

seller.[1] The specter of reciprocity has been raised in merger cases, and the Supreme Court has condemned conglomerate mergers on the theory that they would facilitate reciprocity.[2] Virtually all direct challenges to reciprocity agreements are under § 1 of the Sherman Act.[3] It appears that none have been condemned under § 3 of the Clayton Act.[4] The Federal Trade Commission has also condemned reciprocity agreements under the relatively expansive standards of § 5 of the FTC Act.[5]

Courts have generally analyzed reciprocity much as they have analyzed tie-ins, under the leverage, foreclosure or entry barrier theories. For example, in *Spartan Grain*, the court held that reciprocity should be judged under the *per se* rule used for tie-ins, because both practices involved "the extension of economic power from one market to another market."[6] Other courts have held that illegal reciprocity may be proven under the rule of reason, but requires a showing that the defendant had sufficient market power to force another firm to give it favorable treatment in the market, and then proof of a reciprocity agreement.[7] As in the case of tying arrangements, there is nothing to justify two different standards, and the courts most generally apply a common standard that requires proof of the defendant's market power.[8]

The leverage and entry barrier theories of reciprocity are subject to the same defects and limitations as the corresponding theories of tie-ins. They will not be repeated here.[9] However, the foreclosure theory of tying, and other theories under which tying can facilitate collusion, do not so clearly apply to reciprocity. Indeed, it is hard to see how reciprocity agreements can facilitate collusion. Perhaps more realistically, reciprocity agreements can foreclose the market and raise entry barriers by requiring firms to enter at two levels rather than one.[10] For example, in *Key Enterprises* a hospital permitted home care nurses to serve its discharged patients only if the nurses recommended that the patients purchase durable medical equipment (DME) such as hospital beds and walkers from the hospital's joint venture partner. The theory of the complaint was that an independent supplier of DME could not compete unless it entered with its

§ 10.8

1. See 10 Antitrust Law ¶ ¶ 1775–1779 (1996).

2. FTC v. Consolidated Foods Corp., 380 U.S. 592, 85 S.Ct. 1220 (1965); See also United States v. I.T. & T. Corp., 324 F.Supp. 19 (D.Conn.1970). See § 13.3a.

3. As a result, reciprocity that is imposed "unilaterally" is not a violation, because there is no agreement. See Great Escape v. Union City Body Co., 791 F.2d 532, 538 (7th Cir.1986); United States v. General Dynamics Corp., 258 F.Supp. 36 (S.D.N.Y.1966).

4. Spartan Grain & Mill Co. v. Ayers, 581 F.2d 419, 428 (5th Cir.1978), cert. denied, 444 U.S. 831, 100 S.Ct. 59 (1979), suggested that the language of Clayton § 3 does not apply to reciprocity. The court then concluded that, in any event, Sherman Act and Clayton Act tests would be the same. See 10 Antitrust Law ¶ 1775b (1996).

5. California Packing Corp., 25 F.T.C. 379 (1937) (diversified food processor's use of reciprocity agreements to require suppliers and shipping companies to use its terminal facilities); Mechanical Mfg. Co., 16 F.T.C. 67 (1932) (firm engaged in both meat packing and manufacture of railroad equipment conditioned its use of railroads to ship its meat on railroad's purchase of its railroad equipment). More recently, the FTC has terminated several consent decrees preventing reciprocity. See Diamond Shamrock Corp., 5 Trade Reg. Rep. ¶ 22825 (May 11, 1990); Georgia–Pac. Corp., 103 F.T.C. 203 (1984); Southland Corp., 102 F.T.C. 1337 (1983); Occidental Petroleum Corp., 101 F.T.C. 373 (1983). See also the consent decree in In re Intel Corp. FTC Docket #9288 (1999), under which Intel promised not to withhold its own intellectual property from firms that refused to license their intellectual property to it.

6. Note 4, 581 F.2d at 425. The Ninth Circuit agrees. Betaseed, Inc. v. U and I, Inc., 681 F.2d 1203, 1216–17 (9th Cir.1982).

7. Key Enterprises v. Venice Hospital, 919 F.2d 1550, 1562 (11th Cir.1990), vacated, 979 F.2d 806 (11th Cir. 1992) (defining reciprocity as the use of "market power to unduly influence a second party to treat the first more favorably than the free market would otherwise dictate.... " The court then held that an absolute reciprocity requirement might be per se illegal, but more subtle conditioning would be analyzed under the rule of reason).

8. See Brokerage Concepts v. U.S. Healthcare, 140 F.3d 494 (3d Cir.1998), which concluded that unlawful reciprocity ought to be analyzed under a per se rule but then found lack of sufficient economic power. See also Great Escape, Inc. v. Union City Body Co., Inc., 791 F.2d 532, 537–538 (7th Cir.1986) (requiring proof of market power); *Spartan Grain*, note 4 at 427 ("Market power is generally deemed to be a necessary element of the transaction because without it there would appear to be no adverse effect on competition."); *Key Enterprises*, note 7 at 1562 (requiring market power).

9. See § 10.6.

10. *Key Enterprises*, note 7, 919 F.2d at 1566. See also *Betaseed*, note 6, 681 F.2d at 1220–1221.

own hospital. Since the defendant hospital's patients purchased about 46% of the area's DME used for this purpose, and the defendant seller accounted for some 61% of DME generally, the court found sufficient warrant to condemn the practice under both § 1 (reciprocity) and § 2 (attempted monopolization). Of course, the need for two level entry is an effective deterrent only where it makes entry less likely.[11]

Most firms engage in reciprocity for other reasons, nearly all of which are competitive and efficient. To be sure, the efficiencies that can be obtained by tie-ins are not as obviously attainable by reciprocity agreements. The products come from different sources and move in the market in opposite directions. Thus there is less opportunity for many of the production or transactional efficiencies that justify some tying arrangements.

However, reciprocity agreements can be efficient. By merging two sales into a single transaction they can reduce the costs of using the market. Further, they can yield certain efficiencies in distribution. Suppose that Firm A manufactures baseballs and Firm B makes baseball bats. Both firms operate retail stores in which baseballs and bats are sold. Firm A and Firm B might save on transportation costs if Firm A can sell a load of baseballs to Firm B, deliver them, and return with a load of bats purchased from Firm B. As a result they might negotiate a contract which conditions A's sale of baseballs on its purchase of bats from B.

In addition, reciprocity agreements may reduce the risk of new investments by helping firms guarantee their markets in advance.[12] A firm building a new plant or entering manufacture of a new product will try to purchase inputs from those who agree to purchase its product in return. Reciprocity agreements can also help insure firms against unexpected cancellations, because they increase the cost of canceling. A knows that if he stops buying from B, B will stop buying from A as well.

Reciprocity agreements are often market facilitators, or mechanisms by which a larger firm acts as a broker in smaller related markets. For example, in *Spartan Grain* a large seller of chicken feed discovered that the market for baby chicks was working poorly because hatcheries, which need fertilized eggs, were isolated firms with irregular needs, and the producers of such eggs were equally isolated firms with irregular outputs. Spartan Grain then developed a program under which it would buy up eggs for resale to hatcheries. Since it operated across a large geographic area and served both hatcheries and egg producers, it was in a good position to facilitate such transactions. Of course, its own purpose was to sell more chicken feed, and it refused to act as broker for egg producers not using its feed. Hence the charge of reciprocity.

Reciprocity may also be a quality control mechanism, as it probably was in the *Betaseed* case.[13] A producer of sugar beet seed agreed to purchase sugar beets only from farmers who used its hybrid seed, or substantially equivalent seed. Before condemning such an arrangement as reciprocity, a court should note that the defendant could simply have grown its own sugar beets or contracted with farmers to grow sugar beets for it.

Reciprocity may also enable a firm to price discriminate without violating the Robinson–Patman Act. Suppose that a seller has been selling its product at $3.00 and has a chance to make a large profitable sale at $2.70. If the seller made the sale at that price, the disfavored purchasers might have a secondary-line Robinson–Patman action against him.[14] Instead the seller may make the sale at $3.00 but in return buy a product from the customer at a premium price. Likewise, a cartel member can use a reciprocity agreement to "cheat" on the cartel—by selling at the cartel price but agreeing to buy something in return at a supracompetitive price.[15] A similar arrangement will enable a price-regulated firm to cheat on

11. See § 10.6b1, stating the same limitation respecting tying arrangements.

12. See S. Walters, Reciprocity Reexamined: the Consolidated Foods Case, 29 J.L. & Econ. 423 (1986).

13. Note 6.

14. See § 14.6.

15. See 10 Antitrust Law ¶ 1777b (1996).

the regulatory statute. Analysis of all these functions of reciprocity agreements is the same as the analysis of tie-ins.

The point that reciprocity facilitates cartel cheating is strong, and suggests that reciprocity should be treated much more leniently than tying. To the extent reciprocity agreements have any effect on collusion, they would appear to undermine rather than facilitate it. As § 4.2 notes, collusion, non-cooperative oligopoly and cooperative oligopoly are all facilitated by "single-price" regimes, where transactions are simple, the product is unified and goods are sold at one price to all customers.[16] In concentrated markets, reciprocity serves to enable firms to "cheat" on oligopolies or cartels by making what amounts to secret price cuts. Cartel agreements or market characteristics may prevent a firm from simply cutting price. But the firm may tell a customer that, if the customer takes its product, it will purchase something in return. Since reciprocity agreements are so rarely anti-competitive, a court that condemns one in a concentrated market is very likely shoring up a cartel or oligopoly that might otherwise fall apart.

§ 10.9 Exclusive Dealing

An exclusive dealing arrangement is a contract under which a buyer promises to buy its requirements[1] of one or more products exclusively from a particular seller. Exclusive dealing arrangements have been condemned under § 1 of the Sherman Act and § 3 of the Clayton Act, as well as § 5 of the FTC Act.[2]

§ 10.9a. Anticompetitive Foreclosure and its Variations

10.9a1. The Foreclosure Theory of Exclusive Dealing

Exclusive dealing arrangements have been disapproved under the same, often inadequate "foreclosure" theories that courts have applied in vertical merger cases.[3] For example, if independent gasoline retailers agree to buy all their gasoline needs from one refiner and no one else, the stations are "foreclosed" from other gasoline refiners for the duration of their contracts. In Standard Oil Co. of California v. United States (Standard Stations)[4] the Supreme Court found such contracts illegal when they collectively foreclosed 6.8% of the gasoline market to the defendant's refiner competitors. Since exclusive dealing arrangements were common in the market, the total percentage of independent stations "foreclosed" from the market by *all* refiners who used such contracts was considerably higher.[5]

Did such contracts make the market less competitive? All the arguments against the foreclosure theory presented in chapter 9 on vertical integration apply equally to exclusive dealing. The competitive threat, if any, is generally less in exclusive dealing than in more durable and extensive forms of vertical integration, such as vertical mergers. Unlike mergers, exclusive dealing contracts usually do not govern every aspect of an independent firm's business. Further, exclusive dealing contracts are of limited duration. Every so often, de-

16. In explicit cartels or cooperative oligopolies, cheating by reciprocity would likely start a price war; otherwise the cheater would steal the other firm's market share. In a non-cooperative oligopoly, each firm is equating its own marginal cost and marginal revenue, so across-the-board price cuts are unprofitable. But *selective* price cuts, which could be facilitated through reciprocity agreements, would enable an oligopolist to make more through price discrimination. Furthermore, these sales would come at the expense of other oligopolists, who would then face a lower residual demand curve. They would have to cut price as well. For a fuller explication, see § 4.2.

§ 10.9

1. In antitrust analysis, requirements contracts are generally treated as exclusive dealing. For example, Taggart v. Rutledge, 657 F.Supp. 1420, 1443–1445 (D.Mont. 1987), affirmed mem., 852 F.2d 1290 (9th Cir.1988). *Output* contracts, by contrast, are often treated in antitrust law as exclusive dealerships—or promises by the supplier that its entire output in that area will be sold through a single dealer. See § 11.6d; and see 11 Antitrust Law ¶ 1802 (requirements contracts and exclusive dealing); ¶ 1803 (output contracts) (1998). See also Paddock Pub. v. Chicago Tribune Co., 103 F.3d 42, 47 (7th Cir.1996), cert. denied, 520 U.S. 1265, 117 S.Ct. 2435 (1997) (distinguishing output contract from requirements contract).

2. 15 U.S.C.A. § 45. See FTC v. Brown Shoe Co., 384 U.S. 316, 86 S.Ct. 1501 (1966); and § 10.3e in this volume.

3. See § 9.3c.

4. 337 U.S. 293, 69 S.Ct. 1051 (1949).

5. Id. at 295, 69 S.Ct. at 1053. Only 1.6% of the retail stations had "split pumps"—that is, sold gasoline from two or more different refiners.

pending on contract terms that could range from a few months to many years, the supplier must bid anew against competing suppliers.[6]

Exclusive dealing might foreclose competition inefficiently if the upstream firm has a dominant market position and entry into the downstream market is restricted. As long as new downstream facilities can readily be constructed, effective foreclosure is unlikely. But suppose that geographic location is critical to business survival, and two or three sites for resale locations are substantially better than alternatives. In that case, a dominant upstream firm could "foreclose" competition—thus making entry more difficult—by entering into exclusive dealing contracts with all of the preferred downstream locations.

10.9a2. Raising Rivals' Costs

Many of the foreclosure theories of exclusive dealing become more robust if one views them, not as excluding rivals from a market altogether, but as raising rivals' costs by relegating them to inferior distribution channels.[7] For example, Standard Oil very likely enlarged its monopoly by agreeing with railroads that they would give it preferential scheduling and lower prices than any competing shipper of petroleum products.[8] American Can for a time bought up the full output of can machine makers, thereby forcing rival can makers to resort to inferior technology.[9] Or Toys 'R' Us, the country's largest toy purchaser, forced suppliers to promise that competing discounters would receive only differentiated versions of toys or large bundles that customers would have to take all at once.[10]

10.9a3. Defining Markets to Measure Vertical Foreclosure[11]

In any event, before anticompetitive foreclosure can occur a firm with a relatively large percentage of the upstream market must foreclose a significant percentage of access to the downstream market.[12] To illustrate, suppose that firm X makes 80% of the world's solar-powered wrist watches and enters into exclusive dealing agreements with 100% of the jewelry stores in an area. If jewelry stores were the only places that such watches could be sold, it would be very difficult for competing watch makers to find suitable outlets. But if such watches are efficiently sold through department stores, discount stores, or over the internet, then the restraint might not be all that significant.[13] As a result, it is always important to look at the entire range of distribution channels through which efficient distribution can occur; exclusive dealing that shuts off only one distribution channel might permit ample competition through others.[14]

It is also important to remember that vertically related markets do not necessarily have the same geographic boundaries. For example,

6. The exclusive dealing contracts in the *Standard Stations* case were of varying terms. Many, however, were from year-to-year, requiring a 30 day notice by either party for termination. Id. at 296, 69 S.Ct. at 1053. In such cases competitive bidding for the contracts could be substantial, even though a station carried the gasoline of only one supplier at any given time. See United States v. El Paso Natural Gas Co., 376 U.S. 651, 84 S.Ct. 1044 (1964).

7. See 11 Antitrust Law ¶ 1804 (1998); Interface Group v. Mass. Port Authority, 816 F.2d 9, 11 (1st Cir.1987) (dicta describing hypothetical situations where high foreclosure could raise the costs of rival suppliers forced to deal with inferior dealers). See also C. Stefandis, Selective Contracts, Foreclosure, and the Chicago School View, 41 J.L. & Econ. 429 (1998); K. Baseman, F. Warren–Boulton & G. Woroch, Microsoft Plays Hardball: the Use of Exclusionary Pricing and Technical Incompatibility to Maintain Monopoly Power in markets for Operating System Software, 40 Antitrust Bull. 265 (1995).

8. E. Granitz & B. Klein, Monopolization by "Raising Rivals' Costs:" the Standard Oil Case, 39 J. L. & Econ. 1 (1996).

9. United States v. American Can Co., 230 F. 859; 875 (D. Md. 1916), appeal dismissed, 256 U.S. 706, 41 S.Ct. 624 (1921) ("[F]or a year or two after defendant's formation it was practically impossible for any competitor to obtain the most modern, up-to-date, automatic machinery."). See 11 Antitrust Law ¶ 1801a (1998).

10. Toys 'R' Us, 5 Trade Reg. Rptr. ¶ 24516 (F.T.C. 1998).

11. See 2A Antitrust Law ¶ 570 (rev. ed. 1995).

12. See, e.g., *Paddock*, note 1 (New York Times News Service "competes for column inches of ink not only with other supplemental news services but also with the Associated Press, Reuters," and others; as a result, its output contract giving *Chicago Tribune* exclusive access in the latter's subscription area not anticompetitive).

13. See 11 Antitrust Law ¶ 1802d (1999).

14. See id. at ¶ 1821d4.

suppose that a hospital agrees to use only the services of one particular pathologist. The hospital might have a dominant position in the relevant geographic market that it serves, which may be limited to a single municipality. However, pathologists may be recruited in a regional or even national market. As a result, no single pathologist would be in a position to insist on charging monopoly prices through that hospital.[15]

§ 10.9b. Exclusive Dealing as a Cartel Facilitator

Exclusive dealing may facilitate collusion by denying buyers an opportunity to force sellers to bid against each other. This reduces the opportunities for cartel cheating. For example, if gasoline refiners are colluding, gasoline distributors might be able to force the refiners to bid against each other and reach agreements with individually negotiated secret terms. But if the cartel members agreed to use exclusive dealing contracts with their distributors, thus making them "branded" resellers, then this bidding could be reduced. Of course, exclusive dealing should be condemned under this theory only if (1) the upstream market shows signs of being conducive to collusion; and (2) the exclusive dealing is sufficiently widespread to create the inference that it is being used as a cartel facilitator. Unfortunately, the fact that exclusive dealing is efficient in a market also tends to make it widespread. Firms must either adopt efficient practices or else lose market share to those who do. If upstream markets are highly concentrated and conducive to collusion, but the exclusive dealing itself seems to be efficient, then the policy maker might wish to approve exclusive dealing only for short periods. If exclusive dealing contracts must be re-bid frequently, most of the benefits of exclusive dealing will be retained, but the competitive threat will be greatly diminished.

§ 10.9c. The Difference Between Exclusive Dealing and Tying

Exclusive dealing can actually have a greater anticompetitive impact than tying, depending on the circumstances. For example, suppose that Kodak agreed to supply copy machines to a photocopy store and tied paper and other supplies. The copy store would not be able to use non-Kodak paper in these machines. Unless Kodak also imposed exclusive dealing, however, the store would be free to use Xerox or Toshiba machines, and could use the paper of others in those machines. To the extent the copy store could vary proportions, it might respond to high priced Kodak paper by using the Kodak machines less and the non-Kodak machines more. By contrast, if Kodak imposed exclusive dealing on either machines or paper, then the store would have to take all its requirements of that product from Kodak. In sum, tying arrangements apply to tying products, while exclusive dealing applies to *firms*. The foreclosure caused by tying is less to the extent that a firm can use or sell multiple brands of the tying product.[16]

This fact significantly calls into question Justice Frankfurter's conclusion in *Standard Stations* that exclusive dealing contracts should be dealt with more leniently than tie-ins. While "[t]ying arrangements serve hardly any purpose beyond the suppression of competition," he concluded, exclusive dealing arrangements:

> may well be of economic advantage to buyers as well as to sellers, and thus indirectly of advantage to the consuming public. In the case of the buyer, they may assure supply, afford protection against rises in price, enable long-term planning on the basis of known costs, and obviate the expense and risk of storage in the quantity necessary for a commodity having a fluctuating demand.[17]

While Justice Frankfurter was correct about the efficiency possibility of exclusive dealing,

15. See § 10.9e; Collins v. Associated Pathologists, 844 F.2d 473, 479 (7th Cir.), cert. denied, 488 U.S. 852, 109 S.Ct. 137 (1988) (foreclosure to be assessed in relevant market where pathologists competed for jobs; not relevant market for hospital's services); Balaklaw v. Lovell, 14 F.3d 793 (2d Cir.1994) (same; anesthesiologists). See also 11 Antitrust Law ¶ 1821b (1999).

16. See 11 Antitrust Law ¶ 1800b (1999).

17. 337 U.S. at 305–306, 69 S.Ct. at 1058.

he was wrong about tying. Nevertheless, his observation very largely explains why tying arrangements are said to be illegal per se, while exclusive dealing is generally evaluated under a rule of reason.[18] Section 3 of the Clayton Act provides no basis for the distinction.

Further, it is often difficult to distinguish exclusive dealing from tying. This is particularly true when the scope of the tying product is identical to that of the firm. If by contract a retail gasoline dealer is permitted to display the "Standard" emblem and is required to take all its gasoline for resale from Standard Oil Co., should the arrangement be treated as exclusive dealing or as a tie-in? Likewise, if a dealer agrees to purchase all its tires, batteries and other accessories from Standard, as well as all its requirements of gasoline, the accessories appear to be tied to the gasoline and vice-versa. Justice Frankfurter recognized the artificiality of the distinction in the *Standard Stations* case, and had some difficulty deciding whether "exclusive supply provision[s] * * * should perhaps be considered, as a matter of classification, tying rather than requirements agreements."[19]

In most franchise arrangements, tie-ins and exclusive dealing perform the same economic function. Courts have distinguished the two, however, and apply a more lenient test to exclusive dealing, once they have characterized it as such. The chief difference between exclusive dealing and tying is that in exclusive dealing the court recognizes no distinct "tying" product. A good example is Justice O'Connor's concurring opinion in the *Jefferson Parish* case.[20] Once Justice O'Connor decided that hospital services and anesthesiology were the same "product" and could not constitute a tying arrangement, she dealt with the arrangement as an exclusive dealing contract. In fact, however, a "tying" product exists even in exclusive dealing contracts—namely, the right of the retailer to sell the supplier's merchandise and perhaps to display a sign showing itself to be an "authorized dealer." That right is worth more to the high volume seller than to the low volume seller. As a result, exclusive dealing is probably used to facilitate price discrimination just as tie-ins.[21] That was almost certainly true in *Standard Stations*. Standard had a great deal invested in public recognition of its name. By entering exclusive dealing contracts with stations, permitting them to display the Standard brand, and charging a supracompetitive price for its gasoline, Standard was in effect selling its name as well as its gasoline to the retailer; however, it was selling its name at a price that varied with the amount the retailer sold.[22] Of course, once the court has decided that no tying arrangement exists, because the alleged tying and tied products are actually one, then the plaintiff may have nothing left but an exclusive dealing claim. This often happens in vertical litigation involving franchise arrangements.

§ 10.9d. Efficiency Explanations and Defenses for Exclusive Dealing

The exclusive dealing arrangement stands between the vertical merger and the individual sale as a device for facilitating distribution of a manufacturer's product to the ultimate consumer. Markets are uncertain, some much more uncertain than others.[23] Long-term, flexible contracts can minimize the costs and risks to both parties of dealing with these uncertainties. For example, no retail gasoline dealer

18. See § 10.4 (per se rule for tie-ins) and § 10.9e (rule of reason for most exclusive dealing).

19. *Standard Stations*, 337 U.S. at 305 n. 8, 69 S.Ct. at 1058 n. 8.

20. Jefferson Parish Hosp. Dist. No. 2 v. Hyde, 466 U.S. 2, 44, 104 S.Ct. 1551, 1575–1576 (1984).

21. See § 10.6e.

22. See Krehl v. Baskin–Robbins Ice Cream Co., 664 F.2d 1348 (9th Cir.1982), in which the plaintiff-franchisees were permitted to display the defendant's trademark but also required to sell the defendant's ice cream exclusively. The plaintiffs and the court characterized this as a tying arrangement; however the difference between *Baskin-Robbins* and *Standard Stations* is difficult to discern. See also Queen City Pizza v. Domino's Pizza, 124 F.3d 430 (3d Cir.), cert. denied, ___ U.S. ___, 118 S.Ct. 1385 (1998), which analyzed a requirement that Domino's Pizza franchisees use only pizza dough supplied by Domino's as both tying and exclusive dealing, and dismissed both counts for lack of market power in the upstream market.

23. For an important discussion of the use of vertical integration to avoid market uncertainties, see O. Williamson, Markets and Hierarchies 82–131 (1975).

knows in advance precisely what its sales will be over some future period. Nor may he have anything approaching reliable information about the status of suppliers. Some markets are so uncertain that no reasonable investor will build an outlet unless she has advance assurance of a steady source of supply.[24] If summer travel is brisk, the gasoline retailer needs to know that it can obtain enough gasoline, and relying on the spot market for short-notice purchases can be risky and expensive.

The refiner, by contrast, wants a steady outlet for its product. Customers become accustomed to buying a particular brand at a particular location. A customer's ability to know in advance that a particular station carries a brand he prefers makes the customer better off. The exclusive dealing arrangement gives both refiners and ultimate consumers the advantages of outright refiner ownership of retail stations, but permits the refiner to avoid the high capital costs of investing in stations. The exclusive dealing contract may also provide incentives at the retailer level. If the refiner owns its own stations, the station operator is merely an employee. The independent dealer is a businessman who usually maximizes his profits by selling as much as possible of the refiner's gasoline.

Additionally, vertical integration by contract gives both parties to the agreement an economic interest in productive facilities. For example, the value of a gasoline refinery results from future sales of refined gasoline. By arranging in advance for a steady stream of such sales, the refiner essentially shares the risk of the investment with the gasoline retailers.[25] In general, the more specialized the plant, the greater this risk will be. If the refiner builds without this assurance, retailers can later take advantage of the refiner's sunk costs and bargain for any price sufficient to cover the variable costs of refining gasoline.[26] As a result, the refiner unsure about future demand is likely to build a smaller refinery than it would if the demand were certain, or else not build at all. This situation is exacerbated if information in the market is poor. For example, if I am planning to build a refinery but I do not know what competing refiners are planning to build, I may fear there will be excess refining capacity. By guaranteeing my market through long term requirements contracts, I can spread this risk and reduce my uncertainty.[27]

Finally, from the supplier's viewpoint exclusive dealing or sometimes tying may prevent "interbrand free riding." Free riding is an important reason why suppliers impose resale price maintenance and other vertical restraints.[28] The free rider would otherwise take advantage of the promotional activities undertaken by another dealer of the same brand. Interbrand free riding occurs when a dealer having an ongoing supply relationship with one supplier sells a second brand at the same location and takes advantage of facilities or goodwill contributed by the supplier of the first brand. For example, when Standard licenses a new gasoline station, it may help the dealer with financing, acquisition and maintenance of equipment, certain amenities such as "free" road maps, and most importantly, the large Standard sign at the top of the station. If the dealer were permitted to pump a second brand of "equally good" discount gasoline—even if it were properly distinguished from the true Standard pumps—neither Standard nor

24. See Great Lakes Carbon Corp., 82 F.T.C. 1529, 1656 (1973) ("a prudent refiner will not install [an expensive] facility unless he has in hand, at the time that investment decision is made, a contract for the disposition of the [product] to be produced."); Robinson v. Magovern, 521 F.Supp. 842, 890–91 (W.D.Pa.1981), affirmed, 688 F.2d 824 (3d Cir.1982), cert. denied, 459 U.S. 971, 103 S.Ct. 302 (1982) (young surgeon would logically wish to associate himself with established practice to assure employment). See 11 Antitrust Law ¶ 1811 (1999).

25. See 11 Antitrust Law ¶ 1814 (1998).

26. For one likely instance of this see Great Atlantic & Pacif. Tea Co., v. F.T.C., 440 U.S. 69, 73, 99 S.Ct. 925, 929 (1979), where A & P was able to obtain a very low bid from Borden milk company, allegedly in violation of the Robinson–Patman Act, because Borden had just built an enormous plant in the area in reliance on A & P's continued business, and feared underutilization if it did not retain A & P's account.

27. See W. Liebeler, Antitrust Law and the New Federal Trade Commission, 12 Sw.U.L.Rev. 166, 186–196 (1981); H. Marvel, Exclusive Dealing, 25 J.L. & Econ. 1 (1982).

28. See § 11.3a.

the dealer could segregate all these facilities and amenities supplied by Standard. Invariably, part of Standard's investment would contribute to the sale of a competitor's gasoline. The solution for Standard is to force dealers to sell its gasoline exclusively.[29] The empirical literature suggests that exclusive dealing is most likely to be used in markets that are subject to free riding of this sort.[30] However, exclusive dealing can be costly to the extent it limits customers' ability to compare brands within the same retail store. As a result, a manufacturer may have to trade off efficiency gains against the possibility of lost sales because consumers prefer multiproduct retailers.[31]

For all the reasons outlined above, exclusive dealing is one of the most classic examples of open-ended contracting—that is, of contracting that permits parties to reduce their risk and to account for the fact that they do not know everything about the future.[32] Vertical integration by ownership involves much heavier investment in markets where others are already specialists and capacity may be adequate. Simple contracts that specify quantity are too inflexible to consider the market's uncertain future meanderings.

Justice Douglas, always the champion of the small business, recognized many of the economies that exclusive dealing would generate. His *Standard Stations* dissent recognized the obvious: if the oil companies could not integrate by exclusive dealing, they would do so by outright ownership:

> The Court's * * * [decision] promises to wipe out large segments of independent filling station operators. The method of doing business under requirements contracts at least keeps the independents alive. They survive as small business units. The situation is not ideal from either their point of view or that of the nation. But the alternative which the Court offers is far worse from the point of view of both.
>
> The elimination of these requirements contracts sets the stage for Standard and the other oil companies to build service-station empires of their own.[33]

The statement is one of Justice Douglas' most candid recognitions of the conflict between small business welfare and economic efficiency. If vertical integration gives an oil company a "competitive advantage" but exclusive dealing is unlawful, competition may force the companies to build their own retail stations. Justice Douglas was not willing to make a second admission, however: the "competitive advantage" in this case meant lower prices for consumers.

§ 10.9e. The Legal Standard for Exclusive Dealing Contracts

The district court's opinion in *Standard Stations* had created a virtual *per se* rule against requirements contracts if the percentage of the market foreclosed by the agreement exceeded about 7%. Having concluded that this percentage was high enough, the district court refused to consider evidence concerning "the economic merits or demerits of the present system" and whether the number of dealers had increased or decreased since the exclusive dealing contracts had come into existence.[34] In affirming the district court, the Supreme Court appeared to approve this *per se* approach to exclusive dealing contracts.

The Court retreated from that position, however, in Tampa Elect. Co. v. Nashville Coal Co.,,[35] decided 12 years later. The most significant part of the *Tampa* decision was its defini-

29. See 11 Antitrust Law ¶ 1812 (1998).

30. See J. Heide, S. Dutta, & M. Bergen, Exclusive Dealing and Business Efficiency: Evidence From Industry Practice, 41 J.L. & Econ. 387 (1998).

31. See generally L. Stern, A. El–Ansary & A. Coughlan, Marketing Channels (3d ed. 1996).

32. See I. MacNeil, Contracts: Adjustment of Long–Term Economic Relations Under Classical, Neoclassical, and Relational Contract Law, 72 Nw.U.L.Rev. 854 (1978); D. Carlton Vertical Integration in Competitive Markets Under Uncertainty, 27 J.Indus. Econ. 189 (1979); and, most importantly, the work of Oliver Williamson cited throughout Ch. 9.

33. *Standard Stations*, 337 U.S. at 319–320, 69 S.Ct. at 1066–67.

34. Id. at 298, 69 S.Ct. at 1054.

35. 365 U.S. 320, 81 S.Ct. 623 (1961), on remand, 214 F.Supp. 647 (M.D.Terr.1963).

tion of the relevant market, which reduced effective foreclosure to lower than 1%.[36] As a result, the Court's discussion of the legal standard to be applied can be considered dicta. In an ambiguous but potentially powerful statement, the Court concluded that:

> To determine substantiality [of foreclosure] in a given case, it is necessary to weigh the probable effect of the contract on the relevant area of effective competition, taking into account the relative strength of the parties, the proportionate volume of commerce involved in relation to the total volume of commerce * * * and the probable immediate and future effects which preemption of that share of the market might have on effective competition therein.[37]

As in any case where proof of market share is decisive, a relevant market must be defined.[38] Indeed, that requirement seems implicit even in *Standard Stations*. One cannot produce a percentage of the market foreclosed without defining a relevant market, and there is no reason for thinking that "market" in the context of exclusive dealing means something different than the ordinary relevant antitrust market.

But care must be taken that the *correct* relevant market is used, particularly when the upstream party operates in one geographic market and the downstream party in another. For example, suppose a national company refining and wholesaling gasoline in regional markets enters into exclusive dealing contracts with gasoline stations, as in *Standard Stations*. The first question is, What is the threatened danger to competition? In the typical case, as *Standard Stations* was, the stations promised to sell nothing but Standard's own gasoline. If the perceived threat is foreclosure of suppliers—that is, exclusive dealing makes it impossible for refiners other than Standard to sell gasoline to these stations—then the relevant market is the regional one in which the refiners operate.[39] Likewise, if the threatened harm is collusion at the refiner level, one must look to the refining market. By contrast, if the threatened harm is retailer collusion, then the retail market must be defined.

Likewise, the market share for determining foreclosure is the share of the relevant market that is *foreclosed*, not the share that describes the seller's total sales. For example, suppose that refiner A accounts for 40% of the relevant geographic market for refined gasoline. However, only one-fourth of refiner A's gallonage is sold to independent dealers through exclusive dealing contracts. In that case, the foreclosure percentage is 10%, not 40%.[40] This entails that a plaintiff must determine the extent to which exclusive dealing contracts are imposed on other resellers.[41] One must also subtract out parts of the market that may be denied to competitors for other reasons. Suppose, for example, that half of the gasoline in a region is sold through refiner-owned gasoline stations, which are owned by larger refiners, but that small refiners sell strictly to independents. In that case, the competition among refiners for gasoline retailers must be confined to sales made to independent retailers, and the gasoline sold through the refiner-owned retailers should be subtracted out of the market before the market share calculations are made.

Most lower courts today follow *Tampa*'s suggested rule of reason approach.[42] Foreclo-

36. See § 3.6.

37. 365 U.S. at 329, 81 S.Ct. at 629.

38. For example, Morgan, Strand, Wheeler & Biggs v. Radiology, Ltd., 924 F.2d 1484, 1489–1490 (9th Cir.1991) (exclusive dealing claim dismissed where the plaintiffs failed to define relevant product and geographic markets). On market definition, see Ch. 3.

39. For example, Ryko Mfg. Co. v. Eden Serv., 823 F.2d 1215, 1233 (8th Cir.1987), cert. denied, 484 U.S. 1026, 108 S.Ct. 751 (1988) (looking at degree of foreclosure in supply market).

40. See *Ryko*, note 39, 823 F.2d at 1232 (8% to 10% market share exaggerated foreclosure when plaintiff and only a few other distributors were likely subjected to exclusive dealing).

41. See Chuck's Feed & Seed Co. v. Ralston Purina Co., 810 F.2d 1289, 1295 (4th Cir.), cert. denied, 484 U.S. 827, 108 S.Ct. 94 (1987), (j.n.o.v. for defendant where plaintiff failed to show extent to which exclusive dealing was used in the market as a whole).

42. See Roland Mach. Co. v. Dresser Indus., 749 F.2d 380, 393 (7th Cir.1984) (rule of reason must be applied to exclusive dealing). Some courts suggest that the Supreme Court's decision in Continental T.V., Inc. v. GTE Sylvania, Inc., 433 U.S. 36, 97 S.Ct. 2549 (1977), adopting a rule of reason for vertical nonprice restraints, mandates rule of

sure on the order of 30% to 40% is generally necessary to avoid judgment for the defendant,[43] although several cases decided before *Jefferson Parish* condemned exclusive dealing on lower percentages. The concurring Justices there opined that 30% was insufficient where they could find no additional anticompetitive effects.[44] Exclusive dealing is still condemned where the shares exceed 40% or so.[45] Once foreclosure of a sufficient percentage is found, the court looks at the factors spelled out in the *Tampa* opinion.[46]

The FTC has been somewhat more aggressive. In Toys'R'Us (TRU) it condemned output agreements on market shares of 30% or somewhat less.[47] However, there were some special factors in that case. First, the toy market was highly product differentiated. For example, a Barbie doll probably does not compete very much with a set of Tinker Toys, and even different board games probably do not compete with each other very much. As a result, foreclosure percentages of individual products may have been much higher. Second, the exclusive dealing seemed particularly "naked" in that there appeared to be no provable efficiency justifications for it; TRU simply told major toy manufacturers that as a condition of selling to TRU they must promise not to sell the same toys to certain discounters,[48] or to sell to them only in bundles that consumers would have to purchase as a package.

Some courts appear to apply a two-part test that comes close to per se illegality when foreclosure percentages are sufficiently high. Only if the market share falls below the threshold do these courts look to other factors.[49] Most courts look at actual impact on competition and not merely on the foreclosed market share.[50] Nevertheless, since *Jefferson Parish*, exclusive dealing is rarely condemned on market share foreclosures lower than 30% or 40%.

When shares are sufficiently high, *Tampa*'s rule of reason requires courts to examine numerous other factors, including (1) the duration of the contracts; (2) the likelihood of collusion in the industry, and the degree to which other firms in the market also employ

reason treatment for exclusive dealing. *Chuck's Feed*, note 41 at 1294.

43. For example, Sewell Plastics, Inc. v. Coca–Cola Co. 720 F.Supp. 1196, 1212–1214 (W.D.N.C.1989), affirmed mem., 912 F.2d 463 (4th Cir.1990) (40% insufficient).

44. *Jefferson Parish*, note 20, 466 U.S. at 45, 97 S.Ct. at 1575 (O'Connor, J., concurring): "Exclusive dealing is an unreasonable restraint on trade only when a significant fraction of buyers or sellers are frozen out of a market by the exclusive deal." The concurrers then found 30% coverage inadequate because they could find no anticompetitive effects.

45. For example, Kohler Co. v. Briggs & Stratton Corp., 1986–1 Trade Cas. (CCH) ¶ 67,047, 1986 WL 946 (E.D.Wis.1986) (62% market share sufficient); United States v. Dairymen, Inc., 758 F.2d 654 (6th Cir.), cert. denied, 474 U.S. 822, 106 S.Ct. 73 (1985) (50% sufficient); Oltz v. St. Peter's Community Hosp., 656 F.Supp. 760 (D.Mont.1987), affirmed, 861 F.2d 1440 (9th Cir.1988) (84% of hospital admissions sufficient).

46. See *Chuck's Feed*, note 41 at 1294:

> [T]he application of the "rule of reason" analysis would seem to mean that a court should not look only at the numerical percentage of market foreclosure in order to decide whether or not a particular arrangement is illegal. Rather, after determining that market foreclosure is substantial, the court should consider whether an otherwise unacceptable level of market foreclosure is justified by procompetitive efficiencies.

47. Toys 'R' Us, 5 Trade Reg. Rptr. ¶ 24516 (F.T.C. 1998).

48. TRU's margins on toys were around 30%, while the discount warehouses sold at margins as low as 9%.

49. See *Ryko*, note 39 at 1233: "Where the degree of foreclosure caused by the exclusivity provisions is so great that it invariably indicated the supplier imposing the provisions has substantial market power, we may rely on the foreclosure rate alone to establish the violation. However, where, as here, the foreclosure rate is neither substantial nor even apparent, the plaintiff must demonstrate that other factors in the market exacerbate the detrimental effect of the challenged restraints." Accord Twin City Sportservice, Inc. v. Charles O. Finley & Co., Inc., 676 F.2d 1291 (9th Cir.), cert. denied, 459 U.S. 1009, 103 S.Ct. 364 (1982).

50. For example, Advanced Health–Care Servs. v.Radford Community Hosp., 910 F.2d 139, 151 (4th Cir.1990); Collins v. Associated Pathologists, Ltd., 844 F.2d 473, 478–479 (7th Cir.), cert. denied, 488 U.S. 852, 109 S.Ct. 137 (1988); Interface Group v. Massachusetts Port Authority, 816 F.2d 9, 11–12 (1st Cir.1987).

See also Roland Mach. Co. v. Dresser Indus., 749 F.2d 380, 393–395 (7th Cir.1984), concluding that in order to prove unreasonable exclusive dealing a plaintiff first

> must prove that it is likely to keep at least one significant competitor of the defendant from doing business in a relevant market. If there is no exclusion of a significant competitor, the agreement cannot possibly harm competition. Second, he must prove that the probable (not certain) effect of the exclusion will be to raise prices above (and therefore reduce output below) the competitive level, or otherwise injure competition.

exclusive dealing; (3) the height of entry barriers; (4) the nature of the distribution system and distribution alternatives remaining available after exclusive dealing is taken into account; and (5) other obvious anti-or pro-competitive effects. Among the latter, the most often cited are prevention of free riding and encouragement of the dealer to promote the supplier's product more heavily.[51]

As noted previously, long contracts should generally be regarded as more problematic than short ones, because substantial competition generally emerges when the contracts must be renegotiated. Indeed, a market saturated with exclusive dealing contracts could be fiercely competitive, if the contracts were short term and the parties bid vigorously for the contracts themselves. This is frequently the case for service contracts, where exclusive dealing greatly reduces transaction cost fees. For example, a factory probably does not want to negotiate each day to have its trash hauled away. Rather, it will take competitive bids from trash hauling firms, and the winner will get an exclusive contract with a stated duration, perhaps one year. When the contract expires a new round of bidding will begin. Such a market is likely to operate competitively even though every factory and commercial trash hauler in the area uses a contract that is exclusive over its lifetime.[52]

Likewise, exclusive dealing that "forecloses" a large percentage of one mode of distribution will have little anticompetitive effect if another mode is available.[53] Closely related is the question of entry barriers. Exclusive dealing should be condemned only when it facilitates monopoly pricing, and this is not likely to occur if entry is easy. Of course, meaningful entry must either occur at both levels covered by the exclusive dealing arrangement, or else there must be sufficient free capacity at one level to give a new entrant at the other level a ready source of supply. For example, exclusive dealing between oil refiners and service stations will facilitate monopoly pricing only if prospective competitors cannot easily and quickly enter. If the exclusive dealing is so widespread that anyone wishing to be a refiner must also open a chain of service

51. For example, *Roland Mach.*, note 50 at 394–395:

> "[t]he calculus of competitive effects must also include some consideration of the possible competitive benefits of exclusive dealing. * * * If, as Dresser argues, exclusive dealing leads dealers to promote each manufacturer's brand more vigorously than would be the case under nonexclusive dealing, the quality-adjusted price to the consumer * * * may be lower with exclusive dealing than without, even though a collateral effect of exclusive dealing is to slow the pace at which new brands * * * are introduced."
>
> See also CDC Tech., Inc. v. IDEXX Labs., Inc., 186 F.3d 74 (2d Cir.1999) (no illegality when entry barriers were low).

See also *Ryko*, note 39 at 1234 & n. 17:

> "[The] overall effect on interbrand competition in such cases may be beneficial by focusing the distributor's efforts on one product line and, in turn, removing the "free rider" threat to the manufacturer's own selling efforts Where, as here, the manufacturer engages in promotional activity that is designed to dovetail with the distributor's efforts, an exclusive dealing clause guarantees that the manufacturer's marketing investment will not be lost to other firms. * * * This assurance encourages the manufacturer's investment in marketing activity * * *."

And see *Advanced Health–Care Services.*, note 50, 910 F.2d at 151 (exclusive dealing might increase interbrand competition); Collins v. Associated Pathologists, Ltd., 844 F.2d 473, 478–479 (7th Cir.), cert. denied, 488 U.S. 852, 109 S.Ct. 137 (1988) (same); Empire Volkswagen, Inc. v. World–Wide Volkswagen Corp. 814 F.2d 90, 97 (2d Cir. 1987) (dealer permitted to sell only VW products in its main showroom; limits free riding).

52. See *Twin City*, note 49 (condemning contracts in excess of ten years). Contrast Omega Environmental v. Gilbarco, 127 F.3d 1157, 1164 (9th Cir.1997), cert. denied, ___ U.S. ___, 119 U.S. 46 (1998) (insufficient harm to competition when there were some 500 distributors upon whom exclusive dealing was imposed and 60–day termination notice provisions after the initial year of a distribution contract; as a result, at any time there were numerous distributors for whom manufacturers could bid); *CDC Tech.*, note 51 (contracts terminable on short notice); Paddock Pub. v. Chicago Tribune Co., 103 F.3d 42, 47 (7th Cir.1996), cert. denied, 520 U.S. 1265, 117 S.Ct. 2435 (1997) (contract termination clause made it easy for rivals to bid business away); Barry Wright Corp. v. ITT Grinnell Corp., 724 F.2d 227, 236–238 (1st Cir.1983) (two year contracts approved); *Roland*, note 50, 749 F.2d at 394–395 (agreements that can be terminated on one year notice approved).

53. See 11 Antitrust Law ¶ 1802f (1998); Seagood Trading Corp. v. Jerrico, Inc., 924 F.2d 1555, 1572–1573 (11th Cir.1991) (defendant offered only one of many methods for delivery of restaurant supplies). Accord *Omega*, note 52, 127 F.3d at 1162 ("If competitors can reach the ultimate consumers of the product by employing existing or potential alternative channels of distribution, it is unclear whether such restrictions foreclose from competition

stations, then one must consider whether there are substantial barriers to two-level entry. The difficulty of entry should generally be evaluated under standards similar to those developed in the 1992 Horizontal Merger Guidelines and § 12.6 of this book.

As noted in the discussion of *Toys 'R' Us*,[54] the FTC has employed somewhat more aggressive rules to condemn exclusive dealing or output contracts under the FTC Act than those applied under either the Sherman Act or the Clayton Act.[55] At one time, the FTC Act was held to condemn exclusive dealing without detailed analysis of a relevant market or even computation of foreclosure.[56] The more recent trend on the Commission has been to adhere more closely to Sherman and Clayton Act standards, but to take market imperfections such as product differentiation more seriously.[57] This is consistent with the principle that more aggressive substantive rules are appropriate when remedies are limited and the rules cannot be enforced by private parties.[58]

any part of the relevant market."). Accord *CDC Tech.*, note 51.

54. See text at notes 47–48.

55. See § 10.3e on the use of a more expansive FTC Act standard for tying arrangements.

56. For example, L.G. Balfour Co. v. FTC, 442 F.2d 1 (7th Cir.1971).

57. E.g., Beltone Electronics Corp., 100 F.T.C. 68, 204 (1982) (evaluation of exclusive dealing requires tribunal to define a relevant market and measure foreclosure; and then also look at additional factors, such as "the duration of the contracts, the extent to which entry is deterred, and the reasonable justifications, if any, for the exclusivity."); Toys 'R' Us, note 47 (emphasizing presence of product differentiation in toy market).

58. On this justification for more aggressive antitrust rules under § 5 of the Federal Trade Commission Act, see § 15.2.

Chapter 11

INTRABRAND RESTRAINTS ON DISTRIBUTION

Table of Sections

§ 11.1 Introduction

This chapter deals with two broad categories of vertical integration by contract. One is vertical price fixing, or resale price maintenance (RPM), which is manufacturer or supplier regulation of the price at which a product is resold by independent dealers.[1] The second category is most generally classified as vertical nonprice restraints. Among the most common of these is vertical territorial division, which is supplier regulation of the location or sales territories of its distributors or retailers. Another important vertical nonprice restraint is the customer restriction, which limits the classes of buyers with whom a distributor or other reseller may deal. But vertical nonprice restraints come in numerous other varieties, including restrictions preventing a dealer from selling a particular model, limitations on mail-order sales, limitations on the kinds of contracts that dealers can write with customers, or limitations on the number of dealers that a supplier will permit in a given city or other area.

These restraints are described as "intrabrand," because they regulate a dealer's sales of a single brand without creating limitations on its sales of brands made by other suppliers. By contrast, "interbrand" distribution restraints limit the way downstream firms can use brands made by someone other than the firm imposing the restraint. The principal interbrand distribution restraints are tying arrangements and exclusive dealing, which are the subject of the previous chapter. Intrabrand distribution restraints are governed by § 1 of the Sherman Act. Interbrand distribution restraints are covered by § 3 of the Clayton Act as well.[2] Frequently a supplier uses both kinds of restraints simultaneously. For example, a supplier might provide in its dealer contracts that a dealer may sell only in a designated territory and deal only in the supplier's brand. This would be a combination of a vertical territorial restraint (intrabrand) and exclusive dealing (interbrand). In the balance of this chapter the term "vertical restraint" refers to an intrabrand restraint.

Few areas of antitrust law have provoked more reconsideration of established rules, or more disagreement between courts and commentators, than vertical price and nonprice restraints. Like all practices, they can be governed by three possible legal rules: *per se* illegality, rule of reason analysis, or *per se* legality. Unlike most other practices, however, in this area serious arguments have been made for all three positions.

Equally controversial is the fact that today the two sets of practices are governed by two different legal standards. Minimum RPM is *per se* illegal. By contrast, vertical nonprice restraints have received rule of reason treatment since 1977, and maximum RPM has been governed by the rule of reason since 1997. Many critics believe there is little justification

§ 11.1

1. In this chapter the words "upstream firm," "manufacturer," or "supplier" are used more-or-less interchangeability to refer to the upstream party to a vertical agreement. The words "downstream firm," "distributor," "dealer," "reseller," or "retailer" generally refer to the downstream party. The downstream party is an intermediary between the manufacturer and the end use consumer.

2. Clayton Act § 3, 15 U.S.C.A. § 15, makes it unlawful to lease or sell goods, etc., "on the condition, agreement or understanding that the lessee or purchaser thereof shall not use or deal in the goods * * * of a competitor * * * of the lessor or seller. * * * "

for the different legal treatment accorded minimum RPM and nonprice restraints. In fact, to the extent the effect on competition differs, vertical territorial restraints can actually be more anticompetitive than RPM.[3]

However, a vague Congressional mandate exists for making minimum resale price maintenance illegal. From 1937 until 1975 § 1 of the Sherman Act contained an amendment that permitted states to authorize "fair trade," or resale price maintenance. At one time or another 46 states passed such legislation. The federal "fair trade" enabling statute was repealed, however, because Congress believed that prices were higher in fair trade states than they were in other states.[4]

To be sure, repeal of fair trade is not a clear Congressional preference for a *per se* rule against resale price maintenance. However, it was a clear expression of Congress' general disapproval of resale price maintenance. If our experience with the rule of reason for nonprice restraints is any guide, a rule of reason for RPM would clearly undermine Congress' intent. Since the rule of reason was adopted for nonprice restraints, the vast majority have been upheld. The Supreme Court has said that by repealing the fair trade statute Congress "expressed its approval of a *per se* analysis of vertical price restrictions."[5] Congress has received several proposals to remove minimum RPM from the *per se* classification, but none has ever passed.

3. R. Posner, The Next Step in the Antitrust Treatment of Restricted Distribution: Per Se Legality, 48 U.Chi. L.Rev. 6, 9 (1981); see also Justice White's concurring opinion in Continental T.V., Inc. v. GTE Sylvania Inc.: "It is common ground among the leading advocates of a purely economic approach to the question of distribution restraints that the economic arguments in favor of allowing vertical nonprice restraints generally apply to vertical price restraints as well." 433 U.S. 36, 69, 97 S.Ct. 2549, 2567 (1977).

4. Consumer Goods Pricing Act, 89 Stat. 801, amending 15 U.S.C.A. §§ 1, 45. See Hearings on S. 408 Before the Subcommittee on Antitrust and Monopoly of the Senate Judiciary Committee, 94th Cong., 1st Sess. 174 (1975).

5. *Sylvania*, note 3, 433 U.S. at 51 n.18, 97 S.Ct. at 2558 n.18.

§ 11.2 Perceived Competitive Threats of Minimum RPM and Vertical Territorial Restraints

§ 11.2a. Introduction

Courts have suggested different reasons why RPM should be illegal. One is that it permits a manufacturer to take advantage of its retailers and deny them the freedom to set a price most advantageous to themselves.[1] Another is that RPM is really a manifestation of price fixing among the retailers, who have involved the manufacturer in the agreement so that it can help police the cartel.[2] A variation of the second is that a powerful individual dealer in its territory may insist that minimum prices be imposed on its retailer rivals. Of course, the first explanation applies to one set of circumstances, while the second explanation applies to another.

The first argument seems quite specious as a general proposition. The retailer's mark-up is the price a manufacturer pays to have its product distributed, and a manufacturer should be able to have its product distributed in the most efficient manner—that is, the one that maximizes its profits. Naturally, the manufacturer wants to keep distribution costs as low as possible. Any firm is best off if other firms in the distribution chain behave as competitively as possible.[3] Any profits from a retailer's mark-up accrue to the retailer, not to the manufacturer. Suppose a manufacturer's profit-maximizing price to consumers is $8.00, and the retailers' distribution costs are $1.00.

§ 11.2

1. Simpson v. Union Oil Co., 377 U.S. 13, 20–21, 84 S.Ct. 1051, 1056–57, rehearing denied, 377 U.S. 949, 84 S.Ct. 1349 (1964); United States v. A. Schrader's Son, Inc., 252 U.S. 85, 99, 40 S.Ct. 251, 253 (1920).

2. Dr. Miles Medical Co. v. John D. Park & Sons Co., 220 U.S. 373, 407–08, 31 S.Ct. 376, 384–85 (1911). The antinomy between the two arguments is discussed in R. Posner, Antitrust Policy and the Supreme Court: An Analysis of the Restricted Distribution, Horizontal Merger and Potential Competition Decisions, 75 Col.L.Rev. 282 (1975).

3. See § 9.2b, c.

The manufacturer will wholesale the product for $7.00 and the retailers, if they are competitive, will resell it at $8.00. If the manufacturer sells to its retailers for any price less than $7.00 but forces the retailers to charge $8.00, part of the monopoly profits will accrue to the retailers and be lost to the manufacturer. That is hardly "taking advantage" of retailers.

§ 11.2b. Vertical Restraints as Collusion Facilitators; Powerful Individual Dealers

The second argument noted above is that RPM is really carried out at the instigation of the retailers, who are engaged in price fixing. There are good reasons why retailers would want to involve their suppliers in a cartel. The suppliers may be in a better position to monitor the pricing activities of the retailers, since the manufacturers normally deal with each retailer, but the retailers do not normally deal with each other. In addition, if the manufacturers manage to take advantage of the *Colgate*[4] exception, they will be able to enforce RPM legally.

Such retailer cartels are alleged to come in two kinds. If the manufacturers in the market have no market power, then the retailers of any single manufacturer could not raise the price of the manufacturer's product to monopoly levels. Customers would switch to a different brand. For example, if Sylvania makes 5% of the nation's televisions, a cartel of Sylvania retailers could not charge a monopoly price for Sylvania televisions, any more than Sylvania itself could set a monopoly price. Customers would switch to Sony, Magnavox, Zenith or some other brand. In this situation only an "interbrand" cartel will work—that is, a cartel encompassing enough brands of televisions that the price fixers collectively have significant market power. Likewise, the RPM agreements facilitating the cartel would have to come from all these manufacturers.

By contrast, if Sylvania were a television monopolist, itself capable of charging a monopoly price, then the cartel of Sylvania retailers could likewise charge a monopoly price. The RPM agreements facilitating the cartel need come only from this monopoly manufacturer.[5]

RPM and vertical territorial restrictions can be evidence of retailer collusion only if 1) the manufacturer imposing the restriction is a monopolist in the retailer's area; or 2) the restriction is used by a very high percentage of the manufacturers in the market. Either of these phenomena would support the inference that the retailers subject to the restriction collectively have enough market power to engage in price fixing. In most of the big vertical cases that have come to the Supreme Court, however, the products at issue were produced by manufacturers with relatively small market shares, and there was little evidence that other manufacturers of the same product were imposing similar restrictions.[6]

4. See United States v. Colgate & Co., 250 U.S. 300, 39 S.Ct. 465 (1919), discussed below in § 11.4b.

5. See H. Hovenkamp, Vertical Restrictions and Monopoly Power, 64 Boston Univ.L.Rev. (1984); W. Liebeler, 1983 Economic Review of Antitrust Developments: The Distinction Between Price and Nonprice Distribution Restrictions, 31 UCLA L.Rev. 384 (1983); W. Liebeler, Intrabrand "Cartels" under *GTE Sylvania*, 30 UCLA L.Rev. 1 (1982).

If multibrand dealers had market power locally, they might be able to cartelize a product in which the supplier lacked market power.

6. For example, in Monsanto Co. v. Spray–Rite Service. Corp., 465 U.S. 752, 104 S.Ct. 1464, rehearing denied, 466 U.S. 994, 104 S.Ct. 2378 (1984) the defendant's market share in corn herbicides was 15% and in soybean herbicides was 3%. In Continental T.V., Inc. v. GTE Sylvania Inc., 433 U.S. 36, 97 S.Ct. 2549 (1977), on remand, 461 F.Supp. 1046 (D.Cal.1978), aff'd, 694 F.2d 1132 (9th Cir. 1982), the defendant's national market share was less than 5% and its market share in the restricted territories involved in the litigation was 2.5% and 15%. In United States v. Arnold, Schwinn & Co., 388 U.S. 365, 87 S.Ct. 1856 (1967), defendant's market share ranged from 22.5% to 12.8% during the relevant period. In United States v. Sealy, Inc., 388 U.S. 350, 87 S.Ct. 1847 (1967), the aggregate market share of the manufacturers was 20%. In the FTC Magnavox investigation, which yielded a consent decree, Magnavox's market share was found to be about 9%. Magnavox, 78 F.T.C. 1183 (1971). However, there are cases in which the manufacturer's market share was high enough to warrant a finding of monopoly power. In United States v. General Elec. Co., 272 U.S. 476, 47 S.Ct. 192 (1926), the market share exceeded 80%. Market power has become an issue in several vertical territorial division cases, and some defendants have been found to have substantial market power. See § 11.6b. See generally T. Overstreet, Jr., Resale Price Maintenance: Economic Theories and Empirical Evidence 45–49 (1983); T. Overstreet, Jr., & A. Fisher, Resale Price Maintenance and Distributional Efficiency: Some Lessons from the Past, 3 Contemp. Policy Issues 3 (1985).

Admittedly, retailers engaged in price fixing would profit greatly if manufacturers policed the cartel for them. However, why would the manufacturers agree to participate? The retailers' cartel will reduce output; so the retailers will buy less from the manufacturer. This will force the manufacturer's output below its profit-maximizing level. Even if the manufacturer is a monopolist, a cartel of its independent retailers will charge a price higher than the manufacturer's profit-maximizing price, and reduce output further.[7]

Perhaps the retailers will buy the manufacturers' participation by agreeing to share their monopoly profits. However, the manufacturer can keep *all* the monopoly profits to itself, either by substituting new retailers who behave competitively or else by vertically integrating into retailing. If the manufacturer is a monopolist, vertical integration will enable it to retain all the monopoly profits for itself. If the manufacturer is a competitor and the retailers are engaged in an interbrand cartel, vertical integration will enable the manufacturer to raise its own retail prices up to the level charged by the cartel, while retaining all the monopoly profits itself.[8] If all else fails, the manufacturer can report the cartel to the Department of Justice. Considering the fact that manufacturer participation in a retailer cartel is *per se* illegal under the antitrust laws and can yield treble damages or criminal liability, we cannot presume that manufacturer participation is common.

Analogous reasoning can be applied to manufacturer imposed territorial restrictions. Retailers may find it advantageous to engage in *horizontal* territorial division—in fact, division of territories can be an effective form of price fixing. Each retailer can become a monopolist in its own territory and establish its own profit-maximizing price and rate of output. Thus many of the incentives to cheat on the cartel are removed, and detection of cheating is often easier.[9]

Likewise, the retailers would prefer the territorial restrictions to be imposed from above. The manufacturers are better able to monitor the retailers than the retailers can monitor each other. Further, since 1977 vertical territorial restraints have been analyzed under the rule of reason, while naked horizontal territorial division is illegal *per se*.[10]

But again, the theory does not explain why the manufacturers would participate in the scheme. Any monopoly profits earned by the retailers are taken away from the manufacturers. The manufacturers could earn more by selling to additional outlets in the territories, or by opening their own outlets.

So dealer collusion is not the *presumptive* explanation for vertical restraints. At the same time, the possibility of retailer cartels facilitated by vertical restraints cannot entirely be ignored. To be sure, the argument that suppliers would resist dealer cartels is sound, but it can be pushed to far. Vertically related market participants *always* resist cartels, and some exist anyway. Vertical restraints may facilitate retailer collusion when vertically related firms cannot effectively resist, or where the profit maximizing course of action is to live with the cartel.

For example, suppliers of oil drilling equipment are probably injured by the OPEC oil cartel; they would sell more equipment if oil were produced at the competitive level. But given their lack of access to oil reserves, the equipment manufacturers may have no alternative but to accept the cartel as a condition of doing business. In some situations vertically related firms (whether suppliers or buyers) are in a position to discipline or avoid the cartel effectively, while in other situations they are not.

7. See § 9.2c and accompanying figures, showing that successive monopolists in a distribution chain drive the price higher, and output lower, than the first monopolist's profit-maximizing level. Precisely the same reasoning applies when the upper firm is a monopolist and the resellers operate as a cartel.

8. The best possible position for any firm is to be a nonmember of a cartel in a cartelized market. The firm can sell all it can produce at slightly under the cartel's price with no risk of legal liability. See § 4.1.

9. See § 4.1a.

10. United States v. Topco Assoc., Inc., 405 U.S. 596, 92 S.Ct. 1126 (1972). See § 5.2b4.

A wealth of history shows that dealers have attempted to use RPM imposed by suppliers to facilitate horizontal dealer collusion. Indeed, the *Dr. Miles* decision first condemning RPM was the byproduct of one of the biggest cartels in American history—an agreement by members of national associations of wholesale and retail druggists to fix the price of proprietary medical drugs.[11] In many of the early RPM decisions, there was strong evidence of horizontal as well as vertical collusion.[12] One of the most widely publicized incidents of dealer forced RPM occurred in the 1930's and involved the same industry as *Dr. Miles*. When the manufacturer of Pepsodent toothpaste stopped using RPM, druggists responded *en masse* by relegating Pepsodent to second class distribution or not distributing it at all, and the druggists' trade association campaigned for what amounted to a boycott. The manufacturer gave in and restored RPM.[13]

Effective dealer collusion that suppliers cannot evade is most likely when economies of scope at the *retail* level make single-brand distribution impracticable. For example, toothpaste and other pharmaceuticals are sold more efficiently by stores that sell many brands of toothpaste, as well as other products. If these stores are fixing prices, the manufacturer of a single brand—say, Pepsodent—cannot easily integrate into retailing on its own. This may be true even when the manufacturer is a monopolist in the manufacturing market. For example, the monopolist manufacturer of men's bow ties would probably not find it economical to open its own stores that sell nothing but bow ties. The manufacturer must rely on multi-brand, multi-product men's stores or department stores to distribute its product. As a result the manufacturer cannot integrate vertically in order to circumvent a retailer cartel. If all retailers in a particular retail market are members of the cartel, the bow tie maker may be forced to acquiesce.

There is also evidence that dealer cartels or trade associations have attempted to use RPM as an exclusionary device to restrain the development of lower cost forms of distribution. For example, the movement for "fair trade" was heavily supported by associations of small stores trying to limit the growth of larger, more efficient chains.[14] The thinking was that most customers actually preferred the smaller stores, provided that prices were the same; they would go to larger stores only if retail prices were lower. *Ex post*, one can look back and proclaim the movement unsuccessful, for the chains did in fact move in. But horizontal agreements that delay entry are socially costly, and much of antitrust is concerned with behavior whose harmful effects show up principally in the short run.

Most of the arguments applying to dealer cartels apply even more robustly to single dealers with substantial market power in their local resale markets. Such dealers are most likely to be multibrand stores, and the affected products are most likely to be those that cannot easily be sold by single brand or single product stores. As a result, manufacturers may have little power to discipline a powerful local dealer by integrating vertically.[15]

§ 11.2b1. Dealer Power; Policy Implications

How ubiquitous are dealer cartels, or dealers with enough market power to affect supplier behavior? If dealers with such power are extremely rare, then RPM pursued under this theory may not be worth the costs of expensive rule of reason analysis in many individual cases. RPM should simply be legal. Likewise, if

11. See H. Hovenkamp, Enterprise and American Law, 1836–1937 at 342–345 (1991).

12. See, for example, Continental Wall Paper Co. v. Voight & Sons Co., 148 Fed. 939 (6th Cir.1906), affirmed, 212 U.S. 227, 29 S.Ct. 280 (1909) (refusing to enforce RPM contract between colluding members of manufacturing association and price-cutting reseller); Loder v. Jayne, 142 Fed. 1010 (C.C.Pa.), affirmed, 149 Fed. 21 (3d Cir. 1906) (finding conspiracy among drug manufacturers to fix prices and impose RPM on retailers).

13. T. Overstreet, Jr., & A. Fisher, Resale Price Maintenance and Distributional Efficiency: Some Lessons from the Past, 3 Contemp. Policy Issues 3, 45–50 (1985); R. Larner, Vertical Price Restraints: Per se or Rule of Reason? 123, 131, in Economics and Antitrust Policy (R. Larner & J. Meehan, Jr., eds. 1989).

14. Overstreet & Fisher, note 13 at 46–50.

15. See 8 Antitrust Law ¶ 1604 (1989).

most instances of horizontal collusion can be detected and prosecuted, then the better course of action would be to pursue the dealer cartels directly.

Most of the Chicago School analysis urging *per se* legality has presumed that dealer power is extremely rare. Retail stores generally do not require highly specialized building or other productive assets, and stores selling one set of products can often change or add others readily. In sum entry is easy, and suppliers can quickly find new distribution outlets. Most importantly, manufacturers can always integrate into distribution themselves if resellers persist in charging monopoly prices.

But there is ample experience belying these assumptions. Large multi-brand chain stores almost certainly produce sufficient economies of scale and scope in retailing to give them substantial cost advantages over single-brand stores or small, individual stores. To that extent, entry into the market cannot be presumed to be easy—and not even vertical integration by manufacturers is likely to occur unless the manufacturer's output is broad enough to support brand-specific retailing.

Furthermore, most of the Chicago School analysis has assumed that dealers have little power to change proportions. In fact that is not the case. If there are multi-brand scale economies in retailing, individual retailers may have significant leverage over suppliers simply in the way that they promote individual brands. Dealers with market power may be in a position to give the best display space to price maintained brands, or to instruct their personnel to spend more time and resources promoting those items where profits are highest. Overall, American retailing may be quite competitive. But there is no reason to believe that the large multibrand, multiproduct reseller cannot exert substantial power over its suppliers. Indeed, in some competitive manufacturing markets for products that can be sold only by multiproduct stores, the biggest bottleneck in distribution may be the retailer. In part this is true because retail geographic markets are usually smaller than are wholesale markets. For example, most clothing moves wholesale in a nationwide or even worldwide market. By contrast, retail markets may be limited to a range of, say, thirty to fifty miles.[16]

There is also little reason for thinking that dealer collusion is unusually easy to detect. First of all, horizontal price fixing is illegal *per se*, and for that reason it is ordinarily kept secret. Sometimes our only evidence of price fixing is the devices that facilitate it, such as a pattern of vertical restraints. Second, certain kinds of price fixing may not require an explicit "agreement" among dealers at all, but can be accomplished through informal or tacit communications that are not reachable under § 1 of the Sherman Act.[17] Collusion of this kind can be greatly facilitated by such devices as RPM. Concentrated retail markets are particularly conducive to oligopoly coordination because public advertising is the only effective way of communicating prices. Rivals will know immediately about every price reduction. Third, when the restraints are solicited by a powerful single dealer there is no horizontal cartel agreement at all.

Before dealers are in a position to exercise power over their suppliers, several things must be true. A well designed rule of reason inquiry would look into these things. Unfortunately, since minimum RPM is illegal per se, questions about market position are generally irrelevant once a qualifying price agreement is found.

First, as a general matter the dealer must deal in multiple brands, and this must be necessitated by distributional economies. Manufacturers are able to control resellers who deal exclusively in their own brand, because they have a great deal of leverage over the reseller. Indeed, the manufacturer could deprive the reseller of all its inventory. But when the product must be sold by large multibrand stores, then the tables are often turned. Such resellers can acquire a great deal of leverage over suppliers.

16. On geographic markets, see § 3.6.

17. See § 4.2.

Second, the product must be one that can be sold at a supracompetitive price. This means that the product must have some kind of dominance within a properly defined relevant *retail* product market. The important question is not the product's nationwide market share, assuming it is distributed in a national market, but its share in the municipality or other geographic area where retail customers shop and can seek out alternatives. At the same time, we are not looking for the power to engage in monopolistic exclusionary practices, but merely the power to raise price profitably. A share in the range of 40–50 percent should be sufficient, given that the market is typically subject to both product differentiation and spatial differentiation among sellers—that is, the retailer taking advantage of the restraints is likely to be in a favored position vis-a-vis other retailers.

Importantly, in considering dealer power in this fashion, it is not necessary that the dealer be larger or more powerful than the supplier in any absolute sense. In a distribution system requiring multibrand reselling, the dealer is the bottleneck, and a small neck can restrict the flow from a very large bottle. At the same time, the retailer itself (or cartel of retailers) must have a certain kind of dominance in sales of the good made subject to the challenged restraint. For the same reasons as above, a market share requirement on the order of 50% seems to be about right.[18]

So under a rule of reason analysis a set of rough, presumptive thresholds should be a *brand* that covers about half or more of the sales in the local market (or an aggregation of brands if the restraint covers several), and a *dealer* (or group of dealers) that cover about half of the sales of that brand or brands. The first figure could be less if the same vertical restraints are used on all or most brands of the product in question. For example, if the manufacturers of three brands use RPM, one should aggregate their market shares.

The threat of inefficient, dealer-initiated restraints is stronger if the dealer sells in many different markets, and replacing the dealer would be costly to the supplier. For example, if a nationwide or regional chain of department stores includes fifty or more well-placed stores, a supplier wishing to switch may have to find alternative outlets in all fifty areas. If a fifty-store clothing retailer handling numerous brands announces a policy of no longer dealing with suppliers who also sell to discounters, any particular supplier would have to consider the high costs of losing the chain as the price for violating the policy.[19] In such cases, even a dealer with a relatively small share in a particular local market could be using the restraint anticompetitively. If the dealer is highly desired by customers, RPM could enable it to increase its own market share even as overall output is reduced in a particular market. That is, stores with less prestige compete on price. Once price competition is eliminated, customers will tend to shop at stores which they find most attractive for other reasons.

§ 11.2b2. Manufacturer Collusion and Vertical Restraints

Writers have also argued that vertical restrictions may facilitate collusion at the manufacturer rather than the retailer level. As § 4.1 noted, vertical integration can enable a cartel to police its members more carefully. Sales made to wholesalers or distributors are generally large, secret, and individually negotiated. The cartel member has an incentive to cheat by shading price, providing extra services, engaging in reciprocity,[20] or accepting secret rebates. Since the chances of detection increase with the number of such cheating sales, it is important that each sale be large. Retail prices, by contrast, are generally public, relatively standardized at particular locations, and individual transactions are small. Effective price concessions can be communicated only by public advertising, which competitors will

18. See 8 Antitrust Law ¶ 1604f3 at 61–62 (1989).

19. See, for example, Burlington Coat Factory Warehouse Corp. v. Esprit De Corp., 769 F.2d 919, 922 (2d Cir.1985), where a multimarket retailer may have coerced a manufacturer in this way not to sell to discounters. The court found that the agreement requirement was not met. See § 11.4.

20. On reciprocity, see § 10.8.

see. By imposing RPM or territorial restrictions on retailers, a manufacturers' cartel may be able to monitor prices and number of sales at the retail level.

The manufacturers' cartel will work, however, only if its members collectively control enough of the market to wield monopoly power. Furthermore, price or output verification by vertical restrictions will work only if all cartel members use it. As a result the restrictions are evidence of a manufacturers' cartel only if most manufacturers in the market are using them. Presumptively, at least, if fewer than half of the manufacturers in a properly defined market are using a restraint, it is not likely to be a facilitator of manufacturer collusion. If more than half are using them, then one must look at the concentration level of the users. A Four–Firm Concentration Ratio less than 50%, or a Herfindahl reading less than 1000, suggests a market in which manufacturer collusion is unlikely, although not necessarily impossible.[21]

At least one study of Justice Department and FTC cases has concluded that the use of vertical restraints to support manufacturer cartels is uncommon, although the percentage of cases may have been as little as 4% or as much as 33%.[22] However, when plaintiffs challenge RPM, they do not produce the kind of evidence needed to ascertain whether it is a collusion facilitator. Minimum RPM standing alone is illegal *per se*. Further, tacit, or oligopolistic coordination facilitated by vertical restraints is probably the more serious threat, and such conduct is not directly reachable under § 1.[23] Finally, challenges to particular instances of RPM will not necessarily identify RPM used by other suppliers because the practice itself is kept secret. In sum, we have little way of knowing how often RPM or nonprice restraints are used to facilitate horizontal price fixing or tacit coordination of upstream prices; but the percentage could be substantial, and a figure as high as one-third is certainly not trivial.

§ 11.2c. Foreclosure Effects

Vertical restraints might facilitate a dominant manufacturer's scheme to limit rivals' ability to find suitable dealers. The success of any foreclosure scheme of this kind depends on the height of entry barriers into the dealer market and the market share of the strategizing manufacturer. Further, exclusive dealing or tying are generally more effective than intrabrand restraints in restricting rivals. That is to say, the manufacturer's concern is to make it more difficult for the manufacturers of other brands to retail their product. Exclusive dealing and tying place direct restrictions on a reseller's ability to sell the brands of others. But vertical restraints might be used by suppliers to "compensate" desirable dealers for agreeing to an exclusive dealing arrangement.[24] In such cases, the best course of action is to analyze the competitive effects of the exclusive dealing arrangement itself.[25]

§ 11.2d. Price Discrimination

Vertical restrictions, particularly vertical territorial or product assignments, may be designed to facilitate price discrimination by the manufacturer. Price discrimination occurs when the seller makes higher profits from one set of customers than from another. In order to engage in persistent price discrimination a seller must have a certain amount of market power: assuming the low profit sales are profitable, the high profit sales earn at least some monopoly profit. If the seller had no market

21. The Four–Firm Concentration Ratio is the sum of the market shares of the market's four largest firms. The Herfindahl is the sum of the squares of the market shares of all the firms in the market. Thus a market with ten equal size firms (10% market share each) has a Herfindahl of 1000. See § 12.4.

22. S. Ornstein, Resale Price Maintenance and Cartels, 30 Antitrust Bull. 401, 430–431 (1985). For a critique, see 8 Antitrust Law ¶ 1606f at 104–105 (1989).

23. See § 4.2.

24. See 8 Antitrust Law ¶ 1648c (1989); M. K. Perry & D. Besanko, Resale Price Maintenance and Manufacturer Competition for Exclusive Dealerships, 39 J.Indus. Econ. 517 (1991).

25. On exclusive dealing, see § 10.9.

power, those customers asked to pay a monopoly price would seek out a different seller.[26]

The two most significant practical barriers to price discrimination are the difficulty of identifying and segregating groups of customers willing to pay different prices, and the difficulty of preventing arbitrage. Arbitrage occurs when favored purchasers (those who pay the lower price) resell the product to disfavored purchasers and frustrate the price discrimination scheme.

Vertically imposed territorial or customer restrictions can enable a manufacturer to solve both these problems. For example, suppose that the manufacturer produces a disinfectant used by both hospitals and restaurants. The hospitals have fewer available substitutes for the disinfectant, and they are willing to pay a higher price than the restaurants. The manufacturer could discriminate in price between the two groups of customers by using two different distributors, giving one the exclusive right to sell to hospitals, and the other the exclusive right to sell to restaurants. Alternatively, the manufacturer could engage in "dual distribution," by selling to the hospitals itself but using an independent distributor for the restaurants. In this case the customer restrictions help the manufacturer segregate the customers and prevent arbitrage, because each class of customers deals with a different seller and has little reason to know that a different group of customers is buying the same product from someone else. Both vertical customer restraints and vertical territorial restraints have been used by manufacturers to facilitate price discrimination in this way. For example, in the *Clairol* case the manufacturer produced a hair coloring agent, which it sold in two different bottles, one for solons and one for retail customers. Although the two bottles contained the same ingredients and packaging costs differed by 2¢, Clairol sold the salon version for 46¢ less per bottle. Its restraint system, which survived challenge, forbad distributors of the salon version from making that version available to general retailers.[27]

Should vertical restraints be condemned simply because they facilitate price discrimination? The efficiency effects of such restraints is almost impossible to measure. Price discrimination schemes often increase output and rarely exclude rivals.[28] At the same time, however, price discrimination does not invariably increase output, and it can be costly to administer. As a basic premise, the best answer seems to be that the existence of price discrimination alone should not warrant condemnation of a restraint.

§ 11.2e. Other Theories

Numerous other theories have been offered as to why RPM and nonprice restraints might be harmful to consumers. Developing such models is essential to the policy enterprise of antitrust, and few questions—particularly not this one—should be regarded as settled. But most of the other anticompetitive explanations for vertical restraints are either excessively conjectural, excessively complex, or else not sufficiently robust to cover a wide range of circumstances.[29] Several of these arguments are based on the premise that vertical restraints reduce output, but such results generally do not serve the interests of the supplier unless they are part of a collusion scheme.[30]

26. For the economics of price discrimination, see §§ 14.1–14.3.

27. Clairol v. Boston Discount Center of Berkley, 608 F.2d 1114 (6th Cir.1979). Other likely examples of restraints used for price discrimination are Graphic Prods. Distrib., Inc. v. ITEK Corp., 717 F.2d 1560 (11th Cir. 1983); Davis–Watkins Co. v. Service Merchandise, 686 F.2d 1190 (6th Cir.1982), cert. denied, 466 U.S. 931, 104 S.Ct. 1718 (1984), both of which involved territorial restrictions. See JBL Enterprises, Inc. v. Jhirmack Enterprises, Inc., 698 F.2d 1011 (9th Cir.1983), cert. denied, 464 U.S. 829, 104 S.Ct. 106 (1983), which involved customer restrictions. See Hovenkamp, Vertical Restrictions and Monopoly Power, note 5.

28. See § 14.3.

29. Some of these theories are analyzed in B. White, Black and White Thinking in the Gray Areas of Antitrust: the Dismantling of Vertical Restraints Regulation, 60 Geo. Wash.L.Rev. 1 (1991); W. Grimes, The Seven Myths of Vertical Price Fixing: the Politics and Economics of a Century–Long Debate, 21 Sw. U. L. Rev. 1285 (1992). See also T. Overstreet & A. Fisher, Resale Price Maintenance and Distributional Efficiency: Some Lessons from the Past, 3 Contemp. Policy Issues 3 (1985).

30. See, for example, R. Steiner, Sylvania Economics—a Critique, 60 Antitrust L.J. 41 (1991); W.F. Mueller, The Sealy restraints: Restrictions on Free Riding or Output, 1989 Wis. L. Rev. 1255 (1989).

To be sure, some suppliers' predictions about the consequences of vertical restraints may be wrong, and output may go down rather than up. But antitrust policy is generally not intended to protect firms from their own self-deterring errors.

§ 11.3 Vertical Restraints and Efficiency

§ 11.3a. The Free–Rider Problem

Most instances of RPM or vertical territorial division are not explained by the anticompetitive theories summarized in § 11.2. Most manufacturers use such restrictions not to facilitate price fixing, which reduces output, but to enlarge output by encouraging retailers to market the manufacturer's product more aggressively and efficiently.

Often the manufacturer is attempting to avoid one of the many variations of the "free rider" problem. Suppose that Chrysler Motor Co. has two auto dealerships in Wichita. Dealer A is stocked with a full inventory of cars (which the dealer carries at its own expense), has a large and expensive showroom, many sales agents who spend a great deal of time displaying cars and giving test drives to prospective purchasers, and an excellent service department that makes many pre-sale and post-sale adjustments to new cars. Dealer B, located across town, rents one room in a warehouse, has no inventory, gives no test rides, has no service department, and does all its negotiating over the telephone.[1]

The point-of-sale services given by Dealer A are expensive, and Dealer A must charge about $500 more than it pays for a new car just to cover its distribution costs. By contrast, Dealer B does quite well with a mark-up of $100. What do you do as a new car buyer? Perhaps you will go to Dealer A's large showroom, look at the cars, test drive one or more, collect a good deal of information, and leave, telling the salesperson that you will "think about it." Then you go to Dealer B and place an order for the car you want.

The information you obtained from Dealer A was essential to your decision making. For example, you probably would not have purchased a Chrysler had you not been permitted to test drive one. You avoided paying for the information you gathered, however, by purchasing from a different dealer who did not supply the information and was able to sell the car at a lower price. You and Dealer B in this case took a "free ride" on the point-of-sale information offered by Dealer A.

Unfortunately, Dealer A does not make money giving test drives; the dealer must sell cars. It will not stay in business long if everyone takes advantage of its information system but purchases their cars from Dealer B. Further, if Dealer A goes out of business Chrysler's Wichita sales will decline substantially, because most customers insist on being able to obtain this vital information *somewhere* before they purchase a particular brand of automobile. In order to compete effectively with other automakers, Chrysler must have a mechanism for providing potential customers with test drives and other vital information.

Suppose, however, that Chrysler requires its Wichita dealers to charge the same resale price for various models of automobiles—say, $14,000 for a particular model. Now you as customer have no incentive remaining to make your purchase from the cut-rate dealer, which must charge the same price anyway. You will go to the dealer who does the best job of providing the kind of information and customer service that is important to you when you buy a car. The cut-rate dealer will have to clean up its act or lose business. In fact, with the final output price given, the two dealers will compete with each other, not in price, but in the amount of services they can deliver. Competition between them will drive the level of services up to the point at which their marginal costs equal the maintained price. They will be left with a competitive rate of return, and the auto manufacturer will obtain the amount of services that it has calculated will do the best job of marketing its cars.[2]

1. For a roughly similar story, see United States v. General Motors Corp., 384 U.S. 127, 86 S.Ct. 1321 (1966).

2. See L. Telser, Why Should Manufacturers Want Fair Trade? 3 J.L. & Econ. 86 (1960); R. Bork, The Rule of

Similar analysis applies to vertical territorial restraints. Instead of establishing a resale price, Chrysler might simply terminate Dealer B (the cut-rate dealer) and give Dealer A the exclusive right to retail new Chryslers in Wichita. Now Chrysler can be assured that its customers will obtain the point-of-sale information and services that they want. Dealer A will have a contract with Chrysler, which tells the dealer how much service to provide. The dealer no longer has the disincentive of a cut-rate dealer stealing its customers. Further, Dealer A is not a monopolist: it still competes with other automobile retailers in Wichita, and cannot take a free ride on their services. For example, a customer will not test drive a Ford in order to determine whether she wants to purchase a Chrysler. Nor will the Ford dealer perform warranty maintenance on new Chryslers. The Chrysler dealer who wants to compete with the Ford dealer will do these things for itself. The result is that Chrysler will make more sales in Wichita.

The free rider problem also applies to advertising. If a city contains five dealers in Sony stereo equipment, and one of them advertises that Sony equipment is better than the equipment of other manufacturers, the benefit of the advertising will accrue to all five dealers. No dealer will be willing to pay for the advertising if it is likely to pick up only 20% of the increased purchases that result. Indeed, it may pick up less than 20% because the other Sony dealers, not having to pay for the advertising, may be able to charge a lower price. There may be alternative solutions to this problem: one is a joint advertising venture among the dealers; another is for the manufacturer itself to pay for the advertising and pass on the costs to the dealers; a third is exclusive territories within which all the benefits of the advertising are likely to accrue to a single dealership.

§ 11.3a1. The Economics of Vertical Restraints to Combat Free Riding

Under the free rider theory, manufacturer-imposed RPM or territorial restraints are a mechanism for *increasing* output, not reducing it. When Chrysler (who is not a monopolist) imposes RPM or territorial restraints on its dealers, it has predicted that retail customers will value the point-of-sale information and services more than the cost of providing them.

Figure 1 (following page) illustrates the manufacturer's prediction. Demand curve D represents demand for the product without point-of-sale services. Demand curve D′ represents market demand for the product with the point-of-sale services. At any given level of output, D′ yields a higher price than D, because customers are willing to pay more for the product if the services are provided. If the dealers are forced to sell the product at a certain price, they will continue to compete, not in price, but in delivery of the services. In Figure 1, MC is the marginal cost curve of dealers not providing the services. MC′ is the higher marginal cost curve of dealers who provide the services. Without RPM dealers would tend not to give the services in order to compete in price. Their price would be P and output would be Q. However, if the manufacturer maintained the resale price at level P′ the dealers would compete in services until their marginal costs equaled the maintained price. That would happen when output reached Q′. The difference between Q and Q′ is the number of additional sales that the manufacturer would make as a result of RPM. Essentially the same thing would happen if the manufacturer relied on vertical territorial restraints. The dealer would then be competing with the dealers of other brands. Since customers value the services more than the cost of providing them, competition will drive the level of services up to MC′ and output to Q′.

Reason and the Per Se Concept: Price Fixing and Market Division (part 2), 75 Yale L.J. 373 (1966); R. Posner, The Rule of Reason and the Economic Approach: Reflections on The *Sylvania* Decision, 45 U.Chi.L.Rev. 1 (1977).

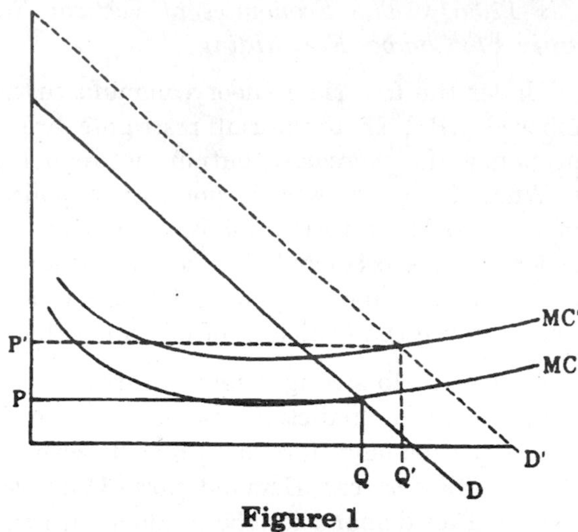

Figure 1

Whether a manufacturer chooses resale price maintenance or some form of nonprice restraint to enhance sales depends on the circumstances. One of the most important circumstances is the relevant legal rule. Since minimum RPM is illegal *per se* but vertical territorial division obtains a rule of reason,[3] some manufacturers undoubtedly have turned to territorial restrictions.

Additionally, however, some products are more conducive to resale price maintenance and others to territorial division. For example, it would not make much sense for a manufacturer of a nonprescription medicine to establish a single store in a large city: convenience and number of outlets is an important element in the marketing of drugs. If the manufacturer wants retailers to provide a certain level of services, such as point-of-sale information, resale price maintenance would be more sensible.

By contrast, restrictions on location may be more useful for big ticket items that involve rather expensive customer services—major appliances, televisions, or automobiles, for example. First of all, numerous locations are relatively less important with such items. Second, prices are often negotiated individually with customers, at least over a relatively narrow range. Third, price competition with other brand manufacturers may be very intense at the retail level (the more expensive the item, the more sensitive customers are to price), making resale price maintenance too inflexible. Likewise, territorial restraints work best for traveling distributors or dealers that must provide on-site information and assistance to their customers. Manufacturers of farm chemicals or seed, for example, commonly assign exclusive territories to their dealers, as do manufacturers that rely on wholesale distributors to retailers.

Exclusive territorial restrictions tend to transfer much more risk to the dealer than does resale price maintenance. The exclusive dealer in a territory has the sole responsibility for selling its manufacturer's product, and if sales decline the blame can quickly be placed. This makes territorial restrictions particularly valuable for products where the amount of dealer contribution to the product's success is particularly high.[4]

§ 11.3a2. The Domain and Efficiency of Vertical Restraints to Combat Free–Riding

After the "free rider" theory of vertical restraints was developed, some true believers wrote as if the theory fully explained all important uses of vertical restraints except the occasional collusion facilitator. But today it seems quite clear that vertical restraints do not effectively deal with all free rider problems. Further, as § 11.3b develops, the free rider model fails to explain some noncollusive vertical restraints. Finally, § 11.3c notes that vertical restraints used to combat free-riding are not necessarily efficient.

First, in many cases involving dealer services, RPM will not effectively eliminate free-riding. To return to the Chrysler example. The discounter may continue to free ride on the full service dealer's services but compete by throwing in some other service or good at the maintained price. For example, suppose Chrys-

3. See § 11.6.

4. See J. Tirole, The Theory of Industrial Organization 190–192 (1988); compare A.P. Minkler, Why Firms Franchise: A Search Cost Theory, 148 J. Institutional and Theoretical Econ. 240 (1992), which emphasizes the use of vertical restrictions in helping suppliers take advantage of the dealer's superior knowledge about local markets.

ler uses a $14,000 maintained price and a wholesale price of $13,500 in order to force dealers to invest $500 worth of dealer services into each sale. Once again, Dealer A offers the test drive, etc. Dealer B competes with Dealer A, not by offering the test drive, but rather by including a "free" $500 television, extended service warranty, or a dealer installed stereo system with each car. You as customer will once again obtain your information from Dealer A, and then go to Dealer B who promises the bigger package at the same price.[5]

Free riding is a much greater problem in some markets than it is in others. As a result the nature of the product can help a court determine whether a particular restraint was designed to combat free rider problems, or was imposed for some other reason. First, free rider problems are greatest in "brand-specific" products, where customers distinguish brands and are not indifferent as to which brand they purchase. For example, a prospective automobile customer is likely to need a test drive in order to help her decide whether to buy a Ford, Chrysler or Toyota. Such point-of-sale services are generally not important in markets for fungible products. As a result, vertical restrictions in the markets for potatoes, lumber, cement, or paper clips should be viewed with greater suspicion.

Second, free rider problems are greatest in markets for technically complex or new products where customer education is particularly important. Although toothpaste is differentiated by brand, it is unlikely that many consumers require elaborate on-site education in order to appreciate its benefits. Personal computers are quite a different matter.

Nevertheless, one must not push this second point too far. Sometimes relatively simple commodities are easily subject to free riding.[6] For example, a person might go to a downtown department store to look at luggage or books or wallpaper in order to identify a model or design that seems right, and then telephone an order to a mail order seller who offers a steep discount.[7] Likewise, one might examine the offering of a local bookstore that sells many titles, or a local music store selling compact disks, but then buy from the internet or a mail order discounter. In such cases it is not the technical sophistication of the product but rather the need for the consumer to obtain information about its look, feel or sound, that creates the opportunity for free riding.

§ 11.3b. Variations on the Free–Rider Problem and Alternative Explanations

§ 11.3b1. Purchase of Preferred Distribution Services; Shelf Space; Quality Certification

Many commodities sold subject to RPM or nonprice restraints seem not to require significant consumer educational services at the point of sale. Among these are toothpaste, candy, blue jeans, men's underwear, pet supplies, and beer. Competitive explanations for vertical restraints in products that appear to require no point-of-sale services have been manifold. The following discussion summarizes those that appear most plausible and that seem to apply to a broad range of situations.

Many of the products sold subject to RPM, but where point-of-sale services seem insubstantial, share one characteristic: economies of scale or scope at the retail level demand that they be sold by multi-brand or multi-product retailers. For example, a store would be unlikely to deal exclusively in Levi's brand blue jeans. Jeans are distributed most efficiently if they can be placed in a large number of stores in a single city. In that case demand in each location will be insufficient to sustain the entire store. As a result Levi's are most generally sold in clothing stores which offer other

5. See R. Pitofsky, In Defense of Discounters: the No–Frills Case for a *Per Se* Rule Against Vertical Price Fixing, 71 Geo. L.J. 1487, 1493 (1983).

6. Some authors believe that product complexity predicts the likelihood of a free rider explanation. P. Ippolito, Resale Price Maintenance: Empirical Evidence from Litigation, 34 J.L. & Econ. 263, 283 (1991).

7. See Alvord–Polk v. F. Schumacher & Co., 37 F.3d 996 (3d Cir.1994), cert. denied, 514 U.S. 1063, 115 S.Ct. 1691 (1995) (finding a conspiracy between "full service" wall paper dealers to force manufacturers to decline to deal with "800 number" dealers who were free-riding on the full service dealers' provision of sample books and installation advice).

brands of blue jeans as well as other types of clothing, or even in department stores that sell a wide array of products.

When Levi Strauss sells its blue jeans through, say, Macy's Department Stores, Levi is effectively purchasing distribution services from Macy's. Importantly, these services are not fungible. Macy's has preferred shelf space in the center of the store, and less satisfactory space hidden in the corners. Further, if Macy's has a very positive image in the eyes of consumers, its handling of a product serves as a kind of certification that the product is good.[8] It hires people to assemble displays, and has considerable discretion about how much expense and effort will go into one particular item's promotion rather than another's.

The amount and quality of shelf space, and the amount that Macy's will spend promoting a particular product is a function of anticipated profitability. If RPM insulates Macy's from price competition for Levi's and enables it to take a relatively high mark-up, Macy's will respond by providing shelf space and promotion up to the point that the expense and opportunity cost of providing these amenities rise to the maintained price. In short, RPM in Levi's will encourage Macy's to sell Levi's a little harder, necessarily at the expense of other items in Macy's stores. The "point-of-sale" services exist, just as much as they would for home computers or automobiles. However, they are more subtle, buried in the retailer's pre-sale decisions about what combination of sales efforts will maximize its profits.[9]

§ 11.3b2. Facilitating Resale Density

Firms also use RPM to obtain high density of distribution. For some relatively inexpensive but space-consuming products, it is more important to manufacturers to have them available on every corner, so to speak, than to have them available at the lowest possible price. In such cases RPM may guarantee relatively high cost outlets a sufficient margin to carry a product.[10] The theory generally requires that different groups of customers have differing amounts of willingness to search or travel longer in order to obtain a lower price. To use a simple illustration, suppose that newspapers could be sold by discounters or large grocery stores at 25¢ but that small convenience stores would not carry them at a price lower than 50¢. Newspapers have two groups of buyers. Group A is willing to pay 50¢ for a newspaper, but they will also walk or drive the extra block or two, or put up with the longer line, in order to buy their newspaper for 25¢. Group B will buy their newspaper from whichever store is closest or most convenient, and not give any thought to the 25¢ higher price. In this situation, without RPM the discounters will sell the newspaper for 25¢ and the convenience stores will sell it for 50¢. The convenience stores will lose all of group A, and this may make carrying newspapers unprofitable. With RPM, both must charge 50¢. Then both groups of customers will shop the convenience stores as much as the discounters. The effect of the RPM may be to make it profitable for both groups of stores to sell the newspaper, thus increasing density of distribution.

§ 11.3b3. Facilitating Supplier Entry

RPM may be especially valuable for a manufacturer that is trying to break into the market for the first time. Once again, widespread exposure is important for the new entrant, and RPM may serve to place the product in the stores of sellers who would not take a risk without RPM. The distribution cost that must be overcome is the cost of dealer uncertainty about whether the new product will produce

8. See H.P. Marvel & S. McCafferty, Resale Price Maintenance and Quality Certification, 15 Rand. J.Econ. 346 (1984).

9. See also O. Williamson, Assessing Vertical Market Restrictions: Antitrust Ramifications of the Transaction Cost Approach, 127 U.Pa.L.Rev. 953 (1979), who argues that RPM can reduce the transaction costs of inducing behavior from dealers, where the dealer and supplier maximize in different ways.

10. T. R. Overstreet, Jr., Resale Price Maintenance: Economic Theories and Empirical Evidence 45–49 (1983); J.R. Gould & L.E. Preston, Resale Price Maintenance and Retail Outlets, 32 Economica 302 (1965). See also P. Ippolito & T.R. Overstreet, Resale Price Maintenance: an Economic Assessment of the FTC's Case Against the Corning Glass Works, 39 J.L. & Econ. 285 (1996) (finding seller density as most likely explanation for resale price maintenance of simple glass items).

enough revenue to cover whatever investment the dealer must make in including it in inventory. The studies finding that RPM used promotionally for this reason have also found that RPM persists in such markets after it has outlived its usefulness—that is, even after the product is well established and dealer uncertainty reduced. The reason given is simple inertia; once parties are protected by RPM and earning a profit, they are reluctant to give it up.[11]

§ 11.3b4. Protection of Dealer Margins; Enforcement of Distribution Contracts

The theories described above seem to explain why RPM or nonprice restraints are efficient (output increasing) in various circumstances. But none of the theories is so general that it could be made to apply to all circumstances involving vertical restraints. Some products need elaborate point-of-sale services, while others do not. Some products need continuing service after the sale has been made, and the traditional inter-dealer free-rider theory does not seem to account for these situations very well. Of course, a general theory is unnecessary. Some manufacturers may employ price or nonprice restraints for one reason, and some for another.

But one theory has been offered that seems very general, and probably applies to a wide range of circumstances. It even applies quite well to service after the sale and, perhaps more importantly, to inter-dealer services, which some products require. For example, a car sold by Dealer A may need to have warranty repairs by Dealer B. Perhaps more extreme, a consumer who buys a complex product from Dealer A may need information about it when she travels to a distant city, and the customer may expect local Dealer B to provide that information without compensation.

Vertical restraints may be mechanisms for enforcing distribution contracts by making termination costly to dealers. Contracts between manufacturers and dealers can apply to the full range of products and dealer services that manufacturers wish their dealers to provide. A supplier "enforces" a contract with a dealer by terminating the dealer or taking some less drastic disciplinary measure, such as reducing the supply of a profitable item. But these enforcement threats are credible only if the dealership in the manufacturer's products is profitable. One conceptual difficulty with the traditional free-rider model is that dealers compete in the giving of nonprice services until their costs rise to the price. Dealers make only a competitive rate of return. A dealer who is earning no more than a competitive return on product A may not be injured very much if its manufacturer terminates the dealer, assuming that the market for products is reasonably competitive. The dealer will simply find another product paying the competitive rate of return. Of course, to the extent the dealer has made irreversible capital investments in product A, these will be lost by the switch and they give the dealer an incentive to adhere to the distribution contract. But if the dealer is a retailer, these investments are not likely substantial.

Resale price maintenance and vertical nonprice restraints may thus serve to ensure that dealers earn positive profits by protecting them from significant intrabrand competition. The effect of the profits is that termination of a dealership is costly to the dealer, thus giving it a powerful incentive to honor the terms of whatever contractual understanding it has with the supplier. The value of this conception of distribution restraints is that it applies across the full range of products and services that we see governed by price and nonprice restrictions.[12]

11. T. Gilligan, The Competitive Effects of Resale Price Maintenance, 17 Rand J.Econ. 544 (1986). See also T. R. Overstreet, Jr., Resale Price Maintenance: Economic Theories and Empirical Evidence (1983).

12. The argument comes from B. Klein & K.M. Murphy, Vertical Restraints as Contract Enforcement Mechanisms, 31 J.L. & Econ. 265 (1988). Compare Business Electronics Corp. v. Sharp Electronics Corp., 485 U.S. 717, 728, 108 S.Ct. 1515, 1521 (1988) (suggesting that vertical non-price restraints ensure that dealers earn enough profits to pay for necessary services). Accord P. Kaufmann & F. Lafontaine, Costs of Control: the Source of Economic Rents for McDonald's Franchisees, 37 J.L. & Econ. 417 (1994). Cf. H.P. Marvel, The Resale Price Maintenance Controversy: Beyond the Conventional Wisdom, 63 Antitrust L.J. 59 (1994) (arguing that, inter alia, resale price

Under this theory, the restraints themselves provide the carrot, while the threat of termination of those who violate the distribution contract is the stick. As noted above, this explanation for vertical restraints seems quite general in that it applies to many product types. It has its own limitations on domain, however. Assuming that dealerships are competitive across brands, vertical restraints may provide sufficient dealer margins only if there is significant product differentiation in the market or the supplier has a very large market share. For example, vertical territorial restraints in the market for electric space heaters will not provide much of a dealer margin if the amount of interbrand competition is significant and consumers have plenty of choices from other brands.[13]

§ 11.3c. Vertical Restraints and Efficiency Reconsidered

Even assuming that RPM or nonprice restraints successfully increase point-of-sale services, is the outcome efficient? Not necessarily. Even a vertical restriction that increases output may sometimes be inefficient. Suppose that a market contains "marginal" customers that need to be educated about a particular good, and numerous "inframarginal" customers who already value the good highly and know how to use it. In this case a seller may increase output by offering point-of-sale services designed to bring the marginal customers into the market, but price the services into the product in such a way that *all* consumers, including the inframarginal ones, must pay for it.

For example, suppose that a computer seller puts up elaborate displays, and offers "free" seminars and a great deal of education from the sales floor to potential customers. The customers most likely to be brought into the market by these activities are those that are thinking about a computer for the first time and have to be convinced of its value. But a much larger group is already hooked on computers and values them highly. If the seller charges all customers the same price, then all end up paying for the education services even though only a small percentage need them.

Figure 2 illustrates. P_1 equals the dealer's marginal cost when few point-of-sale services are offered. Under those conditions demand for the product is D_1. Now suppose that the supplier imposes RPM at P_2, with the result that the dealer provides point-of-sale services that increase its marginal costs up to P_2 as well. The impact of the point of sale services is to move the demand curve out to D_2. But in this case, unlike the case described in § 11.3a above, D_2 and D_1 are not parallel. The two demand curves are relatively close together in the upper range and relatively far apart in the lower range. The upper range customers—those who place the highest value on the product—are really not benefitted very much by the additional services. By contrast, more marginal customers are benefitted a great deal and place a much higher value on the product as point-of-sale services are increased.

maintenance encourages dealers to carry larger inventories).

13. Other good work on the rationales for vertical restraints, some of it fairly technical, includes P. Rey & J. Tirole, The Logic of Vertical Restraints, 76 Am.Econ.Rev. 921 (1985); W. S. Comanor & H. E. Frech III, The Competitive Effects of Vertical Agreements, 75 Am. Econ. Rev. 539 (June 1985) (arguing that vertical restraints can be used to raise rivals costs); S. Ornstein & D.M. Hanssens, Resale Price Maintenance: Output Increasing or Restricting? the Case of Distilled Spirits in the United States, 36 J. Indus. Econ. 1 (1987) (concluding that the "free rider" and other pro-competitive arguments for RPM seem not to apply; the principal effect seemed to be to raise liquor prices and thus transfer wealth to retailers).

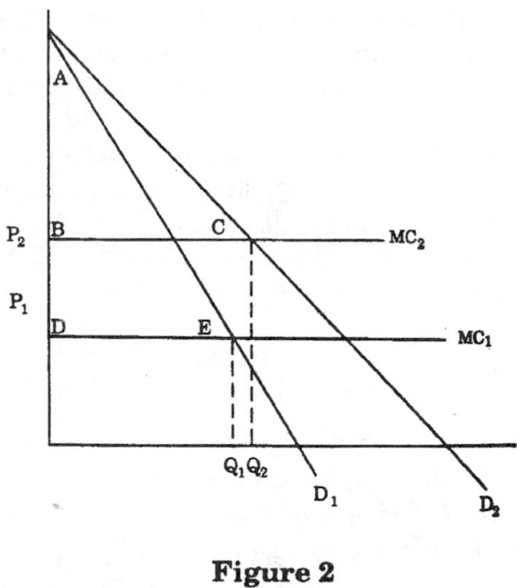

Figure 2

[626a]

Output without the point-of-sale services is Q_1; with them it is Q_2. The manufacturer is better off, for the wholesale price is presumably the same, and the manufacturer profits from higher output. The dealer is presumably better off as well; although it is making only a competitive rate of return, it is making that return on a higher rate of output. By one measure of consumer welfare, output, customers are better off.

But in the Figure 2 case, consumer welfare as measured by consumers' *surplus* is actually lower under resale price maintenance. At price P_1 and without the point-of-sale services, consumers' surplus was triangle A–D–E. At price P_2 and with the services, consumer welfare is triangle A–B–C, which is smaller than A–D–E.[14] Even when RPM forces increased dealer service and higher output, the resulting consumers' surplus can actually be smaller.

Is this observation a useful policy critique of vertical restraints? That is, should we condemn some restraints even if they are shown to increase output? Probably not. Even if the manufacturer were engaged in self-distribution to the retail level, the same problems would show up. For example, a manufacturer-owned Chrysler automobile dealership in high rent New York City would probably have an expensive showroom, even though the principal impact of the showroom is on marginal customers, or those who do significant comparative shopping before making their purchases. The group of more committed Chrysler owners probably do not need the showroom, and they would continue to buy even if the showroom were located in a less well traveled part of the City. But in setting a price the costs of the showroom will be spread across all the customers, not merely the ones whom it has been instrumental in drawing into the market. Indeed, the inframarginal customers may end up paying the higher price, because they are less sensitive to the competition.

In sum, many dealer services are very "lumpy." The optimal package is not the best package for everyone, and invariably one set of customers will end up paying for services or product enhancements that benefit only another set. Such lumpiness is not a monopoly problem, notwithstanding that not every customer is getting the most consumers' surplus possible. In a perfect world perhaps a manufacturer would have different dealers providing differing amounts of service to different classes of customers, and charging accordingly. But in the real world there may not be any way to force the high-service-demanding customers to pay the higher prices for their services, if the low service dealers are present in the area and offering lower prices as well.

One can generalize about the above problem even further: not only distribution, but also most product innovation occurs at the margin of the demand curve. That is to say, the innovation is designed to bring into the market a group of customers that were not in it before. The innovation may not benefit inframarginal customers—indeed, in some cases

14. On consumers' surplus, see § 1.1a. See F.M. Scherer, The Economics of Vertical Restraints, 52 Antitrust L.J. 687 (1983); W.S. Comanor, Vertical Price–Fixing, Vertical Market Restrictions, and the New Antitrust Policy, 98 Harv. L. Rev. 983 (1985); W.S. Comanor & J.B. Kirkwood, Resale Price Maintenance and Antitrust Policy, 3 Contemp. Policy Issues 9 (1985). See also W.S. Comanor, The Two Economics of Vertical Restraints, 21 Sw. U.L.Rev. 1265 (1992); B. White, Resale Price Maintenance and the Problem of Marginal and Inframarginal Customers, 3 Contemp. Policy Issues 17 (1985). The basic theory of the inframarginal consumer comes from A. M. Spence, Monopoly, Quality, and Regulation, 6 Bell J. Econ. 417 (1975).

they may prefer not to have it. Nevertheless, in most cases when the product is priced, all will be asked to pay for it.[15]

A second problem with the observation about the lost welfare of inframarginal customers lies in making it operational. A court would have to distinguish RPM or nonprice restraints that reduced consumers' surplus from those that increased it. Even output cannot be used as a surrogate. In Figure 2 above, output is higher even though consumers' surplus is smaller. The comparison of the size of the two consumers' surplus triangles in Figure 2 depends on fairly accurate information about the location of the two price curves and, more importantly, the shape and the location of the resulting demand curves.

Unfortunately, two things seem to be true today. First, no *general* theory of vertical restrictions explains all of them or tells us whether they are anticompetitive or competitive as a general matter. Second, we have relatively little good information about how often restraints such as RPM are used for procompetitive and how often for anti-competitive reasons. Several studies have looked at litigated RPM cases; but litigated cases probably represent a skewed sample.[16] For example, given the collateral estoppel effects of antitrust actions, the stakes in vertical restraints litigation may be lopsided in favor of the plaintiff; that is, defendants stand to lose more than a particular plaintiff stands to gain. This suggests that plaintiffs will be more aggressive about going to trial, and thus the pool of litigated cases will tend to be more marginal than the overall pool of cases.[17] If so, we would expect the sample of litigated cases to contain relatively fewer cases in which collusion was evident, where the evidence of agreement on a particular price was very strong, and so on. In any event, collusion,[18] powerful dealers, elimination of free riding, and use of vertical restraints to enforce distribution contracts are all reasonable explanations for some litigated cases, but none explains all of them.

§ 11.4 The Agreement Requirement in Vertical Restraints Cases

§ 11.4a. Agreements—Horizontal and Vertical, Price and Nonprice

Both RPM and vertical nonprice restraints are challenged under § 1 of the Sherman Act as contracts, combinations or conspiracies in restraint of trade. Just as with the law of horizontal price fixing,[1] illegal vertical restraints cannot be condemned without evidence of a qualifying agreement among two or more firms to impose the restraint. The agreement need not be with the plaintiff—for example, it could be an agreement with a supplier and the disciplined dealer's competitor.[2] The agreement could also be one among suppliers to impose RPM or vertical nonprice restraints on dealers below. But a purely unilateral decision to impose such restraints is not reachable under § 1.

The conceptual differences between a horizontal agreement and a vertical agreement are significant. For example, competitors meeting together to discuss market prices may provoke considerable suspicion. But a supplier and a dealer are necessarily parties to a buyer-seller

15. For example, a CD player may be designed with a remote control in order to capture marginal consumers, but those not wishing the remote control will have to buy it as well if they wish that particular model.

16. S. Ornstein, Resale Price Maintenance and Cartels, 30 Antitrust Bull. 401, 430–431 (1985); P. Ippolito, Resale Price Maintenance: Empirical Evidence from Litigation, 34 J.L. & Econ. 263, 281–292 (1991).

17. See G. Priest & B. Klein, The Selection of Disputes for Litigation, 13 J.Legal Stud. 1 (1984); Ippolito, note 16, 34 J. L. & Econ. at 272–273.

18. Ippolito, note 16 at 292 agrees with Ornstein, note 16, that collusion at either supplier or dealer level explains only a small number of cases. But neither author takes into account the facts that (1) tacit manufacturer collusion does not count as "collusion"; (2) single powerful dealers can achieve results similar to those achieved by dealer cartels; and (3) since RPM is independently illegal, underlying collusion may never be investigated or discovered. A dealer disciplined for failing to adhere to RPM may or may not know that the RPM was being used to facilitate upstream collusion.

§ 11.4

1. See §§ 4.4–4.6.

2. However, a purely horizontal agreement among suppliers to terminate a dealer for failing to adhere to a vertical restriction is best dealt with as a concerted refusal to deal. See § 5.4.

agreement, and they presumably discuss prices all the time.[3] As a result, in vertical restraints cases the evidentiary focus tends to be the *content* of agreements, while horizontal cases tend to focus on the *fact* of agreement. As § 11.5d notes, when courts determine whether vertical agreements concern "price," they are much stricter than when they make that determination respecting horizontal agreements. A horizontal agreement that merely "affects price" can be illegal per se. By contrast, a vertical agreement does not count as a "price agreement" unless it establishes a rather specific price or price level.

The basic agreement requirement for price and nonprice restraints is the same.[4] Nevertheless, the agreement requirement looms much larger in RPM cases. Since minimum RPM is illegal *per se*, proving a qualifying price "agreement" is often tantamount to establishing the violation. By contrast, most vertical nonprice restraints are legal whether or not there is a qualifying agreement. Indeed, vertical restraints imposing territorial boundaries, store locations, customer restrictions and the like, are often specified in writing in distribution agreements that are signed by both supplier and dealer. The existence of an agreement is therefore not disputed. Only badly advised firms would place resale price maintenance agreements in writing.

§ 11.4b. The Colgate Doctrine

The Supreme Court first stated the agreement requirement for vertical restraints in United States v. Colgate & Co.[5] The *Colgate* decision was the unforeseen result of a badly drafted indictment, which neglected to "charge Colgate * * * with selling its products to dealers under agreements which obligated the latter not to resell except at prices fixed by the company." Rather, the indictment alleged 1) that Colgate entered into sales contracts with retailers; 2) that it separately announced an intention not to make such contracts with retailers who sold for less than Colgate's posted retail prices; 3) that it subsequently refused to deal with price cutters, as it announced. In an era inclined to equate the "agreement" requirement in antitrust with common law contract doctrine, the Court quite easily separated the sales contract on the one hand from Colgate's apparently "unilateral" refusal to deal on the other. The Sherman Act was not designed to "restrict the long recognized right of a trader or manufacturer [to] announce in advance the circumstances under which he will refuse to sell."[6]

Given RPM's great potential to increase efficiency and its relatively small potential for economic harm, the *per se* rule condemning it makes little sense. This may suggest some wisdom in the *Colgate* doctrine. One of the difficulties with *Colgate*, however, is its excessive formalism that sends people looking for qualifying legal "agreements." *Colgate* stands for the controversial proposition that when a manufacturer simply announces its intention not to deal with price cutters and dealers respond by not cutting price, there is no violation because there was no "agreement" between the manufacturer and the price cutting retailer.[7]

Courts have traditionally construed the *Colgate* doctrine narrowly. In order to claim the exception the manufacturer can do no more than announce its intent not to deal with price cutters, and later refuse to deal with a violator. As the Supreme Court held in *Parke, Davis*, if the manufacturer warns, threatens,

3. See 11 Antitrust Law ¶ 1902d (1998).

4. See Parkway Gallery Furniture v. Kittinger/Pennsylvania House Group, 878 F.2d 801, 805 (4th Cir.1989) (agreement requirement is same for price and nonprice restraints, and for rule of reason and per se violations).

5. 250 U.S. 300, 39 S.Ct. 465 (1919).

6. On the relation between *Colgate* and the Supreme Court doctrine of liberty of contract, see E.P. Krugman, Soap, Cream of Wheat and Bakeries; the Intellectual Origins of the *Colgate* Doctrine, 65 St. John's L. Rev. 827 (1991).

7. See United States v. A. Schrader's, Inc., 264 Fed. 175, 183 (N.D.Ohio 1919), reversed, 252 U.S. 85, 40 S.Ct. 251 (1920): "Personally, and with all due respect, * * * I can see no real difference * * * between the Dr. Miles Medical Co. case [refusing to enforce an RPM agreement] and the Colgate Co. case. * * * The tacit acquiescence of the wholesalers and retailers in the prices thus fixed is the equivalent for all practical purposes of an express agreement * * *."

or intimidates its retailers in any way, it is likely to fall out of the exception and into the *per se* prohibition.[8]

Its formalism notwithstanding, the *Colgate* doctrine continues to have a great deal of vitality. In Russell Stover Candies, Inc. v. FTC.[9] the Eighth Circuit reversed a Federal Trade Commission decision that would have emasculated the doctrine. A divided FTC had found that Stover, a large candy manufacturer, fell outside the *Colgate* exception because its announcements of intent not to deal with price cutters and its subsequent refusals to do so established a "course of dealing" that amounted to an agreement. The Commission concluded that "there is no sound legal distinction between coercion resulting from the threat of * * * terminating a franchise and coercion resulting from a communicated policy of terminating supply * * * to dealers who fail to comply with the manufacturer's pricing policies."

In reversing the FTC's decision, the Eighth Circuit conceded that the *Colgate* doctrine might be formalistic. Nevertheless, the doctrine had been created by the Supreme Court and no one but the Supreme Court should overrule it. In *Monsanto*,[10] the Supreme Court expressly refused to overrule *Colgate*, holding that it continues to be "of considerable importance that independent action by the manufacturer * * * be distinguished from price-fixing agreements," since only the latter are subject to the *per se* rule. In fact, the Court went so far as to say that an agreement could not be inferred from the fact that a supplier terminated one dealer in response to a second dealer's complaints about the first dealer's price cutting.

One serious analytic problem with the *Colgate* doctrine as originally developed, is that it seems inimical to the basic rationale for RPM and other vertical restrictions. Such restrictions are a form of vertical integration which enable a manufacturer to achieve optimal distribution of its product. The restrictions should be approved when their potential for creating efficiency is apparent, and condemned only when there is some potential for economic harm.

Colgate, however, is predicated on the natural right of retailers to be free from manufacturers. In order to claim the exception a manufacturer must not become too involved with its retailers. Vertical integration often necessitates a great deal of cooperation and communication between a manufacturer and the retailers who make up its distribution system. One of the chief advantages that a manufacturer obtains from outright ownership of its own retail outlets is the right to operate the stores, displaying and pricing the merchandise as it sees fit. Often the manufacturer is a specialist, while the retailer is a generalist. However, *Colgate* tends to approve RPM only when the level of vertical integration between manufacturer and retailer is very small. The result is that RPM is most available in those situations where it is least valuable—where there is no organized "distribution system" at all.

§ 11.4c. The Rehabilitation of Colgate; Dealer Terminations

One effect of the *per se* rule against RPM and the *Colgate* exception was a rule once adopted by several circuit courts that a supplier could not lawfully terminate a distributor in response to a competing distributor's complaints that the terminated distributor had been cutting prices. In applying the *per se* rule, different courts characterized this conduct in different ways. For example, in Cernuto, Inc. v. United Cabinet Corp.[11] the Third Circuit held that when a supplier terminates a dealer as a result of a competing dealer's complaints, "the restraint becomes primarily horizontal in nature in that one [dealer] is seeking to suppress its competition by utilizing the power of a common supplier." In Spray–Rite Service

8. United States v. Parke, Davis & Co., 362 U.S. 29, 80 S.Ct. 503 (1960).

9. 718 F.2d 256 (8th Cir.1983).

10. Monsanto Co. v. Spray–Rite Svce. Corp., 465 U.S. 752, 763, 104 S.Ct. 1464, 1470 (1984).

11. 595 F.2d 164 (3d Cir.1979). See also Bostick Oil Co. v. Michelin Tire Corp., 702 F.2d 1207, 1213–15 (4th Cir.), cert. denied, 464 U.S. 894, 104 S.Ct. 242 (1983) (supplier pressure placed on dealer after complaint from other dealers created jury issue on agreement).

Corp. v. Monsanto Co.,[12] the Seventh Circuit agreed that such conduct should fall within the *per se* rule, but it developed two different theories than the "horizontal" theory used in *Cernuto*. One theory was that by acting in response to a distributor's complaint, the supplier and distributor were effectively engaged in a *per se* illegal group boycott of a competitor, the terminated distributor. The second theory was that the termination in response to a competitor's price complaint effectively took any attempt by the supplier to control distributor pricing out of the *Colgate* exception, because the conduct could no longer be described as "unilateral."

The Supreme Court affirmed the Seventh Circuit's finding of liability, but held that a court could not infer the existence of an RPM agreement "merely from the existence of complaints, or even from the fact that termination came about 'in response to' complaints." Rather, the evidence must show "a conscious commitment to a common scheme designed to achieve an unlawful objective."[13] In this case the evidence was sufficient to support the jury's finding of a "common scheme" to set resale prices. As the court noted, however, most cases involving allegations that a supplier terminated one dealer in response to another dealer's complaints arose in the context of distribution systems that contained nonprice restrictions. As a result the termination may not have been the result of illegal RPM at all, but was really motivated by a dealer's violation of territorial restraints. Any rule that prevented a "manufacturer from acting solely because the information upon which it acts originated as a price complaint would create an irrational dislocation in the market."

The Supreme Court's conclusion about the relevance of price complaints is hard to dispute. A supplier generally imposes RPM or nonprice restraints in order to combat free riding problems, to force dealers to comply with their distribution contracts or to make an adequate investment in distributing the supplier's product.[14] Furthermore, free riding injures *both* the supplier and dealers who compete with the free rider. As a result, no inference of an agreement can be drawn from the fact that a dealer or retailer complained. The complaining dealer is reporting a violation by a competing dealer that injures the complainant; the supplier is responding by disciplining a violation that injures the supplier. The supplier is acting in its *individual* best interest and no agreement can be inferred.

Since *Monsanto*, some courts have weakened the *Parke, Davis* rule that *any* amount of pressure placed on dealers takes the supplier's action out of the unilateral category. For example, in *Isaksen* the court suggested that even supplier harassment about prices should not make the conduct illegal unless the harassment actually caused the dealer to raise its prices.[15]

The *Monsanto* doctrine applies to dealer initiated restrictions as well as those that originate with the supplier. For example, in *Burlington* a large clothing retailer that sold multiple brands announced that it would no longer handle the brands of suppliers that serviced "off price" retailers as well.[16] Subsequently a

12. 684 F.2d 1226, 1238 (7th Cir.1982). The decision was affirmed on other grounds in *Monsanto*, note 10.

13. *Monsanto*, note 10, 465 U.S. at 768, 104 S.Ct. at 1471.

14. See § 11.3.

15. Isaksen v. Vermont Castings, Inc., 825 F.2d 1158, 1163 (7th Cir.1987), cert. denied, 486 U.S. 1005, 108 S.Ct. 1728 (1988). See also Jeanery, Inc. v. James Jeans, Inc., 849 F.2d 1148, 1158–1159 (9th Cir.1988) (not illegal to advise dealers that they will be terminated if they do not adhere to resale prices).

The courts have also held that discriminatory treatment among dealers, rewarding those who make increased sales, is not a violation of § 1 of the Sherman Act, even though the dealers in question might be able to increase their sales only by cutting their retail prices. For example, Monahan's Marine, Inc. v. Boston Whaler, Inc., 866 F.2d 525 (1st Cir.1989); Alliance Shippers v. Southern Pac. Transp. Co., 858 F.2d 567 (9th Cir.1988). Of course, differential pricing to dealers may violate the Robinson–Patman Act. See § 14.6.

16. Burlington Coat Factory Warehouse Corp. v. Esprit De Corp., 769 F.2d 919 (2d Cir.1985) (discussing *Monsanto*); Garment District v. Belk Stores Servs., 799 F.2d 905, 908–909 (4th Cir.1986), cert. denied, 486 U.S. 1005, 108 S.Ct. 1728 (1988) (discussing both *Colgate* and *Monsanto*). Contrast Ezzo's Inv. v. Royal Beauty Supply, 94 F.3d 1032 (6th Cir.1996) (permitting jury to infer unlawful RPM agreement between manufacturer and distributor in response to complaining dealers, followed by a distributor's order to the plaintiff to sell at suggested retail prices).

supplier terminated its relationship with a discounter in order to retain the larger retailer's business. In applying *Monsanto*, the court noted that a dealer as well as a supplier is generally free to announce unilaterally the conditions under which it will deal.

Since the 1970's, the great majority of restricted distribution cases have been private actions brought mainly by dealers who were terminated or disciplined by suppliers. In some of these cases there was no formal agreement restricting price or imposing nonprice restrictions at all.[17] In others there was a contractually established set of nonprice restrictions.[18] With respect to the latter, an "agreement" requirement was satisfied. However, plaintiffs seldom win cases challenging vertical nonprice restraints. They must generally show a qualifying agreement *about price*. Indeed, as the Supreme Court made clear in *Business Electronics*, the agreement must not merely be one "about price," but it must be an agreement about the particular prices that the disciplined dealer is permitted to charge.[19] What most of the cases have in common is that the plaintiff dealer's termination occurred after communication between the supplier and one or more dealers in competition with the plaintiff.

These cases pose an analytic problem for one simple reason: although the records often uncover agreement-like language, in most cases the conduct that results is perfectly consistent with individual profit-maximizing behavior. What we have is a fairly old contract story. Suppose neighbor A tells neighbor B that a rotting tree on B's property is about to topple onto A's house. A day later B has the tree removed. Have the parties agreed? Probably not, because there was no consideration. Even if A said "I'll sue unless you remove the tree," B's response would not constitute an agreement, for A was not giving anything up. That is, once B removed the tree, A lost the right to maintain a lawsuit anyway. Assuming that the fall of the tree is tortious, it is in B's best interest to remove the tree whether or not A and B have an agreement.

The great majority of dealer termination cases are quite similar. For example, supplier X may have two dealers in a town, A and B. To make the strongest possible case, suppose that A complains with this language: "*B is cutting price, and if you don't make B stop I am going to stop handling your product.*" X then terminates B. Is there an agreement? Ordinarily, X would wish to maximize its sales in the town, and low prices would facilitate this. If that were the entire story, we would expect X to reject A's complaint and favor the low priced dealer. But even if X investigates and then terminates dealer B, we expect that X does so only because it will maximize X's profits.

If X discovers that B has been free-riding, and providing an inadequate level of services itself or making too small an investment in its facility, then A's statement should be regarded as nothing more than informational. To be sure, the threat part of the statement suggests that A did not have the most competent legal advice. But the threat itself mainly reflects that free-riding injures A as well as supplier X.[20] A is simply telling X, that as long as B is permitted to engage in free riding, A finds dealing in X's product to be unprofitable.

Under what circumstances should A's statement plus X's subsequent discipline of B be considered an "agreement?" B would have to show that X's response was sensible (profit-maximizing) *only* on the assumption that A was giving something in return. That is, it must be clear that X would be better off having both A and B as dealers, even with B's current behavior; but that if forced to choose between A and B, X would prefer A. In that case A's threat acts as consideration, for it

17. For example, McCabe's Furniture v. La–Z–Boy Chair Co., 798 F.2d 323 (8th Cir.1986), cert. denied, 486 U.S. 1005, 108 S.Ct. 1728 (1988).

18. For example, Morrison v. Murray Biscuit Co., 797 F.2d 1430 (7th Cir.1986).

19. Business Electronics Corp. v. Sharp Electronics Corp., 485 U.S. 717, 728, 108 S.Ct. 1515, 1521 (1988). See § 11.5d.

20. See for example, Helicopter Support Sys. v. Hughes Helicopter, 818 F.2d 1530 (11th Cir.1987) (mere fact that dealer complains, which suggests that it would benefit from competing dealer's termination, insufficient to establish agreement).

effectively requires X to choose between A and B, even though X's preference is to keep both.

A prerequisite to this finding is A's market power in the downstream market. If dealers such as A are easily found and one is as good as another, then X will not terminate B unless it is in X's independent best interests to do so. So the first step in inferring an agreement in complaint-plus-termination cases is an examination of A's (the complaining dealer's) market position, or the collective position of A and other dealers who have launched or participated in similar complaints.

This determination generally need not involve a full blown inquiry into market power; rather, the court wants to know if A is a highly sought after dealer who is viewed by suppliers as distinctly better than others in the city or region at issue. That is, will the manufacturer pay a certain price to have A as a dealer?[21] Indeed, in some cases the question of market "power" is not really the right one; the term "market position" might be better. For example, suppose that dealer A is a chain store with two hundred outlets across the country, while dealer B is a single store discounter. Dealer A threatens to stop dealing in X's brand unless X terminates B. In that case, A may have little or no market power in the 200 towns where it does business; however, the threat from A forces X to compare the administrative costs of finding substitutes for A in 200 areas, against the losses that result from its termination of B.[22] In such a case it is quite worthwhile to consider whether the termination is in X's best interest in the community of the terminated dealer, or whether it was profit-maximizing only because it forced X to consider this expensive tradeoff.

In such cases, A's power may derive from nothing more than the transaction costs of locating 200 new stores to replace A if A makes good on its threat. If these costs are substantial, they may place dealer A and supplier X in a kind of bilateral monopoly relationship. Indeed, substantial switching costs place the dealer and supplier in precisely the situation described by Ronald Coase in "The Problem of Social Cost."[23] Each has made substantial investments in the status quo. *General* lack of market power notwithstanding, the costs of switching may incline one firm to pay a certain price in lower output in order to maintain the existing relationship. We would expect the firms to reach a solution that maximizes their *joint* profits, and if the costs of permitting multistore dealer A to get rid of a few troublesome price cutters is less than the costs of replacing dealer A, then the profit maximizing solution would involve supplier X's listening to dealer A.[24]

So in determining agreement, one must look at the supplier's *independent* best interest—that is, what would the supplier's best interest be on the assumption that some generic dealer, totally lacking in market power, had made the complaint? For example, Apple Computer Company met this test when it convinced the court that its ban on low price mail order sales was necessary because it believed that optimal customer education required a face to face transaction.[25] In this regard, pro-

21. For example, Lomar Wholesale Grocery v. Dieter's Gourmet Foods, 824 F.2d 582, 594 (8th Cir.1987), cert. denied, 484 U.S. 1010, 108 S.Ct. 707 (1988) (court more likely to find anticompetitive agreement where powerful dealer "forces upon an unwilling supplier more restrictive intrabrand restraints than the supplier would have imposed in serving his own interest in efficient distribution * * * ").

22. See Garment District v. Belk Stores Servs., 799 F.2d 905 (4th Cir.1986), cert. denied, 486 U.S. 1005, 108 S.Ct. 1728 (1988) ("Jantzen, weighting the advantage of selling to 200 Belk [complaining dealer] stores against selling to the Garment District [the plaintiff], opted to drop the Garment District. * * * "; ultimately finding no agreement).

23. 3 J.L. & Econ. 1 (1960). Accord A.J. Meese, Price Theory and Vertical Restraints: A Misunderstood Relation, 45 UCLA L. Rev. 143 (1997).

24. The same situation might occur if the supplier has made a substantial investment in dealer A (but not in dealer B, about whom A's complaint is made), and this investment will be lost if A stops selling the supplier's product.

25. O.S.C. v. Apple Computer, 792 F.2d 1464, 1467–1468 (9th Cir.1986); accord H.L. Hayden Co. of N.Y. v. Siemens Medical Sys., 879 F.2d 1005, 1014 (2d Cir.1989); Parkway Gallery Furniture v. Kittinger/Pennsylvania House Group, 878 F.2d 801 (4th Cir.1989); Trans Sport v. Starter Sportswear, 964 F.2d 186 (2d Cir.1992) (supplier's policy against permitting sales from one dealer to another supported by valid business reasons, such as a concern about dealer free-riding and counterfeiting).

bative evidence should include facts tending to show that the supplier employs the same distribution restraints elsewhere, and that it has disciplined dealers for similar violations where no inference of agreement was warranted. The fact finder should also consider the validity of the reasons advanced for terminating the plaintiff.[26]

The post-*Monsanto* courts have struggled mightily with the issue of when an "agreement" can be inferred from a supplier response to a dealer complaint. They have attempted a variety of formulations. First of all, in some cases involving dealer complaints the complaining dealer was not even soliciting an agreement. For example, suppose Dealer A telephones a supplier and says "Dealer B is certainly advertising low prices; I do not know how B can do this and still perform all its contractual customer service obligations." Thereafter the supplier investigates and terminates B. No agreement was sought and none should be found.[27] Other courts have suggested that no agreement can be inferred if the record suggests that, even though the dealer complained about price, the supplier's concern was not price but rather the level of the terminated dealer's promotional services or investment in the supplier's product.[28] Other courts have said that the termination shall be regarded as unilateral whenever it is justified by independent business reasons, regardless of the price motive of the complaining dealer.[29] As this rule has been applied in some cases, the supplier need produce only a set of plausible explanations why the termination was appropriate; it need not show the particular reason that explains the termination at issue.[30] One court has even held that when Dealer A complains about Dealer B's prices, the supplier's wish not to lose A's business is a sufficient independent reason for terminating B.[31] This seems to be coming very close to establishing an "agreement."

Courts have more readily found an agreement when the complaints came from a group of dealers who appeared to be acting in concert.[32] The horizontal dealer agreement is itself sufficient to meet Sherman § 1's agreement requirement. However, the plaintiff must still prove causation—and causation would generally not be established if the supplier's termination was based entirely on its independent judgment. For example, suppose that Dealers B . . . *n* are disturbed by Dealer

26. For example, McCabe's Furniture v. La–Z–Boy Chair Co., 798 F.2d 323, 329 (8th Cir.1986), cert. denied, 486 U.S. 1005, 108 S.Ct. 1728 (1988) (considering supplier's claim that dealer termination was necessary to assure quality of dealer services).

27. See, for example, Morrison v. Murray Biscuit Co., 797 F.2d 1430, 1439–1440 (7th Cir.1986) (no agreement, where dealer complained about competitor's low prices but did not ask supplier to change any prices or agree with it on prices).

28. Lomar Wholesale Grocery v. Dieter's Gourmet Foods, Inc., 824 F.2d 582, 589 (8th Cir.1987), cert. denied, 484 U.S. 1010, 108 S.Ct. 707 (1988).

29. Dunnivant v. Bi–State Auto Parts, 851 F.2d 1575, 1580–82 (11th Cir.1988) (business justifications for termination undermined conspiracy claim); Houser v. Fox Theatres Mgmt. Corp., 845 F.2d 1225, 1232 (3d Cir.1988) (no agreement, since supplier was acting in independent best interest).

30. See H.L. Hayden Co. of N.Y. v. Siemens Medical Sys., 879 F.2d 1005, 1014 (2d Cir.1989), holding that the termination of a mail order seller did not show a conspiracy with complaining dealers because the supplier could point to "the ineffectiveness of mail order marketing" for its particular product, and the impact on the supplier's reputation when sales were made without "proper installation and servicing."

31. *Garment District*, note 22, 799 F.2d at 909:

> "Jantzen [supplier] was forced to choose between the Garment District [price cutter] and Belk [complaining dealer]. It chose Belk, which was a larger customer. Therefore, even if Jantzen's concern about the Garment's District's image was pretextual, it still had a legitimate, independent reason to terminate their relationship."

Was the interest really "independent?" If I contract to give you my lawn mower in exchange for $100, would one say that there is no agreement because I have an "independent reason" for giving it up—namely, receipt of your $100!

32. Big Apple BMW v. BMW of North Amer., 974 F.2d 1358 (3d Cir.1992), cert. denied, 507 U.S. 912, 113 S.Ct. 1262 (1993) (denying summary judgment against plaintiff's claim of conspiracy among BMW dealers to force distributor to deny plaintiff's application); Arnold Pontiac–GMC, Inc. v. General Motors Corp., 786 F.2d 564, 569 (3d Cir.1986) (same); Lovett v. General Motors Corp., 769 F.Supp. 1506, 1511–1512 (D.Minn.1991), reversed in part, 998 F.2d 575 (8th Cir.1993) ("full price" dealers conspired to eliminate price cutting dealer). But see Valley Liquors v. Renfield Importers, 822 F.2d 656, 661–662 (7th Cir.), cert. denied, 484 U.S. 977, 108 S.Ct. 488 (1987), refusing to infer a conspiracy among dealers from the mere fact that multiple dealers had complained.

A's low prices. B . . . *n* agree with each other to register a complaint to the supplier, whose investigation shows woefully inadequate customer service and other breaches of A's distribution contract with the supplier. In that case, the resulting termination cannot be said to be *caused* by the agreement among dealers. The complaint should be dismissed for lack of cause in fact.[33]

Courts have also found agreements more readily when the supplier *returns* to the dealer after the termination and reports to the effect that "corrective action has been taken."[34] This suggests that there was a kind of quid pro quo in the complaint-response-report sequence.

§ 11.4d. The Agreement Requirement and Antitrust Policy Respecting Vertical Restraints; Restraints Initiated by Powerful Dealers

As a policy matter, can the *Colgate* rule still be defended? The answer, perhaps surprisingly, is yes, but not in the manner that early post-*Colgate* courts articulated it. If one's goal is to eliminate all forms of resale price maintenance, then *Colgate*'s agreement requirement appears quite irrational, for a well behaved supplier can often maintain RPM successfully without ever committing acts constituting an agreement.

But suppose one takes a broader view and wants to distinguish those instances of resale price maintenance or nonprice restraints that are anticompetitive from those that further the independent interests of the supplier by minimizing free riding, maximizing appropriate dealer investment, or that enable the supplier to enforce its dealership contracts.[35] When vertical restrictions are imposed for efficient reasons, they tend to increase supplier output. As a result, they are profitable to the supplier without regard to any agreement that the supplier may have with a competitor or with a vertically related firm. That is to say, when resale price maintenance or a nonprice restriction is imposed without an agreement, then the restriction is output enhancing and should generally be regarded as efficient.

By contrast, suppose a powerful local dealer forces its suppliers to impose RPM on competitors in order to support its own higher resale prices.[36] We could properly infer an "agreement" between the powerful dealer and the various suppliers, for the latter are not acting according to their independent best interest. Independently, they would rather expand their output by selling to the powerful dealer's lower price competitors. They accede to the RPM only to avoid losing the powerful dealer's business. In this case an agreement requirement also helps one distinguish between competitive and anticompetitive uses of vertical restraints.

As a general matter, a supplier's interest lies in maximizing its output, which it does when its dealers supply the optimal mixture of price competition and dealer services. By contrast, a powerful dealer's interest lies in protecting itself from price competition from other dealers. As a result, a restraint initiated by a dealer and that results from powerful dealer pressure placed on a supplier can be regarded as contrary to the supplier's independent best interest. In that case the agreement requirement is clearly met and, if dealer power is proven, anticompetitive effects can be presumed as well.[37]

§ 11.5 Resale Price Maintenance in the Courts: The Per Se Rule and Its Exceptions

§ 11.5a. The Common Law and the Rule in Dr. Miles

In Dr. Miles Medical Co. v. John D. Park &

33. On causation, see § 16.3c.

34. For example, Helicopter Support Sys. v. Hughes Helicopter, 818 F.2d 1530, 1535 (11th Cir.1987). Further, after the supplier reported the corrective action to the dealers, the dealers returned a message thanking the supplier.

35. On these "efficiency" rationales for vertical restraints, see § 11.3.

36. For example, *Garment District*, note 22.

37. See 8 Antitrust Law ¶ 1604 (1989); see also T. Piraino, A Proposed Antitrust Approach to the Conduct of Retailers, Dealers, and other Resellers, 73 Washington L. Rev. 799 (1998).

Sons Co.[1] the Supreme Court held that a contract between a manufacturer and dealer, requiring the dealer to resell the manufacturer's product at a specified price was unenforceable because it was contrary to the policy of the Sherman Act. The Court could not determine why a manufacturer would want to impose such a requirement upon its dealers. It admitted that "the advantage of established retail prices primarily concerns the dealers," who would receive "enlarged profits" as a result. The injury that the Court perceived was that only "favored" dealers would be able to realize these profits. Presumably there were disfavored dealers who could not obtain a fair share of the market unless they cut the resale price.

On this rationale was born the rule that "vertical price-fixing" or resale price maintenance (RPM) is illegal *per se*. The Court found no theory under which the manufacturer would be benefitted by RPM. Since under the Court's theory the end result was higher retail prices, the only thing that accrued to the manufacturer was reduced output, and therefore lower profits. The Court rejected without almost no comment the principal defense given: that the success of Dr. Miles' Medicine depended on the density of its distribution, and the typical pharmacy would be loathe to sell something commonly traded at a discounted price.[2]

The *Dr. Miles* decision followed the traditional common law rule that agreements in restraint of trade, although not affirmatively illegal, were unenforceable among the parties.[3] Indeed, the court made only two brief references to the Sherman Act, and then only to observe that its meaning and that of the common law were probably the same.

The one issue the common law had left unclear was whether resale price maintenance was a qualifying agreement in restraint of trade. By the time of *Dr. Miles,* common law courts had generally held that resale price maintenance agreements were enforceable contracts except in two circumstances: (1) where the supplier had a large market share;[4] and (2) where the RPM was being used as an instrument to facilitate horizontal price fixing.[5] In *Dr. Miles*, the Supreme Court never distinguished between unenforceability and affirmative illegality of RPM agreements, and it neglected to deal with either the market share or horizontal collusion issues in a way that explained RPM's underlying rationale. In any event, although *Dr. Miles* could be read for the proposition that RPM agreements are not enforceable among the parties, it was in fact read for the much broader proposition that such agreements are affirmatively illegal under the Sherman Act, and can be challenged by nonparties (such as terminated dealers) or by the enforcement authorities.[6] This extension was appropriate; Section 7 of Sherman Act, the predecessor to § 4 of the Clayton Act, created a treble damages for anyone injured by a contract in restraint of trade.[7]

The basic rule of *Dr.Miles* persists today,[8] although it took later courts to explain that

§ 11.5

1. 220 U.S. 373, 400, 31 S.Ct. 376, 381 (1911). One year earlier the Dr. Miles Co. had signed a consent decree agreeing not to participate with drug retailers in the horizontal price fixing of drugs. Park was an "aggressive cutter"—a pharmacy that did not participate in the cartel, but instead cut prices. RPM was clearly being used to facilitate horizontal collusion. See Jayne v. Loder, 149 Fed. 21, 25 (3d Cir.1906); and see H. Hovenkamp, Enterprise and American Law: 1836–1937 at ch. 25 (1991).

2. The Court did note: "If there be an advantage to the manufacturer in the maintenance of fixed retail prices, the question remains whether it is one which he is entitled to secure by agreements restricting the freedom of trade on the part of the dealers who own what they sell." 220 U.S. at 407–408, 31 S.Ct. at 384. It then answered in the negative. On the "density of distribution" rationale for RPM, see § 11.3b2.

3. See H. Hovenkamp, *Enterprise*, note 1 at 274.

4. See Grogan v. Chaffee, 156 Cal. 611, 105 P. 745 (1909) (upholding RPM because of supplier's small market share).

5. John D. Park & Sons Co. v. Hartman, 153 Fed. 24, 42 (6th Cir.1907), cert. dismissed, 212 U.S. 588, 29 S.Ct. 689 (1908); Klingel's Pharmacy v. Sharp & Dohme, 104 Md. 218, 64 A. 1029 (1906).

6. In fact, vertical price fixing was virtually ignored by the framers of the Sherman Act. See J. Fortenberry, A History of the Antitrust Law of Vertical Practices, 11 Res. L. & Econ. 133, 209 & n. 161 (R. Zerbe ed. 1988).

7. On private enforcement under § 4 of the Clayton Act, see Ch. 16.

8. In Monsanto Co. v. Spray–Rite Svce. Corp., 465 U.S. 752, 104 S.Ct. 1464, rehearing denied, 466 U.S. 994, 104 S.Ct. 2378 (1984), the Supreme Court was invited to reconsider the *per se* rule for RPM, but refused to do so.

the rule to be applied was *per se*—that is, once an agreement was satisfactorily characterized as RPM, no further economic analysis was necessary to establish its illegality.[9]

§ 11.5b. The Meaning of "Resale"—Consignment Exception

The *Dr. Miles* rule applies only when the supplier sells a good to the dealer and then attempts to regulate the price at which the good is resold. If nothing is resold, then the rule does not apply.[10] For example, suppose a gasoline supplier instructs retail dealers that they may not charge extra money for washing the customer's windows. The restriction would have to be classified as a non-price restraint, for the window wash is not being sold to the dealer and then resold by it; it is merely a service that the dealer provides. Likewise, if the franchisor of a hair cutting salon instructs individual franchisees that a certain type of haircut must cost $12.00, the RPM rule would not apply; nothing is being resold.[11]

In United States v. General Electric Co.,[12] the Court held that the *Dr.Miles* rule does not apply to a consignment agreement in which the retailer is the manufacturer's agent rather than a purchaser and reseller, and title to the merchandise remains with the manufacturer. Once again, nothing was being "sold" to the dealer; thus there was no "resale" to the customer.

Theoretically, everything that can be achieved by a sale and resale can also be achieved by a properly drawn consignment contract. For that reason, firms sometimes attempt to evade *Dr. Miles* by simply relabelling their agreements "consignments" rather than contracts for sale. Historically, courts were rather wooden about applying this consignment, or "agency" exception to the RPM rule, emphasizing such metaphysical questions as when "title" to goods passes from one person to another.[13]

But since the mid 1960s the courts have tried to find viable economic distinctions between resale and consignment agreements, justifying a *Dr. Miles* exception for the latter. In Simpson v. Union Oil Co.,[14] the Supreme Court applied *Dr. Miles* to a "consignment agreement" between a large refiner and its retail gasoline stations. All risks of loss were on the station operators, who leased their stations from the refiner. The operators also faced some risk of lower market prices, since their commissions rose or fell with changes in retail prices. The refiner refused to renew the plaintiff's lease because the plaintiff sold gasoline at less than the refiner's stipulated resale price.

In condemning the arrangement, Justice Douglas expressly approved a bona fide consignment arrangement under which an owner took a single article to a dealer who would sell the article as the owner's agent. However, when such arrangements are used "to cover a vast gasoline distribution system, fixing prices through many retail outlets," then "the antitrust laws prevent calling the 'consignment' an agency * * *." Union Oil's consignment device was nothing more than a "clever manipulation of words."

The *Simpson* rule did not draw the traditional line between bona fide consignment ar-

9. For example, see United States v. Parke, Davis and Co., 362 U.S. 29, 47, 80 S.Ct. 503, 513 (1960).

10. See, e.g., Levine v. Central Fla. Med. Affiliates, 72 F.3d 1538 (11th Cir.), cert. denied, 519 U.S. 820, 117 S.Ct. 75 (1996) (where preferred provider organization negotiated fees with those paying for health care rather than the professionals giving the services there was no resale price maintenance imposed on the professionals). To illustrate, if Blue Cross agrees with General Motors to provide health insurance to a GM employee for $400 monthly, and then BC stipulates a "preferred provider" rate that a physician who wishes to service GM employees may not exceed, there is no RPM. The initial price bargaining is between the payor and the payee of the insurance, and the second one is between BC and the physicians as payor and supplier. See also Mularkey v. Holsum Bakery, 146 F.3d 1064 (9th Cir.1998) (wholesale bakery negotiated its own wholesale price directly with large buyer, 7–Eleven Stores; however the goods are actually distributed through an intermediary, who then unsuccessfully challenged its markup as illegal RPM).

11. See 8 Antitrust Law ¶ 1622 (1989); and Great Clips v. Levine, 1991–2 Trade Cas. ¶ 69671, 1991 WL 322975 (D.Minn.1991) (not unlawful RPM for haircut franchisor to restrict franchisee's pricing of haircuts).

12. 272 U.S. 476, 47 S.Ct. 192 (1926).

13. For example, see *General Electric*, note 12 at 484–485.

14. 377 U.S. 13, 84 S.Ct. 1051 (1964).

rangements and resale agreements. Justice Douglas rested the distinction on whether the producer had a distribution "system" or was simply negotiating a single sale of a single article. For this reason Justice Stewart wrote in dissent that *Simpson* really overruled *General Electric*.[15] *Simpson* effectively held that there was no consignment exception to the *per se* rule for large manufacturers with established distribution networks.

Many courts have agreed. A few years later the very distribution arrangement approved by the Supreme Court in the *General Electric* case was condemned by a district court under the *Simpson* rationale.[16] Other courts have held, however, that when there is an actual agent, not part of a "giant" distribution system, a good faith consignment will still be governed by *General Electric*, even if the seller uses a large distribution network.[17]

Consignment agreements persist in certain situations as an alternative to sale and resale. Two things make consignment attractive to certain retailers. First, consignment can enable a retailer to obtain inventory without tying up capital or credit. Second, under consignment agreements a supplier typically assumes more of the risks of loss, nonsale or price decline than under a resale agreement. For example, sometimes highly perishable products such as bread are distributed to small grocers on consignment. Under the agreement the wholesaler baker comes to the store each morning, dropping off fresh loaves and picking up loaves left unsold from the previous day. The grocer pays only for the loaves that were sold. The baker—who likely has a specialized outlet for "day old" bread—can sell the outdated bread more efficiently than the grocer. By this mechanism most of the risk of nonsale is retained by the manufacturer.

Consignment can also permit certain suppliers to reach a market more efficiently, particularly if market demand for the product is highly uncertain. An unknown artist, for example, may give her painting or sculpture to a retail gallery on consignment. The artist and gallery will agree on a retail price, from which the gallery will take its percentage if the work is sold. If it is not sold within a certain time, the artist and gallery may renegotiate the price or the artist may withdraw the work. By this mechanism the gallery avoids investing its capital in a high risk enterprise. The artist, by contrast, is likely to have more confidence (perhaps unwarranted) in her ability to sell to the public than the gallery does. If the gallery were forced to pay for the painting before resale it would probably demand a much larger discount from the artist's expected resale price than the artist would wish to accept.

Finally, consignment can make certain products sufficiently attractive to dealers who would not carry them otherwise. For example, certain products may be subject to volatile changes in price that make them too risky to be handled by very small dealers. If sales through many small dealers is important, the supplier may respond with a consignment agreement that (a) makes the dealer responsible only for that which she actually sells; and (b) gives her a specified commission on each unit of sale, regardless of changes in the market price. This arrangement is effectively a consignment. Suppose the dealer bought 1000 gallons of gasoline at $1.20 per gallon and later the price dropped to $1.00. The dealer would take a significant loss. Under the above agreement, however, the dealer would make a commission of, say, five cents on each gallon sold, whether the market price was higher or

15. Id. at 21–22, 84 S.Ct. at 1057.

16. United States v. General Electric, 358 F.Supp. 731 (S.D.N.Y.1973); in *Simpson* Justice Douglas had also attempted to distinguish *General Electric* by observing that the light bulbs there were patented, while the gasoline in *Simpson* was not. In his dissent in *Simpson*, J. Stewart found this distinction to be meaningless. 377 U.S. at 26, 84 S.Ct. at 1060. In any event, the district court in the 1973 *General Electric* case felt free to condemn the light bulb consignment arrangement, because GE's patents had expired. On price fixing in patent license agreements, see § 5.5.

17. For example, Mesirow v. Pepperidge Farm, Inc., 703 F.2d 339 (9th Cir.1983), cert. denied, 464 U.S. 820, 104 S.Ct. 83 (1983); Hardwick v. Nu–Way Oil Co., Inc., 589 F.2d 806, 809 (5th Cir.1979), rehearing denied, 592 F.2d 1190 (5th Cir.1979), cert. denied, 444 U.S. 836, 100 S.Ct. 70 (1979); Pogue v. International Indus., Inc., 524 F.2d 342 (6th Cir.1975).

lower than the wholesale price at the time of the transfer of possession.

In a consignment agreement such as this, supplier regulation of the price becomes imperative. Once the dealer's profits are fixed at the five cents commission, the dealer's interest is to sell as much gasoline as possible, without regard to cost. She might even charge five cents per gallon, selling millions of gallons (if the market price is $1.00), but producing no revenues for the supplier.

Consignment's usefulness notwithstanding, making consignment agreements an exception to the *per se* rule against RPM presents a problem. Manufacturers who want to maintain prices can easily change the form of their resale contracts to make them look like consignment agreements. If there is to be a meaningful "consignment" exception to *Dr. Miles,* it should apply when the economics of a particular distribution system justify a relationship in which the manufacturer bears an unusually high proportion of the risk of nonsale. As the Seventh Circuit put it, the function of a consignment agreement should not be merely "to circumvent the rule against price fixing. * * * "[18] The real issues in the consignment cases are not when "title" passes, whether there was a "sale", or whether the retailer was the "agent" of the manufacturer. Even the wholesale bakery could sell its bread to the grocer one day and buy it back the next. The real distinction between consignment and resale rests not on the form of the written contract between the parties, but on the division of risk between them.

In *Illinois Corporate Travel* the court had little difficulty in concluding that a travel agent is not a buyer-reseller of tickets for the airlines.[19] The agents carried no inventory of seats, but simply had access to a computer which committed seats from the airlines' own inventory. There was no risk of non-sale. Equally important to the court was the fact that the market was created and defined totally by the airlines, not the travel agents, and that the market seemed to require consistency in the communication of prices. Finally, the travel agents had very little involvement in the delivery of the service being sold. They printed the tickets, but they had almost nothing to do with providing air transport service itself.[20] However, customers did not merely purchase a "ticket," which is intrinsically worthless; they purchased a ride on an airplane, which the travel agent did not sell. *Illinois Corporate Travel* reflects the trend to limit *Simpson*'s holding that consignment should not be found when the good is distributed through a large distribution system. The array of travel agents used by the national airlines certainly qualifies as a large "system," but the consignment label clearly applies nevertheless.

Only slightly more difficult was the *Ryko* case, where the court found consignment in an arrangement under which independent distributors sold custom made automatic car washes.[21] The equipment varied from one customer to the next. Once the sale was completed, the manufacturer assembled the equipment and delivered it to the distributor. The purchasers paid the manufacturer directly. The distributors did not "buy" the product in any transaction that required them to advance money to the manufacturer; nor did the distributors face any risk of nonsale or market price declines.

18. Morrison v. Murray Biscuit Co., 797 F.2d 1430 (7th Cir.1986).

19. Illinois Corporate Travel, Inc. v. American Airlines, 806 F.2d 722, 725 (7th Cir.1986), after remand, 889 F.2d 751, 752–753 (7th Cir.1989), cert. denied, 495 U.S. 919, 110 S.Ct. 1948 (1990).

20. Id. at 725.

21. Ryko Mfg. Co. v. Eden Servs., 823 F.2d 1215 (8th Cir.1987), cert. denied, 484 U.S. 1026, 108 S.Ct. 751 (1988). See also Belfiore v. New York Times Co., 826 F.2d 177 (2d Cir.1987), cert. denied, 484 U.S. 1067, 108 S.Ct. 1030 (1988) (suggesting consignment where the publisher paid newspaper distributors on a per paper basis and picked up unsold papers the following day, placing all risk of nonsale on the publisher); accord Kowalski v. Chicago Tribune Co., 854 F.2d 168, 172 (7th Cir.1988). And see Miller v. W.H. Bristow, Inc., 739 F.Supp. 1044, 1052–1054 (D.S.C.1990) (following factors are relevant for determining a resale: where middlemen have "all or most of the indicia of entrepreneurs, except for price fixing," where the distribution system is vast, where title passes, where intermediary is responsible for payment immediately upon delivery; where intermediary makes substantial changes in the goods, bears risk of losses, and pays taxes on inventory).

§ 11.5c. Maximum RPM

Although the *per se* rule against minimum RPM has some supporters, few people have had good things to say about the Supreme Court's *Albrecht* decision that *maximum* resale price maintenance is also illegal *per se.*[22] Nevertheless, the *Albrecht* rule lasted thirty years until overruled by the Supreme Court in *State Oil.*[23]

Few Supreme Court decisions had proven more anticompetitive than *Albrecht.* A manufacturer generally establishes maximum resale prices in order to prevent retailers from charging a monopoly price, either because the latter had formed a cartel or because individually they had monopoly power in their respective geographic markets. In *Albrecht,* the dealers (newspaper delivery agents) were monopolists: each had an exclusive territory.[24] Even a small monopolist such as a newspaper carrier has the power to reduce output and raise price. One set of victims of this monopolization was newspaper customers, who must either pay a higher price or cancel their subscriptions. Another victim, however, was the newspaper, which obtained no additional revenues from the higher price but made fewer sales because of the subscription cancellations.

Maximum RPM enables manufacturers to control chronic price fixing by dealers. The feared collusion could be either tacit or express. For example, if a product is fungible and dealers are concentrated and in close proximity, they may be tempted to follow one another's price without competing too aggressively. The result will be oligopoly behavior which serves the dealers well, but reduces the supplier's sales. Maximum RPM can force a dealer to set price closer to the competitive level.

As a general rule, any action by a supplier to reduce the market power of its dealers makes both the supplier and consumers better off. Output will be higher, prices lower and the supplier will obtain larger profits. This is what the defendant was attempting to do in *Albrecht.*[25] Any antitrust policy that places a high value on either efficiency or consumer welfare should approve bona fide maximum RPM agreements. That is, whether one believes the goal of the antitrust laws is either efficiency or stopping monopoly wealth transfers away from consumers,[26] the *per se* rule against maximum RPM is perverse.

The *Khan* case accepted these criticisms and ended the regime of *Albrecht.* Plaintiff Khan's had a lease with defendant State Oil that made it unprofitable for Khan to add more than a 3.25 cents per gallon markup to gasoline, a clear violation of the *Albrecht* rule.[27] But as the Supreme Court observed:

> *Albrecht* was animated in part by the fear that vertical maximum price fixing could allow suppliers to discriminate against certain dealers, restrict the services that dealers could afford to offer customers, or disguise minimum price fixing schemes. The Court rejected the notion (both on the record of that case and in the abstract) that, because the newspaper publisher "granted exclusive territories, a price ceiling was necessary to protect the public from price gouging by dealers who had monopoly power in their own territories."[28]

Further, the Court pointed out that since its *Sylvania* decision in 1977 the Court had been far more sensitive to the question of actual competitive effects of vertical arrange-

22. Albrecht v. The Herald Co., 390 U.S. 145, 88 S.Ct. 869 (1968). Among the most incisive criticism is Blair & G. L. Lang, Albrecht After ARCO: Maximum Resale Price Fixing Moves Toward the rule of Reason, 44 Vand. L. Rev. 1007 (1991); R. Blair & A. Fesmile, Maximum Price Fixing and the Goals of Antitrust, 37 Syracuse L. Rev. 43 (1986); F. Easterbrook, Maximum Price Fixing, 48 U. Chi. L.Rev. 886, 887–890 (1981).

23. *State Oil Co. v. Khan,* 522 U.S. 3, 118 S.Ct. 275 (1997), on remand, 143 F.3d 362 (7th Cir.1998).

24. The territories were exclusive according to the terms of the carrier contracts, probably because they were natural monopolies. See H. Hovenkamp, Vertical Integration by the Newspaper Monopolist, 69 Iowa L. Rev. 451 (1984).

25. See § 9.2.

26. On these alternative goals, see § 2.1a.

27. See Antitrust Law ¶ 1635.1 (current Supp.); and see R.T. Joseph, Vertical Maximum Price Fixing After State Oil Co. v. Khan, 17 WTR–Franchise L.J. 73 (1998).

28. *Khan,* note 23, 118 S.Ct. at 280, referring to *Albrecht,* note 22 at 152–153.

ments.[29] When *Albrecht* was decided both price and nonprice restraints were considered to be unlawful per se, and this fact had disinclined the court to parse out the particular economic effects of maximum resale price maintenance.[30]

The Court then looked at the Seventh Circuit's brief economic analysis of maximum resale price maintenance:

> As Chief Judge Posner wrote for the Court of Appeals in this case: "As for maximum resale price fixing, unless the supplier is a monopsonist he cannot squeeze his dealers' margins below a competitive level; the attempt to do so would just drive the dealers into the arms of a competing supplier. A supplier might, however, fix a maximum resale price in order to prevent his dealers from exploiting a monopoly position.... [S]uppose that State Oil, perhaps to encourage ... dealer services ... has spaced its dealers sufficiently far apart to limit competition among them (or even given each of them an exclusive territory); and suppose further that Union 76 is a sufficiently distinctive and popular brand to give the dealers in it at least a modicum of monopoly power. Then State Oil might want to place a ceiling on the dealers' resale prices in order to prevent them from exploiting that monopoly power fully. It would do this not out of disinterested malice, but in its commercial self-interest. The higher the price at which gasoline is resold, the smaller the volume sold, and so the lower the profit to the supplier if the higher profit per gallon at the higher price is being snared by the dealer."[31]

The Court then considered possible rationales for a per se rule against maximum RPM. First was the oft-stated reason that dealers should have the "freedom" to set their own prices, a freedom that any form of RPM, whether maximum or minimum, impaired. Principally, the Court responded by noting that many suppliers had found it necessary to respond to *Albrecht* by integrating forward into distribution themselves, thus displacing dealers altogether.[32] A decision that forced the elimination of independent dealers altogether in the name of protecting them hardly deserved respect.

Second, the Court noted, *Albrecht* had "also expressed the concern that maximum prices may be set too low for dealers to offer consumers essential or desired services."[33] But the Court noted that such conduct would hurt manufacturers as much as their dealers.[34] Clearly, a supplier might erroneously set resale prices at too low a level, thus depriving even efficient dealers of the margin necessary to support the optimal level of services. But a manufacturer would not ordinarily wish to drive services down to suboptimal levels and certainly has no general interest in driving its own dealers out of business. In any event, even if it occurred the resulting problem would not be one of monopoly.

Third, maximum price fixing might end up channeling distribution through larger, lower cost dealers at the expense of smaller, high cost dealers.[35] But as the Court pointed out, it is hard to see how a manufacturer can benefit by keeping profitable dealers or potential dealers out. And in any event, the injury that is caused to inefficient dealers is not an injury to competition—particularly, in this case, where the overall impact is lower prices and higher output benefitting consumers.[36]

29. *Khan*, 118 S.Ct. at 280–281, referring to Continental T.V. v. GTE Sylvania, 433 U.S. 36, 97 S.Ct. 2549 (1977); see § 11.6.

30. 118 S.Ct. at 281.

31. Id. at 282, quoting 93 F.3d at 1362, and citing R. Bork, The Antitrust Paradox: A Policy at War With Itself 281–282 (1978).

32. 118 S.Ct. at 282. See, e.g., Paschall v. Kansas City Star Co., 727 F.2d 692 (8th Cir.) (en banc), cert. denied, 469 U.S. 872, 105 S.Ct. 222 (1984) (newspaper replaces independent carriers with employee carriers, partially in order to avoid consequences of maximum RPM rule; no § 2 violation).

33. *Khan*, 118 S.Ct. at 282, citing *Albrecht*, 390 U.S. at 152–153.

34. Id. at 282.

35. Id. at 283.

36. See id. at 283, citing Easterbrook, note 22; J. Lopatka, Stephen Breyer and Modern Antitrust: A Snug Fit, 40 Antitrust Bull. 1, 60 (1995); and R. Blair & G. Lang, Albrecht After ARCO : Maximum Resale Price Fix-

Finally, the Court noted the argument that claimed maximum RPM might really be a disguise for minimum RPM. While acknowledging that possibility, the Court concluded that it was best addressed under the rule of reason, which could then separate the sheep from the goats.[37]

The Court then concluded:

> Not only are the potential injuries cited in *Albrecht* less serious than the Court imagined, the per se rule established therein could in fact exacerbate problems related to the unrestrained exercise of market power by monopolist-dealers. Indeed, both courts and antitrust scholars have noted that *Albrecht*'s rule may actually harm consumers and manufacturers. . . .[38]

One important point about the relationship between the rule of reason for nonprice restraints[39] and the *Albrecht* per se rule was that a manufacturer always had to trade off the optimal spacing of its dealers against their propensity to charge high prices. By contrast, with *Albrecht* overruled a manufacturer can impose the kind of territorial division that encourages its dealers to make the maximum commitment to the success of its brand, while using maximum price limitations to ensure that dealers who are not effectively restrained by the competition of others will not charge a high price maximizing their own profits at the expense of both consumers and the manufacturer.

The Court also rejected the argument of the respondent and some amici that *Albrecht* should be overturned only on the basis of expert testimony showing that the per se rule against maximum resale price maintenance has in fact distorted the market. The Court replied:

> Their reasoning ignores the fact that *Albrecht* itself relied solely upon hypothetical effects of vertical maximum price fixing. Further, *Albrecht's* dire predictions have not been borne out, even though manufacturers and suppliers appear to have fashioned schemes to get around the per se rule against vertical maximum price fixing. In these circumstances, it is the retention of the rule of *Albrecht*, and not, as respondents would have it, the rule's elimination, that lacks adequate justification.[40]

The Court made clear that it was not holding that maximum RPM was per se lawful. Rather, like most antitrust practices involving an agreement between two firms, it is to be subjected to the rule of reason.[41] It then remanded to the courts below to reconsider the decision under the rule of reason, although it did not provide any guidance as to the content of such a rule.[42]

In the post-*Albrecht* regime not all rule of reason challenges to maximum price fixing will be alike, but some generalizations are certainly in order. First, *Khan* applies only to *vertical* arrangements imposing maximum prices. Horizontal agreements among suppliers imposing maximum prices on their dealers continue to be treated in the way that naked horizontal price agreements are treated as a general manner—namely, as unlawful per se.[43]

Second, under the rule of reason a relevant market will have to be defined and requisite power proven. The relevant market at issue will depend on the nature of the challenge. For example, if maximum price setting is alleged to be used to facilitate predatory pricing,[44] the

ing Moves Toward the Rule of Reason, 44 Vand. L.Rev. 1007, 1034 (1991).

37. Citing R. Pitofsky, In Defense of Discounters: The No-Frills Case for a Per Se Rule Against Vertical Price Fixing, 71 Geo. L.J. 1487, 1490, n. 17 (1983).

38. *Khan*, 118 S.Ct. at 283.

39. See § 11.6.

40. *Khan*, 118 S.Ct. at 283.

41. Id. at 285.

42. On remand, Judge Posner dismissed the complaint. 143 F.3d 362 (7th Cir.1998). See also Juliano v. Sun Co., 166 F.3d 1205, 1998–2 Trade Cas. ¶ 72325 (3d Cir.1998, unpublished) (dismissing maximum RPM claim); and see W. S. Grimes, Making Sense of State Oil v. Khan: Vertical Maximum Price Fixing Under a Rule of Reason, 66 Antitrust L.J. 567 (1998).

43. E.g., Kiefer–Stewart Co. v. Joseph E. Seagram & Sons, 340 U.S. 211, 71 S.Ct. 259 (1951).

44. See, e.g., Atlantic Richfield Co. v. USA Petroleum Co., 495 U.S. 328, 110 S.Ct. 1884 (1990), on remand, 13 F.3d 1276 (9th Cir. 1994).

relevant market will be the product subject to the restraint. For example, predatory pricing in retail gasoline would require analysis of the extent to which the retail gasoline market and the defendant's position in it make predatory pricing plausible.[45]

By contrast, in the monopsony situation that the Seventh Circuit had discussed,[46] the relevant market would be the one for distribution services, with the allegation being that maximum price fixing is a mechanism for forcing a distributor or reseller to accept less than the competitive return as a reward for reselling the defendant's product.[47]

In either event, one must regard provable, anticompetitive maximum resale price maintenance as rare. The distribution or retail markets in which maximum resale price maintenance agreements are generally not susceptible to predatory pricing, because successful recoupment is almost impossible to show in such markets, which are typically characterized by easy entry and a generally competitive structure.[48] For essentially the same reason, proof of monopsony power in a market for distribution or retailing will not be easy.

§ 11.5d. The Difference Between Price and Non–price Agreements

The plaintiff in a vertical restraints case must prove a qualifying "agreement" between two or more firms.[49] At that point a qualifying minimum price agreement is illegal per se, but a nonprice agreement is assessed under the rule of reason, which is close to a rule of per se legality.[50] As a result, much rests on the plaintiff's ability to prove a qualifying *price* agreement. Superficially, the difference between a "price" agreement and a "nonprice" agreement may seem clear. But the distinction has proved to be one of the most ambiguous and difficult in the law of vertical restraints.

As the previous discussion of the *Monsanto* case illustrates,[51] complaints about free riding or violations of nonprice restrictions are often verbalized as complaints about price. Dealer B free rides on dealer A's expensive point-of-sale services in order to be able to offer a lower price. The lower price is what steals the customers. Furthermore, B's price cutting is often more visible than B's free riding. So when A complains, the language is likely to be of the nature "B is cutting prices."

Suppose a manufacturer plagued with dealer free riding imposes vertical territorial division. Dealer A acquires Massachusetts as its exclusive territory for the manufacturer's product, and dealer B acquires New Hampshire. B persists in making unauthorized sales in Massachusetts. Dealer B can probably make these sales in Massachusetts at a lower price than dealer A charges there, because A bears the burden of promotional and post-sale service expenses in Massachusetts. Further, dealer B is likely to steal customers in dealer A's territory only by underselling A there. That is, customers in A's territory will not be motivated to purchase from a remote dealer unless the dealer gives them a better buy.

Everything about the illustrated distribution practice suggests that it involves "nonprice" restraints. However, when dealer A complains to the supplier that B is violating the restrictions, A will complain about the territorial invasion and the price-cutting simultaneously. Even though the supplier is not concerned with the price that B charges in B's territory, it will discipline B for invading A's territory and cutting prices there.[52]

45. On predatory pricing, see Ch. 8.

46. See *Khan*, 93 F.3d at 1362.

47. See R. Blair & J. Harrison, Monopsony: Antitrust Law and Economics 41–45 (1993).

48. On recoupment in predatory pricing cases, see § 8.4.

49. See § 11.4.

50. See § 11.6.

51. Monsanto Co. v. Spray–Rite Svce. Corp., 465 U.S. 752, 762, 104 S.Ct. 1464, 1470 (1984). See § 11.4c.

52. For example, see Morrison v. Murray Biscuit Co., 797 F.2d 1430, 1439–1440 (7th Cir.1986):

> * * * [I]t is only by price cutting or some equivalent concession that a new dealer can take away the established dealer's customers. As long as the supplier's motive is not to keep his established dealers' prices up but only to maintain his system of lawful nonprice restrictions, he can terminate noncomplying dealers without fear of antitrust liability even if he learns about the violation from dealers whose principal or perhaps only concern is with protecting their prices.

The evidence in *Monsanto* suggested that the defendant had been imposing nonprice rather than price restraints. The plaintiff, Spray–Rite, had argued that it was terminated because it was a price-cutter and other dealers complained about the price-cutting. Monsanto responded that Spray–Rite was terminated not because it was a price-cutter, but because it "lacked technically trained employees capable of promoting Monsanto products." The posture of this argument invited the jury to decide that Spray–Rite was terminated for *either* a price reason or a nonprice reason, and it chose the former. More appropriately, however, Spray–Rite was a price-cutter *because* it lacked adequately trained employees. It was able to charge less because it took a free ride on information provided by the specialists hired by its competitors. Naturally, however, when competing dealers complained, they complained about the phenomenon that appeared to cause their injury: the price-cutting, not the absence of skilled personnel.[53]

The Supreme Court recognized this in its *Business Electronics* decision, where it held that a qualifying "price" conspiracy could not be established simply by dealer complaints about the plaintiff's price cutting. The plaintiff had been an authorized dealer in Sharp electronics products, mainly small devices such as calculators. A competing Sharp dealer complained to Sharp about the plaintiff's low prices and threatened to stop selling Sharp products unless Sharp stopped dealing with the plaintiff. Sharp operated with a system of suggested retail prices. Although both dealers had undercut these prices, the plaintiff's cuts had been steeper and more frequent.

The Supreme Court decided that, although there was an agreement, it was not the right kind of agreement about price. As the Court noted, virtually all dealer complaints about other dealers will be couched in terms of price cutting. "Price cutting and some measure of service cutting generally go hand in hand." As a result, it can be extremely difficult to convince a jury that a dealer termination subsequent to such a complaint is not for reasons related to price:

> Accordingly, a manufacturer that agrees to give one dealer an exclusive territory and terminates another dealer pursuant to that agreement, or even a manufacturer that agrees with one dealer to terminate another for failure to provide contractually-obligated services, exposes itself to the highly plausible claim that its real motivation was to terminate a price cutter.[54]

The Court noted that "vertical nonprice restraints only accomplish [their intended benefits] because they reduce intrabrand price competition to the point where the dealer's profit margin permits provision of the desired services."[55] The court then required that there be a rather specific agreement between the supplier and dealer A (or dealers) about the *price* that dealer B must charge—not merely about the level of services that each dealer must offer. In its words, "a vertical restraint is not illegal *per se* unless it includes some agreement on price or price levels." Thus the rule applied in horizontal cartel cases that agreements "affecting price" are price-fixing conspiracies[56] is much broader than the one applied to vertical agreements. The supplier and at least one dealer must have an agreement, and it must be an agreement about "price or price levels."

In his dissent, Justice Stevens noted that Sharp's distribution scheme did not include non-price restraints. In his mind, that made the majority's argument implausible. A dealer termination following a complaint about the dealer's price cutting might be a plausible way for a supplier to investigate violations of *non*

In the context of transshipping by a price-cutting dealer, see Beach v. Viking Sewing Mach. Co., 784 F.2d 746 (6th Cir.1986), affirming a directed verdict for the defendant.

53. See H. Hovenkamp, Vertical Restrictions and Monopoly Power, 64 Boston Univ.L.Rev. 521 (1984).

54. Business Elecs. Corp. v. Sharp Elecs. Corp., 485 U.S. 717, 728, 108 S.Ct. 1515, 1521 (1988).

55. Ibid. Cf. *Monsanto*, note 51, 465 U.S. at 762–763, 104 S.Ct. at 1470: "The manufacturer often will want to ensure that its distributors earn sufficient profit to pay for programs such as hiring and training additional salesmen or demonstrating the technical features of the product, and will want to see that 'free-riders' do not interfere."

56. For example, United States v. Socony–Vacuum Oil Co., 310 U.S. 150, 60 S.Ct. 811 (1940). See §§ 5.1–5.2.

price restraints; but if there are no such restraints, then this motive cannot be a factor.

But this analysis places the cart before the horse. Vertical nonprice restraints are generally a means to an end, and the end is encouraging dealers to deliver adequate resale services. A supplier can obtain these services in three ways: (1) through price restraints; (2) through non-price restraints; and (3) through other explicit contractual provisions or unilateral communications. The fundamental question was not whether plaintiff Business Electronics was subject to nonprice restraints, but whether it was delivering the services or making the kind of reseller investment that it had bargained to make. If it had entered into no such bargain, then perhaps Sharp was bowing to the price pressures of a powerful reseller. But if Business Electronics had promised to deliver a certain group of resale services and was not in compliance, then the termination was appropriate whether or not vertical nonprice restraints were in place.[57]

Business Electronics conclusion that the prohibition on price restraints should be interpreted narrowly serves to support earlier decisions that merely suggested prices are not illegal.[58] Nor is it illegal for a supplier to communicate suggested retail prices directly to its dealers' customers, whether by advertising or perhaps by printing a price on the box.[59] In most cases of this kind the supplier will be acting unilaterally, so the "agreement" requirement will not be met either.[60] Of course, if a manufacturer uses strong-arm tactics to force dealers to adhere to such prices, then illegal RPM may be found.[61]

But the concept of an "agreement on price or price levels" is not self-defining. Suppose a supplier has two dealers, A and B. B, the larger dealer, does not merely complain about price and present a generalized ultimatum; rather B says to the supplier "Either tell A to stop undercutting our price or we will no longer deal in your product." Clearly, this is an agreement "about price," notwithstanding the fact that it does not name a particular price. Effectively, dealer B is insisting on the right to set the retail price for both A and B, and obtain the supplier's help in doing so.[62] The relevant question is not whether the agreement *names* a particular price, but whether the agreement is one that gives the competing dealer power over a competing dealer's prices, rather than merely about the level of the resale service activities that other dealers perform.

§ 11.5e. Per Se Rule Against RPM; Summary

To summarize briefly, in order to prove a *per se* violation of the antitrust laws, a plaintiff

57. See McCabe's Furniture v. La–Z–Boy Chair Co., 798 F.2d 323, 325–327 (8th Cir.1986), cert. denied, 486 U.S. 1005, 108 S.Ct. 1728 (1988), holding that a dealer's complaint about another free-riding, price cutting dealer, and subsequent termination, should be treated as a nonprice agreement. The court held that even evidence that the supplier was concerned about retail prices should not be given to the jury, so that it could speculate about the cause of the termination.

58. Isaksen v. Vermont Castings, Inc., 825 F.2d 1158, 1162 (7th Cir.1987), cert. denied, 486 U.S. 1005, 108 S.Ct. 1728 (1988) (even harassment of reseller not illegal unless the reseller actually agrees to increase price); Reborn Enters. v. Fine Child, Inc., 590 F.Supp. 1423, 1439 (S.D.N.Y.1984), aff'd per curiam, 754 F.2d 1072 (2d Cir. 1985) (publication of a suggested retail price list and "voluntary adherence" by plaintiff's competitors not an agreement).

59. Jack Walters & Sons Corp. v. Morton Bldg., Inc., 737 F.2d 698, 707 (7th Cir.), cert. denied, 469 U.S. 1018, 105 S.Ct. 432 (1984) ("it is perfectly lawful for a manufacturer to advertise his product to the ultimate consumer, whether or not he sells directly to the consumer, and to mention in that advertisement the retail price of the product"). * * *; Klein v. American Luggage Works, 323 F.2d 787, 790–791 (3d Cir.1963) (legal for manufacturer to pre-ticket items with price).

60. See § 11.4.

61. See *Parke, Davis*, note 9, 362 U.S. at 44, 80 S.Ct. at 511: "When the manufacturer's actions * * * go beyond mere announcement of his policy and the simple refusal to deal * * * he has put together a combination. * * *"); Bender v. Southland Corp., 749 F.2d 1205, 1213 (6th Cir. (1984) ("coercion in the vertical price fixing context is actual or threatened affirmative action, beyond suggestion of persuasion").

62. For that reason the decision in Ben Elfman & Son v. Criterion Mills, 774 F.Supp. 683 (D.Mass.1991) seems wrong. The court found no qualifying price agreement in the threat of a large distributor "make [the plaintiff] raise its prices to our * * * level or drop [it] as a distributor." The court held that this language failed to show that the "defendants agreed to set the prices at which [the complaining distributor] would sell [the defendant's] products."

must show (1) that the arrangement at issue includes a sale and a resale, and is not merely a consignment; (2) that there is a qualifying agreement between two or more distinct firms; and (3) that the agreement is a qualifying "agreement on price or price levels," in the language of the *Business Electronics* decision. In order to win, the private plaintiff will also have to show standing, causation, antitrust injury and damages. These matters are taken up in Chapter 16.

§ 11.6 Vertical Nonprice Restraints and the Rule of Reason

Vertical nonprice restrictions vary with the nature of the product and its distribution system. A manufacturer might specify the locations of its retail outlets and not deal with anyone who resells the product somewhere else. The manufacturer might restrict the number of retailers with whom it will deal in a particular city, sometimes by giving a particular retailer a contractually-guaranteed exclusive right to sell there. Occasionally a manufacturer makes this decision after it has established multiple dealerships in a city, and then it must terminate one or more existing dealerships. Many lawsuits alleging illegal territorial restrictions are brought by such terminated dealers. Territorial restraints are sometimes placed on traveling distributors rather than retailers, with each distributor assigned to a primary or exclusive territory.[1] Sometimes manufacturers assign particular customers to a distributor by size or type, and forbid other distributors from making sales to those customers. Finally, in addition to territorial and customer restrictions are literally hundreds of kinds of restrictions on the way a product is sold. For example, a supplier may require resellers to wear particular uniforms, to display the seller's trademarks in a particular way, to wash vehicles regularly, or to be open evenings or seven days a week. The restrictions in this category are rarely challenged under the antitrust laws, because they seem to have little impact on competition. Such restrictions are an integral part of the franchising system, which accounts for a sizeable percentage of the distribution of goods and services in the United States. As a consequence of these restrictions, all restaurants controlled by a particular franchisor across the country—say, all McDonalds' outlets—may have a certain similarity to one another, in spite of the fact that nearly all are independently owned.

The history of Supreme Court analysis of vertical territorial restrictions is shorter but less consistent than its analysis of RPM. In White Motor Co. v. United States, the Supreme Court refused to condemn a truck manufacturer's vertical territorial restrictions under a *per se* rule.[2] Neither did the Court approve rule of reason analysis, however. Rather, it held that the district court had acted too quickly in fashioning a *per se* rule condemning the practice, and should have waited until after a trial.

In a dissent in *White Motor* Justice Clark noted an important inconsistency in the Court's refusal to condemn vertical territorial restraints under a *per se* rule: *Dr. Miles* had premised its condemnation of RPM on a finding that it eliminated competition among dealers. *Horizontal* territorial division by competitors was clearly illegal *per se* because it eliminated competition among sellers. What sense did it make for the Court to treat vertical price restraints differently from vertical nonprice restraints? Although Justice Clark's observation was apt, it exaggerated the similarities between price and non-price restraints. Dealers who seek territorial restrictions are often seeking spatial dispersion that will protect them from free riding by other dealers in the same brand. This rationale is

§ 11.6

1. In some cases a distributor is permitted to make sales in another distributor's territory, but is required to compensate the latter dealer. See Ohio–Sealy Mattress Mfg. Co. v. Sealy, 585 F.2d 821, 829 (7th Cir.1978), cert. denied, 440 U.S. 930, 99 S.Ct. 1267 (1979). This indicates that the assigned dealer has made an investment in its own territory which will be misappropriated unless compensation is paid.

2. 372 U.S. 253, 83 S.Ct. 696 (1963). The restrictions gave exclusive territories to independent distributors and also reserved certain named customers to the manufacturer.

generally less likely of dealers seeking RPM restrictions.

Justice Clark's argument eventually prevailed for a time. In United States v. Arnold, Schwinn & Co. the Supreme Court declared illegal *per se* all territorial restrictions imposed by a manufacturer on either a distributor or a retailer.[3] No further economic analysis was necessary to convince the Court that territorial restraints in sales transactions were "so obviously destructive of competition that their mere existence is enough" to warrant condemnation. However, the Court distinguished sales from consignment agreements in which the manufacturer "completely retains ownership and risk of loss."[4]

Lower courts revolted against the *per se* rule in *Schwinn* because the value of territorial restrictions in certain distribution systems was obvious. *Schwinn* then became riddled with exceptions.[5]

The *Schwinn* era came to an abrupt end in 1977, when *Schwinn* was expressly overruled by Continental T.V., Inc. v. GTE Sylvania Inc.[6] Sylvania, a struggling television manufacturer with 1% to 2% of the national market sought to improve its market performance by selling exclusively through a small group of carefully selected retailers. Its purpose was to minimize the amount of competition among Sylvania dealers located in the same city, and to enable them to compete better with other brands. Sylvania both limited the number of dealers that could operate in any particular area, and required each dealer to sell its products only from locations specified in its franchise contract. From 1962, when this strategy was implemented, to 1965, Sylvania's share of the television market increased to 5%.

Plaintiff Continental T.V. was a San Francisco retailer who became unhappy when Sylvania licensed an additional dealer in San Francisco. Continental began selling more televisions manufactured by other television makers and opened an unauthorized store in Sacramento. Sylvania responded first by reducing Continental's wholesale credit, and eventually by terminating its franchise.

The Court could have distinguished *Sylvania* from *Schwinn*. For example, Sylvania's market share was much lower than Schwinn's. Such distinctions might justify different outcomes under a rule of reason. However, they could not permit Sylvania to escape from the *per se* rationale developed in the *Schwinn* case. The Supreme Court overruled *Schwinn* and adopted a rule of reason for all nonprice vertical restrictions. The Court then suggested that vertical territorial restraints lessened or eliminated *intrabrand* competition—that is, competition among different distributors or retailers of the same manufacturer. For example, under Sylvania's location clause, there would be fewer Sylvania dealers in Sacramento than if Continental had been permitted to move there. However, Sylvania's increase in market share indicated that vertical restraints could improve *interbrand* competition—competition among different brands of the same product.

The possibility of substantial procompetitive effects warranted taking nonprice restraints out of the *per se* rule, which applies only when judicial experience with a practice suggests that it is almost always anticompetitive. Under the *per se* rule, the Court noted, restraints would be "conclusively presumed to be unreasonable and therefore illegal without elaborate inquiry as to the precise harm they have caused or the business excuse for their use."[7] The possibility that nonprice restraints could improve interbrand competition made such a conclusive presumption inappropriate.

§ 11.6a. Balancing "Intrabrand" and "Interbrand" Competition

Sylvania's rule of reason for nonprice restraints is deceptively easy to formulate. Vertical territorial restraints may lessen competition among the dealers of the manufacturer imposing the restraints. However, they may

3. 388 U.S. 365, 87 S.Ct. 1856 (1967).

4. See § 11.5b.

5. See Continental T.V. v. GTE Sylvania Inc., 433 U.S. 36, 47–48, 97 S.Ct. 2549, 2556–57 (1977).

6. Id.

7. 433 U.S. at 57, 97 S.Ct. at 2561, quoting from *White Motor*.

increase competition among the brands of different manufacturers. The rule of reason requires a court to weigh these two effects against each other and determine whether the net result is competitive or anticompetitive. More commonly, courts say that "a vertical restraint may be reasonable if it is likely to promote interbrand competition without overly restricting intrabrand competition."[8]

However, *Sylvania*'s analysis left unresolved questions and logical riddles. First, what does it mean to say that intrabrand competition is "lessened"? Further, how does a court *balance* an increase in interbrand competition against a decrease in intrabrand competition? Indeed, is it even rational to speak of two different kinds of "competition," intrabrand and interbrand, that somehow pull against each other?

The *Sylvania* court's notion of intrabrand "competition" apparently described a situation in which many sellers of the same brand were wedged into the same market. Its concession in *Sylvania* that "[v]ertical restrictions reduce intrabrand competition" really meant that territorial restrictions can reduce the number of sellers of a particular brand in a particular geographic area. "Intrabrand competition" as the court used the term did *not* refer to a situation in which output is maximized and prices are driven toward marginal cost. A manufacturer who has no market power (such as Sylvania) will not be able to create it by the simple device of giving its dealers exclusive territories. If it already has market power, it will not be able to enlarge it by territorial division, although it might foolishly transfer some monopoly profits to its dealers.

This much seems inescapable: Sylvania was a struggling television manufacturer with a market share of less than 5%. It could not profitably obtain a higher price for televisions by reducing the number it sold. When the manufacturer has no market power, the entire notion that a vertical restriction lessens intrabrand "competition" is empty. To be sure, if the manufacturer miscalculated about the effect of the restriction, the result might be that it would simply sell fewer units—that is apparently what happened in the *Schwinn* case.[9] However, rival manufacturers would immediately make up the difference. Neither Sylvania nor its retailers had the power to lessen competition in any meaningful sense of that word. Today several circuits hold that intrabrand competition cannot be "lessened" at all unless the manufacturer imposing the restraints has market power.[10]

Even when the manufacturer is a monopolist, however, someone must explain how it can increase its profits by dividing territories. More importantly, will these increased profits come from reduced output or increased output? The most plausible explanations for vertical territorial restrictions, even when the manufacturer is a monopolist, is that they ensure dealer compliance with distribution contracts.[11] In that case, the restrictions are designed to increase output—not a very good

8. Continental T.V., Inc. v. G.T.E. Sylvania Inc., 694 F.2d 1132, 1137 (9th Cir.1982).

9. After the territorial restrictions in *Schwinn* were put into effect, the company's market share declined from 22% to 13%, while at least one competitor's sales doubled. 388 U.S. at 368–69, 87 S.Ct. at 1861. Whether the territorial scheme caused the decline or even contributed to it is difficult to say. In any event, a decline in that share range is inconsistent with monopolization; further, although a decline in *output* is consistent with collusion, and even to be expected, a decline in *share* is not, except under the rare case that there was an express cartel, that Schwinn was a high cost manufacturer, and that lower cost cartel members purchased some of its market share. Equally important was the fact that the competitor that experienced the rapid growth, Murray, sold mainly to Sears, Roebuck, a large chain of company owned stores whose locations and distribution methods were completely regulated by the parent company. Ibid. In sum, Schwinn was trying to get its independent dealers to compete more effectively with Sears.

10. JBL Enter., Inc. v. Jhirmack Enter., Inc., 698 F.2d 1011, 1017 (9th Cir.1983), cert. denied, 464 U.S. 829, 104 S.Ct. 106 (1983) (market share of 4.2% or less too small); Graphic Prod. Distrib., Inc. v. Itek Corp., 717 F.2d 1560, 1568 (11th Cir.1983) (defendant's 70% market share sufficient); Valley Liquors, Inc. v. Renfield Importers, Ltd., 678 F.2d 742, 743 (7th Cir.1982) ("balance tips in defendant's favor" if defendant lacks "significant market power"); Muenster Butane v. Stewart Co., 651 F.2d 292, 298 (5th Cir.1981) (market power should have been required, and the requirement "would have saved the litigants and the courts much expense."). See H. Hovenkamp, Vertical Restrictions and Monopoly Power, 64 Boston Univ.L.Rev. (1984).

11. See § 11.3b4.

argument that intrabrand competition has been "lessened."

The second problem with *Sylvania's* rule of reason concerns the court's capacity to measure something as intangible as the balance between interbrand and intrabrand competition. Assuming for argument's sake that a vertical restriction injures intrabrand "competition," can any court really balance the reduced competition in one "market" (Sylvania televisions) against the increased competition in a different market (all televisions)? First of all, the Court could not have been defining "competition" as marginal cost pricing.[12] It would be nonsense to say that the intrabrand effect of the restraints permitted individual sellers to price above marginal cost, while the interbrand effect tended to reduce the prices to marginal cost. Restraints may either be procompetitive or anti-competitive. In either case, *both* kinds of competition (if it is meaningful to speak of two kinds) move in the same direction. If injury to competition is appropriately understood as practices that enable a firm to profit by reducing output and increasing price, then it makes no sense to say that intrabrand competition is reduced while interbrand competition is increased. A restraint that reduces the output of the manufacturer imposing it may indeed reduce intrabrand competition, but in the process it will either reduce interbrand competition as well or else leave it unaffected.[13] A restraint that increases the manufacturer's output will increase interbrand competition—but it must increase intrabrand competition as well, under any sense of that word that is useful for policy. To be sure, an output increasing restraint may result in a smaller number of dealers, or dealers that are more widely dispersed, or perhaps even dealers that have less incentive to cut prices by reducing dealer service. But none of these things count as reduced "competition" unless we give that word a peculiar meaning that looks at the density or placement of dealers rather than the effect of the practice on output.[14]

For the comparison to be sensible at all, the *Sylvania* Court must really have been balancing intrabrand *competition* against overall productive *efficiency*. On the one hand, the restraints could be said to reduce intrabrand competition insofar as product differentiation and the smaller number of Sylvania dealers permitted each to raise price above its marginal cost. On the other hand, the restraints improved the quality of Sylvania's distribution scheme and thus made Sylvania perform better vis-a-vis its manufacturer competitors. The efficiency ("competition") question then reduces to whether the loss in allocative efficiency from reduced dealer *price* competition is outweighed by the gain in productive efficiency that results from improved distribution.

But even assuming this was the Supreme Court's meaning, this balancing test does not provide anything that is very useful to a court. Antitrust tribunals measure both competition and productive efficiency by extremely crude approximations—often little more than hunches guided by a few historically developed presumptions. Even if the *Sylvania* rule of reason could be given a content, no court would be able to use the rule, except perhaps in the clearest of cases.

Some of the difficulties are apparent in the Ninth Circuit's treatment of the *Sylvania* case on remand. The Court dismissed Continental's complaint, after purporting to balance the reduction in intrabrand competition against the increase in interbrand competition. As evidence that Sylvania's restraints on intrabrand competition were not substantial, the Court noted that the territorial restrictions were not "airtight"—any time it wanted Sylvania could add a second dealer to a territory. Further, no Sylvania dealer was terminated in response to a complaint about price-cutting from a competing Sylvania dealer, and there was no evidence that "Sylvania adopted its location clause policy to prevent price discounting * * *." The Court concluded that the restraints improved

12. See §§ 1.1–1.2.

13. That is, in a competitive market an output reducing vertical restraint would simply result in other suppliers' increasing their output to fill the gap.

14. See G. Hay, Observations: *Sylvania* in retrospect, 60 Antitrust L.J. 61 (1991); see generally the articles on Vertical Restraints, parts 1 & 2, 20 J. Reprints Antitrust L. & Econ. (1990).

interbrand competition because any retailer who wished to sell televisions could obtain equivalent units from a different manufacturer, because Sylvania did not prevent its dealers from handling televisions manufactured by competitors and did not adopt its territorial restrictions at the request of retailers other than the plaintiff.[15]

This potpourri of factors may say something about the degree of competition in the retail market for televisions—but it is a long way from "balancing" injury to intrabrand competition against benefits to interbrand competition. In fact, the Court overlooked the factors that would seem most relevant—that Sylvania never had a significant share of any market relevant to the case, and that its market share increased after the restraints were put into place. Increases in output or market share are not good evidence that a practice is monopolistic, particularly when the increase is in the range from 2% of the market to 5%.[16]

Antitrust analysis proceeds by a series of surrogates or shortcuts in reasoning, most of which are cast as rebuttable presumptions. The chief difference between the *per se* rule and the rule of reason lies in the number of presumptions. Given the economics of vertical territorial restraints, the best presumptive rule is that such restraints are legal. The lower courts agree about this. To defeat the presumption a plaintiff should show 1) interbrand collusion at either the dealer or manufacturer level; 2) restraints posed at the behest of a powerful dealer; or 3) that the supplier has market power *and* that the restraints are being used to facilitate intrabrand collusion or inefficient price discrimination.[17]

§ 11.6b. *Sylvania's* Impact in the Lower Courts

The rule of reason has come close to creating complete nonliability for vertical nonprice restraints. If one counts litigated cases, there are no more than a half dozen plaintiff victories.[18] Of course, there could be others that settled at an earlier stage.

Nearly all courts weigh the market power of the firm employing the restraints. Even though the *Sylvania* formulation suggests that vertical restraints reduce "intrabrand" competition—thus suggesting a single brand market—the courts generally formulate market definition in traditional terms. Most courts presume, quite correctly, that before a restraint can have an adverse impact on competition, it must be shown to affect a substantial share of a properly defined relevant antitrust market. The market analysis is less elaborate than in monopolization or merger cases, and there is only vague agreement on market share thresholds[19] or the meaning of market power once it is found. Several decisions found market power lacking without making an explicit determination of market share.[20] In several circuits the defendant's lack of significant market power in the market subject to the challenged restraint appears decisive.[21]

15. Continental T.V., Inc. v. GTE Sylvania Inc., 694 F.2d 1132, 1137 (9th Cir.1982).

16. For further criticism of the rule of reason in restricted distribution cases see R. Posner, The Next Step in the Antitrust Treatment of Restricted Distribution: Per Se Legality, 48 U.Chi.L.Rev. 6 (1981); T.A. Baker, Interconnected Problems of Doctrine and Economics in the Section One Labyrinth: Is *Sylvania* A Way Out? 67 Va.L.Rev. 1457 (1981).

17. See § 11.7.

18. See D.H. Ginsburg, Vertical Restraints: de Facto Legality Under the Rule of Reason, 60 Antitrust L.J. 67 (1991), who counts three plaintiff victories at the circuit level and one remand for trial. The three victories were *Graphic Products*, note 10; Multiflex, Inc. v. Samuel Moore & Co., 709 F.2d 980 (5th Cir.1983); and Eiberger v. Sony Corp. of Amer., 622 F.2d 1068 (2d Cir.1980). Judge Ginsburg also noted Dimidowich v. Bell & Howell, 803 F.2d 1473 (9th Cir.1986), modified, 810 F.2d 1517 (9th Cir.1987), which remanded for trial. See also Kohler Co. v. Briggs & Stratton Corp., 1986–1 Trade Cas. (CCH) ¶ 67,047, 1986 WL 946 (E.D.Wis.1986) (granting preliminary injunction).

19. Compare Assam Drug Co. v. Miller Brewing Co., 798 F.2d 311, 318 (8th Cir.1986) (alleged market share of 19.1% insufficient); *Graphic Products*, note 10 (75% market share sufficient). Market share thresholds are discussed in some detail in 8 Antitrust Law ¶ 1645c (1989).

20. See Murrow Furniture Galleries v. Thomasville Furniture Industries, 889 F.2d 524, 528–529 (4th Cir. 1989); Ryko Mfg. Co. v. Eden Servs., 823 F.2d 1215, 1231 (8th Cir.1987), cert. denied, 484 U.S. 1026, 108 S.Ct. 751 (1988); Bi–Rite Oil Co. v. Indiana Farm Bureau Co–op. Ass'n., 908 F.2d 200, 204 (7th Cir.1990).

21. *Bi–Rite*, note 20 at 204 (7th Cir.); Valley Liquors, Inc. v. Renfield Importers Ltd., 678 F.2d 742, 745 (7th Cir.1982); *Ryko*, note 20 at 1231 (8th Cir.); *Murrow*, note 20, 889 F.2d 528–529 (4th Cir.); Crane & Shovel Sales

If the defendant is found to have sufficient market power, its restraints are not necessarily illegal. At that point the courts generally consider the manufacturer's explanation for the restriction being challenged; if a legitimate business explanation is offered, that fact counts heavily in favor of legality.[22] The proffered defenses are typically that the restraints make dealers more efficient, encourage the optimal range of dealer services, or eliminate free riding. The array of permissible defenses is as varied as the products to which restraints are applied. For example, suppliers may use location clauses to facilitate the inspection of inventory for quality or freshness.[23] They may regulate product safety or integrity by limiting distribution to specified dealers. Restraints may be used to assure dealer efficiency by giving the dealer an unambiguous territory known to customers.[24] Courts have often cited a supplier's need to control dealer free riding as justifying restraints.[25] For example, in the *Rothery* case the court approved a restriction preventing local movers who were franchisees of Atlas, a nationwide moving company, from carrying goods outside the Atlas franchise system unless they started a separate firm that did use Atlas' name, goodwill or other services. As the court noted,

> A carrier agent can attract customers because of Atlas' "national image" and can use Atlas' equipment and order forms when undertaking carriage for its own account* * *. To the degree that a carrier agent uses Atlas' reputation, equipment, facilities, and services in conducting business for its own profit, the agent enjoys a free ride at Atlas' expense.[26]

Sylvania's language notwithstanding, nothing in these lower court decisions comes close to "balancing" interbrand and intrabrand competition. That formulation has simply proved unworkable. Rather the courts appear to adopt a formulation that, at risk of over generalization, looks like this one: *First*, they make sure there is a qualifying vertical nonprice agreement.[27] Then, assuming they find no horizontal agreement, they estimate the defendant's market power in the products or services made subject to the restraint. If that amount falls under roughly 25% or so, they ordinarily dismiss the complaint. As the amount increases beyond 25%, the court insists that the supplier produce a credible and provable justification for the restraint. If such a justification is found, then nothing but a strong, specific showing of anticompetitive effects in the interbrand market will condemn the restraint.[28]

Corp. v. Bucyrus–Erie Co., 854 F.2d 802, 810 (6th Cir. 1988). Other decisions are discussed in 8 Antitrust Law ¶ 1645 (1989).

22. For example, Trans Sport v. Starter Sportswear, 964 F.2d 186 (2d Cir.1992) (supplier's policy against transshipping—sales from one dealer to another—was not shown to be anticompetitive and seemed supported by valid business reasons, such as a concern about dealer free-riding and counterfeiting); Seagood Trading Corp. v. Jerrico, Inc., 924 F.2d 1555, 1570–1571 (11th Cir.1991) (restrictions operated to lower dealers' costs by creating scale economies); *Crane & Shovel*, note 21, 854 F.2d at 810 (exclusive dealer territories strengthened manufacturer's ability to compete against rivals); *Murrow*, note 20 (vertical restriction requiring maintenance of showroom necessary to prevent free riding); H.L. Hayden Co. v. Siemens Medical Sys., 879 F.2d 1005, 1014 (2d Cir.1989) (prohibiting mail order sales in order to reduce free riding); Winn v. Edna Hibel Corp., 858 F.2d 1517, 1520 (11th Cir.1988) (termination of art dealer with questionable reputation as discounter necessary to maintain image of supplier's product).

23. Adolph Coors Co. v. A & S Wholesalers, 561 F.2d 807, 811 (10th Cir.1977).

24. Newberry v. Washington Post Co., 438 F.Supp. 470, 475 (D.D.C.1977) (restraints by dominant newspaper necessary to ensure prompt, undisrupted delivery).

25. O.S.C. Corp. v. Apple Computer, 792 F.2d 1464, 1468 (9th Cir.1986); Muenster Butane v. Stewart Co., 651 F.2d 292, 297 (5th Cir.1981).

26. Rothery Storage & Van Co. v. Atlas Van Lines, 792 F.2d 210, 221 (D.C.Cir.1986), cert. denied, 479 U.S. 1033, 107 S.Ct. 880 (1987).

27. On the "agreement" requirement, see § 11.4; on the difference between price and non-price agreements, see § 11.5d.

28. See, for example, *O.S.C.*, note 25, 792 F.2d at 1467–1468: "Apple [the defendant] met its burden by proffering 'an entirely plausible and justifiable explanation." In this case:

> that the mail order prohibition was imposed to ensure Apple's products were sold only by face-to-face transactions. * * * Apple's market strategy requires sales support such as assessing the needs of prospective purchasers, assembling the particular package to meet those needs, hands-on instruction, education and training, and follow-up servicing. Mail order sales inherently cannot supply that necessary support.

Unfortunately, the courts use such justifications for three different purposes, and are not always clear about which one. First, the business justifications tend to show that the conduct was unilateral rather than subject to an agreement—that is, the justification tends to establish that the restraint was in the *independent* best interest of the supplier.[29] Second, the justification tends to show that the restraint at issue should be considered as "nonprice"—because it justifies the restriction without regard to the restriction's ability to facilitate price fixing. Third, the justification tends to make the restraint substantively permissible under *Sylvania*'s rule of reason. In nearly all cases, however, acceptance of the defendant's justification as legitimate is tantamount to approval of the restraint.

§ 11.6c. Boycott Claims

Many plaintiffs have tried to avoid *Sylvania*'s liability defeating rule of reason by characterizing the supplier's refusal to deal or dealer termination as a boycott.[30] Under appropriate circumstances boycotts, or concerted refusals to deal, can be illegal *per se*. However, the *per se* classification must be limited to horizontal agreements by competitors.[31] The dissenters in *Business Electronics* would have applied the term "boycott" to the agreement between a single complaining dealer and a supplier to terminate the plaintiff dealer—a terminology that the majority rejected.[32] At the very least, the "boycott" claim challenging a dealer termination or nonprice restraint should be reserved for situations involving a *horizontal* agreement—that is, an agreement between two competing suppliers to discipline or terminate a dealer; or an agreement between two or more dealers to compel their supplier to terminate or discipline a third dealer. To apply the "boycott" label to a purely vertical agreement between one dealer and a supplier to terminate a second dealer, deprives *Sylvania*'s rule of reason of all its meaning. In any event, the Supreme Court put the issue to rest in its *NYNEX* decision, holding that an agreement between a single utility and a single supplier of services to the utility could not be unlawful per se.[33] Even if there was no legitimate business reason for the agreement (in this case, to facilitate fraudulent overcharging of regulated rates), the per se rule was apt only if two or more *competing* firms agreed with each other to exclude someone else.[34] In sum, collective *horizontal* action is essential to any claim of a per se unlawful boycott.[35]

When qualifying horizontal agreements are found, courts are much more likely to find a basis for liability under a boycott theory. For example, *Big Apple* denied summary judgment on the plaintiff's claim that BMW denied it a franchise pursuant to an agreement among existing franchisees.[36] Once a horizontal agreement of this kind is found, the court may be tempted to apply the per se rule without any finding of market power. But here a court must tread very carefully. If a supplier has several dealers in a territory and one engages in free riding or equivalent abuses of its supply contract, the others are all likely to complain to the supplier. If they complain independently, there is no horizontal boycott. But dealers are likely to discuss the matter with one another, perhaps verifying that the suspected dealer is really misbehaving. Or perhaps they

29. See § 11.4c.

30. See Dart Indus. v. Plunkett Co., 704 F.2d 496, 499 (10th Cir.1983); Carlson Machine Tools v. American Tool, 678 F.2d 1253, 1258 (5th Cir.1982).

31. See § 5.4.

32. See Business Electronics Corp. v. Sharp Electronics Corp., 485 U.S. 717, 734, 744–748, 108 S.Ct. 1515, 1524, 1530–1533 (1988).

33. NYNEX Corp. v. Discon, 525 U.S. 128, 119 S.Ct. 493 (1998), on remand, 184 F.3d 111 (2d Cir.1999); see § 5.4d.

34. See *NYNEX*, 119 S.Ct. at 498, discussing *Business Electronics*, note 32.

35. See also Electronics Communications Corp. v. Toshiba America Consumer Products, 129 F.3d 240 (2d Cir. 1997) (upholding dismissal on pleadings for failure to state a claim; allegation that Toshiba and Audiovox conspired to sell Toshiba's telephones only through Audiovox under the latter's name; this necessitated cancellation of plaintiff's distributorship).

36. Big Apple BMW v. BMW of North Amer., 974 F.2d 1358 (3d Cir.1992), cert. denied, 507 U.S. 912, 113 S.Ct. 1262 (1993). See also Arnold Pontiac–GMC v. Budd Baer, 826 F.2d 1335 (3d Cir.1987). Compare Bascom Food Prods. Corp. v. Reese Finer Foods, Inc., 715 F.Supp. 616, 630–632 (D.N.J.1989) (where most of the distributors, in the aggregate, owned controlling interest in supplier, distribution restraints from supplier to distributors should be considered unlawful horizontal agreement).

think they can make a more credible claim to the supplier if they speak with one voice. For all these reasons, a per se rule should not automatically be applied to a purely *intra*-brand agreement among dealers to object to the behavior of another dealer. Such agreements should be condemned if they are effectively dealer cartels that have forced the supplier to comply with their wishes, but not if they are simply joint appeals to a supplier reporting the dealers' concerns or communicating the misbehaving dealer's violations. Distinguishing between these can often be accomplished by determining whether the supplier "agreed" with the dealers. If terminating the dealer about whom the complaint was lodged is in the supplier's independent interest, then no agreement with the supplier can be inferred. Although the horizontal agreement among the dealers meets the Sherman Act's agreement requirement, one could think of this situation as lacking causation. The termination was caused, not by the intra-dealer agreement, but by the supplier's independent judgment.

§ 11.6d. Exclusive Dealerships, Sole Outlets, and Refusals to Deal

A firm may designate a single dealer as its distributor in a certain area, and refuse to sell its product to others intending to resell it there. A supplier may even terminate one or more existing dealers in order to create an exclusive dealership.[37] If this act is unilateral, § 1 is not implicated at all,[38] but even an agreement giving a dealer an exclusive right is judged under the rule of reason and is usually legal.[39] Even *Schwinn*,[40] which applied the *per se* rule to nonprice restraints, recognized that exclusive dealerships rarely raise competitive concerns.[41]

Nevertheless, there may be cases where threats to competition are plausible, but only in the presence of properly defined (that is, interbrand) market power. The agreement for an exclusive dealership or sole outlet in a given area cannot be anticompetitive if there is robust interbrand competition.[42] One anticompetitive possibility is the multi-product dealer who has market power in its resale area, while the supplier also has some market power in the same area. If single-product dealers are not cost effective for the product at issue, then the supplier may be stuck with the dealer. If acceding to the dealer's market power is the profit-maximizing alternative for the supplier, then the resulting exclusive arrangement

37. For example, *Crane and Shovel*, note 21; Rutman Wine Co. v. E. & J. Gallo Winery, 829 F.2d 729 (9th Cir.1987).

38. See § 11.4.

39. Golden Gate Acceptance Corp. v. General Motors Corp., 597 F.2d 676, 678 (9th Cir.1979); Ark Dental Supply Co. v. Cavitron Corp., 461 F.2d 1093, 1094 (3d Cir. 1972). Cf. Doctor's Hospital of Jefferson v. Southeast Medical Alliance, 123 F.3d 301 (5th Cir.1997) (upholding an arrangement under which a preferred provider organization designated a single hospital as its supplier of hospitalization services).

40. United States v. Arnold, Schwinn & Co., 388 U.S. 365, 376, 87 S.Ct. 1856, 1864 (1967), on remand, 291 F.Supp. 564 (N.D.Ill.1968). See § 11.6.

41. "[A] manufacturer * * * may select * * * certain dealers to whom, alone, he will sell his goods. If the restraint stops at that point—if nothing more is involved than vertical 'confinement' of the manufacturer's own sales of the merchandise to selected dealers, and if competitive products are readily available to others, the restriction, on these facts alone, would not violate the Sherman Act."

Schwinn, 388 U.S. at 376, 87 S.Ct. at 1864.

At common law exclusive dealerships were called "output contracts." While a "requirements contract" (exclusive dealing) required a dealer to purchase *all* of its requirements of a certain product from the contracting seller, an output contract obligated a supplier to sell all of its output in a specified market through a given dealer.

42. See Packard Motor Car Co. v. Webster Motor Car Co., 243 F.2d 418, 420 (D.C.Cir.), cert. denied, 355 U.S. 822, 78 S.Ct. 29 (1957) ("virtual per se legality" where there is "effective competition * * * at both the seller and buyer levels. * * * "); See Paddock Pub. v. Chicago Tribune Co., 103 F.3d 42, 47 (7th Cir.1996) (wire service's provision to only one newspaper in an area not unlawful when there were numerous competing services); Ron Tonkin Gran Turismo v. Fiat Distribs., 637 F.2d 1376, 1388 (9th Cir.), cert. denied, 454 U.S. 831, 102 S.Ct. 128 (1981) (approving sole outlet arrangement where supplier had a market share of less than 5%, even when the market was confined to foreign automobiles); *Rutman Wine*, note 37, 829 F.2d at 735–736 (sole outlet permissible where no substantial impact on interbrand competition could be shown). A few cases appear to be to the contrary—for example, Beech Cinema v. Twentieth Century–Fox Film Corp., 622 F.2d 1106 (2d Cir.1980) (condemning exclusive distributorship agreement without discussion of market power).

could be anticompetitive.[43] But such facts cannot be presumed and are undoubtedly rare.

§ *11.6e. Dual Distribution*

Sometimes a manufacturer reserves particular territories or customers to itself. A "dual distribution" system is one in which the supplier distributes part of its product through independent resellers and part through its own agents. In some cases the independent dealers and the supplier's company dealers may compete at the resale level; in other cases they may not. In any event, the supplier may wish to control competition between the two by placing territorial or customer restrictions on the various dealers.

Courts were once quite hostile toward vertical restraints imposed in the context of dual distribution. They viewed them as inherently suspect and essentially as horizontal rather than vertical agreements. Since in a dual distribution system the manufacturer both operates its own dealerships and sells its manufactured product to independent dealers, it was seen as imposing the restraints on its own competitors at the resale level.[44] Many oil companies, for example, operate some company-owned retail stations themselves, while they also enter into franchise agreements with independently owned stations. The contracts with the independent stations may contain various territorial or customer restrictions that insulate the manufacturer owned outlets from the competition of the independents.

In *Sylvania,* the Supreme Court suggested in an ambiguous footnote, probably not referring to dual distribution, that some arrangements may present "occasional problems in differentiating vertical restrictions from horizontal restrictions." The latter would clearly be "illegal *per se*."[45] This language has suggested to some courts that they must determine whether restrictions in a dual distribution system are "really" horizontal or vertical.[46]

However, the same analysis generally applies to dual distribution systems as to all other vertical restraints. A manufacturer who has no market power cannot use dual distribution to create it. Furthermore, even a monopoly manufacturer generally cannot increase its market power by insulating its wholly-owned retail outlets, even if the effect is to injure competing, independent retailers. If the manufacturer has market power, any monopoly profits earned at the retailer level could also be earned at the manufacturer level.[47]

Dual distribution networks are even more susceptible to free rider problems than wholly independent networks are. Manufacturer-owned outlets have no incentive to take a free ride, for their profit-and-loss statement is the same as that of their parent. Knowing this, the independent dealers have a strong incentive to free ride: the manufacturer-owned outlet is forced to provide the point-of-sale services and is unlikely to respond to the free rider by cutting services and price itself.

Further, at least one thing suggests that the manufacturer engaged in dual distribution is *not* participating in a retailer cartel: the fact that the manufacturer can and is selling part of its output through its own stores. Any retail cartel would transfer monopoly profits away from the manufacturer and toward the independent retailers. The manufacturer's best response to retailer price fixing is to enter retailing itself and keep the monopoly profits. The manufacturer engaged in dual distribution has already entered. Indeed, the existence of a dual distribution scheme is often evidence that the

43. For further analysis, see 8 Antitrust Law ¶ 1654 (1989).

44. See S. Altschuler, *Sylvania*, Vertical Restraints and Dual Distribution, 25 Antitrust Bull. 1 (1980).

45. 433 U.S. at 58 n. 28, 97 S.Ct. at 2561.

46. For example, Photovest Corp. v. Fotomat Corp., 606 F.2d 704 (7th Cir.1979), cert. denied, 445 U.S. 917, 100 S.Ct. 1278 (1980); Coleman Motor Co. v. Chrysler Motors Corp., 525 F.2d 1338 (3d Cir.1975). Both decisions spoke of a "conspiracy" between the supplier and its wholly owned distributor subsidiary. Such claims of intra-enterprise conspiracy are now forbidden by the Supreme Court's decision in Copperweld Corp. v. Independence Tube Corp., 467 U.S. 752, 104 S.Ct. 2731 (1984). See § 4.7.

47. On the "leverage" theory—that a monopolist one can use vertical arrangements to turn one monopoly into two—see § 7.9; in the context of tying arrangements, see § 10.6a.

manufacturer is trying to combat chronic retailer collusion or poor performance by forcing independent retailers to match its prices and dealer services.

As a general rule the existence of a dual distribution system should be irrelevant to the court's analysis of vertical restrictions. The trend in decisions is toward this view.[48]

§ 11.7 Conclusion: A Rule of Reason for Distribution Restraints

§ 11.7a. *General Policy Concerns*

The reader of this section should note that minimum resale price maintenance remains illegal *per se*. For such agreements, the rule of reason described here would necessitate a substantial but well-advised change in the law. Most price and nonprice restraints are efficient and benefit consumers, and there is little reason for thinking that the impact of price restraints is substantially different than that of nonprice restraints, except in some cases involving substantial dealer power. However, a few vertical restraints may be anticompetitive, and it is quite possible for courts to develop presumptive rules that help them identify this latter set. Finally, although vertical restraints should be governed by a rule of reason, it should generally not be the rule that the Supreme Court suggested in the *Sylvania* decision.

The policy question is complicated by the fact that *economic* policy is not the only kind of policy that counts in a democracy. Although many people believe that economic efficiency should be the exclusive goal of antitrust,[1] most members of the Congresses that have passed the federal antitrust statutes did not share these views. Although the Supreme Court has cited economic concerns as relevant, it has never said that economic efficiency is all that counts, not even in its interpretation of the antitrust laws. Today the principal rationales for a *per se* rule against minimum RPM remain noneconomic—Congress seems to want it that way.[2]

The case for a rule of reason rests on the premise that we need to know to have more information in a particular case than per se analysis provides before we can evaluate the competitive consequences of a vertical restraint. But one additional thing that cannot be overlooked is the value of the rule of reason as a general information collecting device. Both legal policy makers and economists learn a great deal from studying the records of business litigation. Indeed, such records have become a principal source for data about the causes and effects of vertical restraints.[3] Throughout history, economists have learned from lawyers by studying their litigation and the arguments they made after looking at business records. Antitrust need not be an exception.[4] One of the principal difficulties in studies of the relationship between collusion and RPM in litigated cases[5] is that, since the cases proceeded under a *per se* rule, very little evidence was produced about the existence of collusion as an underlying rationale.

Unfortunately, the educational services provided by rule of reason antitrust litigation are extremely expensive, and the rule of rea-

48. See Illinois Corporate Travel v. American Airlines, 889 F.2d 751, 753 (7th Cir.1989), cert. denied, 495 U.S. 919, 110 S.Ct. 1948 (1990) ("dual distribution * * * does not subject to the per se ban a practice that would be lawful if the manufacturer were not selling directly to consumers."); International Logistics Group v. Chrysler Corp., 884 F.2d 904, 906 (6th Cir.1989), cert. denied, 494 U.S. 1066, 110 S.Ct. 1783 (1990) ("erroneous" to characterize dual distribution situation as horizontal); *Ryko*, note 20, 823 F.2d at 1230–1231 (same); St. Martin v. KFC Corp., 935 F.Supp. 898 (W.D.Ky.1996) (franchise arrangement under which franchisor reserved certain territories exclusively to its company owned stores would be considered a vertical rather than a horizontal restraint, for the only injury was to intrabrand competition).

§ 11.7

1. See Ch. 2.

2. See § 11.1.

3. For example, T. Overstreet, Resale Price Maintenance: Economic Theories and Empirical Evidence (1983); P. Ippolito, Resale Price Maintenance: Empirical Evidence from Litigation, 34 J.L. & Econ. 263 (1991).

4. See H. Hovenkamp, Enterprise and American Law: 1836–1937, chs. 22, 23 (1991). Chapter 23 in particular argues that the modern science of industrial organization was developed when economists began to examine the factual basis for arguments that lawyers were already making.

5. For example, Overstreet, note 3; Ippolito, note 3.

son can hardly be justified on this basis alone. But the present state of knowledge seems to permit no alternative. Most of the arguments that all vertical restraints should be illegal per se are based on assumptions that obtain in only a tiny subset of cases. By contrast, arguments for per se legality are driven by simplified assumptions involving competitive markets and modes of distribution, proportions that cannot be varied, and firms that can readily evade upstream or downstream monopolies. Further, they tend to look at long run outcomes. But the real world is never so simple, and in antitrust policy short run concerns are always important.

§ 11.7b. General Efficiency of Vertical Integration Not Decisive

The policy arguments for challenging vertical restraints are broader than those for challenging vertical integration generally. One could believe that nearly all instances of *ownership* vertical integration are efficient, whether they are accomplished by new entry or by merger.[6] Nonetheless, there could still be room for a law of vertical restraints. Some uses of vertical restraints are contrary to the rationales for vertical integration, and vertical integration cannot effectively be used to control them. This point is overlooked by much of the Chicago School literature favoring per se legality for vertical restraints.[7] That literature tends to identify vertical restraints with vertical integration generally, and then argues that virtually all of the latter is competitive.

One example of an inefficient vertical restraint is the restriction created at the behest of the powerful multibrand dealer. If multibrand or multi-product distribution is necessary, manufacturer entry with its own stores will not work. Further, the exercise of dealer power is inconsistent with both the manufacturer's interest and that of its consumers. For example, anticompetitive resale price maintenance imposed on others at the behest of a powerful multibrand dealer cannot be viewed as simply another instance of vertical integration.

Vertical agreements should also be treated differently from vertical ownership for the same reason that price fixing among competitors is treated differently from horizontal mergers. First, agreements are easily entered, and participants can thus take advantage of short-run imperfections in the markets in which they find themselves. To the extent that market imperfections tend to correct themselves over the long run, the most effective anticompetitive restraint may be one that operates only over the short run. Second, vertical agreements are likely to cover only a small part of the price and output decision making of the participants. This means that a firm might be willing to pay the price in reduced efficiency in one area of its business in order to avoid larger costs elsewhere. For example, Levi's, Inc. may sell numerous products to Macy's Department Store, for resale in a large municipality, but only its jeans have the kind of dominance that makes resale price maintenance profitable to Macy's. Macy's may then insist on RPM imposed on competing retailers as a condition of its handling the entire Levi's line. The managers of Levi's must then compare the costs of RPM in jeans against the costs of seeking a new reseller for all of its clothing. More permanent forms of vertical integration do not often force these kinds of tradeoffs.

§ 11.7c. Rejected Approaches

The most plausible situations in which vertical restraints can injure competition are (1) facilitation of supplier collusion; (2) facilitation of dealer collusion; or (3) accommodation of a dominant dealer in its trade area. One might wish to add facilitation of inefficient price discrimination, but price discrimination is not presumptively inefficient and courts are generally unable to distinguish the sheep from the goats.[8]

Two approaches to a rule of reason for vertical restraints appear not to work, al-

6. On vertical integration generally, see Ch. 9.

7. The literature is summarized in § 11.1.

8. See § 11.2c.

though for different reasons. The first approach is to "balance" the increase in interbrand competition with the decrease in intrabrand competition, as the Supreme Court described the rule of reason in the *Sylvania* decision.[9] That rule, quite simply, has no meaning. It suggests that intrabrand competition and interbrand competition are somehow different things, without explaining the differences. For example, if competition exists when prices equal marginal cost, then a restraint that shields dealers within a brand from competing with one another sufficiently to raise price above marginal cost would have to have the same effect with respect to interbrand competition.

The second approach that seems generally unworkable is to consider *ex post* whether the restraint increased or decreased output or market share.[10] Although the answer to this question may produce the theoretically correct result, it is simply impractical in the broad range of cases. Changes in a firm's output or market share can be a function of many things, and in most cases sorting out the causes of a particular change would involve a great deal of conjecture. Furthermore, well intended vertical restraints may simply not work, or they may be badly designed for their intended purpose. Many firms experiment with various types of restraints before they settle on one that is successful.

§ 11.7d. Rule of Reason Inquiry Summarized

A rule of reason inquiry in vertical restraints cases should begin as any rule of reason inquiry does. First, the plaintiff should tell a specific story about why this particular restraint is anticompetitive. Second, the plaintiff must define a relevant market and prove *either* individual market power or the existence of horizontal collusion or collusion-like behavior by a group having market power in that market. Market power is not shown by large market share of a single brand, unless that brand itself has been shown to constitute the relevant market.[11]

In proving a collusion-facilitating vertical restraint, the plaintiff need not necessarily be hampered by the same "agreement" requirement that hinders proof of a Sherman § 1 horizontal conspiracy.[12] In a vertical restraint case the qualifying agreement can be, and usually is, vertical. So for example, suppose that the plaintiff's theory of action is that an oligopoly of upstream suppliers are using vertical restraints as a facilitating device. A court should expect evidence that the upstream market is oligopolistic, that the restrictions at issue are used by all or at least most of the suppliers in the market, and that the restrictions have the effect of facilitating collusion at the upstream level. The qualifying "agreement" itself can be the agreement between the plaintiff and its supplier, or perhaps some other vertical agreement in the same market. Such claims should not be dismissed merely on the grounds that no collusive horizontal agreement can be proven.

A policy toward intrabrand restrictions on distribution concerned with maximizing the welfare of consumers would employ the following principles:

1) Vertical restraints can be used for both competitive and anticompetitive reasons, and the strongly ideological arguments for both extreme positions (*per se* legality and *per se* illegality) fail to take their full range of uses into account.

2) As a general matter, price and nonprice restraints are used for the same purpose and with the same result; in a few cases, such as those involving powerful dealers or where the restraint is being used to facilitate collusion,[13] explicit price restraints might be more anticompetitive. By con-

9. Continental T.V. v. GTE Sylvania Inc., 433 U.S. 36, 97 S.Ct. 2549 (1977). See § 11.6a.

10. See F. Easterbrook, Vertical Arrangements and the Rule of Reason, 53 Antitrust L.J. 135, 163–164 (1984) (advocating such an approach); H. Hovenkamp, Antitrust Policy After Chicago, 84 Mich. L. Rev. 213, 256–259 (1985) (criticizing it).

11. See § 3.3a.

12. See §§ 4.4–4.5.

13. As in the drug cartel cases. See § 11.2b.

trast, territorial restrictions are more often used to combat free riding.

3) Both price and nonprice vertical arrangements are illegal only if the Sherman Act's "agreement" requirement has been met. The requirement may permit some anticompetitive assertions of supplier or dealer power to go unchecked. But properly used, the agreement requirement distinguishes when a supplier is acting in its individual best interest (no agreement; efficient restraint) from when it is acting at the behest of a dealer or group of dealers with market power (agreement; potentially anticompetitive restraint).

4) In order to prove that a particular restraint is anticompetitive, a plaintiff must generally show one of the following: (4a) that it is being used to facilitate dealer (downstream) collusion; (4b) that it is being initiated for anticompetitive purposes by a powerful, multibrand dealer; or (4c) that it is being used to facilitate upstream collusion or oligopoly. These require the following structural prerequisites:

4a) If the argument is that the restraint is being used to facilitate dealer (downstream) collusion, then there must be some reason for thinking that such collusion cannot be effectively disciplined by the manufacturer. A market requiring multibrand reselling ordinarily meets that test, because the supplier could not easily integrate vertically into retailing. Further, the product subject to dealer collusion (over the geographic range that the dealer collusion is said to occur) must either have a substantial market share of a properly defined relevant market; or, if the collusion is said to cover several brands, they collectively must have a substantial market share. In either case, a share of 40–50 percent seems about the proper minimum. Likewise, the dealers involved in the collusion must control at least 50 percent or so of the distribution of this product in this area.[14]

4b) If the argument is that the restraint was developed at the behest of a powerful single dealer dominating the distribution or retail market, then roughly similar analysis is appropriate, although the market share can be a little lower because the single power dealer does not face a coordination problem. In any event, however, the restrained brand or brands should account for about half or more of sales in the dealer's area, and the dealer should account for a third or so of the sales of the relevant brand or brands. The dealer's own market share in the dealer's area could be much smaller, however, if the dealer had additional leverage over the supplier—for example, if the dealer owned a large number of stores across the nation, and was forcing the manufacturer to consider the consequence of losing all these stores at once.[15]

4c) If the plaintiff's argument is that the restraint is being used to facilitate manufacturer (upstream) collusion, then the court should look first for explicit evidence of such collusion. If no such evidence is found, then the court may still condemn the restraint if it finds that the market raises certain danger signals. In making this determination, the court should define the product and geographic market and determine what percentage of firms in that market are using the restraint. If fewer than half are, this claim should ordinarily be dismissed. If more than half are, then the court should determine the market concentration of the users. Ordinarily a Four–Firm Concentration Ratio of less than 50% or an HHI reading of less than 1000 suggests that the restraint is not being used to facilitate manufacturer collusion.

14. These numbers are explained more fully in § 11.2b.

15. See § 11.2b.

The above factors establish no more than *structural preconditions* to anticompetitive vertical restraints. By themselves, they do not establish that a particular restraint is anticompetitive or that collusion is actually occurring. When the preconditions are met, one must still move to factor 5, below. The plaintiff makes a much stronger case, of course, if it can produce more explicit evidence of collusion or dealer domination. For example, if the plaintiff can show *actual* dealer or supplier collusion, with the restraints acting as facilitator, then the practice is illegal *per se* and any other justifications for the restraints are, generally speaking, irrelevant.

5) Once the market share thresholds under either 4(a), 4(b) or 4(c) have been met, the burden should shift to the defendant to show two things: (1) the restraint being challenged serves some, concretely identifiable legitimate business purpose; and (2) no less restrictive alternative to the particular restraint at hand would solve the problem. If the defendant meets this burden, then the restraint should ordinarily be approved, provided that the plaintiff's only evidence is limited to the structural factors outlined above—that is, if it has not produced more explicit evidence of collusion or anticompetitive dealer domination.

Chapter 12

MERGERS OF COMPETITORS

Table of Sections

---

§ 12.1 Introduction: Federal Merger Policy and the 1992 Horizontal Merger Guidelines

A merger occurs when two firms that had been separate come under common ownership or control.[1] The word "merger" has a broader meaning in federal antitrust law than in state corporation law.[2] In many cases a "merger" for antitrust purposes is merely the purchase by one firm of some or all of the assets of another firm. A merger of corporations also occurs when one corporation buys some or all of another corporation's shares. The antitrust laws also use the word "merger" to describe a consolidation: two original corporations cease to exist and a new corporation is formed that owns the assets of the two former corporations.[3]

Today the means by which a merger occurs is largely irrelevant to its legality under the antitrust laws. This was not always so. Before § 7 of the Clayton Act was amended in 1950 the statute applied to stock acquisitions but not asset acquisitions.[4] The result was that stock acquisitions came under the relatively strict test imposed by § 7, which condemns mergers that "may * * * substantially * * * lessen competition, or * * * tend to create a monopoly." Asset acquisitions came under the less restrictive test of § 1 of the Sherman Act, or, if the acquisition produced a monopoly, § 2 of the Sherman Act.[5] Today, § 7 reaches both

§ 12.1

1. "Control" is relevant because leases or contractual arrangements amounting to less than fee simple ownership can be challenged as mergers. See 5 Antitrust Law ¶ 1201 (1980). See also McTamney v. Stolt Tankers & Terminals, 678 F.Supp. 118 (E.D.Pa.1987) (contract to purchase productive assets plus effective control was an "acquisition" for Clayton § 7 purposes). Cf. Lucas Automotive Engineering v. Bridgestone/Firestone, 140 F.3d 1228 (9th Cir.1998) (assuming that long-term exclusive license to manufacture tires under the licensor's name is a merger); Eastman Kodak Co. v. Goodyear Tire & Rubber Co., 114 F.3d 1547, 1997–1 Trade Cas. ¶ 71824 (Fed.Cir. 1997) (dicta: firm's acquisition of exclusive right to enforce a patent can be § 7 violation).

2. See R. C. Clark, Corporate Law 401–498 (1986); H. Henn, & J. Alexander, The Law of Corporations 979–988 (3d ed. 1983). However, see California v. American Stores Co., 872 F.2d 837, 845 (9th Cir.), affirmed on other grounds, 495 U.S. 271, 110 S.Ct. 1853 (1990), holding that state corporate law should be used to determine when an acquisition had occurred. The decision is questioned in Antitrust Law ¶ 1201' (current Supp.).

3. For example, United States v. Rockford Memorial Corp., 717 F.Supp. 1251 (N.D.Ill.1989), affirmed, 898 F.2d 1278 (7th Cir.), cert. denied, 498 U.S. 920, 111 S.Ct. 295 (1990).

4. See Arrow–Hart & Hegeman Electric Co. v. FTC, 291 U.S. 587, 54 S.Ct. 532 (1934). Earlier interpretations, which permitted the FTC to challenge asset acquisitions occurring after its complaint had been filed, are recounted in FTC v. Western Meat Co., 272 U.S. 554, 47 S.Ct. 175 (1926). See especially Justice Brandeis' dissent, id. at 563–564, 47 S.Ct. at 179; and see H. Hovenkamp, Enterprise and American Law: 1836–1937 at ch. 20 (1991) on the legal forms of early mergers; and 4 Antitrust Law ¶ ¶ 902–903 (rev. ed. 1998).

5. See United States v. Columbia Steel Co., 334 U.S. 495, 68 S.Ct. 1107 (1948), which applied the Sherman Act to an asset acquisition. The court noted that the "public policy announced by § 7 of the Clayton Act" should be applied to an asset acquisition that achieved the "same economic results" as a stock acquisition. 334 U.S. at 507 n.7, 68 S.Ct. at 1114. However, it went on to uphold the merger under Sherman Act standards.

stock and asset acquisitions. Further, the Sherman and Clayton Act standards are probably the same.[6] Before 1980, § 7 of the Clayton Act applied only to corporations. It has now been amended to refer to all "persons," whether incorporated or not.

A "horizontal" merger occurs when one firm acquires another firm that manufactures the same product or a close substitute, *and* both firms operate in the same geographic market. In short, the firms were actual competitors before the merger occurred. If the two firms were not actual competitors before the merger, then the merger will be treated either as "vertical" or "conglomerate" depending on the relationship between the firms. These kinds of mergers are discussed in chapters 9 & 13, respectively.

Americans became preoccupied with mergers during a great wave of them between 1895 and 1904, when perhaps as many as fifteen percent of American firms were involved in at least one merger.[7] This great merger movement was traditionally viewed as anticompetitive. In the 1970's and 1980's, however, economic historians began to argue that the mergers were the product of new technology that required greatly increased output, but that consolidation was then necessary because markets could accommodate fewer firms.[8] Subsequent historians then found evidence that, although much of the consolidation was necessary, many mergers were accompanied by practices that seemed inconsistent with purely competitive explanations.[9] Both the motives and outcomes of the great merger movement must be regarded as mixed. The movement produced many failures, but it also gave the United States some of its largest business firms. Finally, it laid the foundations for the generally oligopolistic structure that much of American industry has today.

There is also good evidence that enforcement of the Sherman Act actually *caused* the great merger movement. High fixed costs and high output forced firms to integrate their output, but strict enforcement of Sherman Act § 1 made most collusion illegal. So many firms took the alternative route of merger, since merger enforcement was generally much weaker.[10] Because they took this route, American firms probably developed more efficiently and became much larger. For example, England was much more tolerant of cartels, and thus small firms could collude as an alternative to merger or internal growth. As a result, by the mid-twentieth century many British industries were dominated by inefficiently small, family owned firms.[11] So aggressive American antitrust policy may have had an efficient consequence, although it was not the consequence that its planners had in mind.

Today the great majority of merger cases are brought by the Antitrust Division of the Department of Justice (Division) and the Federal Trade Commission (FTC).[12] A few are brought by private plaintiffs, but their success

6. See *Rockford Memorial*, note 3 at 1258. Historically, the confluence of Sherman Act and Clayton Act standards was also not the case. The Sherman Act was used to condemn a merger already in Northern Securities Co. v. United States, 193 U.S. 197, 24 S.Ct. 436 (1904) (condemning a railroad merger effected by a holding company). However, in *Columbia Steel*, note 5, the Court appeared to require that the merging firms have an intent to monopolize the post-merger market. *Columbia Steel* was one of the causes of Congressional expansion of § 7 in the 1950 Celler–Kefauver Amendments. See S. Rep. No. 1775, 81st Cong., 2d Sess. 4–5 (1949); H.R. Rep. No. 1191, 81st Cong., 1st Sess. 11–12 (1949).

7. See H. Hovenkamp, *Enterprise*, note 4, at chs. 20–25; R. Nelson, Merger Movements in American Industry, 1895–1956 (1959); N. Lamoreaux, The Great Merger Movement in American Business, 1895–1904 (1985); S. Bruchey, Enterprise: the Dynamic Economy of a Free People, ch. 11 (1990).

8. A. Chandler, The Visible Hand: the managerial Revolution in American Business (1977); Chandler, Scale and Scope: Dynamics of Industrial Capitalism (1990); McCraw, Rethinking the Trust Question 1, in Regulation in Perspective: Historical Essays (T.K. McCraw ed. 1981).

9. The practices included nationwide noncompetition covenants and a great deal of pre-emptive contracting, whose principal purpose was to deny competitors access to a needed input. See Hovenkamp, note 4, chs. 20–21; N. Lamoreaux, note 7.

10. See G. Bittlingmayer, Did Antitrust Policy Cause the Great Merger Wave?, 28 J.L. & Econ. 77 (1985).

11. See T. Freyer, Regulating Big Business: Antitrust in Great Britain and America, 1880–1990 (1992).

12. Collectively, the Division and the FTC are frequently referred to below as the "Agencies."

rate has not been high.[13] In 1992 the Division and the FTC jointly issued a set of Guidelines outlining their enforcement policies respecting horizontal mergers. These Guidelines, which replaced previous Guidelines issued in 1968, 1982 and 1984, serve as a useful starting point for testing the legality of mergers.[14] This chapter integrates the discussion of case law, Guidelines and fundamental economic theory in a way that indicates the importance and appropriate domain of each.[15] Importantly, federal merger policy is still governed by the statute and judicial law interpreting it. The Merger Guidelines are only Guidelines and they are not binding on courts. Nonetheless, over the years the courts have paid close attention to the Guidelines, and have followed them more often than not.

§ 12.1a. The Continuing Importance of Market Structure to Merger Analysis

In the 1960's and earlier, industrial organization theory was governed by the "Structure–Conduct–Performance" (S–C–P) paradigm, which suggested that as industries became more concentrated the firms within them would naturally find collusive or oligopolistic conduct more profitable. The result would be poor industry performance.[16] The importance of the S–C–P paradigm was that market structure *entailed* poor performance, because the structure itself made oligopoly conduct inevitable; that is, given a highly concentrated structure, the profit-maximizing strategy for a firm was to behave oligopolistically.

In the 1970's the S–C–P paradigm came under increasing attack from those who argued that (1) high concentration was necessary for firms in many markets to attain available economies of scale and scope; and (2) markets could continue to perform competitively even at high concentration levels.[17] Today, thanks in part to the growing importance of game theory and strategic considerations in industrial organization, there is a new appreciation for the importance of concentration. Most strategies for earning monopoly profits require either a dominant firm or relatively high concentration as a prerequisite. Many of the strategies work much better as concentration levels go up.[18]

Today antitrust enforcers and courts are about as committed as ever to using underlying market structure as a guide in determining the likely competitive consequences of mergers.[19] If anything, merger analysis in the 1990's contains more elaborate inquiry into market structure than merger analysis in the 1960's. Indeed market structure counts more than any other single factor.

Nonetheless, the attacks on the S–C–P paradigm have had three long lasting effects. *First*, mergers in the 1960's were condemned on smaller market shares and in much less concentrated markets than would be required today. *Second*, while the old S–C–P paradigm assumed that high concentration *entailed* poor performance, the new approach tends to view high concentration as merely a *prerequisite* for

13. See § 16.3a.

14. 1992 Horizontal Merger Guidelines, 57 Fed. Reg. 41552 (Sep. 10, 1992); 4 Trade Reg. Rep. (CCH) ¶ 13,104. The Guidelines are also printed as Appendix A in Antitrust Law (current supp.); and in many antitrust casebooks and texts. The 1992 Horizontal Merger Guidelines are the first to be issued jointly by the Department of Justice Antitrust Division and the FTC. Earlier Guidelines were issued by the Department of Justice alone. See generally C.A. James, Overview of the 1992 Horizontal Merger Guidelines, 61 Antitrust L.J. 447 (1993). 61 Antitrust Law Journal 119 et seq (1992) contains a good symposium on the 1992 Guidelines.

15. Those parts of the Guidelines dealing with market definition are analyzed mainly in Chapter 3. Vertical and potential competition mergers continue to be analyzed under standards promulgated in the 1984 Justice Department Guidelines. They are discussed in chapters 9 and 13.

16. Important works include E.S. Mason, Price and Production Policies of Large–Scale Enterprise, 29 Am. Econ. Rev. 61 (1939); H.M. Mann, Seller Concentration, Barriers to Entry, and Rates of Return in Thirty Industries, 1950–1960, 48 Rev. Econ. & Stat. 296 (Aug. 1966); and the first edition of F. M. Scherer, Industrial Market Structure and Economic Performance, ch. 1 (1970). The S–C–P paradigm is discussed more fully in § 1.7.

17. For example, H. Demsetz, Industry Structure, Market Rivalry, and Public Policy, 16 J. L. & Econ. 1 (1973); Y. Brozen, Concentration, Mergers, and Public Policy (1983). Other literature is summarized in R. Posner, The Chicago School of Antitrust Analysis, 127 Univ. Pa. L. Rev. 925 (1979).

18. See generally, T. Bresnahan & R. Schmalensee, eds., The Empirical Renaissance in Industrial Economics, 35 J. Indus. Econ. 4 (1987).

19. See § 12.3.

poor performance. This in itself is a major qualification—some would say a rejection—of the S–C–P paradigm, for it means that evaluation of non-structural evidence is essential to predicting the behavior of the post-merger market. The 1992 Horizontal Merger Guidelines demonstrate this influence by the way in which they take various "non-market-share" factors into account in predicting the consequences of a merger.[20] *Third*, we have become much more sensitive to the impact of economies of scale in production and distribution. That is, the industrial economist of the 1990s is much less likely than the 1960s economist was to assume that breaking up big firms in an industry will make consumers better off. Gains in competitiveness may be more than offset by losses in productive efficiency.[21]

§ 12.1b. The Basic Concerns of Merger Policy: Collusion, Oligopoly and Offsetting Efficiencies

Because the horizontal merger involves two firms in the same market, it produces two consequences that do not flow from vertical or conglomerate mergers: 1) after the merger the relevant market has one firm less than before; 2) the post-merger firm ordinarily has a larger market share than either of the partners had before the merger.[22] Today the principal concern of merger policy is that horizontal mergers may facilitate express or tacit collusion or Cournot-style oligopoly behavior.[23] The 1992 Guidelines use the term "coordinated interaction" to refer to all of these things together.[24] Mergers may additionally create opportunities for price leadership or in some cases eliminate aggressive firms or firms that refuse to cooperate in a cartel.

If mergers produced no beneficial consequences, but only anticompetitive ones, we could justifiably condemn all of them under a *per se* rule. Most mergers are legal, however because they can increase the efficiency of firms by enabling them to attain efficient levels of manufacturing, research & development, or distribution more rapidly than the firms could accomplish by internal growth. Mergers of nondominant firms may actually make markets more competitive by creating more substantial rivals for the dominant firm. Further, mergers may permit firms to acquire productive assets without the social cost that internal growth plus the bankruptcy of some firms might entail. Finally, mergers tend to assign productive assets away from less efficient managers and toward more efficient ones, for the assets are more valuable in the hands of the latter.[25] Alternatively, they may permit the firm to achieve economies in management by eliminating duplication. At least some of these efficiencies are ordinarily passed on to consumers.

Economies of scale can be broadly grouped into two kinds: economies of plant size, and various multi-plant economies. Generally a horizontal merger does not increase plant size,[26] but rather increases the number of plants that are controlled by a single management. This suggests that a merger will not often decrease the costs of operating a single plant,[27] but it may yield substantial multi-

20. See §§ 12.4c, 12.7.

21. For a survey of the S–C–P literature from relatively sympathetic writers, see J. Meehan & R. Larner, The Structural School, its Critics, and its Progeny: an Assessment 179, in Economics and Antitrust Policy (R. Larner & J. Meehan eds. 1989).

22. The post-merger firm could have a constant or smaller market share only on rather unusual assumptions. For example, assume a firm purchased a rival, shut down the rival's only plant, and then reduced its own output to monopoly levels. Its post-merger market share could be smaller than its pre-merger share. See 4 Antitrust Law ¶ 932a (rev. ed. 1998).

23. On collusion and Cournot oligopoly, see § 4.2.

24. 1992 Guidelines, §§ 0.1, 2.1.

25. Although there is some empirical evidence suggesting that takeover targets are underpriced because they are in poorly performing industries, not because the individual firms are badly managed. This suggests in turn that poor performance of the target may explain vertical or conglomerate mergers more frequently than it does horizontal mergers. See R. Morck, A. Shleifer & R. Vishny, "Characteristics of Targets of Hostile and Friendly Takeovers," 114 in Corporate Takeovers: Causes and Consequences (A. Auerbach, ed. 1988).

26. Although there are exceptions. If one farmer purchases an adjacent farm, she may combine and operate them as a single plant. Likewise, if one trucking firm purchases another, the fleets of trucks may be operated together as one.

27. However, substantial empirical evidence suggests that mergers can also create single plant economies, by permitting longer production runs and increased specialization within each plant. For example, if two ball bearing

plant economies. For example, it may be cheaper per unit to purchase 1,000,000 units of some raw material at a time rather than 200,000. Further, the costs per unit of research and development decrease as the number of units a firm produces increase. Likewise, a 30–second television commercial costs as much for a small firm as for a large one, and a one-page grocery store advertisement in a newspaper costs the same, whether it represents the offerings of a single store or of a 100 store chain.

Large horizontal size may also make various forms of vertical integration possible. For example, a large grocery chain with hundreds of retail stores may be able to own its own farms and dairies and operate its own warehouses. This would not be feasible for a single-store firm, which would have to rely on the market.[28]

The kinds of efficiencies that can be achieved by horizontal merger vary immensely from one industry to another. They are largely a function of highly individualized technology and distribution systems. Some industries, such as retail grocers, banks, and trucking companies, may be able to reduce costs significantly and improve consumer welfare by horizontal mergers. Others, such as delicatessens and small French restaurants, may work more efficiently as single-store operations.[29]

Horizontal mergers can create other efficiencies than decreased costs of production or distribution. For example, if horizontal mergers are legal, independent business persons have a "parachute" that they can use if their business does poorly or if they want to retire. Too strong a rule against horizontal mergers may make a small business difficult to sell, particularly if a larger business can be run more efficiently and the small business is languishing as a result. The knowledge that someone can sell out to a larger firm may even encourage entry into a particular market.

The most difficult problem in determining an appropriate merger policy is that the field of mergers cannot be divided into mergers that encourage collusion or increase market power on the one hand, and mergers that create efficiency on the other. Many mergers do both at once. To be sure, there are cases at the extremes where we can confidently predict that the efficiency produced by a particular merger far outweighs the predictable danger of noncompetitive behavior, or vice-versa. But many legally questionable mergers produce ambiguous results.

Further, any theorizing about the efficiency consequences of mergers must be considered in the light of some fairly sobering empirical evidence: as a group, firms that undergo mergers do not improve their market performance. Many experience a decline in profitability.[30] Of course, this fact can be seen as quite irrelevant to merger policy. Such mergers may be bad for consumers, but they are bad for the participating firms as well. To the extent that mergers make the post-merger firms less profitable, they are self-deterring. Antitrust has not generally operated from the premise that it is supposed to save firms from their own bad judgment.

However, the empirical data may be quite relevant if one believes that (1) consumer welfare is an important antitrust goal and (2) firms are not necessarily profit-maximizers, at least not in all circumstances. For example, if firms are persistently structured or operated in such a way that managers are rewarded on the basis of sales or revenues rather than profits, the managers may consummate inefficient mergers. Sales will go up but firm efficiency will go down. Consumers will be no

manufacturers merge, the post-merger firm will be able to make all bearings of one type in one plant, those of a second type in a second plant, etc. See F.M. Scherer and D. Ross, Industrial Market Structure and Economic Performance 164 (3d ed. 1990).

28. See generally 4 Antitrust Law ¶ ¶ 970, 973 (rev. ed. 1998).

29. For a good discussion of the different scale economies available in various industries, see Scherer & Ross, note 27 at 97–151; see also Brozen, note 17.

30. See D. Ravenscraft & F.M. Scherer, Mergers, Sell–Offs, and Economic Efficiency (1987); the findings of this book are summarized briefly in Scherer & Ross, note 27 at 163–174. See also G. Meeks, Disappointing Marriage: A Study of the Gains from Merger (1977), which reaches similar conclusions.

better off in such a market, and they may be worse off, at least in the short run. Conduct is appropriately self-deterring only if the anticipated costs to the actor are sufficient to offset all social losses. For example, driving 100 MPH on city streets is very dangerous to the driver, but it is appropriately illegal nonetheless. Although high speed driving is self-deterring, it is not sufficiently self-deterring to warrant the conclusion that the State need not intervene.

Given that collusion is illegal under the Sherman Act anyway, why do we bother committing resources to evaluating mergers as transactions that *might* facilitate collusion? Why not simply wait until collusion actually occurs? The most important answer is that the Sherman Act has turned out to be a woefully inadequate instrument for going after oligopoly or other collusion-like behavior.[31] Further, of the collusion reachable under § 1, only a small percentage is presumably detected.

Merger policy is the most powerful weapon available in the American antitrust arsenal for combatting tacit collusion or Cournot style oligopoly. Since we cannot go after oligopoly directly under § 1, we do the next best thing. We try to prevent (taking efficiencies and other factors into account) the creation of market structures that tend to facilitate Cournot or collusion-like outcomes.[32]

As § 4.1 notes, much attempted collusion is unsuccessful. But even failed collusion produces harmful consequences. Once the appropriate likelihood of collusion is found, those advocating a merger generally cannot defend it by showing that any collusion that might result will be undermined by cheating or widespread nonprice competition. For example, in *Hospital Corp.* the Federal Trade Commission rejected the argument that even if hospitals would be more likely to collude after a merger, all the gains from collusion would be frittered away through service competition that would accrue to the benefit of consumers.[33]

Consumers are injured by the service competition in this situation, even if the competition effectively reduces the cartel's profits to zero. A very simple example should illustrate. Suppose that under competition most patients occupy shared rooms because they are unwilling to pay the additional cost, say $100 per night, of single rooms. But under collusion the hospitals raise their price by $125 above their costs. At that profit margin, a hospital could enlarge its profits by attracting more patients, and they could do this by giving them a private room at no additional charge. This would particularly be true if the hospital had excess capacity and it could offer the single rooms to patients who might otherwise go elsewhere—say, patients who are planning surgery well in advance. The result would be that a class of patients would get an extra service and the hospital's profits from this particular sale would decline by $100.

Importantly, however, the decrease in the welfare of the cartel member is not matched by a corresponding increase in the welfare of the patient. By assumption, the patient valued the single room less than $100, for he was unwilling to pay for it under competition. In sum, cartel members do sometimes cheat on the cartel by throwing in costly services that steal customers from other cartel members (or bring in marginal customers). Often, however, these additional services are valued by customers at less then their cost. They are effective cheating devices because the customer values them at some amount greater than zero, not because he would be willing to pay the competitive price for them. The underlying rationale of merger policy is that consumers are generally entitled to a market in which both price and the package of services offered is established by competition.

31. See §§ 4.4–4.5.

32. See FTC v. Elders Grain, 868 F.2d 901, 905 (7th Cir.1989), which approved a preliminary injunction against a merger, noting:

> The penalties for price-fixing are now substantial, but they are brought into play only where sellers actually agree on price or output or other dimensions of competition; and if conditions are ripe, sellers may not have to communicate or otherwise collude overtly in order to coordinate their price and output decisions; at least they may not have to collude in a readily detectable manner.

33. Hospital Corp. of Am. 106 F.T.C. 361 (1985), affirmed, 807 F.2d 1381 (7th Cir.1986), cert. denied, 481 U.S. 1038, 107 S.Ct. 1975 (1987).

§ 12.1c. Mergers and Exclusionary Practices; Predatory Pricing; Private Challenges[34]

Since the 1970s merger law has been dominated by an underlying concern with collusion or oligopoly behavior, although the recent trend is to take the possibility of unilateral price increases quite seriously as well.[35] Indeed, the possibility that a merger might facilitate single firm exclusionary practices is not even taken seriously in the Merger Guidelines. The merger to monopoly that might facilitate single-firm exclusionary practices has played only a minor role in horizontal merger policy, and then mainly in litigation brought by private parties. When the private plaintiff challenges a merger, the underlying rationale is most often exclusionary practices such as predatory pricing; when the government challenges a merger, the underlying rationale is generally facilitation of collusion or unilateral price increases in product differentiated markets.[36]

Any merger that creates a post-merger firm large enough to "monopolize" a market is also anticompetitive under the Guidelines standards that the government Agencies employ. For example, the Agencies would almost certainly challenge a merger creating a post-merger firm with a 40% market share in a properly defined relevant market with high barriers to entry. But even a 40% firm would not be a monopolist. As a result, most private merger claims represent a disagreement between the enforcement agencies and private enforcers (who are most often competitors) about the relevant market, ease of entry, or efficiency consequences of the merger. Alternatively, they may represent instances of anticompetitive mergers that the agencies decided not to pursue because the market was too small or the agencies' resources were inadequate. However, there is little evidence that this is happening. In sum, whether the persistence of private suits on monopolistic theories is good or bad depends on how well one thinks the public agencies are doing their job. If they are vigorous in their enforcement, and most competitor suits are complaints about the post-merger firm's increased efficiency, then perhaps the remedy is to eliminate competitor suits altogether.

In sum, while both the enforcement agencies and private plaintiffs have standing to enforce § 7 of the Clayton Act, they generally do so on different substantive theories. The collusion-facilitating and product differentiation theories used by public agencies generally imply that competitors are beneficiaries of the merger: they, as well as the post-merger firm, will be able to charge higher prices. If private enforcement should come at all, it should be from consumers or suppliers—that is, those that are injured by price increases and output restrictions.

If one thinks that the agencies are not sufficiently aggressive or that ideology sometimes prevents them from seeing certain types of anticompetitive consequences, then perhaps it is a good idea to continue to permit competitor challenges to mergers. But assuming that we permit such challenges, what should the substantive standard be? Section 7 condemns mergers that "may" substantially lessen competition. Does that mean that a competitor who fears predatory pricing can challenge the merger on the theory that predatory pricing has now become a structural possibility? Or must the plaintiff also show (perhaps on the basis of subjective evidence) that this particu-

34. On private merger challenges generally, see § 16.3a.

35. See § 12.3.

36. Private firms frequently allege that mergers will facilitate predatory pricing or other exclusionary practices. For example, Cargill v. Monfort of Colorado, 479 U.S. 104, 107 S.Ct. 484 (1986); R.C. Bigelow, Inc. v. Unilever N.V., 867 F.2d 102 (2d Cir.), cert. denied, 493 U.S. 815, 110 S.Ct. 64 (1989); Phototron Corp. v. Eastman Kodak Co., 842 F.2d 95 (5th Cir.), cert. denied, 486 U.S. 1023, 108 S.Ct. 1996 (1988); Ernest W. Hahn, Inc. v. Codding, 615 F.2d 830 (9th Cir.1980), on remand, 501 F.Supp. 155 (N.D.Cal.1980); Remington Prods. v. North American Philips Corp., 717 F.Supp. 36 (D.Conn.1989); Tasty Baking Co. v. Ralston Purina, 653 F.Supp. 1250 (E.D.Pa. 1987); Chrysler Corp. v. General Motors Corp., 589 F.Supp. 1182 (D.D.C.1984).

However, a significant minority of private merger actions are brought by consumers and the underlying theory is that the merger caused a price increase. See, e.g., Midwestern Machinery, Inc. v. Northwest Airlines, Inc., 167 F.3d 439 (8th Cir.1999).

lar post-merger firm is actually bent on predation?

In the case of collusion-facilitating theories, evidence of the first kind is generally all we need. That is, we do not require a showing that the firms in the post-merger market actually intend to fix prices; we simply require proof that the market is more conducive to certain kinds of collusive or oligopoly behavior than it had been before.

But there are two good reasons for thinking that this should not be the standard in cases alleging that the merger will facilitate exclusionary practices. *First*, oligopoly behavior is a more-or-less inherent feature of many highly concentrated markets. As a general matter it would be irrational for firms to behave like competitors in a concentrated market conducive to Cournot behavior. If they did so, they would not be maximizing their short-run profits. By contrast, exclusionary practices, particularly the risky ones such as predatory pricing, are not *inherent* in any market structure. About the most we can say is that under certain market structures predatory pricing may become an option for firms, but firms will not necessarily take the option. Were the contrary true, we could condemn firms of predation without the need to look at the relation between prices and costs. We would simply look at the underlying structural characteristics of the market.[37]

So if we say that certain mergers facilitate collusion, while others facilitate predatory pricing, we are really using the word "facilitate" in two different ways. For that reason, courts are well advised to require private plaintiffs to show not only that a particular merger will make a certain exclusionary practice plausible (or more plausible than it had been before the merger), but also that the firm has a history of engaging in the practice or some fairly specific plans for engaging in the practice in the future, or that the merger *commits* the firm in some way to engaging in the practice.[38]

In the *Cargill* case, the competitor plaintiff did not even survive the first step. The merger was assumed to create a post-merger market share of 21%, and the court concluded that this was not large enough to make predatory pricing plausible, even if it had been properly alleged.[39] The Supreme Court's *Brooke* decision made clear that predatory pricing will not be found unless it can be shown that the payoff, or recoupment, will be sufficiently large to make predation a profitable strategy.[40] Further, this standard applies *even* when predation is being analyzed under the aggressive standards of the Robinson–Patman Act—a standard which, incidentally, is articulated in language virtually identical to the "may substantially lessen competition" language of § 7.[41] *Brooke* thus suggests that when a private plaintiff is challenging a merger on the theory that it will facilitate predation, at the very least the Court must do a full structural analysis such as the one employed in that case in order to determine whether a rational profit-maximizing firm, operating after the merger, would find predation a profitable strategy. This requires a showing of high entry barriers, highly successful oligopoly behavior and other structural features indicating that the payoff to predation will exceed its costs.[42] Indeed, if the private plaintiff is able to make this showing, then it *has* demonstrated that the government enforcement agencies are not doing their job. Any merger satisfying this test should have been condemned on ordinary collusion facilitating grounds.

The *second* reason for applying a higher standard to merger claims alleging future pre-

37. See § 8.4.

38. That is to say, the merger creates the situation where it would be irrational for the firm not to commit an exclusionary practice.

39. Cargill v. Monfort of Colo., 479 U.S. 104, 119, 107 S.Ct. 484, 494 (1986).

40. Brooke Group Ltd. v. Brown & Williamson Tobacco Corp., 509 U.S. 209, 113 S.Ct. 2578 (1993).

41. The Robinson–Patman Act reaches conduct "where the effect * * * may be substantially to lessen competition or tend to create a monopoly in any line of commerce, or to injure, destroy, or prevent competition with any person who either grants or knowingly receives the benefit of such discrimination.* * * " 15 U.S.C.A. § 13(a). For further discussion of *Brook* and of the Robinson–Patman Act in predatory pricing cases, see § 8.8.

42. See §§ 8.4, 8.8.

dation or other exclusionary practices is that the latter practices are *independently* illegal and most often readily detectable. As a result, there is less need for the extra margin of deterrence. We condemn mergers that facilitate oligopoly under a fairly aggressive standard because the oligopoly itself, once it has been achieved, is most generally out of antitrust's reach.[43] To be sure, this is not a complete answer: the social cost of an anticompetitive practice can be minimized if we can reach the practice before rather than after it occurs. But importantly, the other antitrust laws have their own deterrent effects if they are properly applied. The post-merger firm bent on predation must still compare the anticipated benefits against the risk of detection and prosecution.[44] However, the firm in the oligopoly industry is free to set its Cournot price without little antitrust concern.

Suppose the claim is not predatory pricing, but some other kind of exclusionary practice. In such cases private complaints challenging the merger itself must be confined to (a) results that are actually caused by the merger; and (b) results that flow from the *anticompetitive consequences* of the merger. For example, when upstream competitors who use territorial distributors merge, the merger may make one set of distributors superfluous. One distributor can now be used to distribute the product of both pre-merger firms. In this case the termination of the unlucky distributors would be "caused" by the merger, but it would have nothing whatsoever to do with the merger's anticompetitive consequences. This kind of integration could easily result from the merger of two minuscule firms in a highly competitive market.[45]

One kind of claim that seems superficially plausible is that the merger will permit the post-merger firm a greater amount of leverage with downstream or upstream rivals. For example, suppose that a firm making four variations of a differentiated product merges with another firm that makes four variations. Retail shelf space is at a premium, and a retailer often has room for only six or eight variations. The merger may make it easier for the post-merger firm to "monopolize" retailer shelf space by exclusive dealing, or perhaps by insisting that the retailer carry its full line.[46]

Even here there are analytic problems. If the market was properly defined in the first place, such mergers should be illegal under ordinary collusion-facilitating grounds. The firm in the above example "dominates" the shelf space. If the shelf space is essential to distribution, this firm presumably dominates a relevant market as well. Challenges to such mergers generally result from differences of opinion between the enforcement agency and the private plaintiff concerning the scope of the relevant market. But of course, private plaintiffs are entitled to prove relevant markets and anticompetitive effects even if the enforcement agencies disagree.

§ 12.2 Efficiency and Merger Policy

Horizontal mergers can create substantial efficiencies even as they facilitate collusion or enlarge market power. Courts and other policy makers have entertained three different positions concerning efficiency and the legality of mergers:

1) mergers should be evaluated for their effect on market power or likelihood of collusion, and efficiency considerations should be largely irrelevant;

2) mergers that create substantial efficiencies should be legal, or there should be at least a limited "efficiency defense" in certain merger cases;

3) mergers should be condemned *because* they create efficiencies, in order to protect competitors of the post-merger firm.

§ 12.2a. The Dubious Legacy of the Warren Era

The merger policy of the Warren Court in the 1960's adopted the third proposal: it con-

43. See § 4.4.

44. See § 8.4.

45. For elaboration, § 16.3a.

46. See *Bigelow*, note 36 (post merger firm would monopolize shelf space for herbal teas); *Tasty Baking*, note 36 (post-merger firm would use its leverage with retailers to dominate resale of snack cakes and pies).

demned mergers *because* they created certain efficiencies. For example, in Brown Shoe Co. v. United States the Supreme Court held that a horizontal merger between competing retailers of shoes was illegal because the large, post-merger firm could undersell its competitors. The Court concluded that Congress desired "to promote competition through the protection of viable, small, locally owned businesses," and the creation of a large company with lower costs would frustrate this goal. "Congress appreciated that occasional higher costs and prices might result from the maintenance of fragmented industries and markets," the Supreme Court acknowledged, but it "resolved these competing considerations in favor of decentralization."[1]

The district court in *Brown Shoe* had been even more explicit about its reasons for condemning the merger:

> [I]ndependent retailers of shoes are having a harder and harder time in competing with company-owned and company-controlled retail outlets. National advertising by large concerns has increased their brand name acceptability and retail stores handling the brand named shoes have a definite advertising advantage. Company-owned and company-controlled retail stores have definite advantages in buying and credit; they have further advantages in advertising, insurance, inventory control * * * and price control. These advantages result in lower prices or in higher quality for the same price and the independent retailer can no longer compete * * *[2]

Brown Shoe's critics have attacked the opinion for protecting competitors at the expense of consumers.[3] But the identification of antitrust's protected class presents a question of value, not of fact. Further, any such critique must come to terms with the relatively clear legislative history of the 1950 Celler–Kefauver Amendments to § 7. The *Brown Shoe* opinion read it correctly. In 1950 protection of the "viability" of small businesses who were being "gobbled up" by larger companies was much more on Congress's mind than low consumer prices or high product quality.[4]

Brown Shoe and successor cases such as *Von's Grocery*[5] can be criticized, however, not for the goals they chose but for their efficacy in achieving them. *Von's* involved a merger between the third largest and the sixth largest grocery chains in greater Los Angeles. The market was unconcentrated, however, and the combined share of these two chains was 7.5% of sales. Both chains were family owned and operated. The largest firm in the market, which was not a party to the merger, had a market share of only 8%. The market exhibited a "trend" toward concentration with many individual stores being purchased by chains, suggesting that the larger chains were able to undersell the smaller chains and the individual mom-and-pop grocers.

If a medium-sized chain is prevented from acquiring existing stores, it likely will respond by building new stores of its own, particularly if expansion will strengthen its position vis-a-vis larger chains. The result will be that very small chains or single store companies will find themselves unable to compete with larger firms, and unable to sell their stores to competitors. Not only will they lose the power to compete, but they might also lose most of the value of their most substantial capital asset—their stores.[6] It is therefore far from clear that

§ 12.2

1. 370 U.S. 294, 344, 82 S.Ct. 1502, 1534 (1962).

2. United States v. Brown Shoe Co., 179 F.Supp. 721, 738 (E.D.Mo.1959). The Federal Trade Commission took the same position. See In re Foremost Dairies, Inc. 60 F.T.C. 944, 1084 (1962), concluding that efficiencies resulting from a merger were bad because they gave post-merger firms a "decisive advantage" over "smaller rivals."

3. For example, R. Bork, The Antitrust Paradox: A Policy at War With Itself 198–216 (1978; rev. ed. 1993).

4. See D. Bok, Section 7 of the Clayton Act and the Merging of Law and Economics, 74 Harv.L.Rev. 226, 234 (1960); H. Hovenkamp, Derek Bok and the Merger of Law and Economics, 21 J.L.Reform 515 (1988); H. Hovenkamp, Distributive Justice and the Antitrust Laws, 51 Geo. Wash.L.Rev. 1, 23–27 (1982).

5. United States v. Von's Grocery Co., 384 U.S. 270, 86 S.Ct. 1478 (1966).

6. See R. Posner, Antitrust Law: An Economic Perspective 105 (1976).

the rule of *Brown Shoe* and *Von's Grocery* gave small businesses the kind of protection that Congress had in mind.

§ 12.2b. *Assessing the Efficiency Effects of Horizontal Mergers*

§ 12.2b1 *The Welfare "Tradeoff" Model*

The rule that mergers should be condemned because they create efficiency has been abandoned. The opposite position is that mergers should be legal when they create substantial efficiencies—or alternatively, that there should be an "efficiency defense" in merger cases. Although the trail is still somewhat obscure, the courts are heading in the direction of adopting such a rule, and the government's Merger Guidelines explicitly recognize and define an "efficiency defense." Importantly, the rule comes into play *only* after the merger has been found presumptively anticompetitive by structural and behavioral analysis.[7] If a merger poses no competitive threat to begin with, then analysis of possible efficiencies is unnecessary.

The argument for an "efficiency defense" in merger cases is illustrated by the graph in Figure 1.[8] The graph illustrates a merger that gives the post-merger firm measurably more market power than it had before the merger. As a result, the firm reduces output from Q_1 to Q_2 on the graph, and increases price from P_1 to P_2. Triangle A_1 represents the monopoly "deadweight loss" created by this increase in market power.[9]

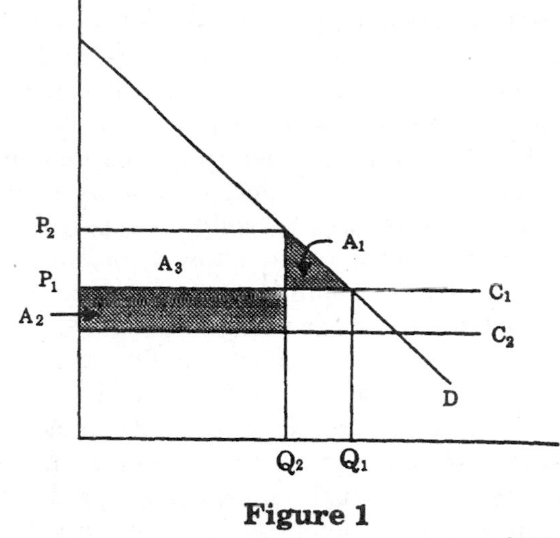

Figure 1

[627a]

At the same time, the merger produces measurable economies, which show up as a reduction in the firm's costs from C_1 to C_2. Rectangle A_2 represents efficiency gains that will result from these economies. If A_2 is larger than A_1 the merger produces a *net* efficiency gain, even though it permits the firm to raise its price above its marginal cost. Furthermore, A_2 is often larger than A_1. The efficiency gains illustrated by A_2 are spread over the entire output of the post-merger firm. The deadweight losses in A_1 are spread over only the reduction in output. If the post-merger firm reduced its output by 10%, each of the 90% of units still being produced would contribute to the efficiency gains; the deadweight loss, however, would accrue over only the 10% reduction.

Williamson concluded that in a market with average elasticities of demand and supply, a merger that produced "nontrivial" economies of 1.2% would be efficient, even if it resulted in a price increase of 10%.[10]

7. See §§ 12.3–12.6.

8. The source is O. Williamson, Economies as an Antitrust Defense: the Welfare Trade–Offs, 58 Amer.Econ.Rev. 18 (1968); see also, O. Williamson, Economies as an Antitrust Defense Revisited, 125 U.Pa.L.Rev. 699 (1977); R. Pitofsky, Efficiencies in Defense of Mergers: Two Years After, 7 Geo. Mason L. Rev. 485 (1999); C. Conrath & N. Widnell, Efficiency Claims in Merger Analysis: Hostility on Humility, 7 Geo. Mason L. Rev. 685 (1999) T. Muris, The Efficiency Defense Under Section 7 of the Clayton Act, 30 Case West.Res.L.Rev. 381 (1980); A.A. Fisher & R.H. Lande, Efficiency Considerations in Merger Enforcement, 71 Calif.L.Rev. 1580 (1983); H. Hovenkamp, Merger Actions for Damages, 35 Hastings L.J. (1984); 4A Antitrust Law ¶¶ 970–976 (rev. ed. 1998).

9. See the discussion of the social cost of monopoly in § 1.3b.

10. Note 8, 58 Amer.Econ.Rev. at 22–23. Compare A.A. Fisher, F.I. Johnson & R.H. Lande, Price Effects of Horizontal Mergers, 77 Calif. L. Rev. 777 (1989), noting that large efficiency gains are needed if a merger creating market power is to result in lower prices. That is, Williamson's welfare "tradeoff" is indifferent to whether the efficiency gains are passed on to consumers as lower prices or retained by the merging firms as increased profits.

Williamson's analysis is vulnerable to some criticism. First, his description of triangle A_1 in the figure as the efficiency costs of a merger probably understates the true social cost. Rectangles A_2 plus A_3 represent potential monopoly profits to the post-merger firm. A profit-maximizing firm will be willing to spend substantial resources in an effort to acquire or retain a certain amount of monopoly power.[11] If a particular merger will give a firm $1,000,000 in additional monopoly profits, the firm will spend up to $1,000,000 in order to accomplish the merger and then retain its monopoly position. It could spend this money in highly inefficient ways, such as espionage, predatory pricing against a potential take-over target, or vexatious litigation. At the extreme, $A_2 + A_3$ are not increased profits to the post-merger firm at all, but funds inefficiently spent in order to give the firm its market position. Importantly, the anticompetitive risk in the merger case is not increased likelihood of single-firm monopoly, but increased likelihood of collusion. The costs of managing a cartel or oligopoly can be quite high in relation to the profits that it produces.[12] A cartel or oligopoly that occasions a price increase of 10% would very likely produce much smaller gains in profitability.[13]

Another problem of the tradeoff model is that it apparently assumes a merger to monopoly. But most collusion facilitating mergers involve firms whose aggregate share is significantly less than 100%. For example, suppose a 20% firm should acquire a 10% firm, greatly increasing the extent of oligopoly performance. In that case, the increased coordination that results from the merger enables *both* the merging and the non-merging firms to increase their prices. However, the efficiency gains are spread across only the output of the two merging firms, which account for only 30% of the market's output.[14]

§ 12.2b2. Must Efficiencies be "Passed On"?

Still another problem of the welfare tradeoff model of merger efficiencies is that it treats all efficiency gains the same way, no matter who gets the benefit. Suppose that two firms selling widgets at a competitive price of $1.00 merge. As a result of the merger the post-merger firm has enough market power to reduce output and increase the price of widgets to $1.05. In addition, the firm's marginal costs drop from $1.00 per widget to 95¢ per widget. In this case the efficiency gains, which are measured across all widgets produced, will probably be larger than the deadweight loss from monopoly pricing, which is measured across only the reduction in output. However, the merger results in an *actual* output reduction and an *actual* price increase for consumers. Although the overall effect of the merger is efficient, the benefits of the increased efficiency accrue mainly to the post-merger firm in the form of higher profits. Such a merger rule would undoubtedly be politically unacceptable, even though the rule promotes efficiency. Several courts have suggested that an efficiency defense should be rejected where the parties cannot show that the gains will be passed on to consumers.[15]

At the same time, a rule requiring *all* efficiency gains to be passed on to consumers is unacceptable as well. First, it would completely undermine the principal motivation for firms to merge in the first place, which is to lower their costs. A rule that forbad firms from pocketing any of the gains of increased

11. See § 1.3c.

12. See § 4.3.

13. The true social cost of Williamson's merger is the sum of (a) the deadweight loss and (b) the resources inefficiently spent in maintaining the cartel or oligopoly facilitated by the merger, less (c) the total wealth accruing to the post-merger firm from the monopoly overcharge and the efficiency gain.

14. For further development, see 4A Antitrust Law ¶ 970e (rev. ed. 1998).

15. FTC v. University Health, 938 F.2d 1206, 1222–23 (11th Cir.1991) (defendant "must demonstrate that the intended acquisition would result in significant economies and that these economies ultimately would benefit competition and, hence, consumers"); United States v. United Tote, 768 F.Supp. 1064, 1084–85 (D.Del.1991) (rejecting efficiency defense in part because there was "no guarantee that these benefits will be passed along" to consumers); American Medical Int'l, 104 F.T.C. 1, 213–20 (1984) (efficiencies defense failed because even assuming "that these cost savings can be realized, AMI does not establish that they will necessarily inure to the benefit of consumers").

merger efficiency would serve as a significant deterrent to efficiency-producing mergers that have crossed the threshold of presumptive legality.[16] Indeed, when two perfect competitors merger, they pocket all of their efficiency gains and nothing is passed on. For example, if two of the nation's 100,000 corn farmers should merge, thus lowering their costs, they will continue to sell at the market price and the market price will not respond to their merger, because they are too small to have any effect. As a result of the merger these firms will increase their output; they will not cut their price.[17]

A more acceptable rule that takes both economic and political concerns into account is that the defendants must show that efficiencies created by the merger are sufficiently large to keep post-merger prices at or below pre-merger levels.[18] For example, if a merger threatens monopoly or oligopoly raising the price from the pre-merger level of $1.00 to $1.10, efficiencies must be sufficient to drive the post-merger price back to the $1.00 range or lower. A 1997 revision to the efficiency statement in the 1992 Merger Guidelines states that the enforcement agency will consider "whether cognizable efficiencies likely would be sufficient to reverse the merger's potential to harm consumers in the relevant market, e.g., by preventing price increases in that market."[19]

§ 12.2b3. Efficiencies Must be "Merger–Specific" and "Extraordinary"

The welfare tradeoff model analyzed in § 12.2b1 has force only because we assume that the efficiencies in question could not readily be obtained by means other than merger. But many efficiency gains can be attained by other means, although perhaps less readily. For example, a merger may result in the termination of an inefficient CEO and his replacement by a more aggressive one, but stockholders or an attentive Board of Directors could do the same thing, and probably will do so eventually.[20] A merger might facilitate a firm's simplification of its distribution system or specialization of its plants, but these things would very likely happen without the merger as well. They might simply take longer.

Questions about the availability of alternative routes to efficiency are vexing, and explain why the efficiency defense has been successful so infrequently.[21] Suppose that the claimed efficiency is that the acquirer needs to modernize and the cheapest way to do so is to acquire another firm's recently built modern plant.[22] Unquestionably, modernization is efficient and anything that reduces the cost of modernization must be efficient as well. But the defense makes sense only if the acquired firm's plant has excess capacity;[23] if it does not, then the post-merger firm must continue to use the old plants as well or perhaps reduce output to the level previously produced by the acquired firm alone. The argument might be that adding to the existing modern plant is cheaper than building a second free-standing plant, but adding would require the two firms to be one. However, then we would want to know why the *acquired* firm cannot simply enlarge its capacity on its own: that is, competition rather than merger most usually solves

16. Of course, efficiency producing mergers in more competitively structured markets would still be pursued, for these mergers would never cross the threshold of presumptive illegality in the first place.

17. See 4A Antitrust Law ¶ 971 (rev. ed. 1998); T. Muris, The Government and Merger Efficiencies: Still Hostile After All These Years, 7 Geo. Mason L. Rev. 729 (1999); P. Yde & M. Vita, Merger Efficiencies: Reconsidering the "Passing-on" Requirement, 64 Antitrust L.J. 735 (1996).

18. See 4A Antitrust Law ¶ 971d (rev. ed. 1998).

19. See 1992 Horizontal Merger Guidelines, with 1997 revision to § 4.0, efficiencies statement. Reprinted as Appendix A in Antitrust Law (current Supp.).

20. See FTC v. Owens–Illinois, Inc., 681 F.Supp. 27, 53 (D.D.C.), vacated as moot, 850 F.2d 694 (D.C.Cir.1988) (accepting this defense).

21. For a description of the various types of merger economies, querying which ones are merger specific and which are not, see 4A Antitrust Law ¶ ¶ 973, 975 (rev. ed. 1998).

22. For example, United States v. Rice Growers Assn. of Cal., 1986–2 Trade Cas. ¶ 67287, 1986 WL 12561 (E.D.Cal.1986).

23. Furthermore, we want to be sure that the excess capacity is not a result of collusion.

such problems.[24]

One plausible alternative to merger is a joint venture, particularly where the efficiency gains are in such activities as research and development. Joint participation in R & D can be highly efficient and, if properly limited, need not raise significant concerns about coordination of prices or output. The same thing is frequently true of intellectual property licensing, which can enable firms to share a technology while continuing to compete with each other in other ways.[25]

Finally, one must keep in mind that the concentration standards for assessing mergers[26] are premised on the proposition that all mergers produce some efficiency gains. As a result, they take into account what one might consider to be the "ordinary" efficiency gains that result from any merger.[27] The kinds of efficiencies that qualify for the defense must be "extraordinary," going beyond the expected savings that attend any business consolidation.

In any event, if a merger poses a significant competitive threat, the proponents of the merger will have the burden not only of showing that significant and extraordinary economies will result, but also that these economies could not readily be attained by means other than the merger.

§ 12.2b4. Problems of Identification and Measurement

A final problem with the welfare tradeoff model is that courts are simply unable to make the measurements that its analysis would require. Efficiencies, Judge Posner has written, are an "intractable subject for litigation."[28] Courts are not up to measuring marginal costs or elasticities of supply or demand with anything approaching the precision required by such an "efficiency defense." Our knowledge that mergers can produce both economies and monopoly pricing is fairly secure. However, quantifying either of these in a particular merger case is impossible. Most mergers found illegal under current law probably create efficiencies. They are condemned, however, because no court is capable of balancing the increase in market power or the potential for collusion against the economies achieved. Judges must necessarily make decisions based on the information they can obtain and understand. When a merger involves companies having a small share of the market, they infer that the potential for monopolistic pricing or collusion is trivial; therefore, the merger must be calculated to increase the efficiency of the post-merger firm. If the merger involves firms large enough to threaten competitive pricing significantly, however, then the measurement problem quickly becomes insoluble unless we create some simplifying rules. Such rules could not involve any kind of precise "balancing" of harm to competition vs. efficiency gains. Rather, they should operate so as to create a complete defense when both "substantial" and "merger specific" economies are shown. In this case, "substantial" means that the efficiencies be great enough to warrant an inference that post-merger prices will be no higher than pre-merger levels, with the burden of proof on the defendant.

In all events, it is important to distinguish between real efficiencies and mere pecuniary efficiencies or gains. For example, a merger may have favorable tax consequences that re-

24. Cf. United States v. Rockford Memorial Corp., 717 F.Supp. 1251, 1290–91 (N.D.Ill.1989), aff'd, 898 F.2d 1278 (7th Cir.), cert. denied, 498 U.S. 920, 111 S.Ct. 295 (1990) (rejecting argument that merger would lead to efficient standardization of procedures where hospitals independently could have achieved standardization); FTC v. Staples, 970 F.Supp. 1066, 1090 (D.D.C.1997) (rejecting proffered defense that merger among office superstores was justified by lower purchase prices for inventory; finding in part that the savings could have been realized without the merger); United States v. Ivaco, 704 F.Supp. 1409, 1425–27 (W.D.Mich.1989) (non-horizontal or more limited joint venture could have achieved same efficiency results with less injury to competition). See generally R. Pitofsky, Proposals for Revised United States Merger Enforcement in a Global Economy, 81 Geo. L.J. 195, 242 (1992).

25. See generally 4A Antitrust Law ¶ 973c (rev. ed. 1998).

26. See § 12.4b.

27. See, e.g., FTC v. Staples, 970 F.Supp. 1066, 1090 (D.D.C.1997) (rejecting savings in employee health insurance costs as a qualifying efficiency); and see 4A Antitrust Law ¶ 974a (rev. ed. 1998).

28. Posner, note 6, at 112.

duce a firm's costs.[29] But in this case the tax savings to the firm are offset by tax revenue loses to the government, and cannot be counted as a qualifying gain from the merger. Likewise, in *Owens–Illinois*[30] the court correctly rejected the argument that the merger must be efficient because the acquiring firm was offering some $20 more per share for the acquired firm then the current trading price, providing an enormous gain to shareholders. Higher stock prices could reflect efficiency, but they could also flow from the increased market power of the post-merger firm.

Most of the courts that have considered the efficiency defense have been skeptical. Most have rejected evidence of efficiencies,[31] while a few have recognized the defense.[32]

§ 12.2b5. Benefit and Threat in Different Markets

When firms operate in multiple markets the anticompetitive threat may occur in one market while the efficiency gains show up in a different market. Recognizing an efficiency defense in such a case seems inconsistent with the language of § 7 of the Clayton Act, which condemns a merger "where in any line of commerce or ... in any section of the country, the effect ... may be substantially to lessen competition...."[33] Further, recognizing an efficiency defense in such a case forces merger policy to permit an injury to consumers in the product where the anticompetitive threat occurs, but benefitting a different set of consumers in the market where the efficiencies are realized.[34]

In some cases the problem goes away if the firms can structure a partial divestiture, and the government so insists. For example, if the two firms manufacture widgets and gidgets and the merger promises anticompetitive effects in the widget market and efficiency gains in the gidget market, the government might condition its approval on a divestiture of one or more widget plants. Of course, this will not be possible when the two products are manufactured in the same plants, or when they are complements, such as leather and beef, that cannot be separated. In such cases the merger must be condemned, with a possible exception for situations where the market in which efficiencies result is significantly larger than the market in which competition is threatened.[35]

§ 12.3 Estimating Anticompetitive Consequences I: Mergers Facilitating Unilateral Price Increases

§ 12.3a. Introduction

The anticompetitive consequences of mergers can be grouped under two general headings. Under the first comes mergers that permit the post-merger firm to make a significant price increase, while other firms in the market either keep their price the same or take a much smaller increase. The second classification, which is discussed in § 12.4, includes mergers that facilitate collusion or other forms of coordinated interaction, thus permitting all firms in the market to increase their price.

§ 12.3b. Merger to Monopoly

The "classic" example of a merger facilitating a unilateral price increase is the merger to

29. See J. Kwoka & F.R. Warren–Boulton, Efficiencies, Failing Firms and Alternatives to Merger: A Policy Synthesis, 31 Antitrust Bull. 431, 433 (1986).

30. Note 20.

31. FTC v. University Health, Inc., 938 F.2d 1206, 1222–1224 (11th Cir.1991); United States v. Rockford Memorial Corp., 717 F.Supp. 1251, 1289–1291 (N.D.Ill.1989), affirmed, 898 F.2d 1278 (7th Cir.), cert. denied, 498 U.S. 920, 111 S.Ct. 295 (1990) (requiring clear and convincing evidence of efficiencies; standard not met); FTC v. Staples, 970 F.Supp. 1066 (D.D.C.1997) (insufficient evidence of efficiencies).

32. See *Owens–Illinois*, note 20, 681 F.Supp. at 53 (accepting defenses that acquiring firm was more efficiently managed than acquired firm, and latter would benefit from improved management; economies of multiplant operations).

33. 15 U.S.C.A. § 18.

34. E.g., United States v. Philadelphia National Bank, 374 U.S. 321, 370, 83 S.Ct. 1715, 1745 (1963) (rejecting defense that a merger that lessened competition in one market should be approved because it increased competition in a different market); United States v. Bethlehem Steel Corp., 168 F.Supp. 576, 618 (S.D.N.Y.1958) (anticompetitive consequences in one region could not be offset against lower prices and reduced freight charges in another region).

35. See generally 4A Antitrust Law ¶ 972c (rev. ed. 1998), which provides illustrations.

monopoly.[1] Such mergers deserve the highest level of antitrust scrutiny, and generally should be condemned even if barriers to entry are low. The need for rivals to be permitted to exist and grow is simply too important in such a market.

Suppose that the antitrust rule were that mergers to monopoly were legal in a market with low entry barriers. As each new entrant came into the market, it could expect an offer to be bought up by the dominant firm. Further, each of those offers would be profitable, for the value of being able to participate in a monopoly would be greater than the value of being a competitive rival against a dominant firm.[2]

§ 12.3c. Dominant Firm's Acquisition of Nascent Rival

Closely related to the merger to monopoly is the monopolist's or near monopolist's acquisition of new rivals as they enter the market.[3] For example, suppose a firm with a 90% market share purchases small firms as they enter into prospective competition. To be sure, economies of scale may explain why the market has a dominant firm, and they may even explain why a small rival will not survive very long. But they do not serve to justify a policy of permitting dominant firms to acquire small rivals. New technologies have often displaced old ones, even when the old ones were subject to significant economies of scale. Further, attainment of further economies rarely justify such mergers. It would be a rare case where a 90% firm could reduce its costs by acquiring a 1% firm, and could not readily attain the same cost reductions by other means.[4]

The most likely explanation of such acquisitions is that the new rival threatens to be an aggressive competitor, or has some technology that the dominant firm wants. But in that case the effect of the merger is to prevent this new technology from developing in competition with that of the dominant firm. Of course, the general policy of the intellectual property laws is to encourage the dissemination of new technology, but in this case a *non*exclusive license will serve that purpose quite adequately. It will permit the dominant firm to have access to the technology at issue, while not denying it to others who might enter into competition with the dominant firm.[5]

§ 12.3d. Unilateral Effects in Product Differentiated Markets[6]

A market is product differentiated when different seller offer distinctive variations. While their products compete with one another to greater or lesser degrees, customers distinguish among them, may have preferences for one variation over another, and may thus be willing to pay more for one variation. Our basic models of cartels and oligopoly assume absolutely undifferentiated products, but in the real world this is the exception rather than the rule. Product differentiation is relevant to the extent that (1) the product produced by one merging firm differs from that produced by another, meaning that the pre-merger competition between them is less than it would be if they produced identical output; and (2) the output of the merging firms differs from that of other firms in the market.

For the most part, Courts have tended to ignore product heterogeneity as a factor in

§ 12.3

1. See 4 Antitrust Law ¶ 911 (rev. ed. 1998).

2. The Coase Theorem predicts that in a well functioning market two firms will bargain their way to a joint maximizing result. Since the monopoly produces greater profits than competition, each new entrant will agree to be bought up by the dominant firm and the market will never become competitive. See R. Coase, The Problem of Social Cost, 3 J.L. & Econ. 1 (1960).

Contrast United States v. Syufy Enters., 903 F.2d 659 (9th Cir.1990), which refused to condemn an exhibitor's acquisition of competing exhibitors when the immediate market share created was nearly 100 percent, but the acquisition was followed almost immediately by entry and dramatic expansion reducing the defendant's share to less than forty percent.

3. See 4 Antitrust Law ¶ 912 (rev. ed. 1998).

4. On the economies defense and the need for "merger specific" economies, see § 12.2b3.

5. See, e.g., United States v. Baroid Corp. 59 Fed. Reg. 2610 (1994) (consent decree conditioning acquisition by large firm of competing technology on the granting of licenses to others).

6. The related theory of unilateral effects resulting from capacity constraints or differential costs is not developed here; see 4 Antitrust Law ¶ 915 (rev. ed. 1998).

merger law, largely because so little is known about the relationship between the degree and nature of product differentiation, and the nature and likelihood of noncompetitive results. Product differentiation has appeared much more prominently in formal economic and policy analysis of mergers. For example, in Edward Chamberlin's model of monopolistic competition,[7] which was prominent from the 1930's through the 1950's, product differentiation was generally thought to be a bad thing that reduced output and raised prices, howbeit without increasing the returns of the firms. They spent all their resources in devising new variations, far in excess of what rational consumers would want if only they knew the cost. But an offsetting consequence of product differentiation is that collusion and oligopoly are more difficult to orchestrate. This serves to mitigate the anticipated anticompetitive effects of a merger.[8]

Chamberlin's original concern about the "monopolistic" results of product differentiation has re-emerged, found its way into the 1992 Horizontal Merger Guidelines, and has become an important part of government merger analysis. Under the right circumstances, product differentiation can give firms a bit of protected space within which supracompetitive price increases can be profitable.

The problem that the Guidelines identify is well known in the economics literature and is best illustrated by a model that economist Harold Hotelling used already in 1929.[9] Figure 2 illustrates. Imagine a row of hot dog vendors spaced out along the beach for sale to sunbathers. In this case we presume that the product itself is identical from one vendor to the next, but the "differentiation" consists in the number of steps that each sunbather must walk in order to purchase a hot dog.[10] Assuming that all hot dogs are sold at the same price, each vendor will be preferred by those sunbathers that are closest to that particular vendor.[11]

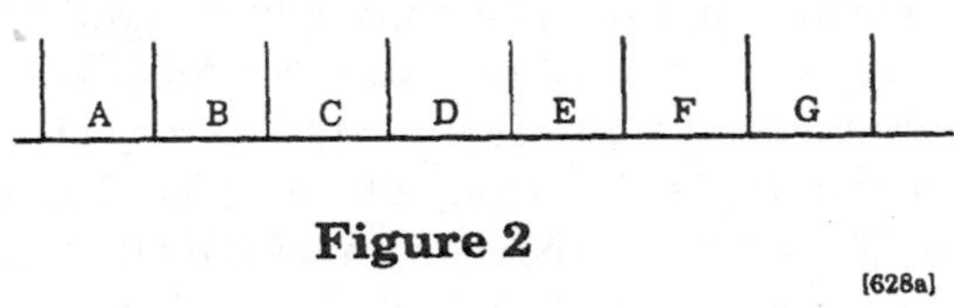

Figure 2

[628a]

Each vendor looks like a monopolist with respect to those sunbathers who are closest to that vendor. That is, all sunbathers closest to A would buy from A, those closest to B would buy from B, and so on. Further, individual vendors might have *some* incentive to increase price, depending on the value that the sunbathers place on the distance they have to walk. That is, their output will not fall to zero in response to a small price increase. For example, if sunbathers valued their steps at 1¢ each, a vendor who increased the hot dog price by 10¢ (others holding their prices constant) would lose those customers for whom the difference in distance between the price increasing vendor and the next nearest vendor was less than ten steps. Whether this price increase would be profitable presents an empirical question, and depends on the location of the sunbathers. If all of the sunbather's in B's area were extremely close to B's stand and relatively far away from the stands of A and C, the price increase would more likely be profitable. By contrast, if all of B's sunbathers were arrayed just inside the boundary line equidistant between B and C, then the price increase would be unprofitable, for B would lose these sunbathers to C.

Now consider the impact of a cartel or a merger between vendor B and vendor C, followed by a joint price increase. To the left of B and the right of C, there are customers who threaten to purchase from either A or D, and that threat would be unchanged. But what about customers arrayed in the area between B and C? While these may have been on the

7. E. Chamberlin, The Theory of Monopolistic Competition (1933).

8. See § 12.5a.

9. H. Hotelling, Stability in Competition, 39 Econ. J. 41 (1929).

10. For a more fully developed example, see 4 Antitrust Law ¶ 914a (rev. ed. 1998); and see T. Campbell, Predation and Competition in Antitrust: the Case of Nonfungible Goods, 87 Col. L.Rev. 1625, 1636 (1987).

11. See J.B. Baker & T.F. Bresnahan, The Gains from Merger or Collusion in Product-Differentiated Industries, 33 J. Indus. Econ. 427, 429 (1985).

competitive margin and would have switched in response to a price increase by *either* B or C standing alone, these customers are very clearly "captured" by cartel BC or post-merger firm BC. That is, they are a relatively great distance from A and D, and thus will be willing to pay more for a hot dog now than they would have been before the cartel or merger came into existence.

Once again, the degree to which the cartel or merger increases the profit-maximizing price of the two firms presents an empirical question, and depends on where the customers are arrayed. If most of the customers are firmly committed to either B or C, but are relatively distant from A or D, the cartel or merger could facilitate a rather large monopoly price increase. By contrast, if the customers are mainly between A and B and between C and D, but not between B and C, then the profit-maximizing post-merger price increase would be relatively lower. Finally, a higher price increase would be profitable the more isolated B and C as a pair are from A and D.

Although the story is a little harder to picture when the firms are spread out in product space rather than geographic space, it is no different in substance. The degree to which a merger in a product differentiated market might facilitate a *unilateral* price increase by the post-merger firm depends on (1) the relative "closeness" in product space of the merging firms to one another; and (2) the relative distance between the post-merger firm's product offering and the offerings of others in the market; and (3) the relative inability of other firms to redesign their products to make them close to the output of the merging firms. This requires the Agencies to consider a variety of factors about the relationship between the two merging firms, between the post-merger firm and other competitors, and between the firms and the customers of each.

Thus there must be a significant number of customers who regard the products of the two merging firms as their first and second market choices.[12] Further, it must be apparent that other firms in the market will not reposition themselves to take advantage of the price increase. For example, in the above illustration if after the BC merger the owner of A either moved or built a second stand wedged between B and C, the price increase consequences of the BC merger would be lost.[13]

Second, the closer the products made by the two merging firms, the more likely that the merger will produce a substantial price increase.[14] However, they need not be the "closest" rivals before the merger can have sufficiently anticompetitive consequences.

As figure 3 (following page) illustrates, suppose that a market has six firms, A through F, making a differentiated product. The firms' products are differentiated, but by different amounts, as indicated by the distances between them. A's marginal cost is $1.00, its current price is $2.00, and at that price it sells 100 units. Its residual price elasticity of demand is–2, which means that a 10% price increase, to $2.20, will yield a 20% demand reduction, to 80 units.[15] Note that this price increase is unprofitable. Pre-increase profits were $100. But post-increase profits are $1.20 per unit, times 80 units, or $96.

12. 1992 Guidelines, § 2.21.

13. See, e.g., State of New York v. Kraft General Foods, 926 F.Supp. 321, 352–358 (S.D.N.Y.1995) (refusing to condemn merger of ready-to-eat breakfast cereal makers on this theory, because one could easily expand its product variety into another's niche); accord United States v. Gillette Co., 828 F.Supp. 78, 84 (D.D.C.1993). See 4 Antitrust Law ¶ 914d (rev. ed. 1998).

14. Id. at § 2.211.

15. A "residual" elasticity of demand is the elasticity facing a single firm rather than the market as a whole. See § 3.9a.

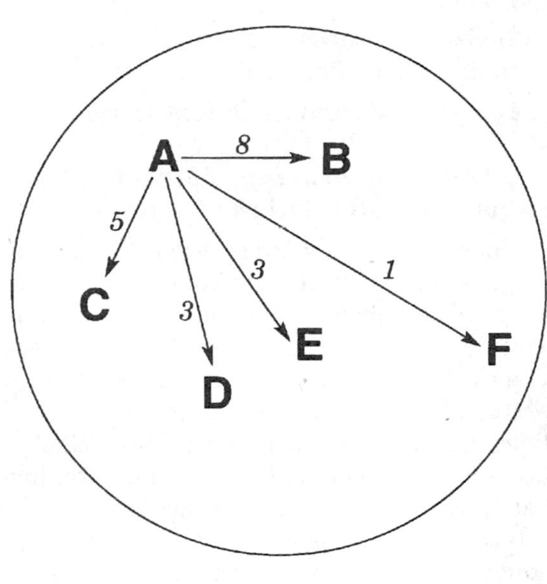

Figure 3

But when firm A raises its price, where do the customers go? Let us assume that of the 20 units that are lost, 8 (40%) go to B, the closest rival, 5 (25%) go to C, the second closest rival, and 3, 3 and 1 units respectively go to rivals D, E & F. This percentage rate at which customers substitute from A to B, or from A to C, is called a "diversion ratio."[16] Assume also that all rivals have the same costs.

In this case an A–C merger would make the price increase profitable. While the price increase to $2.20 reduces A's own profits by $4.00, it increases C's profits by $5.00 (that is, C sells 5 more at a profit of $1.00 each). A merger with B would be even more profitable, since 8 sales, and $8.00 in increased profit, go to B. But the important point is that a merger with *either* B or C would make A's 10% price increase profitable, even though C is only the second closest rival. Thus either merger would be challengeable if we regarded a merger facilitating a 10% price increase as unlawful.[17]

Measuring diversion ratios empirically has turned out to be a fairly manageable problem, particularly in markets where there are electronic records of transactions. For example, if a sporting goods store sells several brands of running shoes and the price of Adidas rises by 10%, scanner data might reveal the number of customers who switched away from Adidas, and the relative numbers that switched to Nike, Saucony, Asics, and so on.

As a result, an economist's predictions of unilateral price effects in product differentiated markets can be at least as robust as predictions about the price consequences of a merger thought to facilitate oligopoly pricing.[18] While the theory of oligopoly and concentration measures such as the HHI have become quite conventional in antitrust merger analysis, the ease with which we use these tools belies the many assumptions that go into our predictions. A great amount of guesswork goes into any theory about the impact of a concentration-increasing merger on the oligopoly game that the firms will play. As a result, the unilat-

16. See J. Baker, Contemporary Empirical Merger Analysis, 5 Geo. Mason L. Rev. 347 (1997); J. Baker, Unilateral Competitive Effects Theories in Merger Analysis, 11 Antitrust 21 (Spring 1997); C. Shapiro, Mergers with Differentiated Products, 10 Antitrust 23, 24 (Spring, 1996); see also C. Vellturo, Evaluating Mergers with Differentiated Products, 11 Antitrust 16 (Spring, 1997).

17. See, e.g., United States v. Interstate Bakeries Corp., 1996–1 Trade Cas. ¶ 71271 at 76190, 1995 WL 803559 (N.D.Ill.1995) (approving consent decree):

> The Complaint alleges that Interstate's acquisition of Continental would likely lead to an increase in price charged to consumers for white pan bread. Following the acquisition, Interstate likely would unilaterally raise the price of its own brands.... Because Interstate and Continental's brands are perceived by consumers as close substitutes, Interstate could pursue such a pricing strategy without losing so much in sales to competing white pan bread brands or to private labels that the price increase would be unprofitable. Interstate could, for instance, profitably impose a significant increase in the price of Wonder white pan bread, since a substantial portion of any sales lost for that product would be recaptured by increased sales of Interstate's other brands.

Id. at 76190. Accord United States v. Kimberly–Clark Corp., 1996–1 Trade Cas. ¶ 71405, 1996 WL 351145 (N.D.Tex.1996).

18. See § 12.4.

eral effects theory of mergers should fare very well in future merger analysis. Its use, however, will always require an expert economist.[19]

§ 12.4 Estimating Anticompetitive Consequences II: Mergers Facilitating Coordinated Interaction

The prevailing concern of merger law today is not to protect small businesses from more efficient rivals but to deter oligopolistic pricing or express collusion. Since many mergers have a significant but unmeasurable potential to create efficiencies,[1] an ideal antitrust policy would condemn mergers when the risk of oligopoly pricing or collusion is substantial and approve them when such risks are minimal.

Economists generally agree that there is a relationship between the size, size distribution and number of firms in a market and the likelihood of collusion. They disagree about the relevant numbers. Furthermore, markets differ from each other. One market containing six firms might be much more susceptible to collusion than another. Nevertheless, both the Merger Guidelines and the courts have tried to develop unitary market *share* rules for prima facie illegality that apply in all industries with a given level of concentration. Then they use several non-market share factors as mitigating or aggravating circumstances on a case-by-case basis. This approach was approved by the Supreme Court in United States v. Philadelphia Nat. Bank.[2] The non-market share factors include:

1) Presence and Height of Entry Barriers[3]

2) Sophistication of Buyers, Suppliers or Others in a Position to Discipline Market Participants[4]

3) Sales Methods, Shipping Costs, Availability of Facilitating Practices[5]

4) Degree of Product Differentiation[6]

§ 12.4a. Measuring Market Concentration: The CR4 and the Herfindahl

Under practically every theory about how mergers can facilitate anticompetitive behavior, market concentration is relevant. If the feared consequence is collusion, it can readily be shown that price fixing is more likely to be successful as the number of price fixers declines. Collusion is particularly more likely to succeed if the colluders can eliminate firms that have been unwilling to participate in the cartel. As the number of cartel members is reduced, the ease with which an agreement can be reached increases; further, cheating becomes a smaller problem and it can often be detected more easily. The ability to eliminate a fringe firm not participating in the cartel can often spell the difference between success and failure, particularly if there are only one or a small number of such firms.[7]

If the feared result is noncooperative oligopoly behavior of the Cournot variety,[8] the inverse relationship between the number of firms and anticompetitive consequences is equally robust. In the orthodox Cournot oligopoly, output goes down and prices go up as the number of firms decreases. More complicated variants generally yield the similar results. For example, the more easily one firm can observe

19. See 4 Antitrust Law ¶ 914e (rev. ed. 1998); and see G. Werden & L. Froeb, The Effects of Mergers in differentiated Products Industries: Structural Merger Policy and the Logit Model, 10 J.L. Econ. & Organ. 407 (1994); J. Baker & T. Bresnahan, The Gains from Merger or Collusion in Product–Differentiated Industries, 33 J. Indus. Econ. 427 (1985). See also G. Werden, Simulating Unilateral Competitive Effects from Differentiated Products Mergers, 11 Antitrust 27 (Spring, 1997); J. Hausman & G. Leonard, Economic Analysis of Differentiated Products Mergers Using Real World Data, 5 Geo. Mason L. Rev. 321 (1997).

§ 12.4

1. See § 12.2.

2. 374 U.S. 321, 355–66, 83 S.Ct. 1715, 1737–43 (1963). The Court compared market share percentages in merger cases in a wide variety of industries and concluded that the percentages in the case before it (combined market share more than 30%) "raise an inference that the effect of the contemplated merger of appellees may be substantially to lessen competition * * *." Id. at 365, 83 S.Ct. at 1742.

3. See § 12.6.

4. See § 12.7a.

5. See § 12.7d.

6. See § 12.5a.

7. For analysis of these factors, see § 4.1.

8. See § 4.2.

the behavior of others, the more easily an oligopoly can be maintained. A small number of rivals is generally easier to observe than a large number, and "cheating" thus easier to detect.[9]

So concentration clearly matters. Nevertheless, the robustness of that conclusion belies much complexity about *how* it matters. The questions are manifold: (1) at what level does the number of firms in the market begin to make a measurable difference in performance? (2) what is the relevance of *variations* in firm size, whether in the market generally or among the merging partners? (3) what index, or measurement device, best captures the market concentration concerns of merger policy? (4) to what extent should differences among markets be taken into account? Although economists agree fairly broadly about the general relevance of concentration, they continue to dispute the answers to all four of these questions. One's position on them affects both the weight given to a particular level of concentration and the choice of a rule, or "index," for measuring concentration.

§ 12.4a1. The Four–Firm Concentration Ratio (CR4)

In the 1960's and 1970's courts and the enforcement agencies most often looked at the "four-firm concentration ratio" (CR4) to determine the degree of danger present in a particular market. The CR4 is computed by adding the market shares of the four largest firms in the market. Thus a market in which the four largest firms have market shares of 30%, 20%, 15%, and 10% has a CR4 of 75%.[10] Such a market was considered highly concentrated, and any merger in that market would be given close scrutiny. If the CR4 was much smaller, such as 25%, then a merger involving firms of somewhat larger market shares might still be legal. Under the original Merger Guidelines issued by the Division in 1968,[11] a merger of two firms of 4% market share each was presumptively illegal in a highly concentrated market (CR4 greater than 75%). If the market was less concentrated, mergers involving firms of 5% each were presumptively illegal. These Guidelines were substantially more tolerant of mergers than Supreme Court case law, which had condemned mergers in unconcentrated markets of firms whose combined post-merger market share was less than 8%.[12]

Conceptually, the CR4 is based on the premise that the four largest firms in the market would collude, while the rest of the market remains competitive.[13] If the four firms made up all, or nearly all, of the market their cartel price would be close to the monopoly price. By contrast, if the four largest firms had only a small market share they could not succeed in getting the price significantly above the competitive level.[14]

Ever since the CR4 was introduced into merger litigation, there has been widespread dispute about how it should be applied. The issues concerned how concentrated a market must be before close scrutiny of mergers is appropriate, and how large the parties must be before the danger to competition is substantial. At one extreme are Supreme Court cases condemning mergers of small firms in unconcentrated markets. At the other extreme are suggestions that mergers are not likely to be harmful unless the combined share of the post-merger firm is 60% or so.[15] In the middle a rather vague consensus emerged that a market in which the CR4 exceeds 75% is conducive to collusion, and that a market in which the CR4 is less than 40% or so is a "safe harbor" in

9. See 4 Antitrust Law ¶ 930 (rev. ed. 1998).

10. Some economists prefer the 8–firm concentration ratio (CR8), which is the sum of the market shares of the eight largest firms. Courts, however, have used the CR4 almost exclusively.

11. U.S. Dep't of Justice Merger Guidelines, reprinted in 1 Trade Reg.Rep. (CCH) ¶ 4430 (1968).

12. E.g., United States v. Von's Grocery Co., 384 U.S. 270, 86 S.Ct. 1478 (1966)(condemning merger where combined market share of merging firms was 7.5% and CR4 was 24.4%); United States v. Pabst Brewing Co., 384 U.S. 546, 86 S.Ct. 1665 (1966), on remand, 296 F.Supp. 994 (E.D.Wis.1969) (condemning merger where firms' combined market share was 4.5% and CR4 less than 30%).

13. See T.R. Saving, Concentration Ratios and the Degree of Monopoly, 11 Int'l. Econ. Rev. 139 (1970); R. Blair & D. Kaserman, Antitrust Economics 236 (1985).

14. See 4 Antitrust Law ¶ 931a1 (rev. ed. 1998).

15. See R. Bork, The Antitrust Paradox: A Policy at War With Itself 221 (1978; rev. ed. 1993).

which most mergers should be legal. There was also general agreement that if the CR4 were 75% or higher, a merger in which the combined market share of the post-merger firm exceeded 12% should be illegal. These figures are admittedly generalizations from a variety of writers whose opinions vary across a wide range.[16] Courts have gravitated toward the same numbers, although there is no unanimity among the judges either.[17]

§ 12.4a2. The Herfindahl–Hirschman Index (HHI)

The enforcement agencies now use the Herfindahl–Hirschman Index (HHI) instead of the CR4 to measure market concentration.[18] The HHI as used in the 1992 Horizontal Merger Guidelines is the sum of the squares of every firm in the relevant market. For example, if a market has 3 firms each with a market share of 25%, 1 firm of 15% and 1 firm of 10%, the HHI would be $25^2 + 25^2 + 25^2 + 15^2 + 10^2 = 2200$. Such a market (which has a CR4 of 90%) is considered highly concentrated under the 1992 Guidelines, which so regard any market with an HHI greater than 1800.

Many economists believe that the HHI describes market structure and dangers of anticompetitive activity more accurately than the CR4 does. For example, the CR4 fails to account for distribution of market shares among the four largest firms. A market in which the four largest firms each have a 20% share has a CR4 of 80%. A market in which the largest firm has 77% and firms 2, 3 and 4 each have 1% also has a CR4 of 80%. This is so because the price charged by a classical cartel is indifferent to the distribution of firm sizes. The cartel of four 20% firms will fix the same price as the cartel of one 77% firm and three 1% firms.

But in a non-cooperative oligopoly[19] the price rises as the disparity in firm size rises, and the HHI reflects this.[20] Our experience also bears this out to some degree. A market with four equal size, equally efficient firms may behave quite competitively. An industry with one giant and several pygmies, however, will likely be conducive to "price leadership," a form of oligopolistic pricing in which the largest firm sets a supracompetitive price and the smaller firms, fearful of retaliation, follow with their own supracompetitive price. The HHI acknowledges that markets with the same CR4 may exhibit widely different degrees of competition. The HHI of the market containing four 20% firms will be around 1700 or 1800, depending on the size of the remaining firms. In the case of the market containing one 77% firm and three 1% firms, the HHI will be around 6000.[21]

The question of variations in firm size is important, but it does not yield answers that are consistent, as the two concentration indices suggest. If the feared threat is price fixing and the industry is subject to scale economies, variations in firm size can make cartel bar-

16. See G. Stigler, The Organization of Industry 58–59 (1983 ed.); for a generally agnostic conclusion, see F.M. Scherer & D. Ross, Industrial Market Structure and Economic Performance 184 (3d ed. 1990).

17. For a table of cases, indicating the market shares of the company, the market structure, and the decision, see 4 Antitrust Law 113–136 (rev. ed. 1998).

18. For the history and early use of the Index, see A.O. Hirschman, The Paternity of an Index, 54 Amer.Econ.Rev. 761 (1964); G. Stigler, A Theory of Oligopoly, 72 J.Pol.Econ. 44 (1964).

19. On non-cooperative, Cournot-style oligopoly, see § 4.2.

20. The HHI is derived from pure Cournot theory. See 4 Antitrust Law ¶ 931d (rev. ed. 1998); and G. Stigler, A Theory of Oligopoly, 72 J.Pol.Econ. 44 (1944). For a simple formulation, see W. Viscusi, J. Vernon & J. Harrington, Economics of Regulation and Antitrust 149–153 (2d ed. 1995).

21. There has been a healthy debate among economists over the relationship between the level of concentration and the size distribution of the firms in facilitating anticompetitive behavior. Earlier empirical studies suggested a positive correlation between the level of concentration in an industry and the amount of monopoly profits. For example, J. Bain, Relation of Profit Rate to Industry Concentration: American Manufacturing, 1936–1940, 65 Q.J.Econ. 293 (1951). However, later economists argued that by using the CR8 as his index of concentration, Bain ignored the fact that asymmetry of firm size within the market may have much more influence than concentration itself on the amount of monopoly pricing. See J. Kwoka, Large–Firm Dominance and Price/Cost Margins in Manufacturing Industries, 44 S.Econ.J. 183 (1977). Other aspects of the debate are summarized in S. Pautler, A Review of the Economic Basis for Broad–Based Horizontal–Merger Policy, 28 Antitrust Bull. 571 (1983).

gains more difficult to reach and enforce. There will be more disagreements about the profit-maximizing price, because firms with different costs compute different profit-maximizing prices. There may also be less agreement about how the output reduction should be allocated.[22] For example, the HHI seems to be superior to the CR4 in predicting that a market in which one firm has a 77% market share and three others have 1% each will perform less competitively than a market with four 20% firms. But the HHI also predicts that a market in which the top four firms have 25%, 20%, 20%, and 15% will perform less competitively than the market with four 20% firms. The HHI in the former will be upwards of 1650, while that of the latter will be somewhere above 1600. *Any* amount of variation in firm size increases the HHI; that is, for any given number of firms, HHI is minimized when all firms are exactly the same size.[23] This prediction is not consistent with the notion that express collusion (or cooperative oligopoly behavior) is most likely to succeed when all the firms are approximately the same size.

If our underlying merger concern is single firm dominance, we would be more suspicious of firms that create or enlarge dominant firms than of mergers that simply make a nondominant firm larger, perhaps decreasing the absolute variation in firm size. For example, if a market contained A=60%, B=20% and C=20%, and B acquired C, the market would be more concentrated in terms of number of firms, but resulting variation in firm size would be less. This particular merger would increase the Cournot equilibrium price, and make collusion easier to manage, but it might reduce the threat of single firm exclusionary practices. Further, if post-merger firm BC was in a better position to be aggressive, the merger might actually increase competition. In sum, the predictive power of either the HHI or the CR4 depends on many assumptions about relative size and behavior, and the assumptions will not obtain across all markets or apply to all firms.

Because the CR4 is derived from a cartel theory, it underestimates the importance of disparities in firm size. By contrast, since the HHI is mathematically derived from a pure Cournot theory, it exaggerates the influence of such disparities. Further, in a Cournot oligopoly the size distribution of firms becomes a function of their marginal costs (firms with higher marginal costs have smaller market shares), and price/cost ratios rise as the disparity in firm size rises.

Is the HHI correct to assume that disparities in firm size yield higher rather than lower market prices in oligopoly markets? That question, it turns out, is extremely complicated and no one knows the answer for sure. Several models of oligopoly pricing actually predict lower prices in a market dominated by a single firm than in an "equivalent" market with the same total number of equal sized firms.[24] In that case the HHI is incorrect to regard disparities in firm size as an aggravating factor. But these models also generally assume that the dominant firm has lower costs than its rivals, and this may not always be the case. Further, dominant firms in markets can facilitate price "leadership," which can be quite different from Cournot oligopoly. In the latter, each firm sets its own profit-maximizing output on the assumption that other firms will not change their behavior. Under price leadership, however, the dominant firm commonly sets the price under the assumption that the followers will match its price, because they fear retaliation. In that case, the price leadership model yields prices and output that approximate the cooperative, or *cartel*, level rather than the lower Cournot oligopoly level. Likewise, if oligopolies are thought of as re-

22. The problems are discussed in § 4.1.

23. This is simply generalized. Suppose a market has n firms with market shares of A each. The HHI will be NA^2. Suppose now that one firm is larger by B, which entails that another firm or group of firms will be smaller by B, since the total must be 100%. Assume that the first firm's market share goes to (A+B) and that the second firm's is now (A−B). When both of these firms were size A, their joint contribution to the HHI was $2A^2$. But now their contribution is $(A + B)^2 + (A-B)^2$, which equals $A^2 + 2AB + B^2 + A^2 - 2AB + B^2$, which is the same as $2A^2 + 2B^2$. So the HHI has increased by $2B^2$.

24. See F.M. Scherer & D. Ross, note 16 at 225–226.

peated games, pricing and output approaching the cartel level may emerge.[25]

All of this underscores that our choice of an index is not only a question of mathematics, but also of the behavioral assumptions we make. One index may in fact be better for some measurement situations, while the other index is better for others.[26] We might use the CR4 to measure concentration in markets where we think the real threat to competition will come from express collusion or cooperative, tacit collusion. But we might want to use the HHI for markets where the perceived threat is Cournot style noncooperative oligopoly behavior.

But as a practical matter such a suggestion is unrealistic. In most industries, predicting the type of behavior that is most likely to occur would involve a great deal of guesswork. Presumably, firms acting in the abstract would prefer cooperative behavior, since it is more profitable.[27] However, their fallback position would be Cournot; so Cournot would express our minimum concern, and the relevant question would be, how successful would the firms be in keeping their prices *above* the Cournot level.

In addition, although the *theoretical* underpinning of CR4 and Cournot are fairly clear, the available empirical evidence is mixed: empirically it has not been shown that the CR4 consistently works better in one type of industry, while the HHI consistently works better in another type.[28]

Ultimately—and importantly—the choice of an index probably does not make all that much difference except in a very few cases. Although the *technical* variations among various indexes are significant, in practice the differences are usually not all that large.[29] Indeed, some studies have found extraordinarily high correlations between the HHI and the CR4 across most American industries, although the variation tends to be greater in markets with higher concentration levels, where merger policy becomes more relevant.[30] Some studies have suggested that we could get along with much simpler structural measures—for example, that the minimum condition for competition in most industries is three or four competitors of approximately equal market position, if the concern is oligopoly, or perhaps a half dozen if the concern is price fixing.[31]

The conclusion that index choice is really not all that important is particularly relevant because a great deal of approximation and guesstimate goes into merger policy to begin with. Most importantly, the "relevant markets" that merger enforcers analyze are only approximations, and the numbers we use to measure market share within these markets carry the degree of approximation even further, especially if there is product differentia-

25. See § 4.2.

26. See Donsimoni, Geroski & Jacquemin, Concentration Indices and Market Power: two Views, 32 J. Indus. Econ. 419, 428 (1984): "[T]here is no such thing as an 'optimal' index of concentration, both because different industries behave differently as well as because no obvious widely accepted normative judgments exist to guarantee its optimality."

27. That is, perfectly cooperative behavior (for example a cartel where the profit-maximizing price is set accurately and no one cheats) yields the single-firm monopoly price. By contrast, Cournot behavior with two or more firms yields a price somewhat less than the single-firm monopoly price, which decreases as the number of firms increases. See § 4.2a.

28. Some empirical studies suggest that likelihood and success of collusion in a market varies with HHI. H. Marvel, Competition and Price Levels in the Retail Gasoline Market, 60 Rev.Econ.Statistics 252 (1978). Others have found that the HHI generally predicts such behavior better than the CR4. Cowling & Waterson, Price–Cost Margins and Market Structure, 43 Economica 267 (1976). However, other studies suggest that the HHI is no more reliable than the CR4. Compare N. Cohen & C. Sullivan, The Herfindahl–Hirschman Index and the New Antitrust Merger Guidelines: Concentrating on Concentration, 62 Texas L.Rev. 453, 490 (1983) (HHI generally no better); J. Kwoka, The effect of Market Share Distribution on Industry Performance, 61 Rev. Econ. & Statistics 101 (1979) (HHI inferior); J. Kwoka, The Herfindahl Index in Theory and Practice, 30 Antitrust Bull 915 (1985) (same).

29. It is logically possible for differences to be large. For example, an HHI of 1800 can describe markets in which the CR4 is as little as 44.73 to as much as 84.48. See D.W. Weinstock, Some Little–Known Properties of the Herfindahl–Hirschman Index: Problems of Translation and Specification, 29 Antitrust Bull. 705, 707 (1984).

30. See Sleuwaegen and Dehandschutter, The Critical Choice Between the Concentration Ratio and the H-index in Assessing Industry Performance, 35 J.Indus.Econ. 193 (1986); J. Kwoka, Does the Choice of Concentration Measure Really Matter?, 29 J.Indus.Econ. 445 (1981).

31. See Kwoka, Id.

tion. For example, we must make fairly absolute decisions, often based on availability of data, whether to use units of output, revenue or plant capacity in calculating market shares.[32] Except perhaps in industries where price is uniform and the product perfectly fungible, each of these tends to distort our conclusions.

The relevant question then becomes whether it is worth the trouble to make the additional inquiry whether HHI or CR4 is the appropriate index for a particular industry. As a general matter, it is not. Perhaps we would wish to make an occasional exception. For example, perhaps we might use the HHI as a general matter but revert to the CR4 in those markets where there has been a history of attempts at collusion, and the attempts seem to have been at least modestly successful. The previous discussion noted that the CR4 is indifferent to the size distribution among the largest four firms, while the HHI places great emphasis on size distribution. Express collusion may be easier to manage in those industries where the size of the colluding firms is more or less the same. As a result, the HHI may tend to be somewhat underdeterrent in an industry where the top four firms have roughly identical market shares of, say, 15%–20%, particularly if those four firms have been moderately successful in managing collusion in the past. In such an industry, it would be a good idea to add some additional factor to our inquiry to take the history of collusion into account. It is far from clear, however, that this additional inquiry requires resort to a specific alternative concentration index such as the CR4. We might just as plausibly say that any merger involving at least one of the significant firms in an industry where there has been a history of collusion should be illegal, and forget about the concentration index.[33]

The HHI also provides more information than the CR4 concerning size disparities *between* the merging firms. If two firms with 20% market shares merge, the result will be a firm with a 40% market share. The same result will obtain from a merger of a 38% firm with a 2% firm. As a general matter, the first merger will have a more serious impact on competition than the second. The first one may double the size of the dominant (or second largest) firm in the market. The second merger will merely make a large firm marginally larger. The CR4 accounts for the result only haphazardly, depending on whether one or both of the merging firms are among the four largest in the industry. The HHI accounts for the difference rather precisely: the first merger increases the market's HHI by 800 points, while the second increases the HHI by only 152 points.[34]

Once again, however, individualized questions about management strategy or specific firm history may provide us with more information than either of the indexes. In the above example the 2% firm acquired by the 38% firm may have been a new, aggressive firm bent on cutting price and becoming larger, and with some promise of doing so. In that case, its acquisition by the largest firm could be quite anticompetitive, to the extent it eliminates a potentially troublesome rival. The 1992 Guidelines acknowledge this by paying special attention to the acquisition of "maverick" firms. Say the Guidelines:

> In some circumstances, coordinated interaction can be effectively prevented or limited by maverick firms—firms that have a greater economic incentive to deviate from the terms of coordination than do most of their rivals (e.g., firms that are unusually disruptive and competitive influences in the market). Consequently, acquisition of a maverick firm is one way in which a merger may make coordinated interaction more likely, more successful, or more complete. For example, in a market where capacity

32. See § 3.7b.

33. See 4 Antitrust Law ¶ ¶ 917, 944b (rev. ed. 1998).

34. To calculate the *increase* in HHI produced by a merger, take the product of the market shares of the merging firms (as whole numbers) and multiply by two. Thus a merger of a 20% firm with a 15% firm produces an HHI increase of 600. Do you see why this is so? Before the merger the two firms represented 20^2 plus 15^2 HHI points. After the merger, however, they represent $(20 + 15)^2$ HHI points. The square of a binomial $(A + B)^2$ equals $A^2 + 2AB + B^2$. The 2AB represents the increase.

constraints are significant for many competitors, a firm is more likely to be a maverick the greater is its excess or divertable capacity in relation to its sales or its total capacity, and the lower are its direct and opportunity costs of expanding sales in the relevant market.* * * A firm also may be a maverick if it has an unusual ability secretly to expand its sales in relation to the sales it would obtain if it adhered to the terms of coordination.[35]

The HHI is also used to establish "safe harbors"—relatively unconcentrated industries in which mergers will not ordinarily be challenged. By accounting for all firms in the market (rather than the top four, as the CR4 does) the HHI can give a measure of total market concentration that indicates to the policy maker whether mergers are likely to be a problem in a particular industry.[36] The 1992 Guidelines indicate that the Division will not challenge any merger in an industry in which the post-merger HHI is less than 1000.[37]

In some respects, the HHI is more difficult to use than the CR4. The latter required measurement of only the four largest firms in the market. The HHI theoretically requires measurement of every firm in the market. The other side of the coin, of course, is that the HHI claims to be a more reliable indicator of overall market concentration *because* it measures every firm. Furthermore, the error that results from miscalculation is very small with respect to the smaller firms in the market. A 5% firm, for example, adds only 25 HHI points, and a 1% firm adds only 1 point. Since the relevant threshold concentration under the HHI is around 1000, an error in the measurement of a small firm makes little difference. For most purposes fringe firms with a market share of 2% or less may safely be ignored.

A more significant problem with the HHI is that an error in measuring the market share of a large firm will distort the measurement substantially. For example, assume that a market contains four firms with market shares of 35%, 15%, 10% and 10%. The CR4 is 70% and the HHI will be around 1700, depending on the size of the other firms in the market. Suppose, however, that the size of the largest firm is erroneously measured as 40%. In that case the four-firm concentration ratio goes to 75%—not a dramatic difference. The HHI, however, jumps to about 2100, and that difference is quite substantial. In fact, a 5 point error in the measurement of the largest firm has about the same impact on the HHI as a 5% error in the measurement of all three of the other firms in the CR4. For this reason precise and careful market definition and share computation is essential to a court relying on the HHI, especially with respect to the largest firms in a fairly concentrated market.

Apropos of the last point, no matter which concentration index one chooses, the conclusions the index produces must be discounted when there is doubt about the quality of the underlying data, or when the market is too "thin" to produce very reliable information. For example, very small markets characterized by large, rather idiosyncratic sales do not provide very reliable numbers—indeed, the numbers may vary widely from one year to the next as firms bid, produce at capacity, and reenter the market with further bids.[38] However, the point can be pushed too far. Markets with high fixed costs and lumpy sales—say, a small number of sales, where each sale is unusually large—can be particularly susceptible to collusion. Cheating is easy to detect as the number of sales that needs to be monitored decreases. So the point is *not* that one should be more tolerant of mergers in such markets; rather, not as much predictive power can be expected from an index such as the HHI.

§ 12.4b. Market Share Thresholds Under the Horizontal Merger Guidelines

The 1992 Guidelines for horizontal mergers rely heavily on industrial organization theory

35. 1992 Guidelines, § 2.12 (footnotes omitted).

36. See R. Posner, Oligopoly and the Antitrust Laws: A Suggested Approach, 21 Stan.L.Rev. 1562, 1602–1603 (1969); S. Calkins, The New Merger Guidelines and the Herfindahl–Hirschman Index, 71 Cal.L.Rev. 402, 419 (1983).

37. 1992 Guidelines, § 1.51.

38. Noting this is United States v. Baker Hughes, 908 F.2d 981 (D.C.Cir.1990).

to establish some prima facie indicators of when the Division or the FTC will challenge a particular merger. In brief, the Guidelines regard any market in which the *post*-merger HHI is below 1000 as "unconcentrated." Such a market has the equivalent of at least 10 equally sized firms. "Mergers resulting in unconcentrated markets are unlikely to have adverse competitive effects and ordinarily require no further analysis."[39]

If the post-merger HHI falls between 1000 and 1800, the market will be deemed "moderately" concentrated. Nevertheless the agencies will be unlikely to challenge a merger that produces an HHI increase of less than 100 points. If the increase is greater than 100 points, however, the likelihood of challenge increases, depending on the presence of non-market-share factors.[40]

Markets where the post-merger HHI exceeds 1800 are regarded as highly concentrated. Even here, however, mergers producing an HHI increase of less than 50 points will not ordinarily be challenged. If the HHI increase falls between 50 and 100 points, then the merger will be regarded as having significant anticompetitive potential, and will be challenged depending on the presence or absence of non-market-share factors. If the HHI increase exceeds 100, the agencies will "presume" that the merger is "likely to create or enhance market power or facilitate its exercise." However, the proponents of the merger can defeat this presumption if they can show, based on the presence or absence of non-market-share factors, that the merger is unlikely to have these anticompetitive consequences. In sum, under the Guidelines' analysis, if the post-merger HHI exceeds 1800 and the HHI increase caused by the merger exceeds 100, the non-market-share factors remain relevant, but the burden shifts to the defendant to show that the merger is not likely to be anticompetitive.

In a market with an HHI above 1800 a dominant firm likely would be prohibited from acquiring any but the smallest of competitors. For example, if a firm with a 30% market share acquired a firm with a 2% share, the increase in HHI would be 120. The Division would probably challenge the merger.

§ 12.4c. Factors Affecting the Significance of Concentration and Market Share Measures

Both concentration measures and estimates of market share are generalized attempts to predict the likelihood of anticompetitive behavior in a market. Often, however, information gleaned from the specific market at issue suggests that the concentration measures overstate or understate the competitive significance of a particular merger.

The 1992 Horizontal Merger Guidelines list two factors in this category: (1) changing market conditions; (2) the degree of difference between products inside and outside the market.

Changing market conditions generally refers to a recent change that is almost certain to have an impact on the market in the future, but which is not yet accounted for in concentration/market share data, which are necessarily historical. For example, if a firm has been losing ground consistently, its patents are about to run out, or its essential mineral reserves are about to be exhausted, then the company's current sales or market share may seriously overstate its competitive capacity for the future. This was the central message of the Supreme Court's *General Dynamics* decision.[41] The government produced evidence that the coal mining companies involved in the merger had combined market shares of 23.2% in Illinois or 12.4% in a larger eastern region of the country, and that the CR4 was 75% in the first area and about 63% in the second. The Court acknowledged that "in the absence of other considerations" these numbers would have justified condemning the merger. In this case, however, General Dynamics owned few coal reserves that were not already committed

39. 1992 Guidelines, § 1.51. For further elaboration, see 4 Antitrust Law ¶ 932 (rev. ed. 1998).

40. See § 12.7.

41. United States v. General Dynamics Corp., 415 U.S. 486, 94 S.Ct. 1186 (1974). See 4A Antitrust Law ¶ 962 (rev. ed. 1998).

to buyers under long term contracts, and its uncommitted reserves were being depleted rapidly.[42] Further, although the acquired firm produced 4.4% of the market's coal, it owned only 1% of the markets coal *reserves*, and the latter number seemed to be a more accurate reflection of the firm's future competitive position. Further, there was "no possibility" that the firm could acquire more reserves. The Court approved the merger.

In cases such as these the court must be fairly certain that the downturn is irreversible and not merely the consequence of poor management or temporary bad luck.[43] Further, the argument should not be considered as a "defense" to a clearly anticompetitive merger. Rather, it should be counted as an argument that current market share overstates the firm's competitive position. In some cases, adjusting for this may involve no more than reducing market share by the amount of the anticipated loss. For example, if a firm owns mines producing 100,000 tons, but one fourth of this capacity will become unproductive in the near future (say, two years), then the best alternative is simply to count the acquiring firm's output as 75,000 tons rather than 100,000 tons. In other cases estimation is more difficult. For example, a firm's current market share may be based on a patent that is about to expire. As soon as that happens, numerous firms will either enter the market or be able to enlarge their own output, but it will be hard to predict the rate or amount by which the defendant's market share will decline.

The 1992 Horizontal Merger Guidelines offer little guidance on such issues. They do note that if the other firms in the market have acquired access to a technology that is not available to the merging firms, then historical market share data may "overstate" the "future competitive significance" of the merging firms in the market.[44] An unstated corollary is that if one of the merging firms has recently acquired access to a technology that will not be available to others, then current market data may tend to *under* state the competitive significance of the merger.

The Merger Guidelines also state that market concentration/market share figures do not adequately account for the *degree* of difference between products inside or outside the market.[45] If products defined as just outside the market are separated widely in product or geographical space from those defined as just inside, then those in the relevant market will have more power to raise price than if the separation is not so wide. What the Guidelines are really telling us here is that cross-elasticities of demand or supply among various products do not exist on a continuum, but may be quite lumpy. Further, the lines that we characterize as "market definition" are fairly arbitrary in the sense that things just inside and things just outside *do* compete. In some cases, how much they compete may be relevant; however, the Guidelines say very little about how such evidence will be taken into account.

§ 12.4d. How Should Concentration Count? Philadelphia Bank

As the previous discussion suggests, predicting the competitive consequences of a merger is hardly an exact science. Several other factors must be taken into account, and each is susceptible to only "soft" measurement.

So does one simply throw them all into a pot and see what kind of stew comes out? In the *Philadelphia Bank* case, the Supreme Court concluded no.[46] Although numerous factors are relevant to predicting the conse-

42. *General Dynamics*, 415 U.S. at 508, 94 S.Ct. at 1199, noting that virtually all proven reserves were depleted or already committed so the company's power to affect the price of coal was severely limited and diminishing.

43. See Olin Corp., 5 Trade Reg. Rep. ¶ 22,857 (FTC, 1990) (mere bad performance not sufficient to justify discounting of market share).

44. 1992 Guidelines, § 1.521.

45. 1992 Guidelines, § 1.522.

46. United States v. Philadelphia Natl. Bank, 374 U.S. 321, 83 S.Ct. 1715 (1963).

quences of a merger, market concentration must be considered more important than others. The Court acknowledged that a prediction of anticompetitive consequences

> is sound only if it is based upon a firm understanding of the structure of the relevant market; yet the relevant economic data are both complex and elusive.* * * [U]nless businessmen can assess the legal consequences of a merger with some confidence, sound business planning is retarded.* * * So also, we must be alert to the danger of subverting congressional intent by permitting a too-broad economic investigation.[47]
>
> [W]e think that a merger which produces a firm controlling an undue percentage share of the relevant market, and results in a significant increase in the concentration of firms in that market, is so inherently likely to lessen competition substantially that it must be enjoined in the absence of evidence clearly showing that the merger is not likely to have such anticompetitive effects.* * *[48]

This language, while not as clear as one might wish, suggests that once the government or other plaintiff has shown minimum concentration levels the merger should be enjoined *unless* there is evidence that the feared anticompetitive effects will not materialize. That means that the defendant has the burden of coming forward with such evidence. This is commonly called the *prima facie* evidence rule: the plaintiff makes a *prima facie* case of illegality by proving high concentration; the defendant then has the burden of rebutting by coming in with evidence unrelated to concentration as such.

Philadelphia Bank's prima facie evidence rule was based at least in part on the Court's conclusion that Congress was concerned about concentration for its own sake, not that Congress had decided that the best predictor of noncompetitive pricing was market concentration. This perspective is important, because it invites us to consider whether the *prima facie* rule is still correct even in a regime where we are inclined to think that economic competition, as measured by marginal cost pricing, ought to be the exclusive goal of merger policy, and that high concentration is bad only when it yields higher prices.[49]

For example, should entry barriers be considered any differently in a regime where low consumer prices is merger law's goal, not merely the preservation of unconcentrated markets? In this particular case, the basic balance should not change all that much. Low entry barriers serve to reduce our concern about mergers under *either* the *Philadelphia Bank* theory that concentration itself was Congress' concern, or the more economic theory that merger policy is concerned about noncompetitive pricing. That is to say, easy entry entails that markets will not be concentrated unless the incumbents are not earning profits.[50] To this extent, there is little basis for deviating from the *Philadelphia Bank* presumptions simply because we no longer think concentration *per se* is an important goal of merger enforcement. To be sure, entry barriers are relevant, but low entry barriers cannot be presumed and it is up to the defendant to provide evidence that they are in fact low.

47. Id. at 362, 83 S.Ct. at 1741.

The Court then noted that Congress' concern was not exclusively efficiency, but also concentration as such. Given these complexities, as well as Congress' clear expression of concern about concentration (rather than entry barriers or other factors), concentration should be the point of entry for merger analysis:

48. Id. at 363, 83 S.Ct. at 1741.

49. A few courts have suggested (rather subtly) that the prima facie evidence rule is eroding. For example, see United States v. Baker Hughes, Inc., 908 F.2d 981, 991–992 (D.C.Cir.1990) (suggesting that defendant's burden in refuting government's *prima facie* case based on concentration should not be heavy). Other courts emphasize the priority of structural considerations. See R.C. Bigelow, Inc. v. Unilever NV, 867 F.2d 102, 110 (2d Cir.1989), cert. denied, 493 U.S. 815, 110 S.Ct. 64 (1989) (structure still starting point for analysis).

50. Provided, that is, that entry barriers are measured under the Bainian formulation: an entry barrier is some condition in the market that permits the incumbent firms to earn monopoly profits while entry is deterred. On the difference between Bainian and Stiglerian entry barriers generally, see § 1.6. On entry barriers in merger cases, see § 12.6.

Although the 1992 Horizontal Merger Guidelines are ambiguous on the point, they seem to be abandoning the government's historical commitment to *Philadelphia Bank*'s prima facie approach.[51] The Guidelines note that they do not purport to assign burdens of proof with respect to any specific issue.[52] The Guidelines' general approach is to consider concentration first, then non-market share signals of anticompetitive effects, then evidence of entry barriers, all apparently on the premise that the government must produce the evidence if these questions become relevant to a merger challenge.[53]

In all events, today the ultimate evil at which horizontal merger policy is directed is facilitation of collusion or collusion-like behavior, not high concentration for its own sake. The priority given to structural evidence should therefore be regarded as a means toward an end. If structural evidence is still the most reliable and easily used basic indicator of likelihood of collusion, then *Philadelphia Bank*'s presumptive rule may continue to make sense. To this end, however, the "structural" rule that merger policy invites may not be anything as elaborate as the HHI or even the CR4. Perhaps the best indicator of likelihood of collusion in a market is the number of effective players, with effectiveness measured in terms of individual firms' realistic ability to upset collusion or oligopoly by cutting price. As that number exceeds eight or ten in the case of express collusion, or five to seven in the case of oligopoly, the likelihood of collusion diminishes rapidly. In markets with numbers of players equal to or less than these, any further reduction makes collusive behavior more likely.

§ 12.5 The Significance of Product Differentiation

§ 12.5a. Product Differentiation as Undermining Collusion

Product heterogeneity has always provoked complexity in the analysis of markets. Most importantly, the perfect competition model does not work very well, and the deviations are difficult to account for systematically.[1] Firms in product differentiated markets face demand curves that slope downward, although perhaps only slightly. At any given output level there will be different customers willing to pay different prices for the output of different sellers. Likewise, substantial product differentiation often entails that different firms have different costs, that they attain scale economies at different levels of output, and that they rely on different sets of inputs in their production processes.

One effect of product differentiation, as developed in § 12.3d, is to enable post-merger firms to exact unilateral price increases when their merger involves two firms that are relatively proximate to each other in product space. But in most other situations the general effect of product differentiation is more benign. As § 4.1 noted, price fixing and cooperative oligopoly behavior can be frustrated if firms are unable to agree on the profit-maximizing cartel price.[2] Product differentiation frustrates collusion in this fashion for two different reasons. First, it may give firms different marginal costs, and firms whose costs differ maximize their profits at different prices. Second, product differentiation may entail that firms face different demand curves and this may give them different profit-maximizing prices. Further, if the firms produce products

51. On this point, see C.A. James, Overview of the 1992 Horizontal Merger Guidelines, 61 Antitrust L.J. 447 (1993).

52. 1992 Guidelines, § 0.1. However, they go on to say that with respect to the efficiency defense and the failing company defense the burden of proof will remain on the firm advocating the merger. Id. at n. 4.

53. 1992 Guidelines, § 0.2.

§ 12.5

1. On the model of perfect competition, see § 1.1.

2. See F.M. Scherer & D. Ross, Industrial Market Structure and Economic Performance 279 (3d ed. 1990): "With perfect [product] homogeneity, there remains only one dimension along which rivalrous actions and counteractions can take place: price. In such a case, oligopolists have a particularly easy task of coordinating their behavior * * * When products are heterogeneously differentiated, the terms of rivalry become multidimensional, and the coordination problem grows in complexity by leaps and bounds." Accord Y. Brozen, Entry Barriers: Advertising and Product Differentiation, 115 in Industrial Concentration: the New Learning (H. Goldschmidt, H. Mann, & J. Weston eds. 1974).

of different levels of quality, a single cartel price will not work. For example, if Mercedes–Benz, Ford and Yugo controlled the automobile market and fixed the same price, nearly all customers would buy Mercedes–Benz until the supply was exhausted. Then, if there was widespread agreement that Fords were superior to Yugos, remaining customers would go to Ford and so on. The only way the cartel could work is if the firms settled on a scale of prices, with individual prices proportional to cost, or else designed to keep market shares stable.

For all these reasons, the most general consensus today is that most of the time product differentiation is a *mitigating* factor in merger analysis.[3] Most of the time the main concern of merger policy is express or tacit collusion, and product differentiation makes collusion harder to maintain.

§ 12.5b. Product Differentiation: When Is a Merger Horizontal?

A merger is strictly "horizontal" only if 1) the two firms involved produce the same product (i.e., consumers cannot distinguish between the products of the two firms, or are completely insensitive to the differences); and 2) the firms sell the product in the same geographic market.

The real world contains few perfectly horizontal mergers. Identical gasoline stations across the street from each other are not exactly in the same market: one will be more attractive to west-bound traffic, the other to east-bound traffic. Nevertheless, a merger between them would almost certainly be treated as "horizontal" for antitrust purposes. Although customers may have preferences, the preferences are not strong enough to prevent substantial numbers of them from making a left turn rather than paying a monopoly price.

Discerning a line between horizontal and non-horizontal mergers that is meaningful for policy purposes is difficult, however. Courts characterize a merger as "horizontal" only after they have decided that the merger partners are in the same product and geographic markets. If they are not, courts characterize the competition between them as merely "potential" and the merger as "conglomerate." At that point, the mode of analysis changes significantly.[4]

The following mergers have been characterized as "horizontal": a merger 1) of a metal can manufacturer and a glass bottle manufacturer; 2) of a company that strip-mined coal and a company that deep-mined coal; 3) of a company that manufactured dry table wines and a company that manufactured sweet, fruity wines; 4) of a firm that manufactured heavy steel products and a firm that manufactured light steel products; 5) of a grocery chain whose stores were located in northeast Los Angeles and a grocery chain whose stores were located in southwest Los Angeles.[5]

It is difficult to generalize about the degree of competition that existed between these pairs of merger partners. In some cases, such as *Continental Can*, cross elasticity of demand between the cans and bottles was high for some customers. The court found that beer bottlers were very sensitive to price and would have responded to a small price increase in cans by switching to bottles, or vice-versa.[6] By contrast, there were other customers who strongly preferred bottles to cans, and for whom the price of bottles would have to go very high before they would consider cans to be satisfactory substitutes.

Courts sometimes look at elasticity of supply when determining the extent to which two companies operate in the same relevant market. For example, United States v. Aluminum Co. of America (Rome Cable) involved the ac-

3. See 4 Antitrust Law ¶ 942 (rev. ed. 1998); B.F. Goodrich Co., 110 F.T.C. 207, 315 (1988): "Differences in product quality may make price differentials necessary to produce a stable market equilibrium, and achieving a consensus on such differentials is likely to be difficult."

4. Potential competition mergers are discussed in the following chapter.

5. United States v. Continental Can Co., 378 U.S. 441, 84 S.Ct. 1738 (1964); United States v. General Dynamics Corp., 415 U.S. 486, 94 S.Ct. 1186 (1974); Coca–Cola Bottling Co., 93 F.T.C. 110 (1979); United States v. Columbia Steel Co., 334 U.S. 495, 68 S.Ct. 1107 (1948); United States v. Von's Grocery Co., 384 U.S. 270, 86 S.Ct. 1478 (1966).

6. 378 U.S. at 451–52, 84 S.Ct. at 1744.

quisition of a company that made copper and aluminum conductor by a much larger firm that made only aluminum conductor. The district court had found that aluminum and copper conductor should be placed in the same market because "there is complete manufacturing interchangeability between copper and aluminum, and manufacturers constantly review their product lines and 'switch readily from one * * * metal to another in accordance with market conditions.' "[7]The Supreme Court reversed, looking largely at demand conditions to hold that aluminum and copper conductor were separate products. The Supreme Court was probably wrong; if input costs were about the same and the firms could quickly substitute from aluminum to copper, or vice-versa, the competition between them was substantial.

In monopoly cases the defendant frequently argues that the relevant market should be larger than the market alleged by the plaintiff. The effect will be to make the defendant's market share smaller. The same strategy is not necessarily best in horizontal merger cases, however. The defendant will argue for a large market if the result is to make the relevant market appear less concentrated and the post-merger firm's market share appear smaller. For example, if a defendant manufacturer of men's cowboy boots acquired a manufacturer of women's cowboy boots, the defendant might argue that the relevant market should be all "footwear." The result would be to place more manufacturers in the relevant market, making it appear less concentrated, and perhaps also to lower the relative market shares of the two merging firms.

The defendant might also try to make the relevant markets much smaller, however—so small that the merger would not appear horizontal at all, but conglomerate. For example, the defendant might argue that men's cowboy boots and women's cowboy boots are really different markets. Therefore the merger should be treated as conglomerate and given the much more lenient potential competition standard.[8] The ideal market definitions for the defendant would be "men's footwear" in one market and "women's footwear" in another. In that case the market would appear unconcentrated and the merging firms' market shares small, *and* the merger would be treated as conglomerate rather than horizontal.[9]

Ideally, a court capable of making the proper measurements would establish a sliding scale measuring the competitive impact of a merger in proportion to the closeness of competition (cross elasticity of demand and supply) between the two firms. Unfortunately, courts are not capable of such precise measurement. They have tended to divide all nonvertical mergers into two kinds: "horizontal" and "conglomerate." Once the court has characterized a merger as "horizontal," the fact that the firms make products that are not precisely similar, or sell them in somewhat different areas, is largely irrelevant. In *Von's Grocery*, for example, the court defined the relevant market as greater Los Angeles and simply added up the market shares of the two grocery chains who were parties to the merger. Once the merger had been classified as horizontal, it was no longer important that virtually all of Von's stores were in the southwest part of the city and all the Shopping Bag stores in the northeast. Surely such a merger did not eliminate as much competition as a merger between two grocery chains all of whose stores were across the street from each other. In fact, Los Angeles was 70 or 80 miles wide, but the lower court found that the average shopper would drive only 10 minutes to buy groceries. The only pairs of Von's and Shopping Bag stores that actually competed with each other were a few pairs toward the

7. 377 U.S. 271, 285, 84 S.Ct. 1283, 1291–92 (1964) (J. Stewart, dissenting). See also Owens–Illinois, 5 Trade Reg. Rep. ¶ 23162 (F.T.C. 1992), which found that the market for glass containers contained several end users who would find substitution difficult—e.g., wine bottles, baby food bottles, etc. But on the supply side, glass bottle manufacturing equipment could be reconfigured in a few hours to permit the supplier to switch from one bottle to the next. See § 3.5 for a more complete discussion of elasticity of supply.

8. On this standard, see § 13.4.

9. This is essentially the position that the defendant argued for in the *Alcoa* (*Rome Cable*) case. See note 7.

middle of the city.[10] The Supreme Court's established framework left it only two alternatives, however: it could have looked at elasticity of supply and considered the likelihood that each chain would have built stores in the other chain's area in response to the second chain's price increase. In that case, it would have treated the merger as "conglomerate" and evaluated it under the potential competition doctrine. The alternative was to ignore the fact that the two chains had stores in different sections of town and treat the merger as purely horizontal. The Court chose the latter alternative.

The Supreme Court's analysis in United States v. Columbia Steel Co.[11] was more convincing. The government challenged United States Steel Corp.'s acquisition of Consolidated Steel as an illegal horizontal merger. Both companies manufactured "steel," but United States Steel fabricated heavy steel products, while Consolidated specialized in lighter products. The bidding record showed that United States Steel bid on approximately 2,400 jobs, while Consolidated bid on about 6,400 jobs. Each was successful about one-third of the time. However, the two companies had bid on the same job only 166 times.[12] Clearly, with respect to those 166 bids the two firms were "competitors." About 8500 jobs were bid by only one of the firms. The court found no "substantial" competition between the firms and dismissed the complaint. This decision seems quite correct from both the demand and supply side of the market. The fact that the firms bid on the same jobs so infrequently suggested that each firm would encounter substantial costs in entering the market of the other, except in a few marginal cases.

The court in such a situation has two choices. Assuming elasticity of supply in the market is high (that is, that United States Steel easily could have produced Consolidated's products out of its existing capacity, and vice-versa), the court can look at the entire output of each company and treat the acquisition as a conglomerate, or potential competition, merger. The alternative is to examine the 166 projects on which both companies bid, and try to define some "market" that described them. In that case the relevant market would represent a trivial percentage of the output of the two firms. Furthermore, the joint-bid projects might not define an area having sufficiently low elasticities of supply and demand (when compared against the capacity and output of other producers) to be considered a relevant market for the purpose of merger law.

§ 12.6 Barriers to Entry in Merger Cases

§ 12.6a. The Appropriate Definition of Entry Barriers for Merger Policy

A barrier to entry is something that permits incumbents to price monopolistically for a socially unacceptable period of time before effective entry restores price and output to the competitive level. If barriers to entry are completely absent, any instance of monopoly pricing will result in immediate entry of sufficient magnitude to restore prices to the competitive level. In this case we can say that the market is not susceptible to monopoly pricing even if is dominated by a single firm or all the firms in the market have organized a cartel. Theoretically, even a merger to monopoly would not result in higher prices in such a market.[1]

The Supreme Court has sometimes cited high entry barriers as a rationale for condemning a particular merger,[2] but has seldom cited low entry barriers as a reason for approving

10. *Von's Grocery,* 384 U.S. at 295–96, 86 S.Ct. at 1492–93. (J. Stewart, dissenting). Justice Stewart concluded that the Von's and Shopping Bag stores actually in competition with each other accounted for "slightly less than 1% of the total grocery store sales in the area."

11. 334 U.S. 495, 68 S.Ct. 1107 (1948).

12. Id. at 515 n. 13, 68 S.Ct. at 1118 n. 13.

§ 12.6

1. On entry barriers generally, see § 1.6.

2. For example, United States v. Phillipsburg Nat. Bank & Trust Co., 399 U.S. 350, 368–69, 90 S.Ct. 2035, 2045–46 (1970), citing state banking regulations that restrict entry as warranting condemnation of a horizontal merger. See also, FTC v. Procter & Gamble Co., 386 U.S. 568, 579, 87 S.Ct. 1224, 1230 (1967), discussed in § 13.4 below.

one. The decision in *Von's Grocery,*[3] for example, has been criticized for ignoring the fact that entry barriers in the retail grocery business were extremely low. As a result monopolistic pricing in that market was unlikely.[4] However, this criticism itself overlooks the fact that monopoly pricing was not the perceived evil of the merger in *Von's Grocery*. The perceived evil was the greater efficiency of the post-merger firm, which would force smaller grocers to go out of business or merge themselves. Superior efficiency is the world's greatest entry barrier, except perhaps for governmental entry restrictions. Few things make entry into a market more difficult than an incumbent's superior ability to produce a good product and sell it at a low price.

In thinking of barriers to entry, it is usually best to focus on output rather than prices as the relevant variable. Setting price is easy to do and prices are easily changed. By contrast, before output is determined one must have a plant, and the size of one's existing plant determines the range over which output can be varied. Under monopoly or collusive pricing, the firms in the market must reduce market-wide output to less than the competitive output. In measuring entry barriers, one must then consider whether sufficient new production can come into the market within a reasonably short time to restore output to the competitive level. Once the competitive level of output is restored, prices will naturally fall to the competitive level as well.

Entry is seldom instantaneous, and it may take considerable time. Incumbent firms will be able to sustain any monopoly pricing scheme until entry occurs of sufficient magnitude to raise output to the competitive level. For the antitrust policy maker, the time question requires a policy choice about how long a period of monopoly pricing is tolerable. We may decide, for example, that monopoly pricing that can last only three months is not worth the commitment of substantial antitrust enforcement resources except in the case of easily formed and quickly abandoned price fixing schemes. If effective entry will occur within three months of a monopoly price increase, the social costs of any monopoly in that market will be smaller than the cost of identifying and enjoining it. In point of fact, however, the courts interpreting the antitrust laws have paid very little attention to this question of time, and there is no general judicial rule on the subject. By contrast, the 1992 Horizontal Merger Guidelines suggest that entry barriers will be considered low for merger purposes when entry will occur "within two years from initial planning to significant market impact."[5]

In one important sense, economists and antitrust policy makers generally have different conceptions of barriers to entry. For the economist a true entry "barrier" is a market factor that prevents entry from occurring in the long run. That is, the economist is generally interested in determining whether there is an *equilibrium* in which entry will or will not occur. Factors that merely delay entry without deterring it indefinitely are generally called "impediments" to entry.[6] By contrast, the antitrust policy maker generally thinks of entry barriers as factors that permit definite periods of monopoly pricing—say, up to two years under the Horizontal Merger Guidelines.[7] Thus the antitrust policy maker's interest is not limited to those situations where the social loss caused by monopoly is infinite (that is, where monopoly pricing will last indefinitely), but where it is too large by some measure which is entirely a function of policy. This book generally uses the antitrust policy maker's definition: a barrier to entry exists if entry

3. United States v. Von's Grocery Co., 384 U.S. 270, 86 S.Ct. 1478 (1966).

4. See R. Posner, Antitrust Law: An Economic Perspective 106 (1976).

5. 1992 Horizontal Merger Guidelines, § 3.2. See J.C. Hilke & P.B. Nelson, The Economics of Entry Lags: A Theoretical and Empirical Overview, 61 Antitrust L.J. 365 (1993) (defending the Guidelines two year standard).

6. See D. Gaskins, Dynamic Limit Pricing: Optimal Pricing Under Threat of Entry, 3 J. Econ. Theory 306 (1971).

7. However, occasionally the Federal Trade Commission has used "barriers" and "impediments" in their technical economic sense. For example, Echlin Mfg., 105 F.T.C. 410, 486 (1985), defining as an "impediment" to entry "any condition that necessarily delays entry into a market for a significant period of time and thus allows market power to be exercised in the interim."

is deterred indefinitely as incumbents earn monopoly profits, *or* if entry is delayed sufficiently long so as to make any resulting monopoly output reduction socially undesirable.

For the antitrust policy maker, the problem of entry barriers revolves around three different issues: *first,* what is a suitable definition of barriers to entry? *second,* what kinds of market characteristics or practices qualify as entry barriers? *third,* what kinds of evidence in addition to the bare presence of these characteristics suggest that entry barriers are high enough to warrant antitrust intervention?

The definition of entry barriers given at the beginning of this section somewhat resembles the definition given by economist Joe S. Bain in the 1960's.[8] Bain tended to regard qualifying barriers to entry as market factors that deterred entry even as the firms already in the market were charging prices above the competitive level.[9] The important difference between Bain's definition and the definition given above is that Bain was interested mainly in long run phenomena—that is, in things that would deter entry indefinitely.

The Bainian approach to entry barriers has some important advantages for antitrust policy purposes. Under it, one can measure the "height" of an entry barrier by the amount of monopoly pricing that will be permitted before entry occurs. For example, if firms in one market can raise prices 50% above cost without encouraging new entry, while firms in another market will encourage new entry as soon as they raise prices 20% above cost, we can say that entry barriers in the first market are higher than entry barriers in the second. We could generally say the same thing about duration. Entry barriers that permit two years worth of monopoly pricing can be said to be more severe than entry barriers that permit only six months of monopoly pricing.

Nevertheless, some features of the Bainian definition of entry barriers seem unacceptable to some economists. First, the definition is circular: it tells us what the *result* of entry barriers is without telling us anything about their substance. Second, the Bainian definition seems to lump socially desirable practices into the category of entry barriers. For example, Bain would define scale economies as an entry barrier. If economies of scale are substantial, a dominant firm may be able to set a price well above its costs without causing new entry, for the residual market will not be large enough for a new firm to bring its costs down to the same level.

The notion that scale economies can be an entry barrier seems irrational, because scale economies are themselves a form of efficiency. If the concept of entry barriers is to be tied to policy, we do not want to define them in such a way that makes efficiency the target of our condemnation.

Largely for this reason, George Stigler redefined the entry barrier as "a cost of producing (at some or every rate of output) which must be borne by a firm which seeks to enter an industry but is not borne by firms already in the industry."[10] The Federal Trade Commission has occasionally adopted a Stiglerian definition of entry barriers. For example, its *Echlin* decision defined entry barriers as "additional long-run costs that must be incurred by an entrant relative to the long-run costs faced by incumbent firms."[11] However, in its

8. J. Bain, Barriers to New Competition: Their Character and Consequences in Manufacturing Industries (1962).

9. "[T]he condition of entry may be evaluated by the extent to which established sellers can persistently raise their prices above a competitive level without attracting new firms to enter the industry." Id. at 5. Or as Bain defined them later, entry barriers measure "the extent to which, in the long run, established firms can elevate their selling prices above the minimal average costs of production and distribution" without "inducing potential entrants to enter the industry." J. Bain, Industrial Organization 252 (1968).

10. G. J. Stigler, The Organization of Industry 67 (1968). See also C. von Weizsacker, A Welfare Analysis of Barriers to Entry, 11 Bell J. Econ. 399, 400 (1980) (an entry barrier is a "cost of producing which must be borne by a firm which seeks to enter an industry but is not borne by firms already in the industry and which implies a distortion in the allocation of resources from the social point of view."); H. Demsetz, Barriers To Entry, 72 Amer. Econ.Rev. 47 (1982) (barrier to entry is something that presents socially preferred entry from occurring).

11. Echlin Mfg., Co., 105 F.T.C. 410, 485 (1985). Other times the FTC has found Stiglerian barriers, although it may not have required them. For example, Owens–Illinois, 5 Trade Reg.Rep. ¶ 23162 (FTC, 1992) (environmental restrictions that applied to new furnaces but exempted existing furnaces a barrier to entry).

subsequent *Flowers* decision, it reverted to a more Bainian definition.[12]

The Bainian definition is generally more consistent with antitrust policy, and most antitrust tribunals continue to use it. High entry barriers are not themselves an antitrust violation. If we had a rule of "no fault" monopolization, under which dominant firms could be penalized simply for having their dominant market positions, then a rule such as Stigler's makes sense. We should not use antitrust policy to punish a firm simply for attaining substantial scale economies. Although they can make entry difficult, scale economies are good for consumers.

But antitrust policy condemns *acts*, and entry barriers are simply one prop on the stage where the acts occur. For example, if the act is a merger, and the feared consequence is collusion or Cournot oligopoly, we want to know whether coordinated interaction such as this will be undermined by effective entry. The collusion itself does not become less harmful simply because the entry barrier, when found, turns out to be the result of economies of scale. In that case, no one is punishing the firms for having attained scale economies; the antitrust policy maker is simply saying that when entry barriers exist, from whatever source, collusion-facilitating practices will not be permitted.[13]

But suppose that the merger in this case is necessary to help the firms attain scale economies? If Firms A and B merge, post-merger AB will be able to take advantage of low cost production processes unavailable to either A or B separately. In that case the antitrust policy may wish to approve the merger, but not on the ground that there is no qualifying barrier to *entry*. Given that the scale economies deter entry, it will not occur. Rather, the AB merger forces the policy maker to consider whether the efficiencies that result from the merger are sufficient to offset any concerns that the merger will be anticompetitive.[14] Indeed, one of the problems with the Stiglerian definition of entry barriers in this context, is that it would force the policy maker to approve the AB merger *whether or not* the merger expanded economies of scale. Under the Stiglerian approach, economies of scale do not count as an entry barrier. If no other barrier were found, the AB merger would be approved even if it created no additional efficiencies.

The Federal Trade Commission in *Echlin* seemed to lose cite of this. Once it had adopted the Stiglerian definition of entry barriers, the Commission concluded that in determining whether the new entrant really did have to incur additional costs, it should view each set of firms (incumbents and entrants) as of the time of their own entry. "The incumbent firm's apparently lower costs merely reflect compensation for the risk it incurred in entering," while the "potential entrant's apparently higher costs will decline * * * if its attempted entry is successful."[15] Under this approach, even the fact that capital costs less for the incumbent firm than for the rival fails to qualify as an entry barrier. Since established firms generally have brighter futures than prospective entrants, they can often obtain capital more cheaply. To be sure, we do not want to "punish" firms because they have overcome the risks of entry and become successful. But defining this value of incumbency as an entry barrier hardly does that. It simply tells firms in such a market that certain practices, such as collusion-facilitating mergers, will receive closer scrutiny.

The one place that the entry barrier itself may become the antitrust violation is if the barrier is "artificial"—that is, if it was erected by the incumbent firm or firms as an entry deterrence device. But in such cases the barrier generally satisfies the Stiglerian definition, provided that the strategic practice is anticompetitive in the first place. For example, brand advertising, bad faith patent, copyright or trademark litigation, and certain kinds of

12. Flowers, 5 Trade Reg. Rep. ¶ 22523 at p. 22,217 & n. 10 (Oliver dissent) (FTC, 1989).

13. See generally R. Schmalensee, Economies of Scale and Barriers to Entry, 89 J.Pol.Econ. 1228 (1981).

14. On the efficiency defense in merger cases, see § 12.2.

15. *Echlin*, 105 F.T.C. at 485–486.

preemptive vertical contracting[16] can all be condemned as erecting "artificial" barriers to entry in a market that would not contain them but for the incumbents' strategic practice. Most barriers of this kind are effective to the extent that they increase the new entrant's per unit costs by a wider margin than they increase the costs of the incumbents.

§ 12.6b. What Constitutes an Entry Barrier

In the final analysis, any merger policy that places a high value on economic efficiency and consumer welfare must designate as "barriers to entry" only those things that permit incumbent firms to engage in monopoly pricing while keeping outsiders from entering the market.

§ 12.6b1. Economies of Scale

As the previous discussion notes, economies of scale are an important entry barrier under the Bainian definition that antitrust most generally employs. Scale economies entail that the firm contemplating entry must always consider, not merely the cost of producing, but also the cost of acquiring enough sales to make its own entry into the market profitable. Most "limit pricing" strategies—under which incumbent firms set price in such a way as to make entry unattractive—depend on the existence of scale economies.[17] If a firm can make one unit per year at the same per unit cost that other firms face in making hundreds of units per year, then pricing strategies of this kind can generally not deter entry. Incumbents could exclude others only by selling their own output at cost or less. Cost prices are, of course, competitive; and below cost prices would be an unpromising entry deterrence strategy.

If economies of scale are substantial, the prospective entrant is forced to consider what the market price will be *after* its own entry is taken into account. For example, assume that minimum efficient operation in a market requires an output of 30 units. When this efficient cost level has been attained, the market would clear at an output of 100 units, assuming the price were competitive. Suppose the market currently contains three firms that are producing 30 units each, and price is about 15% above the competitive level. Will entry occur? Very likely not, even though prices are high. The new firm would have to reach an output level of 30 units in order to produce as efficiently as the incumbents. But any output level in excess of 10 units would mean that output would be too high to be sold at a profitable price. To be sure, if the prospective entrant forced its way in at the efficient level the other firms would lose money. But firms do not enter markets simply to impose losses on rivals. They enter in order to earn profits for themselves, and in this case the prospect of such profits is quite bleak.[18]

For the same reason, in "network" markets where compatibility is essential, a large installed base can serve as a significant deterrent to entry. For example, even if a technically superior operating system to Microsoft Windows were to emerge, a significant impediment to development would be the difficulty in getting other software makers to write software applications for it, and no one wants to do that

16. Such as where the incumbent firms buy up all the available supply of an essential input, or contract with suppliers that they will not sell the input to new entrants. See § 7.10b.

17. For a good summary of the economics literature, see R. J. Gilbert, Mobility Barriers and the Value of Incumbency 475, in Handbook of Industrial Organization (R. Schmalensee & R. Willig, eds. 1989).

18. See, e.g., FTC v. Staples, 970 F.Supp. 1066, 1087 (D.D.C.1997), which found that both the scale economies of operating a very large store, and the scale economies of conducting a multistore operation, operated as effective entry barriers justifying condemnation of an office superstore merger:

A new office superstore would need to open a large number of stores nationally in order to achieve the purchasing and distribution economies of scale enjoyed by the three existing firms. Sunk costs would be extremely high. Economies of scale at the local level, such as in the costs of advertizing and distribution, would also be difficult for a new superstore entrant to achieve since the three existing firms have saturated many important local markets. For example, according to the defendants' own saturation analyses, Staples estimates that there is room for less than two additional superstores in the Washington, D.C. area and Office Depot estimates that there is room for only two more superstores in Tampa, Florida.

for a program that is used by only a few thousand people.[19]

§ 12.6b2. Risk and Size of Investment; Sunk Costs

One important element in the calculus of the prospective entrant is the amount of risk. Federal judges have tended to measure entry barriers by the absolute amount of money that it takes to enter an industry.[20] But there is little reason for thinking that high investment, standing alone, deters entry. American and world capital markets are very efficient. If the investment is promising, it is generally as easy to raise $100,000,000 as $100,000. Indeed, there may be some relevant scale economies in the raising of capital that make it relatively easier to raise the larger amount. High initial investment, standing alone, should not generally be treated as a qualifying entry barrier.

The relevant question for the prospective entrant is not how much it must invest, but rather how much it will lose if the enterprise fails. For this reason, irreversible or "sunk" costs count heavily in its calculus. For example, consider two firms contemplating entry into two markets where the absolute costs of entry are $1,000,000. The first market is general delivery services, which requires the firm to have a general purpose warehouse, some loading equipment such as fork lifts, and some general purpose delivery trucks. If the new business fails, virtually all of these assets can readily be redeployed in other markets, for all of them can be committed to a variety of uses. In such a market the risk of entry is not all that high, even though the firm might have to attain a high volume in order to get its costs down.[21]

By contrast, a second firm must use most of its entry money to build a specialized chemical plant that can be used only for this particular market. If this business fails, the plant will have a salvage value of only 10¢ on the dollar. Given the same initial costs of entry, and scale economies of the same magnitude, entry is much less likely to occur into the second market than the first.

Some courts have recognized the value of asset specificity, or sunk costs, as entry barriers. For example, in *Illinois Cereal Mills* the court noted that corn mills are highly specialized plants that have little salvage value after they are abandoned. This supported the Federal Trade Commission's conclusion that entry barriers into the market were high.[22] The 1992 Horizontal Merger Guidelines define sunk costs as

> the acquisition costs of tangible and intangible assets that cannot be recovered through the redeployment of these assets outside the relevant market, i.e., costs uniquely incurred to supply the relevant product and geographic market.[23]

That is to say, the specialized chemical plant in the above illustration may be capable of being sold, but it will have significant value only to another firm that intends to use it for the same purpose—that is, someone operating within the market. Since firms generally go bankrupt and exit from markets when there is

19. See United States v. Microsoft, 56 F.3d 1448 (D.C.Cir.1995); and see M. Lemley & D. McGowan, Legal Implications of Network Economic Effects, 86 Calif. L. Rev. 479, 502 (1998); J. Farrell & G. Saloner, Installed Base and Compatibility, 76 Am. Econ. Rev. 940 (1986).

20. See for example, Kelco Disposal v. Browning–Ferris Indus. of Vt., 845 F.2d 404 (2d Cir.), affirmed on nonantitrust issue, 492 U.S. 257, 109 S.Ct. 2909 (1989) (high entry barriers found on facts that the cost of entering the market was $300,000, that a firm that controlled 50% of the market and had a 10% return on revenue would realize a profit of only $22,000 annually, and that the market supported only 1 participant in 1980 and 2 from 1981 to 1987); Fruehauf Corp. v. FTC, 603 F.2d 345, 357 (2d Cir.1979) (high entry barriers established by $10—20 million cost of efficient entry). A few decisions correctly state that high cost alone should not be considered an entry barrier. For example, Lomar Wholesale Grocery, Inc. v. Dieter's Gourmet Foods, Inc., 824 F.2d 582, 599–600 (8th Cir.1987), cert. denied, 484 U.S. 1010, 108 S.Ct. 707 (1988) (entry costs of $1.5 million do not create high entry barriers).

21. For example, if it delivers across the city but has only a few stops, the trucks will tend to be emptier than if it has many stops.

22. FTC v. Illinois Cereal Mills, 691 F.Supp. 1131, 1138, 1144 (N.D.Ill.1988), affirmed sub nom., FTC v. Elders Grain, 868 F.2d 901 (7th Cir.1989) (degree of asset specialization suggested high entry barriers); B.A.T. Indus., 104 F.T.C. 852 (1984) (same); United States v. United Tote, 768 F.Supp. 1064 (D.Del.1991) (same); Owens–Illinois, 5 Trade Reg.Rep. ¶ 23162 (FTC, 1992) (same).

23. 1992 Guidelines, § 1.32.

excess capacity, such assets often have little value.

Also important, although probably not as important as the extent of sunk costs, is lead time. As the interval between the decision to enter a market and earliest market impact increases, entry becomes riskier. This is particularly true if the incumbent firms can respond strategically during the entry period. For example, incumbents may be able to increase output, seek out new customers or engage in more aggressive or more directed promotion that will take away much of a market's promise. They may also duplicate the product offering of the new entrant, thus depriving it of a unique market niche.[24] The longer it takes to build a plant, establish a minimum effective distribution network and make a first sale, the greater the risk of entry. Significant sunk expenditures further exacerbates the problem of delay.[25]

§ 12.6b3. Advertising, Promotion, and Customer Loyalty

Brand specific advertising in markets for branded products may constitute an entry barrier in both the Bainian and Stiglerian senses; nonetheless, there is a great deal of dispute about the height or meaningfulness of entry barriers produced by advertising. The debate is actually more psychological than economic, since it pertains to the "staying power" of brand advertising. Simply put, if the effect of advertising dissipates very soon after the advertising occurs, then advertising is not much of a barrier to entry. The incumbent firm will have to keep on advertising in order to retain its lead, and prospective entrants can match the effect of the incumbent firm's advertising by spending an equivalent amount themselves.[26] Of course, there are economies of scale in advertising—the large firm can spread its costs over more output—but that is a barrier that comes from the scale economies rather than the advertising itself.

By contrast, if advertising has a cumulative effect that builds up over time, then the well established firm may have a distinct advantage over new entrants.[27] Advertising costs are generally "sunk"—that is, once spent, the money cannot be recovered when the firm fails. Thus, if advertising has a cumulative, or capital, value, it may constitute a substantial entry barrier. Of course, the height of the entry barrier caused by advertising is also open to dispute, and once again depends on that portion of advertising expenditures that have a kind of built up or cumulative value.[28]

Virtually the same analysis applies to things like customer loyalty, or goodwill. To the extent the effects accumulate, they can raise entry barriers.[29] The only question of any real importance is how high such barriers are. In the great majority of cases, they are probably insignificant. But there are important exceptions. In markets where the product is complex, with many intricacies unfamiliar to the customer, and particularly where the product costs little relative to the customer's overall budget, goodwill and reputation count for a

24. This happened in Brooke Group Ltd. v. Brown & Williamson Tobacco Corp., 509 U.S. 209, 113 S.Ct. 2578 (1993). See § 8.8.

25. *Illinois Cereal*, 691 F.Supp. at 1145 (took nine years for another firm to build a new plant, suggesting high entry barriers); FTC v. PPG Indus., 628 F.Supp. 881, 885 (D.D.C.) (planning time of two to six years suggested high entry barriers), affirmed in part, reversed in part on other grounds, 798 F.2d 1500 (D.C.Cir.1986); FTC v. Owens–Illinois, Inc., 681 F.Supp. 27, 51 (D.D.C.), vacated as moot, 850 F.2d 694 (D.C.Cir.1988) (two year lead time with significant sunk expenditures entailed high entry barriers).

26. The empirical evidence indicates that prices are more competitive in markets where advertising is unrestricted. See H. Beales & T. J. Muris, State and Federal Regulation of National Advertising 7–33 (1993).

27. Making this point was the FTC's opinion in the Procter & Gamble merger case. 63 F.T.C. 1465, 1581 (1963).

28. Economists commonly address the basic issue by considering whether advertising has a fixed as well as a variable cost component. If advertising is nothing other than a variable cost, then its effect applies to current sales and dissipates almost as soon as the advertising stops. See General Foods Corp. 104 F.T.C. 204, 344 (1984), which addresses the same issue in the context of predatory pricing. Numerous other cases are discussed in E. Mensch & A. Freeman, Efficiency and Image: Advertising as an Antitrust Issue, 1990 Duke L.J. 321.

29. For example, FTC v. Coca–Cola Co., 641 F.Supp. 1128, 1137 (D.D.C.1986), vacated mem., 829 F.2d 191 (D.C.Cir.1987) (customer preferences for branded soft drinks created entry barrier).

great deal. The customer must trust the seller because the relative cost of doing a complete product valuation oneself are rather high. By contrast, if the customer is in as good a position to evaluate the product or service as the producer is, then goodwill counts for much less.

Further, the entire problem of goodwill in antitrust analysis is wrapped up in more basic questions of product quality. A firm acquires goodwill with a positive value only to the extent it produces a good product, and the production of a good product is always a substantial entry barrier. For this reason courts have been reluctant to make expansive use of goodwill as a qualifying entry barrier.[30]

§ 12.6b4. Product Differentiation

Product differentiation, particularly when coupled with large amounts of brand advertising, can deter entry by denying potential competitors an opportunity to locate a profitable niche in the market. The principal cause of entry into product differentiated markets is the entrant's perception that the market contains an unfilled niche, or spot where its own differentiated offering will be more attractive to a certain set of consumers than the offerings of established firms. Under this theory, incumbent firms can deter entry by filling the product space with numerous variations. This was the basic claim in the unsuccessful attack launched by the Federal Trade Commission on the Ready–to–Eat breakfast cereals industry.[31] Under the theory, product differentiation and brand advertising feed on each other to produce the entry barrier.[32] The advertising both announces the varied product offerings and creates the impression that differentiation is much more substantial than it may be in fact.[33] As Joe Bain once opined, "the psychology of consumers is very evidently such that they are frequently susceptible to the blandishments of product-differentiating sellers. * * *"[34]

But several economists have been suspicious of the notion that either advertising or product differentiation constitute qualifying entry barriers. The basic Chicago School position has been that advertising is valuable precisely to the extent that it communicates information to consumers, and product differentiation is valuable to the extent that product variety satisfies consumer taste. So if either of these things must be counted as a barrier to entry, it counts in exactly the same way that producing a superior product is an entry barrier. Any time incumbents are giving customers what they want, new entrants will have a tougher time finding profits.[35]

§ 12.6b5. Government Entry Restrictions

Virtually all sides agree that government regulation, licensing and entry restrictions collectively create among the greatest and most effective entry barriers. Some forms of regulation are entry barriers in the Stiglerian sense—particularly grants of monopoly rights (which make the cost of entry by the next firm infinitely high) or regulatory standards that grandparent in existing plants. For example, if an environmental statute exempts existing plants from expensive compliance, new firms will face a cost that existing firms do not face. Such regulations are entry barriers only in the short run. Eventually, the old plants must be replaced and the new ones will need to comply. But in this case the short run could be a period of several years or even decades.

30. But see Henry v. Chloride, Inc., 809 F.2d 1334, 1342 (8th Cir.1987) (brand loyalty an entry barrier).

31. Kellogg Co., 99 F.T.C. 8 (1982). See R. Schmalensee, Entry Deterrence in the Ready–to–Eat Breakfast Cereal Industry, 9 Bell J.Econ. 305 (1978).

32. For example, in W. Comanor & T. Wilson, Advertising, Market Structure, and Performance, 49 Rev. Econ. & Statistics 423 (1967); H.M. Mann, Seller Concentration, Barriers to Entry, and Rates of Return in Thirty Industries, 1950–1960, 48 Rev. Econ. & Stat. 296 (1966).

33. See generally, J. Ferguson, Advertising and Competition: Theory, Measurement, Fact (1974); R. McAuliffe, Advertising, Competition and Public Policy: Theories and New Evidence (1987).

34. J. Bain, *Barriers to New Competition*, note 8 at 216.

35. See Y. Brozen, Entry Barriers: Advertising and Product Differentiation, 115 in Industrial Concentration: the New Learning (H. Goldschmidt, H. Mann, & J. Weston eds. 1974). See also H. Demsetz, Accounting for Advertising as a Barrier to Entry, 52 J.Bus. 345 (1979).

The role of government regulation in creating entry barriers is often used as part of an argument for the inefficiency of regulation. Regulation, after all, creates and encourages monopoly. But there is no necessary connection between the efficiency of regulation and its role in creating entry barriers. Regulation that is quite efficient in that it is a suitably tailored correction for a real market failure might nevertheless entail restrictions on entry, or requirements that increase the cost, risk or minimum efficient scale of new entry. By contrast, very poorly constructed regulatory policies might permit free entry.

Not all forms of government regulation effectively deter entry. As a result, one cannot automatically reason from the presence of regulation to the presence of entry barriers. For example, a truck driver must generally have a commercial drivers' license, but the license is given quite readily to those who pass a test and pay a small fee. There is no reason for thinking that the license requirement itself serves to deter entry. Regulation serves as an entry barrier only if it has some kind of limiting or "bottleneck" effect.

The fact that an entry barrier originates from the government may have an effect on our antitrust analysis. Indeed, in some cases regulated industries are simply exempted from the application of the antitrust laws altogether.[36] Often, however, government regulation is evaluated in exactly the same way that other entry barriers are—that is, as creating a set of circumstances that make certain kinds of antitrust violations possible. For example, in its *Hospital Corporation* decision, the Seventh Circuit noted that a regulatory requirement that hospitals obtain a "certificate of need" could operate as a substantial entry barrier.[37] In this case collusion that resulted from a merger would lead to an output reduction and excess capacity. But in proving need, a firm desiring to enter the market needed to show that the existing hospitals were currently operating at capacity. Thus the collusion itself could create the entry barrier.

In order to constitute a barrier to entry, a regulation need not deter entry expressly or even define conditions under which entry can occur, as in the *Hospital Corporation* case. Sometimes regulation discourages entry simply because compliance is subject to scale economies. For example, if an air cleaning device is required by law but works effectively only on very large plants, then the large plant may be necessary for effective market entry. A great deal of economics literature argues that certain regulatory regimes such as OSHA and the federal environmental regulations deter entry by increasing the operating costs of relatively small firms.[38]

§ 12.6c. Evidence Required to Prove Entry Barriers or Their Absence

Operating under the prima facie illegality rule of *Philadelphia Bank,*[39] the government has historically taken the position that it must show a relevant market and sufficiently high concentration levels to warrant condemnation of the merger. Then the defendant may rebut this evidence with a showing that entry barriers are so low that collusive or oligopoly pricing is not likely. In *Baker Hughes,* the court rejected the government's contention that this evidence must show that such entry would be "quick and effective" in disciplining any attempt at supracompetitive pricing.[40] The court

36. See ch. 19.

37. Hospital Corp. of Am. v. FTC, 807 F.2d 1381, 1387 (7th Cir.1986), cert. denied, 481 U.S. 1038, 107 S.Ct. 1975 (1987); United States v. Rockford Memorial Corp., 717 F.Supp. 1251 (N.D.Ill.1989), affirmed, 898 F.2d 1278 (7th Cir.), cert. denied, 498 U.S. 920, 111 S.Ct. 295 (1990) (same).

38. See M.T. Maloney & R.E. McCormick, A Positive Theory of Environmental Quality Regulation, 25 J.L. & Econ. 99 (1982); G.R. Neumann & J.P. Nelson, Safety Regulation and Firm Size: Effects of the Coal Mine Health and Safety Act of 1969, 25 J.L. & Econ. 183 (1982); P. Pashigian, The Effect of Environmental Regulation on Optimal Plant Size and Factor Shares, 27 J.L. & Econ. 1 (1984); A. Bartel & L. Thomas, Direct and Indirect Effects of Regulation: A New Look at OSHA's Impact, 28 J.L. & Econ. 1 (1985). See also J.B. Wiener, Global Environmental Regulation: Instrumental Choice in Legal Context, 108 Yale L.J. 677 (1999) (discussing many of the issues as they affect worldwide decision making).

39. United States v. Philadelphia National Bank, 374 U.S. 321, 83 S.Ct. 1715 (1963). See § 12.4d.

40. United States v. Baker Hughes, 908 F.2d 981, 983–987 (D.C.Cir.1990).

suggested that such a standard would "require of defendants a degree of clairvoyance alien to section 7, which * * * deals with probability, not certainties." But this is a peculiar reading of § 7, which condemns mergers that "may lessen" competition; it does not exonerate mergers that "may not lessen" competition. That is, the lack of certainty works to the advantage of the government or plaintiff, not to the defendant. In this particular case, concentration levels were above 4000 HHI and the defendant's post merger market share may have been as much as 70%.[41]

But that criticism does not resolve the underlying dispute about what must be shown to refute claims of anticompetitive consequences when market concentration levels are high. Clearly, there must be some kind of showing that entry would be "effective." Otherwise the whole entry barrier inquiry becomes meaningless. A showing that entry would be "quick" is also important, provided that quick is interpreted to refer to the minimum length of time that monopoly pricing is tolerable as a policy matter. If we make the policy decision that collusive or oligopoly pricing is not a problem when it will be disciplined by new entry in two years or less, then "quick and effective" entry should refer to entry that will occur within two years or less, and that will have a substantial impact on the incumbents' abilities to keep the market price above the competitive level.

In explaining how its decision squared with the *Philadelphia Bank* presumptions, the *Baker Hughes* court suggested that it would be "anomalous" to place a high burden on defendants seeking to show low entry barriers when, because of high concentration, it was easy for the government to establish a *prima facie* case.[42] But the truth seems quite to the contrary. A *prima facie* case is easy to establish when a relatively quick look indicates that a merger is highly likely to be anticompetitive. In that case we want defendants to come forward with *more* compelling evidence that the merger will not have the feared anticompetitive consequences.

One kind of evidence that courts have frequently viewed as important is historical evidence of entry or its absence.[43] In fact, a history of previous entry may or may not be important, depending on the circumstances. On the one hand, the best evidence that entry is possible is actual entry. On the other, the fact that entry by firm number *n* occurred is not necessarily good evidence that entry by firm number *n + 1* will occur, since the latter firm generally faces a market in which market output is higher than the former firm faced. That is to say, when firm *n + 1* considers entry, the output of firm *n* must be added to that of previous incumbents, and so on.[44]

Of course, these considerations are relevant only in markets that are fairly concentrated and where there are at least modest scale economies. If a market contains 100 firms and low levels of output can be efficient, then entry by additional firms will not likely have much measurable impact on the market price. Firm *n + 1*'s position will not differ measurably from firm *n*'s. Likewise, ongoing entry and exit from a market is quite good evidence that entry barriers are low, at least if the firms that are exiting are not the same as those that are

41. Id. at 983 & n.3. There was some ambiguity about market shares because different data measured them in different years.

42. Id. at 992.

43. E.g., Anti–Monopoly v. Hasbro, 958 F.Supp. 895 (S.D.N.Y.), aff'd, 130 F.3d 1101 (2d Cir.1997), cert. denied, ___ U.S. ___, 119 S.Ct. 48 (1998) (frequent entry into board game industry undermined any inference that market power could be exercised there); accord United States v. Waste Management, 743 F.2d 976, 983 (2d Cir.1984).

44. For example, suppose that market demand elasticity is around one, that price before firm *n* contemplates entry is $1.00, and that firm *n* 's entry will increase market output by roughly 10%. Price will then drop to roughly 90¢, assuming that other firms hold their output constant. When firm *n* computes the profitability of entry, it must look at this *post*-entry price. After all, it will make its profits only in the post-entry market. If firm *n* believes the 90¢ price at entry will be profitable, it will enter. But then when firm *n + 1* looks at the same market, its calculus will be somewhat different. Assuming it is planning to be the same size as firm *n*, its own output will increase total market output by about 9%, and this will drive prices down to roughly 82¢, assuming once again that the incumbents hold their own output constant. Entry that might have been profitable at the 90¢ price may not be profitable at the 82¢ price. So in this case the fact that *n* entered is not particularly good evidence that *further* entry will occur.

entering and at least some of the entering firms achieve substantial size.

The absence of historical entry is good evidence of high entry barriers only when the industry is sufficiently profitable to make entry worthwhile in the first place. If the industry is competitive, or if the market is shrinking and firms are losing money, then entry is not likely to occur even if barriers are low.[45]

When a court looks at historical evidence of entry it must consider not only the fact of entry but also its scale.[46] Markets may often have small niches or pockets where new firms can carve out a tiny position for themselves without much affect on competitive conditions in the market as a whole. In some markets, for example, there are two or three dominant players with market shares exceeding 30%. In addition there is a significant fringe of firms with 1% market shares, and entry into the fringe is quite common. However, none of the fringe firms ever grows to be a major competitor with the dominant firms. This was the situation in *Waste Management*,[47] where numerous firms had entered the market but none had attained significant size. The court found low entry barriers and dismissed the complaint.

Why might repeated small scale entry with no threat to dominant firms occur? The two most likely reasons are that (1) the new entrants have low entry costs but steeply rising marginal costs; or (2) the market has small pockets that are readily served by small firms, while the market as a whole is subject to substantial economies of scale.

Government regulation can create the first situation. For example, suppose that the sovereign imposes heavy regulatory burdens subject to scale economies on any firm with non-owner employees, but leaves single-person entrepreneurs free of regulation. In that situation one might see two or three large firms supplying the service, and a revolving door filled with sole proprietors coming in and out. But the sole proprietors may never pose much of a threat to the larger firms, particularly if the small firms have higher costs.

The more likely story in *Waste Management* was that full service trash hauling required a fairly large operation able to serve a variety of needs and to cover a wide area. Nevertheless, there were small firms who could serve particular customers such as apartment buildings. In that case the profit maximizing strategy for the larger firms might be to set price at the cartel or oligopoly level to the market as a whole, but leave the small pockets to a fringe of tiny firms. In such a market, entry into the fringe is not particularly good evidence that any attempt by the dominant firms to charge monopoly prices will be effectively disciplined.[48]

Incidentally, the stories told above suggest that the markets in cases such as *Waste Management* were defined too broadly. In both, the large scale firms could raise price above the competitive level without (a) risking substantial incursions by the fringe, or (b) losing too many customers to the fringe. In that case, the entry that is being observed is not entry into the market in question—the output of the dominant firms—at all, but rather into an adjacent market occupied by the tiny firms. So perhaps the relevant market should have been "full service trash disposal" or some other grouping of sales from which tiny entrants were excluded.

Should the likelihood of entry be measured by subjective or objective evidence? In many cases, objective evidence is the only kind that is available. Further, economists are generally more favorably disposed toward objective evidence because they tend to treat ease of entry as an ongoing market condition. What any particular firm plans to do is really not all that important. By contrast, courts have sometimes sought subjective evidence. For example, in the *Country Lake* case the court relied on statements from outside firms that they would

45. See Echlin Mfg., Co., 105 F.T.C. 410, 485 (1985) (absence of entry where incumbents were not doing well did not suggest high entry barriers).

46. On this point, see R. Schmalensee, Ease of Entry: Has the Concept Been Applied Too Readily?, 56 Antitrust L.J. 41 (1987).

47. Note 43.

48. See *Echlin Mfg.*, note 45, which found significant entry barriers because, although several firms had entered, they were small, making up about 2% of market, and the shares of dominant firms remained unchanged.

enter the market quickly in response to a monopoly price increase there.[49]

Such evidence should generally not be taken at face value, however. As an abstract proposition, any entrepreneur will look with interest in any market where prices have increased to monopoly levels. Often entry barriers emerge only upon inspection. Indeed, some of them, such as high capital costs, may not be discovered until someone actually applies for a loan. Furthermore, statements from competitors need to be discounted when the competitors themselves have an interest in seeing the merger approved. Higher prices resulting from a merger in an adjacent geographic area may permit firms in the first area to raise their prices as well. Finally, although testimony that a firm would enter is arguably evidence of low entry barriers, testimony that a firm would not enter is not very good evidence of high barriers. Entry can come from too many sources, including firms in adjacent markets (both product and geographic) and "firms" that do not even exist at the time the question is asked.

Often the most reliable evidence of entry barriers is objective, based on empirical studies from industrial organization economists and others who are knowledgeable about the industry in question. Such experts generally assume that the relevant decision makers are profit maximizers, and then consider whether entry would be a profitable strategy in the market at issue.[50] The 1992 Horizontal Merger Guidelines generally follow this approach.

§ 12.6d. Entry Barrier Analysis Under the 1992 Horizontal Merger Guidelines

The 1984 Merger Guidelines contained a rather uninformative statement on entry barriers that gave great weight to their absence, without defining them in any detail: "If entry into a market is so easy that existing competitors could not succeed in raising price for any significant period of time, the Department is unlikely to challenge mergers in that market."[51]

One unforeseen consequence of this thin discussion was that the Justice Department's antitrust division began to lose many of its own cases. Even though the markets at issue were highly concentrated, the courts did not find significant entry barriers. For example, in *Waste Management*,[52] the court held that a horizontal merger challenged by the Division did not violate § 7 because barriers to entry in the solid waste disposal industry were very low. The combined market share of the merging firms was 48.8%, which the court acknowledged to be *prima facie* illegal.[53] The court also noted that the Supreme Court has never held that evidence of low entry barriers could be used to rebut a showing of *prima facie* illegality. Nevertheless, in this instance entry barriers were so low that people had been known to enter the market at issue by working out of their homes. Citing the Division's own Guidelines against it, the court concluded that if the Division "routinely considers ease of entry as relevant to determining the competitive impact of a merger, it may not argue to a court addressing the same issue that ease of entry is irrelevant."[54]

In contrast, the statement on entry barriers contained in the 1992 Horizontal Merger Guidelines is more detailed and much more explicit about the kinds of things needed to prove or disprove high entry barriers. The guiding question in the 1992 Guidelines is

49. United States v. Country Lake Foods, 754 F.Supp. 669, 679 (D.Minn.1990).

50. A few examples, at various degrees of generality, are M. Lieberman, Excess Capacity as a Barrier to Entry: An Empirical Appraisal, 35 J.Indus. Econ. 607 (1987); M. Spence, Notes on Advertising, Economies of Scale, and Entry Barriers, 95 Q.J.Econ. 493 (1980); R. Schmalensee, Entry Deterrence in the Ready–to–Eat Breakfast Cereal Industry, 9 Bell J.Econ. 305 (1978).

51. 1984 Guidelines, 49 Fed.Reg. at 26,832.

52. United States v. Waste Management, Inc., 743 F.2d 976 (2d Cir.1984).

53. See § 12.4d, discussing United States v. Philadelphia National Bank, 374 U.S. 321, 364–366, 83 S.Ct. 1715, 1742–1743 (1963).

54. Other cases that the Division lost on the entry barriers issue include United States v. Baker Hughes, 908 F.2d 981, 983 (D.C.Cir.1990); United States v. Calmar, 612 F.Supp. 1298 (D.N.J.1985); United States v. Country Lake Foods, 754 F.Supp. 669, 678 (D.Minn.1990).

whether profitable entry could occur within two years, of sufficient magnitude to drive prices back down to pre-merger levels.

Part of the Guidelines' analysis of entry conditions is really included in its basic market definition.[55] The Guidelines include in the market firms that can easily and economically shift to manufacturing the relevant product, or that can easily begin shipment of an existing competitive product into the relevant geographic market. The Guidelines refer to such firms as "uncommitted" entrants—that is, firms that can move into competition with the merging firms with relatively little risk or costly redeployment of resources. These are included in the market itself.[56]

Under the rubric of entry barriers, the Guidelines then include "committed" entrants—that is, firms for which the level of investment and entrepreneurial risk needed to compete with the merging firms is more substantial.[57] This group also includes firms that are not even in existence at the time the merger is evaluated, but that could come into existence in response to monopoly pricing.

The 1992 Guidelines evaluate entry barriers by considering whether the merging firms could profitably maintain a price increase above premerger levels.[58] If the output reduction necessary to support such a price increase would be undermined by new entry, then entry barriers are said to be low. This implies that the Guidelines have adopted a Bainian rather than a Stiglerian definition of entry barriers.[59]

The 1992 Merger Guidelines define entry barriers in terms of timeliness, likelihood, and sufficiency. Timely entry includes "only those committed entry alternatives that can be achieved within two years from initial planning to significant market impact."[60] Significant market impact means generally that the firm must build its plant, arrange its distribution system and markets, get the kinks worked out of its system, and begin adding its output to that of the market. The time taken to win government licensing approval must also be counted. The Guidelines note, however, that if the good at issue is durable, customers in the market might alter their purchasing decisions in anticipation of the new firms' entry with its own durable good. In that case the new entrant would not actually have to be producing. Presumably, however, there would have to be evidence of customer orders or other changes in customer behavior that indicate that the new firm's presence is already a substantial factor, even though it has not yet begun selling its product.[61]

In measuring likelihood, the Guidelines note that entry can be counted as "likely" only if the prospective entrant anticipates that it will be profitable. This implies that the Agencies will rely entirely on objective criteria in determining whether entry will effectively discipline monopoly pricing.[62] Indeed, the Guidelines later emphasize that they will evaluate entry "without attempting to identify who might be potential entrants."[63] The Guidelines then make the following important observation:

> Firms considering entry that requires significant sunk costs must evaluate the profitability of the entry on the basis of long term participation in the market, because the underlying assets will be committed to the market until they are economically depreciated. Entry that is sufficient to counteract the competitive effects of concern will cause prices to fall to their premerger levels or lower. Thus, the profitability of such committed entry must be deter-

55. Market definition analysis under the 1992 Guidelines is discussed in § 3.8.

56. 1992 Guidelines, §§ 1.0 & 1.32.

57. Entry is defined as "new competition that requires expenditure of significant sunk costs of entry and exit." 1992 Guidelines, § 3.0.

58. 1992 Guidelines, § 3.0.

59. On the two definitions, see § 12.6a.

60. 1992 Guidelines, § 3.2. Timeliness has been relevant in previous decisions. For example, Weyerhaeuser, 106 F.T.C. 172, 287 (1985), which concluded that entry that took five years would not be sufficiently timely for antitrust purposes.

61. 1992 Guidelines, § 3.2.

62. On objective vs. subjective criteria, see § 12.6c.

63. 1992 Guidelines, § 3.1.

mined on the basis of premerger market prices over the long-term.[64]

For this reason entry is sufficiently "likely" only if it would have been profitable at premerger prices.[65] In making this determination, the Guidelines develop the concept of "minimum viable scale," which is the smallest scale of operation that the new entrant must achieve in order to be profitable at premerger prices. The entrant's own output at minimum viable scale must be added to the market's existing output in order to determine the market clearing price.[66] If minimum viable scale requires the addition of so much output that price drops to a level too low to be profitable, then qualifying entry is not likely to occur.

Finally, entry will be deemed "sufficient" only if it would be on a large enough scale to drive prices back to pre-merger levels. This discussion is apparently intended to correct the problem that showed up in the *Waste Management* case.[67] Although entry occurred frequently, it was always at a very small scale that appeared to have little impact on the larger firms in the market. Sufficient entry, as the Guidelines note, could result from the entry of a single firm, or from the effects of the entry of several firms. As a general matter, entry that meets the likelihood test described above will also meet the "sufficiency" test. But the Guidelines note that there may be situations when essential inputs are constrained and the entrant will not be able to get its output up sufficiently to restore prices to premerger levels.[68]

These new entry provisions seem well calculated to add some rigor to entry barrier analysis in concentrated markets, where new entrants must consider the impact of their own entry on market prices. They also suggest that ease of entry will not be presumed in a great variety of cases, but will have to be established. No matter how the burden of proof is formally assigned, a sizeable part of the burden of coming forward with the relevant evidence will lie with the merging firm or firms.

§ 12.7 Other Factors Affecting the Competitive Consequences of Mergers

Predicting the likely competitive consequences of a merger does not necessarily end with an examination of market concentration and the market shares of the merging firms. Indeed, it ends at that point only if concentration is so low, or the market shares so small, that the merger clearly poses no threat. Upwards of that point, however, the decision maker must look further at market factors other than those affecting concentration per se.

One of these non-market-share factors is ease of entry, which was discussed in the previous section. Others include the power and sophistication of trading partners, the adequacy of irreplaceable materials, excess capacity, marketing and sales methods, the history of anticompetitive practices in the industry, and perhaps any "trend" toward concentration in the market.

§ 12.7a. Sophistication and Power of Trading Partners

Courts have sometimes cited the presence of powerful or sophisticated buyers or suppliers as militating against the likelihood of any exercise of market power by a merging firm.[1] For example, *Country Lake* held that a merger

64. 1992 Guidelines, § 3.0.

65. 1992 Guidelines, § 3.3.

66. Thus the ultimate question is whether the entrant's output would be sufficient to enable the entrant to break even at pre-merger prices. While the standard concept of minimum efficient scale (MES) is generally expressed in units of output per time period, minimum viable scale is expressed as a minimum market share needed to break even. See J.A. Ordover & J.B. Baker, Entry Analysis Under the 1992 horizontal Merger Guidelines, 61 Antitrust L.J. 139, 143 (1992).

67. Note 52. See § 12.6c.

68. The new entrant's product may also be so differentiated from that of incumbents that it does not sufficiently reduce the market price. Such entry will likewise be regarded as not "substantial." See Ordover & Baker, note 66, at 145.

§ 12.7

1. The argument comes from H. Hovenkamp, Mergers and Buyers, 77 Va. L. Rev. 1369 (1991). See also 4 Antitrust Law ¶ 943 (rev. ed. 1998).

of dairies was not likely to injure competition because, although that market was concentrated, the vertically related market containing food distributors, who purchased the dairies' milk and resold it to grocers, was even more concentrated. Three distributors controlled ninety percent of the whole. "This concentration gives significant market power to these distributors because no dairy * * * could afford to lose their business which would happen if the dairy imposed a price increase unrelated to normal market conditions."[2] Further, if the dairies should collude, "individual grocers could easily unite to purchase through a large distributor," which would then be able to turn to a large supplier outside the government's proposed geographic market.

At least five large milk purchasers in the proposed market were

> sensitive to and carefully monitor changes in fluid milk prices. They believe they would recognize price increases that are not based on normal market conditions. They declared that a substantial increase in milk prices would prompt them to aggressively negotiate a reduction or to seek a substitute or replacement supplier of fluid milk. If competitive prices could not be found within the [relevant market,] the purchasers would seek supplies from outside dairies.[3]

Large, sophisticated buyers can be particularly effective in combatting collusion if they can force sellers to make secret bids or negotiate nonpublic price reductions—that is, if the buyers are able to force cartel members to cheat on the cartel in a way that minimizes the risks of detection. The 1992 Merger Guidelines note that large buyers are particularly likely to encourage cartel cheating if they are negotiating large, long-term contracts.[4]

A merger is to be evaluated by its impact on all buyers, however, not just on the larger more sophisticated ones. For example, in *Archer–Daniels–Midland* the court upheld a merger after noting the presence of powerful buyers who forced the sellers to bid against each other in secret.[5] But there was also a larger group of smaller, less powerful buyers, who were generally constrained to accept the sellers' offerings at the posted list prices. The legality of the merger should have been evaluated by its impact on the latter group of buyers, for the merger may "lessen competition" as to them. The 1992 Guidelines provide as much by noting that where price discrimination is a realistic possibility, the enforcement agencies may draw smaller relevant markets to demarcate the groups of customers who can be forced to pay a higher price.[6]

Further, one must not generalize too quickly from the existence of powerful or knowledgeable vertically related firms to the conclusion that monopoly profits cannot be earned in the market under consideration. In *all* cases, knowledgeable suppliers (or buyers) are likely to restrain monopoly pricing only to the extent that it serves their own interests. The entire proposition that knowledgeable suppliers or buyers will restrain pricing rests on the assumption that doing so is more profitable than simply profiting from any monopoly structure that already exists. This may not always be so.

Suppose, for example, that dairies producing fluid milk threaten to monopolize that market in a particular region.[7] The result will be reduced output of milk and higher milk prices to customers. Middlemen, or distributors who purchase the milk and deliver it to

2. United States v. Country Lake Foods, 754 F.Supp. 669, 679 (D.Minn.1990). See also FTC v. Elders Grain, Inc., 868 F.2d 901, 905 (7th Cir.1989) ("concentrated and knowledgeable buying side" makes seller collusion more difficult); FTC v. Donnelley, 1990–2 Trade Cas. ¶ 69239, 1990 WL 193674 (D.D.C.1990) (merger probably not anticompetitive, given sophistication of the relatively small number of customers for one aspect of the post-merger's firm's printing output). Accord United States v. Baker Hughes, 908 F.2d 981, 986 (D.C.Cir.1990); Owens–Illinois, 5 Trade Reg.Rep. ¶ 23162 (FTC, 1992). Contrast FTC v. University Health, 938 F.2d 1206, 1213 n. 13 (11th Cir. 1991), which rejected the claim that the buyers, large sophisticated health insurers, would discipline any price increases by hospitals. The insurers were found to have little choice but to pay the bills of their insureds, who made the claims.

3. *Country Lake*, 754 F.Supp. at 679.

4. 1992 Guidelines, § 2.12.

5. United States v. Archer–Daniels–Midland, 781 F.Supp. 1400, 1415 (S.D.Iowa 1991).

6. See 1992 Guidelines, § 1.12. On market definition in the presence of price discrimination, see §§ 3.8c, 3.9b.

7. See *Country Lake*, note 2.

stores, will also be injured, however, because the milk monopoly will produce less milk in response to lower customer demand at the monopoly retail price. The distributors will experience the volume reduction but not the higher profits on the milk that is still sold.

If one considers this situation as static, then it is clearly in the distributors' best interest to undermine the retail monopoly, either by integrating into milk production for themselves or else by finding others willing and able to enter the milk production market in competition with the monopoly. But such a solution tends to eliminate monopoly from the market altogether and, from the distributor's position, that is not necessarily the most profitable solution. It may be more profitable for the milk producers and the distributors to come to an agreement maintaining the monopoly but dividing its profits in such a way that both would be better off than they would be under a more competitive regime.

To the extent such an alternative is available, one cannot trust the presence of knowledgeable suppliers or buyers in a market to eliminate monopoly; they may simply preserve the monopoly but use it to their advantage. As a general rule, the *distributors'* preferences in the preceding example must be ranked in this order:

(1) *worst* : the suppliers monopolize or cartelize their market and all the monopoly profits accrue to the suppliers; in this case, the distributors experience only the output loss.

(2) *better* : both the suppliers' and the distributors' markets are competitive; the distributors obtain the full benefit of competition in the upstream market, but earn no monopoly profits.

(3) *still better* : the suppliers' market is monopolized or cartelized, but the suppliers and distributors share the profits.

(4) *best* : the suppliers' market is competitive and the distributors' market is monopolized, with all monopoly profits accruing to the distributor.[8]

Which of these occurs in any given case is an empirical question, and depends on a variety of factors. Importantly, however, the distributors facing a supplier cartel (situation 1) will perhaps at best achieve only situation two by vertically integrating into supply itself or setting up other suppliers in the business. Where it is possible, suppliers and distributors might be expected to negotiate for situation (3). In that case, the supply market will continue to be monopolized, and the suppliers and distributors will share the monopoly profits there.

Alternative merger Guidelines promulgated by the National Association of Attorneys General in 1987 and revised in 1992 have responded to some of these concerns.[9] These Guidelines, which state the criteria that state attorneys general will use to challenge mergers affecting their state,[10] observe that powerful buyers cannot be relied upon to discipline collusion if they "find it more profitable to preserve the monopoly in the primary market * * * than to force competition there." Further, "[t]his is most likely when both buyer and seller market levels are highly concentrated and each side has significant power to force the other side to behave competitively." In that case "forbearance on both sides, which results in preservation of the monopoly and sharing of its profits, is a more profitable result than aggressive behavior that will eliminate monopoly profits at both levels."[11]

§ 12.7b. Adequacy of Irreplaceable Raw Materials

Many scarce natural resources such as coal, oil, and copper are in a practical sense irre-

8. The fact that situation (4) is better for the distributor than situation (3) derives from the fact that any single monopolist in a distribution chain can reap the maximum benefits of monopoly in that chain.

9. NAAG Horizontal Merger Guidelines (1987), 4 Trade Reg. Rep. (CCH) ¶ 13,405; Revised Horizontal Merger Guidelines (1993), reprinted in 64 Antitrust & Trade Reg. Rep. (BNA) #1608, (Special Supp., Apr. 1, 1993).

10. When states Attorneys General challenge mergers they are treated as private plaintiffs; however, they have the power to act as parens patriae in behalf of consumers within their states. See California v. American Stores, 495 U.S. 271, 110 S.Ct. 1853 (1990). See § 15.4.

11. 1992 NAAG Horizontal Merger Guidelines § 5.4 n. 56.

placeable, and often most of the known reserves that can be profitably produced at current market prices are already owned by other firms. If a firm is running out of such reserves its market share of current production may overstate its position as a continuing force in the market. For example, in the *General Dynamics* case,[12] the Supreme Court found that the current market shares of merging coal producers exaggerated their market power when their reserves were depleted and they could not acquire more.

Some caution is in order, however. A firm with only 1% of the world's sand could probably produce 100% of the world's silicone computer chips from now until eternity. Any blanket rule that a firm's irreplaceable reserves rather than its current output be used in estimating market share would cut far too broadly. The court should find initially that a firm's reserve holdings are irreplaceable and depleted, *and* that as a result its output in the relevant market (here, silicone computer chips) will decline substantially in only a few years.

The 1992 Guidelines statement on depleted inputs is brief, but to the point. The Guidelines note that the agencies will calculate market share using "the best indicator of firms' future competitive significance."[13]

§ 12.7c. Excess Capacity

Excess capacity occurs when firms' current output is less than the optimal output that their plants are designed to produce. To say that a firm has excess capacity thus entails that the firm could increase its output at per unit costs no higher than (and perhaps lower than) its current costs. Excess capacity held by a firm's active competitors will confine the firm's ability to increase price. As soon as it does so, the competitors will respond with an output increase.

One way to address this problem is to define market share in terms of the capacity held by rivals, rather than their current output. Although that may be the theoretically best approach to the existence of excess capacity, relevant capacity is often harder to measure than output or sales.[14] Another way is to define markets in the conventional way (on the basis of units of output or dollars of revenue) but then consider market wide excess capacity as a mitigating factor to be weighed in favor of the merger.

The entire problem is further complicated by the fact that excess capacity may serve another, not so propitious function. Firms who are engaged in express or tacit collusion may carry excess capacity in order to punish cartel cheaters. One of the most effective of such punishments is temporary bursts of selling at the competitive price.[15] However, in order to support such punishment the cartel members may have to carry excess capacity sufficient to make the threat that cheaters will be disciplined credible. In that case, the excess capacity may really be a collusion facilitating device. Likewise, market-wide excess capacity may be a signal that the market is already subject to collusion, and that the firms have successfully reduced their output below pre-cartel levels. Approving a merger would simply make the cartel more robust.[16]

How does one tell whether a particular instance of excess capacity tends to mitigate in favor of the merger, because it makes disciplining of post-merger price increases more likely; or tends to mitigate against the merger because it is a sign of collusion? In some cases the decision maker will not be able to tell, and then the best solution is probably not to count excess capacity one way or the other. In other cases, collusion will leave telltale signs: facilitating devices, rigid market shares, apparent price leadership or lockstep pricing, and so on.[17] In the presence of such evidence, excess

12. United States v. General Dynamics Corp., 415 U.S. 486, 94 S.Ct. 1186 (1974). See 4A Antitrust Law ¶ 962 (rev. ed. 1998).

13. 1992 Guidelines, § 1.41.

14. See § 3.7b.

15. See § 4.1.

16. See FTC v. Elders Grain, 868 F.2d 901, 905–906 (7th Cir.1989), which noted the possibility.

17. See §§ 4.4–4.6.

capacity should never be regarded as a mitigating factor.

By contrast, if the excess capacity is held by firms that are clearly aggressive—or "mavericks," in the language of the 1992 Merger Guidelines—then the excess capacity could be used to limit collusion. In that case the central question is whether the firm being acquired is the maverick, or whether it is a third party. In the former case, the merger is more likely to be anticompetitive because it will dispose of a feisty rival who has the capacity to frustrate collusion. In the latter case, the continued presence of the maverick makes successful collusion less likely.[18]

§ 12.7d. Marketing and Sales Methods

Some pricing and sales practices are more conducive to price leadership or price fixing than others. The 1982/1984 Merger Guidelines were criticized for considering all markets to be "auction" markets, in which every seller competes for every buyer and the buyers have complete, easily available information about the offerings of competing sellers.[19]

The amount of competition in a market varies with the way price information flows. A Chicago physician may have a great deal of market power in the Chicago market, even though there are several competitors in her specialty. Often people in need of emergency surgery find comparison shopping very expensive. Since most customers are likely to enter this market only once or at least infrequently, the seller does not need to worry about pricing her product low enough to keep the buyer.

At the other extreme is a market like the New York Stock Exchange or the Chicago Board of Trade, where every buyer has virtually complete information about the offering price of every seller, and vice-versa. If the current price of IBM stock is 130, a seller who offers his shares at 140 will not make the sale.

The 1992 Horizontal Merger Guidelines consider have been a little more responsive to the problem than the 1982/84 Guidelines were. The context of the Guidelines' discussion is the degree to which the availability of certain sales and marketing information enables a cartel or oligopoly to detect cheaters:

> The detection and punishment of [cheaters] may be facilitated by existing practices among firms, themselves not necessarily antitrust violations, and by the characteristics of typical transactions. For example, if key information about specific transactions or individual price or output levels is available routinely to competitors, it may be difficult for a firm to deviate secretly. If orders for the relevant product are frequent, regular and small relative to the total output of a firm in a market, it may be difficult for the firm to deviate in a substantial way without the knowledge of rivals and without the opportunity for rivals to react. If demand or cost fluctuations are relatively infrequent and small, deviations may be relatively easy to deter.[20]

Of course, in some cases the use of a particular pricing or sales method, or of price or output information exchanges, may be so offensive that it constitutes a violation of § 1 of the Sherman Act.[21] In other cases, the use of such practices may be sufficiently suspicious that it justifies condemning the merger even where the ordinary structural thresholds are not satisfied. This question is taken up in § 12.8.

§ 12.7e. History of Collusion or Facilitating Practices

In predicting the likelihood of collusion in a

18. On this point, see 1992 Guidelines § 2.12. Technically, a maverick firm is one whose profit-maximizing rate of output is higher than any share that other firms would tolerate in a cartel or oligopoly equilibrium. As a result, the mere existence of the firm in the given situation undermines the cartel or oligopoly outcome. Mavericks are more likely to exist when there are significant differences among firms in a market—for example, they have widely differing costs, capacities or scale economies, and thus maximize their profits at different output levels.

19. R.B. Harris & T.M. Jorde, Market Definition in the Merger Guidelines: Implications for Antitrust Enforcement, 71 Calif.L.Rev. 464, 476–79 (1983).

20. 1992 Guidelines, § 2.12.

21. See §§ 4.4–4.5.

market, one cannot ignore history.[22] The 1984 Merger Guidelines stated that the government would be more likely to challenge a merger if the firms in the market had previously "been found to have engaged in horizontal collusion. * * * "[23] An occasional court has also suggested that a history of attempts at collusion weigh against approval of a merger.[24]

The 1992 Guidelines refine the standard a little further: "It is likely that market conditions are conducive to coordinated interaction when the firms in the market previously have engaged in express collusion and when the salient characteristics of the market have not changed appreciably since the most recent such incident." The Guidelines add that express collusion by the same firms in a different geographic market will be given equivalent weight.[25]

Of course, elaborate efforts to fix prices may also be evidence that more tacit kinds of collusion or oligopoly behavior have not been successful. By contrast, the absence of evidence of collusion may suggest only that collusion by express agreement is unnecessary: the sellers have managed quite successfully to coordinate prices without express collusion. This suggests that the absence of historical evidence of collusion should generally be ignored. Further, since express collusion is just as much a merger policy concern as oligopoly, and since a reduction in the number of players makes collusion more likely to occur, previous attempts at collusion should always be regarded as an aggravating factor.

§ 12.7f. "Trends" Towards Concentration

In *Brown Shoe*[26] and *Von's Grocery*,[27] the Supreme Court cited an industry-wide trend toward concentration as a rationale for condemning the mergers. If the court approved these mergers, it reasoned, it would be forced to approve other similar mergers in the future. This "domino theory" has been relied on by courts to condemn many mergers.

The significance for merger policy of a "trend" toward concentration in the relevant market has been hotly debated.[28] The 1992 Horizontal Merger Guidelines ignore it, even though it is a well established element in Supreme Court antimerger policy.

What does a "trend" toward concentration indicate? Most of the time it indicates that larger firms have developed economies of scale or scope. Suppose, for example, that a market contains 50 firms, each with 2% of the market and having costs of $4.00 per unit. Two firms merge and achieve economies that reduce the costs of the post-merger firm to $3.60. What will happen next? The larger firm with the lower costs is likely to expand output. The smaller competitors will lose business unless they can achieve the economies themselves, and perhaps the quickest way is by merger. The industry will exhibit a "trend" toward concentration (and merger) until it reaches a new equilibrium in which all firms have either exploited the available economies or exited from the market.

Any rule that identifies such a trend toward concentration as justifying condemnation of mergers is probably calculated to protect small businesses at the expense of consumers. This almost certainly explains the Supreme Court's citation of a trend toward concentration in *Brown Shoe* and *Von's Grocery*. In his

22. See also § 12.8, which discusses the relevance of observed anticompetitive consequences.

23. 1984 Guidelines, § 3.44.

24. For example, FTC v. Elders Grain, 868 F.2d 901, 906 (7th Cir.1989) (merger which reduces number of players in a market historically prone to collusion is unlawful).

25. 1992 Guidelines, § 2.1. See K. Arquit, Perspectives on the 1992 U.S. Government Horizontal Merger Guidelines, 61 Antitrust L.J. 121, 131–133 (1992).

26. Brown Shoe Co. v. United States, 370 U.S. 294, 346, 82 S.Ct. 1502, 1535 (1962).

27. United States v. Von's Grocery Co., 384 U.S. 270, 277, 86 S.Ct. 1478, 1482 (1966) ("Congress sought to preserve competition among many small businesses by arresting a trend toward concentration in its incipiency before that trend developed to the point that a market was left in the grip of a few big companies.")

28. Supporting condemnation of mergers in markets exhibiting a trend toward concentration: D. Bok, Section 7 of the Clayton Act and the Merging of Law and Economics, 74 Harv.L.Rev. 226, 310 (1960); opposing it: R. Bork, The Antitrust Paradox: A Policy at War With Itself 205–206 (1978). Other literature is discussed in 4 Antitrust Law ¶ 932e (rev. ed. 1998).

Von's Grocery dissent Justice Stewart criticized the majority for trying to use Clayton § 7 to "roll back the supermarket revolution."[29] Grocers were merging because multistore companies were achieving economies in buying, advertising and other forms of coordination that were generally not available to smaller chains or individual stores.

The irony of using a "trend" toward concentration to condemn a merger under these circumstances is that the rule often damages the fortunes of the very small businesses it was designed to protect. If multi-store economies are substantial in the grocery business, firms will procure additional stores. If they cannot acquire existing stores they probably will build new ones of their own. The result will be that small operators will still have to face the more efficient operation of their bigger competitors but will have no easy way of exiting the market when things go bad. The "trend" toward concentration that the Court cited should have been used to support, rather than condemn, the mergers at issue.

§ 12.7g. Aggressiveness of Acquired Firm

One thing structural indexes do very poorly is provide us with indicators of the competitiveness of particular firms in the market. Some firms are much more aggressive rivals than others, even if they are small. In amending the Clayton Act in 1950, Congress expressed a concern with mergers that eliminated a rival that was a "substantial factor in competition."[30] Judicial decisions have noted the aggressiveness of the acquired rival only infrequently. However, in the 1964 *Aluminum Co.* decision, the court noted that Rome Cable had been a particularly aggressive and innovative competitor, despite its small market share.[31] The enforcement agencies have incorporated these concerns to some degree in the 1992 Guidelines, which show particular concern with the acquisition of "maverick" firms that have a history of frustrating attempts at collusion.[32]

§ 12.8 Observed Anticompetitive Consequences

Price-fixing and tacit collusion are costly to a firm, because (1) the firm risks losing a customer if it refuses to make a price cut; and (2) the facilitating and enforcement devices are costly to develop and employ.[1] In a competitive market firms should be quite willing to deviate from the terms of sale offered by others, provided that the underlying sale remains profitable. A refusal to deviate suggests a perception that collusion or oligopoly behavior is worth its costs.

Suppose that a merger's competitive consequences are somewhat ambiguous on the standard market structure analysis, or even suggest that the merger is legal. Nonetheless, the firms in the market (either after the merger or both before and after) engage in a variety of practices that show that the market is not performing very competitively. For example, suppose that the firms follow a routine practice of publishing list prices once a month, all of which are nearly identical, and then refuse to negotiate discounts from those list prices, at least to certain classes of customers.[2] Or suppose that the firms have persistently followed a practice of price leadership under which a

29. 384 U.S. at 288, 86 S.Ct. at 1488: "[T]he [majority's] opinion is hardly more than a requiem for the so-called 'Mom and Pop' grocery stores * * * that are now economically and technologically obsolete in many parts of the country."

30. See H.R. Rep. No. 1191, 81st Cong., 1st Sess. 8 (1949).

31. United States v. Aluminum Co. of America (Rome Cable), 377 U.S. 271, 280–281, 84 S.Ct. 1283, 1289–1290 (1964) (" * * * Rome was an aggressive competitor. It was a pioneer in aluminum insulation and developed one of the most widely used insulated conductors. * * * Preservation of Rome, rather than its absorption by one of the giants, will keep it 'as an important competitive factor,' * * * ").

32. See 1992 Guidelines, § 2.12.

§ 12.8

1. On facilitating devices, see § 4.4b.

2. For example, United States v. Archer–Daniels–Midland, 781 F.Supp. 1400 (S.D.Iowa 1991) (sellers in post-merger market announced prices quarterly and did not deviate except to large buyers; however, the court concluded that the evidence failed to indicate sufficient coordination to warrant condemnation, in spite of high concentration. Court apparently overlooked that firms might give price discounts to large buyers, but oligopolistic prices to smaller ones.).

given firm announces the price increase and the others follow; or if the others fail to follow the leader quietly rescinds the increase. Should the merger be condemned on the basis of such evidence alone?

First of all, Clayton § 7's "may substantially lessen competition" language does not require a given market structure or a given set of proofs about market concentration, firm market share, entry barriers or anything else. Rather, it requires fairly convincing evidence of a likelihood that a merger will "lessen" competition. Market structure evidence is the surrogate for bad performance, not the other way around. Further, if any amount of collusion or collusion-like behavior is occurring, a horizontal merger tends to make that behavior more successful. Alternatively, the merger itself may bring the behavior into existence. In both these cases the merger has lessened competition.[3]

One good sign that a market is not performing competitively is the systematic willingness of sellers to engage in costly nonprice competition, coupled with a general unwillingness to reduce the price. Such behavior is costly, since the firm risks losing a sale; so it must have an explanation. In a competitive market, a seller should be indifferent as between offering a price cut of $1.00 or the inclusion of a service that costs $1.00, assuming there are no collateral costs. Under tacit or express collusion, however, the inclusion of the extra service may be a way of cheating on the cartel price without being detected.

Another sign of failure of competition is the existence of multiple pricing regimes.[4] If a market is competitive, prices tend to hover around marginal cost, or a little above average variable costs. They change in response to cost changes, which are generally gradual, or else when there are temporary dislocations in the market, such as temporary shortages or surpluses in relation to demand. By contrast, in an oligopoly prices are maintained "artificially" at a higher than competitive level. At least in a cooperative oligopoly, this maintenance depends on certain assumptions about what rivals will do. But even in non-cooperative oligopolies, firms make assumptions about rivals' responses and set their own prices accordingly.[5]

Oligopolistic firms seldom have perfect information about what motivates the pricing decisions of others. In general, a good strategy in a cartel or oligopoly that faces cheating by one member is to cut prices themselves. Such a price cut may be costly to the cartel members, but it is also costly to the cheater. As a result, the assurance of retaliatory price cutting tends to make cheating unprofitable, if the threat of retaliation is credible.[6] In order for this threat to be credible, the intending cheater must perceive a high likelihood that other firms will immediately retaliate in response to any price cut. How can the other cartel members achieve this high likelihood if they find it difficult to determine whether another firm's price cut is the result of depressed market conditions or of cheating?[7] The answer is that the firm learns from experience that other firms will shoot first and ask questions later. Indeed, the price cut is very likely the optimal response to *both* a depressed market and cheating, which makes it a particularly robust strategy. Further, the price cut does not need to be predatory, and this tends to make it more credible. A mere cut to the competitive level is quite costly to a firm that cheats once or twice and then pays by earning only competitive profits for an indefinite period of time.[8] To be sure, retaliatory price cut-

3. See 4 Antitrust Law ¶ 917 (rev. ed. 1998).

4. The term is from J.B. Baker & T.F. Bresnahan, Empirical Methods of Identifying and Measuring Market Power, 61 Antitrust L. J. 3, 13 (1992). For a more technical discussion, see E. Green & R. Porter, Noncooperative Collusion Under Imperfect Price Information, 52 Econometrica 87 (1984).

5. On the difference between cooperative and noncooperative oligopoly, see § 4.2.

6. See § 4.1a3.

7. Cheating would typically result in higher output, while price reductions reflecting a depressed market would not. But one oligopolist may not easily determine the output of others.

8. The 1992 Horizontal Merger Guidelines, § 2.12, recognize the point. In order for punishment to be credible it "may not need to be any more complex than temporary abandonment of the terms of coordination by other firms in the market."

ting by the non-cheaters seems costly—but the important point is that it is less costly than attempting to maintain the price.

In an oligopoly where the firms do not have perfect information about each other, we would expect periods of oligopoly pricing to be punctuated by occasional price "wars," where prices are cut deeply for a short period of time. When the cheater finally begins raising its price again, other firms will follow the price up as well. Competitive markets do not have price "wars." Oligopolistic markets do. Distinguishing a qualifying price war from the ordinary changes in price that occur in competitive markets requires some econometric modelling, but it is by no means impossible and may often be quite easy.[9] Evidence of multiple pricing regimes, such as periodic price wars, should raise a presumption that a further reduction in the number of effective players in this market is anticompetitive.[10]

Observed noncompetitive consequences are particularly important to the evaluation of mergers in markets that may be defined as too large. As noted in § 3.4, the 1992 Horizontal Merger Guidelines may sometimes lead policy makers to commit the "*Cellophane*" fallacy by focusing too closely on high cross elasticity of demand at current market prices, and not taking into account that if a market is already subject to collusion, cross elasticity of demand will be high. The 1992 Guidelines suggest that if there is evidence that collusion or collusion-like behavior is already occurring, the Agency will attempt to determine what the price would have been absent the collusion, and compute from that point.[11] But there seems to be a better solution: if there is evidence of such behavior, the merger should be condemned without further difficult inquiries into what the competitive price might have been and what would be the cross-elasticity of demand at that price.

Suppose, for example, that on the basis of similar technology and geological proximity the tribunal defines a provisional market as including the output of firms A, B, C, D and E. At current prices the demand of these firms seems highly cross-elastic with the output of firms X, Y and Z. If the firms in the first group increased price further, they would lose too many sales. But suppose that the evidence also suggests one of the following: (1) in the past A, B, C, D & E have fixed prices; or (2) A, B, C, D & E follow a practice of publishing quarterly price lists and seldom deviating from them, and their prices seem to move in lockstep fashion, except for possible discounts to a few large customers. Under the Guidelines approach, the Agency would then try to determine what the competitive price would be for the output of A, B, C, D & E. Then it would determine whether cross-elasticity of demand with the output of X, Y and Z is also high at that lower price. If it is not, then A, B, C, D and E would define a relevant market.

The better approach is to ignore the second step. Once we know that the firms in the provisional market are behaving noncompetitively vis-a-vis one another, we can assume that the refusal to compete is worth its costs. We have already defined a relevant market, and it includes only A, B, C, D & E. Further, any merger among them will exacerbate the anticompetitive performance.

§ 12.9 The "Failing Company" Defense and Related Factors Affecting Firm Viability

The failing company defense exonerates a merger that would otherwise be illegal under § 7. The legislative history of the 1950 Celler–Kefauver Amendments to § 7 makes clear that Congress intended some kind of exemption for acquisitions of "failing" companies.[1] However,

9. See J.B. Baker & T. Bresnahan, note 4 at 13–15; M. Porter, On the Incidence and Duration of Price Wars, 33 J. Indus. Econ. 415 (1985); J.B. Baker, Identifying Cartel Policing Under Uncertainty: the U.S. Steel Industry 1933–1939, 32 J. L. & Econ. S47 (1989).

10. See generally A. Jacquemin & M.E. Slade, Cartels, Collusion, and Horizontal Merger 416–473, 1 Handbook of Industrial Organization (R. Schmalensee & R. Willig eds. 1989).

11. 1992 Horizontal Merger Guidelines, § 1.11.

§ 12.9

1. S.Rep. No. 1775, 81st Cong., 2d Sess. 7 (1950). See P.M. Laurenza, Section 7 of the Clayton Act and the Failing Company: An Updated Perspective, 65 Va.L.Rev.

the legislative history gives little guidance on the important questions of how "failing company" should be defined and what the scope of the defense ought to be.

The history of the failing company defense indicates that it was probably designed to protect the creditors, owners or stockholders, and employees of small businesses. In that case, the defense is more concerned with distributive justice than with efficiency. So regarded, the defense does a poor job of achieving its objective. To be sure, the failing company defense can be beneficial to a small, "failing company" acquired by a larger firm and saved from bankruptcy. However, application of the defense can seriously injure a small business that competes with a failing company acquired by a more efficient firm. For example, the merger at issue in Brunswick Corp. v. Pueblo Bowl–O–Mat, Inc.[2] was a good candidate for the failing company defense,[3] although the Supreme Court never reached that issue. The plaintiff was a relatively small bowling alley operator. Its competitor was also a small operator who was in deep financial trouble. The competitor was acquired by Brunswick Corp., one of the giants in the industry. The acquisition saved the failing company that was acquired, but it injured the (equally small) plaintiff, who then faced a much more formidable competitor than it had before.

Notwithstanding Congress' historical concerns, a strong argument can be made that a narrowly applied failing company defense is economically efficient. The defense could serve to keep facilities in production that would otherwise be shut down. Of course, one of the goals of the bankruptcy laws is to permit firms to re-emerge as successful competitors. However, only a small percentage of failing firms are reorganized successfully in bankruptcy to re-emerge as productive entities.[4] At the same time, the relevant question is not what happens to the bankrupt *firm*, but what happens to its productive assets. Even if the firm ceases production, its assets might stay on the market after being resold to new investors or creditors. Productive assets are likely to be dismantled or taken out of production altogether only when the market contains excess capacity and the assets are highly specialized.

The failing company defense could be efficient when it (1) enables a failing firm and its creditors to avoid the high administrative costs of bankruptcy; and (2) it keeps on the market productive assets that are worth keeping in production and would likely be taken out of production were it not for the merger. Offsetting these is the social cost of any monopoly pricing that flows from the merger itself, less the social cost that would flow from any monopoly created if the failing firm simply went out of business.

Can the acquisition of a failing firm be efficient, even if it creates a monopoly? It can, but it is important to keep four alternative possibilities distinct: (1) the "failing firm" actually survives or is rehabilitated (perhaps in bankruptcy) and the market continues to be competitive; (2) the failing firm is acquired by other owners who continue to operate it as a competitive firm; (3) the failing firm exits from the market and its productive assets are dismantled, giving the remaining viable firm a monopoly; or (4) the failing firm is acquired by the remaining viable firm, giving it a monopoly.

Both (3) and (4) are "monopoly" solutions. Both presumably are inferior as a matter of policy to either (1) or (2). So the first warning to the policy maker is that *before* deciding to accept the failing company defense and permit (4), one must make sure that (1) and (2) are not viable alternatives.[5]

947 (1979); and see 4A Antitrust Law ¶¶ 951–954 (rev. ed. 1998).

2. 429 U.S. 477, 97 S.Ct. 690 (1977). See § 16.3.

3. See P. Areeda, Antitrust Violations Without Damage Recoveries, 89 Harv.L.Rev. 1127 (1976).

4. See M. Bradley & M. Rosenzweig, The Untenable Case for Chapter 11, 101 Yale L.J. 1043, 1075 (1992); R.K. Rasmussen, The Efficiency of Chapter 11, 8 Bankr. Dev's J. 319 (1991).

5. On (1), see FTC v. Tenet Healthcare Corp., 17 F.Supp.2d 937 (E.D.Mo.1998), reversed on other grounds, ___ F.3d ___, 1999 WL 512108 (8th Cir. 1999) (defense not met where firm was still profitable and still able to service its debt, although its patient load had declined); United States v. Ivaco, 704 F.Supp. 1409 (W.D.Mich.1989) (defense not met where failure was merely possible). On (2),

But suppose it is clear that if the failing company defense is disallowed, and alternative (4) thus prohibited, the result will be alternative (3). The firm's assets will be taken off the market. In most cases (4) is a more efficient solution than (3). For example, suppose that output before the failing firm's exit from the market was 60 units for the dominant firm and 40 units for the failing firm. When the failing firm exits from the market, the remaining firm will produce at the profit-maximizing, or monopoly level, which we assume to be 80 units. In this case, it would be a social waste to require that the failing firm's assets be dismantled, and the remaining firm be required to increase its capacity from 60 units to 80 units by means of new construction. In short, the failing company defense permits a firm to reduce the cost of obtaining productive assets. At least a part of these gains will be passed on to consumers, even if the firm at issue is a monopolist.[6]

Indeed, even if the monopolist did not need to add capacity, the result of alternative (4) would likely be efficient. If a firm operates out of a single plant, it will increase output until marginal cost equals marginal revenue. By contrast, if a firm operates out of two plants it will take the horizontal sum of the marginal cost functions for each plant in order to compute a total marginal cost function for equating marginal cost and marginal revenue. It will then allocate this figure, which gives total output, between the two plants in a way that equates marginal cost in the two. Unless one plant alone has excess capacity at the monopoly output, this will generally produce a higher total output than operation out of a single plant.[7] Even a monopolist operating both plants will have a higher output at the profit-maximizing level than a monopolist operating only a single plant.[8]

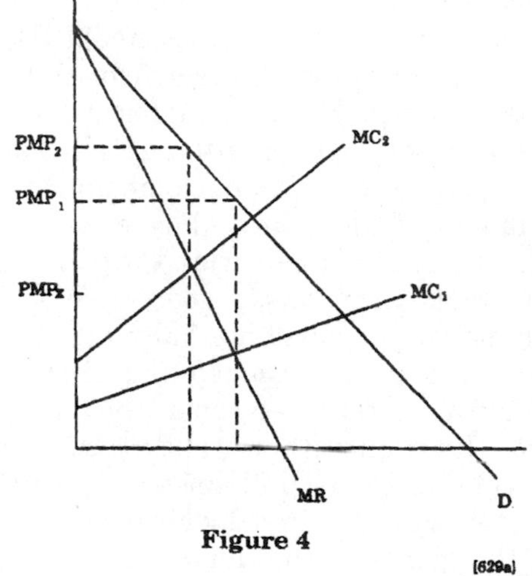

Figure 4

The failing company defense is well established in antitrust case law, although a qualifying "failing company" has been found only a few times.[9] Citizen Publishing Co. v. United

see FTC v. Harbour Group Invs., 1990–2 Trade Cas. ¶ 69,247, 1990 WL 198819 (D.D.C.1990) (failing company defense not applicable where the parties could not show that they had explored all less anticompetitive alternatives, including alternative sources of needed financing).

6. See J. Kwoka & F. Warren–Boulton, Efficiencies, Failing Firms, and Alternatives to Merger: A Policy Synthesis, 31 Antitrust Bull 431, 445 (1986).

7. See W. Shughart & R. Tollison, The Welfare Basis of the "Failing Company" Doctrine, 30 Antitrust Bull. 357 (1985), which uses a model presented in A. Koutsoyiannis, Modern Microeconomics 186–189 (2d ed. 1979). Similar economic arguments can be found in T. Campbell, The Efficiency of the Failing Company Defense, 63 Tex. L. Rev. 251 (1984) (arguing that it is sometimes efficient); F. McChesney, Defending the Failing–Firm Defense, 65 Neb. L.Rev. 1 (1985); R.D. Friedman, Untangling the Failing Company Doctrine, 64 Tex. L. Rev. 1375 (1986). And see E.O. Correia, Re–Examining the Failing Company Defense, 64 Antitrust L.J. 683 (1996) (proposing significant relaxation of defense's requirements).

8. Figure 4 illustrates. MC_1 is the marginal cost function for a single plant, yielding a profit maximizing price of PMP_1. MC_2, which is precisely twice as high, is the *combined* marginal costs of the firm operating two identical plants. MC_2 produces a profit maximizing price of PMP_2, which is *double* the profit maximizing price of the firm running two identical plants, but considerably less than double PMP_1. The firm operating the two identical plants maximizes its profits from the joint output at PMP_x, which is half of PMP_2, and considerably less than PMP_1. The important variable is the steepness of the marginal cost curves. If the curves are steep, as in the figure, the monopolist maximizing its profits from the two plants together tends to cut output in each plant back into a range where marginal costs are much lower. By contrast, if the marginal cost curves are relatively flat, the gains from operating the two plants are much smaller. The illustration applies to two identical plants, but can be generalized to any pairing.

9. See Union Leader Corp. v. Newspapers of New England, Inc., 284 F.2d 582, 589–590 (1st Cir.1960), cert. denied, 365 U.S. 833, 81 S.Ct. 747 (1961) (stating failing company defense but in fact finding no injury to competition); FTC v. Great Lakes Chem. Corp., 528 F.Supp. 84, 96–98 (N.D.Ill.1981) (approving merger that would benefit

States assessed the requirement that before the failing company defense can be used, the defendant must show 1) that the acquired firm is almost certain to go bankrupt and cannot be reorganized successfully; and 2) that no less anticompetitive acquisition (i.e., by a smaller competitor or a noncompetitor) is available as an alternative.[10] The 1992 Horizontal Merger Guidelines generally adopt this position:

> A merger is not likely to create or enhance market power or facilitate its exercise if the following circumstances are met: 1) the allegedly failing firm would be unable to meet its financial obligations in the near future; 2) it would not be able to reorganize successfully under Chapter 11 of the Bankruptcy Act;[11] 3) it has made unsuccessful good-faith efforts to elicit reasonable alternative offers of acquisition of the assets of the failing firm[12] that would both keep its tangible and intangible assets in the relevant market and pose a less severe danger to competition than does the proposed merger; and 4) absent the acquisition, the assets of the failing firm would exit the relevant market.[13]

The fourth factor is an addition from the 1984 Guidelines, and suggests that the enforcement agencies are going to give assertions of the failing company defense even closer scrutiny than they have received in the past.

In addition to the failing company defense, the 1992 Guidelines also acknowledge a "failing division" defense, which might arise when a multidivisional firm decides to abandon a single, unprofitable market.[14] The Guidelines state:

> A similar argument can be made for "failing" divisions as for failing firms. First, upon applying appropriate cost allocation rules, the division must have a negative cash flow on an operating basis. Second, absent the acquisition, it must be shown that the assets of the division would exit the relevant market in the near future if not sold. Due to the ability of the parent firm to allocate costs, revenues, and intracompany transactions among itself and its subsidiaries and divisions, the Agency will require evidence, not based solely on management plans that could be prepared solely for the purpose of demonstrating negative cash flow or the prospect of exit from the relevant market. Third, the owner of the failing division also must have complied with the competitively-preferable purchaser requirement of Section 5.1 [the failing company defense].[15]

failing firm, its shareholders, and economy); Granader v. Public Bank, 281 F.Supp. 120 (E.D.Mich.1967), cert. denied, 397 U.S. 1065, 90 S.Ct. 1503 (1970) (defense accepted where bank failure would injure the public and alternative offers were unacceptable); United States v. M.P.M., 397 F.Supp. 78, 96 (D.Colo.1975) (defense accepted where failure was almost certain and attempts to find alternative transactions had failed).

10. 394 U.S. 131, 138, 89 S.Ct. 927, 931 (1969). The Newspaper Preservation Act, 15 U.S.C.A. §§ 1801–1804, permits "joint operating agreements" between two newspapers in the same city, and contains a weaker version of the "failing company" requirement. In order to enter into a JOA, the parties must show that at least one of the two newspapers "is in probable danger of financial failure * * *." See Michigan Citizens for an Independent Press v. Thornburgh, 868 F.2d 1285 (D.C.Cir.), affirmed by an equally divided Court, 493 U.S. 38, 110 S.Ct. 398 (1989), noting that the Act created a much broader defense than the antitrust failing company doctrine, and vested broad discretion in the Attorney General to approve newspaper joint ventures under the Act. See 4A Antitrust Law ¶ 955 (rev. ed. 1998).

11. 11 U.S.C.A. §§ 1101–1174.

12. The Guidelines note that "Any offer to purchase the assets of the failing firm for a price above the liquidation value of those assets—the highest valued use outside the relevant market or equivalent offer to purchase the stock of the failing firm—will be regarded as a reasonable alternative offer."

Cf. Olin Corp. v. FTC, 986 F.2d 1295, 1306–1307 (9th Cir.1993), cert. denied, 510 U.S. 1110, 114 S.Ct. 1051 (1994) (a preferable purchaser is required even though the acquired assets would have exited from the market if no purchaser could be found); Dr Pepper/Seven–Up Cos. v. FTC, 991 F.2d 859, 864–66 (D.C.Cir.1993) (rejecting FTC's refusal to allow failing company defense where it appeared that no other firm was interested in acquiring the allegedly failing company).

13. 1992 Merger Guidelines, § 5.1.

14. A few courts have acknowledged that the failing company defense might extend to a failing division. FTC v. Great Lakes Chem. Corp., 528 F.Supp. 84, 96 (N.D.Ill. 1981). See also Joseph Ciccone & Sons v. Eastern Indus., 537 F.Supp. 623, 629–630 (E.D.Pa.1982), concluding that the transfer of a plant that had been closed is legal under this defense. The acquired firm had already ceased doing business.

15. 1992 Merger Guidelines, § 5.2. See also 4A Antitrust Law ¶ 953e (rev. ed. 1998) (speaking of "failing subsidiary").

§ 12.10 Partial Acquisitions and Acquisitions "Solely for Investment"

Section 7 of the Clayton Act condemns the acquisition of the "whole or any part" of the stock or assets of another firm if the requisite anticompetitive effects result. However, the section does "not apply to persons purchasing * * * stock solely for investment * * *."

The antitrust laws are concerned with the effects of certain practices on competition, not with the ownership of corporations. Legal "control" of a corporation should therefore not necessarily be the threshold for considering partial acquisitions under the Clayton Act, and the Supreme Court has said as much.[1] As a general rule a person has legal control of a corporation if he owns and votes 50% or more of its shares. Realistically, however, ownership of far less than 50% will enable someone to have effective control of a corporation. In the case of a large corporation, ownership of 15% to 20% of the shares by one person could make him an enormous shareholder with tremendous influence in the buying, selling, entry and exit decisions of the corporation—particularly if all other shareholders were substantially smaller. The Supreme Court has not wasted much time deciding whether one company owned enough shares to have legal "control" of another company. More often than not, it has assumed control when the percentage of shares held was substantial. In United States v. E.I. du Pont de Nemours & Co.,[2] for example, it assumed that du Pont had substantial influence on General Motors' buying decisions even though du Pont owned only 23% of GM's shares.

Competition can be threatened, however, even if the acquiring firm's interest is so small that it has no influence at all over the acquired firm's decisions. Suppose that firms A and B are competitors and A acquires 15% of the shares of B. Clearly the competitive game has acquired a new twist. Under the rules of competition, A would like nothing better than to force B out of the market through A's greater efficiency. As a result of the partial acquisition, however, A suddenly has a strong financial interest in B's welfare. The risks of tacit or explicit collusion may increase dramatically.

There is one additional good reason for carefully scrutinizing stock acquisitions of less than a controlling interest. Granted that there is no "control," there is also no opportunity for the creation of efficiency. Mergers, you will recall, receive rather complex rule of reason treatment because they pose serious dangers of noncompetitive behavior on the one side, but have the potential to create substantial economies on the other. If A acquires 5% of the shares of its competitor B, A may not have enough equity to "control" B. Neither, however, will the firms have common management or other bases for obtaining the kinds of economies that make mergers socially valuable. In this case, the potential for social harm may be somewhat attenuated because the ownership interest is small—but the potential for social good has been reduced to nearly zero. That suggests a presumptive rule of condemnation.

Section 7 contains an explicit exemption for "persons purchasing * * * stock solely for investment and not using the same by voting or otherwise to bring about * * * the substantial lessening of competition." The exemption appears to give the fact finder the difficult job of determining whether a purchase was intended "solely for investment." The courts, however, have leaned toward a different position: if the purchase has a measurable anticompetitive effect, then it will not be considered "solely for investment," regardless of the subjective intent of the purchaser.[3] The result is that the "solely for investment" exception is really not much of an exception at all. Any stock purchase may be challenged on the grounds that

§ 12.10

1. Denver & Rio Grande West. R.R. v. United States, 387 U.S. 485, 501, 87 S.Ct. 1754, 1763 (1967) ("control" does not determine Clayton Act issue).

2. 353 U.S. 586, 77 S.Ct. 872 (1957). See also United States v. General Dynamics Corp., 415 U.S. 486, 94 S.Ct. 1186 (1974), where the acquiring firm owned 34% of the acquired firm's shares, but the parties agreed that there was "effective control."

3. See, e.g., Gulf & West. Indus. v. Great A & P Tea Co., 476 F.2d 687, 693 (2d Cir.1973).

it may substantially lessen competition. If it does so, then the "solely for investment" exception will not apply. If it does not substantially lessen competition, then the merger is not illegal in the first place. The exemption of acquisitions solely for investment has done nothing to simplify judicial evaluation of partial acquisitions.[4]

The problems presented by partial asset acquisitions are different than those presented by partial stock acquisitions. First, asset exchanges are the very heart of a market economy. If Xerox Corp. buys a Ford truck to make its deliveries, Xerox has acquired an "asset" from the Ford Motor Company. All firms, even competitors, exchange assets routinely as part of their business. The vast majority of such asset acquisitions pose no antitrust problems, particularly if they are purchases from the inventory of another firm. Antitrust policy becomes concerned with partial asset acquisitions when the asset that changes hands represents a measurable and relatively permanent transfer of market share or productive capacity from one firm to another.

Even here, however, partial asset acquisitions deserve somewhat different antitrust treatment than partial stock acquisitions. For example, if A purchases an unused plant from its competitor B, that purchase would not give A a continuing interest in B's welfare. In fact, a substantial asset acquisition might not affect competition very much at all. Suppose that A and B are the only competitors in a market. A owns two plants and B three. If A purchases one of B's plants, the result will be that A owns three plants and B two, and market concentration may be about the same after the acquisition as it was before.[5] If A had purchased 33% of B's shares, however, the effect on competition would probably be substantial.

An efficient market demands relatively free exchange of productive assets among competitors. In general, the more specialized the assets, the more essential it becomes that the assets can be purchased by a competitor. If a firm finds itself with more trucks than it needs, it may be able to sell them to a variety of other firms. However, if a business uses a specialized machine to grind optical lenses, the only available buyer may be another firm that makes similar lenses. Any rule that forbids too many transactions among competitors could cause a great amount of social waste.

The effect on competition of *total* asset acquisitions, however, is generally about the same as that of total stock acquisitions. For example, if A's rival has only one productive asset, a single plant, which A purchases, the transaction is likely to be as anticompetitive as a complete merger between the two firms. In fact, this was a common mechanism by which firms avoided application of § 7 before its 1950 Amendments, when the statute applied only to acquisitions of stock.[6]

Once again, the difficult problem for the policy maker is where to draw the line between legal and illegal asset acquisitions. One answer is that § 7 condemns only those acquisitions which "may * * * substantially * * * lessen competition." The trouble with that solution, however, is that analysis of whether an acquisition lessens competition requires an expensive study of the relevant markets and the competitive position of the firms involved.

Nevertheless, no shorter analysis has yet appeared that will effectively separate harmless from dangerous asset acquisitions. In general, if the asset acquisition appears on its face not to affect industrial concentration or the market share of its buyer, the acquisition will be treated as outside the scope of § 7. If it does tend to enlarge the market share or productive capacity of the acquiring firm, or if it increases concentration in the industry, then its effects on competition must be assessed.[7]

4. See 5 Antitrust Law ¶ 1204 (1980).

5. Indeed, horizontal partial asset acquisitions may *reduce* market concentration. Suppose A owns 8 plants, each of which produces 10% of the market. B owns 2 plants, each of which produces 10% of the market. A sells one plant to B. Pre-merger concentration measured under the HHI is $80^2 + 20^2$, or 6800. Post-merger concentration is $70^2 + 30^2$, or 5800.

6. See § 12.1.

7. Certain asset acquisitions may tend to increase concentration or give the acquiring firm a larger market share even though the asset acquisition itself does not increase productive capacity. Acquisition of a trademark,

§ 12.11 Interlocking Corporate Directors or Officers

An interlock of corporate directors or officers occurs when one person serves as director or officer of two different corporations. Such interlocks may be illegal under § 8 of the Clayton Act when the companies stand in such a relationship that an agreement eliminating competition among them would be an antitrust violation.[1] The statute then includes "safe harbor" thresholds, however, that exempt relatively small interlocks.[2]

If the standards are met, the legality of an interlock is determined by the status of a competition-eliminating agreement under *any* of the antitrust laws. That is to say, the interlock is illegal if price fixing agreements between the two corporations would be illegal, even though a merger between the two firms would probably be legal because market structure requirements are not satisfied.[3] So-called vertical interlocks are generally legal under the statute, since vertically related firms are not competitors.[4] Court have also held that interlocks of subsidiaries owned by the same parent are not covered.[5] This seems to be an implication of the Supreme Court's conclusion in *Copperweld* that corporations united by common ownership cannot be conspiring entities under § 1 of the Sherman Act.[6]

for example, would fall into this category. Section 7 should apply. See United States v. Lever Bros. Co., 216 F.Supp. 887, 889 (S.D.N.Y.1963), holding that a trademark is an "asset" for § 7 purposes; but in this case that the acquisition did not lessen competition.

§ 12.11

1. See 15 U.S.C.A. § 19: "No person shall, at the same time, serve as a director or officer in any two corporations (other than banks, banking associations, and trust companies) that are—

(A) engaged in whole or in part in commerce; and

(B) by virtue of their business and location of operation, competitors, so that the elimination of competition by agreement between them would constitute a violation of any of the antitrust laws. * * *"

2. The statute exempts interlocks unless each firm has $10 million in capital, surplus or other undistributed profits. Even then, firms are exempted if (1) the competitive sales of either are less than $1 million annually; (2) competitive sales of either are less than 2% of that corporation's sales; or (3) the competitive sales of each corporation are less than 4% of that corporation's sales. Note the difference between (2) and (3). Under (2) an interlock is exempted if one firm's competitive sales are less than 2% of that firm's sales, even if 100% of the sales of the other firm are competitive. Under (3) an interlock is exempt if for both firms, say, 3.8% of sales are competitive. Finally, the statute provides that the dollar thresholds shall be changed annually by a percentage equal to the percentage change in the Gross National Product. See Antitrust Law ¶ 1301' (current Supp.).

3. United States v. Sears, Roebuck & Co., 111 F.Supp. 614 (S.D.N.Y.1953) (forbidding one person from serving as director of both Sears and Goodrich, both of which sell tires).

4. Paramount Pictures Corp. v. Baldwin–Montrose Chemical Co., 1966 Trade Cas. ¶ 71678 (S.D.N.Y.).

5. Pocahontas Supreme Coal Co. v. Bethlehem Steel Corp., 1986–1 Trade Cas. ¶ 67,111, 1986 WL 957 (S.D.W.Va.1986), affirmed, 828 F.2d 211 (4th Cir.1987).

6. Copperweld Corp. v. Independence Tube Corp., 467 U.S. 752, 104 S.Ct. 2731 (1984). See § 4.7.

Chapter 13

CONGLOMERATE MERGERS

Table of Sections

§ 13.1 Introduction: Competition and Conglomerate Mergers

A merger that is neither horizontal nor vertical is generally called "conglomerate." Although the word "conglomerate" suggests a union of completely unrelated products or activities, antitrust law has been relatively unconcerned with so-called "pure" conglomerate mergers. Most of the conglomerate mergers subject to antitrust scrutiny are between firms that stand in a relatively close market relationship to each other. For example, mergers between firms that manufacture the same product but sell it in different geographic markets are called "market extension" mergers. Mergers between firms that sell different products that are somehow identified or related to each other are called "product extension" mergers.

In *Winslow*,[1] the Supreme Court held that the Sherman Act did not apply to a conglomerate merger—in this case, a merger among manufacturers of different types of shoe making machinery into the United Shoe Machinery Corp. One of the merging firms made lasting machines, another welt-sewing machines and a third outsole-stitching machines. These products were complementary, not competing. A shoe maker that wanted a fully automated factory would need at least one of each. Justice Holmes concluded that no competition was eliminated among the merging firms, and that "[i]t is as lawful for one corporation to make every part of a steam engine and to put the machine together as it would be for one to make the boilers and another to make the wheels. * * * "[2]

Whether Congress ever intended to broaden § 7 to include conglomerate mergers is unclear. The legislative history of original § 7 gives virtually no indication of Congressional concern. Further, its language applied only to competition "between" the acquiring and acquired firms, thus suggesting a concern only

§ 13.1

1. United States v. Sidney W. Winslow, 227 U.S. 202, 33 S.Ct. 253 (1913).

2. Id. at 217–218, 33 S.Ct. at 254–255.

with horizontal mergers.[3] A little evidence, not particularly convincing, suggests that Congress did intend to include conglomerate mergers in the coverage of amended § 7 in 1950.[4] Whatever Congress intended, the reach of § 7 to such mergers is now clearly established. Courts have generally interpreted § 7 as being concerned with mergers that threaten "competition," however, and not with mere size as such (although courts have occasionally come close to condemning mere size). Injury to competition is unlikely unless a particular kind of market relationship exists between the merging firms, or between the post-merger firm and its customers or competitors.

Today, conglomerate mergers are not generally regarded as the competitive threat that they were perceived to be in the 1970s. The high point of American corporate diversification was 1975, but since that time large firms have shown a general tendency to strip themselves of truly unrelated product or service lines and concentrate on their most central line of products.[5]

At the same time, most of the theories under which conglomerate mergers are challenged have either fallen into disrepute or been characterized as unmanageable or excessively speculative. The 1980s and 1990s have witnessed a great reduction in cases challenging such mergers. Except for a few challenges by the Federal Trade Commission,[6] there has been very little activity.[7]

§ 13.2 Conglomerate Mergers and Efficiency

In general, the closer the market relationship between two firms, the greater the efficiencies that can be obtained by merger. By definition, conglomerate mergers involve firms that are not competitors and that do not have a significant buyer-seller relationship with each other. As a result, the efficiencies available from conglomerate mergers may not be as large as the efficiencies that can be obtained from horizontal mergers that enable the post-merger firm to attain minimum optimal size or significant multiplant or distributional economies. Likewise, conglomerate mergers do not produce efficiencies of the same magnitude as vertical mergers that facilitate distribution savings by eliminating market transactions.

Nonetheless, conglomerate mergers can yield efficiencies, depending on the relationship between the merging firms. For example, if the two firms produce related, complementary products that are commonly purchased together, such as laundry soap and bleach, the post-merger firm might be able to distribute the two products together more cheaply than two independent firms could each distribute them before.

Product extension mergers can also enable a firm to save money on advertising, by working two related products into the same advertisement. Further, name recognition derived from advertising can sometimes be spread to additional products. For example, a firm such as Procter & Gamble may spend a great deal of money obtaining recognition of its name for a half dozen related household cleaning products. Once consumer recognition is established, however, P & G might easily be able to add a seventh product to the list. The benefits of past advertising that has created a favorable impression of the first six products in the minds of consumers will spread to the seventh product as well.[1]

3. Clayton Act, Pub. L. No. 63–212, ch. 323, § 7, 38 Stat. 730, 731–732 (1914).

4. See J. Brodley, Potential Competition Mergers: A Structural Synthesis, 87 Yale L.J. 1, 43–44 (1977).

5. See F.M. Scherer & D. Ross, Industrial Market Structure and Economic Performance 90–91 (3d ed. 1990).

6. In re Roche Holding Ltd., 5 Trade reg. Rep. (CCH) ¶ 22879 at 22563 (1990) (consent decree); In re Atlantic Richfield Co., 5 Trade Reg. Rep. (CCH) ¶ 22878 at 22562 (1990) (same); In re Institut Merieux, SA, 5 Trade Reg. Rep. (CCH) ¶ 22779 at 22,505 (1990) (same).

7. But see Alberta Gas Chems. Ltd. v. E.I. Du Pont De nemours & Co., 826 F.2d 1235, 1254 (3d Cir.1987), cert. denied, 486 U.S. 1059, 108 S.Ct. 2830 (1988), where a dissenter would have condemned a privately challenged merger on potential entrant grounds.

§ 13.2

1. Efforts to attach pre-existing goodwill or name recognition to a new product will generally be more successful if advertising has a durable, or capital, quality that lasts a long time. See § 12.6b3.

Similar efficiencies can accrue from market extension mergers. If firms selling the same product in different geographic areas merge, the post-merger firm might be able to coordinate buying of materials, marketing, transportation, and production much more efficiently than each firm alone could do.

In addition are several economies of scale or scope that are available to larger or diversified firms. Research and development can have spillover benefits into a number of areas that might be unrelated in the market.[2] Larger firms can hire their own accountants, economists, statisticians, lawyers and other specialists, while smaller firms must buy these services in the marketplace. In short, certain economies can be achieved by "pure" size, regardless of whether the products of the merging firms are related. This is so because certain kinds of inputs (such as accounting services) are generic to a wide variety of products.

The conglomerate firm can often raise capital internally, without relying on the market. An independent firm short of money must generally enter the capital market, disclose information to outsider lenders or equity buyers, and permit outsiders to evaluate the risks and rewards of investment. Further, the firm must incur all the transaction costs that dealing on the capital market entails. The conglomerate, by contrast, is more likely to be operating in some areas that need capital and in others that are producing excess revenue. It may be able to internalize the entire process of financing new development, simply by shifting money from one division to another.[3]

Courts have long recognized that conglomerate mergers can create efficiency. They have not always been sympathetic, however. The post-merger firm's increased efficiency has sometimes become the rationale for condemning, rather than upholding, a merger. For example, in F.T.C. v. Procter & Gamble Co., the Supreme Court condemned a merger between a major producer of household detergents and cleansers and a major producer of household liquid bleach. One of the reasons the Court cited was that Procter & Gamble could take advantage of "volume discounts" in advertising and therefore market bleach more cheaply than competing bleach producers could.[4] Likewise in Allis-Chalmers Mfg. Co. v. White Consolidated Indus.,[5] the Third Circuit condemned a merger between a company that made electrical equipment and a company that made rolling mills, used in the manufacture of steel. The rolling mills required elaborate electric hook-ups, and generally a purchaser of a rolling mill needed to obtain its electrical hook-up from a different seller. The merger enabled the post-merger firm to become "the only company capable of designing, producing and installing a complete metal rolling mill." The creation of a company that could deliver the entire package, the court concluded, "would raise higher the already significant barriers to the entry of others into the various segments of the metal rolling mill market." Clearly the "entry barrier" that the Court had in mind was the post-merger firm's increased efficiency. Nothing is a more effective barrier to entry than a firm's capacity to produce a high quality product at a low price, or to provide improved service to its customers.

2. See R.R. Nelson, The Simple Economics of Basic Scientific Research, 67 J.Pol.Econ. 297 (Jun.1959). The "Nelson hypothesis" is that research and development is more profitable for diversified firms than for more homogeneous ones.

3. For the same reason, firms often diversify to reduce risk. For example, they might develop some high profit areas that are quite vulnerable to economic recession, but buy "insurance" by investing in other areas that, while less profitable in the peaks, are relatively more secure in bad economic times. On the relationship between corporate size, diversity and risk, see F.M. Scherer & D. Ross, Industrial Market Structure and Economic Performance 127–130 (3d ed. 1990). For further discussion of the kinds of efficiency that can be achieved by conglomeration, see Y. Brozen, Concentration, Mergers, and Public Policy 350–58 (1982).

4. 386 U.S. 568, 579, 87 S.Ct. 1224, 1230 (1967).

5. 414 F.2d 506, 515–518 (3d Cir.1969), cert. denied, 396 U.S. 1009, 90 S.Ct. 567 (1970). See also Parrish's Cake Decorating Supplies v. Wilton Enters., 1984–1 Trade Cas. ¶ 65,917, 1984 WL 2942 (N.D.Ill.1984), modified, 1985–1 Trade Cas. ¶ 66630, 1985 WL 25751 (N.D.Ill.1985), which enjoined a merger on the theory that the parent company would give the acquired firm low interest money and promotional services that would give it an advantage over rivals.

Today, courts are less likely to condemn a merger merely because it increases the efficiency of the post-merger firm. Nevertheless, the courts have never developed a general "efficiency defense" in conglomerate merger cases. Although economists can produce dozens of reasons why conglomerate mergers produce efficiency, measurement of the cost savings that result from a particular merger is extremely difficult, certainly in litigation.[6]

Rather, antitrust law searches for ways to identify those mergers that threaten competition. These are condemned, even though they may produce significant economies. Mergers that are unlikely to increase the market power of the post-merger firm and that will probably not facilitate collusion, oligopoly behavior or inefficient exclusionary practices are generally left alone.

§ 13.3 Perceived Dangers to Competition

Courts have perceived two broad categories of dangers to competition from conglomerate mergers. First, the conglomerate merger, like the horizontal merger, may facilitate collusion or oligopoly pricing by eliminating *potential* (rather than actual) competition between the merging firms. Most of the case law condemning product extension and market extension mergers relies on this rationale, which is discussed below in § 13.4.

Second, conglomerate mergers have been condemned because courts believed they would facilitate inefficient exclusionary practices directed at outsiders, such as reciprocity, tying or predatory pricing. The risk that a conglomerate merger will increase the likelihood of such practices is usually more imagined than real. Further, while the precedent for condemning conglomerate mergers on these grounds is well established, most of it is quite old and no longer used.

6. On the efficiency defense in horizontal merger cases, see § 12.2.

§ 13.3a. Reciprocity

Reciprocity, or reciprocal dealing, occurs when Firm A buys from Firm B and Firm B buys from Firm A.[1] Most reciprocity is purely fortuitous, or at least noncontractual. Firms commonly consider it "good business" to buy from their customers when they have the opportunity, provided that price and quality are competitive. For example, if Bethlehem Steel Corp. provides Ford Motor Company with steel, executives at Bethlehem are likely to buy trucks from Ford.

Economically, reciprocity functions in much the same way as the tying arrangement.[2] A firm cannot enlarge its monopoly profits by nondiscriminatory reciprocity. For example, if a firm is already selling widgets at their profit-maximizing price it cannot increase its profits by forcing customers to sell it gidgets in return at less than the competitive price. The customers will treat the loss on gidgets as an increase in the price of widgets.

Reciprocity can facilitate price discrimination. Suppose that a firm with a certain amount of market power has been selling widgets at $3.00 but has a chance to fill a very large order at a price of $2.80. If it is prevented by customer outrage or the Robinson–Patman Act from making the sale at $2.80, it might agree with the large buyer to a $3.00 price but purchase something from the large buyer in return, paying a supracompetitive price. This type of reciprocity is common, and often buyers and sellers use it to "get together" on a price. It generally facilitates transactions and is procompetitive.

Reciprocity agreements might also be used to avoid statutory price regulation. For example, Firm A might sell a price-regulated product to Firm B at the regulated price but buy something from Firm B in return. The reciprocal product would be priced at more than or less than the competitive price, depending on the relationship between the regulated firm's price and Firm A's profit-maximizing price in the regulated product.

§ 13.3

1. On reciprocity, see § 10.7; and 10 Antitrust Law ¶¶ 1775–1779 (1996).

2. See generally Ch. 10.

But the great majority of reciprocity agreements are pro-competitive. Sometimes reciprocity reduces direct operating costs, such as when Firm A can deliver a truckload of material to Firm B's plant and return with a load of B's product rather than with an empty truck. Reciprocity can also reduce transaction costs and uncertainty costs by limiting the number of outside firms with which a company deals.[3] Finally, reciprocity often serves to undermine collusion by enabling firms to "cheat" on the cartel or oligopoly price. A cartel member or oligopolist may be unable to reduce the cartel price in order to obtain a sale, but it might be willing to buy something back from the buyer at an inflated price. Such "cheating" is probably a common rationale for reciprocity in oligopolistic markets. By the same token, condemning a merger in an oligopolistic market on the ground that it might facilitate reciprocity probably operates to facilitate, rather than undermine, oligopoly behavior in that market.[4]

In spite of reciprocity's efficiency, courts have often viewed it with skepticism. They have termed reciprocity "coercive" when a firm refuses to buy from others who refuse to buy from it. Such coercive dealing has been analogized to tying arrangements and has been condemned under both § 5 of the FTC Act and § 1 of the Sherman Act.[5]

Mergers can facilitate two different varieties of reciprocity. First, a merger of two firms often increases the amount of reciprocal dealings that the two firms have with each other. For example, if a truck manufacturer purchases its own steel mill, the manufacturer likely will obtain its steel from the steel mill, and the steel mill will obtain its trucks from its parent truck plant. In such a case, the two firms stand in a buyer-supplier relationship with each other, and the union is a vertical merger.[6] The reciprocity that results is "intra-enterprise" once the merger occurs. As a result, the reciprocity itself generally raises no antitrust issues, although the resulting foreclosure of rivals may.

The second kind of reciprocity exists between the post-merger firm and other buyers or suppliers who were not a party to the merger. Conglomerate mergers generally increase the potential for reciprocity because the post-merger firm sells in more markets than it did before the merger. This creates more avenues through which reciprocity can occur.

In FTC v. Consolidated Foods Corp.,[7] the Supreme Court condemned a merger under § 7 on the theory that the merger facilitated reciprocity with third parties. Consolidated Foods operated food processing plants as well as wholesale and retail food stores. It acquired Gentry Inc., which manufactured dehydrated onion and garlic that were commonly used in processed food. During the ten years following the acquisition, Consolidated frequently urged its suppliers of processed food to purchase their dehydrated onion and garlic from Gentry. The Court found "that the 'reciprocity' made possible by such an acquisition is one of the congeries of anticompetitive practices at which the antitrust laws are aimed."

Justice Douglas rejected the view that post-acquisition evidence of actual, coercive reciprocity was necessary to condemn a merger on this ground. Such a rule would permit acquisitions to "go forward willy-nilly, the parties biding their time until reciprocity was allowed fully to bloom." No one "acquiring a company with reciprocal buying opportunities is entitled to a 'free trial' period." Rather, the acquisition can be condemned immediately if there is a "probability" that reciprocity will occur. Then Justice Douglas concluded:

> We do not go so far as to say that any acquisition, no matter how small, violates § 7 if there is a probability of reciprocal buying. Some situations may amount only to *de minimis*. But where, as here, the acquisition is of a company that commands a substantial share of the market, a finding of probability of reciprocal buying by the

3. See § 10.8.

4. Ibid.; and see 10 Antitrust Law ¶ 1777b (1995).

5. Ibid.

6. See § 9.4.

7. 380 U.S. 592, 594, 85 S.Ct. 1220, 1221–22 (1965).

Commission * * * should be honored if there is substantial evidence to support it.[8]

Consolidated Foods appears to hold that if reciprocal buying is "probable," and if the acquired company "commands a substantial share of the market," the merger is illegal under § 7. This standard would condemn almost any merger in which substantial reciprocity is likely to occur.[9] Further, the *Consolidated Foods* standard condemns reciprocity-facilitating mergers before it is clear that reciprocity will occur, or whether it will be anticompetitive when it does occur. But not only is reciprocity almost always efficient, the occasional instance of anticompetitive reciprocity can be reached under § 1 of the Sherman Act. The doctrine of *Consolidated Foods* was formulated at a time when the Supreme Court believed that tying arrangements contained almost no potential for good and were certain to cause harm. They responded with a virtual *per se* rule.[10] Justice Douglas' broad observation that reciprocity is one of the "congeries of anticompetitive practices at which the antitrust laws are aimed" reveals the same attitude toward reciprocity agreements.[11]

When a court scrutinizes reciprocity under the Sherman Act, it can balance the efficiency effects of a particular reciprocity agreement against any competitive injury. The Clayton § 7 standard, which condemns a merger because of its potential for reciprocity, pre-empts the opportunity for this kind of case-by-case analysis. Further, it ignores the fact that the merger itself may create substantial efficiencies. The standard assessed in *Consolidated Foods* condemns *all* instances of "substantial" reciprocity that will "probably" occur. Firms generally have been able to defend only by showing that reciprocity would not occur—not by showing that there are compensating efficiencies or that reciprocity, if it occurs, will not be anticompetitive.

Current policy is to the contrary. Although the 1968 Merger Guidelines[12] still noted reciprocity as a rationale for challenging conglomerate mergers, the 1984 Guidelines say nothing. The government enforcement agencies have not challenged a merger under the reciprocity theory in several years and seem disinclined to do so now.

§ 13.3b. Leverage and Tie–Ins

Conglomerate mergers can sometimes facilitate tying arrangements. A film manufacturer's merger with a film processor, for example, might make it easier for the firm to tie film processing to film sales.

The important question for the antitrust policy maker is, Why § 7? Both § 3 of the Clayton Act and § 1 of the Sherman Act reach actual tying arrangements with substantial overdeterrence to spare. Should a merger be condemned simply because it increases the probability that a firm will engage in tying? As Chapter 10 notes, Supreme Court decisions since the late 1970's have been far less hostile toward tying arrangements than earlier decisions, and have acknowledged their potential to create efficiencies.[13] This reduces even further the need to condemn conglomerate mergers simply because they make tying possible. Further, § 3 of the Clayton Act contains the same "may * * * substantially * * * lessen competition" language as § 7, and should permit direct analysis of the competitive effects of any tying that might actually result.

§ 13.3c. Strategic Pricing and Entry Deterrence

A firm generally cannot "finance" predatory pricing in one market by raising prices in

8. Id. at 598–600, 85 S.Ct. at 1224–25.

9. See United States v. International Tel. & Tel. Corp., 306 F.Supp. 766 (D.Conn.1969). If a company can point to a history of taking competitive bids for all relevant purchases, and of accepting the lowest bid, then reciprocity will be merely fortuitous. See J. Bauer, Challenging Conglomerate Mergers Under Section 7 of the Clayton Act: Today's Law and Tomorrow's Legislation, 58 B.U.L.Rev. 199, 231 (1978).

10. See Northern Pacif. Rwy. Co. v. United States, 356 U.S. 1, 6, 78 S.Ct. 514, 518 (1958). See the discussion of efficiency and tying arrangements in § 10.5e.

11. *Consolidated Foods*, 380 U.S. at 594, 85 S.Ct. at 1221.

12. Department of Justice 1968 Merger Guidelines, §§ 19, 20, 4 Trade Reg. Rep. (CCH) ¶ 13101.

13. For example, Jefferson Parish Hosp. Dist. No. 2 v. Hyde, 466 U.S. 2, 104 S.Ct. 1551 (1984).

another market. A profit-maximizing firm will already be selling in each market at its profit-maximizing price for that market.[14] However, predatory behavior may be more rewarding for the multi-market seller. By predating a rival into submission in one market, for example, the firm can "send a message" to competitors in other markets.[15] Thus a dominant firm selling in three different geographic or product markets might predate against a rival in one market and at the same time warn competitors in the other two markets that they should not cut prices. Predatory pricing might be more rational in such a case, because the predator could reap post-predation monopoly profits in three different markets instead of one.

Courts have occasionally cited the possibility of predatory pricing as a reason for condemning a merger. In general, the theory has not been the one outlined above. Rather they have suggested that the merger introduced into the market a giant firm with a deep pocket that could afford extended periods of loss selling.[16]

Such theories stretch § 7 liability beyond any reasonable limit. *All* mergers produce a firm that is larger after the merger than before. Likewise, by definition all conglomerate mergers increase the number of markets in which the post-merger firm sells. If the predatory pricing rationale is not to become a *per se* rule against mergers, some principled way must be found for determining when the dangers of predatory pricing or other price-related strategic behavior are sufficient to warrant condemnation.

Most economists today believe that true predatory pricing is quite rare. No empirical data suggests that predation by multi-market firms is unusually common. To be sure, one result of any merger can be a price reduction. But the reduction results from the merger's increased efficiency, not from its predation.[17] To condemn a merger too quickly on the grounds that it might facilitate predatory pricing would undermine the most central goal of the antitrust laws—high quality and low consumer prices. If predatory pricing occurs, it can be condemned under the more appropriate standards of § 2 of the Sherman Act or the Robinson–Patman Act.[18] At a minimum, however, before any merger is condemned on the theory that it might facilitate predatory pricing, the court must ensure that the structural prerequisites for predatory pricing are present;[19] further, there must be other evidence that predation is really on the agenda of the post-merger firm.[20] The 1984 Merger Guidelines, under which the Antitrust Division continues to analyze conglomerate mergers, generally ignore the possibility of predatory pricing as a rationale for condemning conglomerate mergers.

Somewhat more subtle is the possibility that a conglomerate merger might increase the firm's ability to deter entry, thus facilitating monopoly pricing. For example, product differentiation may deter entry, and conglomerate mergers may be a way of achieving more substantial product differentiation.[21] The 1992 Horizontal Merger Guidelines briefly address this concern in their consideration of mergers in product differentiated markets.[22] Although the 1992 Guidelines expressly apply to "horizontal" mergers, classifying mergers in product differentiated markets is a question of degree.[23] As the Guidelines suggest, a merger of firms producing "adjacent" products in a product differentiated market may facilitate a post-merger price increase, if remaining rivals

14. See § 8.8.

15. See § 8.3b.

16. See Reynolds Metals Co. v. FTC, 309 F.2d 223, 229–230 (D.C.Cir.1962); United States v. Aluminum Co. (Cupples), 233 F.Supp. 718, 727 (E.D.Mo.1964), affirmed mem., 382 U.S. 12, 86 S.Ct. 24 (1965); and see Purex Corp. v. Procter & Gamble Co., 596 F.2d 881, 887–88 (9th Cir.1979), appeal after remand, 664 F.2d 1105 (9th Cir. 1981), cert. denied, 456 U.S. 983, 102 S.Ct. 2256 (1982).

17. See H. Hovenkamp, Merger Actions for Damages, 35 Hastings L.J. 937 (1984).

18. See generally Ch. 8.

19. See § 8.4.

20. See § 16.3a.

21. On product differentiation and entry deterrence, see § 7.8.

22. See § 12.3d of this book.

23. See id., § 12.5b.

offer a product that is substantially different from that of the post-merger firm.

§ 13.4 Mergers of Potential Competitors

Most conglomerate mergers, particularly the product extension and market extension varieties, are analyzed under two versions of the "potential competition" doctrine.

"Potential" competition is a misnomer. Potential competition is really actual competition assessed from the supply side rather than the demand side. As Chapter 3 indicated, a firm's market power is limited by two things: consumer response to a price increase *and* new entry by competitors in search of higher profits. A firm's knowledge that its price increase will flood the market with new sellers is competition just as "actual" as its knowledge that a price increase will cause a loss of many customers.

The separate standard for potential competition mergers developed at a time when antitrust policy makers equated "competition" with a large number of firms in a market. Within that paradigm, "competition" did not exist in a market with only one producer, even though the producer had absolutely no power to raise price above marginal cost without causing substantial new entry. Today antitrust law has generally adopted the economist's more useful definition of competition as that set of market conditions that drives prices toward marginal cost. In this sense, the "potential competition" doctrine survives as a relic of an earlier era.[1]

The potential competition merger is best viewed as a very special case of the horizontal merger. The merger is condemned, if at all, because of its tendency to facilitate oligopolistic pricing or collusion in the post-merger market. The chief difference between the potential competition merger and the conventional horizontal merger is that the former focuses almost exclusively on elasticity of supply and the conditions of entry. The cross-elasticity of demand between the products produced by the merging firms is sufficiently low that they are regarded as being in separate relevant markets.

The Supreme Court first applied the term "potential competition" to a merger in United States v. El Paso Natural Gas Co.[2] The case illustrates the imperceptible distinction that often exists between "actual" and "potential" competition. El Paso was the only out-of-state supplier of natural gas to California, and it sold more than 50% of the gas consumed there. In 1956 El Paso began acquiring the stock of Pacific Northwest, a natural gas company that had bid to make sales into California but had never actually sold gas there. El Paso and Pacific Northwest had often competed for California contracts, however, and El Paso had occasionally revised a bid downward in order to retain customers who had gotten more favorable offers from Pacific Northwest. The Court condemned the merger, observing that "unsuccessful bidders are no less competitors than the successful one," and that the "presence of two or more suppliers" gave the buyers a choice, even though only one of the suppliers could ultimately be chosen.

A natural gas pipeline serving a single city might be a natural monopoly. In that case, the market would be served most efficiently by a single supplier at any given time. The market itself is "contestable," however.[3] Dozens of suppliers could offer bids for the opportunity to build the pipeline, and if there were true competition among the bidders, the resulting price would be competitive. El Paso had simply won all past bids. For future bids El Paso still had to contend with the competition of Pacific Northwest, until the merger eliminated Pacific

§ 13.4

1. For some insights into the two meanings of "competition" see D. Dewey, Monopoly in Economics and Law (1959); E. Mason, Monopoly in Law and Economics, 47 Yale L.J. 34 (1937); and see H. Hovenkamp, Book Review, 33 Hastings L.J. 755, 762 (1982).

2. 376 U.S. 651, 84 S.Ct. 1044 (1964). In the same year the Supreme Court held that the potential competition doctrine applied to a joint venture between noncompetitors. United States v. Penn–Olin Chem. Co., 378 U.S. 158, 84 S.Ct. 1710 (1964), on remand, 246 F.Supp. 917 (D.Del. 1965). Joint ventures and competition are discussed in chapter 5.

3. On "contestable" markets, see § 1.4b.

Northwest as a competitor. Pacific Northwest was an "actual" competitor, even though it was not making any sales into the California market.

A more typical potential competition case is FTC v. Procter & Gamble Co.,[4] in which the Supreme Court condemned P&G's acquisition of Clorox. P&G manufactured a wide variety of household products including cleansers and detergents, but not bleach. Clorox manufactured only bleach. In spite of evidence that P&G never intended to enter the bleach market on its own, the Court found that P&G was the "most likely entrant" into the market. Its acquisition of Clorox, however, foreclosed any possibility of *de novo* entry. Furthermore, the bleach market itself was concentrated, with Clorox controlling 50% of the national market, and the top two firms together controlling 65%.[5]

The Supreme Court did little to clarify the theory of potential competition in the *P&G* case. Justice Douglas was more concerned with the possibility that the post-merger firm would obtain advertising discounts and injure competitors by its lower costs than any likelihood that the merger would facilitate collusion among bleach producers. Such collusion, of course, would be a benefit, not a detriment, to other bleach firms in the market. It would injure consumers, who would either pay a higher price for bleach, or else find a less satisfactory substitute.

§ 13.4a. The Perceived Potential Entrant Doctrine

The Supreme Court articulated a more complete theory of potential competition mergers in 1973, in United States v. Falstaff Brewing Corp..[6] The government challenged a merger between Falstaff, the nation's fourth largest brewer, which made no sales in New England, and Narragansett, the largest regional brewer in New England, having about 20% of that market.

The government pleaded that Falstaff was a potential entrant into the New England market. Had it entered that market *de novo*, or else by a "toe-hold" acquisition of a smaller firm in the New England market, the result would have been increased competition. The district court dismissed the complaint, finding that Falstaff would never have entered the market unless it could have acquired an important brewer with an established distribution network.

The Supreme Court reversed, but rejected the theory offered by the government. The important factor, concluded the Court, was not whether Falstaff subjectively planned to enter the New England market, but whether beer producers in New England *believed* that Falstaff was a potential entrant and behaved more competitively in order to deter its entry.

This "perceived potential entrant" doctrine as formulated in *Falstaff* begins with a "target" market that is highly concentrated and conducive to monopolistic or oligopolistic pricing. The incumbent sellers' inclination to raise prices is restrained, however, by the presence of a large and capable firm poised on the "edge" of the market, eager to enter should the market appear profitable enough. A firm on the "edge" of the market could be either a maker of a related or complimentary product, as in the *P&G* case, or else it could be the seller of the same product in a different geographic market, as in the *Falstaff* case. Thus the perceived potential entrant's presence has the effect of keeping prices lower and output higher than they would otherwise be.

The restraint on pricing disappears, however, if the large firm on the edge of the market acquires one of the larger firms within the market. The target market will still be conducive to oligopoly pricing, but now there is no longer a firm on the edge of the market, threatening to enter if prices rise too high. As a result, output in the target market may be reduced and prices will rise. If the theory is correct, such a merger would fall within the

4. 386 U.S. 568, 87 S.Ct. 1224 (1967).

5. However, there were some 200 smaller producers, many of whom undoubtedly could have increased output in response to a price increase.

6. 410 U.S. 526, 93 S.Ct. 1096 (1973), mandate conformed to, 383 F.Supp. 1020 (D.R.I.1974).

language of § 7 condemning mergers the effect of which "may be substantially to lessen competition * * *."

The plausibility of the perceived potential entrant doctrine is controversial, however. Most applications of the doctrine rest on a complex theory of "limit pricing." Under the theory, the firms within the market charge a price lower than their short-run profit-maximizing price in order to deter the entry of the firm sitting on the edge of the market. Whether such a limit pricing strategy is profitable for an incumbent with market power is debatable.[7] In this case, the limit pricing is carried out not by a unitary monopolist but by a small group of firms in a concentrated market. In *Falstaff*, for example, the acquired firm was the leading seller of beer in New England; however, it still had only 20% of the market. Absent an express agreement, coordination of a "limit price" among five or more sellers seems all but impossible.[8]

That hurdle aside, the perceived potential entrant theory applies only under well-defined conditions. First, the target market must be concentrated and must appear conducive to oligopolistic pricing. Second, the acquiring firm must either be the only perceived potential entrant, or else the number of perceived potential entrants must be sufficiently small that the elimination of the acquiring firm will affect pricing in the market. Finally, the merger itself must not increase competition within the target market significantly, or else the doctrine would be counterproductive.

If a market is already behaving competitively, the presence of a potential entrant will have no effect on output and pricing in the market. Courts generally have been consistent in requiring that the target market be highly concentrated and conducive to oligopoly before the perceived potential entrant doctrine will apply.[9]

A market is conducive to collusion or oligopoly pricing only if it contains substantial barriers to entry. If entry is easy and a new entrant can operate as cheaply as an incumbent, any monopoly price will result in competitive entry. Entry barriers in potential competition cases present a paradox, however. They must be present, or else the market will perform competitively and the presence of any potential entrant will be irrelevant. However, an acquiring firm cannot itself be barred by the entry barriers, or it could not reasonably be perceived as a potential entrant. For example, if local law permitted only three banks in a community and three already existed, no outside bank could be a perceived potential entrant. It would have to enter, if at all, by acquiring one of the three banks already in the market.[10]

In Tenneco, Inc. v. FTC[11] the Second Circuit refused to condemn a merger between Tenneco, a large manufacturer of auto parts, which did not manufacture automobile shock absorbers, and Monroe, a leading shock absorber manufacturer. The court found "substantial" barriers to entry in the replacement shock absorber market, the most significant of which it identified as "economies of scale." Minimum efficient scale for a plant in the industry was 6,000,000 units annually, which was about 10% of annual total sales. The court also identified as barriers "the need for technology and marketing skills peculiar to the industry" and high start-up costs that would result from the "significant time lag" between a firm's decision to build a plant and its attainment of a profitable share of the market.

The court found that Tenneco had actively considered entering the shock absorber market but would not enter *de novo* because start-up costs were too high in proportion to earnings during the early years. In short, the entry barriers may have explained why the target market was not performing competitively, but

7. See § 8.3b.

8. See G. Stigler, The Organization of Industry 20–22 (1983 ed.); 5 Antitrust Law ¶ 1120b (1980).

9. See United States v. Marine Bancorporation, 418 U.S. 602, 630–31, 94 S.Ct. 2856, 2874–75 (1974).

10. See Marine Bancorporation, 418 U.S. at 628, 94 S.Ct. at 2873.

11. 689 F.2d 346 (2d Cir.1982).

they also excluded Tenneco from consideration as a potential entrant.[12]

The perceived potential entrant doctrine makes sense only if the number of potential entrants is limited. If a market contains three firms but a dozen are sitting on the edge, the elimination by merger of one of the firms on the edge will not affect performance in the market. Eleven potential entrants remain. In *Procter & Gamble* the Supreme Court based its holding in part on a finding that "the number of potential entrants was not so large that the elimination of one would be insignificant."[13]

The Court provided no guidelines, however, for determining how few potential entrants there must be, or how likely it must be that any or all of them would enter in response to a price increase. Some scholars regard this kind of measurement as far beyond the capacity of any court. Richard Posner concluded that there "is no practical method of ranking, even crudely, the potential competitors in a market for the purpose of identifying a set of most likely or most feared entrants."[14] Simply to say that the doctrine applies only to the "most likely" *de novo* entrant will not do—for as soon as the "most likely" entrant is eliminated by merger, another most likely entrant will take its place. About the best a court can do is compare the target market before and after the merger. In some cases, it might try to determine whether the acquiring firm did in fact restrain prices before the merger took place, and whether any similar firm was restraining them after the merger occurred. Simply stating the phenomenon that needs measurement, however, suggests how unmanageable the problem is.[15]

Finally, a merger should not be condemned on potential competition grounds if the merger substantially increases actual competition in the target market. This often happens when the acquired company is not the dominant firm in the market. Suppose that an oligopolistic market contains four firms with market shares of 50%, 25%, 15%, and 10%. The market is clearly conducive to price leadership; furthermore, the supracompetitive pricing might be restrained by the perceived presence of a large firm on the edge of the market. The market could behave less competitively if the outside firm acquired the largest firm in the market. But what if it acquired one of the smaller firms? In United States v. Marine Bancorporation, Inc. the Supreme Court approved a market extension merger between a bank in Seattle, Washington, and another bank in Spokane, across the state. The Spokane bank controlled less than 18% of the target market. Their merger might have eliminated a perceived potential entrant; however, the trial judge concluded that the merger would "substantially" *increase* actual competition in the Spokane banking market.[16]

This situation should be distinguished from the one in *Philadelphia Bank*. There, the Supreme Court rejected the defense that although a horizontal merger lessened competition in one market (small loans), it increased competition in another market (large loans).[17] In *Marine Bancorporation,* the government alleged a lessening of "potential" competition in the Spokane banking market, but the court found an increase of actual competition in the *same* market. Given the elusive nature of the potential competition doctrine, any merger shown to increase actual competition substantially should be approved on that ground

12. For a case finding both high entry barriers and a likely entrant see Yamaha Motor Co., Ltd. v. FTC, 657 F.2d 971 (8th Cir.1981), cert. denied, 456 U.S. 915, 102 S.Ct. 1768 (1982). The court found high entry barriers in the relevant market (small outboard boat motors), but it also found that the acquiring firm was well established in other markets around the world. For an incorrect application of the theory, see Mercantile Texas Corp. v. Board of Governors, 638 F.2d 1255, 1268 (5th Cir.1981), approving a finding that the acquiring firm could be a potential entrant because "no significant barriers to entry existed in the target market." In that case, however, the target market would have been performing competitively before the merger occurred.

13. 386 U.S. at 581, 87 S.Ct. at 1231.

14. R. Posner, Antitrust Law: An Economic Perspective 122–23 (1976).

15. See 5 Antitrust Law ¶ 1130 (rev. ed. 2000) (forthcoming).

16. 418 U.S. 602, 616, 94 S.Ct. 2856, 2867 (1974).

17. United States v. Philadelphia Nat. Bank, 374 U.S. 321, 83 S.Ct. 1715 (1963).

alone, and the potential competition doctrine forgotten.

§ 13.4b. "Actual" Potential Entrant Doctrine

The perceived potential entrant doctrine discussed above condemns certain mergers when the acquiring firm was perceived by incumbents in the target market to be a likely entrant. The theory has a weaker variation which has never been approved by the Supreme Court, although it has been used by a few lower courts. The "actual potential entrant" doctrine holds that even though a merger has no current effect on competition in the target market, it should be condemned because the acquiring firm could and probably would have come into the target market in a more competitive way, such as by *de novo* entry or by a "toe-hold" acquisition of a smaller firm. This alternative method of entry would have increased competition.

The actual potential entrant doctrine does some violence to the language of § 7, which condemns mergers only when they "may substantially lessen competition." The actual potential entrant doctrine condemns a merger because it fails to increase competition, not because it damages existing competition in any way.[18] In *Falstaff* the Supreme Court left "for another day" the question whether § 7 should condemn a merger that would "leave competition in the marketplace exactly as it was, neither hurt nor helped," and that could be challenged only "on grounds that the company could, but did not, enter *de novo* or through a 'toe-hold' acquisition * * *."[19]

In *Marine Bancorporation* the Supreme Court declined a second opportunity to adopt the actual potential entrant doctrine. It held that at the very least the government must show that the suggested alternative method of entry was feasible and that, if used, would have produced "deconcentration of [the target] market or other significant procompetitive effects."[20]

Since *Marine Bancorporation*, some circuit courts appear to have made the requirements even stricter. For example, in BOC Int'l, Ltd. (British Oxygen) v. F.T.C.[21] the Second Circuit required a showing of a "reasonable probability" that the acquiring firm would have entered the market anyway in the "near future," whether by acquisition of a smaller firm (a "toe hold" acquisition) or by *de novo* entry. The Fourth Circuit has gone even further, holding that entry of the outside firm by an alternative and more competitive route must appear "certain."[22]

Just as problematic as the degree of certainty of entry that must be proven, is the kind of evidence that can be used to prove likely entry. As noted above, the courts have tended to prefer subjective evidence—that is, evidence that a firm did or did not contemplate entry, or contemplated it and decided not to enter. The Federal Trade Commission has generally adhered to that position as well.[23] One thing to be said in favor of subjective evidence is that it is not prepared in contemplation of the litigation at hand. Objective evidence, by contrast, generally consists of models prepared by economists deciding whether entry by an outsider would be profitable, or whether it would be more profitable than available alternatives. These models generally involve a great deal of speculation. A firm with capital to invest generally has numerous alternatives for expansion; the fact that all are profitable does not mean that the firm will undertake all of them. Such a study would have to show that entry into the subject market is clearly more profitable than other available alternatives, or that entry there is

18. For example, In re B.A.T. Indus., 104 F.T.C. 852, 920 (1984) (actual potential entrant doctrine focuses on "future injury because a currently noncompetitive industry will not become as competitive as it might have as a consequence of the merger. * * * ").

19. United States v. Falstaff Brewing Corp., 410 U.S. 526, 537, 93 S.Ct. 1096, 1103 (1973).

20. 418 U.S. at 633, 94 S.Ct. at 2875.

21. 557 F.2d 24, 29 (2d Cir.1977).

22. FTC v. Atlantic Richfield Co., 549 F.2d 289, 295 (4th Cir.1977).

23. See in re B.A.T. Indus., 104 F.T.C. 852, 927–928 (1984) (concluding that the "best" evidence "is likely to be subjective.")

much easier to accomplish.[24] Many kinds of evidence have been offered as objective proof of likelihood of entry, including high profits in the target market,[25] the advantage to the alleged potential entrant of filling a gap in its product line,[26] familiarity with the technology or distribution system,[27] or historical situations where the same firm has entered in other geographical areas.[28]

It strains credulity to think that courts can reliably make findings of likelihood of entry based on this kind of evidence. Many stock traders would give anything for the ability to predict when and how a particular firm was going to enter a new market. Yet fact finders are asked to determine whether it was "certain," merely "probable," or "uncertain" whether a firm would have entered a new market by another route had it not entered by merger. Further, the rule sensibly applies only after the court has determined that the *perceived* potential entrant doctrine does not apply—that is, that the firms operating in the target market had not behaved more competitively because they feared entry by the acquiring firm. For these reasons the Federal Trade Commission and the Department of Justice have both set high evidentiary standards for proof of likelihood of entry.[29] The actual potential entrant doctrine should join reciprocity and tying[30] in the scrap heap of defunct merger theories.[31]

§ 13.5 Conglomerate Mergers and the Antitrust Division Guidelines

Commentators have criticized the judicial standards for conglomerate mergers as confusing, ambiguous, often irrelevant to the competitive results of the acquisition, and impossible for courts to administer.[1] Courts have responded to the criticism by assessing formidable evidentiary requirements which often have frustrated both the government and private plaintiffs.

The most recent government Guidelines covering potential competition mergers are those issued in 1984. More recent Guidelines issued in 1992 apply only to horizontal mergers.[2] However, the 1992 Guidelines contain a more elaborate analysis of market definition than the 1984 Guidelines do, particularly respecting entry barriers, which are crucial to the analysis of potential competition mergers.[3] Since questions of market definition are more-or-less universal to all forms of mergers, it seems sensible that potential competition mergers should be analyzed under the market definition and entry barrier analysis developed in the 1992 Guidelines, while the substantive standards of the 1984 Guidelines continue to apply.

The 1984 Antitrust Division's Merger Guidelines are significant for conglomerate merger law for several reasons. First, they reiterate that the government still regards certain product extension and market extension mergers as theoretically anticompetitive, notwithstanding the fact that few such mergers are being challenged. Second, the Guidelines offer simplified standards for evaluating potential competition mergers. Third, they ignore virtually all rationales for condemning conglomerate mergers except potential competition. Reciprocity is never mentioned.

24. See 5 Antitrust Law ¶¶ 1121–1123 (1980).

25. *B.A.T.*, note 23.

26. In re Brunswick Corp., 94 F.T.C. 1174, 1268–1270 (1979), modified, 96 F.T.C. 151 (1980), affirmed, Yamaha Motor Co. v. FTC, 657 F.2d 971 (8th Cir.1981), cert. denied, 456 U.S. 915, 102 S.Ct. 1768 (1982).

27. *Brunswick*, 94 F.T.C. at 1261. See also United States v. Siemens Corp., 621 F.2d 499, 507 (2d Cir.1980), citing a lack of evidence that the alleged entrant had technical competence in the target market.

28. *B.A.T.*, note 23 at 939.

29. In the FTC, see *B.A.T.*, note 23 at 926–928; in the Justice Department, see U.S. Dept. of Justice, Antitrust Division, Antitrust Enforcement Guidelines for International Operations § 3.3 (1988), reprinted in 4 Trade Reg. Rep. (CCH) ¶ 13109.

30. See § 13.3a, b.

31. The actual potential competition doctrine has been used to condemn some mergers, however. See Yamaha Motor Co. v. FTC, 657 F.2d 971, 977–78 (8th Cir.1981), cert. denied, 456 U.S. 915, 102 S.Ct. 1768 (1982).

§ 13.5

1. See J. Brodley, Potential Competition Mergers: A Structural Synthesis, 87 Yale L.J. 1 (1977).

2. See § 12.1 of this book.

3. On entry barrier analysis in the 1992 Guidelines, see § 12.4b.

The Government is not likely to challenge a potential competition merger if the HHI in the target market is below 1800.[4] Nor will it challenge a potential competition merger if entry into the target market is easy. If there are more than three perceived potential entrants, the Division will be unlikely to challenge the merger. Elimination of one potential entrant in that case would not affect competition in the market. As noted above, these considerations concerning likelihood of entry should be addressed under the more detailed analysis of entry barriers presented in the 1992 Horizontal Merger Guidelines. For example, the likelihood of entry should be measured in terms of the profitability of entry at post-entry prices, the length of time entry takes to occur, and the difficulty that the prospective entrant will have in attaining scale economies.[5]

The 1984 Merger Guidelines purport to treat all potential competition mergers under "a single structural analysis analogous to that applied to horizontal mergers."[6] This is consistent with the observation made earlier that "potential" competition is really actual competition viewed from the supply side. The Guidelines generally avoid separate doctrines for "perceived" and "actual" potential competition. Nevertheless, the Guidelines note one important distinction between perceived and actual potential entrants. Under the Guidelines the actual potential entrant doctrine continues to have "independent importance" because often entry-deterrent "limit" pricing will not be feasible for the firms in the market. In cases where limit pricing will not work a merger can be condemned, if at all, only under the actual potential entrant doctrine.

The 1984 Guidelines have had little impact on the law of potential competition mergers, mainly because there have been so few cases since that date. Although the Guidelines attempt to rationalize potential competition merger doctrine, the appearance of simplicity is beguiling. Even under the 1984 Guidelines, the Antitrust Division appears willing to attempt certain predictions that will be extraordinarily difficult to make in court. For example, the Guidelines indicate that the Agency is likely to attack a merger if the likelihood of "actual entry by the acquiring firm" was "particularly strong." The Guidelines do not say how strong "particularly strong" is, or how the Division will attempt to establish such a likelihood.[7]

4. For a description of the Herfindahl–Hirschman Index (HHI) and its use see § 12.4a2.

5. All these subjects are taken up in § 12.6.

6. 49 Fed. Reg. at 26,834.

7. For criticism of the 1982 Guidelines' lack of clarity in identifying a likely entrant see J. Brodley, Potential Competition Under the Merger Guidelines, 71 Calif.L.Rev. 376, 389–401 (1983). The 1984 Guidelines were not responsive to the criticism.

Chapter 14

PRICE DISCRIMINATION AND THE ROBINSON–PATMAN ACT

Table of Sections

§ 14.1 Introduction: Price Discrimination

Price discrimination occurs when a firm makes two sales at two different rates of return. More technically, two sales are discriminatory when they have different ratios of price to marginal cost.[1] Discriminatory pricing must be distinguished from *differential* pricing, which occurs whenever the same product is sold to two buyers at different prices. The sale of the same product at two different prices can be nondiscriminatory if the price difference is proportional to the different marginal costs of serving two different customers.[2] Likewise, two sales at the same price can be economically discriminatory if marginal costs for the two sales differ. For example, a seller who charges the same delivered price to a buyer one mile away and another buyer 100 miles away is price discriminating if it costs the seller more to transport the product 100 miles than to transport it a mile.

§ 14.1

1. While this definition is technically correct, it may not always be useful for the policy maker. In some markets nearly all costs are fixed and marginal cost is nearly zero or at least very low. For example, patent and copyright licensees generally pay a royalty based on output or revenue, so licensees who sell a great deal pay a discriminatorily high price, assuming the cost of negotiating the license is the same for all.

2. For example, suppose X produces widgets for a marginal cost of $10.00, incurs $2.00 in delivery costs in selling them to A, and $3.00 in delivery costs in selling them to B, and charges A a delivered price of $12.00 and B $13.00. X is not price discriminating.

The buyer who pays the lower price or produces the lower rate of return to the seller is called the "favored" purchaser. The buyer who gives the seller the higher rate of return or who pays the higher price is called the "disfavored" purchaser. If the favored purchaser is paying a competitive price (marginal cost), the disfavored purchaser must be paying a price higher than marginal cost, and giving the seller monopoly profits. For this reason, the ability to price discriminate is evidence that the seller has a certain amount of market power.[3]

§ 14.2 Price Discrimination and Competition

Price discrimination would not occur in a perfectly competitive market in equilibrium. Any purchaser asked to pay a price above marginal cost would walk away from that seller and find someone willing to sell at the competitive price. In such a hypothetical market all sales would be made at marginal cost.

In the real world markets are in constant flux, however. They are shocked regularly by wars, famines, fads, elections, and the weather. Further, no one has complete knowledge of all market conditions at any given time, and different buyers and sellers have different amounts and kinds of information. As a result, sporadic price discrimination is a daily occurrence in even the most competitive markets. One day a farmer may sell corn for $4.00 a bushel. During the night news breaks about a particularly large harvest in a different state and several buyers decide to postpone their purchases. The first buyer who appears in the morning and the farmer himself may not know of the news, and they will complete a sale at $4.00. Later in the day, however, the second and third customers walk away. Eventually the farmer learns that the market price has dropped to $3.70. He sells to the next customer at that price. He has discriminated between two purchasers on the same day; however, this is an absolutely common occurrence in the most competitive of markets. It happens even in the stock market, where information about market prices can be obtained very cheaply. Nevertheless, prices fluctuate hourly in a way that bears little relation to the short-run marginal costs of the sellers.

Competitive markets change constantly not only through time, but also in space. Suppose that firm A sells in three cities. In one of them a competitor opens a new plant and the immediate result is a large supply in that city in relation to demand. The price in that city will drop first, and the price in the other two cities will drop some time later. Likewise, if there is a sudden surge of demand in one city the immediate result will be a price increase there, which will encourage more of the product to flow into that city until the balance between supply and demand is restored once again. Competitive markets *tend* toward an equilibrium in which all sales are made at marginal cost. In the process of arriving at that equilibrium, however, a certain amount of price discrimination is essential. The low price in Chicago and the high price in St. Louis causes goods to flow from Chicago to St. Louis until the balance is once again restored. If a seller is forbidden from raising price in response to increased demand in St. Louis, unless she also raises prices in Chicago where demand has not increased, the result will be shortages in one city and surpluses in the other.

The kind of price discrimination characteristic of competitive markets is usually termed *sporadic* because it varies daily and is often unpredictable. One day a particular buyer will be favored, the next day disfavored. By contrast, *persistent* price discrimination occurs when a seller with market power systematically divides customers into classes and obtains different rates of return from them.

The complete absence of sporadic price discrimination in a market is not a sign of healthy competition. Much more likely, the firms in the market are coordinating their prices. When sellers fix prices, the first thing they are concerned about is "concessions"—the result of hard competitive bargaining between individual buyers and sellers that is reflected in slightly different prices or other

3. See § 3.6e.

terms for each negotiated transaction. The nature of a cartel is to require all sales within a certain category to be made on the same terms. The result is generally a rigid price structure. Thus *sporadic* price discrimination is generally consistent with competition on the merits, and inconsistent with cartelization. Indeed, our concern with collusion often causes us to favor markets where purchases are negotiated individually and privately, so that cartel members cannot verify the terms of sale. The sporadic price discrimination that results can upset the cartel or oligopoly.[1]

§ 14.3 Price Discrimination and the Monopolist: Perfect Price Discrimination

Sporadic price discrimination is an everyday occurrence in competitive markets. However, persistent price discrimination requires that a seller (or group of sellers) have market power.[1] Price discrimination is persistent when a seller or group of sellers establish a policy of obtaining a higher rate of return from some customers than from others. In a competitive market disfavored purchasers will simply seek out a different seller willing to sell to them at the competitive price.

All markets contain different customers who place different values on a seller's product. Both orthodontic braces and bridge supports are made of steel, for example, but orthodontists may be willing to pay much more than bridge builders for a pound of steel. We refer to the bridges builders as "high elasticity" customers and the orthodontists as "low elasticity" customers. This simply tells us that in response to a given price increase, a much higher percentage of sales will be lost in the bridge support market than in the market for orthodontic braces. The ideal situation for a seller is to be able to sell every unit to every customer at the customer's reservation price, which is the maximum amount that customer is willing to pay for that unit. This is *perfect* price discrimination.

Figure 1 illustrates the difference between competitive pricing, nondiscriminatory monopoly pricing, and perfect price discrimination. The figure shows the demand curve, marginal cost and marginal revenue curves of a seller with market power. In a perfectly competitive market a seller would produce $Q_{(c)}$ output and sell at price $P_{(c)}$—the point at which its marginal cost curve crosses the demand curve. Output beyond that point could not be sold at a price sufficient to cover the additional costs. In a perfectly competitive market triangle 1–3–6 is consumers' surplus: the excess value that accrues to consumers because they are able to purchase the product at a lower price than the value they place on it.[2]

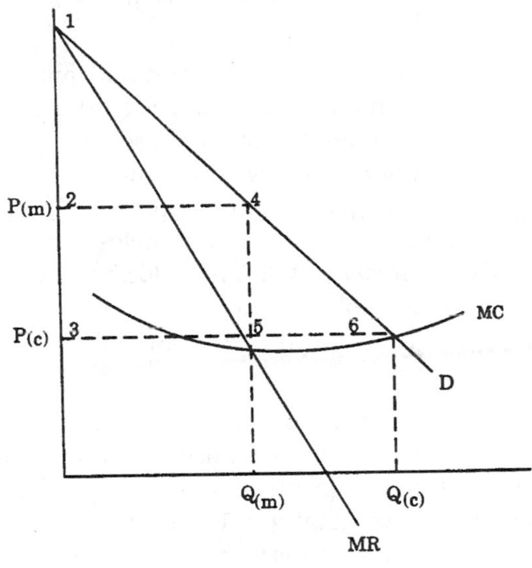

Figure 1

[630a]

The monopolist, however, will reduce its output to $Q_{(m)}$, where its marginal cost and marginal revenue curves intersect, and sell at price $P_{(m)}$, which is its nondiscriminatory profit-maximizing price. $P_{(m)}$ is the price that will maximize the seller's profits if the seller is unable to price discriminate. The output re-

§ 14.2

1. See § 4.1. However, evidence of systematic, persistent price discrimination in a market with multiple sellers likewise suggests a cartel. See R. Posner, Antitrust Law: An Economic Perspective 62–65 (1976).

§ 14.3

1. On proving market power from price discrimination, see § 3.6e.

2. See § 1.1.

duction from $Q_{(c)}$ to $Q_{(m)}$ causes the traditional deadweight loss of monopoly, equal to the area of triangle 4–5–6. Consumers' surplus is reduced to the area of triangle 1–2–4. Rectangle 2–3–5–4 has traditionally been thought of as monopoly profits.[3]

The monopolist charging its nondiscriminatory profit-maximizing price does not make all the money theoretically possible from its position. First, the monopolist loses sales to customers located between points 4 and 6 on the demand curve in Figure 1. Any sale that can be made at price $P_{(c)}$ or higher is profitable to the seller. In reducing output to the profit-maximizing level the monopolist forgoes these profitable sales. Second, high preference customers, located between points 1 and 4 on the demand curve, have reservation prices even higher than $P_{(m)}$.

If the monopolist can identify and charge each customer its reservation price, the monopolist will be able to capture these profits as well. Customers located on the demand curve near point 6 will pay a price approaching the competitive price (which is nonetheless profitable). By contrast, customers located near point 1 on the graph will pay a price that could be far higher than the nondiscriminatory profit-maximizing price.[4]

Perfect price discrimination has two important results. First, the area of traditional monopoly profits, or producers' surplus, is increased to all of triangle 1–3–6. Everything that would be consumers' surplus in a competitive market may become monopoly profits under perfect price discrimination. Second, output under perfect price discrimination is restored to $Q_{(c)}$, the same as under perfect competition. For this reason perfect price discrimination is often said to be as efficient as perfect competition, even though one result of perfect price discrimination is that customers are far poorer and the seller far richer.[5]

§ 14.4 Imperfect Price Discrimination

Perfect price discrimination never exists in the real world.[1] The costs of determining each customer's reservation price and structuring the market to enable the seller to charge that price would be prohibitive. About the best most sellers can do is identify and segregate two or more groups of customers who place different values on the product, and price discriminate among these groups. Furthermore, a price discrimination scheme can be frustrated by arbitrage. Arbitrage occurs when favored purchasers resell the product to disfavored purchasers at some price that is profitable to the favored purchasers but less than the disfavored purchasers were asked to pay.

Arbitrage generally works only when the discriminatory prices are also different prices. For example, if buyers one mile and 100 miles from the seller pay the same delivered price, there is likely price discrimination in favor of the more remote purchasers. However, that purchaser will not be able to resell the product to the disfavored purchaser because the higher costs that occasioned the price discrimination have already been sunk. There is no "spread" in the price between the two purchasers. By contrast, if one buyer pays $1.00 for salt and another buyer pays $1.10, arbitrage may be possible. The first buyer might resell the salt to the second buyer at some price between $1.00 and $1.10.[2] Before arbitrage will work, however, the transaction costs of the arbitrage must be less than the price difference. The favored and disfavored purchasers must find each other, negotiate an arbitrage price and perhaps reship the product from the favored purchaser's location to the disfavored purchas-

3. But see § 1.3c.

4. See H. Hovenkamp, Market Power and Secondary–Line Differential Pricing, 71 Geo.L.J. 1157, 1162–66 (1983).

5. Perfect price discrimination is as efficient as perfect competition, provided that it costs the seller nothing to engage in price discrimination.

§ 14.4

1. For a moderately technical but readable discussion of price discrimination in everyday markets, see L. Phlips, The Economics of Price Discrimination (1983).

2. If there are several favored buyers they will compete with each other to make arbitrage sales to disfavored buyers. The competition will drive the arbitrage price down to the sum of the price paid by the favored buyers plus the transaction costs of the arbitrage.

er's location. If the costs of these maneuvers in the above example exceed 10¢, arbitrage will not occur.

In perfect price discrimination, output is restored to the competitive level. The same thing is not true of imperfect price discrimination. In fact, sometimes output under imperfect price discrimination is actually smaller than output under nondiscriminatory monopoly pricing.[3] Suppose that a monopolist has marginal costs of $1.00 per unit and a profit-maximizing price of $1.50. In studying the market, the monopolist has managed to identify three groups of customers who have different reservation prices. One group, the marginal customers, are willing to pay $1.00 but no more. A second group, the medium preference customers, are willing to pay $1.50. A third group, high preference purchasers, are willing to pay any amount up to $2.00. Sales to all three groups will be profitable, but will the seller make all three sets of sales? Perhaps not. Although the medium preference group is willing to pay $1.50, it may be difficult to segregate them from the low preference customers. Furthermore, the middle group may be quite cost conscious: they will opt for the $1.00 version of the product if it is available. In this case the seller may decide that he will make more money if he offers the product only in $1.50 and $2.00 versions and forgets about the relatively unprofitable group of marginal buyers. In short, the seller may price discriminate, but only *within* the group of customers who are willing to pay the profit-maximizing price or higher. In this case output will be no higher than under nondiscriminatory monopoly pricing.[4] Further, if price discrimination within that group is imperfect, output will be lower. For example, if any person whose reservation price is less than $2.00 is mistakenly placed in the $2.00 group, that sale will not be made, even though this particular buyer would have been willing to pay $1.50.

§ 14.5 Price Discrimination and Antitrust Policy

14.5a. The Social Cost of Price Discrimination

All forms of persistent price discrimination transfer wealth away from consumers and toward sellers. If antitrust policy is concerned with such wealth transfers, then price discrimination presents an antitrust problem.[1]

The question is more complex if economic efficiency is the exclusive goal of the federal antitrust laws. Some commentators have argued that price discrimination should not be an antitrust concern because it does not produce losses in output as other monopolistic practices do.[2] As noted earlier, however, only perfect price discrimination maintains output at the competitive level. Under imperfect price discrimination output is always lower.

Further, price discrimination can generate substantial social losses, equivalent to the efficiency losses that can result from all forms of monopoly. First is the deadweight loss caused by reduction in output. Since all imperfect price discrimination results in output at less than the competitive level, and all real world price discrimination is imperfect, it necessarily follows that persistent price discrimination produces a certain amount of deadweight loss. However, price discrimination in this case reflects monopoly power that already exists; it does not cause monopoly power. A firm does not generally increase the amount or duration of its market power by price discriminating, although it may earn more from the market power it already has.[3]

A second kind of social loss comes from exclusionary practices: the actions that the

3. See J. Robinson, The Economics of Imperfect Competition 188–195 (1933).

4. See H. Hovenkamp, Market Power and Secondary Line Differential Pricing, 71 Geo.L.J. 1157, 1167–71 (1983).

§ 14.5

1. See ch. 2.

2. For example, R. Bork, The Antitrust Paradox: A Policy at War With Itself 304–08 (1978, rev. ed. 1993).

3. While the text statement is intuitively true, it may be technically meaningless. Devices for defining market power, such as the Lerner Index, do so on the assumption that the firm is *not* engaged in price discrimination. For the price discriminator there is no single ratio of price to marginal cost from which the Lerner Index can be derived. On the Lerner Index, see § 3.1a.

price-discriminating monopolist takes in order to obtain or maintain its market power. Just as any other monopolist, the price discriminating monopolist must deter competitive entry into its high profit markets (that is, the markets containing the disfavored purchasers). The social cost of exclusionary practices varies with the activity; however, many such practices are inefficient.[4] There is a presumptive reason for thinking that the cost of exclusionary practices are higher for the price discriminating monopolist than for the monopolist who does not discriminate. A monopolist will price discriminate only if the discrimination is more profitable than nondiscriminatory pricing. Since the profit potential is larger, the discriminating monopolist will be willing to spend more on exclusionary practices.

Finally, imperfect price discrimination can produce one large social cost in addition to both the monopoly deadweight loss and the cost of the exclusionary practices. In order to price discriminate the monopolist must undergo the expense of identifying different groups of customers who have different reservation prices, segregating them, perhaps creating different distribution systems, and disguising the product in such a way as to prevent arbitrage. These efforts may well be a pure social loss.[5]

None of these conclusions suggests that price discrimination should be an antitrust offense, although a few courts have condemned price discrimination under § 2 of the Sherman Act.[6] As a general matter, a monopolist may lawfully set its profit-maximizing price, and price discrimination is not itself an "exclusionary" practice.[7] Further, the costs of preventing price discrimination without any accompanying exclusionary conduct would almost certainly outweigh any benefits, particularly if the market is competitive or oligopolistic. Indeed, as the following discussion indicates, a policy of preventing price discrimination in oligopolistic markets may serve to perpetuate monopoly prices.

14.5b. The Social Cost of Preventing Price Discrimination in Concentrated Markets

Almost any policy of preventing price discrimination in oligopolistic markets would be socially harmful. Indeed, two of the most damaging effects of the Robinson–Patman Act are that it (1) makes cartel "cheating" more difficult by penalizing individual price cuts; and more generally, (2) destroys the incentive for oligopolists to compete more aggressively by pursuing marginal sales.

As the discussion of collusion showed,[8] price fixers have strong incentives to cheat on the cartel by charging a lower price. Most cartel cheating takes the form, not of across-the-board price cuts, but rather of fairly discreet sales made at a lower price than the cartel price generally. The more such sales are made, the less will be the damage done by the cartel, and the more likely that it will simply fall apart.

When firms sell in an oligopolistic market, the story is only a little more complicated. In a non-cooperative Cournot oligopoly,[9] for example, each firm equates its own marginal cost and marginal revenue, yielding a price that can be significantly higher than the competitive level. The firms in such an oligopoly generally have no incentive to cheat by making across the board price cuts. They are already

4. On the social costs of monopoly, see § 1.3.

5. The question is complex. The costs of the price discrimination scheme could be more than offset by the gains in consumer surplus that accrue to customers as a result of the price discrimination. For example, suppose a monopolist has a non-discriminatory profit-maximizing price of $1.50 and marginal costs of $1.00. A group of customers that can be easily segregated is willing to pay prices ranging from $1.10 to $1.35, and the monopolist charges them $1.10. In that case, sales to the second group—which would not occur under single price monopoly—create consumers' surplus that might exceed the costs of the price discrimination scheme.

See also § 10.6e for an argument that price discrimination accomplished by means of variable proportion tying arrangements should generally be legal, particularly in the franchise setting.

6. E.g., United States v. United Shoe Machinery Corp., 110 F.Supp. 295, 340, 341 (D.Mass.1953), affirmed per curiam, 347 U.S. 521, 74 S.Ct. 699 (1954). See § 7.4; and see 3 Antitrust Law ¶ 721 (rev. ed. 1996).

7. See § 6.3.

8. See § 4.1.

9. On non-cooperative oligopoly behavior, see § 4.2.

maximizing their profits, assuming that other firms hold their output constant. Any across-the-board cut would result in lower profits.

But selective cuts are an entirely different matter. If the oligopolist can cut price selectively by bidding for each sale independently as it comes along, without regard to the price charged other customers, then the oligopoly market structure might nevertheless produce the competitive price.[10] Indeed, if the oligopolists are able to make each new sale without worrying about the impact of the price on previous or subsequent customers, they will compete the price for that sale right down to marginal cost. But in that case, at least some of the low priced sales will come out of the output of the other oligopolist. The second oligopolist will have no choice but to cut its own price selectively, or else it will lose its market position. Will the two firms be able to eliminate the discriminatory cuts? Perhaps, but only by an understanding that looks more like an "agreement," and even then they will still have the incentive to cheat if they can do so secretly.[11]

All of this is to say that adhering to the Cournot price is a robust strategy *only* if the firms are unable to engage in price discrimination by negotiating secret price concessions. A policy against price discrimination, such as the Robinson–Patman Act, may prevent a firm from negotiating different contract prices with different buyers. In the process, the Act may serve to make non-cooperative oligopolies more stable, just as it makes cartel cheating more difficult.

§ 14.6 The Robinson–Patman Act and Price Discrimination

14.6a. General Interpretation

§ 14.6a1. Legislative History and Effectiveness in Achieving Goals

Section 2 of the Clayton Act, amended in 1936 by the Robinson–Patman Act, makes it "unlawful for any person * * * to discriminate in price between different purchasers of commodities of like grade and quality * * * where the effect * * * may be substantially to lessen

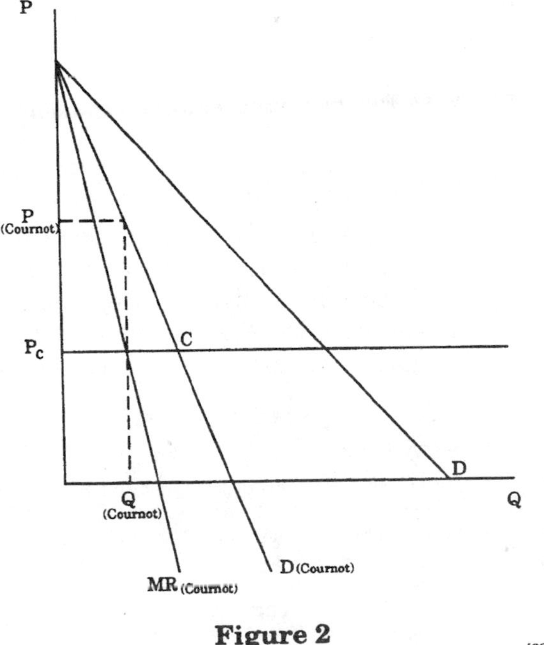

Figure 2

[631a]

10. Figure 2 illustrates for a two person oligopoly (duopoly). Two equal size firms divide a market in half. Each then faces one half of the demand curve, or an effective demand equal to the line labeled $D_{Cournot}$, and marginal revenue denoted by $MR_{Cournot}$. The oligopolist will then maximize its profits by producing at $Q_{Cournot}$ and charging price $P_{Cournot}$. In this equilibrium condition, neither oligopolist will profit from cheating with an *across-the-board* price cut. However, discriminatory price cuts are profitable. The oligopolist could earn more by expanding its output to point C, which it could do by charging the additional customers some price between the oligopoly price and the competitive price (P_c).

The impact of these price cuts on the oligopoly depends entirely on how selectively they can be made. If the increased sales come only from customers unwilling to pay the oligopoly price, then the other oligopolist will not be injured by the price cuts. For example, assume that the competitive price is $1.00 and the Cournot price is $1.30. The oligopolist maintains the $1.30 price to all customers willing to pay $1.30, but charges varying prices down to $1.00 to customers unwilling to pay $1.30. In that case the other oligopolist would lose no sales. It could still make its full "entitlement" of sales at the Cournot price, thus maintaining its output at $Q_{Cournot}$. It could also make selective price cuts to customers unwilling to pay $1.30.

But in a true life oligopoly, the individual participants are generally unable to distinguish a customer who is willing to pay the $1.30 price from one who is not. Customers always want to buy for less, even if they are willing to pay more. If the oligopolist is able to make a large sale at a price of, say, $1.15, and the terms of sale will not be publicized, he will have every incentive to make it.

11. For further analysis of oligopoly pricing, see § 4.2.

competition or tend to create a monopoly * * *."[1]

Welfare losses caused by price discrimination were not on the mind of Congress in 1936. Rather, they were concerned that small businesses, particularly small retailers, were rapidly losing market share to large "chain stores" that were able to underbuy and thus to undersell the small operators.[2] This Congressional concern with small business welfare has substantially colored judicial interpretation of the Act. For example, a small business is injured by a larger firm's lower price whether or not the lower price results from true economic price discrimination by a firm with market power. *Low* prices, not discriminatory prices, are the chief evil condemned by the Act. For that reason the Robinson–Patman Act cannot be understood as designed to encourage allocative efficiency or to maximize consumer welfare. It was designed to protect small businesses from larger, more efficient businesses. A necessary result is higher consumer prices.

A statute is not bad, however, simply because it manifests a distributive rather than an efficiency concern and requires consumers to pay the bill. Many statutes do that, and one function of the legislative process is to protect people whom the free market protects poorly. Rather, criticism of the Robinson–Patman Act focuses on two things. First, although the Act was designed to protect small business, it has not done so very well. Often small businesses have run afoul of the act. For example, the statute has been applied against cooperatives of small businesses designed to enable members to purchase (and therefore to resell) at a lower price, so they could compete more effectively with larger stores.[3]

Secondly, while the Robinson–Patman Act is quite hostile toward economic competition, it is nevertheless disguised as an antitrust law. Furthermore, its inconsistencies with the other antitrust laws are so substantial that businesses have often complained that they can comply with the Robinson–Patman Act only by violating the other antitrust laws, or vice-versa. The Supreme Court has responded by trying to interpret the Act so as to make it consistent with the other antitrust laws.[4] The result, however, has done some violence to the Robinson–Patman Act and to its legislative history.

The Robinson–Patman Act has done an extraordinarily poor job of identifying those forms of price discrimination that most economists consider to be inefficient. At the same time, it has often been used to condemn efficient practices that were really evidence of healthy competition.[5] The Act has been widely castigated by critics who see it as doing far more harm than good to the competitive process. The Department of Justice has not enforced the Act since 1977, and the Federal Trade Commission has greatly reduced its enforcement as well.[6]

As the discussion in § 14.3 suggests, persistent price discrimination cannot occur unless the seller has market power. However, the Robinson–Patman Act does not require a showing of the defendant's market power. This failure, plus the fact that the "cost justification" defense has been very narrowly con-

§ 14.6

1. 15 U.S.C.A. § 13(a).

2. The Bill originally proposed was entitled the "Wholesale Grocers' Protection Act." See H.C. Hansen, Robinson–Patman Law: A Review and Analysis, 51 Fordham L.Rev. 1113, 1123 (1983); see also Federal Trade Commission, Final Report on the Chain–Store Investigation, S. Doc., No. 4, 74th Cong., 1st Sess. (1935). For a more detailed account of the statute and its legislative history see F.M. Rowe, Price Discrimination Under the Robinson–Patman Act (1962); and 14 Antitrust Law ¶ 2302 (1999).

3. See Mid–South Distrib. v. FTC, 287 F.2d 512 (5th Cir.), cert. denied, 368 U.S. 838, 82 S.Ct. 36 (1961); Standard Motor Prod., Inc. v. FTC, 265 F.2d 674 (2d Cir.), cert. denied, 361 U.S. 826, 80 S.Ct. 73 (1959).

4. E.g., Great A. & P. Tea Co. v. FTC, 440 U.S. 69, 80 n. 13, 99 S.Ct. 925, 933 n. 13 (1979); United States v. United States Gypsum Co., 438 U.S. 422, 458, 98 S.Ct. 2864, 2884 (1978), appeal after remand, 600 F.2d 414 (3d Cir.), cert. denied, 444 U.S. 884, 100 S.Ct. 175 (1979).

5. Among the most clever critiques of the statute is W. F. Baxter, A Parable, 23 Stan.L.Rev. 973 (1971).

6. See U.S. Dep't of Justice, Report on the Robinson–Patman Act (1977); Hansen, note 2, at 1174–86. The FTC does continue some enforcement. See T. Calvani, Government Enforcement of the Robinson–Patman Act, 53 Antitrust L.J. 921 (1985).

strued,[7] has yielded a large measure of over-deterrence.[8] Many defendants condemned by the Act were not monopolists engaged in true price discrimination at all. Their differential prices were either nondiscriminatory or else part of the normal give-and-take of the competitive market process.[9] Alternatively, they were efforts by oligopolists to compete by "cheating" on the oligopoly price. By condemning the resulting discrimination, the Robinson–Patman Act effectively supported the oligopoly.

§ 14.6a2. The Robinson–Patman Act's Theory of Competitive Injury

The theory of injury embodied in the Robinson–Patman Act is an intellectually hostile, impenetrable swamp. On the one hand, the Supreme Court has held that the "antitrust injury" requirement for antitrust standing applies to the Act.[10] This suggests a requirement of some kind of injury to "competition." Courts have assessed such a requirement in "primary-line" Robinson–Patman cases, which involve a form of predatory pricing.[11] In its *Brooke* decision,[12] the Supreme Court emphasized that the "may substantially lessen competition" language of the Act required a showing that competition was or would likely be injured by the defendant's practices. This required a showing that the practice would create or perpetuate either monopoly or oligopoly. The Court then crafted a set of rigorous substantive rules designed to weed out cases where these threats were not sufficiently apparent.

By contrast, the courts continue to recognize secondary-line Robinson–Patman claims brought in robustly competitive markets where antitrust law's ordinary "antitrust injury" requirement could never be met. In *Hasbrouck* the Supreme Court characterized the market at issue as "highly competitive," but then gave no further thought to the question, which was not before it, about how price discrimination could ever injure "competition" in such a situation.[13] Likewise, many circuits hold that the injury required by the statute is not an injury to economic competition at all, but merely an injury to a competitor.[14] As a result, there is a major anomaly in the way that the same statutory language is interpreted in primary-line as opposed to secondary-line situations. The courts generally reach this result by observing that primary-line (predatory pricing) cases under the statute are covered by the language of the original 1914 provision, while "secondary-line" cases are covered by the 1936 amendments.[15] Further, the 1936 Amendments added the following italicized language to its prohibition. It is unlawful for a seller

> to discriminate in price between different purchasers of commodities of like grade and quality, ... where the effect of such discrimination may be substantially to lessen competition or tend to create a monopoly in any line of commerce, *or to injure, destroy, or prevent competition with any*

7. See § 14.6f1.

8. See H. Hovenkamp, Market Power and Secondary–Line Differential Pricing, 71 Geo.L.J. 1157 (1983).

9. E.g., FTC v. Morton Salt Co., 334 U.S. 37, 68 S.Ct. 822 (1948), where there was no allegation that the defendant was a monopolist in the sale of table salt; and United States v. Borden Co., 370 U.S. 460, 82 S.Ct. 1309 (1962), where the defendant was in intense competition in the sale of milk.

10. See J. Truett Payne Co. v. Chrysler Motors Corp., 451 U.S. 557, 101 S.Ct. 1923 (1981). On antitrust injury generally, see § 16.3; and see 14 Antitrust Law ¶ 2371c (1999).

11. See § 8.8.

12. Brooke Group Ltd. v. Brown & Williamson Tobacco Corp., 509 U.S. 209, 113 S.Ct. 2578 (1993).

13. Texaco, Inc. v. Hasbrouck, 496 U.S. 543, 548, 110 S.Ct. 2535, 2538 (1990).

14. E.g., Chroma Lighting v. GTE Products Corp., 111 F.3d 653, 655 (9th Cir.), cert. denied, ___ U.S. ___, 118 S.Ct. 357 (1997). See also George Haug Co. v. Rolls Royce Motor Cars, 148 F.3d 136 (2d Cir.1998) ("hornbook law" that one need not allege an injury to competition in a secondary-line Robinson–Patman Act case); J.F. Feeser, Inc. v. Serv–A–Portion, Inc., 909 F.2d 1524, 1533 (3d Cir.1990), cert. denied, 499 U.S. 921, 111 S.Ct. 1313 (1991) (act "intended to justify a finding of injury to competition by a showing of injury to a competitor victimized by the discrimination "); Hasbrouck v. Texaco, Inc., 842 F.2d 1034, 1040 (9th Cir.1987), affirmed, 496 U.S. 543, 110 S.Ct. 2535 (1990). ("injury to competitors may be probative of harm to competition").

15. On the difference between primary-and secondary-line injury, see § 14.6c.

person who either grants or knowingly receives the benefits of such discrimination, or with customers of either of them . . .[16]

This language, according to the Ninth Circuit interpretation, "shifts the focus of the statute from protecting competition to protecting individual disfavored buyers from the loss of business to favored buyers."[17] However, the Ninth circuit seemed to read the italicized statutory language as if it condemned price discriminations that "injure . . . any person. . . ." But the language reaches only those price discriminations that "injure . . . *competition* with any person." The distinction is important when a manufacturer awards a successful dealer by giving it a price concession that is not given to less successful dealers. A manufacturer who creates such a reward system is not injuring competition but advancing it, even though individual dealers may be injured. Acknowledging this fact does more justice to the Supreme Court's insistence that the Robinson–Patman Act be interpreted in such a fashion that it not conflict unnecessarily with the more general goals of the antitrust laws.[18]

§ 14.6b. The Meaning of Price "Discrimination" Under the Act

The Robinson–Patman Act is frequently called a "price discrimination" statute, but that is a misnomer. The Act directly condemns price *differences*, and only indirectly and haphazardly reaches economic discrimination.[19] For example, two sales at the same price can be discriminatory if marginal costs are different. Two sales at the same price do not violate the Robinson–Patman Act.[20] By contrast, sales at two different prices are nondiscriminatory if the price difference is proportional to the difference in marginal costs of servicing the two customers. However, a pair of sales at different prices makes out a *prima facie* case under the Robinson–Patman Act. Although the Act does contain an affirmative "cost justification" defense that permits a defendant to show that sales at different prices were nondiscriminatory, the defense has been so narrowly construed that it is almost impossible to use. It has not rescued many defendants.[21]

§ 14.6c. Primary– and Secondary–Line Violations

The Robinson–Patman Act includes two offenses that are very different from each other, although both are covered by the same statutory language. "Primary-line" differential pricing is really a form of predatory pricing directed at the defendant's competitors. The basic theory is that the defendant uses high prices in one market to offset or "subsidize" predatory pricing in a different market.[22]

By contrast, "secondary-line" price discrimination refers to a firm's differential pricing policies as between customers in the same market. The perceived victims of secondary-line discrimination are the seller's disfavored purchasers, who are also generally the plaintiffs in private, secondary-line actions.[23] The theory of injury is generally that the defendant's lower price sales to the plaintiff's competitor (the favored purchaser) placed the plaintiff at a competitive disadvantage and caused it to lose business.[24] This theory neces-

16. 15 U.S.C.A. § 13(a) (emphasis added).

17. *Chroma Lighting*, 111 F.3d at 655.

18. 14 Antitrust Law ¶ ¶ 2331, 2333 (1999). A minority of courts have assessed a requirement of injury to competition as it is generally defined in antitrust generally. See Boise Cascade Corp. v. FTC, 837 F.2d 1127, 1143–1144 (D.C.Cir.1988) (competitive harm under Act requires injury to competition).

19. See Falls City Indus., Inc. v. Vanco Beverage, Inc., 460 U.S. 428, 444 n. 10, 103 S.Ct. 1282, 1293 n. 10, on remand, 705 F.2d 463 (7th Cir.1983); FTC v. Anheuser–Busch, Inc., 363 U.S. 536, 549, 80 S.Ct. 1267, 1274 (1960), on remand, 289 F.2d 835 (7th Cir.1961): "[A] price discrimination within the meaning of [the statute] is merely a price difference."

20. See Carroll v. Protection Maritime Ins. Co., Ltd., 512 F.2d 4 (1st Cir.1975).

21. See § 14.6f1.

22. Primary-line violations are treated in § 8.8.

23. The statute also recognizes so-called "third-line" and "fourth-line" injury, which occur further down the distributional chain. The basic theory of action is the same. See Perkins v. Standard Oil Co. of California, 395 U.S. 642, 89 S.Ct. 1871 (1969); 14 Antitrust Law ¶ 2334 (1999); F.M. Rowe, Price Discrimination Under the Robinson–Patman Act 195–205 (1962).

24. See, for example, J. Truett Payne Co. v. Chrysler Motors Corp., 451 U.S. 557, 101 S.Ct. 1923 (1981), on remand, 670 F.2d 575 (5th Cir.), rehearing denied, 677 F.2d 117 (11th Cir.), cert. denied, 459 U.S. 908, 103 S.Ct.

sarily requires the plaintiff to show that it competes with the favored purchaser.[25]

It should not escape notice that secondary-line price discrimination is a purely vertical practice and operates entirely as an "intrabrand" restraint.[26] The supplier simply charges two different dealers in its own brand different prices. As the Chapter 11 discussion of intrabrand restraints observes, however, such restrictions are virtually never anticompetitive, and few have been condemned since the Supreme Court began assessing them under a rule of reason.[27]

§ 14.6d. Jurisdictional and Technical Requirements

The Robinson–Patman Act is a morass of technical requirements that often hide or subvert its basic purpose. Although detailed elaboration is beyond the scope of this discussion, knowledge of a few details is helpful.[28]

Unlike the Sherman Act, which applies to all transactions "affecting commerce" up to Congress's full constitutional power, the Robinson–Patman Act requires the seller to be "engaged in" interstate commerce and that one of the discriminatory sales itself be made in interstate commerce.[29] As a result, one of the discriminatory sales must have crossed a state line. This conclusion has generated a great deal of litigation about when the "flow" of commerce stops. For example, suppose that a company manufactures a good in Illinois and ships it to sales agents in Minnesota, where it is sold to different customers at different prices. The general consensus is that if the goods were shipped in Illinois with these particular customers in mind, then the interstate commerce requirement has been met. However, if the good is shipped into Minnesota for resale by dealers to any unknown customer who happens to come along, then the relevant sales are entirely within the state of Minnesota, and the Robinson–Patman Act will not reach the transaction.[30] This suggests in turn that most retail sales are outside the statute's jurisdiction. Typically the seller and retail buyer are located in the same state, and the identity of the buyer is not known when the good crosses the state line.

The statute expressly applies to sales, not to leases, even though price discrimination is as common in leasing as it is in sales.[31] Perhaps more importantly, the statute applies only to the sale of "commodities," and therefore ignores business services.[32] This limitation

212 (1982); J.F. Feeser, Inc. v. Serv–A–Portion, Inc., 909 F.2d 1524, 1535–1538 (3d Cir.1990), cert. denied, 499 U.S. 921, 111 S.Ct. 1313 (1991); Edward J. Sweeney & Sons, Inc. v. Texaco, Inc., 637 F.2d 105 (3d Cir.1980), cert. denied, 451 U.S. 911, 101 S.Ct. 1981 (1981).

25. However, the courts are split on the question whether the requirement that the favored and disfavored purchaser compete is "jurisdictional" or merely part of the statute's substantive coverage. See Godfrey v. Pulitzer Pub., 161 F.3d 1137 (8th Cir.1998), cert. denied, ___ U.S. ___, 119 S.Ct. 1575 (1999) (requirement not jurisdictional); Mayer Paving and Asphalt Co. v. General Dynamics Corp., 486 F.2d 763 (7th Cir.1973), cert. denied, 414 U.S. 1146, 94 S.Ct. 899 (1974) (requirement jurisdictional). However, for most cases this may be a tempest in a teapot. If a complaint fails to allege a jurisdictional element it is ordinarily dismissed under Fed.R.Civ.Proc. 12(b)(1); if it fails to allege an essential substantive element of the statute, it is ordinarily dismissed for failure to state a claim under rule 12(b)(6). See 14 Antitrust Law ¶ 2333b (1999).

26. On intrabrand restraints, see Ch. 11.

27. See § 11.6.

28. The statute is covered comprehensively in 14 Antitrust Law Ch. 23 (1999); and F.M. Rowe, note 23.

29. Gulf Oil Corp. v. Copp Paving Co., 419 U.S. 186, 200–201 & n. 17, 95 S.Ct. 392, 401–402 & n. 17 (1974), on remand, 618 F.2d 91 (9th Cir.1980) (Robinson–Patman Act's "in commerce" requirement generally requires one of the two transactions upon which the discrimination claim is based to have crossed a state line).

30. See Taggart v. Rutledge, 657 F.Supp. 1420, 1438–1440 (D.Mont.1987), affirmed mem., 852 F.2d 1290 (9th Cir.1988); Zoslaw v. MCA Distrib. Corp., 693 F.2d 870, 880 (9th Cir.1982), cert. denied, 460 U.S. 1085, 103 S.Ct. 1777 (1983); Walker Oil Co. v. Hudson Oil Co. of Missouri, 414 F.2d 588 (5th Cir.1969), cert. denied, 396 U.S. 1042, 90 S.Ct. 684 (1970), and Cliff Food Stores, Inc. v. Kroger, Inc., 417 F.2d 203 (5th Cir.1969); Indiana Grocery v. Super Valu Stores, 647 F.Supp. 254 (S.D.Ind.1986). Contra: Rio Vista Oil, Ltd. v. Southland Corp., 667 F.Supp. 757, 762–764 (D.Utah 1987).

31. Export Liquor Sales, Inc. v. Ammex Warehouse Co., 426 F.2d 251, 252 (6th Cir.1970), cert. denied, 400 U.S. 1000, 91 S.Ct. 460 (1971) (Act does not apply to lease of real property). Likewise, consignment contracts are not covered. Seaboard Supply Co. v. Congoleum Corp., 770 F.2d 367, 373 (3d Cir.1985) (mere sales agent not a purchaser). See 14 Antitrust Law ¶ 2312 (1999).

32. 14 Antitrust Law ¶ 2314 (1999); Ball Memorial Hospital v. Mutual Hospital Ins., 784 F.2d 1325, 1340 (7th Cir.), rehearing denied, 788 F.2d 1223 (7th Cir.1986) (Act does not apply to medical services); Alliance Shippers v. Southern Pacif. Transp. Co., 673 F.Supp. 1005, 1006

is particularly irrational because price discrimination in service markets is much more prevalent than in the sale of goods. For example, a patient walking into a doctor's office is likely to have very poor information about the price that the doctor charges other people for various procedures. Furthermore, the doctor need not worry about arbitrage: the favored patient cannot resell the service to a disfavored patient.

The statute requires two different sales to two different purchasers at two different prices. One sale and an offer to sell at a higher or lower price is not a violation of the Act.[33] The two sales must be consummated within a reasonable time of each other.[34] Whether a parent and its subsidiary, or affiliated corporations, are two "different" purchasers has perplexed the courts. Some cases suggest that corporations related by ownership are not "different" and therefore differential sales to them do not violate the statute.[35] The same question has arisen when there were two legal sellers related by ownership. For example, in *Caribe* the First Circuit held that when a parent corporation sold at one price and a wholly owned subsidiary sold at a different price, the two were in fact a single seller, making Robinson–Patman liability possible.[36]

In order to fall within the statute, the different sales at different prices must be of products of "like grade and quality."[37] The requirement has given rise to substantial litigation. Physical differences between two items will often take them out of the "like grade and quality" requirement, and they can freely be sold at different prices provided the differences are recognized and appreciated by consumers.[38] The courts have held, however, that mere differences in the way a product is packaged[39] or advertised will not defeat the requirement. Thus if a producer manufactures and sells a high-priced "name brand" which is advertised, and a chemically identical but unadvertised "house brand" at a lower price, the two sales may violate the statute, even though the seller may have incurred substantial advertising costs for the name brand but not for the house brand.[40]

Section 2(a) of the Act applies to "indirect" as well as "direct" price discrimination. "Indirect" discrimination refers to a seller's provision of different services to different customers—for example, if the seller gives the favored buyer better credit terms,[41] delivery, stocking

(C.D.Cal.1986), affirmed, 858 F.2d 567 (9th Cir.1988) (Act does not apply to freight shipping). See also Advo v. Philadelphia Newspapers, 51 F.3d 1191, 1195 (3d Cir. 1995) (dictum; print advertising not a commodity).

33. See 14 Antitrust Law ¶ 2312 (1999); S & W Constr. & Materials Co. v. Dravo Basic Materials Co., 813 F.Supp. 1214, 1223 (S.D.Miss.1992), aff'd, 1 F.3d 1238 (5th Cir. 1993) (discriminatory quotations or offers not actionable); Vollrath Co. v. Sammi Corp., 1990–1 Trade Cas. ¶ 68955 at 63,136, 1989 WL 201632 (C.D.Cal.1989), aff'd, 9 F.3d 1455 (9th Cir.1993), cert. denied, 511 U.S. 1142, 114 S.Ct. 2163 (1994) (mere offers not actionable, and actual sales were not discriminatory); Terry's Floor Fashions, Inc. v. Burlington Indus., 763 F.2d 604, 615 (4th Cir.1985).

34. See Xeta, Inc. v. Atex, Inc., 852 F.2d 1280 (Fed.Cir. 1988) (requiring sales "during the same time period"); 14 Antitrust Law ¶ 2313 (1999).

35. See 14 Antitrust Law ¶ 2311 (1999); Parrish v. Cox, 586 F.2d 9 (6th Cir.1978); Brown v. Hansen Pub., 556 F.2d 969 (9th Cir.1977). The Supreme Court's decision in Copperweld Corp. v. Independence Tube Corp., 467 U.S. 752, 104 S.Ct. 2731 (1984), may have laid the issue to rest. In *Copperweld* the Supreme Court held that a parent and its wholly-owned subsidiary could not be "conspiring entities" under § 1 of the Sherman Act. See § 4.7. See H. Shelanski, Comment, Robinson–Patman Act Regulation of Intra-Enterprise Pricing, 80 Calif. L. Rev. 247 (1992).

36. Caribe BMW v. Bayerische Motoren Werke Aktiengesellschaft, 19 F.3d 745 (1st Cir.1994).

37. See 14 Antitrust Law ¶ 2315 (1999).

38. But see Bruce's Juices v. American Can. Co., 87 F.Supp. 985, 987 (S.D.Fla.1949), modified, 190 F.2d 73 (5th Cir.1951), cert. dismissed, 342 U.S. 875, 72 S.Ct. 165 (1951), holding that a small difference in the shape of cans sold to consumers was irrelevant, because both "gave substantially identical performance."

39. But see A.A. Poultry Farms v. Rose Acre Farms, 881 F.2d 1396, 1407–1408 (7th Cir.1989), cert. denied, 494 U.S. 1019, 110 S.Ct. 1326 (1990) ("like grade and quality" requirement not met in a set of sales of eggs where the seller picked the sizes and timing of sales, in order to eliminate surplus, as compared with a set of sales where the buyer picked the sizes and timing of sales).

40. FTC v. Borden Co., 383 U.S. 637, 86 S.Ct. 1092 (1966). Compare Texaco, Inc. v. Hasbrouck, 496 U.S. 543, 556 n. 14, 110 S.Ct. 2535, 2543 n. 14 (1990), suggesting in dicta that branded and unbranded gasoline should be considered products "of like grade and quality" for purposes of the statute. See 14 Antitrust Law ¶ 2315d (1999).

41. However, if a seller applies the same standards in determining how much credit to accord different buyers, then the statute is not violated, notwithstanding that some buyers get better terms than others. Thomas J.

or storage, advertising, brokerage allowances, return privileges, or other favorable terms that put one buyer in a better position than another. Such discriminations are legal, however, if they are "functionally available" to all buyers, even though some buyers did not take advantage of them.[42]

When courts analyze such "indirect" discrimination they look from the buyer's point of view, not the seller's. Thus if a seller provides delivery of carload lots at one rate, but requires smaller buyers to pay a higher delivery rate, courts will not begin by looking at the seller's costs. Rather they will ask whether the carload lot buyer effectively obtained the commodity at a lower price. If so, the burden shifts to the defendant seller to show that the lower price delivery was "cost justified."

The Act explicitly accounts for the fact that some customers require different services than others. Section 2(c) prohibits sellers from giving buyers allowances in lieu of brokerage or commission fees unless the services for which the fees would ordinarily be due were actually performed. However, the Supreme Court once held it illegal for a broker to reduce his commission in order to bring the parties together, if the result was a discriminatorily low-priced sale.[43] Likewise, § 2(d) of the Act permits a seller to give "allowances" to buyers who perform certain services themselves, such as promotion, handling or hauling, which the seller would otherwise perform. The statute requires that the allowances be made available "on proportionally equal terms to all other customers competing in the distribution of such products or commodities."[44] Section 2(e) of the statute prohibits a seller from furnishing facilities or services to a buyer for processing, handling or resale of the commodity unless it makes the facilities available to all buyers on proportionally equal terms.[45]

Suppose a buyer performs for itself some distribution function that the seller performs for other buyers. For example, some buyers may act as suppliers to their individual retail stores, while other buyers require direct delivery to each store. Sellers have generally been able to offer discounts to buyers in the first group, but only if the same discount is made available to other buyers willing to perform the same functions for themselves.[46]

In Texaco, Inc. v. Hasbrouck, . the plaintiffs, who were retail gasoline dealers, complained that Texaco sold gasoline cheaper to wholesale distributors than to them.[47] Texaco argued first that the price difference was merely an offset to cover the fact that the distributors, who delivered gasoline to numerous stations, were performing distribution functions that the plaintiffs did not perform. Further, it argued, the availability requirement was met because the same discount was available to any other gasoline *distributor*, even though it was not available to the retailers. However, in this case the price difference was more than sufficient to offset the distribution costs. As a result, the distributors' stations were able to charge lower prices than the direct purchasing stations for the same gasoline. The Supreme Court concluded that, although functional discounts were fully appropriate in principle, the resulting price differential must be one "that merely accords due recognition and reimbursement for actual

Kline, Inc. v. Lorillard, Inc., 878 F.2d 791 (4th Cir.1989), cert. denied, 493 U.S. 1073, 110 S.Ct. 1120 (1990).

42. On functional availability, see DeLong Equip. Co. v.Washington Mills Abrasive Co., 887 F.2d 1499, 1516–1517 (11th Cir.1989), cert. denied, 494 U.S. 1081, 110 S.Ct. 1813 (1990).

43. FTC v. Henry Broch & Co., 363 U.S. 166, 80 S.Ct. 1158 (1960). See 14 Antitrust Law ¶ 2362 (1999).

44. See 14 Antitrust Law ¶ 2363 (1999); and see George Haug Co. v. Rolls Royce Motor Cars, 148 F.3d 136, 145 (2d Cir.1998) (payment of rental for one franchisee's location but not that of the plaintiff, a competing franchisee, could be a § 2(d) violation).

45. See Portland 76 Auto/Truck Plaza v. Union Oil Co. of Cal., 153 F.3d 938 (9th Cir.1998), cert. denied, ___ U.S. ___, 119 S.Ct. 1454 (1999) (defendant upgraded one franchisee truckstop's station but not the plaintiffs; concluding that leasehold was not a qualifying "facility" for purposes of § 2(e)). See 14 Antitrust Law ¶ 2363 (1999).

46. For example, Boise Cascade Corp., 107 F.T.C. 76, 212 (1986), remanded on other grounds, 837 F.2d 1127 (D.C.Cir.1988); FLM Collision Parts, Inc. v. Ford Motor Co., 543 F.2d 1019, 1026 (2d Cir.1976), cert. denied, 429 U.S. 1097, 97 S.Ct. 1116 (1977).

47. 496 U.S. 543, 110 S.Ct. 2535 (1990).

marketing functions."[48] The match between the favored purchasers' distribution costs and the discount did not have to be precise, but it did have to be reasonably calculated to cover the avoided distribution costs and no more. As a result, functional discounts must be justified, albeit by standards that are less stringent than those that apply to the "cost justification" defense, discussed below.[49]

Sales to agencies of the federal government are exempt from the statute. In 1983, however, the Supreme Court decided that the Act applies when the low price sale is made to a state or local government agency, if the agency resells the commodity in competition with the disfavored purchasers. The Supreme Court assumed without deciding that a sale to a state or local government agency for internal consumption is exempt.[50]

§ 14.6e. Violations by Buyers

Section 2(f) of the statute makes it illegal for a *buyer* "knowingly to induce or receive a discrimination in price which is prohibited" by the Act. For many years § 2(f) was interpreted to mean that a large buyer could not put undue pressure on a seller to grant the buyer a discount that was not given to other, smaller buyers. In such cases the buyer was viewed as the violator, and the seller a more-or-less innocent victim.[51] The Congress which passed the Robinson–Patman Act was actually more concerned about pressure to discriminate from large buyers than from sellers: the statute was substantially directed at the buying practices of large chain stores. In Great Atlantic & Pacific Tea Co. v. FTC (A&P),[52] however, the Supreme Court held that a buyer could not violate § 2(f) unless he actually received "a discrimination in price which is prohibited * * *." That is, a buyer could not violate the statute unless the seller were violating it as well. If the seller had a good faith belief that it was only "meeting competition," then the seller could assert one of the affirmative defenses recognized by the Act and discussed in § 14.6f. In that case the buyer could not be in violation either, even though the seller incorrectly believed he was meeting competition because the buyer provided false information.

The *A&P* holding seems quite inconsistent with Congress' original intent.[53] For example, suppose small grocers were buying milk at $1.50 a gallon and a large chain store suddenly announced that it would like to make a large purchase at $1.35. The chain store would probably be condemned under the intent of the Act's framers, if the effect was that some seller sold to the chain store at $1.35, while selling to other stores at $1.50. Under the *A&P* holding, however, if the chain requested competitive bidding for a large purchase and received a low bid of $1.35, its purchase at that price would not violate the statute even though the seller also sold to other, smaller stores at $1.50. The bidding seller could raise the "meeting competition" defense. Since the seller did not violate the Act, the buyer could not be violating it either.[54]

§ 14.6f. Affirmative Defenses

The Robinson–Patman Act contains two affirmative defenses,[55] both of which become rel-

48. Id. at 560, 110 S.Ct. at 2544.

49. See Justice Scalia's concurring opinion, Id. at 579, 110 S.Ct. at 2555.

50. Jefferson County Pharmaceutical Ass'n, Inc. v. Abbott Laboratories, 460 U.S. 150, 103 S.Ct. 1011, rehearing denied, 460 U.S. 1105, 103 S.Ct. 1808 (1983), on remand, 709 F.2d 8 (5th Cir.1983). See 14 Antitrust Law ¶ 2354 (1999), which also discusses a special statutory exemption for purchasing cooperatives.

51. FTC v. Fred Meyer, Inc., 390 U.S. 341, 88 S.Ct. 904 (1968).

52. 440 U.S. 69, 99 S.Ct. 925 (1979). Cf. Automatic Canteen Co. v. FTC, 346 U.S. 61, 70, 73 S.Ct. 1017 (1953) (buyers' liability would not apply if seller could raise the cost justification defense; "a buyer is not precluded from inducing a lower price based on cost differences that would provide the seller with a defense."). See 14 Antitrust Law ¶ 2361b1 (1999).

53. See Justice Marshall's dissent. Id. at 86, 99 S.Ct. at 935.

54. On buyers' violations, see 14 Antitrust Law ¶ 2361 (1999).

55. Actually, the statute has a third defense, which has not been asserted as often. Section 2(a) permits price differences that result from "changing conditions affecting the market for or marketability of the good concerned. * * * "This defense effectively permits a seller to engage in price discrimination with respect to perishable goods that might otherwise spoil, obsolete goods for which the market is dwindling, and the like. See A.A. Poultry Farms v. Rose Acre Farms, 683 F.Supp. 680, 691 (S.D.Ind.1988),

evant only after the plaintiff has made out a *prima facie* case. In both, the defendant has the burden of proof.

§ 14.6f1. "Cost Justification" Defense

The "cost justification" defense of § 2(a) of the Act provides "that nothing herein contained shall prevent [price] differentials which make only due allowance for differences in the cost of manufacture, sale, or delivery" of commodities. The defense has the potential to turn the Act at least halfway into a true economic price discrimination statute. Under it differential prices would not be condemned if the differences were in direct proportion to the differences in marginal costs of serving two customers.[56]

The cost justification defense has not saved many defendants from liability, however. It has been so rigidly construed by courts that it virtually requires the defendant to show affirmatively that lower prices to a particular purchaser were proportional to the lower costs of serving that purchaser. The Supreme Court has rejected expensive, detailed cost studies, because they did not divide purchasers into sufficiently homogenous categories or did not account for every aspect of cost difference.[57] The ironic result has been to force many sellers to engage in true economic discrimination by charging the same price to different groups of buyers, even though the costs of serving them differ. Pricing in proportion to cost would threaten them with Robinson–Patman liability; however, they can always avoid liability by charging all buyers the same price.

Under the statute *marginal* cost is probably not the correct measure for determining whether a low price sale was cost justified. The defense applies only to lower prices that reflect savings in the "cost of manufacture, sale, or delivery * * *."[58] Likewise, where average total cost is higher than marginal cost and disfavored purchasers are charged a price sufficient to cover average total cost, a seller will probably not be able to "cost justify" an additional sale made at short-run marginal cost. That is, all relevant costs will have to be averaged over all customers to whom they apply.[59] This outcome can be particularly anticompetitive. First, the Act prevents sellers from producing at capacity when they can make additional sales only at a lower price than current sales.[60] Second, the Act prevents selective price cuts even when the lower prices are higher than incremental costs—that is, it prevents firms with substantial fixed costs from engaging in marginal cost pricing.

Different buyers invariably impose different costs on a seller. A customer who tries on six pairs of shoes before he makes a purchase is more expensive to serve than a customer who purchases the first pair. When goods are delivered, the differences can become even more pronounced. The delivery agent may have to walk up a flight of steps in one location but not in another. One location may be further away or be surrounded by congested traffic. These things and others can make it

affirmed, 881 F.2d 1396 (7th Cir.1989), cert. denied, 494 U.S. 1019, 110 S.Ct. 1326 (1990) (perishable eggs); Comcoa, Inc. v. NEC Tel. Co., 931 F.2d 655 (10th Cir.1991) (obsolete equipment). See 14 Antitrust Law ¶ 2353 (1999).

56. See 14 Antitrust Law ¶ 2351 (1999).

57. See United States v. Borden Co., 370 U.S. 460, 82 S.Ct. 1309 (1962); Allied Accessories & Auto Parts Co. v. General Motors Corp., 825 F.2d 971, 977 (6th Cir.1987), appeal after remand, 901 F.2d 1322 (6th Cir.1990) (rejecting study using average costs across classes to justify shipping cost savings, where individual customers' costs were not separately given).

Cost studies were accepted in Coastal Fuels of Puerto Rico v. Caribbean Petroleum Corp., 990 F.2d 25 (1st Cir.1993) (accepting facts tending to show that system of volume discounts was cost justified; approving denial of preliminary injunction); OKI Distrib. v. Amana Refrigeration, 850 F.Supp. 637, 648 (S.D.Ohio 1994) (alternative holding approving manufacturer's volume discount program; granting summary judgment against dealer plaintiff); FTC v. Standard Motor Prod., Inc., 371 F.2d 613 (2d Cir.1967); Morton v. National Dairy Prods. Corp., 414 F.2d 403 (3d Cir.1969), cert. denied, 396 U.S. 1006, 90 S.Ct. 560 (1970).

58. Interpreting this language, the FTC once held that a return on capital was not an applicable "cost" saving. Thompson Prod., Inc., 55 F.T.C. 1252, 1265–1266 (1959). See 14 Antitrust Law ¶ 2351b (1999).

59. See Standard Oil Co., 49 F.T.C. 923, 942 (1953), reversed on other grounds, 233 F.2d 649 (7th Cir.1956), affirmed, 355 U.S. 396, 78 S.Ct. 369 (1958). See 14 Antitrust Law ¶ 2351a (1999).

60. The law of predatory pricing generally recognizes that sales of this sort are competitive, not anticompetitive, because they permit firms to operate at full capacity. See § 8.6.

more costly to deliver products to one buyer than to another. About the best any seller can do is find a rational scheme for grouping buyers according to the costs that they impose on the seller. The cost justification defense can do no more.

Furthermore, in a competitive market no seller could long get away with charging a higher price if the price did not reflect the higher costs of serving certain classes of customers. As a result a market power requirement, rather than a "cost justification" defense with the burden on the defendant, would be a much more satisfactory way of initially determining whether differential prices were really discriminatory.[61]

§ 14.6f2. "Meeting Competition" Defense

Section 2(b) of the Robinson–Patman Act also permits a defendant to rebut a *prima facie* case of violation by showing that its lower price "was made in good faith to meet an equally low price of a competitor * * *."[62] This "meeting competition" defense has traditionally required the seller to have actual knowledge that a particular competitor had offered a lower price on an identical or similar product. For example, if a seller had been selling widgets to X at $2.00, but learned that a competitor had offered X widgets at $1.80, then the seller could match the $1.80 offer rather than lose the sale.

In FTC v. A.E. Staley Mfg. Co.[63] the Supreme Court held that the "meeting competition" defense could be raised only by someone who had "first-hand" knowledge of an actual offer of a lower price from an actual competitor. If such an offer did not exist, the seller could not raise the meeting competition defense. *Staley* therefore suggested that it was a seller's responsibility to "investigate or verify" any information about a lower-price offer from a competitor.[64] Additionally, *Staley* held that a seller could not "meet" a competitor's general price structure or schedule, but could "meet competition" only on a transaction-by-transaction basis.

In United States v. United States Gypsum Co.[65] the defendants, who were competitors, were charged with illegally exchanging information about resale prices. The defense raised was that the sellers needed to "investigate or verify" rumored lower price bids from competitors, and the only way they could do so was to ask the competitor.

The defense raised in the *Gypsum* case further illustrates the anticompetitive potential of the Robinson–Patman Act. A great deal of law under § 1 of the Sherman Act forbids price information exchanges among competitors, if the exchange influences price.[66] In *Gypsum* the defendants presented what appeared to be a bona fide defense: in order to comply with the "meeting competition" defense of the Robinson–Patman Act, they were obliged to verify that a competitor had in fact given a lower bid to a particular customer. In short, compliance with the Robinson–Patman Act required violation of the Sherman Act. The Supreme Court, concluding that the Robinson–Patman Act must be harmonized with the policies of the other antitrust laws,[67] held that "meeting competition" required only "good faith," not actual knowledge. Under *Gypsum* a

61. Even with its market power established, however, a defendant should still be permitted to cost justify sales at different prices. That is, market power is a *prerequisite* for persistent price discrimination, but it is not proof of persistent price discrimination. See Hovenkamp, note 8 at 1176.

62. See 14 Antitrust Law ¶ 2352 (1999).

63. 324 U.S. 746, 65 S.Ct. 971 (1945).

64. See Id. at 758–59, 65 S.Ct. at 977. The defendants in *Staley* had made their low price sales "in response to verbal information received from salesmen, brokers, or intending purchasers, without supporting evidence, to the effect that in each case one or more competitors had granted or offered to grant like discriminations." In affirming the FTC's decision that this information was not good enough to sustain the "good faith" meeting competition defense, the Court cited an "entire lack of a showing of diligence * * * to verify the reports * * * or to learn of the existence of facts which would lead a reasonable and prudent person to believe that the granting of a lower price would in fact be meeting the equally low price of a competitor." Id.

65. 438 U.S. 422, 98 S.Ct. 2864 (1978), appeal after remand, 600 F.2d 414 (3d Cir.1979), cert. denied, 444 U.S. 884, 100 S.Ct. 175 (1979).

66. For example, United States v. Container Corp. of America, 393 U.S. 333, 89 S.Ct. 510 (1969), discussed in § 5.3.

67. *Gypsum,* 438 U.S. at 458, 98 S.Ct. at 2884.

seller is entitled to believe a customer if the customer says "I can get it cheaper from your competitor," and the seller has no particular reason to doubt the customer's word. If later it turns out that the customer was lying or mistaken, the seller will not be held liable, provided that he acted in good faith.[68]

Another element of the *Staley* holding was substantially undermined in Falls City Industries, Inc v. Vanco Beverage, Inc.,[69] when the Supreme Court unanimously decided that a seller could meet the lower general price structure in a different market, without necessarily meeting competition on a customer-by-customer or sale-by-sale basis. The Supreme Court found "no evidence that Congress intended to limit the availability of [the meeting competition defense] to customer-specific responses." Rather Congress "intended to allow reasonable pricing responses on an area-specific basis where competitive circumstances warrant them."

This new broader application of the "meeting competition" defense has the potential to create a significant hole in Robinson–Patman enforcement. *All* sales are made at a price calculated by the seller to "meet competition." Even the absolute monopolist cannot charge an infinite price for its product. When the monopolist calculates its profit-maximizing price as $2.00, it has concluded that at a price of $2.10 too many customers will purchase something else instead. More to the point, why would a seller who has just sold 50 gallons of milk to one store for $1.50 per gallon agree to sell 1,000 gallons of milk to another store for $1.35? Any reasonable seller would do so for only one reason: if it refuses the buyer may look elsewhere. Since the seller has calculated that he can profitably make the larger sale at the lower price, he will generally suspect that someone else could do it as well. The Supreme Court's suggestion in *Vanco Beverage* that the "very purpose" of the meeting competition defense "is to permit a seller to treat different competitive situations differently" makes good economic sense.

68. Several decisions have accepted the defense. See, e.g., Bristol Steel & Iron Works v. Bethlehem Steel Corp., 41 F.3d 182 (4th Cir.1994) (approving jury verdict finding the defense to have been met); Bryant Corp. v. Outboard Marine Corp., 1995–1 Trade Cas. ¶ 70,903, at 74,011, 1994 WL 745159 (W.D.Wash.1994), affirmed, 77 F.3d 488 (9th Cir.1996) (defendant actually saw rival's price list and then consulted in house counsel; defense met). But see Rose Confections, Inc. v. Ambrosia Chocolate Co., 816 F.2d 381, 391–393 (8th Cir.1987) (defense rejected where seller did not carefully verify that competitor's prices were in fact lower, but relied on "assumption or speculation."). See 14 Antitrust Law ¶ 2352e (1999).

69. 460 U.S. 428, 103 S.Ct. 1282, on remand, 705 F.2d 463 (7th Cir.1983).

*

Part III

ANTITRUST AS A REGULATORY INSTITUTION

Chapter 15

PUBLIC ENFORCEMENT OF THE FEDERAL ANTITRUST LAWS

Table of Sections

§ 15.1 Public Enforcement Generally; The Antitrust Division

The public enforcement of the federal antitrust laws is largely in the hands of the Antitrust Division of the Department of Justice (Division) and the Federal Trade Commission (FTC). Technically, only the Division has authority to engage in public enforcement of the Sherman Act. However, the FTC may bring actions challenging unfair methods of competition under § 5 of the Federal Trade Commission Act, which has been interpreted to include everything in the Sherman Act, plus a few practices that are not covered by the Sherman Act.[1] The Division and the FTC have concurrent authority to enforce the Clayton Act. Since the jurisdiction of the two agencies overlaps, they have developed clearance procedures for notifying each other before conducting investigations or filing actions. If both are found to be pursuing the same inquiry, the two agencies decide which will handle it, based generally on considerations of expertise, staff availability, and so on. If the matter involves likely criminal activity it will generally be referred to the Division, since the FTC does not have criminal jurisdiction.

Both the Division and the FTC occasionally issue written Guidelines, outlining their enforcement position on various matters. The most prominent of these, the 1992 Horizontal Merger Guidelines issued jointly by the Division and the FTC, are discussed in detail elsewhere.[2] In addition, the Division has issued numerous other enforcement guidelines, some of them in conjunction with the FTC.[3] The Division also issues Business Review Letters, evaluating business conduct contemplated by private parties.[4] Such a letter may state the Division's intention to challenge or not to challenge the conduct as of the date of the letter; but the Division is not bound to state its intent and often refuses to do so. The Division also participates as amicus curiae in private

§ 15.1

1. 15 U.S.C.A. § 45(a); FTC v. Cement Institute, 333 U.S. 683, 694, 68 S.Ct. 793, 800 (1948).

2. See §§ 3.8, 12.1.

3. The most important of these Guidelines are printed as appendices to the *Antitrust Law* treatise (current Supp.); all of them can be found in volume 4 of Trade Regulation Reporter (CCH), where they are continuously updated.

See United States v. Heffernan, 43 F.3d 1144, 1148 (7th Cir.1994) (interpreting sentencing guidelines in a criminal antitrust case; distinguishing bid-rigging from ordinary price-fixing; former gets stiffer penalty).

4. 28 C.F.R. § 50.6 (1999).

antitrust actions, sometimes in behalf of defendants.[5] This practice has sometimes been criticized as falling outside the Division's jurisdictional authority to "prevent and restrain" antitrust violations.[6]

The Division's main antitrust enforcement activity is the launching of investigations and, if necessary, the subsequent pursuit of criminal or civil litigation. Investigations are initiated as a result of private complaints, inquiries conducted at the instigation of the Division itself, or as a result of private reporting, such as premerger notification.[7] In the initial stage, called the "preliminary inquiry," investigations are based solely on public information. If warranted, the Division then proceeds to a formal investigation, under which it may question individuals or subpoena documents. Thereafter the Division may drop the inquiry, terminate through settlement, or file a criminal or civil antitrust action in federal district court.

15.1a. Criminal Enforcement

The Division generally files criminal actions only for clear, intentional violations of the law. The great majority of these are for explicit price fixing or bid rigging. In United States v. United States Gypsum, the Supreme Court held that the Division must prove criminal intent in order to obtain a criminal conviction.[8] This generally requires a showing either that the conduct had an anticompetitive effect and that the defendants knew of these probable effects, or else that the conduct was intended to produce anticompetitive effects, whether or not they actually occurred. A growing body of law has attempted to parse the meaning of these requirements. It seems clear that an effect on competition need not have occurred, provided that the defendants actually, subjectively intended that it occur.[9] In *Cinemette*, the court held that motion picture "split" agreements, a form of horizontal product division in which exhibitors agree not to bid competitively for the same film, could be the subject of a criminal indictment even though the practice was illegal per se in some circuits but not in others.[10] The court rejected the argument that because of the "uncertain legal status" of such agreements, no criminal intent could be inferred. Thus it seems that if the defendants do have an intent to injure competition they can be charged with a crime, even if the practice is not clearly illegal *per se*. By contrast, if the alleged violation is clearly illegal *per se*, several courts have held that intent to enter into the conspiracy is all that is required; no showing must be made of a distinct intent to injure competition as such.[11]

The Division itself has taken the position that criminal violations have these "typical" characteristics:

> (1) the conduct involves agreement among actual, potential, or apparent competitors (except for monopolization involving independently illegal acts, such as bribery or physical violence); (2) that agreement is inherently likely to raise (or, in the case of monopsony, to lower) price and restrict output without the promise of any significant integrative efficiency benefit; (3) the agreement is generally covert or fraudulent; and (4) the conspirators generally are

5. See Interview with William F. Baxter, Assistant Attorney General, Antitrust Division, 51 Antitrust L.J. 23 (1982).

6. See § 4 of the Sherman Act, 15 U.S.C.A. § 4.

7. See § 15.3.

8. 438 U.S. 422, 98 S.Ct. 2864 (1978).

9. United States v. Gravoly, 840 F.2d 1156, 1161 (4th Cir.1988).

10. United States v. Cinemette Corp. of Am., 687 F.Supp. 976 (W.D.Pa.1988). See Viking Theatre Corp. v. Paramount Film Distributing Corp., 320 F.2d 285 (3d Cir.1963), affirmed per curiam by an equally divided court, 378 U.S. 123, 84 S.Ct. 1657, 12 L.Ed.2d 743 (1964) (refusing to apply per se rule); Admiral Theatre Corp. v. Douglas Theatre Co., 585 F.2d 877 (8th Cir.1978) (same); United States v. Capitol Serv., 756 F.2d 502 (7th Cir.), cert. denied, 474 U.S. 945, 106 S.Ct. 311 (1985) (split agreements illegal per se). See 12 Antitrust Law ¶ 2013c (1999).

11. United States v. Brown, 936 F.2d 1042 (9th Cir. 1991); United States v. Suntar Roofing, Inc., 709 F.Supp. 1526, 1540 (D.Kan.1989), affirmed, 897 F.2d 469 (10th Cir.1990); United States v. Gillen, 599 F.2d 541, 545 (3d Cir.), cert. denied, 444 U.S. 866, 100 S.Ct. 137 (1979). See also United States v. Cargo Serv. Stations, 657 F.2d 676, 683 (5th Cir.1981), cert. denied, 455 U.S. 1017, 102 S.Ct. 1712 (1982): "* * * if price fixing is inevitably an unreasonable restraint of trade, the intent to fix prices is equivalent to the intent to unreasonably restrain trade."

aware of the probable anticompetitive consequences of their conduct.[12]

For criminal violations of the Sherman Act, corporate defendants may be fined up to $10,000,000, or individuals up to $350,000.[13] Further, individuals may receive prison sentences of up to 3 years in addition to or instead of a fine.[14] Additionally, however, the Criminal Fines Improvements Act of 1984[15] provides that for violations generally committed since 1984, a fine may be measured by double the gain to the violators or the loss to the victim, or by the antitrust damages provisions, whichever is greater. Although fines measured in this manner may be greater than those explicitly authorized by the Sherman Act, they may be less than the provable treble damages in a private antitrust civil action.[16]

15.1b. Civil Enforcement

For civil investigations, the Division commonly issues Civil Investigative Demands (CIDs), which are subpoenas that can be issued to any person believed to have information pertaining to the investigation, and requiring documents, oral testimony, or answers to interrogatories.[17] Information obtained as a result of a CID may sometimes be shared with the FTC for its own investigation, or may occasionally be disclosed to Congress. Otherwise, it must be kept confidential and is expressly exempt from inquiries made under the Freedom of Information Act.[18]

Most civil antitrust investigations leading to challenges result in consent decrees, which are binding out-of-court settlements approved by the court. Consent decrees permit defendants to avoid the consequences of § 5(a) of the Clayton Act, which provides that a judgment in an antitrust case against a defendant becomes prima facie evidence of guilt in a subsequent private action based on the same violation.[19] Consent decrees can later be enforced by the Division, just as any court judgment can, although they cannot form the basis for an antitrust action by a private plaintiff.[20] Consent decrees are generally interpreted as contracts, and not by reference to the underlying law.[21] In recent years the Division has consented to the modification or termination of many older consent decrees that are now considered to have gone too far, or where the defendants' position has changed materially—for example, if the market has become much more competitive or the defendant is no longer the dominant player.[22]

12. Department of Justice, International Operations Antitrust Enforcement Policy 22 (Nov. 10, 1988), reprinted at 4 Trade Reg. Rep. (CCH) ¶ 13,109 (superceded). On criminal liability of corporations generally, see V. Khanna, Corporate Criminal Liability: what Purpose Does it Serve?, 109 Harv. L. Rev. 1477 (1996); D. Fischel & A. Sykes, Corporate Crime, 25 J. Legal Stud. 310 (1996).

13. 15 U.S.C.A. §§ 1, 2, 3. These numbers are periodically revised to reflect inflation as well as a general view that criminal penalties should not be significantly less than applicable civil damages awards.

14. 15 U.S.C.A. §§ 1, 2.

15. See 18 U.S.C.A. §§ 3621–3624; Criminal Fines Improvements Act of 1987 (re-enacted), 101 Stat. 1279, 1289.

16. On damages measurement, see Chapter 17.

17. See Antitrust Civil Process Act, 15 U.S.C.A. §§ 1311–1314.

18. 15 U.S.C.A. § 1314(g).

19. 15 U.S.C.A. § 16(a). However, the statutes provides that "Nothing contained in this section shall be construed to impose any limitation on the application of collateral estoppel." * * *

20. Blue Chip Stamps v. Manor Drug Stores, 421 U.S. 723, 750, 95 S.Ct. 1917, 1932 (1975) (non-parties may not enforce consent decree; securities case); Data Processing Fin. & Gen. Corp. v. IBM, 430 F.2d 1277 (8th Cir.1970) (per curiam; same; antitrust case). However, private plaintiffs may sometimes act as intervenors in actions requesting termination of consent decrees. See, e.g., United States v. IBM Corp., 163 F.3d 737 (2d Cir.1998) (rejecting intervenor's objection that IBM continued to have significant market power in computer market; approving termination of 1954 consent decree).

21. But the consent decree often incorporates antitrust terms of art, and these are ordinarily interpreted according to antitrust principles. See, e.g., United States v. Microsoft Corp., 980 F.Supp. 537 (D.D.C.1997), rev'd, 147 F.3d 935 (D.C.Cir.1998) (relying heavily on antitrust law to interpret 1995 consent decree that would have forbidden Microsoft from bundling Windows 95 and Internet Explorer if the two were "separate products" for tying purposes; circuit court ultimately concluded that they were a single product). See Antitrust Law ¶ 1746.1 (current Supp.).

22. For example, *IBM*, note 20; United States v. Western Elec. Co., 900 F.2d 283 (D.C.Cir.1990) (partial removal of line-of-business restriction in 1983 consent decree, given changing market circumstances); United States v. Columbia Artists Mgmt., Inc., 662 F.Supp. 865, 869–870 (S.D.N.Y.1987) (terminating decree forbidding joint venture among booking agencies).

Remedies for civil violations can include injunctions, as well as dissolution or divestiture for illegal mergers or occasionally monopolization. Just as any private plaintiff, the United States Government is also entitled to recover treble damages for injuries it suffers as a result of an antitrust violation—as, for example, in the case of federal government purchases subject to price fixing.[23]

§ 15.2 The Federal Trade Commission

The Federal Trade Commission is a regulatory agency established during the Wilson Administration in 1914.[1] The Commission consists of five Commissioners appointed by the President subject to Senate confirmation for seven-year terms. The FTC has authority to enforce the substance of all of the antitrust laws. This includes direct authority with respect to the Clayton Act and the Robinson–Patman Act. With respect to the Sherman Act, the FTC has no direct enforcement authority, but its authority to challenge "unfair methods of competition" under § 5 of the FTC Act[2] has been interpreted to include all practices condemned under the Sherman Act.

Further, in *Sperry & Hutchinson*, the Supreme Court held that the FTC has authority "to define and proscribe an unfair competitive practice, even though the practice does not infringe either the letter or the spirit of the antitrust laws."[3] As the Supreme Court later explained in *Indiana Dentists*, the "standard of 'unfairness' under the FTC Act is, by necessity, an elusive one, encompassing not only practices that violate the Sherman Act and the other antitrust laws but also practices that the Commission determines are against public policy for other reasons. * * * "[4]

As the *Indiana Dentists* statement suggests, the precise scope of the FTC's authority to "expand" the meaning of the Sherman Act is unclear and controversial. Further, it has come under increased scrutiny in recent years. Earlier cases had indicated that the FTC was entitled to condemn tying arrangements in the absence of market power[5] or exclusive dealing without a showing of likely injury to competition.[6] More recently, however, courts have

23. 15 U.S.C.A. § 15(a).

§ 15.2

1. For a brief history, see M. Sklar, The Corporate Reconstruction of American Capitalism, 1890–1916 at 328–332 (1988). See also G. Henderson, The Federal Trade Commission: A Study in Administrative Law and Procedure (1924); T. McCraw, Rethinking the Trust Question, in Regulation in Perspective: Historical Essays 25–55 (T. McCraw, ed. 1981).

The jurisdiction of the FTC includes "corporations," but then defines corporation as an association "organized to carry on business for its own profit or that of its members...." 15 U.S.C.A. §§ 44, 45. In California Dental Assn. (CDA) v. FTC, ___ U.S. ___, 119 S.Ct. 1604 (1999) the Supreme Court agreed with numerous previous FTC and many circuit court decisions that this definition was sufficient to reach an incorporated *non*profit trade association if one of the association's purposes was to further its members' profits. Further, there is:

> no apparent reason to let the statute's application turn on meeting some threshold percentage of activity for this purpose, or even satisfying a softer formulation calling for a substantial part of the nonprofit entity's total activities to be aimed at its members' pecuniary benefit. To be sure, proximate relation to lucre must appear; the FTC Act does not cover all membership organizations of profit-making corporations without more, and an organization devoted solely to professional education may lie outside the FTC Act's jurisdictional reach, even though the quality of professional services ultimately affects the profits of those who deliver them.
>
> ... Through for-profit subsidiaries, the CDA provides advantageous insurance and preferential financing arrangements for its members, and it engages in lobbying, litigation, marketing, and public relations for the benefit of its members' interests. This congeries of activities confers far more than de minimis or merely presumed economic benefits on CDA members; the economic benefits conferred upon the CDA's profit-seeking professionals plainly fall within the object of enhancing its members' 'profit.' ...

119 S.Ct. at 1611.

2. 15 U.S.C.A. § 45.

3. FTC v. Sperry & Hutchinson Co., 405 U.S. 233, 239, 92 S.Ct. 898, 903 (1972).

4. FTC v. Indiana Fed'n of Dentists, 476 U.S. 447, 454, 106 S.Ct. 2009, 2016 (1986). In *California Dental*, note 1 at 1608, n. 3, the Supreme Court declined to comment on the difference in coverage between FTCA § 5 and Sherman § 1, noting only that the FTC had relied on Sherman Act Law in adjudicating the horizontal restraint case before it. The Court therefore did not intimate one way or the other whether § 5 of the FTC Act might condemn a horizontal restraint that the Sherman Act did not condemn.

5. Atlantic Refining Co. v. FTC, 381 U.S. 357, 369–371, 85 S.Ct. 1498, 1506–1507 (1965).

6. FTC v. Brown Shoe Co., 384 U.S. 316, 321, 86 S.Ct. 1501, 1504 (1966).

looked at expansive efforts by the FTC more critically. For example, in *Boise Cascade* the court upset FTC condemnation of a delivered pricing system used in common by several sellers, but where there was no evidence of an agreement among them.[7] The court concluded that the FTC had an obligation to show either an agreement or else evidence that noncollusive use of the system had a measurable anticompetitive effect. The Commission's decision in the *Dupont (Ethyl)* case met a similar fate.[8] The Commission challenged various "facilitating practices" alleged to yield collusion-like results in the absence of a Sherman § 1 price-fixing agreement. In overturning the Commission's decision condemning the practices, the court concluded that

> "before business conduct in an oligopolistic industry may be labelled 'unfair' within the meaning of § 5 a minimum standard demands that, absent a tacit agreement, at least some indicia of oppressiveness must exist such as (1) evidence of anticompetitive intent or purpose on the part of the producer charged, or (2) the absence of an independent legitimate business reason for its conduct."[9]

There are two views about the wisdom of the FTC's use of § 5 to go beyond the substance of the antitrust laws generally. One view looks to the substance of those laws, with their central concern for competition. If the case law under the antitrust laws defines our concerns for competition correctly, then it is wrong for the FTC to go further. In effect, it would turn antitrust into the regulation of "unfair" rather than anticompetitive trade practices. This suggests that the decisions noted above, condemning tying and exclusive dealing without any showing of harm to competition, are incorrect.[10]

But there is an alternative view, perfectly consistent with the proposition that the FTC's antitrust concern should be limited to identifying practices that are economically anticompetitive. The FTC is a regulatory agency, which is more specialized than courts and not as bound by strict rules of procedure and evidence. Further, its general remedy, at least in most cases, is a "cease and desist" order. Findings of violations of the FTC Act that are not also antitrust violations will not support subsequent private actions for treble damages. As a result, application of the FTC Act to practices that do not violate the other antitrust laws are appropriate when (1) the practice seems anticompetitive but is not technically covered by the antitrust laws; and (2) the social cost of an error seems to be relatively small.

A good example is the use of the FTC Act to go after facilitating practices in oligopoly industries in the absence of an express agreement. Today there is widespread consensus that such practices can produce anticompetitive results, and that the Sherman Act's "agreement" requirement limits courts' ability to deal with the range of concerns that we associate with firms' coordination of price or output.[11] Further, if the FTC's remedy is limited to prospective injunction against certain facilitating practices, such as advance price announcements or use of a common delivered pricing or basing point pricing scheme, then the social cost of an error is likely to be rather small. That is to say, advance posting of prices may produce certain economies even in a tightly oligopolistic industry prone to price leadership, but the threat to competition seems significantly larger.

Another example is an unaccepted solicitation or offer to conspire to fix prices, which would not satisfy the Sherman § 1 "agreement" requirement but could nevertheless be anticompetitive. For example, an unaccepted solicitation can inform other firms of the offer-

7. Boise Cascade Corp. v. FTC, 637 F.2d 573, 579–582 (9th Cir.1980). On reaching oligopoly behavior without proof of a qualifying agreement, see § 4.6.

8. E.I. du Pont De Nemours & Co. v. FTC, 729 F.2d 128, 139–142 (2d Cir.1984).

9. 729 F.2d at 139–140.

10. See *Atlantic Refining*, note 5; and *Brown Shoe*, note 6.

11. See § 4.4.

or's willingness to engage in tacit, rather than express, collusion.[12]

The ordinary remedy in an FTC action is a cease and desist order—although this may amount to forced dissolution or divestiture in the case of a merger. The FTC has authority to assess civil penalties, but only for violations of previously given cease and desist orders, or explicit violations of FTC rules and practices.[13]

Although the Commission receives many private complaints and acts upon them as it deems appropriate, only the FTC itself can initiate its proceedings. The FTC has its own procedures for collecting and presenting evidence, generally governed by Section 5(b) of the FTC Act[14] and the Federal Administrative Procedure Act.[15] The initial adjudicative proceeding is given to an Administrative Law Judge (ALJ), who makes a preliminary decision. During this process the FTC provides its own complaint counsel, which generally has the burden of proof, just as the plaintiff in civil litigation. After the ALJ has issued a preliminary decision, it is either approved or disapproved by the Commission itself. If the Commission's decision is adverse to the respondent, it may seek review by the federal courts of appeals.[16] The court is generally obliged to accept the FTC's fact findings if they are supported by substantial evidence in the record as a whole.[17] While courts generally give great weight to the Commission's interpretation of the *law*, they are not bound by it.

12. See Antitrust Law ¶ 1419.1 (current supplement).

13. See 15 U.S.C.A. § 45(*l*) & (m). In one highly publicized case the FTC asked a private defendant to disgorge unlawful monopoly profits earned from a conspiracy to monopolize the market for a drug. See 75 Antitrust & Trade Regulation Rep. 701 (BNA, Dec. 24, 1998) (discussing *Mylan* decision).

14. 15 U.S.C.A. § 45(b).

15. 5 U.S.C.A. § 554.

16. Preliminary injunctions are generally appealed to a federal district court.

17. See RSR Corp. v. FTC, 602 F.2d 1317, 1320 (9th Cir.1979), cert. denied, 445 U.S. 927, 100 S.Ct. 1313 (1980).

§ 15.3 The Process of Premerger Notification

The Hart–Scott–Rodino Antitrust Improvements Act of 1976 requires premerger notification of certain mergers, as well as a waiting period that permits either the Division or the FTC to collect information about the proposed acquisition.[1] The Act is administered by both agencies under complex rules. This section offers only a simple and very brief summary.[2] Generally speaking, transactions are reportable if they satisfy three tests: (1) they must be "in commerce;" (2) the parties must be of a specified minimum size; and (3) the transaction itself must be of a certain minimum size.[3] The "in commerce" provision generally reflects Clayton Act § 7's requirement that limits its provisions to transactions in or affecting interstate commerce. The size-of-the-parties test requires that one of the acquiring or acquired persons have annual net sales or total assets of $100 million or more, and that the other have net sales or total assets of $10 million or more.[4] The transaction test requires that as a result of the transaction the acquiring firm would hold either 15% of either voting securities or assets in the acquired firm, *or* voting securities and assets valued at $15 million or more.

The effect of these rules is that most stock or asset acquisitions must be reported where one of the parties has sales or assets of $100 million or more, the other has sales or assets of $10 million or more, and the transaction itself is valued at $15 million or more. There

§ 15.3

1. 15 U.S.C.A. § 18a.

2. For further information, see 4A Antitrust Law ¶ 990d (rev. ed. 1998). Implementing regulations are codified in 16 C.F.R. §§ 801–803 (1996), as modified, 61 Fed. Reg. 13,666 (1996). The procedures themselves are subject to frequent technical modification or comment, which is ordinarily published in the Federal Register. See, e.g., 62 Fed Reg. 58449–01 (1997) (proposed modification, FTC). See also ABA, The Merger Review Process: a Step-by-Step Guide to Federal Merger Review (1995); FTC, Introductory Guides to the Premerger Notification Program (1991); ABA, Premerger Notification Practice Manual (2d ed. 1991); FTC, Premerger Notification Source Book (1987). See generally L. Mullenix, The Premerger Notification Program of the Federal Trade Commission, 57 Antitrust L.J. 125 (1988).

3. See 16 C.F.R. § 801.11(c)(1),(2) (1996).

4. 15 U.S.C.A. § 18a(a)(2). The rule contains exceptions for non-manufacturing firms.

are exceptions for acquisitions of goods or real property in the ordinary course of business, acquisitions solely for investment, and most intra-firm transactions (such as transactions among wholly owned subsidiaries of a common parent).

Once a transaction is found to be reportable, all parties to the transaction must file a "Notification and Report Form,"[5] together with a filing fee. The ordinary waiting period after filing is 30 days, but in the case of cash tender offers it is reduced to 15 days. During this period the proposed transaction cannot be consummated, nor can the merging companies begin to consolidate their operations.

The penalties for failing to file are substantial, up to $10,000 per day for the firm and each of its managerial officers who had the responsibility to file. The agencies have been quite aggressive about seeking out unreported transactions.[6]

§ 15.4 "Quasi–Public" Enforcement: The States' Attorneys General

In addition to the public agencies, states' attorneys general have authority to enforce the federal antitrust laws. The states are considered private persons when they seek enforcement of the federal antitrust laws, however.[1] As a result, they act in a dual role. Insofar as the relationship between the state attorneys general and federal law is concerned, the states are simply a special case of the private plaintiff, and most of the restrictions on private enforcement apply to them.[2] But the states attorneys general are also public agencies insofar as their responsibility to their own political constituencies is concerned.

The most common kind of state antitrust enforcement is the treble damage suit seeking overcharge damages for price fixing.[3] As a private party, the state is governed by such rules as the indirect purchaser rule, which prohibits those who did not deal directly with a cartel member from recovering damages under federal law.[4] States also enforce the merger laws, and in California v. American Stores[5] the Supreme Court held that a state may obtain divestiture as a remedy for a disapproved merger, even though the merger had previously been approved by the Federal Trade Commission.

The Hart–Scott–Rodino Antitrust Improvements Act of 1976 permits states to bring parens patriae actions in behalf of natural persons[6] residing in the state, for damages arising under the Sherman Act.[7] If such actions are litigated to a final judgment, a private action by the natural persons in whose behalf the action was brought is barred, unless they have exercised a right to opt out. The violation and injury are established as in any private antitrust action. However both the computation of damages and the way that the payment is satisfied differ. First, the Act permits more liberalized proof of damages through sampling methods that may not actually show the amount by which each individual plaintiff was injured.[8] Second, the damages may be paid directly to the state as a civil penalty or by some other method approved by the court.

Since 1983, when the Multistate Antitrust Task Force of the National Association of At-

5. The form itself can be found at 16 C.F.R. § 803 (1996) (appendix), and is subject to periodic revision.

6. See United States v. Sara Lee Corp., 1996–1 Trade Cas. ¶ 71,301, 1996 WL 120857 (D.D.C.1996) ($3.1 million penalty); United States v. Equity Group Holdings, 1991–1 Trade Cas. (CCH) ¶ 69320, 1991 WL 28878 (D.D.C.1991) (consent decree; $850,000 penalty).

§ 15.4

1. See, for example, California v. American Stores, 495 U.S. 271, 110 S.Ct. 1853 (1990) (treating state as private citizen for purpose of interpreting right to divestiture in merger challenge).

2. On private enforcement, see Chapter 16.

3. See § 17.5.

4. See § 16.6.

5. Note 1.

6. I.e., excluding corporations and other business firms.

7. 15 U.S.C.A. § 15c-h.

8. See, for example, In re Mid–Atlantic Toyota Antitrust Litig., 525 F.Supp. 1265, 1285 (D.Md.1981), aff'd sub nom. Pennsylvania v. Mid–Atlantic Toyota Distribs., 704 F.2d 125 (4th Cir.1983) (approving proof of damages by statistical sampling; just compensation clause challenge premature).

torneys General (NAAG) was created, there has been increasing coordination of private enforcement by the states.[9] In part, this has been a response to perceptions by those in several states that the federal government was less aggressive about enforcing the antitrust laws than it had been before. This perception was widespread during the two Reagan Administrations (1981–1989). These coordinated efforts have included major challenges to alleged price fixing,[10] resale price maintenance,[11] tying arrangements,[12] joint ventures with alleged anticompetitive effects,[13] and boycotts in the insurance industry.[14]

The state attorneys general have also coordinated their merger enforcement efforts. In particular, they have jointly issued their own horizontal merger Guidelines, originally released in 1987, and revised in 1992.[15] These Guidelines are somewhat more aggressive against mergers than the corresponding federal Guidelines.[16] For example, the NAAG Guidelines generally define markets more narrowly than do the federal guidelines. Further, they recognize some goals other than efficiency as legitimate parts of antitrust enforcement policy. For example, mergers that transfer wealth away from consumers can be condemned under the NAAG Guidelines even if the merger itself creates efficiency savings larger than the monopoly price increase.[17] A problematic aspect of the NAAG Merger Guidelines is that under them the states can effectively impose a policy concerning the *structure* of interstate industries that is inconsistent with federal policy—provided, of course, that the federal courts will cooperate. For example, a single state could seek divestiture or injunction against an acquisition where most of the productive assets of the acquiring and acquired firms are located in different states.[18] NAAG has also issued vertical restraints Guidelines that are considerably more aggressive against vertical practices than are the corresponding (but now withdrawn) federal Guidelines.[19]

Finally, of course, the states' attorneys general are heavily involved in enforcing the antitrust laws of their particular states, most of which are similar to federal antitrust law. These statutes are generally beyond the scope of this volume, but a brief discussion focusing on issues of federalism is contained in § 20.8.[20]

9. See M.F. Brockmeyer, The State of State Antitrust Enforcement, 59 Antitrust L.J. 25 (1990). A good example is the massive antitrust litigation filed by nineteen states against liability insurers. Hartford Fire Ins. Co. v. California, 509 U.S. 764, 113 S.Ct. 2891 (1993).

10. For example, In re Minolta Camera Products Antitrust Litigation, 668 F.Supp. 456 (D.Md.1987).

11. In re Panasonic Consumer Elecs. Products Antitrust Litig., 1989–1 Trade Cas. ¶ 68613, 1989 WL 63240 (S.D.N.Y.1989) (approving settlement).

12. In re Mid–Atlantic Toyota Antitrust Litigation, 605 F.Supp. 440 (D.Md.1984) (approving settlement).

13. New York v. Visa, U.S.A., Inc., 1990–1 Trade Cas. (CCH) ¶ 69016, 1990 WL 75047 (S.D.N.Y.1990) (approving settlement).

14. *Hartford*, note 9.

15. NAAG Horizontal Merger Guidelines (1987), 4 Trade Reg. Rep. (CCH) ¶ 13,405; Revised Horizontal Merger Guidelines (1993), reprinted in 64 Antitrust & Trade Reg. Rep. (BNA) #1608, Special Supp., (Apr. 1, 1993). For a survey and analysis of state merger enforcement, see R. Lande, When Should States Challenge Mergers: a Proposed Federal/State Balance, 35 New York Law School L. Rev. 1047 (1990). On the state guidelines, see D.W. Barnes, Federal and State Philosophies in the Antitrust Law of Mergers, 56 Geo.Wash.L.Rev. 263 (1988).

16. See Chapter 12, particularly § 12.1.

17. On this issue, see § 12.2b.

18. In the acquisition challenged in California v. American Stores, note 1, 27% of the acquired firm's (Lucky Stores) assets were located outside of California. State of California, Petition for Writ of Certiorari 3.

19. NAAG Vertical Restraints Guidelines (1988), 4 Trade Reg. Rep. ¶ 13,400.

20. See also 14 Antitrust Law, Ch. 24 (1999); H. Hovenkamp, State Antitrust in the Federal Scheme, 58 Ind. L.J. 375 (1983); ABA Antitrust Section, Monograph No. 15, Antitrust Federalism: the Role of State Law (1988); ABA Antitrust Section, State Antitrust Practice and Statutes (2d.ed.1998)

Chapter 16

PRIVATE ENFORCEMENT

Table of Sections

§ 16.1 Introduction: § 4 of the Clayton Act

This chapter is concerned mainly with enforcement of the federal antitrust laws by private persons. It includes a few issues, such as statute of limitation,[1] jury trial, summary judgment, use of experts, and collateral estoppel[2] that are relevant to both public and private enforcement of the antitrust laws.[3] These discussions are placed here for convenience, and because most questions have risen in the context of private antitrust litigation.

Section 4 of the Clayton Act provides that "Any person injured in his business or property by reason of anything forbidden in the antitrust laws may sue * * * and shall recover three-fold the damages * * * sustained and * * * a reasonable attorney's fee."[4]

The simplicity of § 4's language belies the complexity of the many questions it has raised. One problem with the statute is its unrealistic breadth. In a market economy a simple price fixing agreement has effects that injure everyone. Witness the impact of the OPEC cartel, which resulted in higher prices not only of petroleum, but of everything that required energy for its manufacture—industrial products, agricultural products, even other natural resources. The result threw several national economies into disarray.[5]

The difference between a large cartel like OPEC and a small price fixing conspiracy among local concrete producers is one of degree, not of nature. By its language, § 4 appears to give a cause of action to every person who is injured by a cartel or overcharging monopolist. The courts have concluded that the statute cannot be as broad as it purports to be, however, and they have devised ways to limit its scope. Chief among these limitations are the "antitrust injury" doctrine and other requirements of standing and causation, and the indirect purchaser rule established in Illinois Brick Co. v. Illinois.[6]

Although private antitrust actions were filed soon after the passage of the Sherman Act, the number of such cases was not large until the 1950s. The number of private filings increased rapidly through the 1960s and exploded in the 1970s. While the number of private filings leveled off in the 1980s, it increased again in the 1990s. The private antitrust action continues to be the principal mechanism by which the antitrust laws are enforced. As many as 90% of antitrust cases are brought by private plaintiffs.[7]

§ 16.2 Permissible Plaintiffs—Who Should Enforce the Antitrust Laws?

Many persons lack standing to bring an action under § 4, even though they have been injured by someone else's antitrust violation. Market injuries have a way of rippling through the economy. For example, monopolization of a raw material can cause reduced demand for products made of that material. Suppliers of machinery for making those products may also face reduced demand, and some employees may lose their jobs. If bankruptcies result, creditors may not be paid, leases may be pre-

§ 16.1

1. § 16.7.

2. § 16.8a, b, c, d.

3. On public enforcement, see the previous chapter.

4. 15 U.S.C.A. § 15.

5. See International Ass'n of Machinists v. OPEC, 649 F.2d 1354 (9th Cir.1981), cert. denied, 454 U.S. 1163, 102 S.Ct. 1036 (1982) (act of state doctrine precluded antitrust lawsuit by labor union against OPEC).

6. 431 U.S. 720, 97 S.Ct. 2061 (1977), discussed below in § 16.6.

7. See S. Salop & L. White, Private Antitrust Litigation: An Introduction and Framework 3, in Private Antitrust Litigation: New Evidence, New Learning (L. White, ed. 1988.). An earlier study is R. Posner, A Statistical Study of Antitrust Enforcement, 13 J.L. & Econ. 365 (1970). Data for the 1970s are summarized in 46 Antitrust & Trade Reg. Rep. (BNA) 360 (Mar. 1, 1984). For a classification of private filings in the first half of the century, see H. Clark, The Treble Damage Bonanza: New Doctrines of Damages in Private Antitrust Suits, 52 Mich. L.Rev. 363 (1954). For a detailed analysis of private antitrust cases filed in five federal districts from 1973 through 1983, see L. White, The Georgetown Study of Private Antitrust Litigation, 54 Antitrust L.J. 59 (1985).

maturely terminated, and taxes may go uncollected.

Some decision must be made about the amount of antitrust enforcement that the law should permit. If the exclusive purpose of the antitrust laws is to maximize the efficiency of the market system of allocating resources, the optimal level of enforcement will leave the largest amount of social wealth intact after all costs of violations, enforcement and penalties are paid.

Private enforcement is subject to the law of diminishing returns—the more there is, the less deterrence will be obtained per enforcement dollar. If a rule that gave direct purchasers a treble-damages action for cartel overcharges deterred 90% of price fixing, then any rule that additionally gave a cause of action to indirect purchasers, creditors, or employees could not do more than deter the remaining 10%. However, lawsuits by these more remote victims would be more costly to litigate than suits by direct purchasers. Furthermore, there are many more indirect purchasers than there are direct purchasers, so they might file many more lawsuits. The amount of increased efficiency in the form of deterrence of price fixing could be very low in proportion to the increased costs of litigation.[1]

A perfect deterrence system designed to maximize social wealth would locate that point at which the marginal social cost of an additional quantum of enforcement is equal to its marginal social value.[2] If every dollar in increased litigation costs produced by a broader standing rule yielded only 75¢ in social gains, then the broader rule is inconsistent with the proposition that the goal of the antitrust laws is to maximize social wealth.[3] Of course, it may be quite consistent with some alternative goal, such as providing compensation to injured victims or minimizing monopoly wealth transfers away from consumers.

These theoretical observations do not provide us with much help in determining the proper range of permissible plaintiffs, but they do suggest some guidelines for any scheme of private antitrust enforcement whose goals are deterrence and efficiency:

1) enforcement rights (standing) should be granted first to those who can discover violations most accurately and readily, whose incentive to bring an action is high, and whose injuries are most likely to result from the anticompetitive consequences of the violation;

2) the rights should be given first to those for whom litigation costs are smallest;

3) denial of standing is most appropriate when we can point to injured persons other than the immediate plaintiff who better fit the criteria in (1) and (2) above.

The Clayton Act's provision of mandatory treble damages plus attorney's fees to prevailing plaintiffs has put extraordinary pressure on courts to develop intelligible limits on antitrust enforcement rights. These statutory provisions encourage litigation by people for whom the amount of recovery discounted by the probability of success would otherwise be marginal. For example, a common law breach of contract action providing single damages and no attorneys fees might not be worth the risk; but if the action could be turned into an antitrust violation, the outcome may look much more appealing. Thus plaintiffs are continually tempted to turn every claimed business tort or contract breach into an antitrust violation as well.

Unfortunately, the courts have never been able to create an intelligible theory of private antitrust standing capable of being applied across the full range of potential cases. The law remains haphazard and inconsistent. One reason is that neither Congress nor the courts has articulated a rationale for private enforce-

§ 16.2

1. On the indirect purchaser rule, see § 16.6.

2. For elaboration, with reference to the computation of optimal damages, see § 17.1. "Social cost" and "social value" are the relevant variables. Although the cost of bringing an antitrust suit is high for the private plaintiff, the total costs of operating the judicial system are far higher.

3. Too broad a rule might deter companies from engaging in efficient, marginally legal practices that might nevertheless be open to challenge. See K. Elzinga & W. Breit, Antitrust Penalty Reform: An Economic Analysis (1986).

ment. The above framework suggests that the purpose of private antitrust enforcement is to maximize social wealth by deterring inefficient practices and permitting efficient ones. However, courts have generally analyzed antitrust standing requirements in terms of compensation to victims. Once a court permits compensation as a permissible objective the door is opened to many rationales that are even more difficult to quantify than allocative efficiency itself—such as justice, fairness, or the preservation of opportunities for small business.

§ 16.3 Antitrust's Special Requirement of Competitive Injury

Many practices illegal under the antitrust laws produce compensating efficiencies. Courts condemn them either because the anticompetitive effects are clear, while the efficiencies are ambiguous and incapable of measurement, or else because the anticompetitive effects appear to outweigh the efficiencies. Mergers and joint ventures in particular may simultaneously create efficiencies and increase the market power of the participating firms. Vertical integration, whether by contract or merger, has an even greater capacity to produce efficiencies, and an even smaller potential to be anticompetitive.

Increased market power creates a social cost while increased efficiency creates a social gain. But both can impose private losses. To characterize a certain practice as "efficient" is not to conclude that the practice benefits everyone, but only that aggregate benefits are greater than aggregate injuries.[1] As a general rule, increased market power injures purchasers while it benefits competitors. However, increased efficiency benefits purchasers while it injures competitors or potential competitors. An antitrust policy dominated by efficiency concerns will attempt to distinguish purely private losses from those that coincide in some way with losses to society as a whole.

16.3a. "Antitrust Injury"; Private Merger Challenges

16.3a1. Mergers Alleged to Facilitate Exclusionary Practices

The Supreme Court took the above stated concerns into account in Brunswick Corp. v. Pueblo Bowl–O–Mat, Inc.[2] The plaintiff owned several bowling alleys and the defendant was a major national manufacturer of bowling equipment and operator of alleys. It sold bowling equipment to independent alleys on credit, and sometimes acquired alleys that were in financial trouble. Over a ten-year period the defendant had taken over several defaulting alleys that competed with the plaintiff. Most of these acquired alleys would probably have gone out of business had they not been acquired by Brunswick. The plaintiff challenged the acquisition of two of the alleys under § 7 of the Clayton Act, claiming that its market share would have increased had the competing alleys been permitted to go out of business.

The *Brunswick* plaintiff's theory of action reaches the heart of the debate about whom the antitrust laws should protect: competition and consumers, or competitors. Horizontal mergers can facilitate monopolistic or collusive pricing by increasing concentration in the market. Consumers will pay higher prices, but the post-merger firm's output reduction and price increase will benefit other firms already in the market. They can charge higher prices under the "umbrella" created by the larger, post-merger firm.

But mergers can also increase the efficiency of the merging partners. Increased efficiency benefits consumers but invariably injures competitors. The plaintiff in *Brunswick* formerly had a languishing, spiritless rival. After the merger it faced a rejuvenated and aggressive competitor. Whether or not the merger was illegal, the plaintiff's injury was caused by

§ 16.3

1. This is because the standard for efficiency in antitrust policy is not Pareto efficiency, but rather *potential* Pareto efficiency, sometimes called Kaldor–Hicks efficiency. See § 2.3c; and H. Hovenkamp, Distributive Justice and the Antitrust Laws, 51 Geo.Wash.L.Rev. 1, 8–12 (1982). An outcome is Pareto efficient only if it produces no losers. But it is Kaldor–Hicks efficient if aggregate gains, measured by willingness to pay, exceed aggregate losses.

2. 429 U.S. 477, 97 S.Ct. 690 (1977). On § 7 and mergers, see Chapter 12.

increased competition from the post-merger firm, not by the market's increased proclivity toward monopoly pricing.

In denying recovery, the Supreme Court observed that many antitrust violations could cause "losses which are of no concern to the antitrust laws." In order to recover, a plaintiff must show not only that an antitrust law has been violated and the plaintiff injured. It must also show "*antitrust* injury, which is to say injury of the type the antitrust laws were intended to prevent and that flows from that which makes defendants' acts unlawful." Such an injury should "reflect the anticompetitive effect * * * of the violation * * *."[3] Today "antitrust injury" has been established as a requirement for private actions under virtually all of the antitrust laws. It has become an essential element of private plaintiff standing.[4]

The antitrust injury doctrine applies only to private antitrust actions. The *Brunswick* opinion contrasted the "prophylactic" nature of Clayton § 7 with the "remedial" nature of § 4, the provision authorizing private damages actions. Section 7 was designed to reach mergers while the danger to competition was in its "incipiency," and somewhat uncertain.[5] By contrast, § 4 requires a private plaintiff to show actual injury. Since the merger contains two different potentials for injury—one from the post-merger firm's increased market power and the other from its increased efficiency—it becomes important for the plaintiff to identify how it was injured.[6]

The Supreme Court's *Cargill* opinion elaborated on these ideas.[7] The plaintiff, a producer of boxed beef for resale, sought to enjoin a merger of two of its competitors. Among the claims were that the merger (1) might facilitate oligopoly pricing; (2) might enable the post-merger firm to achieve economies of multi-plant production which the plaintiff could not match; and (3) would permit the post-merger firm to lower prices below pre-merger levels. The Supreme Court did not find an adequate allegation that the post-merger firm would engage in predatory pricing.[8]

On the first theory, the claim should be dismissed not for failure of antitrust injury, but for failure of injury-in-fact. A competitor is generally benefitted by collusion or oligopoly pricing in its market, for it will be able to increase its own prices as well. The Court dismissed claims (2) and (3) for failure of antitrust injury: the purpose of merger policy is not to prevent mergers that create efficiencies, but to prevent mergers that result in price increases.[9] Both *Brunswick* and *Cargill* stand for the general proposition that competitors may not challenge mergers on the theory that the post-merger firm will be more efficient than its constituents had been before, or that the post-merger firm will compete more aggressively than its pre-merger partners.

One question that *Cargill* did not address is the legitimacy of competitor challenges to mergers on the theory that the merger will facilitate exclusionary practices such as predatory pricing. At the very least, such claims are plausible only if the structural prerequisites for the feared practice are met.[10] In most cases of marginally illegal mergers they are not. For example, a merger of a 20% market share firm and a 10% firm in a relatively concentrated market would generally be illegal under the merger standards that the Antitrust Division

3. Id. at 489, 97 S.Ct. at 697.

4. A few courts have debated whether antitrust injury is an element of standing or should be regarded as an analytically distinct requirement, but the debate seems quite inconsequential. See Local Beauty Supply v. Lamaur, 787 F.2d 1197, 1201 (7th Cir.1986) (noting the differences among courts).

5. See Chapter 12.

6. On the relationship between antitrust injury and the efficiency concerns of the antitrust laws, see W. Page, The Chicago School and the Evolution of Antitrust: Characterization, Antitrust Injury, and Evidentiary Sufficiency, 75 Va.L.Rev. 1221 (1989); W. Page, The Scope of Liability for Antitrust Violations, 37 Stan.L.Rev. 1445 (1985); R. Blair & J. Harrison, Rethinking Antitrust Injury, 42 Vand. L.Rev. 1539 (1989); H. Hovenkamp, Merger Actions for Damages, 35 Hastings L.J. 937 (1984).

7. Cargill v. Monfort of Colo., 479 U.S. 104, 107 S.Ct. 484 (1986).

8. *Cargill*, 479 U.S. at 118–119, 107 S.Ct. at 493–494.

9. *Cargill*, 479 U.S. at 117, 107 S.Ct. at 492: "The logic of *Brunswick* compels the conclusion that the threat of loss of profits due to possible price competition following a merger does not constitute a threat of antitrust injury."

10. See *Cargill*, 479 U.S. at 119 & n. 15, 107 S.Ct. at 494 & n. 15.

and Federal Trade Commission apply today.[11] However, the 30% firm that results is still too small to engage in predatory pricing under the structural standards applied by most courts.[12] A competitor suit challenging this merger on the claim of threatened predatory pricing should ordinarily be dismissed. The same can be said of mergers in markets where entry barriers are low.

But suppose the structural prerequisites for predatory pricing have been met. Predatory pricing is a risky, expensive enterprise that likely occurs in only a small percentage of the markets where it is plausible. Should competitors be able to stop mergers with efficiency-creating potential merely by showing that the merger created a firm *capable* of engaging in predatory pricing? So far, no court has gone quite this far. However, the *Tasty Baking* opinion did permit a plaintiff to proceed when the merger allegedly created post-merger market shares ranging as high as 78%, and the defendant had left behind memoranda declaring its intentions to "take competition out and then increase price."[13]

At the least, a competitor seeking to enjoin a merger on the theory that it will facilitate predatory pricing[14] must show both that the post-merger market structure is such that the alleged practice is a plausible (that is, profit-maximizing) strategy for the post-merger firm; and additionally that the firm actively intends to pursue this strategy. Evidence of the latter could include evidence (1) that the firm has employed the same strategy in other situations; or (2) memoranda or other testimony stating its intent to do so in the post-merger market.

16.3a2. Takeover Targets as Antitrust Plaintiffs

One set of firms who are almost never the victims of antitrust injury are the targets of hostile takeovers. Suppose that Firm A has made an offer to Firm B's shareholders to buy their shares at an attractive price. If firm A receives enough commitments, it will acquire a controlling interest in Firm B and may reorganize Firm B and dismiss its directors and managers. The directors and managers of Firm B can be expected to take evasive actions to avoid such a takeover, including an antitrust challenge to the resulting merger.

But no matter how you look at such a transaction, Firm B is not an appropriate private plaintiff. *First*, if the basis of the challenge is that post-merger Firm AB will have monopoly power or the increased ability to collude, Firm B will be the beneficiary rather than victim of the merger and will not suffer injury-in-fact.[15] *Second*, loss of employment by Firm B's officers is certainly an injury, but it is not in any way an injury caused by a decrease in competition in the post-merger market. That injury has nothing to do with the purposes of the antitrust laws and would occur not matter what the merger's competitive effects. Currently the courts disagree about whether takeover targets have standing to enforce the antitrust laws against the merger.[16]

Could a takeover target *ever* be the victim of antitrust injury? Suppose the merger will

11. See § 12.4b.

12. See § 8.4a.

13. Tasty Baking Co. v. Ralston Purina, 653 F.Supp. 1250, 1271 (E.D.Pa.1987). See also Bigelow v. Unilever N.V., 867 F.2d 102 (2d Cir.), cert. denied, 493 U.S. 815, 110 S.Ct. 64 (1989), finding plausible a claim that the defendant would use its increased market power following the merger to deny competitors access to shelf space in supermarkets. Contrast Phototron Corp. v. Eastman Kodak Co., 842 F.2d 95, 102 (5th Cir.), cert. denied, 486 U.S. 1023, 108 S.Ct. 1996 (1988) (insisting on sufficient evidence of future predation to establish a "substantial likelihood" of anticompetitive injury).

14. Or perhaps that it will facilitate some other exclusionary practice, such as the foreclosure of access to supermarket shelves. See *Bigelow*, note 13.

15. See F. Easterbrook and D. Fischel, Antitrust Suits by Targets of Tender Offers, 80 Mich.L.Rev. 1155 (1982). Contra J. Brodley, Antitrust Standing in Private Merger Cases: Reconciling Private Incentives and Public Enforcement Goals, 94 Mich. L. Rev. 1, 79–106 (1995).

16. Denying standing: Anago v. Tecnol Medical Products, 976 F.2d 248 (5th Cir.1992); H.H. Robertson Co. v. Guardian Indus. Corp., 1986–1 Trade Cas. ¶ 66,911, 1986 WL 31687 (3d Cir.1986); Hayden v. Bardes Corp., 1989–1 Trade Cas. ¶ 68,477, 1989 WL 61957 (W.D.Ky.1989). Granting standing: Marathon Oil Co. v. Mobil Corp., 669 F.2d 378, 383–384 (6th Cir.1981), cert. denied, 455 U.S. 982, 102 S.Ct. 1490 (1982); A. Copeland Enters. v. Guste, 1989–2 Trade Cas. (CCH) ¶ 68,712, 1988 WL 129318 (E.D.La.1988).

eventually be condemned, but in the meantime the acquiring firm will be able to acquire all of the acquired firm's trade secrets, thus depriving the acquired firm of its ability to compete. *Consolidated Gold Fields*[17] granted standing on this theory. A possible flaw in the theory is that the claimed result would occur even if the market shares of the two firms were less than 1% each but the merger were reversed for some other reason. That is, the injury claim might have little to do with the competitive effect of the merger. On the other hand, theft of trade secrets that disabled one of only three or four firms in a market could have a significant competitive impact. In sum, § 7 does not provide a remedy for theft of trade secrets by merger, unless the theft can be shown to have a real impact on post-merger competition.

16.3a3. Consumer Plaintiffs

The preferred plaintiff in a merger case is the consumer, who is benefitted by the merger's increased efficiency but injured by its post-merger price increase. Nevertheless, consumer challenges are relatively infrequent. We condemn mergers under a prophylactic standard that presumably prevents nearly all of them that have any reasonable chance of causing a price increase. As a general matter, if a merger is followed by a significant price increase and is challenged within four years of its occurrence (the statute of limitation period)[18] there is no reason why a consumer cannot challenge it. Naturally, the plaintiff will still have to prove that the merger was unlawful and—a more difficult task—that the merger caused the price increase.[19]

16.3b. "Antitrust Injury" Beyond § 7; Per Se Violations

Brunswick's contrast of § 7's prophylactic reach with the remedial nature of § 4 suggested that the antitrust injury doctrine applied only to mergers, not to other antitrust violations.[20] In J. Truett Payne Co. v. Chrysler Motor Corp.,[21] however, the Supreme Court applied the doctrine to a private action alleging illegal price discrimination under the Robinson–Patman Act. The Court held that a plaintiff winning a price discrimination suit was not entitled to "automatic" damages based on the difference between the higher price it paid and the lower price paid by others. Rather, the plaintiff must show that the price discrimination affected retail prices and thus caused it actual injury. Although the Court declared this conclusion to be "governed by" *Brunswick*, the decision seems to require proof of injury-in-fact rather than antitrust injury. The Court really said that notwithstanding the Robinson–Patman Act's prophylactic "may * * * substantially * * * lessen competition" language, the plaintiff seeking damages must show actual, present injury.

The Robinson–Patman Act contains the same prophylactic language as Clayton § 7. But what about antitrust violations whose immediate injury is much more apparent, such as *per se* violations of § 1 of the Sherman Act? Some courts initially decided that antitrust injury should be presumed in the case of *per se*

17. Consolidated Gold Fields PLC v. Minorco, S.A., 871 F.2d 252 (2d Cir.1989).

18. See § 16.7.

19. See Midwestern Machinery v. Northwest Airlines, 167 F.3d 439 (8th Cir.1999) (permitting consumer to challenge acquisition on grounds of increased price; rejecting district court's view that once the acquired firm' stock was dissolved and it ceased to exist as an independent entity, the merger qua merger could no longer be challenged); Community Pub. v. DR Partners, 139 F.3d 1180 (8th Cir.1998) (permitting challenge by advertising purchasers to newspaper merger). But see City of Pittsburgh v. West Penn Power Co., 147 F.3d 256 (3d Cir.1998), which denied standing to a municipality to challenge a merger of two electric utilities when one of the utilities would have entered the City in competition with the other but for the fact that it had not yet received the necessary permit. But that conclusion seems wrong, unless one thinks there was very little chance that the permit would have been granted, and in this case there was not. The court thus permitted a monopoly utility to acquire a nascent rival (see § 12.3c) in order to stave off competition that would probably have occurred as soon as the utility received the requisite permission to enter.

20. See Engine Specialties, Inc. v. Bombardier Ltd., 605 F.2d 1 (1st Cir.1979), on rehearing, 615 F.2d 575 (1st Cir.1980), cert. denied, 446 U.S. 983, 100 S.Ct. 2964 (1980) (emphasizing prophylactic nature of § 7).

21. 451 U.S. 557, 101 S.Ct. 1923 (1981), on remand, 670 F.2d 575 (5th Cir.1982), rehearing denied, 677 F.2d 117 (11th Cir.1982), cert. denied, 459 U.S. 908, 103 S.Ct. 212 (1982). See 14 Antitrust Law ¶ 2371 (1999).

violations.[22] But not all injuries caused by *per se* violations result from the anticompetitive consequences of the violation. For example, a joint venture of physicians which includes an agreement about the maximum fees they will charge might be condemned as price fixing under the *per se* rule.[23] If the physicians were sued by a competitor who was injured because she had to compete with the defendants' lower fees, however, the defendants should prevail under *Brunswick*. The plaintiff is not injured by price fixing but by the increased efficiency that results from the joint venture. Alternatively, if the plaintiff claims that the so-called maximum price fixing agreement is really a disguise for minimum price fixing, then the plaintiff has not been injured at all.

In *USA Petroleum* the Supreme Court extended the antitrust injury doctrine to a claim of maximum resale price maintenance, which was unlawful *per se* at the time.[24] The plaintiff, a gasoline retailer, claimed that a gasoline refiner was imposing maximum resale prices on dealers in competition with the plaintiff. The Supreme Court assumed that these prices were not predatory. The Court began with the observation that many instances of maximum RPM could be efficient. It continued:

> The per se rule is a method of determining whether § 1 of the Sherman Act has been violated, but it does not indicate whether a private plaintiff has suffered antitrust injury. * * * The per se rule is a presumption of unreasonableness based on "business certainty and litigation efficiency." * * *
>
> The purpose of the antitrust injury requirement is different. It ensures that the harm claimed by the plaintiff corresponds to the rationale for finding a violation of the antitrust laws in the first place.[25]

The Court then held that the rationale for permitting dealers to complain about maximum RPM imposed upon *themselves* was that such price setting restrained their ability to compete as they saw fit. But a *competitor* of such a dealer would be benefitted rather than injured by the RPM:

> Respondent was *benefitted* rather than harmed if petitioner's pricing policies restricted ARCO sales to a few large dealers or prevented petitioner's dealers from offering services desired by consumers such as credit card sales. Even if the maximum price agreement ultimately had acquired all of the attributes of a minimum price-fixing scheme, respondent still would not have suffered antitrust injury because higher ARCO prices would have worked to USA's advantage.[26]

The Supreme Court's conclusion is fully consistent with *Brunswick*'s basic rationale; nevertheless, it raises an important problem when the alleged *per se* violation produces no anticompetitive injury at all. While maximum RPM was unlawful per se at the time of *USA Petroleum*, the rule was under widespread criticism, and it is difficult to identify realistic circumstances under which it is anticompetitive.[27] Suppose a supplier imposes maximum RPM on individual dealers in order to force them to charge only a competitive markup. The dealers are clearly injured "by reason of" an antitrust violation. But the basis of their claim is lost monopoly profits—something that *Brunswick* appears to prohibit. Importantly, if a dealer in such circumstances cannot sue for maximum RPM, then who can?[28]

One possibility that the *USA Petroleum* opinion acknowledged is that maximum RPM might be used to facilitate a kind of predatory pricing. Suppose a vertically integrated oil re-

22. For example, Lee–Moore Oil Co. v. Union Oil of California, 599 F.2d 1299, 1303 (4th Cir.1979) ("quite rare" that per se violation would not cause antitrust injury).

23. See Arizona v. Maricopa County Medical Society, 457 U.S. 332, 102 S.Ct. 2466 (1982). See § 5.6.

24. Atlantic Richfield Co. v. USA Petroleum Co., 495 U.S. 328, 110 S.Ct. 1884 (1990). Since that time, the per se rule against maximum RPM has been overruled. See § 11.5c.

25. 495 U.S. at 342, 110 S.Ct. at 1891, 1893.

26. 495 U.S. at 336, 110 S.Ct. at 1890.

27. See § 11.5c.

28. See Jack Walters & Sons Corp. v. Morton Bldg., 737 F.2d 698 (7th Cir.), cert. denied, 469 U.S. 1018, 105 S.Ct. 432 (1984), holding that a dealer who claimed that its price-cost margins had been reduced by illegal maximum RPM did not suffer antitrust injury.

finer decided to use predatory pricing to drive out independent gasoline dealers. In carrying out this scheme, the refiner could not simply sell to its own dealers at a below cost price, for the dealers would simply maintain the price at the market level and pocket the revenue resulting from the higher margin. The refiner would have to use maximum RPM to ensure that the predatory wholesale price was carried through to a predatory retail price.

If such a case should arise, competitors of the predator would be victims of antitrust injury. Retail dealers bound by the maximum RPM agreements would probably not be injured at all. That is, they would still presumably be obtaining a competitive markup, and their volume would increase during the predatory pricing scheme. In any event, those who suffered injury would have to prove predatory pricing, including a reasonable likelihood that the conduct, if permitted to run its course, would likely create a monopoly.[29]

16.3c. Causation, Injury-in-fact, Antitrust Injury Distinguished

The previous discussion should make clear that "injury" and "antitrust injury" are not the same thing. A private antitrust plaintiff must establish three quite independent requirements: (1) that it suffered an injury; (2) that its injury was caused by an antitrust violation; and (3) that the injury qualifies as "antitrust injury." Unfortunately, courts have not always kept the three requirements distinct. For example, in its *Matsushita* decision the Supreme Court observed that rivals could not recover from a cartel to increase prices, since competitors would be benefitted, not injured, by such a conspiracy. For that proposition it cited *Brunswick*.[30] But the *Brunswick* plaintiff was injured in fact; it was simply not a victim of antitrust injury. By contrast, the rival in the *Matsushita* illustration was not injured at all.

General standing doctrine requires a private plaintiff to prove injury-in-fact. Indeed, those with no cognizable injury at all may lack standing under Article III of the Constitution.[31] In that case the independent standing requirements of the Clayton Act become superfluous. Nonetheless, Congress has the power to grant the right to sue even to those with negligible injuries. As the discussion of the indirect purchaser rule in § 16.6 indicates, not only standing but even substantial damage recoveries may sometimes be given to plaintiffs whose actual injuries are very small.

A plaintiff must also show that the injuries were caused by the antitrust violation. Courts have articulated the causation requirement in different ways. In *Zenith* the Supreme Court required only that the violation be a "material cause" of the plaintiff's injury.[32] Under this requirement, if a plaintiff's business misfortunes resulted from many causes, it need show only that the defendant's antitrust violation was one of them. Cases following *Zenith* generally do not require the plaintiff to rank the causes and show that the antitrust violation somehow predominated among them.[33] Other

29. On remand, the Ninth Circuit found that the prices imposed on the defendant's dealers could have been predatory and reinstated the plaintiff's case. USA Petroleum Co. v. Atlantic Richfield Co., 972 F.2d 1070 (9th Cir.1992), superseded on rehearing, 13 F.3d 1276 (9th Cir.1994). Problematically, the court did not require the plaintiff to show a "dangerous probability of success" in the market at issue, a requirement usually imposed in predatory pricing cases under the Sherman Act. The court found the requirement unnecessary, given that RPM is illegal *per se*. As a result, the decision is probably overruled by Spectrum Sports v. McQuillan, 506 U.S. 447, 458–460, 113 S.Ct. 884, 892 (1993). See § 8.4.

30. Matsushita Elec. Indus. Co. v. Zenith Radio Corp. 475 U.S. 574, 586, 106 S.Ct. 1348, 1355 (1986). See also *J. Truett Payne*, note 21.

31. See America West Airlines v. Burnley, 838 F.2d 1343 (D.C.Cir.1988) (identifying constitutional standing as requiring injury fairly traceable to the defendant's unlawful acts, and likely to be redressed by the requested relief.).

32. Zenith Radio Corp. v. Hazeltine Research, Inc., 395 U.S. 100, 114 n. 9, 89 S.Ct. 1562, 1571 n. 9, on remand, 418 F.2d 21 (7th Cir.1969), cert. denied, 397 U.S. 979, 90 S.Ct. 1105 (1970).

33. For example, Affiliated Capital Corp. v. City of Houston, 735 F.2d 1555, 1564 (5th Cir.1984), cert. denied, 474 U.S. 1053, 106 S.Ct. 788 (1986); Weiman Co. v. Kroehler Mfg. Co., 428 F.2d 726, 729 (7th Cir.1970); Fishman v. Wirtz, 1981–2 Trade Cas. (CCH) ¶ 64378, 1981 WL 2153 (N.D.Ill.1981). See also Amerinet v. Xerox Corp., 972 F.2d 1483, 1494 (8th Cir.1992), cert. denied, 506 U.S. 1080, 113 S.Ct. 1048 (1993) ("in order to provide sufficient evidence of causation [the plaintiff] need only establish that [the defendant] violated the antitrust laws, that [the defendant's] alleged violations had a tendency to injure

courts have assessed a stronger requirement that the violation be shown to be a "substantial factor" in the plaintiff's loss—apparently meaning that the violation must be the most important cause, or at least among the most important.[34]

Is one articulation of the test better than the other? In most cases the difference is probably more semantic than real. Further, the plaintiff seeking damages will eventually have to separate out those damages caused by the antitrust violation from those caused by other factors.[35] This will require not only a ranking of causes, but also some assignment of weights to each one. One might doubt whether the plaintiff who can do no better than meet *Zenith* "substantial factor" test has any claim for damages at all. Finally, if it seems quite clear that the antitrust violation was at best an insubstantial factor in the plaintiff's loss, then causation will fail under either test.[36]

Both the "material cause" test and the "substantial factor" test properly apply only when the plaintiff's injury can be measured by degrees, such as loss of profits or market share. But many cases involve alternative causes; that is, the plaintiff alleges one thing and the defendant claims another. For example, in the typical dealer termination case the termination was likely effected for either a legal reason (perhaps the dealer was not paying its bills) or an illegal one (perhaps there was an RPM agreement with a complaining dealer).[37] The fact finder will simply have to determine which alleged cause is controlling.

Finally, even severe injury-in-fact and causation do not entail antitrust injury. For example, an efficiency creating joint venture or merger may drive less efficient rivals out of the market altogether. But such firms are injured by more competition in the market, not less.

16.3d. Antitrust Injury and Damages Claims

An interesting if controversial corollary of the antitrust injury doctrine is that a plaintiff may not claim as damages profits it would have earned as a result of an antitrust violation. For example, suppose a plaintiff dealer sues its supplier, claiming that the latter is imposing unlawful resale price maintenance on all its dealers. Assuming the dealer can prove unlawful resale price maintenance, how should damages be computed? It the damages evidence proceeded on the assumption that the plaintiff could set its retail price freely while the supplier continued to impose RPM on other dealers, the plaintiff's damages could be very large. It would be able to undersell the other dealers and presumably take much of their market share. By contrast, if the supplier were forced to stop imposing RPM on all of its dealers, then the plaintiff might be no better off than it was before. Other dealers would cut price as well, and the plaintiff would end up with a much smaller margin. The Seventh Circuit concluded in *Isaksen* that damages must be based on the assumption that the defendant would stop imposing RPM on all of its dealers.[38]

[the plaintiff's] business, and that [the plaintiff] suffered a decline in its business 'not shown to be attributable to other causes.' ").

34. For example, Motive Parts Warehouse v. Facet Enter., 774 F.2d 380, 388 (10th Cir.1985); Port Terminal & Warehousing Co. v. John S. James Co., 695 F.2d 1328, 1331 (11th Cir.1983). See also St. Louis Convention and Visitors Commission v. NFL, 154 F.3d 851, 863 (8th Cir.1998) (mere evidence that teams would have moved in a "freely competitive" market insufficient; must also be evidence tending to show that an NFL team would have wanted to move to St Louis but for an alleged restraint); Massachusetts School of Law at Andover v. ABA, 107 F.3d 1026 (3d Cir.), cert. denied, ___ U.S. ___, 118 S.Ct. 264 (1997) (unaccredited law school could not show that ABA criteria tying accreditation to professors' salaries caused it any injury, for it did not compete in the same market, or for professors with the same qualifications, as ABA-accredited law schools did).

35. See § 17.6c.

36. For example, *Amerinet*, note 33 (plaintiff's business failure seemed inevitable whether or not it was victimized by antitrust violation); Argus v. Eastman Kodak, 801 F.2d 38 (2d Cir.1986), cert. denied, 479 U.S. 1088, 107 S.Ct. 1295 (1987) (same); Catlin v. Washington Energy Co., 791 F.2d 1343 (9th Cir.1986) (plaintiff already showing most of its losses before alleged violation occurred).

37. See § 11.5.

38. Isaksen v. Vermont Castings, 825 F.2d 1158 (7th Cir.1987), cert. denied, 486 U.S. 1005, 108 S.Ct. 1729 (1988). Cf. Johnson v. Pacific Lighting Land Co., 817 F.2d 601 (9th Cir.1987), cert. denied, 484 U.S. 1062, 108 S.Ct.

Isaksen does little more than state a basic common law principle of damages: the plaintiff is entitled to be put into the position it would have been had there been no violation, not in the position it would have been in had the illegal RPM been imposed only on others. This constraint limits the collection of damages by dealers upon whom illegal RPM has been imposed. Indeed, in the great majority of RPM cases, dealers as well as the supplier are better off as a result of the RPM. That is, output is probably higher than it would be in the absence of RPM, or dealer markups are higher at the same level of output. For example, in *Isaksen* the plaintiff wished to recover as damages the earnings it could have obtained from free-riding on the promotional efforts of others who were obedient to their RPM agreements. RPM properly calculated to combat dealer free riding should result in increased output, and thus increased dealer profits. In such cases the dealer whose claimed damages must be based on its earnings in the absence of any RPM whatsoever has very likely suffered no damages at all.[39]

The point that plaintiffs may not be permitted to reap the fruit of antitrust violations can be pushed too far. In the *Todorov* case defendant radiologists denied hospital staff privileges to the plaintiff neurologist, who wished to administer head scans there.[40] The radiologists had exclusive privileges at the hospital, and the Eleventh Circuit reasoned that they were in fact a cartel that the plaintiff wished to join. The court concluded that denial of the right to participate in a cartel is not antitrust injury.

But that conclusion seems completely counterproductive. Assuming the worst, suppose that the plaintiff had every intention of joining the cartel and charging an explicitly-agreed-upon price.[41] After his entry, the cartel would have one more member, and existing members would have to further reduce their output in order to accommodate him. The cartel would become less stable, and its profit-maximizing price would probably decline. More importantly, if one physician applied to join the cartel, anticipating its monopoly profits, others could be expected to follow suit. Few antitrust rules could be more anticompetitive than one permitting a cartel to exclude potential entrants from its market.

16.3e. Injunctive Relief

In its *Cargill* decision the Supreme Court held that the "antitrust injury" doctrine applies equally to suits seeking an injunction (or presumably divestiture) and suits seeking damages.[42] A few earlier decisions had held to the contrary, contrasting the "threatened loss or damage" requirement of § 16 of the Clayton Act,[43] which covers injunctive relief, with the actual injury requirements of § 4's damages provision.[44]

But the logic of *Cargill* on this point seems inescapable. The "threatened" injury requirement of § 16 may indeed require a smaller showing of the *amount* or even the fact of injury than is needed to prove damages under § 4. However, the kind of injury that is relevant to the inquiry is nonetheless injury that results from the impact of the challenged practice on competition. Just as a competitor may not obtain damages for the injuries that result from an efficiency-creating joint venture, so too it may not enjoin such a venture on the theory that it will be injured by the resulting efficiencies. The difference in proof of injury

1020 (1988), holding that sellers of fruit to a cartel whose scheme backfired, with the result that the fruit later had to be sold at low prices, could not claim as damages the high prices that they would have earned had the cartel been successful (applying state antitrust statute similar to Sherman Act).

39. On vertical restraints and free-riding, see § 11.3a.

40. Todorov v. DCH Healthcare Authority, 921 F.2d 1438 (11th Cir.1991).

41. There was apparently no evidence to support these assumptions.

42. Cargill v. Monfort of Colo., 479 U.S. 104, 107 S.Ct. 484 (1986). See § 16.3a.

43. 15 U.S.C.A. § 26.

44. See, for example, Christian Schmidt Brewing Co. v. G. Heileman Brewing Co., 753 F.2d 1354, 1356–1358 (6th Cir.), cert. dismissed, 469 U.S. 1200, 105 S.Ct. 1155 (1985) (since § 16 is "designed to stop anticompetitive behavior in its incipiency," a "lower threshold for standing" is required than for § 4).

has to do not with the nature of the injury, but rather with § 4's separate requirements that the injury be quantifiable sufficiently to permit damages measurement.[45]

16.3f. Plaintiffs Unaffected by Injury to Competition; Pleading Requirements

Properly used, the antitrust injury doctrine can serve the useful function of requiring the plaintiff to show at an early stage the precise relationship between its injury (or threatened injury) and the amount of competition in the market. The result may expose those complaining of a rival's increased efficiency; it may also serve to uncover breach of contract claims or other common law claims disguised as antitrust suits. Although many plaintiffs may have been wronged in some abstract or common law sense, or perhaps even by violation of some other federal statute, they do not have an *antitrust* claim unless their injury results from a practice designed to increase price, decrease output, or eliminate rivals with monopoly as a goal.

For example, in *McDonald* the plaintiff sold its closely held corporation to the defendant, for a price that depended on the corporation's earnings during the subsequent five years.[46] During that period the corporation sustained losses, and the plaintiff's price was accordingly quite small. It then challenged the sale as an illegal merger in the market for the electronic devices that the corporation produced. But even assuming the merger was illegal, the plaintiff's injury had nothing to do with the amount of competition in the market. Indeed, if the merger had facilitated collusion its earnings would have been higher than if the market were competitive. The plaintiff was simply trying to turn a contract claim into an antitrust violation.

Another example is the Seventh Circuit's *Nelson* decision, which granted standing to a mentally disabled plaintiff who claimed that one consequence of an illegal merger of medical clinics was that no local facility would serve him.[47] The plaintiff had formerly visited one of the merging clinics, but had filed a medical malpractice action against it and switched to the other clinic. After the merger the firm refused to serve the plaintiff, and there were no other convenient clinics. In granting standing, the court observed that one of the threats of an illegal merger is an anticompetitive output reduction, and a patient denied service is clearly the victim of an output reduction. True enough, but a monopoly output reduction rations output on the basis of *price*. That is to say, the monopolist reduces output profitably by raising price and foregoing those customers unwilling to pay more. It does not reduce output by eliminating, say, all left-handed customers, or all those with whom dealing has been difficult. To be sure, the plaintiff may have been wronged, but his injury had nothing to do with the anticompetitive consequences of an illegal merger.

Closely related to the plaintiff unaffected by changes in market competition is the substitute monopolist, or the plaintiff who alleges that it rather than the defendant should be the occupant of a monopolized market. Suppose that the plaintiff owned a valid patent giving it monopoly protection in a profitable market, but that the defendant managed to acquire the patent by wrongful means. Assuming the patent theft is wrongful, the market is no less competitive after the theft than it had been before—only the identity of the monopolist has changed. Judge Posner concluded in

45. Another important difference is that § 4 requires proof of injury that has already occurred. By contrast, one may obtain an injunction against injury that is merely threatened in the future, provided that it is antitrust injury. See *Zenith*, note 32, 395 U.S. at 140, 89 S.Ct. at 1585.

46. McDonald v. Johnson & Johnson, 722 F.2d 1370 (8th Cir.1983), cert. denied, 469 U.S. 870, 105 S.Ct. 219 (1984). See also Stamatakis Indus. v. King, 965 F.2d 469 (7th Cir.1992), holding that the lost sales resulting when the plaintiff's employee defected, started a new firm and then "conspired" with customers to steal plaintiff's business, did not constitute antitrust injury. The theft of customers would have occurred regardless of the amount of competition in the market. Further, it would have been irrational for customers to conspire to create a monopoly, for they would then be its victims.

47. Nelson v. Monroe Regional Med. Center, 925 F.2d 1555 (7th Cir.), cert. denied, 502 U.S. 903, 112 S.Ct. 285 (1991).

Riegel Textile that the question which claimant owned the monopoly was a "matter of indifference," insofar as antitrust is concerned.[48]

Monopolies are profitable, and firms can be expected to go to some lengths to preserve them, perhaps even risking an occasional breach of contract or tort suit. But if the plaintiff's only claim is of the nature "I, rather than the defendant, was entitled to be the monopolist," then the plaintiff is not a victim of antitrust injury.

As most other good points, however, this one can be pushed to far. To change the facts of *Riegel Textile* a bit, suppose that firm A owned a patent monopoly for widgets and firm B patented gidgets, which competed with widgets. Firm A then managed to steal firm B's patent. In such a case the theft of a valid patent would not simply be a transfer of a monopoly from one firm to another; it would be the perpetuation of a monopoly (control of both widgets and gidgets by firm A) where there might otherwise have been competition. In this case the claim would be of unlawful merger.[49] Consumers would of course have standing, but so would firm B, who has been unlawfully deprived of a right to compete in the market in question.

§ 16.4 Statutory and Judicial Rules Limiting Antitrust Standing

Clayton § 4 requires a plaintiff to be a "person," which includes natural persons, corporations, and unincorporated associations recognized by federal, state or foreign law. Municipalities, states and foreign governments are all permissible plaintiffs.[1]

16.4a. "Business or Property"

Section 4 requires the antitrust plaintiff to show injury to its "business or property." Most private plaintiffs have alleged injury to some business interest that they owned. They therefore claimed injury to both their "business" *and* their "property." In Reiter v. Sonotone Corp.,[2] however, the Supreme Court granted a damages action to a retail consumer who allegedly paid a higher price for a product because of a price fixing conspiracy. The consumer was injured in her "property" but not in her business. Today the term "property" in § 4 is nearly co-extensive with the common law concept: property is anything in which a person claims a legally recognized ownership interest. In *Reiter* the Supreme Court suggested only personal injuries as not included in § 4's concept of "business or property." It did not explain how an antitrust violation might cause personal injuries.[3]

48. Brunswick Corp. v. Riegel Textile Corp., 752 F.2d 261 (7th Cir.1984), cert. denied, 472 U.S. 1018, 105 S.Ct. 3480 (1985) (the defendant allegedly borrowed the unpatented technology from the plaintiff on a trial basis and then patented it). See also Almeda Mall v. Houston Lighting & Power Co., 615 F.2d 343 (5th Cir.), cert. denied, 449 U.S. 870, 101 S.Ct. 208 (1980) (denying standing to firm wishing to replace one monopoly supplier of electricity with another); contrast Fishman v. Wirtz, 807 F.2d 520 (7th Cir.1986), granting standing to plaintiff who wished to be owner of monopoly professional basketball team rather than defendant. See Judge Easterbrook's dissent at 563.

49. See 4 Antitrust Law ¶ 912d (rev. ed. 1998) (dominant firm's acquisition of rival's intellectual property an unlawful merger).

§ 16.4

1. However, foreign governments are generally restricted to recovery of actual rather than treble damages. 15 U.S.C.A. 15(b). On foreign suits, see Pfizer v. Government of India, 434 U.S. 308, 318–320, 98 S.Ct. 584, 590–591 (1978). Although the United States as purchaser is not a "person" under the statute, a special provision permits it to seek treble damages. 15 U.S.C.A. § 15(a).

2. 442 U.S. 330, 99 S.Ct. 2326 (1979), on remand, 602 F.2d 179 (8th Cir.1979). See 2 Antitrust Law ¶ 361 (rev. ed. 1995).

3. Suppose, however, that firms with good safety records are excluded from a project by an illegal boycott; as a result, firms with poorer safety records participate, and someone is killed. See Hamman v. United States, 267 F.Supp. 420, 432 (D.Mont.1967), denying Clayton § 4 recovery under this theory for loss of consortium. The court held that the loss was not injury to "business or property," even though state law recognized a property right in consortium. Compare In re Multidistrict Vehicle Air Pollution, M.D.L., 481 F.2d 122 (9th Cir.), cert. denied, 414 U.S. 1045, 94 S.Ct. 551 (1973) (denying standing under "target area" test to farmers' claim that a conspiracy among automobile manufacturers to delay development of auto emission controls resulted in increased air pollution and a decline in agricultural production).

See also the numerous actions filed against the tobacco companies, now settled, claiming that an antitrust conspiracy to suppress information about the health effects of smoking resulted in excessive payments for health insurance or health care costs. See, e.g., Texas v. American Tobacco Co., 14 F.Supp.2d 956 (E.D.Tx.1997). The claims are analyzed at 12 Antitrust Law ¶ 2023d (1999).

The concept of "business or property" has sometimes been construed narrowly by lower courts. For example, in Reibert v. Atlantic Richfield Co.[4] the Tenth Circuit held that an employee discharged in the wake of a personnel consolidation brought about by a merger had no cause of action under Clayton § 7, the merger provision, because employment was not "business or property" within the meaning of § 4. A job is clearly a legally recognized property interest, however, and other courts have granted standing when the target of the antitrust violation was the labor market itself.[5] Employee termination does not usually support a damages action under the antitrust laws—but the lack of a "business or property" interest has nothing to do with the denial of standing. Today we would say that Reibert's claim should have been dismissed for failure of antitrust injury. That is, the consolidation was efficient and, in any event, had nothing to do with the amount of competition in the market.

16.4b. Market Relationships; "Direct Injury" and "Target Area" Tests[6]

Section 4 is designed to redress market injuries, or the injuries that accrue to market participants when the market becomes less competitive. Further, the claim of injury must not be so tenuous that damages will be extremely difficult to prove, or will simply be "duplicative" of the injury suffered by others.

Courts have identified certain favored and disfavored classes of antitrust plaintiffs under Clayton § 4. Favored plaintiffs include customers and competitors of the violator. Disfavored plaintiffs include nonpurchasers, most potential competitors, employees of the violator, and stockholders, creditors, landlords, and employees of victims. Standing is sometimes denied to people in the favored categories and sometimes granted to those in the disfavored categories, but in each case there must be a good reason for deviating from a presumption that favors customers and competitors and disfavors most others.

Unfortunately, judicial rules of standing have not been articulated as clearly as the previous paragraph suggests. Rather than identifying preferred classes as such, courts have taken a more conceptual approach, borrowed from various causation doctrines of tort law. The prevailing tests for plaintiff standing in private antitrust damages actions are the "direct injury" test, which purports to measure whether the relationship between the defendant's violation and the plaintiff's injury was "direct" or "indirect"; and the "target-area" test, which tries to identify persons who are in the "target area" of a violation. Both tests have involved courts in endless verbal games, and neither has produced a reliable set of predictive tools calculated to give consistent results. In recent years many courts have either abandoned them or at least placed less emphasis on their verbal formulations.

16.4b1. "Direct Injury"

The "direct injury" test originated in Loeb v. Eastman Kodak Co.[7] The court denied standing to a stockholder in a corporation allegedly victimized by an antitrust violation. The holding was based on two rationales. First, the stockholder's injury was only an "indirect" consequence of the antitrust violation; the direct consequence was the injury to the corporation itself. Second, the court concluded that § 7 of the Sherman Act (Clayton § 4's predecessor) was not intended by Congress to "multiply suits" by conferring standing on thousands of stockholders "when their wrongs could have been equally well and far more economically redressed by a single suit in the name of the corporation."

Measure of the "directness" of an injury, as courts knew from their experience in tort law, would yield complicated metaphysical problems and no clear predictive rule. At the extremes it is perhaps easy to characterize an injury as "direct" or "indirect"—but in the middle are hundreds of cases in which the plaintiff's injury is clear but the chain of

4. 471 F.2d 727 (10th Cir.), cert. denied, 411 U.S. 938, 93 S.Ct. 1900 (1973).

5. See § 16.5b.

6. See 2 Antitrust law ¶ ¶ 360–365 (rev. ed. 1995) & current Supplement.

7. 183 Fed. 704, 709 (3d Cir.1910).

events between the act and the injury contains several, sometimes improbable links. The *Loeb* court's alternative observation was more sensible: that the corporation is a more efficient enforcer than its individual stockholders and should have the same information and incentives to sue.[8] However, *Loeb* became known for its "indirect injury" language, and courts have often relied on it to deny standing to the employees, franchisors, landlords and stockholders of victims, as well as to people in several other categories.[9]

16.4b2. "Target Area"

The "target area" test was designed to eliminate some of the uncertainties of the direct injury test. As the Ninth Circuit formulated the test in Conference of Studio Unions v. Loew's Inc.,[10] the plaintiff must "show that he is within that area of the economy which is endangered by a breakdown of competitive conditions in a particular industry." The court then held that a labor union and its members were not the target of an alleged conspiracy between major motion picture producers and a second union to drive smaller motion picture companies out of business.

The target area test has proved just as problematic as the direct injury test. If standing under the target area test is limited to the defendant's *intended* victims, then the range of potential plaintiffs is often very small. However, if standing is expanded to include all persons whose injury is "foreseeable," then the target area test will often be unduly broad: when a firm is driven from business, it is certainly foreseeable that its employees and their union, its creditors, stockholders, suppliers and landlord will all be injured. All of these participate to some degree in that part of the economy that is threatened by the violation.[11]

16.4b3. Supreme Court Attempts at a More Useful Alternative

Both the direct injury and target area tests for standing give a strong preference to consumers who suffer overcharge injuries or competitors injured by exclusionary practices. Occasionally courts even suggest that standing should be limited to these two classes of plaintiffs. But in Blue Shield of Virginia v. McCready,[12] the Supreme Court granted standing to a health insurance purchaser who alleged that her insurance provider conspired with psychiatrists to exclude psychologists from her health policy's coverage.

The intended victims of the alleged conspiracy were clearly the psychologists. However, the defendant easily could foresee that any exclusion of psychologists from policy coverage would also injure purchasers of psychologists' services. Thus although Ms. McCready was not the "target" of the antitrust conspiracy, her injury was plainly foreseeable.

Without explicitly adopting either the "direct injury" or "target area" test, the Supreme Court granted standing by noting that

8. Indeed, this was the basis for the general rule adopted by courts already in the nineteenth century that shareholders lacked common law standing to sue for injuries to their corporation. See H. Hovenkamp, Enterprise and American Law, 1836–1937 at ch. 4 (1991).

9. See, e.g., Solinger v. A. & M. Records, Inc., 718 F.2d 298 (9th Cir.1983) (no standing for shareholder); Jones v. Ford Motor Co., 599 F.2d 394 (10th Cir.1979) (same; employee); Billy Baxter, Inc. v. Coca–Cola Co., 431 F.2d 183 (2d Cir.1970), cert. denied, 401 U.S. 923, 91 S.Ct. 877 (1971) (same; franchisor); Southaven Land Co., Inc. v. Malone & Hyde, Inc., 715 F.2d 1079 (6th Cir.1983) (same; landlord). See D. Berger & R. Bernstein, An Analytical Framework for Antitrust Standing, 86 Yale L.J. 809 (1977).

10. 193 F.2d 51, 54–55 (9th Cir.1951), cert. denied, 342 U.S. 919, 72 S.Ct. 367 (1952).

11. Some circuits have developed alternatives to the "indirect injury" and "target area tests." For example, the Sixth Circuit's "zone of interests" test, also borrowed from tort law, seeks to determine whether the plaintiff's injury "arguably comes within the zone of interests protected by the [antitrust] laws." Malamud v. Sinclair Oil Corp., 521 F.2d 1142, 1152 (6th Cir.1975). The Sixth Circuit later suggested that *Associated General Contractors* undermined that test. Southaven Land Co. v. Malone & Hyde, 715 F.2d 1079 (6th Cir.1983). On the *Associated* case, see § 16.4b3. The Third Circuit has used a "balancing test comprised of many constant and variable factors" because there is "no talismanic test capable of resolving all § 4 standing problems." Bravman v. Bassett Furn. Indus., Inc., 552 F.2d 90, 99 (3d Cir.1977), cert. denied, 434 U.S. 823, 98 S.Ct. 69 (1977). In Blue Shield of Virginia v. McCready, 457 U.S. 465, 477, n. 12, 102 S.Ct. 2540, 2547 n. 12 (1982), the Supreme Court expressly refused to "evaluate the relative utility of any of these possibly conflicting approaches toward the problem of remote antitrust injury."

12. 457 U.S. 465, 102 S.Ct. 2540 (1982).

plaintiff McCready was "within that area of the economy" that had been endangered by the "breakdown of competitive conditions" resulting from the alleged violation. Further, she was a victim of antitrust injury.[13] That is, her injury was a natural result of diminished competition in the market for medical services.

The Court then appeared to add one restriction to a broad rule granting standing to all plaintiffs who could allege antitrust injury, and whose injury-in-fact was both foreseeable and not *de minimis* : the injury must be "inextricably intertwined with the injury the conspirators sought to inflict on psychologists * * *."[14] The Court's "inextricably intertwined" language is empty rhetoric, however, and not well designed to achieve consistency in standing cases. A stockholder's injuries seem "inextricably intertwined" with the demise of the corporation in which he owns shares. The terminated employee of an antitrust victim certainly suffers injuries that are "inextricably intertwined" with those suffered by her employer. The *McCready* case did little to clarify the law of antitrust standing, except to reaffirm that sometimes persons who are not the target of the violator may be antitrust plaintiffs. Furthermore, the Court paid little attention to the fact that another group of potential plaintiffs, the psychologists, were the direct target of the alleged conspiracy. Certainly they knew that the defendant had excluded them from its insurance coverage, and they had a strong incentive to sue.[15] Ms. McCready was only the second-best plaintiff.[16]

The Court soon backtracked from *McCready* in Associated General Contractors of California, Inc. v. California State Council of Carpenters,[17] which denied standing to a labor union alleging that defendant association of contractors coerced various of its contractor members into dealing only with nonunion firms. The intended victims of the boycott were thus contractors who stood to lose building contracts unless they agreed to the association's demands.

In holding that the union had not been "injured in its business or property," the Court treated the complaint as alleging an injury in the market for building projects, not in the labor market itself.[18] The outcome is easily rationalized if one considers first that employees ordinarily lack standing to sue for injuries that accrue to their employers, and secondly that in this case the plaintiff was not even the employees, but rather the union that represented them.

Nevertheless, the Court went on to note numerous difficulties in the plaintiff's complaint. First, the allegations were vague, and failed to identify precisely who was injured and how they were injured. Second, recognizing an antitrust damages action such as this one would present several problems of tracing and apportioning damages. Third, given that the real target of the alleged boycott was a group of contractors, the labor union was only a second-best plaintiff.[19] Finally, there did not seem to be antitrust injury. Indeed, it was "not clear whether the Union's interest would be served or disserved by enhanced competition" in the contracting market.[20]

After two important Supreme Court decisions the law of standing in private antitrust

13. Id. at 479, 102 S.Ct. at 2548.

14. Id. at 484, 102 S.Ct. at 2551.

15. In fact, the psychologists had sued. See Virginia Academy of Clinical Psychologists v. Blue Shield of Va., 624 F.2d 476 (4th Cir.), on remand, 501 F.Supp. 1232 (E.D.Va.1980), cert. denied, 450 U.S. 916, 101 S.Ct. 1360 (1981).

16. On second-best plaintiffs, see § 16.5d.

17. 459 U.S. 519, 103 S.Ct. 897 (1983).

18. The Court noted that there was:

> no allegation that any collective bargaining agreement was terminated as a result of the coercion, no allegation that the aggregate share of the contracting market controlled by union firms has declined, and no allegation that the Union's revenues in the form of dues or initiation fees have decreased.

459 U.S. at 542, 103 S.Ct. at 911.

19. "[T]he existence of an identifiable class of persons whose self-interest would normally motivate them to vindicate the public interest in antitrust enforcement diminishes the justification for allowing a more remote party such as the Union to perform the office of a private attorney general." 459 U.S. at 539. On second-best plaintiffs, see § 16.5d.

20. Ibid. Indeed, more strenuous competition in the contractor market probably would have benefitted low cost contractors, which would likely be nonunionized.

actions is far from clear. None of the generalized, conceptual tests adequately predicts whether a particular plaintiff will be granted standing. Further, although they leave the older "direct injury" and "target area" tests somewhat in doubt, neither was overruled.[21]

Nevertheless, one can draw a few generalizations that do in fact provide guidance. First, antitrust injury is a *sine qua non* for standing, as are both causation and injury-in-fact. Standing is never granted if one of these is found lacking, and the more tenuous the evidence the more likely the case will be dismissed on standing grounds. Second, consumers and competitors of the violator are presumptively granted standing. A weaker presumption of standing or perhaps no presumption either way attaches to boycott victims other than the immediately intended targets. This accounts for *McCready*. Other classes of victims, such as landlords, employees, stockholders, and creditors of victims, are presumptively denied standing. But the presumptions are rebuttable, and in close cases the court will determine whether there is another highly motivated group of potential plaintiffs in a position to enforce the antitrust laws more efficiently.

In addition, the court should also consider whether the particular plaintiff is in a unique position to discover an antitrust violation earlier than other potential plaintiffs would. In that case, granting standing could minimize the duration, and thus the social cost, of antitrust violations.[22]

16.4c. The Preferred Position of Consumers and Competitors

Consumers have always been antitrust's preferred plaintiffs. Even critics whose notions of appropriate private enforcement are most restrictive recognize the value of consumer suits. An important goal of antitrust policy is low prices and high quality output for consumers; the ideological dispute is mainly between those who believe that consumer welfare is the *only* goal of antitrust policy, and those who believe other goals should be included as well.[23] Ever since Reiter v. Sonotone Corp.[24] permitted an end use consumer to claim damages from a cartel, this proposition seems to be well established. The principal limitation is the rule of *Illinois Brick v. Illinois*, which limits damage actions for cartel and monopoly overcharges to direct purchasers.[25]

But the term "consumer" standing does not fully capture the set of interests it is designed to cover. "Standing by vertically related firms" would be more appropriate, for within the concept of consumer standing must be included intermediate purchasers such as retailers, as well as suppliers. What all these parties have in common is that their injury results from a monopoly overcharge (or monopsony underpayment)[26] that is the main focus of federal antitrust policy.

The courts have had somewhat more difficulty with suits by suppliers than with suits by consumers. For example, the *Dry* decision denied standing to a physician suing a hospital that allegedly agreed with staff physicians to reduce referrals to the plaintiff.[27] The court emphasized that the physicians was neither consumer nor competitor of the hospital. Clearly, however, he was a supplier to the hospital, and a boycott directed at suppliers can be just as anticompetitive as one directed at customers.[28]

21. See Amey, Inc. v. Gulf Abstract & Title, Inc., 758 F.2d 1486, 1496–1497 (11th Cir.1985), cert. denied, 475 U.S. 1107, 106 S.Ct. 1513 (1986), holding that the "target area" test survives *Associated General Contractors*; McDonald v. Johnson & Johnson, 722 F.2d 1370, 1373 (8th Cir.1983), cert. denied, 469 U.S. 870, 105 S.Ct. 219 (1984) (rejecting earlier tests); Merican v. Caterpillar Tractor Co., 713 F.2d 958, 965 (3d Cir.1983), cert. denied, 465 U.S. 1024, 104 S.Ct. 1278 (1984) (criticizing target area test).

22. See generally § 16.5.

23. See Ch. 2.

24. 442 U.S. 330, 99 S.Ct. 2326 (1979). See § 16.4a.

25. Illinois Brick v. Illinois, 431 U.S. 720, 97 S.Ct. 2061 (1977). See § 16.6.

26. On monopsony, see § 1.2b.

27. Dry v. Methodist Medical Center of Oak Ridge, 893 F.2d 1334 (6th Cir.1990).

28. Contrast Sweeney v. Athens Regional Medical Center, 709 F.Supp. 1563 (M.D.Ga.1989), granting standing to nurse midwife alleging a conspiracy among medical clinics and physicians to limit plaintiff's access to patients at the clinics.

The class of relevant consumers (and suppliers) is often broader than the court acknowledges. Reconsider *McCready*.[29] The Supreme Court went to some lengths to extend antitrust standing to the "indirect" victim of a boycott whom it treated as neither consumer nor competitor of the defendant psychiatrists' services. Rather McCready was viewed as claiming injury from a boycott designed to exclude psychologists from participation in the market for insured health care. But the Court could have reached the same destination far more quickly by simply observing that McCready was in fact a consumer of health insurance, and the alleged conspiracy was nothing other than an agreement to reduce the quality of her policy from one that included psychologists' services to one that did not. Viewed in this way, *McCready* presents a fairly easy case of consumer standing. For example, suppose automobile manufacturers should agree with each other and suppliers of plastic seat covers to stop using leather seat covers. Is their agreement a "boycott" of leather seat cover producers or a cartel reducing the quality of the product? For antitrust purposes it is both, and under McCready both classes of victims should have standing.

As *McCready* suggests, boycott claims often raise issues of standing. When boycotts are directed at competitors or immediate consumers, standing is clear and generally not contested.[30] But often courts overlook ways in which boycott victims are really consumers or suppliers. For example, *Reazin* held that a hospital could challenge an agreement among health insurers to terminate their relationship with the hospital even though the hospital itself was neither a consumer of health insurance nor a competitor in the health insurance market; rather it was a supplier of medical services to consumers of health insurance.[31] But there is another way of viewing the case: the hospital sold health care services to the insurers, which purchased them on behalf of their patients. Viewed in this way, *Reazin* involved a boycott of a supplier to the insurers themselves. Likewise, in *Pennsylvania Dental* the court granted standing to Blue Shield, a health insurer, to sue dentists who allegedly boycotted its prepaid dental plan.[32] The immediate victims of the conspiracy were the dentists' patients, for whom the prepaid dental plan became unavailable. Blue Shield sold insurance to the dentists' patients, the insureds. Blue Shield did not offer any dental services itself, and was thus not a competitor with the defendant dentists. Nor, in the court's view, was it a purchaser of dentists' services. Rather, it was merely a supplier of insurance services to the insureds. Once again, the court overlooked the fact that a health insurer *is* a purchaser; indeed, its prepaid plan was simply a way of purchasing dental services in large blocks, and in advance of immediate need.

Competitor lawsuits have frequently been attacked as a principal cause of antitrust overdeterrence.[33] Nevertheless, competitor standing is so well established in antitrust case law that it is seldom questioned except when the plaintiff lacks antitrust injury. Competitors are often in a unique position to enforce the antitrust laws. They may know of a violation much earlier than consumers. Indeed, consumers may never find out at all. Further, injuries to competitors are concentrated while consumer injuries are often diffuse. As a result, consumer suits present many problems of free

29. Note 11.

30. See 2 Antitrust Law ¶ 370 (rev. ed. 1995); Z Channel Limited Partnership v. Home Box Office, 931 F.2d 1338 (9th Cir.1991); Fishman v. Estate of Wirtz, 807 F.2d 520, 533–535 (7th Cir.1986) (competitor has standing to challenge concerted refusal to deal between rival and supplier of stadium facility); Los Angeles Memorial Coliseum Commn. v. NFL, 791 F.2d 1356 (9th Cir.1986), cert. denied, 484 U.S. 826, 108 S.Ct. 92 (1987) (granting standing to football team to challenge concerted refusal by other teams).

31. Reazin v. Blue Cross & Blue Shield of Kansas, 899 F.2d 951, 963 (10th Cir.1990), citing *McCready* for the proposition that "an antitrust plaintiff need not necessarily be a competitor or consumer" of the boycotting defendants. See *McCready*, 457 U.S. at 472, 102 S.Ct. at 2544.

32. Pennsylvania Dental Assn. v. Medical Serv. Assn. of Pa., 815 F.2d 270 (3d Cir.), cert. denied, 484 U.S. 851, 108 S.Ct. 153 (1987).

33. See § 2.2c; and E.A. Snyder & T.E. Kauper, Misuse of the Antitrust Laws: the Competitor Plaintiff, 90 Mich. L. Rev. 551 (1991); W. Page Optimal Antitrust Penalties and Competitors' Injury, 88 Mich. L. Rev. 2151 (1990).

riding and organizational cost that competitor suits do not.

Weighed against these factors is the powerful argument that competitors lack the proper set of incentives. They are injured by rival firms' efficiency at least as often as they are injured by anticompetitive practices. Many competitor suits are nothing more than complaints about the business methods of a more efficient rival. The best solution to this problem is aggressive use of the antitrust injury doctrine, not total abandonment of the competitor lawsuit.

§ 16.5 Special Problems of Antitrust Standing

16.5a. The Unestablished Business as Antitrust Plaintiff

Among the most problematic of plaintiffs is the unestablished business—the person who was denied an opportunity ever to compete in the first place.

Any policy of promoting competition through private antitrust enforcement must protect entry into markets. Further, the prospective entrant is often an easier target than the incumbent. The prospective entrant has fewer unrecoverable sunk costs and is in a better position to consider alternative markets. For that reason many practices such as strategic exclusionary behavior[1] are directed primarily at new entrants or prospective entrants.

At the same time, courts are often skeptical about claims that someone was excluded from a market before ever making her first sale—particularly if the claim seeks damages for lost anticipated profits.[2] A high percentage of new businesses in the United States fail each year, nearly all for reasons having nothing to do with the antitrust laws.[3]

In balancing these considerations, courts have tended to grant standing to unestablished businesses, but only upon a fairly substantial showing of previous commitment. For example, courts often insist that the prospective entrant have obtained some kind of property interest, have some sunk costs or other investment in entry before the requisite "injury" can be inferred. Occasionally they have found the plaintiff's clear intent to enter a certain market to be sufficient. More often they have required more, such as contracts with prospective purchasers, a commitment of financing, or substantial funds spent in marketing research or advertising. In general, the more the unestablished business has at stake in a certain market, the more likely the court will find a sufficient basis for standing.[4]

Likewise, courts dealing with claims by unestablished businesses can be expected to play close attention to causation. Often the causation issue is couched in terms of the plaintiff's degree of "preparedness" to enter the market. For example, a plaintiff who has not yet obtained regulatory approval to enter a market, located trained personnel, or obtained essential patent licenses will not likely succeed in claiming that market access was denied by an incumbent's exclusionary practices.[5] As long as substantial hurdles to entry remain, it is difficult for the plaintiff to show that it would have entered successfully but for the antitrust violation.

16.5b. Employees

When considering the antitrust standing of employees, two questions must be considered:

§ 16.5

1. See § 7.3.

2. On damage recoveries by unestablished rivals, see § 17.6c, which argues that lost anticipated profits should generally be denied, and plaintiffs restricted to damages based on loss of investment.

3. Cochran, Small Business Mortality Rates: A Review of the Literature, 19 J. Small Bus. Mgmt. 50 (1981).

4. See Neumann v. Vidal, 710 F.2d 856 (D.C.Cir.1983), on remand, 594 F.Supp. 139 (D.D.C.1984), affirmed, 786 F.2d 424 (D.C.Cir.1986); Hayes v. Solomon, 597 F.2d 958, 973 (5th Cir.1979), cert. denied, 444 U.S. 1078, 100 S.Ct. 1028 (1980); Note, Unestablished Businesses and Treble Damage Recovery Under Section Four of the Clayton Act, 49 U.Chi.L.Rev. 1076 (1982).

5. For example, Cable Holdings of Ga. v. Home Video, 825 F.2d 1559, 1563 (11th Cir.1987) (cable company not equipped to expand into new territory); Jade Aircraft Sales v. City of Bridgeport, 1990–2 Trade Cas. (CCH) ¶ 69225, 1990 WL 128573 (D.Conn.1990) (no standing where prospective business lacked local zoning approval and federal regulatory approval). Contrast, Central Telecommunic. v. TCI Cablevision, 800 F.2d 711, 727–729 (8th Cir.1986) (granting standing where the plaintiff had acknowledged expertise and experience).

(1) is the alleged antitrust violation occurring in the labor market or in a product or service market where the employee works? and (2) does the employee work for the victim of the antitrust violation or for the violator?[6]

When the alleged antitrust violation occurs in the labor market, then the employee is a participant and ordinarily has standing just as any other market participant.[7] For example, suppose a group of labor unions, employers and other organizations organize a boycott of non-union employees. Someone denied access to the job market as a result of that boycott is the boycott's intended victim and would ordinarily have antitrust standing.[8]

By contrast, when the alleged antitrust violation occurs in the product or service market where the employee works, the employee is almost always denied standing. For example, if a firm shuts down or reduces its output because it is the victim of a boycott in the product market, the firm itself likely has a cause of action. But employees of the firm do not, for the courts consistently hold that their injuries are entirely derivative of the injuries of their employer.[9] Courts often formulate their decisions in terms of the "direct injury" or "target area" tests,[10] but the result is virtually always the same.

A few courts have considered one exception to these rules: namely, complaints by employees of the violator rather than the victim. Suppose the plaintiff alleges that he lost his job because he refused to participate in his employer's antitrust violation. For example, the employee refuses to submit a rigged bid, knowing bid rigging to be a felony, and loses his job as a result. In Bichan v. Chemetron Corp.[11] the Seventh Circuit denied standing under both the indirect injury and target area theories, holding that an action should be granted "to those who, as consumers or competitors, suffer immediate injuries with respect to their business or property," and denied to those "whose injuries were more indirectly caused by the antitrust conduct." In this case, which involved an alleged price fixing conspiracy, the target of the violation was the conspirator's customers, not its employees.

Bichan's loss of employment was arguably an "indirect" result of the antitrust violation. He was also not the "target" of a price fixing conspiracy. But did the two tests for standing produce the correct result? An employee terminated because he refuses to participate in an antitrust violation could be a highly efficient enforcer of the antitrust laws. He certainly has the motivation. More importantly, he has better knowledge than almost any potential plaintiff of the fact of the violation. If the cartel is successful it will not be detected by consumers, the preferred plaintiffs. Giving a plaintiff in Bichan's position the right to sue brings evidence of the existence of a cartel into the open at an early stage, before it has had a chance to cause significant harm.

The Ninth Circuit granted standing in a similar case, *Ostrofe*,[12] noting that although the terminated plaintiff himself may not

6. There may also be a question about whether the plaintiff is in fact an employee. See Garot Anderson Marketing, Inc. v. Blue Cross and Blue Shield United of Wisconsin, 772 F.Supp. 1054, 1062 (N.D.Ill.1990), granting standing where the plaintiffs were not employees but rather independent agents.

7. See 2 Antitrust Law ¶ 376 (rev. ed. 1995).

8. Whether the alleged boycott is exempt from the antitrust laws presents a different issue. See § 19.7a. Cf. Brown v. Pro–Football, 518 U.S. 231, 116 S.Ct. 2116 (1996) (no standing issue, but considering claim by professional football players against team agreement suppressing their salaries during collective bargaining negotiations).

9. For example, Sharp v. United Airlines, 967 F.2d 404 (10th Cir.), cert. denied, 506 U.S. 974, 113 S.Ct. 464 (1992) (employees lacked standing to sue competitor for exclusionary practice injuries that accrued to their former employer.); Adams v. Pan American World Airways, 828 F.2d 24 (D.C.Cir.1987), cert. denied, 485 U.S. 961, 108 S.Ct. 1225 (1988) (same); Province v. Cleveland Press Pub. Co., 787 F.2d 1047 (6th Cir.1986) (same). See 2 Antitrust Law ¶ 376.

10. See § 16.4b.

11. 681 F.2d 514, 517–20 (7th Cir.1982), cert. denied, 460 U.S. 1016, 103 S.Ct. 1261 (1983).

12. Ostrofe v. H.S. Crocker Co., Inc., 670 F.2d 1378 (9th Cir.1982), vacated and remanded, 460 U.S. 1007, 103 S.Ct. 1244 (1983), affirmed on remand, 740 F.2d 739 (9th Cir.1984), cert. dismissed, 469 U.S. 1200, 105 S.Ct. 1155 (1985). See Comment, Discharged Employees: Should They Have Antitrust Standing Under Section Four of the Clayton Act?, 34 Hastings L.J. 839 (1983).

have sustained antitrust injury in the strictest sense from the conspiracy to fix prices, his refusal to cooperate with the conspiracy nonetheless helped vindicate the rights of customers and competitors in that market. Affording standing to sue to such an employee discharged because he refused to cooperate in an antitrust violation by his employer encourages exposure of such schemes by persons best situated to know of their existence.[13]

Antitrust enforcement generally becomes more efficient when violations are detected and challenged at an early stage. The wisdom of the *Ostrofe* decision lies in its unstated acknowledgement that even standing rules such as the antitrust injury rule are means to arriving at the optimal amount of antitrust enforcement. The social costs of collusion may be reduced by giving a particular class of plaintiffs an incentive to blow the whistle, even though they do not satisfy established antitrust criteria for standing.[14]

16.5c. Derivative Injuries and "Duplicative Recovery"

Courts also generally require that the injured business or property belong to the plaintiff and not to someone else. Occasionally, however, ownership of a particular property interest is ambiguous. In Hawaii v. Standard Oil Co. of California,[15] for example, the Supreme Court held that a state could not assert a damages claim for economic injuries to its citizens, or for injury to its general economy, if it was not itself a purchaser or competitor of the defendant. At that time, § 4 did not authorize a state's use of the common law doctrine of *parens patriae*, under which a governmental entity could bring an action asserting injuries to citizens within its protection. Since the citizens themselves had causes of action, the Court reasoned, any damages action brought by the State asserting the same injuries, or some more general injury to the state's economy, would yield duplicative recoveries. Section 4 was subsequently amended to permit *parens patriae* actions by states' attorneys general on behalf of natural persons residing in the state.[16]

The concept of "derivative" injury is slippery. The mere fact that an antitrust violation injures different groups of market participants does not entail that one group's injuries are merely derivative of the other. For example, predatory pricing directed initially at competitors will, if successful, yield higher prices for consumers. In this case we would not say that the competitors' injury is merely derivative of the consumers' injury. Both are participants in the immediate market. Further, their injuries are measured differently: consumers by the monopoly overcharge and competitors by loss of business opportunity.

Ideally, we would reserve the term "derivative" injury for those who claim the selfsame injury as someone else, and usually by their participation in some market other than the market that is the focus of the antitrust violation. A good example is the corporate shareholder, who will lose her investment when her stock becomes worthless as a result of another firm's antitrust violation. In this case, the loss of value in the shares is nothing other than the loss of business assets or potential profits that the corporation itself has experienced. We acknowledge this by saying that the shareholders' loss is entirely derivative of the loss suffered by the corporation itself, and generally deny standing to the shareholder. Roughly similar considerations apply to the landlords of antitrust victims, to their creditors, tax collectors, and customers with long-term contracts.

13. *Ostrofe*, 740 F.2d at 746–747.

14. Compare Donahue v. Pendleton Woolen Mills, 633 F.Supp. 1423 (S.D.N.Y.1986), granting standing to commission salesmen allegedly terminated because they objected to their employer's resale price maintenance imposed on dealers. But in this case, granting employee standing is unnecessary to expose the antitrust violation, for it is already known to the dealers upon whom the RPM is imposed. The Sixth Circuit's decision in Fallis v. Pendleton Woolen Mills, 866 F.2d 209, 211 & n. 4 (6th Cir.1989), denying standing on analogous facts, seems correct. Cf. Vinci v. Waste Management, 80 F.3d 1372 (9th Cir.1996) (denying standing to employee complaining about his employer's alleged scheme to drive rivals out of business; in this case, the rivals themselves would have an adequate incentive to sue).

15. 405 U.S. 251, 92 S.Ct. 885 (1972).

16. 15 U.S.C.A. § 15c.

In brief, when a firm is forced out of business in some market, its exit causes dislocations in numerous related markets where it does business. A court uses the term "derivative" to express its intuition that a particular damage claim is insufficiently distinguished from the claim of another to warrant a separate grant of standing.[17]

The Supreme Court's *McCready* decision is modestly helpful.[18] The Court permitted a health insurance consumer to sue her insurer for participating in an agreement with psychiatrists to exclude the services of clinical psychologists from medical policy coverage. In this case the psychologists were the competitors of the psychiatrists. Further, the psychologists had already maintained their own action.[19] Indeed the district court had considered the psychologists' and McCready's claim together, and had granted the psychologists standing while denying standing to McCready. The Supreme Court reversed the latter decision.[20] The psychologists had suffered one kind of injury—loss of profits in their profession—and McCready had suffered quite another, namely, reduced coverage on her health insurance policy.

Court have often used the term "duplicative recovery" as a rationale for denying standing to a particular class of plaintiffs. The term implies that an antitrust violation produces some identifiable total amount of injury, and that under § 4 the defendant's liability cannot exceed three times that amount.

But few antitrust violations produce an easily demarcated "pool" of injuries. Most produce ripples whose injurious effects spread through the economy, becoming more attenuated as they go further from the primary victim. Courts generally use the term "duplicative recovery" only to suggest that a certain amount of liability seems like too much, measured by some standard of common sense or fairness that is not articulated. Injury is always measured by the plaintiff's losses, not by the defendant's gains, and there is no natural correlation between the amount of injury an antitrust violation causes and its profitability to the violator. Consider an unsuccessful predatory pricing scheme which produces substantial losses for both the predator and its competitor victims. Some competitors may be driven from business, thereby injuring suppliers with long-term contracts, employees and their dues-collecting unions, customers, creditors, landlords and federal, state and local governments which stand to lose tax revenues. To decide that the failing competitor ought to have a cause of action against the predator, but that the landlord, the victim's employees or the state seeking lost taxes should not, may be reasonable. But the problem is not "duplicative recovery." There is no pool of unjust earnings that will be overdrawn; the unsuccessful scheme produces no monopoly profits at all. Nor is there any relationship between the amount of the defendant's illegal gain and the injuries to the various victims. Each victim has its own distinct injury. The competitor, who probably has a cause of action, will be able to recover lost profits and perhaps its lost business investment. Employees, tax collectors and landlords will probably be denied standing. Recovery by these victims would not be "duplicative," but it would yield a large amount of damages—more than many defendants would be capable of paying, and probably more than Congress envisioned when it passed § 4.

The only coherent meaning of "duplicative recovery" is recovery by one person for injuries sustained by another person who has also been able to recover. For example, if a private party obtained redress for its injuries and later

17. See Southwest Suburban Bd. of Realtors, Inc. v. Beverly Area Planning Ass'n, 830 F.2d 1374, 1378 (7th Cir.1987), concluding that "Merely derivative injuries sustained by employees, officers, stockholders, and creditors of an injured company" are insufficient to create antitrust injury or confer standing. See also Lovett v. General Motors Corp., 975 F.2d 518, 521 (8th Cir.1992) (sole owner of closely held corporation lacks standing to sue for injuries that accrued to business).

18. Blue Shield of Va. v. McCready, 457 U.S. 465, 102 S.Ct. 2540 (1982). See § 16.4b3.

19. See Virginia Acad. of Clinical Psychologists v. Blue Shield of Va., 624 F.2d 476 (4th Cir.), on remand, 501 F.Supp. 1232 (E.D.Va.1980), cert. denied, 450 U.S. 916, 101 S.Ct. 1360 (1981).

20. *McCready*, 457 U.S. at 470 n.4, 102 S.Ct. at 2543 n. 4.

a state suing as *parens patriae* obtained damages for the selfsame injury, the two recoveries would arguably be duplicative.[21] The term "duplicative recovery" may therefore have some meaning in the context of the indirect purchaser rule, discussed in § 16.6. A direct purchaser is permitted to recover the entire monopoly overcharge, even though most of the overcharge may have been passed along to the direct purchaser's customers. Some state antitrust laws, however, permit indirect purchaser lawsuits. Suppose that an indirect purchaser recovers for its own passed-on injuries after the defendant has already paid the direct purchaser an amount sufficient to cover the injuries of direct and indirect purchasers all the way down the distribution chain. This recovery is appropriately characterized as duplicative.[22]

16.5d. Second Best Plaintiffs

If not all those injured by an antitrust violation have an action, then prospective plaintiffs must be ranked. Courts must grant standing to some classes of plaintiffs who are well placed to enforce the antitrust laws, while denying it to those who are not so well placed. In the process of denying standing, courts often observe that the plaintiff in the present case was only second best to some other class of persons who was in a better position to sue.[23]

Denying recovery to a "second-best plaintiff" will permit an antitrust violation to go unchallenged if the plaintiff thought to be better in fact lacks the appropriate incentives or entitlements to sue. Courts should not automatically assume an alternative plaintiff is superior simply because it occupies a more proximate position in the market. Alternative plaintiffs might have a very small stake, be co-conspirators, otherwise under the control of the violator, or fearful of suing lest they should lose a valuable contract.

For example, in the Insurance Antitrust Litigation,[24] the court held that purchasers of insurance had standing to challenge a conspiracy by reinsurers (sellers of secondary insurance to insurers) to reduce policy coverage notwithstanding that the primary insurers, with whom the reinsurers dealt directly, would have appeared to suffer the more direct injury. In this case

> [t]he theoretical possibility that such entities could have sued must be discounted by the power the allegations attribute to the London reinsurers. The 1400 [primary insurers] could not withstand this power. As they caved in to it, they are unlikely to desire to challenge it in court.

Finally, a plaintiff cannot be "second best" if the plaintiff characterized as best lacks standing. For example, *Pinney Dock* counted in favor of the plaintiff competitor's standing the fact that customers with the largest incentive to sue would be indirect purchasers, whose damages actions would be barred by the *Illinois Brick* indirect purchaser rule.[25]

16.5e. Pari Delicto; Declaratory Judgment Actions

At common law contracts in restraint of trade were unenforceable. However the doc-

21. As a consequence, the parens patriae statute prohibits recovery by both. See § 15.4 of this volume.

22. See H. Hovenkamp, State Antitrust in the Federal Scheme, 57 Ind.L.J. 375 (1983).

23. For example, see Bodie–Rickett and Assoc. v. Mars, 957 F.2d 287 (6th Cir.1992), holding that a broker of snack foods who lost commissions when a candy manufacturer consolidated its distribution under a single broker lacked standing. The theory of the complaint was that the consolidation was anticompetitive because it was intended to undermine the marketing efforts of rival snack food manufacturers; but with respect to such a theory the manufacturers themselves were better plaintiffs.

24. In re Insurance Antitrust Litigation, 938 F.2d 919, 926 (9th Cir.1991), affirmed in part, reversed in part, 509 U.S. 764, 113 S.Ct. 2891 (1993). Compare Westchester Radiological Assoc. P.C. v. Empire Blue Cross & Blue Shield, 659 F.Supp. 132, 137 (S.D.N.Y.1987), granting standing to radiologists to attack alleged monopolization by the defendant insurer. The immediate victims were rival insurers, while the radiologists were neither competitors of insurers nor purchasers of insurance. However, the court granted standing because the alleged conduct "may indeed not be sufficiently injurious to the competing insurers for them to undertake the time and expense of litigation." This conclusion suggests that the underlying antitrust claim is dubious, but the court was correct to grant standing.

25. Pinney Dock & Transport Co. v. Penn Central Corp., 838 F.2d 1445, 1462–1463 (6th Cir.), cert. denied, 488 U.S. 880, 109 S.Ct. 196 (1988). On the indirect purchaser rule, see § 16.6.

trine of *in pari delicto* ("at equal fault") may forbid a firm from obtaining antitrust damages when it was a participant in the very agreement now alleged to constitute an antitrust violation. Historically, the Supreme Court had concluded that the right to prevent restraints of trade should trump the *pari delicto* concern with preventing recoveries by guilty plaintiffs.[26] Today, the court is more likely to consider whether the plaintiff was a full and equal participant in the contract alleged to be an antitrust violation, or whether it was imposed upon him.[27]

In any event, even a participant in a contract can ordinarily get a judicial *declaration* that a contract is in restraint of trade and thus unenforceable. Such an action could proceed under the federal Declaratory Judgment Act when its requirements are met.[28] In Blackburn v. Sweeney[29] the Seventh Circuit permitted a participant in a horizontal territorial division scheme to obtain declaratory relief that the agreement was not enforceable. The court held that *pari delicto* did not foreclose a claim for purely declaratory relief. However, such a claim was not one under Clayton § 4, and thus the plaintiff was not entitled to damages.

§ 16.6 The Indirect Purchaser Rule

16.6a. Hanover Shoe and Illinois Brick

In Hanover Shoe, Inc. v. United Shoe Machinery Corp.[1] the Supreme Court held that a direct purchaser from a monopolist could claim the entire monopoly overcharge as damages, even though the purchaser passed most of the overcharge on to its customers. The Court acknowledged that much of a monopoly overcharge is passed down the distribution chain and absorbed by the consumer. However, lawsuits by indirect purchaser consumers would be impractical. There might be thousands of such purchasers, each with only a "tiny stake in a lawsuit."

A decade later in Illinois Brick Co. v. Illinois[2] the Supreme Court followed *Hanover Shoe* in deciding that, since the direct purchaser has an action for the entire monopoly overcharge, the indirect purchaser should have none. It did not matter that the indirect purchaser could show that part of the overcharge had been passed on and that it had been injured as a result.

A monopoly overcharge at the top of a distribution chain generally results in higher prices at every level below. For example, if production of aluminum is monopolized or cartelized, fabricators of aluminum cookware will pay higher prices for aluminum. In most cases they will absorb part of these increased costs themselves and pass part along to cookware wholesalers. The wholesalers will charge higher prices to the retail stores, and the stores will do it once again to retail consumers. Every person at every stage in the chain likely will be poorer as a result of the monopoly price at the top.

Theoretically, one can calculate the percentage of any overcharge that a firm at one distributional level will pass on to those at the next level. However, the computation requires knowledge of the prevailing elasticities of supply and demand, and obtaining that information is beyond the technical competence of

26. Perma Life Mufflers v. International Parts Corp., 392 U.S. 134, 88 S.Ct. 1981 (1968). See 2 Antitrust Law ¶ 390 (rev. ed.).

27. E.g., Sullivan v. National Football League, 34 F.3d 1091 (1st Cir.1994), cert. denied, 513 U.S. 1190, 115 S.Ct. 1252 (1995) (fact issue whether plaintiff had been an active and soliciting participant in a contract rule restraining the sales of stock in NFL teams); General Leaseways v. National Truck Leasing Assn., 830 F.2d 716, 722 (7th Cir.1987) (applying pari delicto to bar the plaintiff, who was found to be not merely a member of the association that had negotiated a territorial restraint, but also who had "approved and supported the location restriction and even pressed for its enforcement" in other contexts).

28. See 28 U.S.C.A. § 2201. On declaratory judgment actions, see 10B C.A. Wright, A.R. Miller & M.K. Kane, Federal Practice and Procedure §§ 2755–2764 (civ.3d 1998).

29. 53 F.3d 825 (7th Cir.1995).

§ 16.6

1. 392 U.S. 481, 88 S.Ct. 2224 (1968).

2. 431 U.S. 720, 97 S.Ct. 2061 (1977); see 2 Antitrust Law ¶ 371 (rev. ed. 1995); and see Lucas Automotive Engineering v. Bridgestone/Firestone, 140 F.3d 1228 (9th Cir.1998) (applying indirect purchaser rule so as to preclude indirect purchaser's challenge to a merger).

courts.[3]

Nevertheless, examination of the relationship between demand elasticities and pass-on can provide some guidance about the proper scope of the indirect purchaser rule. For simplicity we consider only demand elasticities and ignore elasticity of supply. We also assume that any monopoly overcharge is spread over an entire relevant market and has absolutely no effect on possible substitute products in a different market.[4]

Finally, we assume that the cartelized product is a variable cost item to all firms in the distribution chain. If the cartelized product is a fixed cost item to a particular firm—for example, if a pizza parlor pays a monopoly price for its delivery truck—the monopoly overcharge will not show up in the firm's short-run marginal cost curve, which includes only variable costs. In a competitive market, in which prices are driven to marginal cost, a pizza parlor that paid a monopoly price for a delivery truck might have to absorb the entire monopoly overcharge itself. If the monopoly overcharge was in anchovies, however, the marginal cost of any pizza with anchovies would rise.[5] Further, if the cartelized product is a fixed cost item, it is less likely that all purchasers in an affected market will buy it. For example, if manufacturers make their plants out of bricks, and the lifetime of a plant is fifty years, a cartel would have to function for fifty years before every manufacturer in the market fell victim to it. If it existed for only three or four years, as most cartels do, it would have imposed higher costs on only a small percentage of the firms in the market. These firms would have to compete with other firms that were not subject to the cartel.

Figures 1, 2, and 3 illustrate the pass-on problem in three different markets. In each, MC represents the marginal cost curve faced by every firm in the market when it purchases the product at a competitive price. MC´ is the higher marginal cost curve each firm faces because of a cartel or monopoly operating at a higher level in the distribution chain.

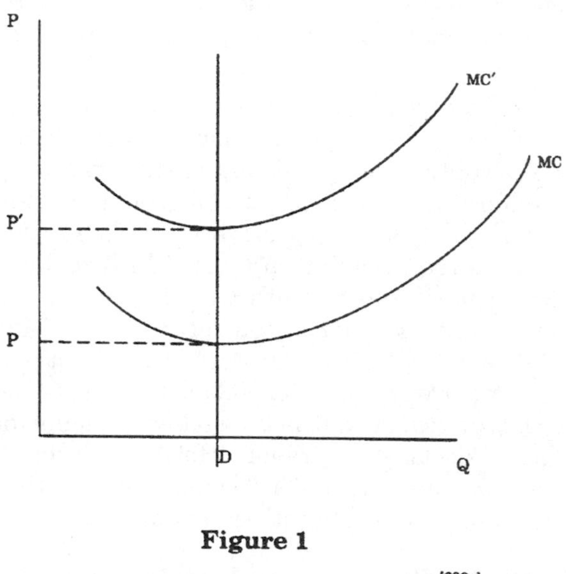

Figure 1

[632a]

In Figure 1 the market demand curve is perfectly inelastic—that is, exactly the same number of sales will be made in the entire market when price = MC´ as when price = MC. (Remember, in a competitive market price always tends toward marginal cost.) In such a market a firm could pass on 100% of the overcharge and continue producing at the same rate as it did before the cartel came into

3. For the relevant formulas, see W. Landes & R. Posner, Should Indirect Purchasers Have Standing to Sue Under the Antitrust Laws? An Economic Analysis of the Rule of *Illinois Brick*, 46 U.Chi.L.Rev. 602 (1979).

4. For some suggestions about how courts should deal with pass-on problems in real world markets, see J. Harris & L. Sullivan, Passing on the Monopoly Overcharge: A Comprehensive Policy Analysis, 128 U.Pa.L.Rev. 269 (1979); W. Landes & R. Posner, The Economics of Passing On: A Reply to Harris and Sullivan, 128 U.Pa.L.Rev. 1274 (1980).

5. The discussion also assumes that each firm uses a rigid proportion of the cartelized product. This is not always the case: a pizza parlor might respond to a monopoly price increase in anchovies by putting fewer anchovies and more cheese on its pizzas. Likewise, a price-regulated utility might be entitled to pass on to its customers the full amount of any cartel overcharge. However, in response to a cartel price increase in oil, the utility might burn less oil and more coal. These possibilities make pass-on much more difficult to calculate. See R. Cooter, Passing on the Monopoly Overcharge: A Further Comment on Economic Theory, 129 U.Pa.L.Rev. 1523 (1981).

existence. It would not be injured by the cartel.

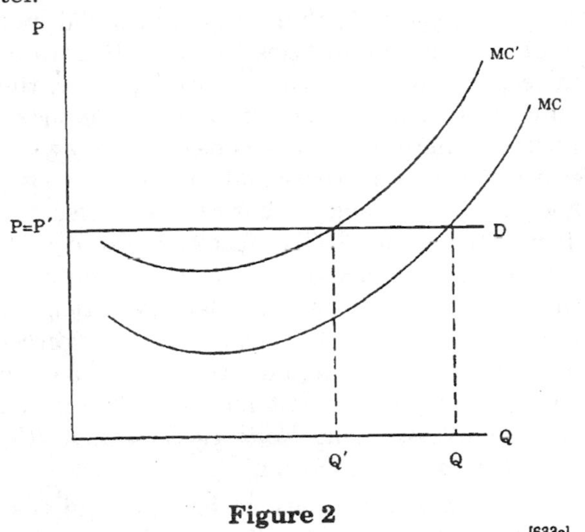

Figure 2

[633a]

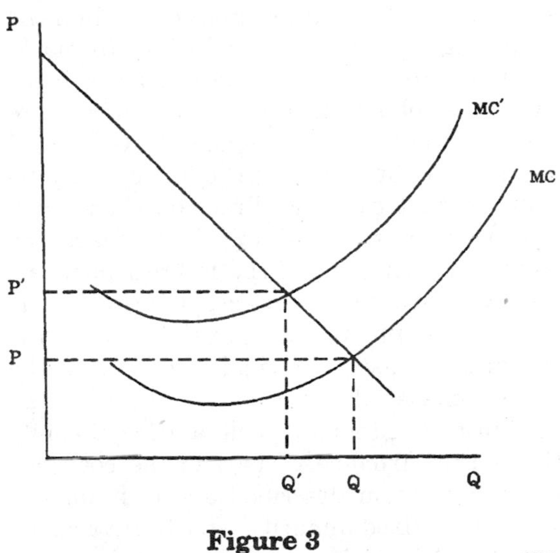

Figure 3

[634a]

Figure 2 illustrates the situation of a single firm whose demand is perfectly elastic. If the firm increased its price even modestly, demand would fall to zero.[6] In that case the firm will respond to the cartel price increase by reducing output from Q to Q´. However, it will continue to charge the same price, effectively absorbing the entire monopoly overcharge. None would be passed on to consumers.

Most real world markets are of the type illustrated in Figure 3. The market demand curve slopes downward, and each firm in the market tends to produce at a level at which its marginal cost equals the market price. When marginal cost is MC, market output is Q and price is P. When the firms must pay a cartel price for a variable cost item, however, their marginal costs rise to MC´, output is reduced to Q´ and price rises to P´.

The reduction in output produces lost profits to the firms, while the increase in price represents that part of the overcharge that is passed on to consumers. Other consumers are injured because they substitute a different product.

16.6b. Exceptions to the Illinois Brick Rule

16.6b1. Pre-existing Contracts

Occasionally the demand conditions facing a particular firm resemble Figure 1 more than Figure 3. Suppose that a direct purchaser executes a 10–year contract to sell 1000 widgets per year at a price 10% higher than its costs. A year later, the firm's supplier enters into a cartel and raises the price of an input to monopoly levels. In that case the direct purchaser can pass on the entire monopoly overcharge for purchases under that contract.

Courts have generally recognized an exception to *Illinois Brick* for *fixed-quantity, fixed-mark-up* contracts that existed *before* the cartel price took effect. Indirect purchasers buying under such contracts can show that the entire monopoly overcharge was passed on to them; hence they should have the action for damages. It follows that the direct purchaser should not have a damages action for purchases and resales made under such contracts.[7]

6. Figure 2 illustrates the unlikely situation of a single perfect competitor paying a monopoly overcharge for a product, while all other competitors in the same market buy the product at a competitive price.

7. In re Beef Industry Antitrust Litigation, 600 F.2d 1148 (5th Cir.1979), cert. denied, 449 U.S. 905, 101 S.Ct. 280 (1980), on remand, 542 F.Supp. 1122 (N.D.Tex.1982), affirmed, 710 F.2d 216 (5th Cir.1983), cert. denied, 465 U.S. 1052, 104 S.Ct. 1326 (1984); Comment, A Legal and

Most courts have held that this exception to the *Illinois Brick* rule applies only when the pre-existing contract is fixed *both* as to markup and quantity. If an indirect purchaser has a simple "cost-plus" contract, such as a requirements contract, it will respond to the cartel price increase by reducing the amount it purchases. In that case the direct purchaser will lose profits; thus the injury will be shared by the direct purchaser and the indirect purchaser. A few courts found an exception to *Illinois Brick* for the "functional equivalent" of a cost-plus contract—usually a rigid formula that the direct purchaser always uses in computing the resale price.[8] Although such a rigid formula satisfies the "fixed-cost" part of the cost-plus contract exception described above, it fails to satisfy the "fixed-quantity" part. Invariably, demand will be reduced when the price rises, and the direct purchaser will make fewer sales.

In *UtiliCorp*, the Supreme Court rejected this "functional equivalent" exception to *Illinois Brick*, since the utility's customers were not obliged in advance to purchase a particular quantity.[9] The *UtiliCorp* plaintiffs were customers of a price regulated natural gas utility that had allegedly purchased gas at illegal monopoly prices. In a related case, the Seventh Circuit had held that the indirect purchasing consumers would have the damages action because (a) a price regulated utility is entitled under its cost-plus regulatory regime to pass on the full amount of any monopoly overcharge; and (b) at the regulated price, the price elasticity of demand for a good such as natural gas is extremely low—that is, customers would not likely reduce their purchases by significant amounts in response to the monopoly or cartel overcharge.[10]

In rejecting the Seventh Circuit's analysis, the Court concluded that the question of the utility's ability to pass on the overcharge was much more complex than the basic regulatory scheme suggested. State regulators did not uniformly permit utilities to raise their rates in response to gas price increases. Rather, the outcome varied from one situation to the next. Further, there was often considerable lag between the price increase and the rate increase, and the utility had to absorb the difference during the interval. The fact that these injuries did in fact accrue to the utility entailed that it be permitted its own damage action. In that case, however, if "we were to add indirect purchasers to the action, we would have to devise an apportionment formula. This is the very complexity that *Hanover Shoe* and *Illinois Brick* sought to avoid."[11]

There are some reasons for thinking that the "cost-plus" exception to *Illinois Brick* has been crafted too narrowly. The indirect purchaser who buys under a "cost-plus" contract bears the full brunt of the overcharges with respect to the purchases that it makes. The direct purchaser's injury is not an *overcharge* injury at all, but an injury that results from loss of sales. For example, suppose that manufacturer A sells widgets to B at a competitive price of $1.00. B in turn sells them to C under a cost-plus-ten-percent contract that says nothing about the quantity C may purchase. At the competitive price, C purchases 100 units at $1.10. Thereafter, A enters a cartel and increases the price of widgets to $1.30. B adds 10% and charges C $1.43, but C reduces its purchases from 100 units to 80 units.

A couple of things are worth noting about this set of transactions. First, B actually makes more per unit under the cartel than under competition, because the "percent-plus" term in the contract permits its own markup to be based on the monopoly price. Under

Economic Analysis of the Cost–Plus Contract Exception in *Hanover Shoe* and *Illinois Brick*, 47 U.Chi.L.Rev. 743 (1980).

8. See *Beef*, Id., 600 F.2d at 1165. The plaintiffs were unable to prove that a rigid formula was in fact used, however, and eventually their claim was dismissed. See 710 F.2d 216 (5th Cir.1983).

9. Kansas & Missouri v. UtiliCorp United, 497 U.S. 199, 218, 110 S.Ct. 2807, 2818 (1990). The contracts at issue in *UtiliCorp* were not cost-plus, but the markup was set by regulatory agencies that presumably applied the same markup formulas to all purchases.

10. Illinois ex rel. Hartigan v. Panhandle E. Pipe Line Co., 852 F.2d 891, 697–899 (7th Cir.1988) (en banc).

11. *UtiliCorp.*, 497 U.S. at 210, 110 S.Ct. at 2814. Finally, the court noted that many utilities are by law required to pass antitrust damage recoveries on to their customers in the form of rebates. Id. at 212, 110 S.Ct. at 2815.

competition B assessed a 10¢ markup per widget; under collusion B charges a 13¢ markup. Indeed, the percentage price increase is the same for B as it is for the cartel. Of course, if the cartelized product was only one of many inputs into the resold product, then the proportionate increase in profits would be smaller.

Second, if B is injured by the cartel, it is *not* with respect to the 80 units that C actually continues to purchase. B's injury accrues from the fact that C has reduced its purchases from 100 units. That is, B's injury equals the profits it would have made on the unsold 20 units. B has thus not suffered an *overcharge* injury at all, but an injury that results from lost volume. Most damages actions involving exclusionary practices are based on lost market share or sales volume (unless the plaintiff was driven from business altogether). Damages are generally predicated on lost profits. If B were given a damage action based on lost profits in this case, there would be no apportionment problem: B could sue for lost profits and C could sue for the overcharge with respect to the widgets that it actually purchased.[12] Indeed, on the above facts B would have a difficult time justifying *overcharge* damages at all—every cent of monopoly overcharge that it actually paid was collected from C, plus an additional 3¢.

Any damage *allocation* problem in the above illustration is the difficulty of distinguishing between the amount of injury that accrues to B when C reduces its demand in response to the cartel and the amount that accrues to C from the same reduction. Because neither B nor C has an overcharge action with respect to unpurchased units, however, this "allocation" problem is a fake. The situation is more analogous to the monopolist who (1) excludes a competitor and (2) thereafter charges a monopoly price. The competitor has a cause of action based on its lost profits and investment; the consumers have an action for the monopoly overcharge. Neither damage measure duplicates the other, and there is nothing to be allocated.

16.6b2. *Injunction Suits*

A second important exception to *Illinois Brick* is indirect purchaser actions seeking only an injunction. The measurement difficulties that prompted the indirect purchaser rule apply only to calculation of the *amount* of a particular purchaser's damages. The fact of damages can be inferred. Likewise, equity suits create no risk of duplicative recovery: it costs a defendant no more to comply with 10 identical injunctions than to comply with one. Lower courts generally have held that an indirect purchaser may seek an injunction against a cartel.[13]

16.6b3. *Cases Involving Vertical Agreements or Control*

A third exception to *Illinois Brick*, which is really no exception at all, involves a middleman who is really part of the antitrust conspiracy. Suppose a cartel member sells to A, who resells to B, but A is also part of the price fixing conspiracy. B is not really an indirect purchaser, but a direct one. He should have a damages action.[14] One result of this rule is that indirect purchasers are encouraged to name their direct sellers as co-defendants in order to avoid dismissal at an early stage of the litigation. In fact, some courts have held that plaintiffs seeking to establish that direct purchasers were members of the conspiracy must name them as parties.[15] This rule seems sensible, at least where naming them is practicable. If they are not named they will not be bound by any legal conclusion that they are

12. For further elaboration, see H. Hovenkamp, The Indirect–Purchaser Rule and Cost–Plus Sales, 103 Harv. L. Rev. 1717, 1721–23 (1990).

13. Campos v. Ticketmaster, 140 F.3d 1166 (8th Cir. 1998), cert. denied, ___ U.S. ___, 119 S.Ct. 865 (1999) (indirect purchasers damage claim rejected, but could continue suit for injunction); Mid–West Paper Products Co. v. Continental Group, Inc., 596 F.2d 573, 589–94 (3d Cir. 1979).

14. See Arizona v. Shamrock Foods Co., 729 F.2d 1208 (9th Cir.1984), cert. denied, 469 U.S. 1197, 105 S.Ct. 980 (1985) (parens patriae suit in behalf of dairy consumers alleging conspiracy involving both grocery stores and dairy producers).

15. See *Campos*, note 13, 140 F.3d at 1171 n. 4.

parties, will not have an opportunity to contest the allegation, and could even become plaintiffs themselves in a subsequent suit against the same defendants.

Closely related to the vertical co-conspirator exception is an exception for intermediaries whose behavior or prices are controlled by the cartel. For example, if cartel members sell through commission-earning brokers, the damage action would still belong to consumers. In this case the brokers are not purchasers at all, but mere agents of the cartel members.[16] In this same general camp belong direct purchasers who resell under a resale price maintenance scheme. Suppose that manufacturer A imposes RPM on unwilling dealer B, who then charges the maintained price to the consumer, C. B cannot be treated as a co-conspirator. Nevertheless, C should have the damage action. The ordinary remedy for dealers forced to engage in RPM is damages based on lost profits, not overcharge damages. Second, the fact that A imposed RPM on dealer B does not entail that B has suffered any *overcharge* injury at all; that is, although A imposed RPM on B, it did not necessarily charge B unlawfully high prices. In order to do the latter it would have to be successfully convicted of monopolization or horizontal collusion as well. So the ordinary remedy in such cases is a lost profits damages action for dealer B and an overcharge damages action for consumers.[17]

The same result should follow when the manufacturer is engaged in collusion and using RPM as a facilitator.[18] In that case the dealer/direct purchaser probably has an action for the cartel overcharge, but the consumer has a damage action for the illegal RPM itself. That is, with respect to the RPM agreement it is a direct purchaser from a party.

As the previous illustrations suggest, the *Illinois Brick* rule applies in only limited ways to vertical restraints cases. In the case of RPM, the firm imposing the RPM is not necessarily charging the dealer a higher price at all; so nothing in *Illinois Brick* would bar a consumers' damage action challenging the RPM agreement. *Illinois Brick* would presumably apply, however, if the distribution chain included a fourth level. Suppose A imposed RPM on B who resold to C at the maintained price. C then resold to D at a higher price reflecting the overcharge. The principles of *Illinois Brick* suggest that C may have an overcharge action against A, but that D's damages action should be barred. It would present the same apportionment problems that *Illinois Brick* contemplates. By contrast, vertical nonprice restraints, exclusive dealing or other vertical practices not involving the explicit setting of price do not ordinarily present *Illinois Brick* problems. Damages are almost always based on lost profits.[19]

16.6c. Monopsony; Buyers' Cartels

The indirect purchaser rule applies with equal force to sellers who deal indirectly with a monopsonist or buyer's cartel.[20] However, not all antitrust violations involving suppressed buying prices have short-run monopsony profits as their goal. They may be attempts to drive suppliers out of business. In Amarel v. Connel,[21] the court held that *Illinois Brick* did not bar a lawsuit by rice producers directed at rice buyers to whom the producers sold through intermediaries. The allegation in the complaint was not collusion but rather an attempt by the defendant to drive the plaintiffs out of business by predatory buying. This offense supposedly occurs when a firm that dominates a buying market but who wishes to

16. See Florida Power Corp. v. Granlund, 78 F.R.D. 441 (M.D.Fla.1978).

17. Accord Link v. Mercedes–Benz of N. Am., 788 F.2d 918 (3d Cir.1986). However, the court also held that the dealers and the consumers must be joined together in a single suit. Id. at 932.

18. On the use of RPM to facilitate manufacturer collusion, see § 11.2b2.

19. But see Laurel Sand & Gravel v. CSX Transp., 924 F.2d 539 (4th Cir.1991), cert. denied, 502 U.S. 814, 112 S.Ct. 64 (1992), which incorrectly applied *Illinois Brick* so as to deny standing to an indirect purchaser claiming a vertical refusal to deal. The denial of standing may have been appropriate, but not on *Illinois Brick* grounds.

20. For example, Zinser v. Continental Grain Co., 660 F.2d 754 (10th Cir.1981), cert. denied, 455 U.S. 941, 102 S.Ct. 1434 (1982). On monopsony, see § 1.2b; and 12 Antitrust Law ¶ ¶ 2011–2012 (1999).

21. 1986–2 Trade Cas. (CCH) ¶ 67233, 1986 WL 10613 (N.D.Cal.1986), at p. 61,177.

dominate a vertically related market as well uses low buying prices to drive the upstream firms out of the market. Damages for such exclusionary practices are ordinarily based on lost profits, so *Illinois Brick* should not bar recovery. At the same time, however, the substantive claim looks dubious. As a general matter it would be more profitable for a monopsonist to impose inframarginal returns on suppliers than to drive them out of the market.[22]

16.6d. Policy Implications of the Indirect Purchaser Rule; State Indirect Purchaser Statutes

Is the indirect purchaser rule a good one? Commentators have argued both sides with vehemence.[23] Several states responded to *Illinois Brick* by amending their own antitrust statutes to allow damages actions by indirect purchasers.[24]

Attitudes toward the indirect purchaser rule track ideology closely. Those who believe that antitrust enforcement should be concerned exclusively with efficiency generally support *Illinois Brick*. Those who believe that antitrust should be concerned with full compensation to victims generally disapprove. Both positions are ideologically consistent. Permitting indirect purchaser actions would increase the costs of litigation and may result in overdeterrence.[25] However, the *Illinois Brick* rule clearly deprives injured parties of their claim to damages.

The most serious criticism of the indirect purchaser rule is that it appears inconsistent with § 4's mandate that damages should be designed to compensate plaintiffs. In the great majority of situations the indirect purchaser rule gives the entire damage action to the person who suffered the smaller injury—or, in some cases, no injury at all.

The main reason this is true is that the elasticity of substitution for direct purchasers is often much higher than it is for indirect purchasers. For example, retailers' shelf space is a highly elastic commodity—it will hold ketchup or breakfast cereal, depending on what earns more profits at the moment. The customer, by contrast, must generally have one or the other. To illustrate, suppose the manufacturers of washing machines collude, increasing their price by 30%. Most washing machine consumers continue to purchase, but overall demand goes down by 20%. How does the appliance dealer respond to this decline in demand for washing machines? Probably by assigning relatively less floor space and other resources to washing machines and relatively more to refrigerators, microwaves, or dishwashers. To be sure, the substitution is inefficient in the sense that the dealer's product mix is not the same as it would be under competition. But the difference is not likely to be all that large, particularly if numerous products compete for a relatively small amount of dealer shelf space.

To state this another way, with respect to end use consumers the difference in utility between the first choice (washing machines) and the second choice (washboards) when both are competitively priced is likely to be quite large; if it is not large, then collusion will

22. In addition, the difference between "undercharge" damages in a monopsony case and lost profit damages may be more rhetorical than real. The plaintiff's revenue varies with the undercharge, and profits equal revenue less costs; the two measures of damages might be identical. However, one important difference between undercharge damages and lost profit damages is that the latter would also include loss of output. That is, the plaintiff seeking undercharge damages would an amount (before trebling) equal to the undercharge on each unit actually sold. The plaintiff winning lost profits would presumably obtain an additional amount reflecting the smaller number of sales made at the monopsony price.

23. See the articles cited in notes 3, 4 and 12 above.

24. See 14 Antitrust Law ¶ 2412d (1999).

25. However, in certain cases recognition of indirect purchaser actions actually may result in underdeterrence. Suppose that the minimum monetary injury a person must suffer before he would sue is $100. If a direct purchaser were able to have the entire damages action, he could claim $1000 in damages. However, he sold to two distributors who sold to 12 stores, each of whom sold to 50 customers. No one's net injury exceeds $50. Unless a consumer class action is practicable, the defendant might never be sued at all.

See also W. Page, The Limits of State Indirect Purchaser Suits: Class Certification in the Shadow of *Illinois Brick*, 67 Antitrust L.J. 1 (1999) (arguing that state indirect purchaser provisions present insurmountable problems of class certification and counsel against such provisions).

probably not be successful, for too many customers will substitute away. With respect to intermediaries, however, the difference between the cartelized product and some substitute may be much smaller, depending on the degree of specialization in the intermediaries' production or distribution plant.[26]

As noted previously, several states have amended their antitrust statutes to permit indirect purchaser damage actions. In California v. ARC America Corp.,[27] the Supreme Court held that these statutes were not preempted by federal antitrust law.

Importantly, the existence of a state statute in no way limits or controls damage measurement under federal law. That is, the state statute cannot mandate that the damages be "allocated," for that would reduce the direct purchaser's federal right. Thus a direct purchaser proceeding under federal law will be entitled to treble the entire monopoly overcharge, while the indirect purchaser proceeding under state law will be entitled to treble the overcharge that was passed on to it. At the margin, this regime could produce six-fold rather than treble damages. Further, the damages could be awarded in a single federal proceeding. For example, direct purchasers could sue for damages under federal law while indirect purchasers sued for an injunction under federal law (one of the *Illinois Brick* exceptions) and attached a pendant state law claim for damages.[28]

16.6e. The Umbrella Plaintiff

Remotely related to the indirect purchaser is the buyer injured by "umbrella pricing" made possible by someone else's antitrust violation. Suppose that X, Y & Z fix the price of widgets at $1.50. The competitive price is $1.00. X, Y & Z control 85% of the market and Q, who is not part of the conspiracy, sells the remaining 15%.

The cartel will create a price "umbrella" under which Q will be able to raise her price to some level just under $1.50 and sell all she can produce.[29] Suppose that P buys widgets from Q at $1.45. Clearly P has been injured by the cartel. P has no cause of action against Q, for Q has done nothing illegal. Instead P sues X, Y & Z, claiming that their cartel caused P's overcharge injuries.

In Mid–West Paper Products Co. v. Continental Group, Inc.[30] the Third Circuit rejected such a theory as speculative. It then analogized the umbrella claim to the indirect purchaser rule and concluded that computation of damages would present problems analogous to those in computing pass-on in indirect purchaser actions. In the *Beef Industry*[31] antitrust litigation, however, the Fifth Circuit permitted "inverted umbrella" sellers to recover from a buyer's cartel which depressed the wholesale price of beef.

Mid–West Paper's comparison of umbrella actions with indirect purchaser actions was not particularly apt. To be sure, both actions may yield a form of "duplicative" recovery, but the two forms are quite different from each other. Indirect purchaser damages actions may yield duplicative recoveries when a defendant is forced to pay overcharge damages twice—once to the direct purchaser for the full overcharge and a second time to the indirect

26. For example, an intermediary with a dedicated plant that can make only a particular chemical may not have much room to substitute; if the price of an input goes to monopoly levels, it will merely bear an output loss. By contrast, the retail grocer selling 10,000 items with another 5000 competing to be placed on the shelves, will barely notice the effects of collusion in a particular item. She will simply raise price, probably according to a generalized formula; when sales drop she will reduce the shelf space allocated to the cartelized item and give the space to something else.

27. 490 U.S. 93, 109 S.Ct. 1661 (1989). For further discussion of the decision, see § 20.8.

28. See, e.g., City of St. Paul v. FMC Corp., 1991–1 Trade Cas. ¶ 69305, 1990 WL 265171 (D.Minn.1990).

29. See § 4.1. Eventually the fringe may grow so large that its presence will undermine the cartel. Further, the existence of the fringe performs one valuable social function even while the cartel exists. The existence of any fringe, no matter how inefficient, will reduce the cartel's profit-maximizing price. See Note, Standing At the Fringe: Antitrust Damages and the Fringe Producer, 35 Stan. L.Rev. 763, 773 (1983).

30. 596 F.2d 573, 583–87 (3d Cir.1979). Accord California v. Standard Oil Co., 691 F.2d 1335 (9th Cir.1982), cert. denied, 464 U.S. 1068, 104 S.Ct. 972 (1984).

31. See note 7.

purchaser for the passed-on overcharge. By contrast, the umbrella action yields a duplicative recovery because the umbrella plaintiff is seeking to recover monies that never accrued to the defendants, but rather to a non-conspiring competitor.

Further, computation of overcharge injuries from umbrella pricing need be no more difficult than computation of overcharge injuries in direct purchaser actions. Assuming that X, Y, Z and Q all operate in the same market and produce fungible products, they would have the same competitive price. A direct purchaser from X, Y or Z would have to show the difference between the competitive price and the price she actually paid. A purchaser from noncartel member Q would have to show precisely the same thing. The fact that Q may have charged a lower price than the cartel will not complicate computation: P will merely recover the difference between the competitive price (which is the same for Q as it is for X, Y, and Z) and the price Q actually charged.

Whether or not denial of umbrella actions is appropriate, the solution to this problem does not rest on the premise that the damages are unusually difficult to compute, or that the plaintiff will recover profits that never accrued to the defendants. Rather, the rationale is that if direct purchaser actions for treble damages provide sufficient deterrence, recognition of umbrella actions would result in overdeterrence.[32]

Damages measurement can become unacceptably speculative for umbrella purchasers in a product differentiated market—particularly if there is a substantial difference between Q's product and that sold by the cartel. Suppose a cartel of coffee bean producers increases the price of coffee. Q sells tea, the price of which rises as the coffee price rises. However, coffee and tea are only imperfect substitutes. One is tempted to say that, to the degree imperfections exist the price of tea will rise less than the price of coffee rises; so the tea purchaser should have a damage action against the cartel for the overcharge he actually paid. The problem with this rule is that it is difficult to draw the line. Milk, orange juice and soda pop may also experience price rises in response to the coffee price increase, but the link will be difficult to establish. Denial of standing to those who purchased imperfect substitutes seems to be the appropriate solution. Once again, however, the rationale is the same as that applied in standing cases generally—that causation and damages are almost impossible to prove. The difficulty of computing pass-on is irrelevant.[33]

32. See W. Landes, Optimal Sanctions for Antitrust Violations, 50 U.Chi.L.Rev. 652, 668 n. 30 (1983). For an argument that actions by umbrella purchasers would not result in overdeterrence and should be permitted, see R.D. Blair & V.G. Maurer, Umbrella Pricing and Antitrust Standing: An Economic Analysis, 1982 Utah L.Rev. 763.

33. For a more general and technical discussion, see R. Blair and R. Romano, Distinguishing Participants from Nonparticipants in a Price–Fixing Conspiracy: Liability and Damages, 28 Am. Bus. L.J. 33 (1990).

§ 16.7 The Antitrust Statute of Limitation[1]

Antitrust damage actions are governed by a four year statute of limitation.[2] The period begins to run when the cause of action "accrues," which is generally when the plaintiff has suffered an injury and damages are sufficiently ascertainable to warrant a suit. The latter requirement becomes important when damages appear only long after a violation occurs. For example, certain exclusionary practices such as fraudulent patent enforcement or perhaps raising rivals' costs[3] may have effects that will not become apparent until several years later. Courts commonly say that if the injury is known but the damages are still speculative, the statute of limitation will not run.[4] But the mere fact that damages are

§ 16.7

1. For a fuller discussion, see 2 Antitrust Law ¶ 338 (rev. ed. 1995).

2. 15 U.S.C.A. § 15b. Injunction suits are not governed by the statute, but laches may apply, with courts typically applying a judge-made four year limitation. E.g., IT & T v. GTE, 518 F.2d 913, 926–929 (9th Cir.1975).

3. See §§ 7.10, 7.11.

4. See Zenith Radio Corp. v. Hazeltine Research, Inc., 401 U.S. 321, 339, 91 S.Ct. 795, 1448 (1971) ("refusal to award future profits as too speculative is equivalent to holding that no cause of action has yet accrued for any but those damages already suffered. In these instances, the

uncertain is insufficient to prevent the statute from running.[5] In applying this rather nebulous distinction the Ninth Circuit contrasted "uncertain damages, which prevent recovery" from "uncertain extent of damage, which does not prevent recovery." It explained that

> The former denotes failure to establish an injury, while the latter denotes imprecision with regard to the scope of extent of the injury. The question of whether there is a right to recovery is not to be confused with the difficulty in ascertaining the scope or extent of the injury.[6]

The rationale for the distinction is clear enough. Once the damages are sufficiently known to warrant a lawsuit, it is socially costly to permit them to keep accruing. The plaintiff must then have an incentive to bring its lawsuit promptly. As a result, the rule is best stated as follows: if the plaintiff has sufficient knowledge of its damages to provide proof of damages in an antitrust action, the statute will run.[7] But if damages are so uncertain that any proof of damages at trial would likely fail, then the statute will not run.

Several courts have also held that if the defendant's antitrust violation consists of a series of "overt acts," each act starts the statute anew. For example, if a group of conspirators meets frequently to adjust the cartel price or output, each new meeting will restart the statute.[8] Other courts have held that the statute does not run on conspiracy claims until the last payment for goods delivered under the conspiracy has been made.[9] However, if the allegation is of refusal to deal, the statute begins to run once the refusal becomes final; it cannot be restarted by the plaintiff's later, renewed request.[10] By contrast, if the refusal is open-ended or the circumstances suggest that a later request would be appropriate, then the later request will start the statute anew.[11]

These rules are supported by an underlying logic. In a cartel or concerted refusal case, each new act is a distinct violation. For example, suppose a cartel forms in 1990 and meets every year through 1999 to adjust price and output. The 1999 meeting is independently illegal, whether or not the cartel existed at all in the earlier years. As a result, each meeting is a new violation restarting the statute of limitation, but plaintiffs will be limited to recovering damages for the four years prior to their filing.[12]

By contrast, a dealer termination, merger, or exclusionary practice is a single unlawful

cause of action for future damages, if they ever occur, will accrue only on the date they are suffered. * * * ").

5. Brunswick Corp. v. Riegel Textile Corp., 752 F.2d 261, 271 (7th Cir.1984), cert. denied, 472 U.S. 1018, 105 S.Ct. 3480 (1985), (Sometimes "the plaintiff may be able to show that his future losses were so speculative at the time of exclusion that a judge or jury would not have been allowed to award damages * * *, in which event the plaintiff may and indeed must wait to sue. * * * But unless special circumstances preclude, as excessively speculative, an award of damages based on predicted as distinct from realized losses * * * the statute of limitations is not tolled simply in order to wait and see. * * *").

6. Pace Indus. v. Three Phoenix Co., 813 F.2d 234, 240 (9th Cir.1987).

7. On the requirements for proof of damages, see § 17.4.

8. See Pennsylvania Dental Assn. v. Medical Serv. Assn. of Pa., 815 F.2d 270 (3d Cir.), cert. denied, 484 U.S. 851, 108 S.Ct. 153 (1987), holding that each meeting furthering the participation in a boycott restarted the statute.

9. See United States v. A–A–A Elec. Co., 788 F.2d 242, 245 (4th Cir.1986) (applying the five year statute of limitation for criminal actions). The five year criminal statute of limitation is found in 18 U.S.C.A. § 3282.

10. Kaw Valley Elec. Co–op. v. Kansas Elec. Power, 872 F.2d 931, 934 (10th Cir.1989) ("if the initial refusal is final the statute of limitations begins to run and no new cause of action is created when the victim makes subsequent futile efforts to deal. * * * "); David Orgell v. Geary's Stores, 640 F.2d 936, 938 (9th Cir.), cert. denied, 454 U.S. 816, 102 S.Ct. 92 (1981) (same).

11. Midwestern Waffles v. Waffle House, 734 F.2d 705, 715 (11th Cir.1984); LaSalvia v. United Dairymen of Ariz., 804 F.2d 1113 (9th Cir.1986), cert. denied, 482 U.S. 928, 107 S.Ct. 3212 (1987).

12. See Klehr v. A.O. Smith Corp., 521 U.S. 179, 117 S.Ct. 1984, 1991 (1997) (a case brought under the federal RICO statute, which employs the antitrust law statute of limitation):

> Antitrust law provides that, in the case of a "continuing violation," say a price fixing conspiracy that brings about a series of unlawfully high priced sales over a period of years, "each overt act that is part of the violation and that injures the plaintiff," e.g., each sale to the plaintiff, "starts the statutory period running again, regardless of the plaintiff's knowledge of the alleged illegality at much earlier times." ... But the commission of a separate new overt act generally does not permit the plaintiff to recover for the injury caused by old overt acts outside the limitations period.

act with a finite end, although its pricing consequences may last far into the future. The merger provides the clearest example. Suppose that two firms merged in 1990 and immediately increased price from $1.00 to $2.00. Further, this price increase is durable, and in 1997 the post-merger firm is still charging it. Significantly, however, after the merger occurred the post-merger firm is a single entity and is entitled to charge any price it pleases, so far as the antitrust laws are concerned. That is to say, the 1997 price can be said to be unlawful, not as an independent act, but only because the 1990 merger was unlawful. In that case, assuming that the merger was adequately known to consumers, the statute of limitation began to run in 1990 and the right to challenge the merger was lost four years later. A contrary rule would make post-merger firms subject to infinite periods of challenge, thus undermining our general policy of favoring mergers.[13] In any event, § 7 of the Clayton Act makes it unlawful to "acquire"—it does not make each subsequent price charged by the post-merger firm independently unlawful.[14]

The antitrust statute of limitation also excepts fraudulent concealment, which occurs when the defendant conceals the violation from the plaintiff in spite of the plaintiff's due diligence in looking for it. Thus, for example, the statute of limitation would generally not run on a price-fixing conspiracy until sufficient objective evidence became available to give injured parties a basis for knowing of the conspiracy's existence.[15] Some courts have reached this conclusion by characterizing certain antitrust violations, such as secret price-fixing, as inherently "self-concealing."[16] Others reject that characterization and require some kind of "affirmative act" directed toward concealment of the underlying violation.[17] In any event, fraudulent concealment will not serve to toll the statute if the plaintiff had actual knowledge of the violation. And in its *Klehr* decision, which applied the antitrust statute of limitation to a RICO claim, the Supreme Court went one step further. It held that the doctrine of fraudulent concealment does not apply in any event if the plaintiff could have discovered the violation by exercising due diligence.[18]

The statute of limitation governing private actions can also be tolled by the filing of a government action, which stops the running of the civil statute during its pendency and for one year thereafter.[19] This tolling provision applies only to proceedings "instituted by the United States,"[20] and only with respect to a private suit "based in whole or in part on any matter complained of" in the government suit.

13. See Midwestern Machinery v. Northwest Airlines, 167 F.3d 439, 442 n. 3 (8th Cir.1999) (dicta; statute of limitation would apply to consumer's post-acquisition merger challenge, lest a merger be opened up to "continual challenge under section 7"). Accord Grand Rapids Plastics, Inc. v. Lakian, ___ F.3d ___, 1999 WL 604199 (6th Cir.1999) (statute of limitation ran from date discriminatory contracts were formed, notwithstanding Subsequent Payments); Eichman v. Fotomat Corp., 880 F.2d 149, 160 (9th Cir.1989) (continuing payments under lease alleged to be part of unlawful tying arrangement at time of lease's creation did not restart statute).

14. See *IT & T* case, note 2; *Midwestern Machinery*, note 13.

15. Pinney Dock & Transp. Co. v. Penn Central Corp., 838 F.2d 1445, 1470–1480 (6th Cir.), cert. denied, 488 U.S. 880, 109 S.Ct. 196 (1988). See also E.W. French & Sons v. General Portland, 885 F.2d 1392 (9th Cir.1989) (secret bids communicated in plain envelopes were effectively concealed from outsiders to the conspiracy); accord Ohio ex rel. Montgomery v. Louis Trauth Dairy, 1996–1 Trade Cas. ¶ 71396, 1996 WL 343440 (S.D. Ohio 1996) (cartel members' practice of submitting "complementary" bids, so that buyer would think that there were numerous bidders when in fact the bidders had preselected the winner, was sufficient act of fraudulent concealment). See generally Note, A reevaluation of Fraudulent Concealment and Section 4B of the Clayton Act, 68 Tex. L.Rev. 649 (1990). See 3 Antitrust Law ¶ 338d (rev. ed. 1995).

16. See State of New York v. Hendrickson Bros., 840 F.2d 1065, 1084 (2d Cir.), cert. denied, 488 U.S. 848, 109 S.Ct. 128 (1988). For the most detailed, but fairly inconclusive discussion, see Colorado v. Western Paving Constr. Co., 630 F.Supp. 206 (D.Colo.1986), affirmed, 841 F.2d 1025 (10th Cir.), cert. denied, 488 U.S. 870, 109 S.Ct. 179 (1988).

17. Supermarket of Marlinton v. Meadow Gold Dairies, 71 F.3d 119, 122–124 (4th Cir.1995), appeal after remand, 161 F.3d 3 (4th Cir.1998).

18. *Klehr*, note 12, 117 S.Ct. at 1993.

19. 15 U.S.C.A. § 16(i).

20. See Minnesota Mining & Mfg. v. New Jersey Wood Finishing Co., 381 U.S. 311, 321–322, 85 S.Ct. 1473, 1478–1479 (1965) (tolling provision applies to FTC action brought under § 7 of the Clayton Act). Lower courts have extended the tolling provision to proceedings brought under § 5 of the FTC Act as well. Donahue v. Pendleton Woolen Mills, 633 F.Supp. 1423, 1441 (S.D.N.Y.1986).

The circuit courts are divided on whether a private antitrust suit is tolled by the pendency of federal administrative proceedings. In *Mount Hood*, the Ninth Circuit held that the statute was tolled as to the plaintiff's antitrust claim while the plaintiff's own proceeding before the Interstate Commerce Commission was pending.[21] The ICC had primary jurisdiction over the case,[22] and the court reasoned that, had the plaintiff gone into court first, "the court would have been compelled to dismiss or stay the suit" pending disposition by the ICC. The plaintiff should therefore not be penalized for taking the same course of action that the government would later have forced him to take. In disagreeing, the Seventh Circuit held that the plaintiff should have *filed* his antitrust suit first, because the statute would then be satisfied even if the court recognized primary jurisdiction in the federal agency.[23]

§ 16.8 Disposition of Issues; Summary Judgment; Expert Testimony; Tagalong Suits

16.8a. Jury Trial

The Seventh Amendment creates a right to a jury trial in nearly all federal court damages actions. Jury trials have been widely criticized as unnecessarily cumbersome and inconsistent in their results. These criticisms seem particularly relevant in antitrust litigation, which is often complex.[1] In the *Japanese Electronic Products* case, the Third Circuit responded to these concerns by creating what amounted to a "complexity exception" to the Seventh Amendment.[2] The court found that the Seventh Amendment right to a jury had to be balanced against the Fifth Amendment Due Process clause's right to a fair trial, and that the latter amendment's concerns were more "fundamental" than the Seventh Amendment right.[3]

The Fifth Circuit took a somewhat different approach in *Cotten*,[4] holding that, even if there were a complexity exception to the Seventh Amendment, it would not be applied to a case simply because the litigants' strategies had made the case extremely complex by the joinder of numerous causes of action covering many issues. The opinion suggests that often the first culprit in federal litigation complexity is the Federal Rules of Civil Procedure, which encourage all parties and issues to be combined into a single proceeding. The result certainly creates some litigation efficiency, but often at the expense of simplicity. One effect may be irrational outcomes.

16.8b. Summary Judgment

Federal Rule of Civil Procedure 56(c) provides that any party may move for a partial or total summary judgment, which shall be granted

> if the pleadings, depositions, answers to interrogatories, and admissions on file, together with the affidavits, if any, show that there is no genuine issue as to any material fact and that the moving party is entitled to a judgment as a matter of law.[5]

The federal courts' basic attitude toward summary judgment in antitrust suits has changed considerably over the last several decades. In Poller v. CBS[6] the Supreme Court concluded that "summary judgment proce-

21. Mount Hood Stages v. Greyhound Corp., 616 F.2d 394, 399–400 (9th Cir.), cert. denied, 449 U.S. 831, 101 S.Ct. 99 (1980).

22. On primary jurisdiction, see § 19.4.

23. *Brunswick*, note 5 at 269.

§ 16.8

1. See R. Posner, The Federal Courts: Crisis and Reform 130 (1985).

2. In re Japanese Elec. Prods. Antitrust Litigation, 631 F.2d 1069 (3d Cir.1980).

3. Id. at 1085: "[W]hen the jury is unable to determine the normal application of the law to the facts of a case and reaches a verdict on the basis of nothing more than its own determination of community wisdom and values, its operation is indistinguishable from arbitrary and unprincipled decisionmaking." The Ninth Circuit declined to find any exception to the Seventh Amendment right in United States Financial Securities Litigation, 609 F.2d 411 (9th Cir.1979), cert. denied sub nom. Gant v. Union Bank, 446 U.S. 929, 100 S.Ct. 1866 (1980).

4. Cotten v. Witco Chem. Corp., 651 F.2d 274 (5th Cir.1981), cert. denied, 455 U.S. 909, 102 S.Ct. 1256 (1982).

5. For elaboration on the workings of Rule 56, see 10A/10B C. Wright, A. Miller & M. Kane, Federal Practice and Procedure §§ 2711—2741 (Civil, 3d., 1998 & West Supp.).

6. 368 U.S. 464, 473, 82 S.Ct. 486, 491 (1962).

dures should be used sparingly in complex antitrust litigation where motive and intent play leading roles, the proof is largely in the hands of the alleged conspirators, and hostile witnesses thicken the plot." That language was much too quickly read by numerous lower courts to indicate that summary judgment should be used sparingly in *all* antitrust cases, not merely in those where intent is an important element, proof is in the hands of the defendants, and there are conflicts in witness testimony.[7] But the statement itself is relatively clear. *Poller*'s hostility to summary judgment correctly applied only in those cases where motive or intent were "leading" considerations in the determination of legality, or where necessary evidence had to be taken by force through testimony from hostile witnesses, such as the defendant's employees.

Nonetheless, the Supreme Court's 1986 *Matsushita* decision ended federal judicial hostility toward summary judgment in antitrust cases, and has inclined many lower courts to prefer summary disposition of antitrust litigation.[8] The plaintiffs, American manufacturers of televisions, claimed that the defendants, Japanese firms, had conspired to fix television prices in Japan and the United States. In order to eliminate rivals they allegedly also conspired to charge predatorily low prices in the United States. Extensive discovery produced little evidence of the latter agreement,[9] the defendants' share of the world market was not dominant, and the alleged predation scheme had taken some twenty years. All these facts tended to show that predatory pricing was implausible in this market.[10]

The Court concluded that "When the moving party has carried its burden under Rule 56(c), its opponent must do more than simply show that there is some metaphysical doubt as to the material facts." Instead, "[w]here the record taken as a whole could not lead a rational trier of fact to find for the non-moving party, there is no genuine issue for trial. * * *"

In particular,

> [I]f the factual context renders respondents' claim implausible—if the claim is one that simply makes no economic sense—respondents must come forward with more persuasive evidence to support their claim than would otherwise be necessary. * * *[11]
>
> Respondents correctly note that "[o]n summary judgment the inferences to be drawn from the underlying facts * * * must be viewed in the light most favorable to the party opposing the motion." * * * But antitrust law limits the range of permissible inferences from ambiguous evidence in a § 1 case. Thus, in Monsanto Co. v. Spray–Rite Service Corp., 465 U.S. 752, 104 S.Ct. 1464 (1984), we held that conduct as consistent with permissible competition

7. For example, Industrial Bldg. Materials, Inc. v. Interchemical Corp., 437 F.2d 1336, 1340 (9th Cir.1970); American Mfrs. Mut. Ins. Co. v. American Broadcasting–Paramount Theatres, 388 F.2d 272, 279–280 (2d Cir.1967), cert. denied, 404 U.S. 1063, 92 S.Ct. 737 (1972). See also S. Calkins, "Equilibrating Tendencies in the Antitrust System, with Special Attention to Summary Judgment and to Motions to Dismiss," 185, 205 in Private Antitrust Litigation: New Evidence, New Learning (L. White, ed. 1988).

8. Matsushita Elec. Indus. Co. v. Zenith Radio Corp., 475 U.S. 574, 106 S.Ct. 1348 (1986). See also Celotex Corp. v. Catrett, 477 U.S. 317, 322, 106 S.Ct. 2548, 2552 (1986), a nonantitrust case which includes the Court's most succinct statement on Rule 56(c)'s standard:

> the plain language of Rule 56(c) * * * mandates the entry of summary judgment, after adequate time for discovery and upon motion, against a party who fails to make a showing sufficient to establish the existence of an element essential to that party's case, and on which that party will bear the burden of proof at trial.

See also two important pieces by a federal judge who has pioneered the use of summary judgment in antitrust cases: W.W. Schwarzer, Summary Judgment and Case Management, 56 Antitrust L.J. 213 (1987); W.W. Schwarzer, Summary Judgment Under the Federal Rules: Defining Genuine Issues of Material Fact, 99 F.R.D. 465 (1984).

9. Proof of the conspiracies to fix high prices, standing alone, would not permit the plaintiffs to win, for they would generally be benefitted by higher prices. Further, the Court held that the jurisdiction of the American antitrust laws would not extend to the Japanese defendants' agreement to raise prices in Japan. 475 U.S. at 582–583, 106 S.Ct. at 1353–1354.

10. Predatory pricing generally requires a dominant market position. See § 8.4a. Likewise, the longer predation takes, the less likely that it will be profitable. See § 8.7.

11. The Court noted that "there is a consensus among commentators that predatory pricing schemes are rarely tried, and even more rarely successful." 475 U.S. at 589, 106 S.Ct. at 1357.

as with illegal conspiracy does not, standing alone, support an inference of antitrust conspiracy, * * * To survive a motion for summary judgment or for a directed verdict, a plaintiff seeking damages for a violation of § 1 must present evidence "that tends to exclude the possibility" that the alleged conspirators acted independently. Respondents in this case, in other words, "must show that the inference of conspiracy is reasonable in light of the competing inferences of independent action or collusive action that could not have harmed respondents. * * * "[12]

In the wake of *Matsushita*, the percentage of antitrust cases resolved by summary judgment (most often on the defendant's motion) increased dramatically.[13]

Matsushita plus the general language of Rule 56(c) have the following implications for antitrust cases:

(1) If there are no disputed fact questions, then a judgment on the basis of legal questions alone is appropriate.

(2) If the party opposing summary judgment (most often, but not always, the plaintiff) argues that there is at least one disputed fact question, then resolution of those questions in the opponent's favor must be sufficient to create antitrust liability on any claim that is to survive a motion for summary judgment. Other claims should be resolved by summary judgment.

(3) Any disputed fact question, in addition to meeting the requirement of (2) must also be sufficiently in dispute that reasonable minds could find it either way. Mere "metaphysical doubt" on one side of the issue is insufficient to withstand a motion for summary judgment.

One confusing aspect of *Matsushita* is its handling of the particular question made subject to the motion for summary judgment in that case: the existence of a qualifying antitrust "conspiracy." The opinion's most important conclusion about conspiracy claims is not limited to summary judgment at all. This is the conclusion that evidence of conduct that is equally consistent with unilateral and collusive behavior does not create an inference of conspiracy. Rather, the evidence must " 'tend[ ] to exclude the possibility' that the alleged conspirators acted independently."[14]

Importantly, *Matsushita* does not assess a general summary judgment requirement that a disputed fact exists only if the opponent's version tends to "exclude the possibility" that the proponent's version is correct. A factual dispute exists if the plaintiff's and the defendant's version of the facts are inconsistent and a reasonable person could find either way. The *Matsushita* statement about conspiracy must be read as a limitation on the fact finder's province with respect to *conspiracy* claims, and not as a special set of instructions for summary judgment.

For example, suppose that in response to lower wholesale prices for oil, several gasoline dealers failed to lower retail prices. This evidence is consistent with the proposition that the dealers are conspiring with each other, but it may also be consistent with unilateral behavior or behavior that, while oligopolistic, does not meet the Sherman Act's "agreement" requirement.[15] In that case, *Matsushita* instructs that the fact finder will not be permitted to infer a conspiracy. When the claim is conspiracy, the evidence must tend to show that the defendants' behavior is rational (profit-maximizing) only on the theory that they are conspiring.

This restriction on *Matsushita*'s meaning for summary judgment is essential if the decision is not to be used to evade the constitu-

12. *Matsushita*, 475 U.S. at 585–588, 106 S.Ct. at 1355–1356. See Ezzo's Invs. v. Royal Beauty Supply, 94 F.3d 1032, 1036 (6th Cir.1996) (citing this standard and finding a fact issue precluding summary judgment in a case alleging both a horizontal and a vertical conspiracy).

13. Calkins, note 7 at 208–211.

14. *Matsushita*, note 8, 475 U.S. at 588, 106 S.Ct. at 1356. See generally, S. DeSanti & W. Kovacic, Matsushita: Its Construction and Application by the Lower Courts, 59 Antitrust L.J. 609 (1991); T. Jorde & M. Lemley, Summary Judgment in Antitrust Cases: Understanding Monsanto and Matsushita, 36 Antitrust Bull. 271 (1991).

15. See § 4.2.

tional province of the jury.[16] When a jury decides fact questions in civil antitrust cases it generally applies a "preponderance of the evidence" standard. A rule that sifted all evidence through a higher standard, such as "more likely than not" or "tends to exclude the possibility" would effectively require an antitrust plaintiff to survive scrutiny from the bench first at a standard higher than the jury itself would be asked to apply. But *Matsushita* should not be read that broadly.[17]

Likewise, insofar as it applies to conspiracy claims, *Matsushita* addresses only the question whether the conspiracy existed, not whether it was anticompetitive under the circumstances. Although the latter might be a fact question as well, it is not the same question, and may not be an appropriate question for the jury at all if the claim is of a *per se* violation. For these reasons the Eleventh Circuit erred in Palmer v. BRG of Ga.,[18] when it granted the defendant's motion for summary judgment respecting an explicit, written horizontal territorial division agreement. In granting the motion, the court had noted that the conduct was "as consistent with permissible competition as with an illegal conspiracy." As an abstract proposition that might be true; certain territorial division agreements are pro-competitive, particularly if they are ancillary to other business activities. But this is an entirely distinct question from that of the agreement's existence, and it may require answers to numerous questions of fact, such as the defendant's market share, the purpose of the agreement, the essentiality of the territorial division to any efficiency-creating joint venture, and the like.[19] Further, insofar as these are fact questions, they would ordinarily be addressed by the jury under the ordinary "preponderance" standard—not under the heightened standard applied to claims of conspiracy based on circumstantial evidence.

In reversing the Eleventh Circuit, the Supreme Court concluded that it was

> doubtful whether the standards announced in *Matsushita* * * * apply in situations * * * where the direct evidence of concerted action is manifest in explicit written agreements between dominant firms allocating and monopolizing the market.[20]

Does *Matsushita*'s heightened "more likely than not" standard apply in other situations than those involving conspiracy claims? Perhaps, but one must tread carefully if the jury's role is not to be obstructed. In *Morristown* the Sixth Circuit appeared to apply the standard to a predatory pricing claim, holding that evidence equally consistent with competitive and predatory pricing would be insufficient to support summary judgment.[21] But once again, this question seems to go more to the nature of the evidence from which predatory pricing can be inferred than to the nature of summary judgment generally. For example, most courts hold that prices above average total cost are nonpredatory as a matter of law. The question whether the defendant's prices exceeded average total cost over the period of claimed preda-

16. See In re Petroleum Products Antitrust Litigation, 906 F.2d 432, 438 (9th Cir.1990) (noting tension between *Matsushita* and constitutional right to jury trial).

17. In *Petroleum Products*, note 16, the court finally concluded that:

> where an antitrust plaintiff relies entirely upon circumstantial evidence of conspiracy, a defendant will be entitled to summary judgment if it can be shown that (1) the defendant's conduct is consistent with other plausible explanations, and (2) permitting an inference of conspiracy would pose a significant deterrent to beneficial procompetitive behavior. Once the defendant has made such a showing, the plaintiff must come forward with other evidence that is sufficiently unambiguous and tends to exclude the possibility that the defendant acted lawfully.

906 F.2d at 440. At first glance, the second requirement seems to turn a question of fact into one of policy. That is, the jury is not being asked whether the social costs of finding a conspiracy are high, but whether a conspiracy in fact existed. But requirement (2) may be nothing more than an acknowledgement that in concentrated markets anticompetitive behavior does not require a classical "agreement." In order to compensate, the court will permit "agreement" to be inferred more readily when oligopoly seems clear, and the offsetting dangers that competitive behavior will be deterred are minimal.

18. 874 F.2d 1417 (11th Cir.1989), amended, 893 F.2d 293 (11th Cir.), reversed, 498 U.S. 46, 111 S.Ct. 401 (1990).

19. See generally Ch. 5.

20. *Palmer*, 498 U.S. at 84, 111 S.Ct. at 422.

21. Morristown Block & Concrete v. General Shale Prods. Corp., 829 F.2d 39 (6th Cir.1987).

tion should be addressed by the jury under ordinary preponderance of the evidence rules.[22] By contrast, some courts insist on evidence of intent, especially where the defendant's prices are lower than average total cost but above average variable cost. However, intent evidence is inherently ambiguous because both competitive intent and predatory intent can be expressed as an intent to harm rivals. With respect to this question, a higher standard may be in order—an expression of intent that is as consistent with competition on the merits as it is with predation (for example, "I will always try to underbid my rival") should not be permitted to create an inference of the latter.

In its *Brooke* decision, the Supreme Court seemed to come down in favor of a heightened standard in predatory pricing cases.[23] That case, as *Matsushita* began with the premise that predatory pricing claims are inherently implausible, and thus require close scrutiny at the summary judgment stage. The important difference, however, is that in *Matsushita* the Court applied summary judgment to the claim of a *conspiracy* to fix prices. In *Brooke*, by contrast, no conspiracy was claimed and the Court applied summary judgment to the predation claim itself.[24] The best reading of *Brooke* is not that the Court applied a heightened summary judgment standard; rather it produced a strict list of structural prerequisites for predatory pricing claims, and then held that summary judgment is appropriate if the record fails to include evidence that the prerequisites were met.[25] However, with respect to each individual prerequisite, such as high entry barriers, or a competitive market structure, ordinary summary judgment standards presumably apply.

In *Kodak* the Supreme Court qualified its *Matsushita* holding on summary judgment.[26] Importantly, *Kodak* was not a conspiracy case. The core factual issue in dispute was whether absence of market power in a primary market (photocopiers) entailed absence of market power in aftermarkets (repair services and replacement parts).[27] Even under *Matsushita*, one would ordinarily expect that such a question would first be classified as one of law or of fact. If the question were one of law, then it would never be given to the fact finder at all and summary judgment would be appropriate, assuming that there were not other disputed fact issues. But if the basic question were one of fact, then it would be decided by the jury under an ordinary preponderance of the evidence standard.

In *Kodak*, some evidence seemed inconsistent with the proposition that lack of market power in the primary market entailed lack of market power in aftermarkets. For example, when Kodak took over service and repair business formerly given by independent firms, it charged much higher prices; further it was able to engage in price discrimination in providing service and replacement parts. The ability to price discriminate is generally a sign of market power.[28]

Thus an important issue in *Kodak* concerned the relationship between economic theory and the division of litigation questions into fact and law. More precisely, at what point does an economic theory become so robust that the conclusions compelled by the theory should be regarded as settled as a matter of law? The

22. On predatory pricing rules, see Ch. 8.

23. Brooke Group Ltd. v. Brown & Williamson Tobacco Corp., 509 U.S. 209, 113 S.Ct. 2578 (1993). The decision involved a judgment as a matter of law, following a jury trial, but the standard is the same as the summary judgment standard.

24. For further analysis, see § 8.8.

25. See *Brooke*, 509 U.S. at 225, 113 S.Ct. at 2589:

If market circumstances or deficiencies in proof would bar a reasonable jury from finding that the scheme alleged would likely result in sustained supracompetitive pricing, the plaintiff's case has failed. In certain situations—for example, where the market is highly diffuse and competitive, or where new entry is easy, or the defendant lacks adequate excess capacity to absorb the market shares of his rivals and cannot quickly create or purchase new capacity—summary disposition of the case is appropriate.

26. Eastman Kodak Co. v. Image Technical Services, 504 U.S. 451, 112 S.Ct. 2072 (1992). The opinion was written by Justice Blackmun, one of the dissenters in *Matsushita*.

27. The decision is discussed further at § 3.3a (market power) and § 10.3b (tying arrangements).

28. See § 3.9b.

lower court had approved summary judgment after almost no discovery, concluding that the economic theory was so robust that it should be regarded as a principle of law: one who lacks market power in the primary market cannot have market power in aftermarkets. *Kodak* effectively held that this economic proposition was not quite as unassailable as the district court thought. As a result, the issue was to be treated as one of fact and, at least on the record as established, summary judgment was inappropriate. As the Court explained,

> The Court's requirement in *Matsushita* that the plaintiffs' claims make economic sense did not introduce a special burden on plaintiff's facing summary judgment in antitrust cases. The Court did not hold that if the moving party enunciates any economic theory supporting its behavior, regardless of its accuracy in reflecting the actual market, it is entitled to summary judgment. *Matsushita* demands only that the nonmoving party's inferences be reasonable in order to reach the jury, a requirement that was not invented, but merely articulated, in that decision. If the plaintiff's theory is economically senseless, no reasonable jury could find in its favor, and summary judgment should be granted. Kodak, then, bears a substantial burden in showing that it is entitled to summary judgment. It must show that despite evidence of increased prices and excluded competition, an inference of market power is unreasonable.[29]

At least one circuit decision has interpreted *Kodak* so as to deny summary judgment to a conspiracy claim whose facts were far more similar to *Matsushita*'s than to *Kodak* In *Big Apple* the Third Circuit denied a defendant's motion for summary judgment on the plaintiff's claim that the defendants BMW dealers and their distributor had conspired to deny a dealership to the plaintiff.[30] The evidence suggested that the distributor consulted with the competing dealers before denying the plaintiff a dealership, but also that both the distributor and the dealers feared that the plaintiff would be a free rider on the sales efforts of the established dealers. Further, the plaintiffs' reputation as a low service deep discounter was inconsistent with the image that BMW wished to project. On this evidence, the *Matsushita* court might have gone either way but probably would have granted summary judgment.[31] The Third Circuit found that the additional considerations raised in *Kodak* justified denial of summary judgment.

The most important tension between *Kodak* and *Matsushita* concerns the appropriateness of summary judgment when prevailing economic theory renders the plaintiff's claim implausible in some fundamental way. *Matsushita* held that when plaintiffs' claims are based on economically implausible theories "more persuasive evidence" is required than "would otherwise be necessary. * * * "[32] This raises two questions. *First*, when is an economic theory so robust that claims contrary to it must be regarded as in some sense "implausible?" *Second*, assuming that the first requirement is met, what kind of evidence is required to overcome the implausibility problem?

On the first issue, economic theories come into and out of fashion, just as legal theories do. Certainly the mere fact that an economic theory is asserted and seems rational does not entail that claims contradicting the theory are implausible. After a time, some theories prove to have a great deal of explanatory power and perhaps survive substantial attempts to falsify them. Then they may be regarded as so robust, or so well established within antitrust doctrine, that claims in contradiction should be regarded as fundamentally implausible. Where the line between the robust and the not-so-robust should be drawn is hard to say. Importantly, however, the predatory pricing theory

29. *Kodak*, 504 U.S. at 469, 112 S.Ct. at 2083.

30. Big Apple BMW v. BMW of North Amer., 974 F.2d 1358 (3d Cir.1992), cert. denied, 507 U.S. 912, 113 S.Ct. 1262 (1993).

31. A dissenting opinion in *Big Apple* found the evidence equally consistent with conspiracy and unilateral conduct—thus indicating that, under *Matsushita*, summary judgment should have been granted. 974 F.2d at 1384.

32. *Matsushita*, note 8, 475 U.S. at 585, 106 S.Ct. at 1355. On expert testimony, see § 16.8c.

asserted in *Matsushita* was fundamentally inconsistent with certain propositions that had been settled as a matter of law in at least some circuits. For example, the defendants' aggregate market share was less than fifty percent and the alleged predatory pricing had occurred over some twenty years. Several circuit courts have held that the structural prerequisites for predatory pricing could not be established on these facts.[33] Likewise, in *Brooke*[34] the Court cited substantial evidence that a rational firm in the defendant's position would not have attempted predatory pricing, for recoupment of the investment in predation was unlikely.[35]

By contrast, the *Kodak* proposition that lack of market power in a primary market entails lack of market power in aftermarkets for service or repair parts is a variation of the Chicago School critique of the leverage theory; but in fact the theory rests on certain informational assumptions that may not apply in imperfect markets. In a perfectly competitive primary market, consumers with good information would not purchase a product whose sellers insisted on obtaining monopoly prices for subsequent repair. But in *Kodak* the primary market was not perfectly competitive, and consumers did not necessarily have the kind of information that they needed. Importantly, *Kodak* did not hold that summary judgment would never be appropriate in such a case; it held merely that summary judgment was not yet appropriate in a case where the factual record was very thin and the defendants were relying on the economic theory standing virtually alone in support of their motion.

Economic theories must be evaluated for both their truth and their robustness. Some theories are discarded when they are simply proven false as a general proposition. Other theories are invariably true when their assumptions obtain, but their assumptions do not always obtain. Within antitrust economics, the great majority of seriously regarded theories fall into this second category. The theories are not likely to be disproved, but there may be considerable dispute about the frequency with which the theory accounts for behavior, given that the theory's assumptions do not always obtain.

The second question is, When the economic theory *is* robust, what extra factual showing is necessary before the plaintiffs can proceed with a claim inconsistent with the theory? Neither *Matsushita* nor *Kodak* is very helpful here. In *Matsushita* the plaintiffs had not produced such facts, and in *Kodak* the underlying theory was not found sufficiently robust. The safest answer is that a sliding scale is in order, but that if a theory is regarded as so robust that it is regarded as settled as a matter of law, then *no amount* of inconsistent factual evidence will be permitted. For example, today most circuits hold that illegal monopolization cannot be established unless the defendant is found to have some minimum share of a properly defined relevant market—say, 60%. Suppose that the plaintiff claims monopolization, but the defendant's market share is only 10%. However, the defendant offers a great deal of evidence of other kinds that the defendant has the power to control price or that its exclusionary practices are indeed anticompetitive.[36] Most courts would grant summary judgment once it appeared that no factual dispute existed about the defendant's low market share.[37]

Finally, the *Kodak* decision tells us little about the dividing line between summary judgment and trial. Since that was the issue in *Matsushita*, that decision still stands. Rather, *Kodak* concern was with the dividing line between summary judgment granted early and summary judgment granted late. Nothing in the decision is inconsistent with the proposition that Kodak may *still* be entitled to summary judgment—but only after full inquiry by discovery is made into questions about Kodak's market power in aftermarkets. If those questions can be answered from documentary

33. See § 8.4.

34. Note 23.

35. See § 8.8.

36. For example, the defendant has high returns or has the ability to engage in price discrimination; or other firms in the market follow its behavior, giving it more effective clout than its market share suggests.

37. See 2A Antitrust Law ¶ 542c (rev. ed. 1995).

evidence or uncontested statements in depositions and do not depend on the testimony of witnesses whose credibility must be ascertained or on conflicting sets of plausible facts among which a choice must be made, summary judgment is still appropriate.

The all important message of *Kodak* then, is not that judges must abandon *Matsushita* and revert to a *Poller*-like standard of preferring trial. Post-*Kodak* decisions such as *Brooke* effectively undermine that proposition. Rather, *Kodak's* point is that summary judgment should not be granted too hastily until the plaintiff has had a chance to produce all the facts it needs to make its case.

16.8c. Judicial Control of Expert Testimony

An important implication of *Matsushita*[38] is that summary judgment is appropriate unless there are disputed issues of *fact*. Affidavits stating the opinions of experts do not automatically constitute assertions of fact. One sad fact of life today is that a qualified expert can be found to give practically any opinion, no matter how weakly supported by the accepted standards of the relevant discipline.[39] Confining expert opinions to received orthodoxy would be reactionary and regressive; but at the very least, the opinion must be supported by facts sufficient to enable others, including other experts, to draw a conclusion one way or the other. Indeed, a footnote statement in *Matsushita* went even a step further, suggesting that expert opinion should not be given great weight if it conflicts with established economic theory.[40]

Thus, for example, the economic expert who recites his credentials and publications and then simply asserts by affidavit that "barriers to entry in this market are high" has not raised a fact question with respect to entry barriers. Rather, he must say something like "entry barriers are high because a new plant costs $100,000,000, takes six years to build and is highly specialized; most costs are unrecoverable in the event of failure, and those currently operating in the market are protected by numerous patents."[41] At this point the opponent may take issue with these asserted facts, or may contest the proposition that these facts indicate high entry barriers. But these possibilities merely illustrate that the affidavit *creates* a fact issue, not that it resolves it. As the Fifth Circuit has noted in a nonantitrust case:

> [T]here is a level of conclusoriness below which an affidavit must not sink if it is to provide the basis for a genuine issue of material fact * * * Indeed, "unsupported * * * affidavits setting forth 'ultimate or conclusory facts and conclusions of law' are insufficient to either support or defeat a motion for summary judgment." * * * "Without more than credentials and a subjective opinion, an expert's testimony that 'it is so' is not admissible. * * * "[42]

38. See note 8.

39. See, e.g., In re Brand Name Prescription Drugs Antitrust Litigation, 1999 WL 33889 (N.D.Ill.1999), which blasted a Nobel prize economist for his handling of a case and then ruled against his client. The testimony was partially rehabilitated in In re Brand Name Prescription Drugs Antitrust Litigation, 186 F.3d 781 (7th Cir.1999). See generally 3 Modern Scientific Evidence: the Law and Science of Expert Testimony (D. Faigman, D. Kaye, M. Saks, J. Sanders, eds., West Group, 1999).

40. Speaking of expert testimony that the defendant had sold televisions at less than cost, the court concluded that even "the expert opinion evidence of below-cost pricing has little probative value in comparison with the economic factors * * * that suggest that such conduct is irrational." *Matsushita*, 475 U.S. at 594 & n. 19, 106 S.Ct. at 1360 n. 19.

41. See 2 Antitrust Law ¶ 322f (rev. ed. 1995).

42. Orthopedic & Sports Injury Clinic v. Wang Labs., 922 F.2d 220, 224 (5th Cir.1991), citing and quoting previous Fifth Circuit decisions. Accord Evers v. General Motors Corp., 770 F.2d 984, 986 (11th Cir.1985) (nonantitrust case) ("a party may not avoid summary judgment solely on the basis of an expert's opinion that fails to provide specific facts from the record to support its conclusory allegations").

Compare M & M Medical Supplies and Service v. Pleasant Valley Hospital, 981 F.2d 160 (4th Cir.1992) (en banc), cert. denied, 508 U.S. 972, 113 S.Ct. 2962 (1993), which found an expert affidavit sufficient to create an issue of market power. The affidavit cited the relevant facts to support its conclusions, but did not append the data itself. The court held that the affidavit could later be supplemented through testimony, interrogatories, and so on. Of course, the stage of the litigation is relevant to the requisite content of an affidavit. If an affidavit is offered to defeat a motion for summary judgment, there may not be a further opportunity for the expert to give testimony. The

Or as the Supreme Court said in *Brooke*,

> When an expert opinion is not supported by sufficient facts to validate it in the eyes of the law, or when indisputable record facts contradict or otherwise render the opinion unreasonable, it cannot support a jury's verdict. * * * Expert testimony is useful as a guide to interpreting market facts, but it is not a substitute for them.[43]

The federal court system attempts to control expert testimony by two different mechanisms. *First*, as described in the previous subsection, Federal Rule of Civil Procedure 56 permits judges to grant summary judgment after concluding that the expert's testimony fails to create a triable fact dispute on an essential issue. *Second*, the Federal Rules of Evidence, but particularly rule 702, permit judges to screen expert testimony for admissibility, under the standard that the evidence must "assist the trier of fact."[44]

In theory, these two approaches to judicial treatment of expert testimony are quite different. Summary judgment, which is frequently used in antitrust litigation, assumes that the expert's testimony is admissible but concludes that the testimony is not sufficiently credible, not sufficiently on point, or undermined by the expert's own statements. As a result, it does not create the requisite fact issue. When a court considers a motion for summary judgment it examines the entire record, and expert testimony that has not been excluded is in the record and is entitled to be considered. Nevertheless, the antitrust court may apply criteria that effectively give the economic testimony little or no weight, as occurred in both the *Matsushita* and *Brooke* cases discussed previously. Significantly, this summary judgment critique of expert testimony generally focuses on the strength and pointedness of the expert's conclusions.

By contrast, exclusion of an expert's testimony under the Federal Rules of Evidence removes the excluded portion from the record completely. The Supreme Court's *Daubert* decision established criteria for determining whether an expert's methodology is admissible under the constraints of Federal Rule of Evidence 702.[45] According to the Supreme Court, the *Daubert* inquiry is supposed to focus, not on the expert's conclusions, but rather on the expert's methodology. In practice, however, the line between "methodology" and "conclusions" has been very difficult to locate.[46]

Under *Daubert*, the party opposing a particular expert's proffered testimony typically

court should decide the summary judgment motion on the basis of what the record contains, not on what the expert might add later.

43. 509 U.S. at 242, 113 S.Ct. at 2598. Compare *Matsushita*, note 8 at 594 n. 19: "expert opinion evidence * * * has little probative value in comparison with the economic factors" that may dictate a particular conclusion.

44. See Federal Rule of Evidence 702:

> If scientific, technical, or other specialized knowledge will assist the trier of fact to understand the evidence or to determine a fact in issue, a [qualified] witness . . . may testify thereto in the form of an opinion or otherwise.

Rules 703–706 are also explicitly relevant to expert testimony.

45. *Daubert v. Merrill Dow Pharmaceuticals,* 509 U.S. 579, 113 S.Ct. 2786 (1993). For further elaboration, see Antitrust Law ¶ 322.1 (current Supp.). See also *General Elec. Co. v. Joiner*, 522 U.S. 136, 118 S.Ct. 512 (1997), on remand, 134 F.3d 1437 (4th Cir.1998), which held that a district court's decision whether to admit expert testimony under *Daubert* is to be reviewed under an abuse of discretion standard, and was entitled to exclude an expert's testimony providing insufficient evidence of causation. That decision, which gives considerable leeway to the trial judge, may be quite relevant in antitrust cases in which expert economists are called upon to provide evidence causally linking an alleged antitrust violation and the plaintiff's injuries.

See also Kumho Tire Co. v. Patrick Carmichael, ___ U.S. ___, 119 S.Ct. 1167 (1999), which applied *Daubert* criteria to all experts, not just "scientific" experts. *Kumho* might be most relevant to antitrust cases when the testimony comes from an industry expert who is not a scientist.

46. Nevertheless, it is quite appropriate that an expert's testimony could be admissible under *Daubert* criteria but nevertheless fail to create a fact issue enabling the expert's client to avoid summary judgment. See Rebel Oil Co. v. Atlantic Richfield Co., 146 F.3d 1088, 1097 (9th Cir.), cert. denied, ___ U.S. ___, 119 S.Ct. 541 (1998);

> The district court's conclusion at summary judgment that [an expert's] testimony was not legally sufficient evidence to create a question of material fact regarding whether ARCO priced its gasoline below its costs is not inconsistent with its conclusion following the *Daubert* hearing that [the same expert's] methodology was sound. An expert witness may be qualified to testify even though the expert's conclusions are legally incorrect.

presents a motion *in limine* to suppress it for failing to satisfy the admissibility criteria of the Federal Rules of Evidence. The effect of granting the motion is that this testimony is not entitled to be considered at all, and thus is not part of the case's record. *Daubert* instructs that when the court evaluates the expert's testimony, it should consider the following criteria:

1. Whether the proffered scientific evidence "can be (and has been) tested."[47]

2. "Whether the theory or technique has been subjected to peer review and publication," although the Court added that "[p]ublication (which is but one element of peer review) is not a sine qua non of admissibility; it does not necessarily correlate with reliability...."[48]

3. "[I]n the case of a particular scientific technique, the court ordinarily should consider the known or potential rate of error...."[49]

4. "[T]he existence and maintenance of standards controlling the technique's operation...."[50]

5. "General acceptance" in the relevant scientific community; a "reliability assessment does not require, although it does permit, explicit identification of a relevant scientific community and an express determination of a particular degree of acceptance within that community."[51]

To these the lower courts have added a few additional criteria, such as the particular experience of the expert in question,[52] or whether the expert is proposing to testify about research done personally and independent of the litigation.[53]

Not many antitrust decisions have excluded testimony offered by an economist under *Daubert* In *Tuscaloosa* the city alleged that producers of chlorine for drinking water treatment had conspired to fix prices.[54] There was no explicit evidence of a price-fixing conspiracy, but the plaintiffs offered an economist and a statistician who testified that the defendant's market behavior revealed the existence of an antitrust conspiracy. Mainly, the economist testified that the chlorine market was characterized by a small number of firms, a homogenous product, identical or highly similar costs, low demand elasticity,[55] and a sealed-bid/auction style of determining price which is conducive to collusion because "cheating" by a cartel member is so readily detected.[56] The economist also noted that the defendants published their list prices, and in non-bid sales refused to deviate from these prices.[57] Finally, he concluded that there was a pattern of identical bidding, of selective refusals to bid, and of using bids to "signal" the price to other rivals that suggested collusive pricing. Among the facts upon which the economist relied were repeated instances in which firms submitted identical bids. The statistician added to this mainly the facts that the bids seemed to follow

47. *Daubert* note 45, 509 U.S. at 593: "Scientific methodology today is based on generating hypotheses and testing them to see if they can be falsified; indeed, this methodology is what distinguishes science from other fields of human inquiry." Quoting M. Green, Expert Witnesses and Sufficiency of Evidence in Toxic Substances Litigation: The Legacy of Agent Orange and Bendectin Litigation, 86 Nw.U.L.Rev. 643, 645 (1992).

48. Ibid.

49. Ibid.

50. Ibid.

51. Id., adding "a known technique which has been able to attract only minimal support within the community" ... may properly be viewed with skepticism...."

52. *Joiner v. General Electric Co.*, 78 F.3d 524, 532 (11th Cir.1996), rev'd on other grounds, 522 U.S. 136, 118 S.Ct. 512 (1997).

53. *Daubert v. Merrell Dow Pharmaceuticals*, 43 F.3d 1311, 1317 (9th Cir.), cert. denied, 516 U.S. 869, 116 S.Ct. 189 (1995). See also *Khan v. State Oil Co.*, 93 F.3d 1358, 1365 (7th Cir.1996), rev'd on other grounds, 522 U.S. 3, 118 S.Ct. 275 (1997) ("As we have emphasized in cases involving scientific testimony—and the principle applies to the social sciences with the same force that it does to the natural sciences—a scientist, however reputable, is not permitted to offer evidence that he has not generated by the methods he would use in his normal academic or professional work, which is to say in work undertaken without reference to or expectation of possible use in litigation.").

54. *City of Tuscaloosa v. Harcros Chemicals*, 877 F.Supp. 1504 (N.D.Ala.1995), rev'd, 158 F.3d 548 (11th Cir.1998).

55. Id. at 1513–1514.

56. Id. at 1514.

57. Ibid.

a pattern in which the firms honored one another's prior claim on certain customers and that prices in the alleged cartel region were significantly higher than prices outside the region.[58] All of this evidence, it should be noted, adopts theory that is quite conventional in neoclassical economics and is "consistent" with the proposition that the defendants were colluding.

The trial judge excluded the testimony, mainly because of the expert's opinion that "conscious parallelism (or tacit collusion) is conspiratorial."[59] However, *Daubert* admonishes that the decision to exclude must be based on the methodologies that the expert employs, not on the conclusions that he draws. In reversing, the Eleventh Circuit noted that the economist had employed methodologies that were quite conventional in economics, and concluded that the district court had confused the basic question of admissibility with the question of sufficiency to prove a legal conspiracy. While the expert's evidence did not do the latter, it certainly "aided the trier of fact," whose job it was to look at the entire record and decide whether a conspiracy had occurred.

The *Phosphide* decision comes closer to *Daubert* rationale for excluding expert testimony not meeting the standards of that discipline.[60] The plaintiff's were seeking damages for price-fixing, and their expert sought to establish damages by using the "before-and-after" method which is commonly used in such cases. In using this method the economist seeks to obtain data about prices in the market during the period immediately before a cartel allegedly came into existence, and also the period immediately after it collapsed. By using a regression analysis the expert can come up with an estimated non-cartel price for the market, and also estimate the amount by which the cartel price exceeded the non-cartel price.[61] But in this case the expert had not done an acceptable job of analyzing the market effects of the cartel.[62] While the generally accepted "before-and-after" method attempts to minimize the effects of market changes by taking price data from both the pre-cartel and post-cartel periods, the expert had taken price data from the period after the cartel fell apart, but not from the period prior to its existence.[63] To be sure, limitations on the availability of data might sometimes prevent an expert from looking at both periods in order to reduce the chance of pricing deviations not fully explained by the cartel. In such a case one might try to compensate by examining data from a longer period, taking more complete data from within the given period, or supplementing the "before-and-method" with some alternative.[64] The expert had not done any of these things. Further, he had apparently not run an acceptable regression analysis on the data at all, but had simply taken a weighted average of prices during the two periods being compared.[65]

In sum, the expert had simply violated too many of the conventions of his own discipline without giving any explanation of why these deviations were necessary. In such a case *Daubert* exclusion makes clear that significant defects in the expert's testimony and not in the summary judgment record as a whole accounts for the failure.

16.8d. Tagalong Suits; Offensive Collateral Estoppel

Clayton § 5(a) provides that a judgment against an antitrust defendant in an action brought by or on behalf of the United States government may sometimes be admissible as prima facie evidence against the same defendant in a subsequent private suit.[66] The provision applies only where the government judg-

58. Id. at 1516.

59. *Tuscaloosa* case, note 54 at 1526.

60. Aluminum Phosphide Antitrust Litigation, 893 F.Supp. 1497 (D.Kan.1995).

61. See § 17.5.

62. The plaintiff's expert was described by the court as an "expert for hire" who was a full time forensic economist and had testified in some 121 cases, 42 of them antitrust cases. *Phosphide*, 893 F.Supp. at 1499.

63. See id. at 1502 & n. 11.

64. See § 17.5b1.

65. See *Phosphide*, 893 F.Supp. at 1504.

66. 15 U.S.C.A. § 16a. See 2 Antitrust Law ¶ ¶ 336–337 (rev. ed. 1995).

ment is final[67] and the action was brought under the antitrust laws.[68] It does not apply to consent judgments or to decrees entered before any testimony was taken. Finally, the prima facie evidence rule applies only to matters that were put in issue, explicitly decided and necessary to the outcome. Even then, the statute creates only a rebuttable presumption in the plaintiff's favor as to the matters to which § 5(a) applies.

These restrictions on § 5(a) have turned it into a relatively feeble instrument in comparison with another tool that came into prominence in the late 1970's: offensive collateral estoppel. In Parklane Hosiery Co. v. Shore,[69] the Supreme Court held that a defendant who had a full and fair opportunity to litigate issues in one proceeding could be precluded from relitigating them in a later collateral proceeding to which it is also a party.[70] *Parklane* established four broad requirements that must be met before offensive collateral estoppel could be applied. *First*, it should not be used if the plaintiff "could easily have joined in the earlier action." An alternative rule would permit plaintiffs who could more efficiently join in an earlier action to wait and see, taking advantage of offensive collateral estoppel if the first plaintiff won, but not being bound by a judgment to which they were not parties if the first plaintiff lost.[71] *Second*, offensive collateral estoppel should not be used if the defendant's stake in the first litigation was very small. In general, parties invest more in litigation as the stakes are higher. *Third*, if a series of litigations had produced inconsistent adjudications, the subsequent plaintiff should not be permitted to choose among them. So offensive collateral estoppel is not appropriate if "the judgment relied upon as a basis for the estoppel is itself inconsistent with one or more previous judgments in favor of the defendant." And *fourth*, offensive collateral estoppel should not be used if "the second action affords the defendant procedural opportunities unavailable in the first action that could readily cause a different result."[72] Finally, the trial judge has broad discretion in deciding whether offensive collateral estoppel is appropriate under the circumstances. Once it applies, however, it is more than a presumptive rule: it simply prevents the defendant from relitigating an issue found against it in the earlier proceeding.

The doctrine of offensive collateral estoppel is not only more powerful than Clayton § 5(a), it also has a broader domain. While § 5(a) applies only when the first suit is brought by the government, offensive collateral estoppel can be brought when the first claim was brought by a private plaintiff.[73] Further, the first suit need not even be brought under the federal antitrust laws, provided that the underlying factual issues are the same.[74]

67. All appeals must be concluded or the time for appeal must have expired. See International Shoe Mach. Corp. v. United Shoe Mach. Corp., 315 F.2d 449, 457 (1st Cir.), cert. denied, 375 U.S. 820, 84 S.Ct. 56 (1963).

68. As a result, proceedings brought under § 5 of the Federal Trade Commission Act are generally not covered. See In re Antibiotic Antitrust Actions, 333 F.Supp. 317, 322 (S.D.N.Y.1971). However, since the FTC has jurisdiction to enforce the Clayton Act directly, some courts have held that such proceedings are covered. Purex Corp. v. Procter & Gamble Co., 453 F.2d 288, 289–291 (9th Cir. 1971), cert. denied, 405 U.S. 1065, 92 S.Ct. 1499 (1972).

69. 439 U.S. 322, 99 S.Ct. 645 (1979).

70. Those in "privity" with the defendant in the first proceeding are also covered. For example, see Randustrial Corp. v. Union Rubber Co., 1986–2 Trade Cas. (CCH) ¶ 67308, 1986 WL 13353 (N.D.Ohio 1986) (parent and 90% owned subsidiary in privity for purposes of offensive collateral estoppel).

71. See Premier Elec. Constr. Co. v. NECA, 814 F.2d 358, 365–366 (7th Cir.1987), finding that to permit members of class actions who opt out of the class to later use offensive collateral estoppel would encourage a multiplicity of such suits. "The more class members who opt out may benefit from preclusion, the more class members will opt out. Preclusion thus may increase the number of suits, undermining the economy the district court hoped to achieve."

72. *Parklane*, 439 U.S. at 330–331, 99 S.Ct. at 651–652.

73. For example, GAF Corp. v. Eastman Kodak Co., 519 F.Supp. 1203 (S.D.N.Y.1981), applying offensive collateral estoppel as to Berkey Photo v. Eastman Kodak Co., 603 F.2d 263 (2d Cir.1979), cert. denied, 444 U.S. 1093, 100 S.Ct. 1061 (1980).

74. For example, Grip–Pak v. Illinois Tool Works, 694 F.2d 466, 469 (7th Cir.1982), cert. denied, 461 U.S. 958, 103 S.Ct. 2430 (1983) (offensive collateral estoppel applies in principle to state court trade secret action; but state court finding that a suit was "not malicious" did not preclude a subsequent federal claim that the suit violated the antitrust laws).

§ 16.9 Equitable Relief

The problem of equitable relief comes up in numerous antitrust contexts. For example, the Supreme Court has held that private plaintiffs may, under appropriate circumstances, obtain a divestiture order after a successful merger challenge.[1] Likewise, the discussion of the indirect purchaser rule noted that while indirect purchasers may not obtain damages under federal antitrust law, they are ordinarily permitted to have an injunction, which does not require proof of passed-on damages.[2]

In any event, § 16 of the Clayton Act permits private plaintiffs to:

> have injunctive relief ... against threatened loss or damage by a violation of the antitrust laws ... when and under the same conditions and principles as injunctive relief against threatened conduct that will cause loss or damage is granted by courts of equity.... [3]

In general, this rule permits an antitrust plaintiff to have an injunction whenever a damage remedy would be inadequate—perhaps because damages are insufficient to correct the wrong, or perhaps because damages cannot be measured with sufficient accuracy to entitle the plaintiff to any damages relief. Nevertheless there must be "threatened loss or damage," and this loss must fit within the definition of "antitrust injury."[4]

In *Marshfield Clinic* the Seventh Circuit concluded that while plaintiff Blue Cross was unable to prove any damages from the defendant's market division scheme, it was still entitled to an injunction, reasoning:

> Even though * * * the district judge was correct that Blue Cross has failed to come up with evidence that would authorize an award of damages for the division of markets, this does not justify withholding an injunction—rather the contrary. Inadequacy of a plaintiff's remedy at law, that is, his damages remedy, is normally * * * a prerequisite to the entry of an injunction. And a common reason why the damages remedy is inadequate is that the plaintiff is unable to quantify the harm that the defendant's practice has inflicted or will inflict on him.[5]

This does not mean that a plaintiff who *can* recover damages is disabled from seeking an injunction as well. Rather, the injunction covers only *future* violations, for which damages are of course not recoverable. As a result, one receives damages for the consequences of previous violations and an injunction for threatened future violations.

Further, as the Seventh Circuit observed, the plaintiff who prevails on the equity claim but not the damages claim, is nevertheless entitled to a statutory attorney's fee.[6]

§ 16.10 Compulsory Arbitration

Historically, the courts refused to enforce contracts requiring the parties to arbitrate antitrust claims. However, in Mitsubishi Motors Corp. v. Soler Chrysler–Plymouth,[1] the Supreme Court enforced an obligation in an international contract to submit an antitrust dispute to arbitration. Since then, the lower courts have seen little reason for treating domestic disputes differently. Most have enforced domestic contract clauses requiring arbitration of antitrust claims,[2] provided that the rights or

§ 16.9

1. California v. American Stores, 495 U.S. 271, 110 S.Ct. 1853 (1990).

2. See § 16.6b2.

3. 15 U.S.C.A. § 26. See 2 Antitrust Law, Ch. 3E (rev. ed. 1995).

4. See § 16.3, discussing the Supreme Court's decision in Cargill v. Monfort of Colo., 479 U.S. 104, 107 S.Ct. 484 (1986).

5. Blue Cross and Blue Shield United of Wisconsin v. Marshfield Clinic, 152 F.3d 588, 591 (7th Cir.1998), cert. denied, ___ U.S. ___, 119 S.Ct. 804 (1999).

6. Id., 152 F.3d at 595, but adding: "Blue Cross is not, however, entitled to fees and costs allocable to claims and theories that neither succeeded, nor contributed to the limited victory that it has obtained."

§ 16.10

1. 473 U.S. 614, 105 S.Ct. 3346 (1985). See 2 Antitrust Law ¶ 324b (rev. ed. 1995).

2. E.g., Swensen's Ice Cream Co. v. Corsair Corp., 942 F.2d 1307 (8th Cir.1991).

liabilities of third parties were not involved.[3]

3. On this point, see Coors Brewing Co. v. Molson Breweries, 51 F.3d 1511 (10th Cir.), on remand, 889 F. Supp. 1394 (d.Colo.1995) (arbitration clause encompasses vertical antitrust dispute between contract parties, but not one alleging a horizontal conspiracy with another firm who was not a party to the contract containing the arbitration clause).

Chapter 17

DAMAGES

Table of Sections

---

§ 17.1 Antitrust Damages Actions and Social Welfare

§ 17.1a. Introduction: the Role of Efficiency in Damages Theory

The marriage between economics and federal antitrust policy becomes rocky when it reaches the law of damages. With the exception of market definition issues, most of the economics applied in substantive antitrust analysis is heavily conceptual and written by academics who were not contemplating litigation. By contrast, an economically sophisticated law of damages requires empirical studies to be made within the context of litigation and with specific application to the facts placed before the court. For the economist, empirical studies invariably mean statistics, regression analysis and other forms of higher mathematics. The result can be a nightmare for the judge, who must ultimately instruct the jury in such a way that their decision will not be arbitrary.

Sections 17.1—17.3 of this chapter deal with various conceptual issues relating to the economics of "optimal" antitrust damages. Then, beginning with § 17.4, the discussion turns to how damages are measured in actual antitrust lawsuits. One thing that should be apparent is that the gap between theory and practice is substantial.

Certain complexities in the law of damages limit the contribution of theoretical economics. The economics revolution in antitrust has been concerned chiefly with the "quality" of antitrust injury. It has helped policy makers determine when certain practices, such as vertical integration, are beneficial to society and when they are harmful; or alternatively, whether the plaintiff is complaining about anticompetitiveness or efficiency. But the law of damages has the much more difficult task of *quantifying* injury. The difference between saying that a certain practice is harmful and quantifying the amount of harm can be significant.

Most of the law continues to be based on concepts of justice and compensation that are inconsistent with any notion that the purpose of antitrust enforcement (including private enforcement) is to deter conduct only to the extent that it is inefficient. But the economics revolution in the substantive law of antitrust cannot be ignored in the law of damages, or nearly everything given with one hand will be taken back by the other. The availability and amount of damages determines the amount of antitrust enforcement that exists. More importantly, it affects the cost-benefit calculus any firm undertakes when it considers whether to undertake a risky, probably efficient practice whose legality is uncertain and which is likely to injure certain competitors. The great majority of antitrust cases are filed by private plaintiffs,[1] and most of these include a damage claim. As a result, most antitrust enforcement comes from private parties whose personal motive is not optimal efficiency or the maximization of consumer wealth, but rather their own economic gain.

The basic economic ideology of antitrust policy today is that antitrust should maximize the wealth of society by condemning practices when they permit inefficient output reductions and price increases, and by approving practices when they are competitive. With respect to damages, however, economists have offered antitrust policy makers a far more difficult proposition: that the damages for a particular offense should be calculated so as to make the offense unprofitable if it is inefficient, but not if it is efficient.[2] The "antitrust injury" doctrine developed by the Supreme Court in Brunswick Corp. v. Pueblo Bowl–O–Mat, Inc.[3] gives ambiguous support for this doctrine, although academic writings have carried the doctrine further than anything the Supreme Court stated.[4]

Many practices alleged to violate the antitrust laws are efficient. Others are inefficient and have few socially redeeming virtues. Still others may simultaneously increase both the efficiency of the participants and their market power. A perfectly designed antitrust policy would exonerate the first set of practices, condemn the second set, and condemn the third set only when the social cost of the restraint exceeds its social value. A theory of damages based on the same principle would make them unprofitable when they are inefficient but leave them alone when they are not.

§ 17.1b. Deterrence and Damages

One superficially plausible way of making damages measurement easier is to establish a relatively high floor for damage recoveries and no ceiling. If all presumptions were in the plaintiff's favor, if the rankest speculation was permitted to go to the jury, and all ambiguities were resolved in favor of the plaintiff's estimates, we could confidently predict that dam-

§ 17.1

1. See Reiter v. Sonotone Corp., 442 U.S. 330, 344, 99 S.Ct. 2326, 2333–34 (1979), citing Annual Report of the Director of Admin. Office of U.S. Courts 78, Table 28 (1978); and see S. C. Salop & L.J. White, Economic Analysis of Private Antitrust Litigation, 74 Geo.L.J. 1001, 1005–1006 (1986), showing data through 1984, and indicating that in most years about 90% of filings are private.

2. See W. Breit & K. Elzinga, Antitrust Penalty Reform: An Economic Analysis 3–29 (1986); W. M. Landes, Optimal Sanctions for Antitrust Violations, 50 U.Chi. L.Rev. 652 (1983); H. Hovenkamp, Treble Damages Reform, 33 Antitrust Bull. 233 (1988).

3. 429 U.S. 477, 97 S.Ct. 690 (1977). See § 16.3.

4. For example, see W. Page, Antitrust Damages and Economic Efficiency: An Approach to Antitrust Injury, 47 U.Chi.L.Rev. 467 (1980).

ages would always be large enough to deter the violations. The same result might be achieved by establishing a scale of very high minimum damages, or by changing the multiplier—say, from treble damages to tenfold damages.

If antitrust enforcement by means of damages actions were costless, if courts never made an error in identifying a certain activity as an antitrust violation, *and* if all antitrust violations so identified were inefficient, without compensating efficiencies, then a case could be made for penalties far in excess of the expected profitability of any illegal act.[5] Such high penalties would certainly deter. Further, when deterrence is costless and *never* deters an efficient practice, then overdeterrence is not a substantial social concern.

If any one of the above propositions fails to obtain, however, deterrence itself becomes a socially costly commodity. Private antitrust enforcement is not costless, but in fact quite expensive. Furthermore, there is good reason to believe that it is subject to declining marginal utility and increasing marginal cost. If there were only a small amount of enforcement it would be directed at egregious, probably *per se* violations, such as price fixing, which are relatively easy to prove. As the law provides for increasing amounts of enforcement (perhaps by increasing the damages multiplier), however, the enforcers will attempt to reach increasingly marginal activity whose social costs are more ambiguous. Furthermore, proving a violation and injury in such circumstances will cost more. As the amount of enforcement increases the benefits may continue to increase, but at a decreasing rate. Likewise, as the amount of enforcement increases the costs will rise at an increasing rate. Eventually the marginal cost and marginal benefit curves will intersect. Enforcement beyond that point would be inefficient: the amount of social gain claimed by the additional enforcement would be less than the additional costs of providing it.[6]

An optimal antitrust enforcement policy would enforce to the point that the marginal cost of enforcement equaled the marginal ben-

5. In a public enforcement system the large fine may reduce enforcement costs, because fewer prosecutions would be necessary to achieve a given level of deterrence. For example, a one in ten chance of paying a $1000 fine should theoretically have about the same deterrent effect as a one in one thousand chance of paying a $100,000 fine. If people are not risk neutral and transaction costs are positive, however, some care must be taken in determining the proper trade-off between the probability and the size of an expected penalty. See W. Breit & K. Elzinga, Antitrust Penalty Reform: an Economic Analysis 7 (1986); M. Polinsky & S. Shavell, The Optimal Tradeoff Between the Probability and Magnitude of Fines, 69 Amer.Econ.Rev. 880 (1979); M.K. Block and J.G. Sidak, Why Not Hang a Price Fixer Now and Then? 68 Geo.L.J. 1131 (1980). See generally R. Posner, Economic Analysis of Law § 7.2 (5th ed. 1998).

In a private enforcement system such as that created by § 4 of the Clayton Act, however, an increase in the size of the expected fine will increase, not decrease, the probability of having to pay the fine, because there would be more private enforcement. More private plaintiffs would bring actions, for as the expected return rises more lawsuits at the margin would become profitable. In short, there would not be a "trade-off" between the probability and the magnitude of the expected penalty at all, but both would increase together. Of course, some other mechanism could be used to reduce the amount of private enforcement, such as narrowing standing to a smaller group of people or radically shortening the limitation period. But calibrating damages by such methods would almost certainly be impossible.

6. See K. Elzinga & W. Breit, The Antitrust Penalties: A Study in Law and Economics 9–12 (1976). Figure 1 below shows the marginal social cost of deterrence (the sum of all costs to the enforcer, the defendant and the rest of society) rising and the marginal social benefit (the sum of all benefits to both the private plaintiff and the rest of society) falling. The optimal amount of deterrence is point 0. Any enforcement beyond point 0 would yield a higher degree of competition, but the social value of the greater competition would be outweighed by the social cost of the additional deterrence.

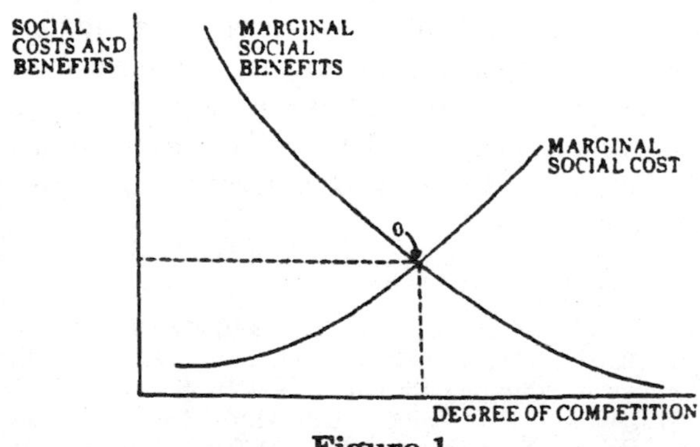

Figure 1

efit. However, locating the intersection of marginal enforcement cost and marginal benefit is possible only in a vague and most general way. At the extreme, some people have argued that the cost of *any* amount of private enforcement exceeds its benefit—that is, that the marginal social cost curve never intersects the marginal social benefit curve at all, but is higher at all places.[7] This would be true if inefficient antitrust violations never occurred, or if the costs of proving the existence of even a simple price fixing conspiracy were higher than the amount of social benefit that condemnation of the conspiracy would produce.

But others believe that the current level of antitrust enforcement falls short of the intersection with marginal benefit—that society would be wealthier if there were more antitrust enforcement. They would propose more enforcement, usually by means such as broader rules of standing, damages actions for indirect purchasers, broader parens patriae actions, easier and more frequent use of class actions, changes in certain presumptions and burdens of proof, more rules of *per se* illegality, and perhaps even changing the damages multiplier from treble to some higher number.[8]

Even if courts could identify antitrust violations with absolute precision and every activity branded as an antitrust violation were inefficient, an unlimited amount of enforcement would nevertheless not be optimal. Sooner or later the cost of enforcement would exceed the benefits.

The social costs of enforcement loom larger when we consider that courts are not always able accurately to distinguish competitive from anticompetitive conduct. The more private enforcement there is, the more likely that the enforcement, at the margin, will be in areas where courts are prone to error. For example, predatory pricing is a "marginal" offense. The costs of litigating it are relatively high, as is the likelihood that the court will make an error.[9] A likely result is many potential defendants (not merely the ones involved in litigation) avoid aggressive pricing for fear of litigating a predatory pricing case, even though they might eventually win. Although the antitrust laws provide costs and attorneys fees for prevailing plaintiffs, they make no similar provision for prevailing defendants. The social cost of the rule against predatory pricing must include not only the costs of litigating the two or three cases in which predation is proved, but also the dozens of cases in which the defendants eventually prevail. The more ambiguous the offense, the larger these costs become.

§ 17.1c. Using Damages to Minimize the Social Cost of Antitrust Violations

As Gary Becker once noted, the costs of harmful conduct and the system of preventing it are of three kinds: 1) the costs imposed by the conduct itself; 2) the costs of detecting, apprehending and determining the guilt of alleged violators; 3) the costs of imposing sanctions on condemned violators.[10] An optimal antitrust policy would minimize the sum of these three costs. However, the costs are not independent of each other. Sometimes one cost will rise as another declines. For example, the substantive law of antitrust is calculated so as to minimize costs of the first type: a well-designed antitrust policy will condemn socially costly acts and approve socially beneficial ones. By contrast, the *per se* rule is designed to

7. For example, L. Thurow, The Zero–Sum Society 145–148 (1980); a somewhat more moderate position is R. Bork, The Antitrust Paradox: A Policy at War With Itself (1978; rev. ed. 1993).

8. E.g., R. Lande, Are Antitrust "Treble" Damages Really Single Damages?, 54 Ohio St. L.J. 115 (1993) (arguing against proposals to limit antitrust damages and, more generally, that treble damages are often insufficient); L. Sullivan, Monopolization: Corporate Strategy, the IBM Cases, and the Transformation of the Law, 60 Tex.L.Rev. 587 (1982); R. Pitofsky, The Political Content of Antitrust, 127 U.Pa.L.Rev. 1051 (1979). In the special context of merger enforcement, see J. Brodley, Antitrust Standing in Private Merger Cases: Reconciling Private Incentives and Public Enforcement Goals, 94 Mich. L. Rev. 1 (1995) (arguing for broader private plaintiff standing in numerous areas).

9. See Ch. 8.

10. G. Becker, Crime and Punishment: An Economic Approach, 76 J.Pol.Econ. 169, 181 (1968); an application of Becker's argument to antitrust damages actions is W. Schwartz, An Overview of the Economics of Antitrust Enforcement, 68 Geo.L.J. 1075 (1980).

minimize costs of the second type—in this case, the costs of operating the system that determines when the antitrust laws have been violated. Expansive use of the *per se* rule (either of legality or illegality) might well reduce costs of the second type substantially; however, the reduction would probably cause an increase in costs of the first type. For example, if too many practices are declared *per se* legal without elaborate inquiry into their rationale and likely effect, underdeterrence and socially costly antitrust violations will be encouraged. By contrast, if too expansive a rule of *per se* illegality is used, the result will be overdeterrence and some socially beneficial practices will be condemned.

The same thing generally applies to punishment costs. Too expansive a law of damages will encourage too many private plaintiff filings, give plaintiffs an incentive to litigate longer, and to hold out for higher settlements. The result will be increased costs of the second type. At the same time, an overexpansive law of damages and the excessive filings caused thereby will dissuade firms from engaging in competitive practices calculated to injure competitors but which might later be characterized as antitrust violations. This will also increase costs of the first type. The greater the room for misinterpretation, or the greater the uncertainty about the law, the greater these social costs become.

Finally, antitrust law, just as all other areas of law, must deal with the problem of marginal deterrence.[11] Deterrence works because people find certain kinds of punishment unpleasant, and some kinds more unpleasant than others. For example, large fines are less pleasant than small fines and long prison sentences are less pleasant for most people than short ones. The marginal deterrence argument says, quite simply, that if both robbery and murder are punishable by death, the person who has just committed a robbery will have no disincentive to kill his victim as well. The chances of detection might be less once the victim is out of the way, and the punishment will be no greater. By contrast, if robbery is punishable by ten years in prison and murder by death, then the person who has just committed a robbery will be forced to balance the decreased chances of detection that might result from killing the victim against the greatly increased expected cost of punishment.[12]

The marginal deterrence argument applies to antitrust. For example, there is probably a correlation between the size of a cartel's monopoly overcharge and the chance of detection: a cartel which pushes the price of widgets from a competitive level of $1.00 to $1.20 is less likely to be detected than a cartel that pushes the price up to $2.50.[13] Since private damages actions yield three times the monopoly overcharge, the "fine" that a violator must pay if it is caught will be substantially larger if the price increase is larger. When the cartel members calculate the increased probability of detection *and* the increased size of the expected fine, they may well decide to be content with the relatively small $1.20 cartel price. The result is that the cartel will probably impose smaller losses on society.[14] However, if all instances of price fixing were punished by a fine of $1,000,000, then the cartel would consider only the increased likelihood of detection and might well conclude that the larger monopoly overcharge would be better. If the probability of detection does not vary with the amount of the overcharge, a uniform fine of $1,000,000 would give the cartel no legal incentive to charge a lower rather than a higher cartel price.

11. For the history of marginal deterrence in the common law tradition, see H. Hovenkamp, The Marginalist Revolution in Legal Thought, 46 Vand. L. Rev. 305 (1993).

12. See G. Stigler, The Optimum Enforcement of Law, 78 J.Pol.Econ. 526, 527 (1970); Block and Sidak, note 5, at 1134.

13. See M.K. Block, F.C. Nold & J.G. Sidak, The Deterrent Effect of Antitrust Enforcement, 89 J.Pol.Econ. 429, 431 (1981).

14. However, the social cost of a cartel includes 1) the monopoly deadweight loss; 2) the cartel's enforcement costs; and 3) the length of time the cartel exists. If (3) goes up as (1) goes down, the welfare effect of the change may not be positive.

§ 17.2 The Optimal Deterrence Model for Antitrust Damages

§ 17.2a. *Victim's Losses v. Violator's Gains*

The rationale for private antitrust damage actions could be either compensation or deterrence. The goal of an enforcement system based on compensation is to restore injured parties to their position had the violation not occurred. The goal of an enforcement system based on deterrence is to identify some optimal level of violations that should be eliminated, and make that level of violations unprofitable by imposing costs on prospective violators.

An *economic* model for assessing the optimal level of antitrust damages will employ a deterrence rationale, making conduct unprofitable precisely to the extent that it is inefficient. As a result, there is a correlation between the expected profitability of harmful conduct and the proper measure of damages needed to deter it.

But there may be little correlation between the expected profitability of inefficient conduct and the amount of harm caused to injured plaintiffs. For example, the profitability of predatory pricing depends on the number of sales that the successful predator eventually makes at a monopoly price, multiplied by the amount of the monopoly overcharge.[1] This number likely bears no relation to the losses suffered by the competitor driven out of business by the predation. There may be a better correlation between the profitability of the post-predation monopoly pricing and the amount of the injury to the monopolist's customers. Here, however, the monopoly profits must be reduced by the costs that the predator encountered during the predatory period. The consumer's overcharge injuries reflect no such discount.

Courts have not often taken sides in the theoretical battle over whether compensation or deterrence should be the goal of private antitrust enforcement. The Supreme Court has said that *both* compensation and deterrence are legitimate goals of private treble damages actions.[2] But the goals of compensation and deterrence are inconsistent with each other, certainly in the face of our present system of legal rules and the high costs of enforcement. Forced payment of compensation, multiplied by three, to every person who could show he was injured by an antitrust violation would almost certainly yield outrageous overdeterrence. By contrast, optimal deterrence can be achieved only by our refusal to compensate some people whose injuries were in fact caused by antitrust violations.[3]

In the vast majority of litigated cases, damages are assessed and computed in ways far more consistent with a compensation model than with any deterrence model.[4] Arguably, in consumer actions for overcharge injuries there is some reasonable relationship between the way damages are measured and the optimal level of deterrence. In competitor actions for injuries caused by exclusionary practices, however, the existing case law simply admits of no such correlation. For all practical purposes the law of damages in competitor actions is based on compensation rather than deterrence.

§ 17.2b. *Optimal Damages for Overcharge Injuries*

Consider first the relatively simple situation of the single-firm monopolist charging its short-run profit-maximizing price. In Figure 2, on the following page, the competitive price would be P_c and output Q_c, but the monopolist reduces output to Q_m and raises price to P_m.

§ 17.2

1. See § 8.4.

2. See Pfizer, Inc. v. Government of India, 434 U.S. 308, 314, 98 S.Ct. 584, 588, rehearing denied, 435 U.S. 910, 98 S.Ct. 1462 (1978); Brunswick Corp. v. Pueblo Bowl–O–Mat, Inc., 429 U.S. 477, 485–86, 97 S.Ct. 690, 695–96 (1977). The Court came a little closer to declaring a preference for deterrence in Illinois Brick Co. v. Illinois, 431 U.S. 720, 746, 97 S.Ct. 2061, 2075, rehearing denied, 434 U.S. 881, 98 S.Ct. 243 (1977), when it said that the two-thirds of the treble damages above the compensatory amount were designed to supplement public enforcement by the creation of "private attorneys general."

3. See W. Schwartz, Private Enforcement of the Antitrust Laws: An Economic Critique 28–32 (1981).

4. See §§ 17.5–17.6.

Rectangle 2–3–5–4 represents a wealth transfer from consumers to the monopolist, while triangle 4–5–6 represents the traditional "deadweight loss" caused by the monopolist's output reduction. Traditionally economists have identified triangle 4–5–6 as the social cost of monopoly, while they have considered rectangle 2–3–5–4 as a transfer payment that has no effect on the overall wealth of society.[5]

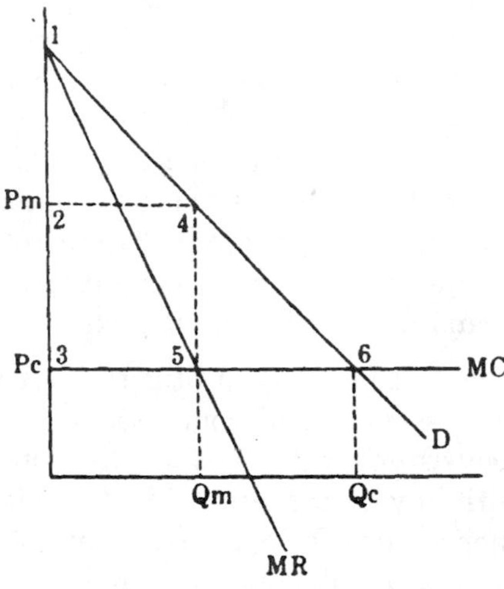

Figure 2

If the demand curve is perfectly linear and the firm's marginal costs are constant, line 3–5 is the same length as line 5–6, and the deadweight loss triangle is precisely one half the size of the wealth transfer rectangle.[6] Assuming the rectangle represents $1000, the monopoly makes the monopolist $1000 richer, the customers who continue to buy $1000 poorer, and generates a lost value, which does not accrue to anyone, of $500.

Assume that the antitrust laws give an action for treble damages and that the possibility of detection and successful prosecution is precisely 1 in 3. The expected costs of a violation to a violator are the amount of damages times the damages "multiplier" (3, in the case of the federal antitrust laws) multiplied again by the likelihood that the violator will have to pay the damages, in this case ⅓. In this hypothetical case the damages multiplier and the risk of detection cancel each other out and the expected cost of the violation will equal whatever damages the legal rule compels. This analysis initially ignores the cost to the defendant of litigating the antitrust claim, and of paying the plaintiff's costs and attorney's fees if the plaintiff should prevail.

Even though triangle 4–5–6 is the efficiency loss created by the monopoly, a damages policy designed to maximize efficiency would *not* set damages equal to the deadweight loss triangle: that is, the optimal rule would not require the defendant merely to pay damages equal to the social cost of his activity. The expected cost of the violation on that basis is $500, while the expected gain from the activity is $1000. The violator will engage in the activity even though it is socially costly. The damages payment is a transfer payment made after the fact. If the social cost of this monopoly is $500, payment of the $500 to the plaintiff does not in any way correct or "eliminate" the social cost of the monopoly. The purpose of the deterrence model is to ensure that an inefficient monopoly will never occur in the first place.

By contrast, a rule that measured damages by either the amount that the violator gained or by the amount that purchasers lost would reduce the expected value of the monopolization to zero. In this case, if the expected level of the fine were $1001.00 no profit-maximizing firm would engage in the illegal activity.[7]

The problem becomes more complicated when we consider a possibility that is frequently addressed in earlier chapters of this book: that an antitrust violation simultaneously increases both the efficiency and the market power of the participants. For example, a horizontal merger or joint venture involving firms that dominate a relevant market may give the

5. See §§ 1.2–1.3.

6. This is because if the demand curve is linear, the marginal revenue curve will also be linear and its slope will be exactly double that of the demand curve. See § 1.2a.

7. The analysis assumes that the firms are risk neutral. If they are risk averse, a lower fine would be sufficient. See M. Polinsky & S. Shavell, The Optimal Tradeoff Between the Probability and Magnitude of Fines, 69 Amer.Econ.Rev. 880 (1979).

firms the power to increase price by reducing output. At the same time, it may permit them to lower their costs. Courts are generally incapable of "balancing" the increased market power that might arise in such circumstances against the increased efficiencies. Rather, they condemn mergers and joint ventures that create a substantial danger of monopoly pricing, and generally ignore offsetting efficiencies, except in the clearest circumstances.[8]

However, the one person or group of persons arguably in a position to measure the efficiencies and assess their value are the participants themselves. This raises the possibility that, although the substantive law of antitrust cannot "net out" efficiencies and increased market power, perhaps the law of damages can. Consider Figure 3, which illustrates the consequences of a merger or joint venture of competitors that simultaneously gives the participants increased market power and increased efficiency. Before the joint venture, the firms faced costs of C_2, output was equal to Q_c, and price equal to P_c. After the inception of the joint venture the firms acquire substantial market power, but their average costs drop from C_2 to C_1. They now determine price and output by the intersection of their new, lower marginal cost curve and their marginal revenue curve. They reduce output to Q_{m1} and raise the price to P_{m1}.[9]

In this case, triangle 4–5–7 represents the deadweight loss produced by the firms' increased market power, while rectangle 2–3–6–5

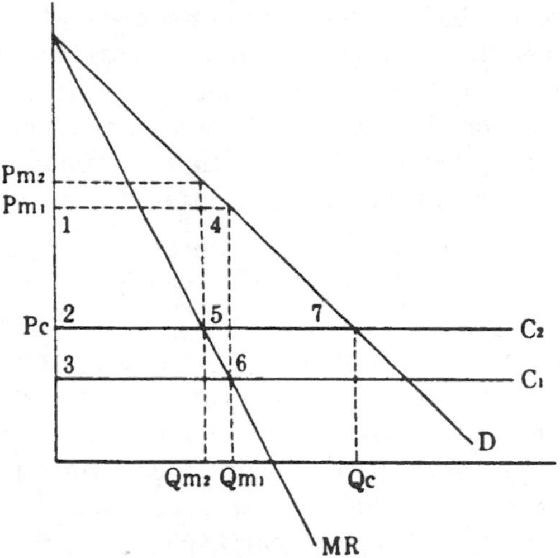

Figure 3

represents the efficiency gains achieved by their increased productive efficiency. The merger or joint venture will be efficient on balance if rectangle 2–3–6–5 is larger than triangle 4–5–7.[10] The merger is characterized as "efficient" in this case *even* though price P_{m1} is higher than price P_c, because the additional cost to consumers is merely a wealth transfer, not a social loss. That is, the merger or joint venture may be efficient, but most of the benefits of the increased efficiency accrue to the participating firms, not to consumers.[11]

Suppose that the area of rectangle 1–2–5–4 (the monopoly wealth transfer) is 1000, the area of triangle 4–5–7 (the deadweight loss) is 400, and the area of rectangle 2–3–6–5 (the efficiency gain) is 500. In this case the gain to the participants from the merger or joint ven-

8. See § 12.2.

9. See W. M. Landes, Optimal Sanctions for Antitrust Violations, 50 U.Chi.L.Rev. 652 (1983).

10. See O. Williamson, Economies as An Antitrust Defense: the Welfare Trade–Offs, 58 Amer.Econ.Rev. 18 (1968).

11. However, some of the benefits of the efficiency will accrue to consumers even if price P_{m1} is higher than price P_c. If no efficiencies were created the market price would be determined by the intersection of the original cost curve, C_2, and the marginal revenue curve. In that case the monopoly price would be P_{m2} in Figure 3; and output would be reduced to Q_{m2}.

It is also possible that a merger or joint venture that simultaneously creates market power and efficiencies will yield a profit-maximizing price lower than the former, competitive price. This would occur when the amount of market power created by the venture is relatively small and the increased efficiencies are substantial, as Figure 4 (on the next page) illustrates. Many marginally illegal horizontal mergers probably fall into this category. For example, under the 1992 Horizontal Merger Guidelines a merger between a firm with a 20% market share and a firm with a 5% market share in a market whose HHI exceeds 1800 would probably be illegal. However, the post-merger firm might not exercise substantially more market power than the pre-merger firm. Whether the threat of collusion were higher would depend on other factors in the market. See §§ 12.4c, 12.7. If the available efficiencies are extraordinarily large, perhaps even a merger to monopoly could yield a price reduction. See A.A. Fisher, R.H. Lande, and W. Vandaele, Afterward: Could a Merger Lead to Both A Monopoly and a Lower Price? 71 Calif. L.Rev. 1697 (1983).

ture is 1500. The loss to consumers who continue to purchase from the participants is 1000, and the loss to consumers who substitute away is 400. Total losses are 1400. On balance, the venture is efficient even though consumer losses are substantial.

If the participants' expected damages are limited to the monopoly overcharge paid by customers who continue to buy from the firms, then *any* cost reduction produced by the venture will make the venture profitable. For example, if 1–2–5–4 is $1000, and the expected damages award to be paid to consumer plaintiffs is also $1000, then the joint activity will be profitable to the participants even if the area of rectangle 2–3–6–5 is equal to $1.00. It would not matter that the area of the deadweight loss triangle 4–5–7 might be many times $1.00, and thus the net effect of the venture inefficient. An expected damages award equal to the overcharge would not deter any joint activity that produced an efficiency savings, even if the savings were dwarfed by the deadweight loss.

But suppose that the expected damages is not merely the overcharge, but the sum of the overcharge and the deadweight loss: rectangle 1–2–5–4 plus triangle 4–5–7. The venture will be profitable to the participants *only* if rectangle 2–3–6–5 is larger than triangle 4–5–7. Since the venture is efficient under the same circumstances, a rule of damages that gave plaintiffs a cause of action for the overcharge plus the deadweight loss would make the venture profitable if it were efficient, but unprofitable if it were inefficient. Firms would undertake only efficient ventures. For example, if the monopoly overcharge rectangle were $1000, the deadweight loss triangle $400, and the efficiency gain rectangle $450, the expected damages cost of the venture would be $1400 but the expected gain would be $1450. The venture would be beneficial to society *and* profitable to the participants. They would pursue the venture.

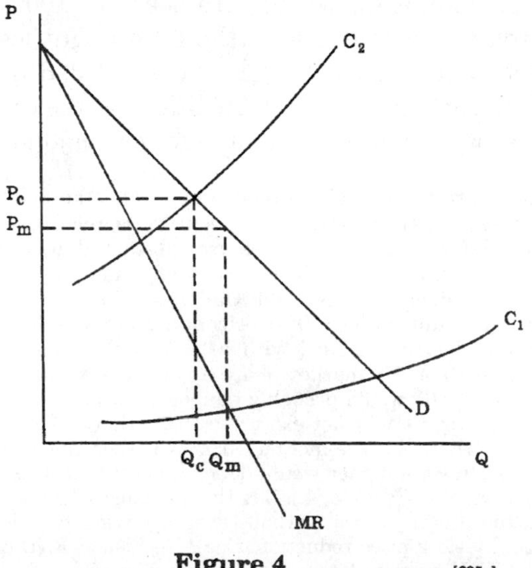

Figure 4 [635a]

As noted above, this assessment of expected damages was premised on the firm's belief that the probability of detection and successful prosecution was one in three. Precisely the same reasoning would hold if the arrangement was absolutely public, so the probability of "detection" were one, but the firms were uncertain about whether the contemplated activity violated the antitrust laws. For example, the blanket licensing agreement at issue in Broadcast Music, Inc. (BMI) v. Columbia Broadcasting System, Inc.[12] was a public price-affecting agreement among sellers who were

12. 441 U.S. 1, 99 S.Ct. 1551, on remand, 607 F.2d 543 (2d Cir.1979). See also National Society of Professional Engineers v. United States, 435 U.S. 679, 98 S.Ct. 1355 (1978), which involved a public agreement among engineers not to bid against each other for contracts; and FTC v. Superior Court Trial Lawyers Assn., 493 U.S. 411, 110 S.Ct. 768 (1990), which involved a public agreement among public defense lawyers to withhold legal services until they received higher fees. In the latter two cases the defendants predicted incorrectly that their agreements would not violate the antitrust laws.

treated as competitors. The arrangement created substantial efficiencies; however, it may also have increased the market power of the licensors, and it did permit them to price discriminate.[13] If *ex ante* BMI had predicted a one-in-three chance that the blanket licensing arrangement would be condemned in an antitrust treble damages action, then it would have undertaken the blanket licensing venture anyway if the efficiencies gained by the venture exceeded the deadweight loss, assuming that the expected penalty would be based on the overcharge plus the deadweight loss. However, if the efficiencies had been less than the deadweight loss, BMI would have foregone the venture. In the *BMI* case there was likely *no* monopoly overcharge: that is, the transactional efficiencies created by the joint venture dwarfed the increased market power so substantially that the joint venture's profit-maximizing price for blanket licenses was lower than the price that would have existed in a competitive market for individual licensing agreements.[14]

At this point it is possible to state a general rule: the best measure of damages for overcharge injuries caused by monopoly pricing should equal the amount of the overcharge plus the deadweight loss. This should be the proper amount even if the agreement among the firms is naked price fixing with no efficiency creation whatsoever. In that case, overdeterrence is not a problem. However, the creation of any efficiency will throw upon the defendants the obligation to compare the efficiency gains produced by their venture against the social losses. Such a rule would permit efficient conduct, even if the conduct is an antitrust violation, but would effectively deter inefficient antitrust violations.

If the costs of litigation, including attorney's fees, are considered, the basic analysis remains the same. Since prevention and enforcement costs are a deadweight loss, the effect of inclusion of these costs is simply to enlarge the deadweight loss that must be balanced against the efficiency gains. For example, if the monopoly overcharge is $1000, deadweight loss from monopoly pricing $400, litigation costs and attorney's fees $50, and efficiency savings $500, the efficiency savings will exceed the sum of deadweight loss and enforcement costs by $50 and the agreement will be profitable. However, if the anticipated litigation costs exceed $100, the agreement will not be profitable; likewise, it would be inefficient. This suggests that the rule requiring defendants to pay costs and attorneys' fees is correct.

§ 17.2c. Optimal Damages for Exclusionary Practices

An "exclusionary practice" is designed by the perpetrator to discipline or exclude rivals so that it can attain or maintain monopoly power. These practices include monopolization and attempt to monopolize, predatory pricing, some concerted refusals to deal and tying arrangements in which the effect is to exclude a rival from the market for the tied product, exclusive dealing, and other forms of vertical integration including vertical restraints. These restraints have in common that they may drive another firm out of business, prevent it from expanding output, or deter it from entering in the first place. The optimal deterrence model suggests that these practices should be condemned if they gave the perpetrator the ability to earn monopoly profits and there were no compensating efficiencies.

But exclusionary practices may be efficient. Further, they may simultaneously be efficient and increase the market power of the participating firms. Courts cannot easily distinguish between competitive and anticompetitive exclusionary behavior, however. Allegations of predatory pricing are often complaints about greater efficiency resulting in lower prices.[15] Tying arrangements, refusals to deal, exclusive dealing and territorial division might all be mechanisms by which a firm improves the efficiency of its production or distribution system. All these practices are efficient if the gains from the increased efficiency exceed any deadweight loss caused by increased market power. By the same token, however, both the

13. See § 5.2.

14. See Figure 4 in note 11.

15. See § 8.4e.

increased efficiency and the increased market power will impose private costs—the former generally upon competitors, the latter generally upon consumers.

An antitrust policy designed to deter inefficient exclusionary practices but permit efficient "exclusionary" practices would assess penalties by looking at the net welfare effect of the practice. Although a court could not quantify efficiency and market power and balance them, the law of damages could arguably be used to shift the obligation to balance to the defendant. If the penalty is the monopoly overcharge plus the monopoly deadweight loss, the practice will be unprofitable if the deadweight loss is greater than the resulting efficiencies, but profitable if the deadweight loss is less than the efficiencies. In short, the damages rule should be the same in exclusionary practices cases as it is in overcharge cases.

The optimal deterrence model's application to the law of exclusionary practices is thus a radical departure from the existing law of damages. Under all prevailing antitrust damages rules for exclusionary practices in lawsuits brought by competitors, the measure of damages is based on the plaintiff's business losses, not on the defendant's monopoly gains and the size of the deadweight loss. Indeed, there is probably no useful correlation between the amount of an injured competitor's lost profits and other consequential damages, and the amount of the monopoly overcharge and deadweight loss caused by the defendant. An efficient practice, which produced no monopoly overcharge and deadweight loss at all, and an inefficient, monopolizing practice might both drive a competing firm out of business. The victim's losses might be precisely the same whether or not the practice was efficient. In one case, however, optimal damages would be zero, in the other very large.

A review of the discussion of the social cost of monopoly in § 1.3 suggests why there is no useful correlation between the amount of an injured competitor's lost profits and the size of the deadweight loss triangle plus the monopoly overcharge. The deadweight loss triangle represents the social cost of monopoly *pricing*—that is, of raising the price to a monopolistic level, with the result that certain persons make inefficient substitutions to different products. By contrast, the injury to the victim of an exclusionary practice such as predatory pricing is a cost of monopolizing *conduct*. If the anticipated return from a particular monopoly is $1,000,000 per year, the firm will be willing to spend any amount up to $1,000,000 per year in acquiring or maintaining its monopoly position. Some of this may be spent in inefficient ways, and thus must be included in the social cost of monopoly.

This analysis reveals the highly static nature of the optimal deterrence model. Under the model no damages are due until after the defendant has engaged in a certain period of monopoly pricing. Suppose a dealer is terminated because its supplier and other suppliers in the same market are in the process of forming a cartel, and are using vertical integration to the retail level to monitor output prices. The terminated dealer is in a relatively good position to know what is going on at the time of its termination. Customer-victims of the cartel may not know until later, after the cartel has succeeded in reducing output and raising price. Indeed, they may never know at all. However, the terminated dealer would not have an action for *damages* until the cartel began operating. Furthermore, the longer the terminated dealer waited before it announced the existence of the cartel and commenced the lawsuit, the greater the damages would be—i.e., since the dealer's damages are measured by the injury suffered by *other* members of society (customers of the cartel) and its own losses are already sunk, the dealer would have an incentive to have those damages be as large as possible.

One radical solution to this problem is to eliminate competitor lawsuits altogether.[16] If the only activities that should be illegal under the antitrust laws are those that are calculated to result in monopoly performance, and if the optimal damages for all instances of monopoly

16. See F. Easterbrook, Predatory Strategies and Counterstrategies, 48 U.Chi.L.Rev. 263, 331 (1981), which proposes this rule for predatory pricing cases; see also F. Easterbrook, On Identifying Exclusionary Conduct, 61 Notre Dame L. Rev. 972 (1986).

performance equal the overcharge plus the deadweight loss, then the best enforcers of the antitrust laws in all instances are customers. Although this might result in a much more efficient level of antitrust enforcement within a static model, it would also eliminate the entire "early warning" system that is now facilitated by competitor lawsuits.[17]

The "early warning" argument cannot be disregarded. The kind of monopoly with which antitrust is concerned is generally "short-run," or of finite duration. Its social cost is a function of its duration. Competitor victims of exclusionary practices are often injured long before consumers are—particularly in cases involving such practices as predatory pricing, where the competitor injury occurs during one time period and consumer injury occurs only later. Further, competitors and other non-consumers, such as terminated employees, are often in a position to detect antitrust violations that may never be detected by consumers.[18] These are values of non-consumer lawsuits that cannot be disregarded, notwithstanding that competitors often have the wrong set of incentives.[19]

The optimal deterrence model for exclusionary practices has other, more analytic shortcomings. It is based on a low estimate of the social cost of monopoly. As § 1.3 noted, the social cost of the kind of monopoly that concerns antitrust consists of three parts: 1) the monopoly "deadweight" loss; 2) the expenses that the monopolizing firm incurs in excluding rivals; and 3) the loss of irreversible investment made by wrongfully excluded rivals. The optimal deterrence model as stated takes costs of the first two types into account, but not costs of the third type. A properly defined model should include the costs to *all* of the victims of a monopolistic practice except those costs that are incurred by the violator.

For example, assume that a challenged practice produced (1) monopoly overcharges of $100, (2) efficiency gains of $60, (3) a deadweight loss of $50, and (4) loss of competitor investment of $30. The optimal deterrence model indicates damages equal to $150 (overcharge plus deadweight loss). This would make the practice profitable, since it produces profits of $160 (overcharge plus efficiency gain). But the practice is in fact inefficient, because it also caused $30 in loss of competitor investment. A properly defined deterrence model should include as damages the sum of overcharges, deadweight loss *and* loss of competitor investment caused by the exclusionary practice.

The optimal deterrence model suggests damages of zero for failed attempts. Suppose an anticompetitively intended exclusionary practice fails to create a monopoly. Perhaps the dominant firm underestimated ease of new entry or the strength of a rival. For example, the firm attempted predatory pricing but quickly found that the costs exceeded any anticipated benefits. The failed attempt produces no monopoly overcharge, and thus it produces no deadweight loss. Clearly, however, rivals could have been injured. Suppose a firm engaging in predatory pricing forces one rival to shut down, but four other rivals remain, and prices stay as competitive as they had been before. Although the attempt fails, the unrecoverable investments of the rival forced to exit are a social cost of this particular attempt to monopolize. The exiting competitor should be permitted a lawsuit in this case, but damages should be based on the lost investment.[20]

§ 17.2d. The Optimal Deterrence Model in Litigation

The case for adopting the optimal deterrence model wholesale becomes quite weak when we consider the difficulties of using it in litigation. The model requires a court to account for several variables that are usually impossible to measure. For example, the entire discussion of optimal deterrence was predicated on a given probability than an antitrust

17. See § 2.2c; and H. Hovenkamp, Antitrust's Protected Classes, 88 Mich.L.Rev. 1, 31 (1989).

18. See § 16.5b.

19. See generally Hovenkamp, *Protected Classes*, note 17; H. Hovenkamp, Antitrust Policy and the Social Cost of Monopoly, 78 Iowa L. Rev. 371 (1993).

20. See § 16.5a; and see S. Shavell, Deterrence and the Punishment of Attempts, 19 J. Legal Stud. 435 (1990).

violation would be detected. For example, the treble damages rule that we actually have is justified by an assumption that the risk of detection and successful prosecution is precisely one in three.

But administering such a rule requires us to know the probability of detection and successful prosecution *ex ante*. Not only do we have no reliable information about the probability of detection, but it is clear that different antitrust violations produce widely different probabilities of detection. For example, the probability of detection of a corporate merger or of a public joint venture is virtually 100%. The probability of detection of secret price fixing agreements is certainly much lower, or else there would be far fewer such agreements.[21]

But even *within* the class of secret price fixing agreements known by the participants to be illegal, the probability of detection varies with the nature of the agreement. A cartel with a dozen members may be easier to detect than one with three members (unless the government scrutinizes three firm markets much more carefully). A cartel in a market with thousands of small buyers may avoid detection more easily than a cartel with a small number of large, knowledgeable buyers. A cartel in an industry where the costs are well known to outsiders is certainly easier to detect than a cartel in an industry in which costs are unknown. A cartel containing firms with widely differing sizes and levels of efficiency is calculated to invite defection, and the probability of detection may rise as the number of defections increases. A cartel that finds it necessary to incorporate certain facilitating devices, such as basing point pricing, that are hard to disguise from the public, is certainly more likely to be detected than one that can get along without such devices.[22] Finally, it has been argued that the probability of detection varies with the amount of the monopoly price increase—the higher the increase, the greater the likelihood of detection.[23]

Even assuming that through some miracle we could compute the probability of detection for all the various kinds of cartels and then produce some weighted "average" probability of detection, such as one in three, we still would not have adequate information upon which to assess optimal penalties. For example, if we concluded that the average probability of detection of all cartels was one in three, and created a treble damages rule, firms would respond by creating a larger number of cartels for which the probability of detection is less than one in three, and a much smaller number of cartels for which the probability of detection was greater than one in three. As soon as that happened, the weighted average and damages multiplier would have to be computed again.[24]

Our usable knowledge of probability of detection is so scant that any argument that the damages multiplier is used to offset the probability of detection must admit that the choice of treble damages or any other multiplier is an absolute shot in the dark. Treble damages is probably outrageously overdeterrent with respect to some offenses, such as mergers, and underdeterrent with respect to some others, such as naked collusion.

Second, computing optimal damages requires information about the size of the monopoly overcharge *and* of the deadweight loss. Courts have some experience at guessing the size of the overcharge; measuring the size of the deadweight loss is next to impossible. Courts often estimate the overcharge caused by monopoly pricing, for this is the principal basis for damages in consumer-brought antitrust cases. The court takes the price the plaintiff actually paid for the product and subtracts from it the price that would have been charged for the product in a competitive market.

21. There have been some attempts to estimate the probability of detection of cartels overall. See P. Bryant & E. Eckard, Price Fixing: the Probability of Getting Caught, 48 Rev. Econ. & Stat. 531 (1991), which estimates very roughly that between 13% and 17% of cartels are detected and successfully prosecuted.

22. See § 4.6.

23. See M.K. Block, F.C. Nold & J.G. Sidak, The Deterrent Effect of Antitrust Enforcement, 89 J.Pol.Econ. 429, 431 (1981).

24. See H. Hovenkamp, Treble Damages Reform, 33 Antitrust Bull. 233 (1988).

Occasionally there will be another market with a firm and cost structure similar to the market at issue, from which the court can draw some inferences about the competitive price. For example, if St. Louis shoe retailers are convicted of price fixing, the court might look at the Kansas City retail market for shoes in order to determine what the competitive price of shoes should be. If the costs in the Kansas City market are the same as in the St. Louis market, or if any differences can be quantified, then the court will have some fairly reliable information about the competitive price. But often such information is unavailable, because the cartel is nationwide and the structure of foreign markets is too different to invite comparison, because the product is custom-made, or else because there simply are no markets similar enough to support such comparisons. Courts generally respond to these difficulties by saying that once violation and fact of injury are established, the plaintiff and court need only develop an approximation of the amount of the overcharge.[25]

Calculation of the deadweight loss makes calculation of the overcharge look easy. If a demand curve is perfectly linear the monopoly overcharge is equal to twice the deadweight loss, but real world demand curves are seldom linear. As a result, the relationship between deadweight loss and overcharge is not constant but varies from case to case. Furthermore, it presents an empirical question that is certainly beyond courtroom measurement. About the only thing that can be said with any confidence is that when the demand curve is concave the amount of the monopolist's *output reduction* from the competitive level will be larger than it would be if the curve were linear. By contrast, if the demand curve is convex, then the amount of the output reduction from the competitive level will be smaller than it would be if the curve were linear.[26] However, deadweight loss is not a function merely of the output reduction, but also of the amount of consumers' surplus above the output reduction. In order to measure it, the court would have to determine the price that would have existed in a competitive market, reconstruct the demand curve faced by the monopolist, and then compute the size of the deadweight triangle.

The difficulties of applying the optimal deterrence model in litigation suggest that, at least for the time being, courts should retain the system under which damages are calculated on the basis of the plaintiff's losses rather than the defendant's gains. First of all, whether deterrence or compensation is the underlying goal of private antitrust enforcement, a powerful case can be made that the framers of the antitrust laws intended damages as compensation. Most obviously, § 4 of the Clayton Act authorizes a private plaintiff to sue and "recover three-fold the damages by him sustained * * *."[27]

However, an economic as well as a legislative case can be made for compensatory measurement. The view that the purpose of private damages actions is to deter does not necessarily dictate that damages be based on some formula other than computation of the plaintiff's losses. Within a deterrence system, the amount of any potential transfer from defendants to plaintiffs serves both as the potential defendants' incentive to avoid the activity and as the potential plaintiffs' incentive to bring the action. Presumably, a plaintiff's incentive to sue is not strictly a function of the amount of its losses—that is, if all antitrust recoveries were regulated at $1,000,000 many plaintiffs would continue to sue, including some whose injuries were less than $1,000,000 and some whose injuries were far greater. At the time of suit the plaintiff's injuries are "sunk," and the potential recovery must be treated simply as a prospect of future income. Nevertheless, if optimal deterrence damages were so low that plaintiffs were unwilling to undergo the costs and risks of litigation, then optimal deterrence damages

25. See § 17.5.

26. See J. Robinson, The Economics of Imperfect Competition 144 (2d ed. 1969).

27. 15 U.S.C.A. § 15. On the legislative history respecting damages actions, see Hovenkamp, Antitrust's Protected Classes, note 17 at 21–30, 41–48.

would not optimally deter: too few lawsuits would be filed.

Further, there is no reason to believe that compensatory measurement is worse than any other kind of measurement in estimating the optimal amount of damages. Any "optimal damages" rule applied in litigation will end up being so capricious that the resulting recoveries will have only a random relationship with the optimal level of deterrence. In that case, if all rules for estimating damages are equally good (or equally bad), then a strong case can be made that the damages formula should attempt to maximize social wealth in some other way. Two possibilities come to mind. One is to maximize social wealth by reducing the costs of litigation. For example, a rule that all antitrust damages recoveries will be $1,000,000 would eliminate damages "computation" entirely. Once standing, violation and antitrust injury had been established, the plaintiff would be entitled to collect its $1,000,000 and go home.

The alternative rule, which intuitively seems to increase the wealth of society far more, is the compensation rule. At the very least, the compensation rule attempts to quantify the private losses (discounted by gains) of successful plaintiffs. Further, the sum of all private losses, reduced by gains, is the social cost of any activity. Second, if people place any value at all on "redress" or "restoration," then compensatory measurement increases social wealth in a way that cannot be overlooked. Third, our democratic policy as expressed in § 4 of the Clayton Act commands it.

§ 17.3 The Rationale for Treble Damages

Section 4 of the Clayton Act grants a prevailing plaintiff "three-fold the damages * * * sustained."[1] Treble damages for antitrust violations were hardly new with the federal antitrust laws. Already in 1623 the English Statute of Monopolies provided that any person injured by a monopoly "shall recover three times so much as the damages that he sustained by means or occasion of being so hindered * * *."[2] Few legal rules are more firmly rooted in history than treble damages recovery for victims of antitrust violations.

Although the Sherman Act and later the Clayton Act both provided for treble damages, the Congressional Record suggests that the members of Congress spent very little time debating the issue. Indeed, the members of Congress probably did not believe there would be a great deal of private antitrust enforcement.[3]

The rationales given for treble damages in private antitrust actions are manifold. Perhaps the oldest is that the antitrust violator deserves to be punished for his crimes, and mere payment of single damages is not punishment enough. This moral argument has gradually given way to an argument based on general deterrence: since not all antitrust violations are detected, a rule providing only single damages would make antitrust violations profitable.[4]

As the previous section suggests, there is no precise correlation between a particular damages rule and the amount of deterrence provided. Viewed in the most favorable light, the treble damages rule must be characterized as a guess that single damages provides too little deterrence and would permit too many antitrust violations to go unchallenged. Likewise, some higher multiplier, such as tenfold damages, would yield overdeterrence and flood the dockets with unmeritorious actions filed by people seeking a quick settlement from a risk averse defendant. There will never be anything approaching a perfect fit.[5]

§ 17.3

1. 15 U.S.C.A. § 15.

2. 21 Jac. 1, c. 3 (1623).

3. 21 Cong. Rec. 2569 (1890). Senator Sherman originally proposed double damages. After a few amendments, the final proposal for treble damages was modelled largely after the English Statute on Monopolies. H. Thorelli, The Federal Antitrust Policy 212 (1955); H. Hovenkamp, Antitrust's Protected Classes, 88 Mich. L. Rev. 1 (1989).

4. See § 17.2.

5. For a more general discussion, see R. Lande, Are Antitrust "Treble" Damages Really Single Damages?, 54 Ohio St. L.J. 115 (1993).

One thing is clear, however. The treble damages rule has different effects in different areas of substantive antitrust law. Some antitrust violations, such as clandestine price fixing, are quasi-criminal or even criminal in character. A large amount of deterrence and perhaps even moral outrage expressed by punitive damages is appropriate. Other antitrust violations such as mergers generally take place only after the parties have made some kind of calculation that the act is legal. The line between efficiency-creating and efficiency-destroying practices is difficult to locate, and overdeterrence comes with much higher social costs. Furthermore, the case for "punishment" is far weaker.

Congress has entertained proposals that would limit the scope of treble damages recovery in antitrust litigation. For example, one proposal would have provided for treble damages in cases involving *per se* antitrust violations, but single damages for rule of reason violations.[6] A second proposal would have permitted single damages for lost profits, but treble damages for monopoly overcharges.[7] Neither proposal passed.

Although segregating antitrust violations for different damages multipliers is a good idea and might reduce excessive litigation in certain substantive areas, the distinction between *per se* and rule of reason violations is not the appropriate place to draw the line. Nor is the distinction between overcharge and lost profit damages. The most plausible rationale for multiple damages is that they provide a proper deterrent in situations where the chances that the defendant will be caught are relatively small. In that case, however, use of the same multiplier would be overdeterrent in situations where the chances of detection are very high.

The best place to draw the line between different damage multipliers is between "clandestine" or secret violations on one side, and "public" violations on the other. Price fixing, predatory pricing, improper patent infringement suits and some other exclusionary practices would generally fit into the former category in which the secrecy of the violation indicates a damages multiplier. However, mergers and joint ventures of public record, refusals to deal, resale price maintenance and other vertical restraints would fit into the latter category, in which single damages would be more appropriate. Most mergers are reported in the press or on the internet when they occur. In such cases the inference is strong that the parties undertaking the action did not believe they were violating the antitrust laws. Further, the probability of detection is 100%.

Most vertical restraints must also be characterized as more public than clandestine. Although the "offense" in such cases is not always obvious to the public, the victim (and most frequently the subsequent plaintiff) is usually a party to the agreement in which the offense was contained. For example, the general public may not have very good knowledge about the "tying arrangement" under which a franchisor requires its franchisees to lease their locations from the franchisor as a condition of obtaining the franchise. However, the plaintiff in such cases is invariably the franchisee, not consumers, and the franchisee is a party to the agreement containing the tying arrangement.[8] Detection of violators in such situations is not a problem, assuming that the franchisee is the person who bears the cost of the violation.

The second problem with dividing treble and single damages actions between *per se* and

6. See the draft of Reagan Administration Legislation on Antitrust, Patents, and Joint Research and Development Ventures, 44 Antitrust & Trade Regulation Report (BNA) 1272 (June 30, 1983), which would abolish treble damages and grant only single damages except with respect to "agreements or practices the nature or necessary effect of which is so plainly anticompetitive that they are deemed unreasonable and therefore illegal without elaborate study in each individual case as to the precise harm they have caused or the business justification for their use * * *."

7. Antitrust Remedies Improvements Act of 1986, Trade Reg. Rptr. (CCH), Report 744 at 21–22 (Feb. 24, 1986). Both proposals are discussed in H. Hovenkamp, Treble Damages Reform, 33 Antitrust Bull. 233 (1988). For a survey of alternatives, see E.D. Cavanagh, Detrebling Antitrust Damages: An Idea Whose Time Has Come?, 61 Tul.L.Rev. 777 (1987).

8. E.g., Queen City Pizza v. Domino's Pizza, 124 F.3d 430 (3d Cir.), rehearing denied, 129 F.3d 724 (3d Cir. 1997), cert. denied, ___ U.S. ___, 118 S.Ct. 1385 (1998). See § 10.6e.

rule of reason antitrust violations is the complex problem of "characterization" that accompanies a judicial decision whether to apply the rule of reason. For example, although explicit, clandestine price fixing is *per se* illegal, not all agreements among competitors that affect price are illegal *per se*, and it often takes the Supreme Court to tell us which rule should be applied. Likewise, today both the rule of reason and the *per se* rule are applied to tying arrangements, vertical restraints cases, and concerted refusals to deal, depending on the circumstances. Whether a particular act was undertaken in public or in secret with the intent to withhold information from the public, however, is a question of fact.

Finally, a policy of providing treble damages for clandestine activities concealed from the public, and single damages for public activities, would give firms an incentive to "go public" with activities that may be efficient but whose legality is open to some doubt. Exchanges of price information, long-term contractual arrangements, and joint ventures are less likely to be anticompetitive if the public (and the government enforcement agencies) know about them from their inception and are thus able to keep a watchful eye.

§ 17.4 How Accurately Must Damages Be Measured?

Any discussion of the accuracy required in measurement of antitrust damages must begin with one premise: the use of private damages actions to enforce the antitrust laws will be undermined by an unrealistic requirement of precision. When a potential plaintiff calculates the chances that antitrust litigation will be successful, he takes into account the risk that he will not be able to prove damages, or that he will not be able to prove an adequate amount of damages. If the probability that he can successfully make out standing, the substantive violation, and antitrust injury is high, but his estimate of damages will likely be thrown out of court, then the action may not be promising.[1] Any system of antitrust enforcement that takes private damages actions seriously must permit plaintiffs to estimate damages by mechanisms that are reasonably within their reach.

Computation of damages often involves more speculation than determining that a particular act is anticompetitive and should be condemned. For example, proof that a price fixing conspiracy existed and even that it raised the price of some product may be relatively easy to establish, but quantifying the increase can be very difficult. In this case, the overcharge is the difference between the price that would have prevailed in a competitive market and the price actually charged by the cartel. In the competitive market, firms presumably would have sold at marginal cost; however, marginal cost would normally be somewhat higher in the competitive market than it was in the cartelized market.[2] The result is that precise quantification of the cartel overcharge requires not merely knowledge of the defendants' marginal costs—a fact normally out of reach of most courts—but knowledge of what their marginal cost would have been at competitive rates of output. Any legal rule that required the plaintiff to establish this figure with even modest precision would effectively be a rule of nonrecovery.

The Supreme Court has responded to these difficulties by setting a relatively high standard for proof of the *fact* of an antitrust violation and resulting injury, but a lower standard for proof of the amount of damages. As the

§ 17.4

1. Many plaintiffs who did or perhaps could have established a violation have been frustrated by their inability to show damages with sufficient precision. See, e.g., Blue Cross and Blue Shield United of Wisconsin v. Marshfield Clinic, 152 F.3d 588 (7th Cir.1998), cert. denied, ___ U.S. ___, 119 S.Ct. 804 (1999) (plaintiff could not prove damages, but was entitled to an injunction); United States Football League v. NFL, 644 F.Supp. 1040, 1051–1054 (S.D.N.Y.1986), affirmed, 842 F.2d 1335 (2d Cir.1988) (jury could not find actual damages without undue speculation about which losses were caused by defendant's violation and which were caused by its own business decisions and fortunes; nominal damages approved). A particularly good discussion of the kind and degree of permissible speculation or uncertainty is R.D. Blair & W.H. Page, "Speculative" Antitrust Damages, 70 Wash. L. Rev. 423 (1995).

2. That is to say, in the relevant decision making range marginal cost is typically rising, and would thus be higher at the competitive output than the cartel output.

Supreme Court put it in Story Parchment Co. v. Paterson Parchment Paper Co., "there is a clear distinction between the measure of proof necessary to establish the fact that petitioner has sustained some damage and the measure of proof necessary to enable the jury to fix the amount."[3]

The need for relaxed standards of measurement is augmented by the fact that the uncertainty is often caused by the defendant's control of essential information. In price fixing cases, for example, the relevant cost data that will establish the relationship between the defendant's costs and the cartel price are not only exclusively in the control of the defendants, but thoughtful firms engaged in price fixing may have distorted or destroyed these data. Once again, the Supreme Court has responded that the "risk of the uncertainty" in damages measurement which was created by the defendant's own wrongdoing must ultimately fall on the defendant itself.[4]

This proposition can be carried to extremes, however: the defendant's unlawful acts are presumably responsible for the difference between the plaintiff's actual position and its position had the violation not occurred. Measurement of that difference is certain to require some speculation, even if the defendant produces all relevant evidence. A rule that saddled the defendant with the entire risk of uncertainty of measurement would open the door to unlimited speculation by plaintiffs. At the very least, a defendant who cannot rebut a plaintiff's damages claims with facts must be permitted to challenge their plausibility.

Courts have not gone so far as to throw the entire burden of uncertainty upon the defendant. Rather they have required the plaintiff to establish at least a reasonable basis for belief that its damages equal some particular amount. Then the defendant may give evidence that various elements of the plaintiff's claim should be reduced or eliminated. As the Supreme Court assessed the plaintiff's requirement, "while the damages may not be determined by mere speculation or guess, it will be enough if the evidence show the extent of the damages as a matter of just and reasonable inference, although the result be only approximate."[5] This effectively forces the plaintiff and defendant to share the risk of uncertainty. In extreme cases—where it is clear at an early stage that any proof of damage will be highly speculative—the court may dismiss the complaint. The Supreme Court has cited the speculative nature of damage claims as one basis for denying antitrust standing.[6]

The general trend in the lower courts, where most of the antitrust law of damages is made, has been to impose rather strict standards for proof of violation and fact of injury, but to allow greater latitude for estimates of the amount. One result is that well-prepared plaintiffs come into court with economic experts armed with computer-created models that often rest on many debatable but plausible assumptions. *If* the plaintiff had stayed in business but for the antitrust violation, and *if* its share of the market had persisted, *if* the overall market continued to grow at its pre-violation rate, and *if* the rate of return were not changed substantially by new entry, then the plaintiff would have made this amount of profits. The problem with such models is that any particular assumption, taken alone, may be plausible. However, the models frequently compound one "plausible" assumption upon another with the result that the final outcome must be characterized more as "possible" than

3. Story Parchment Co. v. Paterson Parchment Paper Co., 282 U.S. 555, 562, 51 S.Ct. 248, 250 (1931). Accord Coastal Fuels of Puerto Rico, Inc. v. Caribbean Petroleum Corp., 79 F.3d 182, 200 (1st Cir.), appeal after remand, 175 F.3d 18 (1st Cir.1999).

4. See Eastman Kodak Co. v. Southern Photo Materials Co., 273 U.S. 359, 379, 47 S.Ct. 400, 408 (1927):

> * * * a defendant whose wrongful conduct has rendered difficult the ascertainment of the precise damages suffered by the plaintiff, is not entitled to complain that they cannot be measured with the same exactness and precision as would otherwise be possible.

See also Bigelow v. RKO Radio Pictures, 327 U.S. 251, 265, 66 S.Ct. 574, 580 (1946).

5. *Story Parchment*, note 3, 282 U.S. at 563, 51 S.Ct. at 250.

6. Associated General Contractors v. California State Council of Carpenters, 459 U.S. 519, 543–544, 103 S.Ct. 897, 911–912 (1983). See § 16.4.

plausible.[7] Then the line between plausibility and speculation becomes rather difficult to locate. Perhaps nowhere is this more true than in the case of damages actions by precluded firms—plaintiffs who allege that they were prevented by the defendant's violation from ever entering business in the first place. The merits of such damages actions are discussed in § 17.6e.

§ 17.5 Measuring Damages for Overcharge Injuries

17.5a. Introduction; Basic Conceptual Problems

An "overcharge" injury is the injury suffered by a customer who paid a monopoly price for a product purchased from an illegal monopolist or cartel. The term "overcharge injury" may also describe the injury suffered by a seller for whom the price was suppressed by a monopsonist or buyer's cartel,[1] or the injury suffered by the purchaser of an illegally tied product.[2]

The basic common law rule of compensatory damages is that a plaintiff is entitled to an award of damages that will restore him to the position in which he would have been but for the violation. Antitrust generally follows this rule, with the important difference that once the damages are computed, they are trebled. According to the classic formulation for antitrust damages, the plaintiff is entitled to treble the difference between the price he actually paid or received and the price that would have prevailed in a competitive market.[3]

The difference between the price actually paid and the competitive price is not necessarily the correct amount to restore the purchaser to the position in which it would have been absent the violation. When the price is raised to monopoly levels the purchaser will often take actions, such as substituting a different product for part of the monopoly product, that will reduce its total damages. As a result, at least in those situations where the victim is itself a business, lost profits rather than the monopoly overcharge might be a more correct measure of damages.[4] In fact, it has been suggested that the Supreme Court adopted the "overcharge" method of computing damages in Chattanooga Foundry and Pipe Works v. Atlanta only because the plaintiff was unable to show lost profits.[5] The plaintiff was a municipal waterworks that paid a monopoly price for underground pipe. There were no measurable lost profits because the utility passed all its costs on to Atlanta's residents in the form of higher water rates.[6] Not being able to show lost profits—at that time considered the ordi-

7. For some of the problems produced by strings of plausible assumptions see Litton Systems, Inc. v. AT & T, 700 F.2d 785, 822–24 (2d Cir.1983), cert. denied, 464 U.S. 1073, 104 S.Ct. 984 (1984); Malcolm v. Marathon Oil Col., 642 F.2d 845, 858 (5th Cir.1981), rehearing denied, 651 F.2d 1016 (5th Cir.), cert. denied, 454 U.S. 1125, 102 S.Ct. 975 (1981). An event whose chance of occurrence is 50–50 is undoubtedly "plausible." However, the chance that five such events will all fall in the plaintiff's favor is
$\frac{1}{2} \times \frac{1}{2} \times \frac{1}{2} \times \frac{1}{2} \times \frac{1}{2} = \frac{1}{32}$, or 3%.

§ 17.5

1. For example, see American Crystal Sugar Co. v. Mandeville Island Farms, Inc., 195 F.2d 622 (9th Cir.), cert. denied, 343 U.S. 957, 72 S.Ct. 1052 (1952); In re Beef Industry Antitrust Litigation, 600 F.2d 1148 (5th Cir. 1979), cert. denied, 449 U.S. 905, 101 S.Ct. 280 (1980). On monopsony, see § 1.2b.

2. See generally Ch. 10.

3. See Chattanooga Foundry & Pipe Works v. Atlanta, 203 U.S. 390, 396, 27 S.Ct. 65, 66 (1906): "* * * the difference between the price paid and the market or fair price * * *;" see also Reiter v. Sonotone Corp., 442 U.S. 330, 340, 99 S.Ct. 2326, 2331 (1979), on remand, 602 F.2d 179 (8th Cir.1979).

4. However, in 1979, in Reiter v. Sonotone Corp., Id., the Supreme Court recognized that consumers may have damages actions for violations of the antitrust laws. The lost profits measure of damages would be inappropriate for them.

5. Note 3; and see L. Sullivan, Handbook of the Law of Antitrust 788 (1977); J. Harrison, The Lost Profits Measure of Damages in Price Enhancement Cases, 64 Minn. L.Rev. 751, 760 (1980).

6. Actually, to say there were *no* lost profits is not quite correct. Presumably the Atlanta waterworks sold less water when it raised its rates. Thus it might have suffered lost profits even though its rate of return on sales remained constant. However, many utilities face very low elasticities of demand, and the amount of sales lost may have been very small. Furthermore, the monopoly overcharge in the Atlanta waterworks case was in a durable item—steel pipe—whose costs would be calculated into the utility's rate base. Most price-regulated utilities receive a rate designed to give them their operating expenses plus a "fair rate of return" on the capital invested in fixed-cost materials. In that case an overcharge in a fixed-cost item could actually increase the utility's gross profitability, although its rate of return would remain the same.

nary measure of damages in all antitrust cases—the plaintiff sought recovery of the overcharge instead.

Today the overcharge method of computing damages is well established. Although both measures of damage are difficult to compute, overcharges remain easier to calculate in most cases than are lost profits, and the amount of speculation is usually less. The case has been made for a return to the lost profits method of damages computation in overcharge actions, particularly when the injured buyers include both direct and indirect purchasers.[7] But courts have declined the invitation, and the Supreme Court's adoption of the indirect purchaser rule in Illinois Brick Co. v. Illinois[8] makes such a rule unlikely.

The concept of *overcharge* is not self-defining, however. The total amount of monopoly profits in a sale is the difference between the actual price and the seller's marginal cost. The overcharge "caused" by a particular antitrust violation could be considerably less if the market was not performing competitively before the violation occurred. For example, markets conducive to cartelization are likely candidates for oligopoly price leadership or tacit collusion.[9] As a result, the pre-cartel price may not have been a competitive price at all but a monopoly price. At the extreme, a newly formed cartel might decide not to increase its price at all from the pre-cartel, oligopoly level, but merely to organize the market better so that sales will be assigned to the lowest-cost provider.[10] In that case the "overcharge"—as measured by the difference between the pre-cartel and cartel prices—would be zero. However, the "overcharge" as measured by the difference between the cartel price and the competitive price might be quite substantial.

The same situation applies to single-firm monopolists. In Berkey Photo, Inc. v. Eastman Kodak Co.,[11] the plaintiff claimed damages both as competitor and as direct purchaser from the defendant. With respect to the latter, the Second Circuit observed that the defendant Eastman Kodak had already been a monopolist before it engaged in the exclusionary practices alleged to be illegal. A monopolist whose position is lawfully created is generally entitled to charge a monopoly price.[12] As a result, damages should not equal the entire difference between the monopoly price and a competitive price, but rather "the price increment caused by the anticompetitive conduct that originated or augmented the monopolist's control over the market."

This constraint may overlook the fact that not all illegal, anticompetitive conduct raises the monopolist's profit-maximizing price. Many of the exclusionary practices undertaken by the monopolist must be characterized as "mobility barriers"—that is, they are designed not to enable the monopolist to charge a higher price but to prevent its monopoly position from eroding.[13] The cost of monopoly is a function both of the amount of the overcharge and inefficient substitutions, and of the duration of the monopoly. Some exclusionary practices such as sabotage, vexatious litigation, or patent fraud may have little effect on the monopolist's short-run profit-maximizing price

7. See Harrison, note 5 above.

8. 431 U.S. 720, 97 S.Ct. 2061 (1977); see § 16.6.

9. See § 4.2.

10. Such a cartel would be efficient, but nonetheless illegal. Other cartels might operate to make the cartel price more consistent, without necessarily increasing the price. For example, an agreement to engage in basing point pricing might be actionable under the antitrust laws, even though the agreement operated to make tacit price leadership more effective, rather than to enable the sellers to charge a higher price. See In re Plywood Antitrust Litigation, 655 F.2d 627 (5th Cir.1981), cert. dismissed, 462 U.S. 1125, 103 S.Ct. 3100 (1983). The court recognized some of the difficulties in computing a monopoly overcharge, or even in determining whether there was any overcharge at all. It awarded the plaintiffs treble the amount of the "phantom freight" they were forced to pay—that is, the difference between the actual freight from the true shipping point and the freight as billed from the basing point. 655 F.2d at 635.

11. 603 F.2d 263 (2d Cir.1979), cert. denied, 444 U.S. 1093, 100 S.Ct. 1061 (1980). Quotation at p. 297. Accord City of Vernon v. Southern Cal. Edison Co., 955 F.2d 1361, 1371–1372 (9th Cir.), cert. denied, 506 U.S. 908, 113 S.Ct. 305 (1992); Allegheny Pepsi–Cola Bottling Co. v. Mid–Atlantic Coca–Cola Bottling Co., 690 F.2d 411, 415 (4th Cir.1982); Litton Sys. v. Honeywell, 1996–2 Trade Cas. ¶ 71559 (C.D.Cal.). See 3 Antitrust Law ¶ 657b, 1996 WL 634213 (rev. ed. 1996).

12. See § 6.1.

13. See generally ch. 7; S. Salop, Strategic Entry Deterrence, 69 Amer.Econ.Rev. 335 (1979).

but may greatly increase the duration of the monopoly by enabling the monopolist to deter competitive entry. In such cases, however, the proper measurement of damages under the rule in *Berkey Photo* is zero. One example of such conduct is predatory entry deterrence by the monopolist. Suppose that Firm A is a monopolist which for some time has charged a monopoly price of $1.00 for widgets. When Firm B, an aspiring entrant, appears on the scene, Firm A drops its price below short-run marginal cost until Firm B is driven from the market. Then it restores the price to the pre-entry level. In such a case, the proper measure of damages in an action brought by a customer is the difference between the price that the customer is forced to pay and the price that the customer would have paid in a market in which Firm B would have been permitted to enter. It is manifestly *not* the difference between the price Firm A was charging as a legal monopolist and the price that it charged after the predation had done its work.

It may also be difficult for an expert to estimate the damages caused by the particular "anticompetitive conduct that originated or augmented the monopolist's control over the market."[14] We can at least *conceptualize* the difference between a marginal cost price and a price dictated by the intersection of the monopolist's marginal cost and marginal revenue curves. However, assuming that a monopolist was alleged to have committed two or three different exclusionary practices—perhaps predatory pricing, vexatious litigation, and patent fraud—it may be impossible to determine how to assign part of the monopolist's price increase to the patent fraud, part to the vexatious litigation, etc. But this division would be essential to damages recovery if one alleged practice were found to be illegal while the others were not.

The great majority of consumer actions for overcharge damages allege price fixing, not illegal monopolization. Cartel members, unlike monopolists, enjoy no presumption that they already had market power before the illegal act was committed. As a result, the damages rule for price fixing cases is somewhat clearer: the plaintiff is entitled to the difference between the "competitive" price and the cartel price, multiplied by the number of units purchased, multiplied by three.

§ 17.5b. Methods of Measurement: "Yardstick" and "Before-and-After"

Assuming that the cartel price less marginal cost in a competitive market is the correct determinant of overcharge damages, courts would be unable to quantify damages very precisely. They usually cannot measure marginal cost directly. But courts have developed two surrogates for the competitive price. Under the "yardstick" approach the price that prevails in a different market, similar to the cartelized market but presumed to be competitive, becomes the surrogate for the competitive price. Under the "before-and-after" method the price that prevailed in the cartelized market before the cartel came into existence or after it fell apart is presumed to be the competitive price. These two approaches have been used by courts not only to estimate overcharges but also to estimate lost profits in competitor antitrust suits.

17.5b1. Yardstick Method

The yardstick method of estimating damages was approved by the Supreme Court in

14. The Second Circuit's proposal in *Berkey Photo* itself suggests the complexity of damages determination that would follow:

> The wrongful conduct rule indicates that a purchaser can recover for an overcharge paid to a violator of § 2 only to the extent that the price he paid exceeds that which would have been charged in the absence of anticompetitive action. An intermediate step in the analysis may be an attempt to estimate what the monopolist's market share would likely have been but for the illegitimate conduct; it would then be possible to gauge approximately what price the defendant would have been able to charge with that degree of market control.

603 F.2d at 298. See also Hanover Shoe, Inc. v. United Shoe Mach. Corp., 392 U.S. 481, 88 S.Ct. 2224, rehearing denied, 393 U.S. 901, 89 S.Ct. 64 (1968), holding that a monopolist in shoe machinery violated the Sherman Act by refusing to sell its machines, but offering them only under lease. The plaintiff was awarded the "excess of leasing costs over what it would have cost to own the same machines had they been available for purchase." Presumably, however, the defendant's profit-maximizing price was the same regardless of whether it sold the machines or leased them. In that case Hanover's damages would be zero.

1946, in Bigelow v. RKO Radio Pictures, Inc.[15] Under the yardstick method the plaintiff identifies some geographic market that is as similar as possible to the cartelized market, but for the conspiracy. Obviously, the yardstick method has certain inherent limitations. If the conspiracy is worldwide, there will be no other terrestrial geographic market with which the cartelized market can be compared. Even if the conspiracy is nationwide, the problems of comparison are substantial. Different countries tax and subsidize businesses in different ways and, as a result, firms in different countries can face very different costs.[16]

The ideal conspiracy for the yardstick approach is a local cartel where a nearby market can be found which has the same basic cost structure. Adjustments must probably be made for differences in taxes and regulatory fees, costs of transportation, and different wage and salary rates. However, if these differences can be isolated and quantified, an expert economist or accountant should be able to produce a "reconstructed" price that would have prevailed in the cartelized market if it had the same level of competition as exists in the yardstick market.

A good illustration of the method in practice is Greenhaw v. Lubbock County Beverage Assoc.,[17] which involved a price fixing conspiracy among liquor retailers in Lubbock County, Texas. In estimating damages the plaintiff's expert compared prices in Lubbock County during the conspiracy period with those that prevailed in Dallas, which was presumably competitive. First, the expert developed a ratio that reflected cost differentials between the two markets, and from this ratio calculated what were described as "should have been" prices for the defendants' products during the conspiracy years. From these prices the expert was then able to estimate that the cartel overcharged purchasers by about 7.74%. This percentage of the defendants' total sales during the conspiracy period equaled the aggregate monopoly overcharge.

§ 17.5b2. *Before–and–After Method*

While the "before-and-after" method of estimating damages has a longer pedigree than the yardstick method,[18] it can involve even more speculation.[19] Under the before-and-after method, the plaintiff produces evidence about the market price before the alleged cartel was formed or after it ceased to exist, or both. From these data the fact finder is then asked to reconstruct a competitive price during the conspiracy period. Damages are the difference between this reconstructed price and the actual price charged by the cartel.

If the market in which the cartel occurred is concentrated and conducive to price leadership or tacit collusion, a good deal of monopoly overcharge may be built into the pre-cartel price to begin with. As a result, the before-

15. 327 U.S. 251, 66 S.Ct. 574, rehearing denied, 327 U.S. 817, 66 S.Ct. 815 (1946). *Bigelow* applied the yardstick method not to estimation of monopoly overcharge, but to estimation of lost profits. See § 17.6.

16. American anti-dumping legislation currently mandates such international price/cost comparisons, however, for determining both liability and damages. 15 U.S.C.A. § 72. See L. Schwartz, American Antitrust and Trading with State–Controlled Economies, 25 Antitrust Bull. 513 (1980).

17. 721 F.2d 1019, 1026 (5th Cir.1983), rehearing denied, 726 F.2d 752 (5th Cir.1984). See also National Farmers' Org. v. Associated Milk Producers, 850 F.2d 1286, 1294–1298 (8th Cir.1988), cert. denied, 489 U.S. 1081, 109 S.Ct. 1535 (1989) (permitting different geographic area to be used as a yardstick, in spite of numerous differences, but no alternative method seemed any better); Metrix Warehouse, Inc. v. Daimler–Benz Aktiengesellschaft, 828 F.2d 1033, 1044 (4th Cir.1987), cert. denied, 486 U.S. 1017, 108 S.Ct. 1753 (1988) (requiring "reasonable comparability" between plaintiff's market and yardstick market); Home Placement Serv. v. Providence Journal Co., 819 F.2d 1199, 1205–1206 (1st Cir.1987) (same).

18. See Eastman Kodak Co. v. Southern Photo Materials Co., 273 U.S. 359, 378–79, 47 S.Ct. 400, 408 (1927); Story Parchment Co. v. Paterson Parchment Paper Co., 282 U.S. 555, 561, 51 S.Ct. 248, 250 (1931). Like the yardstick method, the before-and-after method was developed to estimate lost profits rather than overcharge injuries. However, today it is used to estimate both. See *Home Placement*, note 17 at 1205 & n. 7 (discussing both methods; finding before-and-after method inadequate for plaintiff who was driven out of business before it was able to compile a record of profits).

19. For a criticism of the before and after method, see Isaksen v. Vermont Castings, Inc., 825 F.2d 1158, 1165 (7th Cir.1987), finding that simple before and after comparison is inadequate, at least when "other causal factors are at work." See also Aluminum Phosphide Antitrust Litigation, 893 F.Supp. 1497 (D.Kan.1995) (criticizing and refusing to admit expert's "before-and-after" damage model for methodological failures).

and-after method may not really measure the difference between the cartel price and a truly "competitive" price at all. More importantly, markets change greatly through time, and the before-and-after model must be adjusted to account for these changes. This problem cannot be solved by the simple device of discounting all dollars to the same value to account for inflation or the Consumer Price Index. The price of some products will rise by much more than the index, while the price of other products will rise by much less. If a substantial change in supply conditions or consumer preference causes a shift in the supply curve or demand curve of the cartelized product, the before-and-after method may substantially overstate or understate the true measure of damages.

For example, using the before-and-after method to estimate the impact of a uranium cartel would exaggerate the monopoly overcharge if the estimator failed to consider that during the same period a cartel in crude oil also came into existence. The price increase for oil would have pushed the price for uranium up even absent the uranium cartel. In this case, the creation of the oil cartel effectively shifted the demand curve for the uranium to the right. If the before-and-after method is to be accurate, it must take the shift into account.[20]

If changes in the demand for uranium unrelated to the existence of the cartel are random, however, they will tend to cancel each other out, provided that we look at a long enough time period. If it is possible to have evidence of the market price *both* before the cartel came into existence and after it broke up, then the measurement is likely to be more accurate. Nevertheless, even the most optimistic assessment of the before-and-after method of estimating damages must conclude that it yields only rough approximations of the price that would have prevailed had the conspiracy not occurred.

Both the yardstick and before-and-after methods of measuring overcharge damages can be facilitated by econometric techniques such as regression analysis. The example that follows, which uses a single linear regression in order to estimate damages, is far simpler than any likely to be encountered in litigation. It is presented in order to illustrate the technique. If a regression model is to be used to estimate damages in litigation, an expert should be employed to create the model, estimate the damages, and usually to defend the model in court. The other side may offer its own expert to testify against the proposed model or offer an alternative model more favorable to its position.[21]

Suppose that macaroni manufacturers are accused of fixing the content of macaroni by agreement at 50% semolina and 50% farina. They do this in order to reduce their demand for durum wheat, from which semolina is made, and thus to depress its price.[22] They are sued for treble damages by growers and sellers of durum wheat. It has been established that the conspiracy existed and was effective during the harvest and buying seasons of 1994, 1995, and 1996. Now the difference between the depressed price and the competitive price must be estimated for those years. Data about production and price have been produced for a ten year period, 1990–1999. All prices have been adjusted to constant dollars.

The evidence shows that during the ten years in question the market price of durum wheat was as follows:

20. The illustration is taken from Uranium Antitrust Litigation, 617 F.2d 1248 (7th Cir.1980).

21. Regression models are also used to estimate lost profits as a result of illegal exclusionary practices. See R.C. Hoyt, D.C. Dahl & S.D. Gibson, Comprehensive Models for Assessing Lost Profits to Antitrust Plaintiffs, 60 Minn. L.Rev. 1233 (1976). Good discussions of such models can be found in W. Breit & K. Elzinga, Antitrust Penalty Reform: An Economic Analysis 63–67 (1986); J. Greenfield & M. Polinsky, The Use of Economists in Antitrust Litigation (A.B.A. Mono. 1984).

22. See National Macaroni Mfrs. Assoc., 65 F.T.C. 583 (1964), affirmed, 345 F.2d 421 (7th Cir.1965). See also Petruzzi's IGA Supermarkets, Inc. v. Darling–Delaware Co., Inc., 998 F.2d 1224, 1238 (3d Cir.1993) (approving similar technique). Cf. In re Plastic Cutlery Antitrust Litigation, 1998–1 Trade Cases ¶ 72,107 (CCH), 1998 WL 135703 (E.D.Pa. 1998) (describing multiple regression technique for estimating damages in price-fixing case).

1990:	$4.50/	bushel	
1991:	$5.00	"	
1992:	$4.00	"	
1993:	$3.00	"	
1994:	$4.00	"	(conspiracy year)
1995:	$3.00	"	(conspiracy year)
1996:	$5.00	"	(conspiracy year)
1997:	$5.00	"	
1998:	$3.00	"	
1999:	$3.50	"	

It is certainly not apparent from these price data how much the conspiracy depressed the price of durum wheat. Although the price of durum may have been lower than average during the conspiracy years, it was not outrageously low, and it was equally low during some nonconspiracy years. Furthermore, in 1996, which was a conspiracy year, the price was substantially higher than it was in several of the nonconspiracy years.

The average price of durum over the ten years was $4.00. Plotting the price of durum for the ten years on the graph in Figure 5 reveals the inconclusiveness of the price data.

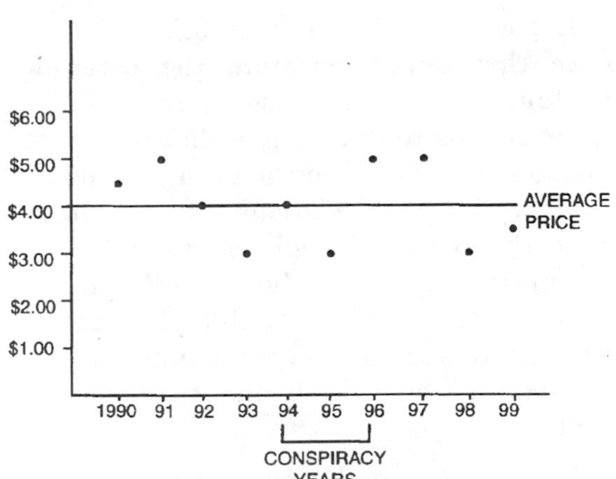

Figure 5

However, the record reveals that the defendants agreed to depress the price of durum during the three conspiracy years because harvests were very bad and the output of durum was much lower than usual. During the ten years in question the harvests of durum were as follows:

1990:	4.7	million	bu.	
1991:	3.7	"	"	
1992:	4.8	"	"	
1993:	7.1	"	"	
1994:	2.9	"	"	(conspiracy year)
1995:	4.6	"	"	(conspiracy year)
1996:	2.6	"	"	(conspiracy year)
1997:	4.2	"	"	
1998:	6.5	"	"	
1999:	6.1	"	"	

The price of durum, like the price of everything else, is a function of the available supply. To be sure, other things, such as consumer tastes or federal regulation and taxation, also affect the price of durum. Likewise, the price of durum will be affected by the price of other products. For example, if the price of a complementary product such as olive oil increases sharply, then the price of durum may decrease. Generally, people who use macaroni products also use olive oil in some constant proportion. A disastrous olive crop might reduce the available supply of olive oil, causing a sharp increase in the olive oil price. If durum is plentiful, however, the chief result of the olive oil shortage will be to reduce demand for durum, and its price will fall. Conversely, if the price of a *substitute* product rises sharply, then the demand for durum will increase and its price will rise. For example, if durum and farina were substitutes in the manufacturing of macaroni, people would respond to a shortage of farina by switching to durum, and the demand for durum would increase.

But let us suppose that these other factors are not notably present. Although consumer taste and the available supply of complementary and substitute products may have had some effect on the price of durum, these effects were both small and were probably unsystematic. If they were truly random, their effects would tend to cancel each other out. So we can say with some confidence that the price of durum during the period 1990–1999 varied inversely with the amount of durum produced in any given year.

Figure 6 shows the relationship between the price and supply of durum during the seven *nonconspiracy* years. Only the nonconspiracy years are plotted, because we want to establish a price function for the nonconspiracy years and then measure how much the price deviated from that function during the conspiracy years.

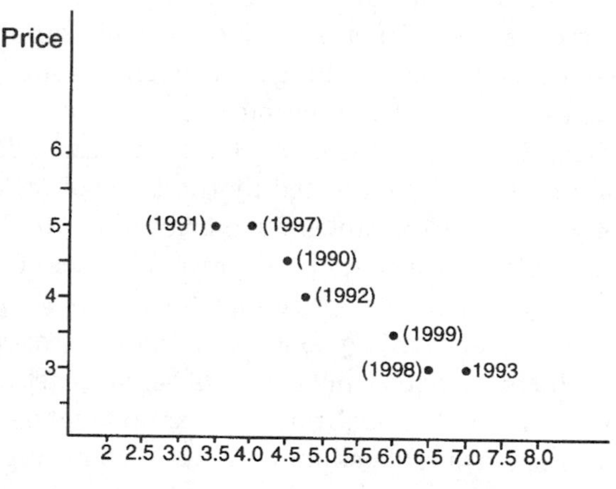

Figure 6

Figure 6 suggests that the size of the harvest and the market price in the nonconspiracy years varied inversely and that the relationship between them may be close to linear—that is, that price rose roughly proportionately to decrease in harvest size. If we could draw a constant curve that accurately described the relationship between price and harvest size in Figure 6, we might have a basis from which to estimate damages during the nonconspiracy years.

The method most generally used to construct such a curve in simple linear regression analysis is identification of a straight line of least squares—that is, a straight line such that the sum of the squares of each datum's deviation from the line is as small as possible. The equation that represents the data in Figure 6, assuming it is a straight line, is:

$$Y = a + bX + E,$$

in which X and Y are the variables, a and b are constants that will determine the slope of the line, and E is the error, or "disturbance," which reflects the amount that each datum on the graph deviates from the line when it is drawn. When the line is properly drawn the sum of the squares of the individual disturbances will be the smallest possible number; furthermore, the amount of error caused by datum entries that are below the line will precisely cancel out the amount of error caused by entries that are above the line; so the net error will be zero.

Importantly, linear regression does not *prove* that deviations from the determined function are random. Rather, linear regression will enable us to draw a line that represents a function determined by a given set of data, *assuming* that all deviations from the function are both relatively small and random. When the function is drawn, the upward and downward deviations will cancel each other out; however, this is because we assumed randomness, and not because the line establishes randomness.

Many of the problems that arise in damages litigation using regression models concern the assumption that a particular disturbance is random. For example, in the earlier illustration about the OPEC cartel's being created during the existence of a uranium cartel, the OPEC cartel would almost certainly have to be treated as a significant nonrandom disturbance: its effect could have been to raise the noncartel price of uranium substantially. In that case the effect of the OPEC cartel on the market for uranium must be computed separately.

If we cannot identify any substantial, nonrandom factors other than supply that might influence the price of durum, our price function will have a slope to conform to the data entered in the graph in Figure 6, such that the sum of the squares of the disturbances, $\Sigma(E^2)$ is, as small as possible. The formula for such a line consists of the following pair of equations:

$$\text{(I) } \Sigma(Y) = Na + b\Sigma(X)$$

$$\text{(II) } \Sigma(XY) = a\Sigma(X) + b\Sigma(X^2),$$

in which N equals the number of data in the sample.[23]

In Figure 6, on the preceding page, the price information was plotted on the X axis and harvest information was plotted on the Y axis; so X = price, and Y = quantity. From the price and harvest information presented above, we can determine the following:

X	Y	XY	X^2
4.50	4.7	21.15	20.25
5	3.7	18.5	25
4	4.8	19.2	16
3	7.1	21.3	9
5	4.2	21	25
3	6.5	19.5	9
3.50	6.1	21.35	12.25
$\Sigma(X) = 28$	$\Sigma(Y) = 37.1$	$\Sigma(XY) = 142$	$\Sigma(X^2) = 116.5$

Substituting these values into the pair of equations above gives us:

$$\text{(I) } 37.1 = 7a + 28b$$

$$\text{(II) } 142 = 28a + 116.5b$$

Multiplying (I) by 4 gives:

$$\text{(I) } 148.4 = 28a + 112b$$

and subtracting (II) from (I) yields:

$$6.4 = -4.5b;$$

$$\text{or } b = -1.42$$

and substituting this into (I) yields a = 10.98.

This means that the function is

$$Y = 10.98 - 1.42X$$

23. There is nothing particularly magic about drawing a function that minimizes the sum of the *squares* of the distances from the plotted data. One could as easily use absolute values, the absolute value of the cubes of the data, or the data raised to the fourth power. Statisticians used least squares largely as a matter of convention. The pair of equations given in the text for producing the line of least squares is derived rather easily. See T. Mirer, Economic Statistics and Econometrics 87–88 (1983); L. Lapin, Quantitative Methods for Business Decisions 88–105 (4th ed. 1988).

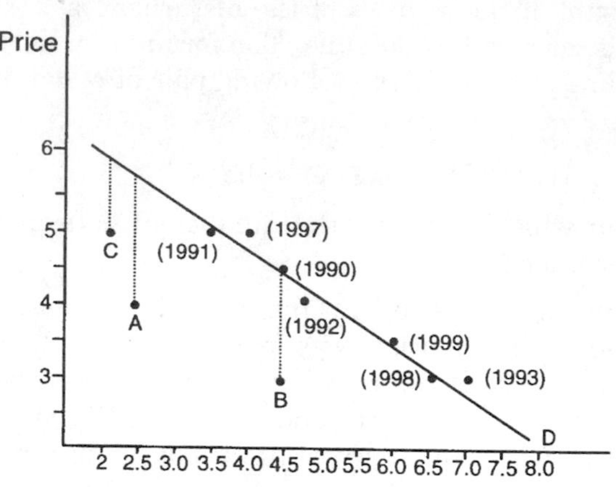

Figure 7

Figure 7 gives the resulting demand curve (D), superimposed over the same data that appeared in Figure 6. Now we can enter the data from the three conspiracy years and measure the amount that the actual price in those years deviated from the "reconstructed" price exhibited on the regression function. Points A, B and C on Figure 7 show the price-harvest size coordinates for the three conspiracy years. Point A reveals that during the first year of the conspiracy the price of durum was depressed about $1.70 per bushel from the competitive price. Point B reveals that during the second year the price was depressed about $1.50. Point C shows that during the third conspiracy year price was depressed about 85¢. Damages for each of those years should equal the amount each plaintiff sold multiplied by the deviation from the reconstructed "competitive price" curve. This amount, of course, must then be trebled.

§ 17.6 Damages for Exclusionary Practices

§ 17.6a. When Are Damages Due?

Any opportunity for monopoly profits naturally attracts new investment. Firms inside the market will try to increase output, and firms outside will try to enter. The monopolist or aspiring monopolist may respond by various acts designed to discourage such competition. These acts include the "exclusionary practices" identified by courts as supporting a Sherman § 2 monopolization or attempt offense.[1] Acts thought to facilitate monopoly pricing also include tying arrangements in which the injury falls upon a competitor in the tied product market, and exclusive dealing contracts, concerted refusals to deal and other concerted conduct. More problematically, they may also include mergers, resale price maintenance and nonprice restraints.

In all these cases, the plaintiff generally claims damages for what may be loosely characterized as lost profits. The basis of the loss may be a reduction in market share, a smaller markup per unit sold, an existing firm's loss of investment or business assets, or preclusion from entry into a profitable business. In most such cases, the measure of damages is so imprecise that "loss of the opportunity to do business" would describe the plaintiff's loss more accurately than "lost profits," which suggests a sum that is quantifiable with a fair amount of precision.

When a plaintiff proves the existence of a price fixing conspiracy and demonstrates that she purchased the cartelized product, the inference is strong that the plaintiff suffered anticompetitive injury. In the case of exclusionary practices, the inference of anticompetitive injury is more ambiguous, even if the fact of the antitrust violation is clearly established. Under the "antitrust injury" doctrine developed in Brunswick Corp. v. Pueblo Bowl-O-Mat, Inc.,[2] the plaintiff may recover damages only for anticompetitive injury—that is, injury which "flows from that which makes defendants' acts unlawful."

This ambiguity in the relationship between conduct and injury in exclusionary practices cases results from two things. First, the phenomenon that governed the *Brunswick* decision itself was the "incipiency" test under

§ 17.6

1. See Chs. 6–8.

2. 429 U.S. 477, 489, 97 S.Ct. 690, 697 (1977). See § 16.3.

which conduct is evaluated under the Clayton Act. Practices such as mergers, tying arrangements and exclusive dealing are illegal when they merely "tend to" create a monopoly, or where their effect "may be" substantially to lessen competition.[3] Under the incipiency test, conduct is often condemned on the theory that if it were allowed to continue, monopoly might emerge at some future time, even though it has not done so yet. The most extreme form of the incipiency test is applied to mergers. Even under the relatively lenient standards established in the 1992 Horizontal Merger Guidelines, the threshold of illegality for mergers is far lower than will support any inference that the post-merger firm is a monopolist or is actually engaging in collusion or an exclusionary practice.[4]

The incipiency test raises the likelihood that conduct condemned under the Clayton Act has not caused any anticompetitive injury at all at the time of litigation. In such cases injunctive relief might be appropriate: the private plaintiff might wish to protect itself from threatened anticompetitive conduct. However, damages based on anticompetitive injury will not be owing until anticompetitive injury has actually occurred.[5]

The second problem with private damages actions for exclusionary practices is more pervasive, and is a function of severe limitations on the judicial fact-finding process. By definition, anticompetitive acts cause *public* injuries. Competition is that state of affairs that maximizes social wealth, and any deviation from competition impoverishes society as a whole. But private plaintiffs do not sue in order to vindicate public injuries. They wish to vindicate private injuries—their own. Unfortunately, both efficiency-creating and efficiency-destroying practices can cause substantial private injuries. The problem is particularly acute when the plaintiff and defendant are competitors, for nothing succeeds like efficiency in injuring one's competitors.[6]

If one principle can be said to underlie the "antitrust injury" doctrine developed in *Brunswick*, it is that a plaintiff should be able to recover damages only if its own private injury and injury to the public coincide in some way. Many efficiency-creating practices are of marginal legality at the time they are undertaken. A rule that permitted a plaintiff to recover for all injuries once an antitrust violation is shown to have occurred could yield outrageous overdeterrence. That in turn could encourage firms to avoid efficient, aggressive conduct that might subsequently be characterized as an antitrust violation.

§ 17.6b. Damages for Lost Sales and Market Share

In most cases involving exclusionary practices the plaintiff seeks compensation for what is generally characterized as "lost profits."[7] Such actions include competitor lawsuits alleging illegal monopolization, attempt to monopolize or predatory pricing, tying arrangements or exclusive dealing, illegal mergers, concerted refusals to deal, and violations of the Robinson–Patman Act. Also included are actions brought by firms who deal with or formerly dealt with the defendant, such as terminated distributors or retailers. The latter lawsuits

3. For example, see Brown Shoe Co. v. United States, 370 U.S. 294, 317, 82 S.Ct. 1502, 1520 (1962), noting that the Celler–Kefauver amendments to § 7 of the Clayton Act were designed to arrest mergers "at a time when the trend to a lessening of competition * * * was still in its incipiency."

4. See § 12.4.

5. See § 16.9; and P. Areeda, Antitrust Violations Without Damage Recoveries, 89 Harv.L.Rev. 1127 (1976). See also Blue Cross and Blue Shield United of Wisconsin v. Marshfield Clinic, 152 F.3d 588, 591 (7th Cir.1998), cert. denied, ___ U.S. ___, 119 S.Ct. 804 (1999) (awarding an injunction when plaintiff could show causation but not damages because there was no way of measuring the latter).

6. See § 2.2c; and H. Hovenkamp, Merger Actions for Damages, 35 Hastings L.J. (1984).

7. For example, H.J., Inc. v. ITT, 867 F.2d 1531, 1549 (8th Cir.1989) ("the present value of profits lost as a result of [the defendant's] improper actions"); Sciambra v. Graham News, 841 F.2d 651, 657 (5th Cir.1988) (lost profits, or going concern value as an alternative for firms excluded entirely from the market). See also Los Angeles Memorial Coliseum Commission v. National Football League, 791 F.2d 1356, 1367 (9th Cir.1986) ("A plaintiff's antitrust damages are to be calculated 'by a comparison of profits, price and values as affected by the conspiracy, with what they would have been in its absence under freely competitive conditions.' ").

often allege illegal vertical price or nonprice restraints. However, they might also allege any one of the antitrust violations listed above.

Once standing, violation, causation and antitrust injury have been established,[8] computation of damages in such cases is generally the same regardless of the nature of the substantive violation. However, the nature of the violation and the pre-litigation relationship between the defendant and plaintiff will be a factor in the court's decision about how much of the plaintiff's injury was caused by the defendant's violation and how much resulted from the plaintiff's own actions or from other causes.

Actions for "lost profits," or loss of the opportunity to do business, are generally of three kinds: 1) actions in which the plaintiff continues to be a going concern but alleges that it lost sales or market share as a result of the defendant's violation, or that the antitrust violation increased its cost of doing business; 2) actions in which the plaintiff alleges that it was put out of business by the violation;[9] 3) actions in which the plaintiff alleges that the violation precluded it from ever entering business in the first place.

In all cases the principle underlying the computation of damages is that the plaintiff is entitled to be put in a position, ignoring trebling, that it would have been in had the anticompetitive conduct not occurred. This generally means that the court must entertain certain assumptions that cannot be established with anything approaching certainty—for example, that the plaintiff's business would have continued to do as well as it did before the violation occurred.

When the plaintiff was established in business before the violation occurred and remains in business thereafter, courts generally estimate the plaintiff's loss by one of three methods: the "before-and-after" method, the "yardstick" method, or the "market share" method. The first two of these methods are also used to estimate overcharge damages, and are discussed in that context in § 17.5b as well.

§ 17.6b1. Before-and-After Method

In the "before-and-after" method the court looks at the plaintiff's business before the violation occurred, during the violation period, and after the violation ended, and estimates the amount that the violation reduced the plaintiff's profits. In its simplest form the theory looks at the plaintiff's net profits before and after the injury period, discounts all dollars to their present value, and gives the plaintiff a sum that, before trebling, will bring its earnings during the injury period up to the same average level as its earnings during the noninjury periods.[10] For example, suppose that the plaintiff establishes that the defendant engaged in predatory pricing during the years 1995–1998. The plaintiff's profits for the period 1992–1999, in constant dollars, were as follows:

1992:	$60,000	
1993:	$50,000	
1994:	$60,000	
1995:	$35,000	(violation year)
1996:	$20,000	(violation year)
1997:	($5,000)	(violation year)
1998:	$10,000	(violation year)
1999:	$50,000	

The plaintiff's average profits during the nonpredatory years were $55,000. Before trebling, the plaintiff is entitled to an amount that will bring its profits up to $55,000 for each of the predatory years—$20,000 for 1995, $35,000 for 1996, $60,000 for 1997, and $45,-000 for 1998. The plaintiff's damages will be

8. See Ch. 16.

9. For example, Sciambra v. Graham News Co., 841 F.2d 651, 657 (5th Cir.1988) (terminated dealer).

10. See Story Parchment Co. v. Paterson Parchment Paper Co., 282 U.S. 555, 566, 51 S.Ct. 248, 251–52 (1931); Bigelow v. RKO Radio Pictures, 327 U.S. 251, 266, 66 S.Ct. 574, 580 (1946); Godix Equipment Export Corp. v. Caterpillar, Inc., 948 F.Supp. 1570, 1584 (S.D.Fla.1996), aff'd, 144 F.3d 55 (11th Cir.1998) (approving before-and-after method of calculating lost profits in principle, but disapproving it in this case because plaintiff had failed to establish causation). See generally E. Timberlake, Federal Treble Damage Antitrust Actions § 21.05 (1965); C. Goetz, The Basic Rules of Antitrust Damages, 49 A.B.A. Antitrust L.J. 125 (1980); A.L. Parker, Measuring Damages in Federal Treble Damages Actions, 17 Antitrust Bull. 497 (1972).

$160,000 x 3, or $480,000.[11]

Obviously, the above example ignores dozens of contingencies that could affect profitability in any market. At one time courts were generally of the view that the highly contingent nature of the before-and-after approach rendered such damages estimates far too speculative.[12] In Bigelow v. RKO Radio Pictures,[13] however, the Supreme Court held that any imprecision in the calculation of damages was the result of the defendant's wrongful conduct; therefore the defendant should bear the risk of any uncertainty of measurement.

If the contingencies affecting the plaintiff's profitability are random or unknown, the before-and-after method is as likely to understate as to overstate the plaintiff's loss. As a result, simple use of the method without consideration of truly random or completely unknown contingencies does not really transfer the risk of uncertainty to the defendant but rests it equally on both parties. However, the advantage is clearly with the plaintiff if the plaintiff is permitted to have every plausible assumption respecting a nonrandom element in its favor.

Information about the plaintiff's performance during the noninjury years may force some adjustment of the before-and-after computation. For example, if the plaintiff's profits and market share were decreasing steadily even before the violation, then a mere average of the plaintiff's performance in a half-dozen pre-violation years will overstate the damages. The reverse might be true if the plaintiff's profits and market share had been steadily increasing.[14] Likewise, if a larger buyer or seller entered or exited the market during the injury period, or if the demand curve for the product shifted dramatically during the injury period, these adjustments must be taken into account.[15] For example, if a slide rule manufacturer was injured by a competitor's antitrust violation at the same time that electronic calculators were introduced into the retail market, it would be inappropriate to attribute the entire decline in the plaintiff's sales to the antitrust violation.[16]

Accommodation of all requisite factors has made the before-and-after method complex, and its use often requires higher forms of mathematics such as multiple and nonlinear regression analysis and—most importantly—a qualified economic or statistical expert.

The extreme complexities of lost profits studies using the before-and-after method can be seen in a series of cases alleging monopolization and predatory pricing against American Telephone and Telegraph Co.[17] In *Litton* the damages study took two years and covered a giant host of variables. It also made a number of assumptions that the defendant challenged unsuccessfully—such as, that the plaintiff would have received its operating certificate promptly absent the defendant's objections,

11. For one application, see Blanton v. Mobil Oil Corp., 721 F.2d 1207, 1216 (9th Cir.1983), cert. denied, 471 U.S. 1007, 105 S.Ct. 1874 (1985). The court approved the jury determination, notwithstanding the possibility that some of the losses could have resulted from things other than the antitrust violation.

12. See Timberlake, note 10 at § 21.01.

13. 327 U.S. 251, 264, 66 S.Ct. 574, 579 (1946).

14. However, businesses that are initially successful frequently exhibit a profit or market share growth rate during the early years that they will not sustain indefinitely. For example, see Volasco Prods. Co. v. Lloyd A. Fry Roofing Co., 308 F.2d 383, 391 (6th Cir.1962), cert. denied, 372 U.S. 907, 83 S.Ct. 721 (1963), where the court refused to believe that the plaintiff's business would have continued indefinitely to grow at a rate of 247% per year.

15. See Isaksen v. Vermont Castings, Inc., 825 F.2d 1158, 1165 (7th Cir.1987), cert. denied, 486 U.S. 1005, 108 S.Ct. 1728 (1988) (before-and-after method overstated damages when overall market demand for woodstoves diminished during violation period, for reasons having nothing to do with the violation. "All [the plaintiff] did to prove damages was to compare his average profits for several years before and several years during the period of unlawful activity. *Post hoc ergo propter hoc* is not a valid methodology of damage calculation, especially when it is apparent that other causal factors are at work.") See also R.C. Hoyt, D.C. Dahl & S.D. Gibson, Comprehensive Models for Assessing Lost Profits to Antitrust Plaintiffs, 60 Minn.L.Rev. 1233, 1236 (1976).

16. In such a case the market share method would be more appropriate. The relevant question is not how much the plaintiff's gross sales declined, but how much its share of the slide rule market declined. On the market share method, see § 17.6b3.

17. Litton System, Inc. v. AT & T, 700 F.2d 785 (2d Cir.1983), cert. denied, 464 U.S. 1073, 104 S.Ct. 984 (1984); see also MCI Communications Corp. v. AT & T Co., 708 F.2d 1081 (7th Cir.), cert. denied, 464 U.S. 891, 104 S.Ct. 234 (1983).

that the plaintiff would have invested far more in research and development than it had actually planned on investing, that the growth rate of AT & T's competitors in the terminal equipment market would be steadily upward, and that the plaintiff would continue to face the same costs that the defendant faced.[18] The Second Circuit found all these assumptions supportable in the record, and affirmed a jury verdict which, after trebling, amounted to some $92,000,000.

However, an equally complex lost profits study by the Southern Pacific Communications Co., which operated long-distance microwave systems that competed with AT & T's long distance service, foundered because it failed to account for the growing market share of satellite communication, and the increasing tendency of large purchasers of long distance service to build their own internal microwave systems. Furthermore, the study appeared to project a rate of growth that exceeded the plaintiff's capacity.[19]

§ 17.6b2. Yardstick Method

The "yardstick" method of estimating lost profits can sometimes simplify the court's calculations, although it can be used only in limited situations. Under the yardstick approach the plaintiff attempts to identify a firm similar to the plaintiff in all respects but for the impact of the antitrust violation. For example, in *Bigelow*,[20] the plaintiff compared its own revenue during the injury period with that earned by a comparable theater operated by one of the defendants. In such circumstances, *if* the markets of the two firms are identical, and *if* the plaintiff's firm and the firm used for comparison stand in the same relative position in those markets, offer the same product mix, have comparable managements and are comparable in all other respects, then the fact finder may infer that the two would have had comparable revenues or profits but for the violation.

The above statement of the "yardstick" methodology gives some indication of its inherent weaknesses. To the extent that either the markets or firms being compared are dissimilar, the yardstick theory will not produce a trustworthy estimate of what the plaintiff would have earned but for the defendant's conduct. The method therefore works best in markets that are both local and relatively homogeneous.[21]

Furthermore, the firm used as a basis for comparison ought not be owned by the defendant, as it was in *Bigelow*, unless such a firm is the only one sufficiently similar to the plaintiff *and* the inference is strong that the defendant-owned firm's profits do not reflect the consequences of the antitrust violation. Consider two examples. If the defendant was engaged in predatory pricing, it is likely that its own business will show lower profits or else losses during the predatory period. In that

18. *Litton*, 700 F.2d at 822–24.

19. Southern Pacific Communications Co. v. AT & T Co., 556 F.Supp. 825, 1060 (D.D.C.1982), affirmed, 740 F.2d 1011 (D.C.Cir.1984). Other courts have also been critical of speculative damage assumptions. See McGlinchy v. Shell Chem. Co., 845 F.2d 802, 806–807 (9th Cir.1988) (rejecting expert's damage study for not carefully examining underlying market conditions, and which projected that growth of sales would exceed 40% annually while expenses would remain constant); Olympia Equip. Leasing Co. v. Western Union Tel. Co., 797 F.2d 370, 382–383 (7th Cir.1986), cert. denied, 480 U.S. 934, 107 S.Ct. 1574 (1987) (severely criticizing expert damage study as nothing more than advocacy); Metrix Warehouse, Inc. v. Daimler–Benz Aktiengesellschaft, 828 F.2d 1033, 1044 (4th Cir.1987), cert. denied, 486 U.S. 1017, 108 S.Ct. 1753 (1988) (expert damages study failed to separate out losses caused by lawful conduct).

20. Note 13. See R. Blair & A. Esquibel, An Econometric Approach to Constructing a Yardstick Model of Damages in Lost Profit Cases, 72 Den. Univ. L. Rev. 113 (1994).

21. See Home Placement Serv. v. Providence Journal Co., 819 F.2d 1199, 1205 & n. 7 (1st Cir.1987) (rejecting yardstick approach when there was inadequate evidence that the plaintiff firm and yardstick firm operated in similar situations and conducted their business in a similar manner); National Farmers' Org. v. Associated Milk Producers, 850 F.2d 1286, 1294–1298 (8th Cir.1988) (approving yardstick measure notwithstanding numerous differences in two markets, particularly since differences tended to underestimate, rather than overestimate, plaintiff's damages); *Metrix Warehouse* case, note 19 at 1044 n. 21 (approving method generally); Rose Confections, Inc. v. Ambrosia Chocolate Co., 816 F.2d 381, 393–394 (8th Cir. 1987) (rejecting study comparing West Coast market and dissimilar midwestern market); Jay Edwards, Inc. v. New England Toyota Distributor, 708 F.2d 814, 821 & n. 6 (1st Cir.), cert. denied, 464 U.S. 894, 104 S.Ct. 241 (1983) (approving use where jury apparently took differences between plaintiff and yardstick dealer into account).

case use of the defendant's firm as a yardstick would understate the plaintiff's damages. By contrast, if the offense was a concerted refusal to deal it is possible that the defendant has made more money as a result of the violation, and use of its profits as a yardstick would overstate the plaintiff's damages. In many cases the problem can be solved by making sure that the plaintiff's outlets and the defendant's outlet used for measurement are in distinct markets. Even then, however, use of one of the defendant's stores as a yardstick is questionable unless profits and losses for each of the defendant's stores can be easily separated.[22]

§ 17.6b3. Lost Market Share.

The third measure of damages for lost profits is generally referred to as the "market share" theory. Actually that term is a misnomer insofar as it suggests that use of the theory invariably requires calculation of the impact of the antitrust violation on the plaintiff's market share. The theory might more appropriately be called the "lost output" theory, because frequently it purports to measure the *absolute* reduction in output suffered by the plaintiff, rather than its percentage decline of some relevant market.

Theoretically, the market share approach can be useful when the antitrust violation is internal to a market, but the market as a whole was also influenced by external shocks during the violation period. For example, suppose that the plaintiff establishes an illegal boycott in the retail gasoline market during a certain period. During the same period, however, the OPEC cartel tripled the price of gasoline, and demand dropped substantially as a result. Under the before-and-after method, it would be impossible to attribute part of the plaintiff's lost profits to the defendants and part to OPEC. Further, the yardstick method might not be available because there is no second market whose characteristics are sufficiently similar.

Presumably, however, the OPEC cartel affected all gasoline sellers proportionately—that is, they all suffered a loss of sales that varied with their volume. As a result their relative shares of the overall market were not affected by OPEC, even though their absolute volume was. If the plaintiff can show that during the violation period its market share dropped from 7% to 3%, it may be possible to separate out the impact of OPEC and compute the damages on the basis of lost market share.[23]

In practice, the market share method often operates as a variant of either the before-and-after or yardstick theories. For example, in Zenith Radio Corp. v. Hazeltine Research, Inc.[24] the plaintiff convinced the court that its market share of the Canadian television market, which was in fact 3%, would have been 16% but for the antitrust violation. The plaintiff arrived at the 16% figure by showing that the Canadian and American television markets were similar and that its market share of the American market varied upwards from 16% during the violation period. Thus the market share approach adopted in *Zenith* was little more than a variation on the yardstick approach.

22. See Timberlake, note 10, at § 21.12.

23. See General Leaseways, Inc. v. National Truck Leasing Ass'n., 830 F.2d 716, 726 (7th Cir.1987) (approving jury verdict awarding zero damages on market share study); Dolphin Tours, Inc. v. Pacifico Creative Serv., 773 F.2d 1506, 1511–1513 (9th Cir.1985) (market share study good enough to avoid summary judgment).

24. 401 U.S. 321, 91 S.Ct. 795, rehearing denied, 401 U.S. 1015, 91 S.Ct. 1247 (1971). See also Multiflex, Inc. v. Samuel Moore & Co., 709 F.2d 980, 996–97 (5th Cir.), rehearing denied, 716 F.2d 901 (5th Cir.1983), cert. denied, 465 U.S. 1100, 104 S.Ct. 1594 (1984). The plaintiff sold its hydraulic hose bundles to two groups of customers, end users and manufacturers of equipment that employed the hoses. The defendant allegedly attempted to monopolize the second market but not the first. The plaintiff's expert produced a study indicating that the plaintiff's share of the end user market, in which the violations had little or no effect, was 80%. However, its share of the equipment market, which was affected by the violation, was 63%. Then the expert produced a formula correlating the plaintiff's profits with market share, and estimated the lost profit that resulted from the 17% loss of market share in the affected market. The court approved this method of estimating damages, but finally rejected the model because it failed to segregate Sherman § 1 damages, in which the court found no liability, from Sherman § 2 damages, where it had.

Once the court has identified a certain loss of market share as the result of the antitrust violation, then it must devise an empirical formula that links market share in the relevant market to profitability. Profits are not always proportional to market share. For example, sometimes one firm will be much more profitable than another firm of the same size, and often a firm twice as big as a second firm will not earn twice the profits. Furthermore, such a formula will not generally take into account relevant economies of scale. Nevertheless, the amount of deviation with respect to such a formula may be within the range of error permitted by the courts in estimating damages.

Another problem of the *Zenith* market share approach is that it does not consider the substantial stochastic elements in the determination of any particular firm's market share. The fact that a firm was successful in obtaining a 16% share of one market is not good evidence that it would obtain a 16% share of a different market, even if the two markets are similar. Although *minimum* firm size in a market might be predetermined by relevant economies of scale, the individual sizes of particular firms in that market is largely a matter of chance. To take an example, suppose that 100 firms start out in a new market (home computers) in which minimum efficient scale is 5%. The firms go through a long period of competition, mergers, antitrust violations, lobbying, advertising and innovation. What will be the market structure after 20 years?

Assuming no tacit or express collusion, it is likely that there would be no remaining firms with a market share substantially less than 5%. That means twenty or fewer firms would survive. Which twenty? *Ex ante*, there is no way to tell, unless some of the starters were obviously more efficient or innovative than others. Furthermore, after this market reaches equilibrium we would probably not find a market with twenty firms of the same size. More likely there would be fewer than twenty firms. Some might have market shares on the order of 30%, others of 15%, and others of 10%. The fact that Zenith was fortunate enough to achieve a 16% share of the American market tells us very little about what share it would acquire in a different market.[25]

One answer to this criticism of the market share theory is that if the determinants of individual market share are truly random, the plaintiff's share in the Canadian market was equally likely to be less than or more than its actual share of the American market. In that case, however, assuming that we were faced with a market in which several equal-sized firms all entered the business at the same time, it would be more plausible to select the mode among the existing firms as the size that Zenith most likely would have reached but for the violation. This number could be either far larger or far smaller than Zenith's 16% share of the American market.[26]

A more acceptable variation of the market share theory is evidence about how much a plaintiff's output has been reduced as a result of a particular antitrust violation. If the plaintiff can point to particular sales which it lost as a result of the defendant's violation, and if the plaintiff can then show its rate of profit per sale, damages will be relatively easy to compute. For example, in Rangen, Inc. v. Sterling Nelson & Sons[27] the defendant violated the Sherman Act and the Robinson–Patman Act by bribing state officials to accept the defendant's bids for sale of fish food, rather than the bids of the plaintiff or other competitors. The plaintiff was able to show that when the bribery had not been a factor, its bids were successful about one-fourth of the time. From this the court inferred that the plaintiff's loss of sales equaled one-fourth of the volume covered by bids that the plaintiff lost to the defendant as a result of the bribery. Lost prof-

25. See F.M. Scherer & D. Ross, Industrial Market Structure and Economic Performance 141–46 (3d ed. 1990).

26. However, some of the determinants of market share may be internal to the firm. For example, if Zenith's 16% share of the American market was a result of good management, and if the same management would be responsible for entry into the Canadian market, then *ex ante* Zenith might have an advantage over competitors in the Canadian market.

27. 351 F.2d 851 (9th Cir.1965), cert. denied, 383 U.S. 936, 86 S.Ct. 1067 (1966).

its were estimated on the basis of this lost sales volume.

Sometimes a combination of the "before-and-after" and "market share" method of computing damages can yield a reasonable estimate, particularly when the plaintiff operates in several markets but the antitrust violation occurs in only one. For example, Moore v. Jas. H. Matthews & Co.[28] was a competitor-brought tying arrangement case. The plaintiff, which manufactured grave markers, successfully established that the defendant cemeteries illegally required purchasers of cemetery lots to purchase their grave markers and installation from the cemeteries as well. The Ninth Circuit approved evidence that in cemeteries not subject to grave marker ties the plaintiff had been able to attain a market share of 50%, while its share in the restricted cemeteries was only 4%. In addition, when three cemeteries settled out of court and agreed to discontinue the restrictions, the plaintiff's share of sales in those cemeteries rose to 50%. Therefore the plaintiff was entitled to damages based on the difference between the market share it actually obtained in the restricted cemeteries, and the 50% share it likely would have obtained absent the violation.

17.6c. Damages and Disaggregation

Several courts have held that if part of the plaintiff's loss in profits was caused by unlawful conduct and part by lawful conduct, the plaintiff is entitled to collect damages only for the former.[29] This requirement can place a heavy burden on the plaintiff, as one court noted:

> The way Memorex [one of the plaintiffs] structured its damage claim there was no basis in the record for the jury to determine what the effect on damages would be if it found one or more of the challenged acts lawful. Thus, if one of [defendant] IBM's acts was not a violation of the antitrust laws, much of the damage claim would become invalid.[30]

The one available escape valve from such a high standard of economic proof may be a rule that places the "burden of disaggregation" on the defendant. That is, if there is no way that either party can separate those damages elements caused by wrongful conduct from those caused by conduct held to be lawful, then the plaintiff will be permitted to recover for both. Whether such a rule actually exists is doubtful.[31] Whether it should exist is even more dubious. Just as a strict rule requiring a plaintiff to separate out damages caused by illegal acts would impose an impossible burden on the plaintiff, so would a similar rule imposed upon the defendant create an impossible burden. It would permit plaintiffs consistently to recover for both antitrust violations as well as injuries caused by efficiency and competition on the merits.

28. 682 F.2d 830, 836–37 (9th Cir.1982). In *Bigelow*, note 13, the plaintiff submitted damages evidence under both the before-and-after and yardstick theories. The measurement under the before-and-after theory was $125,000, under the yardstick theory $116,000, and the jury returned a verdict of $120,000.

29. See Coastal Fuels of Puerto Rico, Inc. v. Caribbean Petroleum Corp., 79 F.3d 182, 200 (1st Cir.), appeal after remand, 175 F.3d 18 (1st Cir.1999) (vacating common damages award for monopolization and price discrimination violations when only the latter verdict was upheld); Multiflex, Inc. v. Samuel Moore & Co., 709 F.2d 980, 997 (5th Cir.), rehearing denied, 716 F.2d 901 (5th Cir.1983), cert. denied, 465 U.S. 1100, 104 S.Ct. 1594 (1984); MCI Communications Corp. v. AT & T Co., 708 F.2d 1081, 1160–63 (7th Cir.), cert. denied, 464 U.S. 891, 104 S.Ct. 234 (1983); Coleman Motor Co. v. Chrysler Corp., 525 F.2d 1338 (3d Cir.1975). See Comment, Segregation of Antitrust Damages: An Excessive Burden on Private Plaintiffs, 72 Calif.L.Rev. 403 (1984).

30. ILC Peripherals Leasing Corp. v. IBM Corp., 458 F.Supp. 423, 434 (N.D.Cal.1978), affirmed per curiam sub nom. Memorex Corp. v. IBM Corp., 636 F.2d 1188 (9th Cir.1980), cert. denied, 452 U.S. 972, 101 S.Ct. 3126 (1981). See also City of Vernon v. Southern Cal. Edison Co., 955 F.2d 1361, 1371 (9th Cir.), cert. denied, 506 U.S. 908, 113 S.Ct. 305 (1992) (city charged utility with denying access to transmission lines, filing discriminatory rates, group boycott; only the first may have been antitrust violation); United States Football League v. NFL, 842 F.2d 1335, 1378–1379 (2d Cir.1988); Metrix Warehouse, Inc. v. Daimler–Benz Aktiengesellschaft, 828 F.2d 1033, 1044 (4th Cir.1987), cert. denied, 486 U.S. 1017, 108 S.Ct. 1753 (1988); Farley Transp. Co. v. Santa Fe Trail Transp. Co., 786 F.2d 1342, 1350–1352 (9th Cir.1985).

31. See the *MCI* case, note 29 above, at 1161–63; City of Mishawaka v. American Elect. Power Co., 616 F.2d 976 (7th Cir.1980), cert. denied, 449 U.S. 1096, 101 S.Ct. 892 (1981), rehearing denied, 450 U.S. 960, 101 S.Ct. 1421 (1981); R.S.E. Inc. v. Pennsylvania Supply, Inc., 523 F.Supp. 954, 964–65 (M.D.Pa.1981).

The problem of assigning a particular amount of damages to a particular exclusionary practice can be made more tractable if the plaintiff bases its damage claim on something other than lost profits. For example, suppose the plaintiff alleges that a competitor monopolist 1) failed to predisclose new technology; and 2) engaged in "sham" enforcement of an invalid patent.[32] The plaintiff then loses on the first claim but wins on the second. Attributing a given profit or market share loss to one or the other of these practices could be impossible, unless the effects appeared in different markets or at different times. However, in the latter case the plaintiff *could* show that it incurred certain costs in litigating against the defendant. In *Premier Electric*, the court held that litigation costs may be recovered as antitrust damages when the underlying violation is use of "sham" litigation to raise rivals' costs.[33] This measure of damages is much more plausible. Indeed, lost competitor investment rather than lost anticipated profits provides a better estimator of competitor injuries for a variety of reasons.[34]

17.6d. Terminated Dealers and Firms Driven From Business

When the plaintiff alleges that it was driven completely out of business by the defendant's activity, a new level of uncertainty must be considered. If the plaintiff's demise was gradual, then computation of damages during the years of decline will involve the methods outlined above. In addition, however, the plaintiff will be entitled to an award that will compensate for the loss of its business. If the plaintiff's demise is sudden, as it might be in a dealer termination case, then the plaintiff is entitled only to the latter sum.

Courts generally estimate damages for the destruction of a business by two different methods: the discounted present value of anticipated profits, or the "going-concern" method, which essentially asks what the business was worth to a reasonable buyer before the violation occurred.

In most cases involving the complete destruction of a business, the court attempts to determine the plaintiff's profitability before the impact of the antitrust violation, and from this evidence of profits to project a stream of future profits. Then, under the first approach this stream of future profits will be discounted to its present value. Under the second approach, the evidence of profits will be used to estimate the "going concern" value of the business.[35] In any case, loss of future profits and loss of going concern value are *alternative* measures of injury. The value of the business as a going concern is nothing more than the present value of its profits, plus its salvageable assets. A court should therefore award either the present value of lost future profits or the market value of the business as a going concern absent the violation, but not both.[36]

The easiest cases involving destruction of a business occur when the plaintiff has had a long period of established profitability and is then terminated immediately by the defendant. If the plaintiff made $100,000 per year for ten years before termination, then his damages equal the present value of a future stream of income of $100,000 per year.[37] Alternatively,

32. See § 7.11.

33. Premier Electrical Constr. Co. v. National Elec. Contractors Assn., 814 F.2d 358, 371–372 (7th Cir.1987). See also Kearney & Trecker Corp. v. Cincinnati Milacron, Inc., 562 F.2d 365 (6th Cir.1977) (awarding costs of defending anticompetitive patent infringement suit as antitrust damages).

34. See § 17.6e.

35. For example, Graphic Prods. Distribs. v. Itek Corp., 717 F.2d 1560, 1580 (11th Cir.1983) (measuring going concern value by comparing FMV of business before and after antitrust violation).

36. Sciambra v. Graham News Co., 841 F.2d 651, 657 (5th Cir.1988) (lost profits and going concern are alternative measures); Graphic Products Distributors, Inc. v. Itek Corp., 717 F.2d 1560, 1579 (11th Cir.1983); Arnott v. American Oil Co., 609 F.2d 873, 886–87 (8th Cir.1979), cert. denied, 446 U.S. 918, 100 S.Ct. 1852 (1980). See A.S. Joslyn, Measures of Damages for the Destruction of a Business, 48 Brook.L.Rev. 431 (1982); R.R. Rulon, Proof of Damages for Terminated or Precluded Plaintiffs, 49 A.B.A. Antitrust L.J. 153 (1980).

37. In the case of terminated dealers, many of which are sole proprietorships, courts sometimes look at the age of the plaintiff and measure how long it is likely that the plaintiff would have stayed in business. Thus in *Graphic Products*, id., the court determined from the age of the plaintiff's principals that they would likely work for ten more years. From this the jury estimated the present value of ten years of future profits, and the Eleventh

the "going concern" value of the business is the fair market value of a business capable of producing $100,000 per year in profits.

Few cases are that simple. In most, the plaintiff attempts to show that the business was likely to increase and therefore the loss of future profits was actually greater than the record of past profits indicates.[38] The defendant may answer that the plaintiff's business was actually in decline and that the plaintiff would probably have gone out of business even if the antitrust violation had not occurred.[39] Needless to say, in all such cases the computation of the plaintiff's damages is at least as complex as it is in the situation when the plaintiff remains a going concern.

In dealer termination cases, the plaintiff usually alleges that it was terminated for noncompliance with an illegal restriction, such as resale price maintenance or an unlawful territorial restraint. The plaintiff may be able to show that it would have made more profits during its period of operation had the restraint not been imposed. The court may give an award for the shortfall in past profits and augment the projection of future profits to account for the effect of the restraint.[40] However, in its *Isaksen* and *Local Beauty* decisions, the Seventh Circuit held that damages may not be based on the ability of the plaintiff to profit from an antitrust violation imposed on others.[41] The plaintiffs in both cases claimed their dealerships were terminated because they refused to participate in the defendants' resale price maintenance schemes. The plaintiffs' damages theories were based on the premise that they would be free to set their own price, while RPM would continue to be imposed on other dealers. The court concluded that "damages based on profits made by a plaintiff because of the existence of an antitrust violation are not recoverable."[42] One implication of *Local Beauty* is that in estimating the plaintiffs damages the court must subtract out all the effects of an antitrust violation, not merely those that injured the plaintiff. To take an obvious example, if a competitor successfully challenges a merger, its damages should be based on profits in the pre-merger market, not in the more concentrated post-merger market.

The going concern measure of damages for destruction of a business also begins with an estimate of future profits, and then capitalizes that estimate, using a multiple that accounts for such factors as the degree of risk, the established growth rate of the particular market, the nature of the arrangement between the plaintiff and its supplier, and the economic

Circuit affirmed. 717 F.2d at 1582 n. 42. But see Mid–Texas Communications Sys., Inc. v. AT & T Co., 615 F.2d 1372, 1391–92 (5th Cir.), rehearing denied, 618 F.2d 1389 (5th Cir.1980), cert. denied, 449 U.S. 912, 101 S.Ct. 286 (1980), where the court held that the plaintiff (in this case an ongoing concern) could not project lost profits twenty-seven years into the future. This concern with the sole proprietor's age apparently assumes that the business has no sale value when the proprietor retires. If a business is truly a "going concern" replacement of its manager will not ordinarily affect its value. Of course, a franchise might be made nontransferable by the franchisor. In that case the business might end when the current franchisee retires. But such a case is the exception rather than the rule.

See also Simpson v. Union Oil Co., 411 F.2d 897, 908–10 (9th Cir.), reversed per curiam on other grounds, 396 U.S. 13, 90 S.Ct. 30 (1969), where the court held that the plaintiff sole proprietor's claim for 24 years of future profits overlooked the fact that there was no reason he could not seek other employment or another business opportunity. See also Arnott v. American Oil Co., 609 F.2d 873, 887 (8th Cir.1979), cert. denied, 446 U.S. 918, 100 S.Ct. 1852 (1980): "The duration of the period during which the plaintiff might be expected to profit will vary from case to case; it is susceptible of no precise formulation, and must be left to the processes of the jury * * *."

38. For example, see Terrell v. Household Goods Carriers' Bureau, 494 F.2d 16, 23 n. 12 (5th Cir.), cert. denied, 419 U.S. 987, 95 S.Ct. 246 (1974), where the court upheld a damages award for future profits even though the business had never earned a profit.

39. See General Electric Credit Corp. v. Grubbs, 478 F.2d 53, 58–59 (5th Cir.), cert. denied, 414 U.S. 854, 94 S.Ct. 153 (1973), appeal after remand, 513 F.2d 783 (5th Cir.), cert. denied, 423 U.S. 947, 96 S.Ct. 363 (1975).

40. Eiberger v. Sony Corp. of America, 622 F.2d 1068, 1081–82 (2d Cir.1980); Pitchford v. PEPI, Inc., 531 F.2d 92 (3d Cir.1975), cert. denied, 426 U.S. 935, 96 S.Ct. 2649 (1976), on remand, 435 F.Supp. 685 (1977), affirmed, 582 F.2d 1275 (3d Cir.1978), cert. denied, 440 U.S. 981, 99 S.Ct. 1790 (1979); Greene v. General Foods Corp., 517 F.2d 635, 660–62 (5th Cir.1975), cert. denied, 424 U.S. 942, 96 S.Ct. 1409 (1976).

41. *Isaksen*, note 15; Local Beauty Supply v. Lamaur, 787 F.2d 1197 (7th Cir.1986).

42. *Local Beauty*, 787 F.2d at 1202–1203; see also Jack Walters & Sons Corp. v. Morton Bldg., 737 F.2d 698 (7th Cir.), cert. denied, 469 U.S. 1018, 105 S.Ct. 432 (1984), which implies similar analysis of maximum RPM claims; and Indiana Grocery v. Super Valu Stores, 864 F.2d 1409 (7th Cir.1989) (same). See also § 16.3d.

outlook. Measurement on the basis of expected future profits and measurement by loss of going concern value are equivalent, and should generally yield similar results.[43]

17.6e. Damages for Precluded Entry

Few claims for damages are more difficult to assess than the plaintiff's allegation that an antitrust violation destroyed its "business" even before it made its first sale. Plaintiffs in such cases often claim lost future profits. Such claims must be taken with a grain of salt, however, for as many as 90% of small businesses fail during the initial years of operation.[44]

The failure rate aside, quantifying the amount of profits that would likely be earned by a firm that has never completed entry into the business is a truly extraordinary task. Clearly, the "before-and-after" approach is inapplicable: there was no "before" and there will be no "after."[45] The "yardstick" approach of measuring damages requires the fact finder to locate a firm similar to the plaintiff's in a similar market. However, in this case there is no "similar" firm. As a result even these poor estimators of damages are of little value.

At the same time, the vulnerability of unestablished firms makes them particularly easy targets for antitrust violations. In fact, many strategic, entry-deterring practices are designed to foreclose rivals before entry is accomplished.[46] Any rule that barred recovery by unestablished firms would encourage incumbents to deter competitors early, when they are easy targets *and* when the incumbents could be free of damages liability. As a result, a well-designed deterrence policy must permit some kind of redress by unestablished firms injured by anticompetitive practices.

These countervailing considerations—the poor profit prospects and problems of proof on the one hand, and the easy susceptibility of unestablished businesses to antitrust violations on the other—suggest two premises for any antitrust damages policy concerning the unestablished business: 1) unestablished businesses should be able to enforce the antitrust laws by means of damages actions; however 2) lost anticipated profits is not the best measure of damages.

The initial hurdle that most plaintiffs confront in cases of precluded entry is not damages but standing. This issue is discussed in § 16.5a. If a court finds the requisite injury and grants standing, it is generally willing to consider a claim for lost profits under more-or-less the same standards as those applied to established firms driven out of business.[47]

Estimation of lost profits in such situations is so speculative that the court's decision can be no more than arbitrary. *Ex ante*, no one could predict the market share or sales volume that could be attained by a prospective business, and no estimate of future profits can be made without some estimate of volume of sales.

A far more judicious approach, which would permit enforcement by precluded plaintiffs but guard against overdeterrence, is to award precluded entrants their sunk costs, plus the fair market value of any contractual obligations which they have already received but will be

43. See Tire Sales Corp. v. Cities Serv. Oil Co., 637 F.2d 467 (7th Cir.1980), cert. denied, 451 U.S. 920, 101 S.Ct. 1999 (1981); Taxi Weekly, Inc. v. Metropolitan Taxicab Bd. of Trade Inc., 539 F.2d 907, 914–15 (2d Cir.1976).

44. Cochran, Small Business Mortality Rates: A Review of the Literature, 19 J. Small Bus. Mgmt. 50 (1981); Comment, Unestablished Businesses and Treble Damage Recovery Under Section Four of the Clayton Act, 49 U.Chi.L.Rev. 1076, 1079 (1982).

45. See Coastal Fuels of Puerto Rico, Inc. v. Caribbean Petroleum Corp., 79 F.3d 182, 200 (1st Cir.), appeal after remand, 175 F.3d 18 (1st Cir.1999) (not rejecting use of before-and-after approach completely, but concluding that it "requires an appraisal of the reliability of a firm's track record, and the length of that track record is one factor to consider ...").

46. For example, strategic pricing is probably used much more often to keep prospective rivals out of the market than to bankrupt firms already in business. See § 8.3b; O. Williamson, Predatory Pricing; A Strategic and Welfare Analysis, 87 Yale L.J. 284 (1977); O. Williamson, "Antitrust Enforcement: Where It Has Been; Where It Is Going," in J. Craven, ed., Industrial Organization, Antitrust, and Public Policy 41–68, 53 (1983).

47. See Central Telecommunic. v. TCI Cablevision, 800 F.2d 711, 730 (8th Cir.1986), cert. denied, 480 U.S. 910, 107 S.Ct. 1358 (1987); *Dolphin Tours*, note 23 at 1511; Terrell v. Household Goods Carriers' Bureau, 494 F.2d 16 (5th Cir.), cert. dismissed, 419 U.S. 987, 95 S.Ct. 246 (1974).

unable to perform as a result of the antitrust violations.[48] "Sunk" costs refer here to investments that the plaintiff reasonably made into the business and which it will not be able to recover as a result of the violation. For example, a prospective entrant who has purchased a delivery truck will presumably be able to sell the truck and should recover only its net loss. By contrast, pre-opening advertising expenses, the cost of obtaining financing, losses caused by early termination of leases, wages and service fees paid for pre-opening activities are all "property" interests compensable under § 4 of the Clayton Act.[49]

§ 17.7 Contribution Among Joint Violators

Contribution is the right of one guilty defendant to force other participants in the same offense to pay a share of the damages award. Many states have adopted contribution rules for tort law, either by statute or by common law rule.[1] In Texas Industries, Inc. v. Radcliff Materials, Inc.,[2] however, the Supreme Court decided that neither the antitrust statutes nor the federal common law implied a right to contribution in federal antitrust cases. The current antitrust rule, therefore, is that a single defendant may have to pay the entire damages award, even though several co-conspirators participated in the violation that caused the plaintiff's injury.

The wisdom of a contribution rule in antitrust has been controversial, with a fair amount of literature on both sides of the question.[3] The current rule of no contribution injects some arbitrariness into private enforcement of the antitrust laws. Theoretically, at the plaintiff's whim one defendant can be held liable for far more than treble the damages that it caused. Another, equally at fault, goes away free. This has prompted arguments that a no contribution rule is overdeterrent, because under it a single firm may be liable for very large damages. The answer, of course, is an argument that a no contribution rule is really underdeterrent, because some firms known to be guilty will not pay anything.

Both of the above judgments can be made only after the fact, however. At the time a firm decides whether to commit an antitrust violation it does not know whether it will have to pay damages for an injury actually caused by a co-conspirator, or whether the co-conspirator will have to pay. However, a no contribution rule may distort antitrust enforcement to the disadvantage of some potential defendants and the advantage of others. For example, if plaintiffs generally sue the largest available defendant rather than the smaller ones, the effect of a no contribution rule would be overdeterrence with respect to large firms and underdeterrence with respect to small ones.

However, the no contribution rule of *Texas Industries* reduces the overall costs of antitrust enforcement by encouraging defendants to settle before trial.[4] For example, suppose

48. But see R.D. Blair & W.H. Page, "Speculative" Antitrust Damages, 70 Wash. L. Rev. 423, 452 (1995) (criticizing this basis for awarding damages). See also W. B. Tye, S. H. Kalos & A. L. Kolbe, How to Value a Lost Opportunity: Defining, Proving and Measuring Damages from Market Foreclosure, 17 Res. L. & Econ. 83 (1995). Courts have held that completed contracts are protected "property" under § 4 of the Clayton Act. North Tex. Producers Ass'n v. Young, 308 F.2d 235, 243 (5th Cir. 1962), cert. denied, 372 U.S. 929, 83 S.Ct. 874 (1963); Peller v. International Boxing Club, 227 F.2d 593, 596 (7th Cir.1955).

49. See Duff v. Kansas City Star Co., 299 F.2d 320 (8th Cir.1962); and Flintkote Co. v. Lysfjord, 246 F.2d 368, 389–394 (9th Cir.), cert. denied, 355 U.S. 835, 78 S.Ct. 54 (1957) (holding that lost profits were too speculative for nascent firm, but awarding invested costs). Courts can and have facilitated such a rule by distinguishing between "business" and "property" interests under § 4 of the Clayton Act. The precluded entrant's sunk costs and the value of its completed contracts are property interests. Its anticipated future profits, however, are uncertain "business" interests in which no property rights have been established. See Comment, Unestablished Businesses and Treble Damage Recovery Under Section Four of the Clayton Act, 49 U.Chi.L.Rev. 1076, 1094–97 (1982).

§ 17.7

1. See W. Keeton, D. Dobbs, R. Keeton & D. Owen, Prosser & Keeton on Torts § 50 (5th ed. 1984).

2. 451 U.S. 630, 101 S.Ct. 2061 (1981). See also Minpeco, SA v. Conticommodity Servs., 677 F.Supp. 151 (S.D.N.Y.1988) (dismissing contribution cross-claim).

3. See M. Polinsky & S. Shavell, Contribution and Claim Reduction Among Antitrust Defendants: An Economic Analysis, 33 Stan.L.Rev. 447 (1981).

4. See F. Easterbrook, W. Landes & R. Posner, Contribution Among Antitrust Defendants: A Legal and Economic Analysis, 23 J.L. & Econ. 331 (1980).

that X, Y, and Z are co-conspirators sued by P. X, Y, and Z predict that if P wins it will collect $6,000,000 in damages, and that P's chances of winning are 50%. For each defendant, the expected liability is $1,000,000 (one-third of 50% of $6,000,000). The value of P's expected award is $3,000,000.

If X settles with P for $1,000,000, the law of claim reduction provides that P's future award will be reduced by that amount, to $5,000,000. P still has a 50% chance of winning. Now the expected liability of Y and Z is $1,250,000 (each has a 50% chance of paying the $5,000,000 judgment, and there is a 50% chance that it will have to be paid). The first settlor comes out better than the two other firms.

The second settlor will come out second best. The expected liability to firms Y and Z is $1,250,000 each. P's expected recovery is $2,500,000 ($5,000,000 discounted by the 50% chance it will lose). Now suppose that Y settles for $1,250,000. If P later recovers from Z, the $5,000,000 will be reduced to $3,750,000 to reflect the settlement with Y. Z's expected liability is $1,875,000.

The result will be a race among the parties to settle. The eagerness of the defendants to settle first may yield higher settlements than would occur otherwise. In the example above, for instance, the first settlor will pay $1,000,000, while the second settlor can expect to pay $1,250,000. The firms will bid against each other to be the first settlor, and the initial settlement may well be more than $1,000,000. Once the first defendant has settled, the remaining defendants will bid against each other for the right to settle next.

A contribution rule, depending on its type, can discourage defendants from settling. In the same case, suppose that X settles early for $1,000,000, leaving P with a 50% chance of recovering $5,000,000 from Y and Z. If Y ends up paying a $5,000,000 damages award, Y will have a cause of action against Z for $2,000,000 and against X for $1,000,000 (that is, for an amount such that the total payment of all three defendants is the same.) In this case, Y's and Z's expected loss is $1,000,000 each, after discounting for the 50% likelihood of P's success. X, however, is in a less fortunate position. The $1,000,000 already paid is sunk costs that it is certain to lose. Its expected additional losses are $500,000, giving it expected total losses of $1,500,000. A contribution rule that does not create a special incentive for early settlement can make early settlors worse off (disregarding litigation costs) than nonsettlors. Thus any contribution rule that does not create an exception for early settlors is calculated to increase the costs of private antitrust enforcement.[5]

Finally, any right of contribution in antitrust cases will impose one additional social cost—the cost of litigating the contribution claims themselves. If its guilt has not been established in a prior proceeding to which it was a party, a defendant in a contribution case may still defend on the merits. A formula will still have to be developed for computing the relative liability of each co-conspirator. One possibility, for example, is liability in proportion to market share. However, such a rule would force the parties to a contribution case to determine a relevant market and calculate each co-defendant's share of it, even though this determination may not have been made in the earlier proceeding.

Most arguments for a right of contribution in antitrust rest on the lack of fairness or justice in any rule that forces one guilty party to pay for the offenses of another party who is equally guilty. If consumer welfare and efficiency are the principle goals of antitrust, however, the current rule of no right of contribution among antitrust defendants may be a good one, for it achieves the same total level of deterrence and reduces litigation costs.

5. The incentive to settle can be restored by a contribution rule that frees any settling defendant from future contribution liability. Some states apply such rules to tort defendants who settle in good faith. See West's Ann.Calif.Code Civ.Proc. § 877. This is in effect a no contribution rule for good faith settlors.

Chapter 18

ANTITRUST AND THE PROCESS OF DEMOCRATIC GOVERNMENT

Table of Sections

§ 18.1 Regulation, Rent–Seeking and Antitrust Immunity

18.1a. Introduction

This chapter, the following chapter on federal regulation, and chapter 20 on state and local regulation (the "state action" doctrine) all deal with variations of the same question: Given that the democratic process often produces anticompetitive results, when should the federal antitrust laws intervene? Although the technical rules differ from one area to the next, the conclusions in these three chapters converge on the same principle: Antitrust intervention is not appropriate when the wrong being challenged is the policy choice of a sovereign government. Rather, antitrust applies when private parties are able to evade or manipulate the democratic process in such a way as to give themselves effective, unsupervised control over a market. Whether the antitrust dispute arises in the context of petitions to the government (this chapter), federal regulation (chapter 19) or regulation by state and local government (chapter 20), this underlying principle is the same.

The approach that antitrust takes in these areas is clearly not a solution to the problem of regulatory "capture," or even an attempt at a solution. The democratic process contains many flaws, but curing them is not antitrust's assignment. Congress never intended the antitrust laws to be used for this purpose, and they are very poorly designed for it. For example, the antitrust laws are concerned mainly with competition and economic efficiency. Although government policy is also concerned with competition and efficiency, governmental concerns range far wider, and governments constantly balance distributive, moral, and economic concerns. So if Congress wanted to draft "anticapture" legislation it could do so, but one would hardly imagine that this legislation would forbid "monopoly" or "combinations in restraint of trade" while saying nothing explicitly about abuses of governmental process.

We ordinarily think of markets as taking care of themselves. The state must establish a few basic working rules, such as those of contract law, but beyond that decisions about prices, entry, exit or product design are left to the market's participants. Every time the government intervenes, private firms and individuals lose some of this discretion. To be sure, not every intervention is anticompetitive. For example, the government can correct market failures, and may sometimes make markets function better than they would if left unattended. But many government interventions are undoubtedly anticompetitive, in the sense that price, output or product quality would have been more favorable to consumers if the government had simply let things alone. The basic question addressed by *Noerr–Pennington*, the subject of this chapter, is this: Are those injured by anticompetitive requests for governmental intervention entitled to an antitrust remedy against those who sought the intervention?

Importantly, antitrust itself is a form of market intervention. So called *laissez faire*, or letting things alone, is never really an option. The sovereign must always make a choice, even if the choice is to develop institutions that will let private decision making determine price, output and quality. Regulating competition is assuredly a form of regulation, just as much as regulating prices. For example, federal prohibition of a merger or a resale price maintenance contract is a form of interference in the market: it prevents a market choice that the participants would otherwise make.

One additional consideration is important. The antitrust laws are concerned mainly with preserving competition and economic efficiency in the production and distribution process. By contrast, economic efficiency is almost never the exclusive goal of government process. Indeed, in many cases it is not even an articulated goal. An antitrust policy that condemned regulation too readily merely because it was inefficient might undermine legitimate, alternative goals of regulation.

Keeping these facts in mind will help you identify the common elements developed in the three quite different doctrinal frameworks described in these three chapters on antitrust and regulation. In all three, antitrust tries to identify circumstances when the relevant sovereign is not effectively in charge of the challenged conduct. This could happen because essentially private activity was never properly exposed to governmental scrutiny. It could also happen because regulatory regimes leave "gaps," where there is room for private firms to exercise their discretion and perhaps behave anticompetitively. Or it could be because the invocation of the regulatory process was really a subterfuge. Compliance with regulatory processes can be very expensive. If a firm can discover how to force rivals to endure these expenses, it can perhaps shield itself from their competition or even drive them from the market.

In sum, all three sets of issues concerning the relation between antitrust and government regulation—federal regulation (chapter 19), state and local government regulation (chapter 20), and the right to petition the government (this chapter)—revolve around one thing: private power that the regulatory process has not effectively constrained.

18.1b. Regulatory Intervention and the Right to Seek It

Every natural person and business corporation in the United States has a right to "petition" the government for what it wants. This right is guaranteed even to those who want something extremely anticompetitive, such as a statutory monopoly, absolute freedom from price competition, or the forced removal of one's rivals from the market.[1] This right ap-

§ 18.1

1. See United Mine Workers v. Pennington, 381 U.S. 657, 670, 85 S.Ct. 1585, 1593 (1965) ("*Noerr* shields from the Sherman Act a concerted effort to influence public officials regardless of intent or purpose."); Kottle v.

plies at every level of government, state, federal and local, and to all three branches.[2] The petitioning right includes the right to go before a regulatory agency in the executive branch; the right to lobby Congress, a state legislature or city council; and the right to bring or defend a case in court. The right's basic source is the First Amendment, although courts have found it in the legislative intent and policy of the Sherman Act as well. The breadth of the right derives from the fact that the "state action" doctrine of the Fourteenth Amendment[3] is extremely broad, applying to every level of government and every government branch and agency.[4]

18.1c. The General Irrelevance of Regulatory Capture

Regulatory "capture" occurs when one particular interest group is able to obtain favors from a legislative body or regulatory agency. To the extent that benefits accruing to the favored interest group are less than the costs imposed upon others, regulatory capture is inefficient. The extent of "capture" in the regulatory process is widely disputed, but some people believe that nearly all regulation represents capture.[5] The associated behavior is often called "rent-seeking," or the seeking of supracompetitive profits that can result from governmental intervention in the market.

The literature on rent-seeking behavior is rich, and there are many theories that explain how it may occur. The most influential have been based on economic theories of collective action developed by Buchanan, Tullock and Olsen.[6] Under the theory, small interest groups of relatively homogenous individuals are more effective at getting their message heard than larger, more diffuse groups. In the latter the tendency to shirk is strong, since each individual's contribution weighs less heavily. As a result, producer groups, which are small and have high stakes per person, are much more effective lobbyists than consumer groups, which are large. Further, for producers the impact of regulation in their area of livelihood is significant, while for consumers the impact of regulation respecting a single product or service is often quite small.

For example, when a regulatory agency considers a proposal to increase taxicab fares, the owners of taxicab companies have much more at stake individually than do taxicab riders, for whom the increase represents a tiny share of income. Further, there are relatively few taxicab companies and they have homogenous interests. By contrast, passengers are numerous and their needs vary widely. We can expect that taxicab owners and operators will show up in large numbers, that they will generally speak with one voice, and that they will conduct a well-financed campaign in favor of their interests. By contrast, consumers may not participate at all, or they will be represented by only a few under-financed and often

Northwest Kidney Centers, 146 F.3d 1056 (9th Cir.1998), cert. denied ___ U.S. ___, 119 S.Ct. 1031 (1999) (*Noerr* protected kidney dialysis monopolist's successful use of administrative process to exclude intending rival from market); Zimomra v. Alamo Rent–A–Car, 111 F.3d 1495 (10th Cir.), cert. denied, ___ U.S. ___, 118 S.Ct. 365 (1997) (*Noerr* protection for firms that lobbied city council to impose airport use fee on auto rental companies).

2. For example, *Kottle*, id. (state administrative agency); King v. Idaho Funeral Serv. Ass'n., 862 F.2d 744 (9th Cir.1988) (*Noerr* immunizes report by antitrust defendants to state licensing agency concerning competitor's illegal activities); Smith v. Combustion Engineering, 856 F.2d 196 (6th Cir.1988), cert. denied, 489 U.S. 1054, 109 S.Ct. 1316 (1989), rehearing denied, 490 U.S. 1032, 109 S.Ct. 1772 (1989) (*Noerr* immunizes antitrust defendant's participation in police investigation of competitor).

3. Not to be confused with the "state action" exemption in the antitrust laws. See ch. 20.

4. Whether *Noerr* applies to petitions directed at *foreign* governments is unresolved, although the trend is to offer at least some protection. See Coastal States Mktg., Inc. v. Hunt, 694 F.2d 1358, 1364–1372 (5th Cir.1983) (applying a *Noerr*-like immunity); United States v. AMAX, Inc., 1977–1 Trade Cas. (CCH) ¶ 61467, 1977 WL 1413 (N.D.Ill.1977). For further discussion, see § 21.2d.

5. For example, Toward a Theory of the Rent–Seeking Society (J. Buchanan, R. Tollison & G. Tullock, eds. 1980). A more moderate view is R. Posner, Theories of Economic Regulation, 5 Bell.J.Econ. & Mgmnt.Sci.335 (1974). For critiques of the literature, see D. Farber & P. Frickey, Law and Public Choice: a Critical Introduction (Chicago: Univ. of Chicago Press, 1991); H. Hovenkamp, Legislation, Well–Being and Public Choice, 57 Univ. Chicago L. Rev. 63 (1990).

6. J. Buchanan and G. Tullock, The Calculus of Consent (1962); M. Olsen, Jr., The Logic of Collective Action: Public Goods and the Theory of Groups (1965).

idiosyncratic spokespersons. Within this model, most regulation ends up benefitting the firms that are regulated rather than the consumers that it is declared to protect.

To the extent regulatory capture occurs, it represents a clear shortcoming in democratic policy making. The government might serve its citizens well if it compensated for capture or corrected for the biases it produces.[7] But to conclude that the State should do something about regulatory capture does not entail using the *antitrust* laws to get the job done. The antitrust laws are concerned about the regulation of economic, or private, markets. Regulatory capture occurs in the political market, and the two markets are much more different than they are similar.

Further, identifying the dividing line between beneficial and harmful regulation presents a problem that is both technically difficult and ideologically loaded. The identification problem is technically difficult because it presents complex questions such as whether a market is really a natural monopoly, whether there are other market failures that justify intervention, whether the intervention at issue is appropriate to the problem, whether the costs of regulation (including both government administrative costs and private losses) are more than offset by the gains, and so on.[8] The question is also ideologically loaded because it goes to the heart of such fundamental political issues as whether regulation ought to incorporate concerns other than efficiency, such as consumer protection, universal service, relief for small businesses, or other values.

Even assuming that courts could correctly identify the set of values that legitimize regulation in our constitutional democracy, they are not up to the task of parsing out good from bad regulation in the general run of cases. At least when the court is applying the rather general antitrust laws, its duty is much more limited. The court must make sure that the regulation is really government *regulation*—that is, that it is not simply a mechanism for cloaking what are really private anticompetitive acts. So when the plaintiff complains that it has been injured by activities subject to regulation, the only appropriate question for the antitrust court is whether the injury was caused by the government's regulatory decision or by the inadequately supervised conduct of a private party. In this sense, *Noerr–Pennington* immunity, federal regulatory immunity, and the "state action" immunity all address the same question: When is the challenged conduct "private," and when does it come from the government itself? Antitrust liability can appropriately attach only to the former.

7. But see E. Elhauge, Does Interest Group Theory Justify More Intrusive Judicial Review?, 101 Yale L.J. 31 (1991) (arguing that judicial review striking down instances of capture is inappropriate).

8. For an overview of some of the problems see C. Sunstein, After the Rights Revolution: Reconceiving the Regulatory State (1990).

§ 18.2 The Scope of Antitrust's Petitioning Immunity

18.2a. Petitions for Legislative or Executive Action Generally

Eastern Railroad Presidents Conference v. Noerr Motor Freight[1] involved an antitrust claim by truckers that railroads had organized a campaign intended to encourage shippers to use railroads rather than trucks for their shipping. Two different aspects of the campaign were challenged. First, the railroads had allegedly petitioned state government officials for legislation that disadvantaged the truckers.[2] Second, the campaign had allegedly presented the trucking companies in a false light, thus upsetting some of their customers. Many of the criticisms of trucking were publicly made by third parties, who appeared to be independent but were actually engaged by the railroads and financed by them.[3] The Court held two things: first, the direct petition to the government for legislation was immune from

§ 18.2

1. 365 U.S. 127, 81 S.Ct. 523 (1961).

2. Id. at 129–130, 81 S.Ct. at 525. For example, the railroads lobbied against a bill that would have permitted trucks to carry heavier loads, and then persuaded a governor to veto it; they also lobbied for laws that increased taxes on heavily loaded trucks.

3. 365 U.S. at 129, 81 S.Ct. at 525.

antitrust liability since Congress never intended the antitrust laws to interfere with the ordinary political process.[4] Second, the railroad statements presenting the truckers in a false light were also immune because they were in fact part of the general plan to make a case to the government for the legislation that the antitrust defendants desired.[5]

Under *Noerr*, a firm that makes misleading or even untruthful claims to the government in order to get the government to injure the petitioner's competitors has antitrust immunity both (1) for any injury caused by the government response itself; and (2) for any consequences that flow from the fact that the public heard the misleading claims and responded by transferring their business away from the competitors. One basis for this doctrine is that in a government petitioning process all sides are entitled to have their say. If the railroads were presenting the trucking industry falsely, the truckers were in a position to correct the record—provided, of course, that they had the opportunity and resources to do so.

18.2b. Petitions to Governments Acting as Market Participants

Three years after *Noerr*, the Supreme Court held in United Mine Workers v. Pennington[6] that the defendant's efforts to influence a government agency to purchase its coal rather than the coal of competitors was immune. Once again, the conduct was a petition to the government, although in this case the government was acting as a potential buyer, rather than a maker of laws. Perhaps unfortunately, in applying *Noerr* the *Pennington* Court noted that the government agent making the purchasing decisions was not alleged to be a "co-conspirator" with the antitrust defendants. This dicta set litigants off on a long, dead-end road toward identifying an exception to *Noerr* for government actions resulting from "conspiracy" with private firms. Only a few courts actually found such a conspiracy,[7] and the Supreme Court's *Columbia* decision,[8] refusing to find conspiracy in a city council's acceding to one firm's request for an anticompetitive ordinance, seems to rule out most conspiracy claims. The Court noted that identifying "conspiracy" between private persons and public officials is both impracticable and beyond the scope of the antitrust laws. It is impracticable because every time one or more government decision makers respond favorably to a private request they can be said to "conspire" with the private party; so all legislation or favorable agency action becomes a "conspiracy." The one perhaps workable limitation that comes to mind is liability for activities such as bribery that are independently illegal.[9] But in that case the legal process of the state—generally the best sovereign for regulating state and local political activity—can be brought to bear.

The *Columbia* court recognized a possible exception to the "state action" defense for situations where the government is a "commercial participant" in the market at issue.[10]

4. Id. at 135–137, 81 S.Ct. at 528–528.

5. Id. at 142, 81 S.Ct. at 532. ("[T]hat the railroads' campaign was intended to and did in fact injure the truckers in their relationships with the public and with their customers can mean no more than that the truckers sustained some direct injury as an incidental effect of the railroads' campaign to influence governmental action and that the railroads were hopeful that this might happen."). Accord Massachusetts School of Law at Andover v. ABA, 107 F.3d 1026 (3d Cir.), cert. denied, ___ U.S. ___, 118 S.Ct. 264 (1997) (*Noerr* protected ABA's petition to states to adopt its law school accreditation standards even though the injury of the plaintiff unaccredited law school was of two types: (1) under the resultant state law, graduates from unaccredited law schools could not take bar exam; and (2) the declaration that a law school was not accredited operated of its own force as a stigma in the marketplace).

6. 381 U.S. 657, 85 S.Ct. 1585 (1965).

7. For example, Affiliated Capital Corp. v. City of Houston, 735 F.2d 1555 (5th Cir.1984) (en banc), cert. denied, 474 U.S. 1053, 106 S.Ct. 788 (1986).

8. City of Columbia & Columbia Outdoor Advertising v. Omni Outdoor Advertising, 499 U.S. 365, 111 S.Ct. 1344 (1991). For the facts, see § 18.3. The "state action" elements of the decision are discussed in Ch. 20.

9. *Columbia*, 499 U.S. at 382–383, 111 S.Ct. at 1355–1356.

10. *Columbia*, 499 U.S. at 374, 111 S.Ct. at 1351. "* * * [I]mmunity does not necessarily obtain where the State acts not in a regulatory capacity but as a commercial participant in a given market." This leaves open the possibility that a private seller who bribes a government procurement agent to accept the briber's product has entered into a qualifying "conspiracy." Whether it is an antitrust violation is another matter.

Whether it intended to do the same for *Noerr* petitioning is unclear. Some lower courts have created a market participant exception to *Noerr*, effectively holding that when the government is participating as buyer or seller, it is to be treated as a private party, not a political entity.[11] Other courts have rejected a commercial exception, applying *Noerr* even when the government is the buyer.[12] As the *Greenwood* case noted, applying any "commercial exception" to *Noerr* would be extremely "difficult, if not impossible * * * where the government engages in a policy decision and at the same time acts as a participant in the marketplace."[13]

Conceding *Greenwood*'s point, not all government purchase decisions are policy decisions. As the Supreme Court made clear in *Superior Court Trial Lawyers*,[14] the mere fact that a concerted refusal to deal is cast as a request of the government to do something does not in and of itself invoke *Noerr* immunity. As a result, there may be no way to avoid the hard decision that *Greenwood* wanted to avoid. If A tells the state "buy my office paper because it is made from recycled pulp," and the government responds for that reason, the government has made a policy decision reflecting its environmental concerns; *Noerr* immunity should follow. If A says "buy my office paper because I am the lowest bidder," and the price turns out to be the result of a rigged bid, no policy decision is implicated and *Noerr* should provide no shield in a subsequent antitrust suit.

In *Superior Court Trial Lawyers*[15] the Supreme Court limited *Pennington* and condemned a concerted boycott of legal services where the purchaser and immediate target of the boycott was the government itself. A group of trial lawyers representing indigent criminal defendants and paid by the District of Columbia collectively agreed to withhold their services until the District agreed to raise the rate of payment. When the District raised the rates, the boycott came to an end.

A number of observations about *Trial Lawyers* are relevant. First, a boycott of the same type directed at private customers would have been *per se* illegal.[16] Second, in this case the government was the customer. The principle that the government can be a victim of an antitrust violation and, in appropriate cases an antitrust plaintiff, is explicitly recognized by statute[17] and by case law that stretches back almost a century.[18] It would be quite irrational to decide that the government is a victim of an antitrust violation when it buys price-fixed goods, but that *Noerr* protects a group of private sellers agreeing with each other that they will withhold their services until they obtain a higher price. In sum, *Trial Lawyers* can be read for the narrow proposition that *Noerr* does not apply when the government is acting as a participant in a *private* market and the antitrust violation results from a privately initiated restraint that interferes with the ordinary process of competitive bargaining.

But *Pennington* still retains its vitality in many other areas involving government purchases. For example, suppose that competing

11. For example, George R. Whitten, Jr., Inc. v. Paddock Pool Builders, Inc., 424 F.2d 25, 33 (1st Cir.), cert. denied, 400 U.S. 850, 91 S.Ct. 54 (1970); Federal Prescription Serv. v. American Pharmaceutical Assn., 663 F.2d 253, 263 (D.C.Cir.1981), cert. denied, 455 U.S. 928, 102 S.Ct. 1293 (1982).

12. Greenwood Utilities Comm'n. v. Mississippi Power Co., 751 F.2d 1484 (5th Cir.1985); In re Airport Car Rental Antitrust Litig., 693 F.2d 84, 88 (9th Cir.1982), cert. denied, 462 U.S. 1133, 103 S.Ct. 3114 (1983); Independent Taxicab Drivers' Employees v. Greater Houston Transp. Co., 760 F.2d 607, 612–613 (5th Cir.), cert. denied, 474 U.S. 903, 106 S.Ct. 231 (1985).

13. *Greenwood*, 751 F.2d at 1505.

14. FTC v. Superior Court Trial Lawyers Assn., 493 U.S. 411, 110 S.Ct. 768 (1990).

15. Note 14. See also Continental Ore Co. v. Union Carbide, 370 U.S. 690, 82 S.Ct. 1404 (1962), which refused to apply *Noerr* where the antitrust defendant had been appointed by the Canadian government as its agent for the regulation of vanadium sales in Canada, and then used this power to attempt to exclude competing vanadium sellers from the Canadian market. The Supreme Court characterized this as purely commercial activity, to which *Noerr* apparently did not apply.

16. See § 5.4.

17. 15 U.S.C.A. § 15a (United States as plaintiff); 15 U.S.C.A. § 15c-h (states as plaintiffs).

18. See Chattanooga Foundry & Pipe Works v. Atlanta, 203 U.S. 390, 27 S.Ct. 65 (1906) (permitting municipality to bring damage action for price fixing).

manufacturers of military aircraft launch campaigns to convince the Defense Department that their particular model is best suited to the government's needs. This campaign may involve many of the same irregularities found in the *Noerr* campaign by railroads against truckers, but the campaign is probably immune notwithstanding that the government is acting as purchaser rather than neutral decision maker. Importantly, in this case the rival manufacturers have the opportunity to respond, and the government is not being boycotted or otherwise coerced into making a decision for one company over the other.[19]

As the Federal Trade Commission described this distinction in the *Trial Lawyers* case:

> Permitting a price-fixing boycott directed at the government as buyer does not foster the *Noerr* goal of free exchange of information between people and the government. At the same time, prohibiting such conduct does not interfere with anyone's ability to choose to sell his services to the government or to make his views on the appropriate price known to the government.[20]

So the appeal to the government buyer or seller has to be calculated to invoke a *policy* decision of the government. Further, as the Supreme Court noted, the antitrust injury caused by the trial lawyers' boycott resulted from the boycott itself, a private act, and not from the government's response:

> The restraint of trade that was implemented while the boycott lasted would have had precisely the same anticompetitive consequences during the period even if no legislation [raising the lawyers' fees] had been enacted. In *Noerr*, the desired legislation would have created the restraint on the truckers' competition; in this case the emergency legislative response to the boycott put an end to the restraint.[21]

This suggests the following outcomes:

1. *Sellers engage in secret price-fixing against a government purchaser* : no immunity; no "petition" to the government is being made, and the injury is caused entirely by the private conduct.

2. *Seller engages in predatory pricing against competitors, where government is the customer*. Once again, there is no petition to the government, which probably does not even know that the price is predatory; the injury is caused by the predation, not by government action. To be sure, the injury is caused by the government's decision to accept the lowest bid, but this cannot be interpreted as a decision to condone predatory pricing.

3. *Sellers publicly boycott government purchaser until they receive higher prices*. *Noerr* provides no exemption, for the sellers are not treating the government as a government; they are using marketplace (not political) coercion. Further, the restraint itself results from purely private action. The government response in agreeing to pay higher prices does not create the restraint, but puts the restraint at an end. This is essentially the *Trial Lawyers*' case, which found no immunity.

4. *A group of sellers of steel electric conduit band together to convince the government that steel conduit is a better choice than plastic conduit in government buildings*. *Noerr* provides immunity, even if some of the information provided to the

19. Finding *Noerr* immunity under similar circumstances are In re Airport Car Rental Antitrust Litigation, 521 F.Supp. 568 (N.D.Cal.1981), affirmed, 693 F.2d 84, 87–88 (9th Cir.1982), cert. denied, 462 U.S. 1133, 103 S.Ct. 3114 (1983) (immunity for an alleged conspiracy among car rental agencies to convince airport officials to give the conspirators preferred space within the airport, while other car rental companies were relegated to more remote areas); Greenwood Utils. Commn. v. Mississippi Power Co., 751 F.2d 1484, 1505 (5th Cir.1985) (immunity for power company that had convinced a government agency selling electric power to sell to it rather than the plaintiff).

20. Superior Court Trial Lawyers, 107 F.T.C. 562, 598 (1986), vacated, 856 F.2d 226 (D.C.Cir.1988), reversed, 493 U.S. 411, 110 S.Ct. 768 (1990).

21. *Superior Court Trial Lawyers*, 493 U.S. at 425, 110 S.Ct. at 776. See also Premier Electrical Construction Co. v. National Electrical Contractors Assn., 814 F.2d 358, 376 (7th Cir.1987) ("If the injury is caused by persuading the government, then the antitrust laws do not apply. * * * If the injury flows directly from the" petitioning"—if the injury occurs no matter how the government responds to the request for aid—then we have an antitrust case.").

government is false. In this case, the conspirators are seeking a policy decision. The government may or may not solicit evidence from both sides of the question, but if it fails to do so that is a failure of government process. The restraint is created, if at all, only when the government decides to listen to the private petitioners.

5. *A firm that deals with the government tells a government official "our employees will not vote for you, or we will give financial support to your opponent in the upcoming election, unless you buy more from us."* The results of such a proposal or threat might certainly be anticompetitive, but any restraint has occurred in the *political* rather than the private market. It is thus exempt.

As a general matter, the motive of the antitrust defendants is irrelevant. That is to say, if the defendants qualify for *Noerr* immunity on the basis of objective criteria, the immunity obtains even though the motive is highly anticompetitive.[22] Some courts do hold that evidence of motive can be important to determining whether the antitrust defendant's petitioning activity is a "sham." That question is taken up in § 18.3.

In sum, laws specifically designed to address corruption of political markets, such as laws against bribery, conflict of interest laws, or laws regulating or limiting the spoils system, are the appropriate vehicles for challenging governmentally produced anticompetitive results. But the domain of antitrust is *private* markets. Care must be taken to distinguish private from public wrongs, even though at the margins the distinction may be ambiguous and difficult to draw.

18.2c. Petitions for Adjudicative Action

The right to petition the government also includes the right to file a lawsuit or to bring a complaint before an agency acting in a quasi-judicial capacity. Although the basic petitioning immunity is the same for judicial action as for legislative or executive action, the details are different. Since adjudicative claims do not involve governments as either purchasers or as the direct victims of antitrust violations, the petitioning immunity is subject to fewer exceptions in the adjudicatory context. Furthermore, the adjudicative process has stricter "rules of conduct" that define the boundaries of acceptable behavior. For example, it is one thing to provide false information in the rough and tumble of a legislative campaign where communication lines are generally open. It is quite another to provide false information in a judicial setting, where an opponent may not have either the access or the resources to counter the challenge, and truthfulness is required by the rules of judicial procedure.

In Walker Process Equipment v. Food Machinery & Chemical Corp., the Supreme Court held that the wrongful filing of a civil suit could constitute an antitrust violation.[23] Walker, the antitrust plaintiff, had alleged that Food Machinery, the antitrust defendant, had fraudulently obtained a patent by lying in its patent application about prior uses that would have made the patent invalid.[24] Food Machinery then filed a patent infringement suit against Walker, but the suit was ultimately dismissed. Walker counterclaimed that the infringement suit itself violated § 2 of the Sherman Act. The Court held that if Food Machinery had knowingly obtained its patent by fraud and then filed an infringement suit, this suit would be stripped of its "exemption from the antitrust laws."[25] *Walker Process* failed to explore most of the fundamental issues raised by *Noerr*—indeed, it never cites *Noerr*. But implicitly at least, the Court held that certain kinds of lawsuits did not qualify for petitioning

22. *Greenwood*, note 12, 751 F.2d at 1499 ("[N]or does the possibility that the companies had selfish or anticompetitive ends in mind when seeking to influence the government deprive them of *Noerr–Pennington* protection."); Razorback Ready Mix Concrete Co. v. Weaver, 761 F.2d 484 (8th Cir.1985) (same; adjudication).

23. 382 U.S. 172, 86 S.Ct. 347 (1965).

24. Id. at 174, 86 S.Ct. at 349. The patent act prevents a firm from patenting something that has been sold in the U.S. for more than a year prior to the patent application. 35 U.S.C.A. § 102(b). For further discussion see § 7.11a of this book.

25. *Walker Process*, 382 U.S. at 175–177, 86 S.Ct. at 349–350.

immunity—perhaps when the lawsuit was badly motivated from the start because the plaintiff (later the antitrust defendant) knew that it had no basis in fact for its legal claim.

The Supreme Court tied *Noerr* and judicial petitions together in California Motor Transport Co. v. Trucking Unlimited,[26] where the plaintiffs alleged that the defendants had agreed with each other to deny the plaintiffs trucking licenses by instituting a series of lawsuits or objections before an administrative agency (the Interstate Commerce Commission) "with or without probable cause, and regardless of the merits of the cases."[27] In fact, most of the suits were not baseless; the firms had won 21 out of 40.[28]

First, the Supreme Court noted that the *Noerr* petitioning immunity applied in principle to petitions to all branches of government, and to requests for adjudicative as well as legislative action. Second, however, Justice Douglas' opinion found an exception to *Noerr* for petitions to the government that are merely a "sham," defined as "forms of illegal and reprehensible practice which may corrupt the administrative or judicial processes."[29] The Court also identified a pattern of "baseless, repetitive claims," made without regard to their merits, as constituting a sham. The Court noted the plaintiffs' allegation that the defendants had used procedural devices, not to win, but to delay and tie up the process, and thus "bar their competitors from meaningful access to adjudicatory tribunals and to usurp that decisionmaking process."[30] These various statements sent lower courts on a twenty-five year expedition to discover the appropriate boundaries of "sham" petitioning.

26. 404 U.S. 508, 92 S.Ct. 609 (1972).

27. Id. at 512, 92 S.Ct. at 612.

28. *Trucking Unlimited*, 1967 Trade Cas. ¶ 72928 at 84744 (N.D.Cal.1967); see E. Elhauge, Making Sense of Antitrust Petitioning Immunity, 80 Calif. L.Rev. 1177, 1184 (1992).

29. 404 U.S. at 513, 92 S.Ct. at 613.

30. Id. at 512, 92 S.Ct. at 612.

§ 18.3 The "Sham" Exception in Legislative and Adjudicative Contexts

The Supreme Court's decisions in *Walker Process*[1] and *California Motor Transport*[2] suggested that petitioning that was a mere "sham" would fail to qualify for *Noerr* immunity. Neither opinion explained precisely what a "sham" petition might be, although *California Motor Transport* suggested that "conspiracies" between a private firm and a public official, or attempts to bribe an official, should be regarded as shams.[3] Indeed, both cases found that *Noerr* immunity failed to apply even though the petitions to the government at issue were "legitimate" in the sense that the petitioners were seeking governmental action of some kind.

The emergent meaning of "sham" is a petition to the government that is nothing more than a subterfuge designed to harass a rival. That is, the rival's injury is intended to result not from the governmental action, for no such action is really anticipated, but rather from the petitioning process itself. Thus, for example, a firm that engages a rival in costly litigation that it has no chance of winning, simply to exhaust the rival's resources, is engaging in a sham. The injury results not from an adverse judicial decision but rather from the litigation process itself.

Suppose a private party really does wish government relief, but uses some kind of improper or perhaps even illegal means to obtain it. Several cases have considered applying the term "sham" to such conduct—particularly to allegations of bribery of a government official, or allegations that the governmental decision maker somehow "conspired" with a private party to exclude the plaintiff from a market.[4]

§ 18.3

1. Walker Process Equipment v. Food Machinery & Chemical Corp., 382 U.S. 172, 86 S.Ct. 347 (1965).

2. California Motor Transport Co. v. Trucking Unlimited, 404 U.S. 508, 92 S.Ct. 609 (1972).

3. *California Motor Transport*, 404 U.S. at 512–513, 92 S.Ct. at 612–613.

4. For example, Affiliated Capital Corp. v. City of Houston, 735 F.2d 1555, 1565 (5th Cir.1984) (en banc), cert. denied, 474 U.S. 1053, 106 S.Ct. 788 (1986) (mayor appeared to knuckle under to the "political clout" of the defendant CATV company; when an expert hired by the City reported favorably to the plaintiff's position, the expert was fired).

But the Supreme Court's *Columbia* decision defined "sham" strictly to apply only to those situations where the antitrust defendant's petition to the government is nothing more than a pretext, intended not to obtain government action but to harass a rival through the petitioning process itself.[5] The private antitrust defendant, a well established firm that sold outdoor billboards was faced with competition by the antitrust plaintiff, a newcomer. The defendant allegedly relied on his close relations with the city council and succeeded in obtaining an ordinance that prohibited the newcomer's billboards from being built, but grandparented in its own existing signs.

In finding that there was no sham, the Court ruled out virtually any possibility of claiming a "conspiracy" between a government official and a private party, where the alleged conspiracy was nothing other than a conspiracy to pass a certain statute, take a certain enforcement action, or otherwise engage in activities officially performed by the state. The only exception that the Court recognized to *Noerr* petitioning immunity was a market participant exception, where the government itself participated in the market being restrained. But the Court said little about the nature or scope of such an exception. Further, it seems that such an exception would not be counted as a "sham," but merely as a situation where *Noerr* immunity would not apply.[6] In this case, no matter how corrupt or unfair the process may have been, the antitrust defendant really did intend to obtain, and actually obtained, legislation favoring itself at the expense of the antitrust plaintiff.

One criticism of the now established definition of the "sham" exception is that many instances of governmental petitioning include *both* legitimate and the illegitimate processes. That is to say, the antitrust defendants in *Noerr* and perhaps *Columbia*, intended to use the *process* of petitioning to discourage or exclude rivals, just as much as the sought after governmental decision. In such cases of dual effective, is there a sham?

The qualified answer seems to be no, although the boundaries are not as clear as first appears. If the petitioner reasonably desires governmental action, and if there is an objectively reasonable chance that he will obtain it, then the conduct is not a "sham" notwithstanding that the rival will be injured more by the process than by the government decision itself. *Noerr* itself spoke of the "incidental effect" of petitions to the government that were in fact intended to obtain governmental relief.[7]

Indeed, in many situations where the governmental decision is not readily predictable, the rival will likely be injured as much by the process as by the outcome. This is so for the simple reason that the rival's willingness to spend on the process is driven by the cost of an adverse governmental decision. For example, suppose that a requested governmental decision will exclude the rival from a market calculated to be worth $100,000. The rival will be willing to spend any amount of money up to $100,000 in order to defeat the requested decision. At the margin, then, it may be a matter of indifference whether the decision is forthcoming. If the strategizing firm's principal goal is to raise its rivals' costs by $100,000, then either the litigation expenditures or the outcome will do the trick.[8]

But let us begin with the premise that if a substantial element (not necessarily the exclusive element) in the antitrust defendant's motive is to obtain the requested relief from the government, then the conduct at issue is not a

5. City of Columbia & Columbia Outdoor Advertising v. Omni Outdoor Advertising, 499 U.S. 365, 381, 111 S.Ct. 1344, 1354 (1991), on remand, 974 F.2d 502 (4th Cir.1992) (although the defendant sought to exclude its rival from the market, it did so "not through the very process of lobbying, or of causing the city council to consider zoning measures, but rather through the ultimate product of that lobbying and consideration, viz., the zoning ordinances").

6. Id. at 374–375, 111 S.Ct. at 1351; see also Municipal Util. Bd. of Albertville v. Alabama Power Co., 934 F.2d 1493 (11th Cir.1991), appeal after remand 21 F.3d 384 (11th Cir.1994) holding that *Columbia* ruled out a conspiracy claim involving a public official.

7. *Eastern Railroad Presidents Conference v. Noerr Motor Freight*, 365 U.S. 127, 142, 81 S.Ct. 523, 532 (1961).

8. On use of petitioning to raise rivals' costs, see § 7.10.

sham. The case law certainly seems to be pointing in that direction, and the First Amendment may compel it. This may entail that some antitrust defendants will get away with badly motivated petitions even when the government takes no action. That outcome may simply be one of the prices that we pay for democracy.

18.3a. Use of Abusive Methods; False Information

The *Columbia* decision reiterates that it is not antitrust's purpose to police the political process and correct its shortcomings:

> Any lobbyist or applicant, in addition to getting himself heard, seeks by procedural and other means to get his opponent ignored. Policing the legitimate boundaries of such defensive strategies, when they are conducted in the context of a genuine attempt to influence governmental action, is not the role of the Sherman Act.[9]

But are there any limits to the abuse of political process that the Sherman Act might correct? Suppose a petitioner uses falsified information in making a request to a legislative body or agency for something that will harm a rival. Worse yet, suppose a court litigant relies on false information in order to obtain a decision injuring a rival. Does *Noerr* protect either or both?

At the onset, one must distinguish between false information used to affect the outcome, and false information intended to raise a rival's costs. False information used for the second purpose can be a "sham" because the underlying motive of the person using it is simply to harass the rival. For example, if a firm falsifies its cost figures simply because it knows the rival must spend thousands of dollars uncovering the "mistakes," the sham exception would apply.

The hard case is the firm that uses false information in order to obtain the requested result. The term "sham" as the Court defined it in *Columbia* does not fit. Several pre-*Columbia* courts found at least the possibility of a "sham."[10]

Before the antitrust laws are applied to such uses of false information a few limitations are important.[11] *First*, the user of the information must have known that it was false. Someone who is merely careless may be subject sanctions, at least in the judicial or agency context[12] but innocent misrepresentations cannot form the basis of an antitrust violation. This is clear enough when the antitrust offense requires intent, measured by a subjective test, as in the law of attempt to monopolize. But even when the conduct is measured by objective criteria, innocent misrepresentations are not reasonably calculated to create monopolies, although they may inadvertently do so.

Second, if the charge is that the adverse government decision was procured by false information, then there must be at least a minimal showing that the false information was material to the government's decision.[13] Such a showing may not be difficult in a case involving a judicial decision, where the fact finder gives reasons supporting its conclusions. It may be much more difficult in a political context, where there are a large number of voters and little way of determining what actually motivated each one.[14]

9. *Columbia*, note 5, 499 U.S. at 381, 111 S.Ct. at 1355. Accord, Allied Tube & Conduit Corp. v. Indian Head, 486 U.S. 492, 508 & n. 10, 108 S.Ct. 1931, 1941 & n. 10 (1988).

10. For example, Woods Exploration & Producing Co. v. Aluminum Co., 438 F.2d 1286, 1296–1298 (5th Cir. 1971), cert. denied, 404 U.S. 1047, 92 S.Ct. 701 (1972); Litton Sys. v. AT & T, 487 F.Supp. 942, 944 (S.D.N.Y. 1980); Outboard Marine Corp. v. Pezetel, 474 F.Supp. 168 (D.Del.1979).

11. See 1 Antitrust Law ¶ 203f (rev. ed. 1997).

12. One example is the sanctions imposed by Federal Rule of Civil Procedure 11. See 2 Antitrust Law ¶ 323e (rev. ed. 1995).

13. The Ninth Circuit's decision in Clipper Exxpress v. Rocky Mountain Motor Tariff Bureau, 690 F.2d 1240, 1261–1262 (9th Cir.1982), cert. denied, 459 U.S. 1227, 103 S.Ct. 1234 (1983), seems incorrect on this point. The court held that the use of false information could be an antitrust violation even if the government agency was not actually influenced by the information. The court noted that no such limitation applied to the law of perjury. Why is that relevant?

14. See Kottle v. Northwest Kidney Centers, 146 F.3d 1056, 1061–1062 (9th Cir.1998), cert. denied, ___ U.S. ___,

Third, the false information must be of a kind that is peculiarly in the control of the antitrust defendant. If the party opposing the user of false information can readily and cheaply disprove the false claims, then the false information is not reasonably calculated to create a monopoly, however annoying it may be in the meanwhile.[15]

Fourth, the allegedly false information must really be false; not merely a matter of interpretation or something about which reasonable minds could differ.

But none of this really resolves the basic question: under the definition of "sham" given at the beginning of this section, the use of false information to obtain a desired result from the government decision maker is not a "sham" at all. There are good reasons for adhering to this definition. First, if the false information is being used merely to increase the rivals' burdens in defending against the claims, or to delay a decision on the rival's request, then the orthodox "sham" exception applies.[16] Second, if the false information really forms the basis of a government decision that would otherwise have been different, and if the victim can later establish these facts, then there will almost always be a remedy under the laws of perjury, abuse of process, libel or slander, and the like. As a general matter, regulation of the judicial process ought to be left to the laws and rules designed to control those processes, not to the antitrust laws.

18.3b. Baselessness in the Adjudicative Setting; Successful Claims

One problem with applying the term "sham" to judicial claims is that not every cause of action is a sure winner; indeed, most cases that go to court are not. Further, different minds may have different opinions about when it is worthwhile to proceed. The mere fact that a person loses is certainly not sufficient evidence that the claim was brought in bad faith.

In *Premier Electrical*, Judge Easterbrook attempted an economic test:

> If the expected value of a judgment is $10,000 (say, a 10% chance of recovering $100,000) the case is not "groundless"; yet if it costs $30,000 to litigate, no rational plaintiff will do so unless he anticipates some other source of benefit. If the other benefit is the costs litigation will impose on a rival, allowing an elevation of the market price, it may be treated as a sham.[17]

There are several things to note about this test. First, "sham" is to be evaluated by a purely objective test; the question is not the state of mind of the person who brought the suit, but rather whether the suit's expected value exceeds its anticipated costs. Second, Judge Easterbrook makes clear that even litigation that is not absolutely "groundless" could be a sham. Indeed, even litigation that the plaintiff ultimately wins could be a sham if, *ex ante*, its expected value is less than its costs.

Third, and more problematically, the benefits of litigation may come from other sources than the judgment itself, and one must consider what these are. *Premier Electrical* suggests that litigation could be used to raise a rivals' costs. But there could be quite legitimate reasons for bringing a lawsuit even when anticipated costs exceed immediate benefits. To call these lawsuits a "sham" would be inappropriate. For example, a commercial lender may spend $1000 noisily collecting a $300 debt. It does so, not because it is attempting to monopolize the money lending business, but because it wants to send the right message to its small

119 S.Ct. 1031 (1999) (noting the "radically diverse" character of the executive branch and its administrative agencies, which entails that the legal standard would have to vary with the nature of the particular agency and of the proceedings in which the allegedly false or misleading information was submitted).

15. See First American Title Co. v. South Dakota Land Title Assn., 714 F.2d 1439, 1447 (8th Cir.1983), cert.denied, 464 U.S. 1042, 104 S.Ct. 709 (1984).

16. See Litton Sys. v. AT & T, 487 F.Supp. 942, 956–58 (S.D.N.Y.1980) (allegation that filing of false information delayed decision on plaintiff's request could define a "sham").

17. Premier Electrical Constr. Co. v. National Elec. Contractors Assn., 814 F.2d 358, 372 (7th Cir.1987).

debtors.[18] If it began to write off delinquent $300 debts because of the high cost of collection, numerous small debtors would default. If the $1000 spent against debtor A also convinces debtor B, C and D that they had better pay up, then the litigation is profitable notwithstanding that it cost more than the anticipated recovery in the case involving A.

Fourth, implementing Judge Easterbrook's test in an antitrust lawsuit would be extraordinarily difficult, particularly if one takes the above described "general deterrence" goals of litigation into account. Suppose that a firm has a 2% chance of winning a patent infringement suit worth $10,000,000 if it does win, and litigation costs $500,000. In this case, the expected value of the recovery ($200,000) is much less than expected costs. But once again, the patent infringement suit may be designed to send a message to other rivals that the firm in question intends to enforce its patents, even if its claims are rather marginal.

In deciding whether this lawsuit is a sham, the fact finder would have to determine (a) the percentage chance that the claimant would win; (b) the amount of the recovery; (c) the cost of bringing suit; (d) the value of the message sent to other rivals. No court has attempted these computations (including the Seventh Circuit in *Premier Electrical*), and it is not likely that one will.

Rather, the courts have asked fundamentally the same question, although in less explicit terms: would a reasonable person have brought this lawsuit with the expectation of winning? Whether that question must be answered subjectively or objectively has been a matter of dispute. Some circuits found subjective evidence of intent to be indispensable.[19] Others required objective baselessness, with baselessness being a question of law.[20] The Professional Real Estate decision discussed below very largely resolves the issue in favor of requiring objectively measured baselessness.

The substantive question of what constitutes a sham has also perplexed the courts. The *Westmac* court concluded that when the challenged litigation "raises a legal issue of genuine substance," there is at least "a rebuttable presumption that it is a serious attempt to obtain a judgment on the merits instead of a mere sham. * * * "[21] That test may sound more helpful than it is in fact. *All* litigation is presumptively brought in good faith, in the sense that the antitrust plaintiff must later produce *some* evidence of sham. What the *Westmac* court probably should have said is that the presumption becomes much stronger when the litigation raises an issue of substance. In the particular context of patent infringement suits, several courts have noted the uncertainty attending claims of patent validity and infringement; any rule that was too aggressive against those bringing infringement suits would defeat the purpose of the patent laws.[22] Several courts hold that there is a strong presumption that patent infringement suits are well brought, and that the presumption can be defeated only by "clear and convincing" evidence of sham.[23]

Should the presumption of a well brought claim be conclusive when the suit is successful? In *California Motor Transport*, the Supreme Court appeared to say no. That decision found that the plaintiffs properly alleged that a pattern of repetitive claims, half of which the

18. Raising rivals' costs would certainly not be the reason. First, the debtor is not the creditor's competitor. Second, raising the debtor's costs is contrary to the creditor's interests.

19. In re Burlington Northern, 822 F.2d 518, 528 (5th Cir.1987), cert. denied, 484 U.S. 1007, 108 S.Ct. 701 (1988) ("determinative issue is * * * whether [the suit] was significantly motivated by a genuine desire for judicial relief."); Greenwood Util. Commn. v. Mississippi Power Co., 751 F.2d 1484 (5th Cir.1985).

20. Columbia Pictures Indus. v. Professional Real Estate Investors, 944 F.2d 1525 (9th Cir.1991), affirmed, 508 U.S. 49, 113 S.Ct. 1920 (1993); accord Westmac v. Smith, 797 F.2d 313 (6th Cir.1986), cert. denied, 479 U.S. 1035, 107 S.Ct. 885 (1987).

21. *Westmac*,, 797 F.2d at 317–318.

22. See, for example, Handgards v. Ethicon (Handgards I), 601 F.2d 986 (9th Cir.1979), cert. denied, 444 U.S. 1025, 100 S.Ct. 688 (1980).

23. *Handgards*, id. The plaintiff later prevailed under this test. Handgards v. Ethicon (Handgards II), 743 F.2d 1282 (9th Cir.1984), cert. denied, 469 U.S. 1190, 105 S.Ct. 963 (1985). See also Loctite Corp. v. Ultraseal, Ltd., 781 F.2d 861 (Fed.Cir.1985); FMC Corp. v. Manitowoc Co., 654 F.Supp. 915 (N.D.Ill.), affirmed, 835 F.2d 1411 (Fed.Cir. 1987).

antitrust defendant won, were in fact a "sham."[24] But there is an alternative explanation. There were apparently many shams among the twenty or so lawsuits that the *California Motor* antitrust defendants lost.[25] The gist of the claim was that the antitrust defendant had brought the suits without regard to merit, and won some by happenstance while it lost others. In *Burlington*, the Fifth Circuit concluded that the "determinative inquiry is not whether the suit was won or lost, but whether it was significantly motivated by a genuine desire for judicial relief."[26] However, then the court went on to note that it was "highly unlikely" that a meritorious suit would not be motivated by a genuine desire for relief.

In *Professional Real Estate*, the Supreme Court made the presumption that a successful suit is not a sham virtually conclusive, holding that "litigation cannot be deprived of [*Noerr*] immunity as a sham unless the litigation is objectively baseless."[27] The antitrust plaintiff Professional Real Estate (PRE) operated hotels and rented videodiscs containing motion pictures to patrons. The antitrust defendant, Columbia Pictures, sued PRE for violating Columbia's exclusive right to "perform" its copyrighted motion pictures, under the relatively novel question whether the watching of a rented videodisc in a hotel room is a "performance." Columbia's copyright infringement case was hardly airtight. However, in other lawsuits filed by Columbia the Third Circuit had held that the watching of video cassettes in private screening rooms constituted a "performance."[28] PRE counterclaimed, alleging that the suit itself was a "sham." The Ninth Circuit first agreed with PRE on the underlying merits, holding that the viewing of videos in a hotel room is not a "performance."[29] However, it later agreed with the district court that since Columbia was "expecting a favorable judgment" in its copyright suit, that suit could not be a "sham." It dismissed PRE's antitrust counterclaim, approving the district court's refusal to permit PRE to engage in further discovery into questions concerning Columbia's motive in bringing the lawsuit in the first place.

In agreeing with the Ninth Circuit, the Supreme Court concluded that an "objectively reasonable effort to litigate cannot be sham regardless of subjective intent."[30] The Court then gave this two part test:

> First, the lawsuit must be objectively baseless in the sense that no reasonable litigant could realistically expect success on the merits. If an objective litigant could conclude that the suit is reasonably calculated to elicit a favorable outcome, the suit is immunized under *Noerr*, and an antitrust claim premised on the sham exception must fail.[31] Only if challenged litigation is objectively meritless may a court examine the litigant's subjective motivation. Under this second part of our definition of sham, the court should focus on whether the baseless lawsuit conceals "an attempt to interfere directly with the business relationships of a competitor," * * *[32]

The court then suggested that the common law tort of "malicious prosecution" captured most of the concerns that were relevant to identifying a "sham." "[T]he plaintiff [must]

24. California Motor Transport Co. v. Trucking Unlimited, 404 U.S. 508, 513, 92 S.Ct. 609, 613 (1972).

25. See the district court's opinion, 1967 Trade Cas. (CCH) ¶ 72,928 at 84,744 (N.D.Cal.1967).

26. *Burlington Northern,* note 19 at 527–528.

27. Professional Real Estate Investors v. Columbia Pictures Industries, 508 U.S. 49, 113 S.Ct. 1920 (1993).

28. See Columbia Pictures Industries v. Redd Horne, 749 F.2d 154 (3d Cir.1984); Columbia Pictures Industries v. Aveco, 612 F.Supp. 315 (M.D.Pa.1985), affirmed, 800 F.2d 59 (3d Cir.1986).

29. 866 F.2d 278 (9th Cir.1989).

30. Ibid.

31. The Court noted in a footnote:

> A winning lawsuit is by definition a reasonable effort at petitioning for redress and therefore not a sham. On the other hand, when the antitrust defendant has lost the underlying litigation, a court must "resist the understandable temptation to engage in post hoc reasoning by concluding" that an ultimately unsuccessful "action must have been unreasonable or without foundation."

PRE, 508 U.S. at 60 n. 5, 113 S.Ct. at 1928 n. 5 (quoting Christiansburg Garment Co. v. EEOC, 434 U.S. 412, 421–422, 98 S.Ct. 694, 700–701 (1978)).

32. 508 U.S. at 50, 113 S.Ct. at 1922, quoting *Noerr*, at 144.

prove that the defendant lacked probable cause to institute an unsuccessful civil lawsuit and that the defendant pressed the action for an improper, malicious purpose."[33] In this context, probable cause requires no more than a "reasonabl[e] belie[f] that there is a chance that [a] claim may be held valid upon adjudication."[34] Further, since "the absence of probable cause is an essential element of the tort, the existence of probable cause is an absolute defense."[35] In this case, given that other circuits had supported the antitrust defendant, and that there was widespread criticism of the Ninth Circuit's rule that playing a recorded movie in a hotel room was not a "performance,"[36] it certainly could not be said that Columbia's suit had been brought without probable cause. Once the suit had been found to be supported by probable cause, then it could not be a sham. As a result the lower court correctly refused discovery into Columbia's subjective intentions in filing the lawsuit.

Beyond these observations, the Court was not clear about what constitutes "baselessness." The case at hand concerned questions of law exclusively. But what if the alleged "sham" involved false allegations of fact as well? The Court expressly refused to decide that issue.[37] This limitation considerably narrows the scope of the *Professional Real Estate* holding. In the great majority of lawsuits challenged as shams, the antitrust plaintiff is complaining about omissions or misrepresentations of fact in the original plaintiff's allegations, not merely about a suit based on a novel or controversial legal theory. For example, in a patent infringement suit challenged as a sham, the antitrust plaintiff typically claims, not that the lawsuit is brought on a bad legal theory, but that the infringement plaintiff had or should have had factual information indicating that the patent was not valid or that the antitrust plaintiff was not infringing on the patent.[38]

In concurring, Justice Stevens objected to the Court's equation of "objectively baseless" with reasonably expected "success on the merits." That concern is more than fanciful. Clever lawyers can almost always come up with novel legal claims where there is a reasonable, objectively measured chance for success. However, the size of the victory would be too small to warrant pursuing suit.[39] Justice Stevens then suggested that:

> The label "sham" is appropriately applied to a case, or series of cases, in which the plaintiff is indifferent to the outcome of the litigation itself, but has nevertheless sought to impose a collateral harm on the defendant by, for example, impairing his credit, abusing the discovery process, or interfering with his access to governmental agencies. It might also apply to a plaintiff who had some reason to expect success on the merits but because of its tremendous cost would not bother to achieve that result without the benefit of collateral injuries imposed on its competitor by the legal process alone.

18.3c. Single or Repetitive Claims

California Motor Transport defined sham in terms of "* * * a pattern of baseless, repet-

33. Id. at 61, 113 S.Ct. at 1929.

34. Ibid., citing Hubbard v. Beatty & Hyde, 343 Mass. 258, 262, 178 N.E.2d 485, 488 (1961); Restatement (Second) of Torts § 675, Comment e, pp. 454–455 (1977).

35. 508 U.S. at 62–63, 113 S.Ct. at 1929.

36. See 1 P. Goldstein, Copyright: Principles, Law and Practice § 5.7.2.2, pp. 616–619 (1989); 2 M. Nimmer & D. Nimmer, Nimmer on Copyright § 8.14[C][3], pp. 8–168 to 8–173 (1992); and see Video Views v. Studio 21, 925 F.2d 1010, 1020 (7th Cir.), cert. denied, 502 U.S. 861, 112 S.Ct. 181 (1991) (refusing to follow Ninth Circuit).

37. We "need not decide here whether and, if so, to what extent *Noerr* permits the imposition of antitrust liability for a litigant's fraud or other misrepresentations" before a tribunal. *PRE*, 508 U.S. at 61, n. 6, 113 S.Ct. at 1928 n. 6.

38. See Nobelpharma v. Implant Innovations, 141 F.3d 1059 (Fed.Cir.), cert. denied, ___ U.S. ___, 119 S.Ct. 178 (1998) (finding liability where patentee knew or should have known that patent was unenforceable); International Technologies Consultants v. Pilkington PLC, 137 F.3d 1382 (9th Cir.1998) (infringement suit based on expired patents a possible antitrust violation). Contrast Repeat–O–Type Stencil Manufacturing Corp. v. Hewlett–Packard Co., 141 F.3d 1178 (9th Cir., unpublished), cert. denied ___ U.S. ___, 119 S.Ct. 338 (1998) (antitrust complaint dismissed where infringement suit found not to be objectively baseless).

39. Justice Stevens noted Farrar v. Hobby, 506 U.S. 103, 113 S.Ct. 566 (1992), which involved ten years of litigation and two appeals to obtain one dollar in relief. See Justice O'Connor's concurring opinion at 575–576.

itive claims * * * which leads the factfinder to conclude that the administrative and judicial processes have been abused."[40] The Court was only describing the kinds of evidence that tends to show sham—a single baseless claim might be an oversight, but multiple claims cannot be so easily excused. At the time the first claim is rebuffed, the claimant should have been given reasons why it was improper. A firm which brings the same baseless claim a second time is more likely bringing the suit to harass.

A few courts have held quite categorically that a single baseless lawsuit cannot be a "sham."[41] But one lawsuit can be very expensive, and with proper pleading can tie up the parties' resources for many years. As a result, to conclude categorically that a single lawsuit is never a "sham" would give firms carte blanche to use complicated, drawn out litigation strategically without fear of antitrust consequences. If the lawsuit was manifestly unreasonable, that fact should emerge either before the lawsuit is filed or while it is in progress. Further, sometimes "sham" takes the form of repetitive filings or demands made *within* a single lawsuit. The majority of circuits passing on the issue now hold that a single lawsuit can, under appropriate circumstances, be an antitrust violation.[42] Other courts have recognized that a single lawsuit can be a sham, but only if it involves "serious misconduct."[43] In *Professional Real Estate,*[44] the Supreme Court made only a few passing references to "repetitiveness," but the clear implication was that repetition is not decisive either way. Rather, the fact that claims were brought repetitively is a piece of objective evidence to be used to determine bad faith.

The other side of the coin is that plurality of lawsuits does not necessarily prove sham. This is clearly true where the suits are brought in different jurisdictions. For example, state laws differ, so a loss on an issue in one state court does not dictate a loss on the same issue in the courts of a different state. Even where there is conflict among the federal circuit courts, a firm might be entitled to seek the ruling of a second federal court, if principles of collateral estoppel do not foreclose it.

Ultimately the meaning of repetitive claims presents a fact question, just as the question of substantive reasonableness itself.[45] The fact that challenged claims are repetitive can be of great importance, especially if the first dismissal gave the claimant objectively sound reasons for thinking that the subsequent claim is without merit.

18.3d. Threat to Sue; Ex Parte Statements

Suppose a firm who believes its patent or copyright has been infringed by a rival writes a letter: "either stop selling this (product or process), or else I will sue." Clearly, the writing of such letters by dominant firms could chill competition. Is the letter itself protected under *Noerr*?

The answer must be yes, even though a threat to sue involves no petition to the government at all. Our entire dispute resolution process is designed to encourage people to resolve their differences if possible before litigating; and to settle out of court once litigation has been filed. A rule that held that litigation is protected but that the pre-litiga-

40. California Motor Transport Co. v. Trucking Unlimited, 404 U.S. 508, 513, 92 S.Ct. 609, 613 (1972). See also Ernest W. Hahn v. Codding, 615 F.2d 830 (9th Cir.), on remand, 501 F.Supp. 155 (N.D.Cal.1980) (multiple claims a sham).

41. E.g., Loctite Corp. v. Fel–Pro, 1978–2 Trade Cas. ¶ 62204, 1978 WL 1385 (N.D.Ill.1978).

42. Clipper Exxpress v. Rocky Mountain Motor Tariff Bureau, 690 F.2d 1240, 1255 (9th Cir.1982), cert. denied, 459 U.S. 1227, 103 S.Ct. 1234 (1983); Feminist Women's Health Center v. Mohammad, 586 F.2d 530, 543 n. 12 (5th Cir.1978), cert. denied, 444 U.S. 924, 100 S.Ct. 262 (1979); MCI Communic. v. AT & T, 708 F.2d 1081, 1155 (7th Cir.), cert. denied, 464 U.S. 891, 104 S.Ct. 234 (1983).

43. Razorback Ready Mix Concrete Co. v. Weaver, 761 F.2d 484, 487 (8th Cir.1985). The court found no serious misconduct, and did not specify what it might be.

44. Note 27.

45. See, e.g., USS–POSCO Indus. v. Contra Costa Cty. Bldg. & Constr. Trades Council, 31 F.3d 800, 811 (9th Cir.1994) (repetitive nature of claims, even if some are upheld, is relevant to whether defendant had a "policy of starting legal proceedings without regard to the merits and for the purpose of injuring a market rival").

tion "demand letter" is not would encourage firms to litigate first.[46]

Of course the threat of *baseless* litigation should not be given any more protection than the baseless litigation itself.[47] Likewise, a threat to sue by someone who has no intention of suing should be denied protection, for the simple reason that such a threat does *not* constitute a petition to the government, no matter how broadly defined. For the same reasons, statements made by one party to litigation to an opponent's customers, to the media, or other private persons should not be protected. Suppose, for example, that a plaintiff in litigation sends a copy of the complaint to the defendant's customers. The sending of a document to a private person is not a petition to the government. Of course, if the plaintiff's purpose is to warn customers that they themselves will be legally liable for purchasing the defendant's product, then the letter would fall into the category of threats to sue, and should enjoy *Noerr* immunity if the lawsuit itself arguably has merit.

In any event, very few non-exempt activities will be antitrust violations. A letter to an opponent's customers describing the contents of ongoing litigation is nothing more than a form of negative advertising, and advertising itself—even the negative kind—violates the antitrust laws only rarely. For example, if the letter is alleged to be an attempt to monopolize, then the other elements of that offense must be proven as well.[48]

18.3e. Petitions for Invalid Legislation and Administrative Rules

The right to petition exists even if what the petitioner seeks subsequently turns out to be unconstitutional or unlawful. For example, suppose a taxicab firm requests a new municipal ordinance giving it a monopoly on travel from downtown to the airport. The ordinance is passed but is later held invalid under the "state action" doctrine because it was inadequately authorized by state law.[49] *Ex ante*, reasonable minds could differ on the issue of the legality of the ordinance, and in this case the members of the city council apparently thought it was valid. The right to petition would lose much of its meaning if we attached a kind of strict liability to petitioners for ordinances subsequently found invalid.[50]

But to make the case a little stronger, suppose that the petitioner knew at the time the petition was made that the requested ordinance or administrative rule was unconstitutional or invalid. Once again, if the legislative body or agency accepts the petition, *and the injury is caused by the resulting rule*, then it would seem that *Noerr* should apply. In this case, the *cause* of the injury is the government's passage of the rule, which injures the plaintiff during the time it is in force.[51]

As noted above, however, petitioning activity is a "sham" when it is intended, not to obtain the explicitly requested response, but when the process itself is intended to impose burdens on rivals. The fact that the sought-for ordinance or rule is unconstitutional could cer-

46. See Coastal States Marketing v. Hunt, 694 F.2d 1358, 1367 (5th Cir.1983) ("The litigator should not be protected only when he strikes without warning. If litigation is in good faith, a token of that sincerity is a warning that it will be commenced and a possible effort to compromise the dispute."). Accord Virginia Panel Corp. v. MAC Panel Co., 133 F.3d 860 (Fed.Cir.1997), cert. denied, ___ U.S. ___, 119 S.Ct. 52 (1998) ("The antitrust laws do not preclude patentees from putting suspected infringers on notice of suspected infringement").

47. CVD v. Raytheon Co., 769 F.2d 842, 850 (1st Cir.1985), cert. denied, 475 U.S. 1016, 106 S.Ct. 1198 (1986) (applying same standard to threat to sue and lawsuit itself).

48. See § 18.4.

49. See § 20.4.

50. See In re Airport Car Rental Antitrust Litig., 521 F.Supp. 568, 583–585 (N.D.Cal.1981), affirmed, 693 F.2d 84 (9th Cir.1982), cert. denied, 462 U.S. 1133, 103 S.Ct. 3114 (1983) (*Noerr* immunity could exist even if requested action was invalid under "state action" doctrine); Greenwood Utilities Commn. v. Mississippi Power Co., 751 F.2d 1484, 1500 (5th Cir.1985):

> * * * in the administrative context, an ultimate determination that agency action sought was unauthorized by statute should not remove protection for petitioning conduct directed to the agency to obtain that action. * * * [A] contrary result would * * * chill petitioning activity. * * *

51. See *Airport Car Rental*, note 50, 521 F.Supp. at 574: "If plaintiff suffered injury, it resulted from the acts of public officials declining to lease space to plaintiff * * * and not the joint action of the defendants. * * *"

tainly be evidence of sham. If any reasonable person acquainted with the law should know that the requested act is unlawful, the probability is increased that the request itself is not intended to elicit the government act, but only to harass the rival.

§ 18.4 The Relation Between Unprotected Petitioning and the Substantive Offense

A few courts have written as if "sham" petitioning were in and of itself an antitrust offense. It is not. If it were, then every common law or statutory abuse of process would violate the antitrust laws.[1]

"Sham" petitioning constitutes the *conduct* element in an antitrust offense. But in most cases the claimed violation is a rule of reason offense such as monopolization or attempted monopolization. If the offense is attempt, it includes three elements: specific intent to create a monopoly in a defined relevant market, conduct, and a "dangerous probability of success" in creating the monopoly.[2] The "sham" petitioning itself satisfies only the second element.[3]

One illustration should suffice. Suppose that Farmer Brown, who grows corn, files repetitive, baseless, absolutely unfounded lawsuits against his neighbor Farmer Green. Both raise corn, and the effect of the lawsuits, which Farmer Green finances out of her own pocket, is that she goes out of business or is unable to plant corn for the season. Farmer Brown has very likely been guilty of tortious abuse of process under state law. But he has not violated the antitrust laws. Between them, Farmers Brown and Green grow one millionth of the corn produced in the relevant market, and there is not the faintest chance that Farmer Brown threatens a monopoly of corn or any other product. To be sure, the lawsuit may raise Farmer Green's costs, but that does Farmer Brown no good, since he must still compete with numerous other growers.

In *Professional Real Estate*, the Supreme Court addressed this concern decisively:

> Of course, even a plaintiff who defeats the defendant's claim to *Noerr* immunity by demonstrating both the objective and the subjective components of a sham must still prove a substantive antitrust violation. Proof of a sham merely deprives the defendant of immunity; it does not relieve the plaintiff of the obligation to establish all other elements of his claim.[4]

§ 18.5 Corruption of Private Decision Making Bodies

In Allied Tube & Conduit Corp. v. Indian Head,[1] the Supreme Court considered whether *Noerr* immunity extended to "petitions" made to a private standard-setting organization that had a great deal of influence on legislation. Indian Head, a maker of plastic conduit, alleged that Allied and other firms who manufactured steel conduit corrupted the processes of the National Fire Protection Association (NFPA) by packing a meeting with its own agents. NFPA was not a governmental entity, but rather a standard-setting association made up of private business firms. The defendants were able to obtain a decision from the standard-setting association disapproving plastic conduit for building construction. NFPA had no authority to pass legislation, of course, but its recommendations were closely followed by numerous state and local governments, which incorporated them into building codes.

In the *Allied Tube* case itself, the plaintiffs had claimed injury as a result of the stigma attached to plastic conduct as a result of the anti-plastic rule. With respect to such injuries, there was no relevant petition to the govern-

§ 18.4

1. See Rickards v. Canine Eye Registration Found., 783 F.2d 1329 (9th Cir.), cert. denied, 479 U.S. 851, 107 S.Ct. 180 (1986) (finding that a sham lawsuit violated § 2 notwithstanding the lack of defendant's market power).

2. See § 6.5.

3. See Neumann v. Reinforced Earth Co., 786 F.2d 424, 428 (D.C.Cir.), cert. denied, 479 U.S. 851, 107 S.Ct. 181 (1986) ("even if the litigation was a sham," the plaintiff "must still prove the other elements of an illegal attempt to monopolize").

4. Professional Real Estate Investors v. Columbia Pictures Industries, 508 U.S. 49, 113 S.Ct. 1920 (1993).

1. 486 U.S. 492, 108 S.Ct. 1931 (1988).

ment. The Supreme Court began with the proposition that *Noerr* immunity might apply to petitions to private bodies, but only if the petition were nothing more than a kind of indirect attempt to obtain a subsequent governmental action. That is to say, *Noerr* does not exempt petitions to private bodies if the body itself then makes rules that are enforced through voluntary compliance or some other means:

> * * * where * * * an economically interested party exercises decision-making authority in formulating a product standard for a private association that comprises market participants, that party enjoys no *Noerr* immunity from any antitrust liability flowing from the effect the standard has *of its own force in the marketplace.*[2]

For example, suppose that the great majority of retailers have a policy of selling electric appliances only if they meet standards promulgated by a trade association's private testing laboratory. A member of the association corruptly obtains a decision from the laboratory board disapproving the plaintiff's product, and numerous stores then decide not to sell that product. *Noerr* plays no role in such a case: no governmental action was sought, and none was obtained.[3]

A much more problematic case arises if (1) the antitrust defendant corrupted the private standard-setting body; (2) the body responded with the anticompetitive rule; (3) local governments enact the anticompetitive rule into law simply on the basis of the standard-setting body's recommendation; and (4) the plaintiff's only injury results from the effect of the enacted laws themselves. Most of the concerns that *Noerr* evokes seem to apply. The failure is one of political process, not of market process. That is, in this case local governments are insufficiently attentive to the biases and distortions that might make recommendations from private trade associations unreliable.[4]

But the problem cannot be disposed of quite this easily. In many areas private rule making takes place in highly technical areas where expertise is necessary and the cost of making fact determinations is extremely high. Furthermore, government officials are generalists and, especially at the local level, do not command the resources necessary to make their own inquiries into the reasonableness of professional recommendations. Following the private decision without a detailed inquiry into the merits is not a result of inattentiveness; it may be inherent in governmental process in technical areas of policy making.

The question then becomes whether those private market participants engaged in standard setting or rule making have a kind of "fiduciary duty" to the public—and, if so, whether the duty is to be enforced by the antitrust laws. As the degree of government abdication grows stronger, so does the case for denying *Noerr* immunity. Suppose, for example, that the state simply passes a statute stating "the standard for electric installations in this state is that promulgated by the National Fire Protection Association." In that case, corruption of NFPA that results in the exclusion of plastic conduit should not enjoy *Noerr* immunity even if the injury results entirely from subsequent government "enactment" of the NFPA standard. The government's "pre-commitment" has effectively made its act nothing more than ministerial. Of course, in most situations the government's prior commitment will be much more ambiguous, involving perhaps a historical pattern of following the private association's recommendations with little debate, but with no statutory commitment to do so.

2. Id. at 510, 108 S.Ct. at 1942 (emphasis added).

3. See id. at 502, 108 S.Ct. at 1938.

4. See Sessions Tank Liners v. Joor Mfg., 17 F.3d 295 (9th Cir.), cert. denied, 513 U.S. 813, 115 S.Ct. 66 (1994) (where the only injury from the defendant's private standard setting resulted when the standards were adopted by various governments, *Noerr* applied).

Chapter 19

ANTITRUST AND FEDERAL REGULATORY POLICY

Table of Sections

---

§ 19.1 Antitrust and Regulation in a Federal System

This chapter is concerned with the relationship between federal antitrust policy and other forms of federal regulation. Then chapter 20 on the "state action" doctrine considers the relation between federal antitrust and the regulatory policies of state and local government. At first glance, the questions raised in these two chapters seem quite different from one another. After all, federal regulation and the federal antitrust laws are passed by the same level of government, and Congress has the authority to repeal, amend or create exceptions to the antitrust laws any time it wishes. By contrast, the relationship between federal statutes and state and local government regulation is governed by the Supremacy Clause of the Constitution,[1] which demands that state and local law give way to valid, inconsistent federal law.

But ultimately these differences are more apparent than real. The "state action" doctrine was developed at a time when sensitivity

§ 19.1

1. U.S. Const. Art. VI, § 2.

toward federalism in our constitutional system was very high. As a result, the Supreme Court was reluctant to run roughshod over legitimate and clearly articulated state interests. Indeed, as we shall see in the next chapter, states and their subdivisions do have a broad power to "repeal" the antitrust laws within regulated industries, provided that they express their designs carefully and carry them out with sufficient attentiveness. As a result, the main differences between the relationship of federal antitrust and federal regulatory policy on the one hand, and federal antitrust and state and local regulation on the other, has to do with the way the doctrines are articulated. The substance is most generally quite similar.

§ 19.2 Regulation, Deregulation and Antitrust Policy

19.2a. The Scope of Regulation and the Domain of Antitrust

Government regulation is ubiquitous and takes many different forms, many of which have little to do with antitrust policy or even with competition as such. For example, OSHA regulates job safety, Title VII regulates race discrimination and sexual harassment in employment relations, and various agencies regulate product quality and safety. None of these regulatory regimes is on an obvious collision course with the antitrust laws. The relationship between antitrust and regulation generally becomes problematic when the regulatory regime (a) controls price; (b) restricts entry (or gives incumbent firms an advantage over new or potential entrants); or (c) requires or permits some practice that antitrust law ordinarily prohibits.

Further, regulation varies in nature and intensity from one regime to another. In some highly regulated markets, firms may have little power to make pricing, entry or expansion decisions on their own; everything must be subjected to close scrutiny by a regulatory agency. In others, the intensity of regulation is not as high, or the domain of decisions subjected to agency scrutiny is smaller, or both.

To state a general principle, the less the regulatory regime interferes with the workings of the market, the more room for antitrust. Intervention under the antitrust laws is generally appropriate with respect to market decisions that (a) are actually or potentially anticompetitive; and (b) are made according to the discretion of private firms without effective agency supervision.

This general principle suggests that the "deregulation" movement which began in the 1970s should lead to an increased role for antitrust in the regulated industries. Precisely that seems to be happening. As industries (such as interstate air travel, trucking or telecommunications) move from price regulation to price competition, the law of collusion, boycott and predatory pricing picks up where agency price regulation left off.

19.2b. The Rationales for Deregulation

19.2b1. Expanded Confidence in Competition and Markets

The Deregulation movement finds its theoretical foundations in two distinct areas of economic theory. The first area, which has its origins in neoclassical price theory and the Coase Theorem,[2] argues that traditional economics has underestimated the role that competition plays in highly concentrated or even natural monopoly markets. The area of inquiry most explicitly concerned with limiting the role of classical regulation is called the theory of "contestable markets." Contestable market theory emphasizes that competition *for* the market is, or can be, competition just as much as competition *in* the market, and can yield competitive pricing. The precondition for such competition is quick and costless entry.

Contestable market theory tends to emphasize the cost of *exit* from the market as the all important entry barrier that might lead to inefficient pricing. The real question for the prospective entrant is not How much does it cost to get in? but rather How much of my

2. See R. Coase, The Problem of Social Cost, 3 J. L. & Econ. 1 (1960) (two persons who have a conflict over some input or resource use will bargain their way to the joint maximizing result).

investment will be lost if I have to get back out? If the answer to the second question is zero (or something close to zero), then so-called "hit and run" entry is possible, and a market should perform competitively even though it has only a single incumbent at any given time.

The favorite example of a contestable market is the passenger airline industry, and airline rate deregulation was accompanied by a great deal of contestable market rhetoric. Air travel was thought to be contestable because, even though airplanes are large and expensive, they are easily transferrable. If the only incumbent operator from Omaha to Natchez is charging a monopoly price, a competitor should be able to swoop into Omaha and undercut the incumbent's price. If entry is instantaneous and the full costs of entry will be recovered upon exit, such entry will occur any time the incumbent charges a price even slightly above its costs. As a result, a perfectly contestable market—one where entry is instantaneous and the net cost of entry and subsequent exit is zero—should yield competitive pricing even though at any given instant there is only a single seller.[3]

Contestable market theory has certainly had positive effects for antitrust analysis. For example, it has re-emphasized the role of competitive bidding for single-seller franchises, and the need for antitrust to take ease of entry more seriously in certain areas, such as merger enforcement. By and large, however, the theoretical preconditions for robust contestability are seldom met, and "imperfectly" contestable markets do not seem to perform nearly as well as imperfectly competitive markets. That is to say, once the conditions for perfect contestability fail, such markets deviate from competitive pricing much more quickly than do traditional, imperfectly competitive markets with multiple sellers. As § 1.4b notes, even in the airline industry, once touted as the most contestable of major markets, the theory gives a poor accounting of reality. Although airplanes and routes may be contestable, gate space in major terminals is not. Indeed, it is oversubscribed, often monopolized, and subject to severe restrictions on expansion. As a practical matter, an airplane cannot swoop into Omaha and rescue overcharged passengers by simply presenting itself on the runway. It must regularize its operations sufficiently so that travellers can count on its presence and its schedule, and perhaps make suitable connections. All of these things require a gate at a minimum, and perhaps other things, such as a hub and a reservation system, that are not so obviously contestable. Importantly, the *least* contestable essential input determines the contestability of the whole. As a result, air routes served by single carriers tend to charge high prices, which come down as the number of carriers go up. That is to say, if we take our air system as a package, warts and all, the system performs more like the ordinary competitive market system than like a perfectly contestable market. For example, mergers in the airline industry that reduce the number of firms flying a particular route almost always generate higher prices—a proposition generally inconsistent with contestability theory.[4]

3. The economics of contestable market theory are explored more fully in § 1.4b. For fuller treatment of the relationship between contestable market theory and deregulation, see 1A Antitrust Law ¶ 241b (rev. ed. 1997).

4. See E. Kim & V. Singal, Mergers and Market Power: Evidence from the Airline Industry, 83 Am. Econ. Rev. 549 (1993) (concluding both that such mergers led to increased prices and that these were not offset by efficiency gains). Some have argued for "reregulation" of the airline industry, as well as other industries thought to be deregulated too hastily. However, the arguments generally mix economic and non-economic concerns. See, for example, R.D. Cudahy, The Coming Demise of Deregulation, 10 Yale J. Reg. 1 (1993); P. Dempsey, The Social and Economic Consequences of Deregulation (1989).

One contestable market theorist, who has worked for the Division, conceded that it generally concludes that relevant airline markets are not larger than city-pair routes—effectively, a concession that the markets are not contestable. R. Willig, Antitrust Lessons from the Airline Industry: the DOJ Experience, 60 Antitrust L.J. 695, 697–698 (1992). The author notes:

> During the late 1970s and early 1980s, many observers, including this author, thought that air travel provided real examples that approximated the conditions of perfectly contestable markets. * * *
>
> Today, the conventional wisdom holds that network effects are crucial to the way the airline business works ..; it is common knowledge that airport space at key network nodes is scarce, and that critical airport assets may be controlled in a concentrated fashion by particular carriers, which may possess market power over travelers as a result.

Seemingly affirming the traditional theory of competition, deregulation of prices has yielded the greatest improvements in competitively structured markets capable of being served by multiple firms simultaneously. Good examples are trucking, the wholesaling of electric power or natural gas through networks of lines, or long distance telecommunications. In such markets one of two things is generally true. First, regulation was very likely a "mismatch" from the beginning.[5] That is, there was really no need to regulate trucking rates when the markets were always capable of accommodating numerous firms who could bid against each other for sales. Second, changes in technology may have facilitated deregulation. For example, when long distance phone calls were all made over a network of wires interconnected to the local telephone system, competition for long distance markets may not have been feasible. But with the rise of microwave and then satellite communication, the long distance part of the telephone network became much more competitively structured. Our current system, with competitive long distance and monopoly local service, reflects the new structure. At the time of this writing, it seems clear that the near future will provide competitive local service as well.

19.2b2. Public Choice: Decreased Confidence in the Regulatory Process

A second branch of economic theory, called public choice, argues that many instances of regulation are the result of legislative or agency "capture" by special interest groups. The regulation was passed, not because it was efficient, but because small, homogeneous interest groups are disproportionately effective at getting their message through, often at the expense of larger more heterogenous groups such as consumers. The result is legislation that represents the interests of the few rather than the many.[6]

One difficulty with public choice theories of regulation is that they have little regard for the relationship between economic theory and the rationales for regulation. If interest group politics explains the development of rate regulation for railroads, electric utilities, or taxicabs, why was steel production, grocery sales or shoe repair not regulated as well? By far the most rational explanation is that regulation of railroads, electricity rates and even taxicabs was a response to prevailing economic theories of natural monopoly or other forms of market failure. It was not merely that the electric utilities had better lobbyists or a better political organization than the steel manufacturers. To be sure, the theories of regulation may have been wrong, or they may now be outmoded, but they were very likely the most robust theories available at the time the regulatory regime in question was passed. This explanation also explains the rise of deregulation in the late 1970s and 1980s. Deregulation did not occur because the lobbying efforts for the regulated firms suddenly fell apart. Rather, it occurred because theories about the nature and robustness of competition, such as contestable market theory,[7] as well as their own experience with regulation, convinced policy makers that regulation in many areas was not worth its costs. Under the prevailing theory at any given time, the regulation that was passed was perceived to be in the public interest.[8]

Nonetheless, Public Choice theory, and the more specific theory of regulatory capture,

5. See S. Breyer, Regulation and its Reform, ch. 12 (1982).

6. See § 18.1c; for surveys of the literature, especially insofar as it affects legal policy, see D. Farber & P. Frickey, *Law and Public Choice: a Critical Introduction* (Chicago: Univ. of Chicago Press, 1991). For specific application to regulation, see G. Stigler, The Theory of Economic Regulation, 2 Bell J. Econ. & Mgt. Sci. 3 (1971); R. Posner, Theories of Economic Regulation, 5 Bell J. Econ. & Mgt. Sci. 335 (1974). For good historical perspective on regulation and deregulation, see R. Vietor, Contrived Competition: Regulation and Deregulation in America (1994); The Regulated Economy: A Historical Approach to Political Economy (C. Goldin & G. Libecap, eds. 1994); E. Sanders, "The Regulatory Surge of the 1970s in Historical Perspective, in Public Regulation: New Perspectives on Institutions and Policies" (E. Bailey, ed., 1987); T. K. McCraw, Prophets of Regulation (1984).

7. See §§ 1.4b, 19.2b1.

8. For elaboration, see H. Hovenkamp, Enterprise and American Law, 1836–1937, chs. 10–13 (1991); H. Hovenkamp, Regulation History as Politics or Markets (reviewing The Regulated Economy: A Historical Approach to Political Economy) (C. Goldin & G. Libecap, eds.), 12 Yale J. Reg. 549 (1995). For a survey of other literature, see M. Levine & J. Forrence, Regulatory Capture, Public Interest, and the Public Agenda: Toward A Synthesis, 6 J. L., Econ. & Org. 167 (1990); for a more pessimistic view, see G. Priest, The Origins of Utility Regulation and the "Theories of Regulation" Debate, 36 J.L. & Econ. 289 (1993).

may explain excessive or badly designed regulation. In the process, such theory may drive powerful arguments for deregulation or for redesign of a regulatory regime. As a general matter, however, an antitrust tribunal is not charged with second guessing Congress or any other legislative body on matters of regulatory policy. Even imperfect regulatory regimes are generally to be taken at face value. As a result, the theory of regulatory capture guides antitrust mainly at the margins. If certain regulatory regimes seem to be anticompetitive, then antitrust scrutinizes the conduct carefully to ensure that the regulatory mandate is really being carried out and not too much is being left to private discretion.

This observation is critical to understanding the role of antitrust in a complex, regulated economy such as our own. Antitrust generally presumes that competitive markets are better than noncompetitive ones. But it also acknowledges two additional things. First, market failures exist that may require public intervention into the market. Second, the prerogative of recognizing market failures and fashioning a corrective belongs in the first instance to legislatures and executives, not to courts. As a result, antitrust does not generally interpose its own theory of the appropriate nature or domain of regulation, even if the antitrust decision maker thinks the regulation is excessive or ill-advised.[9]

§ 19.3 The Role of Antitrust in the Regulated Market

As an abstract proposition, antitrust in the regulated industries can be seen as serving the following goals: (1) to help ensure that the regulatory regime achieves its economic goals, whatever those goals may be; (2) to make markets perform more competitively, given the regulatory regime that happens to control them; and (3) to scrutinize private conduct that is not effectively reviewed or controlled by the regulatory regime. The less room there is for competition and private discretion, the less the role for antitrust.

19.3a. Express or Implied Repeal

The case for limiting the role of antitrust in the regulated industries is strongest when the federal regulatory statute *expressly* exempts firms from antitrust liability. For example, the Shipping Act of 1984 contains a set of antitrust-like provisions that apply to common carriers regulated by the Federal Maritime Commission, and expressly prohibits private antitrust actions based on activities within the jurisdiction of that agency.[1] Likewise, federal statutes regulating railroads and trucking permit firms to engage in joint rate making without running afoul of the antitrust policy against collusion.[2]

In other cases, a federal agency has the authority to grant antitrust immunity as an administrative decision, although such authority will not generally be presumed.[3] As a general matter, such "exemptions from antitrust laws are strictly construed,"[4] and an antitrust court can, under appropriate circumstances, second guess both the agency's interpretation

9. See 1A Antitrust Law ¶ 241b,c (rev. ed. 1997).

§ 19.3

1. See 46 U.S.C.A. § 1701–1720. The antitrust exemption appears at 46 U.S.C.A. § 1706(c)(2). See Seawinds v. Nedlloyd Lines, 80 B.R. 181 (N.D.Cal.1987), affirmed, 846 F.2d 586 (9th Cir.), cert. denied, 488 U.S. 891, 109 S.Ct. 226 (1988) (applying the exemption).

2. Motor Carrier Act of 1980, 49 U.S.C.A. § 10706(b)("A rail carrier * * * that is a party to an agreement of at least two rail carriers * * * that relates to rates * * * shall apply to the Commission for approval of that agreement. * * * If the Commission approves * * * the Sherman Act, the Clayton Act, the Federal Trade Commission Act * * * do not apply * * * with respect to making or carrying out the agreement"); Staggers Rail Act of 1980, 49 U.S.C.A. § 10706(a) (same).

3. E.g., Coal Exporters Ass'n of U.S. v. United States, 745 F.2d 76 (D.C.Cir.1984), cert. denied, 471 U.S. 1072, 105 S.Ct. 2151 (1985) (Interstate Commerce Commission—now, the Surface Transportation Board—incorrectly interpreted its authorization to grant an immunity); Advanced Micro Devices v. Civil Aeronautics Board, 742 F.2d 1520 (D.C.Cir.1984) (same). See 1A Antitrust Law ¶ 243 (rev. ed. 1997).

4. FMC v. Seatrain Lines, 411 U.S. 726, 733, 93 S.Ct. 1773 (1973) (construing exemption language narrowly so as to cover operating agreements but not mergers); Springfield Terminal Rwy. Co. v. Canadian Pacific Limited, 133 F.3d 103 (1st Cir.1997) (ICC—now Surface Transportation Board—had authority to approve railroad mergers, but this did not operate to immunize alleged predatory pricing not arising out of the merger).

of the law as well as its fact determinations.[5]

Most regulatory statutes say nothing at all about the impact of the regulatory regime on antitrust jurisdiction. In these cases, any limitation on or exemption from antitrust must be considered as implied rather than express. Once again, the domain of such exemptions is narrow. As the Supreme Court has said, "Repeals of the antitrust laws by implication from a regulatory statute are strongly disfavored, and have only been found in cases of plain repugnancy between the antitrust and regulatory provisions."[6]

19.3b. The Relation Between Federal Regulation and Antitrust Jurisdiction: Two Views

The traditional approach to antitrust in the regulated industries viewed regulation as a closed box, and a particular market as either inside or outside of the box. A market was either "regulated" or "unregulated." If the former, antitrust was generally unwelcome or at least seriously confined. Within this paradigm, the antitrust tribunal was generally called upon to determine the "pervasiveness" of the regulatory regime. If it was deemed to be pervasive, then all activities within that regime were presumptively exempt from antitrust scrutiny.[7] This approach is built on a rather optimistic model of agency decision making. In an ideal regulatory regime, an agency considering a regulated firm's request would determine all relevant social and economic implications, including the impact on competition. Such a model would be efficient, because the entire record could be developed comprehensively, showing all effects of regulation in a single elaborate proceeding. Many policies respecting public decision making work on such a model. For example, the Federal Rules of Civil Procedure have liberal rules about joinder of issues and parties into a single litigation. Comprehensive public decision making, which resolves all disputed issues in a single proceeding, may seem more cost-effective than piece-by-piece analysis, and more likely to produce consistent results.

But the deregulation movement has changed our perceptions of both the nature and the domain of regulation. First, real world decision making is never as comprehensive or elegant as the previous paragraph suggests. Invariably, agencies do *not* pass on every relevant issue. No matter how "thick" the underlying regime, the agency does not collect all relevant information and consider all relevant factors. Indeed, often it may not consider certain antitrust-related issues at all. As a result, some elements of a regulated firm's conduct are supervised by a regulatory agency, while others are not.

In this regard, the lustre that regulation wore during the Progressive Era and New Deal has been tarnished considerably.[8] Today we think of regulation as expensive, unwieldy, and highly imperfect insofar as its stated goal is to mimic market behavior. As a result, when market forces are working properly, we want them to have free rein, even *within* the regulated market.

Second, today we are more inclined to think of *all* markets as "regulated" to some degree. Antitrust is a form of "regulation"—that is, of sovereign intervention into the marketplace to force a solution different from the one that unrestrained private bargaining would produce. Viewed in this way, even property, tort and contract rules established under the common law are a form of regulation.

Within this perspective, which is heavily influenced by the deregulation movement, the whole question of antitrust involvement be-

5. For example, *Coal Exporters*, note 3 (agency misinterpreted its statute); Arizona Pub. Serv. Co. v. United States, 742 F.2d 644 (D.C.Cir.1984) (ICC fact finding of absence of market dominance incorrect).

6. United States v. Philadelphia National Bank, 374 U.S. 321, 350–351, 83 S.Ct. 1715, 1735 (1963); 1A Antitrust Law ¶ 243 (rev. ed. 1997).

7. See Hughes Tool Co. v. Trans World Airlines, Inc., 409 U.S. 363, 93 S.Ct. 647, (1973) (finding pervasive scheme); Otter Tail Power Co. v. United States, 410 U.S. 366, 93 S.Ct. 1022 (1973) (no pervasive regulatory scheme for wholesale electric power; so no immunity); *Philadelphia Natl. Bank*, note 6, 374 U.S. at 352, 83 S.Ct. at 1735 (same).

8. For a historical glimpse, See T. McCraw, Prophets of Regulation (1984).

comes much more particularized, in two different senses. First, the pervasiveness of the general regulatory regime is relatively unimportant.[9] Second, we generally do not divide the territory into "regulated" and "unregulated" aspects of a firm's behavior. Rather, we consider whether the activity is or should be "regulated by the agency" or "regulated by the antitrust laws." What we really want to know is whether the conduct being challenged was instigated by a public regulatory agency, or perhaps approved after a fairly full review of the merits; or whether the challenged restraint resulted from the essentially unsupervised conduct of a private firm. If the latter, then it should be regarded as "market" conduct and the antitrust laws should presumptively apply. If the private conduct being challenged was "neither compelled nor approved" by the regulatory body, then any claim of antitrust immunity is greatly weakened.[10] In such cases, the court will generally deny the immunity unless application of the antitrust laws would create a "clear repugnancy" between the regulatory statute at issue and federal antitrust policy.[11]

For example, in its *MCI* decision the Seventh Circuit concluded that the "mere pervasiveness" of a regulatory scheme does not create an antitrust immunity with respect to conduct that was "voluntarily initiated" and carried out.[12] Rather, the existence of an immunity depended on a showing that *either* "the activities that are the subject of MCI's complaint were required or approved by the [agency], pursuant to its statutory authority, in a way that is incompatible with antitrust enforcement" or whether the "activities were so pervasively regulated 'that Congress must be assumed to have forsworn the paradigm of competition.' "[13]

In sum, whether the regulatory regime is "pervasive" is not nearly as important as is the answer to questions such as (1) whether the conduct being challenged was within the jurisdiction of the agency; (2) whether it was actually presented to the agency for review; (3) whether the agency appropriately reviewed potential anticompetitive consequences; (4) whether application of the antitrust laws in this particular instance would create inconsistent mandates or would frustrate the operation of the regulatory process; and (5) whether the agency has special expertise not generally available to antitrust tribunals to evaluate a particular claim.

For example, in *Gordon* the Supreme Court held that antitrust scrutiny over alleged fixing of brokerage commissions would collide with the New York Stock Exchange's authority to set the rules governing how brokerage rates should be set.[14] By contrast, in Sound v. AT & T the court found no inconsistency between application of the antitrust laws to the defendant's alleged exclusionary practices against those wishing to interconnect their devices to its telephone lines.[15] In this case the Federal Communications Commission did indeed have a "public interest" standard under which to determine whether AT & T was to interconnect specific pieces of equipment made by competitors to its lines. However, the FCC had not been particularly aggressive about enforcing the standard. More importantly, the standard articulated in the Sherman Act, which condemned anticompetitive exclusionary practices, was found to be in harmony with, rather than inconsistent with, the public interest standard employed by the FCC.[16]

9. See 1A Antitrust Law ¶ 243e (rev. ed. 1997).

10. National Gerimedical Hosp. v. Blue Cross, 452 U.S. 378, 101 S.Ct. 2415 (1981) (immunity denied where no regulatory agency was empowered to supervise the challenged conduct).

11. Id. at 389, 101 S.Ct. at 2422.

12. MCI Communic. Corp. v. AT & T, 708 F.2d 1081 (7th Cir.1983), cert. denied, 464 U.S. 891, 104 S.Ct. 234 (1983). Accord Northeastern Tel. Co. v. AT & T, 651 F.2d 76, 82–83 (2d Cir.1981), cert. denied, 455 U.S. 943, 102 S.Ct. 1438 (1982); Southern Pacific Communic. Co. v. AT & T, 740 F.2d 980, 1000 (D.C.Cir.1984), cert. denied, 470 U.S. 1005, 105 S.Ct. 1359 (1985).

13. *MCI*, 708 F.2d at 1102.

14. Gordon v. New York Stock Exchange, 422 U.S. 659, 95 S.Ct. 2598 (1975).

15. Sound, Inc. v. AT & T, 631 F.2d 1324 (8th Cir. 1980).

16. Accord Midland Telecasting Co. v. Midessa Television Co., 617 F.2d 1141 (5th Cir.), cert. denied, 449 U.S. 954, 101 S.Ct. 361 (1980) (no conflict between regulatory standard designed to promote competition in cable mar-

Judicial deference to an agency may be in order when both the agency and the antitrust court seem to have jurisdiction over a claim, but the agency appears to have specialized expertise that the court lacks. This problem is considered in § 19.4. Likewise, certain industries have *express* antitrust exemptions drafted into the regulatory statute. A few of these are considered briefly in § 19.7.[17]

19.3c. Requisite Regulatory Oversight; "State Action" Compared

How much regulatory oversight is necessary to make particular conduct immune from antitrust scrutiny? The Supreme Court has had little to say on that question in the context of federally regulated industries. However, as the following chapter notes, the Court has said a great deal concerning the amount of "active supervision" that a *state* regulatory agency must engage in before private activity qualifies for the state action exemption. There is no obvious reason why the standard should be any different. That is, once we have concluded that the regulatory regime itself has been properly authorized and is operating within its jurisdiction, we want to assure ourselves that private conduct has been reviewed with the suitable degree of attentiveness. This question should be about the same for both federal and state agencies.[18]

A few decisions have looked to the Supreme Court's "state action" decisions in determining the degree of scrutiny that is appropriate when federal regulation is in question. For example, in *American Agriculture Movement*[19] the Seventh Circuit relied on *Ticor Title Insurance*,[20] a state action decision involving state regulatory agencies, to query into the degree of supervision required of a federal agency:

> [I]mmunity is proper when the relevant agency's scrutiny and approval of the challenged practice is active, intrusive and appropriately deliberative. Put another way, an antitrust court, before relinquishing jurisdiction over allegedly anticompetitive activities, must be convinced that the agency has exercised its independent judgment in reflecting upon and approving the activity at issue.[21]

This required a level of scrutiny that "focuses on the extent to which an administrative agency has actually exercised its supervisory powers over the particular practices at issue."[22] In sum, that inquiry is essentially the same, whether the source of the regulation is the federal government or the states or their properly authorized subdivisions.

§ 19.4 Procedure in Areas of Divided Authority; Primary Jurisdiction

The "primary jurisdiction" doctrine, as its name implies, is not an antitrust exemption but a jurisdictional mechanism for proceeding with a case that may involve an antitrust claim. When a regulatory regime completely ousts the antitrust court, the regulatory agency's jurisdiction over the claim is said to be "exclusive." This happens in some markets because the statute provides an express exemption from antitrust, and in other markets because the court implies an exemption.

ket, and standard articulated by the antitrust laws). Contrast Finnegan v. Campeau Corp., 915 F.2d 824, 830–831 (2d Cir.1990), which held that the Williams Act and antitrust imposed different standards with respect to a charge that competing bidders for a firm's stock agreed not to bid against each other. In this case the SEC had expressly permitted such agreements, provided that they were disclosed, and not fraudulent or manipulative."

17. For detailed coverage, see 1A Antitrust Law ¶ 251 (rev. ed. 1997).

18. On the "active supervision" requirement of the state action doctrine, see § 20.5.

19. American Agriculture Movement v. Board of Trade, City of Chicago, 977 F.2d 1147 (7th Cir.1992).

20. FTC v. Ticor Title Ins. Co., 504 U.S. 621, 112 S.Ct. 2169 (1992), on remand, 998 F.2d 1129 (3d Cir.1993). See § 20.5b.

21. *American Agriculture Movement*, 977 F.2d at 1166, relying on *Ticor Title*, 504 U.S. at 633–634, 112 S.Ct. at 2177. The court found the scrutiny inadequate.

22. *American Agriculture Movement*, 977 F.2d at 1158. Compare United States v. Rockford Memorial Corp., 898 F.2d 1278, 1285 (7th Cir.), cert. denied, 498 U.S. 920, 111 S.Ct. 295 (1990) (mere fact that hospital market was regulated did not serve to immunize a merger); Wheat Rail Freight Rate Antitrust Litigation, 759 F.2d 1305, 1313 (7th Cir.1985), cert. denied, 476 U.S. 1158, 106 S.Ct. 2275 (1986) (immunity for rate-making practices where the ICC had reviewed and approved them).

But even where courts have some jurisdiction to resolve antitrust disputes in a regulated market, some deference to the regulatory agency may be in order. This is particularly true of cases where complex facts need to be determined and the agency is better situated than the court to make these determinations.[1] Further, the agency may be in a much better position than the court is to evaluate how the antitrust claim fits into the entire regulatory picture.

In Ricci v. Chicago Mercantile Exchange, the Supreme Court elaborated on the rationale and process of the primary jurisdiction doctrine.[2] Ricci, a broker, claimed that he had been denied a seat on the Exchange as a result of a concerted refusal to deal involving the Exchange itself and at least one Exchange member. The Commodity Exchange Commission had oversight of the exchange and its rule making, and the plaintiff was alleging violations of the Commodity Exchange Act as well as the Sherman Act. The Supreme Court held that the antitrust court should stay its hand until the Commission had had a chance to decide. Importantly, this was not an exclusive jurisdiction case: the Commission did not have the power to confer antitrust immunity. Rather, it was to determine what the Exchange policies were and whether they had been violated in this case. If the rule had been violated, then there was nothing to prevent the antitrust litigation from proceeding. If the rule had not been violated, then perhaps the antitrust dispute could proceed in any event, but first the court would have to determine whether use of the antitrust laws to condemn conduct permitted under a rule approved by the Commission created a fundamental inconsistency justifying a limited antitrust exemption.[3]

Where the primary jurisdiction doctrine operates, it can have two effects. In some cases a federal court will simply stay its proceedings pending an agency resolution of a particular issue.[4] In other cases the antitrust suit will be dismissed without prejudice and the antitrust plaintiff effectively told to take its case to the agency first.[5] If the plaintiff files its antitrust claim in court on time, and the court defers to the regulatory agency, then the statute of limitation has been tolled even though agency resolution will run beyond the four year limit.

Where the plaintiff has not filed an antitrust suit but waits an agency determination, the circuit courts differ on the question whether the four year antitrust statute of limitation is tolled during the pendency of the agency action. The trend seems to be against tolling.[6] In tolling the statute while the administrative action was pending, the *Ninth Circuit* expressed concern that a contrary rule would force plaintiffs to do just the opposite of what the primary jurisdiction doctrine encompassed: it would make them go to court first, even though the dispute was better suited for resolution by the regulatory agency.[7] Most of the courts that have refused to toll the statute of limitation have relied on stricter interpretations of the statute of limitation itself, which requires that the antitrust action be filed within four years of its accrual. Further, some have suggested that tolling would be appropriate if the plaintiff is required to file its administra-

§ 18.4

1. E.g., Mt. Hood Stages, Inc. v. Greyhound Corp., 616 F.2d 394, 399 (9th Cir.), cert. denied, 449 U.S. 831, 101 S.Ct. 99 (1980); United States v. General Dynamics Corp., 828 F.2d 1356, 1362 (9th Cir.1987). Both cases deferred to the agencies to make complex fact determinations, and tolled the statute of limitation in the meanwhile.

2. 409 U.S. 289, 93 S.Ct. 573 (1973).

3. Id. at 307, 93 S.Ct. at 583.

4. Segal v. AT & T, 606 F.2d 842 (9th Cir.1979) (staying proceeding pending FCC resolution of administrative claims).

5. For example, Sea–Land Serv. v. Alaska R.R., 1980–2 Trade Cas. (CCH) ¶ 63481 at 76527, 1980 WL 1881 (D.D.C.1980), affirmed on other grounds, 659 F.2d 243 (D.C.Cir.1981), cert. denied, 455 U.S. 919, 102 S.Ct. 1274 (1982).

6. Mt. Hood Stages, Inc. v. Greyhound Corp., 616 F.2d 394, 399–400 (9th Cir.), cert. denied, 449 U.S. 831, 101 S.Ct. 99 (1980) (tolling statute); Higgins v. New York Stock Exchange, 942 F.2d 829, 833–834 (2d Cir.1991) (refusing to toll statute, unless invocation of agency claim is jurisdictional prerequisite to antitrust filing); Community Elec. Serv. v. National Elec. Contractors Ass'n., 869 F.2d 1235, 1241 (9th Cir.), cert. denied, 493 U.S. 891, 110 S.Ct. 236 (1989) (same; refusing to toll); Brunswick Corp. v. Riegel Textile Corp., 752 F.2d 261, 269–270 (7th Cir. 1984), cert. denied, 472 U.S. 1018, 105 S.Ct. 3480 (1985) (refusing to toll).

7. *Mt. Hood Stages*, note 6, 616 F.2d at 399–400.

tive action as a prerequisite to filing its antitrust claim.[8]

Also problematic is the weight that the antitrust court must give to the fact findings made by the regulatory agency. In *Ricci*, the Supreme Court suggested that issues actually determined in the agency proceeding would not have to be relitigated in the subsequent judicial proceeding—that is, there should be a kind of res judicata or collateral estoppel as between the agency and the court.[9] Often this could be a peculiar outcome to say the least, because very likely the antitrust plaintiff was not a party in the agency proceeding. Often, when a competitor, consumer or other aggrieved person complains to a regulatory agency, the parties to the inquiry that results are the agency and the firm against which the complaint is brought. The complainant itself is merely a witness. To bind a non-party to an adverse judgment of the agency would violate due process. Of course, if the complainant is a party, collateral estoppel or res judicata could apply.[10] A better way to view the matter in such cases is that the court should give some deference to the agency's expertise, but cannot consider itself bound by the judgment. By contrast, if the complainant wins in the regulatory agency, then there may be a good case for nonmutual, or "offensive" collateral estoppel. The antitrust defendant, or the firm that lost in the regulatory proceeding, *was* a party there, and could be bound to the extent that an issue was the same, was fully and fairly litigated and essential to the outcome.[11] Even then, courts may refuse to apply offensive collateral estoppel if the agency had different burdens of proof than the court, used different rules of evidence, or had substantially different procedures.[12]

One important corollary of *Ricci* is that the antitrust tribunal need not wait for agency resolution if that resolution will have no bearing one way or the other on the antitrust dispute.[13] Likewise, if the principal questions at issue are legal, and the agency has no competence that the courts themselves lack, then yielding jurisdiction is unnecessary.[14] A few courts also hold that deference is inappropriate where the agency does not have the power to give the kinds of remedies that the antitrust plaintiff is seeking.[15] But such a rule generally goes too far—no agency has the power to award the full panoply of damages available in private plaintiff civil antitrust litigation. Indeed, the agency's purpose is not to decide civil liability as to a particular plaintiff, but only whether the regulated firm has violated the provisions of the regulatory regime.

§ 19.5 Market Power Offenses in Regulated Markets

Often antitrust doctrine in the regulated industries has a slightly different look from

8. See *Higgins*, note 6; *Community Elect.*, note 6.

9. *Ricci*, 409 U.S. at 305, 93 S.Ct. at 582.

10. See Aunyx Corp. v. Canon U.S.A., 978 F.2d 3 (1st Cir.1992), cert. denied, 507 U.S. 973, 113 S.Ct. 1416 (1993) (dealer who was a party, and who lost conspiracy claim before International Trade Commission, could not bring subsequent federal court antitrust suit).

11. City of Anaheim v. Southern Cal. Edison Co., 1990–2 Trade Cas. ¶ 69246, 1990 WL 209261 (C.D.Cal. 1990) (no offensive collateral estoppel where price/cost issues addressed by agency did not include all elements of an attempt to monopolize claim).

12. See, for example, Borough of Ellwood City v. Pennsylvania Power Co., 570 F.Supp. 553, 560 (W.D.Pa.1983) (declining to apply offensive collateral estoppel because agency did not have jurisdiction over federal antitrust claims, could not give the relief requested, and was willing to accept defenses that would not have been accepted to an antitrust claim). See also Exxon Corp. v. Fischer, 807 F.2d 842, 845–846 (9th Cir.), modified on other grounds, 817 F.2d 1429 (9th Cir.1987) (applying collateral estoppel; assessing requirements as "(1) whether the [agency] was acting in a judicial capacity; (2) whether the issue presented to the district court was actually litigated before the [agency]; and (3) whether its resolution was necessary to the [agency's] decision").

13. International Travel Arrangers, Inc. v. Western Airlines, 623 F.2d 1255 (8th Cir.), cert. denied, 449 U.S. 1063, 101 S.Ct. 787 (1980) (agency's determination of "unfair competition" under regulatory provision would not dispose of antitrust claims).

14. *Ricci*, note 2, 409 U.S. at 305–306, 93 S.Ct. at 582–583 (agencies not to be presumed better than courts at resolving purely legal issues); ICC v. Big Sky Farmers & Ranchers Marketing Co–op., 451 F.2d 511, 515 (9th Cir. 1971) (same).

15. Long Lake Energy Corp. v. Niagara Mohawk Power Corp., 700 F.Supp. 186, 189 (S.D.N.Y.1988) (primary jurisdiction of agency not recognized where agency did not have power to award treble damages and legislative history suggested that Congress did not intend regulatory regime to cut off antitrust damage actions).

antitrust in ordinary competitive markets. The presence of a regulatory regime may have a great impact on how market power or entry barriers are measured. Some substantive doctrines, such as the essential facility doctrine, appear to have a larger place in regulated than in unregulated markets.[1]

The measurement of market power in regulated markets can be complicated by two distinct factors. First, regulated markets are often natural monopolies in which marginal costs are very low and marginal cost pricing would be unprofitable to the firm. In such cases technical formulations like the Lerner Index do not provide a very good indication of market power, insofar as antitrust policy is concerned.[2] The Lerner Index assumes that healthy competition occurs when price equals marginal cost. But in a natural monopoly market, price can be higher than marginal cost, thus producing a positive reading on the Index, and yet the firm could be losing money because it is not recovering its fixed costs.[3]

The second factor is the presence of regulation itself, which may do two different things. First, it may give the firm an exclusive right to deal in a defined area. Second, regulation may designate the price at which a firm must sell. On the one hand, courts have said that market power is measured by a dominant share of a relevant market. On the other, they have defined market power as the ability to control prices. A price regulated public utility may be thought to have substantial market power under the market share test, but perhaps no market power at all under the test of power to control price. Some courts have held that dominant market share is relatively less important to the assessment of market power in the case of a regulated public utility than for dominant firms generally.[4] Other courts have noted that price regulation may limit substantially a firm's power over price. As the Fifth Circuit put it, in appropriate circumstances price regulation could be an "adequate replacement" for the lack of rivalry among firms.[5]

The latter conclusion must be qualified, however. First, price regulation seldom drives prices to marginal cost. In many price regulated industries a marginal cost price would be unprofitable, for there would not be enough revenues to cover fixed costs. To the extent that public utility prices are above marginal cost, the utility has an incentive to enlarge its market share at the expense of rivals, *even* if such an enlargement is inefficient—that is, even if the firm is not the lowest cost supplier to the new area, or if expansion entails the shutting down of equally efficient plants owned by others.[6] That is to say, the public utility may "monopolize" not by setting a higher price but by increasing its service area at the regulated price. As a result, the most meaningful measure of market power for antitrust purposes is generally the "power to exclude competition."[7] For example, the great

§ 19.5

1. On essential facilities, see § 7.7. On special problems of antitrust actions against regulated dominant firms, see 3A Antitrust Law ¶¶ 785–787 (rev. ed. 1996).

2. On the Lerner Index, see § 3.1a.

3. On natural monopoly, see § 1.4b. In fact, the question is much more complicated than the text discussion indicates. Although the natural monopoly firm might be losing money at a price above marginal cost, it does face a downward sloping demand curve and might be able to profit further by reducing output more. Further, marginal cost pricing might still be the best determinant of the efficient rate of output, although some other means would have to be devised for ensuring that the firm recovered its fixed costs. See R. Coase, The Marginal Cost Controversy, 13 Economica (n.s.) 169 (1946).

4. MCI Communic. Corp. v. AT & T, 708 F.2d 1081, 1106–1108 (7th Cir.), cert. denied, 464 U.S. 891, 104 S.Ct. 234 (1983) (market share "inaccurate or misleading" mechanism for measuring market power of regulated monopoly).

5. Almeda Mall v. Houston Lighting & Power Co., 615 F.2d 343, 354 (5th Cir.), cert. denied, 449 U.S. 870, 101 S.Ct. 208 (1980).

6. See H. Averch & L.L. Johnson, Behavior of the Firm Under Regulatory Constraint, 52 Am. Econ. Rev. 1052 (1962); 2 A. Kahn, The Economics of Regulation: Principles and Institutions 106–108 (rev. ed. 1988). The empirical robustness of the so-called "Averch–Johnson" effect has been controversial. For a summary of empirical tests, see K. Train, Optimal Regulation: the Economic Theory of Natural Monopoly 61–67 (1991), concluding that the theory holds up quite well under empirical testing, generally finding overinvestment in capital among price regulated firms; for other studies, see R. Sherman, The Averch and Johnson Analysis of Public Utility Regulation Twenty Years Later, 2 Rev. Indus. Org. 178 (1985).

7. See Illinois ex rel. Hartigan v. Panhandle E. Pipe Line Co., 730 F.Supp. 826, 904–907 (C.D.Ill.1990), af-

majority of antitrust cases brought against AT & T prior to its breakup were interconnection cases in markets that were price regulated. The effect of AT & T's "exclusionary practices" was to enlarge the scope of its activity at the regulated price.[8]

Importantly, even "regulated" firms are not regulated in all aspects of their operations. For example, although the retail delivery of electricity remains for the most part a price regulated monopoly, the generation and wholesaling of electricity is quite competitive, and market power can at least presumptively be measured by the traditional criteria.[9]

Entry barriers also deserve special consideration in the regulatory framework.[10] Government restrictions remain one of the most ubiquitous sources of entry barriers, taking forms as diverse as absolute restrictions against entry, certificates of need, licensing requirements, and the like. These entry restrictions explain why the so-called "essential facility" doctrine in monopolization cases[11] has found such widespread application in markets subject to regulation. Regulation creates essential facilities by the simple device of limiting entry. Indeed, the essential facility doctrine formed one of the doctrinal bases for numerous lawsuits against AT & T and the eventual divestiture of the telephone company.[12] For example, the *MCI* case involved a challenge to AT & T's refusal to grant certain interconnections to MCI, so that MCI could tie its long distance communications to the nationwide telephone network. The court held that AT & T's refusal was governed by the essential facility doctrine:

> "Such a refusal may be unlawful because a monopolist's control of an essential facility (sometimes called a "bottleneck") can extend monopoly power from one stage of production to another, and from one market into another. Thus, the antitrust laws have imposed on firms controlling an essential facility the obligation to make the facility available on nondiscriminatory terms."[13]

The *MCI* court then identified four elements necessary to establish an essential facility claim, all of which may apply to the operator of a monopoly utility that interconnects with more competitive markets:

> (1) control of the essential facility by a monopolist; (2) a competitor's inability practically or reasonably to duplicate the essential facility; (3) the denial of the use of the facility to a competitor; and (4) the feasibility of providing the facility.[14]

The essential facility doctrine has been applied to access to telephone listings for preparation of telephone directories,[15] the connection of terminal equipment to telephone lines,[16] interconnections with railway lines,[17] and interconnection with electric transmission lines.[18] In

firmed 935 F.2d 1469 (7th Cir.1991), cert. denied, 502 U.S. 1094, 112 S.Ct. 1169 (1992) (finding market power in firm's ability to deny others access to its pipelines).

8. E.g., Sound, Inc. v. AT & T, 631 F.2d 1324 (8th Cir.1980) (refusal to interconnect with price regulated product); MCI Communic. Corp. v. AT & T, 708 F.2d 1081 (7th Cir.), cert. denied, 464 U.S. 891, 104 S.Ct. 234 (1983) (same).

9. See Town of Concord v. Boston Edison Co., 915 F.2d 17 (1st Cir.1990), cert. denied, 499 U.S. 931, 111 S.Ct. 1337, rehearing denied, 500 U.S. 930, 111 S.Ct. 2047 (1991) (refusing to infer market power in generation from a natural monopoly in retailing).

10. On entry barriers, see §§ 1.6, 12.6.

11. See § 7.7.

12. United States v. AT & T, 552 F.Supp. 131 (D.D.C. 1982), aff'd mem. sub nom., Maryland v. U.S., 460 U.S. 1001, 103 S.Ct. 1240 (1983).

13. MCI Communic. Corp. v. AT & T, 708 F.2d 1081, 1132 (7th Cir.), cert. denied, 464 U.S. 891, 104 S.Ct. 234 (1983).

14. Id. at 1132–1133.

15. Bellsouth Advertising & Publishing Corp. v. Donnelley Information Pub., 719 F.Supp. 1551 (S.D.Fla.1988), affirmed, 933 F.2d 952 (11th Cir.1991) (disapproving summary judgment), reversed after remand on nonantitrust grounds 999 F.2d 1436 (11th Cir.1993).

16. United States v. Western Elec. Co., 673 F.Supp. 525 (D.D.C.1987) (refusing to remove business restrictions from earlier consent decree as long as regional telephone companies retained dominant control of networks, which were essential facilities).

17. Delaware & Hudson Rwy. Co. v. Consolidated Rail Corp., 902 F.2d 174, 180 (2d Cir.1990) (disapproving summary judgment).

18. See City of Malden, Mo. v. Union Elec. Co., 887 F.2d 157 (8th Cir.1989) (finding no liability where dealing would have been impractical under the defendant's regulatory tariff).

1999, however, the Supreme Court refused to decide whether the antitrust essential facility doctrine was the correct test under the 1996 Telecommunications Act for a dominant telephone exchange's duty to interconnect.[19] What all these cases share in common is that regulatory policy, whether historical or current, was the source of the claimed essential facility.

§ 19.6 Antitrust Damages Actions and Regulated Rates: the *Keogh* Doctrine

The *Keogh* doctrine is named after a 1922 Supreme Court decision holding that private plaintiffs may not claim treble damages for overcharge injuries resulting from price-fixing, when the challenged prices were rates that had been filed before a regulatory agency.[1] Such challenges could come only from the government.[2] The Court gave four reasons for its decision. First, the regulatory scheme permitted the recovery of damages in a proceeding before the agency, and Congress would not likely have intended to give duplicate remedies. Second, one purpose of agency regulation was to prevent rate discrimination, but discrimination would result if a two-track system of remedies permitted different consumers to obtain different effective rates. Third, damages recovery would depend on a showing that a hypothetical lower rate was the correct one, and that this rate would have been approved by the agency. Whether the agency would actually have approved this lower rate could be better determined in the first instance by the agency itself, rather than by a court. Finally, the customer would not be injured by the higher rate because, assuming that all customers were charged the same higher rate, the rate would simply be passed on to their customers.[3]

None of these arguments had much to be said for them at the time they were originally made, and they are even less sensible today. First, statutory schemes create duplicate remedies all the time, and many things that violate a regulatory rule also violate the antitrust laws. On the second rationale, the Court's observation was either wrong or no longer applicable: rate discrimination is in fact an inherent feature of regulated pricing. But in any event, modern joinder provisions such as class actions would generally result in widespread damages recoveries. Further, injunctive relief would apply to all customers. And, in any event, the Court's second argument would apply to unregulated firms as much as regulated ones. Customers that obtain damages from price fixers get a lower effective price than customers who fail to obtain them. The Court's third argument was simply reasoning in a circle. The whole issue is whether the regulatory agency did an adequate job of overseeing the rate-making process in the first instance. Finally, the Court's fourth argument was really one that final consumers, rather than intermediate purchasers should have the damages action in those situations where the direct purchasers were intermediaries.[4] In any event, many utility customers *are* end use consumers, but *Keogh* denies a damages action to them as well.

These criticisms and others notwithstanding, in Square D Co. v. Niagara Frontier Tariff Bureau,[5] the Supreme Court affirmed its sixty-

19. AT&T Corp. v. Iowa Utilities Board, 525 U.S. 366, 119 S.Ct. 721 (1999). The 1996 Telecommunications Act requires dominant carriers to interconnect, but leaves it to the FCC to determine when interconnection is required and what the terms of connection will be. See 1A Antitrust Law ¶ 251k (rev. ed. 1997).

§ 19.6

1. Keogh v. Chicago & Northwestern Rwy., 260 U.S. 156, 43 S.Ct. 47 (1922). The doctrine is not restricted to antitrust challenges, but operates generally so as to protect the power of the agency to set or approve rates. See, e.g., AT & T v. Central Office Tel., 524 U.S. 214, 118 S.Ct. 1956, rehearing denied, ___ U.S. ___, 119 S.Ct. 20 (1998) (non-antitrust case; state law tortious interference and contract claims brought by reseller of defendant's SDN telephone services barred by filed-rate doctrine); on the relation between the filed rate doctrine and state antitrust law or state regulation, see 14 Antitrust Law ¶ 2411i (1999).

2. *Keogh*, 260 U.S. at 162, 43 S.Ct. at 49.

3. Id. at 164–165, 43 S.Ct. at 50.

4. The Court later adopted the contrary rule in Illinois Brick Co. v. Illinois, 431 U.S. 720, 97 S.Ct. 2061, rehearing denied, 434 U.S. 881, 98 S.Ct. 243 (1977). See § 16.6.

5. 476 U.S. 409, 106 S.Ct. 1922 (1986). See also County of Stanislaus v. PG & E, 114 F.3d 858 (9th Cir.1997), cert. denied, ___ U.S. ___, 118 S.Ct. 854 (1998) (filed-rate doctrine precluded claims that defendant gas pipeline puryear old *Keogh* holding, conceding that it may have been "unwise as a matter of policy," but noting that Congress had had ample opportunity to fix the problem and had never done so.

Indeed, some courts have extended *Keogh* to partially deregulated markets where the agency at issue has only limited power to review or veto a filed rate. For example, in *Wheat Rail* the Seventh Circuit applied the *Keogh* doctrine even though the ICC was operating under a statute that permitted it to challenge a filed rate only after it found that the filers had market dominance.[6] This seems an unwarranted expansion of a rule conceded to be a bad one on policy grounds. An overworked agency may bother to make such inquiries only rarely, and under *Keogh* customers themselves cannot challenge the filed rate in damages actions.[7]

Most courts hold that *Keogh* does not apply to *competitor* suits—for example, suits challenging filed rates as predatory pricing.[8] First, of the original rationales given for *Keogh* only the third, the primacy of agency rate determination, would apply to a competitor suit. Indeed, even that argument is weak because the agency generally scrutinizes rates to see if they are too high, making sure that cost figures are justified. It much less frequently scrutinizes tariff requests to see if the requested rates are too low. Second, a doctrine as indefensible as *Keogh* should be narrowly construed.

Of course, even in a competitor suit the doctrine of primary jurisdiction might apply.[9] That is, the court might permit the regulatory agency to assess the reasonableness of the challenged rate in the first instance.

§ 19.7 Particular Exemptions

A detailed survey of specific regulatory exemptions accorded under federal law is beyond the scope of this volume.[1] What is offered here is a brief description of the most important antitrust exemptions, with particular attention to the labor exemption and the insurance exemption.

19.7a. Miscellaneous Express Exemptions

Agricultural cooperatives are granted an antitrust exemption in § 6 of the Clayton Act[2] and the Capper–Volstead Act.[3] The statutes permit agricultural producers to agree with each other to set price and output, but in *Borden* the Supreme Court held that agreements between producers and non-producers were not exempt.[4] Likewise, although the exemption applies to price-fixing, it does not apply to exclusionary practices such as predatory pricing.[5]

chased so much gas that it exhausted its pipeline capacity, forcing plaintiff purchasers to purchase gas elsewhere).

6. In re Wheat Rail Freight Rate Antitrust Litigation, 759 F.2d 1305 (7th Cir.1985), cert. denied, 476 U.S. 1158, 106 S.Ct. 2275 (1986) The ICC has been abolished and replaced by the Surface Transportation Board.

7. A few courts have found *Keogh* not to apply to rates that the regulatory agency disapproved after consideration. For example, Litton Sys. v. AT & T, 700 F.2d 785, 820 (2d Cir.1983), cert. denied, 464 U.S. 1073, 104 S.Ct. 984 (1984).

8. Barnes v. Arden Mayfair, 759 F.2d 676 (9th Cir. 1985); City of Kirkwood v. Union Elec. Co., 671 F.2d 1173, 1178 (8th Cir.1982), cert. denied, 459 U.S. 1170, 103 S.Ct. 814 (1983). But contra, Pinney Dock & Transport Co. v. Penn Central Corp., 838 F.2d 1445 (6th Cir.), cert. denied, 488 U.S. 880, 109 S.Ct. 196 (1988).

9. See § 19.4.

§ 19.7

1. For more detailed analysis, see 1A Antitrust Law ¶¶ 249–251 (rev. ed. 1997). In addition to the immunities discussed in the text, see the Charitable Donation Antitrust Immunity Act of 1997, which provides that "the antitrust laws, and any State law similar to any of the antitrust laws, shall not apply to charitable gift annuities or charitable remainder trusts." 15 U.S.C. § 37(a). And see Ozee v. American Council on Gift Annuities, 143 F.3d 937 (5th Cir.1998), cert. denied, ___ U.S. ___, 119 S.Ct. 1454 (1999) (provision immunized an agreement among universities and other charities suppressing competition in such annuities).

2. 15 U.S.C.A. § 17.

3. 7 U.S.C.A. § 291–292.

4. United States v. Borden Co., 308 U.S. 188, 60 S.Ct. 182 (1939) (denying exemption for dairy price fixing agreement involving dairy cooperative, processors, distributors and a labor union). Compare National Broiler Marketing Association v. United States, 436 U.S. 816, 98 S.Ct. 2122 (1978), refusing to extend the exemption to non-farmer processors of agricultural products.

5. Maryland & Virginia Milk Producers Assn. v. United States, 362 U.S. 458, 80 S.Ct. 847 (1960).

Today ocean common carriers are regulated by the Federal Maritime Commission (FMC) under the Shipping Act of 1984.[6] Under that Act ocean shippers may file a common tariff, or rate, with the FMC. The rates are then presumptively exempt from the antitrust laws. If part of the conduct is alleged to fall outside the broad 1984 Shipping Act exemptions and is claimed to violate the antitrust laws, the private plaintiff may bring a court action for the non-exempt part.[7]

Although banking does not enjoy a general antitrust exemption, several federal statutes regulating banking provide antitrust-like regulations. These standards may take precedence over antitrust standards when a violation is alleged. For example, the Bank Merger Act of 1960 (amended in 1966), provides for special procedures to be used in evaluating bank mergers, although the substantive standard to be applied mimics that of Clayton Act § 7.[8] Likewise, bank tying arrangements requiring loans to be joined with insurance, title examination fees, legal services, or other services, are governed by a variety of federal statutes.[9] These provisions can be more aggressive than the law of tie-ins generally, for they do not require a showing of the bank's market power in the tying product or of anticompetitive effects in the tied product market.[10]

Amateur athletic associations receive a partial antitrust exemption through the Amateur Sports Act,[11] when they determine who can claim amateur status. Further, the Sports Broadcasting Act, permits football, baseball, basketball, or hockey leagues to deal for all league members in selling television rights, provided that telecasting is not limited in any city other than "the home territory of a member club of the league on a day when such club is playing a game at home."[12] In *Chicago Professional Sports* the Seventh Circuit held that this statute did not justify a National Basketball Association rule limiting the number of times individual teams could sell television right to certain stations—that is, the statute authorizes teams to make joint sales, but not to prevent their members from making individual sales.[13]

19.7b. Antitrust and Federal Labor Policy

One of the unexpected results of passage of the Sherman Act was its aggressive use against labor unions.[14] Indeed, in the early years of antitrust enforcement the Sherman Act was employed much more effectively against labor than against restraints in product markets. Of the first thirteen antitrust violations found by American courts during the period 1890–1897, twelve were challenges to labor strikes, while only one was a challenge to an agreement among manufacturers.[15] Al-

6. 49 U.S.C.A. App. §§ 1701–1720.

7. See American Assn. of Cruise Passengers v. Carnival Cruise Lines, 31 F.3d 1184 (D.C.Cir.1994).

8. 12 U.S.C.A. § 1828(c). The FDIC once promulgated its own set of "merger guidelines" for mergers within its jurisdiction. See 53 Fed. Reg. 39,803 (1988).

9. The principal statute is the Bank Holding Company Act of 1970. 12 U.S.C.A. §§ 1971–1978.

10. For example, Dibidale of Louisiana, Inc. v. American Bank & Trust Co., 916 F.2d 300, 305–306 (5th Cir. 1990), opinion amended and reinstated on rehearing, 941 F.2d 308 (5th Cir.1991); Parsons Steel, Inc. v. First Ala. Bank, 679 F.2d 242, 245 (11th Cir.1982). But see Doe v. Norwest Bank Minnesota, 107 F.3d 1297 (8th Cir.1997) (refusing to condemn tie that had no anticompetitive consequences whatsoever).

One important limitation on the coverage of the Bank Holding Company Act is that it does not prohibit tying arrangements unless they are "unusual" in the banking industry. See, e.g., Quintana v. First National Bank of Santa Fe, 125 F.3d 862, 1997-2 Trade Cas. ¶ 71949 (10th Cir.1997) (bank's requirement that father pay off a son's loan in default before he could receive a new loan was a common banking practice and thus did not violate anti-tying provisions of Bank Holding Co. Act); Norte Car Corp. v. FirstBank Corp., 25 F.Supp.2d 9 (D.P.R.1998) (dismissing tying claim under Bank Holding Company Act where most of the challenged practices were common in the banking industry).

11. 36 U.S.C.A. §§ 371 et seq. See Behagen v. Amateur Basketball Assn., 884 F.2d 524 (10th Cir.1989), cert. denied, 495 U.S. 918, 110 S.Ct. 1947 (1990) (olympic committee's determination of amateur status not subject to antitrust laws under Amateur Sports Act).

12. 15 U.S.C.A. §§ 1291–1295.

13. Chicago Professional Sports Limited Partnership v. NBA, 961 F.2d 667, 670 (7th Cir.), cert. denied, 506 U.S. 954, 113 S.Ct. 409 (1992).

14. For example, Loewe v. Lawlor (Danbury Hatters case), 208 U.S. 274, 28 S.Ct. 301 (1908) (union organized secondary boycott violated Sherman Act).

15. See H. Hovenkamp, Enterprise and American Law, 1836–1937 at 229 (1991).

though labor leaders argued that the framers of the Sherman Act never intended it to cover labor strikes as a form of "price-fixing," there is very little in the legislative history of that statute to support their claims. However, in 1914 a Progressive Congress responded by enacting § 6 of the Clayton Act, which provided that "[t]he labor of a human being is not a commodity or article of commerce," and that the Sherman Act should not be interpreted to forbid the organization and legitimate operation of labor unions.[16] Section 6 proved to be a weak instrument, and the Supreme Court continued to permit Sherman Act injunctions against labor boycotts;[17] so in 1932 Congress passed the Norris–LaGuardia Act, which deprives the federal courts of jurisdiction to issue injunctions in labor disputes, unless independently unlawful acts are threatened or committed.[18]

In order to claim this so-called "statutory" exemption from the labor laws, a labor union must act "in its self-interest" and it may not "combine with non-labor groups."[19] The question of when an agreement is with a "non-labor" group has generated some dispute. Some cases are clear. For example, building contractors organizing a boycott could not ordinarily claim the labor exemption, because their interests are normally aligned with employers rather than employees.[20] However, the Supreme Court has generally interpreted the concept of "labor group," or labor organization broadly. For example, it has held that orchestra leaders, who are in a position to select individual musicians, were a labor group rather than an employer group, particularly since orchestra leaders and musicians often competed with each other in the same labor market.[21] And in *H.A. Artists* the Supreme Court held that an agreement between actors and independent theatrical agents who represented them was not a combination with a non-labor group.[22] Although the agents were self-employed, they were an essential part of the mechanism by which the actors obtained their employment; as a result, they should be considered a labor organization.

But even some agreements between labor organizations and non-labor groups are exempt under the so-called "nonstatutory exemption." The nonstatutory exemption generally applies in a collective bargaining situation where the union has entered into a contract with an employer that imposes potentially anticompetitive limitations on other contractors, competitors or suppliers in the employers' market. These latter are not labor groups; so the statutory exemption itself would not ordinarily apply. In *Jewel Tea,* the Supreme Court exempted an agreement between a butchers' union and an association of grocers limiting the butchers' working hours.[23] The lower court had refused an exemption, noting that the association of grocers was not a labor organization, and that the agreement interfered with the natural competition that would otherwise occur among grocers to offer increased services.[24] In reversing, a deeply divided Supreme Court seemed to find the fact of an agreement with a non-labor group relatively unimportant. More important, the heart of the agreement at issue went to working conditions, which are a legitimate subject of collective bargaining. This exempted the agreement notwithstanding the involvement of a non-union group and the negative impact on competition.

The Supreme Court's important decision in Connell Construction Co. v. Plumbers & Ste-

16. 15 U.S.C.A. § 17. Section 20 of the Clayton Act, passed at the same time, was designed to prevent the issuance of federal injunctions against strikes or labor boycotts. 29 U.S.C.A. § 52.

17. See Duplex Printing Press Co. v. Deering, 254 U.S. 443, 41 S.Ct. 172 (1921); and see H. Hovenkamp, *Enterprise*, note 15, at 229–238.

18. 29 U.S.C.A. §§ 101 et seq.

19. United States v. Hutcheson, 312 U.S. 219, 232, 61 S.Ct. 463 (1941).

20. Altemose Construction Co. v. Building & Constr. Trades Council, 751 F.2d 653, 657 (3d Cir.1985), cert. denied, 475 U.S. 1107, 106 S.Ct. 1513 (1986).

21. American Federation of Musicians v. Carroll, 391 U.S. 99, 88 S.Ct. 1562, rehearing denied, 393 U.S. 902, 89 S.Ct. 64 (1968).

22. H.A. Artists & Assocs. v. Actors' Equity Assn., 451 U.S. 704, 101 S.Ct. 2102 (1981).

23. Local 189, Amalgamated Meat Cutters v. Jewel Tea Co., 381 U.S. 676, 85 S.Ct. 1596 (1965).

24. 331 F.2d 547 (7th Cir.1964).

amfitters Local Union No. 100[25] suggests the limits of the nonstatutory exemption. A union picketed a general contractor in order to win an agreement that the general contractor would give subcontracting jobs for plumbing and other work only to firms represented by that union. The picketing union was not seeking to organize the general contractor itself. A divided (5–4) Supreme Court found the conduct not to be exempt. The principal impact of the solicited agreement was not on wages and hours, but on entitlement to bid to be a subcontractor—that is, the sought for agreement would have limited competition among plumbing subcontractors to those that had a particular union contract. To put it another way, the union was not attempting to regulate the wages and working conditions of the affected subcontractors, but rather was seeking to exclude them from the market altogether. The distinction is quite subtle, since the principal way a union gets what it wants is by striking and boycotting.

In the wake of *Connell* courts have attempted to craft an exemption that incorporates the concerns of earlier decisions, without permitting labor unions to go too far in limiting competition in nonlabor markets. They generally require three things before the nonstatutory exemption can be claimed: (1) the restraint on trade contained in the agreement must be one that affects primarily the parties; (2) the subject matter of the agreement must be what is normally considered a mandatory subject of collective bargaining—that is, wages, hours, working conditions, and the like; and (3) the provision must be the subject of arms length bargaining. The *Connell* boycott violated at least (1) and (2). First, it seriously affected subcontractors who were not bargaining with the union at all. Second, the primary issue was not wages, hours and working conditions, but the basic right to bid as a subcontractor.

Other courts have held in *Connell*-like situations that, although a union may not attempt to exclude non-union sub-contractors from the market altogether under these circumstances, they *may* boycott or bargain to ensure that all sub-contractor employees are paid a specified minimum wage or have specified minimum working conditions.[26] Although these cases are often difficult to parse, they contain the germ of an important principle: unions should not be permitted to "monopolize" a market any more than capitalists. A union of, say, electrical subcontractors may have a legitimate interest in ensuring that employees of other subcontractors are paid the same wages that the union members are paid. Their motive is not so much to protect these other employees as to ensure that the other subcontractors do not have a cost advantage over their own employer. But the union is not entitled to insist that organization by that particular union be a prerequisite for a particular subcontractor's right to be a market participant.

The courts have generally declined to apply the nonstatutory exemption to agreements occurring outside the context of bargaining between a union and an employer. For example, in *Detroit Auto Dealers* the court found no exemption for an agreement among car dealers to restrict showroom hours.[27] Although employees wanted the agreement, the agreement itself was not a direct result of collective bargaining by employees. By contrast, Powell v. NFL[28] applied the nonstatutory exemption to an agreement among NFL players and NFL teams that limited a player's ability to be a "free agent," or to sign freely with a different team than his current one.

Finally, in a significant expansion of the non-statutory exemption, in 1996 the Supreme Court immunized an agreement among employers to set the maximum wage they would

25. 421 U.S. 616, 95 S.Ct. 1830 (1975).

26. California Dump Truck Owners Assn. v. Associated Gen. Contractors, 562 F.2d 607 (9th Cir.1977); Utilities Serv. Engr. v. Colorado Bldg. & Constr. Trades Council, 549 F.2d 173 (10th Cir.1977).

27. Detroit Auto Dealers Assn. v. FTC, 955 F.2d 457, 467 (6th Cir.), cert. denied, 506 U.S. 973, 113 S.Ct. 461 (1992).

28. 888 F.2d 559 (8th Cir.1989), cert. denied, 498 U.S. 1040, 111 S.Ct. 711 (1991). Accord Wood v. NBA, 809 F.2d 954 (2d Cir.1987).

pay to a certain class of employees.[29] The facts were idiosyncratic, however, and the Court was careful to make clear that its holding was limited. The agreement was among NFL football teams to set the maximum salaries of certain new players. While the union and the teams had bargained after the collective bargaining agreement expired, the bargaining had reached a technical impasse, or situation where the parties had presumably bargained in good faith, but irreconcilable differences remained.[30] The Supreme Court found this agreement reasonable, but only because the employers (the teams) had reached it in the context of collective bargaining with the players' union. As the Court pointed out, the logic of multi-employer collective bargaining demanded that *both* sides be able to agree about the various issues that would be brought to the bargaining table. Finally, a contrary interpretation subjecting the practice to antitrust scrutiny would:

> require antitrust courts to answer a host of important practical questions about how collective bargaining over wages, hours and working conditions is to proceed—the very result that the implicit [i.e., nonstatutory] labor exemption seeks to avoid. And it is to place in jeopardy some of the potentially beneficial labor-related effects that multiemployer bargaining can achieve. That is because unlike labor law, which sometimes welcomes anticompetitive agreements conducive to industrial harmony, antitrust law forbids all agreements among competitors (such as competing employers) that unreasonably lessen competition among or between them in virtually any respect whatsoever.[31]

As the court noted, the National Labor Relations Board supervised the entire collective bargaining process, and the principal card that the players held was their ability to strike if the teams did something that injured them excessively. But this was all part of the give-and-take of collective bargaining—a process into which antitrust courts must be loathe to interfere.[32]

19.7c. The McCarran–Ferguson Act and the Insurance Exemption

The federally created exemption for insurance is unique in one important respect: although the exemption is created by federal law, the source of the regulation at issue is the states. However, the federal source of the exemption makes it different from and more expansive than the more limited immunity for "state action" discussed in the following chapter. This sub-section closes with a brief discussion of possible repeal of the federal insurance exemption, and considers whether the "state action" doctrine would be sufficient protection for the insurance industry.

Traditionally the business of insurance was considered peculiarly local in character. For example, in Paul v. Virginia the Supreme Court held that insurance was not interstate commerce at all, but a purely intrastate matter.[33] Likewise, in Allgeyer v. Louisiana,[34] the Supreme Court greatly limited state power to regulate insurance contracts made in another state. But in the wake of Wickard v. Filburn,[35] which greatly expanded Congressional control of transactions that merely "affect" interstate commerce, the Supreme Court held in *South–Eastern Underwriters* that insurance too could be brought under federal control via the antitrust laws.[36] That case condemned agreements under which insurance companies that did not join a trade association were subjected to discriminatory treatment, denied risk data, and agents that dealt with non-member insurers were refused business by the member insurer defendants.

By the time of *South–Eastern Underwriters*, insurers had already developed procedures calling for the common production of insur-

29. Brown v. Pro Football, 518 U.S. 231, 116 S.Ct. 2116 (1996).

30. See 1A Antitrust Law ¶ 257b2 (rev. ed. 1997).

31. *Brown*, 116 S.Ct. at 2122.

32. Id. at 2123.

33. Paul v. Virginia, 75 U.S. (8 Wall.) 168, 183 (1868).

34. 165 U.S. 578, 17 S.Ct. 427 (1897).

35. 317 U.S. 111, 63 S.Ct. 82 (1942).

36. United States v. South–Eastern Underwriters Assn., 322 U.S. 533, 64 S.Ct. 1162 (1944).

ance forms by agreement among rival insurers, "pooling" of risks in order to avoid catastrophic losses, and the like. All these agreements were inherently challengeable under Sherman § 1. From the perspective of insurers, then, application of the antitrust laws threatened the very nature of their industry and they petitioned Congress for relief. In 1945 Congress enacted the McCarran–Ferguson Act,[37] which was roughly intended to preserve the status quo before the *South–Eastern Underwriters* decision, although not necessarily to reverse the outcome in that case: states were left free to regulate the "business of insurance," and insofar as it was subject to state regulation it was exempt from the antitrust laws. However, the statute contains an exception for acts of "boycott, coercion, or intimidation"—a phrase that came straight out of the *South–Eastern Underwriters* decision.[38]

Most of the litigation concerning the insurance exemption has involved three different questions: what kinds of activities are encompassed within the "business of insurance?" When is the business of insurance effectively "regulated" by state law, and thus exempt? and When does coercive activity amount to a "boycott, coercion, or intimidation," and thus fall outside of the exemption?

19.7c1. "Business of Insurance"[39]

The McCarran exemption applies only to activity that constitutes the "business of insurance." Often insurance companies perform a variety of services. For example, title insurance companies do title searches and prepare title reports as well as writing title insurance.[40] Many health insurers are heavily involved in the direct provision of health care or pharmaceuticals through prepaid health plans. Some life insurance companies are in the business of selling other kinds of investments or perhaps even lending money or drafting legal documents.[41] When an insurance company has its thumbs in many pies, the antitrust tribunal may have to consider whether the challenged activity constitutes the "business of insurance." The Supreme Court has identified three criteria for making that determination. First, the practice must have "the effect of transferring or spreading a policy holder's risk. * * * " Second, the practice must be "an integral part of the policy relationship between the insurer and the insured." Third, the practice should be "limited to entities within the insurance industry." The Court then added that "[n]one of these criteria is necessarily determinative in itself. * * * "[42]

Applying these criteria, the courts have had little difficulty in concluding the following: reinsurance—or insurance purchased by insurance companies to protect themselves from catastrophic events—is part of the business of insurance.[43] By contrast, a divided Supreme Court held that a health insurer's agreement with pharmacies for filling the prescriptions of its insureds was not part of the business of insurance; first, the pharmacies were not parties to the insurance policy; further, these agreements did not serve to spread risk, in the way that an insurance policy does.[44] Likewise,

37. 15 U.S.C.A. §§ 1011–1015.

38. *South–Eastern Underwriters*, 322 U.S. at 535, 64 S.Ct. at 1164.

39. See 1 Antitrust Law ¶ 219b (rev. ed. 1997).

40. See Ticor Title Ins. Co., 5 Trade Reg. Rep. ¶ 22744 (FTC 1989) (title searching by title insurance companies, as opposed to the issuance of the title policy itself, not part of the business of insurance). Accord United States v. Title Ins. Rating Bureau of Ariz., 700 F.2d 1247 (9th Cir.1983), cert. denied, 467 U.S. 1240, 104 S.Ct. 3509 (1984) (setting of escrow fees for real estate transfers not part of business of insurance).

41. See Perry v. Fidelity Union Life Ins. Co., 606 F.2d 468 (5th Cir.1979), cert. denied, 446 U.S. 987, 100 S.Ct. 2973 (1980) (lending money not part of business of insurance).

42. Union Labor Life Ins. Co. v. Pireno, 458 U.S. 119, 129, 102 S.Ct. 3002, 3008 (1982), following Group Life & Health Ins. Co. v. Royal Drug Co., 440 U.S. 205, 99 S.Ct. 1067 (1979).

43. In re Insurance Antitrust Litigation, 723 F.Supp. 464 (N.D.Cal.1989), reversed on other grounds, 938 F.2d 919 (9th Cir.1991), affirmed in part, reversed in part sub nom. Hartford Fire Insurance v. California, 509 U.S. 764, 113 S.Ct. 2891 (1993).

44. *Royal Drug*, note 42. However, a lower court held that an insurer's own operation of a pharmacy for its insured was part of the business of insurance, for no third parties were involved. Klamath–Lake Pharmaceutical Assn. v. Klamath Med. Serv. Bureau, 701 F.2d 1276 (9th Cir.), cert. denied, 464 U.S. 822, 104 S.Ct. 88 (1983). Compare Ocean State Physicians Health Plan v. Blue Cross & Blue Shield of R.I., 883 F.2d 1101 (1st Cir.1989), in *Pireno*[45] the Court held that peer review of medical claims for reasonableness does not fall within the business of insurance. In that case the insurer asked one set of chiropractors to assess the reasonableness of the plaintiff chiropractors' treatments of the insured patients. The Court found this activity not to be part of the transfer of risk inherent in insurance, but merely a mechanism by which the insurance company attempted to reduce its costs. For largely analogous reasons, some lower courts have found that insurer limitations to specific kinds of providers are not part of the business of insurance. For example, a health policy might provide that only psychiatrists with M.D. degrees, not psychologists, may give covered treatment for mental or nervous conditions.[46] Likewise, a health insurer may exclude coverage for services provided by chiropractors or other health care professionals who do not have M.D. degrees, and these exclusions may not be part of the business of insurance.[47]

One might dispute the wisdom of such policy limitations and even suspect that they are sometimes anticompetitive. Nevertheless, the conclusion that they are not part of the "business of insurance" is strained at best. Supposedly, if one wishes to have coverage for psychologists' services, he can obtain it by purchasing a different health insurance policy and perhaps paying more. Inherent in the business of insurance is the underwriter's determination of which risks it will insure for a certain premium. For example, the home insurer's decision not to include flood insurance for homes within flood plains is unquestionably part of the "business of insurance." But an inherent part of risk determination is the control of payments for losses. In a properly functioning market, one would expect competition to determine whether or not psychologists or chiropractors would be included in health insurance coverage. If the market is imperfect—for example, if M.D. holding physicians have captured the state insurance agency—the result might be bad. But that does not take the conduct out of the "business of insurance." Taken to its logical conclusion, an insurer could not place any limitations at all on the qualifications of providers without losing its antitrust exemption. For example, I, a Blue Cross insured, might "prescribe" a trip to Bermuda for myself, to relieve the stress of reading numerous antitrust decisions. I could then ask Blue Cross to pay for the trip as a legitimate medical expense. Blue Cross might respond to such suspected abuses by providing it will not cover (1) prescriptions written by the insured for him or herself; or (2) medical treatments given at the advice of people who are not physicians. It strains credulity to say that these limitation decisions are not part of the "business of insurance."

Equally problematic is the extent to which horizontal agreements *among* insurers fall into the general classification of the "business of insurance." The efficient provision of insurance requires a great deal of joint activity. For example, risk data are more reliable as the "pool" of people from whom the data are taken grows larger. As a result, insurers can compute risks more accurately if they can share data about specific risks. Indeed, many insurers cannot write certain kinds of coverage at all if they cannot use data collected by other insurers in computing their premiums. Likewise, agreements about the content of the insurance policy performs a kind of product standardization that often works to consumers' best interests. In most states so-called "forms development" is a process in which all insurers in the affected market participate. One result is that the consumer shopping for, say, automobile insurance compares products that are in most respects identical, and is not mired in numerous technical variations in cov-

cert. denied, 494 U.S. 1027, 110 S.Ct. 1473 (1990) (operation of HMO, including signing on of participating physicians, all part of business of insurance).

45. Note 42.

46. Virginia Academy of Clinical Psychologists v. Blue Shield of Virginia, 624 F.2d 476 (4th Cir.1980), cert. denied, 450 U.S. 916, 101 S.Ct. 1360 (1981) (finding that the decision to exclude was not part of the business of insurance).

47. Health Care Equalization Committee v. Iowa Medical Society, 851 F.2d 1020 (8th Cir.1988) (decision to exclude not part of business of insurance); Hahn v. Oregon Physicians Serv., 689 F.2d 840 (9th Cir.1982), cert. denied, 462 U.S. 1133, 103 S.Ct. 3115 (1983) (same).

erage that make price comparison all but impossible.

But once the data has been gathered and the forms produced, should insurers be able to agree about premiums—that is, should they be permitted to fix prices? The courts agree that if the state regulation contemplates joint rate-making, such rate-making is clearly within the "business of insurance" and thus antitrust exempt.[48] So the legality of joint rate making is generally left up to the state regulators, whose policy varies greatly from state to state and depending on the type of insurance.

19.7c2. "Regulated by State Law"

McCarran also exempts the business of insurance only "to the extent" that the business is "regulated by state law." Importantly, "regulated by state law" for McCarran purposes means much less than the kind of state regulation necessary to qualify for the "state action" immunity, discussed in the next chapter. If that were not the case, the McCarran exemption would become superfluous. Indeed, the state need not actively "regulate" at all; it need only pass a statute that purports to regulate. It makes no difference that the state regulation is not actively enforced, or that the state agency simply rubber stamps the insurance companies' requests.[49] If a statue exists, and the relevant agency or commissioner has jurisdiction over the practice under scrutiny, the "regulation" requirement is met. One important exception is that if a certain activity is not within the jurisdictional reach of the states, then it cannot be "regulated by the states" under McCarran. Accordingly, it loses its exemption. In *Hartford*[50], the Supreme Court suggested that foreign reinsurers might be out of the jurisdictional reach of state regulation. If that were so, then they would not be "regulated" for McCarran purposes. The Court remanded to the Ninth Circuit for that determination.

19.7c3. Acts of Boycott, Coercion or Intimidation

The McCarran antitrust exemption does not apply to acts of boycott, coercion or intimidation.[51] The Supreme Court has generally held that the term "boycott" must be understood in its Sherman Act sense, which includes a wide variety of refusals to deal, both absolute and conditional.[52] For example, the Court held in *St. Paul* that a particular kind of agreement among liability insurers to cover medical malpractice only if both the event and the claim occurred while insurance was in force constituted a "boycott."[53] Under the policy proposal there would be no coverage if (a) the loss occurred during the pre-insurance period but the claim was made during the insurance period; or (b) the loss occurred during the insurance period but the claim was made during the post-insurance period. The impact of the provision would make it more costly for insureds to switch insurers. To this end, it could be an effective collusion facilitating device.

Importantly, the allegation in *St. Paul* was not that the four insurers had agreed to write such coverage limitations into their forms. Such an agreement would have been exempt "forms development," a common part of the regulated business of insurance. For example, if insurers jointly propose a policy form that excludes flood losses from home owners' coverage, that proposal cannot be considered a

48. Owens v. Aetna Life & Casualty Co., 654 F.2d 218 (3d Cir.), cert. denied, 454 U.S. 1092, 102 S.Ct. 657 (1981); In re Workers' Compensation Insurance Antitrust Litigation, 867 F.2d 1552 (8th Cir.), cert. denied, 492 U.S. 920, 109 S.Ct. 3247 (1989).

49. See FTC v. National Casualty Co., 357 U.S. 560, 78 S.Ct. 1260 (1958) (mere enactment of standard sufficient; no administrative supervision needed); Seasongood v. K & K Ins. Agency, 548 F.2d 729 (8th Cir.1977); Ohio AFL–CIO v. Insurance Rating Bd., 451 F.2d 1178, 1184 (6th Cir.1971), cert. denied, 409 U.S. 917, 93 S.Ct. 215 (1972).

50. Note 43, 509 U.S. at 784 n. 12, 113 S.Ct. at 2902 n. 12.

51. 15 U.S.C.A. § 1013(b); see 1 Antitrust Law ¶ 220 (rev. ed. 1997).

52. In *Hartford*, note 43, the Supreme Court rejected the argument that only absolute refusals to deal "on any terms" qualified as boycotts. Rather, "[t]he refusal to deal may * * * be conditional, offering its target the incentive of renewed dealing if and when he mends his ways." 113 S.Ct. at 2911.

53. St. Paul Fire & Marine Ins. Co. v. Barry, 438 U.S. 531, 98 S.Ct. 2923 (1978).

"boycott" of those wishing to purchase flood insurance. Rather, the allegation in *St. Paul* was that the defendants had agreed that three of the four would no longer write malpractice insurance at all in this market, leaving the fourth as the only insurer willing to serve the plaintiff's needs. This, of course, considerably increased the bargaining power of the fourth firm.

St. Paul also made clear that a qualifying boycott could be directed at either policy holders or at other insurers—that is, the exception applied to both vertical and horizontal boycotts. Suppose the insurers go further than simply agreeing with each other to exclude flood coverage from their policy. Suppose that one or more insurers in the area are willing to write policies including flood coverage. The dominant insurers then take various cartel "enforcement" actions against these recalcitrants—for example, they deny them membership in a trade association, or collectively deprive them of risk data ordinarily shared by all insurers. Courts have generally concluded that these activities directed at competing insurers also constitute a boycott, just as much as concerted refusals to deal directed at customers.[54]

In *Hartford*,[55] the Supreme Court found that the McCarran–Ferguson Act did not exempt alleged agreements among primary insurers to reduce their policy coverages so as to eliminate losses that occurred outside the policy period, or upon which claims were made outside the policy period, and losses caused by certain forms of "sudden and accidental" pollution. Although a simple agreement to develop a new insurance form with reduced coverage was exempt "business of insurance," the plaintiffs[56] alleged that the defendants entered collateral agreements with two other entities. The first was an agreement with Insurance Services Office (ISO) that the latter would not supply risk data for risks that the conspirators no longer wished to cover. Several non-conspiring insurers would have continued to write the larger risks, but they could not do so without adequate risk data. Secondly, the defendant insurers allegedly agreed with foreign sellers of *re* insurance that the reinsurers would not provide their services to the non-conspiring insurers either. In finding a boycott the Court noted:

> It is * * * important * * * to distinguish between a conditional boycott and a concerted agreement to seek particular terms in particular transactions. A concerted agreement to terms (a "cartelization") is "a way of obtaining and exercising market power by concertedly exacting terms like those which a monopolist might exact." The parties to such an agreement (the members of a cartel) are not engaging in a boycott, because: "They are not coercing anyone, at least in the usual sense of that word; they are merely (though concertedly) saying 'we will deal with you only on the following trade terms.' "[57]

The critical distinction for the Court was whether the agreement at hand covered only the terms of the contract under negotiation, or whether it reached further. For example, if a group of tenants agreed with each other that they would not renew their leases unless they received lower rents from the landlord, they would be negotiating the contract at hand. They would not be "boycotting" anyone. However, if the tenants also refused to engage in unrelated transactions—for example, if they refused to sell their landlord food or other supplies until he lowered the rents—this latter agreement would be a boycott.[58] "[T]his ex-

54. See *Workers Compensation Insurance*, note 48 (boycott to exclude from trade association insurers who charged lower prices than defendants). Compare Nurse Midwifery Assocs. v. Hibbett, 549 F.Supp. 1185, 1191–1192 (M.D.Tenn.1982) (agreement to deny medical malpractice coverage to plaintiff midwives could be a boycott).

55. Note 43.

56. Several states' attorneys general, in addition to private plaintiffs.

57. 509 U.S. at 802, 113 S.Ct. at 2912.

58. The *Hartford* dissenters—Justice Souter, joined by Justices White, Blackmun and Stevens—would have interpreted "boycott" somewhat more broadly to include a cartel's enforcement activities generally. For example, if the reinsurers agreed with each other not to write reinsurance for certain risks, that would not be a boycott. But if the reinsurers and the defendant insurers agreed among themselves that the reinsurers would not write reinsurance for the non-conspiring insurers, then the term "boycott" was appropriate. 509 U.S. at 785, 113 S.Ct. at 2903.

pansion of the refusal to deal beyond the targeted transaction * * * gives great coercive force to a commercial boycott: unrelated transactions are used as leverage to achieve the terms desired."[59] Applying this definition, the Court found that the plaintiffs' allegations contained several qualifying "boycotts." For example, the reinsurers allegedly refused to write reinsurance on any policy given by a firm that also wrote policies containing the coverages that the defendants wanted removed from the market.

The courts are divided on the issue whether insurance company termination of its own agencies or agents can constitute a boycott, if the termination is pursuant to an agreement with a third party.[60] Since resale price maintenance is not generally an issue in insurer vertical restraints (nothing is being purchased and resold), most such agreements would be treated as vertical nonprice restrictions in any event, and most would thus be legal even if they are not immune.[61]

19.7c4. Continuing Vitality of McCarran–Ferguson

Does McCarran–Ferguson continue to perform a useful function? or does it do more social harm than good? The statute was passed at a time when insurance was considered to be largely a state-centered business, and had traditionally been thought to be out of Congress' power to regulate under the Commerce Clause. But today most insurance is provided by relatively large companies that operate in many states under a wide array of standards. Transactions in which the insured or its property are in one state and the underwriter in another are quite common. As a result, the argument for individual state regulation to the exclusion of federal regulation is much weaker today than it was in the 1930's and earlier. Indeed, the multistate nature of the business suggests that federal regulation, and the resulting uniformity of rules, would be preferable

More to the point here, the consequence of simply repealing McCarran–Ferguson would be that the insurers—just as any other business subject to state regulation—would have to claim their antitrust immunity under the "state action" doctrine. To this author, that seems to be a step in the right direction. The "state action" doctrine, unlike the McCarran exemption, immunizes private parties for regulated conduct only when the state clearly articulates its regulatory policy and actively supervises private decision making that occurs within the regulatory framework. One of the most serious problems with McCarran is that it effectively immunizes purely private, collusive actions undertaken and performed with little effective state oversight. Further, under the "state action" exemption, a state's intention to use its regulatory regime to *displace* the antitrust laws must be made manifest. Under *McCarran*, the presence of any state regulation creates an insurance antitrust exemption, whether or not exemption is the state's wish. A state might very well determine that certain issues, such as joint production of policies, be left to the actively supervised joint efforts of the insurers; but that other issues, such as rate-making or exclusion of others from the market, be left open for antitrust analysis in appropriate cases.

59. Compare Eastern States Retail Lumber Dealers' Assn. v. United States, 234 U.S. 600, 34 S.Ct. 951 (1914), a Sherman Act case not involving insurance, where lumber retailers agreed with each other that they would not purchase lumber from wholesalers that also engaged directly in retailing. The *Hartford* Court noted that the *Eastern States* agreement was "a boycott because [the defendants] sought an objective—the wholesale dealers' forbearance from retail trade—that was collateral to their transactions with the wholesalers." 113 S.Ct. at 2912.

60. See Card v. National Life Ins. Co., 603 F.2d 828 (10th Cir.1979) (no boycott when one agent was terminated in response to complaints from another agent); Malley–Duff & Assocs. v. Crown Life Ins. Co., 734 F.2d 133 (3d Cir.1984) (could be a boycott for insurer to conspire with one agency to terminate a second agency and transfer its business to first agency).

61. See Ch. 11.

Chapter 20

ANTITRUST FEDERALISM AND THE "STATE ACTION" DOCTRINE

Table of Sections

§ 20.1 Introduction; Preemption

In the United States, individual states and even local governments make regulatory policy. Under the Supremacy Clause of the Federal Constitution,[1] the federal government undoubtedly has the power to preempt much of this state and local regulation. In some markets, such as the regulation of labor relations, it has chosen to do so. But nothing in the federal *antitrust* laws even hints that Congress intended to preempt state and local law simply because that law interferes with competitive markets.

State and local governments are not free to regulate without any restraint whatsoever. Nevertheless, the mere fact that state law is inconsistent with federal antitrust policy is generally not enough to preempt the state or local law. This is often the case where the state or local law regulates more intensively than federal antitrust law does. For example, *Exxon* upheld a state statute forbidding vertical integration by petroleum refiners into retailing, notwithstanding that federal antitrust law generally permits vertical ownership.[2] *Pinney Dock* upheld a state antitrust statute with no effective statute of limitation, even though this may have permitted an antitrust action to survive longer than permitted by the federal four year statute.[3] Finally, state antitrust laws

§ 20.1

1. U.S. Const. Art. VI, § 2.

2. Exxon Corp. v. Governor of Maryland, 437 U.S. 117, 98 S.Ct. 2207 (1978). Contrast, State ex rel. Van de Kamp v. Texaco, 193 Cal.App.3d 8, 219 Cal.Rptr. 824 (1985), affirmed, 46 Cal.3d 1147, 252 Cal.Rptr. 221, 762 P.2d 385 (1988), which held that a federal consent decree permitting a merger prevented condemnation of the merger under California antitrust law, because the federal consent decree "occupied the field," in this case regulating the details of the merger.

3. Pinney Dock & Transp. Co. v. Penn Central Corp., 838 F.2d 1445 (6th Cir.), cert. denied, 488 U.S. 880, 109 S.Ct. 196 (1988).

that permit indirect purchasers to sue for damages have been upheld, notwithstanding that federal law limits damage recoveries to direct purchasers.[4]

Where state law permits something that the federal antitrust laws prohibit, the preemption question becomes more complex. Once again, mere inconsistency is not enough. Federal decisions considering preemption have generally focused on two issues: *first*, does the state statute under challenge compel what amounts to a *per se* violation of the federal antitrust laws, or merely something that is arguably a violation under the rule of reason? *second*, to what extent does the challenged statute vest discretion to make anticompetitive decisions in private parties who are not adequately supervised by the state itself? That is, the federal antitrust laws are generally concerned with *privately* initiated restraints, not those compelled by or effectively controlled by the government.

The statute at issue in the *Midcal Aluminum* case failed this test.[5] It required producers and wholesalers of alcoholic beverages to publish resale price schedules, and then required dealers to sell at these prices. This appeared to establish *per se* illegal resale price maintenance and left the determination of resale prices to the unsupervised discretion of the producers and wholesalers.[6] As a result, the Sherman Act preempted the state statute.

To be sure, one essential element of *per se* illegal RPM was missing in *Midcal* : there was no "agreement" between the manufacturer/wholesalers and the retailers to charge a specific set of resale prices.[7] Rather, the statute ordered retailers to charge the prices specified by the manufacturers and wholesalers. The Court simply noted that the statute brought about a result that precisely duplicated the result of a resale price maintenance agreement. A few years later, in *Fisher v. Berkeley*, the Supreme Court took the agreement requirement more seriously, holding that landlord compliance with a rent control ordinance did not amount to an "agreement" between the landlord and the regulatory agency.[8] As a basic matter, it seems clear that obedience of the law should not be found to constitute an "agreement" between the government and a private party for antitrust purposes. Of course, the manufacturers and wholesalers in *Midcal* were only obeying the law as well, but in that case the statute effectively gave one set of private persons the power to control the pricing decisions of another set of private persons. In the private arena, this could have been accomplished only by agreement, extortion or other form of coercion. In the *324 Liquor* case the Supreme Court held that a statute that authorized one set of private firms (liquor wholesalers) to establish the prices to be charged by another set (liquor retailers) created a "hybrid" restraint, which effectively substituted for the "contract, combination * * *, or conspiracy" requirement of § 1 of the Sherman Act.[9]

4. California v. ARC America Corp., 490 U.S. 93, 109 S.Ct. 1661 (1989), on remand, 940 F.2d 1583 (9th Cir. 1991). On indirect purchasers under federal law, see § 16.6. State antitrust laws and their indirect purchaser provisions are discussed more fully in § 20.8.

5. California Retail Liquor Dealers Assn. v. Midcal Aluminum (Midcal), 445 U.S. 97, 100 S.Ct. 937 (1980).

6. The Court essentially confirmed this result in 324 Liquor Corp. v. Duffy, 479 U.S. 335, 107 S.Ct. 720, on remand, 69 N.Y.2d 891, 515 N.Y.S.2d 231, 507 N.E.2d 1087 (1987), which struck down as preempted a statute that permitted liquor wholesalers to control retailers' prices directly. The Court emphasized that under the statute "private actors are granted a degree of private regulatory power. * * * " Id. at 345 n. 8, 107 S.Ct. at 726 n. 8. But see Massachusetts School of Law at Andover v. ABA, 107 F.3d 1026, 1036 (3d Cir.), cert. denied, ___ U.S. ___, 118 S.Ct. 264 (1997), which found *Parker* immunity in a scheme under which state simply adopted the law school accreditation recommendations, of the ABA and, in many cases, forbad graduates from unaccredited law schools from sitting for the state's bar exams. Adoption was usually made without any substantive review or debate.

7. On the agreement requirement in resale price maintenance cases, see § 11.4.

8. Fisher v. Berkeley, 475 U.S. 1150, 106 S.Ct. 1806 (1986). Since then, the Supreme Court and lower courts have consistently held that the term "conspiracy" does not apply to the transaction that occurs between a legislative body and those seeking to have a statute passed, or those complying with it. See City of Columbia, Columbia Outdoor Advertising v. Omni Outdoor Advertising, 499 U.S. 365, 374, 111 S.Ct. 1344, 1350 (1991); Englert v. City of McKeesport, 872 F.2d 1144, 1150 (3d Cir.), cert. denied, 493 U.S. 851, 110 S.Ct. 149 (1989).

9. *324 Liquor*, note 6, 479 U.S. at 345 & n. 8, 107 S.Ct. at 726 & n. 8. Accord Canterbury Liquors & Pantry v. Sullivan, 999 F.Supp. 144 (D.Mass.1998) (state statute requiring liquor wholesaler to post prices and then adhere

If the challenged statute does not compel what amounts to a *per se* violation, then it is usually not preempted. In Rice v. Norman Williams Co.[10] the Supreme Court upheld a California statute permitting manufacturers of liquor to "authorize" particular importers of liquor to bring their brands into the state, but exclude others. The Court treated this arrangement as giving state sanction to vertical territorial division, which is analyzed under the rule of reason and only rarely illegal.[11] It then held that, when a state statute is challenged on its face, it "may be condemned under the antitrust laws only if it mandates or authorizes conduct that necessarily constitutes a violation of the antitrust laws in all cases, or if it places irresistible pressure on a private party to violate the antitrust laws in order to comply with the statute."[12]

The relation between preemption and the "state action" exemption, discussed in subsequent sections of this chapter, remains somewhat ambiguous. In a footnote in the *Rice* case, the Supreme Court stated that, because it failed to find preemption in that case, it was unnecessary to consider whether the challenged statute qualified for the "state action" exemption.[13] This suggests that the Court first considers whether a particular state or local statute is preempted by the federal antitrust laws; if the answer is no, then the statutory scheme will be upheld. If the answer is yes, then the scheme must be considered further to determine whether it qualifies for the "state action" exemption.

But other Supreme Court decisions cast doubt on this sequence. For example, in the *Boulder* case the Supreme Court applied the "state action" doctrine to an ordinance temporarily restraining the territorial expansion of a cable television company pending further study.[14] That statute, it would seem, compelled the equivalent of a vertical territorial restraint or perhaps monopolization, both rule of reason violations. Indeed, it left much less room for private decision making than did the statute in *Rice*, which permitted private liquor firms within the state to select liquor importers for exclusion. Nevertheless, in *Boulder* the Supreme Court went straight to the "state action" question, without considering preemption.[15]

Nevertheless, the same fundamental concern underlies both preemption and the "state action" doctrine—namely, that states will authorize unsupervised private conduct that impairs competition. A more forthright approach would be to merge the two—in effect, to hold that the "state action" doctrine *defines* the scope of federal antitrust preemption of the potentially anticompetitive regulatory schemes of state and local government.

Under such an approach, consideration of whether the challenged statute compels a *per se* violation or not should generally be reserved for the merits of the antitrust case itself. The exemption (or preemption) question should focus only on whether the state's policy is clearly articulated, and whether private decisions with anticompetitive potential are adequately su-

for 30 days constituted a hybrid restraint with state imposition substituting for agreement requirement; and thus and a per se violation of Sherman Act).

10. 458 U.S. 654, 102 S.Ct. 3294 (1982).

11. See § 11.6.

12. *Rice*, 458 U.S. at 661, 102 S.Ct. at 3300. See also Battipaglia v. New York State Liquor Auth., 745 F.2d 166 (2d Cir.1984), cert. denied, 470 U.S. 1027, 105 S.Ct. 1393 (1985) (upholding state statute requiring liquor wholesalers to post their prices and then adhere to them, under the theory that the statute compelled only an exchange of price information, which is governed by the rule of reason); contra Miller v. Hedlund, 813 F.2d 1344 (9th Cir. 1987) (striking down similar statute on the theory that an agreement among competitors to *adhere* to posted prices would be illegal *per se*); and see *Canterbury*, note 9 (agreeing with *Miller*).

13. *Rice*, note 10, 458 U.S. at 662 n.9, 102 S.Ct. at 3300 n. 9.

14. Community Communic. Co. v. City of Boulder, 455 U.S. 40, 102 S.Ct. 835 (1982). See § 20.6.

15. However, then Associate Justice Rehnquist's dissent urged at some length that preemption was the relevant concern. 455 U.S. at 59, 102 S.Ct. at 845. Justice Rehnquist argued among other things that the statute should not be considered preempted because the mere passage of an ordinance did not meet § 1's "contract, combination, or conspiracy" requirement. 455 U.S. at 65 n.1, 102 S.Ct. at 848 n. 1. He then argued that rule of reason statutes should not be preempted, for such inquiries would amount to a kind of substantive due process evaluating the substantive merits of economic regulation.

pervised by an agency of the state or the local government imposing the regulation.

For example, suppose a state statute designated a single retailer for gasoline in the state, and gave the retailer absolute discretion to determine the suppliers with whom it would deal. Such a statute may be seen as facilitating only rule of reason antitrust violations (monopolization, supplier selection, vertical territorial restraints). Under the *Rice* analysis, a court might be tempted to say that the statute is not preempted, so further inquiry is unnecessary. Nevertheless, its anticompetitive potential is significant, and its most problematic component is the unsupervised discretion it gives to the private retailer. A better analytic approach would be to apply the "state action" doctrine directly. If the statute gives private parties the authority to engage in anticompetitive acts that would generally violate the antitrust laws, then the statute is preempted if governmental supervision is lacking or inadequate.

§ 20.2 Federalism and the Policy of the "State Action" Doctrine

The "State Action" doctrine exempts qualifying state and local government regulation from federal antitrust, even if the regulation at issue compels an otherwise clear violation of the federal antitrust laws. The term "state action" should not be confused with the same term as it is used in constitutional cases interpreting the Fourteenth Amendment and the Bill of Rights. In such cases, the term "state action" is interpreted broadly. Many actions that would be constitutional "state action" for Fourteenth Amendment purposes would not qualify for the "state action" antitrust exemption because they were insufficiently articulated as state policy or insufficiently supervised by a state agency. For example, a state regulatory agency that simply authorized private collusion in violation of its own statutory mandate would certainly be engaged in "state action" for Fourteenth Amendment purposes. But such an agency rule would not qualify for the "state action" antitrust exemption because the rule was not articulated in the state's policy and the private conduct that resulted was unsupervised. In the balance of this chapter, the term "state action" refers only to the antitrust doctrine. The term "*Parker*" doctrine or immunity also refers to the antitrust state action doctrine.[1]

20.2a. The Historical Basis of the "State Action" Doctrine

The preemption discussion in § 20.1 leaves federal antitrust in an embarrassingly strong position. Taken literally, it suggests that state and local government statutes that fix prices, divide markets or create exclusive rights are preempted by federal law. But no one has ever made a serious argument that Congress intended to use the Sherman Act to displace all forms of state and local regulation of prices and entry. Indeed, that construction would be inconsistent with the general structure of the federal constitution, which contemplates that the federal government and the states will simultaneously regulate the economy.[2] Under this regime, states and local governments acting under state authorization regulate hundreds of markets. These include land use, taxi fares, waste disposal by private firms, and utilities, to name only a few.

The "state action" doctrine itself rests on a fictional reading of the legislative history of the antitrust laws. In Parker v. Brown, which first recognized the doctrine, the Supreme Court upheld a California statute that limited the production of raisins by California farmers, with allocation decisions made by private participants in the industry, supervised by state officials.[3] The Court found that when Congress passed the Sherman Act in 1890 it never intended the statute to undermine the

§ 20.2

1. The term comes from Parker v. Brown, 317 U.S. 341, 63 S.Ct. 307 (1943).

2. See generally, F. Easterbrook, Antitrust and the Economics of Federalism, 26 J.L. & Econ. 23 (1983); M.B. Garland, Antitrust and State Action: Economic Efficiency and the Political Process, 96 Yale L.J. 486 (1987); W. Page, Antitrust, Federalism, and the Regulatory Process: A Reconstruction and Critique of the State Action Exemption after Midcal Aluminum, 61 B.U.L.Rev. 1099 (1981).

3. *Parker*, note 1 at 350–352, 63 S.Ct. at 313–315. See 1 Antitrust Law ¶ 221 (rev. ed. 1997).

regulatory power of state and local governments. But the prevailing view of federal power under the Commerce Clause in 1890 was that Congress could not have done this even had it wished to. Under that view, which the Supreme Court confirmed in its 1895 *E. C. Knight* decision, the federal government had no power to regulate markets that were perceived to be purely intrastate.[4] By the same token, extraterritorial state regulation was unconstitutional.[5] Under this regime of "dual federalism," any form of regulation that was within the regulatory power of state and local government was outside the reach of the federal antitrust laws. Small wonder that the Supreme Court could find no evidence that the Sherman Act's framers intended to control state and local regulation.

What really made the *Parker* exemption necessary was the Supreme Court's decision in Wickard v. Filburn[6] only a year before *Parker*. *Wickard* held that Congressional authority extended to all economic matters in or affecting interstate commerce, and thus made application of federal antitrust to such local matters as zoning or taxicab fares thinkable. The result could have been that federal antitrust would be used to undermine all state economic regulation, something that the inventors of our federal system did not contemplate.[7]

The "state action" exemption thus stands for the proposition that federal antitrust should not be used to intrude too deeply into state regulatory process. For example, if the state decides to regulate intrastate trucking rates or a city grants an exclusive right to operate a cable television system, these acts should not be challengeable as price fixing or monopolization under federal law.

20.2b. Conflicts Between Federal Antitrust and State Regulation; Alternative Solutions

One could take a variety of approaches to the problem of allocating decisionmaking affecting competition between state government and federal antitrust. One approach is an efficiency test: efficient, or competitive state or local regulation should be permitted, but harmful regulation should be found inconsistent with federal antitrust policy. Such a rule has an intuitive appeal. First, it furthers a general federal policy of making efficiency the principal goal of antitrust enforcement.[8] At the same time, it ensures that federal and state policy will be harmonious.

But an efficiency rationale for antitrust federalism suffers from the general problems that (1) distinguishing efficient from inefficient regulation is difficult or impossible in a wide range of cases; and (2) no governmental entity, including the federal government, operates under the constraint that only efficient regulation is permissible. Regulation may also be used to transfer wealth or to address noneconomic concerns that standard techniques for measuring efficiency (such as cost-benefit analysis) simply fail to take into account. Finally, the "efficiency" rationale does not take the concept of "federalism" seriously. The whole point of federalism is that state and sometimes local governments are entitled to have their own regulatory policy *even if that policy conflicts with federal policy*.

A second approach would be "jurisdictional": if the state regulates a purely intrastate market, its regulation is exempt from antitrust scrutiny, but if the market has substantial interstate spillovers, then federal antitrust scrutiny is appropriate. The principal problem with such an approach is that it leaves very little room for state regulation, except in a few isolated circumstances. Today it seems clear that many local markets have substantial interstate spillovers. For example, even municipal land use regulation or regulation of taxicab rates can have effects on the movement of

4. See United States v. E.C. Knight Co., 156 U.S. 1, 15 S.Ct. 249 (1895); H. Hovenkamp, Enterprise and American Law, 1836–1937, ch. 20 (1991).

5. See Wabash, St. Louis & Pacific Rwy. Co. v. Illinois, 118 U.S. 557, 7 S.Ct. 4 (1886) (state has no power to regulate interstate railroad shipment). See Hovenkamp, *Enterprise*, ch. 13.

6. 317 U.S. 111, 63 S.Ct. 82 (1942).

7. See generally H. Hovenkamp, State Antitrust in the Federal Scheme, 58 Ind.L.J. 375 (1983).

8. See generally Ch. 2.

people or the sale of goods into and out of the state. At the same time, however, there is an argument to be made that if local regulation of a market has no spillovers, or harmful effects outside the state, the federal antitrust laws should not interfere. Such an approach preserves the status of individual states as laboratories for economic experiments. Those that persist in harmful anticompetitive regulation will lose investment to those that do not.[9]

A third approach would be to conceive of the federal antitrust laws as a means of combatting regulatory "capture" at the state or local level.[10] Many regulatory regimes are created at the behest of producers or other small interest groups. Far from being in the consumers' best interest, such regulatory programs injure consumers by sheltering the regulated firms from new entry or from price or quality competition with their rivals. As a general matter, we expect such regulation to occur because the number of producers are relatively small and their interests are homogeneous. As a result they are very effective at making their case to governmental decision makers. By contrast, consumers are numerous and their interests are often very diffuse; so they make much poorer lobbyists.[11]

An "anti-capture" theory of antitrust federalism would attempt to separate those instances of bona fide state and local regulation in the public interest—that is, regulation that deals effectively with clear market failures—from regulation which does no more than feather the nests of the regulated firms. Under this theory, the federal antitrust laws should be used to distinguish between pro-consumer and captured regulatory regimes.

A serious problem with the capture theory of antitrust federalism is that, although the theory of regulatory capture may explain many instances of regulation, it is not easy for a court to distinguish efficient from socially harmful regulation. Those who have argued most vehemently for the capture theory of regulation generally believe that all, or nearly all, instances of regulation fall into this camp. By contrast, the traditional progressive liberal position has seen most regulation as being in the interest of the consumer. Further, people with different ideologies have very different views about what constitutes a market failure and how it should be identified. As a result, they have widely differing ideas about when regulation is justified. Finally, most regulatory regimes are mixed. That is, the markets to which they are applied may be in need of regulation, but the regulation itself does not fit the need precisely and, although much of it benefits consumers, some parts benefit producers as well.[12] *Fourth*, economic efficiency has never been held by anyone to be the exclusive goal of regulation. Indeed, states regulate for a number of reasons.

More fundamentally, a capture theory of regulation would represent a very substantial intrusion of federal power into state regulatory decision making. It would mandate federal preemption of state and local regulation, not because the latter was in conflict with any express federal provision, but simply because it conflicted with a more general federal mandate for competitive markets. In the process, federal antitrust would become a regulator of state *political* process—something that no framer of the Sherman Act publicly contemplated or probably desired. As a general premise, one should not infer lightly that Congress intends to interfere with state political processes when the state itself is not violating the federal constitution.

Finally, a fourth approach would consider whether the relevant decision maker is financially interested in the outcome of a regulatory

9. See H. Hovenkamp & J. MacKerron, Municipal Regulation and Federal Antitrust Policy, 32 UCLA L. Rev. 719 (1985); F. Easterbrook, note 2 at 34–45; E. Elhauge, The Scope of Antitrust Process, 104 Harv. L.Rev. 667, 730 (1991).

10. See J. Wiley, A Capture Theory of Antitrust Federalism, 99 Harv. L. Rev. 713 (1986). See also § 18.1c.

11. For a brief discussion of public choice theory, see § 19.2b2; see also D. Farber & P. Frickey, Law and Public Choice (1991); H. Hovenkamp, Legislation, Well–Being and Public Choice, 57 Univ. Chi. L. Rev. 63 (1990).

12. On the manifold nature and variety of regulation, see C. Sunstein, After the Rights Revolution: Reconceiving the Regulatory State (1991).

decision.[13] Indeed, this may come very close to what the Supreme Court has done in fact, and it is certainly reflected in the "active supervision" prong of the "state action" test, when private conduct is at issue.[14] When the issue is whether a municipality or other governmental subdivision enjoys the immunity, or when private conduct does not need supervision, then the "interested decisionmaker" approach does not explain the case law quite as well.

The approach that federal antitrust policy has in fact taken to state and local regulatory policy is characterized by three different values:

(1) the approach gives the states wide jurisdictional latitude to regulate as they see fit, provided that they take the regulatory enterprise seriously; and

(2) state and local regulation qualifies (or fails to qualify) for the *Parker* exemption without regard to its efficiency or anticompetitiveness.

(3) but federal policy is extremely hostile toward *private* power or discretion in regulated markets, where the power cannot effectively be disciplined by competition.

The stated policy of the federal antitrust laws is not to interfere with the *substance* of state regulation. As the Supreme Court observed in *Ticor Title Insurance*, the purpose of the "state action" doctrine is not "to determine whether the State has met some normative standard," but rather to consider "whether the State has exercised sufficient independent judgment and control so that the details of the rates or prices have been established as a product of deliberate state intervention, not simply by agreement among private parties."[15]

Nevertheless, the notion that the *Parker* exemption takes a non-normative approach to state regulation is false. One federally mandated normative principle continues to ring loud and clear: anticompetitive acts committed by unsupervised private parties will not be tolerated. So the normative principle is that private decision making must be reserved for traditional economic markets, where competition will control inefficiency and prevent monopoly. Once the state interferes in the market with its own awesome power to create monopoly or dictate price, then it must also act as the effective decision maker for acts with anticompetitive potential.

The classical principles of federalism embodied in our constitution are concerned with leaving to the states a great deal of power to regulate their local or intrastate economies. Furthermore, in a country where interstate mobility is easy, such a regime is at least presumptively efficient: states that persist in economically harmful regulation will pay a price in terms of lost customers or lost business firms. To be sure, too much weight can be given to this presumption of efficiency. The fact that mobility is legal does not entail that moving from one state to another is either physically easy or inexpensive. But even the conclusion that local regulation is inefficient does not defeat the basic presumption: except where Congress has declared a contrary intent, the regulation of local economic relations is left to the states and their subdivisions as the states see fit.

Of course, if the *Parker* exemption is found not to apply, then standard concerns about competitiveness and efficiency may be relevant to determining the substantive legality of the activity challenged under the federal antitrust laws.

§ 20.3 Basic Qualifications for Exemption

Federal antitrust immunizes state and local regulation from its prohibitions, without inquiring into anticompetitiveness, provided that:

1. The challenged activity is authorized by a "clearly articulated" state regulatory policy; and

13. Elhauge, note 9. For the same idea applied to petitioners to the government, see E. Elhauge, Making Sense of Antitrust Petitioning Immunity, 80 Calif. L.Rev. 1177 (1992).

14. See § 20.5.

15. FTC v. Ticor Title Ins. Co., 504 U.S. 621, 635, 112 S.Ct. 2169, 2177 (1992), on remand, 998 F.2d 1129 (3d Cir.1993). The Court was speaking of the supervision requirement of the "state action" doctrine; see § 20.5.

2. Any private conduct authorized by the state policy is "actively supervised" by an appropriate governmental agency.

This test is "non-substantive" in the sense that the state is free to regulate in as anticompetitive a manner as it pleases, provided that it takes its own regulatory policy seriously and ensures that private firms act consistently with the stated policy. About the only qualification to attach is that the active supervision requirement does not permit the state to have a "regulatory policy" of permitting private actors to do whatever they please.

Although this two-part test was first articulated in full bloom in the *Midcal* decision,[1] it developed through several intervening decisions. In Goldfarb v. Virginia State Bar,[2] the Supreme Court held that the adoption and enforcement of minimum fee schedules for lawyers was not immune from antitrust attack because the scheme amounted to "essentially . . . private anticompetitive activity," in contrast to the publicly created quota program at issue in *Parker*. Although a state statute gave the state supreme court power to regulate the practice of law, and the court in turn carried this function out through the local bar associations, nothing in the authorizing scheme compelled the setting of minimum fees. A few years later, in Bates v. State Bar, the Court qualified *Goldfarb* and found a *Parker* exemption in a rule prohibiting lawyer advertising, promulgated and enforced directly by the state supreme court.[3] In this case, the court, an arm of the state itself, made the relevant rule and enforced it.

Goldfarb had suggested that the *Parker* exemption would not apply unless the state actually compelled the private activity at issue. The Court reiterated that view in Cantor v. Detroit Edison Co., denying immunity to a regulated utility's policy of providing "free" light bulbs to customers.[4] The mere fact that the state's public utility commission had approved a tariff[5] including the policy was insufficient.

However, the Supreme Court subsequently rejected the position that only activities compelled by the state qualified for *Parker* immunity. The two-part *Midcal* test does not require compulsion, and in *Hallie* the Supreme Court unanimously held that conduct need not be compelled when the relevant actor is a municipality rather than a private party; authorization is sufficient.[6] In *Southern Motor Carriers* the Court extended this holding to private actors.[7] The decision involved so-called "rate bureaus," or joint rate-making by price regulated firms, challenged as simple price fixing. Under the state statutory scheme in question, a trucking company could choose either to participate in a rate bureau and submit a joint rate proposal with competitors, or else it could propose its own rate tariff individually to the regulatory agency. The Court concluded that "[a]s long as the State clearly articulates its intent to adopt a permissive policy, the first prong of the *Midcal* test [clear authorization] is satisfied."[8] Indeed, under the circumstances a mere authorization requirement would be more competitive than a compulsion requirement. Under compulsion, trucking firms would be *required* to collude—that is, to agree in advance on rates before submitting a joint

§ 20.3

1. California Retail Liquor Dealers Assn. v. Midcal Aluminum, 445 U.S. 97, 105, 100 S.Ct. 937, 943 (1980). It was initially proposed in 1 P. Areeda & D. Turner, Antitrust Law ¶ 213 (supervision), ¶ 214 (authorization) (1978).

2. Goldfarb v. Virginia State Bar, 421 U.S. 773, 791–792, 95 S.Ct. 2004, 2015–2016 (1975).

3. Bates v. State Bar of Arizona, 433 U.S. 350, 97 S.Ct. 2691 (1977). See also New Motor Vehicle Board v. Orrin W. Fox Co., 439 U.S. 96, 99 S.Ct. 403 (1978), upholding a statute that required a state agency to approve the location of new automobile dealerships. The Court found that the state's policy of limiting competition was "clearly articulated and affirmatively expressed." Id. at 109, 99 S.Ct. at 411.

4. Cantor v. Detroit Edison Co., 428 U.S. 579, 96 S.Ct. 3110 (1976).

5. A "tariff" is a document that a regulated firm files with its regulatory agency, requesting that it be required to charge certain prices, offer certain packages of services, have certain policies respecting treatment of customers, and the like. Once the tariff has been approved by the agency, the firm is legally obliged to follow the tariff.

6. Town of Hallie v. City of Eau Claire, 471 U.S. 34, 105 S.Ct. 1713 (1985). See § 20.6.

7. Southern Motor Carriers Rate Conference v. United States, 471 U.S. 48, 105 S.Ct. 1721 (1985).

8. Id. at 60, 105 S.Ct. at 1728.

proposal to the regulatory agency. But under the permissive policy, any firm that wanted to deviate downward was free to file its own separate tariff request. That tended to make the filed tariffs more competitive.

The *Southern Motor Carriers* Court emphasized that compulsion could be evidence of authorization.[9] Nevertheless, it now seems clear that the effective requirement is *authorization*, not compulsion.

§ 20.4 Authorization

In applying the "state action" exemption, the court must first consider whether the challenged conduct has been properly authorized by the state. Then it must consider whether any private decision-making under the authorized scheme is adequately supervised by public officials. These two requirements are taken up in this and the following sections.

Authorization must come from the state itself, not from a municipality or other governmental subdivision, and not from a subordinate agency of the state. In *Lafayette*, four members of a deeply divided Supreme Court agreed that a municipality could not authorize anticompetitive conduct, even if the conduct was legal under state law.[1] A fifth member, Chief Justice Burger, agreed, but only if the conduct at issue was proprietary (that is, done for profit) rather than governmental. The Court later clarified its meaning in the *Boulder* decision.[2] The City of Boulder, Colorado, attempted to justify its ordinance restricting the expansion of a private cable television company by noting that the city was a "home rule" municipality, having essentially all the regulatory power of the state. Home rule provisions are created by state law, and designed to increase the regulatory power of designated municipalities. Sometimes they appear in state constitutions, but they may also be statutory. The Supreme Court found home rule to be inadequate state authorization for *Parker* purposes, noting that although the home rule provision itself came from the state, the substance of the provision did not authorize any particular ordinance that the municipality might pass. Rather, it was merely neutral, effectively giving the City of Boulder carte blanche to regulate its CATV system as it pleased. *Boulder* also held that, however a state might wish to allocate regulatory power between itself and its subdivisions, only the federal government and the states had any type of sovereignty recognized in the federal constitution. That is, insofar as federal antitrust is concerned, a municipality may engage in anticompetitive acts only if it has an authorization from its state.

Likewise, *Southern Motor Carriers* concluded that joint rate making would not be found exempt merely because a *regulatory agency* authorized it. The authorization had to appear in some fashion in the *state* statutory scheme creating the agency and enumerating its powers.[3] But this analysis creates some problems in identifying exactly who the state is. The state acts only through its agencies and officials, and a legislature is an "agency" of the state in as real a sense as an administrative agency charged with regulating trucking. Today it seems quite clear that the legislature and the state's supreme court are the "state itself" for *Parker* authorization purposes.[4] Most, but not all, regulatory agencies are part of the executive branch; but decisions such as *Southern Motor Carriers* should not be read for the proposition that the Governor's Office is not part of the state for *Parker* purposes. Rather, one must distinguish between primary and subordinate government agencies. But even here is considerable ambiguity. For example, the Ninth Circuit has found that the state Director of the Department of Transportation

9. 471 U.S. at 61–62, 105 S.Ct. at 1729.

§ 20.4

1. City of Lafayette v. Louisiana Power & Light Co., 435 U.S. 389, 98 S.Ct. 1123 (1978).

2. Community Communications Co. v. City of Boulder, 455 U.S. 40, 102 S.Ct. 835 (1982).

3. Southern Motor Carriers Rate Conference v. United States, 471 U.S. 48, 105 S.Ct. 1721, on remand, 764 F.2d 748 (11th Cir.1985).

4. Cases finding that a state's highest court is part of the state itself are Bates v. State Bar of Arizona, 433 U.S. 350, 51 Ohio Misc. 1, 97 S.Ct. 2691 (1977); Hoover v. Ronwin, 466 U.S. 558, 104 S.Ct. 1989 (1984).

should be treated as the "state itself" for *Parker* purposes.[5]

In finding the line between the "state itself" and its subordinate agencies the courts have focused on three questions:

(1) whether the agency, office, or board at issue has quasi-legislative powers, or is merely instructed to carry out certain functions; if the latter, then the agency is probably not the state itself.[6]

2) Whether the decision makers in the agency, office or board are composed entirely of government officials with no financial interests in the regulated market, or whether representatives of the regulated market are included; if the latter, then the agency, office or board is usually not part of the state itself.[7]

3) Whether the agency is governed or answerable in some explicit fashion to the legislature, governor, or state supreme court; if not, then the agency is less likely to be found part of the state itself.[8]

Assuming that the authorization has come from the appropriate source, exactly what must be authorized and how unambiguous must the authorization be? As the *Boulder* decision noted, mere neutrality is not "authorization." Those defending the regulatory regime being challenged must point to something suggesting that the state contemplated the activity being challenged and decided to permit it. At the same time, most of the details of the regulatory scheme itself may be left to the state agency or governmental subdivision that carries it out. In the context of municipal regulation, it is sufficient that the challenged effects "logically would result" from the authorizing language in the statute. Thus, if state legislation authorizes a city to provide sewage treatment services, and permits it to decline service to areas outside the city, it is reasonably foreseeable that the city would insist on annexation before agreeing to supply sewage treatment services to adjacent areas.[9] In *Columbia* the Supreme Court went much further, holding that authorization for the creation of a virtual monopoly in the provision of billboards could be inferred from a state grant of power to regulate land use.[10] Today the great majority of decisions hold that, once authorization to regulate in a particular market are found, the creation of an exclusive franchise or right to conduct business in that market falls within the authorization.[11] The *Boulder* home rule provision failed this test because it did not involve state authorization to regulate in a *particular* market; rather, home rule provisions simply give municipalities a blanket regulatory power.

5. Charley's Taxi Radio Dispatch v. SIDA of Haw., 810 F.2d 869, 875 (9th Cir.1987); see also Automated Salvage Transport v. Wheelabrator Environmental Systems, 155 F.3d 59 (2d Cir.1998) (Connecticut Resources Recovery Authority (CRRA), a state agency, was the state itself for Parker purposes); Benton, Benton & Benton v. Louisiana Pub. Facilities Authority, 897 F.2d 198 (5th Cir.1990), cert. denied, 499 U.S. 975, 111 S.Ct. 1619 (1991) (Louisiana Public Facilities Authority, a public financing authority in charge of issuing tax exempt bonds, was part of the state itself); Board of Governors of Univ. of N.C. v. Helpingstine, 714 F.Supp. 167, 176 (M.D.N.C.1989) (state university part of state itself).

6. *Southern Motor Carriers*, note 3.

7. See Cine 42nd Street Theater Corp. v. Nederlander Org., 790 F.2d 1032 (2d Cir.1986); Massachusetts Board of Registration of Optometry, 5 Trade Reg. Rep. ¶ 22,555 (F.T.C. 1988); Washington State Elec. Contractors Ass'n. v. Forrest, 930 F.2d 736, 737 (9th Cir.), cert. denied, 502 U.S. 968, 112 S.Ct. 439 (1991).

8. See Bolt v. Halifax Hospital Medical Center, 891 F.2d 810, 824 (11th Cir.), cert. denied, 495 U.S. 924, 110 S.Ct. 1960 (1990); Fuchs v. Rural Elec. Convenience Coop., 858 F.2d 1210, 1217–1218 (7th Cir.1988), cert. denied, 490 U.S. 1020, 109 S.Ct. 1744 (1989).

9. Town of Hallie v. City of Eau Claire, 471 U.S. 34, 105 S.Ct. 1713 (1985).

10. City of Columbia, Columbia Outdoor Advertising v. Omni Outdoor Advertising, 499 U.S. 365, 372–373, 111 S.Ct. 1344, 1350 (1991), on remand, 974 F.2d 502 (4th Cir.1992) (the "very purpose of zoning regulation is to displace unfettered business freedom in a manner that regularly has the effect of preventing normal acts of competition, particularly on the part of new entrants."). Other decisions concerning state authorization in the context of municipal regulation are discussed in § 20.6.

11. See, for example, Earles v. State Bd. of Certified Public Accountants of Louisiana, 139 F.3d 1033, 1043 (5th Cir.), cert. denied, ___ U.S. ___, 119 S.Ct. 444 (1998) (state statute authorizing CPA Board to "[a]dopt and enforce all rules and regulations, bylaws, and rules of professional conduct" was sufficient authorization for Board rule forbidding CPA's from selling securities); Hillman Flying Serv. v. Roanoke, 652 F.Supp. 1142, 1145–1146 (W.D.Va. 1987), affirmed mem., 846 F.2d 71 (4th Cir.1988). See 1 Antitrust Law, ¶ 225 (rev. ed. 1997).

In *Southern Motor Carriers*, the Court made clear that authorization does not require that the state engage in micro-management of the regulatory agency's decision-making.[12] In that case, a general statute enabling the agency to supervise the rate-making process was all that was needed for authorization of joint rate-making. Likewise, in *Municipal Utilities Board* the Eleventh Circuit held that a state statute authorizing cooperation among electric utilities to prevent waste was sufficient authorization for what amounted to a horizontal territorial division arrangement.[13] The utilities divided the state into service areas and agreed not to compete with each other across the division lines.

Decisions such as *Municipal Utilities Board* are troublesome, however, because they fail to distinguish between competitive and anticompetitive responses to the state mandate. To be sure, territorial division schemes are one way for competitors to prevent duplication of facilities; but there may also be less anticompetitive ways that would permit the utilities to engage in true competition for new customers. *Municipal Utilities Board* seems to say that, if the state authorizing statute articulates a certain goal, then any mechanism for achieving that goal, no matter how anticompetitive, will be found to be "authorized" for purposes of *Parker*. This pushes the concept of authorization very far, particularly when we are speaking of the activities of private parties.[14]

Plaintiffs have often argued that, even though a state statute supplies a kind of general authorization, the particular conduct in the case at hand could not have been authorized. For example, suppose that the complaint alleges that a government official entered into a "conspiracy" with one or more private persons to deny market access to the plaintiff. Surely, no state authorizing statute should be construed to authorize its agencies or subdivisions to engage in conspiracies. True enough. But upon inspection, nearly all the conspiracy claims amount to petitioning and governmental response. Uniformly, the courts hold that a private citizen's request that a government agency undertake a certain action, and the agency's affirmative response, cannot be construed as a "conspiracy."[15] Further, such a holding would undermine the constitutional right to petition the government, embodied in antitrust's *Noerr–Pennington* doctrine.[16]

In other cases, the claim is of the nature that, although certain conduct was authorized, the state officials went beyond that point and engaged in unauthorized conduct as well.[17] Some of these cases fall in the area of individual conduct that was probably not part of the official policy of either the state or the agency carrying it out. Some of the cases involve state agencies that violated the state authorizing statutes under which they operated.[18]

Should such situations become antitrust violations, simply because they may have anti-

12. *Southern Motor Carriers*, note 3 at 63–64, 105 S.Ct. at 1729–1731.

13. Municipal Utilities Board of Albertville v. Alabama Power Co., 934 F.2d 1493 (11th Cir.1991), after remand, 21 F.3d 384 (11th Cir.1994), cert. denied, 513 U.S. 1148, 115 S.Ct. 1096 (1995).

14. Compare Consolidated Gas Co. of Fla. v. City Gas Co., 912 F.2d 1262 (11th Cir.1990), reversed per curiam on nonantitrust grounds, 499 U.S. 915, 111 S.Ct. 1300 (1991) (regulatory scheme for natural gas did not authorize horizontal territorial division agreements).

15. See City of Columbia & Columbia Outdoor Advertising v. Omni Outdoor Advertising, 499 U.S. 365, 383–384, 111 S.Ct. 1344, 1356 (1991), on remand, 974 F.2d 502 (4th Cir.1992). See § 20.6; and 1 Antitrust Law ¶ 224d (rev. ed. 1997).

16. See Ch. 18.

17. Surgical Care Center of Hammond v. Hospital Service Dist., 171 F.3d 231 (5th Cir.1999) (state statute authorized hospital district to enter into joint ventures, but this did not include an anticompetitive concerted refusal to deal; "Not all joint ventures are anticompetitive. Thus, it is not the foreseeable result of allowing a hospital service district to form joint ventures that it will engage in anticompetitive conduct."). See also DiVerniero v. Murphy, 635 F.Supp. 1531 (D.Conn.1986) (police harassment of franchisee's competitors not authorized); Anheuser–Busch, Inc. v. Goodman, 745 F.Supp. 1048, 1051–1052 (M.D.Pa.1990) (authority to regulate sale of liquor did not include the creation and enforcement of anticompetitive restraints on pricing).

18. For example Fisichelli v. Town of Methuen, 653 F.Supp. 1494, 1500 (D.Mass.1987), appeal dismissed, 884 F.2d 17 (1st Cir.1989). ("In the instant case, a clearly articulated and affirmatively expressed state policy allows the issuance of industrial revenue bonds. Nevertheless, the state has not authorized government officials to use industrial revenue bonds in furtherance of an illegal conspiracy to restrict competition to benefit the personal financial interests of government officials.").

competitive consequences? Many state law violations, it is worth noting, have consequences for competition. The trend in decisions is that state law irregularities should not be turned into federal antitrust violations, particularly where the state law itself provides a remedy.[19]

This conclusion seems unescapable. When a state regulates, it naturally contemplates that agencies or private actors will make mistakes or even engage in wilful violations of the regulatory scheme. The relevant question is then whether state law can be brought to bear so as to correct or punish these violations. If every imperfection in compliance with a state regulatory scheme instantly becomes a federal antitrust violation, then the state scheme loses its integrity. For example, suppose that a state statute authorizes an agency to regulate, but the agency official makes secret deals favoring one firm at the expense of others. The first question that the federal antitrust tribunal should ask is whether state law creates an effective remedy for those victimized by this official's illegal act. If so, federal antitrust has no place.

In the context of private action, the authorization question becomes a little easier. Private firms are inherently self-interested actors, and with respect to them the exemption should be fairly strictly construed. Several courts have held that, if a private actors exceeds the authorization, the result is denial of *Parker* immunity.[20] In particular, the courts are less willing to infer that the state intended to displace competition when the authorized parties are private actors. If the statute is neutral on the question and there appear to be both competitive and non-competitive ways of operating under the statute, the court may insist on the former.[21]

§ 20.5 Active Supervision

In *Midcal* the Supreme Court held that the state could not simply authorize private actors to create and implement *per se* illegal resale price maintenance without effective state oversight.[1] If the state's policy is to permit private actors to do anticompetitive things, so be it; but the state must ensure that private decision makers are acting in accordance with state policy and not doing additional anticompetitive things that fall outside the scope of state authorization. In *324 Liquor* the Court clarified that holding, striking down a statute that required liquor retailers to resell liquor at a price 12% above a price posted by the wholesaler, but with no agency supervision of the prices that wholesalers posted.[2] Effectively, the statute gave wholesalers the unsupervised discretion to set retail prices.

The law of active supervision has focused on three issues. Two have been addressed, although not conclusively settled, by Supreme Court decisions. The three issues are (1) When is supervision required? (2) What kind of su-

19. For example, Kern–Tulare Water Dist. v. City of Bakersfield, 828 F.2d 514, 522 (9th Cir.1987), cert. denied, 486 U.S. 1015, 108 S.Ct. 1752 (1988) (Federalist notion of respect for states as sovereigns entails that "[w]here ordinary errors or abuses in exercise of state law * * * serves to strip the city of state authorization, aggrieved parties should not forego customary state corrective processes.").

20. In re Insurance Antitrust Litigation, 938 F.2d 919, 931 (9th Cir.1991), affirmed in part, reversed in part on other grounds, 509 U.S. 764, 113 S.Ct. 2891 (1993) (state insurance regulations did not authorize private conspiracies); Sweeney v. Athens Regional Medical Center, 709 F.Supp. 1563, 1576 (M.D.Ga.1989) (regulatory provisions given to hospitals and their boards did not authorize anticompetitive refusals to deal); Reynolds Metals Co. v. Commonwealth Gas Servs., 682 F.Supp. 291, 294 (E.D.Va. 1988) (pipelines' refusal to transport gas of other producers not authorized).

21. See Wicker v. Union County Gen. Hosp., 673 F.Supp. 177, 185 (N.D.Miss.1987) (statute authorizing hospital's staff to terminate physicians for reasons relating to patient care did not permit them to make terminations in order to reduce the amount of competition); Reazin v. Blue Cross & Blue Shield, 663 F.Supp. 1360, 1419 (D.Kan. 1987), affirmed in part and remanded in part, 899 F.2d 951 (10th Cir.), cert. denied, 497 U.S. 1005, 110 S.Ct. 3241 (1990) (statutes regulating dominant health insurer and permitting it to file tariffs did not authorize elimination of competing insurers); Medic Air Corp. v. Air Ambulance Authority, 843 F.2d 1187, 1189–1190 (9th Cir.1988) (statute giving private firm a monopoly in dispatching of air ambulances did not authorize it to discriminate against the plaintiff ambulance service).

§ 20.5

1. California Retail Liquor Dealers Assn. v. Midcal Aluminum (Midcal), 445 U.S. 97, 100 S.Ct. 937 (1980). For a discussion of the facts, see § 20.1.

2. 324 Liquor Corp. v. Duffy, 479 U.S. 335, 107 S.Ct. 720, on remand, 69 N.Y.2d 891, 515 N.Y.S.2d 231, 507 N.E.2d 1087 (1987).

pervision is required? and (3) Who must do the supervising?

20.5a. When is Supervision Required?

Active supervision is required whenever the conduct being challenged is that of a private party.[3] Indeed, the Supreme Court's principal concern in establishing the requirement was that states not simply use *Parker* to give parties carte blanche to do what they wish. When the State itself is the relevant actor, then "supervision" is clearly not required, because there is no relevant entity above the state to do the supervising.

In the *Hallie* case the Supreme Court also held that state supervision is not required when the conduct being challenged is that of a governmental subdivision such as a municipality operating under state authority.[4] That is, the *Parker* doctrine does not require a state both to authorize municipal regulation and to supervise, or review, that regulation once it is in place; municipal governments are trusted to doing their own supervising. This rule is not limited to situations when municipalities are engaged in traditional "governmental" functions, but also applies when they act as entrepreneurs in private markets, in competition with private sellers.[5] Thus, if the actor is "governmental," supervision is not required.

An ambiguity that arises in the context of the authorization requirement re-emerges in slightly different form when we examine supervision. Once again, the line between governmental and private action is not always clear. Actions taken directly by a state legislature, state court or city council are obviously governmental and need not be supervised. But the government often acts through private, or at least quasi-private decision makers. For example, Hass v. Oregon State Bar considered whether a state bar association should be counted as the "state" and thus be exempt from supervision by some higher agency.[6] On the one hand, the bar was an association of lawyers motivated in substantial part by self-interest. On the other, the bar had certain governmental powers, such as the power to make agency-style rules; it was chartered as a *public* corporation; three of its fifteen board members were required to be non-lawyers; it was subject to the open meetings law that applied to state agencies generally. The court concluded that the bar was the "state," and supervision of its activities was unnecessary.

Understand the meaning of the *Hass* rule. A state may grant its bar association the power to set legal fees. Since the bar association itself is a public agency, no one above the bar association in the governmental hierarchy must supervise this fee setting process. The effective result could be an unsupervised cartel of lawyers with the authority, not only to set their own fees by agreement, but also to discipline, perhaps even disbar, those who cheated on the cartel by charging lower prices.[7]

A rule that permits private, self-interested decision makers to control access to markets is inconsistent with federal antitrust policy and is certainly not mandated by the federalism concerns of the *Parker* doctrine. As a principle of government, federalism is concerned with protecting the sovereignty of states, not with protecting individual rights—

3. *Midcal*, note 1, 445 U.S. at 105–106, 100 S.Ct. at 943–944; Southern Motor Carriers Rate Conference v. United States, 471 U.S. 48, 58–59, 105 S.Ct. 1721, 1727–1728 (1985).

4. Town of Hallie v. City of Eau Claire, 471 U.S. 34, 47, 105 S.Ct. 1713, 1720 (1985). On the question of state agencies rather than municipalities, the Court suggested the answer: "In cases in which the actor is a state agency, it is likely that active supervision would * * * not be required, although we do not here decide that issue." Id. at 46 n. 10, 105 S.Ct. at 1720 n. 10.

5. See Wall v. City of Athens, 663 F.Supp. 747, 762 (M.D.Ga.1987), aff'd 976 F.2d 649 (11th Cir.1992) (city acting as supplier of water services; no supervision required of authorized decisions).

6. 883 F.2d 1453 (9th Cir.1989), cert. denied, 494 U.S. 1081, 110 S.Ct. 1812 (1990). See also Earles v. State Bd. of Certified Public Accountants of Louisiana, 139 F.3d 1033 (5th Cir.), cert. denied, ___ U.S. ___, 119 S.Ct. 444 (1998) (Board regulating certified public accountants counted as state, notwithstanding that board membership was almost entirely CPAs).

7. Accord Cohn v. Bond, 953 F.2d 154 (4th Cir.1991), which held that supervision was not required with respect to the decisions of the medical staff of a public hospital terminating the privileges of a chiropractor. Once again, the medical staff were market participants themselves.

and particularly not a "right" to engage in anticompetitive conduct in economic markets. Thus before a body can qualify as part of the "state itself," and not be in need of supervision, the effective decision makers must be economically independent of the conduct that they are regulating. A municipal government generally (although perhaps not always) meets such criteria, as perhaps does a regulatory agency containing salary-paid officials. To be sure, both regulatory officials and local politicians can be "captured," even though they are not individual participants in the private market at issue. But capture is still not the same thing as direct economic interest. Different interest groups can vie with each other to capture the employee official. "Capture" is not a foregone conclusion, and we presume that most government officials do their jobs well. Most importantly, capture itself is ultimately not an antitrust problem but a political one.[8]

The question of the need for supervision is also relevant in another context: in certain cases the conduct at issue is clearly that of private parties, but the statute leaves no room for discretion. For example, in *Municipal Utilities Board* the court approved a territorial division scheme among electric utilities. The original territories had been drawn up under legislative supervision, but future customer allocations had to be made by the private parties. For such situations, the statute provided that if a prospective customer's property should overlap the service areas of two or more of the utilities, the customer should go to the utility within whose territory the customer had the largest amount of property. Thus, although the private utilities divided new customers, they did so according to a legislatively crafted formula that permitted them no discretion. There was nothing to supervise.[9]

The key to solving the supervision problem is to make the analysis specific to the conduct being challenged. The antitrust tribunal should look at the challenged conduct and determine first whether the person engaged in the conduct is a private party. If not, supervision is not required. If the actor is private, then the court must consider whether the act was a matter over which the private actor had some discretion. If the answer is no—if the private actor was simply following a statutory mandate that compelled a certain outcome—then there is nothing to supervise. But if the act was one about which the private actor had a variety of choices, then the choice selected must be effectively supervised by a qualifying state agency.

20.5b. What Kind of Supervision is Required?

Governmental supervision comes in many types and levels of scrutiny. For example, an appellate court "supervises" lower courts by reviewing substantive rulings for legal errors and reversing incorrect decisions. By contrast, an understaffed licensing agency might routinely grant licenses to do business upon application, "rubber-stamping" them without making any substantive investigation into their truthfulness, and reviewing them only when a complaint brings some problem to light, or perhaps not even then. Further, some agencies may not even be empowered to second-guess the merits of private conduct; they can object only to procedural deviations. Indeed, with respect to some activities, the agency may have jurisdiction only to accept reports. For example, in some markets sellers are required to report the prices they charge or the quantities they sell. But the agency that receives the report has no authority to regulate either price or output.

Today it is clear that mere reporting, or agency supervision that extends only to process, does not satisfy the "active supervision" requirement. The Supreme Court so held in Patrick v. Burget, which refused to find adequate supervision in a state-authorized medi-

8. On this point, see E. Elhauge, The Scope of Antitrust Process, 104 Harv. L. Rev. 667 (1991).

9. Municipal Utilities Board of Albertville v. Alabama Power Co., 934 F.2d 1493, 1497 (11th Cir.1991), appeal after remand, 21 F.3d 384 (11th Cir. 1994), cert. denied, 513 U.S. 1148, 115 S.Ct. 1096 (1995).

cal peer review scheme.[10] The plaintiff was a physician who had been disciplined by the physician-controlled peer review board of a public hospital. Under state law a public agency had the power to require reports of staff terminations, and to review denials of hospital staff privileges for procedural irregularities, but it had no power to review the substantive decisions themselves. The Court held that active supervision "requires that state officials have and exercise power to review particular anticompetitive acts of private parties and disapprove those that fail to accord with state policy."[11]

Patrick left open the possibility that judicial review in the state courts could satisfy the active supervision requirement, but the court's decision-making power would have to extend to the merits of the private decision itself. In this case, it appeared that the Oregon state courts had never inquired into the merits of a peer review decision and no state statute authorized such an inquiry; so the supervision requirement was not met. Although *Patrick* acknowledged that in principal the "active supervision" requirement could be met by judicial review in the state courts (as opposed to a specialized agency), the decision says little about the minimum content of such supervision. For example, it is unclear whether the standard of review in such a case need be no higher than the standard often applied to court review of public agency actions—that is, whether the decision is supported by evidence in the record—or whether some stricter standard of review is required.[12]

Supervision involves two quite different questions: what the supervising agency or court is *empowered* to do, and what it does in fact. For example, suppose a rate regulating agency is authorized to review requests for rate increases, determine whether they are reasonably based on increased costs, and approve or disapprove the request depending on what it finds. Such a scheme would certainly qualify as active supervision. But suppose that in fact the agency is underfunded and simply lacks the resources to investigate such requests. Suppose further that for an extended period of time it has followed a practice of simply rubber-stamping all such requests. Alternatively, the regulatory statute may state that the requested rate will go into effect, say, thirty days after the application unless the agency raises an objection; but in fact the agency never objects. Is "active supervision" for federal antitrust purposes established by the fact that the agency has the authority to supervise, or must it be "actively" supervising as well?

In *New England Motor* the First Circuit essentially found the former, holding that state agencies regulating trucking rates met the supervision requirement simply by virtue of the fact that they were *authorized* to review rates and that they were "staffed and funded" to some degree. In one particular case the state agency had never in its history rejected a rate request, and had never even "requested financial information to support collectively set rates."[13]

But in *Ticor Title* the Supreme Court disagreed with *New England Motor* and found supervision inadequate in a similar situation.[14] The defendants were firms that performed title searches of real property, prepared escrow documents, and sold title insurance. They jointly proposed rates to state insurance regulators through rate bureaus.[15] The state regulatory schemes included a "negative option" provision—that is, proposed rates became effective automatically after a specified time period, commonly thirty days, unless the agency

10. Patrick v. Burget, 486 U.S. 94, 108 S.Ct. 1658, rehearing denied, 487 U.S. 1243, 108 S.Ct. 2921 (1988).

11. Id. at 101, 108 S.Ct. at 1663.

12. One court found that judicial review was not adequate when the review standard was merely whether the private peer review decision had been arbitrary and capricious. Shahawy v. Harrison, 875 F.2d 1529 (11th Cir. 1989). But see Lender's Serv. v. Dayton Bar Ass'n., 758 F.Supp. 429, 438–439 (S.D.Ohio 1991) (finding adequate supervision in a review proceeding governing disciplined attorneys that included both substantive review of the merits and numerous procedural safeguards).

13. New England Motor Rate Bureau v. FTC, 908 F.2d 1064 (1st Cir.1990).

14. FTC v. Ticor Title Ins. Co., 504 U.S. 621, 112 S.Ct. 2169 (1992), on remand, 998 F.2d 1129 (3d Cir.1993).

15. For the definition of a rate bureau, see § 20.3.

voiced an objection. But the history of attentiveness of the regulatory agencies was quite embarrassing. Some of them checked the proposals for mathematical accuracy, but some did not even do that. The agencies only infrequently requested additional data in support of a rate increase proposal. Although the agencies were required by law to audit the insurers' costs periodically, very few of the audits were performed. In sum, regulation amounted to little more than a legalized cartel.

The Court found that this record failed to meet the active supervision test. In rejecting the *New England Motor* test[16] the Court observed:

> Where prices or rates are set as an initial matter by private parties, subject only to a veto if the State chooses to exercise it, the party claiming the immunity must show that state officials have undertaken the necessary steps to determine the specifics of the price-fixing or rate-setting scheme. The mere potential for state supervision is not an adequate substitute for a decision by the State.[17]

Justice Scalia concurred, noting first that the outcome seemed correct in light of earlier supervision cases. But he feared that the decision would greatly increase the number of antitrust challenges in state-regulated industries, where lack of resources and, consequently, inadequacy of oversight were common problems.[18]

Justice Scalia's point is worth noting. Although *Ticor* seems precisely consistent with the principles that drive the *Parker* doctrine, the result may be many more antitrust challenges to state agency decisions. Even the relatively diligent agency goes through periods where funding is low or volume of business is unusually high. The result may be that individual private tariff requests are approved without a hard look. Equally serious is the possibility that every agency's procedures, including those in the particular case, will become the subject of antitrust discovery.

In dissent, Chief Justice Rehnquist complained that the majority's position would necessitate substantive review of the quality of state regulation. The Chief Justice predicted that joint rate making could become so dangerous that many regulated firms would abandon it.[19] In that case, the workload on agencies would become even greater. More tariff applications would have to be reviewed, since each firm would be submitting its own. Of course, that result is not necessarily bad. It all depends on what one thinks of the entire enterprise of joint rate proposals. The higher costs of making and supervising individual tariffs may be more than offset by the increased rate competition that results.[20]

Of course, a fundamental problem is that joint tariffs are necessary only in markets where otherwise competing firms operate—thus suggesting that prices should be set by competition rather than regulation in the first place. As the previous chapter notes, many industries of this sort have gone through deregulation, which gives individual firms much greater discretion to set competitive prices.[21]

20.5c. Who Must Supervise?

The Supreme Court has generally spoken of supervision of private conduct as coming from the state itself. But in those cases, such as *Midcal*[22] and *Patrick*,[23] the state was the relevant party and the source of the supervision was not an issue.[24] The better rule is that the level of government imposing the regulation is also the one that should do the supervising. If the regulation at issue is from the state, then supervision is ordinarily carried out

16. Note 13.

17. *Ticor*, 504 U.S. at 638, 112 S.Ct. at 2179.

18. 504 U.S. at 639–643, 112 S.Ct. at 2180–2182.

19. *Ticor*, 504 U.S. at 643–644, 112 S.Ct. at 2182.

20. The more fundamental question, of course, is whether groups of otherwise competing firms in a position to submit joint rate proposals need to be price regulated in the first place; or is price regulation of such markets simply a consequence of regulatory capture?

21. See § 19.2.

22. Note 1.

23. Note 10.

24. See also *Hallie*, note 4 at 46 n. 10, 105 S.Ct. at 1720 n. 10, stating that "where state or municipal regulation of a private party is involved * * * active state supervision must be shown. * * * "

by the state agency charged with enforcing the regulatory regime. By contrast, if the regulation is municipal, then the municipality should supervise, either through its city council directly or perhaps by a commission or agency.

For example, suppose a city regulates taxicab fares through a scheme in which taxicab companies present evidence of cost increases and request corresponding rate increases. No purpose would be served by a federal antitrust policy that required a state agency, rather than a municipal agency, to review these requests and pass judgment on them. Such a regulatory regime could be very cumbersome, and could put the state in the peculiar position of having to carry out the various, perhaps inconsistent regulatory policies of its various municipalities and other political subdivisions. Indeed, in many instances it would result in a situation where the government entity doing the supervision is less accountable politically to those affected, and this certainly is not the goal of antitrust's "state action" doctrine. Many lower court decisions have suggested that, in assessing supervision, one looks primarily to the supervision applied by the governmental entity imposing the regulation.[25]

§ 20.6 The Special Problem of Municipal Antitrust Liability

In the *Lafayette* decision, the Supreme Court embarked on a trouble-filled voyage which thankfully appears to be over.[1] In a claim against municipalities alleging unlawful tying arrangements and other Sherman Act violations, a thoroughly fractured Supreme Court held that (a) the basic *Parker* doctrine does not automatically apply to municipalities; and (b) for a municipality the consequences of not receiving the exemption may be that the municipality has *violated* the antitrust laws, and is thus subject to treble damages and attorneys fees as any other defendant.

Five *Lafayette* Justices appeared to agree with the basic proposition that governmental subdivisions do not automatically qualify for the "state action" exemption. However, one of the five, Chief Justice Burger, would have limited that conclusion to situations when the municipality was acting in a "proprietary" capacity—that is, when it was participating in a market as buyer or seller, and not merely regulating it. In an opinion by Justice Brennan, the four Justice plurality noted that the federal constitution recognizes the federal government and the states as sovereigns; it gives no special recognition to municipalities or other state subdivisions.[2] Today, *Lafayette*'s basic proposition that municipal regulation is not automatically exempt from federal antitrust scrutiny is beyond dispute.

Another *Lafayette* implication, treble damages for municipalities, was subsequently undermined by statute. The Local Government Antitrust Act (LGAA), passed in 1984, provides that "no damages, interest on damages, costs, or attorney's fees may be recovered * * * from any local government, or official or employee thereof acting in an official capacity."[3] The right to an injunction is not restricted, and a prevailing plaintiff in an injunction action may recover attorneys fees.[4] The statute gives similar protection for suits "against a person based on any official action directed by a local government, or official or employee thereof acting in an official capacity."[5]

25. Tri-State Rubbish, Inc. v. Waste Management, Inc., 998 F.2d 1073 (1st Cir.1993) (municipal, as opposed to state, supervision, is permissible); Riverview Invs. v. Ottawa Community Improvement Corp., 769 F.2d 324 (6th Cir.1985) (looking for municipal supervision of municipally created public finance program). Other cases are discussed in 1 Antitrust Law ¶ 226d (rev. ed. 1997).

§ 20.6

1. City of Lafayette v. Louisiana Power & Light Co., 435 U.S. 389, 98 S.Ct. 1123 (1978).

2. 435 U.S. at 410, 98 S.Ct. at 1135.

3. 15 U.S.C.A. §§ 34–36. See Thatcher Enters. v. Cache County Corp., 902 F.2d 1472, 1477–1478 (10th Cir.1990) (barring damage award against municipality and its officials).

4. See Lancaster Community Hosp. v. Antelope Valley Hosp. Dist., 940 F.2d 397, 404 n. 14 (9th Cir.1991), cert. denied, 502 U.S. 1094, 112 S.Ct. 1168 (1992).

5. See Montauk–Caribbean Airways, Inc. v. Hope, 784 F.2d 91, 94–95 (2d Cir.), cert. denied, 479 U.S. 872, 107 S.Ct. 248 (1986) (defining official action broadly to include all official activities taken under city's home rule power, and not merely activities specifically authorized by state law).

The statute leaves some questions unanswered. For example, is a person acting in her "official capacity," and thus immune from damages when she enters into a conspiracy with a private person or perhaps accepts a bribe? Likewise, are private parties exempt from damages if their actions are merely authorized by a local ordinance but not compelled by it?[6] In all events, it seems clear that a private party claiming the LGAA damages immunity must show that its activities were either compelled or that they were adequately supervised, just as private conduct generally must be supervised.[7] Finally, although one court has held to the contrary,[8] the LGAA does nothing to preempt state antitrust laws, which may apply to municipalities or private parties regulated by them. Whether the states wish to create a "*Parker*" exemption from their own antitrust laws is entirely up to them.[9]

The LGAA thus removes the most severe antitrust remedies but leaves unanswered the underlying question of when a municipality may claim the *Parker* exemption. In two subsequent cases the Supreme Court addressed that question, and in the process has almost entirely removed the apparition that haunted local governments in the wake of *Lafayette* and *Boulder*.

In *Hallie*, the Supreme Court came to two important conclusions that it had resisted earlier.[10] First, although municipal conduct qualifies for *Parker* immunity only if it meets the authorization, or "clear articulation," requirement, no legislature could "be expected to catalog all of the anticipated effects" of its delegation of regulatory authority. The true test should be whether the challenged activity "logically would result" from or be a "foreseeable result" of the state delegation.[11] In this case the city had proposed to annex four adjacent towns, and then give the residents of those towns access to its sewage treatment facility only if they agreed to use the city's entire sewage system. Such a decision was found to be a foreseeable consequence of a state grant of authority to the city to operate a sewage treatment facility and sewage system. Indeed, most post-*Hallie* decisions have found that municipal creation of a monopoly is a foreseeable consequence of a state grant of authority to regulate in a particular market.[12]

Of course, this foreseeability test can be pushed only so far. A home rule provision, such as the one at issue in the *Boulder* case, permits a municipality to regulate all of its local markets. It is thus certainly "foreseeable" that a home rule city would regulate land use, cable television, taxicabs, or all the numerous and diverse markets that large municipalities ordinarily regulate. But *Hallie* did not purport to overrule *Boulder*'s conclusion that a home rule provision does not effectively "authorize" anything.

Assuming then that *Boulder* remains good law, it appears that before a municipality can meet the authorization requirement the state must have given a *market specific* grant of regulatory power. A generic power to regulate, such as is contained in a home rule provision, is insufficient. However, once a city enjoys such a market specific grant, the regulatory

6. Finding an exemption under such circumstances is Sandcrest Outpatient Services, P.A. v. Cumberland County, 853 F.2d 1139 (4th Cir.1988) (statute permitted, but did not compel, private parties to object to another firm's provision of emergency services).

7. *Sandcrest*, note 6 at 1143; and City Communications, Inc. v. City of Detroit, 660 F.Supp. 932 (E.D.Mich. 1987) (no damages exemption under LGAA where private cable company could not show that its activities were supervised by municipality).

8. Driscoll v. City of New York, 650 F.Supp. 1522 (S.D.N.Y.1987).

9. See 14 Antitrust Law ¶ 2411c (1999).

10. Town of Hallie v. City of Eau Claire, 471 U.S. 34, 105 S.Ct. 1713 (1985).

11. 471 U.S. at 42, 105 S.Ct. at 1718.

12. For example, City of Columbia & Columbia Outdoor Advertising v. Omni Outdoor Advertising, 499 U.S. 365, 111 S.Ct. 1344, 1350 (1991) (grant of power to zone foreseeably led to municipal creation of de facto billboard monopoly); Sterling Beef Co. v. City of Fort Morgan, 810 F.2d 961 (10th Cir.1987) (state authorization to municipality to regulate gas production and pipelines foreseeably resulted in municipal creation of pipeline monopoly). See also Southern Disposal v. Texas Waste Management, 161 F.3d 1259 (10th Cir.1998) (exclusive contract a foreseeable result of state authorization to municipality to regulate waste disposal, notwithstanding that Oklahoma had a constitutional provision prohibiting "exclusive franchises" unless approved by the voters; but prior state case law had concluded that an exclusive trash agreement did not violate this provision).

decisions that arguably flow from regulation in the area meet the test. One apparent exception is if the local government's regulatory action is manifestly contrary to the state grant of regulatory authority. For example, a few courts have held that a state grant of authority to regulate did not authorize the municipality to engage in anticompetitive or unfair exclusionary practices.[13] As a general matter, however, questions about whether a municipality goes beyond its regulatory authority, or violates its regulatory mandate, should be addressed under state law. The source of municipal power to regulate comes from the state, and the state courts are the best forums for deciding when a municipality has overstepped. A contrary result would turn every municipal violation of its regulatory power into the basis for a federal antitrust challenge.[14]

Earlier cases had also found lack of authorization for municipalities to enter into "conspiracies" with private firms or individuals to exclude others.[15] But the Supreme Court destroyed the basis for such claims in its *Columbia* decision.[16] In that case the defendant Columbia Outdoor Advertising (COA) was a well established firm with good political connections in the City. The plaintiff, Omni, was a new entrant. In response to Omni's entry, COA was able to get its friends on the City Council to pass a new ordinance restricting most billboard construction, but grandparenting in COA's existing billboards. In Omni's Sherman Act suit, a jury found a qualifying "conspiracy" between COA and city officials to deny market access to Omni.

The Supreme Court absolutely refused to find any conspiracy exception to the basic authorization requirement. The Court noted,

> ["C]onspiracy" means nothing more than an agreement to impose the regulation in question. Since it is both inevitable and desirable that public officials often agree to do what one or another group of private citizens urges upon them, such an exception would virtually swallow up the *Parker* rule: All anticompetitive regulation would be vulnerable to a "conspiracy" charge.[17]

Even in the case of governmental "corruption," the Court noted, the "conspiracy" charge cannot remove the antitrust immunity. First, the question whether a particular official act was "corrupt," or not in the public interest, was subject to widespread dispute; as a result, there could not be a meaningful objective test for corruption.[18] Further, even assuming explicit corruption, such as bribery, that fact alone would not determine whether the underlying action was within the scope of the municipality's authority. The bribe, of course,

13. Surgical Care Center of Hammond v. Hosp. Svce. Dist., 171 F.3d 231 (5th Cir. 1999), cert. petition filed (statute permitting joint ventures did not authorize anticompetitive exclusion); Laidlaw Waste Sys. v. City of Fort Smith, 742 F.Supp. 540 (W.D.Ark.1990) (statute authorizing city to regulate waste disposal did not authorize discriminatory treatment in taking bids from private providers for monopoly franchise).

14. On this point, see § 20.4.

15. For example, Affiliated Capital Corp. v. City of Houston, 735 F.2d 1555 (5th Cir.1984), cert. denied, 474 U.S. 1053, 106 S.Ct. 788 (1986) (en banc) (finding a conspiracy); Westborough Mall v. City of Cape Girardeau, 693 F.2d 733 (8th Cir.1982), cert. denied, 461 U.S. 945, 103 S.Ct. 2122 (1983) (reversing summary judgment for defendant on conspiracy charge).

16. City of Columbia & Columbia Outdoor Advertising v. Omni Outdoor Advertising, 499 U.S. 365, 111 S.Ct. 1344 (1991).

17. Id. at 375, 111 S.Ct. at 1351.

18. Id. at 377, 111 S.Ct. at 1352. "If the city of Columbia's decision to regulate * * * 'billboard jungles' * * * is made subject to *ex post facto* judicial assessment of 'the public interest,' with personal liability of city officials a possible consequence, we will have gone far to 'compromise the States' ability to regulate their domestic commerce.' "Compare Interface Group v. Massachusetts Port Authority, 816 F.2d 9 (1st Cir.1987), refusing to interpret state authorization to make rules as authorizing only "reasonable" rules:

> To hold otherwise would impose the antitrust laws' treble damage liability upon agencies that may have done no more than to misjudge difficult questions of state law or make administrative errors having nothing to do with antitrust policy. It would force antitrust courts to review state administrative law disputes.

816 F.2d at 13.

Several courts have held that once the municipality qualifies for the "state action" exemption, analyzed under an objective test, the subjective motivations of city decision makers is irrelevant. Buckley Construction, Inc. v. Shawnee Civic & Cultural Dev. Authority, 933 F.2d 853, 856 (10th Cir.1991); Traweek v. City & County of San Francisco, 920 F.2d 589, 592 (9th Cir.1990); Consolidated Television Cable Serv. v. City of Frankfort, 857 F.2d 354, 362 (6th Cir.1988), cert. denied, 489 U.S. 1082, 109 S.Ct. 1537 (1989).

would presumably be a state law violation, and would presumably give the victim a damages action. Once again, state enabling acts to municipalities do not "authorize" bribery; however, to turn every act of bribery or similar corruption into a federal antitrust violation deprives the states of their power to regulate their own political conduct.[19]

As noted previously,[20] the *Hallie* decision also established that, with respect to the municipality's own actions, "active supervision" was not required.

Read together, *Hallie* and *Columbia* leave very little room for municipal antitrust violations. They have come quite close to emasculating the threat that *Lafayette* originally imposed. Indeed, the Court's *Columbia* opinion recognized only the possibility of a "market participant" exception to its decision that municipalities have an antitrust immunity for all state-authorized regulation.[21]

It takes a fairly extreme situation to find antitrust liability under *Columbia*, and even then there are doubts. One possible exception is activity that is not even remotely close to being authorized. For example, suppose that a state statute explicitly requires a municipality to take competitive bids for all street repair jobs. A municipality then gives an exclusive five-year franchise to a single firm to do all street repairs, awarding the franchise without any competitive bidding whatsoever. In this case, the municipal activity is clearly unauthorized, but very likely there is also a state law remedy. One of the most important lessons of the *Columbia* decision is that, in the first instance, the problem of controlling local governments that violate or exceed their state-created regulatory powers lies with the state itself, not with federal law, and certainly not with a federal statute that was never designed to regulate political markets.

§ 20.7 The Relationship Between Petitions to the Government and the "State Action" Doctrine

The *Noerr–Pennington* doctrine creates an immunity for private persons or interest groups who petition the government for legislation or other action favorable to them, but unfavorable to consumers or competitors of the petitioner.[1] *Noerr* questions frequently arise in "state action" litigation, which often involves the political relationship between a government entity and one or more private parties. The questions of *Parker* and *Noerr* immunity are usually answered independently. The presence or absence of a *Parker* immunity does not determine the existence of a *Noerr* immunity, or vice-versa.

A private actor can be immune even though the governmental act he is requesting violates the "state action" doctrine, provided that the challenge is to the passage of the statute or ordinance at issue. For example, suppose that physicians petition for a state statute that gives them carte blanche to exclude competing physicians from staff privileges without regard to good faith and without any state supervision. The statute itself would fail the *Parker* test, as the Supreme Court's *Patrick* case tells us.[2] Nevertheless, *Noerr* would shield the physicians from antitrust liability with respect to the petitioning itself, as well as injury caused by the passage of the statute. However, if after the petitioning physicians acted under the statute to dismiss a physician and she sues, they could be held liable if the underlying statutory scheme failed to qualify for the *Parker* exemption. Thus, for example, in *Cantor* the Supreme Court held that, whether or not a utility had *Noerr* immunity to petition the government for a tariff authorizing a tying

19. *Columbia*, 499 U.S. at 378, 111 S.Ct. at 1353. Compare Boone v. Redevelopment Agency, 841 F.2d 886, 890 (9th Cir.), cert. denied, 488 U.S. 965, 109 S.Ct. 489 (1988) (local government did not lose *Parker* immunity simply because its officials may have been corrupted).

20. See § 20.5a.

21. *Columbia*, 499 U.S. at 374–375, 111 S.Ct. at 1351: "* * * [I]mmunity does not necessarily obtain where the State acts not in a regulatory capacity but as a commercial participant in a given market."

§ 20.7

1. See Ch. 18.

2. Patrick v. Burget, 486 U.S. 94, 108 S.Ct. 1658, rehearing denied, 487 U.S. 1243, 108 S.Ct. 2921 (1988). See § 20.5b.

arrangement of electricity and lightbulbs, once the scheme was being carried out *Noerr* lost its relevance.[3]

Often the best approach to determining the scope of the two immunities is to consider causation. If the defendant's alleged violation lies in asking the government to do something, and the government is then the cause of the plaintiff's harm, then *Noerr* applies. By contrast, if the private actor's own conduct is the cause of the plaintiff's harm, and the injury is not merely collateral to protected petitioning activity, then *Noerr* is generally not a defense.

One of the more vexing sets of cases involve tariff filings by regulated firms. Suppose a regulatory regime requires a regulated firm to file a tariff with respect to each change in its prices or sales policies. The firm files a tariff that effectively excludes a competitor from some part of the market, and the tariff is approved. Once the tariff is accepted by the regulatory agency, the regulated firm has no choice but to obey the tariff. In response to an antitrust suit, the regulated firm claims both *Noerr* and *Parker* immunities.

In this case two doctrines must be considered separately. Under *Noerr,* one must consider whether the routine, statutorily mandated filing of a tariff by a regulated firm qualifies as a "petition" to the government. Today some circuits hold that a routinely filed tariff is *not* a qualifying petition,[4] while others hold that it is.[5]

But as the FTC held in *New England Motor Transport*, to conclude that mere tariff filings are protected petitioning would "virtually eliminate" the active supervision requirement of the "state action" doctrine.[6] Although the Supreme Court's *Ticor* decision did not address the *Noerr* issue, the outcome of that case seems quite inconsistent with the proposition that a filed rate is a *Noerr*-protected petition to the government.[7] The challenged acts in *Ticor* were tariffs that had been properly filed with state agencies, but the court found no *Parker* immunity because the regulatory agencies had not exercised enough "supervision" in determining whether to approve or disapprove the tariffs. Since the tariffs themselves, once passed, became incumbent on the firms, a *Noerr* exemption would make a *Parker* exemption superfluous. Any challenge must be to the tariffs themselves and not to discretionary private acts taken under the tariffs.

Once it is determined that a filed tariff is not a protected petition to the government, *Parker* immunity might nevertheless remain. However, that question must be resolved independently, under the principles that *Ticor* gives us.[8]

§ 20.8 The Relation Between State and Federal Antitrust Law

This book is not generally concerned with the substance of state antitrust laws, but a brief discussion is necessary to explain the relation between federal policy and the existence of state laws.

Nearly all the states have antitrust laws, some of which actually antedate the Sherman Act.[1] Indeed, until the Sherman Act was

3. Cantor v. Detroit Edison Co., 428 U.S. 579, 601, 96 S.Ct. 3110, 3123 (1976).

4. For example, Litton Sys. v. AT & T, 700 F.2d 785, 807 (2d Cir.1983), cert. denied, 464 U.S. 1073, 104 S.Ct. 984 (1984); City of Kirkwood v. Union Elec. Co., 671 F.2d 1173, 1181 (8th Cir.1982), cert. denied, 459 U.S. 1170, 103 S.Ct. 814 (1983).

5. Clipper Exxpress v. Rocky Mountain Motor Tariff, 690 F.2d 1240, 1253–1254 (9th Cir.1982), cert. denied, 459 U.S. 1227, 103 S.Ct. 1234 (1983); MCI Communic. v. AT & T, 708 F.2d 1081, 1155 (7th Cir.), cert. denied, 464 U.S. 891, 104 S.Ct. 234 (1983).

6. New England Motor Rate Bureau, 5 Trade Reg. Rep. ¶ 22,722 (F.T.C. 1989), vacated on other grounds, 908 F.2d 1064 (1st Cir.1990).

7. FTC v. Ticor Title Ins. Co., 504 U.S. 621, 627–628, 633–634, 112 S.Ct. 2169, 2174, 2177 (1992).

8. See § 20.5b. On *Noerr* protection for tariff filings, see 1 Antitrust Law ¶ 210 (rev. ed. 1997); on the relation between the *Noerr* and *Parker* immunities see 1 id. at ¶ 229.

§ 20.8

1. On the early use of state law against anticompetitive practices, see H. Hovenkamp, Enterprise and American Law: 1836–1937, chs. 20 & 21 (1991); J. May, Antitrust Practice and Procedure in the Formative Era: the Constitutional and Conceptual Reach of State Antitrust Law, 1880–1918, 135 Univ. Pa. L. Rev. 495 (1987). On state antitrust law generally, see 14 Antitrust Law Ch. 24 (1999).

passed competition policy in the United States was governed exclusively by state law, although the original models were based on state corporation laws rather than state laws explicitly concerned with restraints on trade or monopoly.[2] Many, but not all, state antitrust statutes are virtual carbon copies of the Sherman Act. In fact, many state courts hold that federal case law interpreting the federal antitrust laws should be regarded as precedential for that state's antitrust law.[3]

The Supreme Court has consistently held that nothing in the federal antitrust laws or any other body of federal law indicates that Congress intended to displace state antitrust law.[4] Although this proposition is true as a general matter, several areas of potential conflict remain. These can be roughly divided into the following categories:

1) conflicts arising because of the extraterritorial impact of particular applications of state antitrust law;

2) conflicts arising because of express conflict between state antitrust law and some federal law, whether antitrust or non-antitrust.

As a basic proposition, application of state antitrust law is constitutional even though the decision has some impact on interstate commerce.[5] As a result, there is considerable overlap in the situations to which state law and federal law apply. The case for a state application of its own antitrust laws to activities affecting interstate commerce is strongest when the state law is modelled after the federal law. If the extraterritorial impact is very large, however, and the state law requirements differ so significantly from federal requirements that federal policy is undermined, then the state law may be struck down.[6] Further, application of state law may be improper if doing so would effectively force inconsistent rules on a nationwide and networked market, such as professional sports.[7] Finally, some states limit their own statutory coverage to intrastate activities.[8]

The Commerce Clause is not the only limitation on state antitrust's extraterritorial reach. There are also concerns about legislative and adjudicative jurisdiction. However, neither has created significant limits on the jurisdictional reach of state antitrust laws. As a hypothetical principle, the due process clause forbids a state from applying its law to a

2. H. Hovenkamp, *Enterprise* note 1 at ch. 20.

3. For the complete and updated text of all of the state statutes, see 6 Trade Reg. Rep. ¶ 30,000. See also ABA Antitrust Law Section, State Antitrust Practice and Statutes (2d ed. 1998), which contains summaries and analysis written by experts in each of the states.

4. Indeed, Senator Sherman himself argued that the Sherman Act was designed

> to supplement the enforcement of the established rules of the common and statute law by the courts of the several states in dealing with combinations. * * * It is to arm the Federal courts within the full limits of their constitutional power that they may co-operate with the State courts in checking, curbing, and controlling the most dangerous combinations that now threaten the business, property, and trade of the people of the United States. * * *

21 Cong. Rec. 2456–2457 (1890). See H. Hovenkamp, State Antitrust in the Federal Scheme, 58 Ind. L.J. 375, 378–379 (1983).

See also Harolds Stores v. Dillard Department Stores, 82 F.3d 1533, 1543 (10th Cir.), cert. denied, 519 U.S. 928, 117 S.Ct. 297 (1996), which rejected a federal copyright defense to a state antitrust claim where the Act that allegedly violated the state law would also have violated the federal Copyright Act; as a result, there was no need to consider preemption.

5. For example Exxon Corp. v. Governor of Maryland, 437 U.S. 117, 98 S.Ct. 2207 (1978) (state statute affecting interstate commerce permissible, where there was no federal requirement of uniformity across the entire nation). See Leader Theatre Corp. v. Randforce Amusement Corp., 186 Misc. 280, 283, 58 N.Y.S.2d 304, 307 (Sup.Ct.1945), affirmed 273 App.Div. 844, 76 N.Y.S.2d 846 (1948): "It is now well established that states * * * can enact and implement legislation which affects interstate commerce, when such commerce has significant local consequences."

6. See Edgar v. MITE Corp., 457 U.S. 624, 102 S.Ct. 2629 (1982) (striking down state anti-takeover statute).

7. E.g., Partee v. San Diego Chargers Football Co., 34 Cal.3d 378, 383, 194 Cal.Rptr. 367, 668 P.2d 674, 678 (1983) (en banc), cert. denied, 466 U.S. 904, 104 S.Ct. 1678 (1984)(state antitrust law should not be applied to rules of national sports league where uniform governance was essential). See also Hebert v. Los Angeles Raiders, Ltd., 23 Cal.App.4th 414, 29 Cal.Rptr.2d 540 (Cal.App.1991) (same)

8. E.g., Mass. Ann. Laws, Ch. 93, § 3, limiting that state's antitrust reach to activities that "occur and have their competitive impact primarily and predominantly within the commonwealth and at most, only incidentally outside New England." See also Abbott Laboratories v. Durrett, 1999 WL 424338 (Ala.1999) (limiting reach of Alabama antitrust statute to intrastate activities).

transaction with which the state had no contact whatsoever. For example, the due process clause would prevent a Florida purchaser from suing a New York monopolist in a California court under California law, if neither the transaction nor the parties had anything to do with California.[9] But in a case of even minimal contact with the state, application of that state's law would probably not be a due process violation.[10] Likewise, the limits of adjudicative, or personal, jurisdiction are generally reached only when the defendant has virtually no contact with the forum state.

Questions concerning the relation between state antitrust policy and federal law implicate the Supremacy Clause relatively more often. The easy case concerns the state law that purports to permit something that federal antitrust prohibits. The great *Northern Securities* railroad case first established that the fact that a merger was legal and had been approved under the law of a particular state had nothing to do with its legality under federal antitrust law—to that extent, state law was preempted.[11]

But most cases are far less clear. Identifying relevant conflicts is not easy, and requires careful consideration of the intent behind the federal law. For example, in Exxon v. Governor of Maryland,[12] the Supreme Court upheld a state statute requiring oil companies to price uniformly to gasoline stations, in spite of the fact that the federal Robinson–Patman Act[13] permits differential pricing under certain conditions. The Court noted that the state was not requiring anyone to violate the Robinson–Patman Act. Further, nothing in the Act manifested a congressional intent to prevent the states from placing stricter limits on differential pricing than the federal government did. Today it seems well established that preemption occurs only when there is absolute conflict—"that is, when compliance with both state and federal law is impossible," or when the state law "stands as an obstacle to the accomplishment and execution of the full purposes and objectives of Congress."[14]

The most difficult preemption challenge facing state antitrust in recent years involves the various state statutes that have been amended or interpreted by state courts to permit indirect purchasers to sue for overcharge damages in price-fixing cases. In Illinois Brick Co. v. Illinois, the Supreme Court held that under federal law the full damages action goes to the direct purchaser, with nothing left for the indirect purchaser.[15] In California v. ARC America Corp., the Supreme Court held that state indirect purchaser statutes were not preempted by federal law.[16]

Although state indirect purchaser provisions do not expressly violate federal antitrust laws, they do raise some damage liability problems that seem at least superficially inconsistent with federal policy. Suppose that a cartel raises the price of widgets from a competitive price of $1.00 to a cartel price of $1.50. The direct purchaser is a retailer, who resells the product to consumers, taking a more or less standard markup. As a result, of the 50¢ increase, 49¢ is passed on to the customer while only 1¢ is absorbed by the retailer. The *Illinois Brick* rule provides that the retailer has the

9. See Phillips Petroleum Co. v. Shutts, 472 U.S. 797, 105 S.Ct. 2965 (1985), on remand, 240 Kan. 764, 732 P.2d 1286 (1987), cert. denied, 487 U.S. 1223, 108 S.Ct. 2883 (1988) (due process clause prevents state from applying its law to transactions with which it had virtually no contact); Home Insurance Co. v. Dick, 281 U.S. 397, 50 S.Ct. 338 (1930) (same).

10. Allstate Ins. Co. v. Hague, 449 U.S. 302, 101 S.Ct. 633 (1981). See L. Weinberg, Choice of Law and Minimal Scrutiny, 49 U.Chi.L.Rev. 440, 448 (1982). Cf. St. Joe Paper v. Superior Court, 120 Cal.App.3d 991, 175 Cal. Rptr. 94, cert. denied, 455 U.S. 982, 102 S.Ct. 1489 (1982) (personal jurisdiction case; applying California substantive law where cartel in Michigan and Florida sold to distributors outside California, and these distributors then sold to California indirect purchasers).

11. Northern Securities Co. v. United States, 193 U.S. 197, 346, 24 S.Ct. 436, 460 (1904). On preemption generally, see § 20.1.

12. Note 5.

13. 15 U.S.C.A. § 13(b); see ch. 14.

14. California v. ARC America Corp., 490 U.S. 93, 101, 109 S.Ct. 1661, 1665 (1989), on remand, 940 F.2d 1583 (9th Cir.1991).

15. Illinois Brick v. Illinois, 431 U.S. 720, 97 S.Ct. 2061, rehearing denied, 434 U.S. 881, 98 S.Ct. 243 (1977). See § 16.6.

16. Note 14. On state law indirect purchaser provisions, see 14 Antitrust Law ¶ 2412d (1999).

full treble damage action based on a 50¢ overcharge, even though it successfully passed on 49/50 of that overcharge to its own customers. A state indirect purchaser provision then typically provides that the end-use customer will have a treble damage action for the 49¢ overcharge that was passed on to it. Importantly, the existence of the state law in no way diminishes the direct purchasers' entitlement under federal law. That is to say, the combination of the *Illinois Brick* rule at the federal level and a state indirect purchaser statute raises the prospect of near sixfold damages, assuming that nearly all of the overcharge has been passed on. Indeed, in approving the California indirect purchaser statute the Supreme Court noted that there was no contention "that the state indirect purchaser statutes themselves seek to limit the recovery direct purchasers can obtain under federal law."[17] Further, as the Supreme Court noted, state law liability in excess of federal liability is quite common. "Ordinarily, state causes of action are not preempted solely because they impose liability over and above that authorized by federal law. * * * "[18]

There is one other situation when state antitrust law may stand "as an obstacle to the accomplishment and execution of the full purposes and objectives of Congress."[19] This occurs when a plaintiff maintains a state antitrust action not because the relief offered is superior, but because maintaining a distinct lawsuit has strategic value. Under the liberal consolidation provisions of the Federal Rules of Civil Procedure, numerous federal antitrust suits involving the same defendants and claims will be joined together in a single proceeding, at least at the pretrial stage. Although this procedure is efficient, it is particularly beneficial to a defendant who can now respond to discovery and other requests once rather than a dozen times. One way a plaintiff can avoid transfer is to stay out of federal court altogether. However, the federal courts have exclusive jurisdiction over federal antitrust claims, so the plaintiff will have to proceed under state law. In this situation the "nuisance value" of a separately maintained state antitrust suit, with its own separate schedule, discovery orders and the like, can be substantial. Such a proceeding could put increased pressure on the defendant to give the state law plaintiff an attractive individual settlement offer.[20]

A few courts have held that separately maintained state antitrust actions of this sort should be treated as "artfully pled" federal claims, thus making them subject to removal to federal court by defendants.[21] Other courts have refused to do so,[22] noting that changing a state law claim into a federal claim, even if the state law claim is being employed for strategic reasons, is tantamount to preemption—something that Congress never intended. Quite clearly, if state law provides any kind of relief that federal law fails to provide, then the state law complaint cannot be read as an "artfully pled" federal complaint. Perhaps in the case where the state law claim is identical to the federal claim in every respect we might wish to

17. *ARC America,* 490 U.S. at 105 n.7, 109 S.Ct. at 1667 n.7.

18. Id. at 105, 109 S.Ct. at 1667. Under *Illinois Brick*, indirect purchasers are permitted a claim for an injunction, since no damage pass-on need be computed. One device for indirect purchasers who wish to avail themselves of a federal forum is a federal action for an injunction, and a pendent state law claim under a state indirect purchaser law for damages. At least one court has permitted such a claim to proceed. City of St. Paul v. FMC Corp., 1991–1 Trade Cas. ¶ 69,305, 1990 WL 265171 (D.Minn. 1990).

19. *ARC America*, note 14, 490 U.S. at 101, 109 S.Ct. at 1665.

20. See H. Hovenkamp, State Antitrust in the Federal Scheme, note 4 at 405–431. For a case like that described in the text, see Three J Farms, Inc. v. Alton Box Board Co., 1979–1 Trade Cas. (CCH) ¶ 62423, 1978 WL 1459 (D.S.C.1978), reversed on other grounds, 609 F.2d 112 (4th Cir.1979), cert. denied, 445 U.S. 911, 100 S.Ct. 1090 (1980). That federal court, in observing the large additional cost of litigating the one additional state law claim, concluded that allowing it to proceed "would destroy the effectiveness of the Judicial Panel on Multidistrict Litigation. * * * " The judge concluded that the plaintiff's purpose in filing the state antitrust claim was "to harass the defendants by requiring them to fight on two fronts, produce two sets of documents, endure discovery on the same issues in courts 1,500 miles apart, all in the hope of obtaining a settlement from the defendants out of economic necessity. * * * "

21. *Three J Farms*, note 20.

22. California v. California & Hawaiian Sugar Co., 588 F.2d 1270 (9th Cir.1978), cert. denied, 441 U.S. 932, 99 S.Ct. 2052 (1979).

say that removal to federal court is possible. But even the plaintiff's wish to have a home forum must be regarded as legitimate if the underlying body of state law is legitimate.

Chapter 21

THE REACH OF THE FEDERAL ANTITRUST LAWS

Table of Sections

§ 21.1 Local Activities: Federal Antitrust and Interstate Commerce

§ 21.1a. The Sherman Act's Jurisdictional Reach

The federal antitrust laws were enacted under the Commerce Clause of the Constitution, which gives the federal government authority to regulate commerce among the several states. The Sherman Act tracks this language, condemning restraints on trade or commerce "among the several states. * * *"[1] At the time the Sherman Act was passed, the Supreme Court took a relatively narrow view of Congressional power under the Commerce Clause, and generally limited it to transactions or goods that actually moved across state lines. In *E.C. Knight*, the Court held that manufacturing was not the same thing as commerce, and denied Sherman Act jurisdiction to a trust, or merger, involving sugar refineries located in several states.[2] In the Court's eyes, the fact that most of the sugar was destined for interstate shipment did not place production restrictions in the flow of interstate commerce. By contrast, in the railroad cartel cases, which involved the fixing of rates for interstate railroad traffic, no one doubted Sherman Act jurisdiction.[3]

After the New Deal, the Supreme Court's views about federal power over commerce changed dramatically. In Wickard v. Filburn,[4] which was not an antitrust case, the Court concluded that Congress could reach economic acts that merely "affected" interstate commerce, and that the effect did not need to be all that substantial. Two years later the Court

§ 21.1

1. 15 U.S.C.A. § 1.

2. United States v. E.C. Knight Co., 156 U.S. 1, 33, 15 S.Ct. 249, 262 (1895). For further analysis of this case and its role in early federal antitrust policy, see H. Hovenkamp, Enterprise and American Law, 1836–1937 at ch. 20 (1991); C. McCurdy, The Knight Sugar Decision of 1895 and the Modernization of American Corporation Law, 1869–1903, 55 Bus. Hist. Rev. 304 (1979).

3. United States v. Trans–Missouri Freight Assn., 166 U.S. 290, 17 S.Ct. 540 (1897).

4. 317 U.S. 111, 63 S.Ct. 82 (1942).

held that in enacting the Sherman Act, Congress went "to the utmost extent" of its power to regulate interstate commerce.[5] Under *Wickard*'s recently developed "affecting commerce" test, this meant that the Sherman Act reached almost any market or transaction with more than a trivial impact on interstate commerce.[6]

For example, in Burke v. Ford[7] the Court held that the Sherman Act reached an intrastate horizontal territorial division scheme among liquor wholesalers because the result would be fewer liquor sales and thus "fewer purchases from out-of-state distillers." Likewise, in *Hospital Building* it held that the Sherman Act reached a concerted refusal to deal allegedly orchestrated by one hospital to prevent another hospital's relocation within the same region.[8] It was enough that the plaintiff hospital purchased supplies from out of state, accepted the payments of out-of-state health insurers, borrowed from out-of-state banks, and had financial dealings with its out-of-state parent corporation. The Court suggested that commerce clause jurisdiction would be invoked even if the effects on interstate competition were so insubstantial that they did not greatly injure a business or even affect the price in some interstate market.[9] This is consistent with general Supreme Court doctrine that in looking for commerce jurisdiction the *existence* of interstate effects, not their magnitude, is the relevant concern. The effects need not be "substantial," or even large; anything more than *de minimis* is sufficient.[10] Under this test, few decisions since 1980 have found jurisdiction lacking.[11] Further, most cases denying jurisdiction do so on the basis of inadequacies in pleading. Often the implication is that better drafting of the complaint and a more searching factual inquiry would have turned up the requisite effects. This is reflected by the fact that the commerce jurisdiction issue is resolved frequently on a motion to dismiss.[12]

In McLain v. Real Estate Board,[13] the Supreme Court once again found Sherman Act jurisdiction, this time over a claim that realtors in a single locality in a single state fixed real estate commissions. The Supreme Court spoke as follows:

> [I]t would be sufficient for petitioners [antitrust plaintiffs] to demonstrate a substantial effect on interstate commerce generated by respondents' brokerage activity. Petitioners need not make the more particularized showing of an effect on interstate commerce caused by the alleged conspiracy * * * [In that case], jurisdiction would be defeated by a demonstration that the alleged restraint failed to have its intended anticompetitive effect. * * * [L]iability may be established by proof of *either* an unlawful purpose or an anticompetitive effect. * * *[14]

This ambiguous passage suggests first that the plaintiff needs to show only that the antitrust defendant's general business activity has an effect on interstate commerce. One need not make the more particularized showing that the alleged restraint itself affects inter-

5. United States v. South–Eastern Underwriters Assn., 322 U.S. 533, 558, 64 S.Ct. 1162, 1177 (1944).

6. See Mandeville Island Farms v. American Crystal Sugar Co., 334 U.S. 219, 238, 68 S.Ct. 996, 1007, 92 L.Ed. 1328, rehearing denied, 334 U.S. 835, 68 S.Ct. 1343 (1948) (Sherman Act reached intrastate sugar beet cartel where beets were turned into sugar within the state, and the sugar was then exported across state lines).

7. 389 U.S. 320, 321–322, 88 S.Ct. 443, 444 (1967).

8. Hospital Building Co. v. Trustees of the Rex Hospital, 425 U.S. 738, 96 S.Ct. 1848 (1976).

9. Id. at 745–746, 96 S.Ct. at 1853.

10. See also Apex Hosiery Co. v. Leader, 310 U.S. 469, 485, 60 S.Ct. 982, 987 (1940) ("the nature of the restraint and its effect on interstate commerce and not the amount of the commerce").

11. The few exceptions include: Mitchell v. Frank R. Howard Memorial Hosp., 853 F.2d 762, 765 (9th Cir.1988), cert. denied, 489 U.S. 1013, 109 S.Ct. 1123 (1989) (mere allegations that small hospital accepts a few payments from out of state insurers or purchases supplies from out of state insufficient); Heille v. City of St. Paul, 671 F.2d 1134 (8th Cir.1982) (purchase of out of state equipment by garbage haulers demonstrated only a "remote nexus" with interstate commerce).

12. For example, Doe v. St. Joseph's Hospital, 788 F.2d 411 (7th Cir.1986), on remand, 113 F.R.D. 677 (N.D.Ind.1987); Seglin v. Esau, 769 F.2d 1274 (7th Cir. 1985) (dismissing complaints for failure to plead commerce clause jurisdiction).

13. 444 U.S. 232, 100 S.Ct. 502, on remand, 614 F.2d 535 (5th Cir.1980).

14. Id. at 233, 100 S.Ct. at 504.

state commerce. But if one reads on, the Court's meaning seems to be that jurisdiction should be found even if the restraint was unsuccessful. That is, a requirement that the restraint itself affects commerce would prohibit antitrust plaintiffs from challenging restraints that had no impact on interstate commerce because they did not succeed.

Interpretation of *McLain* has divided the circuit courts on the question of jurisdiction where the defendant's general business activities clearly have an interstate impact, but the restraint itself appears not to. Some circuits granted jurisdiction,[15] while others did not.[16] The First Circuit interpreted *McLain* in a fashion designed to capture both of the concerns articulated in the previously quoted paragraph:

> [*McLain*] emphasizes that a plaintiff need not prove that a defendant's unlawful activities actually affected interstate commerce, but it goes on to suggest that defendant's business still must be so closely connected with interstate commerce that it is logical, as a matter of practical economics, to believe that the unlawful activity will affect interstate commerce.[17]

Many antitrust lawyers had hoped that the Supreme Court would clarify this issue in its *Summit* decision, but the outcome was disappointing.[18] The plaintiff was an eye surgeon who alleged that he had developed a new procedure that permitted simpler eye surgery not requiring a second surgeon. He alleged that a peer review board declared him incompetent and revoked his surgical privileges at Midway Hospital; and then threatened further to exclude him from the profession in the entire Los Angeles area. The defense raised to Pinhas' antitrust claim was that the boycott of a single surgeon's practice could have no substantial interstate impact in such a large market. The Ninth Circuit reversed the district court's dismissal of the complaint, holding that it was enough for the plaintiff to show that the hospital's activities generally affected commerce; no additional showing that the particular restraint affected commerce was needed.

As the facts are stated above, *Summit* seems to be an easy case. Unquestionably, the overall market for eye surgery in the Los Angeles area would satisfy the "affecting commerce" test. The defense raised really had to do with the *de minimis* quantity of the alleged restraint in relation to the size of the market as a whole. In a very large market the removal of one provider can hardly be said to have a substantial impact.

But in looking at violations such as concerted refusals to deal, one cannot estimate the effect on interstate commerce simply by looking at the victim's market share in relation to the whole market. The victim in such cases is the "competitive fringe," and its output is bound to be small in relation to the whole.[19] If there really was a concerted refusal to deal designed to exclude surgeons such as low cost Pinhas from a poorly functioning market, then its impact must be measured by the effect of the underlying cartel, not the effect on the excluded surgeon.

To dress the situation up in different facts, suppose the makers of steel conduit have agreed with each other to fix prices and to exclude from the market any rival that threatens to upset the cartel. Their particular concern is the makers of possible low cost alterna-

15. For example, Shahawy v. Harrison, 778 F.2d 636 (11th Cir.1985); Western Waste Serv. v. Universal Waste Control, 616 F.2d 1094 (9th Cir.), cert. denied, 449 U.S. 869, 101 S.Ct. 205 (1980).

16. Furlong v. Long Island College Hospital, 710 F.2d 922 (2d Cir.1983).

17. Cordova & Simonpietri Ins. Agency v. Chase Manhattan Bank, 649 F.2d 36, 45 (1st Cir.1981). The First Circuit adhered to this rule in Wells Real Estate v. Greater Lowell Bd. of Realtors, 850 F.2d 803 (1st Cir.), cert. denied, 488 U.S. 955, 109 S.Ct. 392 (1988). See also Hamilton Chapter of Alpha Delta Phi v. Hamilton College, 128 F.3d 59 (2d Cir.1997) (complaint against college housing policies that alleged that college solicited student applications from around the world and that more than half of the students came from other states sufficient to state claim under Sherman Act's "affecting commerce" jurisdiction). Other decisions are discussed in 1A Antitrust Law ¶ 266 (rev. ed. 1997).

18. Summit Health v. Pinhas, 500 U.S. 322, 111 S.Ct. 1842 (1991).

19. On competitive fringe producers, see § 4.1b.

tives, such as plastic conduit.[20] When firm X, a low cost producer of plastic conduit appears on the scene, the steel conduit makers exclude X by predatory pricing, manipulating a standard-setting organization so as to keep plastic conduit off of a list of approved building products, or some other exclusionary practice. When they are charged with an antitrust violation, they claim that the restraint lacked a sufficient impact on interstate commerce because X, the incipient rival, had a market share of only 1% and all its sales to that point were within a single state. The market would not be noticeably different without X than with X.

But clearly the *impact* of the restraint is not measured by the removal of X's market share. The restraint's true impact is the perpetuation of the steel conduit cartel. *All* new rivals are going to start out small. So it was in the *Summit* case. If Dr. Pinhas' story was really correct and he was removed from the market because he produced a better service at a lower price, then the impact of the restraint is not measured by the removal of one surgeon from a market that presumably contained hundreds. Rather, it is measured by the effect of the perpetuation of the lower quality, higher priced product, whose producers will be able to exclude each small rival that appears, free of antitrust constraint.

The Supreme Court's indecisive discussion in *Summit* left the waters only slightly less muddy than they had been before. The Court's general economic analysis is at least consistent with the propositions (1) that effect on commerce is to be judged by the impact of the *restraint* on interstate commerce, not merely the impact of the defendant's activities generally; and (2) in the case at hand the restraint had a more than sufficient impact.

The Supreme Court also analyzed at some length the relationship between the overall activities of the defendant hospital and its physicians and interstate commerce.[21] This analysis suggests that one can establish impact on interstate commerce by looking at the defendants' general activities rather than the impact of the restraint itself; but unfortunately the Court was not clear.[22] The Court also analyzed the impact of the restraint itself, noting that the specific surgical services at issue were often performed on out-of-state patients, and that these were paid for by out-of-state insurers and other third-party payers.[23] It appeared to conclude that "proper analysis focuses, not upon actual consequences, but rather upon the potential harm that would ensue if the conspiracy were successful."[24]

The dissent regarded *McLain*'s language relying on the defendant's general business activities to establish commerce jurisdiction as ill-conceived dicta. It then contrasted the general price fixing conspiracy in that decision with the concerted refusal to deal aimed at a single victim in the present case.[25] But once again, that seems to focus the inquiry much too narrowly. In *McLain* the plaintiffs were buyers of real property who alleged a market wide injury resulting from a commission fixing conspiracy. But suppose that the plaintiff had been a price-cutting real estate broker who alleged that she had been denied access to the multiple-listing book because she was a commission cutter. Would the impact of the restraint then be judged by the consequences of the removal of a single real estate broker from the New Orleans area?

One important difference between the two cases is that in *McLain* the alleged conspirators were all of New Orleans' real estate brokers. In *Summit*, the alleged conspirators were

20. The facts are borrowed rather loosely from Allied Tube & Conduit Corp. v. Indian Head, 486 U.S. 492, 108 S.Ct. 1931 (1988). See § 18.5.

21. By contrast, the four dissenters opined that the Sherman Act "commands a judicial inquiry into the nature and potential effect of each particular restraint." *Summit*, 500 U.S. at 334, 111 S.Ct. at 1849.

22. Id. at 330–332, 111 S.Ct. at 1847–1848.

23. Ibid.

24. Id. at 330, 111 S.Ct. at 1847.

25. Said the dissent:

> The economic effects of a price-fixing scheme are felt throughout the market in which the prices are fixed; the economic effects of "black-balling" a single supplier are not felt throughout the market from which he is theoretically excluded but, at most, within the subportion of that market in which he was, or could be, doing business. * * *

Id. at 338, 111 S.Ct. at 1851.

the members of the supervisory staff at a single hospital. But that difference hardly seems decisive. If Midway hospital were a perfect competitor with other Los Angeles hospitals, then the exclusion of Pinhas would have no impact on the conspiring surgeons' ability to maintain their prices. If Midway surgeons were themselves able to charge monopoly prices, then the restraint would be profitable and the impact on interstate commerce clear. Alternatively, there were allegations that the defendants threatened to deny Pinhas employment in the entire Los Angeles area, if Pinhas persisted in his procedures. This suggested a conspiracy covering the entire municipal area.

Of course, Pinhas' allegations may simply have been wrong. Perhaps he was disciplined because he was incompetent. In that case Midway's board made the correct decision whether or not it was a competitor with other hospitals. But this question goes to the merits of the antitrust dispute, not to jurisdiction. If the restraint were anticompetitive *at all*, it was so because it either (1) perpetuated higher prices or reduced services at Midway, which was sufficiently differentiated from other hospitals so as to be able to get away with such behavior; or (2) perpetuated a similar conspiracy citywide.

In *Summit*, the Supreme Court also suggested the following:

> We have no doubt concerning the power of Congress to regulate a peer-review process controlling access to the market for ophthalmological surgery in Los Angeles. Thus, respondent's claim that members of the peer-review committee conspired with others to abuse that process and thereby deny respondent access to the market * * * has a sufficient nexus within interstate commerce to support federal jurisdiction.[26]

As noted previously, courts, including the *Summit* Court, often say that when Congress passed the Sherman Act it "left no area of its constitutional power unoccupied."[27] But does this literally mean that any practice is within the jurisdiction of the rather general antitrust laws simply because Congress, by specific legislation, would have the constitutional power to regulate that practice? If that is the test, there are few areas that are so local that they fall outside the Sherman Act's reach. The four dissenters thought, in contradiction to longstanding precedent, that the relevant question was "not whether Congress could reach the activity before us here if it wanted to, but whether it has done so via the Sherman Act."[28] Of course, that statement implies that the Sherman Act reaches to something less than Congress' full jurisdictional power, and the Supreme Court has consistently stated the contrary.

§ 21.1b. Jurisdictional Reach of Other Antitrust Provisions

As originally enacted, the substantive provisions of the Clayton Act reached only persons and conduct that were actually "in commerce." This jurisdictional statement is narrower than the "in or affecting commerce" interpretation given to the Sherman Act. As a result, the Clayton Act provisions did not reach as far as the Sherman Act provisions.[29] The relevant substantive provisions are Clayton Act § 2, as amended by the Robinson–Patman Act,[30] Clayton Act § 3, which covers exclusive dealing and tying,[31] and Clayton Act § 7, which covers mergers.[32] However, in 1980 § 7 was amended to reach persons "engaged in commerce or in any activity affecting commerce. * * * " That Section now presumably reaches just as far as

26. *Summit*, 500 U.S. at 330, 111 S.Ct. at 1848.

27. *Summit*, id. at 329 & n. 10, 111 S.Ct. at 1846 & n. 10, quoting United States v. Frankfort Distilleries, 324 U.S. 293, 298, 65 S.Ct. 661, 664 (1945).

28. Id. at 333, 111 S.Ct. at 1849.

29. See Gulf Oil Corp. v. Copp Paving Co., 419 U.S. 186, 95 S.Ct. 392 (1974), on remand, 618 F.2d 91 (9th Cir.1980) (narrower reach for Robinson–Patman Act, Clayton § 2(a)); United States v. American Bldg. Maintenance Inds., 422 U.S. 271, 95 S.Ct. 2150 (1975) (narrower reach for Clayton § 7). See 1A Antitrust Law ¶ 267 (rev. ed. 1997).

30. 15 U.S.C.A. § 13. On the peculiar meaning of "in commerce" used in Robinson–Patman act cases, see § 14.6d.

31. 15 U.S.C.A. § 14.

32. 15 U.S.C.A. § 18.

the Sherman Act—that is, to the utmost limits of Congress' power.

When originally enacted, § 5 of the Federal Trade Commission Act was likewise limited to transactions that were "in commerce."[33] However, in 1975 that statute was amended so as to cover all transactions "in or affecting" commerce.[34] FTCA § 5 now also reaches to the full extent of Congressional power to regulate interstate commerce.[35]

§ 21.2 Antitrust's Global Reach

This section is concerned with the power of the federal courts to use the federal antitrust laws to reach activities that occur abroad, that contain a measure of foreign government involvement, or that raise actual or potential conflicts with the law of a foreign sovereign.[1] Such conflicts pose significant problems for United States antitrust policy for two reasons. *First*, American antitrust policy is more aggressive than the policy of many other countries, often condemning activities that other sovereigns regard as legal. *Second*, where antitrust is concerned, American enforcers and courts have been quite willing to assert American authority over activities occurring abroad, and not particularly accommodating of the conflicting policies of foreign nations. As a result, scholars of conflict of laws and international law sometimes find American application of its law to activities abroad excessive and perhaps even jingoistic.[2]

An often overlooked factor in this analysis is the crucial difference between purely "private" law and public policy. In areas of law thought to be private, such as common law, where only "private" rights are thought to be vindicated, concerns for the conflicting policies of foreign nations weigh very heavily. By contrast, American "public" policy is entitled to be given as much weight by an American court as is the policy of a foreign sovereign, at least where American interests covered by the policy are substantially affected.[3] Indeed, to the extent the federal antitrust laws represent the public economic policy of the United States, there may be little room for considerations of comity at all.[4] Although the courts have seldom articulated the problem in this way, it is generally consistent with the outcomes. A case (1) where there is a substantial effect on American commerce, (2) which does not invoke the Act of State doctrine,[5] and (3) which does not involve an act compelled by a foreign sovereign on its own soil, is only rarely dismissed simply because the American court feels it must act in a neighborly fashion with respect to the different policies of another nation.

§ 21.2a. Extraterritorial Jurisdiction: Basic Doctrine

During the first half of the nineteenth century federal courts were reluctant to apply federal antitrust too aggressively to acts committed in a foreign country. As Justice Holmes summarized in his *American Banana* opinion, the "general and almost universal rule is that the character of an act as lawful or unlawful must be determined wholly by the law of the

33. See FTC v. Bunte Bros., 312 U.S. 349, 61 S.Ct. 580 (1941) (narrower reach for FTC Act as originally passed).

34. 15 U.S.C.A. § 45(a)(2).

35. See Indiana Federation of Dentists, 101 F.T.C. 57, 161–164 (1983), vacated on other grounds, 745 F.2d 1124 (7th Cir.1984), reversed, 476 U.S. 447, 106 S.Ct. 2009 (1986).

§ 21.2

1. For more detailed coverage, see 1A Antitrust Law Ch. 2F (rev. ed. 1997); W. Fugate, Foreign Commerce and the Antitrust Laws (5th ed. 1996). See also U.S. Dept of Justice and Federal Trade Commission, Antitrust Enforcement Guidelines for International Operations (1995), 59 Fed. Reg. 52810–03 (1994), 1994 WL 568227 (F.R.), reprinted in Antitrust Law (current Supp.), and many other places.

2. A good example is Justice Scalia's dissent in Hartford Fire Insurance Co. v. California, 509 U.S. 764, 812–816, 113 S.Ct. 2891, 2917–2919 (1993).

3. On this distinction, see S. Weintraub, The Extraterritorial Application of Antitrust & Security Laws: An Inquiry into the Utility of a "Choice–of–Law" Approach, 70 Tex.L.Rev.1799, 1818 (1992).

4. See J. Castel, The Extraterritorial Effects of Antitrust Laws, 179 Recueil des Cours D'Academie de Droit International 9, 110 (1983); H. Maier, Extraterritorial Jurisdiction at a Crossroads: An Intersection Between Public and Private International Law, 76 Am.J.Int'l. L. 280, 289 (1982). On comity, see § 21.2b.

5. See § 21.2c.

country where the act is done."[6] But Holmes's categorical statement was subsequently limited[7] and later effectively overruled in 1945, in Judge Hand's *Alcoa* decision.[8]

Justice Holmes' foreign legality test in *American Banana* served as an effective mechanism for preventing the Sherman Act from "governing the world," so to speak. In *Alcoa*, Judge Hand realized that every restraint on trade has numerous effects that can spill into a wide variety of markets. As a result, the Sherman Act should not empower every person capable of suing in federal court and asserting an injury caused by an antitrust violation. Rather, the plaintiff must show that the challenged acts "were intended to affect [U.S.] imports and did affect them."[9] Since this test was developed, the United States Supreme Court has approved it, and consistently grants jurisdiction in cases where a qualifying effect on United States commerce is found.[10]

In 1982 Congress effectively enacted Judge Hand's test in the Foreign Trade Antitrust Improvements Act (FTAIA).[11] That Act, which is stated as a denial of jurisdiction accompanied by exceptions, provides that the Sherman Act will *not* reach:

> conduct involving trade or commerce (other than import trade or import commerce) with foreign nations unless—
>
> (1) such conduct has a direct, substantial, and reasonably foreseeable effect—
>
> (A) on trade or commerce which is not trade or commerce with foreign nations, or on import trade or import commerce with foreign nations; or
>
> (B) on export trade or export commerce with foreign nations, of a person engaged in such trade or commerce in the United States;
>
> and
>
> (2) such effect gives rise to a claim under the provisions of this Act, other than this section.
>
> If this Act applies to such conduct only because of the operation of paragraph (1)(B), then this Act shall apply to such conduct only for injury to export business in the United States.

By its terms, *import* trade or commerce is not covered, by this jurisdiction limiting provision.[12] With respect to those, the *Alcoa* effects test presumably still governs.[13] The Act follows earlier case law in not requiring a *subjective* intent to affect American domestic commerce; rather, intent is measured, if at all, by an objective doctrine: foreseeability. The requisite effect must be direct, substantial and "reasonably foreseeable."[14]

Courts interpreting the statute have generally required the plaintiff to show an injury, not merely to the plaintiff itself, but an injury to the trade or commerce of the United States.[15] Read together, subsections (A) and

6. American Banana Co. v. United Fruit Co., 213 U.S. 347, 356, 29 S.Ct. 511, 512 (1909).

7. For example, United States v. Sisal Sales Corp., 274 U.S. 268, 47 S.Ct. 592 (1927) (fact of foreign legislation controlling production did not oust federal antitrust jurisdiction with respect to effects within the United States).

8. United States v. Aluminum Co. of America, 148 F.2d 416, 443–444 (2d Cir.1945).

9. *Alcoa*, note 8 at 443–444. Judge Hand also debated whether the Sherman Act might reach a foreign act that was intended to affect United States commerce but in fact had no such effect. He concluded that he did not have to decide the issue. Ibid.

10. For example, Continental Ore Co. v. Union Carbide, 370 U.S. 690, 705, 82 S.Ct. 1404, 1414 (1962); *Hartford* case, note 2.

11. 15 U.S.C.A. § 6a.

12. The Court concluded as much in *Hartford*, note 2, 509 U.S. at 796 & n. 23, 113 S.Ct. at 2909 & n. 23.

13. See, for example, Restatement (Third) of Foreign Relations Law § 415 (1987), which provides for jurisdiction over:

> (2) agreements made outside of the United States, and conduct or agreements carried out predominantly outside of the United States, if a principal purpose is to interfere with U.S. trade and commerce and there is "some effect" on such trade;
>
> (3) any other agreement or conduct if it has a "substantial effect" on U.S. trade and the exercise of jurisdiction is not "unreasonable."

14. See H.R. Rep. No. 686, 97th Cong., 2d Sess. 9 (1982), noting that the relevant inquiry as to intent was "an objective one," whose purpose was "to avoid—at least at the jurisdictional stage—inquiries into the actual, subjective motives of defendants."

15. See McGlinchy v. Shell Chem. Co., 845 F.2d 802, 813–815 (9th Cir.1988) (jurisdictional effects lacking); Caribbean Broadcasting Sys. v. Cable & Wireless, 148 F.3d 1080 (D.C.Cir.1998) (complaint alleged sufficient effects to meet FTAIA requirements).

(B) mean that the requisite effect must be on one of the following:

(1) an American domestic market;

(2) a market for importing goods into the United States; or

(3) a market for exporting goods from the United States, but only if the injury occurs to the exporting business within the United States.

Under (3), foreign firms who receive American exported goods abroad would generally not have a cause of action for injuries suffered abroad. For example, suppose a concerted refusal to deal orchestrated by foreign firms in a European country excluded an American export to that country. Under (3), the American exporter who lost business would have a cause of action, but the European importer of the American goods (assuming that it had no injured domestic American interests) would not have an antitrust action under American law. It would have to turn to the competition laws of its own jurisdiction.

Perhaps more interestingly, (3) also prohibits a foreign firm with no American domestic interests from suing an American firm for a restraint allegedly created by the American firm which injured export commerce. For example, *Eurim–Pharm* denied jurisdiction to a European drug distributor challenging territorial restraints in Europe allegedly imposed by an American firm engaged in exporting drugs there.[16]

In *Hartford*,[17] the Supreme Court had no difficulty concluding that an agreement among foreign reinsurers and domestic insurers, under which the foreign reinsurers would refuse to cover American domestic insurance policies insuring certain risks, met the effects test as the Court had traditionally applied it. Although the agreements at issue were negotiated at Lloyds of London, their only purpose was to regulate the coverage of policies insuring American risks. If there was any effect at all, it would be felt within the United States. Justice Scalia, who dissented on comity issues,[18] agreed that *stare decisis* required preservation of the effects test. However, he believed that these decisions conflicted with the general proposition that Acts of Congress should not be interpreted so as to apply extraterritorially unless there is clear language stating a contrary intent.[19] Further, "boilerplate" language stating that the statute applies to "any activity in commerce" is not sufficient intent to the contrary.[20] Justice Scalia believed that the commerce provision in the Sherman Act constituted such "boilerplate." However, the Sherman Act, unlike most federal statutes passed under the commerce clause, expressly applies to contracts, combinations and conspiracies "in restraint of trade or commerce * * * with foreign nations."[21] Why that language should be regarded as "boilerplate" is difficult to appreciate.

Finally, in *Nippon* the First Circuit concluded that a criminal indictment under § 1 of the Sherman Act could reach a price-fixing conspiracy that occurred entirely in Japan, but where the price fixed product was to be shipped into the United States.[22] The one fact that "sticks out like a sore thumb," the court concluded was that the civil and criminal provisions of the Sherman Act are based "on the same language in the same section of the same statute...."[23] This suggested that if the effects test was sufficient for civil liability, it should be sufficient for criminal liability as well. Lest one think that this pushes extrater-

16. Eurim–Pharm GmbH v. Pfizer, 593 F.Supp. 1102 (S.D.N.Y.1984). Other decisions are discussed in 1A Antitrust Law ¶ 273 (rev. ed. 1997).

17. Note 2. The facts are discussed more fully in § 19.7c.

18. See § 21.2b.

19. *Hartford*, 509 U.S. at 814, 113 S.Ct. at 2918, there is a "long-standing principle of American law 'that legislation of Congress, unless a contrary intent appears, is meant to apply only within the territorial jurisdiction of the United States.' "

20. Id., relying on EEOC v. Arabian American Oil Co., 499 U.S. 244, 111 S.Ct. 1227 (1991), holding that federal employment discrimination laws did not apply abroad.

21. 15 U.S.C.A. § 1.

22. United States v. Nippon Paper Indus. Co., 109 F.3d 1 (1st Cir.1997), cert. denied, ___ U.S. ___, 118 S.Ct. 685 (1998) subsequently the government was unable to prove the conspiracy. ___ F.Supp.2d ___, 1999 WL 515827 (D.Mass.1999).

23. Id. at 4.

ritorial antitrust liability too far, it should be remembered that the sovereign into which a price-fixed good is shipped suffers the injury, while the sovereign in which the price-fixing agreement is made suffers none unless the cartelized good is sold there as well. Further, in this case the conduct at issue was unlawful under the law of both sovereigns.[24]

§ 21.2b. Prudential Constraints on Extraterritorial Reach

The test derived from *Alcoa*, which looks to intent and anticompetitive effects in the United States, was designed to express the outer limits of an American court's power to reach activity abroad. But a court may sometimes decline jurisdiction even though the basic requirements for jurisdiction have been met. This notion is said to be driven by concerns of *comity*, or our desire to live peacefully with and accommodate the interests of other nations.[25]

One can debate whether these concerns of comity are "jurisdictional" at all. Comity is sometimes described in jurisdictional language. But judges have at least some discretion in determining whether comity considerations require dismissal of an antitrust suit, and at least some suits are dismissed when basic jurisdictional requirements have been met. So if comity provisions are "jurisdictional"—dealing with the basic power of a court to act—they are so in a rather odd sense.[26] More often, courts say that comity considerations indicate that they should decline to exercise jurisdiction that they are presumed to have. For example, in *Hartford* the Supreme Court expressed this notion in its rejection of the argument that "the District Court should have declined to exercise such jurisdiction under the principle of international comity."[27] By contrast, the dissenters viewed the comity analysis as "jurisdictional" in the sense that it plays into the court's decision whether it has subject matter jurisdiction at all.[28]

In *Hartford,* the Supreme Court held that concerns of comity did not require dismissal of an antitrust suit where there was no actual conflict between American antitrust and the domestic policy of the foreign sovereign. Under a long standing tradition of self-regulation, insurance agreements reached at Lloyds of London were legal even if they were collusive and, at least arguably, even if they excluded other non-parties from participating in the market. However, nothing in British policy *compelled* such agreements. As a result, there was no conflict between American antitrust policy and British policy respecting the regulation of its insurance firms.[29] By contrast, Justice Scalia's dissent found that comity should have required dismissal, notwithstanding substantial effects on American interests. He argued that, by abdicating insurance regulation to the states in the McCarran–Ferguson Act, Congress had indicated that its own interest in insurance was insubstantial. But this conclusion seems to overlook the considerations of federalism inherent in McCarran–Ferguson's passage.[30] When Congress allocates power between itself and the states, as our federal system often invites it to do, it is not necessarily abdicating the national interest as a whole, and one should ordinarily not presume such.

Perhaps more importantly, by relying on several tort cases brought by injured foreign seamen, Justice Scalia indicated that he was taking a distinctly "private" view of antitrust enforcement. Justice Scalia found the basis for his comity analysis principally in Romero v.

24. For further treatment of extraterritorial criminal jurisdiction, see 1A Antitrust Law ¶ 272i (rev. ed. 1997).

25. Whether comity principles limit the reach of the FTAIA remains to be seen. The Supreme Court did not address that issue in the *Hartford* case. 509 U.S. at 798, 113 S.Ct. at 2910.

26. On these point, see 1A Antitrust Law ¶ 273c (rev. ed. 1997).

27. *Hartford* case, note 2 at 2909–2910. Accord Mannington Mills, Inc. v. Congoleum Corp., 595 F.2d 1287, 1294 (3d Cir.1979) (once court finds jurisdiction, it must still consider whether comity precludes its exercise).

28. See *Hartford*, 509 U.S. at 796, n. 24, 817–818, 113 S.Ct. at 2910 n. 24, 2920.

29. Id. at 821, 113 S.Ct. at 2910: there is no conflict "where a person subject to regulation by two states can comply with the laws of both," citing Restatement (Third) Foreign Relations Law § 403, Comment e.

30. See § 19.7c.

International Terminal Operating Co.[31] That case involved a tort claim by a foreign sailor against his own foreign vessel, which happened to be sitting in United States waters when the sailor's on-the-job injury occurred. The Jones Act creates federal jurisdiction for unlawful acts that occur in American waters, but it asserts no substantive provisions.[32] Comity concerns hardly loom as large in such a case, where no American interests were injured or even explicitly covered by a statute, as in an antitrust case where domestic injuries were likely in the millions of dollars and the restraint was intended from the onset to affect insurance policies covering American risks. Indeed, the entire notion that application of the Sherman Act is akin to a foreign seaman's invocation of the Jones Act jurisdictional provision in a suit against a foreign vessel contradicts long held views that the Sherman Act expresses a substantive economic policy of the United States, and that plaintiffs enforcing the Act are acting as "private attorneys general."[33] Perhaps Justice Scalia would reject these views, but he did not discuss them. Significantly, the challenged agreements involving Lloyds of London were to restrain reinsurance coverage *only* on insurance policies written in the United States and covering losses that occurred in the United States.

The leading case detailing the relationship between basic Sherman Act jurisdiction and the concerns of comity is *Timberlane*.[34] A Honduran lumber company, owed money to the Honduran branch of an American bank. The bank placed liens on the company's property and allegedly bribed a Honduran government official to foreclose on the liens, thereby closing down the lumber operation. During the time these transactions were pending, the Honduran lumber company had sold some of the affected property to Timberlane, an American company, which lost its interest as a result of the foreclosure. Timberlane then alleged that the bank and others had used the foreclosure as part of a conspiracy to exclude Timberlane from the Honduran lumber market. The effects test for Sherman Act jurisdiction was supposedly met, since the plaintiff alleged that but for the foreclosure it would have entered the Honduran market and shipped lumber into the United States.

The story of the *Timberlane* case is important because (1) it is quite far-fetched; (2) it finds an antitrust conspiracy by accusing one or more Honduran officials of misconduct; (3) while misconduct was alleged, the validity of the foreclosed lien was never denied; and (4) the plaintiff was only a potential entrant into the Honduran market to begin with.[35] If the case had been entirely domestic, involving a plaintiff from one state and lumber company and bank in a different state, the complaint would likely have been dismissed, perhaps for lack of standing,[36] or perhaps under the *Noerr–Pennington* doctrine.[37] But the Ninth Circuit used the case to develop an elaborate "jurisdictional rule of reason" for determining when a court should hear an antitrust case challenging conduct abroad. The test required the court to consider the following three questions:

1. Did the alleged restraint affect, or was it intended to affect, United States foreign commerce?

2. Is the alleged restraint "of such a type and magnitude so as to be cognizable as a violation of the Sherman Act?"[38]

3. Do considerations of international comity counsel against exercising jurisdiction in this case? This question involves consideration of the following factors:

   a. The degree of conflict with foreign law or policy;

31. 358 U.S. 354, 79 S.Ct. 468 (1959). See *Hartford*, 509 U.S. at 810–814, 113 S.Ct. at 2917–2919.

32. 46 U.S.C.A. § 688.

33. See Illinois Brick Co. v. Illinois, 431 U.S. 720, 746, 97 S.Ct. 2061, 2075, rehearing denied, 434 U.S. 881, 98 S.Ct. 243 (1977).

34. Timberlane Lumber Co. v. Bank of Am., 549 F.2d 597 (9th Cir.1976) (*Timberlane I*), on remand, 574 F.Supp. 1453 (N.D.Cal.1983), affirmed, 749 F.2d 1378 (9th Cir. 1984), cert. denied, 472 U.S. 1032, 105 S.Ct. 3514 (1985) (*Timberlane II*).

35. On unestablished businesses, see § 16.5a.

36. See §§ 16.4–16.5.

37. See ch. 18.

38. *Timberlane II*, 749 F.2d at 1383.

b. The nationality or allegiance of the parties, and their place of doing business;

c. The extent to which either state could expect compliance with its judicial orders;

d. The effects on the various sovereigns involved;

e. Whether there was an explicit intent to harm or otherwise affect United States commerce, and the foreseeability of such an effect;

f. The relevant weight to be given to any conduct that occurred inside the United States.[39]

This test has generally been well received.[40] Nevertheless, one must question the wisdom and practicability of any test that lists numerous factors that are to be balanced in some unspecified way, with little direction as to how things should be measured or weights assigned. The degree of conflict with foreign law cannot be measured in pounds, and the relevant weight to be given to conduct in the United States cannot be measured in inches. Even if they could be, we could still not balance pounds against inches. Further, the test seems extraordinarily complex given the insubstantiality of the complaint. At the very least, before launching into such a test a court should inquire whether the antitrust claim should be dismissed on more readily apparent grounds.

In general, the *Timberlane* test seems to have all of the advantages and shortcomings of balancing tests generally. They sound superficially sensible; they virtually *always* give a judge something to point back to in order to rationalize a decision; but they are totally indeterminate except to the extent that an earlier decision has a factual story that is almost on point. *Timberlane* itself reveals the worst features of the test. A minor dispute over the propriety of enforcing a valid foreign lien in that country's own judicial system, and where the impact on United States commerce was negligible at best,[41] was tied up in the Ninth Circuit for ten years.[42] In *Hartford* the Supreme Court found no conflict at all between foreign and American policy. As a result, it concluded, there was no occasion to pass on the merits of the *Timberlane* test.[43] The latter is to be invoked only where there is *some* conflict that must be evaluated.

A more categorical approach seems to be in order. First, at least a quick look at the merits, standing, antitrust injury, causation, or other issues is in order.[44] If a similar domestic suit would be dismissed on one of these grounds, then the suit involving foreign interests will suffer the same fate. Next, basic jurisdiction should be determined under the effects provisions developed in decisions such as *Alcoa*, or in the FTAIA if the restraint concerns exports. Beyond that, concerns for comity should become decisive only when the conflict with the articulated policy of a foreign government is strong, although perhaps not strong enough to permit an Act of State or foreign sovereign compulsion defense,[45] or when the Department of State or another agency takes the trouble to intervene.

Questions about the wisdom of *Timberlane*'s balancing test may have been mooted by the passage of the Foreign Trade Antitrust Improvement Act, discussed previously. There is some reason for thinking that Congress in-

39. 549 F.2d at 614 (*Timberlane I*). For further analysis of the test and a summary of the court's findings on each of these factors, see 1A Antitrust Law ¶ 273c2 (rev. ed. 1997).

40. For example, Trugman–Nash v. New Zealand Dairy Bd., 954 F.Supp. 733 (S.D.N.Y.1997) (applying *Timberlane* and concluding that its multi-factor test is "controlling law in the Second Circuit."). Other decisions include Montreal Trading v. Amax, 661 F.2d 864 (10th Cir.1981), cert. denied, 455 U.S. 1001, 102 S.Ct. 1634 (1982); Zenith Radio Corp. v. Matsushita Elec. Indus. Co., 494 F.Supp. 1161, 1187 (E.D.Pa.1980).

41. The entire Honduran lumber industry accounted for 0.1% of the United States lumber market, or about 4% if restricted to pine lumber, which the plaintiff wished to ship. Further, the plaintiff was no more than a potential entrant into the Honduran market.

42. Others have criticized the *Timberlane* test as too open-ended and indeterminate. See Weintraub, note 3 at 1819–1824.

43. See *Hartford*, note 2.

44. On these various elements of private plaintiff standing, see §§ 16.4–16.5.

45. See §§ 21.2c, d.

tended that Act to state the *only* test for the Sherman Act's extraterritorial reach. On the one hand, the House Report seems clear that a court may continue to "employe notions of comity" or consider "the international character of the transaction" in determining whether to adjudicate a case.[46] Elsewhere, however, the Report suggests that the traditional effects test, modified to emphasize that the concern is with "foreseeable" effects, should be decisive.[47] Perhaps most importantly, however, the language of the FTAIA makes no provision for the *independent* comity concerns that *Timberlane* raises. Finally, although the statute does not apply to import trade, it would be quite bizarre to conclude from it that comity concerns continue to be relevant with respect to American imports, where American interests are strongest, but not with respect to foreign commerce that does not involve imports. The *Hartford* decision did not address any of these issues.

§ 21.2c. The Act of State Doctrine

The Act of State doctrine is based on the long-standing principle that:

> Every sovereign state is bound to respect the independence of every other sovereign state and the courts of one country will not sit in judgment on the acts of the government of another, done within its own territory.[48]

Full treatment of the Act of State doctrine is beyond our purpose.[49] This section summarizes the doctrine briefly and examines the most important decisions applying it to antitrust disputes.

As a general principle, the Act of State doctrine distinguishes between "public" and "commercial" acts of the foreign sovereign, and refuses to recognize the latter as qualifying "Acts of State."[50] If adjudication of an antitrust case requires the court to pass judgment on the validity of a foreign non-commercial act, then the federal court will decline jurisdiction. For example, in Hunt v. Mobil Oil Corp.[51] the court held that the Act of State doctrine barred adjudication of the Hunt brothers' claim that Mobil Oil Company and others conspired to have the government of Libya expropriate the Hunts' oil producing properties in that country. Even though the government of Libya was not a party, the court reasoned, adjudicating the dispute required consideration of both Libya's motive and the legality of its sovereign act of expropriation.[52] Likewise, in IAM v. OPEC[53] the court found that the Act of State doctrine barred a claim against OPEC members, including sovereign nations as defendants,[54] for price-fixing of petroleum products. The court observed that although United States antitrust policy is extremely hostile toward collusion, many other nations do not share this commitment. As a result, condemnation of the cartel would be tantamount to condemnation of a sovereign act that was legal under the domes-

46. H.R. Comm. on the Judiciary, H.R. Rep. No. 97–686, 97th Cong., 2d Sess. (1982), at 13.

47. Id. at 7–8.

48. Underhill v. Hernandez, 168 U.S. 250, 252, 18 S.Ct. 83, 84 (1897). Compare W.S. Kirkpatrick & Co. v. Environmental Tectonics Corp., 493 U.S. 400, 409, 110 S.Ct. 701, 707 (1990) (under Act of State doctrine "the acts of foreign sovereigns taken within their own jurisdictions shall be deemed valid."); Restatement (Third) Foreign Relations § 443 (1987): a U.S. court should refrain from "sitting in judgment on * * * acts of a governmental character done by a foreign state within its own territory and applicable there."

49. For fuller treatment, see 1A Antitrust Law ¶ 274b (rev. ed. 1997).

50. Alfred Dunhill of London, Inc. v. Republic of Cuba, 425 U.S. 682, 697–698, 96 S.Ct. 1854, 1863 (1976) (Act of State doctrine barred claim of expropriation, for the latter is a public act). Cf. Virgin Atlantic Airways Limited v. British Airways, 872 F.Supp. 52 (S.D.N.Y.1994) (act of state doctrine did not preclude antitrust claim against British Airways because it was no longer publicly owned; no British law compelled the challenged conduct, which could be adjudicated without inquiry into any British Act or the conduct of any one government official).

51. 550 F.2d 68 (2d Cir.), cert. denied, 434 U.S. 984, 98 S.Ct. 608 (1977).

52. The Restatement (Third) Foreign Relations § 443 (1987) expressly includes within the Act of State doctrine judicial challenges "examining the validity of a taking by a foreign state of property within its territory. * * * "

53. International Assn. of Machinists & Aerospace Workers v. Organization of Petroleum Exporting Countries, 649 F.2d 1354 (9th Cir.1981), cert. denied, 454 U.S. 1163, 102 S.Ct. 1036 (1982).

54. The plaintiffs named thirteen Arab and middle eastern countries as defendants.

tic law of the place where it was enacted, and that had not been condemned under international law. Although the Ninth Circuit very likely reached the correct result in the *OPEC* case, the Act of State analysis falls short in important respects. First, the OPEC cartel, where governments themselves were the sellers, seemed to be "commercial" under generally accepted definitions. Second, the prices that were fixed applied extraterritorially to sales made elsewhere, and the Act of State doctrine is generally limited to Acts committed on the soil of the sovereign whose act is called into question.

In *Kirkpatrick*, the Supreme Court's considered whether the Act of State doctrine barred an antitrust complaint that did not directly challenge the validity of a foreign act.[55] The plaintiff was an unsuccessful bidder for a Nigerian contract. It claimed that the successful bidder had bribed a Nigerian official in order to win the contract, and that the resulting agreement violated the Robinson–Patman Act. Bribery was illegal under Nigerian law. The district court had dismissed the complaint under the Act of State doctrine, holding that the antitrust inquiry would have to investigate the motives of the foreign government, and this "would result in embarrassment to the sovereign or constitute interference in the conduct of foreign policy of the United States."[56] In affirming the Third Circuit's reversal, the Supreme Court appeared to confine the Act of State doctrine to lawsuits that required the court to declare a foreign sovereign act invalid, not lawsuits that might merely embarrass a foreign sovereign. More importantly, the Court severely limited the discretion of a judge simply to dismiss a case on comity or Act of State grounds if the case might produce uncomfortable relations with a foreign sovereign:

Courts in the United States have the power, and ordinarily the obligation, to decide cases and controversies properly presented to them. The act of state doctrine does not establish an exception for cases and controversies that may embarrass foreign governments, but merely requires that, in the process of deciding, the acts of foreign sovereigns taken within their own jurisdictions shall be deemed valid.[57]

§ 21.2d. Foreign Sovereign Compulsion; Petitions to Foreign Governments

American courts will also refuse to base liability on the acts of private individuals or firms that were compelled by a foreign sovereign to be performed in that sovereign's territory. The courts have construed the doctrine rather strictly. If conduct is merely authorized,[58] not compelled, the defense cannot be raised; nor can it if the foreign sovereign compels extraterritorial acts.[59]

The doctrine of foreign sovereign compulsion leads to an important auxiliary question, which is at least implied in most sovereign compulsion cases: what if the foreign government "compelled" the defendant to act as a result of the defendant's own petition to the foreign government. To put it another way, does a private firm have a right to petition a foreign government for an anticompetitive policy or rule, and have antitrust immunity for all injuries that result from the foreign government's enactment of the requested policy? The *Noerr–Pennington* doctrine, discussed in Chapter 18, creates a robust exception for petitions directed at governmental entities within the United States, whether federal, state or local. But the First Amendment does not protect petitions directed to foreign governments, and the *Noerr* doctrine is rooted in First Amend-

55. W.S. Kirkpatrick & Co. v. Environmental Tectonics Corp., 493 U.S. 400, 110 S.Ct. 701 (1990).

56. 659 F.Supp. at 1392–1393.

57. *Kirkpatrick*, 493 U.S. at 409, 110 S.Ct. at 707. See also Filetech, S.A. v. France Telecom, 157 F.3d 922 (2d Cir.1998) (mere fact that conflict is alleged in complaint is insufficient to establish that comity requires dismissal).

58. Continental Ore Co. v. Union Carbide & Carbon Corp., 370 U.S. 690, 82 S.Ct. 1404 (1962) (if private person acting as agent of Canadian government had discretion, sovereign compulsion would not apply); Mannington Mills, Inc. v. Congoleum Corp., 595 F.2d 1287, 1293 (3d Cir. 1979) (if the foreign government action "rises no higher than mere approval, the compulsion defense will not be recognized." And, "[t]he defense is not available if the defendant could have legally refused to accede to the foreign power's wishes.").

59. *Continental Ore*, note 58, id.

ment concerns. Nevertheless, concerns of comity suggest substantial deference for private petitioning to foreign governments as well as domestic ones. In *Continental Ore*,[60] the Supreme Court suggested in a dictum that a *Noerr*-like immunity might apply to foreign government petitions, but ultimately decided the case on different grounds. In *Coastal States*, the Fifth Circuit held that *Noerr* would apply to a petition to a foreign government,[61] and the government's Antitrust Guidelines for international operations state that they will treat petitions to foreign governments in largely the same way that the case law treats domestic petitions.[62] Other decisions have either suggested that *Noerr* does not apply to petitions to foreign governments, or else that the protection given is less expansive.[63]

§ 21.2e. Foreign Sovereign Immunity

Foreign sovereign immunity is relevant when the foreign government itself, or one of its agencies or instrumentalities, is sued. Historically, courts relied heavily on statements of the executive branch, particularly the State Department, in determining whether foreign sovereigns should have immunity. But in 1976 United States policy concerning lawsuits against foreign sovereigns was codified in the Foreign Sovereign Immunities Act.[64] The Act grants sovereign immunity for "governmental" actions of a foreign government, but not for their commercial actions.[65] Under the Act, sovereign immunity is generally *denied* for (1) commercial activities carried on in the U.S. by a foreign state; (2) acts performed in the U.S. in connection with a foreign sovereign's commercial activities elsewhere; and (3) acts committed outside the U.S. in connection with commercial activities elsewhere if the act causes a "direct effect" in the United States. Thus the statute was designed to integrate the effects test for extraterritorial jurisdiction to some degree.

In IAM v. OPEC the district court held that the activities of the OPEC oil cartel were governmental rather than commercial, and thus qualified for immunity.[66] The court reasoned that natural resource policy is so central to sovereign policy that the production of rules establishing the terms and conditions under which oil can be removed and sold was inherently a sovereign rather than a commercial act. This interpretation reads the statute rather loosely, since the FSIA expressly provides that the status of an act as "commercial" must be judged by the "nature of the conduct" rather than its purpose.[67] In any event, the Ninth Circuit affirmed the outcome, but relied

60. Note 58.

61. Coastal States Marketing, Inc. v. Hunt, 694 F.2d 1358, 1366 & n. 27 (5th Cir.1983).

62. DOJ and FTC, Antitrust Enforcement Guidelines for International Operations, note 1 at § 3.34:

> Whatever the basis asserted for *Noerr-Pennington* immunity (either as an application of the First Amendment or as a limit on the statutory reach of the Sherman Act, or both), the Agencies will apply it in the same manner to the petitioning of foreign governments and the U.S. Government.

63. For example, *Timberlane I*, note 34, 549 F.2d at 608 (assuming that use of foreign judicial proceedings could constitute antitrust violation, even though domestic use would be protected; significantly, the proceedings were being used to enforce a lien assumed to be valid); Dominicus Americana Bohio v. Gulf & W. Indus., 473 F.Supp. 680, 690 (S.D.N.Y.1979) (corruption of foreign government officials might result in federal antitrust liability); Occidental Petrol. Corp. v. Buttes Gas & Oil Co., 331 F.Supp. 92, 108 (C.D.Cal.1971), aff'd per curiam, 461 F.2d 1261 (9th Cir.), cert. denied, 409 U.S. 950, 93 S.Ct. 272 (1972) (refusing to apply *Noerr* to attempts to persuade nondemocratic sovereigns).

64. 28 U.S.C.A. § 1602 et seq. See H. Hovenkamp, Sovereign Immunities Act Jurisdiction and Antitrust Policy, 15 U.C. Davis L. Rev. 839 (1982); H. Hovenkamp, Can a Foreign Sovereign Be an Antitrust Defendant? 32 Syracuse L. Rev. 879 (1981).

65. Under the Act, an activity is commercial if it is "either a regular course of commercial conduct or a particular commercial transaction or act." The characterization of conduct as commercial is to be determined "by reference to the nature of the course of conduct or particular transaction or act, rather than by reference to its purpose." 28 U.S.C.A. § 1603(d). See M. Kane, Suing Foreign Sovereigns: A Procedural Compass, 34 Stan.L.Rev. 385 (1982).

66. IAM v. OPEC, note 53, 477 F.Supp. 553 (C.D.Cal. 1979).

67. 28 U.S.C.A. § 1603(d). The *IAM* holding on this issue was very likely overruled by Republic of Argentina v. Weltover, 504 U.S. 607, 112 S.Ct. 2160 (1992) (sovereign's issuance of bonds was commercial act, for it was similar to that of any private firm seeking financing).

instead on the Act of State doctrine.[68] In Outboard Marine Corp. v Pezetel,[69] the court found that a Polish governmental organization engaged in the manufacture and sale of golf carts was not immune. That activity was clearly commercial. By contrast, in *Millicom* the court found sovereign immunity from an antitrust challenge to a Costa Rican law preventing the plaintiff from selling cellular phone service there.[70]

§ 21.3 Judicial Jurisdiction and Antitrust

General doctrines of federal jurisdiction and procedure are outside the scope of this book. However, the doctrine of personal jurisdiction as applied in antitrust cases contains a few idiosyncracies that warrant brief separate treatment.[1]

Any modern analysis of personal jurisdiction must begin with the Supreme Court's observation in *International Shoe* that

> due process requires only that in order to subject a defendant to a judgment in personam, if he be not present within the territory of the forum, he have certain minimum contacts with it such that maintenance of the suit does not offend "traditional notions of fair play and substantial justice."[2]

Under this rationale, a state may use its own "long-arm" statute to reach persons located outside the state's territory if there are sufficient minimum contacts between the litigation or the person and the forum state. The "minimum contact" must be sufficient to show that the defendant had "purposefully availed" itself of the privilege of conducting business or other activities that invoked the protection of the sovereign's laws.[3] Second, the assertion of jurisdiction must be fair and reasonable under the circumstances, with fairness measured by looking at "the burden on the defendant, the interests of the forum state, and the plaintiff's interest in obtaining relief."[4] Mere foreseeability of a possible future contact is generally not enough.[5]

Personal jurisdiction in antitrust cases is governed by all of these principles.[6] As a basic matter, Federal Rule of Civil Procedure 4 permits the federal district court to assert personal jurisdiction based on the defendant's conduct with the federal district where the court sits, or on the basis of state contacts by invoking the state's long-arm statute.[7] The Rule provides that service of process may be made "in the manner prescribed by the law of the state in which the district court is held."[8]

However, the relevant sovereign in a federal antitrust case is the federal government, not the state. This means that *International Shoe*'s concerns about minimum contacts with the forum "state" should be understood as applying to the United States as a whole. Federal Rule of Civil Procedure 4 limits the service of process from a federal district court to persons who have had the requisite minimum contacts with the state itself. In the case of antitrust, however, § 12 of the Clayton Act contains its own service of process provision, limited to corporations, that permits an action to be brought and process to be served wherev-

68. *IAM*, note 53. See § 21.2c.

69. 461 F.Supp. 384 (D.Del.1978).

70. Millicom Int'l Cellular, S.A. v. Republic of Costa Rica, 995 F.Supp. 14 (D.D.C.1998).

§ 21.3

1. See generally H. Hovenkamp, Personal Jurisdiction and Venue in Private Antitrust Actions in the Federal Courts: A Policy Analysis, 67 Iowa L.Rev. 485 (1982).

2. International Shoe Co. v. Washington, 326 U.S. 310, 316, 66 S.Ct. 154, 158 (1945).

3. See Burger King Corp. v. Rudzewicz, 471 U.S. 462, 474, 105 S.Ct. 2174, 2183 (1985).

4. Asahi Metal Ind. Co. v. Superior Court of Cal., 480 U.S. 102, 107 S.Ct. 1026 (1987) (unreasonable for United States court to assert jurisdiction over a firm who had simply sold valve stems in Taiwan, with the knowledge that the stems would be used in tires that would eventually be sold in the United States).

5. Ibid. See also World-Wide Volkswagen Corp. v. Woodson, 444 U.S. 286, 100 S.Ct. 559 (1980) (although a defendant who sold cars elsewhere might foresee that one of them would someday be driven into Oklahoma, this "foreseeability" was insufficient to create the requisite minimum contacts there).

6. See 4 C. Wright & A. Miller, Federal Practice and Procedure §§ 1067, 1067.1 (2d ed. 1987).

7. See Chrysler Corp. v. Fedders Corp., 643 F.2d 1229, 1238 (6th Cir.), cert. denied, 454 U.S. 893, 102 S.Ct. 388 (1981).

8. See F.R.Civ.Proc. 4(c), (e).

er the corporation "is an inhabitant" or wherever "it may be found or transacts business."[9] This provision has suggested to many federal courts that process may be served "worldwide," with aggregate contacts with the forum established by reference to the United States as a whole, and not the particular state where the federal district court is located.[10]

Although jurisdiction based on aggregate national contacts seems consistent with the requirements of *International Shoe* and subsequent personal jurisdiction decisions, it can lead to some instances of substantive unfairness. For example, several courts have held that venue in federal antitrust cases can be established under the general venue statute,[11] as an alternative to the venue provision of § 12 of the Clayton Act, which limits suit to those districts where a corporation resides, is found, or transacts business. The general venue statute provides that an alien defendant may be sued in any district.[12] This creates the possibility of a scenario something like this. A foreign company makes certain transactions in Maine, but nowhere else in the United States. A federal antitrust plaintiff then sues the foreign corporation in a federal district court in Arizona, basing personal jurisdiction on aggregate contacts with the United States as a whole, and venue on the foreign venue provision. At least one federal court has approved such a procedure.[13] Significantly, however, the doctrine of forum non conveniens may apply so as to require transfer or even dismissal if an alternative forum is substantially more convenient.[14]

Another interesting question of personal jurisdiction that arises with some frequency in federal antitrust cases is the court's power to obtain jurisdiction over a parent corporation based on the activities of its separately incorporated subsidiary. Suppose, for example, that a Japanese corporation owns a subsidiary incorporated in the United States. The Japanese company does no business in or with United States firms except through this subsidiary. The antitrust plaintiff can quite easily obtain personal jurisdiction over the subsidiary, based on its territorial contacts, but can the plaintiff obtain jurisdiction over the parent as well? Several courts have found jurisdiction over the parent lacking where the parent refrained from managing or otherwise interfering in the subsidiary's business activities.[15] Rather, as some decisions have put it, the parent must be sufficiently involved with the subsidiary's activities that it can be said to be the "alter ego" of the subsidiary.[16] This does not necessarily require that the parent be engaged in micromanagement of the subsidiary's activities, but there must be "significant and continuing interference [by the parent] in and supervision over the subsidiaries' affairs. * * * "[17]

9. 15 U.S.C.A. § 22.

10. For example, Amtrol, Inc. v. Vent–Rite Valve Corp., 646 F.Supp. 1168, 1172 (D.Mass.1986) ("where a defendant is served pursuant to a congressional authorization of worldwide service of process, due process requires only that the defendant's aggregate contacts with the United States as a whole are such that 'maintenance of the suit does not offend traditional notions of fair play and substantial justice.' ") (quoting *International Shoe*); Centronics Data Computer Corp. v. Mannesmann, 432 F.Supp. 659 (D.N.H.1977) (same); *Chrysler Corp.*, note 7, 643 F.2d at 1238 (same). Other cases are discussed in 1A Antitrust Law ¶ 271 (rev. ed. 1997).

11. 28 U.S.C.A. § 1391.

12. 28 U.S.C.A. § 1391(d).

13. Go–Video v. Akai Elec. Co., 885 F.2d 1406 (9th Cir.1989). See also Monument Builders of Greater Kansas City v. American Cemetery Assn., 1991–1 Trade Cas. ¶ 69323, 1990 WL 269872 (D.Kan.1990).

14. See Capital Currency Exchange v. National Westminster Bank, 155 F.3d 603 (2d Cir.1998) (forum non conveniens required dismissal of antitrust suit when the more convenient forum was a foreign country, and transfer was thus impossible); see 7C C.A. Wright, A.R. Miller, & M.K. Kane, Federal Practice and Procedure §§ 1825 (Civ.2d 1986); 15 id. § 3828 (Juris.2d 1986).

15. For example, Kramer Motors v. British Leyland, 628 F.2d 1175 (9th Cir.), cert. denied, 449 U.S. 1062, 101 S.Ct. 785 (1980).

16. E.g., Frank Sexton Enterp. v. Societe De Diffusion Int. Agro–Alimentaire, 1998–2 Trade Cas. ¶ 72264, 1998 WL 632022 (E.D.Pa.1998) (court could not obtain personal jurisdiction over French firm simply by reaching its wholly owned domestic subsidiary; plaintiff had to show that parent was "alter ego" of subsidiary); Perfumer's Workshop v. Roure Bertrand du Pont, 737 F.Supp. 785 (S.D.N.Y.1990) (similar).

17. Cascade Steel Rolling Mills v. C. Itoh & Co., 499 F.Supp. 829, 838 (D.Or.1980) (finding jurisdiction over Japanese parent, based on operation of American subsidiaries).

The *Copperweld* doctrine, discussed in Chapter 4, holds that a parent and its subsidiary cannot be "conspiring entities" for purposes of § 1 of the Sherman Act.[18] Is this doctrine decisive or even relevant for purposes of determining personal jurisdiction? The jurisdictional idea that reaching a subsidiary is not the same thing as reaching a parent flows from the fact that corporations are individually legal "persons" for the purpose of service of process. As a result, a parent and its subsidiary are two different "persons," and the act of obtaining jurisdiction over one person does not create jurisdiction over someone else. But the *Copperweld* doctrine is based on the conclusion that, once legal formalities are cast aside, the parent and its subsidiaries are in fact a single economic actor. As least one court has noted this anomaly, concluding that "for purposes of jurisdiction and venue the federal courts have not accepted as controlling the perspective of economic reality, which quite clearly and properly * * * links a parent and subsidiary into one enterprise for purposes of Sherman Act liability."[19] But the *Copperweld* analogy is a good one, at least when the parent owns all or a controlling interest in the subsidiary. The notion that corporations are separate legal "persons" is entirely fictional and has virtually nothing to do with the extent to which a parent corporation controls its subsidiaries. A parent that owns all or most of a subsidiary is not a mere absentee stockholder, even if it has taken some pains to isolate itself from the subsidiary's daily operational decisions.[20]

18. See § 4.7.

19. Behr Automotive v. Mercedes–Benz of N. Am., 1986–2 Trade Cas. ¶ 67,261, 61,353, 1985 WL 6417 (E.D.Pa.1985), affirmed, 800 F.2d 1130 (3d Cir.1986) (deciding that further discovery was needed for the jurisdiction question).

20. For a good discussion of these issues, see P. Blumberg, The Multinational Challenge to Corporation Law: the Search for a New Corporate Personality (1993).

Appendix

RESEARCHING ANTITRUST LAW ON WESTLAW®

Analysis

Section 1. Introduction

Federal Antitrust Policy: The Law of Competition and Its Practice provides a strong base for analyzing even the most complex problem involving antitrust law. Whether your research requires examination of statutes, case law, administrative materials, expert commentary or other materials, West books and Westlaw are excellent sources of information.

To keep you abreast of current developments, Westlaw provides frequently updated databases. With Westlaw, you have unparalleled legal research resources at your fingertips.

Additional Resources

If you have not previously used Westlaw or have questions not covered in this appendix, call the West Group Reference Attorneys at 1–800–REF–ATTY (1–800–733–2889). The West Group Reference Attorneys are trained, licensed attorneys, available 24 hours a day to assist you with your Westlaw search questions.

Section 2. Westlaw Databases

Each database on Westlaw is assigned an abbreviation called an *identifier*, which you use to access the database. You can find identifiers for all databases in the online Westlaw Directory and in the printed *Westlaw Database Directory*. When you need to know more detailed information about a database, use Scope. Scope contains coverage information, lists of related databases and valuable search tips. To access Scope, click the **Scope** button after you access the database.

The following chart lists Westlaw databases that contain information pertaining to antitrust law. For a complete list of databases, see the online Westlaw Directory or the printed *Westlaw Database Directory*. Because new information is continually being added to Westlaw, you should also check the Welcome to Westlaw window and the Westlaw Directory for new database information.

Selected Westlaw Databases

Database	Identifier	Coverage
Federal Antitrust and Trade Regulation–Combined Federal Antitrust and Trade Regulation Materials	FATR–ALL	Varies by source
Case Law		
Federal Antitrust and Trade Regulation–Federal Cases	FATR–CS	Begins with 1789
Federal Antitrust and Trade Regulation–Supreme Court Cases	FATR–SCT	Begins with 1790
Federal Antitrust and Trade Regulation–Courts of Appeals Cases	FATR–CTA	Begins with 1891
Federal Antitrust and Trade Regulation–District Courts Cases	FATR–DCT	Begins with 1789
Statutes and Regulations		
Federal Antitrust and Trade Regulation–Code and Regulations	FATR–CODREG	Varies by source
Federal Antitrust and Trade Regulation–U.S. Code Annotated	FATR–USCA	Current data
Federal Antitrust and Trade Regulation–Final, Temporary and Proposed Regulations	FATR–REG	Varies by source
Federal Antitrust and Trade Regulation–Code of Federal Regulations	FATR–CFR	Current data
Federal Antitrust and Trade Regulation–Federal Register	FATR–FR	Begins with July 1980

Administrative Materials		
Consumer Product Safety Commission Materials	FATR–CPSC	Begins with 1981
Federal Antitrust and Trade Regulation–Antitrust Releases	FATR–ANTI	Begins with January 1994
Federal Antitrust and Trade Regulation–Department of Justice Business Review Letters	FATR–BRL	Begins with 1975
Federal Antitrust and Trade Regulation–Federal Trade Commission Decisions	FATR–FTC	Begins with 1959
Federal Antitrust and Trade Regulation–News Releases	FATR–NR	Begins with January 1994
NAAG Antitrust Report	NAAGAR	Begins with January 1995
Texts, Periodicals and Research Tools		
Antitrust and Trade Regulation–Law Reviews, Texts and Bar Journals	ATR–TP	Varies by publication
Andrews Antitrust Litigation Reporter	ANANTILR	Begins with November 1996
Antitrust	ANTITR	Selected coverage begins with 1986 (vol. 1)
Antitrust Law Developments *Antitrust Law Developments* Annual Review of Antitrust Law Developments	ABA–ALD	 Fourth edition 1992–1995, 1997–1998
Antitrust Law Journal	ANTITRLJ	Begins with 1982 (vol. 51)
Restatement of the Law–Unfair Competition	REST–UNCOM	Current data
News, Current Events and Directories		
Antitrust and Trade News	ATRNEWS	Varies by source
Antitrust and Trade Regulation Report	BNA–ATRR	Begins with January 1986
Antitrust Bulletin–Dow Jones	ANTITRBUL	Begins with March 1994
BNA Antitrust and Trade Regulation Daily	BNA–ATD	Begins with September 1988
BNA's Antitrust and Trade Regulation Database	BNA–ATR	Begins with January 1986
Microsoft Trial Transcripts	MICROSOFT–TRANS	Begins with October 1998
Westlaw Topical Highlights–Antitrust	WTH–ATR	Current data
West Legal Directory®–Antitrust and Trade Regulation	WLD–ATR	Current data

Section 3. Retrieving a Document with a Citation: Find and Hypertext Links

3.1 Find

Find is a Westlaw service that allows you to retrieve a document by entering its citation. Find allows you to retrieve documents from anywhere in Westlaw without accessing or changing databases. Find is available for many documents, including case law (federal and state), the *United States Code Annotated®*, the *Code of Federal Regulations*, the *Federal Register*, state statutes, administrative materials, texts and periodicals.

To use Find, simply access the Find service and type the citation. The following list provides some examples:

To Find This Document	Access Find and Type
15 U.S.C.A. § 2	**15 usca 2**
15 C.F.R. § 325.5	**15 cfr 325.5**
MCA Television Limited v. Public Interest Corporation, 171 F.3d 1265 (11th Cir. 1999)	**171 f3d 1265**

For a complete list of publications that can be retrieved with Find and their abbreviations, consult the Publications List. Click the **Publications** button after accessing Find.

3.2 Hypertext Links

Use hypertext links to move from one location to another on Westlaw. For example, use hypertext links to go directly from the statute, case or law review article you are viewing to a cited statute, case or article; from a headnote to the corresponding text in the opinion; or from an entry in a statutes index database to the full text of the statute.

Section 4. Searching with Natural Language

Overview: With Natural Language, you can retrieve documents by simply describing your issue in plain English. If you are a relatively new Westlaw user, Natural Language searching can make it easier for you to retrieve cases that are on point. If you are an experienced Westlaw user, Natural Language gives you a valuable alternative search method.

When you enter a Natural Language description, Westlaw automatically identifies legal phrases, removes common words and generates variations of terms in your description. Westlaw then searches for the concepts in your description. Concepts may include significant terms, phrases, legal citations or topic and key numbers. Westlaw retrieves the 20 documents that most closely match your description, beginning with the document most likely to match.

4.1 Natural Language Search

Access a database, such as Federal Antitrust and Trade Regulation–Cases (FATR–CS). If the Terms and Connectors Query Editor is displayed, click the **Natural Language** tab. In the *Natural Language Description* text box, type a Natural Language description such as the following:

what is the test for predatory pricing under the sherman act

4.2 Next Command

Westlaw displays the 20 documents that most closely match your description, beginning with the document most likely to match. If you want to view additional documents, click your right mouse button and choose **Go to Next, 10 Documents** from the pop-up menu.

4.3 Natural Language Browse Commands

Best Mode: To display the best portion (the portion that most closely matches your description) of each document in your search result, click the **Best Section** arrow at the bottom of the window.

Standard Browsing Commands: You can also browse your Natural Language search result using standard Westlaw browsing commands, such as citations list, Locate, page mode and term mode. When you browse your Natural Language search result in term mode, the five portions of each document that most closely match the concepts in your description are displayed.

Section 5. Searching with Terms and Connectors

Overview: With Terms and Connectors searching, you enter a query, which consists of key terms from your issue and connectors specifying the relationship between these terms.

Terms and Connectors searching is useful when you want to retrieve a document for which you know specific details, such as the title or the fact situation. Terms and Connectors searching is also useful when you want to retrieve documents relating to a specific issue. If the Natural Language Description Editor is displayed when you access a database, click the **Terms and Connectors** tab.

5.1 Terms

Plurals and Possessives: Plurals are automatically retrieved when you enter the singular form of a term. This is true for both regular and irregular plurals (e.g., **child** retrieves *children*). If you enter the plural form of a term, you will not retrieve the singular form.

If you enter the nonpossessive form of a term, Westlaw automatically retrieves the possessive form as well. However, if you enter the possessive form, only the possessive form is retrieved.

Automatic Equivalencies: Some terms have alternative forms or equivalencies; for example, *5* and *five* are equivalent terms. Westlaw automatically retrieves equivalent terms. The *Westlaw Reference Manual* contains a list of equivalent terms.

Compound Words, Abbreviations and Acronyms: When a compound word is one of your search terms, use a hyphen to retrieve all forms of the word. For example, the term **cross-claim** retrieves *cross-claim*, *cross claim* and *crossclaim.*

When using an abbreviation or acronym as a search term, place a period after each of the letters to retrieve any of its forms. For example, the term **f.t.c.** retrieves *ftc, f.t.c., f t c* and *f. t. c.* Note: The abbreviation does not retrieve *federal trade commission*, so remember to add alternative terms to your query such as **"federal trade commission"**.

The Root Expander and the Universal Character: When you use the Terms and Connectors search method, placing the root expander (!) at the end of a root term generates all other terms with that root. For example, adding the ! to the root *allocat* in the query

allocat! /s customer

instructs Westlaw to retrieve such terms as *allocate, allocated, allocation* and *allocating.*

The universal character (*) stands for one character and can be inserted in the middle or at the end of a term. For example, the term

withh*ld

will retrieve *withhold* and *withheld*. Adding three asterisks to the root *elect*

elect* * *

instructs Westlaw to retrieve all forms of the root with up to three additional characters. Terms such as *elected* or *election* are retrieved by this query. However, terms with more than three letters following the root, such as *electronic,* are not retrieved. Plurals are always retrieved, even if more than two letters follow the root.

Phrase Searching: To search for an exact phrase, place it within quotation marks. For example, to search for references to *monopoly power*, type **"monopoly power"**. When you are using the Terms and Connectors search method, you should use phrase searching only if you are certain that the terms in the phrase will not appear in any other order.

5.2 Alternative Terms

After selecting the terms for your query, consider which alternative terms are necessary. For example, if you are searching for the term *resident*, you might also want to search for the term *non-resident.* You should consider both synonyms and antonyms as alternative terms. You can also use the Westlaw thesaurus to add alternative terms to your query.

5.3 Connectors

After selecting terms and alternative terms for your query, use connectors to specify the relationship that should exist between search terms in your retrieved documents. The connectors are described below:

Use:	**To retrieve documents with:**	**Example:**
& (and)	both terms	**recoup! & oligopol!**
or (space)	either term or both terms	**compet! noncompet!**
/p	search terms in the same paragraph	**"tying arrangement" /p overcharg!**
/s	search terms in the same sentence	**restrain! /s trade**
+s	the first search term preceding the second within the same sentence	**burden +s prov* * * proof**
/n	search terms within "n" terms of each other (where "n" is a number)	**vertical! /5 integrat!**
+n	the first search term preceding the second by "n" terms (where "n" is a number)	**summary +3 judgment**
" "	search terms appearing in the same order as in the quotation marks	**"price fixing"**

Use:	**To exclude documents with:**	**Example:**
% (but not)	search terms following the % symbol	**attorney lawyer /5 client /s privileg! % sy,di(work-product)**

5.4 Field Restrictions

Overview: Documents in each Westlaw database consist of several segments, or fields. One field may contain the citation, another the title, another the synopsis and so forth. Not all databases contain the same fields. Also depending on the database, fields with the same name may contain different types of information.

To view a list of fields for a specific database and their contents, see Scope for that database. Note that in some databases not every field is available for every document.

To retrieve only those documents containing your search terms in a specific field, restrict your search to that field. To restrict your search to a specific field, type the field name or abbreviation followed by your search terms enclosed in parentheses. For example, to retrieve a case in the Federal Antitrust and Trade Regulation–Supreme Court Cases database (FATR–SCT) entitled *Nynex Corporation v. Discon, Inc.*, search for your terms in the title field (ti):

ti(nynex & discon)

The fields discussed below are available in Westlaw databases you might use for researching antitrust issues.

Digest and Synopsis Fields: The digest (di) and synopsis (sy) fields, added to case law databases by West's attorney-editors, summarize the main points of a case. The synopsis field contains a brief description of a case. The digest field contains the topic and headnote fields and includes the complete hierarchy of concepts used by West's editors to classify the headnotes to specific West digest topics and key numbers. Restricting your search to the synopsis and digest fields limits your result to cases in which your terms are related to a major issue in the case.

Consider restricting your search to one or both of these fields if

- you are searching for common terms or terms with more than one meaning, and you need to narrow your search; or
- you cannot narrow your search by using a smaller database.

For example, to retrieve federal cases that discuss damages for misappropriating trade secrets, access the Federal Antitrust and Trade Regulation–Cases database (FATR–CS) and type the following query:

sy,di("trade secret" /3 misappropriat! /3 damages)

Headnote Field: The headnote field (he) is part of the digest field, but does not contain topic numbers, hierarchical classification information or key numbers. The headnote field contains a one-sentence summary for each point of law in a case and any supporting citations given by the author of the opinion. A headnote field restriction is useful when you are searching for specific statutory sections or rule numbers. For example, to retrieve headnotes from federal cases that cite 15 U.S.C.A. § 13(b), access the Federal Antitrust and Trade Regulation–Cases database (FATR–CS) and type the following query:

he(15 +5 13(b))

Topic Field: The topic field (to) is also part of the digest field. It contains hierarchical classification information, including the West digest topic names and numbers and the key numbers. You should restrict search terms to the topic field in a case law database if

- a digest field search retrieves too many documents; or
- you want to retrieve cases with digest paragraphs classified under more than one topic.

For example, the topic Monopolies has the topic number 265. To retrieve U.S. district courts cases that discuss sham litigation, access the Federal Antitrust and Trade Regulation–District Courts Cases database (FATR–DCT) and type a query like the following:

to(265) /p sham /5 litig!

To retrieve cases classified under more than one topic and key number, search for your terms in the topic field. For example, to search for cases discussing good will, which may be classified to Good Will (192), Internal Revenue (220) or Trade Regulation (382), among other topics, type a query like the following:

to(good-will)

For a complete list of West digest topics and their corresponding topic numbers, access the Key Number Service: click the **Key Number Service** button or choose **Key Number Service** from the Services menu.

> *Note* Slips opinions, cases not reported by West and cases from topical services do not contain the digest, headnote and topic fields.

Prelim and Caption Fields: When searching in a database containing statutes, rules or regulations, restrict your search to the prelim (pr) and caption (ca) fields to retrieve documents in which your terms are important enough to appear in a section name or heading. For example, to retrieve federal statutes relating to exemptions from antitrust laws, access the Federal Antitrust and Trade Regulation–U.S. Code Annotated database (FATR–USCA) and type the following:

pr,ca(anti-trust /s exempt!)

5.5 Date Restrictions

You can use Westlaw to retrieve documents *decided* or *issued* before, after or on a specified date, as well as within a range of dates. The following sample queries contain date restrictions:

da(1999) & monopol! /5 attempt!

da(aft 1995) & monopol! /5 attempt!

da(9/28/1998) & monopol! /5 attempt!

You can also search for documents *added to a database* on or after a specified date, as well as within a range of dates. The following sample queries contain added-date restrictions:

ad(aft 1996) & monopol! /5 attempt!

ad(aft 11–1–1998 & bef 11–17–1998) & monopol! /5 attempt!

Section 6. Searching with Topic and Key Numbers

To retrieve cases that address a specific point of law, use topic and key numbers as your search terms. If you have an on-point case, run a search using the topic and key number from the relevant headnote in an appropriate database to find other cases containing headnotes classified to that topic and key number. For example, to search for state cases containing headnotes classified under topic 265 (Monopolies) and key number 20(9) (Horizontal, vertical, or conglomerate mergers), access the Federal Antitrust and Trade Regulation–Cases database (FATR–CS) and enter the following query:

265k20(9)

For a complete list of West digest topic and key numbers, access the Key Number Service: click the **Key Number Service** button or choose **Key Number Service** from the Services menu.

> *Note:* Slip opinions, cases not reported by West and cases from topical services do not contain West topic and key numbers.

Section 7. Verifying Your Research with Citation Research Services

Overview: A citation research service is a tool that helps you ensure that your cases are good law; helps you retrieve cases, legislation or articles that cite a case, rule or statute; and helps you verify that the spelling and format of your citations are correct.

7.1 KeyCite

KeyCite is the citation research service from West Group.

KeyCite for cases covers case law on Westlaw, including unpublished opinions.

KeyCite for statutes covers the *United States Code Annotated*® (USCA®), the *Code of Federal Regulations* (CFR) and statutes from all 50 states.

KeyCite Alert monitors the status of your case or statute and automatically sends you updates at the frequency you specify when their KeyCite information changes.

KeyCite provides the following:

- Direct appellate history of a case, including related references, which are opinions involving the same parties and facts but resolving different issues
- Negative indirect history of a case, which consists of cases outside the direct appellate line that may have a negative impact on its precedential value
- The title, parallel citations, court of decision, docket number and filing date of a case
- Citations to cases, administrative decisions and secondary sources on Westlaw that have cited a case
- Complete integration with the West Key Number System® so you can track legal issues discussed in a case
- Links to session laws amending or repealing a statute
- Statutory credits and historical notes
- Citations to pending legislation affecting a federal statute
- Citations to cases, administrative decisions and secondary sources that have cited a statute or federal regulation

7.2 Westlaw As a Citator

For citations not covered by KeyCite, including persuasive secondary authority such as restatements and treatises, use Westlaw as a citator to retrieve cases that cite your authority.

For example, to retrieve federal cases citing the law review article "Predatory Pricing and Related Practices Under Section 2 of the Sherman Act," 88 Harv. L. Rev. 697, access the Federal Antitrust and Trade Regulation–Cases database (FATR–CS) and type a query like the following:

"predatory pricing" /s 88 +5 697

Section 8. Researching with Westlaw—Examples

8.1 Retrieving Law Review Articles

Recent law review articles are often a good place to begin researching a legal issue because law review articles serve 1) as an excellent introduction to a new topic or review for a stale one, providing terminology to help you formulate a query; 2) as a finding tool for pertinent primary authority, such as rules, statutes and cases; and 3) in some instances, as persuasive secondary authority.

Suppose you need to gain more background information on extraterritorial enforcement of federal antitrust laws.

Solution

- To retrieve law review articles relevant to your issue, access the Antitrust and Trade Regulation–Law Reviews, Texts and Bar Journals database (ATR–TP). Using the Natural Language search method, enter a description like the following:

  extra-territorial enforcement of antitrust laws

- If you have a citation to an article in a specific publication, use Find to retrieve it. For more information on Find, see Section 3.1 of this appendix. For example, to retrieve the article found at 32 John Marshall L. Rev. 141, access Find and type

  32 j marshall l rev 141

- If you know the title of an article but not which journal it appeared in, access the Antitrust and Trade Regulation–Law Reviews, Texts and Bar Journals database (ATR–TP) and search for key terms from the title in the title field. For example, to retrieve the article "Criminal Sanctions Under the Sherman Act Arise in the Land of the Rising Sun: How Far Can Sherman Go?" type the following Terms and Connectors query:

ti("sherman act" & "rising sun")

8.2 Retrieving Statutes and Regulations

Suppose you need to retrieve federal statutes dealing with injunctive relief for violations of antitrust laws.

Solution

- Access the Federal Antitrust and Trade Regulation–U.S. Code Annotated database (FATR–USCA). Search for your terms in the prelim and caption fields using the Terms and Connectors search method:

  pr,ca(monopoly & injunct!)

- When you know the citation for a specific rule or statute, use Find to retrieve it. For example, to retrieve 15 U.S.C.A. § 15c, access Find and type

  15 usca 15c

- To look at surrounding statutory sections, use the Table of Contents service. Click a hypertext link in the prelim or caption field. You can also use Documents in Sequence to retrieve the section following § 15c, even if that subsequent section was not retrieved with your search or Find request. Click your right mouse button and choose **Documents in Sequence** from the pop-up menu.
- When you retrieve a statute on Westlaw, it will contain an Update message if legislation amending or repealing it is available online. To display this legislation, click the hypertext link in the Update message.

> Because slip copy versions of laws are added to Westlaw before they contain full editorial enhancements, they are not retrieved with Update. To retrieve slip copy versions of laws, access the United States Public Laws database (US-PL) or a state's legislative service database (XX-LEGIS, where XX is the state's two-letter postal abbreviation). Then type **ci(slip)** and descriptive terms, e.g., **ci(slip) & monopoly**. Slip copy documents are replaced by the editorially enhanced versions within a few working days. Update also does not retrieve legislation that enacts a new statute or covers a topic that will not be incorporated into the statutes. To retrieve this legislation, access US-PL or a legislative service database and enter a query containing terms that describe the new legislation

8.3 Retrieving Case Law

Suppose you need to retrieve federal case law that discusses tying arrangements.

Solution

- Access the Federal Antitrust and Trade Regulation–Cases database (FATR–CS). Type a Natural Language description such as the following:

  tying arrangements

- When you know the citation for a specific case, use Find to retrieve it. (For more information on Find, see Section 3.1 of this appendix.) For example, to retrieve *Datagate, Inc. v. Hewlett–Packard Co.*, 60 F.3d 1421 (1995), access Find and type

  60 f3d 1421

- If you find a topic and key number that is on point, run a search using that topic and key number to retrieve additional cases discussing that point of law. For example, to retrieve cases containing headnotes classified under topic 265 (Monopolies) and key number 17.5(7) (Per se violations), type the following query:

  265k17.5(7)

- To retrieve cases written by a particular judge, add a judge field (ju) restriction to your query. For example, to retrieve cases written by Judge Beezer that contain headnotes classified under topic 265 (Monopolies), type the following query:

  ju(beezer) & to(265)

8.4 Using KeyCite

Suppose one of the cases you retrieve in your case law research is *Farley Transportation Co., Inc. v. Santa Fe Trail Transportation Company*, 786 F.2d 1342 (9th Cir. 1985). You want to determine whether this case is good law and to find other cases that have cited this case.

Solution

- Use KeyCite to retrieve direct history and negative indirect history for *Farley v. Santa Fe Trail*. While viewing the case, click the **KC** button.
- Use KeyCite to display citing references for *Farley*. From the History display, click the **Citations** tab.

8.5 Following Recent Developments

As the antitrust specialist in your firm, you are expected to keep up with and summarize recent legal developments in antitrust law. How can you do this efficiently?

Solution

- One of the easiest ways to stay abreast of recent developments in antitrust law is by accessing the Westlaw Topical Highlights–Antitrust database (WTH–ATR). The WTH–ATR database contains summaries of recent legal developments, including court decisions, legislation and materials released by administrative agencies. When you access WTH–ATR, you will automatically retrieve a list of documents added to the database in the last two weeks. To read a summary of a document, double-click its entry in the list. To view the full text of a document, click the Jump marker preceding its citation while viewing its summary. To search this database, choose **Edit Query** from the Research menu. Delete the existing query and type your new query in either the *Terms and Connectors Query* or *Natural Language Description* text box.
- Another easy way to stay abreast of recent developments in antitrust law is by accessing the BNA Antitrust and Trade Regulation Daily database (BNA–ATD) that is provided by The Bureau of National Affairs, Inc. (BNA). BNA–ATD also contains summaries of recent significant developments that affect antitrust law. After you access BNA–ATD, type **read** in either the *Terms and Connectors Query* or *Natural Language Description* text box and click **Search**. You will automatically retrieve documents from the most recent issue. To run a new search, choose **New Query** from the Research menu. At the Terms and Connectors or the Natural Language Query Editor, type your query.

*

Table of Cases

A

B

Battipaglia v. New York State Liquor Authority, 745 F.2d 166 (2nd Cir.1984)—**§ 20.1, n. 12.**

Baxley–DeLamar Monuments, Inc. v. American Cemetery Ass'n, 938 F.2d 846 (8th Cir.1991)—**§ 3.6, n. 3, 22, 32.**

Baxley–DeLamar Monuments, Inc. v. American Cemetery Ass'n, 843 F.2d 1154 (8th Cir.1988)—**§ 6.2, n. 5; § 10.3, n. 54.**

Beach v. Viking Sewing Mach. Co., Inc., 784 F.2d 746 (6th Cir.1986)—**§ 11.5, n. 52.**

Beech Cinema, Inc. v. Twentieth Century–Fox Film Corp., 622 F.2d 1106 (2nd Cir.1980)—**§ 11.6, n. 42.**

Beech–Nut Packing Co., F.T.C. v., 257 U.S. 441, 42 S.Ct. 150, 66 L.Ed. 307 (1922)—**§ 2.1, n. 77.**

Beef Industry Antitrust Litigation, In re, 907 F.2d 510 (5th Cir.1990)—**§ 4.1, n. 47.**

Beef Industry Antitrust Litigation, In re, 713 F.Supp. 971 (N.D.Tex.1988)—**§ 4.5, n. 17, 28.**

Beef Industry Antitrust Litigation, In re, 710 F.2d 216 (5th Cir.1983)—**§ 16.6, n. 8.**

Beef Industry Antitrust Litigation, In re, 600 F.2d 1148 (5th Cir.1979)—**§ 16.6, n. 7; § 17.5, n. 1.**

Behagen v. Amateur Basketball Ass'n of United States, 884 F.2d 524 (10th Cir.1989)—**§ 19.7, n. 11.**

Behr Automotive, Inc. v. Mercedes–Benz of North America, Inc., 1985 WL 6417 (E.D.Pa.1985)—**§ 21.3, n. 19.**

Belcher Oil Co. v. Florida Fuels, Inc., 749 F.Supp. 1104 (S.D.Fla.1990)—**§ 7.10, n. 23.**

Belfiore v. New York Times Co., 826 F.2d 177 (2nd Cir. 1987)—**§ 6.6, n. 2; § 11.5, n. 21.**

Bell v. Cherokee Aviation Corp., 660 F.2d 1123 (6th Cir. 1981)—**§ 10.4, n. 6, 11.**

Bell Atlantic Business Systems Services v. Hitachi Data Systems Corp., 849 F.Supp. 702 (N.D.Cal.1994)—**§ 4.7, n. 5.**

Bellsouth Advertising & Pub. Corp. v. Donnelley Information Pub., Inc., 933 F.2d 952 (11th Cir.1991)—**§ 7.11, n. 39.**

Bellsouth Advertising & Pub. Corp. v. Donnelley Information Pub., Inc., 719 F.Supp. 1551 (S.D.Fla.1988)—**§ 7.7, n. 7; § 19.5, n. 15.**

BellSouth Corp. v. F.C.C., 162 F.3d 678, 333 U.S.App.D.C. 253 (D.C.Cir.1998)—**§ 6.4, n. 10; § 9.3, n. 16.**

Beltone Electronics Corp., 100 F.T.C. 68 (1982)—**§ 10.9, n. 57.**

Bender v. Southland Corp., 749 F.2d 1205 (6th Cir.1984)—**§ 11.5, n. 61.**

Ben Elfman & Son, Inc. v. Criterion Mills, Inc., 774 F.Supp. 683 (D.Mass.1991)—**§ 11.5, n. 62.**

Benger Laboratories Limited v. R. K. Laros Co., 209 F.Supp. 639 (E.D.Pa.1962)—**§ 5.5, n. 58, 59.**

Benton, Benton & Benton v. Louisiana Public Facilities Authority, 897 F.2d 198 (5th Cir.1990)—**§ 20.4, n. 5.**

Berkey Photo, Inc. v. Eastman Kodak Co., 603 F.2d 263 (2nd Cir.1979)—**§ 1.3, n. 15; § 5.2, n. 21; § 5.4; § 5.4, n. 94; § 6.1, n. 13; § 6.5, n. 12; § 7.5, n. 14; § 7.8, n. 15; § 7.9, n. 3; § 7.13, n. 4; § 16.8, n. 73; § 17.5; § 17.5, n. 11.**

Besser Mfg. Co., United States v., 96 F.Supp. 304 (E.D.Mich.1951)—**§ 7.11, n. 20.**

Betaseed, Inc. v. U and I Inc., 681 F.2d 1203 (9th Cir. 1982)—**§ 10.8, n. 6.**

Bethlehem Steel Corp, United States v., 168 F.Supp. 576 (S.D.N.Y.1958)—**§ 12.2, n. 34.**

B.F. Goodrich Co., 110 F.T.C. 207 (1988)—**§ 12.5, n. 3.**

Bhan v. NME Hospitals, Inc., 929 F.2d 1404 (9th Cir. 1991)—**§ 5.1, n. 22; § 5.4, n. 81.**

Bichan v. Chemetron Corp., 681 F.2d 514 (7th Cir.1982)—**§ 16.5; § 16.5, n. 11.**

Big Apple BMW, Inc. v. BMW of North America, Inc., 974 F.2d 1358 (3rd Cir.1992)—**§ 11.4, n. 32; § 11.6, n. 36; § 16.8, n. 30.**

Bigelow v. RKO Radio Pictures, 327 U.S. 251, 66 S.Ct. 574, 90 L.Ed. 652 (1946)—**§ 17.4, n. 4; § 17.5; § 17.5, n. 15; § 17.6; § 17.6, n. 10, 13.**

Bigelow, Inc. v. Unilever N.V., 867 F.2d 102 (2nd Cir. 1989)—**§ 12.1, n. 36; § 12.4, n. 49; § 16.3, n. 13.**

Billy Baxter, Inc. v. Coca–Cola Co., 431 F.2d 183 (2nd Cir.1970)—**§ 16.4, n. 9.**

Bi–Rite Oil Co., Inc. v. Indiana Farm Bureau Co-op. Ass'n, Inc., 908 F.2d 200 (7th Cir.1990)—**§ 11.6, n. 20.**

Blackburn v. Sweeney, 53 F.3d 825 (7th Cir.1995)—**§ 5.2, n. 31, 37; § 16.5; § 16.5, n. 29.**

Blair Foods, Inc. v. Ranchers Cotton Oil, 610 F.2d 665 (9th Cir.1980)—**§ 6.5, n. 16.**

Blalock v. Ladies Professional Golf Ass'n, 359 F.Supp. 1260 (N.D.Ga.1973)—**§ 5.4, n. 63.**

Blanchard v. Bergeron, 489 U.S. 87, 109 S.Ct. 939, 103 L.Ed.2d 67 (1989)—**§ 2.1, n. 1.**

Blanton v. Mobil Oil Corp., 721 F.2d 1207 (9th Cir.1983)—**§ 17.6, n. 11.**

Blount Mfg. Co. v. Yale & Towne Mfg. Co., 166 F. 555 (C.C.D.Mass.1909)—**§ 5.5, n. 51.**

Blue Chip Stamps v. Manor Drug Stores, 421 U.S. 723, 95 S.Ct. 1917, 44 L.Ed.2d 539 (1975)—**§ 15.1, n. 20.**

Blue Cross and Blue Shield of Ohio v. Bingaman, 1996 WL 677094 (N.D.Ohio 1996)—**§ 8.9, n. 9.**

Blue Cross and Blue Shield United of Wisconsin v. Marshfield Clinic, 152 F.3d 588 (7th Cir.1998)—**§ 16.9, n. 5; § 17.4, n. 1; § 17.6, n. 5.**

Blue Cross & Blue Shield United of Wisconsin v. Marshfield Clinic, 65 F.3d 1406 (7th Cir.1995)—**§ 5.2, n. 36; § 7.7, n. 27; § 8.9, n. 9.**

Blue Shield of Virginia v. McCready, 457 U.S. 465, 102 S.Ct. 2540, 73 L.Ed.2d 149 (1982)—**§ 16.4; § 16.4, n. 11, 12; § 16.5, n. 18.**

Board of Governors of University of North Carolina v. Helpingstine, 714 F.Supp. 167 (M.D.N.C.1989)—**§ 20.4, n. 5.**

Board of Regents of University of Oklahoma v. National Collegiate Athletic Ass'n, 546 F.Supp. 1276 (W.D.Okla. 1982)—**§ 3.3, n. 8.**

Bob Maxfield, Inc. v. American Motors Corp., 637 F.2d 1033 (5th Cir.1981)—**§ 10.1, n. 3.**

BOC Intern., Ltd. v. F. T. C., 557 F.2d 24 (2nd Cir.1977)—**§ 13.4; § 13.4, n. 21.**

Boczar v. Manatee Hospitals & Health Systems, Inc., 993 F.2d 1514 (11th Cir.1993)—**§ 4.7, n. 8.**

Bodie–Rickett and Associates v. Mars, Inc., 957 F.2d 287 (6th Cir.1992)—**§ 16.5, n. 23.**

Bogosian v. Gulf Oil Corp., 561 F.2d 434 (3rd Cir.1977)—**§ 10.4, n. 4.**

Boise Cascade Corp., 107 F.T.C. 76 (1986)—**§ 14.6, n. 46.**

Boise Cascade Corp. v. F.T.C., 837 F.2d 1127, 267 U.S.App.D.C. 124 (D.C.Cir.1988)—**§ 14.6, n. 18.**

Boise Cascade Corp. v. F.T.C., 637 F.2d 573 (9th Cir. 1980)—**§ 4.6; § 4.6, n. 24; § 15.2, n. 7.**

Bolt v. Halifax Hosp. Medical Center, 891 F.2d 810 (11th Cir.1990)—**§ 4.7, n. 8; § 20.4, n. 8.**

Bonjorno v. Kaiser Aluminum & Chemical Corp., 752 F.2d 802 (3rd Cir.1984)—**§ 7.6, n. 17.**

Boone v. Redevelopment Agency of City of San Jose, 841 F.2d 886 (9th Cir.1988)—**§ 20.6, n. 19.**

C

D

E

F

Falls City Industries, Inc. v. Vanco Beverage, Inc., 460 U.S. 428, 103 S.Ct. 1282, 75 L.Ed.2d 174 (1983)—**§ 3.6, n. 31; § 14.6; § 14.6, n. 19, 69.**

Falstaff Brewing Corp., United States v., 410 U.S. 526, 93 S.Ct. 1096, 35 L.Ed.2d 475 (1973)—**§ 13.4; § 13.4, n. 6, 19.**

Famous Brands, Inc. v. David Sherman Corp., 814 F.2d 517 (8th Cir.1987)—**§ 10.7, n. 6.**

Farley Transp. Co., Inc. v. Santa Fe Trail Transp. Co., 786 F.2d 1342 (9th Cir.1985)—**§ 17.6, n. 30.**

Farrar v. Hobby, 506 U.S. 103, 113 S.Ct. 566, 121 L.Ed.2d 494 (1992)—**§ 18.3, n. 39.**

Fashion Originators' Guild of America v. Federal Trade Commission, 312 U.S. 457, 312 U.S. 668, 61 S.Ct. 703, 85 L.Ed. 949 (1941)—**§ 5.4; § 5.4, n. 21.**

Federal Maritime Commission v. Aktiebolaget Svenska Amerika Linien, 390 U.S. 238, 88 S.Ct. 1005, 19 L.Ed.2d 1071 (1968)—**§ 5.4, n. 12.**

Federal Maritime Com'n v. Seatrain Lines, Inc., 411 U.S. 726, 93 S.Ct. 1773, 36 L.Ed.2d 620 (1973)—**§ 19.3, n. 4.**

Federal Prescription Service, Inc. v. American Pharmaceutical Ass'n, 663 F.2d 253, 214 U.S.App.D.C. 76 (D.C.Cir.1981)—**§ 18.2, n. 11.**

Federal Prescription Service, Inc. v. American Pharmaceutical Ass'n, 484 F.Supp. 1195 (D.D.C.1980)—**§ 5.2, n. 33.**

Feist Publications, Inc. v. Rural Telephone Service Co., Inc., 499 U.S. 340, 111 S.Ct. 1282, 113 L.Ed.2d 358 (1991)—**§ 5.5, n. 83.**

Feminist Women's Health Center, Inc. v. Mohammad, 586 F.2d 530 (5th Cir.1978)—**§ 18.3, n. 42.**

Fiberglass Insulators, Inc. v. Dupuy, 856 F.2d 652 (4th Cir.1988)—**§ 6.5, n. 36.**

Fiberglass Insulators, Inc. v. Dupuy, 1986 WL 13356 (D.S.C.1986)—**§ 8.7, n. 5.**

Filetech S.A. v. France Telecom S.A., 157 F.3d 922 (2nd Cir.1998)—**§ 21.2, n. 57.**

Fineman v. Armstrong World Industries, Inc., 980 F.2d 171 (3rd Cir.1992)—**§ 3.5, n. 11; § 7.9, n. 3.**

Finnegan v. Campeau Corp., 915 F.2d 824 (2nd Cir. 1990)—**§ 19.3, n. 16.**

First American Title Co. of South Dakota v. South Dakota Land Title Ass'n, 714 F.2d 1439 (8th Cir.1983)—**§ 18.3, n. 15.**

First Nat. Bank of Ariz. v. Cities Service Co., 391 U.S. 253, 88 S.Ct. 1575, 20 L.Ed.2d 569 (1968)—**§ 4.4, n. 1.**

First Nat. Bank & Trust Co. of Lexington, United States v., 376 U.S. 665, 84 S.Ct. 1033, 12 L.Ed.2d 1 (1964)—**§ 7.2, n. 1.**

Fisher v. City of Berkeley, California, 475 U.S. 1150, 106 S.Ct. 1806, 90 L.Ed.2d 350 (1986)—**§ 20.1; § 20.1, n. 8.**

Fishman v. Estate of Wirtz, 807 F.2d 520 (7th Cir.1986)—**§ 4.7, n. 3; § 7.7; § 7.7, n. 19; § 16.3, n. 48; § 16.4, n. 30.**

Fishman v. Wirtz, 1981 WL 2153 (N.D.Ill.1981)—**§ 16.3, n. 33.**

Fisichelli v. Town of Methuen, 653 F.Supp. 1494 (D.Mass. 1987)—**§ 20.4, n. 18.**

Flintkote Co. v. Lysfjord, 246 F.2d 368 (9th Cir.1957)—**§ 17.6, n. 49.**

Flip Side Productions, Inc. v. Jam Productions, Ltd., 843 F.2d 1024 (7th Cir.1988)—**§ 7.7, n. 22.**

FLM Collision Parts, Inc. v. Ford Motor Co., 543 F.2d 1019 (2nd Cir.1976)—**§ 6.5, n. 15; § 14.6, n. 46.**

Florida Power Corp. v. Granlund, 78 F.R.D. 441 (M.D.Fla. 1978)—**§ 16.6, n. 16.**

Flowers, 5 Trade Reg.Rep. ¶ 22523 (FTC 1989)—**§ 12.6, n. 12.**

FMC Corp. v. Manitowoc Co., Inc., 835 F.2d 1411 (Fed.Cir. 1987)—**§ 7.11, n. 13, 18.**

FMC Corp. v. Manitowoc Co., Inc., 654 F.Supp. 915 (N.D.Ill.1987)—**§ 6.5, n. 35; § 18.3, n. 23.**

Ford v. Chicago Milk Shippers' Ass'n, 155 Ill. 166, 39 N.E. 651 (Ill.1895)—**§ 2.1, n. 48.**

Ford v. Stroup, 113 F.3d 1234 (6th Cir.1997)—**§ 6.2, n. 10; § 6.5, n. 35.**

Ford Motor Co. v. United States, 405 U.S. 562, 92 S.Ct. 1142, 31 L.Ed.2d 492 (1972)—**§ 9.4; § 9.4, n. 15.**

Foremost Dairies, Inc., In re, 60 F.T.C. 944 (1962)—**§ 12.2, n. 2.**

Foremost Pro Color, Inc. v. Eastman Kodak Co., 703 F.2d 534 (9th Cir.1983)—**§ 7.8, n. 15; § 10.4, n. 32.**

Forsyth v. Humana, Inc., 114 F.3d 1467 (9th Cir.1997)—**§ 7.10, n. 13.**

Forsyth v. Humana, Inc., 99 F.3d 1504 (9th Cir.1996)—**§ 3.2, n. 19.**

Fortner Enterprises, Inc. v. United States Steel Corp. (Fortner I), 394 U.S. 495, 89 S.Ct. 1252, 22 L.Ed.2d 495 (1969)—**§ 10.1, n. 6; § 10.2, n. 2; § 10.3; § 10.3, n. 13, 43, 50; § 10.5, n. 30; § 10.6, n. 1, 39.**

Frankfort Distilleries, United States v., 324 U.S. 293, 65 S.Ct. 661, 89 L.Ed. 951 (1945)—**§ 21.1, n. 27.**

Frank Sexton Enters., Inc. v. Societe De Diffusion Internationale, 1998 WL 632022 (E.D.Pa.1998)—**§ 21.3, n. 16.**

Fred Meyer, Inc., F.T.C. v., 390 U.S. 341, 88 S.Ct. 904, 19 L.Ed.2d 1222 (1968)—**§ 14.6, n. 51.**

Freeman Hosp., F.T.C. v., 911 F.Supp. 1213 (W.D.Mo. 1995)—**§ 3.6, n. 27.**

Fruehauf Corp. v. F. T. C., 603 F.2d 345 (2nd Cir.1979)—**§ 3.3, n. 49; § 9.4; § 9.4, n. 21; § 12.6, n. 20.**

F.T.C. v. ______ (see opposing party)

Fuchs v. Rural Elec. Convenience Co-op. Inc., 858 F.2d 1210 (7th Cir.1988)—**§ 20.4, n. 8.**

Furlong v. Long Island College Hosp., 710 F.2d 922 (2nd Cir.1983)—**§ 21.1, n. 16.**

G

GAF Corp. v. Eastman Kodak Co., 519 F.Supp. 1203 (S.D.N.Y.1981)—**§ 16.8, n. 73.**

Garment Dist., Inc. v. Belk Stores Services, Inc., 799 F.2d 905 (4th Cir.1986)—**§ 11.4, n. 16, 22.**

Garot Anderson Marketing, Inc. v. Blue Cross and Blue Shield United of Wisconsin, 772 F.Supp. 1054 (N.D.Ill. 1990)—**§ 16.5, n. 6.**

Garshman v. Universal Resources Holding Inc., 824 F.2d 223 (3rd Cir.1987)—**§ 7.7, n. 18.**

Gasoline Retailers Ass'n, Inc., United States v., 285 F.2d 688 (7th Cir.1961)—**§ 5.2, n. 32.**

Gearhart Industries, Inc. v. Smith Intern., Inc., 592 F.Supp. 203 (N.D.Tex.1984)—**§ 3.7, n. 10.**

Genentech, Inc. v. Eli Lilly and Co., 998 F.2d 931 (Fed.Cir. 1993)—**§ 7.11, n. 47.**

General Dynamics Corp., United States v., 828 F.2d 1356 (9th Cir.1987)—**§ 19.4, n. 1.**

General Dynamics Corp., United States v., 415 U.S. 486, 94 S.Ct. 1186, 39 L.Ed.2d 530 (1974)—**§ 12.4, n. 41; § 12.5, n. 5; § 12.7, n. 12; § 12.10, n. 2.**

H

Hahn v. Oregon Physicians Service, 689 F.2d 840 (9th Cir.1982)—**§ 19.7, n. 47.**

Hairston v. Pacific 10 Conference, 101 F.3d 1315 (9th Cir.1996)—**§ 5.1, n. 22.**

Hallie, Town of v. City of Eau Claire, 471 U.S. 34, 105 S.Ct. 1713, 85 L.Ed.2d 24 (1985)—**§ 20.3, n. 6; § 20.4, n. 9; § 20.5, n. 4; § 20.6, n. 10.**

Hamilton Chapter of Alpha Delta Phi, Inc. v. Hamilton College, 128 F.3d 59 (2nd Cir.1997)—**§ 21.1, n. 17.**

Hamman v. United States, 267 F.Supp. 420 (D.Mont. 1967)—**§ 16.4, n. 3.**

Hand v. Central Transport, Inc., 779 F.2d 8 (6th Cir. 1985)—**§ 10.4, n. 14.**

Handgards, Inc. v. Ethicon, Inc. (Handgards II), 743 F.2d 1282 (9th Cir.1984)—**§ 7.11, n. 19; § 18.3, n. 23.**

Handgards, Inc. v. Ethicon, Inc. (Handgards I), 601 F.2d 986 (9th Cir.1979)—**§ 7.11, n. 19; § 18.3, n. 22.**

Hanover Shoe, Inc. v. United Shoe Machinery Corp., 392 U.S. 481, 88 S.Ct. 2224, 20 L.Ed.2d 1231 (1968)—**§ 6.4, n. 12; § 16.6; § 16.6, n. 1; § 17.5, n. 14.**

Harbour Group Investments, L.P., F.T.C. v., 1990 WL 198819 (D.D.C.1990)—**§ 12.9, n. 5.**

Hardwick v. Nu–Way Oil Co., Inc., 589 F.2d 806 (5th Cir.1979)—**§ 11.5, n. 17.**

Harolds Stores, Inc. v. Dillard Dept. Stores, Inc., 82 F.3d 1533 (10th Cir.1996)—**§ 20.8, n. 4.**

Hartford Fire Ins. Co. v. California, 509 U.S. 764, 113 S.Ct. 2891, 125 L.Ed.2d 612 (1993)—**§ 5.4, n. 26; § 15.4, n. 9; § 21.2, n. 2.**

Hasbrouck v. Texaco, Inc., 842 F.2d 1034 (9th Cir.1987)—**§ 14.6, n. 14.**

Hass v. Oregon State Bar, 883 F.2d 1453 (9th Cir.1989)—**§ 20.5; § 20.5, n. 6.**

Hawaii v. Standard Oil Co. of Cal., 405 U.S. 251, 92 S.Ct. 885, 31 L.Ed.2d 184 (1972)—**§ 16.5; § 16.5, n. 15.**

Hayden v. Bardes Corp., 1989 WL 61957 (W.D.Ky.1989)—**§ 16.3, n. 16.**

Hayes v. Solomon, 597 F.2d 958 (5th Cir.1979)—**§ 16.5, n. 4.**

Health Care Equalization Committee of the Iowa Chiropractic Soc. v. Iowa Medical Soc., 851 F.2d 1020 (8th Cir.1988)—**§ 19.7, n. 47.**

Heatransfer Corp. v. Volkswagenwerk, A. G., 553 F.2d 964 (5th Cir.1977)—**§ 3.5, n. 18; § 7.6, n. 33; § 9.4, n. 22; § 10.3, n. 18; § 10.6; § 10.6, n. 11.**

Hebert v. Los Angeles Raiders, Ltd., 29 Cal.Rptr.2d 540 (Cal.App. 2 Dist.1991)—**§ 20.8, n. 7.**

Hecht v. Pro–Football, Inc., 570 F.2d 982, 187 U.S.App. D.C. 73 (D.C.Cir.1977)—**§ 7.7, n. 10.**

Heffernan, United States v., 43 F.3d 1144 (7th Cir.1994)—**§ 4.1, n. 24; § 15.1, n. 3.**

Heille v. City of St. Paul, Minn., 671 F.2d 1134 (8th Cir.1982)—**§ 21.1, n. 11.**

Helicopter Support Systems, Inc. v. Hughes Helicopter, Inc., 818 F.2d 1530 (11th Cir.1987)—**§ 11.4, n. 20, 34.**

Helix Milling Co. v. Terminal Flour Mills Co., 523 F.2d 1317 (9th Cir.1975)—**§ 7.7, n. 11.**

Henry v. A.B. Dick Co., 224 U.S. 1, 32 S.Ct. 364, 56 L.Ed. 645 (1912)—**§ 2.1; § 2.1, n. 52, 69; § 10.3, n. 2; § 10.6, n. 42.**

Henry v. Chloride, Inc., 809 F.2d 1334 (8th Cir.1987)—**§ 3.1, n. 6; § 8.3, n. 4; § 8.4, n. 13; § 8.5, n. 16; § 8.8, n. 12; § 12.6, n. 30.**

Henry Broch & Company, F.T.C. v., 363 U.S. 166, 80 S.Ct. 1158, 4 L.Ed.2d 1124 (1960)—**§ 14.6, n. 43.**

H.H. Robertson Co. v. Guardian Industries Corp., 1986 WL 31687 (3rd Cir.1986)—**§ 16.3, n. 16.**

Higgins v. New York Stock Exchange, Inc., 942 F.2d 829 (2nd Cir.1991)—**§ 19.4, n. 6.**

Hillman Flying Service, Inc. v. City of Roanoke, 652 F.Supp. 1142 (W.D.Va.1987)—**§ 20.4, n. 11.**

Hirsh v. Martindale–Hubbell, Inc., 674 F.2d 1343 (9th Cir.1982)—**§ 10.6, n. 4, 39.**

H.J., Inc. v. International Tel. & Tel. Corp., 867 F.2d 1531 (8th Cir.1989)—**§ 6.5, n. 6; § 8.7, n. 5; § 17.6, n. 7.**

H.L. Hayden Co. of New York, Inc. v. Siemens Medical Systems, Inc., 879 F.2d 1005 (2nd Cir.1989)—**§ 6.5, n. 35; § 6.6, n. 4; § 11.4, n. 25, 30; § 11.6, n. 22.**

Holmes Products Corp. v. Dana Lighting, Inc., 958 F.Supp. 27 (D.Mass.1997)—**§ 5.6, n. 52.**

Home Ins. Co. v. Dick, 281 U.S. 397, 50 S.Ct. 338, 74 L.Ed. 926 (1930)—**§ 20.8, n. 9.**

Home Placement Service, Inc. v. Providence Journal Co., 819 F.2d 1199 (1st Cir.1987)—**§ 17.5, n. 17; § 17.6, n. 21.**

Hoover v. Ronwin, 466 U.S. 558, 104 S.Ct. 1989, 80 L.Ed.2d 590 (1984)—**§ 20.4, n. 4.**

Hospital Bldg. Co. v. Trustees of Rex Hospital, 425 U.S. 738, 96 S.Ct. 1848, 48 L.Ed.2d 338 (1976)—**§ 21.1, n. 8.**

Hospital Corp. of America, 106 F.T.C. 361 (1985)—**§ 12.1, n. 33.**

Hospital Corp. of America, 106 F.T.C. 207 (1985)—**§ 3.6, n. 28.**

Hospital Corp. of America v. F.T.C., 807 F.2d 1381 (7th Cir.1986)—**§ 12.6, n. 37.**

Houser v. Fox Theatres Management Corp., 845 F.2d 1225 (3rd Cir.1988)—**§ 3.6, n. 7; § 4.5, n. 25; § 11.4, n. 29.**

Hubbard v. Beatty & Hyde, Inc., 343 Mass. 258, 178 N.E.2d 485 (Mass.1961)—**§ 18.3, n. 34.**

Huck Mfg. Co., United States v., 382 U.S. 197, 86 S.Ct. 385, 15 L.Ed.2d 268 (1965)—**§ 5.5, n. 31.**

Hudson's Bay Co. Fur Sales Inc. v. American Legend Co-op., 651 F.Supp. 819 (D.N.J.1986)—**§ 5.2, n. 14; § 10.1, n. 8.**

Hughes Tool Co. v. Trans World Airlines, Inc., 409 U.S. 363, 93 S.Ct. 647, 34 L.Ed.2d 577 (1973)—**§ 19.3, n. 7.**

Hunt v. Crumboch, 325 U.S. 821, 65 S.Ct. 1545, 89 L.Ed. 1954 (1945)—**§ 8.8, n. 22.**

Hunt v. Mobil Oil Corp., 550 F.2d 68 (2nd Cir.1977)—**§ 21.2; § 21.2, n. 51.**

Hutcheson, United States v., 312 U.S. 219, 61 S.Ct. 463, 85 L.Ed. 788 (1941)—**§ 19.7, n. 19.**

Hyde v. Jefferson Parish Hosp. Dist. No. 2, 686 F.2d 286 (5th Cir.1982)—**§ 10.3, n. 71.**

I

I. C. C. v. Big Sky Farmers and Ranchers Marketing Co-op. of Mont., 451 F.2d 511 (9th Cir.1971)—**§ 19.4, n. 14.**

ILC Peripherals Leasing Corp. v. International Business Machines Corp., 458 F.Supp. 423 (N.D.Cal.1978)—**§ 17.6, n. 30.**

ILC Peripherals Leasing Corp. v. International Business Machines Corp., 448 F.Supp. 228 (N.D.Cal.1978)—**§ 10.4, n. 31.**

Illinois Bell Telephone Co. v. Haines and Co., Inc., 905 F.2d 1081 (7th Cir.1990)—**§ 7.7, n. 12.**

J

K

Malamud v. Sinclair Oil Corp., 521 F.2d 1142 (6th Cir. 1975)—**§ 16.4, n. 11.**
Malcolm v. Marathon Oil Co., 642 F.2d 845 (5th Cir. 1981)—**§ 17.4, n. 7.**
Malden, Mo., City of v. Union Elec. Co., 887 F.2d 157 (8th Cir.1989)—**§ 7.7, n. 12; § 19.5, n. 18.**
Malley–Duff & Associates, Inc. v. Crown Life Ins. Co., 734 F.2d 133 (3rd Cir.1984)—**§ 5.4, n. 18; § 19.7, n. 60.**
Mandeville Island Farms v. American Crystal Sugar Co., 334 U.S. 219, 68 S.Ct. 996, 92 L.Ed. 1328 (1948)—**§ 4.1, n. 47; § 21.1, n. 6.**
Mannington Mills, Inc. v. Congoleum Corp., 595 F.2d 1287 (3rd Cir.1979)—**§ 21.2, n. 27, 58.**
Maple Flooring Mfrs.' Ass'n v. United States, 268 U.S. 563, 45 S.Ct. 578, 69 L.Ed. 1093 (1925)—**§ 2.1, n. 76; § 5.3; § 5.3, n. 8.**
Marathon Oil Co. v. Mobil Corp., 669 F.2d 378 (6th Cir.1981)—**§ 16.3, n. 16.**
Marin v. Citizens Memorial Hosp., 700 F.Supp. 354 (S.D.Tex.1988)—**§ 5.4, n. 70.**
Marine Bancorporation, Inc., United States v., 418 U.S. 602, 94 S.Ct. 2856, 41 L.Ed.2d 978 (1974)—**§ 13.4; § 13.4, n. 9, 16.**
Market Force Inc. v. Wauwatosa Realty Co., 906 F.2d 1167 (7th Cir.1990)—**§ 4.5, n. 11.**
Marsann Co. v. Brammall, Inc., 788 F.2d 611 (9th Cir. 1986)—**§ 8.6; § 8.6, n. 6.**
Martino v. McDonald's System, Inc., 86 F.R.D. 145 (N.D.Ill.1980)—**§ 10.6, n. 5.**
Marts v. Xerox, Inc., 77 F.3d 1109 (8th Cir.1996)—**§ 10.3, n. 19; § 10.4, n. 29.**
Maryland and Virginia Milk Producers Ass'n v. United States, 362 U.S. 458, 80 S.Ct. 847, 4 L.Ed.2d 880 (1960)—**§ 19.7, n. 5.**
Massachusetts Board of Registration in Optometry, 110 F.T.C. 549 (1988)—**§ 5.2, n. 32.**
Massachusetts Board of Registration in Optometry, 5 Trade Reg.Rep. ¶ 22555 (FTC 1988)—**§ 4.7, n. 7; § 20.4, n. 7.**
Massachusetts School of Law at Andover, Inc. v. American Bar Ass'n, 107 F.3d 1026 (3rd Cir.1997)—**§ 16.3, n. 34; § 18.2, n. 5; § 20.1, n. 6.**
Mathews v. Lancaster General Hosp., 883 F.Supp. 1016 (E.D.Pa.1995)—**§ 5.4, n. 70.**
Matsushita Elec. Indus. Co., Ltd. v. Zenith Radio Corp., 475 U.S. 574, 106 S.Ct. 1348, 89 L.Ed.2d 538 (1986)—**§ 4.1, n. 43; § 8.3, n. 26; § 8.7, n. 2, 11; § 8.8, n. 30; § 16.3, n. 30; § 16.8, n. 8.**
Matter of (see name of party)
Mayer Paving & Asphalt Co. v. General Dynamics Corp., 486 F.2d 763 (7th Cir.1973)—**§ 14.6, n. 25.**
MCA Television Ltd. v. Public Interest Corp., 171 F.3d 1265 (11th Cir.1999)—**§ 5.5, n. 64; § 10.1, n. 9; § 10.3, n. 44; § 10.6, n. 50.**
McCabe's Furniture, Inc. v. La–Z–Boy Chair Co., 798 F.2d 323 (8th Cir.1986)—**§ 11.4, n. 17, 26; § 11.5, n. 57.**
McDonald v. Johnson & Johnson, 722 F.2d 1370 (8th Cir.1983)—**§ 16.3, n. 46; § 16.4, n. 21.**
McGahee v. Northern Propane Gas Co., 858 F.2d 1487 (11th Cir.1988)—**§ 6.5, n. 35; § 8.3, n. 3; § 8.5, n. 4.**
McGlinchy v. Shell Chemical Co., 845 F.2d 802 (9th Cir. 1988)—**§ 17.6, n. 19; § 21.2, n. 15.**
MCI Communications Corp. v. American Tel. and Tel. Co., 708 F.2d 1081 (7th Cir.1983)—**§ 7.7, n. 6; § 9.3, n. 13; § 17.6, n. 17, 29; § 18.3, n. 42; § 19.3, n. 12; § 19.5, n. 4, 8, 13; § 20.7, n. 5.**
McKenzie v. Mercy Hosp. of Independence, Kansas., 854 F.2d 365 (10th Cir.1988)—**§ 7.7, n. 17.**
McLain v. Real Estate Bd. of New Orleans, Inc., 444 U.S. 232, 100 S.Ct. 502, 62 L.Ed.2d 441 (1980)—**§ 21.1; § 21.1, n. 13.**
McTamney v. Stolt Tankers and Terminals (Holdings), S.A., 678 F.Supp. 118 (E.D.Pa.1987)—**§ 12.1, n. 1.**
Mechanical Mfg. Co., 16 F.T.C. 67 (1932)—**§ 10.8, n. 5.**
Medic Air Corp. v. Air Ambulance Authority, 843 F.2d 1187 (9th Cir.1988)—**§ 20.4, n. 21.**
Medical X–Ray Film Antitrust Litigation, In re, 946 F.Supp. 209 (E.D.N.Y.1996)—**§ 4.5, n. 5.**
Meehan v. PPG Industries, Inc., 802 F.2d 881 (7th Cir. 1986)—**§ 5.5, n. 49.**
Menominee Rubber Co. v. Gould, Inc., 657 F.2d 164 (7th Cir.1981)—**§ 10.7, n. 6.**
Mercantile Texas Corp. v. Board of Governors, 638 F.2d 1255 (5th Cir.1981)—**§ 13.4, n. 12.**
Mercoid Corp. v. Mid–Continent Inv. Co. (Mercoid I), 320 U.S. 661, 64 S.Ct. 268, 88 L.Ed. 376 (1944)—**§ 5.5, n. 9, 18.**
Mercoid Corp. v. Minneapolis–Honeywell Regulator Co. (Mercoid II), 320 U.S. 680, 64 S.Ct. 278, 88 L.Ed. 396 (1944)—**§ 5.5, n. 18.**
Mercy Health Services, United States v., 902 F.Supp. 968 (N.D.Iowa 1995)—**§ 3.6, n. 7.**
Merican, Inc. v. Caterpillar Tractor Co., 713 F.2d 958 (3rd Cir.1983)—**§ 16.4, n. 21.**
Mesirow v. Pepperidge Farm, Inc., 703 F.2d 339 (9th Cir.1983)—**§ 11.5, n. 17.**
Metrix Warehouse, Inc. v. Daimler–Benz Aktiengesellschaft, 828 F.2d 1033 (4th Cir.1987)—**§ 10.7, n. 4; § 17.5, n. 17; § 17.6, n. 19, 30.**
Metro Industries, Inc. v. Sammi Corp., 82 F.3d 839 (9th Cir.1996)—**§ 5.2, n. 53.**
Metzler v. Bear Automotive Service Equipment Co., 19 F.Supp.2d 1345 (S.D.Fla.1998)—**§ 3.3, n. 32; § 7.6, n. 10.**
M & H Tire Co., Inc. v. Hoosier Racing Tire Corp., 733 F.2d 973 (1st Cir.1984)—**§ 5.4, n. 70.**
Michigan Citizens for an Independent Press v. Thornburgh, 868 F.2d 1285, 276 U.S.App.D.C. 130 (D.C.Cir. 1989)—**§ 12.9, n. 10.**
Microsoft Corp., United States v., 1998 WL 614485 (D.D.C. 1998)—**§ 4.1, n. 30; § 6.6, n. 7; § 7.9, n. 11; § 10.4, n. 34.**
Microsoft Corp., United States v., 147 F.3d 935, 331 U.S.App.D.C. 121 (D.C.Cir.1998)—**§ 6.4, n. 7; § 10.5, n. 11.**
Microsoft Corp., United States v., 980 F.Supp. 537 (D.D.C. 1997)—**§ 5.5, n. 44; § 15.1, n. 21.**
Microsoft Corp., United States v., 1995 WL 505998 (D.D.C. 1995)—**§ 5.5, n. 44; § 6.4, n. 7.**
Microsoft Corp., United States v., 56 F.3d 1448, 312 U.S.App.D.C. 378 (D.C.Cir.1995)—**§ 12.6, n. 19.**
Mid–Atlantic Toyota Antitrust Litigation, In re, 605 F.Supp. 440 (D.Md.1984)—**§ 15.4, n. 12.**
Mid–Atlantic Toyota Antitrust Litigation, In re, 525 F.Supp. 1265 (D.Md.1981)—**§ 15.4, n. 8.**
Midcon, In re, 5 Trade Reg.Rep. ¶ 22707 (FTC 1989)—**§ 3.6, n. 37.**
Midland Telecasting Co. v. Midessa Television Co., Inc., 617 F.2d 1141 (5th Cir.1980)—**§ 19.3, n. 16.**
Mid–South Distributors v. F.T.C., 287 F.2d 512 (5th Cir. 1961)—**§ 14.6, n. 3.**

Mid–Texas Communications Systems, Inc. v. American Tel. and Tel. Co., 615 F.2d 1372 (5th Cir.1980)—**§ 17.6, n. 37.**

Midwestern Machinery, Inc. v. Northwest Airlines, Inc., 167 F.3d 439 (8th Cir.1999)—**§ 12.1, n. 36; § 16.3, n. 19; § 16.7, n. 13.**

Midwestern Waffles, Inc. v. Waffle House, Inc., 734 F.2d 705 (11th Cir.1984)—**§ 10.5, n. 22; § 16.7, n. 11.**

Mid–West Paper Products Co. v. Continental Group, Inc., 596 F.2d 573 (3rd Cir.1979)—**§ 16.6; § 16.6, n. 13, 30.**

Midwest Radio Co., Inc. v. Forum Pub. Co., 942 F.2d 1294 (8th Cir.1991)—**§ 7.10, n. 18.**

Miller v. Hedlund, 813 F.2d 1344 (9th Cir.1987)—**§ 5.3, n. 28; § 20.1, n. 12.**

Miller v. Indiana Hosp., 843 F.2d 139 (3rd Cir.1988)—**§ 5.4, n. 70.**

Miller v. W.H. Bristow, Inc., 739 F.Supp. 1044 (D.S.C. 1990)—**§ 11.5, n. 21.**

Millicom Intern. Cellular v. Republic of Costa Rica, 995 F.Supp. 14 (D.D.C.1998)—**§ 21.2, n. 70.**

Minnesota Min. & Mfg. Co. v. New Jersey Wood Finishing Co., 381 U.S. 311, 85 S.Ct. 1473, 14 L.Ed.2d 405 (1965)—**§ 16.7, n. 20.**

Minolta Camera Products Antitrust Litigation, In re, 668 F.Supp. 456 (D.Md.1987)—**§ 15.4, n. 10.**

Minpeco, S.A. v. Conticommodity Services, Inc., 677 F.Supp. 151 (S.D.N.Y.1988)—**§ 17.7, n. 2.**

Mishawaka, Ind., City of v. American Elec. Power Co., Inc., 616 F.2d 976 (7th Cir.1980)—**§ 17.6, n. 31.**

Missouri, State of v. National Organization for Women, Inc., 620 F.2d 1301 (8th Cir.1980)—**§ 5.4; § 5.4, n. 98.**

Mitchell v. Frank R. Howard Memorial Hosp., 853 F.2d 762 (9th Cir.1988)—**§ 21.1, n. 11.**

Mitsubishi Motors Corp. v. Soler Chrysler–Plymouth, Inc., 473 U.S. 614, 105 S.Ct. 3346, 87 L.Ed.2d 444 (1985)—**§ 16.10; § 16.10, n. 1.**

M. Loff Radio Parts, Inc. v. Mattel, Inc., 706 F.Supp. 387 (W.D.Pa.1988)—**§ 10.1, n. 8.**

M & M Medical Supplies and Service, Inc. v. Pleasant Valley Hosp., Inc., 981 F.2d 160 (4th Cir.1992)—**§ 6.5, n. 34; § 16.8, n. 42.**

Molinas v. National Basketball Ass'n, 190 F.Supp. 241 (S.D.N.Y.1961)—**§ 5.4, n. 63.**

Monahan's Marine, Inc. v. Boston Whaler, Inc., 866 F.2d 525 (1st Cir.1989)—**§ 11.4, n. 15.**

Monfort of Colorado, Inc. v. Cargill, Inc., 591 F.Supp. 683 (D.Colo.1983)—**§ 3.7, n. 10.**

Monsanto Co. v. Spray–Rite Service Corp., 465 U.S. 752, 104 S.Ct. 1464, 79 L.Ed.2d 775 (1984)—**§ 2.2, n. 59; § 11.2, n. 6; § 11.4, n. 10; § 11.5, n. 8, 51.**

Montauk–Caribbean Airways, Inc. v. Hope, 784 F.2d 91 (2nd Cir.1986)—**§ 20.6, n. 5.**

Montreal Trading Ltd. v. Amax Inc., 661 F.2d 864 (10th Cir.1981)—**§ 21.2, n. 40.**

Montvale Management Group v. Snowshoe Co., 1984 WL 2949 (N.D.W.Va.1984)—**§ 3.2, n. 25.**

Monument Builders of Greater Kansas City, Inc. v. American Cemetery Ass'n, 1990 WL 269872 (D.Kan.1990)—**§ 21.3, n. 13.**

Monument Builders of Greater Kansas City, Inc. v. American Cemetery Assn. of Kansas, 891 F.2d 1473 (10th Cir.1989)—**§ 6.6, n. 5; § 10.3, n. 51.**

Moore v. Boating Industry Associations, 819 F.2d 693 (7th Cir.1987)—**§ 5.4, n. 70.**

Moore v. Jas. H. Matthews & Co., 682 F.2d 830 (9th Cir.1982)—**§ 17.6; § 17.6, n. 28.**

Moore v. Jas. H. Matthews & Co., 550 F.2d 1207 (9th Cir.1977)—**§ 10.3, n. 5; § 10.4, n. 5; § 10.6, n. 39.**

Moore v. Jas. H. Matthews & Co., 473 F.2d 328 (9th Cir.1972)—**§ 6.2, n. 4.**

Morgan v. Ponder, 892 F.2d 1355 (8th Cir.1989)—**§ 6.5, n. 13; § 8.5, n. 15; § 8.6, n. 4; § 8.7, n. 6.**

Morgan, Strand, Wheeler & Biggs v. Radiology, Ltd., 924 F.2d 1484 (9th Cir.1991)—**§ 3.3, n. 6; § 3.6, n. 7; § 10.9, n. 38.**

Morgenstern v. Wilson, 29 F.3d 1291 (8th Cir.1994)—**§ 3.7, n. 25.**

Morrison v. Murray Biscuit Co., 797 F.2d 1430 (7th Cir. 1986)—**§ 11.4, n. 18, 27; § 11.5, n. 18, 52.**

Morris Run Coal Co. v. Barclay Coal Co., 68 Pa. 173 (Pa.1871)—**§ 2.1; § 2.1, n. 48, 50.**

Morristown Block and Concrete Products Co. v. General Shale Products Corp., 829 F.2d 39 (6th Cir.1987)—**§ 16.8, n. 21.**

Morton v. National Dairy Products Corp., 414 F.2d 403 (3rd Cir.1969)—**§ 14.6, n. 57.**

Morton Salt Co. v. G. S. Suppiger Co., 314 U.S. 488, 62 S.Ct. 402, 86 L.Ed. 363 (1942)—**§ 5.5, n. 9.**

Morton Salt Co., F.T.C. v., 334 U.S. 37, 68 S.Ct. 822, 92 L.Ed. 1196 (1948)—**§ 14.6, n. 9.**

Motion Picture Patents Co. v. Universal Film Mfg. Co., 243 U.S. 502, 37 S.Ct. 416, 61 L.Ed. 871 (1917)—**§ 10.3, n. 8; § 10.6, n. 1.**

Motive Parts Warehouse v. Facet Enterprises, 774 F.2d 380 (10th Cir.1985)—**§ 16.3, n. 34.**

Mozart Co. v. Mercedes–Benz of North America, Inc., 833 F.2d 1342 (9th Cir.1987)—**§ 3.3, n. 37; § 10.3, n. 42, 59.**

Mozart Co. v. Mercedes–Benz of North America, Inc., 593 F.Supp. 1506 (N.D.Cal.1984)—**§ 10.5, n. 3.**

M. P. M., Inc., United States v., 397 F.Supp. 78 (D.Colo. 1975)—**§ 12.9, n. 9.**

Mt. Hood Stages, Inc. v. Greyhound Corp., 616 F.2d 394 (9th Cir.1980)—**§ 16.7, n. 21; § 19.4, n. 1, 6.**

Mt. Lebanon Motors, Inc. v. Chrysler Corp., 283 F.Supp. 453 (W.D.Pa.1968)—**§ 6.5, n. 27.**

Muenster Butane, Inc. v. Stewart Co., 651 F.2d 292 (5th Cir.1981)—**§ 11.6, n. 10, 25.**

Mularkey v. Holsum Bakery, Inc., 146 F.3d 1064 (9th Cir.1998)—**§ 11.5, n. 10.**

Multidistrict Vehicle Air Pollution M.D.L. No. 31, In re, 481 F.2d 122 (9th Cir.1973)—**§ 16.4, n. 3.**

Multiflex, Inc. v. Samuel Moore & Co., 709 F.2d 980 (5th Cir.1983)—**§ 11.6, n. 18; § 17.6, n. 24, 29.**

Multistate Legal Studies, Inc. v. Harcourt Brace Jovanovich Legal and Professional Publications, Inc., 63 F.3d 1540 (10th Cir.1995)—**§ 6.4, n. 16; § 6.5, n. 9; § 7.10, n. 13; § 8.9, n. 1; § 10.5, n. 2.**

Municipal Utilities Bd. of Albertville v. Alabama Power Co., 934 F.2d 1493 (11th Cir.1991)—**§ 18.3, n. 6; § 20.4, n. 13; § 20.5, n. 9.**

Murrow Furniture Galleries, Inc. v. Thomasville Furniture Industries, Inc., 889 F.2d 524 (4th Cir.1989)—**§ 6.6, n. 2; § 11.6, n. 20.**

N

N. A. A. C. P. v. Claiborne Hardware Co., 458 U.S. 886, 102 S.Ct. 3409, 73 L.Ed.2d 1215 (1982)—**§ 5.4, n. 96.**

Nanavati v. Burdette Tomlin Memorial Hosp., 857 F.2d 96 (3rd Cir.1988)—**§ 4.7, n. 8.**

National Ass'n of Pharmaceutical Mfrs., Inc. v. Ayerst Laboratories, 850 F.2d 904 (2nd Cir.1988)—**§ 3.3, n. 11.**

National Bancard Corp. (NaBanco) v. VISA U.S.A., Inc., 779 F.2d 592 (11th Cir.1986)—**§ 3.3, n. 1; § 5.4, n. 53.**

National Broiler Marketing Ass'n v. United States, 436 U.S. 816, 98 S.Ct. 2122, 56 L.Ed.2d 728 (1978)—**§ 19.7, n. 4.**

National Casualty Co., F.T.C. v., 357 U.S. 560, 78 S.Ct. 1260, 2 L.Ed.2d 1540 (1958)—**§ 19.7, n. 49.**

National Collegiate Athletic Ass'n v. Board of Regents of University of Oklahoma, 468 U.S. 85, 104 S.Ct. 2948, 82 L.Ed.2d 70 (1984)—**§ 5.1, n. 8, 16; § 5.6, n. 30.**

National Farmers' Organization, Inc. v. Associated Milk Producers, Inc., 850 F.2d 1286 (8th Cir.1988)—**§ 17.5, n. 17; § 17.6, n. 21.**

National Gerimedical Hospital and Gerontology Center v. Blue Cross of Kansas City, 452 U.S. 378, 101 S.Ct. 2415, 69 L.Ed.2d 89 (1981)—**§ 19.3, n. 10.**

National Lead Co., 49 F.T.C. 791 (1953)—**§ 4.6, n. 29.**

National Macaroni Manufacturers v. F.T.C., 65 F.T.C. 583 (1964)—**§ 4.6, n. 7; § 17.5, n. 22.**

National Organization for Women, Inc. v. Scheidler, 968 F.2d 612 (7th Cir.1992)—**§ 5.4, n. 99; § 7.10, n. 13.**

National Parcel Services, Inc. v. J.B. Hunt Logistics, Inc., 150 F.3d 970 (8th Cir.1998)—**§ 8.7, n. 4.**

National Soc. of Professional Engineers v. United States, 435 U.S. 679, 98 S.Ct. 1355, 55 L.Ed.2d 637 (1978)—**§ 5.1, n. 5; § 5.4, n. 36; § 5.6; § 5.6, n. 10; § 17.2, n. 12.**

Nelson v. Monroe Regional Medical Center, 925 F.2d 1555 (7th Cir.1991)—**§ 16.3, n. 47.**

Nelson, United States v., 52 F. 646 (D.Minn.1892)—**§ 2.1, n. 46, 57.**

Neumann v. Reinforced Earth Co., 786 F.2d 424, 252 U.S.App.D.C. 11 (D.C.Cir.1986)—**§ 7.12, n. 3; § 7.13, n. 13; § 18.4, n. 3.**

Neumann v. Vidal, 710 F.2d 856, 228 U.S.App.D.C. 345 (D.C.Cir.1983)—**§ 16.5, n. 4.**

Newberry v. Washington Post Co., 438 F.Supp. 470 (D.D.C.1977)—**§ 11.6, n. 24.**

Newburgh Moire Co. v. Superior Moire Co., 237 F.2d 283 (3rd Cir.1956)—**§ 5.5, n. 36.**

New England Motor Rate Bureau, 5 Trade Reg.Rep. ¶ 22722 (FTC 1989)—**§ 20.7, n. 6.**

New England Motor Rate Bureau, Inc. v. F.T.C., 908 F.2d 1064 (1st Cir.1990)—**§ 20.5, n. 13.**

New Motor Vehicle Bd. of California v. Orrin W. Fox Co., 439 U.S. 96, 99 S.Ct. 403, 58 L.Ed.2d 361 (1978)—**§ 20.3, n. 3.**

New Wrinkle, Inc., United States v., 342 U.S. 371, 72 S.Ct. 350, 96 L.Ed. 417 (1952)—**§ 5.5, n. 36.**

New York v. Visa, U.S.A., Inc., 1990 WL 75047 (S.D.N.Y. 1990)—**§ 15.4, n. 13.**

New York, State of v. Hendrickson Bros., Inc., 840 F.2d 1065 (2nd Cir.1988)—**§ 16.7, n. 16.**

New York, State of v. Kraft General Foods, Inc., 926 F.Supp. 321 (S.D.N.Y.1995)—**§ 12.3, n. 13.**

Nifty Foods Corp. v. Great Atlantic & Pac. Tea Co., Inc., 614 F.2d 832 (2nd Cir.1980)—**§ 3.2, n. 22.**

Nippon Paper Industries Co., Ltd., United States v., 1999 WL 515827 (D.Mass.1999)—**§ 21.2, n. 22.**

Nippon Paper Industries Co., Ltd., United States v., 109 F.3d 1 (1st Cir.1997)—**§ 21.2, n. 22.**

Nobelpharma AB v. Implant Innovations, Inc., 141 F.3d 1059 (Fed.Cir.1998)—**§ 7.11, n. 33; § 18.3, n. 38.**

Norte Car Corp. v. FirstBank Corp., 25 F.Supp.2d 9 (D.Puerto Rico 1998)—**§ 19.7, n. 10.**

North American Soccer League v. National Football League, 670 F.2d 1249 (2nd Cir.1982)—**§ 5.1, n. 22.**

North Carolina Elec. Membership Corp. v. Carolina Power & Light Co., 780 F.Supp. 322 (M.D.N.C.1991)—**§ 8.7, n. 11.**

Northeastern Tel. Co. v. American Tel. and Tel. Co., 651 F.2d 76 (2nd Cir.1981)—**§ 19.3, n. 12.**

Northern Pac. Ry. Co. v. United States, 356 U.S. 1, 78 S.Ct. 514, 2 L.Ed.2d 545 (1958)—**§ 10.1, n. 5; § 10.3; § 10.3, n. 11, 70; § 10.6, n. 20; § 13.3, n. 10.**

Northern Securities Co. v. United States, 193 U.S. 197, 24 S.Ct. 436, 48 L.Ed. 679 (1904)—**§ 2.1, n. 64; § 7.2, n. 1; § 12.1, n. 6; § 20.8, n. 11.**

Northrop Corp. v. McDonnell Douglas Corp., 705 F.2d 1030 (9th Cir.1983)—**§ 5.2, n. 51.**

North Texas Producers Ass'n v. Young, 308 F.2d 235 (5th Cir.1962)—**§ 17.6, n. 48.**

Northwest Wholesale Stationers, Inc. v. Pacific Stationery and Printing Co., 472 U.S. 284, 105 S.Ct. 2613, 86 L.Ed.2d 202 (1985)—**§ 1.2, n. 15; § 4.1, n. 49; § 5.2, n. 16; § 5.4, n. 13, 74.**

Novatel Communications, Inc. v. Cellular Telephone Supply, Inc., 1986 WL 15507 (N.D.Ga.1986)—**§ 4.7, n. 5.**

Nurse Midwifery Associates v. Hibbett, 918 F.2d 605 (6th Cir.1990)—**§ 4.7, n. 8; § 5.4, n. 70.**

Nurse Midwifery Associates v. Hibbett, 549 F.Supp. 1185 (M.D.Tenn.1982)—**§ 19.7, n. 54.**

NYNEX Corp. v. Discon, Inc., 525 U.S. 128, 119 S.Ct. 493, 142 L.Ed.2d 510 (1998)—**§ 5.4, n. 20, 87; § 9.3, n. 11; § 11.6, n. 33.**

O

Oahu Gas Service, Inc. v. Pacific Resources, Inc., 838 F.2d 360 (9th Cir.1988)—**§ 7.5, n. 16.**

Occidental Petroleum Corp., 101 F.T.C. 373 (1983)—**§ 10.8, n. 5.**

Occidental Petroleum Corp. v. Buttes Gas & Oil Co., 331 F.Supp. 92 (C.D.Cal.1971)—**§ 21.2, n. 63.**

Ocean State Physicians Health Plan, Inc. v. Blue Cross & Blue Shield of Rhode Island, 883 F.2d 1101 (1st Cir. 1989)—**§ 19.7, n. 44.**

Official Airline Guides, Inc. v. F. T. C., 630 F.2d 920 (2nd Cir.1980)—**§ 7.5, n. 2.**

Ohio AFL–CIO v. Insurance Rating Bd., 451 F.2d 1178, 61 O.O.2d 114 (6th Cir.1971)—**§ 19.7, n. 49.**

Ohio ex rel. Montgomery v. Louis Trauth Dairy, Inc., 1996 WL 343440 (S.D.Ohio 1996)—**§ 16.7, n. 15.**

Ohio–Sealy Mattress Mfg. Co. v. Sealy, Inc., 585 F.2d 821 (7th Cir.1978)—**§ 5.2, n. 14; § 11.6, n. 1.**

OKI Distributing, Inc. v. Amana Refrigeration, Inc., 850 F.Supp. 637 (S.D.Ohio 1994)—**§ 14.6, n. 57.**

Oksanen v. Page Memorial Hosp., 945 F.2d 696 (4th Cir.1991)—**§ 4.7, n. 8; § 5.4, n. 70.**

Olin Corp., 5 Trade Reg.Rep. ¶ 22857 (FTC 1990)—**§ 12.4, n. 43.**

Olin Corp. v. F.T.C., 986 F.2d 1295 (9th Cir.1993)—**§ 3.8, n. 8; § 12.9, n. 12.**

Oltz v. St. Peter's Community Hosp., 656 F.Supp. 760 (D.Mont.1987)—**§ 10.9, n. 45.**

Olympia Equipment Leasing Co. v. Western Union Telegraph Co., 797 F.2d 370 (7th Cir.1986)—**§ 7.5, n. 16; § 17.6, n. 19.**

P

Q

R

S

Seasongood v. K and K Ins. Agency, 548 F.2d 729 (8th Cir.1977)—**§ 19.7, n. 49.**
Seawinds Ltd. v. Nedlloyd Lines, B.V., 80 B.R. 181 (N.D.Cal.1987)—**§ 19.3, n. 1.**
Segal v. American Tel. and Tel. Co., Inc., 606 F.2d 842 (9th Cir.1979)—**§ 19.4, n. 4.**
Seglin v. Esau, 769 F.2d 1274 (7th Cir.1985)—**§ 21.1, n. 12.**
Senza–Gel Corp. v. Seiffhart, 803 F.2d 661 (Fed.Cir. 1986)—**§ 5.5, n. 23.**
Serta Associates, Inc., United States v., 296 F.Supp. 1121 (N.D.Ill.1968)—**§ 5.2, n. 26.**
Sessions Tank Liners, Inc. v. Joor Mfg., Inc., 17 F.3d 295 (9th Cir.1994)—**§ 18.5, n. 4.**
Sewell Plastics, Inc. v. Coca–Cola Co., 720 F.Supp. 1196 (W.D.N.C.1989)—**§ 10.9, n. 43.**
Shafi v. St. Francis Hosp. of Charleston, W. Va., 937 F.2d 603 (4th Cir.1991)—**§ 10.3, n. 19.**
Shahawy v. Harrison, 875 F.2d 1529 (11th Cir.1989)—**§ 20.5, n. 12.**
Shahawy v. Harrison, 778 F.2d 636 (11th Cir.1985)—**§ 21.1, n. 15.**
Sharp v. United Airlines, Inc., 967 F.2d 404 (10th Cir. 1992)—**§ 16.5, n. 9.**
Sheldon, People v., 139 N.Y. 251, 34 N.E. 785 (N.Y. 1893)—**§ 2.1; § 2.1, n. 48.**
Siegel v. Chicken Delight, Inc., 448 F.2d 43 (9th Cir. 1971)—**§ 10.3, n. 42; § 10.4, n. 24; § 10.5, n. 22; § 10.6; § 10.6, n. 47.**
Siemens Corp., United States v., 621 F.2d 499 (2nd Cir. 1980)—**§ 13.4, n. 27.**
Silicon Graphics, 5 Trade Reg.Rep. ¶ 23838 (FTC 1995)—**§ 9.4, n. 29.**
Silver v. New York Stock Exchange, 373 U.S. 341, 83 S.Ct. 1246, 10 L.Ed.2d 389 (1963)—**§ 5.4; § 5.4, n. 72.**
Simpson v. Union Oil Co. of Cal., 411 F.2d 897 (9th Cir.1969)—**§ 17.6, n. 37.**
Simpson v. Union Oil Co. of Cal., 377 U.S. 13, 84 S.Ct. 1051, 12 L.Ed.2d 98 (1964)—**§ 11.2, n. 1; § 11.5; § 11.5, n. 14.**
Sinclair Refining Co., F.T.C. v., 261 U.S. 463, 43 S.Ct. 450, 67 L.Ed. 746 (1923)—**§ 2.1, n. 78.**
Sisal Sales Corp., United States v., 274 U.S. 268, 47 S.Ct. 592, 71 L.Ed. 1042 (1927)—**§ 21.2, n. 7.**
Skrainka v. Scharringhausen, 8 Mo.App. 522 (Mo.App. 1880)—**§ 2.1, n. 46.**
SmileCare Dental Group v. Delta Dental Plan of California, Inc., 88 F.3d 780 (9th Cir.1996)—**§ 7.5, n. 13.**
Smith v. Combustion Engineering, Inc., 856 F.2d 196 (6th Cir.1988)—**§ 18.1, n. 2.**
SmithKline Corp. v. Eli Lilly & Co., 427 F.Supp. 1089 (E.D.Pa.1976)—**§ 8.9, n. 3.**
SmithKline Diagnostics, Inc. v. Helena Laboratories Corp., 859 F.2d 878 (Fed.Cir.1988)—**§ 7.11, n. 18.**
Smith Machinery Co., Inc. v. Hesston Corp., 878 F.2d 1290 (10th Cir.1989)—**§ 10.7, n. 6.**
Smith Machinery Co., Inc. v. Hesston Corp., 1987 WL 14498 (D.N.M.1987)—**§ 10.6, n. 5.**
SMS Systems Maint. Ser., Inc. v. Digital Equip. Corp., 1999 WL 618046 (1st Cir.1999)—**§ 3.3, n. 33; § 7.6, n. 10; § 10.3, n. 38; § 10.5, n. 4.**
Socony–Vacuum Oil Co., United States v., 310 U.S. 150, 60 S.Ct. 811, 84 L.Ed. 1129 (1940)—**§ 2.1, n. 81; § 5.2, n. 66; § 5.6; § 5.6, n. 6; § 11.5, n. 56.**
Solinger v. A. & M. Records, Inc., 718 F.2d 298 (9th Cir.1983)—**§ 16.4, n. 9.**
Sound, Inc. v. American Tel. and Tel. Co., 631 F.2d 1324 (8th Cir.1980)—**§ 19.3; § 19.3, n. 15; § 19.5, n. 8.**
Southaven Land Co., Inc. v. Malone & Hyde, Inc., 715 F.2d 1079 (6th Cir.1983)—**§ 16.4, n. 9, 11.**
South–Eastern Underwriters Ass'n, United States v., 322 U.S. 533, 64 S.Ct. 1162, 88 L.Ed. 1440 (1944)—**§ 19.7, n. 36; § 21.1, n. 5.**
Southern Card & Novelty, Inc. v. Lawson Mardon Label, Inc., 138 F.3d 869 (11th Cir.1998)—**§ 10.7, n. 6.**
Southern Disposal, Inc. v. Texas Waste Management, 161 F.3d 1259 (10th Cir.1998)—**§ 20.6, n. 12.**
Southern Motor Carriers Rate Conference, Inc. v. United States, 471 U.S. 48, 105 S.Ct. 1721, 85 L.Ed.2d 36 (1985)—**§ 20.3, n. 7; § 20.4, n. 3; § 20.5, n. 3.**
Southern Pac. Co., United States v., 259 U.S. 214, 42 S.Ct. 496, 66 L.Ed. 907 (1922)—**§ 2.1, n. 75.**
Southern Pacific Communications Co. v. American Tel. and Tel. Co., 740 F.2d 980, 238 U.S.App.D.C. 309 (D.C.Cir.1984)—**§ 7.7, n. 15; § 9.3, n. 14; § 19.3, n. 12.**
Southern Pacific Communications Co. v. American Tel. and Tel. Co., 556 F.Supp. 825 (D.D.C.1982)—**§ 17.6, n. 19.**
Southern Pines Chrysler–Plymouth, Inc. v. Chrysler Corp., 826 F.2d 1360 (4th Cir.1987)—**§ 10.7, n. 6.**
Southland Corp., 102 F.T.C. 1337 (1983)—**§ 10.8, n. 5.**
Southwest Suburban Bd. of Realtors, Inc. v. Beverly Area Planning Ass'n, 830 F.2d 1374 (7th Cir.1987)—**§ 16.5, n. 17.**
Souza v. Estate of Bishop, 821 F.2d 1332 (9th Cir.1987)—**§ 3.7, n. 16; § 4.5, n. 8, 27; § 10.5, n. 2.**
Spartan Grain & Mill Co. v. Ayers, 581 F.2d 419 (5th Cir.1978)—**§ 10.8, n. 4.**
Spectrum Sports, Inc. v. McQuillan, 506 U.S. 447, 113 S.Ct. 884, 122 L.Ed.2d 247 (1993)—**§ 3.1, n. 6; § 3.7, n. 23; § 6.2, n. 16; § 6.4, n. 20; § 6.5, n. 8; § 7.9, n. 9; § 7.11, n. 5; § 8.4, n. 11; § 8.7, n. 5; § 10.4, n. 8; § 16.3, n. 29.**
Sperry & Hutchinson Co., F.T.C. v., 405 U.S. 233, 92 S.Ct. 898, 31 L.Ed.2d 170 (1972)—**§ 2.1, n. 74; § 15.2, n. 3.**
Spray–Rite Service Corp. v. Monsanto Co., 684 F.2d 1226 (7th Cir.1982)—**§ 11.4; § 11.4, n. 12.**
Springfield Terminal Ry. Co. v. Canadian Pacific Ltd., 133 F.3d 103 (1st Cir.1997)—**§ 6.5, n. 35; § 19.3, n. 4.**
Square D Co. v. Niagara Frontier Tariff Bureau, Inc., 476 U.S. 409, 106 S.Ct. 1922, 90 L.Ed.2d 413 (1986)—**§ 19.6; § 19.6, n. 5.**
Stamatakis Industries, Inc. v. King, 965 F.2d 469 (7th Cir.1992)—**§ 16.3, n. 46.**
Standard Motor Products, Inc. v. Federal Trade Commission, 265 F.2d 674 (2nd Cir.1959)—**§ 14.6, n. 3.**
Standard Motor Products, Inc., F.T.C. v., 371 F.2d 613 (2nd Cir.1967)—**§ 14.6, n. 57.**
Standard Oil Co., 49 F.T.C. 923 (1953)—**§ 14.6, n. 59.**
Standard Oil Co., Ind. v. United States, 283 U.S. 163, 51 S.Ct. 421, 75 L.Ed. 926 (1931)—**§ 5.5, n. 66.**
Standard Oil Co. of California v. United States, 337 U.S. 293, 69 S.Ct. 1051, 93 L.Ed. 1371 (1949)—**§ 2.1, n. 87; § 2.3; § 2.3, n. 6; § 10.3, n. 70; § 10.9; § 10.9, n. 4.**
Standard Oil Co. of New Jersey v. United States, 221 U.S. 1, 31 S.Ct. 502, 55 L.Ed. 619 (1911)—**§ 2.1, n. 66; § 3.1, n. 17; § 4.1, n. 17; § 6.1, n. 6; § 6.4, n. 1; § 7.2, n. 1.**
Stanislaus, County of v. Pacific Gas and Elec. Co., 114 F.3d 858 (9th Cir.1997)—**§ 19.6, n. 5.**

T

U

V

W

X

Y

Z

Table of Statutes

UNITED STATES

UNITED STATES CONSTITUTION

Art.	This Work Sec.	Note
I, § 8, cl. 8	5.5	
III	16.3	
VI, § 2	19.1	1
VI, § 2	20.1	1

UNITED STATES CODE ANNOTATED

5 U.S.C.A.—Government Organization and Employees

Sec.	This Work Sec.	Note
554	15.2	15

7 U.S.C.A.—Agriculture

Sec.	This Work Sec.	Note
291—292	19.7	3

11 U.S.C.A.—Bankruptcy

Sec.	This Work Sec.	Note
1101—1174	12.9	11

12 U.S.C.A.—Banks and Banking

Sec.	This Work Sec.	Note
1828(c)	19.7	8
1971—1978	19.7	9

15 U.S.C.A.—Commerce and Trade

Sec.	This Work Sec.	Note
1	2.1	2
1	3.1	7
1	10.4	18
1	11.1	4
1	15.1	13
1	15.1	14
1	21.1	1
1	21.2	21
2	2.1	2
2	3.1	4
2	3.2	17
2	6.1	
2	6.5	

UNITED STATES CODE ANNOTATED

15 U.S.C.A.—Commerce and Trade

Sec.	This Work Sec.	Note
2	6.5	2
2	10.5	31
2	15.1	13
2	15.1	14
3	15.1	13
4	15.1	6
6a	21.2	11
12	2.1	37
12 et seq.	2.1	70
13	3.1	6
13	10.6	39
13	21.1	30
13(a)	8.8	1
13(a)	12.1	41
13(a)	14.6	1
13(a)	14.6	16
13(b)	20.8	13
14	2.1	53
14	3.1	7
14	7.11	55
14	8.9	
14	10.1	1
14	10.4	19
14	10.6	26
14	21.1	31
15	11.1	2
15	16.1	4
15	17.2	27
15	17.3	1
15(a)	15.1	23
15(a)	16.4	1
15(b)	16.4	1
15a	18.2	17
15b	16.7	2
15c	16.5	16
15c—h	15.4	7
15c—h	18.2	17
16	2.1	61
16(a)	15.1	19
16(i)	16.7	19
16a	16.8	66
17	19.7	2
17	19.7	16
18	1.7	21
18	3.1	10
18	3.2	18
18	12.2	33
18	21.1	32
18a	15.3	1
18a(a)(2)	15.3	4
19	12.11	1

UNITED STATES CODE ANNOTATED

15 U.S.C.A.—Commerce and Trade

Sec.	This Work Sec.	Note
22	21.3	9
26	16.3	43
26	16.9	3
34—36	20.6	3
37(a)	19.7	1
41 et seq.	2.1	71
44	15.2	1
45	10.3	61
45	10.9	2
45	11.1	4
45	15.2	1
45	15.2	2
45(a)	15.1	1
45(a)(2)	21.1	34
45(b)	15.2	14
45(*l*)	15.2	13
45(m)	15.2	13
72	17.5	16
1011—1015	19.7	37
1013(b)	19.7	51
1291—1295	19.7	12
1311—1314	15.1	17
1314(g)	15.1	18
1801—1804	12.9	10
4301—4304	5.2	22

18 U.S.C.A.—Crimes and Criminal Procedure

Sec.	This Work Sec.	Note
3282	16.7	9
3621—3624	15.1	15

28 U.S.C.A.—Judiciary and Judicial Procedure

Sec.	This Work Sec.	Note
1391	21.3	11
1391(d)	21.3	12
1602 et seq.	21.2	64
1603(d)	21.2	65
1603(d)	21.2	67

29 U.S.C.A.—Labor

Sec.	This Work Sec.	Note
52	19.7	16
101—110	2.1	62
101 et seq.	19.7	18
113—115	2.1	62

33 U.S.C.A.—Navigation and Navigable Waters

Sec.	This Work Sec.	Note
271(d)(5)	10.3	

35 U.S.C.A.—Patents

Sec.	This Work Sec.	Note
102(b)	7.11	12

UNITED STATES CODE ANNOTATED

35 U.S.C.A.—Patents

Sec.	This Work Sec.	Note
102(b)	18.2	24
261	5.5	52
271(c)	5.5	19
271(d)	5.5	19
271(d)	5.5	24
271(d)	5.5	63
271(d)(5)	3.9	29
271(d)(5)	7.11	56

36 U.S.C.A.—Patriotic Societies and Observances

Sec.	This Work Sec.	Note
371 et seq.	19.7	11

42 U.S.C.A.—The Public Health and Welfare

Sec.	This Work Sec.	Note
4321—4347	1.3	1
11101—11152	5.4	80

46 U.S.C.A.—Shipping

Sec.	This Work Sec.	Note
688	21.2	32
1701—1720	19.3	1
1706(c)(2)	19.3	1

49 U.S.C.A.—Transportation

Sec.	This Work Sec.	Note
10706(a)	19.3	2
10706(b)	19.3	2
41712	8.3	34

49 U.S.C.A.App.—Transportation

Sec.	This Work Sec.	Note
1701—1720	19.7	6

STATUTES AT LARGE

Year	This Work Sec.	Note
1914, Oct. 15, ch. 323	13.1	3
1914, Oct. 15, P.L. 63–212, § 7	13.1	3
1937, Aug. 17, ch. 690	2.1	55
1975, Dec.12, P.L. 94–145	2.1	55
1975, Dec. 12, P.L. 94–145	11.1	4
1987, Dec. 11, P.L. 100–185	15.1	15
1987, Dec. 11, P.L. 100–187	15.1	15

POPULAR NAME ACTS

CIVIL RIGHTS ACT OF 1964

Sec.	This Work Sec.	Note
Tit. VII	19.2	

CLAYTON ACT

Sec.	This Work Sec.	Note
1	2.1	
2	2.1	
2	5.5	
2	8.1	
2	8.8	
2	14.6	
2	21.1	
2(a)	21.1	29
3	2.1	
3	3.1	
3	7.6	
3	7.10	
3	7.11	
3	8.9	
3	9.1	
3	10.1	
3	10.3	
3	10.3	6
3	10.4	
3	10.6	
3	10.6	27
3	10.8	
3	10.8	4
3	10.9	
3	11.1	
3	11.1	2
3	13.3	
3	21.1	
4	2.1	
4	11.5	
4	11.5	7
4	16.1	
4	16.2	
4	16.3	
4	16.3	44
4	16.3	45
4	16.4	
4	16.4	3
4	16.5	
4	16.6	
4	17.1	5
4	17.2	
4	17.3	
4	17.6	
4	17.6	48
4	17.6	49
5(a)	15.1	
5(a)	16.8	
6	2.1	
6	19.7	
6	19.7	
7	2.1	
7	2.2	58
7	2.3	
7	3.1	
7	3.5	
7	3.8	26
7	5.2	
7	5.3	
7	7.2	
7	8.4	
7	9.1	
7	9.4	
7	9.4	3
7	9.4	8
7	10.6	
7	12.1	
7	12.1	1
7	12.1	6
7	12.2	
7	12.7	
7	12.8	
7	12.9	
7	12.10	
7	13.1	
7	13.3	
7	15.3	
7	16.3	
7	16.4	
7	16.7	
7	16.7	15
7	17.6	3
7	19.7	
7	21.1	
7	21.1	29
8	12.11	
12	21.3	
16	2.1	
16	16.3	
16	16.3	44
16	16.9	
20	19.7	16

FEDERAL TRADE COMMISSION ACT

Sec.	This Work Sec.	Note
5	2.1	
5	4.4	
5	4.6	
5	4.6	
5	4.6	12
5	6.6	7
5	7.8	
5	7.11	
5	7.11	11
5	10.1	
5	10.3	
5	10.8	
5	10.9	
5	10.9	58
5	13.3	
5	15.1	
5	15.2	
5	16.7	15
5	16.8	68
5	21.1	
5(b)	15.2	

PATENT ACT

Sec.	This Work Sec.	Note
271(d)	7.11	

ROBINSON–PATMAN ACT

Sec.	This Work Sec.	Note
2(a)	14.6	
2(b)	14.6	
2(c)	14.6	
2(d)	14.6	
2(e)	14.6	
2(f)	14.6	

SHERMAN ACT

Sec.	This Work Sec.	Note
1	1.5	
1	2.1	
1	3.1	
1	4.2	
1	4.4	
1	4.5	
1	4.5	23
1	4.6	
1	4.6	
1	4.7	
1	5.1	
1	5.2	
1	5.4	
1	6.1	
1	6.6	
1	7.5	
1	7.6	
1	7.7	
1	7.10	
1	9.1	
1	9.4	
1	10.1	
1	10.3	
1	10.4	
1	10.8	
1	10.9	
1	11.1	
1	11.2	
1	11.4	
1	11.4	15
1	11.7	
1	12.1	
1	12.7	
1	12.11	
1	13.3	
1	14.6	
1	14.6	35
1	15.2	
1	16.3	
1	17.6	24
1	19.7	
1	20.1	
1	21.2	
1	21.3	
2	3.1	
2	3.8	26
2	4.2	
2	4.7	
2	5.1	
2	6.1	

SHERMAN ACT

Sec.	This Work Sec.	Note
2	6.4	
2	6.5	
2	6.6	
2	7.1	
2	7.5	
2	7.6	
2	7.6	24
2	7.7	
2	7.10	
2	7.11	
2	7.12	
2	8.1	
2	8.5	
2	8.8	
2	9.1	
2	10.3	39
2	10.5	
2	10.5	31
2	12.1	
2	13.3	
2	14.5	
2	17.6	
2	17.6	24
2	18.2	
4	15.1	6
7	2.1	
7	11.5	
7	16.4	

STATE STATUTES

WEST'S ANNOTATED CALIFORNIA CODE OF CIVIL PROCEDURE

Sec.	This Work Sec.	Note
877	17.7	5

FEDERAL RULES OF CIVIL PROCEDURE

Rule	This Work Sec.	Note
4	21.3	
4(c)	21.3	8
4(e)	21.3	8
23(b)(3)	10.4	3
56	16.8	
56(c)	16.8	
56(c)	16.8	8

FEDERAL RULES OF EVIDENCE

Rule	This Work Sec.	Note
702	16.8	

CODE OF FEDERAL REGULATIONS

Tit.	This Work Sec.	Note
16, §§ 801—803	15.3	2
16, § 801.11(c)(1)	15.3	2
16, § 801.11(c)(2)	15.3	3

CODE OF FEDERAL REGULATIONS

FEDERAL REGISTER

*

INDEX

References are to section numbers